Electronic Commerce

Electronic Commerce

Second Edition

Ronald J. Mann
Ben H. and Kitty King Powell Chair in Commercial
and Business Law
Co-Director, Center for Law, Business and Economics
The University of Texas School of Law

Jane K. Winn
Director, Shidler Center for Law, Commerce and Technology
University of Washington School of Law

ASPEN
PUBLISHERS

111 Eighth Avenue, New York, NY 10011
www.aspenpublishers.com

About Aspen Publishers

Aspen Publishers, headquartered in New York City, is a leading information provider for attorneys, business professionals, and law students. Written by preeminent authorities, our products consist of analytical and practical information covering both U.S. and international topics. We publish in the full range of formats, including updated manuals, books, periodicals, CDs, and online products.

Our proprietary content is complemented by 2,500 legal databases, containing over 11 million documents, available through our Loislaw division. Aspen Publishers also offers a wide range of topical legal and business databases linked to Loislaw's primary material. Our mission is to provide accurate, timely, and authoritative content in easily accessible formats, supported by unmatched customer care.

To order any Aspen Publishers title, go to *www.aspenpublishers.com* or call 1-800-638-8437.

To reinstate your manual update service, call 1-800-638-8437.

For more information on Loislaw products, go to *www.loislaw.com* or call 1-800-364-2512.

For Customer Care issues, e-mail *CustomerCare@aspenpublishers.com*; call 1-800-234-1660; or fax 1-800-901-9075.

Aspen Publishers
A Wolters Kluwer Company

For my girls

—R.J.M.

For Peter, Julia, and Lydia

—J.K.W.

Summary of Contents

Contents

Chapter 3.   Protecting Information   193

Section B.   B2B Transactions   331

Preface

This book provides a comprehensive survey of electronic commerce. The premise of the book is that developments in information technology—not only the Internet, but also developments in the technology of managing and analyzing information—have a significant effect on virtually every aspect of commercial transactions. Accordingly, the course covers a broad spectrum of topics. The book is structured around the representation of a technology company. Thus, Part One addresses basic questions about which jurisdictions and judicial regimes can regulate an Internet business. Part Two discusses the context within which Internet businesses operate, with assignments on Setting Up Shop on the Internet and Protecting Information. Part Three covers Electronic Commerce Transactions (with sections on sales, B2B transactions, information transactions, and software licenses), Payments, Lending, and Financing the Technology Company.

As the foregoing suggests, the book confronts the "Law of the Horse" problem proposed by Professor Lessig, *The Law of the Horse: What Cyberlaw Might Teach*, 113 HARV. L. REV. 501 (1999). Specifically, Professor Lessig's famous article challenged the assumption that there needs to be a law school course on electronic commerce if the law of electronic commerce is just the law of every kind of transactional problem, as applied to electronic commerce. Because much of the material in this course in fact is material that also applies to conventional transactions, the criticism is a serious one. There are several responses to that problem. The most obvious response is that there would be value in teaching a course designed to cover the bodies of law relevant to electronic commerce even if the electronic aspects of the transactions did not alter those bodies of law. The reason is that many of our students in fact will practice law in groups devoted for the most part to electronic commerce. If there were horse-law groups in major law firms, we might teach horse law more frequently in law school. (Furthermore, as it happens, one of us teaches at a school that in fact does offer a course in horse law.) More generally, the purpose of a systems-oriented book like this is to teach something like the law of the horse: to teach the law as it applies to a general group of transactions, even if—as a doctrinal matter—that requires the juxtaposition of a broad range of apparently disparate bodies of doctrine. If our students will be forced to bring those legal doctrines together in their practices, it cannot hurt for us to help them start now.

Finally, and most importantly, the premise of this book is one of skepticism toward the thesis that Lessig propounds, at least with respect to transactional law. As the chapters that follow illustrate, there really are a set of basic changes that information technology brings to transactional practice, and—whether or not these changes are truly revolutionary—they do go far beyond adding "e" to every one of the standard transactional forms.

The breadth of coverage necessarily makes the book difficult. Several assignments require students within the course of a day to learn the basics of important areas of substantive law (trademarks, copyright, antitrust, secured transactions). Although that calls for sketchy descriptions of those areas of law, the payoff is a good one: getting the students to see how many different areas of law are relevant to commercial transactions and also to see how advances in technology alter the contexts in which those laws are relevant.

At the same time, the book does not contemplate any required prerequisite courses beyond the typical first-year law school curriculum of such courses as contracts, property, torts, civil procedure, and constitutional law. The goal is to provide a survey introduction of the relevant topics.

The book also does not expect students to have any substantial technical background. It defines technical or industry-specific terms the first time that they appear. You and your students should refer to the glossary at the back of this book if you come upon terms that seem obscure.

Because the purpose of the book is to illuminate the effects of infrastructure development on commerce, portions of the book necessarily focus on developing business and technology practices, even where no significant statutory, case law, or regulatory developments have occurred. The goal is to acquaint the student with the major topics that the student is likely to face in the process of representing information-economy clients. To that end, those business-oriented sections of the book seem important.

The book also reflects a preference for a problem-based method of legal instruction. The philosophy is that learning proceeds best when students are given all of the information they need to solve the problems. The intellectual task is for them to apply the material. Consequently, the share of narrative text is considerably larger than in traditional casebooks, and at the same time excerpts from cases are considerably less extensive. (That is of course no surprise for this topic given the paucity of cases on all but a few topics.) At bottom, the goal is to maximize the value of each page that students are asked to read and to minimize the time students spend studying details that do not directly advance their understanding of the system at hand.

At the same time, this edition of the book differs from the previous edition by including more excerpts and more cases than in the first edition. Many users of this book do not use the problem method, and many of the topics (particularly in the second part of the book) can be covered more effectively by traditional Socratic instruction. Accordingly, the assignments in that part of the book have been lengthened, with a view to accommodating alternate methods of instruction.

A major feature of the text is the Web site for the book (*http://www.utexas.edu/law/faculty/ecommerce*). Among other things, it includes material necessary to work problems (such as policies that the students should locate and examine), updates reflecting the rapid pace of development in the topics that the book discusses, downloadable versions of all the diagrams in the book, the glossary to the book, and links to other sites that might be of interest to you and your students, organized by the assignment to which they are most relevant.

The last major feature of the book is the assignment approach. The material is presented in the form of separate, self-contained assignments. Each assignment is designed to provide adequate material for one 60- to 75-minute class session. Unlike most other law school textbooks, the assignments include no supplementary notes suggesting that the students might profit by consulting cases, law review articles, or other secondary sources. The only things a student needs besides this book, a commercial law statutory supplement, and an Internet connection (to view the Web site) are imagination and a sincere interest in learning how law interacts with businesses and technology to foster or retard economic activity.

If each assignment provides more than an hour of problems, then obviously the material cannot be taught in a typical 3-hour law school course. One approach is to teach this as a 4-hour course. The more common approach doubtless is to delete substantial parts of the book. Conversations with users of the first edition suggest that there is a variety of views regarding exactly what should be covered in an electronic commerce course. These materials are long enough to permit substantial deletions and still suffice for a 3-hour course.

The goal at all points is to provide the students two things: the ability to see the structure of the systems that we cover and the ability to pick up and use new systems that develop in the years to come.

Good luck!

Ronald J. Mann
Jane Kaufman Winn

November 2004
Austin, Texas
Seattle, Washington

Acknowledgments

We have received aid in the preparation of this book from several widely differing groups of people. As a pedagogical matter, the materials in their form owe a great debt to the work of Jay Westbrook and Elizabeth Warren, whose materials on *Debtor-Creditor* law are the precursor to the approach used in these materials (and in the previous textbooks of one of us).

As a matter of substance, we are grateful to Ed Cavazos of Andrews & Kurth LLP and Ann Newton of Haynes and Boone for insight on a variety of issues related to Web-site development and software licenses. The materials on those subjects draw heavily on materials they have provided.

We also owe special thanks to the professors who provided detailed comments on prepublication versions of these materials, particularly Bill Boyd, Dan Hunter, Juliet Moringiello, and Joseph Segui.

For extraordinary clerical assistance in the various stages of publication, we are grateful to Paula Payton and Cathy Brooks. For research assistance of various kinds, we thank Nicole Levin. For assistance with graphics, we thank Alex Grigoras. I also thank several students who provided particularly useful comments, including John Amash, Michael Hopp, Scott Nelson, Travis Seibeneicher, and John Sloat.

Electronic Commerce

Introduction

To think about the role of law in electronic commerce is necessarily to consider the balance between government regulation and freedom of action in the private sector. Juxtaposing that balance with the commercialization of the Internet in 1994 and its rapid growth since that date presents an unusually dynamic policy problem. Perhaps the most perceptive insight on how to place that problem in historical context is Harvard Business School Professor Debora L. Spar's recent book on *Ruling the Waves*. Professor Spar's basic thesis is that society's reactions to important discoveries follow a cyclical historical pattern. Using examples that start with the fifteenth-century reign of Prince Henry the Navigator of Portugal and continue through the rise of the Internet in the twentieth century, she discerns four phases through which the society that exploits those discoveries commonly passes: innovation, commercialization, creative anarchy, and rules. The phase of innovation is the flash point of discovery—Morse's invention of the telegraph, for example. The phase of commercialization is the phase in which pioneers (or pirates, depending on your perspective) move into the new area seeking to exploit its potential: one of Spar's examples discusses the actual pirates who exploited the newly discovered Atlantic in the sixteenth century. The phase of creative anarchy is the phase when the needs of ordinary commerce come into tension with the theretofore freewheeling spirit of the new frontier. Spar's best example of that phase is the 1920's era of radio broadcasting, when competing (and wholly unregulated) radio stations broadcast on overlapping frequencies that made it difficult for any of them to be heard by listeners. The final phase—rules—follows ineluctably as the commercial enterprises unable to suppress anarchy on their own call for government intervention as the best vehicle for bringing order (and profit) to the wild frontier.

Using that framework, it seems plain that the Internet is in the midst of the third phase. As you read through the material for this course, you will see numerous examples of early actors whose businesses provided a major impetus for the growth of the Internet as we know it. But also you will see a set of legal rules that have for the time being often granted those actors broad freedom of action or exemption from rules that govern analogous conduct outside cyberspace. For example, you will read of the immunity granted Internet service providers by the Communications Decency Act and the Digital Millennium Copyright Act (discussed in Assignment 8), of the immunity from taxation granted by the Internet Tax Freedom Act (discussed in Assignment 16), of the rise of unregulated peer-to-peer music sharing (discussed in Assignment 21), and of the general lack of regulation of person-to-person payment providers (discussed in Assignment 29).

In each of those instances, however, you will see also a growing backlash of pressure, as parties who perceive themselves to be harmed by those exemptions seek the establishment of more rigorous regulatory regimes. A major theme of this book is the question of how to transplant existing regulatory regimes to the Internet context or to design new regulatory regimes that are better suited for that context. Because this is a commercial law course, the first question in each instance will be why the businesses that are harmed cannot solve the problems on their own. For example, you might wonder (as you study the topic in Assignment 6) why the government needs to regulate unsolicited commercial e-mail—however annoying it might be—given the obvious market pressures spurring the major Internet service providers to disable those that send it.

Understanding the ability of existing businesses to solve the problems that plague commerce on the Internet must start from a basic understanding of who those businesses are and what they do. Unfortunately, because of the fluidity of the Internet even the types of businesses that are important are changing with rapidity: Who would have predicted in 1998 that one of the most successful Internet companies in 2004 would be a company whose main technology is a search engine? The Internet is populated, and operated, by numerous groups, including (on a by-no-means exclusive list) telecommunications firms, Internet service providers, intermediaries like eBay and PayPal, software firms, content providers and advertisers, retailers, and ordinary users like the readers of this book.

Because the interactions among the members of those disparate groups are too numerous to provide any useful pedagogical focus, this text generally focuses on the Internet retailer, largely because it is a highly visible and readily comprehensible category. Starting from that focus, the regulations and transactions discussed in this text are for the most part those that affect the retailer: the contracts the retailer forms to build a Web site (Assignment 5), to collect information (Assignment 11), to sell products (Assignment 13), to manage relations with its suppliers (Assignments 17 through 19), and to obtain software for its operations (Assignments 22 through 25).

These are not, of course, the only transactional relationships of significance, and they certainly are not the only ones that you will encounter in your years in practice. Indeed, it is likely that many of the transactions you will encounter will involve businesses engaged in endeavors that do not yet exist. If you practice law for only 30 years, your affairs will be as far removed from the early days of the Internet as your affairs are removed from the Cuban missile crisis and the Vietnam War. Your goal throughout should be to build an understanding of how you can structure transactions and the language that guides them to solve the problems that businesses face in developing and marketing their products. That understanding, in turn, should rest on an underlying sensibility for the circumstances in which the work that you and your client are doing *should* resolve those problems, and when intervention by a broader lawmaking authority is appropriate.

Part One

The Background: Regimes for Resolving Disputes

Chapter 1.   The Background: Regimes for Resolving Disputes

This book covers commercial transactions involving the Internet or some other electronic technology. The goal of the book is to help students understand how lawyers should approach the legal and structural issues raised by electronic commerce transactions. Lawyers cannot address the substantive legal and transactional issues in a sensible way until they know what legal regime will govern disputes related to their transactions. Although that topic might be a minor or ancillary issue in the negotiation of the transaction, it is important as a pedagogical matter to introduce that issue before we begin to move through the substantive issues in Parts Two and Three of this book.

This chapter is organized around two basic issues that a lawyer needs to understand to build a successful transaction. The first is foundational: What legal regimes potentially govern the transaction? More specifically, which jurisdictions have the authority to resolve disputes about the transaction and to declare legal rules that would apply to the transaction? The second issue governs the lawyer's relation to the first question. Can a lawyer, by contract, choose the regime that will govern the transaction?

Assignment 1: Jurisdiction and Conflict of Laws

This assignment introduces a basic question for any transaction: What jurisdictions have the power to resolve disputes and to articulate legal rules for the transaction? The Internet, and especially the Internet businesses whose operations are at the core of this book, present a basic problem in resolving those questions. Legal systems traditionally have resolved those questions by considering the physical location of the parties and the conduct involved, so that a party could be sued wherever the party was physically present and would be governed by the law of the place where the party acted. Because of the ambiguity of location of Internet actors and their transactions, those concepts do not apply easily to Internet businesses.

Moreover, the global reach of the Internet, where purely electronic transactions can have effects in many different jurisdictions, makes those questions much more problematic than they were before. First, they create a fundamental lack of symmetry between the regulatory jurisdiction and the underlying market. Legal systems arguably work best when a single jurisdiction can articulate rules that govern all transactions in a single market. The Internet, however, spans the entire globe, and thus its transactions are not necessarily located in any single territorial jurisdiction. Second, exacerbating the first, the Internet lowers the threshold for transnational economic activity. Just a decade ago, only a small number of the largest companies regularly engaged in activities in numerous countries—the number was so small that the term *multinational* is synonymous with that small number of fully global enterprises. However, with the Internet, even a very small company—or a single blogger—can engage in activity that has substantial economic effects in literally hundreds of countries. Because the burdens on those companies of litigating in multiple fora are quite different from the burdens on conventional multinational companies, the tensions of allocating jurisdictional authority will be *both* more common *and* more problematic in the Internet age.

A. Jurisdiction and Internet Commerce

A fundamental concern for any business is to know which governing bodies will adjudicate disputes in which it is involved. For an American business engaged in electronic commerce, that inquiry breaks down into several categories. Among other things, it is important to understand the basic American rules that determine where a company can be sued within the United States and the rules concerning the enforcement of judgments within the United States.

Given the nature of electronic commerce, it also is important to understand the rules other countries apply to those problems.

1.   Minimum Contacts and Internet Commerce

In the United States, the ability of a court to entertain a lawsuit against a defendant depends on personal jurisdiction over the defendant. The rules on personal jurisdiction, in turn, depend on the Due Process Clause of the Fourteenth Amendment. Those rules generally permit courts to exercise jurisdiction in cases in which the defendant has adequate "contact" with the forum in which the court is located. During the decade since commercial interaction on the Internet began, courts have struggled to articulate general rules to determine when the operator of a Web site is subject to suit in a particular forum. Early cases tried to articulate special rules applicable only to Web sites. For example, the prominent early decision in Zippo Mfg. Co. v. Zippo Dot Com, Inc., 952 F. Supp. 1119, 1124 (W.D. Pa. 1997), reasoned that decisions about jurisdiction should turn on a "sliding scale" of how interactive the Web site is: Passive sites might not be subject to widespread jurisdiction, while interactive sites would be subject to jurisdiction more broadly.

More recent cases have retreated from those efforts to articulate Internet-specific rules, instead attempting to examine activity on a case-by-case basis directly under the general principles the Supreme Court has articulated for personal jurisdiction in other contexts. For example, in cases addressing the question whether jurisdiction exists to adjudicate, the cases often consider whether the activity has had a substantial effect in the forum state. The most notable case of that sort is Panavision International, L.P. v. Toeppen, 141 F.3d 1316 (9th Cir. 1998). In that case, a cybersquatter was held subject to personal jurisdiction in California because the target of the cybersquatting scheme was a California entity.

The other common basis for finding jurisdiction over the operator of a Web site is to consider whether the operations of the Web site amount to "availment" of opportunities in the forum state. The case that follows is illustrative of the typical availment analysis.

Neogen Corp. v. Neo Gen Screening, Inc.
282 F.3d 883 (6th Cir. 2002)

RONALD LEE GILMAN, Circuit Judge.
In April of 2000, Neogen Corp. (Neogen), a Michigan corporation, filed suit in the Western District of Michigan against Neo Gen Screening, Inc. (NGS), a Pennsylvania corporation, alleging (1) trademark infringement, (2) federal dilution and unfair competition, (3) violation of the Michigan Consumer Protection Act, (4) violation of the Michigan Pricing and Advertising Act, and (5) unjust enrichment. The district court dismissed the suit in August of 2000 for lack of personal jurisdiction over NGS pursuant to Rule 12(b)(2) of the Federal Rules of Civil Procedure. Neogen has appealed. For the reasons set forth below, we reverse the judgment of the district court and remand the case for further proceedings consistent with this opinion.

BACKGROUND

Neogen is in the business of developing and marketing a range of health care, food, and animal-related products and services, including certain diagnostic test kits. Its principal place of business is in Lansing, Michigan, but Neogen also has places of business in Florida, Illinois, and Kentucky. Neogen alleges that it has used the "Neogen" name and trademark continuously and extensively in interstate commerce, and that it has registered the mark with theU.S. Patent and Trademark Office. Its website is found at www.neogen.com.

NGS performs diagnostic testing of blood samples from newborn infants. A closely held Pennsylvania corporation, NGS has its sole place of business in Pittsburgh. Approximately ninety percent of the 215,000 tests that NGS performed in 1999 were generated through contracts with hospitals and governmental agencies around the world, none of which were located in Michigan. The remainder of the tests performed by NGS in 1999 were done at the request of individual physicians or coroners with whom NGS did not have a prior contract. Such customers not under contract can obtain testing services by telephoning or e-mailing NGS to request information and "filter blood-collection forms." NGS then mails the collection form to the customer, who collects the sample and sends it back to the company in a pre-addressed return envelope for testing. The customer can then obtain the test results through the mail, or on NGS's website with a password provided by the company. Customers pay for the tests by mailing a check to NGS's Pittsburgh office. NGS tested 14 blood samples from Michigan coroners in 1999, and anticipated about the same number for 2000. In earlier years, NGS also received and tested an undisclosed number of samples from Michigan residents.

NGS's only continuous advertising is through its website, www.neogen-screening.com. The website provides information about NGS's services, lists the e-mail addresses of personnel, and allows prospective customers to print blood-collection forms to be mailed along with blood samples to Pittsburgh. NGS's website is internationally accessible. Neogen claims that NGS's contacts with Michigan through its website and its approximately 14 yearly mail-order transactions with Michigan customers subject NGS to the jurisdiction of the United States District Court for the Western District of Michigan.

Based upon its conclusion that the exercise of personal jurisdiction over NGS would violate due process, the district court granted NGS's motion to dismiss pursuant to Rule 12(b)(2) of the Federal Rules of Civil Procedure. . . .

Neogen appeals the dismissal. . . .

II.   ANALYSIS

. . . C.   The district court erred in concluding that Neogen failed to present a prima facie case of personal jurisdiction over NGS

. . . 2.   Neogen has presented a prima facie case that Michigan's "long-arm" statute authorizes limited personal jurisdiction over NGS

Michigan's long-arm statute extends "limited" jurisdiction over nonresident corporations pursuant to Mich. Comp. Laws §600.715, and "general" jurisdiction pursuant to Mich. Comp. Laws §600.711. Limited jurisdiction extends only to claims arising from the defendant's activities that were either within Michigan or had an in-state effect. General jurisdiction, on the other hand, enables a court in Michigan to exercise jurisdiction over a corporation regardless of whether the claim at issue is related to its activities in the state or has an in-state effect.

Mich. Comp. Laws §600.715 extends limited personal jurisdiction over a non-resident corporation in claims "arising out of the act or acts which create any of the following relationships," including: "[t]he transaction of any business within the state" under §600.715(1), "[t]he doing or causing of any act to be done, or consequences to occur, in the state resulting in an action for tort" under §600.715(2), and the "[e]ntering into a contract for services to be performed or for materials to be furnished in the state by the defendant" under §600.715(5).

The "transaction of any business" necessary for limited personal jurisdiction under §600.715(1) is established by the slightest act of business in Michigan. [Quotation marks and citation omitted.] Neogen has presented a prima facie case that NGS transacted business in Michigan when it accepted blood for testing from Michigan, mailed the test results to Michigan, made the results accessible to its Michigan customers on its website, and accepted payment through the mail from Michigan.

The "arising out of" requirement of §600.715 is satisfied because the alleged economic harm and trademark infringement that form the basis of Neogen's suit were directly related to NGS's transaction of business in Michigan. Viewing the allegations in the light most favorable to Neogen, the economic harm of which it complains can be construed as resulting from NGS's conduct of business with Michigan residents over the wires, through the mail, and by use of the Internet.

Neogen has also presented a prima facie case that limited jurisdiction exists over NGS under §600.715(2), based upon Neogen's allegation that the use of NGS's website and tradename in dealing with its Michigan customers has caused an adverse economic effect upon Neogen in Michigan. . . . In addition, Neogen has presented a prima facie case that limited jurisdiction exists under §600.715(5) because NGS's blood-test transactions with Michigan residents constitute "entering into a contract for services to be performed or for materials to be furnished in the state by the defendant." Part of NGS's service is the packaging of the information revealed by the tests. When NGS provided passwords to Michigan customers or mailed them the test results, this constituted the performance of services and the furnishing of materials in the state within the meaning of §600.715(5).

In order to be subject to general jurisdiction in Michigan, a nonconsenting, nonresident corporation such as NGS must have carried on "a continuous and systematic part of its general business" within Michigan. Mich. Comp. Laws §600.711(3). We decline to decide the broader issue of whether general jurisdiction exists under the facts of this case, however, because Neogen has presented a prima facie case that limited jurisdiction is present.

3. The district court erred in concluding that due process would be violated by Michigan's exercise of limited personal jurisdiction over NGS

Although Michigan's long-arm statute authorizes personal jurisdiction over NGS, a court in Michigan cannot exercise its personal jurisdiction in violation of NGS's constitutional right to due process. In order to survive NGS's motion to dismiss, Neogen was required to present a prima facie case that the district court's exercise of personal jurisdiction would not offend due process. Neogen must therefore establish with reasonable particularity sufficient "minimum contacts" with Michigan so that the exercise of jurisdiction over NGS would not offend "traditional notions of fair play and substantial justice." [*International Shoe v. Washington*, 326U.S. 310, 316 (1945).]

The minimum-contacts requirement is met if NGS "purposely avail[ed] itself of the privilege of conducting activities within the forum State." [*Hanson v. Denckla*, 357 U.S. 235, 253 (1958).] "Purposeful availment," the "constitutional touchstone" of personal jurisdiction, is present where the defendant's contacts with the forum state "proximately result from actions by the defendant *himself* that create a 'substantial connection' with the forum State," *Burger King Corp. v. Rudzewicz*, 471U.S. 462, 475 (1985) [emphasis by *Burger King* Court], and where the defendant's conduct and connection with the forum are such that he "should reasonably anticipate being haled into court there." *Id.* at 474 (quoting *World-Wide Volkswagen Corp. v. Woodson*, 444 U.S. 286, 295 (1980)). "This 'purposeful availment' requirement ensures that a defendant will not be haled into a jurisdiction solely as a result of 'random,' 'fortuitous,' or 'attenuated' contacts, or of the 'unilateral activity of another party or a third person.' " *Burger King Corp.*, 471 U.S. at 475.

This court has distilled these due process requirements into a three-part test. In order for a court to assert limited personal jurisdiction over an out-of-state defendant, the following three criteria must be met:

> First, the defendant must purposefully avail himself of the privilege of acting in the forum state or causing a consequence in the forum state. Second, the cause of action must arise from the defendant's activities there. Finally, the acts of the defendant or consequences caused by the defendant must have a substantial enough connection with the forum state to make the exercise of jurisdiction over the defendant reasonable.

S. Mach. Co. v. Mohasco Indus., Inc., 401 F.2d 374, 381 (6th Cir. 1968).

Turning to the first *Mohasco* requirement, NGS contends that it did not purposefully avail itself of the benefits of Michigan law because, rather than reach out to Michigan, it engaged in nothing more than a passive availment of Michigan opportunities. Neogen, however, argues that NGS "purposefully availed" itself of the privilege of acting in Michigan by maintaining an "interactive" website, responding to business inquiries from Michigan residents, mailing completed test results to Michigan customers, and accepting payment by mail from these customers.

A defendant purposefully avails itself of the privilege of acting in a state through its website if the website is interactive to a degree that reveals specifically intended interaction with residents of the state. *Zippo Mfg. Co. v. Zippo Dot Com, Inc.*, 952 F. Supp. 1119, 1124 (W.D. Pa. 1997) (using a "sliding scale" of interactivity to identify Internet activity that constitutes purposeful availment). In *Zippo,* the district court held that the defendant manifested its purposeful availment of the privilege of acting in Pennsylvania when it "repeatedly and consciously chose to process Pennsylvania residents' applications and to assign them passwords," knowing that the result of these Internet contacts would be to perform services for Pennsylvania customers in part through the transmission of electronic messages to Pennsylvania. *Id.* at 1126. Such intentional interaction with the residents of a forum state, the *Zippo* court concluded, is evidence of a conscious choice to transact business with inhabitants of a forum state in a way that the passive posting of information accessible from anywhere in the world is not. *Id.*

The maintenance of NGS's website, in and of itself, does not constitute the purposeful availment of the privilege of acting in Michigan. An Internet website by its very nature can be accessed internationally. By maintaining a website in Pennsylvania, NGS is no more benefitting from the laws of Michigan than from the laws of any other state. The level of contact with a state that occurs simply from the fact of a website's availability on the Internet is therefore an "attenuated" contact that falls short of purposeful availment.

In the present case, NGS's website consists primarily of passively posted information. The website advertises NGS's services and provides basic contact information. Several aspects of the website, however, support a finding of purposeful availment. When Michigan residents purchase NGS's services, for example, NGS provides them with passwords to access their test results on the website from Michigan. The granting of passwords to Michigan residents as part of a contract for NGS's services is an interactive usage showing that NGS has intentionally reached out to Michigan customers and enabled them to use NGS's services from Michigan. Another aspect of the website that supports purposeful availment, even if passive, is the fact that NGS holds itself out as welcoming Michigan business. On the website, NGS states that it will "do a genetic newborn screening test for any parent in any state," and enables Michigan residents to print out the testing form to send along with payment. NGS also posts on its website a chart showing the "results of screening 4,579 infant deaths with unknown cause," including a geographical breakdown of data that expressly includes Michigan. This chart suggests that NGS has used data collected from Michigan residents to complete this study, and holds itself out as having done so.

Whether NGS's website alone would be sufficient to sustain personal jurisdiction in Michigan, however, is a close question that need not be decided in this appeal. This is because NSG's website is not its only contact with the state. The website must be considered alongside NGS's other interactions with Michigan residents. Most significantly, when potential customers from Michigan have contacted NGS to purchase its services, NGS has welcomed their individual business on a regular basis.

The district court did not consider NGS's 14 yearly contracts with Michigan customers to be "purposeful availment." In so doing, it properly rejected Neogen's contention that NGS "must manifest a desire to not do business in Michigan." Rather, "purposeful availment" is something akin to a deliberate undertaking to do or cause an act or thing to be done in Michigan or conduct which can be properly regarded as a prime generating cause of the effects resulting in Michigan, something more than a passive availment of Michigan opportunities. [Citation and quotation marks omitted.] . . .

The district court also erred in concluding that the 14 yearly contracts with Michigan customers were insufficient to establish personal jurisdiction over NGS because they represented an insignificant percentage of NGS's overall business. The proper test for personal jurisdiction is not based on a "percentage of business" analysis as contended by NGS, but rather on whether the absolute amount of business conducted by NGS in Michigan represents something more than "random, fortuitous, or attenuated contacts" with the state. *Burger King*, 471 U.S. at 475.

Neogen's allegations constitute a prima facie showing that NGS's contacts with Michigan customers are more than random or fortuitous events. Although customers from Michigan contacted NGS, and not the other way around, NGS could not mail test results to and accept payment from customers with Michigan addresses without intentionally choosing to conduct business in Michigan. This establishes that NGS chose to contract with customers from Michigan. Additionally, a part of NGS's service is the packaging of the results of the tests that it performs. When NGS mails these test results to its Michigan customers, or sends them a password to be used interactively on its website, NGS reaches out to Michigan to perform its services there. Neogen has therefore alleged facts which, when viewed in the light most favorable to Neogen, support a finding that NGS purposefully availed itself of the privilege of doing business in Michigan.

The second *Mohasco* requirement for the exercise of personal jurisdiction — that "the cause of action must arise from the defendant's activities [in the forum state]" — is also satisfied in the present case. *Mohasco*, 401 F.2d at 381. Neogen claims that the use of NGS's tradename on its website and its business contacts with Michigan residents under that name have caused a variety of economic harms in Michigan. Construing the facts in the light most favorable to Neogen, as we must for the purposes of this appeal, it is possible that NGS's activities in Michigan have caused economic injury to Neogen. Such a causal connection satisfies the "arising from" requirement of *Mohasco*.

Finally, Neogen has alleged sufficient facts to present a prima facie case regarding the third *Mohasco* requirement — that "the acts of the defendant or consequences caused by the defendant must have a substantial enough connection with the forum state to make the exercise of jurisdiction over the defendant reasonable" — because NGS's 14 yearly sales in Michigan constitute a "continuous and systematic" part of its business. [*International Shoe*, 326 U.S. at 317.] NGS anticipates from year to year that it will conduct a given level of sales in Michigan. It conducted 14 tests for Michigan customers in 1999, and predicted a similar number for 2000. Although NGS's tests for individual customers do not represent "continuing relationships and obligations" with those particular customers, its predictable yearly business in Michigan does represent such a continuing relationship with the state overall.

NGS's contact with Michigan customers through the mail and the wires is significant because it constitutes the doing of business there, rather than simply the exchange of information.

Because NGS knew that it was doing business with Michigan customers, and performed part of its services in Michigan by mailing test results there and providing special passwords to Michigan customers, NGS could reasonably anticipate being haled into a court in Michigan. Neogen has therefore overcome NGS's due process challenge by establishing a prima facie case that the exercise of personal jurisdiction over NGS by a court in Michigan does not offend "traditional notions of fair play and substantial justice." [*International Shoe*, 326 U.S. at 316.] . . .

III.   CONCLUSION

For all of the reasons set forth above, we reverse the judgment of the district court and remand the case for further proceedings consistent with this opinion.

Perhaps the most difficult problems face Internet-based businesses that sell goods or services through a Web site. As the introduction suggests, it is much easier for a small business to operate nationwide or globally on the Internet than using a conventional distribution system. At the same time, as the following case notes, a broad nationwide business generally is subject to personal jurisdiction in all of the jurisdictions into which it sells a substantial amount of its products. As you read the following case, consider whether the result would be different for a small Internet-only retailer with a nationwide distribution system.

Gator.com Corp. v. L.L. Bean, Inc.

341 F.3d 1072 (9th Cir. 2003)

Before FERGUSON, BRUNETTI, and TASHIMA, Circuit Judges.
FERGUSON, Circuit Judge.

This case presents the issue of whether the District Court has personal jurisdiction over Defendant-Appellee L.L. Bean, Inc. ("L.L. Bean"), either because L.L. Bean's contacts with California as a result of its sales and other activities in California are "substantial" or "continuous and systematic," or because L.L. Bean sent a cease-and-desist letter to the Plaintiff, Gator.com Corp. ("Gator"), at its office in California. In response to L.L. Bean's motion for dismissal, the District Court determined that it did not have in personam jurisdiction. Because we determine that L.L. Bean's contacts with California, in particular its substantial mail-order and internet-based commerce in the state, are sufficient to support the assertion of general personal jurisdiction, we reverse the District Court's decision and remand for further proceedings.

I.

A.   Factual Background

Defendant/Appellee L.L. Bean is a Maine corporation with its principal place of business in that state. Its corporate offices, distribution facilities, and manufacturing facilities are all located in Maine. L.L. Bean sells clothing and outdoor equipment and maintains stores in Maine, Delaware, New Hampshire, Oregon, and Virginia. In total, L.L. Bean sells over one billion dollars worth of merchandise annually to consumers in 150 different countries.

A very large percentage of L.L. Bean's sales come from mail-order and internet business. The company ships approximately 200 million catalogs each year. In 2000, its website sales accounted for over two hundred million, or about 16 percent, of its total sales. A September 2000 *New York Times* article described L.L. Bean as "an e-commerce star that is out-performing all but a few companies in its categories on the Web." Bob Tedeschi, *L.L. Bean Beats the Current by Staying in Midstream,* N.Y. Times, Sept. 20, 2000, at H7. The same article quoted an L.L. Bean senior executive as stating that "[t]he Web is the fastest-growing, most profitable source of revenue for [L.L. Bean], . . . [a]nd it's been the primary area for generating new customers." *Id.*

L.L. Bean is not authorized to do business in California, has no agent for service of process in California, and is not required to pay taxes in California. However, in the year 2000 alone, L.L. Bean sold millions of dollars worth of products in California (about 6 percent of its total sales) through its catalog, its toll-free telephone number, and its internet website. In the same year, L.L. Bean also mailed a substantial number of catalogs and packages to California residents, targeted substantial numbers of California residents for direct email solicitation, and maintained substantial numbers of "on-line" accounts for California consumers. Like other internet customers, California residents may view and purchase products online as well as interact with L.L. Bean customer service representatives "live" over the internet if they have questions or concerns with an L.L. Bean product.

In addition, L.L. Bean conducts national print and broadcast marketing efforts that include, but according to L.L. Bean do not target, California. L.L. Bean also maintains relationships with numerous California vendors from whom they purchase products. Other than for the year 2000, L.L. Bean has not provided information regarding the contacts its employees have had with California or any purchases of goods from California.

Plaintiff/Appellant Gator.com Corp. is a Delaware corporation with its principal place of business in California. Gator develops and distributes software ("the Gator program") to consumers who purchase goods or services over the internet. The Gator program provides a "digital wallet" which stores computer user passwords to various websites, user personal information, and credit card information. In addition, when a user visits a website on the internet, the Gator program analyzes the Uniform Resource Locator ("URL") associated with that web page. When it recognizes certain URLs that have been pre-selected by Gator, the program displays a pop-up window offering a coupon for a competitor. Gator users who visit L.L. Bean's website are offered coupons for one of L.L. Bean's competitors, Eddie Bauer, via a pop-up window that at least partially obscures L.L. Bean's website.

On March 16, 2001, L.L. Bean's counsel mailed Gator a cease-and-desist letter requesting that Gator stop its pop-up windows from appearing when customers visited L.L. Bean's website. . . .

B.   Procedural History

On March 19, 2001, Gator filed a declaratory judgment action in the District Court for the Northern District of California, requesting a judgment that the Gator program "does not infringe, or dilute, directly or contributorily, any trademark held by [L.L. Bean] and does not constitute unfair competition, a deceptive or unfair trade or sales practice, false advertising, fraud, or any other violation of either federal or state law." On July 16, 2001, L.L. Bean filed a Motion to Dismiss, along with a Declaration of Support, alleging that the District Court lacked personal jurisdiction. On November 21, 2001, after a hearing, the District Court granted L.L. Bean's motion, finding that neither general nor specific jurisdiction existed. On December 21, 2001, Gator filed this timely appeal. . . .

III.

. . . The assertion of personal jurisdiction satisfies due process so long as there are "minimum contacts" with the forum state "such that the maintenance of the suit does not offend 'traditional notions of fair play and substantial justice.' " *Int'l Shoe Co. v. Washington,* 326 U.S. 310, 316 (1945) (quoting *Milliken v. Meyer,* 311 U.S. 457, 463 (1940)). These requirements "give[ ] a degree of predictability to the legal system that allows potential defendants to structure their primary conduct with some minimum assurance as to where that conduct will and will not render them liable to suit." *World-Wide Volkswagen Corp. v. Woodson,* 444 U.S. 286, 297 (1980).

Personal jurisdiction may be either general or specific. General jurisdiction exists when there are "substantial" or "continuous and systematic" contacts with the forum state, even if the cause of action is unrelated to those contacts. *Helicopteros Nacionales de Colombia, S.A. v. Hall,* 466 U.S. 408, 415 (1984). Specific jurisdiction may be asserted "if the case arises out of certain forum-related acts." *Id.* Whether dealing with specific or general jurisdiction, the touchstone remains purposeful availment to ensure that a defendant will not be haled into a jurisdiction solely as a result of random, fortuitous, or attenuated contacts. [Brackets, quotation marks, and citations omitted.] The goal of the "purposeful availment" requirement is to give the corporation "clear notice that it is subject to suit [in the forum State]" so that it "can act to alleviate the risk of burdensome litigation by procuring insurance, passing the expected costs on to customers, or, if the risks are too great, severing its connection with the State." *World-Wide Volkswagen,* 444 U.S. at 297.

We begin with an analysis of whether L.L. Bean's contacts with California were sufficient to confer general jurisdiction.[2] The standard for establishing general jurisdiction is fairly high. [Brackets, quotation marks, and citations omitted.] These contacts with the forum state must be of a sort that approximate physical presence. [Quotation marks and citations omitted]; *but see Int'l Shoe,* 326 U.S. at 316-317 ("[T]he terms 'present' or 'presence' are used merely to symbolize those activities of the corporation's agent within the state which courts will deem to be sufficient to satisfy the demands of due process.") Factors to be taken into consideration are whether the defendant makes sales, solicits or engages in business in the state, serves the state's markets, designates an agent for service of process, holds a license, or is incorporated there. [Quotation marks and citations omitted.] We focus upon the economic reality of the defendant's activities rather than a mechanical checklist. [Ellipses, quotation marks, and citations omitted.] Even if substantial, or continuous and systematic, contacts exist, the assertion of general jurisdiction must be reasonable.

A. Substantial or Continuous and Systematic Contacts Test

In applying the "substantial" or "continuous and systematic" contacts test, courts have focused primarily on two areas. First, they look for some kind of deliberate "presence" in the forum state, including physical facilities, bank accounts, agents, registration, or incorporation. *See Perkins v. Benguet Consol. Mining Co.,* 342 U.S. 437 (1952) (finding general jurisdiction when president of Phi[l]ipines-based corporation maintained office, kept company files, held director meetings, distributed salaries, and conducted other company business in the forum state). In addition, courts have looked at whether the company has engaged in active solicitation toward and participation in the state's markets, i.e., the economic reality of the defendant's activities in the state.

In *Helicopteros,* the Supreme Court considered both of these factors and found no general jurisdiction in Texas. The case involved a defendant whose contacts

---

2. Because we hold that there is general jurisdiction in this case, we do not address whether specific jurisdiction is present on the basis of L.L. Bean's cease-and-desist letter.

consisted of sending its CEO to Houston for meetings, drawing checks on a Houston bank, and purchasing large quantities of helicopters and training for the helicopters from a Texas supplier. *Helicopteros,* 466 U.S. at 416. After noting the absence of traditional presence factors—an agent, license to do business, incorporation, or physical facilities—the Supreme Court also noted that the defendant "never . . . performed . . . operations in Texas or sold any product that reached Texas, [and] never solicited business in Texas." *Id.* at 411.

No Supreme Court cases and only a handful of Ninth Circuit cases have addressed the issue of when and whether general jurisdiction may be asserted over a company that does business on the internet. The most relevant of our cases, [*Bancroft & Masters, Inc. v. Augusta Nat'l, Inc.,* 223 F.3d 1082 (9th Cir. 2000)], held that the defendant's contacts were insufficient to confer general jurisdiction. In addition to not being registered or licensed to do business in California, the defendant in *Bancroft* did not pay taxes or maintain a bank account in California and "target[ed] no print, television, or radio advertising toward California." 223 F.3d at 1086. In addition, the court found that the defendant's website was "'passive,' i.e., consumers cannot use it to make purchases." *Id.* Finally, the court found that neither the defendant's "occasional, unsolicited sales of tournament tickets and merchandise to California residents" nor a few licensing agreements that the defendant had made with California vendors were sufficient to create general jurisdiction, as these contacts "constitute doing business with California, but do not constitute doing business in California." *Id.*

Given the high standard the Ninth Circuit has set, the presence of general jurisdiction in the instant case is a close question. Admittedly, L.L. Bean has few of the factors traditionally associated with physical presence, such as an official agent or incorporation. Nevertheless, we find that there is general jurisdiction in light of L.L. Bean's extensive marketing and sales in California, its extensive contacts with California vendors, and the fact that, as alleged by Gator, its website is clearly and deliberately structured to operate as a sophisticated virtual store in California.

First, L.L. Bean's overall commercial contacts with California meet the continuous and systematic contacts test applied in *Helicopteros.* The facts as alleged by Gator indicate that L.L. Bean meets the first set of factors set out in these cases: it makes sales, solicits business in the state, and serves the state's markets. In addition, unlike the defendant in *Bancroft,* Gator alleges that L.L. Bean "targets" its electronic advertising at California and maintains a highly interactive, as opposed to "passive," website from which very large numbers of California consumers regularly make purchases and interact with L.L. Bean sales representatives. Unlike the defendant in *Helicopteros,* L.L. Bean has not merely made a single "package" purchase from a forum vendor or cashed a check on a forum bank; instead, it ships very large numbers of products to California and maintains ongoing contacts with numerous California vendors. Nor are any of L.L. Bean's contacts occasional or infrequent. L.L. Bean's contacts are part of a consistent, ongoing, and sophisticated sales effort that has included California for a number of years.

In short, even under the heightened standard applied to general jurisdiction, the consistent and substantial pattern of business relations represented by these facts is sufficient to confer general jurisdiction. [Quotation marks and citation omitted.] There is nothing "random, fortuitous, or attenuated" about subjecting L.L. Bean to the authority of the court as L.L. Bean has deliberately and purposefully availed itself, on a very large scale, of the benefits of doing business within the state. *See* [*Burger King Corp. v. Rudzewicz,* 471 U.S. 462, 475 (1985)]; *Asahi Metal Indus. Co. v. Superior Court,* 480 U.S. 102, 112 (1987).[7]

Second, even if the only contacts L.L. Bean had with California were through its virtual store, a finding of general jurisdiction in the instant case would be consistent with the "sliding scale" test that both our own and other circuits have applied to internet-based companies. This test requires both that the party in question "clearly [do] business over the Internet," *Zippo Mfg. Co. v. Zippo Dot Com, Inc.,* 952 F. Supp. 1119, 1124 (W.D. Pa. 1997),[8] and that the internet business contacts with the forum state be substantial or continuous and systematic. Recognizing that an online store can operate as the functional equivalent of a physical store, the test does not require an actual presence in the state. Rather, the nature of the commercial activity must be of a substantial enough nature that it approximate[s] physical presence. [Quotation mark and citations omitted.]

Applying this test, the District of Columbia Circuit recently found general jurisdiction after finding that a defendant online brokerage firm was "through its website . . . doing business in the District of Columbia" where customers could use the website to open accounts, transmit funds to those accounts electronically, use the accounts to buy and sell securities, and enter into binding contracts with the defendant. *Gorman v. Ameritrade Holding Corp.,* 293 F.3d 506, 512-13 (D.C.Cir. 2002) (citing *Zippo,* 952 F. Supp. at 1124). . . .

Under the sliding-scale analysis, L.L. Bean's contacts with California are sufficient to confer general jurisdiction. L.L. Bean's website is highly interactive and very extensive: L.L. Bean "clearly does business over the Internet." *See Zippo,* 952 F. Supp. at 1124. Moreover, millions of dollars in sales, driven by an extensive, ongoing, and sophisticated sales effort involving very large numbers of direct email solicitations and millions of catalog sales, qualifies as "substantial" or "continuous and systematic" commercial activity.

The District Court erred in concluding that there was no general jurisdiction in this case. We now proceed to consider whether assertion of general jurisdiction over L.L. Bean is reasonable.

B. Reasonableness Test

Even if there are sufficient contacts to support general jurisdiction in a particular case, it is still limited by a reasonableness analysis. . . .

---

7. Gator also points to the Supreme Court's decision in Quill Corp. v. North Dakota as supportive of its position. [*Quill* is reprinted in Assignment 16.] *Quill* involved a state's request for a declaratory judgment that an out-of-state mail-order company with no physical presence in the state had sufficient "minimum contacts" with the state to justify the imposition of a sales tax. *See* Quill Corp. v. North Dakota, 504 U.S. 298 (1992). Although the Court eventually concluded that the imposition of a tax would violate the "substantial nexus" requirement of the Commerce Clause, it also concluded, applying the reasoning of *International Shoe* and *Burger King,* that "the imposition of the collection duty on a mail-order house that is engaged in continuous and widespread solicitation of business within a State [would not violate Due Process]." *Id.* at 308, 312.

8. [T]he likelihood that personal jurisdiction can be constitutionally exercised is directly proportionate to the nature and quality of commercial activity that an entity conducts over the Internet. . . . At one end of the spectrum are situations where a defendant clearly does business over the Internet. If the defendant enters into contracts with residents of a foreign jurisdiction that involve the knowing and repeated transmission of computer files over the Internet, personal jurisdiction is proper. At the opposite end . . . a defendant has simply posted information on an Internet Web site which is accessible to [forum resident] users. . . . The middle ground is occupied by interactive Web sites where a user can exchange information with the host computer.

L.L. Bean asserts that three . . . factors cut in its favor: the extent of purposeful interjection, the burden on L.L. Bean of litigating in California, and the availability of an alternative forum. . . .

As discussed above, there is substantial evidence that L.L. Bean has purposefully interjected itself into the California market. Even conceding that this may be a close case for general jurisdiction, this factor does not create a compelling case for unreasonableness. [Quotation marks and citation omitted.] To the contrary, the extensive nature of L.L. Bean's interjection cuts in Gator's favor.

L.L. Bean also argues that defending this litigation would impose a substantial burden on it because its principal place of business and its corporate records and personnel are all located in Maine. This argument lends little support to L.L. Bean's case, given that it is a multi-million dollar company that concedes that its agents regularly do business around the country, including flying to California to meet with vendors. Nor does this case present issues whose disposition will rely on access to L.L. Bean's facilities or records. Moreover, the burden on Gator if it were forced to proceed in Maine would be at least equal to, if not more severe, than the burden faced by L.L. Bean. In short, L.L. Bean presents no evidence that the inconvenience is so great as to constitute a deprivation of due process. [Brackets, quotation marks, and citation omitted.]

Finally, L.L. Bean asserts that because Gator has filed an almost identical declaratory action in the District Court of Oregon, Gator has failed to show that there is no alternative forum available. While this factor does cut in L.L. Bean's favor, it does not make assertion of jurisdiction unreasonable. We therefore find that L.L. Bean has not presented a compelling case that general jurisdiction is unreasonable.

IV.

It is increasingly clear that modern businesses no longer require an actual physical presence in a state in order to engage in commercial activity there. With the advent of "e-commerce," businesses may set up shop, so to speak, without ever actually setting foot in the state where they intend to sell their wares. Our conceptions of jurisdiction must be flexible enough to respond to the realities of the modern marketplace. "As technological progress . . . increase[s] the flow of commerce between States, the need for jurisdiction over nonresidents [undergoes] a similar increase. . . . In response to these changes, the requirements for personal jurisdiction over nonresidents [evolve]." *Hanson v. Denckla,* 357 U.S. 235, 250-251 (1958). Businesses who structure their activities to take full advantage of the opportunities that virtual commerce offers can reasonably anticipate that these same activities will potentially subject them to suit in the locales that they have targeted.

We find that the facts as alleged by Gator demonstrate that L.L. Bean has substantial or continuous and systematic contacts with California sufficient to support a finding of general jurisdiction. The decision of the District Court is reversed and we remand for further proceedings consistent with this opinion.

As this book goes to press, *Gator.com* has just been argued before the Ninth Circuit sitting en banc. One interesting point about the rules for personal jurisdiction, noted in passing by the *Gator.com* court, is the premise that a business that wishes to avoid suit in a particular jurisdiction can simply refrain from doing business there. How simple would that be considering that the technology makes it difficult to verify the physical location of persons with whom the site is interacting?

As a final note, one practical problem related to the personal jurisdiction question is how to effect service of process on entities that can be identified only through their operation of a Web site. On that question, the Ninth Circuit has held (in what appears to be a case of first impression) that in such a case service by e-mail was appropriate under the Federal Rules. Rio Properties, Inc. v. Rio International Interlink, 284 F.3d 1007 (9th Cir. 2002).

2. Judgment Enforcement

If the plaintiff in a dispute arising out of interstate Internet commerce obtains a judgment in either a federal or state court in the United States, and if the defendant does not voluntarily comply with the terms of the judgment, the plaintiff may wish to take steps to enforce the judgment in another jurisdiction. If the judgment was rendered by a federal court, the plaintiff merely has to register the judgment in a federal jurisdiction in which the defendant has assets to begin the process of enforcing the judgment in that jurisdiction. 28 U.S.C. §1963. With regard to a judgment rendered in the courts of one state, the Constitution requires that the courts of other states must give it "Full Faith and Credit." U.S. Const. Art. IV, §1. Full faith and credit does not require automatic acceptance of another state's judgment—for example, the defendant has an opportunity to establish that the rendering state did not have personal jurisdiction—but as a general rule it precludes most challenges to the rendering court's resolution of the underlying dispute.

There is not, however, any uniform national system for giving effect to sister-state judgments. Some states permit the judgments of "foreign" states to be registered in a manner similar to the process for federal-court judgments, but other states require a new lawsuit to give effect to the first state-court judgment. Forty-six states have enacted the 1964 Uniform Enforcement of Foreign Judgments Act. Despite the implication suggested by its name, that statute applies only to the recognition of sister-state judgments, not judgments obtained in foreign countries (or even in federal courts). This law creates a summary procedure for "domesticating" a judgment rendered by the courts of another state, provided that the plaintiff can show that the first proceeding provided due process of law. Once that process has been completed, the plaintiff can enforce the judgment against assets in the new jurisdiction.

3. Cross-Border Issues

Internet transactions, of course, are not confined to parties that reside in the United States. Thus, it is important to consider the circumstances in which courts of another country can exercise jurisdiction over the operator of a Web-based business. On that point, international law imposes substantial limitations on the authority of a country to exercise jurisdiction in disputes between its own citizens and parties that do not reside in that country. Generally, a country has authority to exercise jurisdiction if the dispute involves conduct that took place within its borders or that has or is intended to have a substantial effect within its borders. In addition, a country generally has authority to regulate the behavior of non-resident foreigners either outside or within its territory if the behavior affects the activities and interests of its citizens. In analyzing whether a country can subject a non-resident foreigner to its legal processes, the traditional framework considers whether a country has "jurisdiction to prescribe," "jurisdiction to adjudicate," or "jurisdiction to enforce." Jurisdiction to prescribe refers to the authority of a country to regulate the behavior of non-resident foreigners, whether by legislation, administrative regulation, or judicial precedent. Jurisdiction to adjudicate refers to the authority of a country to subject non-resident foreigners to civil or criminal proceedings in its courts. Jurisdiction to enforce refers to the authority to compel compliance or punish non-compliance with its laws.

(a) Jurisdiction to Prescribe and Adjudicate

Modern approaches to the problem of jurisdiction in cross-border disputes emphasize the need for any exercise of jurisdiction to be reasonable. This is a considerable advance over older approaches, which tolerated what are now labeled "exorbitant" bases of jurisdiction. For example, France has long claimed jurisdiction over any defendant in a dispute in which the plaintiff was French. At the same time, many claim that the United States exercises its authority over affairs too far removed from its realm. For example, complaints about American antitrust law have been commonplace for decades. More recently, to offer an example salient in the context of this course, the World Trade Organization (WTO) has issued a preliminary ruling that American laws regulating offshore gambling are inconsistent with our international trade obligations. So it would be parochial to assume that exorbitant claims of authority are exclusively the province of foreign nations.

Recognizing that historical practice, some argue that France continues to exert exorbitant jurisdiction. In the most prominent example, a French court ruled in November 2000 that Yahoo! had violated French laws that prohibit the dissemination of information about Nazi and holocaust denials by allowing its French customers to access those materials through Yahoo!'s Web site. The court ordered Yahoo! to put filtering systems in place that would block individuals in France from accessing Nazi materials, as recommended by a panel of court-appointed experts. [The court expunged large parts of the opinion of Vinton Cerf (one of the architects of the Internet, and one of the court-appointed experts), presumably because of Cerf's emphasis on the limits of currently available blocking technology. The court also ignored Cerf's observation that the solution proposed by the court would require Yahoo! to violate the European Data Directive, discussed in detail in Assignment 10.]

Yahoo! responded by filing suit against the French plaintiffs in federal court in California, seeking a declaratory judgment that the French court's judgment was not enforceable under U.S. law. Yahoo! argued that the French order was an unreasonable exercise of jurisdiction to prescribe because it violated the First Amendment. The French plaintiffs challenged the authority of the

U.S. court, claiming that the American court had no personal jurisdiction over them. The American court, however, disagreed. It noted that the French plaintiffs had sent cease-and-desist letters to Yahoo! in the United States, demanding that it comply with the judgment of the French court or risk enforcement action being taken against it in the United States. In the court's view, that conduct was adequate to support personal jurisdiction over the French defendants. Yahoo! v. LICRA, 145 F. Supp. 2d 1168 (N.D. Cal. 2001). More recently, the federal court granted Yahoo! a declaratory judgment preventing any enforcement of the French order against Yahoo!'s assets in this country. Finally, the Ninth Circuit held on appeal that the district court did not have personal jurisdiction over the French defendants, thus overturning the declaratory judgment in favor of Yahoo!. Yahoo! v. LICRA, 379 F.3d 1120 (9th Cir. 2004).

Finally, within the European Union (EU), a specific body of law (parallel to our minimum-contacts jurisprudence) establishes a framework for the exercise of jurisdiction by the courts of one country over the citizens of another. That framework starts with the 1968 Brussels Convention, which governs jurisdiction in most civil and commercial matters, including disputes arising in Internet commerce. More recently, that convention was updated by the Brussels I Regulation, which governs relations among all countries in the EU except for Denmark.

In general, both the Brussels Convention and the Brussels I Regulation take a more "formalistic" approach to questions of jurisdiction than U.S. courts are likely to take. For example, Art. 5 of the Brussels Convention and of the Brussels I Regulation both provide that a court located at the place of performance of a contract has jurisdiction to hear disputes involving the contract. The same articles provide for jurisdiction by a court located at the place of the harm caused by tortious conduct. It should be obvious already that any rule that regulates Internet conduct based on its location will be at best unpredictable and at worst arbitrary.

(b)   Jurisdiction to Enforce

When it comes to the enforcement of judgments, U.S. courts have no general obligation to recognize the judgments of foreign courts. Rather, U.S. courts have discretion to honor those judgments under principles of "comity." The standard is one first articulated by the Supreme Court in 1895:

> [W]here there has been an opportunity for a full and fair trial abroad before a court of competent jurisdiction, conducting the trial upon regular proceedings, after due citation or voluntary appearance of the defendant, and under a system of jurisprudence likely to secure an impartial administration of justice between citizens of its own country and those of other countries, and there is nothing to show either prejudice in the court, or in the system of laws under which it was sitting, or fraud in procuring the judgment, or any other special reason why the comity of this nation should not allow it full effect, the merits of the case should not, in an action brought in this country upon the judgment, be tried afresh, as on a new trial or on appeal, upon the mere assertion by the party that the judgment was erroneous in law or in fact.

Hilton v. Guyot, 159 U.S. 113, 203 (1895). Comity is an expression of one nation's respect for its international obligations, balanced against the need to safeguard its own interests and the interest of its own citizens when they have been the subject of legal proceedings in foreign courts. For example, in Hilton v. Guyot itself, the Supreme Court ultimately determined that a judgment rendered against a New York resident doing business in France by a French court was *not* enforceable in the United States. The Court pointed to claims that the French judgment had been obtained by fraud and that French courts would not have given effect to a similar judgment rendered against a French resident doing business in the United States. Similarly, in the Yahoo! case discussed above, the district court ultimately granted Yahoo! a declaratory judgment holding that the French judgment could not be enforced in this country because of First Amendment concerns. Yahoo! v. LICRA, 169 F. Supp. 2d 1181, 1192-1194 (N.D. Cal. 2001).

In state courts, the applicable principles are likely to be those of the Uniform Foreign Money-Judgments Recognition Act, enacted by about 30 states. That statute codifies the common law governing enforcement of foreign judgments and simplifies the procedure a foreign judgment creditor must follow to have a foreign judgment registered in a jurisdiction where the defendant has assets.

The Hague Conference on Private International Law has been working for several years on a draft Convention on Jurisdiction and Foreign Judgments in Civil and Commercial Matters. (The Hague Conference is an intergovernmental organization with more than 50 member states, founded in 1893. The Conference promotes the harmonization of bodies of law that are important in cross-border trade. Among its great successes is the Hague Service Convention, a treaty that governs the service of process on foreign parties in civil and commercial litigation.) The draft treaty, adopted in 1999, would facilitate the enforcement of judgments rendered in one signatory state in the courts of another signatory state. In effect, signatories to such a treaty would undertake to give "full faith and credit" to judgments rendered by other signatory states in much the same manner as the U.S. Constitution requires the courts of each state to give full faith and credit to judgments rendered by another U.S. state. Although many observers agree that this is a good idea in principle, the project has been controversial since it began in 1993. As we write, it remains doubtful that this convention will ever be completed and proposed for adoption.

B.   Conflict of Laws and Internet Commerce

When disputes have a significant relationship to more than one jurisdiction, and the laws of the different jurisdictions that would apply to the dispute are so inconsistent that they would produce different outcomes, then there is a "conflict of laws." In the United States, there have been two attempts to "restate" the law governing conflicts of laws. The first was completed in 1934, the second in 1969. A substantial minority of U.S. jurisdictions still follow the "vested rights" approach of the RESTATEMENT (FIRST) OF CONFLICT OF LAWS. That approach relies on formal rules to determine the applicable law in an objective way; the problem is that the rules are not always easy to apply. For example, the FIRST RESTATEMENT calls for a question of tort liability to be determined under the law of the "place of the wrong," which is defined as the state where the last event necessary to make an actor liable for an alleged tort takes place. RESTATEMENT (FIRST) OF CONFLICT OF LAWS §§377, 378. Although those rules might be relatively clear in simple cases involving personal injury, they are quite imprecise in cases involving business injury in multistate transactions, because it often is arbitrary to locate the injury in one location or another. Similarly, the law of the place of contracting governs issues surrounding contract validity and formation, while questions surrounding breach of the contract are determined by the law of the place the contract is to be performed. RESTATEMENT (FIRST) OF CONFLICT OF LAWS §§311, 358. As suggested above, it is quite arbitrary in Internet situations to determine the place where a contract is formed.

The FIRST RESTATEMENT approach fell from favor among U.S. conflicts academics because of the perception that its highly formalistic rules often led to arbitrary results. Accordingly, conflicts scholars developed a more malleable "governmental interest" approach to the subject, which is to some degree incorporated in the RESTATEMENT (SECOND) OF CONFLICT OF LAWS. That approach focuses on the relation between the subject matter of the dispute and the interests of the different jurisdictions whose law might apply. Ultimately, the SECOND RESTATEMENT allows courts to determine which jurisdiction's law should apply by considering a lengthy list of such factors as the needs of interstate commerce; the relevant policies of the forum where the conflict analysis is being performed; the relevant policies of the other states with a claim to regulate the dispute; the protection of justified expectations; the policies underlying a particular body of law; the need for certainty and predictability of results; and the ease with which the law can be determined and applied. RESTATEMENT (SECOND) OF CONFLICT OF LAWS §6.

Although the SECOND RESTATEMENT approach is popular among U.S. academics, it has not gained universal acceptance from courts in this country. The basic concern—a concern that is of great importance to the business lawyer—is that the rules are so malleable that they make it reasonably simple for a motivated court to justify a determination that its own law should apply to any dispute. Thus, a business lawyer can rarely be sure that a court that has jurisdiction over a dispute (a question that the Supreme Court polices under the Due Process Clause) will not decide to apply its own rules to any dispute presented to it. To get a sense for how malleable interest analysis can be, especially in this context, consider the following opinion.

CAT Internet Services v. Magazines.com Inc.

2001 WL 8858 (E.D. Penn. Jan. 4, 2001)

PADOVA, J.

I. BACKGROUND

Plaintiff CAT Internet Services, Inc. ("CAT") is a Pennsylvania corporation with its principal place of business in Pennsylvania. CAT is an Internet and e-commerce company which owns, licenses, and operates web pages at various domains on the Internet. Plaintiff owns the rights and interest in the domain name www.magazine.com, which it purchased in August 1999. Subsequent to the acquisition, Plaintiff contacted numerous third party vendors to assess interest in converting the site to market and sell conventional, rather than electronic, magazines.

Defendant Magazines.com is a Delaware corporation with its principal place of business in Murfreesboro, Tennessee. Defendant owns the Internet domain address www.magazines.com, through which it sells conventional magazines and magazine subscriptions.

In December 1999, Plaintiff entered into an agreement with a third party, Magazine Mall, Inc., under which the companies agreed to provide links to Internet domain addresses owned and used by Magazine Mall. In January 2000, CAT entered into a similar agreement with E-News. In addition, CAT began discussions with E-News about other possible deals, including selling the domain name to E-News outright, or creating a co-branded site.

Plaintiff alleges that in January 2000, it discovered that the Defendant was utilizing CAT's domain name to redirect Internet traffic to Defendant's web site. . . . On February 28, 2000, Defendant filed a lawsuit in Tennessee state court against CAT, E-News, Magazine Mall, and another party, seeking to enjoin Plaintiff from using its domain name for on-line sales of magazine subscriptions. . . .

Plaintiff further alleges that Defendant has continued to spread false information regarding CAT to its actual and prospective business associates. Plaintiff also alleges Defendant "threatened E-News into refusing to engage in business with CAT by offering to discontinue its lawsuit in Tennessee against E-News if E-News would agree never to engage in any business transaction with CAT again." . . .

III.   DISCUSSION

Defendant claims that Plaintiff . . . fails to state a claim upon which relief can be granted. As a threshold inquiry . . ., the court must first determine which law, Tennessee law or Pennsylvania law, applies to each of the claims asserted. A federal court sitting in a diversity case applies the conflict laws of the state in which it sits. See *Klaxon Co. v. Stentor Elec. Mfg. Co.*, 313 U.S. 487 (1941). Here, the Court applies Pennsylvania's choice-of-law rules. Pennsylvania choice of law analysis consists of two parts. First, the Court examines whether an actual conflict exists. No actual conflict exists where the different laws do not produce different results, and in such a case, courts presume that the law of the forum state applies. A false conflict exists if only one jurisdiction's governmental interests would be impaired by the application of the other jurisdiction's law. In such a case, the law of the impaired district is applied.

If the Court finds there is an actual conflict, it will apply the law of the state that has the greater interest in having its law applied. . . . Courts may consider such issues as the place where the injury occurred; the place where the conduct causing the injury occurred; the domicile, residence, nationality, place of incorporation and place of business of the parties; and the place where the relationship, if any, between the parties is centered. . . .

[Plaintiff] alleges tortious interference with . . . prospective contractual relations. . . .

. . . Plaintiff's prospective contractual relations claim presents an actual conflict between the laws of the two states. Tennessee does not recognize a cause of action for tortious interference with prospective contractual relations. Pennsylvania does recognize a cause of action for tortious interference with prospective contractual relations. Furthermore, the interests of both states are invoked. The Tennessee Supreme Court has chosen not to recognize this tort for two reasons: first, prospective contracts do not involve agreements to be bound, and therefore interference with them does not threaten the integrity of contracting; and second, recognition of the tort would have the tendency to hinder market efficiency. Here, the Defendant would benefit from the Tennessee rule. Pennsylvania, on the other hand, recognizes the tort of interference with prospective contractual relations for the same reasons it recognizes the tort of interference with actual contractual relations; that is, to create predictability and confidence in contracting. Entities contemplating entering into a contract benefit from the Pennsylvania rule.

Having found that a conflict does exist, the Court must next examine which state has the greater interest in having its rule applied, by considering: the place where the injury occurred; the place where the conduct causing the injury occurred; the domicile, residence, nationality, place of incorporation and place of business of the parties; and the place where the relationship, if any, between the parties is centered.

Here, neither state has a monopoly on such interests; however, Pennsylvania has the more significant contacts for purposes of this tort claim. The alleged injury here is damage to Plaintiff's prospective business relationships. When the injury sustained is of a pecuniary nature, the plaintiff's principal place of business is generally considered the place of injury and represents a contact of substantial significance. In this case, the alleged harm to business relationships is centered in Pennsylvania, which is the state of incorporation and the principal place of business of the Plaintiff, and this is a contact of substantial significance. Though Tennessee also has an interest in having its law applied, by virtue of its being the location of the underlying lawsuit, its contacts are not sufficient to outweigh Pennsylvania's interest in the context of this cause of action. The alleged harm here is precisely that envisioned by Pennsylvania law, and Pennsylvania law should apply. . . .

Problem Set 1

1.1. Your client, Tibetan Imports Inc., is a large designer and manufacturer of textile rugs. Tibetan Imports has its U.S. headquarters in Seattle, Washington. A former employee moved to New Mexico and now runs a business (Realrugs.com) that purports to sell antique Persian rugs. Your client is outraged; it claims not only that the rugs are not in fact antiques but also that the rug designs were based on its copyrighted designs. Your client wants to sue Realrugs.com for copyright infringement in Seattle.

(a) Assume that Realrugs.com maintains a Web site that gives a telephone number that prospective customers can call to receive a copy of its paper catalog in the mail. Can Tibetan Imports sue Realrugs.com in Seattle? Does it matter how many rugs Realrugs.com has shipped to Washington?

(b) Assume in addition that the Web site provides forms on which customers can place orders. Can Tibetan Imports sue Realrugs.com in Seattle? Does it matter how many rugs Realrugs.com has shipped to Washington?

(c) Assume in addition that Realrugs.com uses unsolicited commercial e-mail (UCE) to market its services to the public. Does it matter how much UCE has been sent to Washington residents?

(d) Assume in addition that Realrugs.com has a catalog on the Web site that includes images of the allegedly infringing rugs. Can Tibetan Imports sue Realrugs.com in Seattle on a claim that the images in its programs infringe the copyrights of Tibetan Imports? Does it matter if its records do not indicate that Washington residents have viewed the images?

(e) As an aside, assume that a Realrugs.com van hit another car while the driver of that car was driving across New México as part of a move from Georgia to Utah. Can the driver of the car file a personal injury claim against Realrugs.com in Utah after he finally relocates there and hires a personal injury attorney?

1.2.   Student activists in Maine create a Web site (*www.duchampseatspoop. com*) criticizing Duchamps, a multinational chemical company based in Arizona. The site includes message boards with comments posted by individuals opposed to the Duchamps policy of securing patents on the genetic information contained in biological specimens obtained from third-world countries. Duchamps sues the students in federal court in Arizona, claiming trademark dilution in violation of the Lanham Act. Does a federal court in Arizona have jurisdiction over the students?

1.3.   Your friend Donald Branson operates a Web site that publishes reviews of recent texts of Greek and Latin works. Customers pay an annual subscription fee for access to the site. He has a substantial body of customers spread throughout a number of countries. He comes to you quite disgruntled because of a story he just read about the judgment of the High Court of Australia in Gutnick v. Dow Jones & Co. [2001] V.S. Ct. 305 (upholding a verdict against Dow Jones for a story published in the Wall Street Journal alleged to libel an Australian resident). Don is concerned because, based on newspaper accounts of the decision, he is worried that people dissatisfied by his reviews might be able to sue him in any of the countries in which his subscribers are located. What do you have to tell him?

1.4.   Your client, Tibetan Imports, has another problem with a different rug dealer, World Rugs Inc., based in Omaha, Nebraska. It has learned that World Rugs is using a revolutionary new process for adding muted shades to existing rugs to fit each customer's unique décor. Your client claims that this process is its trade secret. It appears that a licensee of its process (flagrantly breaching its contract with your client) shared enough information for World Rugs Inc. to be able to implement the new process. World Rugs Inc. had no actual knowledge that the disclosure to it breached the licensee's agreement with your client. It is clear, though, that a few probing questions before paying for the information would have revealed that the licensee was violating a non-disclosure agreement. Assume that under the law of the State of Washington, a party receiving trade secrets in violation of a duty of confidentiality may be liable to the owner of the trade secret for damages if the receiving party "knew or should have known" that the disclosure constituted a breach of a duty of confidentiality. On the other hand, assume that under the law of Nebraska the receiving party is only liable for damages to the owner of the trade secret if it had actual knowledge and acted in bad faith in receiving the information.

Tibetan Imports wants to sue World Rugs Inc. for violating its trade secret rights. In theory, should it make any difference with regard to the applicable law whether it files the suit in Washington or Nebraska? In practice, is it likely to make any difference? How should a court in either Washington or Nebraska decide which law to apply?

1.5.   For your summer job after your last year in law school, you take a position as an extern at the United Nations Commission on International Trade Laws (UNCITRAL). Your assignment is to write policy papers on issues of interest to the policymakers at UNCITRAL. Your first assignment is to consider a possible UNCITRAL project to develop a World Internet Court. The purpose of the Court would be to provide a uniform adjudicatory process for disputes arising out of activities on the Internet. Your task is to describe (a) the principle benefits of such a court; (b) the types of disputes that appropriately might be heard by it; and (c) any obstacles or problems you see in creating such a court.

Assignment 2: Contractual Choice of Regime

One way to reduce the risk that litigation arising out of cross-border or interstate transactions will occur in a remote or hostile forum is to use contracts that choose a favorable law or forum. A similar but more aggressive approach is to opt out of the judicial system entirely by drafting contracts that require arbitration of any disputes arising out of or related to the contract. Although courts of sovereign nations traditionally have been hostile to contractual limitations on their authority, that hostility has eased during recent decades. Thus, courts in most countries defer to the parties' choice in business transactions, as long as the choice does not offend some important public policy of the forum.

In the context of consumer transactions, however, the trend is less clear. In the United States, courts have extended a similar deference even to transactions that involve consumers. In the European Union, however, a sharp distinction is drawn between the use of such provisions against consumers and against businesses; courts strongly disfavor the use of such terms in transactions with consumers. With the explosion in the volume of cross-border Internet retail trade, the differing perspectives present an increasing prospect for tension. It appears that the European Union is not at all likely to adopt the current U.S. position. Still, criticism of the burdens that unconstrained litigation places on online retail businesses has led the European Union to consider online alternative dispute resolution as a way of accommodating the needs of both consumers and online retailers.

A. Contractual Choice of Law

1. Choice of Law and Interstate Commerce

The topic of choice of law is fundamentally different from the topic of the "conflicts of law" discussed in the preceding assignment. The previous assignment discusses principles that courts use to determine which jurisdiction's law will apply to a particular dispute. Choice of law, by contrast, is a contractual tool that parties use in an attempt to avoid the results courts would reach under applicable conflicts principles. Because conflicts principles are relatively indeterminate, parties to business transactions usually include a choice-of-law clause in their written contracts. Accordingly, the enforceability of those clauses is an important issue for business lawyers.

Courts assessing the validity of choice-of-law clauses start from the perspective that the power to determine what law should apply to a dispute is a core competence of the courts established by national governments. Because nineteenth-century courts generally perceived the use of choice-of-law terms in contracts as a direct assault on their basic functions, they routinely disregarded such provisions. In the twentieth-century, courts in most trading nations have come to accept that choice-of-law terms serve a legitimate function in reducing the legal uncertainty parties to cross-border transactions face when disputes arise. In the United States, this issue is decided by the state courts under the *Erie* doctrine. E.g., Klaxon Co. v. Stentor Electric Mfg. Co., 313 U.S. 487 (1941). Thus, although the enforcement of choice-of-law provisions is not yet routine, a party challenging the enforcement of a choice-of-law provision normally must make a substantial showing to overturn the provision.

Thus, the RESTATEMENT (SECOND) OF CONFLICT OF LAWS provides that a court should respect the choice of the parties to the contract with regard to the applicable law if the issue that the court is considering is one that could have been resolved by an explicit provision in the contract. RESTATEMENT (SECOND) OF CONFLICT OF LAWS § 187(1). For example, most American jurisdictions limit the ability of a merchant to disclaim its liability for personal injury or death caused by the products that the merchant sells. See, e.g., UCC § 2-719(3). If that limitation would apply under traditional conflicts principles, then the parties could not avoid the application of that law by choosing the law of a jurisdiction that would uphold such a disclaimer. Other similar rules would include such things as limits on the enforceability of standard form contracts, special rights of cancellation during a "cooling off" period, and mandatory disclosure or warranty rules applicable to merchants that sell to consumers.

That provision is less important in transactions among businesses, because most of those rules apply only to protect consumers. The issues that arise in most business transactions are issues that freely can be resolved by contract. For those issues, the choice of governing law typically can be justified under two separate rules: if the chosen state bears some reasonable relationship to the transaction; or if the application of the law of the chosen state would not violate a fundamental public policy of the state whose law would be chosen under traditional conflicts principles. RESTATEMENT (SECOND) OF CONFLICT OF LAWS § 187(2).

UCC Article 1 sets out a choice-of-law rule for commercial transactions to which the UCC applies. Before 2001, the UCC choice-of-law rule permitted enforcement of a choice-of-law clause if the transaction bore a reasonable relationship to the state whose law was specified by the parties in their contract. If the parties had not made a choice, the UCC would apply to transactions bearing an appropriate relationship to a state that has enacted the UCC. Former UCC § 1-105(a).

In 2001, however, the American Law Institute and NCCUSL finalized a new version of Article 1, which includes a new provision governing choice-of-law clauses. The provision represents a major and highly controversial rethinking of choice-of-law principles. Of greatest importance for our purposes, revised UCC § 1-301(b) distinguishes between choice-of-law terms in contracts between commercial parties, granting them more freedom in choosing applicable law than did the old UCC § 1-105. Parties are released from the obligation to choose the law of a jurisdiction that bears a reasonable relationship to the transaction. For example, a party in Alabama may agree to buy wheat from a party in North Dakota and the contract may specify New York law to govern a transaction even though neither the parties nor the goods have any relationship to New York. Similarly, in international transactions, a party in New Jersey might agree to buy wheat from a party in Australia and the contract may specify English law even though there is no relationship between England and either the parties or the specific transaction. Parties might do such a thing for various reasons, perhaps because of a forum's more sophisticated treatment of issues related to the transaction, or perhaps because both parties believe that the law of a neutral forum would be preferable. In any event, UCC § 1-301(b) now would give the parties to commercial transactions freedom to make that choice. It is not clear, however, that the provision will gain widespread adoption. At this time, all of the states that have adopted Revised Article 1 have modified that provision in some way to retain the pre-existing rule on choice-of-law clauses.

That same freedom has not, however, been extended to consumer transactions. In that context, for example, the "reasonable relationship" limitation on the choice of law continues. UCC § 1-301(d)(1). Furthermore, a choice-of-law term is unenforceable if it would deprive a consumer of the benefit of any consumer-protection law that would otherwise apply to the transaction based on the principal residence of the consumer or, for a sale of goods, the place where the consumer entered the contract and took delivery of goods. UCC § 1-301(d)(2).

2.   Choice of Law and Cross-Border Commerce

Choice of law in the European Union is governed by the 1980 Rome Convention on the Law Applicable to Contractual Obligations. Article 3 of the Rome Convention contains a general grant of authority to contracting parties to choose the law that will govern their agreements. Article 5 of the treaty, however, articulates a special rule for consumer cases. Specifically, parties generally cannot by contract deprive a consumer of protections provided by "mandatory rules" in the consumer's country of domicile. As the Convention makes plain in Article 3(3), the concept of mandatory rules is similar to the concept from RESTATEMENT (SECOND) OF CONFLICT OF LAWS § 187(1), discussed above.

Given the frequency of travel among nations in the European Union, it is important for the Convention to address transactions that involve parties from different EU countries. Article 5 provides that individuals receive the protections afforded consumers in the country of their residence if the contract was preceded by a specific invitation from the seller to the consumer received in the consumer's country; the seller or its agent received the order in the consumer's country; or the seller arranged for or induced the consumer to travel to the seller's country to purchase goods. By contrast, if the consumer has come to the seller's jurisdiction independently of any action by the seller, then the consumer is bound by the consumer protections that the merchant's jurisdiction provides. For Internet purposes, that contemplates the unsurprising rule that an Internet retailer in the European Union cannot by contract avoid its responsibility to comply with mandatory rules in the jurisdictions from which it receives orders.

B.   Contractual Choice of Forum

1.   *Choice of Forum and Interstate Commerce*

Courts traditionally were no more willing to tolerate contractual preemption of their power to hear a dispute than they were willing to tolerate contractual preemption of their power to decide what law would apply to the dispute. In recent decades, however, the United States Supreme Court at least has adopted a considerably different view for federal courts. The first major development came in The Bremen v. Zapata Off-Shore Co., 407 U.S. 1 (1972). The Court in that case held that choice-of-forum provisions in cross-border commercial disputes would be enforced unless the party resisting enforcement could make a strong case against enforcement. In 1991, the Court extended that rule to consumer transactions. Carnival Cruise Lines, Inc. v. Shute, 499 U.S. 585 (1991). The Court's willingness to defer to contractual choice is evident from the unsympathetic facts of the case, in which the clause appeared on the back of a ticket: a standard form not subject to negotiation by the consumer, and indeed not likely to have been noticed by a typical consumer.

Against the backdrop of the vigorous enforcement of choice-of-forum clauses in *Bremen* and *Carnival Cruise Lines*, it should be no surprise that few federal courts confronted with such terms in online contracts have declined to enforce them. Because *Bremen* and *Carnival Cruise Lines* do not rest on the federal Constitution, state courts are not bound by those decisions. Thus, results in state courts have been less uniform. The following opinion illustrates the factors courts typically consider in assessing the strength of the objections raised by the party seeking to block enforcement of the term.

Groff v. America Online, Inc.

1998 WL 307001 (R.I. Super. Ct. 1998)

CLIFTON, J.
The matter is before the Court on defendant America Online, Inc.'s Motion to Dismiss plaintiff's Complaint on the grounds of improper venue. . . .

FACTS:
According to plaintiff's Complaint, defendant is a "[V]irginia Company" that operates an "on-line" computer service which allows plaintiff "to access and receive information via his personal computer, including access to the Internet, so-called."

Initially, individuals receiving that service were provided, for a set fee, a limited maximum number of hours and were charged additionally for time "on line" beyond the limited maximum. Thereafter, defendant initiated a "flat fee" which allowed for unlimited hours "on line."

The gravamen of plaintiff's complaint is, at the time he accepted defendant's offer for unlimited service, defendant knew they were unable to provide the service and said actions were in violation of the Rhode Island Unfair Trade Practice and Consumer Protection Act, R.I.G.L. (1956) 6-13.1-1, et seq.

Before this action was filed, January 21, 1997, a similar action had been certified as a class [in an Illinois state court] consisting of "all AOL subscribers who were subscribers to AOL on December 1, 1996 or who became subscribers on said date or thereafter." [Plaintiff opted out of that case.] . . .

Defendant . . . argued that . . . the forum selection clause in defendant's contract with its members, including plaintiff . . . requires that this action must be litigated in Virginia.

In support of its Motion, defendant submitted the affidavit dated October 9, 1997 of Randell J. Boe, Assistant General Counsel for defendant, together with an exhibit entitled "Quick Reference Guide — America OnLine 3.0 For Windows 95" consisting of ninety-four (94) pages showing . . . each screen in order that the member sees and interacts with it immediately upon loading the software. . . ."

The affidavit outlines the process each subscriber must follow. The affidavit asserts in paragraph 7 after reading the Terms of Service (TOS) . . . "the user is unable to proceed onto the AOL system or become an AOL member without affirmatively choosing to accept the TOS. The user has the option of clicking 'I Agree' or 'I Disagree' after reading the TOS."

The affidavit states in paragraph 8 "[T]he TOS contains a forum selection clause which expressly provides that Virginia law and Virginia courts are the appropriate law and forum for the litigation between members and AOL."

Plaintiff, in his affidavit dated October 6, 1997, stated in part that "he never saw, read, negotiated for or knowingly agreed to be bound by the choice of law or forum selection clause. . . ."

DISCUSSION:

. . . Historically, courts have looked with disfavor upon forum selection clauses on the basis that such clauses were contrary to public policy or had the effect of ousting proper jurisdiction from a court. However, in *M/S Bremen vs. Zapata Off-Shore Company*, 407 U.S. 1 (1972), the United States Supreme Court held in reversing and remanding the matter for further consideration, that such forum selection clauses were "prima facie valid" [and] should be upheld unless it is shown to be "unreasonable" by the resisting party under the circumstances. That court went further to explain that where a contract is " . . . unaffected by fraud, undue influence or overweening bargain power . . . " the contract should be given its full effect. 407 U.S. at 10.

Under the test enunciated in *M/S Bremen*, the party resisting the motion bears a heavy burden of proof in his attempt to demonstrate unreasonableness.

After *M/S Bremen* was decided, numerous Circuit Courts applied factors in determining if a forum selection clause was unreasonable. Locally, then District Judge (now Circuit Judge) Selya upheld a forum selection clause between defendant (a California corporation) and plaintiff (a Rhode Island resident) seeking recovery, in part, under the same legal theory and statutory basis as here.

Judge Selya analyzed nine factors which other Federal Courts have examined in applying the reasonableness of enforcing a forum selection clause, those being:

1. identity of the law that governs the construction of the contract;
2. place of execution of contract;
3. place where transactions are to be performed;
4. availability of remedies in the designated forum;
5. public policy of the initial forum state;
6. location of the parties, the convenience of the prospective witnesses, and the accessibility of evidence;
7. relative bargaining power of the parties and the circumstances surrounding their dealings;
8. presence or absence of fraud, undue influence or other extenuating (or exacerbating) circumstances; and
9. the conduct of the parties.

Judge Selya wrote further "While each of these factors has some degree of relevance and some claim to weight, there are no hard-and-fast rules, no precise formula. The totality of the circumstances, measured in the interests of justice will and should ultimately control." [*D'Antuano v. CCH Computax System, Inc.*, 570 F. Supp. 708, 712 (D.R.I. 1983).]

Applying the above factors to this matter, under the terms of the agreement, "The laws of the Commonwealth of Virginia, excluding its conflicts-of-law rules, govern the TOS and your membership." It is not clear, in this electronic age, where the last place the contract was executed. Was it when plaintiff clicked the "I agree" button in Rhode Island or where that message was received, at defendant's mainframe in Virginia? The place where the transaction has been or are to be performed appears to take place where defendant's mainframe is located. Given the burden imposed upon plaintiff, this Court is not satisfied that the contract was executed in Rhode Island, or to be performed in Rhode Island.

As to the availability of a remedy, if this matter were brought in Virginia, the Virginia Legislature has enacted [a consumer protection act that provides typical damages for victimized consumers. Thus we need not worry that plaintiff is being required to litigate in a forum that will not entertain the claim.]

While no one can seriously argue that the public policy of Rhode Island to provide a remedy for its citizens is not an important one, it is at least of equal, if not greater importance, that parties to a contract who select Rhode Island as the forum [should have] that agreement . . . enforced by other jurisdictions. Indeed as the Uniform Commercial Code, applicable in Rhode Island provides in part ". . . when a transaction bears a reasonable relation to this state and also to another state or nation, the parties may agree that the law either of this state or of such other state or nation shall govern their rights and duties." [Old UCC § 1-105.]

With the exception of plaintiff, it would appear that all the remaining parties, and evidence is in Virginia. This makes access to evidence, compulsory process of witness, views if necessary, more convenient.

Additionally, plaintiff cannot claim that he is uninformed in the area of contract law. Plaintiff, as pointed out by defendant, has been at the bar in this state for approximately thirty (30) years. . . .

While defendant prepared this contract, plaintiff was under no obligation to agree to the terms. Plaintiff had the option to refuse the service and the contract offered by plaintiff. Although plaintiff, in his affidavit, states "I never saw, read, negotiated for or knowingly agreed to be bound by the choice of law . . . " he does not point to any conduct of defendant or other reason why he could not. Indeed as pointed out in defendant's affidavit and argued in his memorandum, one could not enroll unless they clicked the "I agree" button which was immediately next to the "read now" button or, finally, the "I agree" button next to the "I disagree" button at the conclusion of the agreement.

. . . Here, plaintiff effectively "signed" the agreement by clicking "I agree" not once but twice. Under these circumstances, he should not be heard to complain that he did not see, read, etc. and is bound to the terms of his agreement.

Plaintiff [does not] claim that the forum selection clause was the result of fraud.

Lastly, as to the conduct of the parties, clearly plaintiff had the option not to accept defendant's terms. He did not. He chose to go on line. . . .

CONCLUSION:

Based upon the controlling princip[le]s, plaintiff has the burden of persuading the Court that the forum selection clause in his agreement with defendant was unreasonable. For the reasons stated, this Court is not satisfied that plaintiff has met his burden. Defendant's Motion to Dismiss based upon improper venue is granted.

As a business lawyer, the analysis of that case has to be profoundly troubling, because it involves so many factors as to prevent any lawyer drafting a contract from predicting confidently that any particular contract will — or will not — be enforced. For example, the same clause was found unenforceable in Mark Williams v. America Online, Inc., 43 U.C.C. Rep. Serv. 2d (Callaghan) 1101 (Mass. Super. 2001) (edited version available at the course Web site). Thus, despite the Supreme Court's firm position on the topic, it remains one on which contracting parties must face profound uncertainty.

2. Choice of Forum and Cross-Border Commerce

The Brussels Convention and the Brussels I Regulation (both discussed in Assignment 1), establish the framework within which courts in EU member states review choice-of-forum terms. Generally, if one party to a contract resides in the European Union, then the courts of any member state will uphold a provision in the agreement designating the courts of another member state as the exclusive forum. Brussels I Regulation, art. 23. As you might expect, the most prominent exception relates to consumer contracts. If a merchant targets consumers located in other states that are subject to the Brussels Convention or Regulation, then the merchant's contract cannot deny the consumer the right to sue the merchant in the consumer's local courts. Brussels I Regulation, arts. 15, 16 & 17. Although that approach might seem less favorable to merchants — by denying them the chance to draft an effective clause that chooses the merchant's forum — it does have the virtue of being considerably more predictable than the U.S. rule. Do American merchants really benefit from the unpredictable U.S. rule?

C. Arbitration Clauses

Transactional lawyers often are not content to use clauses that attempt to determine the forum in which a dispute will be resolved or the law that the forum will apply. Rather, they often go so far as to avoid judicial resolution entirely, using clauses that call for resolution of a dispute by binding arbitration. It is beyond the scope of this course to discuss the details of how arbitration works, but it is important to understand that the choice between litigation and arbitration is a difficult one. On the one hand, arbitration often is viewed as being less expensive and more expeditious than conventional litigation. Among other things, an arbitral award generally is enforceable without any substantial judicial review, even in foreign countries. Businesses also often are attracted to the potential for selecting a tribunal with expertise in a particular subject matter. For example, the International Chamber of Commerce has a specialized tribunal with expertise in issues related to letters of credit that is attractive to banks issuing and receiving letters of credit. On the other hand, the shift of complex disputes to arbitration in recent decades has made the arbitration process often as complicated as traditional litigation. Moreover, because arbitral awards typically are not subject to any substantial judicial review, some businesses fear the risk that they will be harmed by arbitrary decisions.

Despite those issues, it certainly is the case that a large share of the contracts drafted by sophisticated lawyers will include a clause that explicitly calls for arbitration. The Internet does not present any particular challenge to those rules: There is no obvious reason why arbitration clauses should be any more problematic in the Internet context than they are in conventional contexts. Still, the importance of arbitration in Internet relations makes it important to discuss the concept at the beginning of this course.

The basic problem is that the costs of conventional litigation between parties connected only by an Internet transaction are likely to swamp any transaction cost savings that could make such arrangements commercially viable. Accordingly, many of the most successful types of commercial enterprises on the Internet rely on arbitral regimes of various kinds. In some cases, it is a matter of online contracting calling for resolution under a traditional arbitral regime (as in the *Brower* case below). In others, private entities have established Internet-specific regimes. For example, the Internet Corporation for Assigned Names and Numbers (ICANN) has established an important regime under the Uniform Dispute Resolution Policy (UDRP) that governs disputes about domain names. (Assignment 4 discusses that system in detail.)

To understand the legal rules that apply to arbitration agreements, the two sections that follow address the enforceability of arbitration clauses first in interstate commerce and then in the European Union.

1. *Arbitration Clauses and Interstate Commerce*

As you might expect based on our discussion of contractual efforts to select law and forum, courts traditionally were hostile to arbitration clauses. In this country, at least, that hostility is fading rapidly. In the United States, the Federal Arbitration Act (FAA) directly mandates the enforcement of an arbitration agreement in any transaction that involves interstate commerce. 9 U.S.C. §§ 1 et seq. In the almost hypothetical case of a transaction that does not involve interstate commerce, the Uniform Arbitration Act (recently revised by NCCUSL, but adopted in one form or another by almost all states) would call for a similar result. The Supreme Court has applied the Federal Arbitration Act with notable vigor, firmly rejecting almost all claims for exceptions or limitations to the general principle that federal and state courts should enforce all arbitration agreements presented to them. For example, the Court has held that the statute applies even to cases filed in state court, as long as the agreement involves interstate commerce. Thus, although it might seem paradoxical as a matter of policy, it is easier to enforce an agreement that obviates judicial consideration entirely than it is to enforce an agreement that specifies a particular forum in which a case will be resolved. Indeed, although the Supreme Court has not yet addressed the question, the lower courts have read recent Supreme Court decisions to suggest that arbitration agreements can be used to deprive a plaintiff of the possibility of a class action. Johnson v. West Suburban Bank, 225 F.3d 366 (3rd Cir. 2000); Bowen v. First Family Financial Services, 233 F.3d 1331 (11th Cir. 2000).

Given the clear enforceability of arbitration agreements under American law, the remaining points of dispute are likely to turn on the question whether the parties have made a contract to arbitrate the dispute in question. Thus, even under the FAA a court at least in theory has jurisdiction to determine whether the arbitration clause in the parties' agreement calls for arbitration of the dispute. But even in that circumstance the court defers to the arbitrator's decision about the arbitrator's power to decide. On that question, the arbitration clause might be drafted narrowly — specifying, for example, that all disputes "arising under" the agreement will be arbitrated. A court interpreting that clause would be likely to hold that it does not extend to claims that are merely "related to" the subject matter of the agreement (such as claims that the agreement violates applicable consumer-protection laws). A broader arbitration clause — providing that all disputes "relating to or arising in connection with the agreement" — will make it more difficult to challenge the use of arbitration.

A common complaint about arbitration agreements is the cost of the tribunal. In some cases, the arbitration agreement will contemplate ad hoc arbitration and include all of the rules for the arbitration in the agreement itself. More commonly, especially in commercial transactions, the agreement will designate a particular institution to conduct the arbitration. Institutions commonly designated in arbitration agreements involving cross-border trade include the Court of Arbitration of the International Chamber of Commerce (ICC) in Paris, the American Arbitration Association (AAA), the CPR Institute for Dispute Resolution, the London Court of International Arbitration (LCIA), the Arbitration Institute of the Stockholm Chamber of Commerce, the Zurich Chamber of Commerce, the Hong Kong Arbitration Center, and the World Intellectual Property Organization. Many of those institutions have their own rules (such as the AAA, the ICC, the CPR Institute, and the LCIA); others use the CPR rules or rules articulated by third parties such as the United Nations Commission on International Trade Law (UNCITRAL).

One drafting point that has been particularly important in cases involving online disputes is the expense of the arbitration process. A business lawyer must have a basic understanding of the different characteristics associated with different arbitration providers. Some providers, like the AAA, are relatively expensive, designed for large commercial transactions. Others, like ICANN, are fast and cheap, designed for low-dollar transactions. The wrong choice might lead not just to a waste of resources in the event of arbitration, but also to invalidation of the entire clause. Building on a suggestion by Justice Ginsburg in her dissent in Green Tree Financial Corp.-Alabama v. Randolph, 531 U.S. 79 (2000), consumer advocates recently have argued that arbitration agreements should be unenforceable if they are unreasonably expensive given the amount likely to be in dispute. As the following case shows, that is merely one example of how overly zealous drafting can undermine the effectiveness of an agreement for arbitration.

Comb v. PayPal, Inc.

218 F. Supp. 2d 1165 (N.D. Cal. 2002)

FOGEL, District Judge.

Plaintiffs seek injunctive relief and related remedies on behalf of a purported nationwide class for alleged violations of state and federal law by Defendant PayPal, Inc. ("PayPal"). PayPal moves to compel individual arbitration pursuant to the arbitration clause contained in its standard User Agreement and the Federal Arbitration Act ("FAA"), 9 U.S.C. § 1, et seq. The Court has read and considered the moving, responding and supplemental papers as well as the oral arguments presented by counsel on August 12, 2002. For the reasons set forth below, the motions will be denied.

I. BACKGROUND

A. CUSTOMER COMPLAINTS

PayPal is an online payment service that allows a business or private individual to send and receive payments via the Internet. A PayPal account holder sends money by informing Paypal [sic] of the intended recipient's e-mail address and the amount to be sent and by designating a funding source such as a credit card, bank account or separate PayPal account. PayPal accesses the funds and immediately makes them available to the intended recipient. If an intended recipient does not have a PayPal account, the recipient must open an account to access the payment by following a link that is included in the payment notification e-mail. PayPal generates revenues from transaction fees and the interest it derives from holding funds until they are sent. [PayPal is discussed extensively in Assignment 29.]

As of January 1, 2001, approximately 10,000 account holders had registered with PayPal. PayPal thereafter experienced a sudden and dramatic increase in its popularity, attracting one million customers over the next five months and 10.6 million accounts (of which 8.5 million were held by private individuals) by September 30, 2001. Currently, PayPal provides services to twelve million accounts, and approximately 18,000 new accounts are opened each day. Plaintiffs allege that while PayPal has experienced a seven-fold increase in revenues and a thirteen-fold increase in users, it only has doubled the number of service representatives available to address customer concerns.

Plaintiffs contend that because PayPal's customer base has exceeded its operational capacity, PayPal has been and continues to be unable to maintain and manage accounts in the manner required by applicable state and federal legislation. Plaintiffs allege in particular that when PayPal investigates a customer's complaint of fraud, it freezes the customer's access to his or her account until the investigation is completed, but at the same time keeps the account open for deposits, a practice which allows PayPal to derive economic benefit from the deposits while preventing customers from accessing even undisputed funds while the investigation is pending. Plaintiffs further allege that PayPal does not provide a toll-free customer service telephone number, does not effectively publish the customer service telephone number it does provide, requires customers to report erroneous transactions by e-mail while not providing a specific e-mail address for that purpose, requires customers to provide numerous and burdensome personal documents before it undertakes an investigation, responds to e-mail inquiries with form letters, refuses to provide details or explanations with respect to its investigations, and provides no procedure by which a customer can appeal the results of an investigation. Plaintiffs also allege that when customers *are* able to contact PayPal representatives, the representatives are combative and rude, refuse to answer specific questions, hang up in the middle of phone calls, provide "canned" responses to individualized problems, require customers to fax information while providing inoperative fax numbers, and refuse to allow customers to speak to managers.

Newspaper articles have reported that disgruntled customers who have been unable to contact anyone at PayPal to resolve their disputes have created their own website providing consumers with difficult-to-find customer service numbers and reporting their own frustrations with PayPal's service. According to these accounts, PayPal has a backlog of over 100,000 unanswered customer complaints, a fact that has led the Better Business Bureau to revoke its seal of approval. Plaintiffs allege that PayPal profits from its alleged acts and omissions because customers either abandon their efforts to recover their money or, in cases in which funds actually are returned, because it retains the interest collected on the funds it has held during the investigation process.

1.   Craig Comb

Plaintiff Craig Comb ("Comb"), who is not a PayPal customer, alleges the following: On February 15, 2002, without his knowledge, consent or authorization, PayPal removed the sums of $110.00 and $450.00 from his bank account. Comb allegedly had difficulty contacting PayPal with respect to the erroneous transfer and finally reached a PayPal representative on February 18, 2002 to report the alleged error. PayPal acknowledged the error and returned the entire $560.00 to Comb's account on February 25, 2002.

PayPal's transfers, however, caused Comb's bank account to have insufficient funds, and the bank charged Comb $208.50 for failing to maintain his required balance. Comb contacted PayPal and requested reimbursement for the insufficient fund penalty and any interest his funds accrued while in PayPal's possession. PayPal allegedly refused to pay either amount, disputing Comb's figures but failing to provide Comb its own figures or documentation of its investigation.

2.   Roberta Toher

Plaintiff Roberta Toher ("Toher") alleges the following: Toher opened a PayPal account sometime in 2000. PayPal failed to provide her with the name, address, and telephone number of a person she should notify in the event of an unauthorized electronic transfer. On February 24, 2002, Toher discovered that PayPal had transferred funds from her checking account to four individuals without her knowledge, consent or authorization. Toher had difficulty locating any telephone number for contacting PayPal. Once she found a telephone number, which was not toll-free, she was placed on hold for a lengthy period of time, and no one answered her call. Toher then located PayPal's e-mail address and reported the error by e-mail.

On or about February 25, 2002, PayPal responded to Toher by e-mail and instructed her to report the erroneous transaction by sending her complaint to either of two e-mail addresses it provided. Toher sent her complaint to one e-mail address, from which it was returned undeliverable, and then to the other address. She also attempted again to contact PayPal by telephone. After Toher again was placed on hold for a lengthy period of time, a PayPal representative instructed her to change her password and report the error by telephone to a different department. Toher called that department's telephone number and spoke with a service representative who informed her that he had verified that the transaction had not been initiated by Toher and that PayPal would send Toher a letter explaining how to report the transaction in writing. During this time, the recipients who erroneously had received the funds e-mailed Toher and inquired as to the reason for the payment.

On or about February 27, 2002, before her complaint had been investigated or resolved, PayPal informed Toher that it intended to take money from her checking account because her bank had declined a different, unrelated transaction. Toher called PayPal and explained that she had filed a claim with respect to the erroneous withdrawal and instructed PayPal to stop removing funds from the checking account. PayPal explained that there was nothing it could do to stop the latter transaction, and Toher was forced to pay a $27.00 fee to her bank to decline all subsequent electronic transactions related to PayPal. Toher contacted PayPal to request for a second time the letter explaining how to report her original claim. PayPal subsequently informed Toher that it would begin processing her claim once she completed and returned a notarized affidavit by mail.

On March 6, 2002, PayPal sent Toher a series of e-mails explaining that because her bank had declined its attempted transfers, PayPal intended to transfer funds from her credit card account. Toher in turn closed and reopened her credit card account to prevent PayPal from accessing her funds. As of the date the instant suit was filed, PayPal had not acknowledged that Toher had reported an erroneous withdrawal or that an error had occurred, nor had it undertaken any investigation with respect to Toher's complaint.

3.   Jeffrey Resnick

Plaintiff Jeffrey Resnick ("Resnick") alleges the following: Resnick registered an account with PayPal and linked his e-mail address *resnickjeff@hotmail.com* (with two "f"s) to that account. He used the account to sell comic books on eBay, an Internet auction service. On January 29, 2002, a third party appropriated Resnick's PayPal user name and password and linked an e-mail account *resnickjefff@hotmail.com* (with three "f"s) to Resnick's PayPal account. The third party sold two Apple Computers on eBay, and the buyers deposited their payment into the fraudulent account. When the buyers did not receive their product, they filed a complaint with PayPal, which without notice or explanation then restricted Resnick's legitimate account.

In late January or early February 2002, Resnick learned that his account had been restricted and contacted PayPal to inquire as to the reason. Once informed of the circumstances, Resnick explained that he had not sold the computers and stated that because the fraudulent account's e-mail address contained three "f"s rather than two, someone must have appropriated his account information. At the time he filed the instant suit, although more than forty-five days had elapsed since he informed PayPal of its error, he had not received any information or documentation with respect to the status of PayPal's investigation, and PayPal had not unrestricted or credited his account.

B.   User Agreement

PayPal customers open an account by completing an online application for a personal, premier, or business account. A prospective customer clicks a box at the bottom of the application page that reads, "[you] have read and agree to the User Agreement and [PayPal's] privacy policy." A link to the text of the User Agreement is located at the bottom of the application. The link need not be opened for the application to be processed. The User Agreement is lengthy, consisting of twenty-five printed pages and eleven sections, each containing a number of subparagraphs enumerating the parties' respective obligations and duties.

PayPal admonishes every customer to read the User Agreement carefully, informs him or her that the Agreement forms a binding contract, and advises the customer to retain a copy of the User Agreement. The User Agreement is a "click-wrap contract," formed when the customer "click[s] 'I Agree,' 'I Accept,' or by submitting payment information through the Service. . . ." User Agreement, ¶ 2.

The User Agreement contains the following arbitration clause:

Arbitration.   Any controversy or claim arising out of or relating to this Agreement or the provision of Services shall be settled by binding arbitration in accordance with the commercial arbitration rules of the American Arbitration Association. Any such controversy or claim shall be arbitrated on an individual basis, and shall not be consolidated in any arbitration with any claim or controversy of any other party. The arbitration shall be conducted in Santa Clara County, California, and judgment on the arbitration award may be entered in any court having jurisdiction thereof. Either you or PayPal may seek any interim or preliminary relief from a court of competent jurisdiction in Santa Clara County, California necessary to protect the rights or property of you or PayPal, Inc. (or its agents, suppliers, and subcontractors) pending the completion of arbitration.

User Agreement, Section II(19).

II.   DISCUSSION

The FAA was enacted to overcome longstanding judicial reluctance to enforce agreements to arbitrate. It applies to all written contracts involving interstate or

foreign commerce and provides in relevant part that arbitration agreements contained within such contracts "shall be valid, irrevocable, and enforceable, save
upon such grounds as exist at law or in equity for the revocation of any contract."
9 U.S.C. § 2. As a result, state laws hostile to arbitration agreements have been
held invalid on the ground that such laws frustrate congressional intent to place
arbitration agreements on the same footing as other contracts.

State law is not entirely displaced from FAA analysis, however. It is undisputed
that "generally applicable contract defenses, such as fraud, duress, or unconscionability, may be applied to invalidate arbitration agreements without contra-
vening § 2." *Doctor's Assocs., Inc. v. Casarotto*, 517 U.S. 681, 686 (1996). Here, the
User Agreement is "governed by and interpreted under the laws of the state of
California . . . [as] applied to agreements entered into and to be performed
entirely within California by California residents." User Agreement, Section II(18).
Because there is no dispute that the contract at issue in this case involves interstate commerce, this Court's role thus is limited to determining whether under
California law (1) a valid agreement to arbitrate exists and, if so, (2) whether the
agreement encompasses the dispute at issue. If both of these requirements are
satisfied, the FAA requires this Court to enforce the subject arbitration clause in
accordance with the terms of the User Agreement.

A.   Agreement to Arbitrate

Even though California has a strong policy favoring arbitration, it is beyond
cavil that arbitration is a matter of contract and a party cannot be required to submit to arbitration any dispute which he has not agreed so to submit. [Brackets,
quotation marks, and citation omitted.] The Court must interpret the parties' written agreement so as to give effect to the parties' mutual intention. If possible, the
Court will determine the parties' intention solely from the language of the agreement itself. Extrinsic evidence is admissible, however, if the offered evidence is relevant to prove the meaning of ambiguous language and such interpretation is
reasonable in light of all the facts, circumstances, and conditions surrounding the
execution of the agreement. Because the existence of the agreement is a statutory
prerequisite to granting the petition, the petitioner bears the burden of proving
its existence by a preponderance of the evidence. [Quotation marks and citation
omitted.]

It is undisputed that Comb's claims are not subject to arbitration. With respect
to Toher and Resnick, [the Court concludes that PayPal submitted adequate evidence of an enforceable agreement to survive a motion to dismiss].

B.   Unconscionability

Plaintiffs argue that even if they did enter into a version of the User Agreement,
the User Agreement and in particular its arbitration clause are unconscionable.
Unconscionability is a defense applicable to contracts generally and thus may be
raised in defense to an arbitration provision. Unconscionability has both procedural and substantive components. The procedural component is satisfied by the
existence of unequal bargaining positions and hidden terms common in the context of adhesion contracts. The substantive component is satisfied by overly harsh
or one-sided results that "shock the conscience." The two elements operate on a
sliding scale such that the more significant one is, the less significant the other

need be. A claim of unconscionability cannot be determined merely by examining the face of the contract; there must be an inquiry into the circumstances under which the contract was executed, its purpose, and effect.

1. Procedural Unconscionability

A contract or clause is procedurally unconscionable if it is a contract of adhesion. A contract of adhesion, in turn, is a standardized contract, which, imposed and drafted by the party of superior bargaining strength, relegates to the subscribing party only the opportunity to adhere to the contract or reject it. [Quotation marks and citation omitted.] Although PayPal does not dispute that the agreement and arbitration clause at issue here meet this definition, it asserts that the instant contract is not procedurally unconscionable because it does not concern essential items such as food or clothing and because Plaintiffs had meaningful alternative sources for the subject services.

Relying upon *Dean Witter Reynolds, Inc. v. Superior Court,* [211 Cal. App. 3d 758] (1989), PayPal argues that the availability of alternative sources is enough to defeat a showing of procedural unconscionability. In *Dean Witter,* however, the California Court of Appeal noted that the party asserting unconscionability was "a sophisticated investor" and that "[t]he record establishe[d] without conflict that other financial institutions offered competing IRA's which lacked the challenged provision." *Id.* at 771. In this case, the amount of the average transaction is $55.00, the vast majority of PayPal customers are private individuals who are not "sophisticated," and there is at least a factual dispute as to whether PayPal's competitors offer their services without requiring customers to enter into arbitration agreements. The *Dean Witter* court explicitly limited its holding, indicating that a claim of procedural unconscionability cannot be defeated merely by "*any* showing of competition in the marketplace as to the desired goods and services. . . ." *Id.* at 772 (emphasis in original). PayPal cites no authority extending *Dean Witter* to circumstances analogous to those presented here. The Court concludes that the User Agreement at issue here satisfies the criteria for procedural unconscionability under California law.

2. Substantive Unconscionability

Even if instant agreement is procedurally unconscionable, it may nonetheless be enforceable if the substantive terms are reasonable. The Court's principal substantive concerns in the present case are a lack of mutuality in the User Agreement and the practical effects of the arbitration clause with respect to consolidation of claims, the costs of arbitration, and venue.

a. Mutuality

Substantive unconscionability has been found in many cases based upon arbitration provisions requiring arbitration of the weaker party's claims but permitting a choice of forums for the stronger party. Considered in isolation, the arbitration clause at issue here appears to permit a mutuality of remedies, providing that "[e]ither you or PayPal may seek any interim or preliminary relief from a court of competent jurisdiction in Santa Clara County, California necessary to protect the rights or property of you or PayPal, Inc. (or its agents, suppliers, and subcontractors) pending the completion of arbitration." User Agreement, Section II(19).

Section V(3) of the User Agreement, however, provides that in the event of a dispute, PayPal "at its sole discretion" may restrict accounts, withhold funds, undertake its own investigation of a customer's financial records, close accounts, and procure ownership of all funds in dispute unless and until the customer is "later determined to be entitled to the funds in dispute." PayPal alone makes the final decision with respect to a dispute.[11] Finally, as noted earlier, the User Agreement "is subject to change by PayPal without prior notice (unless prior notice is required by law), by posting of the revised Agreement on the PayPal website."[12]

A contract may provide a margin of safety that provides the party with superior bargaining strength protection for which it has a legitimate commercial need. However, unless the business realities that create the special need for such an advantage are explained in the contract itself, it must be factually established. [Brackets, ellipses, quotation marks, and citation omitted.] When a contract is alleged to be unconscionable, "the parties shall be afforded a reasonable opportunity to present evidence as to its commercial setting, purpose, and effect to aid the court in making the determination." Cal. Civ. Code § 1670.5. The statutory scheme reflects legislative recognition that a claim of unconscionability often cannot be determined merely by examining the face of the contract, but will require inquiry into its setting, purpose, and effect. [Quotation marks and citation omitted.]

PayPal argues that the User Agreement does not lack mutuality because nothing in the agreement precludes a customer from using the court system to seek any relief related to a restricted account pending the outcome of an arbitration

---

11.   Section V(3) provides:

PayPal, at its sole discretion, reserves the right to close an account at any time for any reason, including but not limited to a violation of this Agreement, upon notice to the User and payment to the User of any unrestricted funds held in custody. PayPal, at its sole discretion, also reserves the right to periodically retrieve and review a business and / or consumer credit report for any account, and reserves the right to close an account based on information obtained during this credit review process.

PayPal, at its sole discretion, also reserves the right to restrict withdrawals from an account for any one of the events listed below. If the dispute covers only a specific transaction, we will only restrict funds related to that particular transaction. If your account is restricted, you will be notified by e-mail and requested to provide information relevant to your account. PayPal will investigate the matter promptly. If the investigation is in your favor, we will unrestrict your account. If the investigation is not in your favor, PayPal may return funds to the sender and unrestrict the remainder of your account, continue the restriction for up to 180 days as to funds necessary to protect PayPal against the risk of reversals, or may close your account by giving you notice and mailing a check for any funds in your account (minus funds that are in dispute) to the address that you have provided. If you are later determined to be entitled to the funds in dispute, PayPal will make an additional payment of those funds to you. Any of the following events may lead to a restriction of your account. . . .[omitting list of nineteen provisions that include "Receipt of potentially fraudulent funds," "Refusal to cooperate in an investigation," "Opening multiple Personal accounts," and "Logging in from a country not included on PayPal's permitted countries list."]. . . .[¶] PayPal will use reasonable efforts to investigate accounts that are subject to a restriction and to reach a final decision promptly.

12.   ¶ 2 provides:
This Agreement is subject to change by PayPal without prior notice (unless prior notice is required by law), by posting of the revised Agreement on the PayPal website. Descriptions of material amendments to this Agreement will be posted in advance on the PayPal website in the "Policy Updates" section that is displayed to you when you log in to your account. You can also set your Preferences to receive e-mail notification of all policy updates. You may review the current Agreement prior to initiating a transaction at any time at our User Agreement page.

proceeding. However, Plaintiffs present evidence that PayPal has frozen customer accounts and retained funds that it alone determined were subject to dispute without notice to the named Plaintiffs. The User Agreement expressly authorizes PayPal to engage in such conduct unilaterally. While in theory a customer may seek provisional relief in the courts, including presumably an order to unfreeze an account, the cost of doing so would be prohibitive in relation to the amounts typically in dispute. For all practical purposes, a customer may resolve disputes only after PayPal has had control of the disputed funds for an indefinite period of time. Although PayPal alone may amend the User Agreement without notice or negotiation, a customer is bound to any and all such amendments for the duration of the customer's relationship with PayPal. PayPal has not shown that "business realities" justify such one- sidedness.

b.   Prohibition against Consolidation of Claims

The subject arbitration clause expressly prohibits PayPal customers from consolidating their claims. Relying upon *Vernon v. Drexel Burnham & Co.,* 52 Cal.App.3d 706 (1975), PayPal argues that such a prohibition cannot render an agreement to arbitrate substantively unconscionable. The arbitration clause in *Vernon,* however, did not preclude consolidation of claims *per se,* and whatever relevance *Vernon* may have in this case is overshadowed by the much more recent decision of the California Court of Appeal in *Szetela v. Discover Bank,* [97 Cal. App. 4th 1094 (2002).] As is th[e] case here, the arbitration agreement at issue in *Szetela* categorically prohibited individual customers from joining or consolidating claims in arbitration. The court determined that a large credit card company could not enforce the prohibition with respect to consumer claims against it because in practice most claims likely would involve consumers seeking the return of small amounts of money, and any remedy obtained by the few consumers who would not be dissuaded from pursuing their rights would pertain only to those consumers without collateral estoppel effect. *Id.* at 1101. The court concluded that such circumstances raise "[t]he potential for millions of customers to be overcharged small amounts without an effective method of redress. . . ." *Id.*

PayPal argues that because federal cases applying the FAA have enforced arbitration clauses containing such prohibitions on collective actions, *Szetela* is irrelevant to the present proceedings. In the Ninth Circuit, however, . . . a federal court properly may consider whether such a prohibition in combination with other provisions and circumstances renders an agreement substantively unconscionable as a matter of state law.

c.   Costs of Arbitration

Plaintiffs claim that the cost of an individual arbitration under the User Agreement is likely to exceed $5,000 and submit declarations stating that such arbitration would be cost-prohibitive for them. PayPal disputes Plaintiffs' calculation of costs, contending that because any arbitration in practice would proceed under the consumer rules of the American Arbitration Association ("AAA"), a customer's only expense would be a filing fee of approximately $125.00.

The arbitration clause itself expressly undercuts PayPal's assertion. It states in pertinent part that "[a]ny controversy or claim arising out of or relating to this Agreement or the provision of Services shall be settled by binding arbitration in accordance with the *commercial* arbitration rules of the American Arbitration

Association" (emphasis added). Further, because the clause is silent as to who bears the cost of arbitration, under California law each party is required to pay a *pro rata* share of the "expenses and fees of the neutral arbitrator, together with other expenses of the arbitration incurred or approved by the neutral arbitrator, not including counsel fees or witness fees or other expenses incurred by a party for his own benefit." Cal. Code Civ. P. § 1284.2.

Unlike the plaintiff in *Green Tree Fin. Corp.-Ala. v. Randolph*, 531 U.S. 79 (2000), who claimed that the unknown and unidentified risk of excessive fees should be sufficient to defeat a valid arbitration clause, the named Plaintiffs here, none of whose individual claims exceeds $310.00, have shown that the costs each of them is likely to incur in commercial arbitration likely would exceed those involved in bringing a collective action. By allowing for prohibitive arbitration fees and precluding joinder of claims (which would make each individual customer's participation in arbitration more economical), PayPal appears to be attempting to insulate itself contractually from any meaningful challenge to its alleged practices. Under these circumstances, the Court concludes that this aspect of the arbitration clause is so harsh as to be substantively unconscionable.

d. Venue

The User Agreement requires that any arbitration take place in Santa Clara County, California. PayPal argues that this venue provision is not unconscionable because forum selection clauses in general are *prima facie* valid, courts have found similar forum selection clauses in arbitration clauses reasonable, and the named Plaintiffs themselves elected to litigate in this Court, thereby undercutting any claim that the contractual forum is burdensome or inconvenient for them.

Although it is true that forum selection clauses generally are presumed *prima facie* valid, a forum selection clause may be unconscionable if the place or manner in which arbitration is to occur is unreasonable taking into account the respective circumstances of the parties. [Quotation marks and citation omitted.] The record in this case shows that PayPal serves millions of customers across the United States and that the amount of the average transaction through PayPal is $55.00. Although PayPal cites to unpublished or out-of-state authority holding that such facts do not warrant a finding of unconscionability, PayPal cites no California authority holding that it is reasonable for individual consumers from throughout the country to travel to one locale to arbitrate claims involving such minimal sums. Limiting venue to PayPal's backyard appears to be yet one more means by which the arbitration clause serves to shield PayPal from liability instead of providing a neutral forum in which to arbitrate disputes.

III. DISPOSITION

Having considered the terms of the User Agreement generally and the arbitration clause in particular, as well as the totality of the circumstances, the Court concludes that the User Agreement and arbitration clause are substantively unconscionable under California law and that arbitration cannot be compelled herein. Good cause therefor appearing, IT IS HEREBY ORDERED that the motions to compel individual arbitration are DENIED.

---

2. Arbitration Clauses and EU Commerce

As with questions of jurisdiction and choice of law, the EU perspective on the use of arbitration agreements in consumer transactions differs markedly from the U.S. perspective, providing more certainty by articulating specific rules for consumer protections. Of relevance here is the European Union's 1993 directive on unfair contract terms. The directive harmonized the law of the EU member states with regard to the types of contract terms that would be denied enforcement in consumer transactions. The directive rests on the premise that agreements including such terms are likely to be the result of overreaching by the party that drafted the agreement. Article 3 of the directive provides that contract terms not individually negotiated will be deemed unfair if they create a significant imbalance to the consumer's detriment between the rights and obligations of the contracting parties. Article 2 of the directive provides that if a contract term is drafted in advance and the consumer has no influence over the substance of the term, then it is always considered not to be individually negotiated, and hence subject to review based on substantive fairness. An annex to the directive contains a list of terms that may be deemed unfair. Among the terms listed in the annex is the following:

> (q) excluding or hindering the consumer's right to take legal action or exercise any other legal remedy, particularly by requiring the consumer to take disputes exclusively to arbitration not covered by legal provisions, unduly restricting the evidence available to him or imposing on him a burden of proof which, according to the applicable law, should lie with the other party to the contract.

Like all EU directives, those provisions are not directly binding in the individual member states of the European Union. Rather, they constitute a directive that the member states adopt implementing legislation. Thus, England has implemented that directive with its Unfair Terms in Consumer Contracts Regulation (SI 1999/2083), and appended the annex to the directive as a "schedule" to the regulation.

Relevant Glossary Entries

Internet Corporation for Assigned Names and Numbers (ICANN)
Uniform Dispute Resolution Procedure (UDRP)

Problem Set 2

2.1. Global Scanners, Inc. is a manufacturer and distributor of scanning systems and related scanning components. It is incorporated in Delaware and has its principal place of business in Texas. It sells directly to consumers by catalog, telephone, and Web site. It also sells its products through distributors located in the United States and 20 other countries. All of its warehouses and offices are in Texas. The company recently was forced to defend a frivolous personal injury lawsuit halfway around the world, in part because a sales representative failed to document an oral agreement. Global Scanners comes to you for assistance in formalizing its contractual relationships through one or more standard contracts. What do you advise Global Scanners to do with regard to forum-selection and choice-of-law clauses? Consider the following specific questions.

(a) Do the concerns differ in consumer and business transactions? Domestic and cross-border transactions? Old UCC § 1-105; UCC § 1-301; RESTATEMENT (SECOND) OF CONFLICTS § 187; Rome Convention art. 3; Brussels I Regulation, art. 23.

(b) The general counsel of Global Scanners indicates that Texas has enacted UCC § 2-719(3), which invalidates any attempt to disclaim liability for personal injury or death in a sale-of-goods transaction with a consumer. He feels that this is extremely unfair and potentially damaging to his company. On the other hand, he does not wish to be exposed to the "eccentricities" of foreign law. Does this affect your analysis?

(c) Mindful of the expense involved in using outside counsel, the general counsel of Global Scanners presents you with model clauses he found on the Internet. They read as follows:

The laws of the State of New York shall govern the interpretation of the Agreement.

Disputes concerning the interpretation of the Agreement may be submitted to the appropriate jurisdiction of the state or federal courts in the State of New York.

What is your advice about these clauses? Is there anything specific that the clauses need to address?

2.2. Your neighbor bought a computer from fell.com, a U.S. manufacturer, and placed the order using its Internet site. When the box containing the computer arrived at her home, she found inside a pre-printed form contract that included a pre-dispute binding arbitration clause that did not specify the arbitrator or rules that would be used in the arbitration or how the costs of the arbitration would be allocated between the parties. The Web site contained prominent banners trumpeting the availability of fell.com's 24/7 telephone support service for its customers. Your neighbor was disappointed with performance of the computer from the day it arrived, and found that it was difficult to get any help from the support service. She contacted her family attorney who thinks the case could be organized as a class action because everyone who bought a fell.com computer from the Web site would have the same breach of warranty claim based on fell.com's failure to live up to the promises posted on its site. She now has asked for your advice. Can she pursue a class-action lawsuit against fell.com? Federal Arbitration Act, 9 U.S.C. § 2.

2.3. Robert Rich, a former executive for one of your most important clients, recently retired and moved to London. He recently spent £1,000 to buy a powerful new personal digital assistant (PDA) from CheapStuff.com, a discount online retailer located in the United States. The clickthrough order agreement included a standard form "terms and conditions" that contained a pre-dispute binding arbitration clause designating the American Arbitration Association as the arbitrator and Atlanta, Georgia as the forum for the arbitration.

He was disappointed with performance of the PDA from the day it arrived, and was unable to get any help from the support service. The final straw came when a malfunction in the synchronization function of the PDA appeared to damage the hard drive of his new laptop computer that he had just purchased for £4,000. He had to pay a computer consultant £2,000 to repair the damage to the PDA and laptop. Robert would like to sue CheapStuff.com and the PDA manufacturer in London to recover his damages. Can CheapStuff.com and the PDA manufacturer force him to participate in arbitration in the United States? EU Unfair Contract Terms Directive; UK Unfair Terms in Consumer Contracts Regulation (SI 1999/2083).

2.4.   A junior associate has revised PayPal's arbitration policy in response to the decision in *Combs*. The revised policy tentatively is posted at the Course Web site. Please review the policy and comment on how well the associate has responded to the concerns that the decision raises.

THE CAMFORD BOOKS PROBLEM

(Part I)

Before you came to law school, you attended undergraduate school on a classics scholarship. Many of your closest friends at the time were fascinated by classical literature, studying and discussing Greek and Latin texts at all hours of the day and night. Some of them have returned to Britain, where they have been operating a classics bookstore with locations in Cambridge and Oxford. Others, like you, ultimately chose to attend a graduate school that held out the promise of a remunerative career. Several of your friends who recently have graduated from business school have decided to establish an Internet business, building on the bookstores of your friends, the purpose of which is to provide any and every product that could be of interest to the enthusiast of classical literature: an interface to purchase texts from bookstores around the world; reviews of recent and forthcoming texts; information about the languages; audio files with recitations of major texts, etc. Showing considerable lack of originality, they have decided to name the business CamfordBooks.com and to establish it at *www.camford.com*.

Because you are the only member of the group to attend law school, they have scheduled a meeting with you today to discuss some basic questions about the organization. In particular, they are at the stage now of locating their offices and incorporating their business. They want to know the extent to which they should be concerned about local laws in various jurisdictions that might apply to their activities. Specifically, they want to know what they should do to ensure that they are not subject to suit in all of the various jurisdictions in which their Web site might reach. What advice would you give them on that point? In answering that question, you should review all of the materials you have studied in this part of the book. (You also should show the care you would show in working for a client who is expected to return. They will return with problems of a similar scope on several occasions as the course progresses.)

THE OXFORD RULES PROBLEM

Part Two

The Context of Electronic Commerce

The commercialization of the Internet has enabled businesses and consumers to operate Web sites that they can use to transact business with other consumers or businesses as adjuncts to brick-and-mortar channels or as free-standing channels for the distribution of goods and services. This part of the book accordingly discusses the various legal problems related to setting up and operating such a site. The first chapter of this part (Chapter 2) discusses the issues related to acquiring and establishing a Web site. The second chapter (Chapter 3) discusses the general problem of information related to Web sites. Because a Web site in substance is little more than a device for collecting and disseminating information, this subject is central to an understanding of the commercial significance of operating a Web site.

Part Two

The Context of Electronic
Commerce

Chapter 2.   Setting Up Shop on the Internet

For a business that conducts transactions on the Internet, the Web site plays the same role as the retail space from which a brick-and-mortar retailer operates. Without a Web site, the Internet business literally does not exist. Accordingly, the first step in the formation of an Internet business is to obtain a domain name, at which the site will be located, and develop a Web site that can be accessed at that name. The purpose of this chapter is to delineate the principal legal and contractual issues you will encounter in that process.

Assignment 3: Trademarks and Domain Names

Put yourself back in 1994, before "Internet" and "World Wide Web" were household phrases, and before personal computers came equipped with Internet browsers and modems as standard equipment. A journalist named Joshua Quittner wanted to assess the Internet awareness of a major American corporation. Starting with McDonald's, he tried unsuccessfully for weeks to get a comment from the public relations office of McDonald's on its Internet strategy. At that point, taking matters into his own hands, he registered the domain name mcdonalds.com himself. He later published a hilarious account of his failed attempts to find anyone employed by McDonald's who thought this might be a problem. When McDonald's finally realized its blunder, it demanded that Quittner turn over the domain name and threatened to sue. Quittner refused to surrender the domain name until McDonald's agreed to donate $3,500 to provide Internet access to one New York City public elementary school. Fast-forward to the twenty-first century and the control of corporate names on the Internet is an important element of business strategy for almost all large firms. Indeed, because retailing on the Internet depends so much more on brand identity than it does in a brick-and-mortar world — where physical location alone is so important — control of corporate names is much more important now than it ever has been before. The first two assignments of this chapter discuss this topic.

The starting point — perhaps surprising at first — is the complete separation of the domain-name registration process from trademark law and trademark rights. (If the process of assigning domain names is unfamiliar to you, we suggest that you consult Appendix A at the back of this text.) That process generally results in an agreement by a registrar to take certain actions on behalf of the registrant, in return for which the registrant pays specified fees to the registrar. The output of that process, the domain name, is thus purely a contract right, capable of extinguishment if the recipient breaches its contract with the registrar. At the same time, a domain name is a valuable asset to the company. As Chapter 7 explains, it is also an asset to a commercial lawyer, in the sense that it is something in which a security interest can be granted and something on which a lender can foreclose.

It also is important that the domain-name registration process itself is a merely administrative function, in which the registrar checks to see if the domain name in question has already been registered to someone else. If it is not, the registrar assigns the name to the registrant and makes a corresponding entry in the domain-name system (DNS). Although trademark owners would have liked a system in which they could hold domain-name registrars liable for trademark infringements committed by individuals using their services, they have been uniformly rebuffed by the courts.

Accordingly, the ability of a trademark holder to control a domain name related to the trademark is resolved to a considerable extent under traditional principles of trademark law, the topic of this assignment. There are a number of new procedural and substantive rules directed specifically at those disputes; those topics are the subject of Assignment 4. Thus, our discussion starts with a summary of basic trademark principles and how they apply to domain names.

A. Trademarks and Trademark Infringement

Trademark law addresses the needs of businesses to identify their products and services to potential customers. A trademark may consist of a word, a combination of words, an abbreviation, a logo or other symbol, an image, a shape, a color, or a sound, so long as it in fact is used to distinguish the goods and services of one producer from those of another. When a mark is used to identify goods or services, consumers of goods and services can associate the mark with certain producers or certain qualities in the goods and services they purchase. At that point — once the mark has acquired "secondary meaning" (to use the relevant legal term) — the mark gains protection under traditional rules of state common law. The basic premise is that unauthorized use of the mark (or any identifying material confusingly similar to the mark) would harm consumers by confusing them about the source of goods and services. Accordingly, courts at that point will enjoin further use of the mark by the junior user of the mark.

In the Internet context, a common question is whether a party can obtain a trademark in a common and generic word simply by appending the phrase ".com" to the word. Courts, following the lead of the Patent and Trademark Office, generally have rejected efforts to obtain such names, reasoning that there can be no secondary meaning in the generic term and that the addition of ".com" or some other top-level-domain indicator should not alter that fact. E.g., In re Oppedahl & Larson, LLP, 2004 WL 1416361 (Fed. Cir. June 25, 2004) (rejecting effort to register "patents.com" as a trademark).

The owner can enhance his rights considerably by registering his mark under the federal Lanham Act. Lanham Act registration provides nationwide protection, even in geographic markets so distant from the current use that the owner could not establish the consumer confusion required for protection under traditional state common-law rules. Once a trademark is registered, the owner may give notice of that fact by using the symbol ®. While a trademark registration application is pending, or while a trademark is protected by common-law trademark, the trademark owner may use the symbols "SM" to indicate a mark for services and "TM" to indicate a trademark for goods.

After review by a government examiner and publication of the application in the Official Gazette of the Patent and Trademark Office (PTO), the trademark generally is registered if it does not conflict with an existing mark and if nobody opposes it. Although the process does not involve the kind of substantive review that a patent application does, it does involve a thorough search for similar marks, and thus is likely to take several months to complete.

A trademark casts a considerable shadow beyond the literal bounds of the mark itself, because the owner of a trademark is entitled to enjoin not only any use of the precise mark but also any use of an identifier that is confusingly similar to the mark. Thus, Microsoft, relying on its interests in the name of its various Windows-identified operating systems, has instituted litigation in numerous countries against parties selling a Linux-based "Lindows" operating system. Although some of that litigation is ongoing, and even though Microsoft lost in a number of jurisdictions, Microsoft's claims were sufficiently plausible to force a variety of changes in the Lindows operation, even though Lindows has adopted a name that plainly is distinct from the names that Microsoft uses. The key question will be whether the name is so similar as to confuse consumers as to the origins of the products.

Trademark law also has expanded in recent years to apply not only to names that are distinct from the trademarked identifier, but also to businesses that are distinct from those in which the mark is used. In that context, statutes and case law gradually have expanded the rights of the trademark owner to include protection even in the absence of confusion, through a property right to prevent "dilution" of the mark. The basic idea is that use of a famous mark, even in a context far from its traditional use, can diminish the value of the mark by reducing its distinctive identification with the existing products on which it is used, by tarnishing the connotations of the existing mark (when the diluting conduct involves products or services of inferior quality), or by limiting the registrant's ability to expand into new markets. For example, in one seminal case a court enjoined the sale of Kodak bicycles. Even in this age of conglomerates, few would expect a "Kodak" bicycle to come from the leading photographic products firm, but an injunction issued to prevent dilution of the mark. Eastman Photographic Materials Co. v. Kodak Cycle Co., 15 [British] R.P.C. 105 (1898).

The concept of dilution first arose in judicial decisions like the *Kodak* case discussed above, but by the 1990s several states had codified the doctrine. It gained definitive footing in 1996, however, with the enactment of Lanham Act § 43(c), 15 U.S.C. § 1125(c), which creates a general federal cause of action for dilution of marks that are "famous." That statute is particularly important in the Internet context, because most of the prominent disputes to date have involved circumstances in which it would have been difficult to prove consumer confusion about the source of the challenged site. For example, in one noted dispute the Hasbro toy company used § 43(c) to challenge an adult-content Web site at candyland.com — a site that few would have associated with Hasbro itself.

At first glance, domain names and trademarks are quite similar—both are indicators that businesses can use to identify themselves to customers. In fact, however, they really are quite different. Most obviously, a trademark can gain protection *only* if it is used to identify goods or services of the trademark owner. Conversely, an individual can obtain a domain name for any number of legitimate reasons completely separate from the distribution of goods and services — I might reserve the name *www.judemann.org* in honor of a deceased pet. In that situation, the use of the domain name might neither establish nor infringe rights under the trademark laws.

As the preceding paragraphs suggest, information about existing marks is crucial to trademark use and development. The United States Patent and Trademark Office (PTO) maintains the federal Trademark Register, which can be searched from the PTO's Web site. If the results of that search are favorable, a potential registrant ordinarily purchases a professional search from a third-party company, which normally would cost several hundred dollars. That search includes not only the federal records, but also state trademark registrations and evidence of common-law marks evident from trade directories, telephone directories, and state assumed-name filings.

B. Initial Interest Confusion

Although trademark law traditionally focused on confusion regarding the source of goods and services, the discussion above illustrates that the "propertization" of trademarks has moved the law in a variety of ways beyond that traditional focus. The Internet has presented its own line of authority on this front, as recent cases — several involving Web sites and the devices people use to find them — have extended trademark law to condemn devices that confuse consumers in a more subtle way. "Initial interest confusion" occurs when a consumer is led to one business not (as in the traditional trademark case) because of confusion about the name that the business places on its goods or services, but in some less direct way because of the consumer's reliance on the business of a competitor. If that seems confusing, the following case illustrates the importance of that concept to electronic commerce.

Playboy Enterprises, Inc. v. Netscape Communications Corp.
354 F.3d 1020 (9th Cir. 2004)

Before B. FLETCHER, T.G. NELSON, and BERZON, Circuit Judges.
T.G. NELSON, Circuit Judge.

Playboy Enterprises International, Inc. (PEI) appeals from the district court's grant of summary judgment in favor of Netscape Communications Corporation and Excite, Inc. PEI sued defendants for trademark infringement and dilution. . . . Because we conclude that genuine issues of material fact preclude summary judgment on both the trademark infringement and dilution claims, we reverse and remand.

I. FACTS

This case involves a practice called "keying" that defendants use on their Internet search engines. Keying allows advertisers to target individuals with certain interests by linking advertisements to pre-identified terms. To take an innocuous example, a person who searches for a term related to gardening may be a likely customer for a company selling seeds. Thus, a seed company might pay to have its advertisement displayed when searchers enter terms related to gardening. After paying a fee to defendants, that company could have its advertisements appear on the page listing the search results for gardening-related terms: the ad would be "keyed" to gardening-related terms. Advertisements appearing on search result pages are called "banner ads" because they run along the top or side of a page much like a banner.[1]

Defendants have various lists of terms to which they key advertisers' banner ads. Those lists include the one at issue in this case, a list containing terms related to sex and adult-oriented entertainment. Among the over-400 terms in this list are two for which PEI holds trademarks: "playboy" and "playmate." Defendants *require* adult-oriented companies to link their ads to this set of words. Thus, when a user types in "playboy," "playmate," or one of the other listed terms, those companies' banner ads appear on the search results page.[3]

PEI introduced evidence that the adult-oriented banner ads displayed on defendants' search results pages are often graphic in nature and are confusingly labeled or not labeled at all. In addition, the parties do not dispute that buttons on the banner ads say "click here." When a searcher complies, the search results page disappears, and the searcher finds him or herself at the advertiser's website. PEI presented uncontroverted evidence that defendants monitor "click rates," the ratio between the number of times searchers click on banner ads and the number of times the ads are shown. Defendants use click rate statistics to convince advertisers to renew their keyword contracts. The higher the click rate, the more successful they deem a banner ad.

PEI sued defendants, asserting that they were using PEI's marks in a manner that infringed upon and diluted them. The district court denied PEI's request for a preliminary injunction, and this court affirmed in an unpublished disposition. On remand, the parties filed cross-motions for summary judgment. The district court granted summary judgment in favor of defendants. We reverse . . .

III. DISCUSSION

A. TRADEMARK INFRINGEMENT . . .

2. PEI's case for trademark infringement.

The core element of trademark infringement, the likelihood of confusion, lies at the center of this case. [Quotation marks and citation omitted.] No dispute exists regarding the other requirements set forth by the statute: PEI clearly holds the marks in question and defendants used the marks in commerce without PEI's permission.

PEI's strongest argument for a likelihood of confusion is for a certain kind of confusion: initial interest confusion. Initial interest confusion is customer confusion that creates initial interest in a competitor's product. Although dispelled before an actual sale occurs, initial interest confusion impermissibly capitalizes on the goodwill associated with a mark and is therefore actionable trademark infringement.

PEI asserts that, by keying adult-oriented advertisements to PEI's trademarks, defendants actively create initial interest confusion in the following manner.

---

1. Not all banner ads are keyed. Some advertisers buy space for their banner ads but only pay to have their ads displayed randomly. Such ads cost less because they are un-targeted and are therefore considered less effective.

3. The search results page lists websites relevant to the search terms pursuant to the search engine's computer program. A user can click on any item in the list to link to the website of the organization listed. Defendants' search results pages for the terms "playboy" and "playmate" include links to PEI's websites.

Because banner advertisements appear immediately after users type in PEI's marks, PEI asserts that users are likely to be confused regarding the sponsorship of un-labeled banner advertisements. In addition, many of the advertisements instruct users to "click here." Because of their confusion, users may follow the instruction, believing they will be connected to a PEI cite. Even if they realize immediately upon accessing the competitor's site that they have reached a site wholly unre-lated to PEI's, the damage has been done: Through initial consumer confusion, the competitor will still have gained a customer by appropriating the goodwill that PEI has developed in its mark. [Quotation marks and brackets omitted.]

PEI's theory strongly resembles the theory adopted by this court in *Brookfield Communications, Inc. v. West Coast Entertainment Corporation,* [174 F.2d 1036 (1999)]. In *Brookfield,* a video rental company, West Coast Entertainment Corporation, planned on using "moviebuff.com" as a domain name for its web-site and using a similar term in the metatags for the site. Brookfield had trade-marked the term "MovieBuff," however, and sued West Coast for trademark infringement. The court ruled in favor of Brookfield. It reasoned that Internet users entering Brookfield's mark (plus ".com") or searching for Brookfield's mark on search engines using metatags, would find themselves at West Coast's website. Although they might "realize, immediately upon accessing 'moviebuff.com,' that they have reached a site operated by West Coast and wholly unrelated to Brookfield," some customers who were originally seeking Brookfield's website "may be perfectly content with West Coast's database (especially as it is offered free of charge)." [174 F.2d at 1057.] Because those customers would have found West Coast's site due to West Coast's "misappropriation of Brookfield's goodwill" in its mark, the court concluded that Brookfield withstood summary judgment. *Id.*

In this case, PEI claims that defendants, in conjunction with advertisers, have misappropriated the goodwill of PEI's marks by leading Internet users to competi-tors' websites just as West Coast video misappropriated the goodwill of Brookfield's mark. Some consumers, initially seeking PEI's sites, may initially believe that unlabeled banner advertisements are links to PEI's sites or to sites affil-iated with PEI. Once they follow the instructions to "click here," and they access the site, they may well realize that they are not at a PEI-sponsored site. However, they may be perfectly happy to remain on the competitor's site, just as the *Brookfield* court surmised that some searchers initially seeking Brookfield's site would happily remain on West Coast's site. The Internet user will have reached the site because of defendants' use of PEI's mark. Such use is actionable.

Although analogies to *Brookfield* suggest that PEI will be able to show a likeli-hood of confusion sufficient to defeat summary judgment, we must test PEI's the-ory using this circuit's well-established eight-factor test for the likelihood of confusion to be certain. [The court considers the eight factors in detail and con-cludes] that the majority favor PEI. Accordingly, we conclude that a genuine issue of material fact exists as to the substantial likelihood of confusion. . . .

[The court also reversed the district court's grant of summary judgment dis-missing PEI's claims for trademark dilution.]

Reversed and remanded.

BERZON, Circuit Judge, concurring.

I concur in Judge Nelson's careful opinion in this case, as it is fully consistent with the applicable precedents. I write separately, however, to express concern that one of those precedents was wrongly decided and may one day, if not now, need to be reconsidered *en banc.*

I am struck by how analytically similar keyed advertisements are to the metatags found infringing in *Brookfield Communications v. West Coast Entertainment Corp.,* 174 F.3d 1036 (9th Cir.1999). In *Brookfield,* the court held that the defendant could not use the trademarked term "moviebuff" as one of its metatags. . . .

Specifically, *Brookfield* held that the use of the trademarked terms in metatags violated the Lanham Act because it caused "initial interest confusion." *Brookfield,* 174 F.3d at 1062-66. The court explained that even though "there is no source confusion in the sense that consumers know [who] they are patronizing, . . . there is nevertheless initial interest confusion in the sense that, by using 'moviebuff.com' or 'MovieBuff' to divert people looking for 'MovieBuff' to its web-site, [the defendant] improperly benefits from the goodwill that [the plaintiff] developed in its mark." *Id.* at 1062.

As applied to this case, *Brookfield* might suggest that there could be a Lanham Act violation *even if* the banner advertisements were clearly labeled, either by the advertiser or by the search engine. I do not believe that to be so. So read, the metatag holding in *Brookfield* would expand the reach of initial interest confusion from situations in which a party is initially confused to situations in which a party is never confused. I do not think it is reasonable to find initial interest confusion when a consumer is never confused as to source or affiliation, but instead knows, or should know, from the outset that a product or web link is not related to that of the trademark holder because the list produced by the search engine so informs him.

There is a big difference between hijacking a customer to another website by making the customer think he or she is visiting the trademark holder's website (even if only briefly), which is what may be happening in this case when the banner advertisements are not labeled, and just distracting a potential customer with another *choice,* when it is clear that it is a choice. True, when the search engine list generated by the search for the trademark ensconced in a metatag comes up, an internet user might *choose* to visit westcoastvideo.com, the defendant's web-site in *Brookfield,* instead of the plaintiff's moviebuff.com website, but such choices do not constitute trademark infringement off the internet, and I cannot under-stand why they should on the internet.

For example, consider the following scenario: I walk into Macy's and ask for the Calvin Klein section and am directed upstairs to the second floor. Once I get to the second floor, on my way to the Calvin Klein section, I notice a more promi-nently displayed line of Charter Club clothes, Macy's own brand, designed to appeal to the same people attracted by the style of Calvin Klein's latest line of clothes. Let's say I get diverted from my goal of reaching the Calvin Klein section, the Charter Club stuff looks good enough to me, and I purchase some Charter Club shirts instead. Has Charter Club or Macy's infringed Calvin Klein's trademark, simply by having another product more prominently displayed before one reaches the Klein line? Certainly not. *See* Gregory Shea, Note, *Trademarks and Keyword Banner Advertising,* 75 S. CAL. L. REV. 529, 554 (2002) (comparing keyed banner advertisements to a customer entering a supermarket, requesting Tylenol, and then being directed to the pain reliever section which includes generic Acetaminophen, along with other generic and name-brand pain relievers); Julie A. Rajzer, Comment, *Misunderstanding the Internet: How Courts are Overprotecting Trademarks Used in Metatags,* 2001 L. REV. MICH. ST. U.C.L. 427, 462-63 (2001) (highlighting the brick-and-mortar world in which Kellogg's Raisin Bran and Post Raisin Bran both appear next to one another on the same aisle).

Similarly, suppose a customer walks into a bookstore and asks for Playboy magazine and is then directed to the adult magazine section, where he or she sees Penthouse or Hustler up front on the rack while Playboy is buried in back. One would not say that Penthouse or Hustler had violated Playboy's trademark. This conclusion holds true even if Hustler paid the store owner to put its magazines in front of Playboy's.

One can test these analogies with an on-line example: If I went to Macy's website and did a search for a Calvin Klein shirt, would Macy's violate Calvin Klein's trademark if it responded (as does Amazon.com, for example) with the requested shirt and pictures of other shirts I might like to consider as well? I very much doubt it.

Accordingly, I simply cannot understand the broad principle set forth in *Brookfield.* Even the main analogy given in *Brookfield* belies its conclusion. The Court gives an example of Blockbuster misdirecting customers from a competing video store, West Coast Video, by putting up a highway billboard sign giving directions to Blockbuster but telling customers that a West Coast Video store is located there. *Brookfield,* 174 F.3d at 1064. Even though customers who arrive at the Blockbuster realize that it is not West Coast Video, they were initially misled and confused. *Id.*

But there was no similar misdirection in *Brookfield,* nor would there be similar misdirection in this case were the banner ads labeled or otherwise identified. The *Brookfield* defendant's website was described by the court as being accurately listed as westcoastvideo.com in the applicable search results. Consumers were free to choose the official moviebuff.com website and were not hijacked or misdirected elsewhere. I note that the billboard analogy has been widely criticized as inapplicable to the internet situation, given both the fact that customers were not misdirected and the minimal inconvenience in directing one's web browser back to the original list of search results.

The degree to which this questionable aspect of *Brookfield* affects this case is not clear to me. Our opinion limits the present holding to situations in which the banner advertisements are not labeled or identified. Whether, on remand, the case will remain so limited is questionable. PEI may seek to reach labeled advertisements as well.

There will be time enough to address the continuing vitality of *Brookfield* should the labeled advertisement issue arise later. I wanted to flag the issue, however, as . . . the issue is a recurring one. Should the question arise again, in this case or some other, this court needs to consider whether we want to continue to apply an insupportable rule.

Given the increasing focus of Internet technology on making the Internet experience relevant to the interests of each particular user, you should ponder the policy implications, underscored in Judge Berzon's concurrence, of a doctrine that has the potential to give a trademark owner control over the experiences that users receive on the Internet when they use a trademarked name to identify something that they seek.

The developing doctrine has the potential to influence a variety of common marketing practices. For example, consider the use of pop-up ads for competitors that appear whenever a browser comes to a well-known site (the technology at issue in the *Gator.com* case in Assignment 1). That technology also has been challenged under the initial interest confusion doctrine. The following case provides a good lesson for the business lawyer, by illustrating that the details of how the technology is implemented can affect the legality of the technology.

U-Haul International, Inc. v. WhenU.Com, Inc.

279 F. Supp. 2d 723 (E.D. Va. 2003)

LEE, District Judge.

THIS MATTER is before the Court on the Plaintiff U-Haul International, Inc.'s ("U-Haul") and the Defendants WhenU.com, Inc.'s, ("WhenU") and Avi Naider's motions for summary judgment . . . .. This case involves pop-up advertising and Plaintiff U-Haul's claim that Defendant WhenU's pop-up advertising infringes upon U-Haul's trademark . . . . U-Haul complains that WhenU's pop-up advertisements, which crowd the computer user's screen and block out U-Haul's website display, in effect, infringe on U-Haul's registered trademark. The issue presented is whether WhenU's computer software, which presents pop-up advertising when the individual computer user searches for goods and services on the Internet, is a form of trademark . . . infringement. . . . Because the computer software at issue does not copy or use U-Haul's trademark the Court concludes that WhenU's pop-up advertising does not constitute trademark . . . infringement . . .; therefore, the Court grants WhenU's motion for summary judgment.

The Court acknowledges that this case is an attempt by a trademark owner and copyright holder to limit annoying pop-up advertising from blotting out its website on the individual computer user's screen. The average computer user who conducts a web search for the U-Haul website would expect the U-Haul website to appear on their computer screen; however, in this case, the computer screen fills with the advertisement of a U-Haul competitor. The user must then click and close the pop-up advertisement window in order to get to their destination, the U-Haul website. While at first blush this detour in the user's web search seems like a siphon-off of a business opportunity, the fact is that the computer user consented to this detour when the user downloaded WhenU's computer software from the Internet. In other words, the user deliberately or unwittingly downloaded the pop-up advertisement software. The foregoing explanation makes it clear that under the circumstances, while pop-up advertising may crowd out the U-Haul's advertisement screen through a separate window, this act is not trademark . . . infringement . . . .

Computer users, like this trial judge, may wonder what we have done to warrant the punishment of seizure of our computer screens by pop-up advertisements for secret web cameras, insurance, travel values, and fad diets. Did we unwittingly sign up for incessant advertisements that require us to click, click, and click again in order to return to our Internet work? The Court, in this opinion, attempts to answer this question; we have invited these pop-up advertisements by downloading free screen savers and other free software from the Internet.

Despite U-Haul's plea, the Court, upon review of the applicable law, concludes that, while pop-up advertisements seize the user's computer screen with a window of advertisement, blocking out the object of your search and your document, requiring you to click several times to clear your computer screen, these advertisements do not consist of trademark . . . infringement . . . .. WhenU's pop-up advertisement software resides in individual computers as a result of the invitation and consent of the individual computer user, and, thus, the advertisements do not use, alter or interfere with U-Haul's trademarks. Alas, we computer users must endure pop-up advertising along with her ugly brother unsolicited bulk email, "spam", as a burden of using the Internet.

I.   BACKGROUND

WhenU.com, Inc., and Avi Naider (collectively "WhenU") distribute a down-loadable software program called "SaveNow" that is generally bundled for distri-bution with other software programs. For example, the pop-up advertisement software is found in many web-based "free" screensaver programs downloaded by individual computer users. Once a user accepts the license agreement, the SaveNow software is delivered and installed on the user's computer. Using a direc-tory of commonly used search phrases, commonly visited web addresses, and var-ious keyword algorithms, the SaveNow program scans the user's Internet activity to determine whether any of the terms, web addresses, or content match the infor-mation in the directory. If the program finds a match, it identifies an associated product or service category. The SaveNow program then determines whether the user's computer should receive a pop-up advertisement that is selected at random from WhenU's clients which match the category of the user's activity. The program will then display a pop-up advertisement on the user's computer screen; this pop-up ad will generally appear in front of all the windows the user may have open at the time. Once the pop-up ad is displayed, the user must either move the mouse and click the ad closed or use the keystrokes "Alt-F4" to close the ad.

To maintain its business, WhenU sells advertising space and opportunities to merchants that want to take advantage of the SaveNow software. However, WhenU does not sell individual web addresses to its advertising clients and does not guarantee to any advertiser that its ad will be shown when a consumer visits a particular website. . . .

II.   DISCUSSION

. . . The Court grants Defendants' motion for summary judgment on Plaintiff's trademark claims because Plaintiff fails to show how a pop-up advertisement appearing in a separate window on an individual's computer obstructing U-Haul's advertisement is a "use" of U-Haul's trademarks in commerce. A plaintiff alleging causes of action for trademark infringement and unfair competition must prove (1) that it possesses a mark, (2) that the defendant used the mark, (3) that the defendant's use of the mark occurred 'in commerce', (4) that the defendant used the mark 'in connection with the sale, offering for sale, distribution, or advertis-ing' of goods or services, and (5) that the defendant used the mark in a manner likely to confuse consumers. 15 U.S.C. §§1114, 1125(a). A fundamental prereq-uisite for claims of trademark infringement pursuant to 15 U.S.C. §1114 and of unfair competition pursuant to 15 U.S.C. §1125(a) is proof that the defendant used one of the plaintiff's protected marks in commerce. A mark is "used in com-merce" in connection with goods when the mark is "placed in any manner on the goods or their containers or the displays associated therewith or on the tags or labels affixed thereto, . . . or on the documents associated with the goods or their sale." 15 U.S.C. §1127. A mark is "used in commerce" in connection with services when the mark is "used or displayed in the sale or advertising of services and the services are rendered in commerce. . . ." Id.

U-Haul contends that the fact that WhenU's pop-up ads appear on the same screen as U-Haul's website and logo is enough to constitute a "use in commerce" under the Lanham Act. U-Haul further argues that WhenU's use of U-Haul's trademark "U-Haul" as part of the process by which its pop-up advertisements are triggered constitutes "use in commerce." U-Haul also contends that When-U's pop-up scheme interferes with the use of U-Haul's Web site by its customers and dealers. As discussed below, however, WhenU's pop-up advertisements do not constitute "use in commerce" of U-Haul's trademarks for four reasons.

First, U-Haul relies on the premise that WhenU's pop-up ads are framed by the U-Haul website; in other words, the argument is that WhenU's ads appear as a single visual presentation as part of U-Haul's website. This position, however, is untenable. When a WhenU ad appears on a user's computer screen, it opens in a WhenU-branded window that is separate and distinct from the window in which the U-Haul website appears. It is important to note that in the Microsoft Windows environment, each program that the user launches generally appears on a separate window on the user's computer screen. In addition, the computer user may have multiple windows open at once; and in many instances, a separate window may pop-up on the user's screen notifying the user of an event: incoming e-mail, completion of a task by the computer, an appointment, etc.

Second, "use" is not established merely because trademarks are simultaneously visible to a consumer. Such comparative advertising does not violate trademark law, even when the advertising makes use of a competitor's trademark. Thus, the appearance of WhenU's ads on a user's computer screen at the same time as the U-Haul web page is a result of how applications operate in the Windows environment and does not consist "use" pursuant to the Lanham Act.

Third, WhenU's inclusion of the U-Haul uniform resource locator ("URL") and "U-Haul" in its directory incorporated into the SaveNow program does not constitute "use" under the Lanham Act. WhenU does not sell the U-Haul URL to its customers. Nor, does WhenU display the U-Haul URL or the words "U-Haul" to the computer user when the ad pops-up. U-Haul fails to adduce any evidence that WhenU uses U-Haul's trademarks to identify the source of its goods or services. WhenU does not place the U-Haul trademarks in commerce; the SaveNow program merely uses the U-Haul URL and "U-Haul". Likewise in the instant case, WhenU's incorporation of U-Haul's URL and "U-Haul" in the SaveNow program is not a trademark use because WhenU merely uses the marks for the "pure machine-linking function" and in no way advertises or promotes U-Haul's web address or any other U-Haul trademark.

Fourth, WhenU's pop-up scheme does not interfere with the use of U-Haul's web site by its customers and dealers because the SaveNow program does not interact with U-Haul's computer servers or systems and the SaveNow program is a user-installed program where the user has made a conscious decision to install the program. U-Haul cites several cases for the proposition that interference with a Web page constitutes a use in commerce; however, Plaintiff's reliance on these cases is misplaced. The cases address situations where the defendants prevented or hindered Internet users from accessing plaintiffs' services. *See People for Ethical Treatment of Animals v. Doughney,* 263 F.3d 359 (4th Cir. 2001) (finding that defendant had prevented users from downloading or using PETA's goods or services through cybersquatting on the domain name "www.peta.org"); *OBH, Inc. v. Spotlight Magazine, Inc.,* 86 F. Supp. 2d 176 (W.D.N.Y. 2000) (holding that defendant's website was likely to prevent or hinder Internet users from accessing plaintiff's services on plaintiff's own web site where defendant cybersquatted on the domain name "thebuffalonews.com").

In this instance, WhenU is not cybersquatting on U-Haul's trademark which serves as its domain name on the Internet. Nor, is a computer user taken to a WhenU website when the user searches for U-Haul's domain name. Furthermore, the SaveNow program does not hinder or impede Internet users from accessing U- Haul's web site in such a manner that WhenU "uses" U-Haul's trademarks. The SaveNow program resides within the user's computer and does not interact or communicate with U-Haul's website, its computer servers, or its computer systems. Further, the SaveNow program does not change the underlying appearance of the U-Haul website. In addition, the SaveNow program is installed by the computer user who can decline to accept the licensing agreement or decline to download the program. Thus, the user controls the computer display the moment the WhenU ad pops up, and the user may also have other programs with pop-up windows notifying the user of an event within the computer system. The SaveNow program is, therefore, no different than an e-mail system that pops a window up when the registered user receives a new e-mail message.

In sum, U-haul fails to establish that WhenU uses U-Haul's trademarks in commerce in violation of the Lanham Act because (1) WhenU's pop-up window is separate and distinct from U-Haul's web site, (2) WhenU does not advertise or promote U-Haul's trademarks through the use of U-Haul's URL or "U-Haul" in its SaveNow directory, and (3) the SaveNow program does not hinder or impede Internet users from accessing U-Haul's web site in such a manner that WhenU "uses" U-Haul's trademarks. Therefore, WhenU is entitled to summary judgment on U-Haul's claims of trademark infringement.

Relevant Glossary Entries

Description meta tag
DNS
Keyword meta tag
Meta tag
Trademark dilution

Problem Set 3

3.1.   Your friend Carl Eben at RiverFront Tools comes to see you today. Carl runs a pneumatic tool company located in central Texas, with customers located around the United States. As his business grows, he has decided that he would like to start marketing his products under an abbreviated name — "RFT." (He admits to you that he is inspired by the general abandonment of the name Federal Express in favor of the shorter FedEx mark. Like Federal

Express, he will continue to use RiverFront Tools on some products, to make sure that he doesn't abandon the RiverFront mark.) He also would like to set up a Web site at *www.rft.com* from which he would sell goods. He has several questions for you. The first question is whether (and when) he should do anything to protect the name "RFT"?

3.2.   Carl goes off to implement your advice and calls you back the next week. It appears that there is a domain name already in existence for *www.rft.com*. The site appears to be owned by Robert "Fats" Taylor, a blues piano player from Memphis, Tennessee. The site includes pictures of Robert (and his mentor Big Maceo Merriweather), an e-mail address to which fans can send requests for copies of Robert's musical recordings, and a page where fans can sign up for a newsletter about Robert's activities. How much of a problem does this pose for Carl? What should Carl do? Lanham Act §§ 32, 43.

3.3.   How would your answer change if Taylor has just started selling shirts emblazoned with a logo consisting of RFT in large, brightly colored letters with the rest of the characters of the full name "Robert 'Fats' Taylor" trailing off in small letters from the large letters?

3.4.   Still later, after Carl has reached an accommodation with Robert and has his Web site up and running at *www.rft.com*, Carl comes to ask about a problem. He discovered from a customer yesterday that searches for RiverFront Tools on all of the major search engines report as the first result *www.cpt.com*, a Web site operated by California Pneumatic Tools. On investigation, this appears to be because California Pneumatic Tools (CPT) has included in its meta tags all of the information that resides on the meta tags at *www.rft.com*. Can Carl do anything about this? Lanham Act §§ 32, 43.

3.5.   A few hours later, even more frustrated, Carl calls you back to report that a search for "RiverFront Tools" on Google produces a link to a street address for RiverFront tools as the top search result, a prominent ad for *www.cpt.com* on the right side of the screen, but no link at all for *www.rft.com*. Does Carl have a valid complaint against Google? Lanham Act §§ 32, 43.

Assignment 4: Cybersquatting

Almost as soon as the Internet was opened to commercial activity, disputes between trademark owners and domain-name registrants began to arise with alarming frequency. The creation of new "generic top level domains" (gTLDs) may usher in another round of such disputes as new territory for domain-name competition becomes available. (If you would like to read more about this topic, see Appendix A at the end of the book.) Thus, owners of valuable trademarks must bear the expense and difficulty of monitoring the Internet to detect infringing activities and to stop so-called "cybersquatters," who occupy domain names related in some noticeable way to a valuable trademark. Because of the volume of those disputes and their importance to trademark owners, specialized rules for resolving those disputes have developed rapidly. This assignment discusses the two most important sets of rules: the dispute-resolution systems promulgated by the Internet Corporation for Assigned Names and Numbers (ICANN) (and formerly by Network Solutions Inc. (NSI)), and, more recently, the 1999 Anticybersquatting Consumer Protection Act (ACPA).

A. Private Responses: NSI and ICANN Dispute-Resolution Policies

From the days of the first disputes between domain-name registrants and trademark owners, trademark owners have put considerable pressure on the domain-name registrars either to screen applications for possible trademark violations or to provide a mechanism for trademark owners to resolve such disputes without litigation. But neither NSI nor ICANN has been willing to increase the amount it charges to the point where those fees would cover the expense of screening applications for potential trademark infringement. In 1995, however, NSI did respond to pressure from trademark owners by issuing a dispute-resolution policy. That policy was designed to address both the demands of trademark owners for simple and effective alternative dispute resolution and the desire of NSI to avoid becoming entangled in questions of trademark law.

The initial NSI policy required applicants to warrant that their registration would not interfere with the rights of any third parties and obligated registrants to use domain names once they were registered. If the complaining party submitted to NSI proof that it had a registered trademark that was identical to the domain name in question, and if the potential domain-name registrant offered no proof that it had registered the same mark, then NSI would place a domain name on "hold." The policy did not, however, provide a process for resolving the dispute. Rather, once a domain name was on hold, NSI would not allow its use until NSI was presented with a court order or arbitrator's award resolving the dispute. That policy caused a considerable outcry among many in the Internet community, who found it to be biased against registrants who had a legitimate interest in the domain name but did not have a registered trademark. Consider, for example, the famous dispute between Marvel Comics (which holds intellectual property related to the character Veronica in the Archie comic strips) and the parent that registered a Web site for a daughter named Veronica.

Shortly after ICANN took over management of the domain-name system, it promulgated a new dispute-resolution policy, which took effect in 1999. As a practical matter, that policy has universal application to disputes involving the generic top-level domains, because all registrars accredited by ICANN to register domain names within the gTLDs must, as part of the registration process, require all applicants for domain-name registration services to agree to follow ICANN's Uniform Dispute Resolution Procedure (UDRP).

Proceedings under the UDRP begin with a complaint by the trademark owner, which is filed with an arbitrator, selected by the trademark owner from a list approved by ICANN. Although the list includes several minor dispute-resolution providers, more than 90 percent of the disputes are handled by the World Intellectual Property Organization (WIPO), the National Arbitration Forum, and the Center for Public Resources.

In most cases, the complaining party will have no opportunity to file additional pleadings, so the complaint should fully document the trademark owner's right to recover under the UDRP. The complaint may be served on the registrant by lodging it with the dispute-resolution service provider. The provider then forwards the complaint to the registrant, using the administrative contact information shown for that domain name. The registrant has 20 days to submit a response.

Unless the domain-name registrant objects, the proceeding is conducted before a single arbitrator and the complaining party pays the fees of the arbitrator. The domain-name registrant can, however, ask for a three-person arbitration panel, but then it must pay half of the fees for the three-person panel. The typical fees are quite modest. For example, as of June 2004, if one domain name is in dispute, the WIPO fee for a single arbitrator is $1,500, for a three-person panel $4,000. The NAF fees are $1,150 and $2,500, respectively. The CPR fees are $2,000 and $4,500, respectively.

The only relief available under the UDRP is cancellation of the domain-name registration or transfer of the registration to the complaining party. The decisions usually are provided in a matter of weeks. They normally come in the form of opinions, which are broadly disseminated and published. The caseload illustrates the magnitude of the problem. By the summer of 2004, the UDRP had been invoked in about 9,000 proceedings involving about 15,000 domain names.

The success of the UDRP doubtless is driven by the favorable results it offers trademark owners (who are choosing the forum). For one thing, the UDRP substantially solves the problem of obtaining personal jurisdiction over the registrant, at least if the trademark owner is willing to accept a resolution limited to the domain name and forgo the possibility of money damages or broader injunctive relief. Also, trademark owners tend to be quite successful under the UDRP. For example, a study by Michael Geist suggests that as of 2002 complainants win about 83 percent of single-member panel cases, and 94 percent of cases in which the registrant fails to respond. Even when a response is filed, complainants win 68 percent of the single-member panel cases.

As a formal matter, the UDRP requires the complaining party to show both that the registrant has no "legitimate interest" in the name and that the registrant has used the name in "bad faith." Part of the reason complainants are so successful under the UDRP doubtless is because the arbitration panels have not consistently required as high a threshold of proof as the language might suggest to the uninformed reader. The following case is illustrative.

Hewlett-Packard Company v. Burgar

Nat'l Arb. Forum Domain Dispute Decision No. FA 0002000093564
(Apr. 10, 2000)

DOMAIN NAME AT ISSUE

The Domain Name at issue is HEWLETTPACKARD.COM, which is registered with Network Solutions, Inc. (NSI).

SUMMARY OF EVIDENCE, ISSUES AND FINDINGS

Hewlett-Packard is a company that owns seventeen U.S. registrations for HEWLETT PACKARD. It uses the mark HEWLETT PACKARD in connection with computer software, computer hardware, computer printers and cartridges, printed materials, Internet services, business services, computer peripherals, and various other computer related services. Hewlett-Packard has used the mark HEWLETT PACKARD since January 1, 1946.

The respondent Jeff Burgar d/b/a Hewlett Club registered the domain name "hewlettpackard.com" on October 17, 1996. Respondent is not a licensed Hewlett-Packard re-seller. He claims to be affiliated with the Pegasus Bookstore located in High Prarie [sic], Alberta, Canada that is a licensed re-seller of [Hewlett Packard] products.

Respondent raises several issues in his response. The first issue concerns jurisdiction to arbitrate. Respondent claims that in order for arbitral jurisdiction to attach, there must be an explicit agreement to arbitrate.

With regard to this issue, the arbitration panel found that the respondent renewed the domain name registration on October 16, 1999. At that time, "Version 4.0" of the NSI Registration Agreement contained the following language:

*DISPUTE POLICY**

> C) Registrant agrees, as a condition to submitting this Registration Agreement, and if the Registration Agreement is accepted by NSI, that the registrant shall be bound by NSI current Dispute Policy.
> D) Dispute Policy Changes or Modifications: Registrant agrees that NSI, in its sole discretion may change or modify the Dispute Policy incorporated by reference herein,

---

* Paragraph formatting of quotation from agreement altered for consistency.

at any time. Registrant agrees that registrant's maintaining the registration of a domain name after changes or modification to the Dispute Policy becomes effective constitutes Registrant's continued acceptance of these changes or modifications.

Registrant agrees that if Registrant considers any such changes or modifications to be unacceptable, Registrant may request that the domain name be deleted from the domain name database.

NSI's [current] policy [calls] for resolution of all Domain Disputes . . . by arbitration pursuant to The Internet Corporation for Assigned Names and Numbers Rules for Uniform Domain Name Dispute Resolution Policy. (ICANN UDRP) Approved on October 24, 1999. Respondent has never requested NSI to delete him as Registrant of the Domain Name in dispute.

Based on the foregoing, the panel finds that jurisdiction to arbitrate does exist.

The next issue to be decided by the panel concerns the elements of a Domain Name Transfer Claim. Specifically, in order to prevail, a Complainant must prove the following:

1. [T]hat the domain name is identical or confusingly similar to a trademark or service mark in which the complainant has rights; and,
2. [T]hat the respondent has no rights or legitimate interests in respect of the domain name; and,
3. That the domain name has been registered and is being used in bad faith.

With regard to the first element, the panel finds that the domain name at issue is identical to the trademark of the Complainant.

With regard to the second element, the panel finds that the respondent has no rights or legitimate interests in respect of the domain name. He is not a licensed dealer of Hewlett-Packard products and has not demonstrated any right except to declare that he is affiliated with the Pegasus Bookstore.

With regard to the third element, the panel finds that the respondent has registered and is using the domain name in bad faith. Evidence of bad faith exists from a finding that the respondent registered the domain name in order to prevent the owner of the trademark or service mark from using the mark in a corresponding domain name and that the respondent has engaged in a pattern of such conduct. Specifically, the respondent has stated that he would transfer the name if he were paid his costs associated with registration and received a public apology from the complainant. This demonstrates to the panel that he has no legitimate right or interest in the domain name. Also, the panel finds that the respondent has engaged in a pattern of such conduct. That pattern of conduct is shown by the fact that the respondent has registered more than 1,300 domain names that correspond to well-known and famous names without any purported right or interest in those names. Some of those domain names include TEXASIN-STRUMENTS.COM; TOMCRUISE3.COM; MARIAHCAREY4.COM; GUN-SNROSES4.COM; DENZELWASHINGTON2.COM; ASHLEYJUDD2.COM; CARMENELECTRA.COM; JOHN TRAVOLA3.COM; MELANIEGRIFFITH2.COM; ELLAMACPHERSON2.COM; and many more. In addition, the Respondent has registered domain names corresponding with the names of Major League Baseball Properties, National Football League, National Basketball Association and National Hockey League [teams]. Many of these entities have filed suit against the respondent for the purported illegal registration and use of said domain names.

DECISION

Having found jurisdiction to arbitrate and having found the elements necessary to grant the relief requested, the panel, by a majority vote, directs that the domain name "HEWLETTPACKARD.COM" be transferred to the Complainant Hewlett-Packard Company.

DISSENTING OPINION [of Professor A. Michael Froomkin]

The complainant is a US corporation with a world-wide presence, and the respondent is a Canadian national. Complainant has used the trademark Hewlett Packard in the US since 1946, and has 18 registrations dating between 1957 and 1997. The complainant established its internet presence under the hp.com domain, registered March 3, 1986.

Respondent, a Canadian, registered the domain name hewlettpackard.com under the name Hewlett Club of Las Vegas, Nevada on Oct. 17, 1996. The respondent has registered some 1300 domains, many of which are names identifying sports teams or other business[es] with which the respondent has no contractual relationships. There is no evidence that these domains have been offered for sale, and respondent alleges that he uses at least some of them to provide free "vanity" web-based e-mail services to thousands of subscribers.

The respondent alleges that he registered hewlettpackard.com for his daughter, who owns the Pegasus bookstore in High Prairie, Alberta, Canada, and which offers certain licensed Hewlett Packard products for sale. He alleges that he knew that Hewlett Packard was using hp.com, and concluded that his daughter could expand into online distribution of the products she sold in her store. Thus, by his own admission, the domain was registered for a business purpose. At complainant's request, NSI placed the domain on "hold" on Dec 4, 1996, and the domain has remained frozen and unusable ever since.

Respondent's first contention is that when faced with a claim that it is without jurisdiction the panel should refuse to decide the matter until the question of arbitrability has been decided by a competent court. I agree with the majority that this panel, whether viewed as engaged in an international arbitration or an administrative procedure, has both the power and the duty to determine whether it has jurisdiction. Respondent's contentions to the contrary fly in the face of the long-held principle that arbitrators must decide jurisdictional issues as an initial matter, and are without merit.

The claim that there is no jurisdiction because the respondent has never agreed to the UDRP is more substantial, but on the facts of this case it fails. When respondent originally registered the domain the NSI dispute policy provided that NSI would place domains on "hold" when requested to do so by any trademark holder with a valid registration in a name identical to the domain. When the respondent most recently renewed his registration, Network Solutions's standard form contract was as quoted by the majority. NSI changed the contract a few days later to require that registrants agree to the UDRP, a new third-party beneficiary arbitration clause. (The record is silent as to what actual notice the respondent may have had. It seems fair to assume, however, that anyone with 1300 domain name registrations, not to mention at least one on hold, kept abreast of the vagaries of the dispute process.)

Given that this term implies agreement by acquiescence, and that the only remedy provided by NSI to one unhappy with the new terms is to forfeit one's registration without a refund, one might reasonably ask if some more overt agreement was required to make the new term effective, or if the term is unconscionable, or if it violates some public policy. However, respondent has failed to identify or argue any relevant public policies, much less what law applies. Furthermore, it is at least arguable that, for the special class of those with domains on hold, the UDRP is actually an improvement over the previous policy since it holds out the prospect of having a matter resolved in their favor as opposed to a seemingly permanent freeze. Finally, in this case it is clear that there are no consumer law issues since the respondent specified he acquired the domain for his daughter's business.

At this point, I must part company with the majority. The UDRP states plainly that a complainant has the burden of demonstrating that the respondent's domain "has been registered and is being used in bad faith". Sec. 4(a)(iii). The issue of registration in bad faith is in part a question of credibility of the respondent's assertion that he obtained the domain name in good faith for his daughter's bookstore. There is no evidence before us contradicting this assertion other than the somewhat suspicious choice of the name "Hewlett Club" as the registrant; the claim of good faith — or, at least, of the absence of any intent to block Hewlett Packard from using its name as it saw fit — receives at least some support from the fact that Hewlett Packard Corp. had chosen to register and use hp.com many years earlier. The majority nevertheless decides that respondent's sworn affidavit is not credible on the apparent grounds that this testimony regarding his daughter from someone with 1300 domains, many of which appear to overlap trademarks, is inherently incredible. Although this reasoning has the attraction of rough justice, it comes dangerously close to making cybersquatting a status offense rather than one that the UDRP instructs us must be based on conduct.

Be that as it may, one thing is clear: the domain name hewlettpackard.com has never been used. The domain has been on hold since shortly after its registration. No email, no ftp, no web access has been possible since that time. Nor has the domain been "used" by being offered for sale "for valuable consideration in excess of documented out-of-pocket costs" unless one would intend the absurdity that the request of an apology in addition to reimbursement for cost is to be evidence of bad faith. This simple fact should suffice to find that the complainant has failed to state a claim under the UDRP.

The majority opinion could be read to suggest that [§] 4(b)(ii) of the UDRP supplies the necessary bad faith use. Section 4(b)(ii) says that evidence of bad faith can be found if respondent has "registered the domain name in order to prevent the owner of the trademark or service mark from reflecting the mark in a corresponding domain name, provided that you have engaged in a patter[n] of such conduct". This seems best understood as a gloss on what constitutes bad faith registration, and extending registration to constitute bad faith use strains the English language. It turns the "and" in [§] 4(a)(iii) into an "or" since multiple registrations become a form of use. This reading does not seem correct, but rather a case of letting the result determine the reasoning. Even if one were to agree that the record in this case supports a finding that the respondent has engaged in a pattern and practice of registering domain names in order to prevent the owner of the correlative trademarks from registering the names (something respondent strenuously denies, and which is currently being litigated in various courts), it does not follow that any domain name registered by the respondent is therefore being used in bad faith if it is on hold, has never been used in any fashion, and has not been offered for sale above cost.

The lack of "use" compels a verdict for the respondent.

Two other elements of the majority decision deserve mention. First, any suggestion that asking for an apology as well as actual costs suffices to make someone a cybersquatter seems well calculated to destroy settlement talks and is a very bad signal to send the bar. Second, although it is certainly the case that the respondent has registered a large number of domain names that resemble other people's trademarks, the examples cited by the majority are mostly "handles" (internal NSI nicknames) rather than domain names, or are personal names which are neither trademarks nor servicemarks and are not covered by the UDRP.

One of the most serious questions in UDRP cases has been the ability of a trademark owner to obtain a domain name that is used for the purpose of criticizing the products of a trademark owner. As the following case suggests, those cases present a close interpretive question under the UDRP. The cases seem to be coalescing around the result this case suggests, that a "cybergriping" site like this one is permissible if the owner refrains from any commercial conduct on the site and refrains from inappropriate (that is, extortionate) efforts to cause the trademark owner to purchase the site.

Wal-Mart Stores, Inc. v. Richard MacLeod d/b/a For Sale

(WIPO Arbitration and Mediation Center Case No. D2000-0662)
(Sept. 19, 2000)

1.   The Parties

The Complainant is Wal-Mart Stores, Inc., a United States corporation with its headquarters in Bentonville, Arkansas, United States of America.

The Respondent is Richard MacLeod d/b/a For Sale, 21 Simpson Avenue, Toronto, ON M8Z1C9, United States of America.

2.   The Domain Name and Registrar

The domain name at issue is wal-martsucks.com. The domain name is registered with Register.com.

3.   Factual Background

The Panel has reviewed the Complainant's Complaint and Respondent's Response. The following facts appear to be undisputed: The Complainant operates over 2,500 stores worldwide. All its trading operations, advertisements and promotions are conducted under the mark "Wal-Mart," and it has used this mark continuously since 1962. Its Internet addresses include walmart.com, wal-mart.com, and walmartstores.com. Its businesses include discount retail stores, grocery stores, pharmacies, membership warehouse clubs, and deep discount warehouse outlets.

Complainant holds registrations for the mark "Wal-Mart" in the United States, Switzerland, the United Kingdom, Denmark, and numerous other countries. The

Respondent has no rights granted by the Complainant in any of the marks involving the word "Wal-Mart".

The Respondent registered the domain name wal-martsucks.com on February 12, 2000.

4.   Procedural Background

Complainant filed its Complaint by email on June 22, 2000. Because of a deficiency noted by the Center (Complainant had failed to comply with Rule 3(b)(xiii)), Complainant filed an Amended Complaint, which was received in hardcopy by the Center on July 10, 2000.

On July 14, 2000, the Center formally commenced this proceeding and notified Respondent that its Response would be due by August 2, 2000. Respondent timely filed its Response, which was received by the Center in hardcopy on July 26, 2000. . . .

On August 4, 2000, the Center appointed a Panel. The Panelist thereafter developed a conflict of interest, and recused himself. On September 6, 2000, the Center appointed David H. Bernstein as a substitute Panelist. Neither party requested a three-member Panel. . . .

5.   Parties' Allegations

The Complainant submits that its mark is famous throughout the United States and all those other countries in which it trades. It further argues that the domain name is identical to its "Wal-Mart" mark because the domain name wholly incorporates "Wal-Mart" and also is confusingly similar to its "Wal-Mart" marks because "Wal-Mart" is so famous that buyers "would be likely to think that any commercial site connected with the domain name wal-martsucks.com, particularly a site selling consumer products," or "any domain name incorporating the Wal-Mart name (or a close approximation thereof)" originates with the Complainant.

The Complainant argues that Respondent has no rights or legitimate interests in respect of the domain name. First, Respondent is not currently using the domain name in connection with any ongoing business. Second, to the best of the Complainant's knowledge, Respondent has no rights to any use of the term Wal-Mart.

The Complainant further submits that the domain name wal-martsucks.com was registered and is used in bad faith. Improper use of the name is shown by the Respondent's attempt to sell the name through the Great Domains website for $530,000 and on Respondent's website for $545,000.

The Respondent focuses his response on the first factor of the ICANN policy, arguing that wal-martsucks.com is neither identical to nor confusingly similar to "Wal-Mart." He relies on *Bally Total Fitness Holding Corp. v. Faber*, 29 F. Supp. 2d 1161 (C.D. Cal. 1998), which concluded that the addition of the word "sucks" prevents any reasonably prudent user from confusing a "sucks" website with an authorized website.

Respondent concedes that his original intention upon registration of wal-martsucks.com was to sell the name for profit, and concedes that this constitutes registration in bad faith, but claims that he had a "change of heart" when he learned of Wal-Mart's abusive employment and consumer practices, so that the website no longer is being "used" in bad faith. He further claims that Wal-Mart cannot prove that it was actually Respondent who offered wal-martsucks.com for sale because Great Domains does not verify sellers. Thus, he claims that Complainant has insufficient evidence to show bad faith. Finally, he suggests that Complainant knew of the availability of the wal-martsucks.com domain name long before he registered it and should have done so when the name was available.

6. Discussion and Findings

The burden for the Complainant under paragraph 4(a) of the ICANN Policy is to prove:

(a)   That the domain name registered by the Respondent is identical or confusingly similar to a trademark or service mark in which the Complainant has rights;

(b)   That the Respondent has no rights or legitimate interests in respect of the domain name; and

(c)   The domain name has been registered and used in bad faith.

Initially, the Panel rejects any suggestion that Complainant's failure to register wal-martsucks.com before Respondent did so precludes this Complaint under any theory, including laches. Trademark owners are not required to create "libraries" of domain names in order to protect themselves, and there are strong policy reasons against encouraging this behavior. Moreover, as human creativity reaches its utmost where disparagement (not to mention money) is involved, any such attempt by a trademark owner would be futile, and thus Respondent has no equitable argument against Complainant.

The second and third elements of the Policy are easily disposed of in this case. Respondent's sole argument with respect to the second element is that he is using wal-martsucks.com to criticize Wal-Mart. Respondent could potentially have a legitimate interest in using wal-martsucks.com as a site critical of Wal-Mart; the Policy specifically provides that "a legitimate noncommercial or fair use of the domain name, without intent for commercial gain to misleadingly divert consumers or to tarnish the trademark or service mark," can establish legitimate rights and interests in a domain name. Policy paragraph 4(c)(iii). In this case, however, Complainant alleges, and Respondent does not deny, that before Complainant initiated the present proceeding, he was using the site solely for the purpose of selling it. While Respondent claims to have had a "change of heart," this change appears to have been driven by his domain name disputes with Complainant, and it is too little, too late.

Respondent admits that he registered the domain name in bad faith. The Panel specifically rejects Respondent's argument that Complainant produced insufficient evidence of bad faith use. Though Respondent questions the reliability of the information on the Great Domains website (Respondent claims that anyone can list a domain name for sale on that site, and thus Complainant has not proven that it is Respondent who offered the name for sale), he never actually denies that it was he who listed wal-martsucks.com on Great Domains, nor does he deny that he offered the domain name for sale on his own site. Indeed, the Respondent's intent is made clear by the name in which he registered the domain name: "For Sale." See Unibanco v. Vendo Domain Sale, Case No. D2000-0671 (WIPO, Aug. 31, 2000). Combined with Respondent's own admission, this is ample evidence of bad faith use. Again, Respondent's newly developed critical use of the site during the pendency of this proceeding is insufficient to erase the prior bad faith use.

The difficult question in this case is whether Complainant has shown that wal-martsucks.com "is identical or confusingly similar to" Complainant's mark under

Paragraph 4(a)(1) of the Policy. In prior cases, this Panel has held that a domain name that incorporates a mark but also adds another word is not "identical" to the mark under the Policy. See, e.g., EAuto, L.L.C. v. Triple S. Auto Parts d/b/a Kung Fu Yea Enterprises, Inc., No. D2000-0047 (WIPO, Mar. 24, 2000). This Panel has also held that incorporating a distinctive mark in its entirety creates sufficient similarity between the mark and the domain name to render it confusingly similar. Id.

Following this reasoning, Complainant contends that consumers are likely to believe that any domain name incorporating the sequence "Wal-Mart" or a close approximation thereof is associated with Complainant. In the ordinary case, when a generic term is appended to the trademark (such as the domain name wal-martstores.com), this would be so. But the fame of a mark does not always mean that consumers will associate all use of the mark with the mark's owner. No reasonable speaker of modern English would find it likely that Wal-Mart would identify itself using wal-martsucks.com. Complainant has no evidence of any potential confusion. The Panel specifically rejects Complainant's argument that consumers are likely to be confused as to the sponsorship or association of a domain name that combines a famous mark with a term casting opprobrium on the mark.

Nevertheless, the Panel understands the phrase "identical or confusingly similar" to be greater than the sum of its parts. The Policy was adopted to prevent the extortionate behavior commonly known as "cybersquatting," in which parties registered domain names in which major trademark owners had a particular interest in order to extort money from those trademark owners. This describes Respondent's behavior. Thus, the Panel concludes that a domain name is "identical or confusingly similar" to a trademark for purposes of the Policy when the domain name includes the trademark, or a confusingly similar approximation, regardless of the other terms in the domain name. In other words, the issue under the first factor is not whether the domain name causes confusion as to source (a factor more appropriately considered in connection with the legitimacy of interest and bad faith factors), but instead whether the mark and domain name, when directly compared, have confusing similarity. Having so concluded, Respondent's use of the domain name wal-martsucks.com meets all three of the conditions necessary to justify a transfer of the domain name to Complainant.

The Panel is cognizant of the importance of protecting protest sites that use a trademark to identify the object of their criticism. The "legitimate interest" and "bad faith" factors should adequately insulate true protest sites from vulnerability under the Policy, especially as the Complainant retains the burden of proof on each factor. Where, as here, a domain name registrant does not use a site for protest but instead offers it for sale for substantially more than the costs of registration, the site does not further the goal of legitimate protest; rather, it constitutes trademark piracy.

7. Decision

For the foregoing reasons, the Panel decides:

(a) that the domain name wal-martsucks.com is identical or confusingly similar to the Wal-Mart trademark in which the Complainant has rights;

(b) that the Respondent has no rights or legitimate interests in respect of the domain name; and

(c) the Respondent's domain name has been registered and is being used in bad faith.

Accordingly, pursuant to paragraph 4(i) of the Policy, the Panel requires that the registration of the domain name wal-martsucks.com be transferred to the Complainant.

B.   Federal Response:
The Anticybersquatting Consumer Protection Act

In 1999, Congress passed the Anticybersquatting Consumer Protection Act (ACPA), codified as Lanham Act § 43(d), 15 U.S.C. § 1125(d). The ACPA creates a new cause of action for trademark owners that can show bad-faith registration or use of a domain name that infringes or dilutes a trademark. The ACPA also simplifies the process of obtaining jurisdiction over a remote defendant by creating a new form of *in rem* jurisdiction over the domain name in the jurisdiction where the registrar who registered the domain name is located. For example, because of NSI's location in Reston, Virginia, federal courts in the Eastern District of Virginia now have jurisdiction to provide relief to trademark owners in cybersquatting cases involving all names registered by NSI.

To establish a claim under the ACPA, the trademark owner must provide the same proof as in a typical trademark case, as well as proof of a bad-faith intention to profit from the registration of the name. The ACPA and UDRP nominally impose different standards of bad faith: The ACPA requires a showing of bad faith in registration, while the UDRP requires proof of bad faith in registration *and* use. But, as the *Hewlett-Packard* case suggests, arbitrators in UDRP cases frequently decide cases in favor of trademark owners without requiring any more concrete showing of bad-faith use than registration of the domain name. Accordingly, there seems to be increasingly little substantive difference between the two avenues for recourse.

There is, however, a substantial difference in the procedures: The UDRP is a wholly summary process that is decided entirely "on the papers." A proceeding under the ACPA is a standard piece of civil litigation, which can involve discovery, motion practice, a trial, and then an appeal. An important point for the business owner, however, is that the UDRP is not the end of the litigation. Even after proceedings under the UDRP have been completed, there is the prospect of further litigation under the ACPA. The key question in that litigation will be the degree of deference that the federal court must afford to the award of the arbitral tribunal. The Third Circuit addressed that question in the case that follows.

Dluhos v. Strasberg
321 F.3d 365 (3rd Cir. 2003)

Before ROTH, FUENTES and ALDISERT, Circuit Judges.
ALDISERT, Circuit Judge.
This appeal requires us to decide whether a dispute resolution under the Internet Corporation for Assigned Names and Numbers' Uniform Domain Name

Dispute Resolution Policy ("UDRP") is entitled to the extremely deferential standard of judicial review set forth in the Federal Arbitration Act ("FAA"), 9 U.S.C. §10(a)(2)-10(a)(3). After Appellant Eric Dluhos registered the domain name www.leestrasberg.com invoking the name of the renowned acting coach, representatives of Lee Strasberg's widow, his eponymous acting institute and his estate instituted administrative proceedings culminating in a National Arbitration Forum dispute resolution that shifted the domain name from Dluhos to the Strasberg parties. Dluhos simultaneously sought relief in the district court, which applied the FAA standards to the NAF panel's order and dismissed the complaint. Dluhos appealed, and we now reverse.

Among Appellant's various contentions, he appeals from the district court's refusal to vacate an order under the UDRP. Constitutional issues are presented, but we must first decide whether the district court properly chose to review the NAF panel's decision under the Federal Arbitration Act's deferential standards for judicial review of arbitration decisions and a separate "manifest disregard for the law" standard, or whether a UDRP dispute resolution proceeding does not qualify as "arbitration" under the FAA and instead falls under broader category of review.

I.

In the district court, Dluhos had filed a complaint against Anna Strasberg, the Estate of Lee Strasberg and the Lee Strasberg Theatre Institute (the "Strasberg defendants"); Mark Roesler and CMG Worldwide Inc. (the "CMG defendants"); and Network Solutions, Inc. The court ruled that he failed to state a claim for which relief may be granted. . . .

Pursuant to a Cooperative Agreement with the federal National Science Foundation (NSF), one of the Appellees, Network Solutions, Inc. (NSI), a private entity, is the exclusive provider of Internet domain name registration services to the public. On June 25, 1999, *pro se* plaintiff Eric Dluhos entered into a domain-name registration agreement with NSI to register the domain name www.leestrasberg.com. The registration agreement required Dluhos to abide by NSI's ever-evolving dispute resolution policy, which incorporated the Internet Corporation for Assigned Names and Numbers' Uniform Domain Name Dispute Resolution Policy as it developed. The UDRP — and thus Dluhos' agreement with NSI — requires a domain-name registrant to submit to a "mandatory administrative proceeding" before an approved dispute resolution service provider to resolve a third party's complaint concerning the registration and use of a particular registered domain name. [UDRP §] 4(a). The National Arbitration Forum is one such approved provider.

Anna Strasberg — the widow of actor and acting coach Lee Strasberg — owns and directs the Lee Strasberg Theatre Institute and serves as the executrix of the Estate of Lee Strasberg. As executrix, she is responsible for Estate-owned trademarks and service marks, which include "The Lee Strasberg Institute" and "Actor by Lee Strasberg." CMG Worldwide, Inc. represents and manages Internet sites for the Estate, the Institute and Anna Strasberg. CMG maintains an official Web sites for the Institute, the Estate and Anna Strasberg at www.strasberg.com.

Dluhos' registration of www.leestrasberg.com came to the attention of Mark Roesler, CMG's chief executive officer. In May 2000, Roesler sent four letters to Dluhos, informing him that his use of the domain name www.leestrasberg.com

violated the Strasberg trademarks and that CMG would take action to have the domain name transferred, potentially through UDRP dispute resolution, if Dluhos would not rescind it.

Having heard nothing from Dluhos, CMG submitted a complaint to the National Arbitration Forum on June 2, 2000. The complaint requested a UDRP dispute resolution proceeding and formally disputed Dluhos' right to use the domain name, alleging that the domain name was "identical or confusingly similar to" a trademark owned by the Estate; that Dluhos had "no rights or legitimate interests" in the name; and that he had registered and used the name "in bad faith." Dluhos had until June 26, 2000 to respond. Rather than participating in the dispute resolution process to which he had agreed when he registered the domain name with NSI a year earlier, Dluhos submitted a letter of limited appearance to the NAF to explain that he would not submit to dispute resolution because he contested the NAF's jurisdiction over the matter. He added that he would instead file a complaint in federal court. On June 27, 2000, he did just that. He filed a complaint against the Strasberg defendants and the CMG defendants with the district court challenging the constitutionality of the dispute resolution process.

Three days later on June 30, 2000, a one-member NAF panel issued an order suspending the NAF/UDRP proceeding in light of the pending federal lawsuit. *See* UDRP §18 (giving panel "the discretion to decide whether to suspend or terminate the administrative proceeding, or to proceed to a decision" while a lawsuit is pending). Because Dluhos failed to serve properly either the Strasberg defendants or the CMG defendants, CMG formally requested in August 2000 that the NAF lift the suspension order and proceed with UDRP dispute resolution. NAF lifted the order when CMG served notice of its request on Dluhos and paid a $150 fee to remove the suspension order.

On October 26, 2000, the NAF panel issued a decision against Dluhos — without his participation — and directed that the domain name www.leestrasberg.com be transferred to the Estate. *See* UDRP §5(e) (mandating that the panel "decide the dispute based upon the complaint" if a registrant declines to participate in the UDRP proceedings).

Dluhos filed an amended complaint in the district court on October 31, 2000, alleging harassment, breach of contract, and violations of his First, Fifth and Fourteenth Amendment rights. Essentially, he challenged the constitutionality of the dispute resolution process, raised First Amendment arguments against enforcement of NSI's dispute resolution policy and asked the district court to restore his right in the domain name www.leestrasberg.com. All defendants promptly filed motions to dismiss for failure to state a claim, and in an August 31, 2001 memorandum and order, the district court granted the defendants' motions. After dismissing all constitutional and §1983 claims against the defendants for want of state action, the district court dismissed the various state law claims against all parties for failure to state a claim for which relief may be granted.

The court then proceeded to review the NAF's decision in favor of the Strasberg and CMG defendants under: 1) 9 U.S.C. §10(a)(2)-10(a)(3) of the Federal Arbitration Act, which authorizes a district court to vacate an arbitration decision if there is "evident partiality or corruption in the arbitrato[r]," or if "the arbitrators were guilty of misconduct . . . in refusing to hear evidence pertinent and material to the controversy"; and 2) the judicially created "manifest disregard of the law" standard, which allows a district court to vacate an arbitration award that "evidences manifest disregard of the law rather than an erroneous interpretation."

The district court reviewed and upheld the NAF's decision under both deferential standards.

Dluhos filed a timely Notice of Appeal. . . .

III.

The Federal Arbitration Act explicitly permits the use of arbitration and specifically authorizes individuals in commercial transactions to contract for arbitration. 9 U.S.C. §§1-10. Congress enacted the FAA in 1925 to offset the "hostility of American courts to the enforcement of arbitration agreements." *Circuit City Stores, Inc. v. Adams,* 532 U.S. 105, 111 (2001). As the FAA evinces the "liberal federal policy favoring arbitration," *Moses H. Cone Mem'l Hosp. v. Mercury Constr. Corp.,* 460 U.S. 1, 24 (1983), the legislation "compels judicial enforcement of a wide range of written arbitration agreements." *Circuit City,* 532 U.S. at 111.

Federal courts primarily invoke the FAA to give effect to contracting parties' expectations for resolving disputes. Accordingly, the FAA revolves around contract interpretation. Because the FAA does not define the term "arbitration," courts and commentators have struggled to do so. [Citation and quotation marks omitted.] Broadly, this Court has essentially concluded that the essence of arbitration . . . is that, when the parties agree to submit their disputes to it, they have agreed to arbitrate these disputes through to completion, i.e. to an award made by a third-party arbitrator. Arbitration does not occur until the process is completed and the arbitrator makes a decision. [Citation and quotation marks omitted.]

Admittedly, this definition does little to assist us in determining which types of dispute resolution fall under the FAA and which do not. . . .

If a dispute-resolution mechanism indeed constitutes arbitration under the FAA, then a district court may vacate it only under exceedingly narrow circumstances. 9 U.S.C. §10. . . . The net result of a court's application of this standard is generally to affirm easily the arbitration award under this extremely deferential standard — a result that is squarely in line with the purpose behind the FAA where courts are tasked with reviewing an arbitration decision.

If, however, a dispute-resolution mechanism does not constitute arbitration under the FAA, then a district court has no jurisdiction to review the result absent an independent jurisdictional hook.

At issue before us then is whether the nonbinding domain name resolution policy (UDRP) proceeding that shifted Appellant's registered domain name to the Strasberg defendants constitutes arbitration under the FAA. If this proceeding qualifies as arbitration under the FAA, then the dispute resolution is subject to extremely limited review. If it does not fall under the FAA umbrella, then the district court lacked jurisdiction to examine — and thus to affirm — the result under the lax FAA review standards.

IV.

We begin our analysis of the FAA's applicability by examining the specific arbitration agreement at issue, a contract-based arrangement for handling disputes between domain name registrants and third parties who challenge the registration and use of their trademarks. In our view, the UDRP's unique contractual arrangement renders the FAA's provisions for judicial review inapplicable.

A.

First, the UDRP obviously contemplates the possibility of judicial intervention, as no provision of the policy prevents a party from filing suit before, after or during the administrative proceedings. *See* UDRP §4(k) (stating that domain-name resolution proceedings shall not stop either party from "submitting the dispute to a court of competent jurisdiction for independent resolution"). In that sense, this mechanism would not fall under the FAA because the dispute will not necessarily be settled by this arbitration. [Citation, brackets, and quotation marks omitted.]

The UDRP was intended to ensure that the parties could seek independent judicial resolution of domain name disputes, regardless of whether its proceeding reached a conclusion.

Indeed, unlike methods of dispute resolution covered by the FAA, UDRP proceedings were never intended to replace formal litigation. Rather, the UDRP contemplates truncated proceedings. It is fashioned as an 'online' procedure administered via the Internet, which does not permit discovery, the presentation of live testimony (absent exceptional circumstances), or any remedy other than the transfer or cancellation of the domain name in question. [Citation and quotation marks omitted.] *See* UDRP § 4(i).

To shove Dluhos' square-peg UDRP proceeding into the round hole of the FAA would be to frustrate this aim, as judicial review of FAA-styled arbitration proceedings could be generously described only as extremely deferential.

B.

Second, because the trademark holder or the trademark holder's representative is not required to avail itself of the dispute resolution policy before moving ahead in the district court, these proceedings do not qualify as the type that would entail a court's compelling party participation prior to independent judicial review — thus removing the proceeding from the warmth of the FAA blanket. Under §4 of the FAA, a district court may "stay the trial of the action until such arbitration has been had in accordance with the terms of the agreement." 9 U.S.C. § 4. Although some courts, relying in part on their inherent equitable powers, have stayed litigation and compelled participation in non-binding procedures so long as there are reasonable commercial expectations that the procedures would settle disputed issues, a UDRP proceeding settles a domain-name dispute only to the extent that a season-finale cliffhanger resolves a sitcom's storyline — that is, it doesn't. [Citation and quotation marks omitted.] It is true that the language of the resolution policy describes the dispute-resolution process as "mandatory," but the process is not mandatory in the sense that either disputant's legal claims accrue only after a panel's decision. [Citation and quotation marks omitted.] Only the domain-name *registrant* is contractually obligated to participate in the proceeding if a complaint is filed. Even then, the panel may "decide the dispute based on the complaint" if the registrant declines to participate. UDRP § 5(e). That Dluhos could do precisely that by eschewing the NAF proceeding and filing suit in district court only demonstrates the dispute resolution policy's outcome's relative hollowness. Indeed, it is not the district court litigation that could be stayed pending dispute resolution, but rather the dispute-resolution mechanism itself. *See* UDRP § 18 (giving arbitration panel "the discretion to decide whether to suspend or terminate the administrative proceeding, or to proceed to a decision" while a lawsuit is pending). And that is exactly what the NAF panel did.

C.

The bottom line is that a registrant who loses a domain name to a trademark holder can effectively suspend a panel's decision by filing a lawsuit in the specified jurisdiction and notifying the registrar in accordance with UDRP § 4(k). [Citation, brackets, and quotation marks omitted.] From that provision, it is evident that the UDRP provides parity of appeal, affording a clear mechanism for seeking judicial review of a decision of an administrative panel canceling or transferring the domain name. [Citation and quotation marks omitted.]

Accordingly, we hold that UDRP proceedings do not fall under the Federal Arbitration Act. More specifically, judicial review of those decisions is not restricted to a motion to vacate arbitration award under § 10 of the FAA, which applies only to binding proceedings likely to "realistically settle the dispute." The district court erred in reviewing the domain name proceeding under limitations of FAA standards.

V.

Because the UDRP — a private covenant — cannot confer federal jurisdiction where none independently exists, the remaining question is whether the Congress has provided a cause of action to challenge its decisions. In the Anticybersquatting Consumer Protection Act, we hold that it has.

The ACPA, 15 U.S.C. § 1114(2)(D)(v), "provide[s] registrants . . . with an affirmative cause of action to recover domain names lost in UDRP proceedings." [*Sallen v. Corinthians Licenciamentos LTDA*, 273 F.3d 14, 27 (1st Cir. 2001).] Under this modern amendment to the Lanham Act, a registrant whose domain name has been "suspended, disabled, or transferred" may sue for a declaration that the registrant is not in violation of the Act, as well as for an injunction returning the domain name. 15 U.S.C. § 1114(2)(D)(v). Congress' authorization of the federal courts to "grant injunctive relief to the domain name registrant, including the reactivation of the domain name or transfer of the domain name to the domain name registrant" gives the registrant an explicit cause of action through which to redress the loss of a domain name under the UDRP.

Once again, we must liberally construe the *pro se* litigant's pleadings, and we will apply the applicable law, irrespective of whether he has mentioned it by name. Although Dluhos did not expressly invoke the ACPA, his allegations and demand for the return of the domain name can reasonably be construed as such a request; Dluhos' end goal is the return of www.leestrasberg.com to him, bringing his cause of action squarely under the ACPA. Dluhos is a registrant, and the domain name has been transferred to the Strasberg defendants via a complaint by the CMG defendants and resulting arbitration.

Accordingly, as to the CMG and Strasberg defendants, we will reverse and remand the case for further proceedings consistent with this opinion. This decision in no way reflects an intimation that the NAP panel erred in its judgment, but merely that UDRP resolutions do not fall under the limited judicial review of the FAA.

Another consideration is that federal courts applying federal trademark law are much more likely to give weight to the First Amendment implications of their decisions than a UDRP panel — to which the First Amendment arguably does not even apply. Essentially, the First Amendment gives federal courts a more direct policy reason for reaching the same result that many UDRP panels struggle to reach through interpretation of the UDRP.

The Taubman Company v. Webfeats

319 F.3d 770 (6th Cir. 2003)

Before: BOGGS, SUHRHEINRICH and CLAY, Circuit Judges.

SUHRHEINRICH, Circuit Judge.

Defendant-Appellant Henry Mishkoff, d/b/a Webfeats, appeals from two preliminary injunctions, respectively entered on October 11, 2001, and December 7, 2001, in the United States District Court for the Eastern District of Michigan, together granting Plaintiff-Appellee the Taubman Company's (Taubman) request to prevent Mishkoff from using six internet domain names because they likely violate Taubman's trademarks in the terms "Taubman," and "The Shops at Willow Bend.". . .

. . . Taubman had failed to demonstrate a likelihood of success on the merits because Mishkoff's use was not "in connection with the sale or advertising of goods or services," and there is no likelihood of confusion among consumers.

I. FACTS

Mishkoff is a resident of Carrollton, Texas, and a web designer by trade. Upon hearing the news that Taubman, a Delaware corporation with its principal place of business in Michigan, was building a shopping mall called "The Shops at Willow Bend," in Plano, Texas, Mishkoff registered the domain name, "shopsatwillowbend.com," and created an internet website with that address. Mishkoff had no connection to the mall except for the fact that it was being built near his home.

Mishkoff's website featured information about the mall, with a map and links to individual websites of the tenant stores. The site also contained a prominent disclaimer, indicating that Mishkoff's site was unofficial, and a link to Taubman's official site for the mall, found at the addresses "theshopsatwillowbend.com," and "shopwillowbend.com."

Mishkoff describes his site as a "fan site," with no commercial purpose. The site did, however, contain a link to the website of a company run by Mishkoff's girlfriend, Donna Hartley, where she sold custom-made shirts under the name "shirtbiz.com;" and to Mishkoff's site for his web design business, "Webfeats."

When Taubman discovered that Mishkoff had created this site, it demanded he remove it from the internet. Taubman claimed that Mishkoff's use of the domain name "shopsatwillowbend.com" infringed on its registered mark, "The Shops at Willow Bend." Taubman filed a complaint on August 7, 2001, claiming, *inter alia,* trademark infringement under the Lanham Act, 15 U.S.C. §1114, asking for a preliminary injunction, and demanding surrender of Mishkoff's domain name.

Mishkoff responsively registered five more domain names: 1) taubmansucks.com; 2) shopsatwillowbendsucks.com; 3) theshopsatwillowbendsucks.com; 4) willowbendmallsucks.com; and 5) willowbendsucks.com. All five of these web names link to the same site, which is a running editorial on Mishkoff's battle with Taubman and its lawyers, and exhaustively documents his proceedings in both the district court and this Court, both through visual scans of filed motions, as well as a first person narrative from Mishkoff. In internet parlance, a web name with a "sucks.com" moniker attached to it is known as a "complaint name," and the process of registering and using such names is known as "cybergriping."

On October 11, 2001, the district court granted Taubman's motion for a preliminary injunction, enjoining Mishkoff from using the first host name, "shopsatwillowbend.com."[2] On October 15, 2001, Taubman filed a motion to amend the preliminary injunction to include the five "complaint names" used by Mishkoff. On December 7, 2001, the district court allowed the amendment and enjoined Mishkoff from using the complaint names.

[Mishkoff appealed in a timely manner.]. . .

III.   ANALYSIS

Mishkoff claims the injunctions preventing his use of the domain name "shopsatwillowbend.com" and the five "complaint names" are inappropriate because Taubman has not demonstrated a likelihood of success on the merits and because the orders represent a prior restraint on his First Amendment right to speak. . . .

B.   Propriety of the Injunctions

1.   Likelihood of Success on the Merits

. . . Mishkoff proposes that, regardless of whether his use of Taubman's marks violates the Lanham Act, any injunction prohibiting his use violates the Constitution as a prior restraint on his First Amendment right of Free Speech. Since Mishkoff has raised Free Speech concerns, we will first explain the interrelation between the First Amendment and the Lanham Act. First, this Court has held that the Lanham Act is constitutional. The Lanham Act is constitutional because it only regulates commercial speech, which is entitled to reduced protections under the First Amendment. *Central Hudson Gas & Elec. Corp. v. Public Serv. Comm'n,* 447 U.S. 557, 563 (1980) (stating that regulation of commercial speech is subject only to intermediate scrutiny). Thus, we must first determine if Mishkoff's use is commercial and therefore within the jurisdiction of the Lanham Act, worthy of lesser First Amendment protections.

If Mishkoff's use is commercial, then, and only then, do we analyze his use for a likelihood of confusion. If Mishkoff's use is also confusing, then it is misleading commercial speech, and outside the First Amendment. *See* 134 Cong. Rec. 31, 851 (Oct. 19, 1988) (statement of Rep. Kastenmeier) (stating that §43 of the Lanham Act only affects misleading commercial speech); *cf. Va. Bd. of Pharmacy v. Va. Citizens Consumer Council, Inc.,* 425 U.S. 748, 771 & n.24 (1976) (stating that

---

2. Taubman sought the injunction under other claims too, including violation of the Anticybersquatting Act. However, the district court granted the injunction based only on the Lanham Act claim. Accordingly, that is the only issue before this Court.

misleading commercial speech is not protected by the First Amendment); *Bonito Boats, Inc. v. Thunder Craft Boats, Inc.,* 489 U.S. 141, 157 (1989) (stating that a trademark owner has at best a quasi-property right in his mark, and can only prevent its use so as to maintain a confusion-free purchasing public) (quoting *Crescent Tool Co. v. Kilborn & Bishop Co.,* 247 F. 299, 301 (2d Cir.1917) (L. Hand, J.)).

Hence, as per the language of the Lanham Act, any expression embodying the use of a mark not "in connection with the sale . . . or advertising of any goods or services," and not likely to cause confusion, is outside the jurisdiction of the Lanham Act and necessarily protected by the First Amendment. Accordingly, we need not analyze Mishkoff's constitutional defenses independent of our Lanham Act analysis. With this backdrop in mind, we proceed to analyze the nature of the two websites.

a.   November 9 Injunction — The "shopsatwillowbend" Website

In regard to the first website, "shopsatwillowbend.com," Mishkoff argues that his use is completely non-commercial and not confusing, and therefore speech entitled to the full protections of the First Amendment. Taubman offers three arguments that Mishkoff is using its name commercially to sell or advertise goods or services. First, Mishkoff had a link to a site owned by Hartley's blouse company, "shirtbiz.com." Second, he had a link to his own site for his web design company, Webfeats. Third, Mishkoff had accepted a $1000 offer to relinquish the name to Taubman.

Although Mishkoff claims his intention in creating his website was non-commercial, the proper inquiry is not one of intent. In that sense, the Lanham Act is a strict liability statute. If consumers are confused by an infringing mark, the offender's motives are largely irrelevant. We believe the advertisements on Mishkoff's site, though extremely minimal, constituted his use of Taubman's mark "in connection with the advertising" of the goods sold by the advertisers. This is precisely what the Lanham Act prohibits.

However, Mishkoff had at least removed the shirtbiz.com link prior to the injunction. A preliminary injunction is proper only to prevent an on-going violation. As long as Mishkoff has no commercial links on either of his websites, including links to shirtbiz.com, Webfeats, or any other business, we find no use "in connection with the advertising" of goods and services to enjoin, and the Lanham Act cannot be properly invoked.

Taubman's assertion that its offer to buy the domain name "shopsatwillowbend.com" from Mishkoff qualifies Mishkoff's use of the mark as "in connection with the sale of goods" is meritless. Although other courts have held that a so-called cybersquatter, who registers domain names with the intent to sell the name to the trademark holder, uses the mark "in connection with the sale of goods," they have also limited their holdings to such instances where the defendant had made a habit and a business of such practices. *See, e.g., E & J Gallo Winery v. Spider Webs Ltd.,* 286 F.3d 270, 270 (5th Cir. 2002) (noting that defendant had made a business practice of selling domain names on eBay for no less than $10,000); *Panavision Int'l, L.P. v. Toeppen,* 141 F.3d 1316 (9th Cir.1998). [Ed.: Assignment 1 discusses the personal jurisdiction holding in *Panavision.*]

In *Panavision,* the defendant, Toeppen, purchased and offered to sell the name "panavision.com" to Panavision for $13,000. *Id.* at 1318. Evidence showed that Toeppen had attempted similar deals with a myriad of other companies, ranging from Delta Airlines to Eddie Bauer. *Id.* at 1319. The Ninth Circuit found Toeppen's intent to sell the domain name relevant in determining that his creation of the site was a commercial use of Panavision's mark. *Id.* at 1325. In contrast, not only has Mishkoff not made a practice of registering and selling domain names, but he did not even initiate the bargaining process here. Although Taubman's counsel intimated at oral argument that Mishkoff had in fact initiated the negotiation process, correspondence in the record supports the opposite conclusion, and shows that Taubman first offered Mishkoff $1000 to relinquish the site on August 16, 2001, and Mishkoff initially accepted it under threat of litigation. Hence, this case is distinguishable from *Panavision.* There is no evidence that Mishkoff's initial motive in selecting Taubman's mark was to re-sell the name. Therefore, we hold his use of the name "shopsatwillowbend.com" is not "in connection with the sale of goods."

Even if Mishkoff's use is commercial speech, i.e., "in connection with the sale . . . or advertising of any goods or services," and within the jurisdiction of the Lanham Act, there is a violation only if his use also creates a likelihood of confusion among customers. 15 U.S.C. §1114(1). Moreover, the only important question is whether there is a likelihood of confusion *between the parties' goods or services.* Under Lanham Act jurisprudence, it is irrelevant whether customers would be confused as to the origin of the websites, unless there is confusion as to the origin of the respective products.

Since its inception, Mishkoff had always maintained a disclaimer on the website, indicating that his was not the official website. . . .

. . . We find the analysis here indistinguishable from the disclaimer analysis in [earlier cases]. Mishkoff has placed a conspicuous disclaimer informing customers that they had not reached Taubman's official mall site. Furthermore, Mishkoff placed a hyperlink to Taubman's site within the disclaimer. . . . Here, a misplaced customer simply has to click his mouse to be redirected to Taubman's site. Moreover, . . . , the customers who stumble upon Mishkoff's site would otherwise have reached a dead address. They would have received an error message upon typing "shopsatwillowbend.com," simply stating that the name was not a proper domain name, with no message relating how to arrive at the official site. Hence, Mishkoff's website and its disclaimer actually serve to redirect lost customers to Taubman's site that might otherwise be lost. Accordingly, we find no likelihood that a customer would be confused as to the source of Taubman's and Mishkoff's respective goods.

b. December 7 Injunction — The "sucks" Site

In regard to Mishkoff's "complaint site," Taubman claims that Mishkoff's use is necessarily "in connection with the sale of goods" because his intent behind the use of the names "taubmansucks.com," *et al.,* is to harm Taubman economically. . . .

. . . Taubman argues that all cybergriping sites are per se commercial and "in connection with the sale of goods.". . . Even if Mishkoff's use is commercial, it must still lead to a likelihood of confusion to be violative of the Lanham Act. 15 U.S.C. §1114(1). In [an earlier case condemning a cybergriping site], the defendant used the plaintiff's trade name as a domain name, without the qualifying moniker "sucks," or any other such addendum to indicate that the plaintiff was not the proprietor of the website. In contrast, "taubmansucks.com" removes any confusion as to source. We find no possibility of confusion and no Lanham Act violation.

We find that Mishkoff's use of Taubman's mark in the domain name "taubmansucks.com" is purely an exhibition of Free Speech, and the Lanham Act is not invoked. And although economic damage might be an intended effect of Mishkoff's expression, the First Amendment protects critical commentary when there is no confusion as to source, even when it involves the criticism of a business. Such use is not subject to scrutiny under the Lanham Act. In fact, Taubman concedes that Mishkoff is "free to shout 'Taubman Sucks!' from the rooftops. . . ." Brief for Respondent, at 58. Essentially, this is what he has done in his domain name. The rooftops of our past have evolved into the internet domain names of our present. We find that the domain name is a type of public expression, no different in scope than a billboard or a pulpit, and Mishkoff has a First Amendment right to express his opinion about Taubman, and as long as his speech is not commercially misleading, the Lanham Act cannot be summoned to prevent it.

2. The Remaining Injunctive Factors

When, as here, a preliminary injunction would infringe upon a constitutional right, the likelihood of success on the merits is often the determinative factor. Even so, the other three factors also suggest that a preliminary injunction is not proper. Because Mishkoff is not using Taubman's mark to peddle competing goods, and because any damages would be economic in nature and fully compensable monetarily, we find no potential for irreparable harm to Taubman that should lead us to uphold the injunctions. Moreover, absent a likelihood of confusion, we find no negative impact on the public interest caused by Mishkoff's use. In fact, due to the Free Speech concerns present, we find the potential for irreparable harm to Mishkoff more likely, and that the public would be negatively impacted, should we *not* dissolve the injunctions.

Lastly, although no economic harm will accrue to Mishkoff should he be prevented from maintaining his sites, there is little potential harm to Taubman, or any other party, as well, because Mishkoff is not a competitor in the marketplace. Accordingly, upon a balancing of the factors for injunctive relief, we dissolve both injunctions.

One final difference between UDRP proceedings and ACPA proceedings is in the available remedies. A trademark owner who prevails under the ACPA is entitled to recover actual damages, including the registrant's profits, or (without proving actual damages) statutory damages ranging from $1,000 to $100,000. On the other hand, because the ACPA involves conventional litigation, it is much more expensive and time-consuming than UDRP proceedings. Also, although the ACPA *in rem* procedure simplifies the process of getting jurisdiction over the domain name, it does not simplify the process of actually locating the domain-name registrant and determining whether that person has any assets worth pursuing. Still, the potential for a recovery of damages could motivate ACPA actions in cases with substantial commercial implications. The following case illustrates the strong remedies the statute provides.

Shields v. Zuccarini

254 F.3d 476 (3rd Cir. 2001)

Before: BARRY, AMBRO and ALDISERT, Circuit Judges.
ALDISERT, Circuit Judge.
John Zuccarini appeals from the district court's grant of summary judgment and award of statutory damages and attorneys' fees in favor of Joseph Shields

under the new Anticybersquatting Consumer Protection Act ("ACPA" or "Act"). In this case of first impression in this court interpreting the ACPA, we must decide whether the district court erred in determining that registering domain names that are intentional misspellings of distinctive or famous names constitutes unlawful conduct under the Act. We must decide also whether the district court abused its discretion by assessing statutory damages of $10,000 per domain name. Finally, we must decide whether the court erred in awarding attorneys' fees in favor of Shields based on its determination that this case qualified as an "exceptional" case under the ACPA. We affirm the judgment of the district court. . . .

I.

Shields, a graphic artist from Alto, Michigan, creates, exhibits and markets cartoons under the names "Joe Cartoon" and "The Joe Cartoon Co." His creations include the popular "Frog Blender," "Micro-Gerbil" and "Live and Let Dive" animations. Shields licenses his cartoons to others for display on T-shirts, coffee mugs and other items, many of which are sold at gift stores across the country. He has marketed his cartoons under the "Joe Cartoon" label for the past fifteen years.

On June 12, 1997, Shields registered the domain name joecartoon.com, and he has operated it as a web site ever since. Visitors to the site can download his animations and purchase Joe Cartoon merchandise. Since April 1998, when it won "shock site of the day" from Macromedia, Joe Cartoon's web traffic has increased exponentially, now averaging over 700,000 visits per month.

In November 1999, Zuccarini, an Andalusia, Pennsylvania "wholesaler" of Internet domain names,[1] registered five world wide web variations on Shields's site: joescartoon.com, joecarton.com, joescartons.com, joescartoons.com and cartoonjoe.com. Zuccarini's sites featured advertisements for other sites and for credit card companies. Visitors were trapped or "mousetrapped" in the sites, which, in the jargon of the computer world, means that they were unable to exit without clicking on a succession of advertisements. Zuccarini received between ten and twenty-five cents from the advertisers for every click.

In December 1999, Shields sent "cease and desist" letters to Zuccarini regarding the infringing domain names. Zuccarini did not respond to the letters. Immediately after Shields filed this suit, Zuccarini changed the five sites to "political protest" pages and posted the following message on them:

> This is a page of POLITICAL PROTEST
>
> — Against the web site joecartoon.com —
>
> joecartoon.com is a web site that depicts the mutilation and killing of animals in a shockwave based cartoon format — many children are inticed [sic] to the web site, not knowing what is really there and then encouraged to join in the mutilation and killing through use of the shockwave cartoon presented to them.
>
> — Against the domain name policys [sic] of ICANN —

---

1. "Wholesaling" refers to the practice of acquiring multiple domain names with the intent to profit from them.

— Against the Cyberpiracy Consumer Protection Act —

As the owner of this domain name, I am being sued by joecartoon.com for $100,000 so he can use this domain to direct more kids to a web site that not only desensitizes children to killing animals, but makes it seem like great fun and games.

I will under no circumstances hand this domain name over to him so he can do that.

I hope that ICANN and Network Solutions will not assist him to attaining this goal.

— Thank You —

Shields's Complaint invoked the ACPA as well as federal and state unfair competition law and sought injunctive relief, statutory damages and attorneys' fees. . . .

[The trial court ordered Zuccarini to transfer the names to Shields, enjoined Zuccarini from using the names, awarded statutory damages of $10,000 for each infringing domain name, and also awarded attorneys' fees and costs in the amount of $39,109.46.] . . .

III.

On November 29, 1999, the ACPA became law, making it illegal for a person to register or to use with the "bad faith" intent to profit from an Internet domain name that is "identical or confusingly similar" to the distinctive or famous trademark or Internet domain name of another person or company. *See* 15 U.S.C. §1125(d). The Act was intended to prevent "cybersquatting," an expression that has come to mean the bad faith, abusive registration and use of the distinctive trademarks of others as Internet domain names, with the intent to profit from the goodwill associated with those trademarks. Under the ACPA, successful plaintiffs may recover statutory damages in an amount to be assessed by the district court in its discretion, from $1,000 to $100,000 per domain name. *See* 15 U.S.C. §1117(d). In addition, successful plaintiffs may recover attorneys' fees in "exceptional" cases. *See id.* at §1117(a). . . .

A.

To succeed on his ACPA claim, Shields was required to prove that (1) "Joe Cartoon" is a distinctive or famous mark entitled to protection; (2) Zuccarini's domain names are "identical or confusingly similar to" Shields's mark; and (3) Zuccarini registered the domain names with the bad faith intent to profit from them. *See* 15 U.S.C. §1125(d)(1)(A).

1.

Under §1125(d)(1)(A)(ii)(I) and (II), the district court first had to determine if "Joe Cartoon" is a "distinctive" or "famous" mark and, therefore, is entitled to protection under the Act. . . .

. . . Shields runs the only "Joe Cartoon" operation in the nation and has done so for the past fifteen years. This suggests both the inherent and acquired distinctiveness of the "Joe Cartoon" name. In addition to using the "Joe Cartoon" name for fifteen years, Shields has used the domain name joecartoon.com as a web site since June 1997 to display his animations and sell products featuring his drawings. The longevity of his use suggests that "Joe Cartoon" has acquired some fame in the marketplace. The New York Times ran a page one story that quoted Shields and cited Joe Cartoon.

Joe Cartoon T-shirts have been sold across the country since at least the early 1990s, and its products appear on the web site of at least one nationally known retail chain, Spencer Gifts. Shields has advertised in an online humor magazine with a circulation of about 1.4 million. The Joe Cartoon web site receives in excess of 700,000 visits per month, bringing it wide publicity. According to Shields, word-of-mouth also generates considerable interest in the Joe Cartoon site. Shields trades nationwide in both real and virtual markets. The web site gives Joe Cartoon a global reach. Shields's cartoons and merchandise are marketed on the Internet, in gift shops and at tourist venues. The Joe Cartoon mark has won a huge following because of the work of Shields. In light of the above, we conclude that "Joe Cartoon" is distinctive, and, with 700,000 hits a month, the web site "joecartoon.com" qualifies as being famous. Therefore, the trademark and domain name are protected under the ACPA.

2.

Under the Act, the next inquiry is whether Zuccarini's domain names are "identical or confusingly similar" to Shields's mark. The domain names — joescartoon.com, joecarton.com, joescartons.com, joescartoons.com and cartoonjoe.com — closely resemble "joecartoon.com," with a few additional or deleted letters, or, in the last domain name, by rearranging the order of the words. To divert Internet traffic to his sites, Zuccarini admits that he registers domain names, including the five at issue here, because they are likely misspellings of famous marks or personal names.[4] The strong similarity between these domain names and joecartoon.com persuades us that they are "confusingly similar." Shields also produced evidence of Internet users who were actually confused by Zuccarini's sites. *See, e.g.,* Pltf's Exh. 22, at [4] (copy of an email stating, "I tried to look up you[r] website yesterday afternoon and a protest page came up. Will I have trouble entering the site at times because of this?").

On appeal, Zuccarini argues that registering domain names that are intentional misspellings of distinctive or famous names (or "typosquatting," his term for this kind of conduct) is not actionable under the ACPA. Zuccarini contends that the Act is intended to prevent "cybersquatting," which he defines as registering someone's famous name and trying to sell the domain name to them or registering it to prevent the famous person from using it themselves. This argument ignores the plain language of the statute and its stated purpose as discussed in the legislative history.

---

4. Zuccarini testified that he was amazed to learn that "people mistype [domain names] as often as they do," and thus variants on likely search names would result in many unintended visitors to his sites.

The statute covers the registration of domain names that are "identical" to distinctive or famous marks, but it also covers domain names that are "confusingly similar" to distinctive or famous marks. *See* 15 U.S.C. § 1125(d)(1)(A)(ii)(I), (II). A reasonable interpretation of conduct covered by the phrase "confusingly similar" is the intentional registration of domain names that are misspellings of distinctive or famous names, causing an Internet user who makes a slight spelling or typing error to reach an unintended site. The ACPA's legislative history contemplates such situations:

> [C]ybersquatters often register well-known marks to prey on consumer confusion by misusing the domain name to divert customers from the mark owner's site to the cybersquatter's own site, many of which are pornography sites that derive advertising revenue based on the number of visits, or "hits," the site receives. For example, the Committee was informed of a parent whose child *mistakenly typed in the domain name for 'dosney.com,'* expecting to access the family-oriented content of the Walt Disney home page, only to end up staring at a screen of hardcore pornography because a cybersquatter had registered that domain name in anticipation that consumers would make that exact mistake.

S. Rep. No. 106-140 (1999), 1999 WL 594571, at *15 (emphasis added).

Although Zuccarini's sites did not involve pornography, his intent was the same as that mentioned in the legislative history above — to register a domain name in anticipation that consumers would make a mistake, thereby increasing the number of hits his site would receive, and, consequently, the number of advertising dollars he would gain. We conclude that Zuccarini's conduct here is a classic example of a specific practice the ACPA was designed to prohibit. The district court properly found that the domain names he registered were "confusingly similar."

3.

The final inquiry under the ACPA is whether Zuccarini acted with a bad faith intent to profit from Shields's distinctive and famous mark or whether his con-|duct falls under the safe harbor provision of the Act. Section 1125(d)(1)(B)(i) provides a non-exhaustive list of nine factors for us to consider when making this determination. . . .

Zuccarini's conduct satisfies a number of these factors. Zuccarini has never used the infringing domain names as trademarks or service marks; thus, he has no intellectual property rights in these domain names. *See id.* at (B)(i)(I). The domain names do not contain any variation of the legal name of Zuccarini, nor any other name commonly used to identify him. *See id.* at (B)(i)(II). Zuccarini has never used the infringing domain names in connection with the bona fide offering of goods or services. *See id.* at (B)(i)(III). He does not use these domain names for a non-commercial or "fair use" purpose. *See id.* at (B)(i)(IV). He deliberately maintains these domain names to divert consumers from Shields's web site. In so doing, he harms the goodwill associated with the mark. He does this either for commercial gain, or with the intent to tarnish or disparage Shields's mark by creating a likelihood of confusion. *See id.* at (B)(i)(V). He has knowingly registered thousands of Internet domain names that are identical to, or confusingly similar to, the distinctive marks of others, without the permission of the mark holders to do so.[5] *See id.* at (B)(i)(VIII). We have already established that Shields's mark is distinctive and famous. *See id.* at (B)(i)(IX).

Zuccarini argues that his web sites were protected by the First Amendment because he was using them as self-described "protest pages." Therefore, he contends, his use falls under the safe harbor provision of §1125(d)(1)(B)(ii), which states that "[b]ad faith intent . . . shall not be found in any case in which the court determines that the person believed and had reasonable grounds to believe that the use of the domain name was a fair use or otherwise lawful." The district court rejected this argument based on its conclusion that Zuccarini's claim of good faith and fair use was a "spurious explanation cooked up purely for this suit." We agree.

Zuccarini used his "Joe Cartoon" web sites for purely commercial purposes before Shields filed this action. Zuccarini was on notice that his use of the domain names was considered unlawful when he received the cease and desist letters from Shields in December 1999. Zuccarini continued to use the infringing domain names for commercial purposes until Shields filed this lawsuit. Zuccarini testified that he put up the protest pages at 3:00 a.m. on February 1, 2000, just hours after being served with Shields's Complaint. Thus, by his own admission, Zuccarini submits that his alleged "fair use" of the offending domain names for "political protest" began only after Shields brought this action alleging a violation of the ACPA. We are aware of no authority providing that a defendant's "fair use" of a distinctive or famous mark only after the filing of a complaint alleging infringement can absolve that defendant of liability for his earlier unlawful activities. Indeed, were there such authority we think it would be contrary to the orderly enforcement of the trademark and copyright laws. . . .

B.

The district court correctly concluded that there is a substantial likelihood of confusion, as well as actual evidence of confusion, between Zuccarini's infringing domain names and the "Joe Cartoon" mark. . . . The district court determined that Shields will suffer damage to his reputation and a loss of goodwill if Zuccarini is allowed to operate his offending web sites. Shields's livelihood and fame depend, in large part, on Internet users being able to access his sites, and he does not want his audience trapped in Zuccarini's sites or put off by images displayed thereon which they may attribute to him. The district court properly determined that Shields would be irreparably harmed if the court did not grant the permanent injunction.

Zuccarini testified that he has more than three thousand web sites and earns between $800,000 and $1,000,000 a year from their use. The court determined that any economic harm from the loss of the five infringing domain names would be trivial. . . . Zuccarini admitted that he is in the business of profiting from the

---

5. During his deposition and at the preliminary injunction hearing, Zuccarini admitted that he registered the variations of "Joe Cartoon," as well as thousands of other domain names, because they are confusingly similar to others' famous marks or personal names — and thus are likely misspellings of these names — in an effort to divert Internet traffic to his sites. He has registered obvious misspellings of celebrities' names, such as gwenythpaltrow.com, rikymartin.com, and britneyspears.com. He has also registered variations on popular product and web site names, like sportillustrated.com, mountianbikes.com, and msnchatrooms.com. Although we do not determine whether Zuccarini's conduct in each of these other cases is itself a violation of the Act, nonetheless his pattern of behavior is consistent with a bad faith intent to profit.

public's confusion and that he does, in fact, profit from this confusion. The district court properly concluded that this injunction would be in the public interest. . . .

IV.

The Act provides for statutory damages for a violation of § 1125(d)(1) "in the amount of not less than $1,000 and not more than $100,000 per domain name, as the court considers just." 15 U.S.C. § 1117(d). Zuccarini argues that § 1117(d) does not apply to him because he registered the offending domain names before the ACPA became law. The district court held that Zuccarini's continued use of the domain names after November 29, 1999 subjects him to the statute's proscriptions and remedies. We agree with the teachings of *Virtual Works, Inc. v. Volkswagen of America, Inc.,* 238 F.3d 264, 268 (4th Cir. 2001) ("A person who unlawfully registers, traffics in, or uses a domain name after the ACPA's date of enactment, November 29, 1999, can be liable for monetary damages. . . .").

In the alternative, Zuccarini argues that he only used the web site for sixty days after the passage of the ACPA and prior to this lawsuit being filed. He implies that, because he only used the web site for a short period of time, the district court's assessment of statutory damages was punitive in nature. Under the statute, the court has the discretion to award statutory damages that it "considers just" within a range from $1,000 to $100,000 per infringing domain name. *See* 15 U.S.C. § 1117(d). There is nothing in the statute that requires that the court consider the duration of the infringement when calculating statutory damages. We conclude that the district court properly exercised its discretion in awarding $10,000 for each infringing domain name.

V.

The ACPA provides that "[t]he court in exceptional cases may award reasonable attorney fees to the prevailing party." 15 U.S.C. § 1117(a). In trademark infringement cases, this court has held that a district court must make a finding of culpable conduct on the part of the losing party, such as bad faith, fraud, malice or knowing infringement before a case qualifies as "exceptional." [Citation and internal quotation marks omitted.] The district court found that Zuccarini acted willfully and in bad faith when he registered the "Joe Cartoon" domain names in an effort to confuse people and to divert Internet traffic to his web sites for his own economic gain. The court found that Zuccarini conducted no bona fide business related to Joe Cartoon and that he had no basis on which to believe his use of the domain names was fair and lawful.

Although the term "bad faith" is written into § 1125(d)(1)(A)(i) such that it is a threshold finding for any violation of the ACPA, we are persuaded that the district court made a proper finding that, under the circumstances, this case qualified as "exceptional" and merited the award of attorneys' fees under § 1117(a). The record indicates that Zuccarini's conduct was particularly flagrant and that he showed no remorse for his actions. The court stated that "based on the egregiousness of Zuccarini's conduct and his lack of contrition, we without hesitation hold that this is an 'exceptional' case and that Shields was entitled to an award of attorneys' fees." The court's interpretation of what constitutes an "exceptional" case under the ACPA is proper.

Relevant Glossary Entries

Cybersquatting
Internet Corporation for Assigned Names and Numbers (ICANN)
National Arbitration Forum (NAF)
Typosquatting
Uniform Dispute Resolution Policy (UDRP)
Wholesaling Domain Names
World Intellectual Property Organization (WIPO)

Problem Set 4

4.1. Archibald Motors (AM), the manufacturer of the famous Xerxes sports car, keeps you on retainer to handle Internet-related matters that arise in connection with its Web site *www.xerxes.com*. AM invests heavily in online marketing to maintain its aggressive image with young drivers, and is very aggressive about protecting the value of its trademark, Xerxes, both online and in the brick-and-mortar world. Among other things, it has registered the mark in the Patent and Trademark Office. As with most major businesses that maintain Web sites, AM has a lot of problems with people it views as cybersquatters.

(a) The marketing manager at AM calls to tell you that Xerxes Jones has just registered myxerxes.com and is using it as a personal home page. On his home page, he describes himself as a direct lineal descendant of Xerxes the famous Persian king. What options does AM have with regard to the myxerxes.com Web site? Is there any additional information you need about Xerxes Jones before you can advise AM with regard to its options? Lanham Act §43(d); UDRP §4.

(b) Assume the same facts as in question (a). A few days after responding to that query, the marketing manager at AM calls to tell you that further investigation has revealed that Xerxes Jones also has registered xerzes.com, but that he is not using the domain name. Does this change anything?

4.2. Shortly after you deal with Xerxes, you get a call from Kate McCulloch at KM Toys. It appears that another person (Mark Trafeli) has registered the name *www.kmtoys.com*. Kate believes that the other person is the son of a disgruntled employee. When you start negotiating with the "squatter" you learn two things. One, the squatter says that he doesn't have a site up yet (even though he registered the name a year ago), but that he is just planning on using it for his hobby, which happens to be making toys. Two, he is willing to sell the name to KM Toys for $2,000.

(a) Suppose that the facts are that Trafeli has no experience making toys and that the initials KM do not appear to resemble his name or the names of any of his immediate family, friends, or pets. Would you advise Kate that you have a good case under the UDRP or the Lanham Act? If she decides to pursue the matter rather than settle it, which avenue would you recommend in the circumstances? UDRP § 4; Lanham Act § 43(d).

(b) In response to your advice in question (a), the client eventually authorizes you to settle the matter for $2,000. Unfortunately, when you go to finalize the deal, Trafeli now wants not $2,000, but $3,000, "paid up front in cash." Ms. McCulloch is understandably irate, but the fact is, $3,000 is still much cheaper than the true cost of litigation. If your client decides to accept the $3,000 offer, what steps would you take to make sure your client doesn't get burned?

4.3. A colleague comes in to ask you about a "personal" matter. He wanted to register his daughter's name as a domain name for her birthday, and discovered to his chagrin that the name already is registered by a company called namezero.com. The company told him that it would be happy to sell him the name for $150. He thinks this is entirely unreasonable, because they have no legitimate claim to the name. Does he have any legal recourse? UDRP § 4; Lanham Act § 43(d).

4.4. Your teenage son operates a Web site called catsdrool.com, generally devoted to expressing the view that dogs are superior to cats in every possible way. Yesterday he was presented with a UDRP complaint from catz.com, seeking a transfer of the name to the owners of catz.com.

(a) Should your son prevail in a UDRP proceeding? UDRP ¶ 4.

(b) If not, can he seek further review in federal court? Federal Arbitration Act §§ 1, 9; Lanham Act §§ 32(2)(D), 43(d).

4.5. Evan Archibald, the heir of the Archibald Motors fortune, just ran into you in the lobby of your office building as he was on his way up to his private club on the 68th floor. He reports to you that while he was golfing in Palm Springs with your local Congressional representative, they tossed around the idea of adding a new provision to the Trademark Counterfeiting Act of 1984 (which criminalizes knowing trademark infringement by counterfeiting goods or services). The new provision also would criminalize the intentional registration of a domain name that infringes a registered trademark or dilutes a famous trademark. He invites you to join him for lunch to discuss this with him further. If he remembers to ask your opinion of such a project, what will you tell him?

Assignment 5: Web-Site Development and Hosting

Once a business decides to establish a presence on the Web and obtains control of the domain name that it wishes to use, it will then proceed to develop a Web site to display at that domain name. In many cases, the business will turn to outside consultants and developers for the technological and logistical expertise involved in designing and implementing a Web site. The transactional lawyer at this point will be asked to prepare an agreement that addresses the important issues raised by the development project. This assignment discusses the principal issues such an agreement must address, focusing on the important business interests of the customer and the developer that such an agreement must accommodate.

A. What Will the Web Site Do?

Different companies pursue different objectives with their commercial Internet sites. At one extreme are "pure play" Internet companies that have no offline presence for dealing with their customers. At the other extreme are "brick and mortar" companies that merely put up a static home page that provides little information about the business and no online interactivity. Most businesses that create commercial Web sites operate somewhere between those two extremes.

1. Informational Sites

A company that has only one place of business, whose customers are largely drawn from the neighborhoods adjacent to the business premises, may have no real economic motive for building a Web site. Such a business is unlikely to increase the traffic in its store by maintaining a Web presence, especially if its customer base depends on word-of-mouth recommendations and prospective customers walking past the store itself. The Web presence of such a company is likely to be nothing more than a way of staking out a claim to a good domain name to prevent anyone else from getting there first, and perhaps to develop some basic familiarity with Web commerce.

Even a business that depends on customer traffic actually going to its physical premises as the backbone of its business may find ways to increase its revenues by using a Web presence. For example, many manufacturers have sophisticated distribution networks for which a Web retail site would not be a useful substitute. Such a business might make an effective marketing tool out of a Web site that contains nothing more than a catalog of its products, a location map, and a link to an e-mail address to receive queries. Maintaining such a simple Web site could be a cost-effective alternative to a large listing in the telephone directories of the communities to which the manufacturer distributes its products or a direct-mail campaign to homes of likely purchasers. For a more complicated business, it might be useful to have a full retail Web site for one portion of the business (such as commercial sales), with only a simple catalog for another portion of the business (such as consumer sales). The Web site for General Electrics (*www.ge.com*) is a good example of such a site.

Another simple but inexpensive way that a Web site can attract new business is to provide an order form that can be printed from the Web site and then used to place an order to the business. For example, *www.dominos.com* includes a menu of Domino's products, together with a search engine that identifies for the user the telephone number of the nearest retail location. Although such a low-tech interface might reflect poorly on the sophistication of a business trying to market high-tech goods or services, it could be helpful for a business operating in a lower-tech market (like the market for pizza).

2. Simple Storefronts

Many businesses that create commercial Web sites expect to take orders from the Web site and then either ship tangible goods to their customers (books, records, electronics, etc.), or permit their customers to download digital media to fulfill the orders (news stories, photographs, data, etc.). When a business decides to build a site with that higher degree of interactivity, the Web-site development and maintenance issues become quite complex. Among other things, computer security becomes a major issue, because the site necessarily will permit outsiders to transmit data to the business's Web server (the computer where the content of the Web site resides). At the same time, the site will be permitting outsiders to retrieve data from the business's computers—assuming that the site will permit potential customers to examine pictures of items for sale or textual descriptions of the items or the terms on which they can be purchased. To permit those simultaneous inflows and outflows of data to occur smoothly without leaving holes for unauthorized data transmissions can be a considerable challenge. The costs of those security problems—and the consequent costs of designing the site to minimize them—are an important part of the costs of a storefront site.

It also is challenging to develop a functional interface between a Web server and other business-software applications. Most companies will use some kind of software to manage personnel matters, production processes, or financial resources; some companies will have many more applications in addition to such basic ones. If a business is using out-of-date ("legacy") applications to perform those functions, the cost of developing an interface between those applications and an Internet storefront may be considerable, or even prohibitive.

It is part of the "conventional wisdom" of modern management that efforts to make "one small change" in a business information system often turn into a much larger effort to "reengineer" large portions of the business's organizational structure and business culture. Another way to look at the same process, however, is to think of it as an example of the problem (not unique to software) of "feature creep," in which projects with an initially clear objective evolve into monstrosities that are overdue, over-budget, and unwieldy. As disquieting as feature creep is to the supervisors of an in-house project, it presents more serious legal problems when a third party is constructing the site under a contract with the site sponsor. If the Web site is a simple affair and the changes sought are modest, they might be implemented without formal modifications of the original agreement. On the other hand, if there are major problems in setting and maintaining the objectives of the project, the business's attorney must hope that the documents governing the relationship provide a workable mechanism for reaching a joint consensus on the objectives of the continuing project.

Many of those problems will be less serious for new businesses that have little or no "brick and mortar" interactions with its customers. Among other things, those businesses may have few problems integrating new Web-enabled applications with older legacy applications because they are less likely to have older legacy systems in the first place. Indeed, startup Internet businesses often can use "commercial off the shelf" (COTS) software application packages that provide electronic-commerce functions at a reasonable price. Some COTS systems are even "turnkey" systems, which are designed to operate as a single system without any further system integration by the purchaser.

The value of COTS e-commerce systems has improved significantly in the last few years. Even in the late 1990s, COTS business software applications often failed to live up to the expectations of the purchasers, typically because they would not support all of the functions that the purchaser needed, so that the company would end up spending considerable amounts on custom software development in order to get the COTS system to meet its needs. More recently, however, as Internet storefront functions become (relatively) standardized, COTS applications tend to be fully adequate for companies that do not need a significant interface with brick-and-mortar operations.

3. Complex Sites

The final level of difficulty arises if a business plans to offer online services that demand significant system resources, such as the delivery of streaming media or network-access services. Delivery of audio or video files demands large-bandwidth network connections and the ability to process huge amounts of data at high speeds. When the business model of an Internet company is focused on delivery of online services, its customers expect those services to be available 7 days a week, 24 hours a day ("24/7"). Its customers also doubtless expect enough bandwidth and processing power to allow all customers to be accommodated at the same time without any noticeable delay. Unfortunately, under current levels of technology, it is very difficult and expensive to maintain that level of service. But, however difficult it may be, failure to invest in sufficient capacity can be disastrous. For example, eBay lost $5 million in sales and $4 billion in market capitalization when a hacker brought down the eBay Web site for just 22 hours in 1999. Although eBay has recovered from this disaster, and even gone on to greater strength as an online business, less well-known Internet companies cannot count on having such good fortune.

B.   Web-Site Development Agreements

1.   Defining and Implementing the Project

The most basic object of a Web-site development agreement as a business proposition is to define the scope of the work that each party will undertake. For several reasons, this task is more difficult here than it is in many other transactional contexts. Most obviously, there is no industry custom or standard as to how a Web site should look. Some Web sites are simple, amounting to little more than a brochure for the firm's products. Others are intricate, providing interactive customer support or retail capabilities. Also, given the novelty of the problem from the perspective of the customer, the customer's expectations may not be well-developed or well-informed at the beginning of the process.

The difficulty in determining the scope of work complicates negotiations about the method of payment. Flat-fee or fixed-cost contracts, for example, present the potential for serious disagreement if the customer ultimately hopes for greater functionality or sophistication than the developer anticipated in establishing a fixed price up front. Thus, the parties often require a developer to prepare a prototype or skeleton site that the customer can approve at an early stage of the process to avoid future disputes.

In short, it is important for the lawyer both to help the client develop a more precise understanding of its wishes and to draft an agreement that implements those wishes in a reasonably precise way. The typical format is to include in the agreement a relatively vague description of the obligations, with attachments that specify more particularly exactly what the developer is to do and exactly when and how the customer is to pay for it, and provisions providing a framework for altering the obligations as the expectations of the parties develop.

SAMPLE PROVISIONS

1.   Description of Services

Developer agrees to provide consulting, world wide web development, and related services ("Services") specified in the Statement of Work attached hereto as Exhibit A, as amended from time to time by Supplemental Statements of Work. The Services shall be provided in accordance with the provisions of this Agreement and the applicable Statement of Work.

2.   Payment for Services

2.1   Customer agrees to pay Developer for the Services in accordance with the Fee Schedule attached hereto as Schedule A or set forth in any Statement of Work. The fees specified in Schedule A or in any Statement of Work are the total fees and charges for the Services and will not be increased during the term of this Agreement except as the parties may agree in writing.

2.2   Invoices. Developer shall invoice Customer for Services rendered during the preceding monthly period. The invoice will detail the work performed during such period. Customer shall pay the invoice within thirty (30) days after receipt.

3.   Statements of Work

When required by either party, the parties may in good faith negotiate Supplemental Statements of Work ("Supplements"), each of which upon signing by both parties shall be deemed part of this Agreement. Such Supplements shall be substantially in the form of Appendix A hereto. Unless otherwise agreed in a Supplement, the following provisions shall govern Supplements generally:

3.1   Definitions. As used in this Agreement and any relevant Statement of Work, the following terms shall be defined as follows:

3.1(a)   "Milestone Schedule" shall mean the schedule for the Services as set forth as part of the relevant Statement of Work.

3.1(b)   "Specifications" shall mean the requirements for the development of the Web Site or other Deliverables as set forth as part of the relevant Statement of Work.

3.1(c)   "Deliverables" shall mean any work designed, created, and/or produced by Developer hereunder in connection with this Agreement and as further set forth as part of the relevant Statement of Work.

(a)   Site Design: How the Site Looks

Users might view a Web site from different hardware platforms (Windows, Macintosh, and Linux computers, cellphones, PDAs, etc.) and with different Web browsers (Explorer, Navigator, Opera, etc.). Unfortunately, because those technologies are not yet standardized, this often means that a Web site will look and perform differently, depending on the manner in which a user accesses the site. The problem is augmented by the differing capabilities of different browsers, which often support different HTML functions. Thus, it is difficult for a developer to design a Web site that will maintain a consistent appearance across different brands of Web browsers. The problem can be resolved in several ways. For example, a customer with a small budget might prefer a lowest-common-denominator approach, in which the developer refrains from using any browser-specific HTML functions. The problem with that approach, however, is that it eliminates multimedia and design options available in sophisticated browsers. Parties concerned about that problem might require the Web site to be compatible with the latest versions of one or more popular Web browsers (Explorer and Navigator, for example). Yet a more expensive approach would be to require the developer to maintain different versions of the Web site, each of which would be fully compatible with different Web browsers.

(b)   Site Performance: How the Site Performs

A separate problem is that the statement of work (SOW) also should reflect concerns about performance issues, such as bandwidth capacities and response time. Although those problems are directly relevant to a hosting agreement (the agreement under which a party with a server hosts the Web site), they are indirectly relevant to the development agreement because the site needs to be developed in a way that will make it usable when it is posted. As long as a significant number of users access Web sites over telephone lines rather than some form of broadband access, multimedia-laden sites will be time-consuming to download. Customers concerned about that problem might include in the SOW specifications that would require low-graphics versions of the site to facilitate access by non-broadband users. In some cases, the customer might even prefer to maintain a text-only version of the site.

(c)   Implementing the Statement of Work

Although the parties normally will not address these issues in great technical detail, they will need to anticipate them. The basic concept is that the developer must convert the content (much of which is supplied by the customer) into a display-ready format, usually by developing software and scripting routines that generate the formats that the customer requires. A common way to implement those provisions is to incorporate by reference a separate document such as a statement of work that addresses these issues. The parties often will negotiate and execute the main portion of the agreement first, leaving negotiation of the SOW itself to subsequent procedures specified in the agreement. The provisions below are typical.

SAMPLE PROVISIONS

3.2   Information to be Supplied to Developer
To implement a Statement of Work, Customer shall supply to Developer the Specifications, Milestone Schedule, pricing, and payment terms (including an estimate of required hours or a fixed price proposal) and any other information that Developer may reasonably require to evaluate the performance of the services proposed by Customer (the "Proposal").

3.2(a)   Within five (5) business days of Developer's receipt of the Proposal, Developer shall respond and either accept the Proposal as a Statement of Work or require changes thereto.

3.2(b)   The parties shall negotiate in good faith with respect to the Proposal, until both parties agree to implement the Proposal, as revised if necessary, as a Statement of Work. Developer shall not be required to commence work pursuant to the Statement of Work until both parties have agreed in writing to the Statement of Work.

3.2(c)   All Services performed hereunder, other than fixed price proposals, shall be compensated pursuant to the Fee Schedule set forth in Schedule A or any applicable Statement of Work.

3.2(d)   The performance of Services required in the Statement of Work shall be completed in accordance with the Milestone Schedule set forth in the Statement of Work, provided Customer shall have delivered all necessary information and materials in a timely fashion, and if not, then Consultant's obligations which are dependent on such information or materials shall be extended to reflect such delay.

3.3 Term. In the absence of an express provision for the duration or early termination of a Supplement, any SOW shall be terminable upon thirty (30) days' written notice of either party without cause.

3.4 Payment. Supplements may call for lump-sum or periodic payment, payment against performance milestones, compensation based upon time and materials, or on a fixed price, or any other arrangement agreed upon by the parties.

(d) The Customer's Obligation to Provide Materials

From the developer's perspective, it is crucial that the customer's obligation to provide content be set forth with clarity. The creation of the content and the decisions about the format and organization of the content on the site likely will be among the most time-consuming parts of the development of the Web site. Because those materials often will be created by the customer, the developer's ability to meet its deadlines will depend on prompt delivery by the customer of the required materials. Thus, the developer typically will include provisions that set forth that obligation specifically. A key question will be whether the customer wishes (as it often will) to retain complete editorial control over the content of the Web site. This will be particularly important in situations in which the site involves use of a valuable trademark owned by the customer. At the same time, the developer might be concerned that material supplied by the customer might (in the view of the developer) be offensive in some way or (perhaps more seriously) violate the IP rights of a third party. A well-drafted agreement will address all of those concerns.

4.   Delivery of Satisfactory Production Materials by Customer to Developer

4.1   Customer shall provide Developer, upon reasonable notice, all necessary materials, data, or documentation pertaining to the Services as set forth in the applicable SOW.

4.2   Customer shall deliver to Developer such materials, data, or documentation in a form satisfactory to Developer. All photographs, images, video, animation, film, illustrations, drawings, charts, maps, indexes and other graphical and visual materials, as well as all music, sound, narration and other audio materials or other works owned or controlled by Customer that are necessary to completion of the Services (collectively "Customer Content") shall be suitable for reproduction and shall be timely delivered to Developer in the form specified in the applicable SOW.

4.3   Developer shall make no changes to the text or appearance or otherwise of any of the Customer Content without the prior written approval of Customer. Customer shall make the final determination of all Customer Content to be used on the Web Site.

4.4   Developer reserves the right to refuse to include Customer Content in the Web Site that Developer deems offensive or otherwise inappropriate.

(e) Delivery and Acceptance

Provisions for acceptance testing of the site are critical in any development agreement. They are particularly crucial in this context, where it is difficult (if not impossible) to specify in advance the precise nature of the product to be delivered. Because the process of designing a Web site is complex and technical, parties normally provide for a thorough and lengthy process of acceptance testing. The point is to give the customer an opportunity to test the software in day-to-day operation, with a variety of hardware and software combinations.

From the customer's perspective, the acceptance scheme can give the customer significant control over the design process if it allows the customer to decide what qualifies as a conforming product and what must be cured. Conversely, a developer will want to limit the customer's ability to reject a product opportunistically. The most typical processes aim to limit conflict on those questions by providing for a staged process of development and approval that results in timely and ongoing feedback rather than a surprise rejection at the conclusion of the process. Whatever the procedure, it will need to include some formal method of dispute resolution if the parties have a material disagreement about some aesthetic or functional aspect of the site.

SAMPLE PROVISIONS

5. Delivery and Acceptance of Deliverables

   5.1 Time and Manner of Delivery. Developer shall deliver each Deliverable at the times and in the manner specified under this Agreement, including any relevant Statement of Work. Notwithstanding the foregoing, if Customer fails to provide Developer with the information or feedback required under the acceptance test procedure set forth herein within the applicable time period, then Developer's obligations that are dependent on such information or approval shall be extended to reflect such delay.

   5.2 Procedure for Acceptance. The procedure for acceptance of any Deliverable shall be as follows:

   5.2(a) Customer shall have thirty (30) days to inspect and test each such Deliverable when received to determine if it conforms to the Specifications.

   5.2(b) If any Deliverable fails to conform to its Specifications, Customer shall give Developer written notice of the failure stating the defect in the Deliverable. Developer shall then have thirty (30) days to remedy such failure or defect and redeliver such Deliverable to Customer.

   5.2(c) After resubmission of the Deliverable by Developer, Customer shall again inspect the Deliverable to confirm that it conforms to Specifications. If the resubmitted Deliverable again fails Customer's acceptance testing, Customer may, in its sole discretion (i) deem the failure to be a material breach of this Agreement; or (ii) accept the Deliverable as a non-conforming Deliverable. If Customer elects (ii), Customer may in its sole discretion either: (aa) withhold a mutually agreed upon offset from the fees payable to Developer for the Deliverable under this Agreement or any applicable Statement of Work; or (bb) invoice and recover from Developer the amount of Customer's reasonable out-of-pocket costs to correct, modify, and/or complete the Deliverable in accordance with the Specifications.

   5.3 Each Deliverable shall be deemed to be accepted upon written notice by Customer to Developer of such acceptance. Customer shall not unreasonably withhold or delay acceptance.

5.4 Except in the instances of Force Majeure or in the case of an extension pursuant to Sections [ ], a failure by Developer to provide Deliverables to Customer within the agreed upon time period shall be a material breach of the Agreement.

2. Ownership

(a) Legal Rules

Intellectual property issues are central to a Web-site development contract, primarily because the Web site often will represent an integration of substantial amounts of IP belonging to both the customer and the developer: the content of the customer and the software technology of the developer. Accordingly, it is important that the agreement deal with the problem expressly.

Many small- and medium-sized brick-and-mortar businesses may never have given any serious consideration to the acquisition or protection of intellectual-property rights in connection with their business operations, so negotiating a Web-site development agreement will force them to focus on these issues for the first time.

The first and most basic question is ownership of the site. With regard to the terms of the site-development contract itself, the company will need to decide as a general matter whether it wants to purchase the developer's output and the intellectual-property rights associated with it or merely obtain a license to use them. That problem can be difficult, because Web-site developers typically try to develop a portfolio of products that they adapt and license to many different customers. It is much more expensive to have a developer create an entirely unique Web site that it will sell outright to the company. If the company is willing merely to license a variation of something the developer plans to use repeatedly, the company then must consider whether it needs to prevent the developer from selling a similar Web site to a competitor of the company.

Once the company decides what interest it wants to have in the site, the next question will be how to document that interest. A Web site is not a tangible object that can be "owned" in the same way as a typewriter or a desk. Rather, the apex of protection generally is acquired under copyright law. Copyright law does not grant the owner any affirmative rights to the software, but it does grant the owner the right to exclude others from any of a variety of specified uses of the software's expressive content. Most importantly for our purposes, the owner of a copyright can prevent others from copying and distributing the software; together, those rights functionally should allow the copyright owner to prevent others from using the software. Copyright Act §106. It also is possible that some of the software might be patented, but patent rules regarding ownership and transfer are sufficiently flexible that they rarely present issues of great difficulty.

In the case of a copyright, the work ordinarily is owned in the first instance by its creator. If the site is developed by an employee, then the employer would own the site as a work made for hire. See 17 U.S.C. §101 (definition of "work made for hire"). In the case where the work is created by a third-party developer, however, the developer ordinarily will own the intellectual property that it creates in the course of development. If the company wishes to own the copyright to its site, it can obtain ownership of the copyright by having the developer transfer the copyright to the company. Because the Copyright Act includes a statute of frauds, that transfer must be in writing and signed by the owner of the copyright. 17 U.S.C. § 204(a). As discussed in more detail in Assignment 35, a prudent copyright owner will record that transfer document promptly in the records of the Copyright Office, to ensure that the developer cannot at a later date transfer the copyright to some other party.

If the company decides that it does not wish to own the work outright, it will obtain some lesser right to use the software, ordinarily in the form of a license. Chapter 4 discusses licenses in considerable detail, but for now it is important to notice the distinction between an "exclusive" and a "nonexclusive" license to use the software. An exclusive license is functionally similar to a transfer of ownership, because it gives the licensee the exclusive right to use the software, and carries with it the right to sue to prevent infringement of the copyright. See Copyright Act §§ 101 (defining "transfer of copyright ownership" to include an exclusive license); 501(b) (permitting exclusive licensees to sue for infringement of a copyright).

A nonexclusive license, on the other hand, simply waives the right of the copyright owner to complain about actions by the licensee that otherwise would constitute infringement. Thus, for example, when a consumer purchases a copy of Microsoft Office it obtains a nonexclusive license that permits it to use the software in ways that Microsoft otherwise could prohibit based on its ownership of the copyright in the software.

(b) Drafting Issues

Working within that legal framework, both parties have important interests that can make resolution of this particular issue difficult or complex. First, customers have a variety of important reasons that motivate them to seek outright ownership of the copyright in their sites. For one thing, customers probably are best placed to modify and update a site over time; ordinarily that activity would violate the developer's exclusive right to create derivative works under Copyright Act § 106(2). More seriously, the customer will have concerns about the developer reusing work created for the customer for another customer, especially if the second customer competes with the customer for whom the work was done in the first instance.

At the same time, as suggested above, the developer has important interests in retaining at least some of the IP related to the site. Modern Web sites involve the application of considerable technological skill to produce complicated software products. If a developer cannot reuse any of the products of that skill, then it will be much more laborious and time-intensive for it to create new sites for subsequent customers. It often will make good sense to permit the developer to reuse the "technological" aspects of the site, but not the content and other material originally provided by the customer.

Because those issues can be resolved in so many different ways, it is difficult to provide standard provisions. The most general compromise is to allow the developer to retain formal copyright ownership, but to grant a nonexclusive license of the software together with adequate assurances about future conduct by the developer and customer to respond to the customer's concerns. For example, the customer will need provisions that require the developer to deliver the site's source code to the customer and that permit the customer to modify the site and create derivative works.

The provisions below provide a variety of ways that such an agreement might be structured, including differing compromises of the relevant issues. From the perspective of the student, these provisions should be viewed as a checklist of relevant negotiating points.

BASIC PROVISIONS

Section 6   Rights in Data and Works

6.1   For purposes of this Agreement, the following terms shall have the meanings set forth below:

6.1(a)   "Custom Work Product" shall mean all designs, discoveries, inventions, products, computer programs, procedures, improvements, developments, drawings, notes, documents, information, and materials made, conceived, or developed by Developer either before or after the Effective Date of this Agreement on behalf of Customer in furtherance of the Site or other Services provided to Customer under the terms of this Agreement, and paid for by Customer. Customer Work Product does not include any preexisting software owned by Developer, nor any Customer Content, as herein defined, nor any third party software products incorporated into the Custom Work Product.

6.1(b)   "Customer Content" shall mean any computer programs, designs, data, video or audio materials, graphics or other materials provided by Customer to Developer pursuant to this Agreement.

6.1(c)   "Intellectual Property" shall mean intellectual property or proprietary rights, including but not limited to copyright rights, moral rights, patent rights (including patent applications and disclosures), rights of priority, mask work rights, and trade secret rights, recognized in any country or jurisdiction in the world.

PRO-DEVELOPER PROVISIONS

6.2   Ownership. Customer agrees that Developer is the owner of all rights, title and interest in and to the Custom Work Product, including, but not limited to page design and layout and associated techniques, CGI or PERL scripting, any software (including all routines and algorithms therein), images or icons developed by Developer or its agents pursuant to this Agreement.

6.3   Customer's Rights. Developer grants to Customer a non-exclusive, worldwide, fully paid license to use the Custom Work Product and the executable form of all software contained therein, and to reproduce, transmit, and distribute it by electronic means solely for Customer's own business use in operating the Web site. This license shall be perpetual and irrevocable except as provided in Section [] below. Customer may not (i) create derivative works based on the Custom Work Product; (ii) modify the Custom Work Product except to update certain modules identified by Developer; (iii) use the Custom Work Product to provide services to third parties; or (iv) rent, lease, market, or sublicense the Custom Work Product to third parties, except pursuant to a separate distribution agreement with Developer.

6.4 Developer's Rights to Customer Content. Customer grants to Developer a non-exclusive, worldwide, perpetual, royalty-free license to reproduce, modify, display, perform, adapt, transmit, distribute, improve, and otherwise use the Customer Content in connection with Developer's performance under this Agreement.

PRO-CUSTOMER PROVISIONS

6.2 Ownership. Unless otherwise specified in a Statement of Work, the Custom Work Product, all Deliverables, and all Intellectual Property Rights therein shall be deemed to be the sole and exclusive property of Customer and all title and interest therein shall vest in Customer and shall be deemed to be a "work made for hire" and made in the course of the Services rendered hereunder. To the extent that any title to any such Custom Work Product may not, by operation of law, vest in Customer or such works may not be considered works made for hire, all right, title and interest therein shall be irrevocably assigned to Customer. All such Custom Work Product shall belong exclusively to Customer with Customer having the right to obtain and to hold in its name copyrights, registrations or such other protection as may be appropriate to the subject matter, and any extensions and renewals thereof. Developer agrees to provide reasonable assistance and cooperation to Customer to acquire, transfer, maintain, perfect, and/or enforce the Intellectual Property rights in the Custom Work Product, including but not limited to execution of assignment of ownership or other documents as may be reasonably required by Customer.

6.3 Developer agrees to: (i) disclose promptly in writing to Customer all Custom Work Product; (ii) cooperate with and assist Customer to apply for, and to execute any applications and/or assignments reasonably necessary to obtain any patent, copyright, trademark, or other statutory protection for the Custom Work Product in Customer's name as Customer deems appropriate; and (iii) otherwise treat all Custom Work Product as Confidential Information, as herein defined. These obligations will survive any expiration or termination of this Agreement.

(To mitigate the effects of that approach on a developer's standard technology library, a developer would request provisions like those that follow.)

PROPOSED MITIGATING ALTERNATIVES FROM DEVELOPER'S PERSPECTIVE:

6.4(a) "Custom Work Product" shall mean computer programs, designs, products, developments, drawings, notes, documents and other materials created by Developer during the term of this Agreement on behalf of Customer in furtherance of the Web site development and other Services that has been delivered to Customer and paid for by Customer, except for Generic Modules. Custom Work Product shall not include any Customer

Content, nor any third-party software products incorporated into the Custom Work Products, nor any Developer Technology, as herein defined.

6.4(b) "Generic Modules" shall mean discrete computer program subroutines that are not specific to the functions of the Custom Work Product but are useful generally in Developer's business and that are designated as "Generic Modules" in a writing signed by both parties.

6.4(c) "Developer Technology" shall mean any and all existing software, technology, know-how, algorithms, procedures, techniques, and solutions associated with the use, design, development, testing, and distribution of the Custom Work Product and improvements to such existing software and related technology, which technology is owned by Developer or its suppliers and used by Developer in the development effort hereunder.

6.5 Developer hereby grants to Customer a perpetual, irrevocable, non-exclusive, worldwide, fully paid license to use, reproduce, modify, display, perform, create derivative works based upon, and to grant end-user customers (either directly or indirectly via distributors, value-added resellers and software developers) sublicenses to use Developer Technology, the Generic Modules, and all Intellectual Property rights contained in the Custom Work Product.

6.6 Developer's Rights. Developer Technology, the Generic Modules, and all Intellectual Property rights contained therein are and will remain the sole and exclusive property of Developer.

6.7 Customer grants to Developer a perpetual, irrevocable, non-exclusive, worldwide, fully paid license to use, reproduce, modify, display, perform, create derivative works based upon, and to grant end-user customers (either directly or indirectly via distributors, value-added resellers and software developers) sublicenses to use the Custom Work Product and all Intellectual Property rights contained therein; provided that Developer may not use the Custom Work Product to create (directly or indirectly) a product for any of the companies listed in Exhibit [ ] [or a direct competitor of Customer] that performs substantially the same functions as the software contained in the Custom Work Product.

6.8 Nothing in this Agreement shall be construed to limit Developer's right to use information in nontangible form retained by Developer as ideas, information and understandings retained in the human memories of its employees, contractors and agents, provided that Developer may only use information of general applicability and not Customer's Confidential Information. This provision shall not be construed to operate to grant Developer any rights under Customer's patents or copyrights.

6.9 Customer will provide reasonable assistance and cooperation to Developer to acquire, transfer, maintain, perfect, and/or enforce the Intellectual Property rights in the Web site (excluding Customer Content) and Custom Work Product, including, but not limited to, execution of a formal assignment or such other documents as may be reasonably requested by Developer. Customer hereby appoints the officers of Developer as Customer's attorneys-in-fact to execute such documents on Customer's behalf for this purpose.

3.   Allocating Risks

As in any contractual relationship, the agreement must address a variety of contingencies that cannot fully be understood by both parties at the time they sign the agreement. Traditionally, most commercial agreements would include (at least) three different types of provisions to deal with such problems. First, it is common for a contract to include a specific representation or warranty about matters that are or fairly ought to be within the knowledge and control of one party. Second, in cases in which the background legal rules permit liability that businesses would regard as excessive, sophisticated parties often will agree to limit their liability to specified amounts. Finally, with respect to future occurrences that the parties regard as fairly chargeable to a specific party, an agreement often will include indemnity provisions under which the responsible party bears the costs associated with such an occurrence.

(a) Representations and Warranties

Representations and warranties generally set the terms of performance to which each party will be held. Given the developer's expertise in technological performance, the customer reasonably will seek a variety of warranties from the developer. For example, the customer often will want not only a specific warranty that the program will comply with the specifications, but also a general warranty that the program will be developed in a timely, professional manner and that the programming will be error- and virus-free. The customer also might seek a warranty that the site will use up-to-date technology, to ensure that the site has the greatest possible functionality. Finally, the customer reasonably would want an assurance that the materials the developer provides to the site do not infringe the IP or other rights of any third party. Conversely, the developer may have sound reasons for wishing to limit many of the warranties that the customer seeks. Customers must understand that a developer's potential exposure to liability on a large and ambitious development project may increase the cost of the project substantially. That is particularly true for topics (like patent liability) as to which it is difficult for the developer to be sure that its product does not infringe.

SAMPLE PRO-DEVELOPER WARRANTY PROVISION

7.   Warranties and Disclaimers

    7.1   Customer represents and warrants that it is authorized by all required authorities [to grant the license to the Customer Content to Developer as set forth in Section [ ] and] that neither the Customer Content nor Developer's exercise of the license granted in Section [ ] hereof infringes upon any copyright, patent, trademark, or other proprietary rights of third parties or any other applicable laws, regulations and non-proprietary third-party rights. Moreover, Customer warrants that the Customer Content contains no material that is unlawful, harmful, fraudulent, threatening, abusive, harassing, defamatory, vulgar, obscene, profane, hateful, racially, ethnically, or otherwise objectionable, including, without limitation, any material that encourages conduct that would constitute a criminal offense, give rise to civil liability, or otherwise violate any applicable laws or regulations.

7.2   Neither Developer nor any of its information providers, employers or agents warrant that the Services or Deliverables provided hereunder will be uninterrupted or error free. Nor does Developer or any of its information providers, employees, or agents make any warranty as to the results to be obtained from the use of the Web site or any other Services provided hereunder. The Services and Deliverables are to be performed and delivered on an "AS IS" basis, without warranties of any kind, either express or implied, including but not limited to warranties of title or implied warranties of merchantability or fitness for a particular purpose.

SAMPLE PRO-CUSTOMER WARRANTY PROVISIONS

7.1   Developer represents and warrants that it is the owner of or otherwise has the right to use and distribute all materials and methodologies used in connection with providing the Deliverables, that such materials and methodologies (other than information or materials supplied by Customer and reproduced accurately in the Deliverables) shall not infringe any copyright or other proprietary right of a third party, and that Developer will comply with all applicable laws and regulations in performance of its obligations hereunder.

7.2   Developer represents and warrants that (a) all of the Services to be performed by it under this Agreement will be rendered using sound, professional practices and in a competent and professional manner by knowledgeable, trained, and qualified personnel; (b) the Deliverables will be configured using the most up-to-date commercially reasonable technical specifications; (c) the Deliverables will operate in conformance with the terms of this Agreement, including without limitation, any applicable Statement of Work; (d) the Deliverables are and will be free of any software disabling devices or internal controls, including, without limitation, time bombs, viruses, or devices of similar nature; and that (e) all Deliverables hereunder will be compatible and operate in conjunction with all software and hardware previously delivered under this Agreement.

(b) Limitations of Liability

Sophisticated businesses also almost always wish to include clear and specific provisions that limit their liability to specific types of damages, often with specific damage caps. In this context, for example, both parties generally would agree to forgo any right to pursue consequential or incidental damages such as lost profits. Similarly, the parties might establish a liability cap tied to the revenues paid under the agreement or to some other arbitrary figure mutually acceptable to the parties. The general premise of all of those provisions is that businesses prefer a contracting environment in which the ultimate downside of a failed relationship is limited to a discrete and predictable sum.

SAMPLE PROVISIONS

8.   Limitations on Liability
8.1   Limitation on Liability. Except for the indemnification obligations set forth in this Agreement, neither party shall be liable to the other for lost profits, lost

opportunities, or special, consequential, or indirect damages under any circumstances.

8.2   Limitation on Developer's Liability. Developer's liability to Customer shall in no event exceed the total amounts paid by Customer to Developer under this Agreement.

8.3   Limitation on Customer's Liability. Customer's liability to Developer for any and all matters related to this Agreement shall not exceed the total of payments due to Developer from Customer hereunder.

(c)   Indemnification

In launching a commercial Web site, a company must take steps to ensure that the content of its Web site does not infringe the intellectual-property rights of others. Using content developed by others may result in more rapid or more professional development of the Web site, but it will require the company either to buy or license rights to that content. Thus, however attractive it might be to develop a site by copying attractive arrangements and devices found on another site, any such copying runs the risk of infringing the intellectual property of the copied site.

One possibility is that the copied site is protected by a patent. It once was difficult to get patents on software or business methods, but in recent years the Federal Circuit has relaxed those rules considerably, so much of the technology on Web sites now is protected by patents. Thus, any technology copied from another Web site has the potential of bringing with it liability for patent infringement.

There also is the possibility of copyright infringement, because any posting of another's copyrighted material on the sponsor's Web site will constitute infringement, if only because posting the material involves copying it. In some cases, the sponsor might avoid that problem by providing a hyperlink to the other material instead of copying it, but often that will not serve the company's needs. The other possibility relates to the limited protections that copyright affords (a topic mentioned above). It is fundamental to copyright law that it protects only the "expression" contained in the protected work. Thus, "copyright protection [does not extend] to any idea, procedure, process, system, method of operation, concept, principle, or discovery" that might be contained in the copied Web site. Copyright Act § 102(b).

Hence, if the company develops its site by copying "ideas" from another site but refrains from copying any "expression" from the other site, the company will not have infringed the copyright of the copied site. It still might have infringed the patent, but it may be able to solve that problem by examining the records of the Patent and Trademark Office to discover any relevant patents. On the copyright question, though, the distinction between "idea" and "expression" is quite vague, but a few rules of thumb are useful. First, if the company copies any substantial amount of narrative text it probably has infringed the copyright (because of the expression inherent in almost any substantial passage of narrative). Second, if the company copies only the functional features that are available on the site, it probably has taken only an "idea," for which it cannot be held responsible. Third, even if nothing visible to the user has been copied, the company will be liable for infringement if it has copied substantial amounts of the underlying software "code" that operates the site.

The serious possibility of liability for copyright infringement in particular invariably is addressed in a contract for the development of a commercial Web site. Depending on which party is responsible for providing content, either or both of the parties may make representations and warranties to the other. If the developer provides content to the company, the company is justified in asking for a warranty from the developer that the content it provides for the company's use does not infringe the rights of third parties. The agreement also typically would require the developer to defend the company from claims of infringement of the rights of third parties and compensation for any damages awarded to compensate for such infringement. Conversely, if the company turns over content to the developer for use in the Web site, the developer is justified in seeking similar assurances from the company.

Finally, given the often limited tangible asset base of Internet-related companies, both the sponsor and the developer will need to consider whether the other party has the resources to make good on its obligations in the event of later allegations of infringement. If either party is thinly capitalized, the other party must understand that its protection in the event of infringement might be illusory.

Indemnification provisions respond to those problems—often in prose that is quite murky at first reading. For what it is worth, you should understand that the provisions set forth below, obscure as they might seem, are shorter (and clearer) by far than many such provisions.

SAMPLE PROVISIONS

9.   Indemnification

9.1   Developer Indemnification. Developer shall indemnify and hold harmless (including payment of reasonable attorneys' fees) Customer, its directors, officers, employees, and agents (each of the foregoing being hereinafter referred to individually as "Indemnified Party") against all liability to third parties arising from or in connection with any acts or omissions of Developer in connection with its performance of this Agreement. This indemnification includes any cause of action brought against the Indemnified Party in relation to the services including, but not limited to, those related to alleged copyright infringement, defamation, products liability, the *[insert name of appropriate state deceptive trade practices statute]*, fraud, or based in whole or in part on any negligent or grossly negligent act or omission of the Indemnified Party, its officers, agents, or employees. Developer's obligation to indemnify the Indemnified Party will survive the expiration or termination of this Agreement by either party for any reason. Developer shall pay for the defense of any such third-party action arising as described herein unless the Indemnified Party and Developer shall mutually agree that the Indemnified Party will pay for the defense.

9.2   Customer Indemnification. Customer shall indemnify and hold harmless (including payment of reasonable attorneys' fees) Developer, its directors, officers, employees, and agents (each of the foregoing being hereinafter referred to individually as "Indemnified Party") against all liability to third parties arising from or in connection with the Customer Materials provided by Customer to Developer as necessary to perform services under this

Agreement, or any acts or omissions of Customer in relation to its dealings with third parties in connection with the performed services under this Agreement. This indemnification includes any cause of action brought against the Indemnified Party in relation to the services including, but not limited to, those related to alleged copyright infringement, defamation, products liability, the *[insert name of appropriate state deceptive trade practices statute]*, fraud, or based in whole or in part on any negligent or grossly negligent act or omission of the Indemnified Party, its officers, agents, or employees. Customer's obligation to indemnify the Indemnified Party will survive the expiration or termination of this Agreement by either party for any reason. Customer shall pay for the defense of any such third-party action arising as described herein unless the Indemnified Party and Customer shall mutually agree that the Indemnified Party will pay for the defense.

C.   Web-Site Hosting

Once the company has built the content for its Web site, the company must decide how to make the Web site accessible on the Internet. If the company does not already have its own internal computer network connected to the Internet, then, at least initially, the company will need to purchase Web-site hosting services from an Internet service provider (ISP). A Web-site hosting agreement may cover a narrow or a wide range of services, so its terms will depend on the business deal reached between the company and the service provider.

A typical arrangement with a Web-site hosting service would include most if not all of the following terms:

- A summary of each party's major obligations to the other;
- A description of the benchmarks or metrics that the parties will use to measure the level of services actually provided, how those standards will be applied, and what periodic reports (if any) the service provider will issue to the company;
- Administrative procedures for making changes in the content or data hosted by the service provider (such as designation of contact persons at each organization and the forms that instructions to the other party should take);
- An agreement from the service provider to maintain databases of customer information and to protect the confidentiality of such data;
- An acknowledgment from the service provider to the company that the service provider has no rights to any data from the Web site;
- An acceptable use policy to ensure that the site is not used in a way that would generate liability for the hosting company;
- An agreement from the service provider to create backup copies of all data and content maintained on the service provider's equipment;
- Whether the service provider will be a "sponsor" of the company's Web site (offering some compensation to the company in return for promoting the service provider's services on the company's site);
- Whether the service provider will help steer traffic to the company's site, such as by referring visitors to the company's site from a popular site maintained by the service provider;

- Dispute-resolution procedures, normally including informal procedures for at least some minor disputes as well as provisions regarding the choice of law and forum for more serious disputes;
- A description of the events that will entitle either party to terminate the agreement, such as failure by the service provider to protect the company's data or to maintain the agreed upon level of services for a significant period of time (such as three months); and
- Establishment of a procedure for either party to terminate the relationship and to "disengage," i.e., for the company to recover its data and content from the service provider.

For present purposes, it is useful to discuss a few of the principal issues in a bit more detail. One of the most central issues in developing a Web-site hosting relationship will be the level of service that will be provided. That topic has a quantitative dimension, under which the company might be allocated a certain amount of storage space for digital media; a certain volume of traffic on the network (which might be specified in terms of hits to the Web site or bits of data transferred over the network); processing services for a certain number of transactions; and access to a certain number of e-mail accounts. It also has a qualitative dimension, which would specify the scope of services and the levels of those services to be provided; the measures that will be used to assess whether those levels are being met; the rights and responsibilities of each party with regard to maintaining the service levels described in the agreement; the specific hardware, software, and network connections that will be used to provide the services; the location of the equipment used to provide the services covered by the agreement; whether the equipment to be used will be purchased, leased, or licensed, and the basis for calculating the price of the services provided.

It can be quite difficult for the parties to reach agreement upon the scope of services to be provided and the levels at which those services will be provided. Even when recognizable benchmarks are readily available, it may be difficult to agree on the specific level at which the benchmark should be set. For example, one of the company's primary concerns will normally be that its Web site should be accessible to visitors 24 hours a day, 7 days a week, and that the site will not crash because too many visitors are trying to access it at the same time. In a perfect world, the service provider might guarantee that the site would be available 99.999 percent of the time during any given period of time such as a calendar month (this standard is referred to as "five nines"). If a company has never entered into a service-level agreement before, it might feel that such a high degree of reliability is not worth the price the service provider would ask to guarantee five-nines uptime.

But the costs of what seem like even minor levels of downtime can be quite high to the company. For example, if the company agreed to a service level of access 99 percent of the time, then it has agreed that its Web site can be down 3.65 days a year. That might not be a problem if the company is maintaining a simple, static home page. But if the company is maintaining a retail Web store and those 3.65 days are prime shopping days, that 1 percent of downtime might be financially crippling to the company's Web efforts. If the company agreed to a service level of 99.9 percent uptime, it is in effect agreeing that its site can be down a little less than 9 hours a year; 99.99 percent translates into

52 minutes of downtime a year; and 99.999 percent, about 5 minutes a year. To put the significance of this level of service into context, many residential telephone-service subscribers in the United States enjoy something like 99.999 percent uptime on their telephone service today. In the current environment, however, many online service providers (if any), cannot guarantee reliability at even a four-nines standard.

At the same time, the ISP will be concerned lest the company place excessive demands on the ISP's services that might cause the ISP to fail to fulfill its obligations to its other customers. The ISP's concern is legitimate in the abstract, but it is quite difficult to quantify in a contractual agreement, because neither the company nor the ISP are likely to have firm understandings of their likely needs even a few years in the future.

Another crucial issue will be how the Web-site hosting provider will charge for its services. At one extreme, the service provider may charge a flat monthly fee to host a simple Web site with limited interactivity. At the other extreme, if the company has purchased Web-site development and hosting services from the same provider and relied heavily on the electronic-commerce expertise of the provider, the company and provider may agree that the provider will receive a percentage of the revenues that the Web site generates.

If the company is buying marketing services from the service provider (such as the right to maintain a link from a site maintained by the service provider), then the company also may pay referral fees for the visitors that arrive at the company's site from the provider's site. Common formulas for calculating these payments would be to charge a flat fee for displaying a link to the company's site, a payment per "click through" for each visitor that actually clicks on the link, or some combination of the two. Conversely, the service provider might give the company a discount off the rates it would otherwise charge for its services if the company displays a link to the service provider or otherwise advertises its relationship with the service provider.

Relevant Glossary Entries

Active Server Pages (ASP)
Applet
Application Service Provider (ASP)
Bandwidth
Brick and Mortar
Commercial off the Shelf (COTS)
Common Gateway Interface (CGI)
Cookie
Deliverables
Feature Creep
Five-Nines Uptime
Legacy System
Outsource
Pure Play
Streaming Media
Turnkey
Web Server

Problem Set 5

5.1.   Carl Eben (familiar to you from Problem Set 3) decided he needed
to build a Web site at the *www.rft.com* domain name he has based on your
work in Problem Set 3. Carl entered into negotiations with Aggie Web
Developers to prepare a new Web site for him. The negotiations quickly
reached a sticking point when Aggie Web Developers refused to agree to do
the site for a fixed fee, insisting instead that all of their contracts are on a
time-and-materials basis. Carl is frustrated because he wants to have the
process carefully budgeted so that he will know in advance precisely how
much it will cost to have the site developed. He seeks your advice. What do
you tell him?

5.2.   A few days later, after working through the pricing problem, Carl
calls with another sticking point. The developers have insisted that before
they sign the agreement, Carl has to produce a variety of exhibits describing
in some detail what the site is supposed to do and say. He has no idea what
he wants to put on the site. That, he says, is why he has hired the developer.
What is your advice on this point?

5.3.   The next day, Carl calls with his last problem. It appears that Aggie is
willing to provide a warranty that the site it develops will not infringe any
copyright of third parties, but it is not willing to provide such a warranty with
respect to patent infringement. On that topic, it is only willing to provide a
warranty that it does not know of any patent infringement. Carl is frustrated.
His perspective is that Aggie should bear the losses caused by any IP
infringement in Aggie's work. Can you understand any basis for Aggie's
position? Compare Copyright Act § 106(1) with Patent Act § 271(a).

5.4.   A few months after the site is finished, Carl discovers to his chagrin
that a competitor named Junior's Power Tools has a very similar site. When
he looks closely, he sees that Junior's site also was developed by Aggie. Can
Carl do anything about this? What do you need to know about the agreement
that Carl signed? Copyright Act §§ 106, 204, 205, 501(b).

5.5.   After you sort out the mess with Junior's and Aggie Web
Development, Carl decides he wants to stop dealing with small-town operators like Aggie and decides to hire Bevo Web Design, a Web-development firm
in Austin, Texas. Bevo explained that it could give Carl a much lower price if
it could start by modifying Carl's existing site instead of creating an entirely
new one. When Carl called Aggie to terminate his account, however, the
account representative at Aggie told him that unless Carl purchased the right
to make a derivative work for an amount equal to the three months of hosting fees, Aggie wouldn't authorize Carl to make any changes in the Web site.
Carl has just called you on the phone to find out if Aggie can really make him
pay more just to let Bevo modify his current site. What should you tell him?
What do you need to know about Carl's development agreement? Copyright
Act § 106(2).

Assignment 6: Controlling Access to a Web Site

If the owner of a Web site could keep the content of the site on a disk, it could prevent others from copying and reusing the information on its site simply by keeping the disk in a secure location. Of course, the purpose of a Web site is to communicate with third parties. Because it is technologically difficult (if not impossible) to distinguish between the types of visitors that the site operator wishes to invite and those that it wishes to exclude, the legal rules that sanction unauthorized access of a Web site are important in determining exactly what conduct is permitted.

The problem is particularly controversial because it underscores the lack of consensus about the appropriate legal characterization of the relationships among the Web-site operator, site visitors, and the global collective enterprise that makes up the Internet. To the extent that an Internet site is a place like a building, you would expect the site operator generally to have the ability to exclude unwanted visitors from the site, notwithstanding the openness of the Internet (the public highways that adjoin cyberspace locations). Conversely, if the Web site is like a software program, you would expect the site operator to have rights under the copyright laws to protect the expression on the site, but no general right to prevent the viewing or copying of factual information.

Buildings and software, however, do not exhaust the potential for metaphors that capture important characteristics of Internet sites. Whatever metaphor seems most illuminating, it must take account of broader public interests than those of the operator and the individual visitor. Taking account of the speech-related concerns, a good metaphor for the Internet would be Speakers' Corner at Hyde Park in London. From that vantage point, the posting of a commercial Web site to the Internet would be equivalent to entering into a public debate. From that perspective, First Amendment principles might limit the rights of an Internet site operator to exclude unwanted visitors just as surely as they limit the rights of a shopping-center operator to exclude unwanted visitors. See PruneYard Shopping Center v. Robins, 447 U.S. 74 (1980) (holding that the federal Constitution did not bar California from recognizing such a right under its state constitution).

Copyright law counsels a similar concern. For example, if posting a commercial site to the Internet is the equivalent of contributing a copy of the site's content to a giant, digital public library, the copyright doctrine of first sale would give the library the right to lend the content to other users free of charge or constraint by the owner. Although book publishers might wish that they could ask librarians to collect a fee from each library patron looking at one of their books, and although some countries grant such a public lending

117

right, American copyright law gives the library as the owner of the copy the right to lend it to others without charge.

All of these metaphors, of course, reflect clumsy efforts to adapt the legal systems that govern conventional interactions to the rapidly changing phenomenon of Internet commercial interactions. We do not yet have a legal framework to govern those interactions, or even the first steps toward a developing cultural consensus about how those interactions should be governed. Thus, it is to be expected that visitors and operators would dispute the nature of that relationship. That dispute will proceed not only in the courts (as summarized in the discussion below), but also in legislatures and administrative agencies (in this country and elsewhere). In all of those arenas, operators will continue to press for implementation of the view that Web sites are private property, to which they are free to condition access. Conversely, those who see the Internet as the public forum of the new millennium will press for unconstrained access without regard to the wishes of the operators. It is plainly too early to tell what balance we will strike among the various concerns. For now, it is enough to underscore the issues and how they affect the relevant commercial interests.

Without a contract to govern their relations, a Web-site operator and a visitor are likely to form very different expectations regarding their respective rights and obligations. As discussed above, the Web-site operator is likely to view the Web site as its private property, much as the physical premises of a brick-and-mortar store are its private property. Thus, the operator may think itself free to exclude unwanted visitors from its Web site or, more likely, to condition access on the visitors' compliance with rules regarding the use of information available at the site.

The visitor, on the other hand, may consider itself free to take any actions that are technologically feasible given the access controls the operator has placed on the site. Thus, from that perspective, the Web-site operator would have no right to prevent any visitor that accesses the site from using any available factual information as the visitor sees fit. The visitor would view any effort to impose a contractual limitation on its use of factual information as an invalid attempt to use contract law to supersede the limited intellectual-property protections for that information, undermining the careful balance those protections strike between public and private interests in ideas and information.

In 2000, litigation about the rights of Web-site operators to restrict access to their sites first began to reach the courts. There are two main fact patterns. In many cases, the unwanted visitors have been commercial competitors collecting information. Thus, in the most famous of the cases, eBay, Inc. v. Bidder's Edge, Inc., 100 F. Supp. 2d 1058 (N.D. Cal. 2000), eBay prevented Bidder's Edge from using automated "bots" to collect information about the auctions being conducted at eBay. The second fact pattern is an unwanted visitor sending e-mails to the company's server. Although most of the cases involve large-scale spam operations, that is not always the situation. The *Hamidi* case reprinted below, for example, involves the annoyance of a disgruntled former employee. The cases decided to date suggest several legal theories under which the operators might challenge the activities of visitors. The remainder of the assignment discusses the most prominent of those theories.

A.   Trespass to Chattels

The first-year law student is familiar with the tort of trespass where it involves the entry to another's real property without permission or right. The related tort of trespass to chattels is defined as an intentional and unauthorized interference with another's possessory interest in personal property. Recognizing that a Web site is not an interest in land, owners of Web sites and servers seeking to exclude unwanted visitors have relied on the doctrine of trespass to chattels. The California supreme court's analysis is the first definitive appellate treatment of the question.

Intel Corp. v. Hamidi
71 P.3d 296 (Cal. 2003)

WERDEGAR, J.

Intel Corporation (Intel) maintains an electronic mail system, connected to the Internet, through which messages between employees and those outside the company can be sent and received, and permits its employees to make reasonable nonbusiness use of this system. On six occasions over almost two years, Kourosh Kenneth Hamidi, a former Intel employee, sent e-mails criticizing Intel's employment practices to numerous current employees on Intel's electronic mail system. Hamidi breached no computer security barriers in order to communicate with Intel employees. He offered to, and did, remove from his mailing list any recipient who so wished. Hamidi's communications to individual Intel employees caused neither physical damage nor functional disruption to the company's computers, nor did they at any time deprive Intel of the use of its computers. The contents of the messages, however, caused discussion among employees and managers.

On these facts, Intel brought suit, claiming that by communicating with its employees over the company's e-mail system Hamidi committed the tort of trespass to chattels. The trial court granted Intel's motion for summary judgment and enjoined Hamidi from any further mailings. A divided Court of Appeal affirmed.

After reviewing the decisions analyzing unauthorized electronic contact with computer systems as potential trespasses to chattels, we conclude that under California law the tort does not encompass, and should not be extended to encompass, an electronic communication that neither damages the recipient computer system nor impairs its functioning. Such an electronic communication does not constitute an actionable trespass to personal property, i.e., the computer system, because it does not interfere with the possessor's use or possession of, or any other legally protected interest in, the personal property itself. The consequential economic damage Intel claims to have suffered, i.e., loss of productivity caused by employees reading and reacting to Hamidi's messages and company efforts to block the messages, is not an injury to the company's interest in its computers — which worked as intended and were unharmed by the communications — any more than the personal distress caused by reading an unpleasant letter would be an injury to the recipient's mailbox, or the loss of privacy caused by an intrusive telephone call would be an injury to the recipient's telephone equipment.

Our conclusion does not rest on any special immunity for communications by electronic mail; we do not hold that messages transmitted through the Internet are exempt from the ordinary rules of tort liability. To the contrary, e-mail, like other forms of communication, may in some circumstances cause legally cogniz-able injury to the recipient or to third parties and may be actionable under vari-ous common law or statutory theories. Indeed, on facts somewhat similar to those here, a company or its employees might be able to plead causes of action for interference with prospective economic relations, interference with contract or intentional infliction of emotional distress. And, of course, as with any other means of publication, third party subjects of e-mail communications may under appropriate facts make claims for defamation, publication of private facts, or other speech-based torts. Intel's claim fails not because e-mail transmitted through the Internet enjoys unique immunity, but because the trespass to chattels tort — unlike the causes of action just mentioned — may not, in California, be proved without evidence of an injury to the plaintiff's personal property or legal interest therein.

Nor does our holding affect the legal remedies of Internet service providers (ISP's) against senders of unsolicited commercial bulk e-mail (UCE), also known as "spam." A series of federal district court decisions . . . has approved the use of tres-pass to chattels as a theory of spammers' liability to ISP's, based upon evidence that the vast quantities of mail sent by spammers both overburdened the ISPs own computers and made the entire computer system harder to use for recipients, the ISP's customers. In those cases, discussed in greater detail below, the underlying complaint was that the extraordinary quantity of UCE impaired the computer sys-tem's functioning. In the present case, the claimed injury is located in the disrup-tion or distraction caused to recipients by the contents of the e-mail messages, an injury entirely separate from, and not directly affecting, the possession or value of personal property.

FACTUAL AND PROCEDURAL BACKGROUND

. . . Hamidi, a former Intel engineer, together with others, formed an organi-zation named Former and Current Employees of Intel (FACE-Intel) to disseminate information and views critical of Intel's employment and personnel policies and practices. FACE-Intel maintained a Web site (which identified Hamidi as Webmaster and as the organization's spokesperson) containing such material. In addition, over a 21-month period Hamidi, on behalf of FACE-Intel, sent six mass e-mails to employee addresses on Intel's electronic mail system. The messages criticized Intel's employment practices, warned employees of the dangers those practices posed to their careers, suggested employees consider moving to other companies, solicited employees' participation in FACE-Intel, and urged employees to inform themselves further by visiting FACE-Intel's Web site. The messages stated that recipients could, by notifying the sender of their wishes, be removed from FACE-Intel's mailing list; Hamidi did not subsequently send messages to anyone who requested removal.

Each message was sent to thousands of addresses (as many as 35,000 accord-ing to FACE-Intel's Web site), though some messages were blocked by Intel before reaching employees. Intel's attempt to block internal transmission of the messages succeeded only in part; Hamidi later admitted he evaded blocking efforts by using different sending computers. When Intel, in March 1998, demanded in writing that Hamidi and FACE-Intel stop sending e-mails to Intel's computer system, Hamidi asserted the organization had a right to communicate with willing Intel employees; he sent a new mass mailing in September 1998.

The summary judgment record contains no evidence Hamidi breached Intel's computer security in order to obtain the recipient addresses for his messages; indeed, internal Intel memoranda show the company's management concluded no security breach had occurred. Hamidi stated he created the recipient address list using an Intel directory on a floppy disk anonymously sent to him. Nor is there any evidence that the receipt or internal distribution of Hamidi's electronic messages damaged Intel's computer system or slowed or impaired its functioning. Intel did present uncontradicted evidence, however, that many employee recipients asked a company official to stop the messages and that staff time was consumed in attempts to block further messages from FACE-Intel. According to the FACE-Intel Web site, moreover, the messages had prompted discussions between "[e]xcited and nervous managers" and the company's human resources department.

Intel sued Hamidi . . . The [trial] court . . . granted Intel's motion for summary judgment, permanently enjoining Hamidi, FACE-Intel, and their agents "from sending unsolicited e-mail to addresses on Intel's computer systems." Hamidi appealed. . . .

The Court of Appeal, with one justice dissenting, affirmed the grant of injunctive relief. The majority took the view that the use of or intermeddling with another's personal property is actionable as a trespass to chattels without proof of any actual injury to the personal property; even if Intel could not show any damages resulting from Hamidi's sending of messages, "it showed he was disrupting its business by using its property and therefore is entitled to injunctive relief based on a theory of trespass to chattels." The dissenting justice warned that the majority's application of the trespass to chattels tort to "unsolicited electronic mail that causes no harm to the private computer system that receives it" would "expand the tort of trespass to chattel in untold ways and to unanticipated circumstances."

We granted Hamidi's petition for review.

DISCUSSION

I. CURRENT CALIFORNIA TORT LAW

Dubbed by Prosser the "little brother of conversion," the tort of trespass to chattels allows recovery for interferences with possession of personal property "not sufficiently important to be classed as conversion, and so to compel the defendant to pay the full value of the thing with which he has interfered." (Prosser & Keeton, Torts (5th ed. 1984) §14, pp. 85-86.)

Though not amounting to conversion, the defendant's interference must, to be actionable, have caused some injury to the chattel or to the plaintiff's rights in it. Under California law, trespass to chattels lies where an intentional interference with the possession of personal property has proximately caused injury. [Citation and quotation marks omitted.] In cases of interference with possession of personal property not amounting to conversion, the owner has a cause of action for trespass or case, and may recover only the actual damages suffered by reason of the impairment of the property or the loss of its use. [Citation and quotation marks omitted.] In modern American law generally, "[t]respass remains as an occasional remedy for minor interferences, resulting in some damage, but not sufficiently serious or sufficiently important to amount to the greater tort" of conversion. (Prosser & Keeton, Torts, supra, §15, p. 90, italics added.)

The Restatement, too, makes clear that some actual injury must have occurred in order for a trespass to chattels to be actionable. Under section 218 of the Restatement Second of Torts, dispossession alone, without further damages, is actionable (see [§218(a) & comment d]), but other forms of interference require some additional harm to the personal property or the possessor's interests in it. ([§218(b)-(d)].) "The interest of a possessor of a chattel in its inviolability, unlike the similar interest of a possessor of land, is not given legal protection by an action for nominal damages for harmless intermeddlings with the chattel. In order that an actor who interferes with another's chattel may be liable, his conduct must affect some other and more important interest of the possessor. Therefore, one who intentionally intermeddles with another's chattel is subject to liability only if his intermeddling is harmful to the possessor's materially valuable interest in the physical condition, quality, or value of the chattel, or if the possessor is deprived of the use of the chattel for a substantial time, or some other legally protected interest of the possessor is affected as stated in Clause (c). Sufficient legal protection of the possessor's interest in the mere inviolability of his chattel is afforded by his privilege to use reasonable force to protect his possession against even harmless interference." [§218 comment e.]. . .

In this respect, as Prosser explains, modern day trespass to chattels differs both from the original English writ and from the action for trespass to land: "Another departure from the original rule of the old writ of trespass concerns the necessity of some actual damage to the chattel before the action can be maintained. Where the defendant merely interferes without doing any harm — as where, for example, he merely lays hands upon the plaintiff's horse, or sits in his car — there has been a division of opinion among the writers, and a surprising dearth of authority. By analogy to trespass to land there might be a technical tort in such a case . . . Such scanty authority as there is, however, has considered that the dignitary interest in the inviolability of chattels, unlike that as to land, is not sufficiently important to require any greater defense than the privilege of using reasonable force when necessary to protect them. Accordingly it has been held that nominal damages will not be awarded, and that in the absence of any actual damage the action will not lie." (Prosser & Keeton, Torts, supra, §14, p. 87.)

Intel suggests that the requirement of actual harm does not apply here because it sought only injunctive relief, as protection from future injuries. But as Justice Kolkey, dissenting below, observed, "[t]he fact the relief sought is injunctive does not excuse a showing of injury, whether actual or threatened." Indeed, in order to obtain injunctive relief the plaintiff must ordinarily show that the defendant's wrongful acts threaten to cause irreparable injuries, ones that cannot be adequately compensated in damages. . . .

The dispositive issue in this case, therefore, is whether the undisputed facts demonstrate Hamidi's actions caused or threatened to cause damage to Intel's computer system, or injury to its rights in that personal property, such as to entitle Intel to judgment as a matter of law. To review, the undisputed evidence revealed no actual or threatened damage to Intel's computer hardware or software and no interference with its ordinary and intended operation. Intel was not dispossessed of its computers, nor did Hamidi's messages prevent Intel from using its computers for any measurable length of time. Intel presented no evidence its system was slowed or otherwise impaired by the burden of delivering Hamidi's electronic messages. Nor was there any evidence transmission of the messages imposed any marginal cost on the operation of Intel's computers. In sum, no evidence suggested that in sending messages through Intel's Internet connections and internal computer system Hamidi used the system in any manner in which it was not intended to function or impaired the system in any way. Nor does the evidence show the request of any employee to be removed from FACE-Intel's mailing list was not honored. The evidence did show, however, that some employees who found the messages unwelcome asked management to stop them and that Intel technical staff spent time and effort attempting to block the messages. A statement on the FACE-Intel Web site, moreover, could be taken as an admission that the messages had caused "[e]xcited and nervous managers" to discuss the matter with Intel's human resources department.

Relying on a line of decisions, most from federal district courts, applying the tort of trespass to chattels to various types of unwanted electronic contact between computers, Intel contends that, while its computers were not damaged by receiving Hamidi's messages, its interest in the "physical condition, quality or value" of the computers was harmed. We disagree. The cited line of decisions does not persuade us that the mere sending of electronic communications that assertedly cause injury only because of their contents constitutes an actionable trespass to a computer system through which the messages are transmitted. Rather, the decisions finding electronic contact to be a trespass to computer systems have generally involved some actual or threatened interference with the computers' functioning. . . .

Following [a California case regarding automated telephone dialing], a series of federal district court decisions held that sending UCE through an ISP's equipment may constitute trespass to the ISP's computer system. The lead case, CompuServe, Inc. v. Cyber Promotions, Inc., [962 F. Supp. 1015, 1021, 1023 (S.D. Ohio 1997)] (CompuServe), was followed by Hotmail Corp. v. Van$ Money Pie, Inc., [1998 WL 388389 (N.D. Cal.)], America Online, Inc. v. IMS, [24 F. Supp. 2d 548 (E.D. Va. 1998)], and America Online, Inc. v. LCGM, Inc., [46 F. Supp. 2d 444 (E.D. Va. 1998)].

In each of these spamming cases, the plaintiff showed, or was prepared to show, some interference with the efficient functioning of its computer system. In *CompuServ*, the plaintiff ISP's mail equipment monitor stated that mass UCE mailings, especially from nonexistent addresses such as those used by the defendant, placed "a tremendous burden" on the ISP's equipment, using "disk space and drain[ing] the processing power," making those resources unavailable to serve subscribers. [Citations omitted.] Similarly, in *Hotmail Corp. v. Van$ Money Pie, Inc.*, the court found the evidence supported a finding that the defendant's mailings "fill[ed] up Hotmail's computer storage space and threaten[ed] to damage Hotmail's ability to service its legitimate customers." America Online, Inc. v. IMS, decided on summary judgment, was deemed factually indistinguishable from CompuServe; the court observed that in both cases the plaintiffs "alleged that processing the bulk e-mail cost them time and money and burdened their equipment." The same court, in *America Online, Inc. v. LCGM, Inc.*, simply followed *CompuServe* and its earlier *America Online* decision, quoting the former's explanation that UCE burdened the computer's processing power and memory.

Building on the spamming cases, in particular *CompuServe*, three even more recent district court decisions addressed whether unauthorized robotic data collection from a company's publicly accessible Web site is a trespass on the company's computer system. The two district courts that found such automated data collection to constitute a trespass relied, in part, on the deleterious impact this activity could have, especially if replicated by other searchers, on the functioning of a Web site's computer equipment.

In the leading case, [eBay v. Bidder's Edge, Inc., 100 F. Supp. 2d 1058 (N.D. Cal. 2000)], the defendant Bidder's Edge (BE), operating an auction aggregation site, accessed the eBay Web site about 100,000 times per day, accounting for between 1 and 2 percent of the information requests received by eBay and a slightly smaller percentage of the data transferred by eBay. The district court rejected eBay's claim that it was entitled to injunctive relief because of the defendant's unauthorized presence alone, or because of the incremental cost the defendant had imposed on operation of the eBay site, but found sufficient proof of threatened harm in the potential for others to imitate the defendant's activity: "If BE's activity is allowed to continue unchecked, it would encourage other auction aggregators to engage in similar recursive searching of the eBay system such that eBay would suffer irreparable harm from reduced system performance, system unavailability, or data losses." Again, in addressing the likelihood of eBay's success on its trespass to chattels cause of action, the court held the evidence of injury to eBay's computer system sufficient to support a preliminary injunction: "If the court were to hold otherwise, it would likely encourage other auction aggregators to crawl the eBay site, potentially to the point of denying effective access to eBay's customers. If preliminary injunctive relief were denied, and other aggregators began to crawl the eBay site, there appears to be little doubt that the load on eBay's computer system would qualify as a substantial impairment of condition or value."

Another district court followed eBay on similar facts — a domain name registrar's claim against a Web hosting and development site that robotically searched the registrar's database of newly registered domain names in search of business leads — in Register.com, Inc. v. Verio, Inc., [126 F. Supp. 2d 238 (S.D.N.Y. 2000)]. Although the plaintiff was unable to measure the burden the defendant's searching had placed on its system, the district court, quoting the declaration of one of the plaintiff's officers, found sufficient evidence of threatened harm to the system in the possibility the defendant's activities would be copied by others: "I believe that if Verio's searching of Register.com's WHOIS database were determined to be lawful, then every purveyor of Internet-based services would engage in similar conduct." Like eBay, the court observed, Register.com had a legitimate fear "that its servers will be flooded by search robots."

In the third decision discussing robotic data collection as a trespass, Ticketmaster Corp. v. Tickets.com, Inc., 2000 WL 1887522 [(C.D. Cal. 2000)] (Ticketmaster), the court, distinguishing *eBay*, found insufficient evidence of harm to the chattel to constitute an actionable trespass: "A basic element of trespass to chattels must be physical harm to the chattel (not present here) or some obstruction of its basic function (in the court's opinion not sufficiently shown here). . . . The comparative use [by the defendant of the plaintiff's computer system] appears very small and there is no showing that the use interferes to any extent with the regular business of [the plaintiff]. . . . Nor here is the specter of dozens or more parasites joining the fray, the cumulative total of which could affect the operation of [the plaintiff's] business."

In the decisions so far reviewed, the defendant's use of the plaintiff's computer system was held sufficient to support an action for trespass when it actually did, or threatened to, interfere with the intended functioning of the system, as by significantly reducing its available memory and processing power. In *Ticketmaster*, the one case where no such effect, actual or threatened, had been demonstrated, the court found insufficient evidence of harm to support a trespass action. These decisions do not persuade us to Intel's position here, for Intel has demonstrated neither any appreciable effect on the operation of its computer system from Hamidi's messages, nor any likelihood that Hamidi's actions will be replicated by others if found not to constitute a trespass.

That Intel does not claim the type of functional impact that spammers and robots have been alleged to cause is not surprising in light of the differences between Hamidi's activities and those of a commercial enterprise that uses sheer quantity of messages as its communications strategy. Though Hamidi sent thousands of copies of the same message on six occasions over 21 months, that number is minuscule compared to the amounts of mail sent by commercial operations. The individual advertisers sued in [the *America Online* cases] were alleged to have sent more than 60 million messages over 10 months and more than 92 million messages over seven months, respectively. Collectively, UCE has reportedly come to constitute about 45 percent of all e-mail. The functional burden on Intel's computers, or the cost in time to individual recipients, of receiving Hamidi's occasional advocacy messages cannot be compared to the burdens and costs caused ISP's and their customers by the ever-rising deluge of commercial e-mail.

Intel relies on language in the *eBay* decision suggesting that unauthorized use of another's chattel is actionable even without any showing of injury: "Even if, as [defendant] BE argues, its searches use only a small amount of eBay's computer system capacity, BE has nonetheless deprived eBay of the ability to use that portion of its personal property for its own purposes. The law recognizes no such right to use another's personal property." But as the *eBay* court went on immediately to find that the defendant's conduct, if widely replicated, would likely impair the functioning of the plaintiff's system, we do not read the quoted remarks as expressing the court's complete view of the issue. In isolation, moreover, they would not be a correct statement of California or general American law on this point. While one may have no right temporarily to use another's personal property, such use is actionable as a trespass only if it has proximately caused injury. [Citation and quotation marks omitted.] "[I]n the absence of any actual damage the action will not lie." (Prosser & Keeton, Torts, supra, §14, p. 87.) Short of dispossession, personal injury, or physical damage (not present here), intermeddling is actionable only if "the chattel is impaired as to its condition, quality, or value, or [¶] . . . the possessor is deprived of the use of the chattel for a substantial time." [Rest. (2d) Torts §218(b), (c).] In particular, an actionable deprivation of use "must be for a time so substantial that it is possible to estimate the loss caused thereby. A mere momentary or theoretical deprivation of use is not sufficient unless there is a dispossession. . . ." [Rest. (2d) Torts §218 comment i.] That Hamidi's messages temporarily used some portion of the Intel computers' processors or storage is, therefore, not enough; Intel must, but does not, demonstrate some measurable loss from the use of its computer system.

In addition to impairment of system functionality, *CompuServe* and its progeny also refer to the ISP's loss of business reputation and customer goodwill, resulting from the inconvenience and cost that spam causes to its members, as harm to the

ISP's legally protected interests in its personal property. Intel argues that its own interest in employee productivity, assertedly disrupted by Hamidi's messages, is a comparable protected interest in its computer system. We disagree.

Whether the economic injuries identified in *CompuServe* were properly considered injuries to the ISP's possessory interest in its personal property, the type of property interest the tort is primarily intended to protect has been questioned. "[T]he court broke the chain between the trespass and the harm, allowing indirect harms to CompuServe's business interests — reputation, customer goodwill, and employee time — to count as harms to the chattel (the server)." [Laura Quilter, *The Continuing Expansion of Cyberspace Trespass to Chattels*, 17 Berkeley Tech. L.J. 421, 429-30 (2002).] "[T]his move cuts trespass to chattels free from its moorings of dispossession or the equivalent, allowing the court free reign [sic] to hunt for 'impairment.'" [Dan L. Burk, *The Trouble with Trespass*, 4 J. Small & Emerging Bus. L. 27 (2000).] But even if the loss of goodwill identified in *CompuServe* were the type of injury that would give rise to a trespass to chattels claim under California law, Intel's position would not follow, for Intel's claimed injury has even less connection to its personal property than did CompuServe's.

CompuServe's customers were annoyed because the system was inundated with unsolicited commercial messages, making its use for personal communication more difficult and costly. Their complaint, which allegedly led some to cancel their CompuServe service, was about the functioning of CompuServe's electronic mail service. Intel's workers, in contrast, were allegedly distracted from their work not because of the frequency or quantity of Hamidi's messages, but because of assertions and opinions the messages conveyed. Intel's complaint is thus about the contents of the messages rather than the functioning of the company's e-mail system. Even accepting *CompuServe*'s economic injury rationale, therefore, Intel's position represents a further extension of the trespass to chattels tort, fictionally recharacterizing the allegedly injurious effect of a communication's contents on recipients as an impairment to the device which transmitted the message.

This theory of "impairment by content" threatens to stretch trespass law to cover injuries far afield from the harms to possession the tort evolved to protect. Intel's theory would expand the tort of trespass to chattels to cover virtually any unconsented-to communication that, solely because of its content, is unwelcome to the recipient or intermediate transmitter. As the dissenting justice below explained,

> Damage of this nature — the distraction of reading or listening to an unsolicited communication — is not within the scope of the injury against which the trespass-to-chattel tort protects, and indeed trivializes it. After all, '[t]he property interest protected by the old action of trespass was that of possession; and this has continued to affect the character of the action.' (Prosser & Keeton on Torts, supra, §14, p. 87.) Reading an e-mail transmitted to equipment designed to receive it, in and of itself, does not affect the possessory interest in the equipment. Indeed, if a chattel's receipt of an electronic communication constitutes a trespass to that chattel, then not only are unsolicited telephone calls and faxes trespasses to chattel, but unwelcome radio waves and television signals also constitute a trespass to chattel every time the viewer inadvertently sees or hears the unwanted program.

We agree. While unwelcome communications, electronic or otherwise, can cause a variety of injuries to economic relations, reputation and emotions, those interests are protected by other branches of tort law; in order to address them, we need not create a fiction of injury to the communication system.

Nor may Intel appropriately assert a property interest in its employees' time. "The Restatement test clearly speaks in the first instance to the impairment of the chattel. . . . But employees are not chattels (at least not in the legal sense of the term)." [Burk, 4 J. SMALL & EMERGING BUS. L. at 36.] Whatever interest Intel may have in preventing its employees from receiving disruptive communications, it is not an interest in personal property, and trespass to chattels is therefore not an action that will lie to protect it. Nor, finally, can the fact Intel staff spent time attempting to block Hamidi's messages be bootstrapped into an injury to Intel's possessory interest in its computers. To quote, again, from the dissenting opinion in the Court of Appeal: "[I]t is circular to premise the damage element of a tort solely upon the steps taken to prevent the damage. Injury can only be established by the completed tort's consequences, not by the cost of the steps taken to avoid the injury and prevent the tort; otherwise, we can create injury for every supposed tort."

Intel connected its e-mail system to the Internet and permitted its employees to make use of this connection both for business and, to a reasonable extent, for their own purposes. In doing so, the company necessarily contemplated the employees' receipt of unsolicited as well as solicited communications from other companies and individuals. That some communications would, because of their contents, be unwelcome to Intel management was virtually inevitable. Hamidi did nothing but use the e-mail system for its intended purpose — to communicate with employees. The system worked as designed, delivering the messages without any physical or functional harm or disruption. These occasional transmissions cannot reasonably be viewed as impairing the quality or value of Intel's computer system. We conclude, therefore, that Intel has not presented undisputed facts demonstrating an injury to its personal property, or to its legal interest in that property, that support, under California tort law, an action for trespass to chattels.

II.   PROPOSED EXTENSION OF CALIFORNIA TORT LAW

We next consider whether California common law should be extended to cover, as a trespass to chattels, an otherwise harmless electronic communication whose contents are objectionable. We decline to so expand California law. Intel, of course, was not the recipient of Hamidi's messages, but rather the owner and possessor of computer servers used to relay the messages, and it bases this tort action on that ownership and possession. The property rule proposed is a rigid one, under which the sender of an electronic message would be strictly liable to the owner of equipment through which the communication passes — here, Intel — for any consequential injury flowing from the contents of the communication. The arguments of amici curiae and academic writers on this topic, discussed below, leave us highly doubtful whether creation of such a rigid property rule would be wise.

Writing on behalf of several industry groups appearing as amici curiae, Professor Richard A. Epstein of the University of Chicago urges us to excuse the required showing of injury to personal property in cases of unauthorized electronic contact between computers, "extending the rules of trespass to real property to all interactive Web sites and servers." The court is thus urged to recognize, for owners of a particular species of personal property, computer servers, the same interest in inviolability as is generally accorded a possessor of land. In effect, Professor Epstein suggests that a company's server should be its castle, upon which any unauthorized intrusion, however harmless, is a trespass.

Epstein's argument derives, in part, from the familiar metaphor of the Internet as a physical space, reflected in much of the language that has been used to describe it: "cyberspace," "the information superhighway," e-mail "addresses," and the like. Of course, the Internet is also frequently called simply the "Net," a term, Hamidi points out, "evoking a fisherman's chattel." A major component of the Internet is the World Wide "Web," a descriptive term suggesting neither personal nor real property, and "cyberspace" itself has come to be known by the oxymoronic phrase "virtual reality," which would suggest that any real property "located" in "cyberspace" must be "virtually real" property. Metaphor is a two-edged sword.

Indeed, the metaphorical application of real property rules would not, by itself, transform a physically harmless electronic intrusion on a computer server into a trespass. That is because, under California law, intangible intrusions on land, including electromagnetic transmissions, are not actionable as trespasses (though they may be as nuisances) unless they cause physical damage to the real property. Since Intel does not claim Hamidi's electronically transmitted messages physically damaged its servers, it could not prove a trespass to land even were we to treat the computers as a type of real property. Some further extension of the conceit would be required, under which the electronic signals Hamidi sent would be recast as tangible intruders, perhaps as tiny messengers rushing through the "hallways" of Intel's computers and bursting out of employees' computers to read them Hamidi's missives. But such fictions promise more confusion than clarity in the law. (See *eBay*, supra, 100 F. Supp. 2d at 1065-1066 [rejecting eBay's argument that the defendant's automated data searches "should be thought of as equivalent to sending in an army of 100,000 robots a day to check the prices in a competitor's store"].)

The plain fact is that computers, even those making up the Internet, are — like such older communications equipment as telephones and fax machines — personal property, not realty. Professor Epstein observes that "[a]lthough servers may be moved in real space, they cannot be moved in cyberspace," because an Internet server must, to be useful, be accessible at a known address. But the same is true of the telephone: to be useful for incoming communication, the telephone must remain constantly linked to the same number (or, when the number is changed, the system must include some forwarding or notification capability, a qualification that also applies to computer addresses). Does this suggest that an unwelcome message delivered through a telephone or fax machine should be viewed as a trespass to a type of real property? We think not: As already discussed, the contents of a telephone communication may cause a variety of injuries and may be the basis for a variety of tort actions (e.g., defamation, intentional infliction of emotional distress, invasion of privacy), but the injuries are not to an interest in property, much less real property, and the appropriate tort is not trespass.

More substantively, Professor Epstein argues that a rule of computer server inviolability will, through the formation or extension of a market in computer-to-computer access, create "the right social result." In most circumstances, he predicts, companies with computers on the Internet will continue to authorize transmission of information through e-mail, Web site searching, and page linking because they benefit by that open access. When a Web site owner does deny access to a particular sending, searching, or linking computer, a system of "simple one-on-one negotiations" will arise to provide the necessary individual licenses.

Other scholars are less optimistic about such a complete propertization of the Internet. Professor Mark Lemley of the University of California, Berkeley, writing on behalf of an amici curiae group of professors of intellectual property and computer law, observes that under a property rule of server inviolability, "each of the hundreds of millions of [Internet] users must get permission in advance from anyone with whom they want to communicate and anyone who owns a server through which their message may travel." The consequence for e-mail could be a substantial reduction in the freedom of electronic communication, as the owner of each computer through which an electronic message passes could impose its own limitations on message content or source. As Professor Dan Hunter of the University of Pennsylvania asks rhetorically: "Does this mean that one must read the 'Terms of Acceptable Email Usage' of every email system that one emails in the course of an ordinary day? If the University of Pennsylvania had a policy that sending a joke by email would be an unauthorized use of their system, then under the logic of [the lower court decision in this case], you commit 'trespass' if you emailed me a . . . cartoon." [Dan Hunter, *Cyberspace as Place, and the Tragedy of the Digital Anticommons*, 91 CAL. L. REV. 439, 508-09 (2003).]

Web site linking, Professor Lemley further observes, "would exist at the sufferance of the linked-to party, because a Web user who followed a 'disapproved' link would be trespassing on the plaintiff's server, just as sending an e-mail is trespass under the [lower] court's theory." Another writer warns that "[c]yber-trespass theory will curtail the free flow of price and product information on the Internet by allowing website owners to tightly control who and what may enter and make use of the information housed on its Internet site." [Edward W. Chang, *Bidding on Trespass: eBay, Inc. v. Bidder's Edge, Inc. and the Abuse of Trespass Theory in Cyberspace Law*, 29 AIPLA Q.J. 445, 459 (2001)]. A leading scholar of Internet law and policy, Professor Lawrence Lessig of Stanford University, has criticized Professor Epstein's theory of the computer server as quasi-real property, previously put forward in the *eBay* case, on the ground that it ignores the costs to society in the loss of network benefits: "eBay benefits greatly from a network that is open and where access is free. It is this general feature of the Net that makes the Net so valuable to users and a source of great innovation. And to the extent that individual sites begin to impose their own rules of exclusion, the value of the network as a network declines. If machines must negotiate before entering any individual site, then the costs of using the network climb." [LAWRENCE LESSIG, THE FUTURE OF IDEAS: THE FATE OF THE COMMONS IN A CONNECTED WORLD 171 (2001)]; see also [Hunter, supra, 91 CAL. L. REV. at 512 ("If we continue to mark out anticommons claims in cyberspace, not only will we preclude better, more innovative uses of cyberspace resources, but we will lose sight of what might be possible").]

We discuss this debate among the amici curiae and academic writers only to note its existence and contours, not to attempt its resolution. Creating an absolute property right to exclude undesired communications from one's e-mail and Web servers might help force spammers to internalize the costs they impose on ISP's and their customers. But such a property rule might also create substantial new costs, to e-mail and e-commerce users and to society generally, in lost ease and openness of communication and in lost network benefits. In light of the unresolved controversy, we would be acting rashly to adopt a rule treating computer servers as real property for purposes of trespass law.

The Legislature has already adopted detailed regulations governing UCE. [CAL. BUS. & PROF. CODE §§17538.4, 17538.45.] It may see fit in the future also to regulate noncommercial e-mail, such as that sent by Hamidi, or other kinds of unwanted contact between computers on the Internet . . .. But we are not persuaded that these perceived problems call at present for judicial creation of a rigid property rule of computer server inviolability. We therefore decline to create an exception, covering Hamidi's unwanted electronic messages to Intel employees, to the general rule that a trespass to chattels is not actionable if it does not involve actual or threatened injury to the personal property or to the possessor's legally protected interest in the personal property. No such injury having been shown on the undisputed facts, Intel was not entitled to summary judgment in its favor. . . .

Concurring Opinion by Kennard, *J.*

I concur.

Does a person commit the tort of trespass to chattels by making occasional personal calls to a mobile phone despite the stated objection of the person who owns the mobile phone and pays for the mobile phone service? Does it matter that the calls are not made to the mobile phone's owner, but to another person who ordinarily uses that phone? Does it matter that the person to whom the calls are made has not objected to them? Does it matter that the calls do not damage the mobile phone or reduce in any significant way its availability or usefulness?

The majority concludes, and I agree, that using another's equipment to communicate with a third person who is an authorized user of the equipment and who does not object to the communication is trespass to chattels only if the communications damage the equipment or in some significant way impair its usefulness or availability.

Intel has my sympathy. Unsolicited and unwanted bulk e-mail, most of it commercial, is a serious annoyance and inconvenience for persons who communicate electronically through the Internet, and bulk e-mail that distracts employees in the workplace can adversely affect overall productivity. But, as the majority persuasively explains, to establish the tort of trespass to chattels in California, the plaintiff must prove either damage to the plaintiff's personal property or actual or threatened impairment of the plaintiff's ability to use that property. Because plaintiff Intel has not shown that defendant Hamidi's occasional bulk e-mail messages to Intel's employees have damaged Intel's computer system or impaired its functioning in any significant way, Intel has not established the tort of trespass to chattels.

This is not to say that Intel is helpless either practically or legally. As a practical matter, Intel need only instruct its employees to delete messages from Hamidi without reading them and to notify Hamidi to remove their workplace e-mail addresses from his mailing lists. Hamidi's messages promised to remove recipients from the mailing list on request, and there is no evidence that Hamidi has ever failed to do so. From a legal perspective, a tort theory other than trespass to chattels may provide Intel with an effective remedy if Hamidi's messages are defamatory or wrongfully interfere with Intel's economic interests. Additionally, the Legislature continues to study the problems caused by bulk e-mails and other dubious uses of modern communication technologies and may craft legislation that accommodates the competing concerns in these sensitive and highly complex areas.

Accordingly, I join the majority in reversing the Court of Appeal's judgment.

Dissenting Opinion of Brown, *J.*

Candidate A finds the vehicles that candidate B has provided for his campaign workers, and A spray paints the water soluble message, "Fight corruption, vote for A" on the bumpers. The majority's reasoning would find that notwithstanding the time it takes the workers to remove the paint and the expense they incur in altering the bumpers to prevent further unwanted messages, candidate B does not deserve an injunction unless the paint is so heavy that it reduces the cars' gas mileage or otherwise depreciates the cars' market value. Furthermore, candidate B has an obligation to permit the paint's display, because the cars are driven by workers and not B personally, because B allows his workers to use the cars to pick up their lunch or retrieve their children from school, or because the bumpers display B's own slogans. I disagree.

Intel has invested millions of dollars to develop and maintain a computer system. It did this not to act as a public forum but to enhance the productivity of its employees. Kourosh Kenneth Hamidi sent as many as 200,000 e-mail messages to Intel employees. The time required to review and delete Hamidi's messages diverted employees from productive tasks and undermined the utility of the computer system. "There may . . . be situations in which the value to the owner of a particular type of chattel may be impaired by dealing with it in a manner that does not affect its physical condition." (Rest. 2d Torts, §218, com. h, p. 422.) This is such a case.

The majority repeatedly asserts that Intel objected to the hundreds of thousands of messages solely due to their content, and proposes that Intel seek relief by pleading content-based speech torts. This proposal misses the point that Intel's objection is directed not toward Hamidi's message but his use of Intel's property to display his message. Intel has not sought to prevent Hamidi from expressing his ideas on his Web site, through private mail (paper or electronic) to employees' homes, or through any other means like picketing or billboards. But as counsel for Intel explained during oral argument, the company objects to Hamidi's using Intel's property to advance his message.

Of course, Intel deserves an injunction even if its objections are based entirely on the e-mail's content. Intel is entitled, for example, to allow employees use of the Internet to check stock market tables or weather forecasts without incurring any concomitant obligation to allow access to pornographic Web sites. A private property owner may choose to exclude unwanted mail for any reason, including its content. . . .

Dissenting Opinion by MOSK, J.

The majority hold that the California tort of trespass to chattels does not encompass the use of expressly unwanted electronic mail that causes no physical damage or impairment to the recipient's computer system. They also conclude that because a computer system is not like real property, the rules of trespass to real property are also inapplicable to the circumstances in this case. Finally, they suggest that an injunction to preclude mass, noncommercial, unwelcome e-mails may offend the interests of free communication.

I respectfully disagree and would affirm the trial court's decision. In my view, the repeated transmission of bulk e-mails by appellant Kourosh Kenneth Hamidi (Hamidi) to the employees of Intel Corporation (Intel) on its proprietary confidential e-mail lists, despite Intel's demand that he cease such activities, constituted an actionable trespass to chattels. The majority fail to distinguish open communication in the public "commons" of the Internet from unauthorized intermeddling on a private, proprietary intranet. Hamidi is not communicating in the equivalent of a town square or of an unsolicited "junk" mailing through the United States Postal Service. His action, in crossing from the public Internet into a private intranet, is more like intruding into a private office mailroom, commandeering the mail cart, and dropping off unwanted broadsides on 30,000 desks. Because Intel's security measures have been circumvented by Hamidi, the majority leave Intel, which has exercised all reasonable self-help efforts, with no recourse unless he causes a malfunction or systems "crash." Hamidi's repeated intrusions did more than merely "prompt[ ] discussions between '[e]xcited and nervous managers' and the company's human resource department"; they also constituted a misappropriation of Intel's private computer system contrary to its intended use and against Intel's wishes.

The law of trespass to chattels has not universally been limited to physical damage. I believe it is entirely consistent to apply that legal theory to these circumstances — that is, when a proprietary computer system is being used contrary to its owner's purposes and expressed desires, and self-help has been ineffective. Intel correctly expects protection from an intruder who misuses its proprietary system, its nonpublic directories, and its supposedly controlled connection to the Internet to achieve his bulk mailing objectives — incidentally, without even having to pay postage. . . .

For these reasons, I respectfully dissent.

I concur: GEORGE, C.J.

B. Misappropriation

A related common-law cause of action that might be available in information cases (like the *Bidder's Edge* case discussed above) is misappropriation. Although the Supreme Court made it clear in Feist Publications, Inc. v. Rural Telephone Service, 499 U.S. 340 (1991), that federal copyright does not provide any substantial protection for compilations of facts (a telephone directory in that case), it still might be possible to raise a state-law claim of misappropriation based on the unauthorized use of collections of facts, based on the (pre-*Erie*) decision of the United States Supreme Court in International News Service v. Associated Press, 248 U.S. 215 (1918). As Assignment 21 discusses more fully, any such cause of action would have to establish that the information collector was free riding on the efforts of the Web-site operator.

C. Other Causes of Action for Unauthorized Access: Breach of Contract and the Computer Fraud and Abuse Act

The *Bidder's Edge* court refers in various places to the "site license" that purports to describe the terms on which customers have access to the Web site. Assignment 13 discusses in more detail how a Web-site owner might ensure that customers have consented to the license with sufficient certainty to create a binding contract. But the question of the visitor's authorization has been squarely disputed in a number of cases in which Web-site owners attempt to repel unwanted access by claiming that the access violates the Computer Fraud and Abuse Act, 18 U.S.C. §1030. As the case below explains, permissibility of access under that statute turns on the question of the visitor's authority, which is in turn a question that the owner of the site can control by the terms of the contract it offers to visitors.

EF Cultural Travel BV v. Zefer Corp.

318 F.3d 58 (1st Cir. 2003)

Before Boudin, Chief Judge, Torruella, Circuit Judge, and Cyr, Senior Circuit Judge.

Boudin, Chief Judge.

Defendant Zefer Corporation ("Zefer") seeks review of a preliminary injunction prohibiting it from using a "scraper tool" to collect pricing information from the website of plaintiff EF Cultural Travel BV ("EF"). . . . This court earlier upheld the injunction against co-defendant Explorica, Inc. ("Explorica"). The validity of the injunction as applied to Zefer was not addressed because Zefer's appeal was stayed when it filed for bankruptcy, but the stay has now been lifted.

EF and Explorica are competitors in the student travel business. Explorica was started in the spring of 2000 by several former EF employees who aimed to compete in part by copying EF's prices from EF's website and setting Explorica's own prices slightly lower. EF's website permits a visitor to the site to search its tour database and view the prices for tours meeting specified criteria such as gateway (*e.g.,* departure) cities, destination cities, and tour duration. In June 2000, Explorica hired Zefer, which provides computer-related expertise, to build a scraper tool that could "scrape" the prices from EF's website and download them into an Excel spreadsheet.

A scraper, also called a "robot" or "bot," is nothing more than a computer program that accesses information contained in a succession of webpages stored on the accessed computer. Strictly speaking, the accessed information is not the graphical interface seen by the user but rather the HTML source code — available to anyone who views the site — that generates the graphical interface. This information is then downloaded to the user's computer. The scraper program used in this case was not designed to copy all of the information on the accessed pages (*e.g.,* the descriptions of the tours), but rather only the price for each tour through each possible gateway city.

Zefer built a scraper tool that scraped two years of pricing data from EF's website. After receiving the pricing data from Zefer, Explorica set its own prices for the public, undercutting EF's prices an average of five percent. EF discovered Explorica's use of the scraper tool during discovery in an unrelated state-court action brought by Explorica's President against EF for back wages.

EF then sued Zefer, Explorica, and several of Explorica's employees in federal court. Pertinently, EF sought a preliminary injunction on the ground that the copying violated the federal Copyright Act, 17 U.S.C. §§101 *et seq.,* and various provisions of the Computer Fraud and Abuse Act ("CFAA"), 18 U.S.C. §1030. The district court refused to grant EF summary judgment on its copyright claim, but it did issue a preliminary injunction against all defendants based on one provision of the CFAA, ruling that the use of the scraper tool went beyond the "reasonable expectations" of ordinary users. . . .

The defendants appealed, but soon after briefing was completed, Zefer filed for bankruptcy and its appeal was automatically stayed. 11 U.S.C. §362(a)(1). Explorica's appeal went forward and in *EF I* a panel of this court upheld the preliminary injunction against Explorica. The panel held that the use of the scraper tool exceeded the defendants' authorized access to EF's website because (according to the district court's findings for the preliminary injunction) access was facilitated by use of confidential information obtained in violation of the broad confidentiality agreement signed by EF's former employees. *EF I*, 274 F.3d at 582-84.

On Zefer's re-activated appeal, the question presented is whether the preliminary injunction is proper as to Zefer. We conclude that it is proper even as to Zefer, which signed no confidentiality agreement, but on relatively narrow grounds. Given the prospect of further proceedings — this appeal is merely from a preliminary injunction — it is helpful to explain where and why our own reasoning differs from that of the district court. . . .

EF argues at the outset that our decision in *EF I* is decisive as to Zefer. But the ground we adopted there in upholding the injunction as to the other defendants was that they had apparently used confidential information to facilitate the obtaining of the EF data. Explorica was created by former EF employees, some of whom were subject to confidentiality agreements. Zefer's position in that respect is quite different than that of Explorica or former EF employees. It signed no such agreement, and its prior knowledge as to the agreement is an open question.

EF suggests that Zefer must have known that information provided to it by Explorica had been improperly obtained. This is possible but not certain, and there are no express district court findings on this issue; indeed, given the district court's much broader basis for its injunction, it had no reason to make any detailed findings as to the role of the confidentiality agreement. What can be gleaned from the record as to Zefer's knowledge certainly does not permit us to make on appeal the finding urged by EF.

What appears to have happened is that Philip Gormley, Explorica's Chief Information Officer and EF's former Vice President of Information Strategy, e-mailed Zefer a description of how EF's website was structured and identified the information that Explorica wanted to have copied; this may have facilitated Zefer's development of the scraper tool, but there is no indication that the structural information was unavailable from perusal of the website or that Zefer would have known that it was information subject to a confidentiality agreement.

EF also claims that Gormley e-mailed Zefer the "codes" identifying in computer shorthand the names of EF's gateway and destination cities. These codes were used to direct the scraper tool to the specific pages on EF's website that contained EF's pricing information. But, again, it appears that the codes could be extracted more slowly by examining EF's webpages manually, so it is far from clear that Zefer would have had to know that they were confidential. The only information that Zefer received that was described as confidential (passwords for tour-leader access) apparently had no role in the scraper project.

EF's alternative ground for affirmance is the rationale adopted by the district court for the preliminary injunction. That court relied on its "reasonable expectations" test as a gloss on the CFAA and then applied it to the facts of this case.

Although we bypassed the issue in *EF I,* the district court's rationale would embrace Zefer as readily as Explorica itself. But the gloss presents a pure question of law to be reviewed *de novo* and, on this issue, we differ with the district court.

The CFAA provision relied upon by the district court states:

> Whoever . . . knowingly and with intent to defraud, accesses a protected computer without authorization, or exceeds authorized access, and by means of such conduct furthers the intended fraud and obtains anything of value, unless the object of the fraud and the thing obtained consists only of the use of the computer and the value of such use is not more than $ 5,000 in any 1-year period . . . shall be punished as provided in subsection (c) of this section.

18 U.S.C. §1030(a)(4). The statute defines "exceeds authorized access" as "to access a computer with authorization and to use such access to obtain or alter information in the computer that the accesser is not entitled so to obtain or alter." *Id.* §1030(e)(6). The CFAA furnishes a civil remedy for individuals who suffer damages or loss as a result of a violation of the above section. *Id.* §1030(g).

At the outset, one might think that EF could have difficulty in showing an intent to defraud. But Zefer did not brief the issue on the original appeal before bankruptcy. In addition, there may be an argument that the fraud requirement should not pertain to injunctive relief. Accordingly, we bypass these matters and assume that the fraud requirement has been satisfied or is not an obstacle to the injunction.

The issue, then, is whether use of the scraper "exceed[ed] authorized access." A lack of authorization could be established by an explicit statement on the website restricting access. (Whether public policy might in turn limit certain restrictions is a separate issue.) Many webpages contain lengthy limiting conditions, including limitations on the use of scrapers.[3] However, at the time of Zefer's use of the scraper, EF had no such explicit prohibition in place, although it may well use one now.

The district court thought that a lack of authorization could also be inferred from the circumstances, using "reasonable expectations" as the test; and it said that three such circumstances comprised such a warning in this case: the copyright notice on EF's homepage with a link directing users to contact the company with questions; EF's provision to Zefer of confidential information obtained in breach of the employee confidentiality agreements; and the fact that the website was configured to allow ordinary visitors to the site to view only one page at a time.

We agree with the district court that lack of authorization may be implicit, rather than explicit. After all, password protection itself normally limits authorization by implication (and technology), even without express terms. But we think

---

3. For example, the "legal notices" on one familiar website state that "you may print or download one copy of the materials or content on this site on any single computer for your personal, non-commercial use, provided you keep intact all copyright and other proprietary notices. Systematic retrieval of data or other content from this site to create or compile, directly or indirectly, a collection, compilation, database or directory without written permission from America Online is prohibited." AOL Anywhere Terms and Conditions of Use, *at* http:// www.aol.com/ copyright.html (last visited Jan. 14, 2003).

that in general a reasonable expectations test is not the proper gloss on subsection (a)(4) and we reject it. However useful a reasonable expectations test might be in other contexts where there may be a common understanding underpinning the notion, its use in this context is neither prescribed by the statute nor prudentially sound.

Our basis for this view is not, as some have urged, that there is a "presumption" of open access to Internet information. The CFAA, after all, is primarily a statute imposing limits on access and enhancing control by information providers. Instead, we think that the public website provider can easily spell out explicitly what is forbidden and, consonantly, that nothing justifies putting users at the mercy of a highly imprecise, litigation-spawning standard like "reasonable expectations." If EF wants to ban scrapers, let it say so on the webpage or a link clearly marked as containing restrictions.

This case itself illustrates the flaws in the "reasonable expectations" standard. Why should the copyright symbol, which arguably does not protect the substantive information anyway, *Feist Publ'ns, Inc. v. Rural Tel. Serv. Co.*, 499 U.S. 340, 344-45 (1991), or the provision of page-by-page access for that matter, be taken to suggest that downloading information at higher speed is forbidden. EF could easily include — indeed, by now probably has included — a sentence on its home page or in its terms of use stating that "no scrapers may be used," giving fair warning and avoiding time-consuming litigation about its private, albeit "reasonable," intentions.

Needless to say, Zefer can have been in no doubt that EF would dislike the use of the scraper to construct a database for Explorica to undercut EF's prices; but EF would equally have disliked the compilation of such a database manually without the use of a scraper tool. EF did not purport to exclude competitors from looking at its website and any such limitation would raise serious public policy concerns. . . .

Lastly, Zefer has alleged that the First Amendment would be offended if the statute were construed to forbid generally the use of scrapers to collect otherwise available information where there was no intent to defraud or harm the target website. Here, the preliminary injunction is premised on EF's misuse of confidential information and Zefer thus far is constrained only in helping a tentatively-identified wrongdoer in exploiting that confidential information. None of Zefer's arguments address this narrowed constraint or suggest to us that it is constitutionally doubtful.

The preliminary injunction is *affirmed* on the limited basis set forth above and as construed by this court. Each side shall bear its own costs on this appeal.

D. Unsolicited Commercial E-mail

Another often unwelcome member of the Internet community is the party that sends "unsolicited commercial e-mail" (UCE), also known as unsolicited bulk e-mail or (more pejoratively) as spam. Senders of UCE obtain huge lists of e-mail addresses, to which they send vast quantities of electronic mail.

Individual recipients of UCE may find it annoying to clear it out of their e-mail inboxes. They also may find it expensive, particularly if they pay for their Internet access based on the volume of data they download or the amount of time they spend online. Similarly, Internet service providers (with thousands or millions of subscribers) find UCE to be a major administrative burden and expense, because failure to find some way to interpose an effective check against UCE substantially lowers the level of service they can provide their subscribers. Thus, in the aggregate, UCE poses a threat to the security and reliability of the Internet because it ties up huge quantities of system resources.

System administrators and legislators have tried a variety of approaches to control UCE. The first of those to gain prominence was the Realtime Blackhole List (RBL) maintained by the Mail Abuse Prevention System (MAPS), a California not-for-profit corporation. MAPS has articulated a set of "Basic Mailing List Management Principles for Preventing Abuse." If it comes to the attention of MAPS that an IP address is sending mail in a way that violates those principles (which UCE often does), MAPS adds the IP address to the RBL. Then, system administrators can use the RBL to block all e-mail coming from that IP address. The system is controversial for a variety of reasons. For one thing, because a large number of system administrators rely on the RBL, MAPS effectively has the power through defining its principles to enforce rules of conduct on large parts of the Internet — rules that are as effective as legislation could be, even though they are articulated by a private body without any sustained opportunity for public debate or review. For another, a listing on the RBL attributable to the activities of one person at an IP address often has the effect of blocking e-mail sent by innocent third parties that use the same IP address. That problem is exacerbated when the party sending the UCE routes its e-mail surreptitiously through the Web server of a third party. In any event, despite the controversy and a variety of challenges brought by parties whose e-mail has been blocked, MAPS and the RBL have been able to withstand all attacks to date.

On the other hand, private technological responses have led to a growing race in which spammers devise new technologies to avoid detection just as rapidly as businesses develop technologies to detect spammers. For example, as this edition goes to press, some of the largest ISPs (America Online, Yahoo!, Earthlink, and Microsoft) have entered into a major alliance to develop technology that would limit the transmission of UCE through authentication of senders. Because most UCE is transmitted through "zombies" — computers controlled by hackers that send UCE without the knowledge of their owners — this technology has great promise. Meanwhile, the percentage of all e-mail traffic that amounts to UCE has risen steadily over the last few years, to the point where as of the summer of 2004 it generally was regarded as constituting approximately 70 percent of all e-mail traffic.

At that point, public outcry forced a federal legislative response. Although dozens of states already had adopted their own statutes, with varying levels of rigor, Congress in 2003 commandeered the field with its enactment of the Controlling the Assault of Non-Solicited Pornography and Marketing Act of 2003 (CAN-SPAM). The statute includes a confusing preemption provision that appears to preempt all state laws specifically directed at UCE, but to permit continued application of laws of general application that regulate such matters as falsity and deception. CAN-SPAM §8(b), 15 U.S.C. §7707(b).

The federal statute imposes several obligations on those that send UCE. Most importantly, it requires that all senders have a functioning e-mail address (or Internet link) through which a recipient can request not to receive future e-mails. It is a violation of the statute if the sender does not stop transmitting such messages within 10 business days after receiving the request. CAN-SPAM §5(a)(3)-(4), 15 U.S.C. §7704(a)(3)-(4). The statute also includes a broad exemption for a "transactional or relationship message," to which the statute generally does not apply. CAN-SPAM §§3(2), 3(17), 15 U.S.C. §§7702(3), (17) (excluding "[t]ransactional or relationship message" from the definition of "[c]ommercial electronic mail message").

The statute does not include a private cause of action for users. Instead, it contemplates enforcement by the Federal Trade Commission as part of its general obligation to prevent unfair business practices, with a limited right for state attorneys general to pursue actions on behalf of their citizenry, and an arguably more important right of action for Internet service providers. CAN-SPAM §7, 15 U.S.C. §7706. The vigor with which Internet service providers might enforce the statute was evidenced by a prominent suit by leading providers brought in the spring of 2004 shortly after the statute became effective.

CAN-SPAM has been criticized as a general federal validation of UCE, primarily because its "opt-out" system of consumer protection pointedly rejects a more protective "opt-in" system, under which it would be permissible to send messages only to those individuals who had agreed to receive them. Consistently with the more proactive attitude discussed in Chapter 1, it should be no surprise that the EU legal system regulates UCE much more aggressively. First, because the European Data Protection Directive (discussed at length in Assignment 10), generally prohibits any processing of personal information without the consent of the person in question, unsolicited commercial e-mail is quite difficult, although not entirely, illegal. More specifically, Article 10 of the 1997 Distance Selling Directive generally prohibits unsolicited automated commercial communications to which consumers object. Some of the EU member states (Austria, Denmark, Finland, Germany, and Italy) have acted under that rule to establish opt-in systems. If a member state adopts an opt-out system, Article 7 of the E-Commerce Directive requires UCE senders to consult registers of people who have opted out before sending UCE transmissions. In the CAN-SPAM statute, by contrast, Congress asks only for a study of the feasibility of an opt-out registry that would parallel the successful do-not-call registry. CAN-SPAM §9, 15 U.S.C. §7708. In June of 2004, the FTC responded to that request with a report indicating that a "do-not-spam" registry would not be useful until further development of the sender-authentication technology discussed above. Absent further technological developments, the FTC reasoned, maintenance of a registry in fact would be harmful because it would provide those who wish to violate the law with a valuable list of active and valid e-mail addresses.

Relevant Glossary Entries

Bot
Database

IP Address
Opt-in
Opt-out
Site License
Spam
Spider
Stockkeeping Unit (SKU)
Unsolicited Commercial E-mail (UCE)
Web Server

Problem Set 6

6.1.   The League of Net Consumers (LNC) is a not-for-profit organization supported largely by dues paid by its members. LNC created a Web site that permits consumers to do price comparisons for popular consumer items. The site organizes information by using the "stockkeeping unit" (SKU) number for each product (assigned by each product's manufacturer). LNC collects price information by sending bots out to (A) find merchants offering products that consumers frequently purchase over the Internet; (B) copy the price and shipping information posted to the merchant's site; and (C) return that information for use on the LNC site. A consumer checking an item on the LNC site can see on the same Web page (I) a description of the item; (II) a list of merchants offering the item; (III) the price to the consumer to obtain the item from each merchant (including shipping and handling charges); and (IV) reviews of the merchant and the product.

Monster Mart, a major brick-and-mortar retailer with an online store at MonsterMart.com, files suit against LNC to stop LNC from copying its price and shipping information and redisplaying that information on the LNC site. Your firm has agreed to take on this matter as a pro bono project. Gwen Hightower, president of the board of trustees of LNC, has asked you whether Monster Mart can force LNC to stop using bots to copy MonsterMart.com price and shipping information for its site. What do you advise Gwen? Is your answer influenced by the non-profit nature of her activities? Be sure to consider the possibility of liability for trespass to chattels, for breach of contract, and for violation of the Computer Fraud and Abuse Act, 18 U.S.C. §1030. (You should refer to the course Web site for a representative site license.)

6.2.   The United States office of the Mouvement d'Emancipation des Nains de Jardin ("MENJ" or Movement for the Liberation of Garden Gnomes) uses bots to trawl the Internet for the names and e-mail addresses of garden gnome aficionados. MENJ sent a bot to *www.GnoMania.com*, a business-to-business Internet marketplace for the global garden gnome industry, copied the names and e-mail addresses of all registered members of the GnoMania.com community, and began a relentless campaign of unsolicited e-mail demanding that garden gnomes be released into their natural habitat and not kept in captivity. (You should assume that the enthusiasts of MENJ are as rational and sensible as is typical for members of similar activist groups.) Among the terms of the www.GnoMania.com site license are prohibitions (A) on accessing the site through automated means without the express permission of the site operators; and (B) on the sending of unsolicited commercial e-mail to the members of the community.

(a) Can the operators of the GnoMania.com Web site obtain an injunction to stop MENJ from using a bot to access its Web site? Is there anything different in this problem from the issues in Problem 6.1?

(b) Can the operators of the GnoMania.com site stop MENJ from sending bulk e-mails to members of its community?

6.3. Gwen Hightower calls you back this morning to find out if you are willing to take on a new pro bono matter. She reports that her Congressman has proposed amending the CFAA to make it clear that "authorization" to access a Web site is defined by the terms of any site license that the Web-site operator has posted. Gwen would like your advice on whether the LNC should take a public position opposing this proposed legislation. Gwen is worried because she has heard that if this proposal is not accepted, its sponsors are ready to introduce legislation to create a new intellectual-property right in collection of facts. Do you have any advice for Gwen on how to prevent either proposal from being enacted into law?

Assignment 7: Liability of the Site Owner

Having discussed the issues relating to establishing a Web site and excluding unwanted users from that site, this assignment addresses the liability of the site owner to third parties arising out of the content on the site. Because that topic is so broad, it is impossible to discuss all of the issues that potentially fall within the scope of that topic here. Rather, this assignment addresses several issues that relate directly to the content conveyed through a Web site or server: liability as a publisher, linking and framing, employees' use of the Internet, and securities regulation.

A. Liability as a Publisher

Potential liability for content has been one of the most visible issues associated with the Internet. Among other things, distributing content over the Internet can expose a company to liability for copyright infringement or defamation, even if the content is only information about products and services offered for sale. [For reasons discussed in the earlier assignments, the Internet has the ability to greatly increase the potential reach of criminal or otherwise harmful activity associated with some forms of speech — such as hate speech or obscenity. This development, in turn, has caused state and federal legislators to devote more attention to statutes designed to curtail harmful speech. Many of these statutes have been challenged (often successfully) on free speech grounds. This assignment, however, focuses primarily on commercial speech and the related topic of speech in a corporate setting.]

Publishers were among the first to establish major Internet operations when the Internet was opened to commercial activity in the mid-1990s. Traditional print publishers and broadcasters usually are aware of the risks of publishing material that infringes the copyright of a third party or that contains statements that are damaging to the reputation of a third party. They also are familiar with rules about misleading advertising that influence the content and format of the advertisements that they display. Thus, professional publishers typically have attorneys conduct a formal pre-publication review of works to limit their exposure to lawsuits related to the content that they publish. They also may carry "media perils" insurance to protect them against those risks.

However, as time has passed, traditional publishing has become less central to the economic potential of the Internet. Commercial activity on the Internet is comprised of thousands of companies (such as retailers) that have no direct interest in publishing as well as many newer forms of publishing entities that "host" content provided by others. Businesses operating under these newer business models must be aware of the ways to minimize their potential liability. In some cases, such as advertising, the issues are relatively simple, in that they require a fairly straightforward application of existing legal rules to online activity. The FTC, for example, has promulgated a working paper that contains guidelines for ensuring that online advertising and associated disclosures are delivered in a format that is not misleading. In other cases, the application of existing legal issues to online activity has become more challenging.

1. Defamation and the Communications Decency Act

Defamation is a tort defined by state law. The Restatement (Second) of Torts §559 defines defamation as (a) a false and defamatory statement concerning another person; (b) that is communicated or "published" to a third party; (c) through fault amounting at least to negligence on the part of the publisher; (d) that causes harm to the person. Some comments are thought to be so pernicious that they are defamatory "per se," so that the plaintiff is presumed to have been harmed. For example, falsely accusing someone of having committed a crime is defamatory per se. In other cases, however, the plaintiff will have to establish actual harm. The tort is committed not only by the one who originally "published" the defamatory statement (either in written form as libel, or in an oral statement as slander), but also by anyone who republishes the defamatory comment with knowledge or reason to know of its defamatory character. RESTATEMENT (SECOND) OF TORTS §581.

Even before the Internet became synonymous with "online," bulletin board services and online services such as America Online, Prodigy, and CompuServe created pre-Internet public networks for personal computers. The perception that it was inappropriate for those networks to be responsible for defamatory material posted by their customers motivated Congress to include important protections for AOL and similar providers in the Communications Decency Act of 1996 (CDA). The next assignment discusses the implications of the statute for ISPs. For now, however, it is important to see that the statute also extends protection in certain cases to the owner of a site.

Batzel v. Smith
333 F.3d 1018 (9th Cir. 2003)

Before CANBY, GOULD, and BERZON, Circuit Judges.

Opinion by Judge BERZON. Opinion concurring in part and dissenting in part by Judge GOULD.

BERZON, Circuit Judge.

...here is no reason inherent in the technological features of cyberspace why ...dment and defamation law should apply differently in cyberspace than ... mortar world. Congress, however, has chosen for policy reasons ...ility for defamatory or obscene speech "providers and users ...vices" when the defamatory or obscene material is "provided" by someone else. This case presents the question whether and, if so, under what circumstances a moderator of a listserv and operator of a website who posts an allegedly defamatory e-mail authored by a third party can be held liable for doing so. . . .

I.

In the summer of 1999, sometime-handyman Robert Smith was working for Ellen Batzel, an attorney licensed to practice in California and North Carolina, at Batzel's house in the North Carolina mountains. Smith recounted that while he was repairing Batzel's truck, Batzel told him that she was "the granddaughter of one of Adolf Hitler's right-hand men." Smith also maintained that as he was painting the walls of Batzel's sitting room he overheard Batzel tell her roommate that she was related to Nazi politician Heinrich Himmler. According to Smith, Batzel told him on another occasion that some of the paintings hanging in her house were inherited. To Smith, these paintings looked old and European.

After assembling these clues, Smith used a computer to look for websites concerning stolen art work and was directed by a search engine to the Museum Security Network ("the Network") website. He thereupon sent the following e-mail message to the Network:

> From: Bob Smith [e-mail address omitted]
>
> To: securma@museum-security.org [the Network]
>
> Subject: Stolen Art
>
> Hi there,
>
> I am a building contractor in Asheville, North Carolina, USA. A month ago, I did a remodeling job for a woman, Ellen L. Batzel who bragged to me about being the grand daughter [sic] of "one of Adolph Hitler's right-hand men." At the time, I was concentrating on performing my tasks, but upon reflection, I believe she said she was the descendant of Heinrich Himmler.
>
> Ellen Batzel has hundreds of older European paintings on her walls, all with heavy carved wooden frames. She told me she inherited them.
>
> I believe these paintings were looted during WWII and are the rightful legacy of the Jewish people. Her address is [omitted].
>
> I also believe that the descendants of criminals should not be persecuted for the crimes of the [sic] fathers, nor should they benefit. I do not know who to contact about this, so I start with your organization. Please contact me via email [. . .] if you would like to discuss this matter.
>
> Bob.

Ton Cremers, then-Director of Security at Amsterdam's famous Rijksmuseum and (in his spare time) sole operator of the Museum Security Network ("the Network"), received Smith's e-mail message. The nonprofit Network maintains both a website and an electronic e-mailed newsletter about museum security and stolen art. Cremers periodically puts together an electronic document containing: e-mails sent to him, primarily from Network subscribers; comments by himself as the moderator of an on-line discussion; and excerpts from news articles related to stolen works of art. He exercises some editorial discretion in choosing which of the e-mails he receives are included in the listserv mailing, omitting e-mails unrelated to stolen art and eliminating other material that he decides does not merit distribution to his subscribers. The remaining amalgamation of material is then posted on the Network's website and sent to subscribers automatically via a listserv. The Network's website and listserv mailings are read by hundreds of museum security officials, insurance investigators, and law enforcement personnel around the world, who use the information in the Network posting to track down stolen art.

After receiving it, Cremers published Smith's e-mail message to the Network, with some minor wording changes, on the Network listserv. He also posted that listserv, with Smith's message included, on the Network's website. Cremers later included it on the Network listserv and posted a "moderator's message" stating that "the FBI has been informed of the contents of [Smith's] original message.". . .

Batzel discovered the message several months after its initial posting and complained to Cremers about the message. Cremers then contacted Smith via e-mail to request additional information about Smith's allegations. Smith continued to insist on the truth of his statements. He also told Cremers that if he had thought his e-mail "message would be posted on an international message board [he] never would have sent it in the first place."

Upon discovering that Smith had not intended to post his message, Cremers apologized for the confusion. He told Smith in an e-mail that "[y]ou were not a subscriber to the list and I believe that you did not realize your message would be forwarded to the mailinglist [sic]." Apparently, subscribers send messages for inclusion in the listserv to securma@x54all.nl, a different address from that to which Smith had sent his e-mail contacting the Network. Cremers further explained that he "receive[s] many e-mails each day some of which contain queries [he thinks] interesting enough to forward to the list. [Smith's] was one of those."

Batzel disputes Smith's account of their conversations. She says she is not, and never said she is, a descendant of a Nazi official, and that she did not inherit any art. Smith, she charges, defamed her not because he believed her artwork stolen but out of pique, because Batzel refused to show Hollywood contacts a screenplay he had written.

Batzel claims further that because of Cremers's actions she lost several prominent clients in California and was investigated by the North Carolina Bar Association. Also, she represents that her social reputation suffered. To redress her claimed reputational injuries she filed this lawsuit against Smith, Cremers, the Netherlands Museum Association, and Mosler, Inc. ("Mosler") in federal court in Los Angeles, California.

[The trial court rejected Cremers's motion that the suit be dismissed under a special California statute (the "anti-SLAPP" statute) directed at harassing litigation. Cremers appealed.]

Batzel . . . alleged in her complaint that Mosler was vicariously liable for her reputational injuries because Cremers was acting as Mosler's agent. This agency relationship arose, according to Batzel, because Mosler gave Cremers $8,000 for displaying Mosler's logo and other advertisements on the Network website and in its listserv. The district court entered summary judgment in favor of Mosler, ruling that, under California law as applied to the undisputed facts, Cremers was not an agent of Mosler and Mosler could not be vicariously liable. Batzel appeals this decision as well.

II

[The court dismissed as untimely Cremers's challenge to the trial court's personal jurisdiction.]

III

. . . [The court of appeals explained that the trial court's refusal to dismiss the lawsuit under the anti-SLAPP statute rested on the trial court's determination that the lawsuit had merit. Accordingly, the court of appeals turned to that question in Part III.C of its opinion.]

To resist a motion to strike pursuant to California's anti-SLAPP law, Batzel must demonstrate a probability that she will prevail on the merits of her complaint. The district court held that Batzel had made such a showing, and absent 47 U.S.C. §230, we would be inclined to agree.

1.   SECTION 230(C)

We begin with a brief survey of the background of §230(c), as that background is useful in construing the statutory terms here at issue.

Title V of the Telecommunications Act of 1996, Pub. L. No. 104-104, is known as the "Communications Decency Act of 1996" [the "CDA" or "the Act"]. The primary goal of the Act was to control the exposure of minors to indecent material. Parts of the Act have since been struck down as unconstitutional limitations on free speech, *see Reno v. ACLU*, 521 U.S. 844 (1997); *United States v. Playboy Ent. Group*, 529 U.S. 803 (2000), but the section at issue here, §230, remains intact.

Section 230 was first offered as an amendment by Representatives Christopher Cox (R-Cal.) and Ron Wyden (D-Ore.). The specific provision at issue here, §230(c)(1), overrides the traditional treatment of publishers, distributors, and speakers under statutory and common law. . . . Absent §230, a person who published or distributed speech over the Internet could be held liable for defamation even if he or she was not the author of the defamatory text, and, indeed, at least with regard to publishers, even if unaware of the statement. *See, e.g., Stratton Oakmont, Inc. v. Prodigy Services Co.*, 1995 WL 323710 (N.Y. Sup. Ct. May 24, 1995) (pre-Communications Decency Act case holding internet service provider liable for posting by third party on one of its electronic bulletin boards). Congress, however, has chosen to treat cyberspace differently.

Congress made this legislative choice for two primary reasons. First, Congress wanted to encourage the unfettered and unregulated development of free speech on the Internet, and to promote the development of e-commerce. . . .

. . . Consistent with these provisions, courts construing §230 have recognized as critical in applying the statute the concern that lawsuits could threaten the "freedom of speech in the new and burgeoning Internet medium." *Zeran v. America Online, Inc.*, 129 F.3d 327, 330 (4th Cir. 1997). "Section 230 was enacted, in part, to maintain the robust nature of Internet communication, and accordingly, to keep government interference in the medium to a minimum." Making interactive computer services and their users liable for the speech of third parties would severely restrict the information available on the Internet. Section 230 therefore sought to prevent lawsuits from shutting down websites and other services on the Internet.

The second reason for enacting §230(c) was to encourage interactive computer services and users of such services to self-police the Internet for obscenity and other offensive material, so as to aid parents in limiting their children's access to such material. *See* §230(b)(4). We recognize that there is an apparent tension between Congress's goals of promoting free speech while at the same time giving parents the tools to limit the material their children can access over the Internet. As a result of this apparent tension, some commentators have suggested that the Fourth Circuit in *Zeran* imposed the First Amendment goals on legislation that was actually adopted for the speech-restrictive purpose of controlling the dissemination of content over the Internet. These critics fail to recognize that laws often have more than one goal in mind, and that it is not uncommon for these purposes to look in opposite directions. The need to balance competing values is a primary impetus for enacting legislation. Tension within statutes is often not a defect but an indication that the legislature was doing its job.

So, even though the CDA overall may have had the purpose of restricting content, there is little doubt that the Cox-Wyden amendment, which added what ultimately became §230 to the Act, sought to further First Amendment and e-commerce interests on the Internet while also promoting the protection of minors. Fostering the two ostensibly competing purposes here works because parents best can control the material accessed by their children with the cooperation and assistance of Internet service providers ("ISPs") and other providers and users of services on the Internet. Section 230(b)(4) describes this goal: "It is the policy of the United States . . . to remove disincentives for the development and utilization of blocking and filtering technologies that empower parents to restrict their children's access to objectionable or inappropriate online material." §230(b)(4). Some blocking and filtering programs depend on the cooperation of website operators and access providers who label material that appears on their services.

Without the immunity provided in Section 230(c), users and providers of interactive computer services who review material could be found liable for the statements of third parties, yet providers and users that disavow any responsibility would be free from liability. *Compare Stratton Oakmont*, 1995 WL 323710 (holding a service provider liable for speech appearing on its service because it generally reviewed posted content), with *Cubby, Inc. v. CompuServe, Inc.*, 776 F. Supp. 135 (S.D.N.Y. 1991) (holding a service provider not liable for posted speech because the provider was simply the conduit through which defamatory statements were distributed).

In particular, Congress adopted §230(c) to overrule the decision of a New York state court in *Stratton Oakmont*, 1995 WL 323710. *Stratton Oakmont* held that Prodigy, an Internet access provider that ran a number of bulletin boards, could be held responsible for libelous statements posted on its "Money Talk" bulletin board by an unidentified person. *Id.* The court relied on the fact that Prodigy held itself out as a service that monitored its bulletin boards for offensive content and removed such content. *Id.* at *2, *4. Prodigy used filtering software and assigned board leaders to monitor the postings on each bulletin board. *Id.* at *1-*2. Because of Prodigy's active role in monitoring its bulletin boards, the court found, Prodigy was a publisher for purposes of state libel law and therefore could be held liable for any defamatory statements posted on the website. *Id.* at *4.

Although *Stratton* was a defamation case, Congress was concerned with the impact such a holding would have on the control of material inappropriate for minors. If efforts to review and omit third-party defamatory, obscene or inappropriate material make a computer service provider or user liable for posted speech, then website operators and Internet service providers are likely to abandon efforts to eliminate such material from their site.

2.   APPLICATION TO CREMERS AND THE MUSEUM SECURITY NETWORK

To benefit from § 230(c) immunity, Cremers must first demonstrate that his Network website and listserv qualify as "provider[s] or user[s] of an *interactive computer service.*" § 230(c)(1) (emphasis added). An "interactive computer service" is defined as "any information service, system, or access software provider that provides or enables computer access by multiple users to a computer server, including specifically a service or system that provides access to the Internet and such systems operated or services offered by libraries or educational institutions." § 230(f)(2).

The district court concluded that only services that provide access to the Internet as a whole are covered by this definition. But the definition of "interactive computer service" on its face covers "*any*" information services or other systems, as long as the service or system allows "multiple users" to access "a computer server." Further, the statute repeatedly refers to "the Internet and *other* interactive computer services," (emphasis added), making clear that the statutory immunity extends beyond the Internet itself. §§ 230(a)(3), (a)(4), (b)(1), (b)(2), and (f)(3). Also, the definition of "interactive computer service" after the broad definitional language, states that the definition "*includ[es]* specifically a service or system that provides access to the Internet," § 230(f)(2) (emphasis added), thereby confirming that services providing access to the Internet as a whole are only a subset of the services to which the statutory immunity applies.

There is, however, no need here to decide whether a listserv or website itself fits the broad statutory definition of "interactive computer service," because the language of § 230(c)(1) confers immunity not just on "providers" of such services, but also on "users" of such services. § 230(c)(1).

There is no dispute that the Network uses interactive computer services to distribute its on-line mailing and to post the listserv on its website. Indeed, to make its website available and to mail out the listserv, the Network *must* access the Internet through some form of "interactive computer service." Thus, both the Network website and the listserv are potentially immune under § 230.

Critically, however, § 230 limits immunity to information "provided by another information content provider." § 230(c)(1). An "information content provider" is defined by the statute to mean "any person or entity that is responsible, in whole or in part, for the creation or development of information provided through the Internet or any other interactive computer service." § 230(f)(3). The reference to "*another* information content provider" (emphasis added) distinguishes the circumstance in which the interactive computer service itself meets the definition of "information content provider" with respect to the information in question. The pertinent question therefore becomes whether Smith was the sole content provider of his e-mail, or whether Cremers can also be considered to have "creat[ed]" or "develop[ed]" Smith's e-mail message forwarded to the listserv.

Obviously, Cremers did not create Smith's e-mail. Smith composed the e-mail entirely on his own. Nor do Cremers's minor alterations of Smith's e-mail prior to its posting or his choice to publish the e-mail (while rejecting other e-mails for inclusion in the listserv) rise to the level of "development." As we have seen, a central purpose of the Act was to protect from liability service providers and users who take some affirmative steps to edit the material posted. Also, the exclusion of "publisher" liability necessarily precludes liability for exercising the usual prerogative of publishers to choose among proffered material and to edit the material published while retaining its basic form and message.

The "development of information" therefore means something more substantial than merely editing portions of an e-mail and selecting material for publication. Because Cremers did no more than select and make minor alterations to Smith's e-mail, Cremers cannot be considered the content provider of Smith's e-mail for purposes of § 230.[19]

One possible solution to this statutorily created problem is the approach taken by Congress in the Digital Millennium Copyright Act ("Digital Act"). The Digital Act includes immunity provisions, similar to those of the Communications Decency Act, that protect service providers from liability for content provided by third parties. The Digital Act, however, unlike the Communications Decency Act, provides specific notice, take-down, and put-back procedures that carefully balance the First Amendment rights of users with the rights of a potentially injured copyright holder. *See* 17 U.S.C. §§ 512(c) and (g). To date, Congress has not amended § 230 to provide for similar take-down and put-back procedures.

The partial dissent does not register any disagreement with this interpretation of the definition of "information content provider" or with the observation that immunity for "publisher[s]" indicates a recognition that the immunity will extend to the selection of material supplied by others. It nonetheless simultaneously maintains that 1) a defendant who takes an active role in selecting information for publication is not immune; and 2) interactive computer service users and providers who screen the material submitted and remove offensive content are immune. These two positions simply cannot logically coexist.

Such a distinction between deciding to publish only some of the material submitted and deciding *not* to publish some of the material submitted is not a viable one. The scope of the immunity cannot turn on whether the publisher approaches the selection process as one of inclusion or removal, as the difference is one of method or degree, not substance.

A distinction between removing an item once it has appeared on the Internet and screening before publication cannot fly either. For one thing, there is no basis for believing that Congress intended a one-bite-at-the-apple form of immunity. Also, Congress could not have meant to favor removal of offending material over more advanced software that screens out the material before it ever appears. If

---

19. As other courts have pointed out, the broad immunity created by § 230 can sometimes lead to troubling results. For example, a service provider that cannot be held liable for posting a defamatory message may have little incentive to take such material down even if informed that the material is defamatory.

anything, the goal of encouraging assistance to parents seeking to control children's access to offensive material would suggest a preference for a system in which the offensive material is not available even temporarily. The upshot is that the partial dissent's posit concerning the limitations of §230(c) immunity simply cannot be squared with the statute's language and purposes, whatever merit it, or a variant of it, might have as a policy matter.

In most cases our conclusion that Cremers cannot be considered a content provider would end matters, but this case presents one twist on the usual §230 analysis: Smith maintains that he never "imagined [his] message would be posted on an international message board or [he] never would have sent it in the first place." The question thus becomes whether Smith can be said to have "provided" his e-mail in the sense intended by §230(c). If the defamatory information is not "*provided* by another information content provider," then §230(c) does not confer immunity on the publisher of the information.

"[P]rovided" suggests, at least, some active role by the "provider" in supplying the material to a "provider or user of an interactive computer service." One would not say, for example, that the author of a magazine article "provided" it to an interactive computer service provider or user by allowing the article to be published in hard copy off-line. Although such an article is available to anyone with access to a library or a newsstand, it is not "provided" for use on the Internet.

The result in the foregoing example should not change if the interactive computer service provider or user has a subscription to the magazine. In that instance, the material in question is "provided" to the "provider or user of an interactive computer service," but not in its role as a provider or user of a computer service. The structure and purpose of §230(c)(1) indicate that the immunity applies only with regard to third-party information provided *for use on the Internet* or another interactive computer service. As we have seen, the section is concerned with providing special immunity for individuals who would otherwise be publishers or speakers, because of Congress's concern with assuring a free market in ideas and information on the Internet. If information is provided to those individuals in a capacity unrelated to their function as a provider or user of interactive computer services, then there is no reason to protect them with the special statutory immunity.

So, if, for example, an individual who happens to operate a website receives a defamatory "snail mail" letter from an old friend, the website operator cannot be said to have been "provided" the information in his capacity as a website service. Section 230(c)(1) supplies immunity for only individuals or entities acting as "provider[s]" or "user[s]" of an "interactive computer service," and therefore does not apply when it is not "provided" to such persons in their roles as providers or users.

The situation here is somewhat more complicated than our letter example, because Smith did provide his e-mail over the Internet and transmitted it to the Network, an operator of a website that is an user of an interactive computer service. Nevertheless, Smith contends that he did not intend his e-mail to be placed on an interactive computer service for public viewing.

Smith's confusion, even if legitimate, does not matter, Cremers maintains, because the §230(c)(1) immunity should be available simply because Smith was the author of the e-mail, without more.

We disagree. Under Cremers's broad interpretation of §230(c), users and providers of interactive computer services could with impunity intentionally post material they knew was never meant to be put on the Internet. At the same time, the creator or developer of the information presumably could not be held liable for unforeseeable publication of his material to huge numbers of people with whom he had no intention to communicate. The result would be nearly limitless immunity for speech never meant to be broadcast over the Internet.

Supplying a "provider or user of an interactive computer service" with immunity in such circumstances is not consistent with Congress's expressly stated purposes in adopting §230. Free speech and the development of the Internet are not "promote[d]" by affording immunity when providers and users of "interactive computer service[s]" knew or had reason to know that the information provided was not intended for publication on the Internet. Quite the contrary: Users of the Internet are likely to be discouraged from sending e-mails for fear that their e-mails may be published on the web without their permission.

Such a scenario is very different from the bulletin boards that Congress had in mind when passing §230. When a user sends a message to a bulletin board, it is obvious that by doing so, he or she will be publicly posting the message. Here, by contrast, Smith claims that he had no idea that the Network even had a listserv. His expectation, he says, was that he was simply sending a private e-mail to an organization informing it of his concern about Batzel's artwork, and, he insists, he would not have sent the message had he known it would be sent on through the listserv. Absent an incentive for service providers and users to evaluate whether the content they receive is meant to be posted, speech over the Internet will be chilled rather than encouraged. Immunizing providers and users of "interactive computer service[s]" for publishing material when they have reason to know that the material is not intended for publication therefore contravenes the Congressional purpose of encouraging the "development of the Internet."

Immunizing individuals and entities in such situations also interferes with Congress's objective of providing incentives for providers and users of interactive computer services to remove offensive material, especially obscene and defamatory speech. Far from encouraging such actions, immunizing a publisher or distributor for including content not intended for Internet publication increases the likelihood that obscene and defamatory material will be widely available. Not only will on-line publishers be able to distribute such material obtained from "hard copy" sources with impunity, but, because the content provider him or herself never intended publication, there is a greater likelihood that the distributed material will in fact be defamatory or obscene. A person is much more likely to exercise care in choosing his words when he knows that those words will be widely read. This is true not only for altruistic reasons but also because liability for defamation attaches only upon publication. In the current case, Smith claimed exactly that: He told Cremers that if he had known his e-mail would be posted, he never would have sent it. The congressional objectives in passing §230 therefore are not furthered by providing immunity in instances where posted material was clearly not meant for publication.

At the same time, Congress's purpose in enacting §230(c)(1) suggests that we must take great care in determining whether another's information was "provided" to a "provider or user of an interactive computer service" for publication. Otherwise, posting of information on the Internet and other interactive computer services would be chilled, as the service provider or user could not tell whether posting was contemplated. To preclude this possibility, the focus should be not on the information provider's intentions or knowledge when transmitting content but, instead, on the service provider's or user's reasonable perception of those intentions or knowledge. We therefore hold that a service provider or user is immune from liability under § 230(c)(1) when a third person or entity that created or developed the information in question furnished it to the provider or user under circumstances in which a reasonable person in the position of the service provider or user would conclude that the information was provided for publication on the Internet or other "interactive computer service."

It is not entirely clear from the record whether Smith "provided" the e-mail for publication on the Internet under this standard. There are facts that could have led Cremers reasonably to conclude that Smith sent him the information because he operated an Internet service. On the other hand, Smith was not a subscriber to the listserv and apparently sent the information to a different e-mail account from the one at which Cremers usually received information for publication. More development of the record may be necessary to determine whether, under all the circumstances, a reasonable person in Cremers' position would conclude that the information was sent for internet publication, or whether a triable issue of fact is presented on that issue.

We therefore vacate the district court's order . . . and remand to the district court for further proceedings to develop the facts under this newly announced standard and to evaluate what Cremers should have reasonably concluded at the time he received Smith's e-mail. If Cremers should have reasonably concluded, for example, that because Smith's e-mail arrived via a different e-mail address it was not provided to him for possible posting on the listserv, then Cremers cannot take advantage of the § 230(c) immunities. Under that circumstance, the posted information was not "provided" by another "information content provider" within the meaning of § 230. . . .

IV

Batzel argues that the district court erred in granting Mosler's motion for summary judgment. According to Batzel, Cremers was acting as Mosler's agent and therefore should be held vicariously liable for Cremers's alleged defamation. We reject this contention.

"Agency is the fiduciary relationship that arises when one person (a 'principal') manifests assent to another person (an 'agent') that the agent shall act on the principal's behalf and subject to the principal's control, and the agent manifests assent or otherwise consents so to act." Restatement (Third) of Agency § 1.01 (Tentative Draft). In order for Mosler to be held vicariously liable for the torts of Cremers on a theory of agency, Mosler must have had the ability to control Cremers's activities.

Batzel failed to present any genuine issue of material fact as to whether Mosler had control over Cremers's management of the Network. The sponsorship agreement executed by Mosler and Cremers requires, in essence, that Cremers include Mosler's trademark in future editions of the Network. It does not give Mosler any right to control what is published by Cremers. The agreement states that Cremers will "maintain ownership and control of all aspects of [the Network's] content and operation." The agreement further states that Mosler "understands that the Museum Security Network is editorially independent and maintains full control of All [sic] editorial content." Cremers also posted on the Network's website a statement that Mosler "understand[s] that the [Network] must remain editorially independent and they respect that." Rather than evincing Cremers's assent to control by Mosler, these statements disclaim control. Without the element of control, Batzel's vicarious liability argument fails.

The fact that Mosler provided Cremers with financial support does not support an inference that Mosler possessed practical control of Cremers's editorial content. Sponsorship alone is insufficient to render the sponsor the guarantor of the truth of all statements made in a publication.

We likewise reject the argument that Mosler's continued sponsorship of the Network after Cremers published Smith's statements should give rise to liability. Although a principal is liable when it ratifies an originally unauthorized tort, the principal-agent relationship is still a requisite, and ratification can have no meaning without it. Because Cremers was not acting as Mosler's agent at the time he published Smith's statements, Mosler's continued funding of the Network did not amount to ratification of the tort.

The district court accordingly did not err in ruling that Mosler cannot be held vicariously liable for Cremers' actions because there was no principal-agent relationship between Mosler and Cremers. We affirm the district court's grant of summary judgment in favor of Mosler. . . .

GOULD, Circuit Judge, concurring in part, dissenting in part:

I respectfully dissent from the majority's analysis of the statutory immunity from libel suits created by § 230 of the Communications Decency Act (CDA). The majority gives the phrase "information provided by another" an incorrect and unworkable meaning that extends CDA immunity far beyond what Congress intended. Under the majority's interpretation of § 230, many persons who intentionally spread vicious falsehoods on the Internet will be immune from suit. This sweeping preemption of valid state libel laws is not necessary to promote Internet use and is not what Congress had in mind.

Congress in 1996 was worried that excessive state-law libel lawsuits would threaten the growth of the Internet. Congress enacted the CDA, which immunizes "provider[s] or user[s]" of "interactive computer service[s]" from civil liability for material disseminated by them but "provided by another information content provider." 47 U.S.C. § 230(c). Under the CDA, courts must treat providers or users of interactive computer services differently from other information providers, such as newspapers, magazines, or television and radio stations, all of which may be held liable for publishing or distributing obscene or defamatory material written or prepared by others. Congress believed this special treatment would "promote the continued development of the Internet and other interactive computer services" and "preserve the vibrant and competitive free market" for such services, largely "unfettered by Federal or State regulation." 47 U.S.C. § 230(b)(1)-(2).

The statute states: No provider or user of an interactive computer service shall be treated as the publisher or speaker of any information provided by another information content provider. 47 U.S.C. § 230(c)(1). Three elements are thus required for § 230 immunity: (1) the defendant must be a provider or user of an "interactive computer service"; (2) the asserted claims must treat the defendant as a publisher or speaker of information; and (3) the challenged communication must be "information provided by another information content provider." The majority and I agree on the importance of the CDA and on the proper interpretation of the first and second elements. We disagree only over the third element.

The majority holds that information is "provided by another" when "a third person or entity that created or developed the information in question furnished it to the provider or user under circumstances in which a reasonable person in the position of the service provider or user would conclude that the information was provided for publication on the Internet or other 'interactive computer service.'" In other words, whether information is "provided" depends on the *defendant's perception* of the *author's intention.* Nothing in the statutory language suggests that "provided" should be interpreted in this convoluted and unworkable fashion.

Under the majority's rule, a court determining whether to extend CDA immunity to a defendant must determine whether the author of allegedly defamatory information — a person who often will be beyond reach of the court's process or, worse, unknown — intended that the information be distributed on the Internet. In many cases, the author's intention may not be discernable from the face of the defamatory communication. Even people who want an e-mail message widely disseminated may not preface the message with words such as "Please pass it on." Moreover, the fact-intensive question of the author's intent is particularly unsuited for a judge's determination before trial, when the immunity question will most often arise.

The majority's rule will be incomprehensible to most citizens, who will be unable to plan their own conduct mindful of the law's requirements. Laypersons may not grasp that their tort liability depends on whether they reasonably should have known that the author of a particular communication intended that it be distributed on the Internet. Laypersons certainly will not grasp *why* this should be the case, as a matter of justice, morality, or politics. Those who receive a potentially libelous e-mail message from another person would seldom wonder, when deciding whether to forward the message to others, "Did *the author* of this defamatory information intend that it be distributed on the Internet?" However, those who receive a potentially libelous e-mail almost certainly would wonder, "Is it appropriate *for me* to spread this defamatory message?" By shifting its inquiry away from the defendant's conduct, the majority has crafted a rule that encourages the casual spread of harmful lies. The majority has improvidently crafted a rule that is foreign to the statutory text and foreign to human experience.

The majority rule licenses professional rumor-mongers and gossip-hounds to spread false and hurtful information with impunity. So long as the defamatory information was written by a person who wanted the information to be spread on the Internet (in other words, a person with an axe to grind), the rumormonger's injurious conduct is beyond legal redress. Nothing in the CDA's text or legislative history suggests that Congress intended CDA immunity to extend so far. Nothing in the text, legislative history, or human experience would lead me to accept the notion that Congress in § 230 intended to immunize users or providers of interactive computer services who, by their discretionary decisions to spread particular communications, cause trickles of defamation to swell into rivers of harm.

The problems caused by the majority's rule all would vanish if we focused our inquiry not on the *author's intent,* but on the *defendant's acts,* as I believe Congress intended. We should hold that the CDA immunizes a defendant only when the defendant took no active role in selecting the questionable information for publication. If the defendant took an active role in selecting information for publication, the information is no longer "information provided by another" within the meaning of § 230. We should draw this conclusion from the statute's text and purposes.

A person's decision to select particular information for distribution on the Internet changes that information in a subtle but important way: it adds the person's imprimatur to it. The recipient of information that has been selected by another person for distribution understands that the information has been deemed worthy of dissemination by the sender. Information that bears such an implicit endorsement[5] is no longer merely the "information provided by" the original sender. 47 U.S.C. §230(c)(1). It is information transformed. It is information bolstered, strengthened to do more harm if it is wrongful. A defendant who has actively selected libelous information for distribution thus should not be entitled to CDA immunity for disseminating "information provided by another."

My interpretation of §230 is consistent with the CDA's legislative history. Congress understood that entities that facilitate communication on the Internet — particularly entities that operate e-mail networks, "chat rooms," "bulletin boards," and "listservs" — have special needs. The amount of information communicated through such services is staggering. Millions of communications are sent daily. It would be impossible to screen all such communications for libelous or offensive content. Faced with potential liability for each message republished by their services, interactive computer service users and providers might choose to restrict severely the number and type of messages posted. The threat of tort liability in an area of such prolific speech would have an obvious chilling effect on free speech and would hamper the new medium.

These policy concerns have force when a potential defendant uses or provides technology that enables others to disseminate information directly without intervening human action. These policy concerns lack force when a potential defendant does not offer users this power of direct transmission. If a potential defendant employs a person to screen communications to select some of them for dissemination, it is not impossible (or even difficult) for that person to screen communications for defamatory content. Immunizing that person or the person's employer from liability would not advance Congress's goal of protecting those in need of protection.

If a person is charged with screening all communications to select some for dissemination, that person can decide not to disseminate a potentially offensive communication. Or that person can undertake some reasonable investigation. Such a process would be relatively inexpensive and would reduce the serious social costs caused by the spread of offensive and defamatory communications.

Under my interpretation of §230, a company that operates an e-mail network would be immune from libel suits arising out of e-mail messages transmitted automatically across its network. Similarly, the owner, operator, organizer, or moderator of an Internet bulletin board, chat room, or listserv would be immune from libel suits arising out of messages distributed using that technology, provided that the person does not actively select particular messages for publication.

On the other hand, a person who receives a libelous communication and makes the decision to disseminate that messages to others — whether via e-mail, a bulletin board, a chat room, or a listserv — would not be immune.

My approach also would further Congress's goal of encouraging "self-policing" on the Internet. Congress decided to immunize from liability those who publish material on the Internet, so long as they do not actively select defamatory or

---

5. By "endorsement," I do not mean that the person who selects information for distribution agrees with the content of that information. Rather, I mean that the person has endorsed the information insofar as he or she has deemed it appropriate for distribution to others. That adds enough to the information to remove it from CDA immunity.

offensive material for distribution. As a result, those who *remove* all or part of an offensive information posted on (for example) an Internet bulletin board are immune from suit. Those who employ blocking or filtering technologies that allow readers to avoid obscene or offensive materials also are immune from suit.

On the other hand, Congress decided not to immunize those who actively select defamatory or offensive information for distribution on the Internet. Congress thereby ensured that users and providers of interactive computer services would have an incentive not to spread harmful gossip and lies intentionally.

Congress wanted to ensure that excessive government regulation did not slow America's expansion into the exciting new frontier of the Internet. But Congress did not want this new frontier to be like the Old West: a lawless zone governed by retribution and mob justice. The CDA does not license anarchy. A person's decision to disseminate the rankest rumor or most blatant falsehood should not escape legal redress merely because the person chose to disseminate it through the Internet rather than through some other medium. A proper analysis of § 230, which makes a human being's decision to disseminate a particular communication the touchstone of CDA immunity, reconciles Congress's intent to deregulate the Internet with Congress's recognition that certain beneficial technologies, which promote efficient global communication and advance values enshrined in our First Amendment, are unique to the Internet and need special protection. Congress wanted to preserve the Internet and aid its growth, but not at all costs. Congress did not want to remove incentives for people armed with the power of the Internet to act with reasonable care to avoid unnecessary harm to others.

In this case, I would hold that Cremers is *not* entitled to CDA immunity because Cremers actively selected Smith's e-mail message for publication. Whether Cremers's Museum Security Network is characterized as a "moderated listserv," an "e-mail newsletter," or otherwise, it is certain that the Network did not permit users to disseminate information to other users directly without intervening human action. According to Cremers, "To post a response or to provide new information, the subscriber merely replies to the listserv mailing and *the message is sent directly to Cremers, who includes it* in the listserv with the subsequent distribution." (Emphasis added.)

This procedure was followed with respect to Smith's e-mail message accusing Batzel of owning art stolen by a Nazi ancestor. Smith transmitted the message to one e-mail account, from which Cremers received it. Cremers forwarded the message to a second e-mail account. He pasted the message into a new edition of the Museum Security Network newsletter. He then sent that newsletter to his subscribers and posted it on the Network's website. Cremers's decision to select Smith's e-mail message for publication effectively altered the messages's meaning, adding to the message the unstated suggestion that Cremers deemed the message worthy of readers' attention. Cremers therefore did not merely distribute "information provided by another," and he is not entitled to CDA immunity.

From the record before us, we have no reason to think that Cremers is not well-meaning or that his concerns about stolen artwork are not genuine. Nor on this appeal do we decide whether his communications were defamatory or harmful in fact. We deal only with immunity. And, in my view, there is no immunity under the CDA if Cremers made a discretionary decision to distribute on the Internet defamatory information about another person, without any investigation whatsoever. If Cremers made a mistake, we should not hold that he may escape all accountability just because he made that mistake on the Internet.

I respectfully dissent.

---

2. Copyright Infringement and the Digital Millennium Copyright Act

Some postings on the Internet are objectionable not because they have offensive content, but because they copy and distribute material protected by the copyright laws. Because copyright infringement occurs under Copyright Act § 106(1) & (3) whenever a work is copied or distributed without permission of the owner — without regard to knowledge of the protected nature of the material — owners of sites where content can be posted have faced considerable difficulty. The problem is that a posting on a Web site necessarily involves a copy of the work.

Thus, it was no surprise in 1993 when a court first held a pre-Internet online service provider liable for copyright infringement after a subscriber had uploaded infringing materials. There, the subscribers' act of uploading and other subscribers' acts of downloading included the making of copies on the provider's system. Playboy Enterprises, Inc. v. Frena, 839 F. Supp. 1552 (M.D. Fla. 1993). In 1995, however, a different court came to the opposite result on substantially similar facts, pointing to the fact that the provider was a mere passive conduit for the content and that there was no human intervention on the part of the provider in the copying activity. Religious Technology Ctr. v. Netcom On-Line Communications Servs., Inc., 907 F. Supp. 1361 (N.D. Cal. 1995). Still, even the *Netcom* court stated that the provider might be liable for infringement if it took steps to facilitate the infringing conduct, such as reviewing files before permitting others to download them, authorizing others to make infringing copies while not actively participating in the copying activity, or automating the collection of infringing copies posted by others and reposting them in a single location to facilitate downloading.

Once again, Congress intervened to resolve this quandary by creating a "safe harbor" from liability. The safe harbor in this context appeared as part of the 1998 Digital Millennium Copyright Act (DMCA). That statute is better known for some of its other provisions — most importantly the provisions that make it a criminal offense to circumvent electronic technologies designed to protect digital media from unauthorized copying, Copyright Act §§ 1201-1205. But it also created a safe harbor for site owners, codified in the lengthy and convoluted Section 512 of the Copyright Act. Section 512(c) applies, for example to the operator of a chat room or bulletin board: the statute protects a "service provider" involved in the "storage at the direction of a user of material that resides on a system . . . controlled . . . by . . . the service provider." Protection under that provision, however, is dependent on the provider's compliance with a scheme for promptly removing infringing material from the Internet. Set out in Section 512(g), the scheme generally contemplates

- Prompt removal by the owner upon receipt of an appropriate notice alleging that material infringes. Section 512(c)(1)(C)
- Prompt notice to the person that posted the allegedly infringing material. Section 512(g)(2)(A)
- Replacement of the material within 10 to 14 business days after receipt of a qualifying counter-notification from the original poster, unless the complaining party has filed suit by that time. Section 512(g)(2)(C).

Perhaps the central question under the statute is the relation between that safe harbor and the preexisting liability for copyright infringement, the topic of the following case.

CoStar Group, Inc. v. LoopNet, Inc.
373 F.3d 544 (4th Cir. 2004)

Before NIEMEYER, MICHAEL, and GREGORY, Circuit Judges.
NIEMEYER, Circuit Judge:
CoStar Group, Inc. and CoStar Realty Information, Inc. (collectively "CoStar"), a copyright owner of numerous photographs of commercial real estate, commenced this copyright infringement action against LoopNet, Inc., an Internet service provider, for direct infringement under §§ 501 and 106 of the Copyright Act because CoStar's copyrighted photographs were posted by LoopNet's subscribers on LoopNet's website. CoStar contended that the photographs were copied into LoopNet's computer system and that LoopNet therefore was a copier strictly liable for infringement of CoStar's rights under § 106, regardless of whether LoopNet's role was passive when the photographs were copied into its system.

. . . [T]he district court entered summary judgment in favor of LoopNet on the claim of direct infringement under § 106. We agree with the district court. Because LoopNet, as an Internet service provider, is simply the owner and manager of a system used by others who are violating CoStar's copyrights and is not an actual duplicator itself, it is not *directly* liable for copyright infringement. We therefore affirm.

I

CoStar is a national provider of commercial real estate information, and it claims to have collected the most comprehensive database of information on commercial real estate markets and commercial properties in the United States and the United Kingdom. Its database includes a large collection of photographs of commercial properties, and CoStar owns the copyright in the vast majority of these photographs. CoStar makes its database, including photographs, available to customers through the Internet and otherwise, and each customer agrees not to post CoStar's photographs on its own website or on the website of a third party.

LoopNet is an Internet service provider ("ISP") whose website allows subscribers, generally real estate brokers, to post listings of commercial real estate on the Internet. It claims that its computer system contains over 100,000 customer listings of commercial real estate, including approximately 33,000 photographs, and that it was, during the district court proceedings, adding about 2200 listings each day, 250 of which include photographs. LoopNet does not post real estate listings on its own account. Rather it provides a "web hosting service that enables users who wish to display real estate over the Internet to post listings for those properties on LoopNet's web site."

When using LoopNet's services, a subscriber fills out a form and agrees to "Terms and Conditions" that include a promise not to post copies of photographs without authorization. If the subscriber includes a photograph for a listing, it must fill out another form and agree again to the "Terms and Conditions," along with an additional express warranty that the subscriber has "all necessary rights and authorizations" from the copyright owner of the photographs. The subscriber then uploads the photographs into a folder in LoopNet's system, and the photograph is transferred to the RAM of one of Loop-Net's computers for review. A LoopNet employee then cursorily reviews the photograph (1) to determine whether the photograph in fact depicts commercial real estate, and (2) to identify any obvious evidence, such as a text message or copyright notice, that the photograph may have been copyrighted by another. If the photograph fails either one of these criteria, the employee deletes the photograph and notifies the subscriber. Otherwise, the employee clicks an "accept" button that prompts LoopNet's system to associate the photograph with the web page for the property listing, making the photograph available for viewing.

Beginning in early 1998, CoStar became aware that photographs for which it held copyrights were being posted on LoopNet's website by LoopNet's subscribers. When CoStar informed LoopNet of the violations, LoopNet removed the photographs. In addition, LoopNet instituted and followed a policy of marking properties to which infringing photographs had been posted so that if other photographs were posted to that property, LoopNet could inspect the photographs side-by-side to make sure that the new photographs were not the infringing photographs. By late summer 1999, CoStar had discovered 112 infringing photographs on LoopNet's website, and by September 2001, it had found over 300. At that time, LoopNet had in its system about 33,000 photographs posted by its subscribers.

CoStar commenced this action in September 1999 against LoopNet, alleging copyright infringement, violation of the Lanham Act, and several state-law causes of action. On cross-motions for summary judgment, the district court concluded that LoopNet had not engaged in direct infringement under the Copyright Act. It left open, however, CoStar's claims that LoopNet might have contributorily infringed CoStar's copyrights and that LoopNet was not entitled to the "safe harbor" immunity provided by the Digital Millennium Copyright Act, 17 U.S.C. §512. When the parties stipulated to the dismissal of all claims except the district court's summary judgment in favor of LoopNet on direct infringement, the district court entered final judgment on that issue in favor of LoopNet. From entry of the judgment, CoStar noticed this appeal.

II

CoStar contends principally that the district court erred in providing LoopNet "conclusive immunity," as a "'passive' provider of Internet" services, from strict liability for its hosting of CoStar's copyrighted pictures on LoopNet's website. The district court based its decision on the reasoning of *Religious Technology Center v. Net-com On-Line Communication Services, Inc.*, 907 F. Supp. 1361 (N.D. Cal. 1995) ("*Netcom*"), which held that an ISP serving as a passive conduit for copyrighted material is not liable as a direct infringer. CoStar asserts that LoopNet is strictly liable for infringement of CoStar's rights protected by §106 of the Copyright Act. According to CoStar, any immunity for the passive conduct of an ISP such as LoopNet must come from the safe harbor immunity provided by the Digital Millennium Computer Act ("DMCA"), if at all, because the DMCA codified and supplanted the *Netcom* holding. Because LoopNet could not meet the conditions for immunity under the DMCA as to many of the copyrighted photographs, LoopNet accordingly would be liable under CoStar's terms for direct copyright infringement for hosting web pages containing the infringing photos.

Stated otherwise, CoStar argues (1) that the *Netcom* decision was a pragmatic and temporary limitation of traditional copyright liability, which would otherwise have held ISPs strictly liable, and that in view of the enactment of the DMCA, *Netcom*'s limitation is no longer necessary; (2) that Congress considered *Netcom* in enacting the DMCA, codifying its principles and thereby supplanting and preempting *Netcom* as the only exemption from liability for direct infringement; and (3) that because LoopNet cannot satisfy the conditions of the DMCA, it remains strictly liable for direct infringement under §§106 and 501 of the Copyright Act. We will address CoStar's points, determining first the nature and applicability of the *Netcom* decision and second the impact of the DMCA on *Netcom*.

A

In *Netcom*, the court held, among other things, that neither the ISP providing Internet access, nor the bulletin board service storing the posted material, was liable for direct copyright infringement under §106 when a subscriber posted copyrighted materials on the Internet. The court observed that "[a]lthough copyright is a strict liability statute, there should still be some element of volition or causation which is lacking where a defendant's system is merely used to use a copy by a third party." 907 F. Supp. at 1370. In responding to the argument that the ISP's computers stored and thereby "copied" copyrighted material on its system for a period of days in rendering its service, the court stated:

> Where the infringing subscriber is clearly directly liable for the same act, it does not make sense to adopt a rule that would lead to the liability of countless parties whose role in the infringement is nothing more than setting up and operating a system that is necessary for the functioning of the Internet. . . . The court does not find workable a theory of infringement that would hold the entire Internet liable for activities that cannot reasonabl[y] be deterred. Billions of bits of data flow through the Internet and are necessarily stored on servers throughout the network and it is thus practically impossible to screen out infringing bits from noninfringing bits. Because the court cannot see any meaningful distinction (without regard to knowledge) between what Netcom did and what every other Usenet server does, the court finds that Netcom cannot be held liable for direct infringement.

Id. at 1372-73.

CoStar argues, in view of the court's explanation, that the *Netcom* decision was driven by expedience and that its holding is inconsistent with the established law of copyright. It maintains that the court made a policy judgment based not on what the law was but on the fact that the Internet would have been crippled as a medium if preexisting law had been applied. It argues further that since the enactment of the DMCA in 1998, the problem identified in *Netcom* has been solved by the DMCA, and consequently there is no longer any need for the courts to continue to uphold this "special exemption" from § 106 liability for ISPs.

While the court in *Netcom* did point out the dramatic consequences of a decision that would hold ISPs strictly liable for transmitting copyrighted materials through their systems without knowledge of what was being transmitted, the court grounded its ruling principally on its interpretation of § 106 of the Copyright Act as implying a requirement of "volition or causation" by the purported infringer. . . . There are several reasons to commend this approach.

"[T]he Copyright Act grants the copyright holder 'exclusive' rights to use and to authorize the use of his work in five qualified ways, including reproduction of the copyrighted work in copies." *Sony Corp. v. Universal City Studios, Inc.*, 464 U.S. 417, 432-33 (1984). And it provides that "[a]nyone who violates any of the exclusive rights of the copyright owner . . . is an infringer of the copyright." 17 U.S.C. § 501. Stated at a general level, "[t]o establish infringement, two elements must be proven: (1) ownership of a valid copyright, and (2) copying of constituent elements of the work that are original." *Feist Publications, Inc. v. Rural Tel. Serv. Co.*, 499 U.S. 340, 361 (1991). A direct infringer has thus been characterized as one who "trespasses into [the copyright owner's] exclusive domain" established in § 106, subject to the limitations of §§ 107 through 118. *Sony,* 464 U.S. at 433; *see also* 17 U.S.C. § 106 (specifying limitations).

While the Copyright Act does not require that the infringer know that he is infringing or that his conduct amount to a willful violation of the copyright owner's rights, it nonetheless requires *conduct* by a person who causes in some meaningful way an infringement. Were this not so, the Supreme Court could not have held, as it did in *Sony,* that a manufacturer of copy machines, possessing constructive knowledge that purchasers of its machine may be using them to engage in copyright infringement, is not strictly liable for infringement. 464 U.S. at 439-42. This, of course, does not mean that a manufacturer or owner of machines used for copyright violations could not have some *indirect* liability, such as contributory or vicarious liability. But such extensions of liability would require a showing of additional elements such as knowledge coupled with inducement or supervision coupled with a financial interest in the illegal copying.

The Copyright Act does not specifically provide for such extended liability, instead describing only the party who *actually engages* in infringing conduct — the one who directly violates the prohibitions. Yet under general principles of law, vicarious liability or contributory liability may be imposed:

> The absence of such express language in the copyright statute does not preclude the imposition of liability for copyright infringements on certain parties who have not themselves engaged in the infringing activity. For vicarious liability is imposed in virtually all areas of the law, and the concept of contributory infringement is merely a species of the broader problem of identifying the circumstances in which it is just to hold one individual accountable for the actions of another.

Sony, 464 U.S. at 435. Under a theory of contributory infringement, one who, with knowledge of the infringing activity, induces, causes or materially contributes to the infringing conduct of another is liable for the infringement, too. [Quotation marks and citation omitted.] Under a theory of vicarious liability, a defendant who has the right and ability to supervise the infringing activity and also has a direct financial interest in such activities is similarly liable. [Quotation marks and citation omitted.]

But to establish *direct* liability under §§ 501 and 106 of the Act, something more must be shown than mere ownership of a machine used by others to make illegal copies. There must be actual infringing conduct with a nexus sufficiently close and causal to the illegal copying that one could conclude that the machine owner himself trespassed on the exclusive domain of the copyright owner. The *Netcom* court described this nexus as requiring some aspect of volition or causation. 907 F. Supp. at 1370. Indeed, counsel for both parties agreed at oral argument that a copy machine owner who makes the machine available to the public to use for copying is not, without more, strictly liable under § 106 for illegal copying by a customer. The ISP in this case is an analogue to the owner of a traditional copying machine whose customers pay a fixed amount per copy and operate the machine themselves to make copies. When a customer duplicates an infringing work, the owner of the copy machine is not considered a direct infringer. Similarly, an ISP who owns an electronic facility that responds automatically to users' input is not a direct infringer. If the Copyright Act does not hold the owner of the copying machine liable as a direct infringer when its customer copies infringing material without knowledge of the owner, the ISP should not be found liable as a direct infringer when its facility is used by a subscriber to violate a copyright without intervening conduct of the ISP.

Moreover, in the context of the conduct typically engaged in by an ISP, construing the Copyright Act to require some aspect of volition and meaningful causation — as distinct from passive ownership and management of an electronic Internet facility — receives additional support from the Act's concept of "copying." A violation of § 106 requires copying or the making of copies. *See* 17 U.S.C. § 106(1), (3); *id.* § 102(a); *Feist Publishing,* 449 U.S. at 361. And the term "copies" refers to "material objects . . . in which a work *is fixed.*" 17 U.S.C. § 101 ("Definitions") (emphasis added). A work is "fixed" in a medium when it is embodied in a copy "sufficiently permanent or stable to permit it to be perceived, reproduced, or otherwise communicated for a period *of more than transitory duration.*" *Id.* (emphasis added). When an electronic infrastructure is designed and managed as a *conduit* of information and data that connects users over the Internet, the owner and manager of the conduit hardly "copies" the information and data in the sense that it fixes a copy in its system *of more than transitory duration.* Even if the information and data are "downloaded" onto the owner's RAM or other component as part of the transmission function, that downloading is a temporary, automatic response to the user's request, and the entire system functions solely to transmit the user's data to the Internet. Under such an arrangement, the ISP provides a system that automatically transmits users' material but is itself totally indifferent to the material's content. In this way, it functions as does a traditional telephone company when it transmits the contents of its users' conversations. While temporary electronic copies may be made in this transmission process, they would appear not to be "fixed" in the sense that they are "of more than transitory duration," and the ISP therefore would not be a "copier" to make it directly liable under the Copyright Act. With additional facts, of course, an ISP could become *indirectly* liable.

In concluding that an ISP has not itself fixed a copy in its system of more than transitory duration when it provides an Internet hosting service to its subscribers, we do not hold that a computer owner who downloads copyrighted software onto a computer cannot infringe the software's copyright. *See, e.g., MAI Systems Corp. v. Peak Computer, Inc.,* 991 F.2d 511, 518-19 (9th Cir. 1993). When the computer owner downloads copyrighted software, it possesses the software, which then functions in the service of the computer or its owner, and the copying is no longer of a transitory nature. "Transitory duration" is thus both a qualitative and quantitative characterization. It is quantitative insofar as it describes the period during which the function occurs, and it is qualitative in the sense that it describes the status of transition. Thus, when the copyrighted software is downloaded onto the computer, because it may be used to serve the computer or the computer owner, it no longer remains transitory. This, however, is unlike an ISP, which provides a system that automatically receives a subscriber's infringing material and transmits it to the Internet at the instigation of the subscriber.

Accordingly, we conclude that *Netcom* made a particularly rational interpretation of § 106 when it concluded that a person had to engage in volitional conduct — specifically, the act constituting infringement — to become a direct infringer. As the court in *Netcom* concluded, such a construction of the Act is especially important when it is applied to cyberspace. There are thousands of owners, contractors, servers, and users involved in the Internet whose role involves the storage and transmission of data in the establishment and maintenance of an Internet facility. Yet their conduct is not truly "copying" as understood by the Act; rather, they are conduits from or to would-be copiers and have no interest in the copy itself. *See Doe v. GTE Corp.,* 347 F.3d 655, 659 (7th Cir. 2003) ("A web host, like a delivery service or phone company, is an intermediary and normally is indifferent to the content of what it transmits"). To conclude that these persons are copyright infringers simply because they are involved in the ownership, operation, or maintenance of a transmission facility that automatically records material — copyrighted or not — would miss the thrust of the protections afforded by the Copyright Act. . . .

B

CoStar rests its position not only on the marginalization of the *Netcom* holding, but also on the assertion that the DMCA rendered *Netcom* no longer necessary — indeed, even codified and preempted *Netcom* — by imposing an exclusive safe harbor for ISPs that fulfill the conditions of the DMCA. CoStar argues that because the DMCA supplanted *Netcom,* LoopNet must rely for its defense exclusively on the immunity conferred by the DMCA. This argument, however, is belied by the plain language of the DMCA itself.

The DMCA was enacted as § 512 of the Copyright Act. The relevant subsection of § 512 provides limitations on liability "for infringement of copyright by reason of the storage at the direction of a user of material that resides on a system or network controlled or operated by or for the service for the [Internet] service provider" if the ISP lacks scienter about a copyright violation by a user, does not profit directly from the violation, and responds expeditiously to a proper notice of the violation. *See* 17 U.S.C. § 512(c)(1). In order to enjoy the safe harbor provided by § 512(c), the ISP must also fulfill other conditions imposed by the DMCA. *See id.* § 512(c), (i). Even though the DMCA was designed to provide ISPs with a safe harbor from copyright liability, nothing in the language of § 512 indicates that the limitation on liability described therein is exclusive. Indeed, another section of the DMCA provides explicitly that the DMCA is *not* exclusive:

> *Other defenses not affected.* — The failure of a service provider's conduct to qualify for limitation of liability under this section shall not bear adversely upon the consideration of a defense by the service provider that the service provider's conduct is not infringing under this title or any other defense.

Id. § 512(*l*). Thus the statute specifically provides that despite a failure to meet the safe-harbor conditions in § 512(c) and (i), an ISP is still entitled to all other arguments under the law — whether by way of an affirmative defense or through an argument that conduct simply does not constitute a prima facie case of infringement under the Copyright Act.

Given that the statute declares its intent not to "bear adversely upon" any of the ISP's defenses under law, including the defense that the plaintiff has not made out a prima facie case for infringement, it is difficult to argue, as CoStar does, that the statute in fact precludes ISPs from relying on an entire strain of case law holding that direct infringement must involve conduct having a volitional or causal aspect. Giving such a construction to the DMCA would in fact "bear adversely upon the consideration" of this defense, in direct contravention of § 512(*l*). We conclude that in enacting the DMCA, Congress did not preempt the decision in *Netcom* nor foreclose the continuing development of liability through court decisions interpreting §§ 106 and 501 of the Copyright Act.

CoStar advances the additional argument that because "Congress 'codified' *Netcom* in the DMCA . . . it can only be *to the DMCA* that we look for enforcement of those principles.". . . CoStar . . . , however, ha[s] this point of statutory construction exactly backward. When Congress codifies a common-law principle, the common law remains not only good law, but a valuable touchstone for interpreting the statute, unless Congress explicitly states that it *intends* to supplant the common law. "The normal rule of statutory construction is that if Congress intends for legislation to change the interpretation of a judicially created concept, it makes that intent specific." *Midatlantic Nat'l Bank v. N.J. Dep't of Envtl. Prot.,* 474 U.S. 494, 501 (1986). . . .

CoStar's argument that the DMCA supplanted and preempted *Netcom* is further undermined by the DMCA's legislative history. Congress actually expressed its intent that the courts would continue to determine how to apply the Copyright Act to the Internet and that the DMCA would merely create a floor of protection for ISPs. . . . [T]he Senate Committee on the Judiciary explained that "rather than embarking upon a wholesale clarification of these doctrines, the Committee decided to leave current law in its evolving state and, instead, to create a series of 'safe harbors,' for certain common activities of service providers." S. Rep. No. 105-190, at 19 (1998). The Ninth Circuit has found this language persuasive, citing it in finding that "[t]he DMCA did not simply rewrite copyright law for the on-line world." *Ellison v. Robertson,* 357 F.3d 1072, 1077 (9th Cir. 2004). Furthermore, the final conference report supports this passage, stating:

> As provided in subsection (l), Section 512 is not intended to imply that a service provider is or is not liable as an infringer either for conduct that qualifies for a

limitation of liability or for conduct that fails to so qualify. Rather, the limitations of liability apply if the provider is found to be liable under existing principles of law.

H.R. Conf. Rep. No. 105-796, at 73 (1998). Thus the DMCA was intended not to change the "evolving" doctrines on ISP liability for copyright infringement, which included *Netcom* and *Frena,* but to offer a certain safe harbor for ISPs. Courts were left free to continue to construe the Copyright Act in deciding the scope and nature of prima facie liability. The legislative "compromise" repeatedly invoked by CoStar and its *amici* was that Congress would not end the debate by importing and fixing copyright infringement liability in the form articulated by *Netcom,* but rather would provide a limited safe harbor immediately necessary to ISPs, and allow the courts to continue defining what constitutes a prima facie case of copyright infringement against an ISP. . . .

It is clear that Congress intended the DMCA's safe harbor for ISPs to be a floor, not a ceiling, of protection. Congress said nothing about whether passive ISPs should ever be held strictly liable as direct infringers or whether plaintiffs suing ISPs should instead proceed under contributory theories. The DMCA has merely added a second step to assessing infringement liability for Internet service providers, after it is determined whether they are infringers in the first place under the preexisting Copyright Act. Thus, the DMCA is irrelevant to determining what constitutes a prima facie case of copyright infringement.

At bottom, we hold that ISPs, when passively storing material at the direction of users in order to make that material available to other users upon their request, do not "copy" the material in direct violation of § 106 of the Copyright Act. Agreeing with the analysis in *Netcom,* we hold that the automatic copying, storage, and transmission of copyrighted materials, when instigated by others, does not render an ISP strictly liable for copyright infringement under §§ 501 and 106 of the Copyright Act. An ISP, however, can become liable indirectly upon a showing of additional involvement sufficient to establish a contributory or vicarious violation of the Act. In that case, the ISP could still look to the DMCA for a safe harbor if it fulfilled the conditions therein.

III

CoStar contends that even under *Netcom*'s construction of copyright infringement liability for ISPs, LoopNet's conduct in this case is more than passive, in that LoopNet screens photographs posted by its subscribers. In CoStar's opinion, this screening process renders LoopNet liable for direct copyright infringement.

LoopNet, like other ISPs, affords its subscribers an Internet-based facility on which to post materials, but the materials posted are of a type and kind selected by the subscriber and at a time initiated by the subscriber. Similarly, users who wish to access a subscriber's information may do so without intervention from LoopNet. A subscriber seeking to post a listing on LoopNet's website containing only *text* fills out a form and agrees to LoopNet's "Terms and Conditions," which include the obligation to respect others' copyrights. Once the subscriber has filled out the form and agreed to the "Terms and Conditions," an identification number is automatically assigned to the listing, and a web page containing the listing and the identification number is automatically created. The web page is then hosted on LoopNet's website to be viewed by users who request the listing.

CoStar does not contend that LoopNet's activity in signing up subscribers with *only* textual property listings is anything other than passive.

To argue that LoopNet loses its status as a passive ISP and therefore becomes liable for direct copyright infringement, CoStar focuses on LoopNet's gatekeeping practice with respect to photographs. To add a photograph to a listing, the subscriber must fill out another form and again agree to the "Terms and Conditions." After expressly warranting that he has "all necessary rights and authorizations from the . . . copyright owner of the photographs," the subscriber uploads the photograph into a folder in LoopNet's system. The photograph is then transferred to the RAM of one of LoopNet's computers for review. A LoopNet employee reviews the photo for two purposes: (1) to block photographs that do not depict commercial real estate, and (2) to block photographs with obvious signs that they are copyrighted by a third party. If the photograph carries a copyright notice or represents subject matter other than commercial real estate, the employee deletes the photograph; otherwise, she clicks a button marked "accept," and LoopNet's system automatically associates the photograph with the subscriber's web page for the property listing, making it available for use. Unless a question arises, this entire process takes "a few seconds."

Although LoopNet engages in volitional conduct to block photographs measured by two grossly defined criteria, this conduct, which takes only seconds, does not amount to "copying," nor does it add volition to LoopNet's involvement in storing the copy. The employee's look is so cursory as to be insignificant, and if it has any significance, it tends only to lessen the possibility that LoopNet's automatic electronic responses will inadvertently enable others to trespass on a copyright owner's rights. In performing this gatekeeping function, LoopNet does not attempt to search out or select photographs for duplication; it merely *prevents* users from duplicating certain photographs. To invoke again the analogy of the shop with the copy machine, LoopNet can be compared to an owner of a copy machine who has stationed a guard by the door to turn away customers who are attempting to duplicate clearly copyrighted works. LoopNet has not by this screening process become engaged as a "copier" of copyrighted works who can be held liable under §§501 and 106 of the Copyright Act.

To the extent that LoopNet's intervention in screening photographs goes further than the simple gatekeeping function described above, it is because of CoStar's complaints about copyright violations. Whenever CoStar has complained to LoopNet about a particular photograph, LoopNet has removed the photograph, and the property listing with which the photograph was associated has been marked. The next time the user tries to post a photograph to accompany that listing, LoopNet conducts a manual side-by-side review to make sure that the user is not reposting the infringing photograph. CoStar and other copyright holders benefit significantly from this type of response. If they find such conduct by an ISP too active, they can avoid it by adding a copyright notice to their photographs, which CoStar does not do. CoStar can hardly request LoopNet to prevent its users from infringing upon particular unmarked photographs and then subsequently seek to hold LoopNet liable as a direct infringer when Loop-Net complies with CoStar's request.

In short, we do not conclude that LoopNet's perfunctory gatekeeping process, which furthers the goals of the Copyright Act, can be taken to create liability for LoopNet as a direct infringer when its conduct otherwise does not amount to direct infringement.

For the reasons given, we affirm the judgment of the district court.

GREGORY, Circuit Judge, dissenting:

While I largely agree with the majority's careful explication of the direct infringement doctrine within the cybersphere post-DMCA, I cannot join the majority's application of that law. First, I disagree with the majority's characterizations of LoopNet as "an analogue to the owner of a traditional copying machine whose customers pay a fixed amount per copy and operate the machine themselves to make copies," and its comparison of the company to "an owner of a copy machine who has stationed a guard by the door to turn away customers who are attempting to duplicate clearly copyrighted works." Specifically, these ill-fitting characterizations lead the majority to the erroneous conclusion that LoopNet is not liable for direct infringement despite its volitional screening process. Because I would hold that LoopNet engages in non-passive, volitional conduct with respect to the photographs on its website such that the *Netcom* defense does not apply, I respectfully dissent.

I

In examining whether LoopNet is a passive provider not subject to direct infringement liability, the majority conducts a comparison of LoopNet's posting processes as to text and images. The majority properly recognizes, and CoStar does not dispute, that when a subscriber posts text to LoopNet's website the process is completely passive. Indeed, whatever text the subscriber enters into LoopNet's form is automatically uploaded to, and immediately accessible on, LoopNet's website. By contrast, when a subscriber wishes to post a photograph on the site, such posting is not automatic or immediate. Instead, the photograph is transferred to LoopNet's computers where one of the company's employees can review the photo to ensure (1) it is an image of commercial real estate, and (2) it is not an obviously copyrighted image.

At this stage of the process the LoopNet employee has a choice, he or she can reject the photograph because it does not comply with the above-noted criteria, or he or she can "accept" the photograph, at which time it becomes accessible on the subscriber's web page to which the text was previously and automatically uploaded. The majority thus finds itself in a bind, namely how is this decision by the LoopNet employee whether or not to "accept" an image akin to the automated posting of text such that it, too, does not constitute direct infringement. The majority attempts to resolve this paradox by first admitting, "LoopNet engages in *volitional conduct to block photographs*," (emphasis added), however, it reasons, "this conduct, which takes only seconds, does not amount to 'copying,' nor does it *add volition* to LoopNet's involvement in storing the copy. The employee's look is so cursory as to be insignificant. . . . In performing this gatekeeping function, LoopNet does not attempt to search out or select photographs for duplication; it merely *prevents* users from duplicating certain photographs." *Id.* (first emphasis added). In so determining that LoopNet's "gatekeeping function" does not expose it to direct infringement liability, I submit that the majority expands the non-volitional defense well beyond *Netcom* and subsequent holdings, and gives direct infringers in the commercial cybersphere far greater protections than they would be accorded in print and other more traditional media.

II

In *Netcom,* the court recognized that traditional strict liability copyright principles were ill-suited to cyberspace. *See* 907 F. Supp. at 1369-73. Bulletin board operators and other ISPs provided a forum for content, a truly open communicative space over which they exercised no control; in a sense, they were publishers who did not — and could not, because of their automated processes — review their own "publications." In recognizing the realities of this new information domain, the *Netcom* court rejected copyright owners' claims against an ISP, reasoning that the ISP did not take any affirmative action that resulted in copying plaintiffs' works other than maintaining a system through which software automatically forwarded subscribers' messages onto Usenet. *See Netcom,* 907 F. Supp. at 1368. The court observed that the ISP did not "initiate[ ] the copying," and its system operated without any human interaction, thus "the mere fact that [the ISP's] system incidentally makes temporary copies of plaintiffs' works does not mean [the ISP] has caused the copying." *Id.* at 1368-69. The *Netcom* court concluded: "Although copyright is a strict liability statute, there should still be some element of volition or causation which is lacking. . . ." *Id.* at 1370. Accordingly, the *Netcom* rule was fashioned to protect computer systems that *automatically* transfer data with no realistic manner by which the operator can monitor content. *See id.* at 1369-70 (stating plaintiff's theory "would result in liability for every single Usenet server in the worldwide link of computers transmitting [the message] to every other computer. These parties, who are liable under plaintiffs' theory, do *no more than* operate or implement a system that is essential if Usenet messages are to be widely distributed." (emphasis added)). . . .

The difference between LoopNet's conduct in this case and the protection originally afforded by *Netcom* is illustrated by examining the *Netcom* court's aforementioned statement that "Netcom did not take any affirmative action that directly resulted in copying plaintiffs' works *other than* by installing and maintaining a system whereby software *automatically* forwards messages received from subscribers onto the Usenet, and temporarily stores copies on its system." 907 F. Supp. at 1368 (emphasis added). Here, however, LoopNet's conduct with regard to the photos is anything but automatic. In contrast to the real estate property descriptions which are *automatically* uploaded to the website without any service provider input, the photos *cannot* appear on LoopNet's site *without* operator approval.

The majority tries to diminish the importance of this fact by arguing that the review is very brief and the reviewer presses a single button. At the heart of the review, however, is an inherently "volitional" action without which the subscriber's photos would not be accessible. For every photograph submitted, a LoopNet employee must determine: (1) is this real estate and (2) does the photo comply — on its face, at least — with our terms and conditions. These inquiries are the antitheses of passive, automatic actions. . . . Here, . . . humans employed by LoopNet limited the content of postings and screened and sometimes edited photos to keep quality consistent, thus taking the case far outside the previously understood scope of coverage for *Netcom*'s volitional defense.

The majority downplays LoopNet's volition, and the break from previous application of the volitional defense, by focusing on the fact that it is *the subscriber,* not LoopNet, who begins the volitional process, *i.e.,* the subscriber is the initial direct infringer. This distinction, however, is illusory, as I believe is demonstrated by analyzing LoopNet's actions through the hypothetical of a more traditional copyright context.

Consider the following example: *LoopNet Magazine* is a for-profit publication freely distributed in curbside boxes that displays commercial real estate listings. *LoopNet Magazine* solicits listings from its readership, but neither the reader who submits the listing, nor the reader accessing the listing pays for the service. Instead, *LoopNet Magazine* subsists on advertising revenue and other products it sells through the publication. Readers may electronically submit textual listings, or those with text and graphics. When *LoopNet Magazine* receives a text listing, its computers automatically transfer the content into the template for the next issue. However, when a reader submits a photograph, he or she must submit a digital image and sign a terms and conditions release stating that he or she has not infringed the copyright of the image submitted. *LoopNet Magazine* employees engage in a quick review of the images to determine that they are, in fact, pictures of real estate and that no obvious copyright has been violated.

Reader X sends *LoopNet Magazine* text describing commercial office space for rent in New York City's renowned Flatiron Building; the text describing the property is, of course, automatically inserted into the *LoopNet Magazine* template and is ready for publication. Reader X has also submitted a photograph of the Flatiron Building, and signs the terms and conditions form. Reader X knows, however, that she has not complied with the terms and conditions because the photo is not hers, rather it is Edward Steichen's 1905 photograph, *The Flatiron. LoopNet Magazine*'s Intern Y receives the photo of the Flatiron Building, notes Reader X has signed the terms and conditions, and evaluates the photo for a few seconds. Intern Y finds the image to be a beautiful depiction of the building, precisely the type of material *LoopNet Magazine* seeks to display, and does not recognize it as the copyrighted Steichen image. However, Intern Y finds that the image was "uploaded in a format that's not correct," so he takes steps to remedy the image "so that it can appear [in the publication] without any technical problems." [Quoting the deposition testimony of LoopNet's CEO.] Once properly formatted, the image appears in the next issue of *LoopNet Magazine,* and Steichen's estate sues both Reader X and *LoopNet Magazine* for direct infringement. Is *LoopNet Magazine* relieved of direct infringement liability because its screening process was most brief, a simple "yes" or "no" inquiry conducted by an intern, followed by a formatting correction? Of course not, but no different is the situation here.

That another person initiated the process which led to LoopNet's infringement is of no consequence. LoopNet remains the pivotal volitional *actor,* "but for" whose action, the images would never appear on the website. Indeed, "volition" is defined as "the act of willing or choosing[;] the act of deciding (as on a course of action or an end to be striven for)[;] the exercise of the will . . . [or] the termination of an act or exercise of choosing or willing[;] a state of decision or choice." *Webster's Third New International Dictionary of the English Language, unabridged* 2562 (1981). Under any analytical framework, LoopNet has engaged in active, volitional conduct; its employees make a conscious choice as to whether a given image will appear in its electronic publication, or whether the image will be deleted from the company's system. Nothing in the brief nature of LoopNet's review makes the company akin to a copy machine owner or a security guard by the owner's door. LoopNet *is* the publisher of *LoopNet Magazine* in cyberform; a volitional copier of images to whom direct infringement liability applies. Because I believe that the *Netcom* volitional defense should focus on passivity and the automated nature of the act — *not* the fact that a user's initial volition somehow exterminates liability for later volitional acts — I would reverse the district court. Accordingly, I respectfully dissent.

B.   Linking and Framing

The defining characteristic of the World Wide Web is the ability to link information from many sources in ways that make it easier for the viewer to access and understand the information. Thus, any substantial site is likely to refer to information that already appears at other sites, by providing a link to that information. Technologically, the links that create the World Wide Web are embedded electronic addresses that point to other Web locations. Generally, links fall into two types: *out-links,* which permit the viewer to move to another site on the Web, and *in-line links,* which in effect pull information into the browser for display from other sources (either on the present site or at another Web site). "Framing" is the process of displaying material from an in-line link within a frame or border on the current Web site. Not surprisingly, there has been considerable litigation about the propriety of including frames or links on one page that use content from another Web site without the consent of the linked or framed site.

To understand how such a dispute could arise, consider a Scottish controversy from the early days of the Internet, a 1996 dispute between the *Shetland Times* and the *Shetland News.* The *News* took verbatim headlines from the *Times* site and placed them on the *News* Web site, and then used those headlines as links to the actual stories on the *Times* site. Readers of the *News* site were able to access the *Times* stories while bypassing the advertising on the front page of the *Times'* own Web site. After a British court issued a preliminary ruling that the *News* was violating the *Times* copyright in the headlines, the parties settled the case. In the settlement, the *News* agreed to provide links only with prominent legends indicating the provenance of the stories and accompanied by the *Times* logo.

Similarly in this country, the Internet news directory service Total News, Inc. was forced in 1997 to discontinue framing at its Web site after six major media companies (including The Washington Post, Time Magazine, and the Cable News Network) brought suit. The Total News Web site provided buttons linked to the plaintiffs' various news sites and displayed the content of the plaintiffs' sites within one frame on the Total News site. At the same time, users still could see the Total News domain name (*www.totalnews.com*), logo, and advertisements. The case settled when Total News agreed to replace the framing presentation format with a more traditional hyperlink that makes jumps between different Web sites more evident to users.

There is surprisingly little discussion of the problem by the appellate courts. The most extended discussion appears in Kelly v. Arriba Soft Corporation, 336 F.3d 811 (9th Cir. 2003). In that case, Arriba Soft (now Ditto.com) operated an Internet search engine that looked for images. It displayed the results of the search in a series of small "thumbnail" images (of degraded quality). If an Arriba user wished to see a full version of the image, it could click on the thumbnail image and receive (framed in the Arriba site) the full image (at its original level of quality). The Ninth Circuit approved the use of the small images (which it characterized as a fair use under Copyright Act § 107).

It is not clear how to extend the reasoning of *Arriba Soft* to the more conventional framing context, because the court specifically declined to resolve the propriety of Arriba's actions in showing the full-quality images — a display that would parallel the conventional framing context. The question, then, is likely to be whether the use is "fair" for purposes of the Copyright Act. That inquiry is sufficiently malleable that it is difficult to predict global outcomes. A few guidelines seem clear, however. For example, friction can be minimized if the linking site clearly notes the true location of the information it displays. By preventing confusion about the source, the linking site might make the use seem more "fair" to a reviewing court. To put it another way, a link that plainly transports the user to the copyright owner's display hardly seems to present a substantial copyright problem. Another consideration is that linking is more likely to be permissible when the linked page is almost completely factual (because the Copyright Act does not provide protection for factual information). Indeed, a broad prohibition on linking would require the demolition of the search engines on which we now rely to surf the Web so effectively.

Linking controversies are more difficult when the target site relies on advertising. In that case, a link to the main or index page of the target site (normally the principal location of advertising content) is less likely to be objectionable to the target site than a link to a page deeper within the Web site (because that deeper link might cause viewers to miss the advertising content). On the other hand, deep linking has great benefits to the linking site, because it allows it to send its viewers directly to the relevant page, saving viewers the time of navigating to that page themselves (as well as the clutter of viewing all the advertisements that the linking site's users might find superfluous). To the extent that activity avoids the advertising content, however, it probably has an adverse market impact that might make the use unfair.

For example, Ticketmaster has been involved in two major disputes, in each of which other sites attempted to provide deep links to pages for purchasing tickets to particular events. Litigation with Microsoft (about a CityWalk page providing content about Seattle) settled when Microsoft agreed to link to the Ticketmaster home page rather than provide deep links into the Ticketmaster site. More recently, Ticketmaster survived a motion for summary judgment in a dispute with Tickets.com. In that case, Tickets.com provided "deep links" to the Ticketmaster site, permitting visitors to Tickets.com access to information in the Ticketmaster site without having to go through the Ticketmaster home page. Ticketmaster filed suit, presenting various claims under federal trademark law. After the district court denied a motion for summary judgment by Tickets.com, Ticketmaster Corporation v. Tickets.com, 2000 U.S. Dist. LEXIS 4533 (C.D. Cal. Mar. 27, 2000), Ticketmaster designed a way to prevent Tickets.com from creating deep links into its Web site. That mooted the dispute technologically, so no appellate resolution of the controversy is likely.

C. Respondeat Superior: E-mail, Weblogs, and Chat Rooms

Businesses that rely in any substantial way on computer technology in the workplace must address the uses of that technology by their employees. Under conventional agency and tort doctrines, including the doctrine of *respondeat superior*, employers may be liable for the conduct of their employees. In this context, that could include anything from messages sent through internal e-mail systems to postings by employees on external Web sites. For example, in Blakey v. Continental Airlines, 751 A.2d 538 (N.J. 2000), the court held that an employee stated a claim against Continental Airlines for sexual harassment based on Continental's failure to prevent other employees from publishing messages on an internal bulletin board that, plaintiff alleged, created a hostile work environment. The Court's view was that the defendant had the same duty to stop that conduct when it learned of it as it would if the comments were made in conventional office spaces. The United States Court of Appeals upheld a similar claim in Meloff v. New York Life Insurance Co., 240 F.3d 138 (2nd Cir. 2001). That case involved an employee terminated because of a dispute over her expense account. An internal e-mail advised other employees that she had been terminated for credit card fraud. The Second Circuit held that the employee's claim of defamation *by the company* warranted trial.

Many of the underlying problems are exemplified by the blog. A "blog" (short for Weblog) is a combination of an open diary and a newspaper column filled with personal opinion, excerpts from other writers, and links to other sites. The number of regular visitors and the number of sites that link to the blog are measures of the success of a blog. The popularity of blogs has been a source of great enthusiasm in cyberspace circles — perhaps the only recent example of continued flowering of the irreverent iconoclasm characteristic of the pre-commercial Internet.

From the perspective of the entities that operate the networks where blogs may appear, the blog can be a source of concern. The problems come in varied forms. The most obvious, given the personalities of many whose blogs are sufficiently interesting to be successful, is the possibility that the blogger will publish defamatory speech. Similarly, the freewheeling character of the blog easily can involve copyright infringement. The blogger might reproduce the entirety of a copyrighted news story rather than providing a link that directs interested readers to the original source. Finally, although not a source of liability to the host, the blogger might inadvertently or intentionally release proprietary information about the company's products or business plans or disclose information in ways or at times contrary to applicable securities laws.

The conceptual problem is that the blogger is at bottom a completely unconstrained disseminator of information. Thus, if the host can be held responsible for the activities of the blogger, the host faces the choice of constraining the activities of the blogger to fit corporate policies or facing liability for activities in which the host would not engage. Constraining the activities of the blogger in a substantial way raises problems of its own. If the entity is a state university for example, constraints based on subject matter or viewpoint might violate the First Amendment. Even if the First Amendment does not apply, constraints might cause low morale or stifle a culture of free inquiry that is important to the entity's mission. In addition, for reasons discussed above, businesses and other institutions that impose constraints on blogs may increase their risks if they actively monitor the content that bloggers post.

Because blogs have arisen so recently, businesses are still struggling to develop optimal responses. Among the most common elements of existing policies are rules that forbid dissemination of proprietary information and require a disclaimer dissociating the company from the content on the blog. Other common provisions include a right to limit the topics discussed on the blog as required by applicable security laws. With respect to content liability, the most typical response is a rule that permits the host to require the blogger to remove material to which the host objects and that requires the blogger to indemnify the company from any liability arising out of the activities of the blogger. In many cases, that rule is supplemented by a broader rule permitting the host to require the blogger to move the blog "off-site" — to another host — upon a request from the host. That response may become more common, as the rise of blogging aggregators (who presumably will be protected by CDA and the DMCA) should make it more common for blogs to be hosted by third parties rather than by employers or employer-supported networks.

D.   Securities Law Problems

The problems discussed above pose yet another set of issues for the public company, because of the pervasive regulation that the federal securities laws impose on the speech of public companies. That problem is particularly important given the reality that the SEC has taken a vigorous approach to these issues, instituting a substantial number of high-profile enforcement actions. Although a detailed discussion is far beyond the scope of this assignment, a summary of a few of the most obvious problems should give a sense of the efforts public companies must take to resolve these problems.

1.   The Duty to Update

One of the most common features of a corporate Web site is a section that contains all of the company's press releases. That poses a difficulty if the company fails to update the site with regularity, because information in a press release — probably long discarded by the press office — often will become misleading over time. If the misleading information remains on the Web site, however, a potential investor that reads it could complain that the company has made a misleading statement to the investor, a potential violation of Rule 10b-5, 17 CFR 240.10b-5. The SEC has imposed fines on several companies for violations of that sort.

The most obvious response to that problem is to manage the corporate Web site more actively, taking care to update and remove information as it becomes inaccurate. Appropriate disclosures also might be useful, indicating that information was thought to be accurate when issued but that investors should not rely on its accuracy after a substantial lapse of time.

2. Forward-Looking Statements

Because a corporate Web site often includes speeches and recent presentations by executives, it often will include forward-looking information about the business's plans. In the real world, predictions contained in such information often will turn out not to be entirely accurate. Disgruntled investors (and the SEC) have an opportunity to seize on the inaccuracy and sue the company under Rule 10b-5. In this context, securities cases for some time have permitted companies to avoid liability if they present the information in a way that "bespeaks caution." The Private Securities Litigation Reform Act of 1995 created a special statutory safe harbor that protects such information if companies present the forward-looking information as prescribed by the statute. 15 U.S.C. 78u-5. To take advantage of those protections, the Web site must be designed in a way to ensure that the forward-looking information always is presented together with the appropriate disclosure.

Relevant Glossary Entries

Deep Links
Frames
Media Perils Insurance
Out-link

Problem Set 7

7.1.   GigaMart.com had its initial public offering in 1999 and its stock is now listed on the Silicon Valley Stock Exchange. In 2001, its stock took a nosedive after an anonymous contributor to a chat room maintained by My-E-Brokeronline.com posted scurrilous rumors about the company.

(a)   Assuming that the allegations are false, does GigaMart.com have any recourse against My-E-Brokeronline.com? Communications Decency Act, 47 U.S.C. § 230(c), Copyright Act § 512.

(b)   Would your answer change if My-E-Brokeronline.com had instituted a program monitoring the quality of communications posted in its chat rooms? 47 U.S.C. § 230(c).

(c)   What if the material was posted to a listserv that My-E-Brokeronline. com used to provide timely and important information to "a select group of its most favored clients"?

7.2.   You have another visit this morning from Carl Eben at RiverFront Tools. Unbeknownst to Carl, one of his customers posted materials to a chat room that Carl maintains on the *www.rft.com* Web site for use by his customers. The materials included some very detailed discussions of the strengths and weaknesses of some new models of pneumatic tools. A few weeks later, Carl is served with a complaint from Pneumatic Tools Consulting (PTC). PTC claims that the content Carl's customer posted to the chat room is from PTC's annual Pneumatic Tools Review, a special report that PTC sells for $1,000 per copy. PTC is suing Carl for copyright infringement. Carl tells you that he knows nothing about copyright law or the DMCA. What can you tell Carl about his potential liability? Is there anything Carl can do (or should have done) to minimize the risk of this kind of liability? Copyright Act §§ 106, 512(c) & (i).

7.3.   PetPortal.com is an Internet portal operated by a leading producer of pet and animal magazines. Among other things, the site includes message boards for pet owners of various kinds, including dogs. One of the members of the "Pooch Partner" community (the message board for dogs maintained at the PoochPortal.com Web site) posted a very unflattering review of Mighty Meaty's new line of dog food products. Because PetPortal.com has designated an agent as required by the safe-harbor take-down provisions of the DMCA, Mighty Meaty sent to Mia Sandoval (PetPortal's designated DMCA agent) a DMCA take-down notice claiming that the unflattering review violates its copyright. Mia immediately removed the review, but later was notified by the Pooch Partner community member that the contents of the review were entirely original and could not possibly infringe the rights of Mighty Meaty.

(a)   Does PetPortal face any liability to its community member for following Mighty Meaty's instructions? Copyright Act § 512.

(b)   Does Mighty Meaty face any liability to the community member? Copyright Act § 512.

7.4.   Same facts as Problem 7.3, but assume now that the material was posted by a PetPortal employee that operates a blog. Would you in that event be concerned about liability for defamation? Copyright Act § 512; 47 U.S.C. § 230(c).

7.5.   RiverFront Tools (RFT) and Ricky's Building Wreckers enter into a linking agreement. Under the terms of the agreement, RFT will display the logo of Ricky's business on the home page of his Web site and provide a hyperlink to Ricky's site, and Ricky will do the same for RFT. The term of the linking agreement is one year, and neither side compensates the other for referrals. After the linking agreement has been in place for several months, Carl found that it has increased the volume of traffic to his site, and seems to be increasing the volume of sales he is doing with first-time customers.

A year after the signing of the linking agreement, Carl is surprised to hear that his competitor, California Pneumatic Tools (CPT) has acquired a stake in Ricky's. After CPT becomes part owner of Ricky's, it insists that Ricky remove the RFT logo and the link to the RFT Web site, and demands that Carl do the same. Carl realizes that he can't force CPT to keep the link from Ricky's site to his, and he realizes he can't use Ricky's logo on his site without permission from CPT (and Ricky). But Carl also feels that he may lose credibility with some of the first-time customers he recently acquired as a result of his linking agreement with Ricky's if he removes the link from his site to Ricky's. Can

Carl keep the hyperlink from his site to Ricky's even if CPT objects after the linking agreement expires? Copyright Act §§ 101 ("display" and "publicly"), 106, 107.

7.6.   Clarissa Janeway at WessexCard International contacts you. She just received a call from someone at the New York Stock Exchange, asking about some unusual movement in her company's stock price. After making a few quick telephone calls and examining the firm's Web site, she discovers that investors recently have taken a great deal of interest in an outdated press release that has been on the firm's Web site for about two years. Because the press release relates to a proposed merger that fell apart years ago, she removed the press release from the site earlier today. The press release was accurate when it was posted. Should she have any concerns? Rule 10b-5.

Assignment 8:   ISP Liability

The operator of a Web site is not the only party with exposure related to content. Indeed, many of the most controversial developments for the Internet have related to whether Internet service providers should be liable for content disseminated through their sites. Accordingly, it is useful to address that topic both to explore potential regulatory regimes and also to give context to the rules that govern the liability of the owner.

A.   The Role of the ISP

The proliferation of Web sites owned and operated by businesses of all sizes does not mean that all of those businesses connect directly to the Internet. To the contrary, the great majority of businesses that have Web sites connect to the Internet through the equipment of a third-party "hosting company." The hosting company itself maintains the hardware and software necessary to transmit and receive communications that are sent to and from the business's Web site. It also typically maintains the domain name's listing on the DNS, so that other computers on the Internet will be able to locate the company's Web site. For simplicity, this assignment generically refers to such a company as an ISP.

That simple reference, of course, ignores the different layers of technological activity necessary to transmit information from the company to the Internet "backbone" and from the backbone to the site of the person communicating with the company's site. To understand the process, consider the example of the University of Texas, which maintains an extensive network of computers that, among other things, are the location of the content displayed at *www.utexas.edu*. That network connects to the Internet through four ISPs: AT&T, Broadwing, Southwestern Bell, and Qwest. Whenever a message is sent from the utexas.edu domain to a location that none of those carriers serve, the carrier attempting to send the message will transmit the message to a point at which the carrier accesses the network of one of the Internet backbone providers. (The major Internet backbone providers are businesses like MCI, Sprint, UUNET, AGIS, and BBN.) Those providers, in turn, will deliver the message to an access point available to an ISP that serves the other party to the transmission. Alternatively, instead of using the backbone, occasionally the sending ISP can transfer the message to the receiving ISP at an Internet exchange point (IXP), points maintained for that purpose by groups of ISPs. Not surprisingly, each party whose facilities are used for the transmission of Internet messages charges fees to justify the investment in constructing and maintaining the backbone, exchange points, and other aspects of the network.

As that discussion suggests, the term "ISP" subsumes a variety of activities: from the wholly anonymous transmission of a backbone provider, to the wholly transmissive service that a commercial ISP provides to a domain like utexas.edu, to the partially content-based activity that a provider like AOL, MSN, or Yahoo! provide to one of their subscribers. For present purposes, the only thing that is important about that technology is that all traffic to and from the ISP's customers passes through the computers of the ISP.

The technical arrangements have two important practical consequences, which are the focus of the remainder of the assignment. First, it means that the ISP necessarily copies and distributes any information sent to or from its customers. Second, it means that the ISP, at least in theory, has an opportunity to filter out and prevent the promulgation of "bad" content. In economic terms, the ISP has the potential to serve as a "gatekeeper" that can prevent wrongful behavior that otherwise could be policed only through monitoring and regulation of the ISP's customers. At least theoretically, that could result in obligations for any party in the chain of transmission. In practical reality, however, backbone providers and other distant intermediaries are not targets for litigation. Rather, the primary targets are the ISPs who directly deal with the alleged malefactors.

B. Liability as a Publisher

As discussed in the preceding assignment, potential liability for content has been one of the most visible problems associated with the Internet. Internet service providers are in a particularly difficult position because they generally have been unable or unwilling to control the behavior of their customers. Because ISPs are easier to locate and more likely to have the assets to pay a damage award than the individuals who post libelous or infringing material on the Internet, plaintiffs upset by such postings often have tried to recover from the ISPs. A great deal of litigation and legislation has arisen out of the resulting conflict — between ISPs who want to be able to sell access to the Internet without assuming responsibility for monitoring their customers' conduct and individuals who want to proceed directly against ISPs for their customers' misconduct.

1. Defamation and the CDA

As discussed in Assignment 7, the CDA enacts a broad exemption from defamation liability for an "interactive computer service." Because the statute was intended to protect pre-Internet bulletin-board operators and "online service providers," its application to the ISP is even plainer than its application to the Web-site operator discussed in Assignment 7. That is not to say, however, that the breadth of the exemption is free from doubt.

Doe v. GTE Corp.

347 F.3d 655 (7th Cir. 2003)

Before BAUER, EASTERBROOK, and DIANE P. WOOD, Circuit Judges.

EASTERBROOK, Circuit Judge.

Someone secreted video cameras in the locker rooms, bathrooms, and showers of several sports teams. Tapes showing undressed players were compiled, given titles such as "Voyeur Time" and "Between the Lockers," and sold by entities calling themselves "Franco Productions," "Rodco," "Hidvidco — Atlas Video Release," and other names designed to conceal the persons actually responsible. All of this happened without the knowledge or consent of the people depicted. This suit, filed by football players at Illinois State University, wrestlers at Northwestern University, and varsity athletes from several other universities, named as defendants not only the persons and organizations that offered the tapes for sale (to which we refer collectively as "Franco"), plus college officials who had failed to detect the cameras (or prevent their installation), but also three corporations that provided Internet access and web hosting services to the sellers. The sellers either defaulted or were dismissed when they could not be located or served. The college officials prevailed on grounds of qualified immunity. The only remaining defendants are the informational intermediaries — large corporations, two-thirds of them solvent. The solvent defendants are GTE Corp. and Genuity Inc. (formerly known as GTE Internetworking), both of which are subsidiaries of Verizon Communications. . . . The district court dismissed all claims against them in reliance on 47 U.S.C. § 230(c). After the judgment became final with the resolution or dismissal of all claims against all other defendants — the defaulting defendants were ordered to pay more than $500 million, though there is little prospect of collection — plaintiffs filed this appeal in order to continue their pursuit of the deep pockets. . . .

According to the complaint, GTE provided web hosting services to sites such as "youngstuds.com" at which the hidden-camera videos were offered for sale. GTE did not create or distribute the tapes, which were sold by phone and through the mail as well as over the Internet. Although the complaint is not specific about just what GTE did, we may assume that GTE provided the usual package of services that enables someone to publish a web site over the Internet. This package has three principal components: (1) static IP (Internet protocol) addresses through which the web sites may be reached (a web host sometimes registers a domain name that corresponds to the IP address); (2) a high-speed physical connection through which communications pass between the Internet's transmission lines and the web sites; and (3) storage space on a server (a computer and hard disk that are always on) so that the content of the web sites can be accessed reliably. Advertisements about, and nude images from, the videos thus passed over GTE's network between Franco and its customers, and the data constituting the web site were stored on GTE's servers. Franco rather than GTE determined the contents of the site, though the complaint raises the possibility that GTE's staff gave Franco technical or artistic assistance in the creation and maintenance of its web site. Sales occurred directly between Franco and customers; communications may have been encrypted (most commercial transactions over the Internet are); and GTE did not earn revenues from sales of the tapes. Franco signed contracts with GTE promising not to use the web site to conduct illegal activities, infringe the rights of others, or distribute obscenity (a promise Franco broke). GTE thus had a contractual right to inspect each site and cut off any customer engaged in improper activity. We must assume that GTE did not exercise this right. Some domain administrators and other personnel maintaining GTE's servers and communications network may have realized the character of Franco's wares, but if so they did not alert anyone within GTE who had the authority to withdraw services. Managers were passive, and the complaint alleges that GTE has a policy of not censoring any hosted web site (that is, that GTE does not enforce the contractual commitments that Franco and other customers make).

The district court's order dismissing the complaint rests on 47 U.S.C. § 230(c), a part of the Communications Decency Act of 1996. This subsection provides:

> (c) Protection for "Good Samaritan" blocking and screening of offensive material.
>
> (1) Treatment of publisher or speaker. No provider or user of an interactive computer service shall be treated as the publisher or speaker of any information provided by another information content provider.
> (2) Civil liability. No provider or user of an interactive computer service shall be held liable on account of — (A) any action voluntarily taken in good faith to restrict access to or availability of material that the provider or user considers to be obscene, lewd, lascivious, filthy, excessively violent, harassing, or otherwise objectionable, whether or not such material is constitutionally protected; or (B) any action taken to enable or make available to information content providers or others the technical means to restrict access to material described in paragraph (1).

These provisions preempt contrary state law. "No cause of action may be brought and no liability may be imposed under any State or local law that is inconsistent with this section." 47 U.S.C. § 230(e)(3). But "[n]othing in this section shall be construed to limit the application of the Electronic Communications Privacy Act of 1986 or any of the amendments made by such Act, or any similar State law." 47 U.S.C. § 230(e)(4). We therefore start with the question whether plaintiffs have a claim under the Electronic Communications Privacy Act. [Assignment 12 discusses that statute in detail.]

Plaintiffs rely on 18 U.S.C. § 2511 and § 2520, two provisions of that statute. Under § 2511(1), "any person who — (a) intentionally intercepts, endeavors to intercept, or procures any other person to intercept or endeavor to intercept, any wire, oral, or electronic communication; (b) intentionally uses, endeavors to use, or procures any other person to use or endeavor to use any electronic, mechanical, or other device to intercept any oral communication" faces civil liability. Section 2520(a) creates a damages remedy in favor of a person "whose wire, oral, or electronic communication is intercepted, disclosed, or intentionally used in violation of this chapter". Franco and confederates intercepted and disclosed oral communications (the tapes have audio as well as video tracks) and thus are liable under § 2511 and § 2520. But what could be the source of liability for a web host?

GTE did not intercept or disclose any communication; and though one could say that its network was a "device" to do so, plaintiffs do not make such an argument (which would be equally applicable to a phone company whose lines were used to spread gossip). Instead plaintiffs say that GTE is liable for aiding and abetting Franco. Yet nothing in the statute condemns assistants, as opposed to those who directly perpetrate the act. Normally federal courts refrain from creating secondary liability that is not specified by statute. Although a statute's structure may show that secondary liability has been established implicitly, it is hard to read § 2511 in that way. Subsection 2511(1)(c) creates liability for those who wilfully disseminate the contents of unlawfully intercepted information. A statute that is this precise about who, other than the primary interceptor, can be liable, should not be read to create a penumbra of additional but unspecified liability.

What is more, GTE's activity does not satisfy the ordinary understanding of culpable assistance to a wrongdoer, which requires a desire to promote the wrongful venture's success. A web host, like a delivery service or phone company, is an intermediary and normally is indifferent to the content of what it transmits. Even entities that know the information's content do not become liable for the sponsor's deeds. Does a newspaper that carries an advertisement for "escort services" or "massage parlors" aid and abet the crime of prostitution, if it turns out that some (or many) of the advertisers make money from that activity? How about Verizon, which furnishes pagers and cell phones to drug dealers and thus facilitates their business? GTE does not want to encourage the surreptitious interception of oral communications, nor did it profit from the sale of the tapes. It *does* profit from the sale of server space and bandwidth, but these are lawful commodities whose uses overwhelmingly are socially productive. That web hosting services likewise may be used to carry out illegal activities does not justify condemning their provision whenever a given customer turns out to be crooked. Franco did not demand a quantity or type of service that is specialized to unlawful activities, nor do plaintiffs allege that the bandwidth or other services required were themselves tipoffs so that GTE, like the seller of sugar to a bootlegger, must have known that the customer had no legitimate use for the service. Just as the telephone company is not liable as an aider and abettor for tapes or narcotics sold by phone, and the Postal Service is not liable for tapes sold (and delivered) by mail, so a web host cannot be classified as an aider and abettor of criminal activities conducted through access to the Internet. Congress is free to oblige web hosts to withhold services from criminals (to the extent legally required screening for content may be consistent with the first amendment), but neither § 2511(a) nor § 2520 can be understood as such a statute.

Section 230(c)(2) tackles this problem not with a sword but with a safety net. A web host that *does* filter out offensive material is not liable to the censored customer. Removing the risk of civil liability may induce web hosts and other informational intermediaries to take more care to protect the privacy and sensibilities of third parties. The district court held that subsection (c)(1), though phrased as a definition rather than as an immunity, also blocks civil liability when web hosts and other Internet service providers (ISPs) *refrain* from filtering or censoring the information on their sites. Franco provided the offensive material; GTE is not a "publisher or speaker" as § 230(c)(1) uses those terms; therefore, the district court held, GTE cannot be liable under any state-law theory to the persons harmed by Franco's material. This approach has the support of four circuits. See *Zeran v. America Online, Inc.,* 129 F.3d 327 (4th Cir. 1997); *Ben Ezra, Weinstein & Co. v. America Online, Inc.,* 206 F.3d 980 (10th Cir. 2000); *Green v. America Online,* 318

F.3d 465 (3d Cir. 2003); *Batzel v. Smith,* 333 F.3d 1018 (9th Cir. 2003) [Assignment 7 reprints *Batzel*]. No appellate decision is to the contrary.

If this reading is sound, then § 230(c) as a whole makes ISPs indifferent to the content of information they host or transmit: whether they do (subsection (c)(2)) or do not (subsection (c)(1)) take precautions, there is no liability under either state or federal law. As precautions are costly, not only in direct outlay but also in lost revenue from the filtered customers, ISPs may be expected to take the do-nothing option and enjoy immunity under § 230(c)(1). Yet § 230(c) — which is, recall, part of the "Communications Decency Act" — bears the title "Protection for 'Good Samaritan' blocking and screening of offensive material", hardly an apt description if its principal effect is to induce ISPs to do nothing about the distribution of indecent and offensive materials via their services. Why should a law designed to eliminate ISPs' liability to the creators of offensive material end up defeating claims by the victims of tortious or criminal conduct?

True, a statute's caption must yield to its text when the two conflict, but *whether* there is a conflict is the question on the table. Why not read § 230(c)(1) as a definitional clause rather than as an immunity from liability, and thus harmonize the text with the caption? On this reading, an entity would remain a "provider or user" — and thus be eligible for the immunity under § 230(c)(2) — as long as the information came from someone else; but it would become a "publisher or speaker" and lose the benefit of § 230(c)(2) if it created the objectionable information. The difference between this reading and the district court's is that § 230(c)(2) never requires ISPs to filter offensive content, and thus § 230(e)(3) would not preempt state laws or common-law doctrines that induce or require ISPs to protect the interests of third parties, such as the spied-on plaintiffs, for such laws would not be "inconsistent with" this understanding of § 230(c)(1). There is yet another possibility: perhaps § 230(c)(1) forecloses any liability that depends on deeming the ISP a "publisher" — defamation law would be a good example of such liability — while permitting the states to regulate ISPs in their capacity as intermediaries.

We need not decide which understanding of § 230(c) is superior, because the difference matters only when some rule of state law *does* require ISPs to protect third parties who may be injured by material posted on their services. Plaintiffs do not contend that GTE "published" the tapes and pictures for purposes of defamation and related theories of liability. Thus plaintiffs do not attempt to use theories such as the holding of *Braun v. Soldier of Fortune,* 968 F.2d 1110 (11th Cir. 1992), that a magazine publisher must use care to protect third parties from harm caused by the sale of products or services advertised within its pages, and we need not decide whether such theories (if recognized by state law and applied to ISPs) would survive § 230(c). Instead, they say, GTE is liable for "negligent entrustment of a chattel," a tort that the *Restatement (Second) of Torts* § 318 encapsulates thus:

> If the actor permits a third person to use . . . chattels in his possession otherwise than as a servant, he is, if present, under a duty to exercise reasonable care so to control the conduct of the third person as to prevent him from intentionally harming others . . . if the actor (a) knows or has reason to know that he has the ability to control the third person, and (b) knows or should know of the necessity and opportunity for exercising such control.

See also Restatement (Second) of Torts § 308. The idea is that if A entrusts his car to B, knowing that B is not competent to drive, then A (if present) must exercise reasonable care to protect pedestrians and other drivers. Plaintiffs want us to treat GTE's servers, routers, and optical-fiber lines as chattels negligently "entrusted" to Franco and used to injure others. But GTE did not entrust its computers, network, or any other hardware to Franco; it furnished a service, not a chattel.

Plaintiffs do not cite any case in any jurisdiction holding that a service provider must take reasonable care to prevent injury to third parties. Consider the Postal Service or Federal Express, which sell transportation services that could be used to carry harmful articles. As far as we can discover, no court has held such a carrier liable for failure to detect and remove harmful items from shipments. That likely is why plaintiffs have not sued any delivery service for transporting the tapes from Franco to the buyers. Similarly, telephone companies are free to sell phone lines to entities such as Franco, without endeavoring to find out what use the customers make of the service. See, e.g., *Anderson v. New York Telephone Co.,* 35 N.Y.2d 746, 361 N.Y.S.2d 913, 320 N.E.2d 647 (1974) (no liability for phone company that furnished service to someone who used the connection to play a defamatory recording to all callers). Again plaintiffs have not sued any phone company.

Yet an ISP, like a phone company, sells a communications service; it enabled Franco to post a web site and conduct whatever business Franco chose. That GTE supplied some inputs (server space, bandwidth, and technical assistance) into Franco's business does not distinguish it from the lessor of Franco's office space or the shipper of the tapes to its customers. Landlord, phone company, delivery service, and web host all *could* learn, at some cost, what Franco was doing with the services and who was potentially injured as a result; but state law does not require these providers to learn, or to act as Good Samaritans if they do. The common law rarely requires people to protect strangers, or for that matter acquaintances or employees. States have enacted statutes to change that norm in some respects; Dram Shop laws are good examples. Plaintiffs do not identify anything along those lines concerning web hosts. Certainly "negligent entrustment of a chattel" is not a plausible description of a requirement that service providers investigate their customers' activities and protect strangers from harm. Nor does the doctrine of contributory infringement, offer a helpful analogy. A person may be liable as a contributory infringer if the product or service it sells has no (or only slight) legal use, see *Sony Corp. of America v. Universal City Studios, Inc.,* 464 U.S. 417 (1984); *In re Aimster Copyright Litigation,* 334 F.3d 643 (7th Cir. 2003), but GTE's web hosting services are put to lawful use by the great majority of its customers. (This is why ISPs are not liable as contributory infringers for serving persons who may use the bandwidth to download or distribute copyrighted music — and indeed enjoy safe harbors under the Digital Millennium Communications Act, discussed in *Aimster,* unless the ISP has actual notice that a given customer is a repeat infringer.) For the same reason, plaintiffs' invocation of nuisance law gets them nowhere; the ability to misuse a service that provides substantial benefits to the great majority of its customers does not turn that service into a "public nuisance."

Maybe plaintiffs would have a better argument that, by its contracts with Franco, GTE assumed a duty to protect them. No third-party-beneficiary argument has been advanced in this court, however, so we need not decide how it would fare. None of the arguments that plaintiffs now make shows that any of the states where their colleges and universities were located requires suppliers of web

hosting services to investigate their clients' activities and cut off those who are selling hurtful materials, so the district court's judgment is
   Affirmed.

The policy instinct implicit in the CDA is widespread. For example, similar provisions appear in Articles 12 through 14 of the EU Directive on Electronic Commerce. As you read the material below, however, you should consider the incentive structure that the statute creates for ISPs and whether that structure optimally regulates defamatory conduct.

2. Copyright Infringement and the Digital Millennium Copyright Act

Copyright infringement presents a similar problem. Whenever infringing material is sent to or from one of the ISP's customers because of the copying and distribution of material inherent in those activities, an ISP can be subject to copyright infringement liability. As discussed in Assignment 7, the Digital Millennium Copyright Act (DMCA) created a broad safe harbor addressed to that problem. Because ISPs do not need to store the material indefinitely, the statute does not include the complex "take-down" scheme discussed in Assignment 7. Their only affirmative obligation is the straightforward duty to terminate the service provided to persistent malefactors. Copyright Act § 512(i)(1)(A). That is not to say, however, that the statute is easy to implement. The following case illustrates, if nothing else, the perils of relying on that statute without first obtaining the advice of able counsel.

Ellison v. Robertson
357 F.3d 1072 (9th Cir. 2004)

Before PREGERSON, THOMAS, Circuit Judges, and OBERDORFER, Senior District Judge.
PREGERSON, Circuit Judge:
   Harlan Ellison appeals the district court's summary judgment dismissal of his copyright infringement action against America Online, Inc. (AOL). The copyright infringement action arose when, without Ellison's authorization, Stephen Robertson posted copies of some of Ellison's copyrighted short stories on a peer-to-peer file sharing network, the USENET.[1] Because AOL provides its subscribers access to the USENET news-group at issue, Ellison brought claims for vicarious and contributory copyright infringement against AOL. AOL moved for summary judgment. It asserted defenses to Ellison's infringement claims and alternatively argued that it qualified for one of the four safe harbor limitations of liability under Title II

---

   1. USENET is an abbreviation of "user network." This term refers to an international collection of organizations and individuals (known as "peers") whose computers connect to one another and exchange messages posted by USENET users. *See Ellison v. Robertson*, 189 F.Supp. 2d 1051, 1053 (C.D. Cal. 2002).

of the Digital Millennium Copyright Act (DMCA). The district court concluded that AOL was not liable for vicarious infringement. Although the court found there to be triable issues of material fact concerning Ellison's contributory infringement claim, it nonetheless granted summary judgment because it held that AOL qualified for the DMCA safe harbor limitation of liability under 17 U.S.C. § 512(a).

We hold that the district court erred in granting AOL's motion for summary judgment. We affirm the district court's holdings as to vicarious and contributory infringement, but we reverse the district court's application of the safe harbor limitation from liability. There are triable issues of material fact concerning whether AOL meets the threshold requirements, set forth in § 512(i), to assert the safe harbor limitations of liability of § § 512(a-d). If after remand a jury finds AOL to be eligible under § 512(i) to assert the safe harbor limitations of §§ 512(a-d), the parties need not relitigate whether AOL qualifies for the limitation of liability provided by § 512(a); the district court's resolution of that issue at the summary judgment stage is sound. We affirm in part, reverse in part, and remand.

FACTS AND PROCEDURAL BACKGROUND

Harlan Ellison is the author of numerous science fiction novels and short stories, and he owns valid copyrights to those works. In the spring of 2000, Stephen Robertson electronically scanned and copied a number of Ellison's fictional works to convert them to digital files. Robertson subsequently uploaded the files onto the USENET news-group "alt.binaries.e-book." Robertson accessed the Internet through his local Internet service provider, Tehama County Online, and his USENET service was provided by RemarQ Communities, Inc. The USENET news-group at issue in this case was used primarily to exchange unauthorized digital copies of works by famous authors, including Ellison.

After Robertson made the infringing copies of Ellison's works accessible to the news-group, the works were forwarded and copied throughout the USENET to servers all over the world, including those belonging to AOL. As a result, AOL's subscribers had access to the news-group containing the infringing copies of Ellison's works. At the time Robertson posted the infringing copies of Ellison's works, AOL's policy was to store and retain files attached to USENET postings on the company's servers for fourteen days.

On or about April 13, 2000, Ellison learned of the infringing activity and contacted legal counsel. On April 17, 2000, in compliance with the notification procedures the DMCA requires, Ellison's counsel sent an e-mail message to agents of Tehama County Online and AOL to notify the service providers of the infringing activity. Ellison received an acknowledgment of receipt from Tehama County Online but received nothing from AOL, which claims never to have received the e-mail.

On April 24, 2000, Ellison filed an action against AOL and others in the United States District Court for the Central District of California. Upon receipt of Ellison's complaint, AOL blocked its subscribers' access to the news-group at issue. AOL thereafter moved for summary judgment, arguing that the undisputed facts did not prove Ellison's copyright infringement claims. AOL alternatively asserted the safe harbor limitations to liability under Title II of the DMCA. On November 27, 2001, Ellison moved for summary judgment of his contributory and vicarious copyright infringement claims against AOL. On March 13, 2002, the district court granted AOL's summary judgment motion and denied Ellison's summary judg-ment motion. The court found that: (1) the evidence failed to establish Ellison's claims of direct and vicarious copyright infringement; (2) whether AOL was liable for contributory copyright infringement presented a triable issue of fact; (3) the evidence showed that AOL met the threshold eligibility requirements of 17 U.S.C. § 512(i) for the safe harbor limitations from liability under OCILLA* . . .; and (4) AOL *qualified* for the safe harbor limitation on liability under 17 U.S.C. § 512(a). Ellison now appeals.

DISCUSSION . . .

II. THE LAW OF COPYRIGHT INFRINGEMENT AND THE DMCA

Ellison alleges that AOL infringed his copyrighted works. As a threshold ques-tion, a plaintiff who claims copyright infringement must show: (1) ownership of a valid copyright; and (2) that the defendant violated the copyright owner's exclu-sive rights under the Copyright Act. 17 U.S.C. § 501(a). We recognize three doc-trines of copyright liability: direct copyright infringement, contributory copyright infringement, and vicarious copyright infringement. To prove a claim of direct copyright infringement, a plaintiff must show that he owns the copyright and that the defendant himself violated one or more of the plaintiff's exclusive rights under the Copyright Act. One who, with knowledge of the infringing activity, induces, causes or materially contributes to the infringing conduct *of another* may be liable as a contributory copyright infringer. [Citations, brackets, and quotation marks omitted.] . . . A defendant is vicariously liable for copyright infringement if he enjoys a direct financial benefit from *another's* infringing activity and has the right and ability to supervise the infringing activity. [Citation and quotation marks omitted.]

Congress enacted the DMCA in 1998 to comply with international copyright treaties and to update domestic copyright law for the online world. Difficult and controversial questions of copyright liability in the online world prompted Congress to enact Title II of the DMCA, the Online Copyright Infringement Liability Limitation Act (OCILLA). 17 U.S.C. § 512. OCILLA endeavors to facilitate cooperation among Internet service providers and copyright owners "to detect and deal with copyright infringements that take place in the digital networked environment." S. Rep. 105-190, at 20 (1998); H.R. Rep. 105-551, pt. 2, at 49 (1998). Congress hoped to provide "greater certainty to service providers con-cerning their legal exposure for infringements that may occur in the course of their activities." *Id.*

But "[r]ather than embarking on a wholesale clarification of" the various doc-trines of copyright liability, Congress opted "to leave current law in its evolving state and, instead, to create a series of 'safe harbors,' for certain common activi-ties of service providers." S. Rep. 105-190, at 19. Under OCILLA's four safe har-bors, service providers may limit their liability for claims of copyright infringement. 17 U.S.C. § 512(a-d). These safe harbors provide protection from

---

* The Online Copyright Infringement Liability Limitation Act (OCILLA) is Title II of the DMCA.

liability for: (1) transitory digital network communications; (2) system caching; (3) information residing on systems or networks at the direction of users; and (4) information location tools. Far short of adopting enhanced or wholly new standards to evaluate claims of copyright infringement against online service providers, Congress provided that OCILLA's "limitations of liability apply if the provider is found to be liable *under existing principles of law.*" S. Rep. 105-190, at 19 (emphasis added).

We thus agree with the district court that "[t]he DMCA did not simply rewrite copyright law for the on-line world." *Ellison,* 189 F. Supp. 2d at 1061. Congress would have done so if it so desired. Claims against service providers for direct, contributory, or vicarious copyright infringement, therefore, are generally evaluated just as they would be in the non-online world.

III. ELLISON'S CLAIMS AGAINST AOL

[After reviewing the record, the court of appeals upheld Ellison's claim for contributory infringement, reasoning that "a reasonable trier of fact could conclude that AOL materially contributed to the copyright infringement by storing infringing copies of Ellison's works . . . and providing the groups' users with access to those copies." It rejected the claim for vicarious infringement, however, explaining that "no jury could reasonably conclude that AOL received a direct financial benefit from providing access to the infringing material."]

IV. AOL AND THE SAFE HARBORS FROM LIABILITY UNDER THE DMCA

A. Threshold Eligibility Under § 512(i) for OCILLA's Safe Harbors

To be eligible for any of the four safe harbor limitations of liability, a service provider must meet the conditions for eligibility set forth in OCILLA. 17 U.S.C. § 512(i). The safe harbor limitations of liability only apply to a service provider that:

> (A) has adopted and reasonably implemented, and informs subscribers and account holders of the service provider's system or network of, a policy that provides for the termination in appropriate circumstances of subscribers and account holders of the service provider's system or network who are repeat infringers; and
> (B) accommodates and does not interfere with standard technical measures.

17 U.S.C. § 512(i)(1). If a service provider does not meet these threshold requirements, it is not entitled to invoke OCILLA's safe harbor limitations on liability. 17 U.S.C. § 512(i)(1).

We hold that the district court erred in concluding on summary judgment that AOL satisfied the requirements of § 512(i). There is at least a triable issue of material fact regarding AOL's eligibility for the safe harbor limitations of liability in this case. Section 512(i)(1)(A) requires service providers to: (1) adopt a policy that provides for the termination of service access for repeat copyright infringers in appropriate circumstances; (2) implement that policy in a reasonable manner; and (3) inform its subscribers of the policy. It is difficult to conclude as a matter of law, as the district court did, that AOL had "reasonably implemented" a policy against repeat infringers. There is ample evidence in the record that suggests that AOL did not have an effective notification procedure in place at the time the alleged infringing activities were taking place. Although AOL did notify the Copyright Office of its correct e-mail address before Ellison's attorney attempted to contact AOL and did post its correct e-mail address on the AOL website with a brief summary of its policy as to repeat infringers, AOL also: (1) changed the e-mail address to which infringement notifications were supposed to have been sent; and (2) failed to provide for forwarding of messages sent to the old address or notification that the e-mail address was inactive. *See Ellison,* 189 F. Supp. 2d at 1057-58. AOL should have closed the old e-mail account or forwarded the e-mails sent to the old account to the new one. Instead, AOL allowed notices of potential copyright infringement to fall into a vacuum and to go unheeded; that fact is sufficient for a reasonable jury to conclude that AOL had not reasonably implemented its policy against repeat infringers.

B.   AOL AND THE LIMITATION OF LIABILITY UNDER § 512(a)

If after remand a jury finds AOL eligible under § 512(i) to assert OCILLA's safe harbor limitations of liability, the court need not revisit whether AOL qualifies for the limitation of liability provided by § 512(a).

The first safe harbor in OCILLA pertains to "transitory digital network communications." 17 U.S.C. § 512(a). Under this section, a service provider would not be liable for copyright infringement:

> by reason of the provider's transmitting, routing, or providing connections for, material through a system or network controlled or operated by or for the service provider, or by reason of the intermediate and transient storage of that material in the course of such transmitting, routing, or providing connections, if—
> (1) the transmission of the material was initiated by or at the direction of a person other than the service provider;
> (2) the transmission, routing, provision of connections, or storage is carried out through an automatic technical process without selection of the material by the service provider;
> (3) the service provider does not select the recipients of the material except as an automatic response to the request of another person;
> (4) no copy of the material made by the service provider in the course of such intermediate or transient storage is maintained on the system or network in a manner ordinarily accessible to anyone other than anticipated recipients, and no such copy is maintained on the system or network in a manner ordinarily accessible to such anticipated recipients for a longer period than is reasonably necessary for the transmission, routing, or provision of connections; and
> (5) the material is transmitted through the system or network without modification of its content.

Id. The definition of "service provider" for the purposes of the § 512(a) safe harbor limitation of liability is "an entity offering the transmission, routing, or providing of connections for digital online communications, between or among points specified by a user, of material of the user's choosing, without modification to the content of the material as sent or received." 17 U.S.C. § 512(k)(1)(A).

Whether AOL functioned as a conduit service provider in this case presents pure questions of law: was the fourteen day period during which AOL stored and retained the infringing material "transient" and "intermediate" within the meaning of §512(a)?; was "no . . . copy . . . maintained on the system or network . . . for a longer period than is reasonably necessary for the transmission, routing, or provision of connections?" The district court appropriately answered these questions in the affirmative. In doing so, the court relied upon on the legislative history indicating that Congress intended the relevant language of §512(a) to codify the result of *Netcom,* 907 F. Supp. at 1361 (provider that stored Usenet messages for 11 days not liable for direct infringement merely for "installing and maintaining a system whereby software automatically forwards messages received from subscribers onto the Usenet, and temporarily stores copies on its system"), and to extend it to claims for secondary liability. We affirm the district court's ruling that AOL is eligible for the safe harbor limitation of liability of §512(a).

To the extent that the DMCA does not offer a wholesale exemption from liability, the framework that it establishes falls within the general category of "gatekeeper" liability. That is to say, because the ISP is the party in the chain that is most easily identified and most likely to be solvent, a good case can be made — at least in cases where infringement is easily verifiable and not plausibly disputable — that the ISP should be obligated to take reasonable steps to prevent the wrongful conduct. What reasons justify a differing framework for defamatory and copyright-infringing speech?

C.   A Note on Gatekeeper Liability

The statutes discussed in the previous section reflect Congress's firm commitment to two intertwined policy perspectives on ISPs. The first is that any active regulatory intervention on the Internet poses an unacceptably high risk of hindering the rapid development of online commerce, with all the attendant benefits. As the Introduction notes, that perspective is characteristic of the early stage of "pioneer" economic territories. The materials in the last two assignments (and in other assignments in the chapters that follow) show that the so-called "growth-of-the-Internet" perspective is not limited to a level-playing-field approach that would discourage new Internet-targeting regulatory initiatives. Rather, the dominant perspective acts to exempt the Internet even from the natural application of existing regulatory regimes.

The second related perspective concerns ISPs directly. Generally, this perspective reflects the idea that an ISP should not be expected to do anything about malfeasance by its customers. Under that perspective, it is reasonable to exempt an ISP from liability for copyright infringement and defamation because the ISP can do nothing about that activity. Thus, any copyright infringement is a technicality and the idea of liability for the transmission of a defamatory "publication" is outmoded.

As technology has developed, however, it is clear in many contexts that an ISP is in a position to hinder wrongful conduct by those whose transmissions pass through its network. As a matter of economic theory, this ordinarily is referred to as "gatekeeper" liability — imposing obligations on an intermediary not because of malfeasance by the intermediary but because of the need for the malefactors to conduct their activities through the intermediary.

The ability of ISPs to deal with malfeasance potentially could be valuable in many contexts. In some cases, this is made clear by market-driven activities of the ISPs themselves. For example, consider the plague of UCE discussed in Assignment 6. A prominent feature of competition among the most successful consumer ISPs is the sophistication and effectiveness of the filters that those ISPs use to prevent UCE from reaching their customers. Indeed, as Assignment 6 notes, it is the ISPs — not the FTC or the aggrieved consumers — that seem to be taking the lead role in litigation against the largest purveyors of UCE.

Another major regulatory issue in Internet commerce is gambling. For obvious reasons, ISPs are convenient targets for regulatory activity in the area: online gambling businesses can locate themselves "offshore," using the Internet to make it difficult for regulatory authorities to locate the individuals or their assets. Conversely, it is not particularly palatable or effective to target the individuals that use the services. One of the most effective responses would be to work through the ISPs. For example, it would be technologically feasible for ISPs to refrain from forwarding traffic to or from specified Web sites. By preventing customers from reaching the sites in question, such a rule might have a more cost-effective impact on unlawful gambling operations than anything that could be implemented against the wrongdoers.

As you work through the problems below, and as you read on through the chapters to come, you should consider whether the applicable legal rules seem to take adequate notice of the potential capabilities of the ISPs to participate in the response to misconduct facilitated by the Internet.

Relevant Glossary Entry

Internet Service Provider (ISP)

Problem Set 8

8.1.   Same facts as Problem 7.1, but now you represent World Hosting & Internet Provider (WHIP), a major provider of hosting services to Web-based businesses. Does WHIP have any potential liability for the message posted in the chat room? Communications Decency Act, 47 U.S.C. §230.

8.2.   A few weeks later, you get another call from your contact at WHIP. On this occasion, the concern relates to *www.freebiemovies.com*, a site for which WHIP provides Internet-related services. WHIP has just been served with a complaint by the Motion Picture Association of America. The complaint contends that WHIP is liable for copyright infringement because copyright-infringing copies of movies have been sent to and from the WHIP site. The general counsel explains to you that all of the content at the site in question resides on servers entirely within the control of FreebieMovies.

(a)   First, assume that WHIP provides both hosting and communications services, so that all content on the Web site resides on a server owned by WHIP, under a contract that permits FreebieMovies to post material to that server. Does WHIP have any potential exposure? Copyright Act §§ 106, 512.

(b)   How does your answer change if the only service provided by WHIP is a communications service? Thus, all content on the FreebieMovies site resides on a server owned and under the exclusive control of FreebieMovies, but all signals to and from the site travel through WHIP's network. Copyright Act §§ 106, 512.

(c)   Does your answer depend on anything about WHIP's information-retention policies — how long it saves copies of information that passes through its network? Copyright Act § 512.

8.3.   You get a call this morning from the general counsel of Wolverine Access, an Internet Service Provider that provides broadband Internet access in Ann Arbor, Michigan, targeting University of Michigan students dissatisfied with the University-provided Internet access. Wolverine has just been served with a demand letter from the Recording Industry Association of America (RIAA). The letter lists 37 customers of Wolverine (about 10 percent of its total customer base), all alleged to have downloaded at least two pieces of copyright-infringing music. Assume for the time being that the RIAA's allegations of infringement are correct as a matter of substantive copyright law (a topic discussed further in Assignment 21), if they could prove the allegations factually. The demand letter states that if Wolverine does not terminate services for those 37 customers immediately, the RIAA will file suit directly against Wolverine charging Wolverine with copyright infringement and seeking "thousands and thousands" of dollars in statutory damages. Wolverine is reluctant to terminate the service of these customers. For one thing, it is worried that its market appeal to college students will be diminished if it gives in too easily to this complaint. What can you tell Wolverine about its potential exposure? Copyright Act §§ 106, 504, 512.

8.4.   Your last project of the week comes from an e-mail from an old college friend who works at NWBell, a major ISP in the Pacific Northwest. Your friend tells you that NWBell has developed technology for a sophisticated "decency" monitor. The monitor would examine all incoming and outgoing traffic for content that is pornographic or otherwise "indecent." The service would work both for e-mail traffic and for Web browsing. Customers would pay five dollars a month for the service, in return for which NWBell would undertake to protect the customers in two ways. First, it would prevent the customers' browsers from reaching any sites displaying indecent content. Second, it would ensure that no e-mail messages including indecent content would be sent to (or transmitted from) the customers' addresses. Your friend wants to know whether you foresee any exposure to the company from this program. What do you say?

8.5.   A few days later, you get a call from Congresswoman Pamela Herring. Because NWBell is in her congressional district, she has heard about this potential program. She is considering the enactment of a bill that would obligate ISPs that serve consumers to provide a service like the one that NWBell is considering. She wants your view on whether such a regulation would be a good idea, asking for a position paper on the subject in three days. (She asks you to assume that the program is technologically feasible.) What would you tell her?

The Camford Books Problem

(Part II)

Your friends at Camford Books are now in the process of setting up their site. As their *de facto* general counsel, they seek advice from you on any Web site–related legal problems that they should consider. "We know books. You know the Web, so just tell us what to do and we'll do it." They have a protected trademark in the name "Camford Books." They have brought a few questions of their own, but welcome any broader advice you might offer.

1. What steps should they take to obtain and protect a domain name?
2. What are the major legal issues they should consider in designing their Web site?
3. They assume that they will post their catalog and a price list on the Internet. Will this make it easier for their competitors to monitor and undercut their prices?
4. They previously have published newsletters with reviews of books in the area, selected from the best reviews published in major newspapers. Should they have any special concerns about continuing that activity on the Internet?
5. They expect their site to include a feature encouraging their customers to post reviews of books that their customers have read, as a resource to other customers considering whether to purchase books.
6. Not surprisingly, given the literary bent of their employees, they expect that several employees will operate blogs. Does that raise any special concerns?
7. What else would you recommend to mitigate other forms of liability that might arise out of operation of the site?

Chapter 3.   Protecting Information

Assignment 9:   Protecting Information: The Basics

Just as businesses can violate the legal rights of others by displaying information, they also can be liable for misusing or failing to protect information that they acquire in the operation of the site. The classic hypothetical is a regrettably familiar one: an online retailer has a database of information about its customers and their transactions. What is the liability of the retailer to its customers if a third party steals the information or if the retailer voluntarily sells the information to a third party? The next three assignments consider that issue from different perspectives. This assignment introduces the topic of information collection on the Internet. It then considers the extent to which a business may be exposed to tort liability if the information is stolen by a third party. Finally, it discusses the existing statutory limitations on voluntary uses the business makes of the information. The next assignment considers the more restrictive statutory scheme in place in the European Union. The third assignment addresses privacy policies and the extent to which a business is liable as a matter of contract.

A.   Clickstream Data, Online Profiling, and Data Warehousing

The open architecture of the Internet has created an environment in which it is much easier to collect data than it used to be. Operators of commercial Internet sites can capture information about individuals in several ways. The most obvious way is to ask individuals for information. For example, some commercial Web sites such as *www.nytimes.com* provide services to customers without charge, but require customers to register to gain access to important portions of the site. When registered customers visit *www.nytimes.com*, they must first log in with a user ID and password. After they log in, their online behavior can be associated with the personal information provided when they registered.

When an individual visitor to a Web site clicks on a link, the individual's computer sends a message to the server hosting the Web site. That message includes some or all of the following "clickstream" information: the visitor's IP address; the Internet location from which the visitor came (known as the referring site); the type of browser software the visitor is using; preferences specified in the browser software by the visitor; the time and duration of the visit; purchase or other transaction information; and the pages requested by the visitor from the site being visited. Often, a Web-site owner can capture clickstream information about its visitors and retain the information for later analysis. Sometimes the analysis is limited to traffic-related issues, such as the number of pages delivered to visitors, how long it took to load a completed page, and how much data was transmitted. Once visitors register and log in, however, clickstream data can be tied to a particular individual. In 1999, Intel embedded identity numbers in its Pentium III personal computer chips that would have made it easier to tie clickstream data more closely to a specific computer (and, by extension, to the user of that computer). The proposal resulted in such a huge outcry from privacy advocates (the "Big Brother Inside" campaign against Intel) that Intel the next year abandoned efforts to develop and market the technology.

Although the particular product developed by Intel to tie individuals to online behavior failed, other technologies can accomplish similar objectives. One of the important advances in networked computing technology in recent years has been the ability to use computer programs (often called applets) to distribute computing processes throughout a network; the applets typically are sent together with text or images from a Web server to a browser running on a personal computer. For example, a Web server can send ActiveX, Java, or JavaScript applets to a computer that requests pages from the site; the applets can help the requesting computer create animations or perform calculations or can even cause the requesting computer to send back to the server copies of information from the visitor's computer. The applet may be (and usually is) sent without the end user's knowledge; the applet's functions normally are not discernible to the ordinary user. For example, an applet could send back to the server a copy of the browser's "history file," which keeps a record of all Web pages the end user has visited recently. That type of undisclosed end-user monitoring resulted in a number of class-action lawsuits against RealNetworks.

A related tool is the "cookie" — a text file that a Web server places on the hard drive of a computer that requests a page from the site. The technology for placing cookies on the hard drives of individual users of Internet browsers was first developed with Netscape version 1.1, with a view to making it easier for individual users to access Web sites without having to reenter identifying information each time. The use of cookies to identify users and track their movements is no longer limited to movements on a single Web site; cookies now can track a user's movements from site to site. Because the cookie files on a user's hard drive are placed there by servers at Web sites that the user visits, they normally will not contain any information identifying the individual user. Still, if the user provides personally identifying information online (by filling out a registration form, for example), the party using the cookie to collect clickstream data may be able to associate the browsing history with a real-world identity.

"Web bugs" are a variation of cookies, but instead of text files they usually are graphic images that are invisible to the visitor to a Web site using them. A Web bug permits someone to monitor who is looking at a Web page or an e-mail message. The operator of the Web bug can collect the same clickstream data that the operator of the Web site hosting the Web bug can. A Web bug is normally a one-pixel-by-one-pixel graphic file that is placed on a Web site or in an e-mail message that uses HTML formatting. It is invisible to the viewer because it is set to match the color of the background and takes up almost no space on a computer monitor anyway. The Web-bug operator obtains the data normally found in cookies by collecting the sites that users are visiting when the Web bug is sent to the users' computers. The simplest way to detect Web bugs ordinarily is to review the HTML source code and discover that the source of an image is a different Web server than the rest of the page. For ordinary users, that is a difficult and cumbersome process. Moreover, unlike cookies, Web bugs ordinarily cannot be prohibited by conventional Internet browser settings.

The term "spyware" — a broad, pejorative term used to describe this technology generally — captures the general view of many in the Internet community that surreptitious collection of information is ethically wrong and that it cannot be justified either by the profits gained by exploitation of the technology or by the benefits such technologies may confer on the individuals about whom information is collected. That aversion to spyware is in tension with the economic value of the information. Marketing companies combining clickstream data and registration or survey information can create a sophisticated "profile" of an individual. That profile can foster predictions about the individual's tastes and proclivities, which in turn can be used to create personalized marketing appeals. Those marketing campaigns include the display of banner ads with content designed to appeal to particular individuals (familiar to any repeat user of a major Internet retailer), as well as e-mail or offline solicitations.

Business groups argue that targeted advertising provides value to both consumers and businesses by reducing the volume of unwelcome advertising and by providing consumers with useful information about products and services likely to be of interest. Privacy and consumer advocates who object to profiling find it problematic that the process is carried on without the knowledge or consent of consumers, who are not normally given any opportunity to "opt-out" or limit what use is made of the profile information once it has been created.

Still, some business organizations are committed to finding a way to use the marketing potential of the Internet and profiling technologies while still respecting the privacy preferences of individuals. For example, some have suggested a move toward permission marketing, electronic marketing campaigns based on "opt-in" by the individual being targeted. At least in the United States, however, there have been few significant moves in that direction.

Individuals who wish to stop the undisclosed and unauthorized collection of information about their online behavior are not powerless. In addition to modifying the cookies settings in browser software, they can manually delete cookies from the hard drive of a computer, or use more sophisticated "cookie-cutter" software that applies different criteria to restrict the types of cookies the user's system will accept. Individuals also can use "identity scrubbers" to remain anonymous while accessing Internet sites. These normally involve routing e-mail and requests for Web content through a third-party service that removes all identifying information before transmitting any message or request. Another option is an "identity manager" application, which ensures that an individual's privacy preferences are consistently enforced. Of course, individuals that choose to use those technologies may find themselves unable to use sophisticated retail sites that depend on that technology for the purchasing process.

A final concept of import here is the data warehouse. Businesses use relational databases to handle the administration of transactional affairs related to such things as customer accounts, employment records, and inventory. A data warehouse, by contrast, is not used to process transactional information, but rather is a huge collection of information collected from a variety of sources, including historical transaction data. Businesses use that warehouse for "mining" in an effort to discover relations between particular customer and transactional characteristics of which the business was not previously aware. When successful, that kind of data mining can give a company a strategic advantage in identifying market trends and directing company resources to the most profitable opportunities. Accordingly, some businesses can even use those databases as revenue sources, by licensing them to other businesses for mining related to the products of the licensee business. All of those operations, of course, can have an adverse effect on the privacy interests of individuals about whom the warehouses include information.

B. Tortious Failure to Protect Data

Not surprisingly, the increasing value of information has led to concerns about the failure of businesses to protect data. This is but one instance of a more general problem — the failure to maintain adequate security — which can cause a variety of problems for Internet-related businesses. One obvious concern is that a site or a server operated without adequate security might result in the transmission of viruses that cause harm in any of a number of ways: to the site (through alteration of its content), to the server (through alteration of its software), to those that visit it. In some cases, the server will be involved in harm in a transitory way — as it is used to facilitate the further transmission of a virus. Similar problems arise when inadequate security might leave the site vulnerable to hackers who wish to harm the site, disrupt its operations, or take information from the site. If a server is disrupted, for example, parties who rely on continuous operation may incur substantial losses, which they may seek to recover from whoever is responsible. For present purposes, we note that the loss of information has been a highly visible problem in recent years, as a number of major entities — OfficeMax, IKEA, CDUniverse, and the federal Department of Commerce to name a few — have found proprietary or personal information on their Web sites freely available to the public. Related to that problem, consider the case of a business whose site is hacked, information compromised, and yet may have little or no incentive to inform the victims whose information was compromised. See Cal. Civ. Code §1798.82 (state-law obligation to notify customers of a breach of security information). Finally, there is growing concern about the possibility of a concerted attack on government and business computers connected to the Internet.

   In cases where third parties cause the harm in question, the third party obviously is subject to civil and criminal sanctions. Given the limited financial responsibility that is typical of those who engage in that activity, the more pressing question for the business or for the regulator is whether liability appropriately might be imposed on some other party — such as the business that failed to maintain the security of its site. As a matter of economic policy, the basic question would be to identify which party is the "least-cost-avoider" of the harms in question. That question suggests the possibility of liability for a variety of parties in the chain. For example, some knowledgeable software experts argue that the security difficulties that plague existing computers are attributable to remediable flaws in software design. If that is true, it would suggest that an appropriate response would be to impose liability on the software designer. This would be a typical products liability claim, much like the liability of a business that sells a lawnmower without incorporating obvious safety features that would prevent harms incident to the operation of the lawnmower.

One complicating feature of imposing liability on the software designer is the need to give the software designer an ongoing incentive to upgrade software to respond to the rapidly advancing technology of malicious software developers. Thus, it is evident that a great part of the harm caused by hackers and viruses relates to flaws for which software developers already had distributed patches that would have prevented the harm — had the patch only been widely implemented. Software designers plausibly can say that their responsibility is satisfied when they have distributed a patch that repairs a flaw. Indeed, designers would argue in contrast, it is entirely proper to impose liability on a business that fails to implement a patch that would have prevented some harm that occurs at the business's server or site. Critics of software designers, on the other hand, argue that a carefully designed software product would not have been vulnerable in the first instance and thus would not require incessant patching.

Another obvious possibility is liability on the part of the owner or host of the site. If the designer of the software that is exploited is not the least-cost avoider, then the operator or host of the site might be the least-cost avoider. This would obviously be true, for example, in cases in which the operator or host of the site failed to implement standard security precautions. This might be true not only in failure-to-patch cases discussed above, but also in cases that challenge the basic programs that the operator has decided to implement.

Again, although there is not yet any substantial judicial analysis of that question, the underlying tort principles are easy to discern. The basic argument would be that the security breaches reflect negligence on the part of the operator of the site. Security experts argue that the overwhelming majority of the incidents in which information has been stolen involve a failure of the site to conform to the best available security technology. Indeed, commercial Web sites fail to conform to available security procedures with such disappointing regularity that a business operating a site often might be able to show — even after a breach of security — that its security procedures were reasonable in the sense that they conformed to industry standards.

The problem is complicated by the difficulty businesses face in developing "reasonable" security systems that would not be found negligent by a factfinder evaluating the system's security after a serious breach of security has occurred. Computer-security standards are developing so rapidly that there is no reliable, standard metric against which businesses can compare their systems. The most that businesses can do is try to identify the "best practices" in their respective industries and do their best to conform to those practices. For example, the federal government has created a Web site posting best practices developed by different government agencies, together with feedback from users who have tried to implement those best practices. Each best-practice document describes the legal and technical standards upon which it is based and an explanation of how to implement the best practice in another organization. Another good source of information is the federal government's National Infrastructure Protection Center (NIPC, pronounced "nip-see"), which provides a clearinghouse of information for private-sector organizations about current developments in computer security, as well as information about appropriate responses to computer security incidents.

A private endeavor along similar lines is the CERT Coordination Center sponsored by the Software Engineering Institute of Carnegie Mellon University. Another is the Internet Engineering Task Force (IETF), a voluntary standards-developing organization whose hallmark is its openness and pragmatism, as summed up in its requirement of "rough consensus and running code." The typical standard-developing process finalizes a standard first and then sends it out for implementation. IETF, in contrast, requires two successful implementations *before* it recognizes a proposed standard. It also does not require unanimity among members of a working group, or even have formal voting procedures. Instead, it allows working-group leaders to proceed based on their sense of the consensus of the members of the working group. If none of those endeavors provide any information, there is always the possibility that industry trade associations can provide useful information.

The coverage of those endeavors is haphazard and spotty at best, but it does provide some opportunity for a business to determine what most businesses in a particular industry are doing. Still, even if a business could determine that its systems are as secure as is typical of the relevant industry, it could not be sure that it would be insulated from liability. First, it always would have to fear the likelihood that evaluation in hindsight — after a breach has occurred — will look critically on a system and conclude that the designers should have understood the deficiencies of the system much more clearly than they in fact could have understood them before the breach. The practices that looked "best" before the breach might look sadly deficient afterward.

More broadly, basic principles of economics suggest that courts will not find businesses innocent solely because of conformance to industry standards. As Learned Hand explained in his classic opinions in The T.J. Hooper, 60 F.2d 737 (2nd Cir. 1932), and United States v. Carroll Towing Co., 159 F.2d 169 (2nd Cir. 1947), compliance with industry standards does not always establish the reasonableness of conduct. In Judge Hand's view, the reasonableness of conduct should be judged as a matter of economics: Would the costs of better protections exceed the likelihood of loss multiplied by the size of the anticipated loss? If businesses in a particular industry systematically underestimate the gravity and likelihood of losses from inadequate security, perhaps *all* businesses in that industry are behaving negligently. Because the harms caused by a loss of information are borne in the first instance by the customers rather than the businesses, there is good reason to think that businesses might not be adequately motivated to invest in systems to prevent such losses. Standard tort theory suggests that tort liability shifting those losses to the party whose inadequate security caused the losses might improve the incentive to invest in security.

On the other hand, several other tort doctrines suggest reasons why businesses might escape liability in many cases. For example, some courts might find it inappropriate to hold a business liable in tort for harms caused by third parties who hack the business's site. The analysis of that line of defense would resemble the defense of a landowner in cases where a tenant tries to hold the landlord responsible for criminal acts of third parties that harm the tenant on the landlord's property. The D.C. Circuit, for example, held in the well-known case of Kline v. 1500 Massachusetts Avenue Apartment Corp., 439 F.2d 477 (D.C. Cir. 1970), that a landlord *is* liable for those activities where the premises are "peculiarly under the landlord's control." Application of a similar principle in this context might make businesses liable for injuries suffered from misconduct that affects information stored on the business's Web site.

Another possible defense is the economic loss rule, which traditionally has denied recovery in tort cases for economic losses in the absence of physical damages. Again, this rule has softened considerably in recent years, particularly in situations in which negligent conduct exposes a class of persons as a group to a predictable type of economic damages. E.g., People Express Airlines v. Consolidated Rail Corp., 495 A.2d 107 (N.J. 1985).

In sum, this is an area that is ripe for judicial development. As you proceed through the assignments that follow, you should consider as a normative matter whether you think it is appropriate to impose tort liability in these situations, and more broadly, whether you think it would be effective. Consider in particular the differing effects of regulation by tort, statute, and contract.

C.   Statutory Obligations to Protect Data

In some cases, the problem will not be that data is stolen from a business, but that a business wishes to use the data itself, for the valuable purposes discussed in the opening pages of this assignment. Although there is little development as yet on the principles that will guide tort liability for failure to protect data, there are decades of thought on the principles that guide statutory liability. The problem is complicated by starkly differing perspectives on the appropriate statutory scheme. One possibility is a broad scheme of fair information practices, which closely regulate the permissible uses that businesses might make of data. Another possibility is a targeted approach that provides specific protections to particularly sensitive types of data. The sections that follow summarize the development of the concept of fair information practices, the cross-cutting development of technological methods for exploiting Internet-related data, and finally the most important statutory scheme regulating Internet-related data, the Children's Online Privacy Protection Act (COPPA).

1.   Fair Information Practices

The concept of fair information practices dates to 1973, when the Secretary of Health, Education, and Welfare released an advisory committee report on *Records, Computers and the Rights of Citizens*. That report recommended the recognition of a code of "fair information practices" based on the following principles:

- There should be no secret collections of personal data.
- There should be a way for a person to find out what information has been collected and how it is used.
- There should be a way for a person to prevent information that was obtained for one purpose from being used or made available for other purposes without the person's consent.
- There should be a way for a person to correct or amend a record of identifiable information about the person.
- Any organization creating, maintaining, using, or disseminating records of identifiable personal data should assure the reliability of the data for their intended use and must take precautions to prevent misuses of the data.

Responding to that report, as well as congressional hearings on the harassment of opponents of the Nixon administration through the use of personal information contained in government computer databases, Congress in 1974 enacted the Privacy Act to prevent misuse of personal information held by the federal government. The Privacy Act incorporates many of the concepts of fair information practices, but applies them only to government databases. Other similar limited-purpose statutes include the Buckley Amendment, 20 U.S.C. §1232g (regulating student records), the Right to Financial Privacy Act of 1978, 12 U.S.C. §§3401 et seq. (regulating bank-account records), the Cable Communications Privacy Act, 47 U.S.C. §551 (regulating information collected from cable-television customers), the Video Privacy Act, 18 U.S.C. §2710 (regulating information about video rentals), the Telephone Consumer Protection Act, 47 U.S.C. §227 (the poorly enforced statute regulating unsolicited telephone calls), the Driver's Privacy Protection Act, 18 U.S.C. §§2721 et seq. (regulating driver's license records), and the Identity Theft and Assumption Deterrence Act, 18 U.S.C. §1028 (regulating identity theft).

In 1980, the Organization of Economic Cooperation and Development (OECD) (an organization of industrialized nations) published its *Guidelines on the Protection of Privacy and Transborder Flows of Personal Data*, which were influenced by the earlier HEW report. The *Guidelines* included principles providing that individuals should be notified when personal data is being collected; that the amount of personal data collected and the uses to which it could be put should be limited; that data collected for one purpose should not later be used for another; that personal data should not be disclosed without the consent of the subject; that it should be kept secure; that individuals should have a means of learning who collected data about them; that individuals should be allowed to access data that has been collected about them and to have corrections made if the data is not accurate; and that there should be some means of holding those who collect personal data accountable for compliance with these principles. The OECD *Guidelines* form the foundation of data protection laws in the European Union and other countries that have laws recognizing general information privacy rights. The next assignment discusses the EU framework to provide a contrast to the U.S. approach.

In recent debates in the United States regarding fair information practices, that long list of factors often is pared down to four basic elements: notice, consent, access, and security. (Another two elements, enforcement and "chain of trust," also appear on some lists; chain of trust refers to the ability to ensure the conduct of third parties to whom the data is transferred.) Although that list is a gross oversimplification of the concept of fair information practices, it is a useful heuristic in evaluating the content of rules governing the collection and use of personal information. For example, the Federal Trade Commission summarized fair information practices as requiring those elements in its June 1998 report to Congress on online privacy. (The most telling omissions from this list when compared with the OECD *Guidelines* are the ideas that the collection of information itself should be limited and that information collected for one purpose should not be used for another.)

In the United States, the Watergate-era political commitment to protecting information faded considerably during the 1980s and 1990s. As a result, during a period when businesses in the United States developed very sophisticated and powerful marketing technologies that depended on the collection and analysis of detailed personal information, Congress passed no major statutes regulating those activities. As a result, few American businesses took any notice of fair information practices while developing the systems they use today to collect and process personal information. Only in the late 1990s, when the collection and use of personal information on the Internet became a controversial topic, did the idea gain significant political support. In recent years, there have been repeated calls for legislation mandating general compliance with fair information practices. Those proposals, however, face staunch opposition from business organizations that have developed substantial businesses that rely on large amounts of personal information, most prominently for marketing purposes (attempting to design products and advertising programs) and credit purposes (attempting to assess credit risk). Congress has enacted new protections in a few areas: for financial records in Gramm-Leach-Bliley and health records in the Health Insurance Portability and Accountability Act. But in the area of the Internet — where data protection is a salient public issue — the only major statutory protection that approaches compliance with conventional fair information practices is for data covered by the COPPA, the subject of the next section.

2. COPPA

Congress passed the Children's Online Privacy Protection Act of 1998 (COPPA), 15 U.S.C. §§6501-6506, in response to general outrage at the practices of operators of Web sites that target children in the collection and use of personal information. The FTC implemented that statute with its Children's Online Privacy Protection Rule (COPPA Rule, 16 C.F.R. pt. 312). Although

COPPA and the COPPA Rule both are limited to children under age 13, the legislation is significant for Internet commerce because it is the first U.S. privacy law that imposes substantial obligations on Web-site operators.

The tipping point that led to COPPA was the FTC's 1998 report on the information practices of operators of Web sites that target children. The survey triggered widespread public outcry over the aggressive and unregulated information practices of businesses operating Web sites targeted at children. The survey pointed out that children are a large and rapidly growing segment of online consumers. Because American children are consumers in their own right and often influence their parents' consumption choices, marketing to American children is a big business supported by the collection and analysis of personal information about children. The aggressive information practices of Web-site operators were troubling because of the ability of those operators to engage children directly and circumvent parental supervision. By engaging children without parental supervision, the operators could encourage children to reveal personal information in a manner that might raise serious safety concerns. The FBI and Justice Department confirmed that predators seeking to identify and contact children for illicit purposes relied heavily on personal information about children that was accessible on the Web.

Moreover, even aside from safety concerns, there is a general sentiment that it is offensive to collect and use personal information from children for marketing purposes. According to FTC survey data, 97 percent of parents whose children use the Internet believed Web sites should not sell or rent personal information relating to children, and 72 percent objected to a Web site's requesting a child's name and address when the child registers at the site, even if the site only uses the information internally.

The 1998 FTC privacy online report revealed that 89 percent of the 212 Web sites covered by the survey (all of which were sites targeting children) collected personal information. Types of personal information commonly collected from children included name, e-mail address, postal address, telephone number, and Social Security number, as well as other personal information like age or date of birth, gender, education, interests, hobbies, or even financial information. Web sites used a variety of techniques to solicit personal information from children. For example, some sites required children to answer questions about their interests in order to register or to become eligible to win prizes. Other sites used "imaginary" characters to request information from children, had children sign a "guest book," solicited information to create home pages for children, invited children to participate in chat and electronic pen-pal programs, required children to register with the site for updates and information, and offered prizes and other incentives for completing surveys and polls. Only 1 percent of the sites in the survey required parental consent to the collection and use of information before collecting or using the information; only 8 percent gave parents the right to force deletion or removal from the server of personal information that the site previously had collected from their children.

The COPPA Rule applies to commercial Web-site operators if their sites target children or if they have actual knowledge that they are collecting information from children. 16 C.F.R. §312.3. The FTC will determine whether a Web site targets children in light of the overall appearance and content of the Web site. 16 C.F.R. §312.2 (definition of "Website or online service directed to children"). An operator of a general Web site could have actual knowledge that personal information has been collected from a child in a variety of ways: for example, it would be evident if an individual lists "elementary school" in response to a query about employment. The COPPA Rule applies to information that might permit someone to identify or contact the child, such as full name, address, e-mail address, telephone number. 16 C.F.R. §312.2 (definition of "Personal information"). The Rule does not apply to non-profit organizations that otherwise are exempt from regulation under the FTC Act. 16 C.F.R. §312.2 (definition of "Website or online service directed to children").

Web sites targeted at children must post a link to a privacy notice on the home page of the Web site and on each page from which they collect personal information from children; operators of general-interest Web sites must post notices on any pages directed at children. 16 C.F.R. §312.4(b). The link to the privacy notice must be clearly and understandably written, 16 C.F.R. §312.4(a) and placed in a clear and prominent location, 16 C.F.R. §312.4(b)(1). The notice must include a variety of specific information listed in the regulation, including a way to contact the operator of the Web site, the types of information being collected, the uses that the operator makes of the information, and a recitation of the rights COPPA grants to children and their parents. 16 C.F.R. §312.4(b)(2).

Web-site operators subject to the COPPA Rule must obtain "verifiable consent" from parents before collecting information from a child. The operator must send a notice to a parent informing the parent that it wishes to collect information from the child and that the parent's consent is required to do this, and then explain how the parent can consent. The notice requesting consent to the collection of information must include the same information as the posted privacy policy. To meet the standard of "verifiable" parental consent, the Web-site operator must make reasonable efforts in light of currently available technology to ensure that the child's parent has actually been notified and has consented. 15 U.S.C. §6502(b)(1)(A)(ii); 16 C.F.R. §312.5.

A Web-site operator also must provide parents with a means of reviewing any personal information collected from their children. The procedure for obtaining that information must not be unduly burdensome; however, it must also ensure that no one but the parent is able to obtain a copy of a child's personal information. 16 C.F.R. §312.6. To limit the ability of operators to coerce the disclosure of information, the statute prohibits Web-site operators from conditioning a child's participation in an activity on the child's disclosing more personal information than is reasonably necessary to participate in the activity. 15 U.S.C. §6502(b)(1)(C); 16 C.F.R. §312.7.

COPPA includes provisions for FTC-approved self-regulatory programs. 15 U.S.C. §6803; 16 C.F.R. §312.10. To qualify, such a program must require members to comply with the substantive requirements of the COPPA Rule (notice; parental consent; parental access; confidentiality, security, and integrity of data); provide an effective, mandatory mechanism for the independent assessment of compliance with the program (such as periodic compliance audits, either of all members or of a random sample of all members, conducted by the sponsoring organization or an independent entity); and provide effective, mandatory enforcement mechanisms (such as publication of disciplinary actions; procedures for consumer redress; levying fines; or referral to the FTC). 16 C.F.R. §312.10(b). Once the FTC has approved a self-regulatory program, compliance with the program creates a "safe harbor" from any FTC enforcement actions under COPPA. 15 U.S.C. §6803(b)(2); 16 C.F.R. §312.10(a). That provision appears to be quite popular with the industry. The FTC already has approved self-regulatory programs submitted by the Children's Advertising Review Unit (CARU) of the Better Business Bureau, the Entertainment Software Rating Board, and TRUSTe.

COPPA does not provide a private cause of action. Rather, enforcement is limited to actions by the FTC or by State attorneys general. 15 U.S.C. §§6504, 6506. Despite — or perhaps because of — the clarity and vigor of COPPA, it is not clear that those enforcement measures will be adequate to force compliance by Web-site operators. In March 2001, the Annenberg Public Policy Center published a report of its study of 162 child-oriented Web sites. It found that 10 percent of the sites were in blatant non-compliance with COPPA and that almost half failed to comply with important elements of the COPPA Rule. The FTC, however, has been responding with some vigor. For example, in July 2000, the FTC sent e-mails to scores of children-targeting Web sites, warning them that they were subject to the requirements of COPPA and that they faced FTC enforcement actions if they did not revise their sites to comply with the law.

The FTC also has imposed substantial fines in enforcement actions against non-complying Web-site operators. For example, the *www.Girlslife.com* Web site targeted girls aged 9 to 14 and offered features such as online articles and advice columns, contests, and pen-pal opportunities. Partnering with *www.BigMailbox.com* and Looksmart Ltd., it also offered children free e-mail accounts and online message boards. The FTC alleged that the defendants had collected personal information from children (including such things as full name and home address, e-mail addresses, and telephone numbers), but had neither posted privacy policies that complied with the Act nor obtained the required consent from parents before collecting their children's personally identifiable information. The Web sites also enabled children to publicly reveal their personal information online without first obtaining parental consent and even provided children's personal information to third parties without prior parental consent. In a settlement of actions against those sites, the FTC not only required the operators to comply with COPPA in the future, but also imposed a total of $100,000 in civil penalties and required deletion of all personally identifying information collected from children online at any time since the effective date of the COPPA Rule.

What is remarkable about COPPA is the unqualified manner with which it mandates compliance with fair information practices. COPPA contrasts with the limited reforms enacted in Gramm-Leuch-Bliley by mandating compliance with fair-information practices in a direct and relatively unqualified way. Accordingly, the costs of complying with COPPA can be substantial. Many children-targeting Web sites have curtailed their services, ceased collecting any personal information, or simply shut down after COPPA. Children, at least, may find that outcome unsatisfying.

Relevant Glossary Entries

ActiveX
Applet
CERT
Clickstream Data
Cookie
Data Warehouse
End user
Firewall
History File
Identity Manager
Identity Scrubber
Identity Theft
Internet Engineering Task Force (IETF)
IP Address
Java
Opt-in
Opt-out
Permission Marketing
Relational Database
Source Code
Spyware
Trojan Horse
Web Bugs
Web Server

Problem Set 9

9.1. Like most Internet retailers, GigaMart accepts credit-card payments for the products that it sells. (Assignment 28 discusses the reasons for the pervasive use of the credit card in Internet transactions.) Martha Mitchell, GigaMart's Webmaster, designed the portions of the Web site that process transactions. To make the shopping experience as convenient as possible for customers, the site saves the credit-card information that shoppers provide so that they can reuse a credit card on repeat visits without having to retype the credit-card number and their address information. To enhance the speed with which the site can retrieve the information when repeat customers try to make purchases from the site, Martha decided to keep the personal information (including credit-card numbers) on the Web server outside GigaMart's firewall. Unfortunately, a hacker breached GigaMart's security and obtained a copy of all of the credit-card numbers and other information in the Web-site customer database.

Alex Anders, GigaMart's inside counsel, telephones you when she becomes aware of the security breach.

(a) What possible liability does GigaMart face because of the unauthorized copying of its customer database? (In answering the question, you should assume that, as between cardholders and their banks, any losses from unauthorized transactions on the credit cards will be borne by the banks that issued the cards. Also, some (but not all) of that loss passes to the merchants that accepted the cards. The basis for those assumptions is explained in Assignment 28.)

(b) Does GigaMart (based in Tennessee) need to notify its customers about the breach? Cal. Civ. Code §1798.82.

9.2.   Alex Anders at GigaMart has heard that someone in the state legislature has decided to try to grab a few headlines by proposing legislation that would mandate the use of firewalls for any business storing credit-card information. She is concerned because she has heard that the proposed legislation will require the use of software that conforms to a specific IETF technical standard for firewalls. The firewall that GigaMart installed does not conform to that particular standard, although it seems to be working perfectly well. In fact, the IETF standard has been adopted by only one of the many significant vendors of firewall technologies. She is not sure why a legislator would try to mandate a technical standard in law and needs to know what she will have to do if this bill actually becomes law. Do you have any constructive advice?

9.3.   Bourgeois Cinema owns the rights to the hugely popular Bitsy Buggy, a cartoon cockroach that appears in a syndicated children's TV show and feature motion pictures. Bourgeois Cinema runs a chain of 500 retail stores (Bug Boutiques) targeting children in shopping malls across the country. It also maintains a Web site for Bitsy Buggy fans, *www.bitsybuggy.com*. The site provides bulletin boards with threaded discussions containing postings on different topics relevant to Bitsy Buggy (such as her off-and-on relationship with Raoul Roach, her cartoon cockroach companion), as well as chat rooms for live online interactions among Bitsy Buggy fans.

Carl Eben has just called you because he discovered that his 11-year-old son has been using these bulletin boards and chat rooms without his permission. Apparently his son signed up for the Bitsy Bug community, intercepted the parental consent form sent to his house by regular mail, forged his father's signature on the consent form, and returned it to Bourgeois Cinema without telling him. Carl discovered the activity when he found over $100 in charges on his most recent credit-card statement for purchases his son had made using the site. Carl wants to know whether Bourgeois Cinema is allowed to entice his son into participating in this online community without Carl actually having consented to it, and what he can do besides contest the charges on his credit card to resolve the problems his son has gotten into here. What should you advise him to do? 15 U.S.C. §6502, 6504; 16 C.F.R. §§312.2-312.8.

9.4.   Mia Katerina at PetPortal.com has called you for advice regarding its Web site targeting children, PupPortal.com. At this time, the site does not collect any personal information from children, so PupPortal has not done anything to comply with COPPA. The marketing managers at PupPortal would like to add online bulletin boards and chat rooms for children to discuss their pets with each other. As part of the plan, PupPortal would like to collect personal information about the children using the service so that PupPortal can develop products and services the children might buy (or convince their parents to buy for them).

Mia has reviewed the information about the COPPA Rule on the FTC's Web site, however, and she doubts that PupPortal could comply with COPPA's requirements without hiring a "chief privacy officer" and pouring about $250,000 to $500,000 a year into compliance. It is unclear how much revenue the site might generate, but even the most wildly optimistic projections don't come anywhere near covering those costs. Her inclination is to tell the marketing people to forget it, but wants your advice first. Is compliance with COPPA likely to be as onerous and expensive as Mia thinks it is? 16 C.F.R. §§312.3, 312.4, 312.5, 312.6, 312.7.

Assignment 10: Data Protection in the European Union

Cross-border issues are particularly difficult for personal information, largely because of the nature of government regulation of information. With respect to ordinary goods, the country of export typically has little concern about what happens in the country into which the goods are sent. Thus, the typical trade problems arise out of regulations imposed by the country of import that make it more difficult for the goods to be sold in that market. With respect to personal information, however, regulations protecting consumers in the country of their residence tend to restrict the ability to transfer the information freely. Thus, there is a great potential for tension in any situation involving substantial commerce between countries with differing views regarding the propriety of commercial use of personal information. The rise of the Internet exacerbates this problem by facilitating a large increase in cross-border commerce that involves individuals and small businesses rather than large multinational corporations.

The previous assignment summarized the relatively laissez-faire attitude of the United States. This assignment discusses the more pro-active protective European perspective on those issues, together with the difficulties that perspective poses for companies that do business in both Europe and the United States.

For the student that worries that the focus on the European Union is parochial, it is important to understand that about three dozen jurisdictions (including Australia, New Zealand, the Canadian province of Quebec, and a variety of countries in Asia), have enacted data-protection laws that conform to the basic pattern established by the OECD *Guidelines* discussed below. For the American lawyer unfamiliar with the basic concept of a "data protection" law, those laws seem unbelievably complex and highly regulatory. From the EU perspective, however, the American system seems to reflect a complete lack of attention to an important social problem. From that point of view, the waves of direct marketing that assault Americans on a daily basis result from an unwillingness to address in a collective way the important issues raised by this chapter. The assignment proceeds by discussing the OECD *Guidelines* on which these statutes typically are based, the EU Directive, the UK statute that implements the directive in the United Kingdom, and finally the efforts to reconcile the U.S. and EU positions through rules to govern businesses that operate on both sides of the Atlantic.

A.   OECD *Guidelines*

In 1978, the Organization for Economic Cooperation and Development (OECD) convened a group of experts to study developments in different countries and to produce guidelines that might form a consensus position on privacy issues, with a view to facilitating harmonization of national laws in this area. In 1980, the OECD published its *Guidelines on the Protection of Privacy and Transborder Flows of Personal Data*. As discussed in Assignment 8, the *Guidelines* are the basic source of the fair-information principles at the heart of debates about commercial use of personal information.

Because of their age, the OECD *Guidelines* often are not easy to apply to contemporary data-collection practices. For example, you will learn in the pages that follow that statutes based on the *Guidelines* typically focus on regulation of the activities of any "data controller." But that concept is difficult to apply to modern organizations that collect information from a variety of sources in open network environments, because there typically will not be any single person or even a single group of people in a position to control the data-collection practices of the organization as a whole. Similarly, there is no *de minimis* threshold on what constitutes a data record, which creates administrative problems of staggering proportions in trying to meet notice, consent, and access requirements whenever a company creates a data "record" with regard to an individual. Similarly, the volume of information now being collected about individuals and the distributed manner in which it is stored create major security problems for programs designed to grant individuals effective rights to access and correct data about themselves.

Those problems have not been a major issue in the United States, because the United States has not forced its businesses to comply with the *Guidelines*. In Europe, however, those shortcomings are significant because to this day the OECD *Guidelines* serve as a source of inspiration for EU data-protection law. Working from the rather antiquated *Guidelines*, the OECD has tried hard to keep the issue of data protection on the agenda of its members, to promote dialogue, and to identify effective strategies to improve information privacy for individuals around the world. The apparent OECD consensus regarding the importance of information privacy and the importance of taking all appropriate steps to increase individual privacy rights is in marked contrast with the sharp divisions within the U.S. debate on information privacy and the tortured progress of information-privacy law reform in the United States. If the apparent OECD consensus is a reliable indicator of the future of law reform in developed and developing countries, then at some point in the not-too-distant future, U.S. businesses may find themselves at a serious disadvantage trying to compete in global markets where consumers expect to have strong data-privacy rights and U.S. businesses are not accustomed to honoring them.

B.   EU Data Protection Directive

European cooperation with respect to regulation of commercial use of information builds in part on principles from the 1953 European Convention on

Human Rights and Fundamental Freedoms. The first major implementation of the *Guidelines* was the Council of Europe's 1981 Convention for the Protection of Individuals with Regard to Automatic Processing of Data, which went into effect in 1985. [The Council of Europe is a 40-country intergovernmental organization that should not be confused with the European Union (EU).]

The watershed event, however, is the European Union's 1995 adoption of the Data Protection Directive (DP Directive), which provides individuals with powerful protections from nonconsensual uses of personal data. (That directive is not to be confused with the 1996 Database Directive, discussed in Assignment 21.) In assessing European law in this area, it is important to understand the limited legal significance of a directive. When the European Union wishes to enact a direct modification of the laws of its member states, it uses a regulation issued under Article 249 of the Treaty on European Union. Directives, however, do not have any immediate effect within the legal systems of the member states. Rather, a directive is a legislative template that, literally, directs member states to assess their existing laws on the topic. If the existing laws of a member state already conform to the requirements of a directive, then the state need take no further action. In the more common situation in which existing law is not entirely consistent with a new EU directive, the member state has a duty to enact legislation to bring its national law into conformity with the substance of the directive. Thus, although the DP Directive provides a good idea of the general tenor of European law in this area, it is not at all the same thing as a federal statute. To get an operative understanding of the legal rules that govern commercial processing of personal information, it is necessary to look at the member-state laws passed in response to the DP Directive. For example, the next section of this assignment examines the applicable UK statute, the 1998 Data Protection Act.

The general purpose of the DP Directive is to harmonize the laws of the 25 member states that govern the rights of individuals with regard to their personal information. When the DP Directive was enacted in 1995, there was a broad range of data-protection laws in the European Union, ranging from the strong laws in place in France, Germany, and the United Kingdom to the complete absence of regulation in countries such as Greece. In that milieu, some countries would not permit personal information to be transferred to member states perceived to have lax data-protection laws; conversely, the member states with lax rules might have become "data havens" attractive to data-processing companies in the same way that tax havens are attractive to high-income individuals and companies. Those problems fostered the view that harmonization of data-protection laws was a necessary condition for the formation of a single Europe-wide market for "information society services." Hence, the DP Directive obligated each member state in the European Union to move by 1998 to enact privacy laws conforming to the provisions of the Directive. (Not surprisingly, some member states missed the 1998 deadline. This is the kind of delay that makes American companies skeptical about whether these laws are enforced in a serious way.)

The Directive starts from the premise that privacy is a fundamental human right, and that any standardization of data-protection laws in Europe must proceed from that point. DP Directive art. 1. Thus, it is no surprise that the major provisions of the Directive cover much the same ground as the 1980

OECD *Guidelines* on fair-information practices. For example, the Directive requires that personal data be collected only for specified, explicit, and legitimate purposes, that collections of data be maintained only to the degree that they are relevant to the purpose for which they were collected, and that data be maintained in an accurate and, where necessary, up-to-date form. DP Directive art. 6. Subject to certain limited exceptions, the Directive reflects an "opt-in" system, under which each individual must provide unambiguous consent to the collection and use of personal information. DP Directive art. 7(a). When collecting information from individuals, the data controller must advise the individual of the purposes for which the information will be used. DP Directive art. 10(b). Finally, the individual must have a reasonable opportunity to access the data and to force the correction or deletion of inaccurate or inappropriately collected information. DP Directive art. 12.

Having established a comprehensive system to protect the privacy rights of individuals in Europe, the Directive goes on to restrict the circumstances under which personal information can be transferred out of Europe. Such transfers may take place only if the target country ensures an "adequate" level of protection. DP Directive art. 25. The adequacy of the level of protection afforded by a third country depends on all the circumstances surrounding the transfer of personal information, and questions about the adequacy of levels of protection may be raised either by member states or the European Commission. In the absence of an adequate level of protection, the transfer of data to a third country may nevertheless be permitted if the individual has unambiguously consented to the transfer, or if the organization receiving the personal information has in place adequate safeguards based on contractual obligations. DP Directive art. 26. As a result of implementing the Directive, many EU member states now require the party receiving the personal data outside the European Union to deposit with the national data-protection agency a copy of the contract governing the transfer. Then, the data-protection agency is aware of the fact of the transfer and of the terms on which it is taking place.

The DP Directive does not specify the enforcement measures to be adopted by member states, requiring only that they adopt "suitable measures" to ensure full implementation of its provisions. The Directive does indicate that suitable measures may include both civil and criminal remedies, but does not require any particular types of civil or criminal remedies. DP Directive art. 24.

The effects that the Directive has on the large number of U.S. companies with European operations have caused considerable controversy. The basic problem is that Article 25 of the Directive prohibits the transfer of personal data from Europe to any country that does not provide "an adequate level of protection" for that data. Given the European perspective that the U.S. legal system is wholly inadequate, the DP Directive posed the prospect of a balkanization of commerce in which U.S. companies with information-sensitive operations would be excluded from Europe. Thus, even before the Directive was finalized in 1995, representatives of the United States and European Union began discussing the U.S. response to the Directive. The position of the United States has been that American law is adequate, which at the time meant that self-regulation by private parties should be an adequate substitute for comprehensive information-privacy legislation. The United States also firmly rejected the persistent EU suggestion that we should have some sort of "Federal Privacy Agency." The intractability of the U.S. position — bolstered by the realization that no President could force Congress to adopt legislation reflecting the policy underpinnings that motivated the DP Directive — eventually led EU negotiators to consider the possibility of self-regulation as an acceptable response. Those problems have not yet been resolved; the closing sections of this assignment discuss the current state of accommodation.

C. UK Data Protection Act of 1998

The data-protection law of the United Kingdom is representative not only of the data-protection laws enacted throughout the European Union in response to the DP Directive, but also of data-protection laws in other parts of the world such as Australia, New Zealand, Hong Kong, Taiwan, and Israel. If the UK law is not fully representative of such laws, it is primarily because it is longer and more complex than the data-protection laws of many other countries. At times, the UK law borders on Byzantine, because its terms are modified by "schedules" containing fundamental "principles" as well as by dozens of "statutory instruments" (which an American lawyer might think of as agency regulations). Merely locating the relevant provision of the UK law can at times be a daunting task; the great length of the statute combined with its many statutory instruments makes reading it a major undertaking. At the same time, the United Kingdom's status as a major U.S. trading partner makes an understanding of the law valuable for those who represent U.S. businesses with interests in the United Kingdom.

Although the United Kingdom first enacted comprehensive privacy legislation in 1984 (the Data Protection Act of 1984, which came into force in 1987), the Data Protection Act of 1998 (the DPA) is the primary statute of relevance now, because that statute brings the United Kingdom's laws on information privacy into conformity with the DP Directive. As you would expect, the DPA builds on the OECD *Guidelines* discussed above, establishing a regulatory framework for the activities of "data controller[s]" and third-party "data processor[s]" with respect to information about "data subject[s]." Generally, a data controller is any party that "determines the purposes for which and the manner in which any personal data are . . . processed." DPA §1(1). A data processor is any third party that "processes the data on behalf of the data controller." DPA §1(1). Finally, the data subject is "an individual who is the subject of personal data." DPA §1(1). The "personal data" to which the statute applies generally include any data that relates to an identifiable individual. DPA §1(1). The term "data" in turn is defined quite broadly, including not only machine-readable information, but any "information relating to individuals that . . . is structured . . . in such a way that specific information relating to a particular individual is readily accessible." DPA §1(1) (definitions of "data" and "relevant filing system").

The heart of the DPA is a requirement that any data controller "comply with . . . data protection principles." DPA §4(4). The principles in question are set out in three Schedules attached to the statute. Part I of Schedule 1 requires compliance with eight principles that generally track the OECD *Guidelines*.

For example, the first principle prohibits any processing of personal data without consent or some other specified justification. The breadth of that provision is enhanced by an expansive definition of "processing" that includes "obtaining, recording or holding the information . . . or carrying out any operation . . . on the information." DPA §1(1). The permissible justifications are set out in detail in Schedules 2 and 3 to the DPA; Schedule 2 articulates general rules, while Schedule 3 articulates special restrictive rules for "sensitive" personal data. In addition to consent (Schedule 2 item 1), the list includes circumstances such as the need to perform a contract to which the data subject is a party (Schedule 2 item 2). For sensitive data, not surprisingly, the circumstances under which processing can be performed without consent are quite narrow. DPA Sch. 3.

In addition to the substantive restrictions on processing, the principles require a variety of other typical fair-information practices. For example, the second principle prohibits the processing of data for any purpose other than the purpose for which it is obtained, and the seventh principle requires adequate technical and organizational measures to prevent inappropriate access to personal data. Data subjects also have general rights to notification whenever personal data is being collected and to access any personal data about themselves. DPA §7; DPA Sch. 1, Part II, ¶¶ 2(1)(a) & 2(3) (interpreting the first principle). To ensure security, the data controller may require persons requesting access to provide reasonable proof of their identity. DPA §7(3). The data controller may also charge a fee for providing access, DPA §7(2)(b), but applicable regulations have set limits that keep the fees quite modest; often they are capped at £2.

The DPA even grants the data subject several rights to control processing of lawfully acquired data. For example, the data subject can require the data controller to cease any processing that "is likely to cause substantial [and unwarranted] damage or substantial distress to him or to another." DPA §10(1). There also is a specific right to stop processing for the purpose of direct marketing, DPA §11, and to prevent the use of automated decisionmaking regarding the subject's "performance at work, his creditworthiness, his reliability or his conduct." DPA §12(1). Similarly, a data subject can require the data controller to correct or destroy any data that the data subject can show to be inaccurate. DPA §14.

Of particular importance for our purposes is the eighth principle, which tracks DP Directive art. 25 in barring any transfer of personal data to a country outside the European Union that does not "ensur[e] an adequate level of protection" for the data. DPA Sch. 1, Part I, eighth principle. The DPA includes an eight-factor test for determining whether any particular country provides an adequate level of protection, DPA Sch. 1, Part II, ¶13, but it is safe to say that the laws of the United States do not satisfy that test. (DPA Sch. 1 Part II, ¶15 requires deference to EU findings on that point; the European Union has made such a finding with respect to the United States.) Thus, within the framework of the DPA, transfers to the United States are permitted only upon compliance with one of the conditions of Schedule 4. DPA Sch. 1, Part II, ¶14 (permitting transfers that otherwise would violate the eighth principle upon satisfaction of one of the conditions of Schedule 4). Schedule 4, in turn, includes relatively narrow conditions such as consent by the data subject (DPA Sch. 4, ¶1), the completion of transactions to which the data subject is a part (DPA Sch. 4, ¶2). The last two sections of the assignment discuss more general ways for American companies to avoid the strictures of the eighth principle.

Finally, the DPA also imposes a general obligation on anyone "processing" personal data to register with the Commissioner. DPA §17(1). Given the broad definition of "processing" mentioned above, that obligation is quite far-reaching. The Information Commissioner also is authorized to investigate the activities of data controllers and to take enforcement action where appropriate. DPA §40. The DPA includes a compensatory civil remedy, DPA §13, and criminal sanctions for serious non-compliance, DPA §21.

Those rules, of course, contrast sharply with the discussion of clickstream data and data warehousing discussed in Assignment 8. To get an understanding of how regulators expect those rules to play out "on the ground" of the Internet, consider the following guidance that the UK Information Commissioner has provided (on its Web site) to UK businesses regarding the application of the DPA to Internet commerce.

INTERNET: PROTECTION OF PRIVACY-DATA CONTROLLERS

In using the Internet for their business dealings, data controllers must take into account the privacy rights of individuals and their own responsibilities under privacy and data protection legislation. The following points should be considered by data controllers in planning their Internet strategies.

Personal data placed on the Internet is available world-wide. In many countries the use of personal data is not protected by legislation. Because of this it is always advisable and will often be essential to obtain consent from individuals before publishing their personal data on your website.

When collecting information via the Internet always inform the user of who you are, what personal data you are collecting, processing and storing and for what purpose. Do this before a user gives you any information, when they visit your site and wherever they are asked to provide information, for example via an on-line application form. It is good practice to ask for consent for the collection of all data and it is usually essential to get consent if you want to process sensitive personal data.

It is good practice for a data controller who sets up a website to provide a statement of its privacy policy. A 'privacy statement' helps individuals to decide whether or not to visit a site and, when they do visit, whether or not to provide any personal information to the data controller.

Always let individuals know when you intend to use 'Cookies' or other covert software to collect information about them.

Never collect or retain personal data unless it is strictly necessary for your purposes. For example you should not require a person's name and full address to provide an on-line quotation. If extra information is required for marketing purposes this should be made clear and the provision of the information should be optional.

Design your systems in such a way as to avoid or minimise the use of personal data.

D.   Accommodations Between the United States and the European Union

Before the DP Directive was enacted in 1995, U.S. companies doing business in the European Union had to work out compliance strategies with the data-protection officials in the countries in which they had operations on a case-by-case basis. The DP Directive's prohibition on data flows out of the European Union to countries lacking an "adequate level of protection" threatened to deprive data-protection officials of the authority to work out ad hoc deals with individual companies. After the European Union made the predictable determination that the United States did indeed lack adequate legal protection, the battle lines were drawn and multinational corporations found themselves about to be caught in the crossfire. When several years of diplomatic pressure from the European Union failed to produce American legislation of the kind that the European Union thought was appropriate, it was necessary to reach some compromise that would permit multinational corporations to keep the lines of communication open between their EU and American divisions.

After a considerable amount of negotiating (and attendant posturing), the United States Department of Commerce and the Commission of the European Union in 2000 agreed upon a framework for a "safe harbor." To qualify for the safe harbor, a U.S. company must self-certify that its procedures for handling the personal information of individuals in Europe conform to the fair-information practices outlined in the safe-harbor agreement, which in turn are based on the provisions of the Directive. If a company that has certified that it complies with the information privacy principles in the safe-harbor agreement fails to comply with those principles, then state and federal regulators — but not regulators from the European Union or its member states — can take enforcement action against the company. The advantage from the perspective of the European Union is that the safe harbor requires a much stronger enforcement mechanism and closer adherence to fair-information practices than any similar programs in the United States.

Considering the great effort that went into negotiations for the safe harbor, it was disappointing that so few companies immediately took advantage of it. Over the years, however, the need for compliance has become more pressing. By the summer of 2004, more than 500 companies had self-certified their compliance. Although that still is probably only a small share of the companies that transfer personal information between Europe and the United States, it includes many of the largest multinationals and thus reflects a considerable "on-the-ground" impact for the safe harbor as far as dominant U.S. business practices go. For the uncertified companies EU citizens have no information about privacy practices except for any privacy policy the company might have posted and no ready way to determine how close the practices articulated in that policy come to a baseline exception of EU-style fair-information practices.

Another avenue for accommodation has relied on Article 26(2) of the DP Directive, which provides that a member state may authorize transfers of personal information out of the European Union to a country that does not ensure an adequate level of protection of information privacy if the data controller inside the European Union "adduces adequate safeguards" with respect to the transferred data. See DPA Sch. 4, ¶8 (permitting a transfer "on terms which are of a kind approved by the Commissioner as ensuring adequate safeguards"). The Directive specifically contemplates "appropriate contractual clauses" as one way of satisfying that provision. DP Directive art. 26(2). In 2001, after negotiations that paralleled the effort to produce the safe-harbor agreement described above, the EU Commission issued a decision setting out standard contractual clauses that parties to international data transfers could incorporate in their agreements to establish that there would be adequate safeguards to protect the personal information after it left the European Union. Among other things, the clauses require the data exporter and data importer to ensure that the data is used only in accordance with the EU DP Directive, and require that the data exporter and data importer assume joint and several liability for compliance with the agreement, so that affected data subjects can obtain relief either in the European Union or in the United States. Those clauses provide relief for companies that want to engage in occasional transactions involving EU data, but do not have sufficient business in the European Union to justify whole-scale compliance through the safe harbor.

The decision requires member states to recognize that companies or organizations using such standard clauses are offering "adequate protection" to the data. The clauses, however, are wholly voluntary. The purpose of issuing them is to simplify negotiations between data controllers wishing to transfer data outside the European Union, the prospective transferees of the data, and the data-protection authorities within the member states that are required to review the proposed transfers and approve them before they can take place. Thus, if someone inside the European Union wants to transfer data to one of the numerous U.S. businesses that does not qualify for the safe harbor, it may still be possible to make the transfer, provided the transferor gets the permission of its national data-protection authority based on having appropriate restrictions on the U.S. use of the data in the contract governing the transfer. See DPA Sch. 4, ¶9 (generally authorizing out-of-country transfers to countries that do not provide adequate protection if "[t]he transfer has been authorised by the Commissioner as being made in such a manner as to ensure adequate safeguards for the rights and freedoms of data subjects"). If the transfer uses the EU-approved clauses, approval will be automatic. See DPA Sch. 4, ¶8 (permitting transfers "made on terms which are of a kind approved by the Commissioner"); DPA Sch. 2, ¶15 (interpreting the eighth principle) (requiring the UK Commissioner to defer to EU determinations regarding adequate protection). The parties simply must deposit the relevant agreement with the relevant national authority.

Relevant Glossary Entries

Cookie
Online Privacy Seal Program
Opt-In
Self-Regulation

Problem Set 10

10.1. Zahida Hussain runs a babysitting agency in Ambridge, England and keeps records on the families who use her service. When the sitters return from working with a family, Zahida de-briefs them on the family's circumstances, entering the information into a filing system she has set up. If Zahida notices that the families are Shiite Muslims, she passes that information on to her uncle, an imam at the local Shiite mosque so that he can check to see if they are members at the mosque. If not, he contacts them to invite them to attend a worship service. Is there anything Zahida and her uncle should be doing differently? DPA §§1, 2, 4, 5, 16-18; Schedules 1, 2 & 3.

10.2. Fred Bloggs (a resident of East London), has constructed a Web site at *www.trulygormless.com*. The Web site (residing on a server in East London) provides advice to the lovelorn and an online dating service. Does Fred have any reason to be concerned if he shares the information he collects from lovelorn visitors to his site with his friend Lardy Dar, who would like to contact them to try to sell them some prime Florida real estate at fire-sale prices? Assuming that he has notified the Commissioner that he is collecting the information, is there anything else that he would need to do to comply with the DPA? DPA §§1, 2, 4, 11; Sch. 1, Part I, first and second Principles; Sch 2, ¶1; Sch. 3, ¶1.

10.3. Textrade.com is a multinational corporation that provides an Internet marketplace for the worldwide textile industry. The servers that support its Web site are located in Texas, but many of its customers live outside the United States. Many of its customers are EU corporations and individuals. The CEO of Textrade.com is a British lawyer who has heard about the safe-harbor agreement related to the DP Directive and would like to take advantage of it. What advice would you give him to help him assess the pros and cons of participating in the safe harbor? DP Directive art. 4; DPA §5.

10.4. Robert Mirobal, president of Native Breeze Flutes, a small family business that manufactures traditional Native American flutes, was recently on a golf vacation in St. Andrews, Scotland. While golfing, he became quite friendly with Diana Llewellyn. When Robert told Diana about some of his products, Diana was very interested in learning more. Thinking that some of his accessories would be useful to her friends that play bagpipes, Diana offered to share with him the names and addresses of all her colleagues in the Great Highland Bagpipers Association, of which she was currently the secretary. Does Robert need to be worried about having Diana e-mail him an electronic copy of the membership directory of the Association (including names, home addresses, spouses' names, telephone numbers, and birth dates of members)? If so, would the safe-harbor clauses provide a potential avenue for relief? DP Directive art. 26; DPA §§4, 11; Sch. 1, Part I, first, second & eighth Principles; Sch. 1, Part II, ¶15; Sch. 4, ¶¶8, 9.

Assignment 11: Internet Privacy Policies and Related Practices

With the surging popularity of Internet commerce has come an unprecedented amount of controversy over privacy issues. If American consumers once were not concerned about the large volumes of personal information American companies were collecting about them, they certainly have awakened to concern about the online collection of personal information. And their concern has not been diminished by frequent media reports about the government's vigorous efforts to use the ill fated "clipper chip" and the Carnivore system to monitor online communications. But most people who have tried to prevent the collection and transfer of personal information have quickly learned the practical consequences of the American approach to privacy law. Scott McNealy, CEO of Sun Microsystems, ably summed up this view in 1999 when he responded to a journalist's concerns about Sun's JINI (a network communication technology that might permit the location of users to be monitored by others): "You have zero privacy anyway. Get over it."

American businesses have invested heavily in marketing technologies that depend on the collection and transfer of vast quantities of personal information in a manner that is fundamentally incompatible with fair information practices. Thus, privacy laws mandating general compliance with fair information practices would have stark economic consequences for many U.S. businesses.

In this environment of growing public concern, contentious debate, and political uncertainty, the Federal Trade Commission (FTC) has taken the regulatory lead. Interestingly enough, the FTC has undertaken this role not in response to any specific legislative mandate, but rather under its general authority to regulate "unfair or deceptive acts" in interstate commerce. 15 U.S.C. §45. In this particular context, the FTC initially adopted an approach strongly favoring self-regulation, through a policy of promoting the voluntary posting of Internet privacy policies. After closely monitoring developments in online privacy for several years, the FTC eventually conceded that the voluntary self-regulatory strategy was a failure, and in the last year of the Clinton Administration called for major new legislation. That legislation has not, however, been enacted. As a result, the privacy rights of U.S. consumers engaged in Internet commerce are for the most part limited to the rights granted in the privacy policies posted on Internet sites. Thus, this assignment explores the process of developing and implementing a privacy policy and the legal consequences that attach to posting a privacy policy on an Internet site.

A.   Privacy Policies

1.   *Online Privacy Practices*

The FTC has closely monitored online information practices since its first workshop on consumer protection in cyberspace in 1995. Thus, FTC surveys on online information practices have been important in public policy debates. The first general conclusions based on that monitoring were published in 1998 in the FTC's inaugural annual report on online privacy. [*http://www.ftc.gov/reports/privacy3/toc.htm*] That report surveyed privacy protection at over 1,400 commercial Internet sites and found the results wholly unsatisfactory. Although the FTC did find that industry-association guidelines already were encouraging members to post notices about their information practices, those guidelines did not often provide any substantive protections regarding data security, consumer access, or enforcement mechanisms. Moreover, the FTC's survey revealed that the Web sites did not even comply with the guidelines that the FTC found inadequate. Among other things, the FTC found that 85 percent of sites collected personal information, but only 14 percent provided any notice to consumers, and a mere 2 percent posted a comprehensive privacy policy.

In July 1999, the FTC issued a second report to Congress, *Self-Regulation and Privacy Online*. [*http://www.ftc.gov/os/1999/07/privacy99.pdf*] That report concluded that progress in the private sector was so rapid that legislation was not needed at the time. The report described the findings of a survey conducted by Georgetown University, noting that the number of Web sites posting at least one disclosure about their information practices had increased to 66 percent, although 93 percent of the sites collected personal information from consumers. Furthermore, only 44 percent of sites posted privacy policy notices, and only 10 percent of sites had notices that implemented the four most fundamental fair information practices — notice, consent, access, and security.

In May 2000, the FTC issued a third report to Congress, *Privacy Online: Fair Information Practices in the Electronic Marketplace*. [*www.ftc.gov/reports/privacy2000/privacy2000text.pdf*] That report studied the 100 busiest Web sites and a random sample of 335 Web sites. Although 88 percent of the sites in the random sample and 100 percent of the busiest sites posted some kind of privacy disclosure, the FTC found that it still was true that few of the policies implemented fair information practices: only 20 percent of the sites in the random sample and 42 percent of the busiest sites. Only 41 percent of the sites in the random sample and 60 percent of the busiest sites met even the basic notice and consent standards. The survey also found that online-privacy seal programs (discussed below as one of the leading forms of self-regulation) were not widely supported, as only 8 percent of the sites in the random sample and 45 percent of the busiest sites displayed an online-privacy program seal. That rather dismal showing finally persuaded the FTC to abandon its reliance on self-regulation. At that point, the FTC turned to recommending legislation that would establish basic privacy protections for consumer-oriented Web sites.

2. Developing a Privacy Policy

Until such a statute is enacted, however, there are no rules that generally require commercial Web-site operators in the United States to post privacy policies of any kind. As the opening assignments of this chapter suggest, the only exceptions are for specialized subject matters, such as child-oriented sites covered by COPPA. Still, businesses often are motivated to post such policies both by the need to satisfy consumers that increasingly expect to see privacy policies and by a general desire to forestall restrictive legislation.

If a company operating a commercial Internet site decides it wants to post a privacy policy, the first step in developing one is to determine what personal information the company collects and what it does with that information. Given the historically lackadaisical attitude to such matters in this country, few U.S. companies can answer those questions without a comprehensive "information audit." An information audit ordinarily requires each division or operating unit of the company to review its current operations to answer some set of questions along the lines of the following:

- What information is being collected?
- Is the information personally identifiable, or does it describe individuals only in the aggregate?
- How is the information being collected? Specifically, is it account information? Directories of customers or business contacts? Web-site registration forms? Cookies? Clickstream data?
- Who has access to the information? How do you ensure that unauthorized persons do not access the information?
- What do you do with the information? Are additional uses contemplated?
- How is the information stored? Is security adequate? Are records-management policies in place to determine when the information should be deleted from the system?
- Is the information being transferred to third parties? If so, what representations and warranties have been given by those third parties regarding their use of the information? Are those undertakings credible?

Once it has conducted such an audit, the company has the information to evaluate its current practices. Managers then can compare the benefits of granting increased information privacy rights to customers (primarily the ability of the company to palliate regulators, consumers, and their advocates) against its likely costs, which may include adverse effects on such things as transaction processing, marketing effectiveness, and revenue streams from information sales. Those issues, of course, are likely to require attention from the highest levels of company management.

When a company's managers have developed a sense of what personal information is being collected, how it is being used, and what changes, if any, it wishes to make in its current procedures, it is in a position to construct a formal privacy policy. A wealth of information about the range of possible policies is available from privacy policies posted on commercial Web sites run by businesses with similar business models, markets, or customers. At one extreme is the 200-word privacy policy of the Center for Democracy and Technology, itself a privacy-rights organization, which explains in a few sentences what little information is collected and what few uses are made of it. For example, it states "CDT does not use cookies." A privacy policy of that rigor can be stated clearly with few words, but is unlikely to be very appealing to commercial Internet site operators. At the other extreme is the 5,000-word privacy policy of NetZero, which provides "free" Internet access services in exchange for collecting personal information from its subscribers that it aggregates and sells to prospective marketers. That policy imposes few substantial restrictions on the activities of NetZero.

To understand the drafting issues involved in a privacy policy, the discussion here focuses on three issues: the types of information that will be collected, the parties with whom the information will be shared or to whom the information will be disclosed, and procedures for revising the policy. The discussion relies on excerpts from the privacy policies in use in the summer of 2004 at Amazon.com, Yahoo.com, and Netzero.net. (Copies of the full terms of those policies are posted on the Web site for this book on the page for this assignment.) As you study these policies, remember that the privacy policy arguably serves as a contractual agreement between the Web-site operator and the user. Of course, the user does not sign it and may not see it, so a privacy policy has questionable validity as a contract that can be enforced by either party. As a practical matter, however, the privacy policy is binding at least on the owner of the site, in that the FTC is likely to view conduct inconsistent with the policy as a deceptive practice by the Web-site operator.

(a) What Information Will Be Collected?

The most basic task is to describe the information that is collected. If the policy is to serve as a contract validating the site's collection of information, the site's policy must describe that information comprehensively. To do so might be easy for primitive Web sites that collect information only when consumers fill out forms. For example, a typical site for a local financial institution's Web site provides on this topic as follows:

> [W]e gather information about you from the following sources:
>
> - Information we receive from you in applications and other forms.
> - Information about your transactions with others and us.
> - Information we receive from consumer reporting agencies, such as credit bureaus and check reporting services.
>
> We use this information to help us make informed decisions about how to best service your accounts and provide the services and products you request.

Other Web sites, however, use sophisticated technology to collect a wide variety of information, the nature of which probably would surprise the typical Web surfer. For those sites, a careful description of the types of information is a major undertaking. Amazon.com's position as a leader in the technology of information collection makes those portions of its policy instructive:

What Personal Information About Customers Does Amazon.com Gather?
The information we learn from customers helps us personalize and continually improve your shopping experience at Amazon.com. Here are the types of information we gather.

- **Information You Give Us:** We receive and store any information you enter on our Web site or give us in any other way. Click here to see examples of what we collect. You can choose not to provide certain information, but then you might not be able to take advantage of many of our features. We use the information that you provide for such purposes as responding to your requests, customizing future shopping for you, improving our stores, and communicating with you.
- **Automatic Information:** We receive and store certain types of information whenever you interact with us. For example, like many Web sites, we use "cookies," and we obtain certain types of information when your Web browser accesses Amazon.com. Click here to see examples of the information we receive. A number of companies offer utilities designed to help you visit Web sites anonymously. Although we will not be able to provide you with a personalized experience at Amazon.com if we cannot recognize you, we want you to be aware that these tools exist.
- **E-mail Communications:** To help us make e-mails more useful and interesting, we often receive a confirmation when you open e-mail from Amazon.com if your computer supports such capabilities. We also compare our customer list to lists received from other companies, in an effort to avoid sending unnecessary messages to our customers. If you do not want to receive e-mail or other mail from us, please adjust your Customer Communication Preferences.
- **Information from Other Sources:** We might receive information about you from other sources and add it to our account information. Click here to see examples of the information we receive.

Information You Give Us
You provide most such information when you search, buy, bid, post, participate in a contest or questionnaire, or communicate with customer service. For example, you provide information when you search for a product; place an order through Amazon.com or one of our third-party sellers; make an Auction bid or purchase; provide information in Your Account (and you might have more than one if you have used more than one e-mail address when shopping with us) or About You; communicate with us by phone, e-mail, or otherwise; complete a questionnaire or a contest entry form; compile Wish Lists or other gift registries; provide employer information when opening a corporate account; participate in Discussion Boards or Amazon.com Chat; provide and rate Reviews; specify a Special Occasion Reminder or a favorite charity in Charity Links; share information with Amazon Friends; and employ other Personal Notification Services, such as Available to Order Notifications. As a result of those actions, you might supply us with such information as your name, address, and phone numbers; credit card information; people to whom purchases have been shipped, including addresses and phone number; people (with addresses and phone numbers) listed in 1-Click settings; e-mail addresses of Amazon Friends and other people; content of reviews and e-mails to us; personal description and photograph in About You; and financial information, including Social Security and driver's license numbers.

Automatic Information

Examples of the information we collect and analyze include the Internet protocol (IP) address used to connect your computer to the Internet; login; e-mail
address; password; computer and connection information such as browser type
and version, operating system, and platform; purchase history, which we sometimes aggregate with similar information from other customers to create fea-
tures such as <u>Purchase Circles</u>, <u>Top Sellers</u>, and <u>Just Like You</u>; the full Uniform
Resource Locator (URL) clickstream to, through, and from our Web site, includ-
ing date and time; cookie number; products you viewed or searched for; zShops
you visited; your Auction history; and the phone number you used to call our
800 number. During some visits we may use software tools such as JavaScript to
measure and collect session information, including page response times, download errors, length of visits to certain pages, page interaction information (such
as scrolling, clicks, and mouse-overs), and methods used to browse away from
the page.

Information from Other Sources

Examples of information we receive from other sources include updated delivery
and address information from our carriers or other third parties, which we use to
correct our records and deliver your next purchase or communication more easily; account information, purchase or redemption information, and page-view
information from some merchants with which we operate co-branded businesses
(such as drugstore.com) or for which we provide technical, fulfillment, advertising, or other services (such as Target.com); search term and search result information from some searches conducted through the Web search features offered
by our subsidiary, Alexa Internet; search results and links, including paid listings
(such as Sponsored Links from Google); and credit history information from credit
bureaus, which we use to help prevent and detect fraud and to offer certain credit
or financial services to some customers.

(b) Who Will Have Access to the Information

The most controversial aspect of any privacy policy is the description of the
uses to which the information will be put. Businesses face many choices in
this context, limited only by the level of dissatisfaction that will be brought
to bear by consumer advocates (frequently) and government regulators (occasionally). Using the example of the local financial institution again, some
businesses, particularly those for whom privacy is an important element of
customer trust, will wish to make strong commitments against third-party use
of the information:

> [We] do not share any customer information with third party marketers offering their
> products and services. While we may offer products and services from third parties,
> such as check printing companies, [we] will control the customer information used
> to make the offers.

Most major retailers, however, will rely in their businesses on the ability to
disseminate information about their customers either to affiliated entities or
to nonaffiliated entities that use it for marketing purposes. The typical style

of these policies is to write with a reassuring tone suggesting that all of the uses are quite narrow and limited, while using language that directly permits broad dissemination of the relevant information.

Aside from the voluntary transfers that arise out of the company's affirmative business plan, companies also are likely to use this opportunity to discuss involuntary transfers — information that is lost through hacking, as discussed above. On that topic, it has become increasingly common for companies to attempt to disclaim any responsibility for such a loss of information, through either a privacy policy or some other policy document posted on the Web site.

Although it does not include all of the features discussed above, the Yahoo.com privacy policy offers a good example:

Information Sharing and Disclosure

- Yahoo! does not rent, sell, or share personal information about you with other people or nonaffiliated companies except to provide products or services you've requested, when we have your permission, or under the following circumstances:
  - We provide the information to trusted partners who work on behalf of or with Yahoo! under confidentiality agreements. These companies may use your personal information to help Yahoo! communicate with you about offers from Yahoo! and our marketing partners. However, these companies do not have any independent right to share this information.
  - We have a parent's permission to share the information if the user is a child under age 13. Parents have the option of allowing Yahoo! to collect and use their child's information without consenting to Yahoo! sharing of this information with people and companies who may use this information for their own purposes;
  - We respond to subpoenas, court orders, or legal process, or to establish or exercise our legal rights or defend against legal claims;
  - We believe it is necessary to share information in order to investigate, prevent, or take action regarding illegal activities, suspected fraud, situations involving potential threats to the physical safety of any person, violations of Yahoo!'s terms of use, or as otherwise required by law.
  - We transfer information about you if Yahoo! is acquired by or merged with another company. In this event, Yahoo! will notify you before information about you is transferred and becomes subject to a different privacy policy.

(c) How Can the Policy Be Changed?

The final topic discussed here — how to change the policy — is not one of the most prominent topics in any privacy policy, but warrants attention because it provides an opportunity to examine a notable example of bad legal advice for a major Internet retailer. The basic problem arises because — given the youth of the Internet and the relevant technologies — the IT and marketing practices of businesses are changing rapidly. Thus, as businesses are presented with profitable or cost-saving opportunities that depend on an alteration of their data-protection practices, they will wish in some cases to revise their privacy policies to permit them to take advantage of those opportunities.

At least theoretically, a company could include a provision in its privacy policy stating that it reserves the right to revise the policy at any time without any notice to its customers. In principle, that would mean that any individual whose personal information was collected while that privacy policy was in effect could not object to the company later modifying its privacy policy in a way that broadened the permitted types of information collection or use. But those kinds of terms are likely to make the entire privacy policy "illusory." In the realm of contract law, if one party offers an illusory promise in exchange for the other party's substantial one, courts often would either find that no contract exists or interpret the terms of the illusory promise to implicitly require reasonable behavior on the part of the party that offered it. RESTATEMENT (SECOND) OF CONTRACTS §76. Application of that doctrine to a privacy policy could result either in a conclusion that the policy is not a binding contract (and thus does not provide the company contractually binding permission for its practices) or (much worse) in a judicial amendment of the policy that prevents "unreasonable" or perhaps "unforeseeable" amendments of the policy by the company. Thus, most companies have not taken that approach.

The most prominent dispute in this context involves Amazon.com, which triggered a firestorm of criticism when it sent notices to all of its customers on September 5, 2000, explaining that it had modified its privacy policy a few days earlier to, among other things, include the following clause:

> As we continue to develop our business, we might sell or buy stores or assets. In such transactions, customer information generally is one of the transferred business assets. Also, in the unlikely event that Amazon.com Inc., or substantially all its assets are acquired, customer information will of course be one of the transferred assets.

In correspondence with the FTC demanding an investigation into those notices, leading privacy advocates pejoratively labeled this statement the "wholesale exception clause." They argued that this statement was deceptive in light of other provisions in the Amazon.com privacy policy stating that certain types of personal information would "never" be shared with third parties.

As a transactional lawyer, you should see that the basic contractual problem was that Amazon.com's maturity as a company required it to take account of the possibility that it might be acquired, and that it might not be able to control its information in the event of an acquisition. The FTC did open an investigation, but eventually determined that in light of Amazon.com's actual information practices, it seemed unlikely that Amazon.com had engaged in unfair and deceptive trade practices. In the meantime, privacy advocates have attempted to keep the issue as visible as possible. The incident unquestionably has tarnished Amazon.com's once sterling reputation as a leader among U.S. Internet businesses for following fair information practices. Amazon.com's privacy policy now provides as follows:

> Our business changes constantly, and our Privacy Notice and the <u>Conditions of Use</u> will change also. We may e-mail periodic reminders of our notices and conditions, unless you have instructed us not to, but you should check our Web site frequently to see recent changes. Unless stated otherwise, our current Privacy Notice applies to all information that we have about you and your account. We stand behind the promises we make, however, and will never materially change our policies and

practices to make them less protective of customer information collected in the past without the consent of affected customers.

Businesses that have regular e-mail contacts with their customers have a simpler solution, in that they can promise to notify the customer. Consider the following example from Yahoo.com: "Yahoo! may update this policy. We will notify you about significant changes in the way we treat personal information by sending a notice to the primary email address specified in your Yahoo! account or by placing a prominent notice on our site."

For what it is worth, Amazon.com's policy on business transfers *now* states as follows:

- *Business Transfers*: As we continue to develop our business, we might sell or buy stores, subsidiaries, or business units. In such transactions, customer information generally is one of the transferred business assets but remains subject to the promises made in any pre-existing Privacy Notice (unless, of course, the customer consents otherwise). Also, in the unlikely event that Amazon.com, Inc., or substantially all of its assets are acquired, customer information will of course be one of the transferred assets.

Other approaches would provide greater protection of personal information, albeit at greater cost to the collector of the information. For example, privacy advocates would prefer that customers have an opportunity to opt out of having their personal information handled under the terms of the new privacy policy. That rule is required by COPPA and the regulations promulgated under Gramm-Leach-Bliley (a privacy statute for financial institutions). 16 C.F.R. 312.5(a)(1) (COPPA regulations); 16 C.F.R. §313.8 (GLB regulations promulgated by the FTC). That approach, however, is not often voluntarily adopted, because it has significant costs in records management. The company would need to establish procedures for segregating data according to the privacy policy that applied to each record, and for ensuring that personal information was handled only according to the terms of the relevant privacy policy. Under such a system, a company would have to be able to administer several privacy policies simultaneously or would have to purge its databases of personal information of those individuals who were unwilling to consent to changes in its privacy policy.

B. Self-Regulation

Privacy policies generally are enforced either through FTC enforcement actions or by class-action lawsuits. Those enforcement mechanisms, however, are relevant only if the companies violate their own policies. Thus, one possible effect of the self-regulatory scheme that the FTC adopted is simply to encourage companies to adopt policies that clearly permit the activity in which they wish to engage. If consumers do not actively monitor the policies, and if consumers will not refuse to use a Web site because of the operator's privacy policies, then there is little reason to adopt a restrictive policy. The obvious problem is the limited market incentive that businesses face to upgrade their privacy packages. On the other hand, self-regulation does offer greater flexibility in the development of specific norms in light of evolving technology. It also shifts the responsibility for developing those norms to private parties that are likely to have a more comprehensive understanding of the relevant technical constraints and possibilities. At the same time, unsupervised self-regulation can provide a false sense of comfort to consumers whose information is in fact being used in ways to which they would not voluntarily consent. Similarly, as you will recall from the discussion in Assignment 6 of the Realtime Blackhole List, self-regulation has the potential to place undue power in the hands of private parties with no claim to a democratic mandate.

To explore fully the concept of self-regulation, it is necessary to look not only at the direct enforcement through litigation, but also at other institutions that have developed to help consumers protect their information. The most important in this context are information intermediaries that evaluate privacy policies (seal programs) and developments in browser technology that allow users to evaluate privacy protections automatically.

1. Seal Programs

The most prominent type of self-regulation has been a series of parallel efforts to develop credible online privacy-seal programs. The three most prominent of those programs are sponsored by the BBB (a program known as BBBOnLine), the American Institute of Certified Public Accountants (a program known as WebTrust), and TRUSTe. The programs are entirely voluntary, supported by subscription fees that members must pay. By 2004, WebTrust had signed up about 40 companies for its seal program; BBBOnLine had over 10,000; and TRUSTe had over 1,000. More recently, the Direct Marketing Association itself, responding to criticism of the activities of its members, has undertaken its own seal program, which permits its members to display a seal indicating that they conform to the DMA's "Privacy Promise to Consumers." Although the DMA site does not indicate how many of its members display their seal, a casual survey suggests that the seal is quite common on Web sites of DMA members.

The main tool of the programs is a "seal" that members display on their Web sites. The seals are designed to inform visitors that the site operator complies with the minimum privacy-policy standards that the seal program requires. Each of those programs also provides an alternative dispute resolution (ADR) mechanism for visitors to sites who believe that an operator has failed to comply with the seal program rules. In addition to the potential for enforcement by visitors, the seal programs themselves are also expected to monitor compliance of their subscribers and impose sanctions for non-compliance, such as withdrawal of the seal, negative publicity, or referral to appropriate government enforcement agencies. Because the level of subscription fees that the programs charge is quite low, none of the programs has funding adequate to support systematic auditing of subscriber sites. Thus, as a practical matter, the only substantial monitoring comes from the subscriber itself or third parties.

The most significant study of those programs is a September 2000 study published by the Privacy Commissioners of Ontario and Australia. This study examined each seal program in terms of the rigor of its policies, its systems for policing compliance with their policies by members of their seal programs, and the efficacy and fairness of its ADR procedures. The benchmark that the Commissioners used in their study was the statement of fair information practices contained in the 1980 OECD *Guidelines*. None of the programs required full compliance with those standards; assessing the extent of compliance, the Commissioners awarded scores on a range of 6.0 to 6.375 on a scale of 8.0. The Commissioners also noted that the effectiveness of those practices that the seal programs do require would be enhanced if applicable law supported the requirements of the seal program. Moreover, the Commissioners concluded that seal-program requirements would be practically effective only when all three parties (the consumer, the site operator, and the seal service) were located in the same jurisdiction. Still, they were guardedly optimistic regarding the role seal programs might play in the growth of Internet commerce.

Privacy advocates in the United States have focused their criticisms on the limited use of the programs. They point out that the thousands of sites that have enrolled in the three major programs are only a small minority of all commercial Internet sites. Although many commercial Internet sites have chosen not to participate in seal programs, the number that does participate has grown rapidly in recent years. The goal of those who support the programs is that the seals will become so pervasive and so visible that companies will be reluctant to abandon the programs for fear that they will become noted for their lax privacy practices.

2. Privacy Enhancing Technologies

If the architecture of Internet commerce could be modified to give individuals more control over how their personal information is collected and used, then reform of U.S. privacy law would not be such an essential element to any program aimed at providing Americans with more information-privacy rights. The concept of "privacy enhancing technologies" (PET) is now attracting quite a bit of attention as one possible mechanism for increasing compliance with fair information practices in electronic commerce.

A leading example of a PET that is beginning to change the way Internet commerce is conducted is a technical standard called the Platform for Privacy Preferences Project (P3P), developed by the World Wide Web Consortium (W3C), one of the leading Internet standard-setting organizations. The general purpose of P3P is to allow a company to create a computer-readable privacy policy that it can post on its Web site. If a site has posted such a policy, then the Web browser of a consumer visiting the site could access the site's P3P encoded privacy policy and compare it with privacy preferences previously set in the consumer's browser. If the site's policies as indicated by its P3P code do not conform to the consumer's privacy standards as coded in the consumer's Web browser, the browser would block the transmission of the consumer's personal information to the site. The problem for the consumer, of course, is that he or she may find access to parts of the Web site blocked as a result. For example, a shopping-cart function that depends on the use of cookies would not function if the consumer's privacy preferences were set to bar the transmission of cookies to the consumer's computer.

Some privacy advocates support P3P because it makes it more practical for consumers to control who can collect personal information from them. Other advocates, however, are not so favorable. One problem should be familiar to you already. As with the Internet generally, there is no central organization overseeing the implementation of the P3P standard. Thus, each company maintaining a commercial Web site that collects personal information will have to make its own decisions about how the company's privacy policy is encoded with P3P codes. Thus, there will be no general system for auditing a company's actual information practices to determine how accurately the P3P codes reflect the written version of the privacy policy, much less the site's actual information practices.

Another problem is that companies that distribute browser software will establish the default settings for P3P programs. Thus, a consumer who wants enhanced privacy will have to alter those settings manually after he or she receives the computer. Microsoft has implemented P3P in version 6.0 of its Internet Explorer browser. (You can see the settings in Tools → Internet Options → Security in your browser.) As currently configured, the browser does permit a consumer the choice to "opt-out" of having personal information collected. Privacy advocates, of course, counter that this is too administratively complex and burdensome; they argue that Microsoft should have a default setting requiring users to "opt-in" to a browser that permits information collection.

Although designers hope that the P3P standard will gain global use, it is likely to be too U.S.-centric to appeal to consumers and organizations outside the United States. Representatives of the European Union have pointed out that the codes are designed in a way that would facilitate transfers of data that are unlawful under EU law. The basic problem is that the center of the P3P development process is U.S. Internet commerce, not Internet commerce as conducted outside the United States. As a result, unless a consumer has sufficient technological sophistication to alter the direct-from-the-factory default settings on the consumer's browser, the browser will tend to encourage consumers to release more personally identifiable information to commercial Internet sites than is permissible under EU law. That outcome is largely consistent with current practices at U.S.-based Web sites. It is at the same time inconsistent with the policy views of privacy advocates and EU regulators: that transfers of personal information are always problematic, should not be facilitated without the express, knowing authorization of the consumer, and always should be limited in scope to the minimum necessary to address a particular task.

Relevant Glossary Entries

Information Audit
Online Privacy Seal Program
Opt-in
Opt-out

Platform for Privacy Preferences (P3P)
Privacy Enhancing Technologies (PET)
Self-regulation
Wholesale Exception Clause
World Wide Web Consortium (W3C)

Problem Set 11

11.1. You represent a large Fortune 50 company with a substantial Internet retail operation. Your client has just been served with a subpoena seeking information from your Web site about purchases of materials possibly related to terrorist planning. The subpoena seeks the release of all of the personal information you have about the relevant customers, including their purchasing history with you, information you have about sites that they have visited, and personal identifying information that would allow the government to locate them. The compliance officer that received the subpoena feels that he has little choice to comply, but wants your advice on whether he will face a risk of litigation from the people whose information he releases. Assuming that the policy is in substance similar to the Yahoo! policy in the assignment, what is your answer?

11.2. A few weeks later, the same company calls you back. The company is about to acquire a large competitor, and the general counsel is worried that his company's privacy policy authorizes uses that are prohibited by the policy of the company that is being acquired. He has two questions for you.

(a) First, he wants your advice on how much the policy will limit his activities. Generally, he freely shares information with third parties that pay him for the opportunity to market goods and services to his customers. Assuming that the acquired company has a policy identical to the Yahoo.com policy in the assignment, would his activities be permissible under that policy?

(b) Second, assuming that his policy is more lenient in important ways, he wants to know if he can continue to handle the information under his own policy once the company is acquired. Assuming that the acquired entity's policy includes the same clause as the Amazon.com site, what do you tell him? How would your answer differ if the company had the relevant clause from the Yahoo.com policy?

11.3. Alfredo Guzman, the Webmaster for RiverFront Tools, Inc. (see Problem Set 5), had been trying to develop a privacy policy for the RiverFront Tools Web site. When he was unable to get the attention of Carl Eben, president of the company, Alfredo simply proceeded on his own. He surveyed other Web sites, found a privacy policy that struck him as fair, edited it, and posted it to the RiverFront Tools site at *www.rft.com*. The privacy policy says that personal information will be treated as private and confidential at all times and will not be shared with any third parties without the prior express authorization of the identified individual.

One of Carl's friends introduced Carl to a salesman with a local information technology company marketing its services that help businesses obtain the "decisionmaking intelligence" they need to survive in today's markets.

The salesman convinced Carl he needed to sign up for the company's data warehouse service. Carl brought the salesman in to meet Alfredo and to teach Alfredo how to upload all the data Alfredo had collected and stored regarding Carl's Web customers to the data warehouse for analysis. After the salesman left, Alfredo told Carl about the privacy policy that had been up on the Web site for over a year, and pointed out that the privacy policy would have to be revised if Carl wanted to use the salesman's data warehouse service. What course of action do you recommend to Carl?

11.4. California Pneumatic Tools (CPT, familiar to you most recently from Problem Set 7) has a Web site for power tool enthusiasts called mypowertools online.com. Last year, CPT signed up for the TRUSTe privacy seal program in order to increase the willingness of visitors to register with the site and disclose information about their power tool preferences. This year, advertising revenue for the site has fallen 90 percent and CPT is no longer able to cover the costs of maintaining the site. It thinks it has two options to keep the site up: charge visitors a subscription fee to access the bulletin boards and chat rooms where power tools enthusiasts can share opinions, or start selling profiles of visitors to power tools manufacturers who would pay a lot of money to know what CPT has learned about its customers. CPT is afraid that if it charges a fee to users, the site will die a rapid death, so it is inclined to sell the profiles instead. But if it revises the privacy policy to disclose that it is selling the profiles and gives visitors the opportunity to opt out of having their information sold, then the site will just as surely die. As a practical matter, what would be the downside to CPT of selling the profiles, not revising the company's privacy policy, and not notifying TRUSTe of the change in its information practices? [A careful analysis of TRUSTe policies (the current version of which is posted at the Web site for this course) will help to inform CPT's choices.]

11.5. Wally Webb is in charge of creating a machine-readable version of PetPortal's privacy policy based on P3P standards. He attended a workshop sponsored by Microsoft and the W3C to learn how to encode the PetPortal Web site with P3P privacy policy information. After he returned from the workshop, he set to work with a "P3P Policy Generator" application similar to those developed by IBM and PrivacyBot.com. First, he analyzed the organization of the Web site, the current privacy policy, and the data-collection functions associated with the different parts of the Web site. He decided to divide the Web site contents into three categories: browsing only, transaction processing, and interactive. The browsing-only category includes informational pages; PetPortal collects only basic clickstream data about users visiting these pages for analysis by the marketing department. In the transaction processing category are the pages where customers can select products, specify a payment mechanism, and submit their orders; PetPortal collects a great deal of personally identifiable information here. In the interactive category are the bulletin boards and chat rooms; PetPortal collects information about the actions of registered users, which it can match up with the registration information to reveal the identity of individuals.

While Wally was loading this information into the Policy Generator program, however, he made several mistakes, which resulted in the coding of all three categories of pages with the privacy policy codes appropriate for the browsing-only category. Several months later, company president Mia Katerina's cousin mentions that he has visited the PetPortal site and in light of what his packet sniffer software disclosed to him about the communications between his personal computer and the PetPortal server, he does not believe that the P3P codes on the site are accurate. Mia sat down with Wally and confirmed the nature of the problem, at which point Wally set about rectifying it immediately. Mia is now calling you to find out whether the company has any exposure for the time when the P3P codes were set incorrectly in light of PetPortal's human readable privacy policy and their actual information practices.

Assignment 12: Theft of Information

A. Electronic Communications Privacy Act

Although the Supreme Court once took a different view, it is now well established that the Fourth Amendment protects citizens against warrantless wiretaps of telephone conversations. Katz v. United States, 389 U.S. 347 (1967). Primarily motivated to provide procedures to permit the constitutional use of wiretaps in criminal investigations, Congress has enacted a variety of statutes limiting the circumstances in which wiretaps are available, which generally appear now in the Electronic Communications Privacy Act of 1986 (ECPA), 18 U.S.C. §§2510-2711. That statute modified and extended the existing Wiretap Act of 1968 (Sections 2510-2521) to include electronic communications. The second title of the ECPA also added an entirely new regulatory program, the Stored Communications Act (Sections 2701-2711), which covers access to certain stored communications. Crucial for our discussion is the oddity that although the primary concern of the Supreme Court and Congress has been government monitoring of electronic communications, the ECPA applies generally to the monitoring of electronic communications by private parties.

As modified by the ECPA, the Wiretap Act generally prohibits the "interception" of specified forms of communication. Interception is defined broadly to include "aural or other acquisition of the contents of any wire, electronic or oral communication through the use of any electronic, mechanical or other device." 18 U.S.C. §2510(4). Electronic communications are broadly defined to include all transmissions of signs, signals, writing, images, sounds, data, or intelligence of any nature that rely on a wire, radio, electromagnetic, photoelectric, or photooptical system. 18 U.S.C. §2510(12). Thus, electronic communications include not only conventional telephone communications, but also e-mail, cellphones, cordless phones, pagers, or satellite communications as well as computer-to-computer communications.

The biggest exception to the ECPA is that it permits the interception and disclosure of electronic communications if any one of the parties to the communication has consented. 18 U.S.C. §2511(2)(d). That is an important point, because states such as Florida, Maryland, and Pennsylvania have more stringent rules that require all parties to consent to monitoring. (For example, even though she did not violate the federal wiretap law, Linda Tripp was indicted for violating the Maryland wiretap statute after she taped telephone conversations with Monica Lewinsky.)

Another exception applies to providers of electronic communication services. Under the ECPA, the provider can monitor communications in the normal course of providing the service, if the monitoring is a necessary incident to providing the service, or if it is necessary to protect the rights or property of the service provider. 18 U.S.C. §2511(2)(a)(i).

Yet another exception is the so-called "ordinary course of business" exception, which permits certain kinds of employer monitoring of employee communications in the workplace. That exception appears indirectly through the interaction of a number of the definitional provisions of the ECPA. Generally, the ECPA applies whenever a communication is "intercept[ed]." An interception occurs only when the contents of a communication are acquired through the use of an "electronic, mechanical, or other device." 18 U.S.C. §2510(4). That term is generally defined quite broadly. For present purposes, however, it is important to note that it excludes

> any telephone or telegraph instrument, equipment or facility, or any component thereof, . . . furnished to the subscriber or user by a provider of wire or electronic communication service in the ordinary course of its business and being used by the subscriber or user in the ordinary course of its business or furnished by such subscriber or user for connection to the facilities of such service and used in the ordinary course of its business.

18 U.S.C. §2510(5)(a).

Thus, "ordinary course" use of telephone equipment is not an unlawful interception, whether the equipment is provided by the subscriber or by the telephone company. To see how the statute works, consider a case in which TelCo provides telephone service to RFT and in which RFT monitors the activities of its employees. In the language of the statute, TelCo is the "provider of [an] electronic communication service" and RFT is the "subscriber." Accordingly, the statute excludes from the range of covered devices any "equipment" or "facility" that TelCo furnishes to RFT that RFT is using in the ordinary course of its business. Thus, if RFT happens in the ordinary course of its business to overhear employee telephone communications using the standard equipment it leases from TelCo, then the ECPA does not apply.

On the other hand, monitoring that does not take place "in the ordinary course of its business" is covered by the ECPA, even if the monitoring uses conventional telephone equipment. The question, then, is what it means for monitoring to take place outside the ordinary course of business. The statute is not particularly clear on that point, but the general intuition seems to be that "ordinary" refers to the nature of business objective, rather than the frequency of the monitoring. Therefore, a consistent practice of monitoring for no particular reason or no justifiable reason probably would not be "ordinary course" — in the absence of some legitimate business objective separate from monitoring. (Of course, even that type of monitoring would be lawful as long as the employer had consent, perhaps obtained as a condition of employment through a general firm policy.) On the other hand, irregular and haphazard monitoring that occurs as a result of some other objective — a switchboard operator occasionally overhearing conversations as calls are transferred — probably would be ordinary.

The Stored Communications Act addresses wire and electronic communications that are stored by service providers. It establishes civil and criminal penalties for granting unauthorized access to or use of stored electronic communications such as voicemail or e-mail. 18 U.S.C. §§2701, 2707. For example, absent some exception, the statute would make it illegal for AOL to allow third parties to view records related to their customer's e-mail transmissions. As with the prohibition on the interception of live communications, exceptions exist for disclosures made with the consent of the originator of the communication; those necessary to or a normal incident of the operation of the communication system; or those made pursuant to a court order. 18 U.S.C. §2702(b).

The cases that follow should give a sense for how the Wiretap Act and the Stored Communications Act apply in the context of the Internet. As you read the next case in particular, consider how you might have advised the businesses involved in these transactions to increase the likelihood that their business plans would be found lawful.

In re Pharmatrak, Inc. Privacy Litigation
(Blumofe v. Pharmatrak, Inc.)

329 F.3d 9 (1st Cir. 2003)

Before LYNCH, Circuit Judge, BOWNES, Senior Circuit Judge, and HOWARD, Circuit Judge.

LYNCH, Circuit Judge.

This case raises important questions about the scope of privacy protection afforded internet users under the Electronic Communications Privacy Act of 1986 (ECPA), 18 U.S.C. §§2511, 2520.

In sum, pharmaceutical companies invited users to visit their websites to learn about their drugs and to obtain rebates. An enterprising company, Pharmatrak, sold a service, called "NETcompare," to these pharmaceutical companies. That service accessed information about the internet users and collected certain information meant to permit the pharmaceutical companies to do intra-industry comparisons of website traffic and usage. Most of the pharmaceutical companies were emphatic that they did not want personal or identifying data about their web site users to be collected. In connection with their contracting to use NETcompare, they sought and received assurances from Pharmatrak that such data collection would not occur. As it turned out, some such personal and identifying data was found, using easily customized search programs, on Pharmatrak's computers. Plaintiffs, on behalf of the purported class of internet users whose data Pharmatrak collected, sued both Pharmatrak and the pharmaceutical companies asserting, inter alia, that they intercepted electronic communications without consent, in violation of the ECPA.

The district court entered summary judgment for defendants on the basis that Pharmatrak's activities fell within an exception to the statute where one party consents to an interception. The court found the client pharmaceutical companies had consented by contracting with Pharmatrak and so this protected Pharmatrak. The plaintiffs dismissed all ECPA claims as to the pharmaceutical companies. This appeal concerns only the claim that Pharmatrak violated Title I of the ECPA.

We hold that the district court incorrectly interpreted the "consent" exception to the ECPA; we also hold that Pharmatrak "intercepted" the communication under the statute. We reverse and remand for further proceedings. . . .

I.

Pharmatrak provided its NETcompare service to pharmaceutical companies including American Home Products, Pharmacia, SmithKline Beecham, Pfizer, and Novartis from approximately June 1998 to November 2000. The pharmaceutical clients terminated their contracts with Pharmatrak shortly after this lawsuit was filed in August 2000. As a result, Pharmatrak was forced to cease its operations by December 1, 2000.

NETcompare was marketed as a tool that would allow a company to compare traffic on and usage of different parts of its website with the same information from its competitors' websites. The key advantage of NETcompare over off-the-shelf software was its capacity to allow each client to compare its performance with that of other clients from the same industry.

NETcompare was designed to record the webpages a user viewed at clients' websites; how long the user spent on each webpage; the visitor's path through the site (including her points of entry and exit); the visitor's IP address; and, for later versions, the webpage the user viewed immediately before arriving at the client's site (i.e., the "referrer URL"). This information-gathering was not visible to users of the pharmaceutical clients' websites. According to Wes Sonnenreich, former Chief Technology Officer of Pharmatrak, and Timothy W. Macinta, former Managing Director for Technology of Pharmatrak, NETcompare was not designed to collect any personal information whatsoever.

NETcompare operated as follows. A pharmaceutical client installed NETcompare by adding five to ten lines of HTML code to each webpage it wished to track and configuring the pages to interface with Pharmatrak's technology. When a user visited the website of a Pharmatrak client, Pharmatrak's HTML code instructed the user's computer to contact Pharmatrak's web server and retrieve from it a tiny, invisible graphic image known as a "clear GIF" (or a "web bug"). The purpose of the clear GIF was to cause the user's computer to communicate directly with Pharmatrak's web server. When the user's computer requested the clear GIF, Pharmatrak's web servers responded by either placing or accessing a "persistent cookie" on the user's computer. On a user's first visit to a webpage monitored by NETcompare, Pharmatrak's servers would plant a cookie on the user's computer. If the user had already visited a NETcompare webpage, then Pharmatrak's servers would access the information on the existing cookie.

A cookie is a piece of information sent by a web server to a web browser that the browser software is expected to save and to send back whenever the browser makes additional requests of the server (such as when the user visits additional webpages at the same or related sites). A persistent cookie is one that does not expire at the end of an online session. Cookies are widely used on the internet by reputable websites to promote convenience and customization. Cookies often store user preferences, login and registration information, or information related to an online "shopping cart." Cookies may also contain unique identifiers that allow a website to differentiate among users.

Each Pharmatrak cookie contained a unique alphanumeric identifier that allowed Pharmatrak to track a user as she navigated through a client's site and to identify a repeat user each time she visited clients' sites. If a person visited *www.pfizer.com* in June 2000 and *www.pharmacia.com* in July 2000, for example, then the persistent cookie on her computer would indicate to Pharmatrak that the same computer had been used to visit both sites. As NETcompare tracked a user through a website, it used JavaScript and a JavaApplet to record information such as the URLs the user visited. This data was recorded on the access logs of Pharmatrak's web servers.

Pharmatrak sent monthly reports to its clients juxtaposing the data collected by NETcompare about all pharmaceutical clients. These reports covered topics such as the most heavily used parts of a particular site; which site was receiving the most hits in particular areas such as investor or media relations; and the most important links to a site.

The monthly reports did not contain any personally identifiable information about users. The only information provided by Pharmatrak to clients about their users and traffic was contained in the reports (and executive summaries thereof). Slides from a Pharmatrak marketing presentation did say the company would break data out into categories and provide "user profiles." In practice, the aggregate demographic information in the reports was limited to the percentages of users from different countries; the percentages of users with different domain extensions (i.e., the percentages of users originating from for-profit, government, academic, or other not-for-profit organizations); and the percentages of first-time versus repeat users. An example of a NETcompare "user profile" is: "The average Novartis visitor is a first-time visitor from the U.S., visiting from a .com domain."

While it was marketing NETcompare to prospective pharmaceutical clients, Pharmatrak repeatedly told them that NETcompare did not collect personally identifiable information. It said its technology could not collect personal information, and specifically provided that the information it gathered could not be *used* to identify particular users by name. In their affidavits and depositions, executives of Pharmatrak clients consistently said that they believed NETcompare did not collect personal information, and that they did not learn otherwise until the onset of litigation. Some, if not all, pharmaceutical clients explicitly conditioned their purchase of NETcompare on Pharmatrak's guarantees that it would not collect users' personal information. For example, Pharmacia's April 2000 contract with Pharmatrak provided that NETcompare would not collect personally identifiable information from users. Michael Sonnenreich, Chief Executive Officer of Pharmatrak, stated unequivocally at his deposition that none of his company's clients consented to the collection of personally identifiable information.

Pharmatrak nevertheless collected some personal information on a small number of users. Pharmatrak distributed approximately 18.7 million persistent cookies through NETcompare. The number of unique cookies provides a rough estimate of the number of users Pharmatrak monitored. Plaintiffs' expert was able to develop individual profiles for just 232 users.

The following personal information was found on Pharmatrak servers: names, addresses, telephone numbers, email addresses, dates of birth, genders, insurance statuses, education levels, occupations, medical conditions, medications, and reasons for visiting the particular website. Pharmatrak also occasionally recorded the subject, sender, and date of the web- based email message a user was reading immediately prior to visiting the website of a Pharmatrak client. Most of the individual profiles assembled by plaintiffs' expert contain some but not all of this information.

The personal information in 197 of the 232 user profiles was recorded due to an interaction between NETcompare and computer code written by one pharmaceutical client, Pharmacia, for one of its webpages. Starting on or before August 18, 2000 and ending sometime between December 2, 2000 and February 6,

2001, the client Pharmacia used the "get" method to transmit information from a rebate form on its Detrol[11] website; the webpage was subsequently modified to use the "post" method of transmission. This was the source of the personal information collected by Pharmatrak from users of the Detrol website.

Web servers use two methods to transmit information entered into online forms: the get method and the post method. The get method is generally used for short forms such as the "Search" box at Yahoo! and other online search engines. The post method is normally used for longer forms and forms soliciting private information.[12] When a server uses the get method, the information entered into the online form becomes appended to the next URL. For example, if a user enters "respiratory problems" into the query box at a search engine, and the search engine transmits this information using the get method, then the words "respiratory" and "problems" will be appended to the query string at the end of the URL of the webpage showing the search results. By contrast, if a website transmits information via the post method, then that information does not appear in the URL. Since NETcompare was designed to record the full URLs of the webpages a user viewed immediately before and during a visit to a client's site, Pharmatrak recorded personal information transmitted using the get method.

There is no evidence Pharmatrak instructed its clients not to use the get method. The detailed installation instructions Pharmatrak provided to pharmaceutical clients ignore entirely the issue of the different transmission methods.

In addition to the problem at the Detrol website, there was also another instance in which a pharmaceutical client used the get method to transmit personal information entered into an online form. The other personal information on Pharmatrak's servers was recorded as a result of software errors. These errors were a bug in a popular email program (reported in May 2001 and subsequently fixed) and an aberrant web browser.

II.

[The district court granted summary judgment for Pharmatrak based on its view that the pharmaceutical companies consent authorized the activities about which plaintiffs complained.]

III.

. . . B. ELEMENTS OF THE ECPA CAUSE OF ACTION

ECPA amended the Federal Wiretap Act by extending to data and electronic transmissions the same protection already afforded to oral and wire communications. The paramount objective of the Wiretap Act is to protect effectively the privacy of communications.

The post-ECPA Wiretap Act provides a private right of action against one who "intentionally intercepts, endeavors to intercept, or procures any other person to

---

11. Detrol is a bladder control medication.

12. An example is the registration page at the New York Times website, which asks for a user's email address, date of birth, income, and other information.

intercept or endeavor to intercept, any wire, oral, or electronic communication." 18 U.S.C. §2511(1)(a); *see* 18 U.S.C. §2520 (providing a private right of action). The Wiretap Act defines "intercept" as "the aural or other acquisition of the contents of any wire, electronic, or oral communication through the use of any electronic, mechanical, or other device." *Id.* §2510(4). Thus, plaintiffs must show five elements to make their claim under Title I of the ECPA: that a defendant (1) intentionally (2) intercepted, endeavored to intercept or procured another person to intercept or endeavor to intercept (3) the contents of (4) an electronic communication (5) using a device. This showing is subject to certain statutory exceptions, such as consent.

In its trial and appellate court briefs, Pharmatrak sought summary judgment on only one element of §2511(1)(a), interception, as well as on the statutory consent exception. We address these issues below. Pharmatrak has not contested whether it used a device or obtained the contents of an electronic communication. This is appropriate. The ECPA adopts a "broad, functional" definition of an electronic communication. *Brown v. Waddell*, 50 F.3d 285, 289 (4th Cir. 1995). This definition includes "any transfer of signs, signals, writing, images, sounds, data, or intelligence of any nature transmitted in whole or in part by a wire, radio, electromagnetic, photoelectric, or photooptical system that affects interstate or foreign commerce," with certain exceptions unrelated to this case. 18 U.S.C. §2510(12). Transmissions of completed online forms, such as the one at Pharmacia's Detrol website, to the pharmaceutical defendants constitute electronic communications.

The ECPA also says that "'contents,' when used with respect to any wire, oral, or electronic communication, includes any information concerning the substance, purport, or meaning of that communication." 18 U.S.C. §2510(8). This definition encompasses personally identifiable information such as a party's name, date of birth, and medical condition. Finally, it is clear that Pharmatrak relied on devices such as its web servers to capture information from users.

C.   Consent Exception

There is a pertinent statutory exception to §2511(1)(a) "where one of the parties to the communication has given prior consent to such interception unless such communication is intercepted for the purpose of committing any criminal or tortious act. . . ." 18 U.S.C. §2511(2)(d). Plaintiffs, of course, bear the burden of establishing a violation of the ECPA. We think, at least for the consent exception under the ECPA in civil cases, that it makes more sense to place the burden of showing consent on the party seeking the benefit of the exception, and so hold. That party is more likely to have evidence pertinent to the issue of consent. Plaintiffs do not allege that Pharmatrak acted with a criminal or tortious purpose. Therefore, the question under the exception is limited to whether the pharmaceutical defendants gave consent to the interception. Because the district court disposed of the case on the grounds that Pharmatrak's conduct fell within the consent exception, we start there.

The district court adopted Pharmatrak's argument that the only relevant inquiry is whether the pharmaceutical companies consented to use Pharmatrak's NETcompare service, regardless of how the service eventually operated. In doing so, the district court did not apply this circuit's general standards for consent under the Wiretap Act and the ECPA. . . .

A party may consent to the interception of only part of a communication or to the interception of only a subset of its communications. Thus, a reviewing court must inquire into the *dimensions of the consent* and then ascertain whether the interception exceeded those boundaries. [Quotation marks omitted; emphasis in original.] Consent may be explicit or implied, but it must be actual consent rather than constructive consent. Pharmatrak argues that it had implied consent from the pharmaceutical companies.

Consent should not casually be inferred. [Quotation marks omitted.] Without actual notice, consent can only be implied when the surrounding circumstances *convincingly* show that the party knew about and consented to the interception. [Quotation marks omitted; emphasis in original.]

The district court made an error of law, urged on it by Pharmatrak, as to what constitutes consent. . . . Moreover, [the existing cases] do not set up a rule, contrary to the district court's reading of them, that a consent to interception can be inferred from the mere purchase of a service, regardless of circumstances. [The existing cases on which Pharmatrak relies] were concerned with situations in which the defendant companies' clients purchased their services for the precise purpose of creating individual user profiles in order to target those users for particular advertisements. . . . These decisions found it would be unreasonable to infer that the clients had *not* consented merely because they might not understand precisely how the user demographics were collected. The facts in our case are the mirror image of those in [the previous cases]: the pharmaceutical clients insisted there be no collection of personal data and the circumstances permit no reasonable inference that they did consent.

On the undisputed facts, the client pharmaceutical companies did not give the requisite consent. The pharmaceutical clients sought and received assurances from Pharmatrak that its NETcompare service did not and could not collect personally identifiable information. Far from consenting to the collection of personally identifiable information, the pharmaceutical clients explicitly conditioned their purchase of NETcompare on the fact that it would *not* collect such information.

The interpretation urged by Pharmatrak would, we think, lead to results inconsistent with the statutory intent. It would undercut efforts by one party to a contract to require that the privacy interests of those who electronically communicate with it be protected by the other party to the contract. It also would lead to irrational results. Suppose Pharmatrak, for example, had intentionally designed its software, contrary to its representations and its clients' expectations, to redirect all possible personal information to Pharmatrak servers, which collected and mined the data. Under the district court's approach, Pharmatrak would nevertheless be insulated against liability under the ECPA on the theory that the pharmaceutical companies had "consented" by simply buying Pharmatrak's product. Or suppose an internet service provider received a parent's consent solely to monitor a child's internet usage for attempts to access sexually explicit sites — but the ISP installed code that monitored, recorded and cataloged all internet usage by parent and child alike. Under the theory we have rejected, the ISP would not be liable under the ECPA.

Nor did the users consent. On the undisputed facts, it is clear that the internet user did not consent to Pharmatrak's accessing his or her communication with the pharmaceutical companies. The pharmaceutical companies' websites gave no indication that use meant consent to collection of personal information by a third party. Rather, Pharmatrak's involvement was meant to be invisible to the user, and it was. Deficient notice will almost always defeat a claim of implied consent. Pharmatrak makes a frivolous argument that the internet users visiting client Pharmacia's webpage for rebates on Detrol thereby consented to Pharmatrak's intercepting their personal information. On that theory, every online communication would provide consent to interception by a third party.

D.   INTERCEPTION REQUIREMENT

The parties briefed to the district court the question of whether Pharmatrak had "intercepted" electronic communications. If this question could be resolved in Pharmatrak's favor, that would provide a ground for affirmance of the summary judgment. It cannot be answered in favor of Pharmatrak.

The ECPA prohibits only "interceptions" of electronic communications. "Intercept" is defined as "the aural or other acquisition of the contents of any wire, electronic, or oral communication through the use of any electronic, mechanical, or other device." *Id.* §2510(4).

Before enactment of the ECPA, some courts had narrowed the Wiretap Act's definition of interception to include only acquisitions of a communication contemporaneous with transmission. *See, e.g., Steve Jackson Games, Inc. v. U.S. Secret Serv.*, 36 F.3d 457, 460-61 (5th Cir.1994) (applying pre-ECPA interpretation to post-ECPA case). There was a resulting debate about whether the ECPA should be similarly restricted. The debate is well described in [Konop v. Hawaiian Airlines, Inc., 302 F.3d 868, 876-79 & n.6 (9th Cir. 2002).] Other circuits have invoked the contemporaneous, or "real-time," requirement to exclude acquisitions apparently made a substantial amount of time after material was put into electronic storage. These circuits have distinguished between materials acquired in transit, which are interceptions, and those acquired from storage, which purportedly are not.

We share the concern of the Ninth and Eleventh Circuits about the judicial interpretation of a statute written prior to the widespread usage of the internet and the World Wide Web in a case involving purported interceptions of online communications. In particular, the storage-transit dichotomy adopted by earlier courts may be less than apt to address current problems. As one court recently observed, "[T]echnology has, to some extent, overtaken language. Traveling the internet, electronic communications are often — perhaps constantly — both 'in transit' and 'in storage' simultaneously, a linguistic but not a technological paradox." *United States v. Councilman*, 245 F. Supp. 2d 319, 321 (D. Mass. 2003).

The facts here do not require us to enter the debate over the existence of a real-time requirement. The acquisition by Pharmatrak was contemporaneous with the transmission by the internet users to the pharmaceutical companies. Both Curtin, the plaintiffs' expert, and Wes Sonnenreich, Pharmatrak's former CTO, observed that users communicated simultaneously with the pharmaceutical client's web server and with Pharmatrak's web server. After the user's personal information was transmitted using the get method, both the pharmaceutical client's server and Pharmatrak's server contributed content for the succeeding webpage; as both Curtin and Wes Sonnenreich acknowledged, Pharmatrak's content (the clear GIF that enabled the interception) sometimes arrived before the content delivered by the pharmaceutical clients.

Even those courts that narrowly read "interception" would find that Pharmatrak's acquisition was an interception. . . . NETcompare was effectively an automatic routing program. It was code that automatically duplicated part of the communication between a user and a pharmaceutical client and sent this information to a third party (Pharmatrak).

Pharmatrak argues that there was no interception because "there were always two separate communications: one between the Web user and the Pharmaceutical Client, and the other between the Web user and Pharmatrak." This argument fails for two reasons. First, as a matter of law, even the circuits adopting a narrow reading of the Wiretap Act merely require that the acquisition occur at the same time as the transmission; they do not require that the acquisition somehow constitute the same communication as the transmission. Second, Pharmatrak acquired the same URL query string (sometimes containing personal information) exchanged as part of the communication between the pharmaceutical client and the user. Separate, but simultaneous and identical, communications satisfy even the strictest real-time requirement. . . .

F.   CONCLUSION

We *reverse* and *remand* for further proceedings consistent with this opinion.

One of the most difficult questions courts have faced relates to how the concept of "interception" applies in the Internet era. The case below presents a controversial understanding of that problem.

United States v. Councilman
373 F.3d 197 (1st Cir. 2004)

Before TORRUELLA, Circuit Judge, CYR, Senior Circuit Judge, and LIPEZ, Circuit Judge.
   TORRUELLA, Circuit Judge.
   The United States appeals from the district court's dismissal of Count One of the Indictment against defendant Bradford C. Councilman ("defendant"). Count One charged defendant with conspiring to engage in conduct prohibited by various provisions of the Wiretap Act, 18 U.S.C. §§2510-2522, in violation of 18 U.S.C. §371. We affirm.

I.   FACTS

Defendant was Vice-president of Interloc, Inc. ("Interloc"). Interloc's primary business was as an online rare and out-of-print book listing service. As part of its services, Interloc provided certain book dealer customers with an electronic mail ("e-mail") address and acted as the service provider. The dealer was provided with an e-mail account ending in "@Interloc.com".

In May 1998, Alibris, a California corporation, acquired Interloc. Defendant was Vice-president, shareholder and employee of Interloc and Alibris. Among defendant's responsibilities was the management of the Internet Service Provider ("ISP") and the book dealer subscription list managed by Interloc.

The parties stipulated to the following facts relevant to the transfer of electronic messages by the Interloc systems. An e-mail message, which is composed using an e-mail program, is transferred from one computer to another on its way to its final destination, the addressee. Building on the principle of store and forward, the message is handed to a Message Transfer Agent ("MTA") which stores the message locally. The message is routed through the network from one MTA to another until it reaches the recipient's mail server, which accepts it and stores it in a location accessible to the recipient. Once the e-mail is accessible to the recipient, final delivery has been completed. The final delivery process places the message into storage in a message store area. Often, a separate Mail Delivery Agent ("MDA") will be required to retrieve the e-mail from the MTA in order to make final delivery.

Interloc's computer facility used a program known as procmail (short for process mail) as its MDA. Procmail operates by scanning and sorting e-mail together with an MTA computer program known as "sendmail."

According to the Indictment, on or about January 1998, defendant directed Interloc employees to write computer code to intercept and copy all incoming communications from Amazon.com to subscriber dealers. The Interloc systems administrator wrote a revision to the mail processing code called procmail.rc ("the procmail"), designed to intercept, copy, and store, all incoming messages from Amazon.com before they were delivered to the members' e-mail, and therefore, before the e-mail was read by the intended recipient. Defendant was charged with using the procmail to intercept thousands of messages. Defendant and other Interloc employees routinely read the e-mails sent to its members seeking to gain a commercial advantage.

The procmail was designed to work only within the confines of Interloc's computer. At all times that MTA sendmail and MDA procmail performed operations affecting the e-mail system, the messages existed in the random access memory (RAM) or in hard disks, or both, within Interloc's computer systems. Each of the e-mails at issue constituted an "electronic communication" within the meaning of 18 U.S.C. §2510(12).

Count One of the Indictment charged defendant with a violation of 18 U.S.C. §371 for conspiracy to violate 18 U.S.C. §2511. Defendant allegedly conspired to intercept the electronic communications, to intentionally disclose the contents of the intercepted communications, in violation of 18 U.S.C. §2511(1)(a), and to use the contents of the unlawfully obtained electronic communication, in violation of 18 U.S.C. §2511(1)(c). Finally, the government alleged that defendant had conspired to cause a person to divulge the content of the communications while in transmission to persons other than the addressees of the communications, in violation of 18 U.S.C. §2511(3)(a). The object of the conspiracy, according to the government, was to exploit the content of e-mail from Amazon.com, the Internet retailer, to dealers in order to develop a list of books, learn about competitors and attain a commercial advantage for Alibris and Interloc.

Defendant moved to dismiss the Indictment for failure to state an offense under the Wiretap Act, as the e-mail interceptions at issue were in "electronic storage," as defined in 18 U.S.C. §2510(17), and could not be intercepted as a matter of law. The district court did not initially grant the motion to dismiss but, upon further briefing by the parties, granted the motion and dismissed Count One. The district court found that the e-mails were in electronic storage and that, therefore, the Wiretap Act could not be violated because the requisite "interception" was lacking.

II. ANALYSIS

A. THE WIRETAP ACT

. . . The issue in this case is whether there was an "intercept" of a communication within the meaning of the Wiretap Act. In cases of statutory construction we begin with the language of the statute. We determine the meaning of a word from the context in which it is used. . . .

We begin our analysis by highlighting the difference between the definitions of "wire communications" and "electronic communications" in the Wiretap Act, mindful that the communications at issue in this appeal are electronic in nature. Under 18 U.S.C. §2510(1), a

> "wire communication" means any aural transfer made in whole or in part through the use of facilities for the transmission of communications by the aid of wire, cable or other like connection between the point of origin and the point of reception furnished or operated by any person engaged in providing or operating such facilities . . . and such term includes any electronic storage of such communication. . . .

18 U.S.C. §2510(1). By comparison, "'electronic communication' means any transfer of signs, signals, writing, images, sounds, data, or intelligence of any nature transmitted in whole or in part by a wire, radio, electromagnetic, photoelectronic or photooptical system." Id. §2510(12). No mention is made of electronic storage of electronic communications.

"Intercept" is defined as "the aural or other acquisition of the contents of any wire, electronic, or oral communication through the use of any electronic, mechanical, or other device." 18 U.S.C. §2510(4).

The statute that defendant is charged with conspiring to violate, 18 U.S.C. §2511, provides criminal penalties to be imposed on "any person who — (a) intentionally intercepts, endeavors to intercept, or procures any other person to intercept or endeavor to intercept, any wire, oral, or electronic communication." 18 U.S.C. §2511(1)(a).

Relying on the language of the statute and the decisions of our sister circuits, the district court held that Congress did not intend for the Wiretap Act's interception provisions to apply to communication in electronic storage. The district court rejected "[t]he Government's position . . . that the Wiretap Act applies to interceptions that take place when the message . . . is 'in transit' or 'in process of delivery.' " Relying on the definition of electronic storage, the district court held that no interception can occur while the e-mails are in electronic storage and therefore, without the requisite interception, the Wiretap Act could not be violated. . . .

The particular problem confronted in this case is what has been called the "contemporaneous" problem in the intercept requirement of the Wiretap Act. See In re Pharmatrak, 329 F.3d 9, 21-22 (1st Cir. 2003). The government argues that given the particular nature of electronic communications and the mechanisms used to retrieve them, 18 U.S.C. §2511(a) is a proper foundation for Count One of the Indictment. . . .

The first case to address the issue of unlawful intercept in the context of electronic communications is Steve Jackson Games, Inc. v. United States Secret Service, 36 F.3d 457 (5th Cir. 1994). There, the plaintiff company sued the Secret Service because the agency had seized a computer used to operate a bulletin board system, but which also contained private, unretrieved electronic mail. Id. at 459. The plaintiff provided its customers with the ability to send and retrieve e-mail, which was stored on the company's hard disk drive temporarily, until the recipient retrieved the e-mail. *Id.* at 458. After seizing the computer, the Secret Service allegedly opened the private e-mails, read them and deleted them. The company sued, alleging, *inter alia,* a violation of the Wiretap Act. *Id.* at 459-60.

The Fifth Circuit held that the seizure of sent but unretrieved e-mail did not constitute an intercept for purposes of 18 U.S.C. §2511(1)(a). *See Steve Jackson Games,* 36 F.3d at 461-62. In reaching that conclusion, it relied on the difference in the definitions of electronic and wire communication and the definition of electronic storage. "Congress' use of the word 'transfer' in the definition of 'electronic communication,' and its omission in that definition of the phrase 'any electronic storage of such communication' (part of the definition of 'wire communication') reflects that Congress did not intend for 'intercept' to apply to 'electronic communications' when those communications are in 'electronic storage.' " *Id.*

In contrast, *Konop v. Hawaiian Airlines, Inc.,* 302 F.3d 868 (9th Cir. 2002), concerned a plaintiff, an employee of Hawaiian Airlines, who operated a secure website which posted criticism of his employer. A vice-president of the airline obtained permission from authorized users to view the website. Plaintiff sued, alleging, *inter alia,* that defendant had violated the Wiretap Act by violating the terms of use of the website and entering a secure website under false pretenses.

The Ninth Circuit, after granting panel rehearing, reversed its earlier position that the electronic communications were covered under the Wiretap Act. It did so because, in its view, the conduct of the defendant did not constitute an intercept as that term is defined. *Konop,* 302 F.3d at 876. Relying on *Steve Jackson Games,* it held that "for a website such as Konop's to be 'intercepted' in violation of the Wiretap Act, it must be acquired during transmission, not while in electronic storage." *Id.* at 878. In doing so, it rejected the position the government takes in this case, that, given the nature of e-mail, the Wiretap Act must apply to en route storage. *Id.* at 879 n.6. "While this argument is not without appeal, the language and structure of the [Act] demonstrate that Congress considered and rejected this argument." *Id.* The court relied, as did the district court in this case, on the expansive definition of the term "electronic storage" in 18 U.S.C. §2510(17)(A). The dismissal of the Wiretap Act claim was affirmed.

The government is correct that the electronic communications at issue here were acquired in a different manner than in *Steve Jackson Games* and *Konop.* Defendant's procmail operated to obtain the e-mails before they were received by its intended recipients. While the e-mail in *Steve Jackson Games* was retrieved from storage in a computer and the website in *Konop* was accessed under false pretenses, the e-mails in this case were accessed by the procmail as they were being transmitted and in real time. However, the presence of the words "any temporary, intermediate storage" in 18 U.S.C. §2510(17) controls. On the facts of this case, it is clear that the electronic communications in this case were in a form of electronic storage. It may well be that the protections of the Wiretap Act have been eviscerated as technology advances. *See United States v. Steiger,* 318 F.3d 1039, 1047-51 (11th Cir. 2003) (holding intercept did not occur because there was no contemporaneous acquisition but commenting that under the narrow reading of the statute few seizures will constitute interceptions under Wiretap Act). As the stipulation reached by the parties states, "[a]t all times that sendmail and procmail performed operations affecting the email messages at issue, the messages existed in the random access memory (RAM) or in hard disks, or both, within Interloc's computer system." When defendant obtained the e-mails, they were in temporary storage in Interloc's computer systems. There was also a stipulation that "[n]either sendmail nor procmail performed functions that affected the emails in issue while the emails were in transmission through wires or cables between computers." This fact places the messages outside the scope of 18 U.S.C. §2511(a), and into temporary electronic storage under 18 U.S.C. §2510(17)(A).

[The panel considers and rejects the view of the government and the dissenting judge that the legislative history requires a contrary interpretation of the statute.]

The Wiretap Act's purpose was, and continues to be, to protect the privacy of communications. We believe that the language of the statute makes clear that Congress meant to give lesser protection to electronic communications than wire and oral communications. Moreover, at this juncture, much of the protection may have been eviscerated by the realities of modern technology. We observe, as most courts have, that the language may be out of step with the technological realities of computer crimes. However, it is not the province of this court to graft meaning onto the statute where Congress has spoken plainly. We therefore affirm the district court's dismissal of Count One of the Indictment on the premise that no intercept occurred in this case, and therefore, the Wiretap Act could not be violated. . . .

LIPEZ, Circuit Judge (Dissenting).

Unlike my colleagues, I believe that the district court erred in dismissing the indictment against Defendant-Appellee Bradford Councilman for violating Title I of the Electronic Communications Privacy Act (ECPA). . . .

I.   THE TECHNOLOGY

The Internet consists of a network of inter-connected computers in which data are broken down into small, individual packets and forwarded from one computer to another until they reach their destinations. Each service on the Internet — e.g., e-mail, web hosting, and instant messaging — has its own protocol for using those packets of data to transmit information from one place to another. I will focus solely on the e-mail protocol. After a user composes a message in an e-mail program, a mail transfer agent ("MTA") formats that message and sends it to another program that "packetizes it" and sends those packets out to the Internet. Computers on the network then pass the packets from one to another; each computer along the route stores the packets in memory, retrieves the address of their destination, and then determines where to send it next based on the packet's destination. At various points the packets are reassembled to form the original e-mail message, copied, and then repacketized for the next leg of the journey. These intermediate computers occasionally retain backup copies of the e-mails that they forward and then delete those backups a short time later. The method of transmission is commonly called "store and forward" delivery.

Once all the packets reach the recipient's mail server, they are reassembled to form the e-mail message. A mail user agent ("MUA"), which in Councilman's case was a program called "Procmail," then determines which user should receive the e-mail and places the message in that user's mailbox. The MUA is controlled by programs called "recipe files." These recipe files can be used in a variety of ways and can, for example, instruct the MUA to deposit mail addressed to one address into another user's mailbox (i.e., to send mail addressed to "help" to the tech support department), to reject mail from certain addresses, or to make copies of certain messages. Once the messages are deposited in a mailbox, the end user simply needs to use an e-mail program to retrieve and read that message. Councilman wrote a recipe file for his MUA that caused all of the messages from Amazon.com to be copied while the MUA was in the process of placing that message into the recipient's mailbox, and to place these copies into his own personal box.

II. THE LEGISLATIVE CONTEXT

Congress passed the 1968 Wiretap Act to "protect[ ] the privacy of wire and oral communications, and [to] delineat[e] on a uniform basis the circumstances and conditions under which the interception of wire and oral communications may be authorized." *Gelbard v. United States*, 408 U.S. 41, 48 (1972) (quoting S. Rep. No. 90-1097, at 66 (1968)). By the mid-1980s, however, technology had outpaced the privacy protections in the Act, creating uncertainty and gaps in its coverage. . . .

. . . Title I of the [ECPA responded to that problem. It] amended the 1968 Wiretap Act and added new protections for electronic and digital technologies. Section 101(c)(1)(A) added "electronic communications" to the existing prohibitions against intercepting wire — which are essentially telephone calls — and oral communications. . . . Congress intended to give the term "electronic communication" a broad definition . . . Section 101(a)(3) added "or other" to the definition of "intercept," which had previously only referred to the "*aural* acquisition of the contents of any . . . communication." Also relevant to this case, albeit not at issue here, Section 101(c)(7) removed a phrase in the Wiretap Act that limited the scope of the Act to communications transmitted on common carriers. This amendment expanded the reach of the Act's protections to private telephone and computer networks, including internal office networks, and cellular phones. The amended Wiretap Act now reads, in pertinent part: "[A]ny person who intentionally intercepts, endeavors to intercept, or procures any person to intercept or endeavor to intercept, any wire, oral or electronic communication . . . shall be punished. . . ." 18 U.S.C. §2511(1).

Congress also recognized that, with the rise of remote computing operations and large databanks of stored electronic communications, the threats to individual privacy extended well beyond the bounds of the Wiretap Act's prohibition against the "interception" of communications. These stored communications — including stored e-mail messages, stored financial transactions, stored medical records, and stored pager messages — were not protected by the Wiretap Act, presumably because the Act had been interpreted to only prohibit the contemporaneous acquisition of a communication. [Brackets, quotation marks, and citation omitted.] Therefore, Congress concluded that "the information [in these communications] may be open to possible wrongful use and public disclosure by law enforcement authorities as well as unauthorized private parties." Sen. Rep. 99-541, at 3 (1986).

Congress added Title II to the ECPA to halt these potential intrusions on individual privacy. This title, which is commonly referred to as the Stored Communications Act, established new punishments for any person who "1) intentionally accesses without authorization a facility through which an electronic communication service is provided; or 2) intentionally exceeds an authorization to access that facility; and thereby obtains, alters, or prevents authorized access to a wire or electronic communication while it is in electronic storage. . . ." 18 U.S.C. §2701(a).

The privacy protections established by the Stored Communications Act were intended to apply to two categories of communications. . . . The first category refers to temporary storage such as when a message sits in an e-mail user's mailbox after transmission but prior to the user retrieving the message from the mail server. Importantly, however, this category does not include messages that are still in transmission, which remain covered by the Wiretap Act. [H.R. Rep. No. 99-647], at 65 (stating that *the Wiretap Act* "prohibits . . . a provider from divulging the contents of a communication while it is in transmission."). The second category includes communications that are retained on a server for administrative and billing purposes. Communications service providers could use stored messages in this category to restore a user's data in the event of a system crash or to recover accidentally-deleted messages.

Defendant-Appellee Bradford Councilman was indicted on July 11, 2001 for violating Title I of the ECPA, the Wiretap Act, but was not charged with violating Title II, the Stored Communications Act. Determining the legality of this indictment requires us to explore the dividing line between these two titles. Councilman claims that the e-mails at issue were stored communications when they were being processed for delivery in his company's computers, and, therefore, they were not the type of "evanescent" transmissions, i.e., telephone calls traveling through a wire, that the Wiretap Act addresses. Under his approach, an e-mail would only be subject to the Wiretap Act when it is traveling through cables and not when it is being processed by electronic switches and computers during transit and delivery. . . .

. . . The government focuses on the temporal nature of Councilman's actions and argues that he violated the Wiretap Act because he copied the e-mails "contemporaneously with their transmission." In other words, he copied them in real time while they were in the process of being delivered. Under its view, an intercept is subject to the Wiretap Act between the time that the author presses the "send" button and the time that the message arrives in the recipient's e-mail box. Accordingly, the Wiretap Act would apply to messages that are intercepted contemporaneously with their transmission and the Stored Communications Act would apply to messages that are accessed non-contemporaneously with transmission.

As I discuss in greater detail in Section V, *infra,* the line that we draw in this case will have far-reaching effects on personal privacy and security. Congress concluded that stored communications, while requiring protection, require fewer privacy protections than those in transit. Therefore, the Wiretap Act includes significant procedural protections which go beyond the requirements of the Fourth Amendment itself and which are not applicable to the Stored Communications Act. First, officers may only obtain wiretap orders for investigations involving federal felonies. *See* 18 U.S.C. §2516(3). Second, in addition to demonstrating that they have probable cause, the officers must provide specific information regarding, *inter alia,* the types of communications that would likely be intercepted, the individuals whose conversations would be intercepted, the steps that the agents took to avoid having to rely on a wiretap, and the steps that they would take to avoid intercepting more information than is necessary. 18 U.S.C. §§2518(1)-(4). Third, unless the court grants a special extension, the wiretap may only last for the shorter of thirty days or as long as is necessary to obtain the necessary evidence. §2518(5). Fourth, the court may require the Government to produce regular reports on the progress of its wiretaps and to keep the tapes and transcripts of those wiretaps under seal. §§2518(6) & 8(a). Fifth, the court must notify the target of the wiretap application — within a reasonable time — that their communications may have been intercepted. §2518(8)(d). Finally, if the officers violate any portion of these rules, the evidence obtained through the wiretap is automatically suppressed, even if the Government's actions did not violate the Fourth Amendment. §2515.

The Stored Communications Act does not contain any of the Wiretap Act's special protections. A federal law enforcement agent could obtain access to such communications simply by obtaining a warrant. 18 U.S.C. §2703(a). The target of the investigation does not need to be informed that the government accessed his or her communications, §2703(b)(1)(A), and a defendant does not have the right, outside of the Fourth Amendment, to seek to suppress communications that were obtained in violation of the Stored Communications Act.

It is also easier for private actors to access private messages under the Stored Communications Act. Section 2702(a) exempts, *inter alia,* "conduct authorized by the person or entity providing a wire or electronic communications service" from the prohibition against unauthorized access. Thus, a private actor like Councilman may open a user's files and may read the e-mails that are stored in that user's mailbox. *But see* 18 U.S.C. §2702 (stating that service providers may not, with certain objections, disclose stored communications that they access). The Wiretap Act does not include any such broad exemption.

III.   COUNCILMAN'S ARGUMENTS

A.   THE PLAIN TEXT

Councilman's primary argument, which was dispositive with the district court and now with my colleagues, is that the plain text of the ECPA exempts electronic communications that are in storage from the purview of the Wiretap Act. In brief, he argues that Congress included the term "electronic storage" in the ECPA's definition of "wire communication" but failed to do so in the definition of "electronic communication." That omission, according to Councilman, indicates that Congress intended to exclude communications that are in storage from the definition of "electronic communication" and, hence, from the scope of the Wiretap Act. Moreover, Congress defined the term "electronic storage" expansively to include "any temporary, intermediate storage of a wire or electronic communication incidental to the electronic transmission thereof." 18 U.S.C. §2510(17). Since the parties stipulated that the e-mails in this case were "in the random access memory (RAM) or in the hard disks, or both, within [Councilman's company's] computer system" at the time of the interception, those e-mails fall under the statutory definition of "in storage."

As so often happens under close scrutiny, the plain text is not so plain. There is no explicit statement from Congress that it intended to exclude communications that are in storage from the definition of "electronic communication," and, hence, from, the scope of the Wiretap Act. Councilman, without acknowledging it, looks beyond the face of the statute and makes a non-textual, inferential leap. He infers that Congress intended to exclude all communications that are in storage from the definition of "electronic communication," regardless of whether they are in the process of being delivered, simply because it did not include the term "electronic storage" in that definition. This inferential leap is not a plain text reading of the statute.

As I discuss in greater detail in Section IV, this inferential leap ignores the rationale behind Congress's inclusion of electronic storage in the definition of "wire communication." Recognizing that telephone calls would no longer be protected by the Wiretap Act after they were stored in voicemail, Congress wanted to expand the scope of the Wiretap Act to embrace these stored communications. Although this decision might indicate that Congress did not intend to use the Wiretap Act to protect e-mails after they have been delivered, it says nothing about Congressional intent regarding e-mails that are still in transmission. Furthermore, my colleagues use that maxim to impute meaning to the statute that the legislative history does not support. Congress included electronic storage in its definition of wire communications because it wanted voicemails to be protected under the Wiretap Act after those messages were delivered. We should not misconstrue this easily understood inclusion of post-delivery voicemail storage as indicating an unstated intention to exclude emails in transmission from the scope of the Wiretap Act. . . .

In short, the plain text of the ECPA does not clearly address the issue of whether a communication is still considered an electronic communication when it is in electronic storage during transmission. Given this ambiguity, I turn to Councilman's arguments regarding Congressional intent and legislative history.

B.   CONGRESSIONAL INTENT AND LEGISLATIVE HISTORY

[Judge Lipez chronicles legislative history that generally establishes that the purpose of the ECPA was to update privacy protections to prevent the provisions of the Wiretap Act from being eroded by technological developments.]

C.   OTHER PRECEDENTS

[Judge Lipez rejects Councilman's reliance on the Fifth Circuit's decision in *Steve Jackson Games* and the Ninth Circuit's decision in *Konop* because neither case involved interception of communications that were stored during the process of transmission. Both cases involved communications that had been stored after transmission was completed.]. . .

IV.   THE GOVERNMENT'S VIEW

According to the Government's view of the ECPA, "an 'intercept' occurs [and the Wiretap Act applies] when one acquires an electronic communication contemporaneous with its transmission." It is irrelevant that the transmission may have been in electronic storage at the time of the acquisition. In my view, this interpretation of the Act is consistent with Congressional intent, precedent, and the realities of electronic communication systems.

The district court seemed to agree with one predicate of the Government's argument when it acknowledged that "technology has, to some extent, overtaken language" and that "[t]raveling the Internet, electronic communications are often — perhaps constantly both 'in transit' and 'in storage' simultaneously." This apt observation should have prompted a different legal conclusion.

All digital transmissions must be stored in RAM or on hard drives while they are being processed by computers during transmission. Every computer that forwards the packets that comprise an e-mail message must store those packets in memory while it reads their addresses, and every digital switch that makes up the telecommunications network through which the packets travel between computers must also store the packets while they are being routed across the network. Since this type of storage is a fundamental part of the transmission process, attempting to separate all storage from transmission makes no sense.

Furthermore, in addition to storing the individual packets during routing, intermediate computers must temporarily store entire e-mail messages during transmission at various points along the route from sender to recipient. The technical specification for this type of e-mail transmission was adopted by the group that was coordinating standards for the Internet in 1982, and this standard for e-mail transmission was in use well before Congress adopted the ECPA in 1986. Therefore, when Congress acted, the fallacy of excluding from the scope of the Wiretap Act a message in storage at the time of interception was well-documented. The government's contemporaneous v. non-contemporaneous dichotomy accommodates this aspect of electronic technology; unlike Councilman's approach, it also makes sense in the real world.

The government's approach is also fully compatible with the portions of the ECPA that Councilman highlights in his argument. In a strange twist of logic, Councilman argues that Congress's broad definition of the term "electronic storage" supports his view that the e-mails at issue in this case were protected by the Stored Communications Act and not by the Wiretap Act. Yet the legislative history demonstrates that Congress adopted this broad definition to *enlarge* privacy protections for personal data, not to exclude e-mails stored during transmission from the strong protections of the Wiretap Act.

Responding to concerns raised in [a report from the Office of Technology Assessment (OTA) on *Electronic Surveillance and Civil Liberties*], Congress wanted to ensure that the messages and by-product files that are left behind after transmission and messages stored in a user's mailbox are protected from unauthorized access. The OTA identified four states during which a stored e-mail message could be accessed: 1) in the sender's terminal; 2) in the recipient's terminal; 3) in the recipient's paper files after the message was printed; and 4) in the service provider's electronic files when retained for administrative purposes. *Electronic Surveillance,* at 45. E-mails in the sender's and recipient's terminals could be accessed by "breaking into" those computers and retrieving the files. *Id.* at 48-49. As discussed in Section II, *supra,* the victim of such an attack had few legal remedies for such an invasion prior to the ECPA. The e-mails retained on the service provider's computers after transmission, which the report noted are primarily retained for "billing purposes and as a convenience in case the customer loses the message," could be accessed and possibly disclosed by the provider. *Id.* at 50. Prior to the ECPA, it was not clear whether the user had the right to challenge such a disclosure. *Id.* Similar concerns applied to temporary financial records and personal data retained after transmission. *Id.* Given that background and evidence in the legislative history that Congress incorporated much of the OTA's report in the legislation, it appears that Congress had in mind these types of pre and post transmission "temporary, intermediate storage of a wire or electronic communication incidental to the electronic transmission thereof," *see* 18 U.S.C. §2510(17), when it established the definition of "electronic storage." There is no indication that it meant to exclude the type of storage used during transmission from the scope of the Wiretap Act.

It is also telling that virtually none of the discussions of electronic storage in House and Senate conference reports occur within the context of message transmission or the Wiretap Act. If, as the District Court and Councilman suggest, Congress intended to narrow the scope of the Wiretap Act by adopting a broad definition of "electronic storage," it would likely have discussed storage during transmission while it discussed the new provisions in the Wiretap Act. . . .

Likewise, there is nothing in the legislative record to indicate that Congress intended to reduce the protection for electronic communications by including the term "electronic storage" in its definition of "wire communication." Instead, as noted earlier, it appears that Congress included that provision in the ECPA simply to expand the protections for voicemails. The government's contemporaneous v. non-contemporaneous approach recognizes that Congress had to specifically include stored voicemails in the definition of "wire communication" to have the Wiretap Act apply to those communications. Without the explicit addition of voicemails to the scope of the Wiretap Act, these communications would have been regulated by the Stored Communications Act. Indeed, that is exactly what happened when Congress removed the explicit reference to "electronic storage" from the definition of "wire communication" in the [USA Patriot Act adopted in 2001]. *See Konop*, 302 F.3d at 878 ("By eliminating storage from the definition of wire communication, Congress essentially reinstated the pre-ECPA definition of 'intercept' — acquisition contemporaneous with transmission — with respect to wire communications."); Robert A. Pikowsky, *An Overview of the Law of Electronic Surveillance Post September 11, 2001*, 94 Law Libr. J. 601, 608 (2002) ("[T]he USA PATRIOT Act amended the statutory scheme and unambiguously brought voicemail under the Stored Communications Act.").

This result creates an analogy between electronic and wire communications: voicemails are to telephone calls in the wire communication context as messages stored in mailboxes are to e-mails in transit in the electronic communications context. The Government's approach to the ECPA is faithful to this analogy. Acquisitions of conversation stored in voicemailboxes, like messages stored in e-mailboxes, do not occur contemporaneously with communications; therefore, neither of these should be treated as intercepts under the Wiretap Act. Telephone wiretaps and acquisitions of e-mails through the use of MUA recipe files, on the other hand, do occur contemporaneously with communications and should be considered intercepts under the Wiretap Act.

V. EXISTING PRACTICES AND PRIVACY PROTECTIONS

The Government observes in its brief that its criminal investigators would stand to gain by the court's adoption of Councilman's interpretation: "If defendant's argument prevails, law enforcement would not violate the Wiretap Act by capturing the email without a wiretap order. Instead, law enforcement could rely on lesser legal process, with lesser judicial oversight, than is required under the Wiretap Act." As discussed in Section II, *supra,* the Stored Communications Act does not require the government to follow the procedures for obtaining a wiretap order. Officers can seize stored records for any crime for which they can get a search warrant; their search can extend to the limits of the Fourth Amendment; they do not need to report the progress of their search to courts; and defendants do not have an extra-constitutional right to suppress evidence from illegal searches.

The Justice Department's current policy guidance memorandum assumes that the type of communications at issue here fall under the purview of the Wiretap Act. Therefore, it has been the Government's position that it had to obtain judicial authorization under the Wiretap Act to seize e-mails contemporaneously with their delivery. That practice would likely change under Councilman's interpretation of the Act. For example, the government states in its brief that "to implement wiretap orders on email accounts, the Federal Bureau of Investigation usually relies on the communication service providers to conduct the acquisitions." The providers use MUA recipe files similar to the one in this case to intercept, copy, and deliver the targeted e-mails to the government as they are being delivered. Under Councilman's narrow interpretation of the Act, the Government would no longer need to obtain a court-authorized wiretap order to conduct such surveillance. This would effectuate a dramatic change in Justice Department policy and mark a significant reduction in the public's right to privacy.

Such a change would not, however, be limited to the interception of e-mails. Under Councilman's approach, the government would be free to intercept all wire and electronic communications that are in temporary electronic storage without having to comply with the Wiretap Act's procedural protections. That means that the Government could install taps at telephone company switching stations to monitor phone conversations that are temporarily "stored" in electronic routers during transmission. *See United States Telecom. Ass'n v. FCC*, 227 F.3d 450, 464 (D.C. Cir. 2000) ("[In a digital telephone network,] a call is broken into a number of discrete digital data packets, each traveling independently through the network along different routes. Data packets are then reassembled in the proper sequence at the call's destination"); United States Congress, Office of Technology Assessment, *Electronic Surveillance in a Digital Age* 33 (1995) (stating that eighty percent of the telephone switches in the United States in 1991 were digital); *see also* 18 U.S.C. §1002 (requiring telephone companies to ensure that the government retains the ability to intercept calls as the company installs new technologies). It could install "packet sniffer" software, computer programs that record the contents of all of the packets traveling through a network, on the servers of Internet Service Providers (ISPs) without having to comply with the Wiretap Act.

In short, Councilman's approach to the Wiretap Act would undo decades of practice and precedent regarding the scope of the Wiretap Act and would essentially render the Act irrelevant to the protection of wire and electronic privacy. Since I find it inconceivable that Congress could have intended such a result merely by omitting the term "electronic storage" from its definition of "electronic communication," I respectfully dissent.

B.   USA Patriot Act of 2001

The U.S. government responded to the events of September 11, 2001 with an unprecedented anti-terrorism campaign. As part of that campaign, President

Bush in October 2001 signed into law the Uniting and Strengthening America by Providing Appropriate Tools Required to Intercept and Obstruct Terrorism Act, Pub. L. No. 107-56 (the USA Patriot Act). Enacted with great haste in the wake of the attacks, the USA Patriot Act changes more than a dozen laws governing counter-terrorism activities by federal law-enforcement officers. The Act includes new anti-money-laundering provisions, which may have a major impact on the work of regulated financial institutions, as well as provisions that enhance the government's right to monitor electronic communications.

Of relevance to this course, the USA Patriot Act modifies key definitions in the Wiretap Act to clarify their applicability to Internet communications. For example, USA Patriot Act §216(a) modifies the statutory constraints on the use of pen registers to clarify that the statute permits not only monitoring of "call processing" (which presumably refers only to telephone calls), but also of "the processing and transmitting of wire or electronic communications" (which presumably refers also to Internet transmissions). USA Patriot Act §216(a) (modifying 18 U.S.C. §3121). The revision permits law enforcement greater latitude in collecting information associated with the addressing functions used in Internet communications. Privacy advocates long had resisted such a change, because Internet addresses often include more information about the thoughts of the communicating parties than do mere telephone numbers, to which the law previously referred.

The Act also enhances the power of law-enforcement officers under the ECPA in two significant respects. First, it substantially broadens the types of information available to law-enforcement officers that obtain warrants, court orders, or subpoenas, adding provisions to permit access to transactional information such as records of session times and durations, temporarily assigned network addresses, and means and source of payments, including credit card or bank account numbers. USA Patriot Act §210 (amending 18 U.S.C. §2703(c)(2) (formerly §2703(c)(1)(C)), 212(b) (generally revising §2703(c)).

Second, it adds a new provision permitting Internet service providers to disclose the contents of communications without the need for any court order or subpoena, if "the provider reasonably believes that an emergency involving immediate danger of death or serious physical injury to any person requires disclosure of the information without delay." USA Patriot Act §212(a)(D) (adding 18 U.S.C. §2702(b)(6)(C)). The statute also adds a new subsection that permits disclosure of transactional information in the same circumstances. USA Patriot Act §212(a)(E) (adding 18 U.S.C. §2702(c)).

Relevant Glossary Entries

Cookie
Uniform Resource Locator (URL)
Web Server

Problem Set 12

12.1. Struggling to increase productivity, your client Ben Darrow recently had the "bright idea" to install "Super Sniffer Employee Watchdog" software on the computer network at his bank in Matacora, hoping to monitor the computer activity of his employees. Only a few days after he installed the program, he learned that Johnny Rocket (one of his top loan officers) was downloading huge graphics files from the Internet. When the Super Sniffer reported the file names and the names of the sites from which the files had been downloaded, Ben was troubled to discover that Johnny had a taste for hardcore pornography. Ben was so upset by this discovery that he marched down the hall to Johnny's office and told him to clear out immediately. A few minutes after Johnny left, Ben got worried that Johnny might try to sue in retaliation. Does Ben have anything to fear? ECPA, 18 U.S.C. §§2510(4), 2510(5), 2511.

    12.2.   Same facts as Problem 12.1, but suppose that instead of monitoring Johnny's activities with the Super Sniffer, Ben instead discovers Johnny's activities by examining the cookies left on his hard drive that show his interactions with Web sites. Does Ben have anything to fear? ECPA, 18 U.S.C. §§2510, 2701, 2707.

    12.3.   Mia Katerina calls one afternoon to discuss a problem related to her PetPortal chat room. Some malicious rumors have started circulating on her chat room recently. She is worried about this, particularly because she has started getting requests to disclose the identity of the posters of the malicious information. It occurred to her that she could refuse to release that information because releasing it would be a criminal offense under the Stored Communications Act. She wants to check with you to see if that is a valid reason for refusing to disclose the information. 18 U.S.C. §§2510, 2701, 2702.

    12.4.   Mia Katerina calls you back a few days later after she has been served with a complaint for a class action filed on behalf of members of the PetPortal community. PetPortal entered into a deal with Animal Internet Monitoring, Inc. (AIM). AIM is working to build a database of all household pets in the country. In that effort, it has entered into similar cooperative arrangements with many sites, including those operated by vendors of pet products, veterinarian services, pet breeders, and others. As part of the deal with AIM, PetPortal will permit AIM to track the behavior of visitors and collect information relevant to its database. In return, AIM will provide PetPortal with periodic reports analyzing trends in the behavior of its visitors, which PetPortal will use to customize the information it displays to visitors. In addition, PetPortal provides links to AIM's site and AIM will link to PetPortal.

    In its privacy policy, PetPortal discloses to visitors that it exchanges the personal information it collects from members of its community with business partners that offer products and services that may be of interest to members. Thus, Mia is shocked to find that the claim asks for statutory ECPA damages of $10,000 for each member of the PetPortal community. Because there are 115,000 community members, that results in a total claim of substantially more than $1 billion. Mia wails, "How can they say that we were engaged in illicit wiretaps of their communications? I disclosed everything in the Privacy Policy. Even when the market was up, this company wasn't worth a billion dollars! What will our CEO say? What will our investment bankers say?"

    (a)   Is there any reassurance you can offer Mia that things aren't really as bad as they seem? Electronic Communication Privacy Act, 18 U.S.C. §§2510(4), 2511, 2520, 2701, 2702, 2707.

(b) Can you think of any reason why the plaintiffs might have omitted a claim under the Computer Fraud and Abuse Act? 18 U.S.C. §1030.

12.5. As generous as always, Carl Eben gave a part-time job to Sonya Nunn's cousin Boris Bota, who recently immigrated to the United States from the central Asian country Zakastan. Like all employees of RiverFront Tools (RFT), Boris received a telephone extension number and e-mail address when he was hired. Carl provides e-mail and Web access to his employees through Lone Star Link, a local Internet service provider.

The operator at Lone Star became quite agitated one day when he realized that Boris was using his Lone Star e-mail account to communicate with Chechen separatist groups in Zakastan. The operator notified local authorities and asked them to look into the matter. While monitoring e-mail communications on the Lone Star system to get an understanding of Boris's activities, the officers noticed an e-mail that Farley Farah sent to his grandmother Kaye Farah, Carl's long-trusted bookkeeper. It appears that Kaye was one of the RFT employees communicating with Boris by e-mail on a regular basis, because she needed to keep track of Boris's hours as a part-time worker. Farley's e-mail mentioned to his grandmother that the RA in his dormitory had just found marijuana in a cupboard in his dorm room, but that he didn't think the RA would rat on him or have him expelled. As it happened, the officer investigating Boris's activities happened to know Farley from some minor altercations during Farley's high-school days. If the officer has Farley arrested for possession of marijuana, does his grandmother Kaye, her employer Carl, or even Boris have any cause of action against Lone Star for permitting the police to monitor its e-mail communications without a court order? Wiretap Act, 18 U.S.C. §2702(b) & (c).

THE CAMFORD BOOKS PROBLEM

(PART III)

Your friends at Camford Books are finalizing the "details" of their Web site. They schedule a meeting with you to discuss how they will treat customer information. They necessarily will collect information about the books that particular customers order. They expect to use that information to design recommendations for books and other products that might be of interest to their customers as they return to the Web site from time to time. Because they are interested in maximizing the profits from their new venture, they also are interested in exploring the possibility that some of that information might be valuable to others. After all, they explain, it is a list of relatively snobbish people from all over the world that are willing to buy things over the Internet, complete with contact information, details about purchases, and even (potentially) details about what items each person views when it visits the Camford site. They would like your general view as to any pitfalls they face in addressing these questions and how they best can comply with their obligations and at the same time protect themselves from liability to third parties.

Part Three

The Influence of Information Technology on Commercial Transactions

Chapter 4.   Transactions in Electronic Commerce

Section A.   Sales of Goods

Discussion of commercial transactions starts with the sale of goods because that activity has for thousands of years been the core of commercial interchange. Before turning to the major issues raised by the rise of the Internet and advances in information technology, a few words about the principal sources of law are warranted.

The major source of law for sales of goods in this country has for almost half a century been Article 2 of the Uniform Commercial Code (UCC), adopted in some form by all states in the country. Unlike all of the other articles of the Uniform Commercial Code, Article 2 has never been revised since its first adoption. Only in 2003 did the American Law Institute (ALI) and the National Conference of Commissioners on Uniform State Laws (NCCUSL) approve substantial amendments to Article 2. Many of those amendments relate directly to electronic transactions. Accordingly, they are discussed throughout the assignments that follow, even though they have not been adopted in any jurisdiction (at least as of the time this book goes to press).

Many sales of goods, particularly in the Internet context, occur across national borders. In many cases, the UNCITRAL Convention on International Sales of Goods (the CISG) governs those transactions. The CISG is a set of provisions similar to the Uniform Commercial Code that apply to private international transactions where each of the contracting party's nations has ratified the accord. The CISG has not yet been updated to accommodate electronic transactions. Accordingly, although it plays an important role in cross-border transactions, this text discusses the specific provisions of the CISG very little.

The amendments to UCC Article 2 were adopted in the shadow of a failed effort to produce a new UCC article — Article 2B — to deal in a comprehensive way with software transactions. After a failed effort to form a consensus on the provisions of Article 2B, NCCUSL on its own promulgated the statute as the Uniform Computer Information Transactions Act (UCITA). That statute received a hostile reaction from state legislatures. It was adopted only by Virginia and Maryland. Recently, NCCUSL has withdrawn support so that statute is unlikely to obtain further adoptions. Accordingly, this text does not discuss UCITA in any substantial detail.

This section closes with specialized assignments (Assignments 15 and 16) on issues related to Internet auctions and taxation, but the core of the section focuses on two fundamental questions of commercial law. The first relates to the problem of assent. Should traditional forms of contracting be modified to deal with the reality that commercial interactions are for the most part now electronic? That material (predominantly in Assignment 13) discusses such problems as "shrinkwrap," "clickwrap," and "browsewrap" contracting.

The second issue is how an individual's consent is to be memorialized. In the electronic world, reliance on a traditional pen-and-ink signature is obviously impractical. Assignment 14 provides a detailed discussion of two recent statutes that deal with that problem. The first is a uniform state law adopted in the last few years by most American states, the Uniform Electronic Transactions Act (UETA). The second is a closely related federal statute, the Electronic Signatures in Global and National Commerce Act (E-SIGN).

Assignment 13: Electronic Contracting I

The mutual assent contractual paradigm applies most easily to a face-to-face retail transaction in which the buyer visits the seller's place of business and agrees to purchase goods that the seller offers for sale. In many cases, of course, the buyer and seller do not meet, but make their arrangements remotely. Indeed, from the earliest days of contract law courts have considered issues related to contracts among merchants that are remote from each other. More recently, courts have struggled with problems associated with the obligations of a manufacturer to a buyer who purchases from a retailer rather than the manufacturer itself. See, e.g., UCC §2-318.

Mail-order merchants played a significant role in the economy even before the rise of the Internet. But the Internet, however, has vastly increased the importance of remote contracting to the ordinary retail consumer. Among other things, as remote contracting becomes more important, businesses have taken more care to ensure that the transactions are conducted on the terms that they desire. Conversely, the increased prevalence of such arrangements has focused courts and academics on the issues that such contracts raise. The result has been a steadily increasing controversy about the propriety of the terms that sellers choose for those contracts.

This assignment has three sections. First, it discusses the problem of delayed presentation of terms. Second, it examines the issues associated with electronic presentation of terms. Finally, it sketches the special mandatory federal rules for mail-order contracts.

A. Delayed Presentation of Terms ("Shrinkwrap")

Remote contracts place special pressure on contract law because of the inevitable separation in time between the moment when the buyer places the order and the moment when the buyer receives the goods. Moreover, when the seller chooses to use a tangible writing to present the terms on which it wishes to do business, those terms ordinarily will not be visible to the buyer until the goods arrive. At least in the context of software products, those terms typically are called "shrinkwrap" terms, because they often are visible to the consumer only when it removes the shrinkwrap that surrounds the product.

When the terms are not presented until the goods arrive, it is important to decide when the contract is formed. Traditionally, a contract is formed by "a bargain in which there is a manifestation of mutual assent to the exchange and a consideration." RESTATEMENT (2D) OF CONTRACTS §17(1). Although courts at one time spent a great deal of effort attempting to determine the precise moment in time at which a contract was formed, in most contexts that has become an irrelevant formality, as modern courts are much more likely to find a contract formed based upon "conduct of both parties which recognizes the existence of . . . a contract." Old UCC §2-204(1).*

In our context, however, it is important to determine when a contract was formed, because of the effect that question can have on determining which terms are part of the contract. For example, if the contract is formed when the buyer places its order to purchase the goods, then the terms that the merchant delivers when it sends the goods are proposals for additions to the contract, which often will not be treated as part of the contract. See, e.g., Old UCC §2-207(2). Conversely, if the contract is formed later, after the buyer has received the goods and had an opportunity to review the seller's terms, those terms are more naturally considered part of the contract. The following case illustrates that problem.

Brower v. Gateway 2000, Inc.

676 N.Y.S.2d 569 (S. Ct. 1998)

MILONAS, J.P., NARDELLI, MAZZARELLI and SAXE, JJ.

MILONAS, Justice Presiding.

Appeal from an order of the Supreme Court (Beatrice Shainswit, J.), entered October 21, 1997 in New York County, which, to the extent appealed from, granted defendants' motion to dismiss the complaint on the ground that there was a valid agreement to arbitrate between the parties.

Appellants are among the many consumers who purchased computers and software products from defendant Gateway 2000 through a direct-sales system, by mail or telephone order. As of July 3, 1995, it was Gateway's practice to include with the materials shipped to the purchaser along with the merchandise a copy of its "Standard Terms and Conditions Agreement" and any relevant warranties for the products in the shipment. The Agreement begins with a "NOTE TO CUS-TOMER," which provides, in slightly larger print than the remainder of the document, in a box that spans the width of the page: "This document contains Gateway 2000's Standard Terms and Conditions. By keeping your Gateway 2000 computer system beyond thirty (30) days after the date of delivery, you accept these Terms and Conditions." The document consists of 16 paragraphs, and, as is relevant to this appeal, paragraph 10 of the agreement, entitled "DISPUTE RESO-LUTION," reads as follows:

> Any dispute or controversy arising out of or relating to this Agreement or its interpre-tation shall be settled exclusively and finally by arbitration. The arbitration shall be conducted in accordance with the Rules of Conciliation and Arbitration of the International Chamber of Commerce. The arbitration shall be conducted in Chicago, Illinois, U.S.A. before a sole arbitrator. Any award rendered in any such arbitration pro-ceeding shall be final and binding on each of the parties, and judgment may be entered thereon in a court of competent jurisdiction.

---

* NCCUSL and the ALI recently have promulgated proposed amendments to UCC Article 2. In this book, unadorned references to Article 2 refer to Article 2 as amended. References to "Old Article 2" refer to the original version of Article 2.

Plaintiffs commenced this action on behalf of themselves and others similarly situated for compensatory and punitive damages, alleging deceptive sales practices in seven causes of action, including breach of warranty, breach of contract, fraud and unfair trade practices. In particular, the allegations focused on Gateway's representations and advertising that promised "service when you need it," including around-the-clock free technical support, free software technical support and certain on-site services. According to plaintiffs, not only were they unable to avail themselves of this offer because it was virtually impossible to get through to a technician, but also Gateway continued to advertise this claim notwithstanding numerous complaints and reports about the problem.

Insofar as is relevant to appellants, who purchased their computers after July 3, 1995, Gateway moved to dismiss the complaint based on the arbitration clause in the Agreement. Appellants argued that the arbitration clause is invalid under [Old] UCC 2-207, unconscionable under [Old] UCC 2-302 and an unenforceable contract of adhesion. Specifically, they claimed that the provision was obscure; that a customer could not reasonably be expected to appreciate or investigate its meaning and effect; that the International Chamber of Commerce ("ICC") was not a forum commonly used for consumer matters; and that because ICC headquarters were in France, it was particularly difficult to locate the organization and its rules. To illustrate just how inaccessible the forum was, appellants advised the court that the ICC was not registered with the Secretary of State, that efforts to locate and contact the ICC had been unsuccessful and that apparently the only way to attempt to contact the ICC was through the United States Council for International Business, with which the ICC maintained some sort of relationship.

In support of their arguments, appellants submitted a copy of the ICC's Rules of Conciliation and Arbitration and contended that the cost of ICC arbitration was prohibitive, particularly given the amount of the typical consumer claim involved. For example, a claim of less than $50,000 required advance fees of $4,000 (more than the cost of most Gateway products), of which the $2000 registration fee was nonrefundable even if the consumer prevailed at the arbitration. Consumers would also incur travel expenses disproportionate to the damages sought, which appellants' counsel estimated would not exceed $1,000 per customer in this action, as well as bear the cost of Gateway's legal fees if the consumer did not prevail at the arbitration; in this respect, the ICC rules follow the "loser pays" rule used in England. Also, although Chicago was designated as the site of the actual arbitration, all correspondence must be sent to ICC headquarters in France.

The IAS court dismissed the complaint as to appellants based on the arbitration clause in the Agreements delivered with their computers. We agree with the court's decision and reasoning in all respects but for the issue of the unconscionability of the designation of the ICC as the arbitration body.

First, the court properly rejected appellants' argument that the arbitration clause was invalid under [Old] UCC 2-207. Appellants claim that when they placed their order they did not bargain for, much less accept, arbitration of any dispute, and therefore the arbitration clause in the agreement that accompanied the merchandise shipment was a "material alteration" of a preexisting oral agreement. Under [Old] UCC 2-207(2), such a material alteration constitutes "proposals for addition to the contract" that become part of the contract only upon appellants' express acceptance. However, as the court correctly concluded, the clause was not a "material alteration" of an oral agreement, but, rather, simply one provision of the sole contract that existed between the parties. That contract, the court explained, was formed and acceptance was manifested not when the order was placed but only with the retention of the merchandise beyond the 30 days specified in the Agreement enclosed in the shipment of merchandise. Accordingly, the contract was outside the scope of [Old] UCC 2-207.

In reaching its conclusion, the IAS court took note of the litigation in Federal courts on this very issue, and, indeed, on this very arbitration clause. In *Hill v. Gateway 2000, Inc.*, 105 F.3d 1147, *cert. denied*, 522 U.S. 808, plaintiffs in a class action contested the identical Gateway contract in dispute before us, including the enforceability of the arbitration clause. As that court framed the issue, the "[t]erms inside Gateway's box stand or fall together. If they constitute the parties contract because the Hills had an opportunity to return the computer after reading them, then all must be enforced" (*id.* at 1148). The court then concluded that the contract was not formed with the placement of a telephone order or with the delivery of the goods. Instead, an enforceable contract was formed only with the consumer's decision to retain the merchandise beyond the 30-day period specified in the agreement. Thus, the agreement as a whole, including the arbitration clause, was enforceable.

This conclusion was in keeping with the same court's decision in *ProCD, Inc. v. Zeidenberg*, 86 F.3d 1447, where it found that detailed terms enclosed within the packaging of particular computer software purchased in a retail outlet constituted the contract between the vendor and the consumer who retained the product. In that case, the Seventh Circuit held that [Old] UCC 2-207 did not apply and indeed was "irrelevant" to such transactions, noting that the section is generally invoked where multiple agreements have been exchanged between the parties in a classic "battle of the forms," whereas *ProCD* (as well as *Hill* and this case) involves but a single form (*id.* at 1452).

The *Hill* decision, in its examination of the formation of the contract, takes note of the realities of conducting business in today's world. Transactions involving "cash now, terms later" have become commonplace, enabling the consumer to make purchases of sophisticated merchandise such as computers over the phone or by mail — and even by computer. Indeed, the concept of "[p]ayment preceding the revelation of full terms" is particularly common in certain industries, such as air transportation and insurance (*id.* at 1149; *ProCD v. Zeidenberg, supra,* at 1451).

While *Hill* and *ProCD,* as the IAS court recognized, are not controlling (although they are decisions of the United States Court of Appeals for the circuit encompassing the forum state designated for arbitration), we agree with their rationale that, in such transactions, there is no agreement or contract upon the placement of the order or even upon the receipt of the goods. By the terms of the Agreement at issue, it is only after the consumer has affirmatively retained the merchandise for more than 30 days — within which the consumer has presumably examined and even used the product(s) and read the agreement — that the contract has been effectuated. . . .

. . . Second, with respect to appellants' claim that the arbitration clause is unenforceable as a contract of adhesion, in that it involved no choice or negotiation on the part of the consumer but was a "take it or leave it" proposition, we find that this argument, too, was properly rejected by the IAS court. Although the parties clearly do not possess equal bargaining power, this factor alone does not invalidate the contract as one of adhesion. As the IAS court observed, with the ability to make the purchase elsewhere and the express option to return the goods, the consumer is not in a "take it or leave it" position at all; if any term of the agreement is unacceptable to the consumer, he or she can easily buy a competitor's product instead — either from a retailer or directly from the manufacturer — and reject Gateway's agreement by returning the merchandise (*see, e.g., Carnival Cruise Lines v. Shute,* 499 U.S. 585, 593-594 . . . The consumer has 30 days to make that decision. Within that time, the consumer can inspect the goods and examine and seek clarification of the terms of the agreement; until those 30 days have elapsed, the consumer has the unqualified right to return the merchandise, because the goods or terms are unsatisfactory or for no reason at all.

While returning the goods to avoid the formation of the contract entails affirmative action on the part of the consumer, and even some expense, this may be seen as a trade-off for the convenience and savings for which the consumer presumably opted when he or she chose to make a purchase of such consequence by phone or mail as an alternative to on-site retail shopping. That a consumer does not read the agreement or thereafter claims he or she failed to understand or appreciate some term therein does not invalidate the contract any more than such claim would undo a contract formed under other circumstances.

[The court went on to hold that the arbitration clause was unenforceable because it was unconscionable. Assignment 2 reprints that portion of the opinion in its general discussion of the enforceability of arbitration clauses.]

———————

The approach of *Brower* and the cases it discusses (*ProCD* and *Hill*) certainly is not the only possible response to the problem. For example, some early cases (most notably Step-Saver Data Systems, Inc. v. Wyse Technology, 939 F.2d 91 (3rd Cir. 1991)) have reached contrary results. The rationale of the contrary cases — suggested in the text above the *Brower* opinion — is that a contract is formed no later than the time the merchant ships the goods, with the merchant's partial performance serving as evidence of a contract. See Old UCC §2-204(1).

The more recent cases, however, have tended to favor the merchants. Those cases, like *Brower,* eschew a functional analysis of the transaction and instead apply a more formal analysis under which the merchant as offeror is "the master of his offer," RESTATEMENT (2D) OF CONTRACTS §30 comment a. Under that analysis, the merchant has an almost unconstrained ability to determine the method by which the offer is to be accepted. To get an insider's understanding of how Article 2 should apply to those cases, consider the views of Jim White (co-author of WHITE & SUMMERS and a member of the Article 2 drafting committee).

James J. White, Contracting Under Amended 2-207, 2004
Wis. L. Rev. xxx

IF YOU TIE YOUR SHOELACES

One of the ways that clever lawyers have tried to escape the reach of Section 2-207 is to assert that the other party's behavior is an acceptance of all of the

terms on the first party's form. For example a form might say that any action —
even in preparation for performance — will be an acceptance of the offeror's
terms. In an act of splendid chutzpah (or unforgivable ignorance), the drafters of
UCITA ruled that one has "manifested assent" (agreed to something) if he "intentionally engage[s] in conduct . . . with reason to know that the other party . . .
may infer from the conduct that the person assents to the term (ital added)."
[UCITA §112(a).] Suppose that your form asserts that my intentional tying my
shoelaces tomorrow morning will be assent to all of your terms. Since I cannot tie
my shoelaces unintentionally and since I have no valet, I'm stuck, not so?

In the infamous *Zeidenberg v. ProCD* the Court suggests the same when it stated
that Mr. Z was stuck with the terms on the box because the offeror was "the master of his offer."[1] The statement is right, but the application is wrong. To say that
the offeror is the master of his offer means only that he may rule out certain things
as acceptance, i.e. that he can limit the universe of things that will be regarded as
acceptances, not that he can expand "acceptance" beyond the universe that a
reasonable person in the offeree's shoes would believe to be acceptance.

The case is not far fetched. Two years ago one of my students brought me a
clear plastic sleeve in which she had received the power cord to her computer. On
its face was the message: "By opening this plastic sleeve, you agree to all of the
terms of the seller's contract and license."

Such terms should not transform behavior that would not normally be an
acceptance into an acceptance, and, in general, they have not.[2] If one limits
Section 112(a) of UCITA to the conventional case where a buyer clicks "I Agree,"
the rule is a tautology, for the click would be regarded by all reasonable people as
an agreement, just as the oral expression of the same words would mean agreement. So in my opinion one can safely tie his shoelaces without fear of making an
unfavorable contract. Conceivably there are cases near the border where such a
term might push an act over the line and make something an acceptance that
would otherwise fail, but I can't identify any such. If Section 112 of UCITA reaches
to your shoelaces, the law is a ass. . . .

TERMS ON OR IN THE BOX

Section 2-207 has done most of its work in industrial contracting. Most of the
2-207 cases are between industrial manufacturers and industrial buyers; the latter
intend to resell or to use the products in their own manufacturing process. A separate contracting practice between consumer and non-consumer end users and
manufacturers has persisted even longer than the industrial contracting process.
Even though the consumer and the industrial practices present similar contract
issues, the two have marched in parallel with little reference by the cases from one
to the similar issues in the other. The case that put Madison on the contract map,
ProCD, Inc. v. Zeidenberg, has changed that.[3] The courts, the drafters of amended

1. 86 F.3d 1447, 1452 (7th Cir. 1996) ("A vendor, as master of the offer, may invite acceptance
by conduct, and propose limitations on the kind of conduct that constitutes acceptance.").
2. *See* Licitra v. Gateway, Inc., 734 N.Y.S.2d 389 (N.Y. City Civ. Ct. 2001) (" . . . if the defendant, as a term and condition of filing a claim, required the consumer to sing "O Sole Mio" in
Yiddish while standing on his or her head in Macy's window, only Mandy Patinkin would qualify to object to the receipt of defective equipment. This cannot be so.").
3. 86 F.3d 1447 (7th Cir. 1996).

Article 2, and particularly the commentators have now awakened to the common issues in the parallel tracks and to the need to reconcile the cases in the industrial forum with those in the retail forum.

Manufacturers of retail goods have long attached contract statements to or included contract documents with new goods. Early examples were warnings, disclaimers or limitation of remedies on sacks of seed or containers of fertilizer.[4] As this is written, nearly all boxed appliances and other boxed electronic hardware sold new at retail include contract documents. Some terms in the box favor the buyer — the limited express warranty and the help line for computer hardware. Some favor the seller — limitations of remedy, restrictions on forum, arbitration clauses and reduction in the limitations period.[5]

Licensors and sellers of software try to protect their intellectual property interests by terms in or on the box or on the software itself. They hope to make the transaction a license and not a sale so to avoid the first sale doctrine. And where the market is divided — some will pay much and other will pay little for the same product — they badly want to keep the buyers in the less expensive market from committing arbitrage, i.e., they hope to prevent purchasers in the cheap market from reselling into the dear market.[6]

The first and still the most prominent case is *ProCD v. Zeidenberg*.[7] . . .

. . . Whatever the merit of the outcome in *ProCD* (Matthew Zeidenberg was surely a naughty boy who should have his hands slapped), Judge Easterbrook's consideration of the Article 2 issues is sloppy. First, he applies Article 2 without considering whether the contract for the use of a database was a "transaction in goods" and so within the scope of Article 2.[8] Second he dismisses Section 2-207 in one sentence: "Our case has only one form; UCC 2-207 is irrelevant."[9] That statement is wrong; nothing in Section 2-207, its comments or the cases limit the

---

4. See Mullis v. Speight Seed Farms, Inc., 505 S.E. 2d 818 (Ga. Ct. App. 1998) (enforcing disclaimer and limitation on seed can which read: "NOTICE TO PURCHASER: [Seller] warrants that, at the time of delivery, the seeds in this container conform to the label description as required under state and federal laws. [Seller] makes no other warranties whether written, oral, statutory, express or implied, including but not limited to warranty of merchantability, fitness for a particular purpose, or otherwise, that would extend beyond such descriptions contained herein. In any event, [seller's] liability for breach of any warranty with respect to such seeds shall be limited to the purchase price. Purchaser assumes the risk for results obtained from use of such seeds, including but not limited to the condition under which the seeds are planted, germinated, or grown."); Dessert Seed Co. v. Drew Farmers Supply, Inc., 248 Ark. 858 (1970) (refusing to enforce limitation of remedies on tomato seed bag which read: "Subject to the limitation of liability herein set forth, we warrant that seeds or bulbs sold are as described on the container, within recognized tolerances. Our liability on this warranty is limited in amount to the purchase price of the seeds or bulbs. In no way shall we be liable for the crop.").

5. Manufacturers of retail goods sold to consumers rarely disclaim the implied warranty of merchantability. In almost all cases, manufactures furnish to consumers some form of express warranty of the goods. Thus, any attempt to disclaim the implied warranty of merchantability would violate the Magnuson-Moss Warranty–Federal Trade Commission Improvement Act. *See* 15 U.S.C. §§2301-12.

6. Matthew Zeindenberg's attempt at arbitrage was at issue in *ProCD*. Having purchased a consumer version of a computer telephone directory, Zeidenberg's corporation made the database (which cost over $10 million to compile) available over the Internet at a price which was much lower than ProCD charged the commercial market. See *ProCD*, 86 F.3d at 1449-50.

7. 86 F3d 1447 (7th Cir. 1996).

8. One can argue that the ProCD contract is not for goods, and that it is governed by the common law rather than by Article 2. In *Hill v. Gateway 2000*, 105 F.3d 1147 (7th Cir. 1997), Judge Easterbrook is saved from repeating this error, for that case deals with a contract for the sale of goods, namely a computer.

9. *ProCD*, 86 F.3d at 1452.

Section to cases with more than one form. Indeed, the second sentence in Comment 1 states a hypothetical case with only one form.

A series of cases involving Gateway's arbitration clause — that is contained in the computer box — have agreed with *ProCD*.[10] But one, *Klocek v. Gateway, Inc.*,[11] goes the other way. In *Klocek*, Judge Vratil applied Section 2-207 and found that the buyer's "act of keeping the computer past five days was not sufficient to demonstrate that plaintiff expressly agreed to the Standard Terms."[12]

Before we turn to amended 2-207's treatment of terms in the box, we should give the Seventh Circuit its due. Judge Easterbrook's discussion of the economics of retail contracting and of the virtue of giving sellers easy ways to discriminate in price between sets of potential buyers deserves more respect than does his careless dismissal of 2-207. When he argues that society is well served by law that makes contracting inexpensive and easy, Judge Easterbrook is right. For a nickel or a dime almost all of us would give up our right to resell software and would agree to arbitrate. If that is so, it hardly makes sense to charge our seller a dollar in contracting costs to make that deal with us. Still the contract law and our conventional understanding deserve some respect; there must be reasons why we persist in looking for "agreement" and why courts routinely reject some behavior as inadequate to show agreement.

But these issues are not new; consider how the drafters of Article 2, now and earlier, have dealt with them. Fifty years ago Professor Llewellyn recognized the challenge to standard contract rules that was presented by terms that are attached to or delivered with the goods. He made only a half-hearted stab at the problem in Comment 7 to 2-313:

> 7. Subsection (2)(b) makes specific some of the principles set forth above when a description of the goods is given by the seller. A description need not be by words. Technical specifications, blueprints and the like can afford more exact description than mere language and if made part of the basis of the bargain goods must conform with them. Past deliveries may set the description of quality, either expressly or impliedly by course of dealing. Of course, all descriptions by merchants must be read against the applicable trade usages with the general rules as to merchantability resolving any doubts.

In urging that the "sole question is whether the language . . . [is] fairly to be regarded as part of the contract. . . ." Professor Llewellyn sounds like amended 2-207. Of course, Llewellyn was addressing express warranties where the problem is complicated by the requirement that an express warranty be "part of the basis of the bargain."

In the Article 2 amendment process the drafting committee dealt with these issues twice. First, it adopted 2-313A. Second, the committee considered and abandoned a subsection in 2-207 specifically addressed to terms in or on the box. The poverty of our imagination is shown by the fact that no one on the drafting committee appears ever to have noticed that the proposed subsection to Section 2-207 and Section 2-313A addressed the same question.

---

10. *See* Westendorf v. Gateway 2000, Inc., 2000 WL 307369 (2000) (arbitration provision shipped with computer); *see also* Brower v. Gateway 2000, Inc., 246 A.D.2d 246 (N.Y. App. Div. 1998) (warranty disclaimer included inside computer packaging); Levy v. Gateway 2000, Inc., 33 U.C.C. Rep. Serv. 2d 1060 (N.Y. Sup. Ct. 1997) (same).

11. 204 F. Supp. 2d 1332 (D. Kan. 2000).

12. *Id.* at 1341.

Section 2-313A is a comprehensive codification of only a piece of the law on express warranties in the box. . . .

. . . If Gateway sells through Circuit City to a consumer, Gateway's warranty in the box to the consumer (remote purchaser) is binding and Gateway's arbitration clause and other limitation of remedies are binding on the consumer under 2-313A(5)(a). So far so good.

What of the same consumer's rights as a third party beneficiary of Gateway's warranty to Circuit City? Neither those warranties nor any limitation on damages for breach of them is addressed in 2-313A. Nothing in 2-313A affects the consumer's rights under the applicable alternative of 2-318 (privity rules). Any right to sue as a third party beneficiary and any bar to such suit for lack of privity are unchanged.

If Gateway sells directly to the consumer, no part of Section 2-313A applies and the parties are back under 2-313 and under cases interpreting that Section. Ironically, a consumer who buys directly from Gateway may not be bound by Gateway's arbitration term under *Klocek*, yet if the same person buys from a retailer, he will be bound by the arbitration clause because of Section 2-313A. So our attempt to codify even this small part of law on terms in the box has not distinguished us.

In 2000, long after 2-313A had been installed and agreed upon, the drafting committee considered a subsection in 2-207 that would have dealt with all terms in the box.[13] The Subsection read as follows:

(b) Terms to which the buyer has not otherwise agreed that are delivered to the buyer with the goods become part of the contract, subject to 2-202, only if:

(1) the buyer does not within [twenty] [thirty] days of their receipt object to the terms and offer to return the goods at the seller's expense,

(2) the terms do not contradict the terms of the parties' agreement, and

(3) taken as a whole, the terms do not materially alter the contract to the detriment of the buyer.

The Subsection was accompanied by a comment which stated that usual terms in the box would not "materially alter the contract to the detriment of the buyer" if they contained an express warranty, a promise of consumer help and the like even if they also limited the buyer's remedies. Note that the word "agreement" defined in 1-201(3) and included in (b)(2) of the proposed Subsection does not include gap fillers provided by Article 2; so a limitation of remedies would not "contradict" an "agreement" that, by law, included the remedies provided by part 7 of Article 2. Such implied terms would be a part of the "contract" but not part of the "agreement."

I thought the proposal gave the sellers what they needed without opening the buyers to onerous terms. For example, an arbitration clause with a $4000 filing fee would materially alter the terms to the buyer's detriment, but arbitration without such a fee would not. Eccentric, finicky buyers could have protected themselves by returning the product. Since eccentrics are scarce, the cost to Gateway of a duty to accept returns would have been inconsequential.

I was wrong. The buyers (represented by Gail Hillebrand from Consumers Union) were tempted but feared that the sellers would agree and then take the

---

13. I confess that it never occurred to me when we were considering the subsection to 2-207 that we should look back at 2-313A. We treated 2-313A as put to bed (after a big fight with sellers and advertisers several years before) and, to my recollection, no one suggested that the two sections might be stepping on one another's toes.

concession away in the legislatures.[14] The sellers . . . were also opposed. So the committee rejected the Subsection four to three. Of course, we will never know the true position either of the buyers and sellers or of their agents; those positions are revealed, if ever, only after a provision has been adopted. Each side may have believed that it would prevail in court. If that was their belief, one is wrong.

The Subsection was replaced by Comment 5 that reads:

> The section omits any specific treatment of terms on or in the container in which the goods are delivered. This Article takes no position on whether a court should follow the reasoning in *Hill v. Gateway 2000*, 105 F.3d 1147 (7th Cir. 1997) (Section 2-207 does not apply to these cases; the "rolling contract" is not made until acceptance of the seller's terms after the goods and terms are delivered) or the contrary reasoning in *Step-Saver Data Systems, Inc. v. Wyse Technology*, 939 F.2d 91 (3d Cir. 1991) (contract is made at time of oral or other bargain and "shrink wrap" terms or those in the container become part of the contract only if they comply with provisions such as are contained in Section 2-207).

The comment leaves courts free to apply 2-207 or to decline to do so. It frees buyers to argue in and sellers to argue out.

Does amended 2-207 apply to cases like *Gateway*? I think it does. Judge Easterbrook never was right about cases with only one form, and his position would be even farther from the truth under amended 2-207. The first four lines of amended 2-207 are comprehensive; they apply to all Article 2 contracts:

> Subject to Section 2-202, if (i) conduct by both parties recognizes the existence of a contract although their records do not otherwise establish a contract, (ii) a contract is formed by an offer and acceptance, or (iii) a contract formed in any manner is confirmed by a record that contains terms additional to or different from those in the contract being confirmed, the terms of the contract are . . .

The difficulty is that these parties think that they are making a binding deal at the time of the first and, often, the only conversation. They are not like industrial buyers and sellers who anticipate negotiations and perhaps a multiple exchange of documents. So it seems to me that the seller must either incorporate the terms in the box into the telephone or e-mail contract or somehow make his term in the box into a modification

Consider *Gateway* under amended 2-207. Since the arbitration clause appears only in Gateway's record, it does not get into the contract under (a). If there is only one record, the clause does not meet (1) for the want of a second record; if there are two records, it fails because the clause will not appear in the buyer's record.

The arbitration clause would make it into the contract under (b) if the parties "agree." Comment 3 invites a court's consideration of the parties' verbal and non-verbal behavior:

> In a rare case the terms in the records of both parties might not become part of the contract. This could be the case, for example, when the parties contemplated an

---

14. In a couple of states secured creditors did not conform to the expectations of consumer debtors when Article 9 was being considered. Local bankers organizations apparently did not regard themselves bound by deals that had been struck during the negotiation of the uniform version of revised Article 9.

agreement to a single negotiated record, and each party submitted to the other party similar proposals and then commenced performance, but the parties never reached a negotiated agreement because of the differences over crucial terms. There is a variety of verbal and nonverbal behavior that may be suggest agreement to another's record. This section leaves the interpretation of that behavior to the discretion of the courts.

Now what behavior might do? If Gateway's agent got the buyer's agreement to the terms in the box as a part of the parties' telephone or e-mail exchange at the time of contracting, that would do. If the buyer agreed that the contract would not be binding until after the delivery — so keeping the contracting process open — that might work also.

An e-mail agreement after the initial contract discussion but before delivery might work if the seller conditioned its delivery on buyer's e-mail agreement to the terms. Of course, technically that e-mail might be a breach of the existing contract, but if the buyer accedes, the resulting e-mail deal would be an effective modification even if one thought a deal had already been struck. The e-mails satisfy the amended statute of frauds.[15] Since consideration is not needed for modifications under 2-209 and since the seller's good faith would arise from its legitimate need for the terms, that would work.

The seller is farther out on a limb if it must rely on a click-through agreement or on a sign on the box. For the reasons stated above, we should not permit the seller to make an act that no rational buyer would regard as an acceptance ("opening this means you agree to Gateway's terms") into one.

The buyer will have a different objection to the click-through agreement. He will understand that his click on the "I agree" is a proper acceptance of the seller's terms. But now the seller's offer is coercive. The buyer has received and spent all evening setting up the computer; he is sitting in his study in International Falls in his underwear with a beer when he has to decide whether to agree to the new terms or go out in the minus 30 temperature and return the computer. Because it is coercive, this offer is more objectionable than a pre-delivery e-mail.

What about the second purchase? If the buyer buys twice from the same seller does his knowledge of the terms from the first sale bind him as to the second? I am not sure. Knowing that my opposite party's form insists on something is normally not enough to bind me if his behavior does not back up his form. Remember the industrial seller whose form always demands arbitration but who always performs in the face of the buyer's silence? There, we require seller to pull up and insist on express agreement to his arbitration term if we are to find an "agreement."[16] But maybe this is different. Unlike the industrial buyer who will express himself with his own form and so implicitly reject seller's terms that are not included on his form, our Gateway buyer makes no explicit or implicit expression of discontent with the seller's terms.

---

15. By substituting "record" for writing the amendments recognize e-mails as sufficient for Section 2-201. *See* U.C.C. §2-103(1)(m). Even without the amended language, the e-mails work under UETA (*see* UETA §2(13)) or [E-SIGN] (*see* 15 U.S.C. §7006(4), (9) (2003)).

16. *See* Avedon Engineering, Inc. v. Seatex, 112 F. Supp. 2d 1090 (D. Colo. 2000) (holding that unilaterally inserted arbitration clause did not materially alter agreement and so became part of the contract where terms were clear and legible, form with clause was routinely used in parties' course of dealing, buyer had at least three chances to read clause, and custom in textile industry was to include arbitration terms in all contracts); *see also* Sethness-Greenleaf, Inc. v. Green River Corp., 65 F.3d 64 (7th Cir. 1995) (Easterbrook, J.) (enforcing payment terms which appeared in over 200 invoices from seller but not in buyer's forms).

What about *ProCD*? Amended Article 2 might treat ProCD differently than it treats Gateway. First, it is probable that amended Article 2 does not apply to ProCD. Even if the data are delivered on a disk that is goods, the contract is for the data and the disk is merely the temporary carrier; it can be discarded once the data are on the buyer's hard drive. So the medium that holds the data is less important than with a book where the medium is the permanent residence of the data. Amended 2-103 and its attending comment support that view. If Article 2 does not reach *ProCD*, Judge Easterbrook can play all he wants in the common law without doing any harm to Article 2.

Even if one applies amended 2-207 to *ProCD*, the result might be different than the Gateway result. Under amended 2-207 a court could conclude that the purchase of a box with a warning on the outside about terms on the inside is an agreement to those terms under 2-207(2). Unlike *Gateway*, this buyer is holding the terms in his hand when he makes the contract to buy. So here the seller avoids the doctrinal conundrum from *Gateway*, namely that normal rules of contracting would find that a contract existed long before the seller's terms show up in International Falls. Particularly if the box in the buyer's hand warns of terms inside, one might conclude here that the buyer's payment shows his agreement to those terms . . .

The concerns that Professor White emphasizes are particularly problematic given the ease with which sellers in an Internet age could make terms available for review, either in the catalogs merchants disseminate or on their Web sites. In addition to Professor White's doctrinal argument summarized above, at least two other contract doctrines — neither widely used to date — are available to protect purchasers from terms of which they are not aware at the time they make a purchase: the doctrine of surprising terms and a right of return.

The doctrine of "surprising" terms appears in Restatement (2d) of Contracts §211(3). That doctrine deals with the situation in which a party becomes bound by a standard agreement, but seeks to avoid some term in the contract that is surprising to the person. The Restatement concludes that the party offering the form contract cannot enforce the term if it "ha[d] reason to believe that the [other party] would not [have agreed] if [it] knew that the writing contained a particular term." RESTATEMENT (2D) OF CONTRACTS §211(3). For example, suppose in the *Brower* case that Gateway knew that its customers would refuse to contract with Gateway if they understood in advance the terms on which disputes with Gateway would be resolved. Under the Restatement rule, those terms would not be part of the contract.

Although that rule would provide considerable protection for purchasers, it has come under sharp attack. Opponents decry the uncertainty it would bring to contracting, because it would allow purchasers to raise complaints when a dispute arose about terms that did not concern them at the time the contract was signed. As it happens, very few courts have followed the Restatement rule. Also, despite considerable discussion of the problem during the multiyear process that attempted to prepare amendments to UCC Article 2, no provision based on Section 211 appeared in the recently promulgated revisions to Article 2. Accordingly, that provision has at best limited value as a reflection of existing law.

An approach less objectionable to merchants appears in Section 209(b) of the Uniform Computer Information Transactions Act. That provision applies only to transactions that involve licenses (usually licenses of software, the principal subject of Chapter 4), not to sales of goods, and in the licensing context applies only in mass-market transactions. Mass-market transactions, in turn, are defined to include consumer transactions and also business transactions conducted on generally standardized terms. UCITA §102(a)(43) and (44).

In the context of mass-market license transactions, the provision applies whenever a licensee/purchaser does not have an opportunity to review the terms before it becomes obligated to pay. UCITA §209(b). The statute includes a detailed description of what it means to make terms available for review on a Web site, and contemplates that the ease (or difficulty) of access and review is part of the inquiry whether an adequate opportunity has been provided. UCITA §§112 and comment 8(b), 211. If the purchaser does not have such an opportunity, UCITA §209(b) grants a right to return the product. Moreover, it also requires the seller to reimburse the purchaser for the expenses of returning the product to the seller and even the expenses of uninstalling the product from the purchaser's systems. UCITA §209(b)(1) and (2). Many observers have criticized that provision, however, urging that contract terms should not be enforceable, at least against consumers, unless they are made available at the time of the decision to purchase.

The Uniform Commercial Code, however, includes no similar provision, and UCITA was adopted in only two jurisdictions before NCCUSL withdrew its support for the statute, so the provision has no direct force even in software and information transactions. Accordingly, at present the situation remains as *Brower* suggests: Although judicial decisions have not been entirely uniform, there is no general rule precluding the enforceability of terms solely because the seller delays the time at which the terms are presented to the buyer.

B. Electronic Presentation of Terms ("Clickwrap" and "Browsewrap")

Another set of problems arises when presentation of the terms is not delayed, but instead is made in an electronic format at the time the consumer decides to make the purchase. The difficulty here lies in determining the extent to which a purchaser has assented to terms that the purchaser could examine at a Web site from which it makes a purchase. Such terms can be presented in several different ways, resulting in a variety of neologisms to describe the contracting practices, building on the term "shrinkwrap" that describes terms that are presented only when the product arrives to the purchaser's location. The most common are "clickwrap" — terms for which the merchant obtains assent by forcing the purchaser to click a button with a mouse — and "browsewrap" — terms for which the merchant purports to obtain implicit assent through the purchaser's opportunity to view the terms while browsing the site. As the following cases suggest, courts have been sensitive to the method by which assent is obtained, but have not been overtly hostile to the electronic medium itself.

Rudder v. Microsoft Corp.

1999 Carswell Ont. 3195 (Ont. Super. Ct.)

WINKLER J.

1 This is a motion by the defendant Microsoft for a permanent stay of this intended class proceeding. The motion is based on [among other things, the claim] that the parties have agreed to the exclusive jurisdiction, and venue, of the courts in King County in the State of Washington in respect of any litigation between them. . . .

2 The Microsoft Network ("MSN"), is an online service, providing, *interalia*, information and services including Internet access to its members. The service is provided to members, around the world, from a "gateway" located in the State of Washington through computer connections most often made over standard telephone lines.

3 The proposed representative plaintiffs in this action were subscriber members of MSN. Both are law school graduates, one of whom is admitted to the Bar in Ontario while the other worked as a legal researcher. They were associated with the law firm which originally represented the intended class. The plaintiffs claim under the *Class Proceedings Act*, 1992, S.O., C.6 on behalf of a Canada-wide class defined as:

> All persons resident in Canada who subscribed for the provision of Internet access or information or services from or through MSN, The Microsoft Network, since September 1, 1995.

This class is estimated to contain some 89,000 MSN members across Canada.

4 The plaintiffs claim damages for breach of contract, breach of fiduciary duty, misappropriation and punitive damages in the total amount of $75,000,000.00 together with an accounting and injunctive relief. The plaintiffs allege that Microsoft has charged members of MSN and taken payment from their credit cards in breach of contract and that Microsoft has failed to provide reasonable or accurate information concerning accounts. The Statement of Claim was served on Microsoft at its offices in Redmond, Washington on January 5, 1998.

5 The contract which the plaintiffs allege to have been breached is identified by MSN as a "Member Agreement". Potential members of MSN are required to electronically execute this agreement prior to receiving the services provided by the company. Each Member Agreement contains the following provision:

> 15.1 This Agreement is governed by the laws of the State of Washington, U.S.A., and you consent to the exclusive jurisdiction and venue of courts in King County, Washington, in all disputes arising out of or relating to your use of MSN or your MSN membership.

The defendant relies on this clause in support of its assertion that the intended class proceeding should be permanently stayed.

6 Although the plaintiffs rely on the contract as the basis for their causes of action, they submit that the court ought not to give credence to the "forum selection clause" contained within. It is stated in support of this contention that the representative plaintiffs read only portions of the Member Agreement and thus had no notice of the forum selection clause. . . .

7 I cannot accede to these submissions. In my view, the forum selection clause is dispositive and there is nothing in the factual record which persuades me that I should exercise my discretion so as to permit the plaintiffs to avoid the effect of the contractual provision. Accordingly, an order will go granting the relief sought by the defendant. My reasons follow.

ANALYSIS AND DISPOSITION . . .

10 The plaintiffs contend, first, that . . . no effect should be given to the particular clause at issue in this case because it does not represent the true agreement of the parties. It is the plaintiff[s'] submission that the form in which the Member Agreement is provided to potential members of MSN is such that it obscures the forum selection clause. Therefore, the plaintiffs argue, the clause should be treated as if it were the fine print in a contract which must be brought specifically to the attention of the party accepting the terms. Since there was no specific notice given, in the plaintiffs' view, the forum selection clause should be severed from the Agreement which they otherwise seek to enforce.

11 The argument advanced by the plaintiffs relies heavily on the alleged deficiencies in the technological aspects of electronic formats for presenting the terms of agreements. In other words, the plaintiffs contend that because only a portion of the Agreement was presented on the screen at one time, the terms of the Agreement which were not on the screen are essentially "fine print".

12 I disagree. The Member Agreement is provided to potential members of MSN in a computer readable form through either individual computer disks or via the Internet at the MSN website. In this case, the plaintiff Rudder, whose affidavit was filed on the motion, received a computer disk as part of a promotion by MSN. The disk contained the operating software for MSN and included a multi-media sign up procedure for persons who wished to obtain the MSN service. As part of the sign-up routine, potential members of MSN were required to acknowledge their acceptance of the terms of the Member Agreement by clicking on an "I Agree" button presented on the computer screen at the same time as the terms of the Member Agreement were displayed.

13 Rudder admitted in cross-examination on his affidavit that the entire agreement was readily viewable by using the scrolling function on the portion of the computer screen where the Membership Agreement was presented. Moreover, Rudder acknowledged that he "scanned" through part of the Agreement looking for "costs" that would be charged by MSN. He further admitted that once he had found the provisions relating to costs, he did not read the rest of the Agreement. An excerpt from the transcript of Rudder's cross-examination is illustrative:

> Q.   314. I will now take you down to another section. I am now looking at heading 15, which is entitled "General", and immediately underneath that is subsection 15.1. Now, do I take it, when you were scanning, you would have actually scanned past this, and you would have at least seen there was a heading that said "General"? Is that fair? Or did you not even scan all the way through?
>
> A.   I did not go all the way down, I can honestly say. Once I found out what it would cost me, that is where I would stop.
>
> Q.   315. So, I take it that you did not read 15.1?
>
> A.   No, I definitely did not read this, no.

Q. 316. I now have 15.4 on the screen, and presumably you did not read that either?

A. No, I did not.

Q. 317. I take it, during the whole signup process that you did, you did the whole thing online on the computer. . . .

A. Yes.

Q. 318 . . . [U]sing the disk? And we will come to the connection. You did not have any voice communication with MSN?

A. No.

Q. 319. Or with Microsoft Corporation?

A. No.

Q. 320. You did not have any written correspondence with them at the time of signup?

A. No.

Q. 321. All right. Now, I take it that, after doing the review of this that you did do, you clicked, "I agree"? Is that what you did?

A. *After I was satisfied with what it was going to cost me, I agreed.*

14 I have viewed the Member Agreement as it was presented to Rudder during the sign up procedure. All of the terms of the Agreement are displayed in the same format. Although, there are certain terms of the Agreement displayed entirely in upper-case letters, there are no physical differences which make a particular term of the agreement more difficult to read than any other term. In other words, there is no fine print as that term would be defined in a written document. The terms are set out in plain language, absent words that are commonly referred to as "legalese". Admittedly, the entire Agreement cannot be displayed at once on the computer screen, but this is not materially different from a multi-page written document which requires a party to turn the pages. Furthermore, the structure of the sign-up procedure is such that the potential member is presented with the terms of membership twice during the process and must signify acceptance each time. Each time the potential member is provided with the option of disagreeing which terminates the process. The second time the terms are displayed occurs during the online portion of the process and at that time, the potential member is advised via a clear notice on the computer screen of the following:

> . . . The membership agreement includes terms that govern how information about you and your membership may be used. To become a MSN Premier member, you must select "I Agree" to acknowledge your consent to the terms of the membership agreement. If you click "I Agree" without reading the membership agreement, you are still agreeing to be bound by all of the terms of the membership agreement, without limitation. . . .

15 On cross-examination, Rudder admitted to having seen the screen containing the notice. In order to replicate the conditions, portions of the cross-examination were conducted while Rudder was being led through an actual sign-up process including the online connection portion. While online, and after having been shown the notice posted above, Rudder responded to questioning as follows:

Q. 372. All right. You see immediately below the printing that we have just read, a rectangular box that says, "MSN Premier Membership Rules"?

A. Yes.

Q. 373. And, below that, a larger white box that says, "Please click MSN Membership Rules and read the membership agreement"?

A. Yes.

Q. 374. Did you read the phrase that I just stated in the big white box?

A. No. What I probably did . . . I can't say for sure . . . is I probably just went to "I Agree", and then "Next".

Q. 375. Did you understand, when you clicked "I Agree" on this occasion, that you were agreeing to was something that was going to govern your legal relationship surrounding your use of MSN?

A. If you are asking me if I made a mental note, or if I had knowledge of that, no, I did not really pay attention to that. That is a common practice when I sign up on anything. Like I said, my main concern is what the costs are.

16 It is plain and obvious that there is no factual foundation for the plaintiffs' assertion that any term of the Membership Agreement was analogous to "fine print" in a written contract. What is equally clear is that the plaintiffs seek to avoid the consequences of specific terms of their agreement while at the same time seeking to have others enforced. Neither the form of this contract nor its manner of presentation to potential members are so aberrant as to lead to such an anomalous result. To give effect to the plaintiffs' argument would, rather than advancing the goal of commercial certainty, . . . move this type of electronic transaction into the realm of commercial absurdity. It would lead to chaos in the marketplace, render ineffectual electronic commerce and undermine the integrity of any agreement entered into through this medium.

17 On the present facts, the Membership Agreement must be afforded the sanctity that must be given to any agreement in writing. The position of selectivity advanced by the plaintiffs runs contrary to this stated approach, both in principle and on the evidence, and must be rejected. Moreover, given that both of the representative plaintiffs are graduates of law schools and have a professed familiarity with Internet services, their position is particularly indefensible . . .

26 The defendant shall have the relief requested.

To get a sense for how the quality of assent can differ depending on how the Web site is arranged, consider the following.

Specht v. Netscape Communications Corporation

2002 WL 31166784 (2nd Cir.)

Before McLAUGHLIN, LEVAL, and SOTOMAYOR, Circuit Judges.
SOTOMAYOR, Circuit Judge.

This is an appeal from a judgment of the Southern District of New York denying a motion by defendants-appellants Netscape Communications Corporation and its corporate parent, America Online, Inc. (collectively, "defendants" or "Netscape"), to compel arbitration and to stay court proceedings. In order to resolve the central question of arbitrability presented here, we must address issues of contract formation in cyberspace. Principally, we are asked to determine whether plaintiffs-appellees ("plaintiffs"), by acting upon defendants' invitation to download free software made available on defendants' webpage, agreed to be bound by the software's license terms (which included the arbitration clause at issue), even though plaintiffs could not have learned of the existence of those terms unless, prior to executing the download, they had scrolled down the webpage to a screen located below the download button. We agree with the district court that a reasonably prudent Internet user in circumstances such as these would not have known or learned of the existence of the license terms before responding to defendants' invitation to download the free software, and that defendants therefore did not provide reasonable notice of the license terms. In consequence, plaintiffs' bare act of downloading the software did not unambiguously manifest assent to the arbitration provision contained in the license terms. . . .

We therefore affirm the district court's denial of defendants' motion to compel arbitration and to stay court proceedings.

BACKGROUND

I. Facts

In three related putative class actions, plaintiffs alleged that, unknown to them, their use of SmartDownload transmitted to defendants private information about plaintiffs' downloading of files from the Internet, thereby effecting an electronic surveillance of their online activities in violation of two federal statutes, the Electronic Communications Privacy Act, 18 U.S.C. §§2510 *et seq.*, and the Computer Fraud and Abuse Act, 18 U.S.C. §1030.

Specifically, plaintiffs alleged that when they first used Netscape's Communicator — a software program that permits Internet browsing — the program created and stored on each of their computer hard drives a small text file known as a "cookie" that functioned "as a kind of electronic identification tag for future communications" between their computers and Netscape. Plaintiffs further alleged that when they installed SmartDownload — a separate software "plug-in" that served to enhance Communicator's browsing capabilities — SmartDownload created and stored on their computer hard drives another string of characters, known as a "Key," which similarly functioned as an identification tag in future communications with Netscape. According to the complaints in this case, each time a computer user employed Communicator to download a file from the Internet, SmartDownload "assume[d] from Communicator the task of downloading" the file and transmitted to Netscape the address of the file being downloaded together with the cookie created by Communicator and the Key created by SmartDownload. These processes, plaintiffs claim, constituted unlawful "eavesdropping" on users of Netscape's software products as well as on Internet websites from which users employing SmartDownload downloaded files.

In the time period relevant to this litigation, Netscape offered on its website various software programs, including Communicator and SmartDownload, which visitors to the site were invited to obtain free of charge. It is undisputed that five of the six named plaintiffs — Michael Fagan, John Gibson, Mark Gruber, Sean Kelly, and Sherry Weindorf — downloaded Communicator from the Netscape website. These plaintiffs acknowledge that when they proceeded to initiate installation of Communicator, they were automatically shown a scrollable text of that program's license agreement and were not permitted to complete the installation until they had clicked on a "Yes" button to indicate that they accepted all the license terms. If a user attempted to install Communicator without clicking "Yes," the installation would be aborted. All five named user plaintiffs expressly agreed to Communicator's license terms by clicking "Yes." The Communicator license agreement that these plaintiffs saw made no mention of SmartDownload or other plug-in programs, and stated that "[t]hese terms apply to Netscape Communicator and Netscape Navigator" and that "all disputes relating to this Agreement (excepting any dispute relating to intellectual property rights)" are subject to "binding arbitration in Santa Clara County, California."

Although Communicator could be obtained independently of SmartDownload, all the named user plaintiffs, except Fagan, downloaded and installed Communicator in connection with downloading SmartDownload. Each of these plaintiffs allegedly arrived at a Netscape webpage captioned "SmartDownload Communicator" that urged them to "Download With Confidence Using SmartDownload!" At or near the bottom of the screen facing plaintiffs was the prompt "Start Download" and a tinted button labeled "Download." By clicking on the button, plaintiffs initiated the download of SmartDownload. Once that process was complete, SmartDownload, as its first plug-in task, permitted plaintiffs to proceed with downloading and installing Communicator, an operation that was accompanied by the clickwrap display of Communicator's license terms described above.

The signal difference between downloading Communicator and downloading SmartDownload was that no clickwrap presentation accompanied the latter operation. Instead, once plaintiffs Gibson, Gruber, Kelly, and Weindorf had clicked on the "Download" button located at or near the bottom of their screen, and the downloading of SmartDownload was complete, these plaintiffs encountered no further information about the plug-in program or the existence of license terms governing its use. The sole reference to SmartDownload's license terms on the "SmartDownload Communicator" webpage was located in text that would have become visible to plaintiffs only if they had scrolled down to the next screen.

Had plaintiffs scrolled down instead of acting on defendants' invitation to click on the "Download" button, they would have encountered the following invitation: "Please review and agree to the terms of the *Netscape SmartDownload software license agreement* before downloading and using the software." Plaintiffs Gibson, Gruber, Kelly, and Weindorf averred in their affidavits that they never saw this reference to the SmartDownload license agreement when they clicked on the "Download" button. They also testified during depositions that they saw no reference to license terms when they clicked to download SmartDownload, although under questioning by defendants' counsel, some plaintiffs added that they could not "remember" or be "sure" whether the screen shots of the SmartDownload page attached to their affidavits reflected precisely what they had seen on their computer screens when they downloaded SmartDownload.

In sum, plaintiffs Gibson, Gruber, Kelly, and Weindorf allege that the process of obtaining SmartDownload contrasted sharply with that of obtaining Communicator. Having selected SmartDownload, they were required neither to express unambiguous assent to that program's license agreement nor even to view the license terms or become aware of their existence before proceeding with the invited download of the free plug-in program. Moreover, once these plaintiffs had initiated the download, the existence of SmartDownload's license terms was not mentioned while the software was running or at any later point in plaintiffs' experience of the product.

Even for a user who, unlike plaintiffs, did happen to scroll down past the download button, SmartDownload's license terms would not have been immediately displayed in the manner of Communicator's clickwrapped terms. Instead, if such a user had seen the notice of SmartDownload's terms and then clicked on the underlined invitation to review and agree to the terms, a hypertext link would have taken the user to a separate webpage entitled "License & Support Agreements." The first paragraph on this page read, in pertinent part:

The use of each Netscape software product is governed by a license agreement. You must read and agree to the license agreement terms BEFORE acquiring a product. Please click on the appropriate link below to review the current license agreement for the product of interest to you before acquisition. For products available for download, you must read and agree to the license agreement terms BEFORE you install the software. If you do not agree to the license terms, do not download, install or use the software.

Below this paragraph appeared a list of license agreements, the first of which was *"License Agreement for Netscape Navigator and Netscape Communicator Product Family* (Netscape Navigator, Netscape Communicator and Netscape SmartDownload)." If the user clicked on that link, he or she would be taken to yet another webpage that contained the full text of a license agreement that was identical in every respect to the Communicator license agreement except that it stated that its "terms apply to Netscape Communicator, Netscape Navigator, and Netscape SmartDownload." The license agreement granted the user a nonexclusive license to use and reproduce the software, subject to certain terms:

BY CLICKING THE ACCEPTANCE BUTTON OR INSTALLING OR USING NETSCAPE COMMUNICATOR, NETSCAPE NAVIGATOR, OR NETSCAPE SMART-DOWNLOAD SOFTWARE (THE "PRODUCT"), THE INDIVIDUAL OR ENTITY LICENSING THE PRODUCT ("LICENSEE") IS CONSENTING TO BE BOUND BY AND IS BECOMING A PARTY TO THIS AGREEMENT. IF LICENSEE DOES NOT AGREE TO ALL OF THE TERMS OF THIS AGREEMENT, THE BUTTON INDICATING NON-ACCEPTANCE MUST BE SELECTED, AND LICENSEE MUST NOT INSTALL OR USE THE SOFTWARE.

Among the license terms was a provision requiring virtually all disputes relating to the agreement to be submitted to arbitration:

Unless otherwise agreed in writing, all disputes relating to this Agreement (excepting any dispute relating to intellectual property rights) shall be subject to final and binding arbitration in Santa Clara County, California, under the auspices of JAMS/EndDispute, with the losing party paying all costs of arbitration. . . .

II. PROCEEDINGS BELOW

In the district court, defendants moved to compel arbitration and to stay court proceedings pursuant to the Federal Arbitration Act ("FAA"), 9 U.S.C. §4, arguing that the disputes reflected in the complaints, like any other dispute relating to the SmartDownload license agreement, are subject to the arbitration clause contained in that agreement. Finding that Netscape's webpage, unlike typical examples of clickwrap, neither adequately alerted users to the existence of SmartDownload's license terms nor required users unambiguously to manifest assent to those terms as a condition of downloading the product, the court held that the user plaintiffs had not entered into the SmartDownload license agreement.

The district court also ruled that the separate license agreement governing use of Communicator, even though the user plaintiffs had assented to its terms, involved an independent transaction that made no mention of SmartDownload and so did not bind plaintiffs to arbitrate their claims relating to SmartDownload.

Defendants took this timely appeal. . . .

Discussion

I.   STANDARD OF REVIEW AND APPLICABLE LAW . . .

The FAA provides that a "written provision in any . . . contract evidencing a transaction involving commerce to settle by arbitration a controversy thereafter arising out of such contract or transaction . . . shall be valid, irrevocable, and enforceable, save upon such grounds as exist at law or in equity for the revocation of any contract." 9 U.S.C. §2. It is well settled that a court may not compel arbitration until it has resolved the question of the very existence of the contract embodying the arbitration clause. [Citations and internal quotation marks omitted.]

The district court properly concluded that in deciding whether parties agreed to arbitrate a certain matter, a court should generally apply state-law principles to the issue of contract formation. Therefore, state law governs the question of whether the parties in the present case entered into an agreement to arbitrate disputes relating to the SmartDownload license agreement. The district court further held that California law governs the question of contract formation here; the parties do not appeal that determination.

II.   WHETHER THIS COURT SHOULD REMAND FOR A TRIAL ON CONTRACT FORMATION

[Although it was not entirely clear that none of the plaintiffs saw the contract terms in question, the court concluded that the record was adequate to resolve the issue of contract formation.]

III.   WHETHER THE USER PLAINTIFFS HAD REASONABLE NOTICE OF AND MANIFESTED ASSENT TO THE SMARTDOWNLOAD LICENSE AGREEMENT

Whether governed by the common law or by Article 2 of the Uniform Commercial Code ("UCC"), a transaction, in order to be a contract, requires a manifestation of agreement between the parties.[13] Mutual manifestation of

---

13. The district court concluded that the SmartDownload transactions here should be governed by "California law as it relates to the sale of goods, including the Uniform Commercial Code in effect in California." It is not obvious, however, that UCC Article 2 ("sales of goods") applies to the licensing of software that is downloadable from the Internet. There is no doubt that a sale of tangible goods over the Internet is governed by Article 2 of the UCC. Some courts have

assent, whether by written or spoken word or by conduct, is the touchstone of contract. Although an onlooker observing the disputed transactions in this case would have seen each of the user plaintiffs click on the SmartDownload "Download" button, a consumer's clicking on a download button does not communicate assent to contractual terms if the offer did not make clear to the consumer that clicking on the download button would signify assent to those terms. [The] common law is clear that an offeree, regardless of apparent manifestation of his consent, is not bound by inconspicuous contractual provisions of which he is unaware, contained in a document whose contractual nature is not obvious. [Citations and internal quotation marks omitted.] . . .

A. THE REASONABLY PRUDENT OFFEREE OF DOWNLOADABLE SOFTWARE

Defendants argue that plaintiffs must be held to a standard of reasonable prudence and that, because notice of the existence of SmartDownload license terms was on the next scrollable screen, plaintiffs were on "inquiry notice" of those terms. We disagree with the proposition that a reasonably prudent offeree in plaintiffs' position would necessarily have known or learned of the existence of the SmartDownload license agreement prior to acting, so that plaintiffs may be held to have assented to that agreement with constructive notice of its terms. It is true that [a] party cannot avoid the terms of a contract on the ground that he or she failed to read it before signing. [Citation and internal quotation marks omitted]. But courts are quick to add: "An exception to this general rule exists when the writing does not appear to be a contract and the terms are not called to the attention of the recipient. In such a case, no contract is formed with respect to the undisclosed term." [Citations omitted.]

Most of the cases cited by defendants in support of their inquiry-notice argument are drawn from the world of paper contracting.

As [those] cases suggest, receipt of a physical document containing contract terms or notice thereof is frequently deemed, in the world of paper transactions, a sufficient circumstance to place the offeree on inquiry notice of those terms. . . .These principles apply equally to the emergent world of online product delivery, pop-up screens, hyperlinked pages, clickwrap licensing, scrollable documents, and urgent admonitions to "Download Now!". What plaintiffs saw when they were being invited by defendants to download this fast, free plug-in called

---

also applied Article 2, occasionally with misgivings, to sales of off-the-shelf software in tangible, packaged formats.

Downloadable software, however, is scarcely a "tangible" good, and, in part because software may be obtained, copied, or transferred effortlessly at the stroke of a computer key, licensing of such Internet products has assumed a vast importance in recent years. Recognizing that "a body of law based on images of the sale of manufactured goods ill fits licenses and other transactions in computer information," the National Conference of Commissioners on Uniform State Laws has promulgated the Uniform Computer Information Transactions Act ("UCITA"), a code resembling UCC Article 2 in many respects but drafted to reflect emergent practices in the sale and licensing of computer information. UCITA, prefatory note (rev. ed. Aug. 23, 2001) (available at *www.ucitaonline.com/ucita.html*). UCITA — originally intended as a new Article 2B to supplement Articles 2 and 2A of the UCC but later proposed as an independent code — has been adopted by two states, Maryland and Virginia.

We need not decide today whether UCC Article 2 applies to Internet transactions in downloadable products. The district court's analysis and the parties' arguments on appeal show that, for present purposes, there is no essential difference between UCC Article 2 and the common law of contracts. We therefore apply the common law, with exceptions as noted.

SmartDownload was a screen containing praise for the product and, at the very bottom of the screen, a "Download" button. Defendants argue that under the principles set forth in the cases cited above, a "fair and prudent person using ordinary care" would have been on inquiry notice of SmartDownload's license terms.

We are not persuaded that a reasonably prudent offeree in these circumstances would have known of the existence of license terms. Plaintiffs were responding to an offer that did not carry an immediately visible notice of the existence of license terms or require unambiguous manifestation of assent to those terms. Thus, plaintiffs' apparent manifestation of consent was to terms contained in a document whose contractual nature [was] not obvious. [Citation and internal quotation marks omitted.] Moreover, the fact that, given the position of the scroll bar on their computer screens, plaintiffs may have been aware that an unexplored portion of the Netscape webpage remained below the download button does not mean that they reasonably should have concluded that this portion contained a notice of license terms. In their deposition testimony, plaintiffs variously stated that they used the scroll bar "[o]nly if there is something that I feel I need to see that is on — that is off the page," or that the elevated position of the scroll bar suggested the presence of "mere[ ] formalities, standard lower banner links" or "that the page is bigger than what I can see." Plaintiffs testified, and defendants did not refute, that plaintiffs were in fact unaware that defendants intended to attach license terms to the use of SmartDownload.

We conclude that in circumstances such as these, where consumers are urged to download free software at the immediate click of a button, a reference to the existence of license terms on a submerged screen is not sufficient to place consumers on inquiry or constructive notice of those terms.   The SmartDownload webpage screen was printed in such a manner that it tended to conceal the fact that it was an express acceptance of [Netscape's] rules and regulations. [Citation and internal quotation marks omitted.] Internet users may have, as defendants put it, "as much time as they need[ ]" to scroll through multiple screens on a webpage, but there is no reason to assume that viewers will scroll down to subsequent screens simply because screens are there. When products are "free" and users are invited to download them in the absence of reasonably conspicuous notice that they are about to bind themselves to contract terms, the transactional circumstances cannot be fully analogized to those in the paper world of arm's-length bargaining. In the next two sections, we discuss case law and other legal authorities that have addressed the circumstances of computer sales, software licensing, and online transacting. Those authorities tend strongly to support our conclusion that plaintiffs did not manifest assent to SmartDownload's license terms.

B.   Shrinkwrap Licensing and Related Practices

Defendants cite certain well-known cases involving shrinkwrap licensing and related commercial practices in support of their contention that plaintiffs became bound by the SmartDownload license terms by virtue of inquiry notice. For example, in *Hill v. Gateway 2000, Inc.*, 105 F.3d 1147 (7th Cir.1997), the Seventh Circuit held that where a purchaser had ordered a computer over the telephone, received the order in a shipped box containing the computer along with printed contract terms, and did not return the computer within the thirty days required by the terms, the purchaser was bound by the contract. *Id.* at 1148-49. In *ProCD, Inc. v. Zeidenberg,* [86 F.3d 1447 (7th Cir. 1996),] the same court held that where an individual purchased software in a box containing license terms which were displayed on the computer screen every time the user executed the software program, the user had sufficient opportunity to review the terms and to return the software, and so was contractually bound after retaining the product. *ProCD*, 86 F.3d at 1452; *cf. Moore v. Microsoft Corp.*, 741 N.Y.S.2d 91, 92 (2d Dep't 2002) (software user was bound by license agreement where terms were prominently displayed on computer screen before software could be installed and where user was required to indicate assent by clicking "I agree"); *Brower v. Gateway 2000, Inc.*, 676 N.Y.S.2d 569, 572 (1st Dep't 1998) (buyer assented to arbitration clause shipped inside box with computer and software by retaining items beyond date specified by license terms); *M.A. Mortenson Co. v. Timberline Software Corp.*, 970 P.2d 803, 809 (Wash.Ct.App.1999) (buyer manifested assent to software license terms by installing and using software), *aff'd*, 998 P.2d 305 (Wash.2000); *see also* [*iLan Sys., Inc. v. NetScout Serv. Level Corp.*, 183 F. Supp. 2d 328, 338 (D. Mass. 2002) (business entity "explicitly accepted the clickwrap license agreement [contained in purchased software] when it clicked on the box stating 'I agree'").

These cases do not help defendants. To the extent that they hold that the purchaser of a computer or tangible software is contractually bound after failing to object to printed license terms provided with the product, *Hill* and *Brower* do not differ markedly from the cases involving traditional paper contracting discussed in the previous section. Insofar as the purchaser in *ProCD* was confronted with conspicuous, mandatory license terms every time he ran the software on his computer, that case actually undermines defendants' contention that downloading in the absence of conspicuous terms is an act that binds plaintiffs to those terms. In *Mortenson*, the full text of license terms was printed on each sealed diskette envelope inside the software box, printed again on the inside cover of the user manual, and notice of the terms appeared on the computer screen every time the purchaser executed the program. *Mortenson*, 970 P.2d at 806. In sum, the foregoing cases are clearly distinguishable from the facts of the present action.

C.   ONLINE TRANSACTIONS

Cases in which courts have found contracts arising from Internet use do not assist defendants, because in those circumstances there was much clearer notice than in the present case that a user's act would manifest assent to contract terms.[16]

After reviewing the California common law and other relevant legal authority, we conclude that under the circumstances here, plaintiffs' downloading of SmartDownload did not constitute acceptance of defendants' license terms. Reasonably conspicuous notice of the existence of contract terms and unambiguous manifestation of assent to those terms by consumers are essential if electronic bargaining is to have integrity and credibility. We hold that a reasonably prudent offeree in plaintiffs' position would not have known or learned, prior to acting on

---

16. Defendants place great importance on *Register.com, Inc. v. Verio, Inc.*, 126 F. Supp. 2d 238 (S.D.N.Y.2000), which held that a user of the Internet domain-name database, Register.com, had "manifested its assent to be bound" by the database's terms of use when it electronically submitted queries to the database. *Id.* at 248. But *Verio* is not helpful to defendants. There, the plaintiff's terms of use of its information were well known to the defendant, which took the information daily with full awareness that it was using the information in a manner prohibited by the terms of the plaintiff's offer. The case is not closely analogous to ours.

the invitation to download, of the reference to SmartDownload's license terms hidden below the "Download" button on the next screen. We affirm the district court's conclusion that the user plaintiffs, including Fagan, are not bound by the arbitration clause contained in those terms.

IV. WHETHER PLAINTIFFS' ASSENT TO COMMUNICATOR'S LICENSE AGREEMENT REQUIRES THEM TO ARBITRATE THEIR CLAIMS REGARDING SMARTDOWNLOAD

[The court of appeals affirmed the conclusion of the trial court that the Netscape Communicator license (to which plaintiffs admittedly agreed) did not apply to plaintiffs' complaint about SmartDownload.]

CONCLUSION

For the foregoing reasons, we affirm the district court's denial of defendants' motion to compel arbitration and to stay court proceedings.

C. Mail-Order Rule

Thus far, remote contracting has not been the subject of any significant federal regulation. The most prominent exception is the FTC's Mail and Telephone Order Merchandise Rule, 16 C.F.R. Part 435 (1996), commonly known as the Mail-Order Rule. That rule effectively incorporates a few standard terms into all contracts for the sale of goods by telephone or mail. More importantly, it provides federal regulatory enforcement for those terms.

First, the rule requires that the seller must have a reasonable basis for believing that it can deliver the goods in the time it promises, or in any event within 30 days. The rule also requires the retailer faced with an unexpected delay (a) to contact the purchaser to explain the cause and expected duration of the delay; and (b) to permit the purchaser to cancel the transaction, with a refund to be paid within seven days.

That rule has gained prominence during recent holiday seasons, as prominent Internet toy retailers (many now defunct) have failed conspicuously to satisfy their promises to deliver goods by Christmas. Although normal contract-law rules might have made the retailers liable for breach of contract, the FTC rule resulted in something that state contract law did not: the swift and highly visible imposition of millions of dollars of fines.

Relevant Glossary Entries

Clickwrap Terms
Shrinkwrap Terms

Problem Set 13

13.1. You purchase a new computer from Fell Computers at *www.fell.com*. When the computer arrives, you open the box and discover a detailed "Welcome Kit," which includes a seven-page "Terms and Conditions" document. The document states that if you are unsatisfied with your purchase for any reason (including implicitly the Terms and Conditions) you may return the computer within the next 30 days for a complete refund (except for any shipping costs you incur). The document also states that all claims related to any defect in the computer must be presented in an arbitration proceeding in New York City under the rules of the American Arbitration Association. This is not inconsistent with any of the information on the Fell Computers Web site (which does not include a link to the terms and conditions on which Fell Computers makes sales), but it certainly was news to you, and quite objectionable — you are sure you would have bought a computer from the competitor Janeway Computers if you had known of this term.

Now that you have the computer, however, you proceed to use it. If you later challenge the enforceability of the arbitration clause, is it enforceable against you? (You should assume for purposes of this problem that in the applicable jurisdiction there are no special rules regarding arbitration clauses; they are at least as enforceable as any other clauses in such a contract.) What do you say? Old UCC §§2-204, 2-207, UCC §2-207; RESTATEMENT (2D) OF CONTRACTS §211.

13.2. Same facts as Problem 13.1, but in this case the terms were presented to you at the Fell Computers Web site. The entire "Terms and Conditions" document was displayed on the screen, and you could not complete the purchase without scrolling to the bottom of the document and clicking on a button that said "Click here to buy." Just above the button was a box in large dark type running all the way across the screen that stated:

> BY CLICKING ON THE BUTTON BELOW, YOU ACKNOWLEDGE THAT YOU HAVE READ THE FOREGOING AND AGREE TO BE BOUND BY IT WITH THE SAME FORMALITY AS IF YOU HAD SIGNED IT IN PERSON.

The screen also included a button that indicated you should "Click here to decline purchase if the terms are unacceptable." You completed the purchase, clicking through the screens as quickly as possible without reading the document. A second copy of the document was enclosed with the computer, but you did not read that one either. Instead, you proceeded to use the computer. Is your answer any different than it was before? Old UCC §§2-204, 2-207, UCC §§2-204(4)(b), 2-207.

13.3. Same facts as Problem 13.2, but this time you did not have to review the terms and conditions to purchase the computer. Rather, the terms and conditions were available only through a link at the bottom of the "Click Here To Buy" page; you did not happen to click on that link, which appeared beneath the following statement in fine print: "By placing your order you agree to fell.com's privacy notice and conditions of use." If you had clicked on the link, you might have seen that the conditions say, among other things, that if a customer returns an order for any reason, the customer must pay the cost of shipping to return plus a 10 percent restocking fee. Assuming that you wish to return the computer, do you have to pay shipping and the restocking fee or not? Old UCC §2-204, UCC §2-204(4)(b).

13.4. Your friend Mia Katerina at PoochPortal calls with a question about their privacy policy. She recently charged a new attorney with the job of reviewing all of the contractual material on her Web site. The attorney noticed that the privacy policy currently appears to visitors only if they click on a link at the bottom of the page. He has proposed altering their site so that the privacy policy appears to every visitor that enters information (ordinarily at the time of any purchase), so that each purchaser from whom the site collected information would be forced to "click-through" consent to the privacy policy. Mia is puzzled as to why you did not originally set up the privacy policy to require such consent. She wants to know if this was inadvertent or intentional. What do you have to say? Is the new attorney's idea a good one?

13.5. Recall the facts of Problem 2.1, in which the general counsel of Global Scanners sought advice on choice-of-law and choice-of-forum clauses. He indicates that it would not be customary in the industry for the parties to sit down and sign documents at a closing, and that obviously consumers do not actually sign contracts for their purchases. He wants to know how to deliver these standard form contracts in a way that will not interfere with the marketing efforts of the company, but at the same time he wants to ensure that they are binding. What do you recommend?

13.6. Shortly after Music Depot (the world's largest musical-instrument retailer) opens its Web site to retail traffic, it is swamped by wholly unexpected demand. Its Web-order processing software initially reports to customers that they should expect shipment normally within 24 hours. After 2,000 orders are received, the interface is revised to provide a more realistic estimate of the shipment date. At that point, Music Depot sends postcards to consumers 201 through 2,000 informing them of the delay and providing a new estimated date for shipment ranging from 2 to 12 weeks.

(a) Assuming that the revised date reflects an honest estimation, has Music Depot violated the law? 16 C.F.R. §435.1.

(b) Would your answer for buyers whose Internet connections were based on telephone lines differ from your answer for buyers whose Internet connections used cable or other methods of Internet access that do not depend on telephone lines? 16 C.F.R. §435.2; compare EU Directive on Distance Selling art. 2(4).

13.7. State Representative Mark Trafeli calls seeking advice. Another representative has just introduced a bill calling for an amendment of the Uniform Commercial Code that would add a new subsection to UCC §2-207 providing as follows: "No contract involving a sale to a consumer shall include any term that is not available in a manner permitting an opportunity for review by the consumer before the consumer becomes obligated to pay for the sale." He wants your views on whether he should support the revision. What do you think? [He mentions that the revision is based on UCITA §§112 and 209(b) and on art. 10(1)(d) of the EU Electronic Commerce Directive, to which you might wish to refer.]

Assignment 14: Electronic Contracting II

The technology for storing and sending information has changed immensely in the past few decades. Those changes have altered in fundamental ways the methods that businesses and consumers use to accomplish transactions. Consider, for example, the change from the world of 1990 in which e-mail was almost unheard of to the world of the early twenty-first century in which many of us strongly prefer e-mail communications to contact in person or by telephone, letter, or telecopy. If the law of contracting is to remain relevant to commercial transactions, it must adapt not only to the remoteness of the transactions, but also to the electronic communications that businesses and consumers now use. This assignment discusses the major topics in which that problem arises.

A. Eliminating Paper Documents

The Statute of Frauds is a traditional contract doctrine requiring certain contracts to be in writing and signed by the party to be bound by the contract. The most common types of contract to which the doctrine applies are contracts related to family matters (such as wills or pre-nuptial agreements), guaranty contracts, contracts for the sale or transfer of land, certain contracts for the sale of goods, and contracts with a term that exceeds one year. See e.g., Old UCC §2-201; RESTATEMENT (2D) OF CONTRACTS §110. Although the writing requirement always has been limited to contracts involving certain subject matters, and has been undermined in recent decades by judicially created exceptions, it has played a part in slowing the use of electronic media to enter contracts.

Similarly, numerous state and federal statutes have supplemented state contract law by requiring one of the parties to the transaction to provide specific written disclosures to the other. The most obvious examples in the commercial law context are the various requirements of the Consumer Credit Protection Act, which includes the Truth-in-Lending Act and the Electronic Fund Transfers Act.

The Uniform Commercial Code always has had a functional notion of a signature, so that a variety of things other than a manual pen-and-ink signature readily would satisfy it. See Old UCC §1-201(39) (defining "Signed" to include "any symbol executed or adopted by a party with present intention to authenticate a writing"). However, at its core that definition relies on the relatively inflexible concept of a "writing," which seems to demand a tangible document. In recent years, however, legislatures at the state and federal level have for the most part abandoned the Statute of Frauds, at least to the point of permitting an electronic record to satisfy any requirement of a written memorial.

The most important enactment in that trend is the Uniform Electronic Transactions Act (UETA), promulgated by the National Conference of Commissioners on Uniform State Laws in 1999 and already adopted by almost 40 states. That statute does not require the use of electronic contracting or records, but it does provide, however, that any party that chooses to use electronic contracting and records should receive the same legal treatment as a party that uses traditional written documentation. The core provision is UETA §7, which states that "[a] contract may not be denied legal effect or enforceability solely because an electronic record was used in its formation." UETA §7(b). More generally, the statute provides that "[a] record or signature may not be denied legal effect or enforceability solely because it is in electronic form." UETA §7(a); see UCC §2-201 (Statute of Frauds satisfied by a record in electronic form).

Shortly after NCCUSL promulgated UETA, Congress enacted a similar provision into federal law in the Electronic Signatures in Global and National Commerce Act (E-SIGN), 15 U.S.C. §§7000-7300. Because UETA will take effect state by state, as the individual legislatures enact it into law, Congress enacted E-SIGN to provide immediate nationwide coverage for UETA's basic principle. The core provision of E-SIGN, parallel to UETA §7, is E-SIGN §101(a):

> [W]ith respect to any transaction in or affecting interstate or foreign commerce —
>   (1) a signature, contract, or other record relating to such transaction may not be denied legal effect, validity, or enforceability solely because it is in electronic form; and
>   (2) a contract relating to such transaction may not be denied legal effect, validity, or enforceability solely because an electronic signature or electronic record was used in its formation.

Because many states already had adopted UETA, and because UETA differs from E-SIGN in some of its details, it seemed likely to the parties working on E-SIGN that many states might prefer to retain UETA. To accommodate that likelihood, E-SIGN does not preempt any state enactment of UETA (at least if the state adopts the official version of UETA). E-SIGN §102(a)(1).

On the global level, the central provisions of UETA and E-SIGN closely track the Model Law on Electronic Commerce promulgated by UNCITRAL in 1996. Specifically, article 5 of that Law (titled "Legal recognition of data messages"), provides: "Information shall not be denied legal effect, validity or enforceability solely on the grounds that it is in the form of a data message." In addition to jurisdictions like the individual United States (which have adopted provisions that are similar to the Model Law), that Law has been directly adopted in more than 20 countries (including France, Korea, and India). Because the Model Law closely tracks the provisions of domestic American law — unlike the CISG (which covers conventional contracts and differs substantially from UCC Article 2), it thus affords considerable uniformity in cross-border transactions.

UETA and E-SIGN also include a media-neutral definition of signature. In UETA, for example, an "Electronic signature" is defined to mean "an electronic sound, symbol, or process attached to or logically associated with a record and executed or adopted by a person with the intent to sign the record." UETA §2(8). A similar definition appears in E-SIGN §106(5).

Although both UETA and E-SIGN reflect a general desire to remove barriers that prevent parties from using electronic communications in their transactions, neither statute reflects a blind confidence in the specific types of communications that parties will choose to use. Thus, most obviously, both statutes state only that contracts and records are not to be held invalid "solely" because they are in electronic form. All rules that invalidate contracts for other reasons apply in full force to electronic contracts. Thus, for example, doctrines of unconscionability (evident in Assignment 2) and problems of assent (discussed in Assignment 13) do not disappear solely because a signature is electronic instead of manual.

Both statutes also include affirmative provisions designed to ensure that businesses provide electronic communications in a readily accessible format. For example, UETA §8 provides rules for how parties must provide information and records to those with whom they are dealing. Under those rules — which apply to all contracting parties (businesses and consumers) — one party cannot rely on information it provided the other party if the sending party "inhibits the ability of the recipient to print or store the electronic record" of the information. For example, if a seller claims that it has provided another party notice that it has goods ready for delivery (as required by UCC §2-503), the notice would be invalid if it was sent in a format that did not permit the recipient to store and print the information. UETA §8(a). The statute reflects a preemptive aversion to technologies (not currently common) that would allow a business to send a communication that the recipient can view but not print. See UETA §8 comment 3.

The drafters of E-SIGN §101(c) took a different approach to that problem, including a considerably more onerous provision, limited however, to transactions with consumers. [E-SIGN §106(a) defines "consumer" as "an individual who obtains, through a transaction, products or services which are used primarily for personal, family, or household purposes."] That provision applies to any law that "requires that information relating to a transaction . . . be provided or made available to a consumer in writing," E-SIGN §101(c)(1); its most obvious application is to the myriad disclosures required by the various titles of the Consumer Credit Protection Act mentioned above. It also could apply, however, in a variety of other circumstances if some particular state or federal law requires a specific written disclosure with respect to some specific term of the transaction (such as an indemnity clause).

Under E-SIGN §101(c)(1), the business providing the disclosure can use an electronic record only if it satisfies three requirements. First, it must provide a clear and conspicuous statement advising the consumer of the procedures related to the electronic record (such things as whether the consumer can insist on a paper notice, the transactions for which electronic notices will be provided, how the consumer can withdraw its consent, and how the consumer can obtain hard copies of the information in question). E-SIGN §101(c)(1)(B). Second, the consumer must affirmatively consent to use of the electronic disclosure. E-SIGN §101(c)(1)(A).

Third, the party providing the disclosure must test the consumer's ability to access information in the format in which notices will be sent; this is to be done by obtaining a consent (or confirmation of consent) "in a manner that reasonably demonstrates that the consumer can access information in the electronic form that will be used to provide the information that is the subject of the consent." E-SIGN §101(c)(1)(C)(ii). That provision should go a long way toward ensuring in a practical way that consumers in transactions governed by E-SIGN receive notices in a format that is accessible to them.

For a merchant trying to determine whether state law or federal law governs its obligations to consumers, the preemption provisions of E-SIGN are remarkably unclear. That is because federal legislators trying to placate states that might wish to follow the UETA model agreed that enactments of UETA would "supersede" federal law that otherwise would preempt state law. See E-SIGN §102(a). The only state law that can "supersede" E-SIGN is UETA in its uniform form; if a state makes any material modification to UETA, then E-SIGN governs. Yet UETA lacks any analog to E-SIGN §101(c), so it would seem that a state enacting a "clean" version of UETA exempts its merchants from complying with E-SIGN §101(c) for contracts subject only to state law. Consumer advocates have argued long and hard against this interpretation of the preempt/supersede provisions of E-SIGN, and, just in case their statutory interpretation arguments do not carry the day, are lobbying states to enact consumer protection laws substantially in the form of E-SIGN §101(c). Given the turmoil, there is every reason to expect judicial explication of those provisions in the near term.

B. Attribution

Another issue raised by electronic contracting is the problem of attribution. In the face-to-face context, attribution is not a serious problem: A person that appears at the merchant's counter, signs documents, and hands over money or accepted property is bound to the contract that those actions implement.

In the electronic context, however, the parties need not meet in person: One of the purposes of Internet retailing is to save consumers the hassle of traveling to the merchant's location. That circumstance can cause problems, however, when one party claims that it is not responsible for a transaction completed in its name in an electronic format. That issue arises in two separate contexts: the use of robotic devices, and the use of signatures as evidence of authorization.

1. Robotic Devices

One development in contracting that has great potential for Internet commerce is the rise of robotic devices for contracting (often called "bots"). In this context, the idea is that a person would program its computer to search for products that it wishes to buy (or persons to whom it can sell) and have the computer enter into transactions upon terms that meet specified conditions. Because the bot should be able to search the Web much more widely and rapidly than an individual, it should enhance the ability of buyers and sellers to find favorable terms for their transactions.

The basic question that those bots present is whether the party that programs the bot and sends it on its way is bound by contracts into which the bot enters. That issue is particularly important given the likelihood in an electronic context that those contracting with the bot often will not realize that they are not interacting with a human individual. In one sense, it is quite simple to conclude the principal that sends the bot on its way is bound by its conduct, just as a person would be bound by a telegram or electronic-mail message that it sends, or by a communication that it sends through punching numeric buttons on a touch-telephone key pad. Thus, for example, comment 1 to UETA §9 explains that "a person's actions include actions taken by human agents of the person, as well as actions taken by an electronic agent, i.e., the tool, of the person." More specifically, UCC §2-204 provides that "[a] contract may be formed by the interaction of electronic agents of the parties, even if no individual was aware of or reviewed the electronic agents' actions or the resulting terms and agreements." UCC §2-204(4)(a).

On the other hand, the spread of robotic contracting is likely to raise new questions, if only because the types of contracting disputes will expand to include disputes that involve things like errors in robot programming or failure of a Web site to provide information in a way that a typical robot readily might understand. You will get a glimpse of those problems in the next section of the text as you learn about the effects information technology already has had on business transactions.

2.   *Signatures*

A more difficult problem relates to the signature. For manual signatures — pen on paper — the common-sense traditional rule is that a person is bound by his signature and is not bound by the signature of others (unless they are acting as agents). UETA §9(a) includes an analogous provision for electronic signatures, binding persons to signatures that actually are theirs. It then goes on to deal with a more difficult problem, how to determine whether a particular transaction truly involved an act of a particular person: Was Alex in fact the person that purchased the book from Amazon.com? As you would expect given its general laissez-faire stance, UETA does not require any particular authentication procedure. Rather, it states only that the act of the person can be demonstrated by, among other things, "a showing of the efficacy of any security procedure applied to determine the person to which the electronic record or electronic signature was attributable." For example, if a merchant could show that it attributed a purchase to a particular individual (Alex) because the purchase was completed after the user logged in with Alex's user ID and password, that would be substantial proof that Alex in fact made the purchase.

Notice, however, what the provision does not say: It does not say that Alex is bound by anything completed through the security procedure, only that proof of the security procedure is one method of establishing that Alex *in fact* was the actor. Thus, if Alex can show that an impostor with her user ID and password in fact was the actor (for example, by showing that the goods were shipped to the impostor rather than Alex), UETA §9(a) would not attribute the act to her. That provision thus provides a relatively limited role for the security procedures. Compare UCC §4A-202(b) (validating payment orders issued by security procedure even if the customer in fact did not issue them). What that means is that merchants must protect themselves by making the systems sufficiently secure that consumers will not practicably be able to disavow transactions. For large transactions, that outcome might lead to secure (user ID/password) systems; for others that involve no extension of credit, there might be almost no security. More broadly, it reflects a general view that placing the risk of loss in those situations on those that deal with consumers is more likely to result in an appropriate level of technological authentication than a rule that places the risk of loss on consumers. The contrary rule in UCC Article 4A reflects the fact that UCC Article 4A is designed for large-dollar payments by sophisticated businesses.

A more intractable issue is the legal effect of the electronic signature. In our daily lives we take many actions that are not intended to be binding contracts — we write post-it notes and leave them on our desks, we initial documents that have passed through our inbox, we write grocery lists. There is a special significance in our culture to the signature as an action that binds us to a particular obligation, as opposed to a writing that simply demonstrates that we have seen or sent the document in question. It is not yet clear how the electronic-contracting realm will distinguish attribution in the sense of acknowledgment of receipt or indication of origin from the formal acceptance of obligation that the signature provides. For example, it is reasonable to think that the sense of legal obligation is imposed much less clearly upon the average person by a Web-site request to "**CLICK HERE IF YOU AGREE**" than it is by a requirement that a person sign a signature line on a written contract.

UETA recognizes the possibility that an electronic act might not be as adequate to bind an individual as a formal written signature, and leaves the issue for later decisionmaking by courts. Despite considerable efforts in the drafting process to develop a provision that at a minimum included safe-harbor specifications of procedures that would produce a conclusively binding signature, the final version of UETA has only an open-ended and general statement that "[t]he effect of an electronic record or signature" — once the record or signature has been attributed to a particular person — "is determined from the context and surrounding circumstances at the time of its creation, execution, or adoption." UETA §9(b). Thus, that provision leaves open the possibility that an action or record attributable to a person under §9(a) would be sufficiently informal that it would not create a binding contract under §9(b).

C.   Mailbox Rule

A common problem in forming conventional contracts is determining the time when a particular communication is effective. Normally, this is resolved by the "mailbox rule," under which the action of a party accepting an offer is effective when it places an acceptance in the mail, even before it is received. Thus, for example, if the party places an acceptance in the mail and the offeror tries to revoke the offer by telephone before the acceptance arrives, the contract is valid and the revocation is ineffective. RESTATEMENT (2D) OF CONTRACTS §66. That rule is an exception to the general rule, under which communications are not effective until they are received — a communication revoking an offer, for example, is not effective until it is received. RESTATEMENT (2D) OF CONTRACTS §42.

Those rules were formulated in a context in which transmissions sent by mail have questionable reliability and contemplate a delay of several days between transmission and receipt. Thus, they do not fit well with a world of e-mail transmissions that often are received within seconds. At the same time, the regularity and universality of mail transmissions to business and residence addresses contrasts, at least for now, with the confusion that can be occasioned by e-mail transmissions that do not go directly to the appropriate individual at the receiving company.

Section 15 of UETA responds to that issue with a detailed provision specifying the time when electronic communications are sent and received. Subsection (a) provides a three-part test for when a communication is sent. First, it must be directed to an address specified by the recipient or in fact used by the recipient for messages of the type in question. Second, it must be sent in a format capable of being processed by the recipient's system. Finally, it must be sent, in the sense that it must "ente[r] an information processing system outside the control of the sender" or "ente[r] a region of the information processing system . . . which is under the control of the recipient." UETA §15(a).

The statute provides a parallel definition of the time of receipt: when "it enters an information processing system that the recipient has designated or uses for the process of receiving electronic records . . . of the type sent," provided that the message "is in a form capable of being processed by that system." UETA §15(b). Most importantly, UETA buttresses that definition by providing that a message is received "even if no individual is aware of its receipt." Like the provisions related to agents, that might seem obvious in light of the preceding definition, but the plain statement of the rule is useful for clarity. See also UCC §2-213(1) (incorporating that rule into the Uniform Commercial Code).

D.   Mistake

One final problem that is unfortunately common for electronic contracting is the mistake. As we all know, any interaction between a human individual and a computer includes the possibility of a mistake. When a mistake happens at a retail counter, it often can be remedied on the spot — "Oh, if that blouse is $240 instead of $24 then I don't want it" — but that often is not practical in an electronic context, because the computer may not be programmed to receive and respond to such a communication.

Traditional contract law is unsympathetic to claims of mistake. For example, the RESTATEMENT provides that a mistake by one party (a "unilateral" mistake) justifies invalidation of the contract only if it is a mistake "as to a basic assumption on which he made the contract," if it "has a material effect on the agreed exchange of performances that is adverse," and if "the effect of the mistake is such that enforcement of the contract would be unconscionable," or "the other party had reason to know of the mistake." RESTATEMENT (2D) OF CONTRACTS §153.

That formulation works well in the context for which it is designed, for example, when a mathematical error causes somebody inadvertently to submit a bid of $100,000 rather than $300,000. It makes less sense for common electronic errors, as when a consumer accidentally clicks a mouse on a button to buy one product when the consumer intends to buy another, or when the consumer clicks a button to buy intending to click a button to quit the transaction. Section 10 of UETA includes a provision to protect the purchaser in that context, which permits the consumer to avoid the transaction if three conditions are met. First, the rule applies only if the Web site fails to "provide an opportunity for the prevention or correction of the error." Thus, a merchant could avoid the rule entirely — protect itself against after-the-fact cancellations — by designing its Web site to provide an adequate opportunity for before-the-fact correction. UETA §10(2). Second, the consumer must promptly notify the seller of the error and the consumer's intention to revoke the transaction. UETA §10(2)(A). Finally, the consumer must promptly return the purchased material without using it. UETA §10(2)(C). [Alternatively, if the merchant so directs, the purchaser might destroy the purchased material — which would make sense for information or other electronic goods. UETA §10(2)(C).]

Relevant Glossary Entries

Electronic Signature
E-Sign

Problem Set 14

14.1. Music Depot is sued in a class action by consumers upset with alleged defects in the recording equipment that they have sold from their Web site. Based on your earlier advice to it, Music Depot's Web site requires all customers that purchase musical instruments to click specifically on a button that indicates their agreement to be legally bound by Music Depot's terms of sale, which include an arbitration clause. The class action claims that the clause is invalid because the Federal Arbitration Act requires such terms to be in writing. Assuming that the Federal Arbitration Act does say that, is the arbitration clause from the Web-site agreement enforceable? E-SIGN §§101(a)(1), 102(a).

14.2. Does it affect your answer if the Music Depot Web site does not afford customers an opportunity to print or save the agreement, but without further ado simply displays the agreement on their screen?

(a) Consider first only the arbitration clause that the Federal Arbitration Act requires to be in writing. E-SIGN §§101(c), 101(e).

(b) Then consider more generally the question whether the format affects the enforceability of the entire agreement. UETA §8.

14.3.   The same plaintiffs also claim that the contract is not enforceable because they did not understand that they were signing a contract. Currently, the contract has a bold-faced notice at the top that says: "***By clicking 'I Accept' at the end of this Agreement, you agree that you understand and accept the terms and conditions of this Agreement.***" After you read the notice, you must scroll down through the agreement to the "I Accept" button at the end, and then use your mouse to click on that button. Do the plaintiffs have a good argument? UETA §9.

14.4.   Cliff Janeway comes to you with a problem related to his rare book store. Last week he tried to purchase from Amazon.com a copy of Samuel Richardson's famous novel *Sir Charles Grandison*. He has been looking for a complete set of the 1780 Dublin edition for some time and was surprised to see a copy in excellent condition at a reasonable price (only $3,000). (He laughed when he saw them charging $39.95 for the two-volume 1995 Everyman edition, knowing that he could get the same book for only $25.) When he completed the purchase and looked at the confirmation e-mail that Amazon.com sent him he discovered to his chagrin that he had purchased not the 1780 edition, but 10 copies of the 1995 edition. As a matter of principle, Cliff doesn't want to pay for the 1995 books. Is he obligated to buy the books? (You should examine the Amazon.com Web site in answering the question.) UETA §§9-10; RESTATEMENT (2D) OF CONTRACTS §153.

14.5.   Last week you received a bill in the mail for a $3,700 order placed at *www.cdnow.com*. When you go to the Web site and look at your account, it appears that there in fact was a $3,700 order placed under your account, shipped to an address in Madison, Wisconsin (far from where you live). On further inquiry, you discover that the order was placed by a former boyfriend of your daughter, who learned your user ID and password from your daughter.

(a)   Are you obliged to pay for the order? UETA §9.

(b)   Would your answer change if you had signed a user agreement at cdnow.com under which you agreed to be bound by all actions taken with your user ID and password? UETA §5(d). (Assume for present purposes that you "signed" the agreement in a manner adequate to make it fully binding on you.)

14.6.   Returning to the facts of Problem 13.3, your frustration with the arbitration clause in the Fell Computers Terms and Conditions leads you to type the following on the shipping form at the site (in the lines for your street address): "My order is conditioned on your waiver of the arbitration clause, to which I expressly do not agree." After typing that language, you proceed to complete the order. Would you be bound by the arbitration clause? UCC §§2-207, 2-211(4).

14.7.   You get another call today from Nikki Levin, the general counsel of Videoland, the operator of *www.videoland.com*, a Web site that sells audio equipment. Because of a technical error, last week it posted a large banner ad on several Web sites, indicating that customers could buy a Sony Playstation II for $35. This was a mistake; there was supposed to be a special sale of Sony Playstation II machines for $350; they normally retail for about $400. The ads were, in a sense, quite successful. Three thousand customers made purchases over the Internet in response.

This is of course a disaster for Videoland, which pays Sony $200 per machine (and, to make matters worse, a $35 (10 percent) referral fee for each of the ad-induced sales). Videoland sent e-mails out yesterday to the people who had ordered machines over the Internet, apologizing for the mistake and offering to honor the sales at the intended price of $350. Today, it received a letter from one disgruntled purchaser (who happens to be an attorney) threatening a class action on behalf of the buyers unless Videoland complies with its contract. Ms. Levin wants to know if Videoland can avoid the contract. What do you tell her? RESTATEMENT (2D) OF CONTRACTS §153; UETA §10.

14.8. Your client Tertius Lydgate has a brokerage account and a cash-management account at My-E-Brokeronline.com. When he opened the account, he agreed to receive all notices related to the account in an electronic form. Thus, he receives his monthly statements and all other formal notices by e-mail from My-E-Brokeronline.com. Among other things, he receives notices of funds transfers made to and from the account, as well as periodic statements regarding the account, both required to be delivered in writing by EFTA §906, 15 U.S.C. §1693d.

Yesterday, his computer crashed permanently. He will not have Internet or e-mail access until he purchases a new computer. Accordingly, he is unable to read or respond to any notices that he receives until that time. He is worried, because he understands that if he receives a notice or a statement of a transfer that is fraudulent and fails to respond promptly he could be responsible for the transfer even if he did not authorize it. (You should trust his understanding of that point, which is based on EFTA §909, 15 U.S.C. §1693g.)

(a) Do you see any way that Lydgate can avoid his agreement to accept electronic notices? E-SIGN §101(c).

(b) What if My-E-Brokeronline.com tells Lydgate that it will cancel his account if he withdraws his consent? E-SIGN §101(c).

Assignment 15:   Internet Auctions

Few of the dot-com startups that received financing during the Internet commerce boom in 1999 achieved their objectives and almost all have now vanished without a trace. By contrast, eBay has been profitable and has continued to grow even after the burst of the speculative bubble in Internet stocks. The service it offers has proven so successful that it has changed the way many people think about computers and the Internet. The success of eBay created a place in the public imagination for a new form of transaction, the "online auction." Although eBay may be the most visible example of a business using online auctions, it is certainly not the only one. Advances in information technology have lowered the cost of conducting auctions, so many businesses that formerly could not have used competitive bidding to lower their overheads or improve their margins are now using online auctions in place of fixed pricing. For example, online auctions are a common tool in private B2B exchanges (discussed in the section of this chapter about transactions among businesses).

Because eBay in effect created a new business model and a new form of transaction from whole cloth, there is remarkably little existing law that applies specifically to the rights and obligations of parties offering or using online auction services. By contrast, the law governing traditional auctions is well settled, and state and local governments regulate the work of professional auctioneers. Filling that void, eBay has created a legal edifice of click-through agreements to govern its rights and obligations and the rights and obligations of "members" of its "community." The biggest concern is that the volume of fraud appears to have grown just as the number of online auction transactions has grown. As you read the materials that follow, consider whether a framework constructed by private agreements and reinforced by conventional fraud detection and prevention measures provides an adequate legal structure for the new marketplaces. What reason is there to think — or doubt — that eBay's incentives to prevent misconduct are adequate?

This assignment starts by providing a background discussion of the basic legal rules developed in the context of traditional auctions, and then proceeds to discuss the existing regulatory framework for auctions, remedies for auction-related fraud, and finally the special position of eBay as the dominant online auction provider.

A.   Traditional Auctions

An auction is defined as buying and selling property through public bidding. In a traditional auction, the auctioneer solicits a succession of increasing

300

bids until the highest bid is finally accepted and a contract formed between the bidder and the seller. This is not the only form auctions can take, however. In a Dutch auction, the seller offers property at successively lower prices until one of the offers is accepted or until the price drops so low that the seller withdraws the property from the sale. A sophisticated set of economic theories regarding auctions shows how different forms of auctions can be optimal in different settings, depending on the number of potential buyers, the verifiability of information related to the value of the good being auctioned, and the existence of related goods to be auctioned at the same time.

For present purposes, however, it is enough to say that the auction is most successfully used in a situation in which a seller cannot obtain a satisfactory outcome through negotiation with a single bidder. The most obvious problem that motivates an auction is the time-constrained seller: An auction produces an immediate liquidation of an asset at a specified time, while a negotiated sale takes an amount of time that is difficult to predict. A more complex situation is the seller that cannot readily determine which of a large number of potential buyers is likely to value the asset most highly. The auction provides a method for selecting among potential buyers that — at a minimum — should produce for the seller a price that exceeds the valuation of the second most-highly-valuing bidder.

The legal rules that govern auctions are a specialized branch of contract law. Under those rules, a contract is formed when the offer from the bidder is accepted by the auctioneer, which is for most purposes regarded as an agent of the seller. Acceptance of a bid is denoted by the fall of the hammer or by any other audible or visible means. UCC §2-328(2). The auctioneer (now acting on behalf of both buyer and seller) then draws up a memorandum of sale. When signed by the auctioneer, that memorandum meets any applicable Statute of Frauds requirement.

The owner of the property to be sold generally has the right to set the terms and conditions under which the auction will take place. The auctioneer, as an agent of the seller, is bound by those terms and conditions. These include the time and place of the auction, the payment terms, and whether any warranty will be offered on the property. It is common to incorporate these terms and conditions into advertisements of the auction and to announce them when the auction takes place. As you would expect, the terms and conditions are binding on bidders even if they have not read the advertisements or heard the announcements.

Once a bid has been accepted, the parties are in the relation of a promisor and promisee in an executory contract of sale. The seller at that point has no right to accept a higher bid. The buyer cannot withdraw its bid. If the highest bidder fails to pay the purchase price, the auctioneer (as agent of the owner) is entitled to refuse to turn over the property. If the high bidder already has possession, the law imposes a lien on the property to secure payment of the purchase price.

A seller may set a reserve price before the sale, which means that no sale will take place unless the auctioneer receives a bid above that price. If the sale is "with reserve," then the seller retains the right to remove the property from the auction at any time before the completion of the sale. If the auction is "without reserve," then the seller has no right to withdraw the item once bidding has begun. On the other hand, a bidder always has the right to withdraw its bid at any time before the auctioneer has accepted it. If the property to be auctioned is tangible goods, then UCC Article 2 applies, which provides the default rule that a sale is "with reserve" unless it has been explicitly made "without reserve." UCC §2-328(3). If a sale is without reserve and the seller fails to turn over the property to the highest bidder after the auction, the buyer has a right of specific performance or may recover damages for breach of contract.

In a voluntary auction, a seller is not allowed to participate unless it has reserved the right to do so by giving prior notice to other prospective bidders. The frequent discussion of this problem in the literature on auctions suggests that sellers often have tried to influence auctions in ways that violate this rule. The most commonly discussed tactic is to arrange for the presence at the auction of persons who bid for the purpose of inflating the value of the property on behalf of those interested in the sale; such bidders often are referred to as "puffers," "sham bidders," or "shills." In the strictest meaning of the word, a puffer is a person who, without having any intention to purchase, is employed by the seller at an auction to raise the price by making bids. Thus, the puffer increases competition among the bidders, while the puffer is secured from risk by a secret understanding with the seller that the seller will not enforce the puffer's bids. The law's response, if a buyer discovers that an owner has directly or indirectly made bids at an auction, is to give the buyer the option of avoiding the sale, or taking the goods at the last good-faith bid received before the sale was completed. UCC §2-328(4).

Interestingly, the rule against seller bidding does not apply if the property was taken from the original owner under duress for the purpose of a forced sale, such as a sheriff's auction. The formal premise for the exception is that the original owner is not the party conducting the sale and thus can bid without an unacceptable risk of conflict. A more satisfactory functional explanation is that it would be normatively unacceptable to tell a borrower losing the family home that it cannot even bid at the auction at which the home is sold.

When the Uniform Commercial Code applies, the UCC's express and implied warranty provisions govern. Thus, in an auction sale subject to the provisions of the UCC, a vendor that does not disclaim its title is held to an implied warranty of title. UCC §2-312. Similarly, the implied warranty of merchantability under the UCC extends to auctioned goods where circumstances support a finding that their owner is a merchant with respect to goods of that kind. UCC §2-314.

The contract between the auctioneer and the vendor determines the scope of the auctioneer's responsibilities to the vendor. For example, the duty to sell a product for more than the reserve price arises entirely from the contract between the auctioneer and the vendor. If the auctioneer fails to live up to the terms of the contract, it is liable to the vendor in damages in the same way as any other agent. The auctioneer is also personally responsible for any loss that is a consequence of negligence, that is, a failure to use ordinary care and skill in the performance of the auctioning duties. Finally, an auctioneer has no implied or apparent authority to warrant what is sold, and so is not ordinarily liable for the condition or quality of the property sold.

B.   Licensing of Auctioneers

The overwhelming majority of American jurisdictions regulate the activities of auctioneers. Most states require auctioneers to obtain a license before conducting any auctions. Regulation of auctioneers may entail screening prospective auctioneers to ensure that they have a basic knowledge of how auctions work. It also is typical to include some provision to compensate the public in the event of defalcation by a licensed auctioneer.

To get a sense for a typical auction statute, consider Texas law. Under Texas law, an auctioneer's license can be issued to anyone who is 18 years old and has either passed a written or oral examination demonstrating knowledge of the auction business and applicable Texas law, or can show proof of employment by a licensed auctioneer for at least one year during which the applicant participated in at least five auctions. TEX. OCC. CODE §1802.052. A license may be revoked if the auctioneer engages in a continued and flagrant course of misrepresentation, fails to account for money belonging to another that was in the auctioneer's possession, or is convicted of a felony or a crime involving moral turpitude. TEX. OCC. CODE §1802.251. Auctioneers pay an annual license fee of $100. The proceeds are deposited in an "auctioneer education and recovery fund," used to compensate individuals defrauded by licensed auctioneers. Claimants must have dealt with a licensed auctioneer and be "aggrieved by an action of the auctioneer as a result of a violation of a contract made by the auctioneer." TEX. OCC. CODE §1802.202(a). The Texas Department of Licensing and Regulation investigates claims against the fund and determines the amount of compensation to which the complainant is entitled; either the auctioneer or the claimant may contest a finding of the Department. Payments out of the fund are limited to $10,000 to any individual or $20,000 in connection with any single auction. After a payment is made to a claimant, the fund is subrogated to the rights of the claimant; the fund then pursues the auctioneer for reimbursement. TEX. OCC. CODE §1802.206. Other states require auctioneers to post a bond to protect buyers and sellers at auctions instead of requiring contributions to a mandatory compensation fund.

Although state and local government licensing requirements are not particularly onerous for traditional auctioneers, it might be challenging for an online auction service such as eBay to obtain an auctioneer's license in every jurisdiction in which subscribers to its service are found. Given that an auction is defined as the sale of property by competitive bid, it might seem that eBay and its competitors are conducting auctions under Texas law. However, an auctioneer is defined as "an individual who sells or offers to sell property at auction, with or without receiving consideration, as a bid caller." TEX. OCC. CODE §1802.001. The eBay online "marketplace" does permit competitive bidding, but eBay is not an "individual" who sells goods by "call[ing]" out bids. The eBay online marketplace uses technology to mediate between buyer and seller; state and local laws regulating auctioneers regulate the behavior of individuals who perform that function. So before a state regulator or local official could act against an online auction service for failing to comply with state auctioneer regulations, it is likely that existing laws would have to be revised to bring online auctions within their scope. As discussed below, the result under current law is consistent with a central element of eBay's legal strategy — to establish that it is not a party to the transactions conducted at its site.

The regulation of auctions is often justified by the high risk that either the seller or a buyer will be defrauded if the auction is not conducted in a responsible, open manner. Several types of auction fraud can take place in Internet auctions as well as brick-and-mortar auctions:

- *Bid shilling*: As discussed above, an individual schemes with someone else or creates a false identity to drive up prices for the benefit of the seller.
- *Bid shielding*: A buyer and a partner artificially inflate bids in order to discourage other bidders, but just before the auction ends, the phony high bid is cancelled, permitting the second highest bidder to win the auction for a lower price.
- Nondelivery of the goods or delivery of nonconforming goods.
- Nonpayment of the purchase price.

To combat fraud, Internet sites encourage users to be vigilant and to learn as much as possible about the party on the other side of the transaction. Most importantly — something that would *not* be practical for typical brick-and-mortar auctions — they provide rating systems to permit parties with no prior relationship and no contact outside the Internet auction site to assess each other's *bona fides*. Under those systems, a buyer new to the system can gain considerable comfort about the reliability of the seller through positive reviews from prior purchasers. Of course, the problem of unreliability is inherently higher in the online context — where the seller is an unknown individual rather than an auctioneer and where the goods are not present in the sight of the buyer at the time of the bid. Moreover, given the difficulty of locating a fraudulent seller or buyer who is remote from the defrauded contracting party, criminal prosecution and civil actions often are ineffective to protect consumers. Rating services are not a perfect remedy for those problems. For one thing, they are vulnerable to manipulation by unscrupulous parties — who may register under multiple aliases and submit positive feedback on themselves or may work with other individuals to inflate each other's positive ratings. But they are considerably more effective than anything available in the traditional context.

While Internet auction sites have operated for several years with relatively little supervision from government regulators, increasing reports of fraud may make it difficult for regulators to continue to adopt a hands-off posture. Furthermore, even if American governments maintain a laissez-faire attitude, not all regulators may be as accommodating. For example, a French court in May 2000 barred *nart.com* from accepting bids from French consumers because it failed to use a state-licensed auctioneer and pay French value-added tax. As state regulators hear increasing numbers of complaints about Internet fraud, it is unclear whether state regulators will continue to address them under general consumer-fraud statutes, or whether states will begin to require Internet auction sites to obtain licenses.

C.   Online Auctions

Although it is by no means the only one, eBay was the first online auction site, and remains the largest and most successful, estimated to have over 90 percent of the market for such services. Pierre Omidyar started eBay in 1995 (so the legend says) as a hobby because his wife collected Pez containers but had trouble finding other like-minded individuals. By 1996, the site was so popular that he quit his day job as a software developer to run the service full time. Although the origins of the name "eBay" are shrouded in mystery, one plausible story is that Omidyar intended to name the site "Echo Bay," but shortened the name to eBay when he found that the domain echobay.com already had been registered. Unlike most dot-com companies, eBay has been profitable ever since its 1998 initial public offering. In 2003, eBay had 105 million registered users, of which 45 million bid or listed products during that year. In the first quarter of 2004, eBay sold merchandise worth more than 8 billion dollars and listed 327 million new items for sale in the first quarter of 2004 (more than 3.5 million new listings a day). The site currently is directed toward about 20 countries.

1.   Auctions on eBay

The prominence and success of eBay suggests that some attention to the design of its product is warranted. Remember, the success of eBay is attributable almost entirely to the structure of the auction system that it has designed. Because much of that system resides in the terms of the agreements eBay offers to its users, there is much of interest here for the commercial lawyer.

The basic premise of the eBay legal system is that an individual that wants to buy or sell goods at eBay must join the eBay "community," which requires agreement to the terms and conditions of the site. Although membership is free and generally available, eBay does bar minors and those who previously have been suspended from eBay. Also, eBay suspends members detected as violators of eBay policies. For example, eBay in 2001 suspended Adam Butle for conducting an auction in which he obtained $400 as the price for selling his soul — an item not permitted to be sold under applicable eBay rules. (Other more conventional forbidden items are such things as human organs, firearms, TV descrambling devices, tobacco, or alcohol.)

Although eBay charges no fees to join or bid in auctions, it is most distinctly interested in profiting from the auctions. Thus, it charges sellers that use eBay's listing services. For most items, sellers pay a nominal fee to list the item in an auction, and then pay 1.25 to 5 percent of the amount of the sale if the auction is successful.

One innovation in the conduct of the auctions is eBay's "proxy bidding" system. When an item is listed for sale, the vendor sets a starting price for the auction and a time for the auction to end, and is given the option to set a reserve price. The eBay system determines the minimum increments for bids based on the starting price; for example, if an item has a starting price of $25, the minimum increment for bids is $1, but if the price of that item rises to $100, then the minimum increment increases to $2.50. If a member wishes to bid on the item, that person indicates the highest price that it is willing to pay. The eBay system then will make bids on the bidder's behalf in minimum increments until the bidder has either submitted the high bid, or is outbid by another bidder. For example, if Bidder A bids $30 for a new item with no bids and a starting price of $10, and there are no other bidders, then eBay will process that as a bid for $10. If Bidder B then arrives and bids $15, eBay will bid $15.50 on behalf of Bidder A. If Bidder B responds by bidding $25, then eBay will submit a slightly higher bid on behalf of Bidder A. If Bidder B then bids $35, Bidder A will receive a notification that it has been outbid.

As the eBay system has matured, the bidding system has become more problematic. Many prospective purchasers watch auctions without bidding until just minutes before they close, hoping to avoid unnecessarily bidding up the price of the item in which they are interested. However, prospective purchasers who wait to bid until the auction is almost over still often find they are outbid in the final seconds. This is called "sniping" by another bidder, and while it may be very upsetting to a losing bidder, it does not violate any eBay policy. Proxy bidding is particularly useful in dealing with that phenomenon. In the example above, if Bidder C appeared and bid $40 thirty seconds before the auction ended, Bidder B would not be able to enter a higher bid before the auction ended unless Bidder B was attentively watching the auction site at that moment. If Bidder B has entered a maximum bid of $50, it can be sure that it will get the item if its $50 maximum bid is higher than the maximum bid of any other competing bidder.

One partial response to the dissatisfaction caused by sniping is eBay's development of various forms of fixed-price sales. Thus, vendors are now permitted to list items for competitive bidding with a "buy it now" price that would end the bidding immediately. This option is particularly appealing to prospective buyers fearful that they will be "sniped" out of a purchase at the last minute.

As a matter of economic theory, it seems unlikely that the proxy bidding system is optimal — it certainly in some cases results in lower sales prices than a more traditional system that permits bidding to continue until a set period passes without further bidding. It does, however, have the signal virtue of accommodating both sufficiently lengthy auctions to permit dissemination of information about the items throughout the community of interested Internet observers and at the same time providing definitive closure to an auction at a preset moment.

Under the eBay user agreement, a member that places a bid is bound to perform on the resulting contract if that bid turns out to be the high bid. For example, if the bid was entered as a typographical error, if a member believes that the description of an item has changed, or if the member is unable to confirm the identity of the seller, then the member may retract the bid without violating eBay's user agreement. In any event, even if the retraction is justified, it will become a part of a member's feedback profile, so that other sellers will be aware of the retraction. Because a seller has the option to block certain members from placing bids, that type of information can be detrimental to a bidder's future operations on eBay.

One obvious problem with an online auction — in which the parties are remote from each other — is the difficulty of providing contemporaneous and reliable payment. In the early days of eBay, sellers often asked for money orders in payment or would require purchasers to wait 10 days to allow personal checks to clear; most sellers on eBay were not merchants and so could not accept credit cards in payment. Person-to-person payment services such as PayPal sprang up to meet the need of eBay buyers and sellers unhappy with the inconvenience and delay caused by paying by check or money order. eBay at one point organized its own online payment processing service (Billpoint), but when Billpoint failed to gain market share, eBay ultimately acquired PayPal. (Assignment 29 discusses these payment services.)

In addition to the framework for the auctions themselves, eBay offers various auction-related services, generally designed to enhance the satisfaction of members of its community with their overall experience. Among other things, these services include:

- **Feedback forum.** Members of the eBay community are allowed to leave comments about each other's performance in transactions in a "feedback profile." After a member's user ID will appear a number in parentheses that indicates the total number of feedback comments a user has received and an indication as to whether the feedback is positive, neutral, or negative. eBay places restrictions on the ability of members of the community to place feedback in others' profiles; for example, only the seller and the winning bidder may leave feedback related to a particular transaction. Once a member has posted feedback, it cannot be retracted. eBay will only remove feedback if it determines the feedback violates one of its own policies, and does not generally remove feedback at the behest of a party who has been criticized.

- **Third-party authentication services for collectibles.** Because of the serious problem of forged or fraudulent collectibles, eBay provides information about third-party authentication services that examine goods offered for sale and provide prospective purchasers with an independent assessment of the seller's claims.

- **Third-party escrow services.** Prospective purchasers of very expensive or valuable items (such as the Honus Wagner baseball card that sold for $1.2 million in July of 2000; the most lucrative sale to date was a $5 million private jet) may ask that the items be placed in escrow. After the purchase price is paid to the escrow agent, the item is shipped to the buyer. If the buyer approves, the funds are released to the seller. If not, the buyer can return the item to the escrow agent for a refund.

- **Third-party dispute-resolution services.** In order to help its members resolve disputes, eBay has hired a dispute-resolution service. Square Trade provides online mediation services without charge to eBay members, or access to a live, human mediator for a nominal $15 charge.

- **Fraud protection insurance.** eBay offers its members without charge coverage of up to $200, with a $25 deductible, for documented instances of fraud. eBay estimates that one in 40,000 listings results in a paid claim.

As you think about those services, you should consider precisely what motivates eBay to limit fraud on its site. Sellers and buyers face ordinary liability to each other for fraud and breach of contract, and the FTC has pursued online sellers for violations of its mail- or telephone-order rules. What reason is there to think greater regulation is appropriate? To the extent that it is, are eBay's market incentives adequate to obviate any need for government intervention?

Although eBay initially targeted individuals, no discussion would be complete without mentioning eBay's recent success as a channel through which businesses can buy and sell supplies and equipment. It is now possible to buy or sell automobiles, trucks, airplanes, telephone switchboards, bulldozers, or cash registers on eBay. Bob Dylan's childhood home in Duluth, Minnesota was sold on eBay in 2001 for $94,600.

2. Contracting Out of Auctioneer Status

To a lawyer, the most provocative aspect of eBay's user agreement probably is its careful explication of eBay's position that it is not in fact auctioning anything. Thus, the User Agreement states plainly that "eBay is only a venue." eBay is careful to make sure that buyers and sellers who use its site must independently evaluate the credibility of the other buyers and sellers with whom they deal. The eBay User Agreement states:

> Although we are commonly referred to as an online auction web site, it is important to realize that we are not a traditional "auctioneer." Instead, our site acts as a venue to allow anyone to offer, sell and buy just about anything, at anytime, from anywhere, in a variety of formats, including a fixed price format and an auction-style format commonly referred to as an "online auction." We are not involved in the actual transaction between buyers and sellers. As a result, we have no control over the quality, safety or legality of the items advertised, the truth or accuracy of the listings, the ability of sellers to sell items or the ability of buyers to buy items. We cannot ensure that a buyer or a seller will actually complete a transaction.

However plausible you might find those assertions, it is plain as a matter of current law that the strategy has been effective in preventing litigation in which parties defrauded in eBay transactions have sought to recover from eBay. The case that follows is the most substantial published opinion on the topic to date. As you contemplate the court's analysis, consider what incentives to monitor activities on its site motivate eBay *after* this decision.

Gentry v. eBay, Inc.

121 Cal. Rptr. 2d 703 (Ct. App. 2002)

O'ROURKE, J.

Lars Gentry, Henry Camp, Mike Hyder, James Conboy, William Pommerening, and Michael Osacky (appellants) appeal a judgment of dismissal entered after the trial court sustained eBay, Inc.'s (eBay) demurrer to appellants' second amended complaint without leave to amend. In that pleading, appellants alleged eBay violated California's Autographed Sports Memorabilia statute (Civ. Code §1739.7) by failing to furnish a certificate of authenticity to persons who purchased autographed sports-related collectibles through its web site. Appellants also alleged eBay was negligent and engaged in unfair business practices under the Unfair Competition Law (UCL) (Bus. and Prof. Code §17200 et seq.) based on its failure to supply such certificates as well as its acts in distributing false certificates, permitting other false representations to be placed on its web site, and making its own false or misleading representations. . . .

. . . [W]e affirm the judgment of dismissal.

FACTUAL AND PROCEDURAL BACKGROUND

eBay promotes itself as the world's largest online marketplace for the sale of goods and services among its registered users. It operates an Internet-based service in which it enables member sellers to offer items for sale to member buyers in what eBay characterizes as either auction-style or fixed price formats. To better enable users to place items for sale on its site, eBay provides descriptions to its users under various product categories and subcategories. For sports items, eBay's web site has a sports product category with the following subcategories: "Sports: Autographs"; "Sports: Memorabilia"; "Sports: Sporting Goods" and "Sports: Trading Cards." eBay's "Sports: Autographs" subcategory is further organized into sub-subcategories to differentiate autographed sports collectibles by particular leagues.

In September 1995, various individuals embarked on a plan to sell faked autographed sports memorabilia to consumers. Specifically, Angelo Marino, Gloria Marino, Gregory Marino, John Marino and Kathleen Marino (the Marino defendants) purchased sporting goods items and photographs from retail stores, forged signatures of professional athletes upon them, and employed Wayne Bray and Donald Frangipani to produce false certificates of authenticity for the items. The Marino defendants then sold most of the forged items to Stanley Fitzgerald and Phil Scheinman, larger dealers who mostly used eBay auctions to eventually sell the forged items to consumers. Stanley Fitzgerald did business as "Stan The Man Memorabilia" and "Stan's Sports Memorabilia." Phil Scheinman did business as "Smokey's Sportscard, Inc."

Appellants are individuals who purchased forged autographed sports items including baseballs, photographs and autographed pieces of paper or "cuts," from Fitzgerald, Scheinman or the Marino defendants through eBay.

Intending to act on behalf of all purchasers of autographed sports collectibles purchased through eBay from September 1, 1995, to the time of trial, appellants sued the Marino defendants, Bray, Frangipani, Fitzgerald, Scheinman and eBay. Their first-amended complaint asserted causes of action against eBay for negligence, violation of the UCL, violation of Civil Code section 1739.7 and for injunctive relief. In that pleading, appellants alleged eBay, having identified itself as an auctioneer in press releases and provided a venue for auctions, "violated California law by either failing to provide a certificate of authenticity expressly warranting the [autographed sports memorabilia] or failing to insure that such a certificate was being provided by any other party to the auction." According to their allegations, during the class period, eBay auctioned thousands of items of sports memorabilia created by the Marino defendants, a substantial number of which were accompanied by fraudulent certificates of authenticity and "expert opinions" produced by Bray and Frangipani. eBay charged placement fees to dealers listing an item for auction, and success fees (percentage fees) when items were sold. Further, appellants alleged, eBay gave customers a false sense of confidence by maintaining a forum that permitted dealers and consumers to give positive or negative feedback to other dealers or consumers, giving endorsements to certain dealers based on the volume of sales and positive feedback ratings, and advising users it may suspend or terminate their account if it finds them to have engaged in fraudulent activity in connection with the web site.

Appellants alleged that as early as 1996, eBay received numerous complaints from consumers and warnings from governmental agencies that a substantial amount of forged sports memorabilia was being auctioned on eBay, but eBay ignored the warnings and allowed the forged sports memorabilia scheme to continue in order to continue to reap millions of dollars in profits for itself.

[After providing appellants several opportunities to amend their complaint to add new allegations, the trial court eventually dismissed the complaint in its entirety.]

DISCUSSION . . .

II.   CLAIM FOR ALLEGED VIOLATION OF THE AUTOGRAPHED SPORTS MEMORABILIA STATUTE (CIV. CODE §1739.7)

. . . Civil Code section 1739.7, entitled Autographed Sports Memorabilia, regulates the sale of autographed sports items, broadly termed "collectibles." (Civ. Code §1739.7(a)(2).) The statute generally forbids dealers of collectibles from representing an item as a collectible "if it was not autographed by the sports personality in his or her own hand." (Civ. Code §1739.7(c). It also places various obligations on such dealers. Specifically, subdivision (b) of the statute requires dealers to provide certificates of authenticity of a prescribed form and content. It provides in part: "Whenever a dealer, in selling or offering to sell to a consumer a collectible in or from this state, provides a description of that collectible as being autographed, the dealer shall furnish a certificate of authenticity to the consumer at the time of sale. The certificate of authenticity shall be in writing, shall be signed by the dealer or his or her authorized agent, and shall specify the date of sale." (Civ. Code §1739.7(b).)

The statute defines a dealer as follows:

"'Dealer' means a person who is in the business of selling or offering for sale collectibles in or from this state, exclusively or nonexclusively, or a person who by his or her occupation holds himself or herself out as having knowledge or skill peculiar to collectibles, or to whom that knowledge or skill may be attributed by his or her employment of an agent or other intermediary that by his or her occupation holds himself or herself out as having that knowledge or skill. 'Dealer' includes an auctioneer who sells collectibles at a public auction, and also includes persons who are consignors or representatives or agents of auctioneers. 'Dealer' includes a person engaged in a mail order, telephone order, or cable television business for the sale of collectibles."

(Civ. Code §1739.7(a)(4).)

. . . Appellants contend they stated a cause of action against eBay under Civil Code section 1739.7 by alleging eBay is an auctioneer that engages in the sale or offer for sale of autographed collectibles in or from this state, provides descriptions of collectibles as being autographed, yet has never furnished the requisite certificates of authenticity under the statute. . . .

As stated, liability as a dealer under Civil Code section 1739.7 requires that the dealer be exclusively or nonexclusively "in the business of selling or offering for sale collectibles in or from this state." (Civ. Code §1739.7(a)(4).) Here, appellants' specific allegations reveal eBay is not in the business of selling or offering to sell the collectibles at issue; rather, it is the individual defendants who sold the items to plaintiffs, using eBay as a venue. In reaching this conclusion, we acknowledge we are required to construe appellants' allegations liberally, with a view towards substantial justice between the parties. . . .

The general allegation that eBay engages in the sale or offer for sale is irreconcilable with other, more specific allegations. These allegations describe the specific operations of the individual defendants, expressly stating that the sellers of the forged items were Fitzgerald or Scheinman through their respective business entities. As appellants alleged, the scheme began with the Marino defendants' conduct in faking autographs of celebrated sports figures on baseballs, photographs and other collectibles and forwarding those items to Fitzgerald or Scheinman, who then placed them for sale on eBay by, in part, designating the appropriate categories contained on the web site. These factual allegations control. . . .

Notwithstanding our conclusion above, we additionally hold, under the facts presented, placing liability upon eBay for failing to provide a warranty under Civil Code section 1739.7 would be inconsistent with and hence preempted by . . . the Communications Decency Act. . . . The operative provision of Section 230 states: "[n]o provider or user of an interactive computer service shall be treated as the publisher or speaker of any information provided by another information content provider." (47 U.S.C. §230(c)(1).) The statute further provides:

"(e) Effect on other laws . . .

"(3) State Law

"Nothing in this section shall be construed to prevent any State from enforcing any State law that is consistent with this section. *No cause of action may be brought and no liability may be imposed under any State or local law that is inconsistent with this section.*" (47 U.S.C. §230(e)(3), emphasis added.)

In [Zeran v. America Online, Inc., 129 F.3d 327 (4th Cir. 1997) [*Zeran*]], the court held section 230, by its "plain language," created a federal immunity to any cause of action that would make interactive service providers liable for information originating with a third-party user of the service. (*Id.* at p. 330.) "Specifically, §230 precludes courts from entertaining claims that would place a computer service provider in a publisher's role. Thus, lawsuits seeking to hold a service provider liable for its exercise of a publisher's traditional editorial functions — such as deciding whether to publish, withdraw, postpone or alter content — are barred." (*Zeran, supra*, at 330.). . .

Subsection (c)(1) of section 230 thus immunizes providers of interactive computer services (service providers) and their users from causes of action asserted by persons alleging harm caused by content provided by a third party. This form of immunity requires (1) the defendant be a provider or user of an interactive computer service; (2) the cause of action treat the defendant as a publisher or speaker of information; and (3) the information at issue be provided by another information content provider. (47 U.S.C. §230(c)(1).)

Appellants concede for purposes of this appeal that eBay is an interactive computer service provider. And appellants do not expressly challenge the application of section 230 to liability based on content placed on eBay's web site by eBay's users or other third parties. Rather, they contend section 230 does not apply because they seek to enforce eBay's independent duty under the statute to furnish a warranty as the " 'provider' of descriptions," not as a publisher. We disagree.

The substance of appellants' allegations reveal they ultimately seek to hold eBay responsible for conduct falling within the reach of section 230, namely, eBay's dissemination of representations made by the individual defendants, or the posting of compilations of information generated by those defendants and other third parties. Under section 230, eBay cannot be "treated as the publisher or speaker" of content supplied by other information content providers. (47 U.S.C. §230(c)(1).) If by imposing liability under Civil Code section 1739.7 we ultimately hold eBay responsible for content originating from other parties, we would be treating it as the publisher, viz., the original communicator, contrary to Congress's expressed intent under section 230(c)(1) and (e)(3).

In connection with appellants' argument relating to the sufficiency of their Civil Code section 1739.7 cause of action, appellants point out they alleged eBay provided its own descriptions of collectibles through its lists of product categories, but also assert, to the extent the individual defendants created the ultimate descriptions of their faked collectibles, eBay provided those descriptions within the meaning of the statute by making them available to the users of its web site. In opposition to eBay's demurrer, they argued:

> It does not matter under [Civil Code section] 1739.7 who 'creates' the original specific description of the memorabilia, because the obligation to furnish a warranty arises when a dealer 'provides' the description in offering or selling the item and the description characterizes the item as being autographed. . . . Therefore, although the specific description of an item originates with the seller, eBay, by making the description available over its auction website . . . then 'provides' the description to its consumers.

While the fact eBay does not create the description may be of no significance to liability under Civil Code section 1739.7 as appellants maintain, it is highly significant for purposes of assessing the application of section 230. Appellants do not dispute the fact, judicially noticed by the trial court, that it was dealers Fitzgerald and Scheinman, not eBay, who chose their own category description for the item offered for sale. Thus, for purposes of applying section 230 immunity, we consider it was the individual defendants who falsely identified the product as authentically autographed in order to place their items on eBay for sale. On the basis of appellants' allegations, holding eBay responsible for providing a warranty under Civil Code section 1739.7 when it merely made the individual defendant's false product descriptions available to other users on its web site, or provided the web site on which the individual defendants designated their collectibles as autographed, puts eBay in the shoes of the individual defendants, making it responsible for their publications or statements. We therefore conclude enforcement of appellants' Civil Code section 1739.7 cause of action is inconsistent with section 230 because it would stand as an obstacle to the accomplishment and execution of the full purposes and objectives of Congress. [Brackets, quotation marks, and citation omitted.]

III.   NEGLIGENCE CAUSE OF ACTION

Apart from the cause of action under Civil Code section 1739, which we have held is barred, appellants' negligence cause of action is based on allegations that eBay itself misrepresented the safety of purchasing items from the individual defendants and knew or should have known the individual defendants were conducting unlawful practices but failed to ensure they comply with the law. In an attempt to plead around section 230 with respect to these causes of action, appellants generally allege eBay was an information content provider in that it was responsible for the creation of information, or development of information, for the online auction it provided through the Internet; that eBay did not act as an Internet service provider; and the information at issue (descriptions of collectibles as autographed) did not concern the publication of obscene or similarly objectionable materials.

These conclusory and argumentative allegations are followed by more specific averments. Appellants more specifically described the information purportedly developed by eBay for its "safety program," identifying it as consisting of a color-coded star symbol, a Power Sellers endorsement, and a Feedback Forum. Appellants alleged:

> eBay encourages its users to rely upon its 'Feedback Forum' prior to engaging in a sales transaction. The Feedback Forum purportedly *allows dealers and consumers* to rate a sales transaction with a compliment (a 'Positive Feedback'), a criticism (a 'Negative Feedback'), or other comments (a 'Neutral Feedback'). eBay has advertised that, 'A positive eBay rating is worth its weight in gold.' A dealer or consumer who achieves a designated level of Positive Feedback is awarded a star symbol display next to the user name, which is color coded to indicate the amount of Positive Feedback received by the user. [¶] . . . In addition to the Feedback Forum, eBay designed a 'Power Sellers' endorsement, which purportedly is an award given to select eBay dealers based on the volume of sales and Positive Feedback ratings. [¶] . . . In reality, however, eBay's 'safety' programs have contributed to enormous damage to autographed sports memorabilia consumers. For example, the Feedback Forum allows anyone to rate a dealer, even if there has never been a sales transaction between the parties. Thus, Fitzgerald and Scheinman have at least hundreds of Positive Feedback ratings which are unrelated to any sales transactions. *Most, if not all, of these Positive Feedback ratings are self-generated or provided by other co-conspiring dealers.* (Bold in original; emphasis added by court.)

None of these allegations place eBay outside the immunity for service providers. As eBay points out, the allegations reveal that eBay's Feedback Forum is comprised of negative or positive information provided by third party consumers and dealers. Likewise, the star symbol and "Power Sellers" designation is simply a representation of the amount of such positive information received by other users of eBay's web site. Appellants' negligence claim is based on the assertion that the information is false or misleading because it has been manipulated *by the individual defendants or other co-conspiring parties.* Based on these allegations, enforcing appellants' negligence claim would place liability on eBay for simply compiling false and/or misleading content created by the individual defendants and other co-conspirators. We do not see such activities transforming eBay into an information content provider with respect to the representations targeted by appellants as it did not create or develop the underlying misinformation. We are constrained from enforcing such liability under California law because it would treat eBay as the publisher or speaker of the individual defendants' materials, and thereby conflict with section 230.

We reach the same conclusion with regard to appellants' general assertion that eBay knew or should have known about the individual defendant's illegal or fraudulent conduct but failed to take steps to ensure they comply with the law. This claim seeks to hold eBay responsible for having notice of illegal activities conducted by others on its web site, and for electing not to take action against those third parties, including by withdrawing or somehow altering the content placed by them. This is the classic kind of claim that *Zeran* found to be preempted by section 230, as one that seeks to hold eBay liable for its exercise of a publisher's traditional editorial functions. Such claims have been uniformly rejected by the courts that have considered them.

Finally, taking as true the fact eBay makes the statement on its web site that a positive eBay rating is "worth its weight in gold," such an assertion cannot support a cause of action for negligent misrepresentation regardless of federal statutory immunity because it amounts to a general statement of opinion, not a positive assertion of fact. An essential element of a cause of action for negligent misrepresentation is that the defendant must have made a misrepresentation as to a past or existing material fact. The law is quite clear that expressions of opinion are not generally treated as representations of fact, and thus are not grounds for a misrepresentation cause of action. [Quotation marks and citations omitted.] Representations of value are opinions. Although the line of demarcation between expressions of fact and opinion can be unclear at times, this is not such a case. This kind of vague, highly subjective statement as to the significance of a positive rating is not the sort of statement that a consumer would interpret as factual or upon which he or she could reasonably rely.

IV. UCL CAUSE OF ACTION

Appellants' UCL cause of action is based upon the same allegations as their negligence claim: that eBay misrepresented the forged collectibles offered for sale in its auctions; failed to furnish certificates of authenticity; was aware of the fraudulent nature of the collectibles but failed to disclose such information to consumers; and "made use of various forms of marketing and advertising to falsely advertise, call attention to, endorse, or give publicity to the sale of forged collectibles . . ." On appeal, appellants argue the sufficiency of only those allegations regarding eBay's safety programs, seeking to distinguish them as statements made by eBay itself. They plead eBay knew or reasonably should have known their marketing and advertising was untrue and/or misleading. For the reasons explained above, because eBay's liability would be based upon the misrepresentations of the individual defendants, to the extent these allegations state a cause of action, it is inconsistent with and barred by section 230.

DISPOSITION

The judgment is affirmed.

———————————

eBay also prevailed in similar litigation in Germany challenging the sale of fraudulent Rolex watches. You should consider the propriety of eBay's ability by contract to design its business in a way that effectively enables it to "opt in" to the CDA's exemption for ISP liability.

Relevant Glossary Entries

Brick and Mortar
Business to Business
Cookie
Dutch Auction
Proxy Bidding
Reserve Price
Reverse Auction
Shill
Sniping
User Agreement

Problem Set 15

15.1(a). Masao Morimatsu was getting ready to move from Clear Lake, Texas to Chicago. Masao had been fond of riding dirt bikes while he lived in Clear Lake, but figured he wouldn't need the dozen or so he had accumulated after he moved to Chicago. He hired Dusty Hall, a professional auctioneer from Amarillo, to sell his collection of dirt bikes by auction. Dusty sold 10 dirt bikes at the auction and turned over the proceeds of $3,000 to Masao. Some of the proceeds were personal checks, and Masao was disgusted when his bank notified him several days after he deposited them that two had bounced. What recourse does Masao have for the bounced checks?

(b) His mood turned even darker when one of the purchasers called him and asked for a refund, complaining that the bicycle was malfunctioning. Do Masao or Dusty have any exposure if the bike in fact is defective? UCC §2-314.

(c) But the worst was when one of the purchasers at the auction called him up to complain that the bike he purchased at the auction had been repossessed by Dirt Bike Chalet, the shop that had sold Masao the bike in the first place. Dirt Bike Chalet claimed that Masao had defaulted on the loan he had been given to buy the bike; the purchaser understandably wanted his money back too. Masao admits last year he bought the bike on credit from Dirt Bike Chalet (signing a standard security agreement and financing statement), and admits that he might have fallen behind in his payments to the store, but doesn't see what relevance that might have to the rights of the purchaser at his auction. Does Masao have any exposure here? If so, what recourse does he have against Dusty? UCC §2-312.

(d)   Which, if any, of the unsatisfied parties can recover from the Texas auctioneer fund? TEX. OCC. CODE §1802.202.

15.2(a).   Nami Morimatsu (Masao's sister) was getting ready to move from Clear Lake, Texas to Minneapolis. She figured she wouldn't need her collection of model trains, so she decided to auction them off using eBay. In all she sold about a dozen Lionel locomotives and cars for a total of about $3,000. She shipped the trains after she received payment from the high bidders, but was disgusted when two of the personal checks she received bounced. What recourse does Nami have against eBay for the bounced checks? (You should refer to the eBay User Agreement, available at the course Web site.)

(b)   She was even more unhappy when one of the high bidders contacted her announcing he would return the locomotive to her and wanted a refund because it was badly rusted on the bottom, a fact that Nami did not disclose in the item description that she posted. Does Nami have to give a refund to the disgruntled purchaser? UCC §2-314.

(c)   The final blow came when one purchaser contacted Nami demanding a refund. The purchaser explained that law-enforcement officers had come to his home and confiscated the locomotive, saying it was stolen property that would be returned to its rightful owner. Assuming that the locomotive in fact was stolen, does Nami have to give a refund to the disgruntled purchaser? UCC §2-312.

15.3.   Clarissa Janeway, who lives in California, bought a football signed by Doak Walker on eBay. She wanted to give the football to her father as a birthday gift, because her father was a big fan of the SMU Mustangs; he had attended SMU as an undergraduate many years ago when Walker won the Heisman trophy. After her father showed it to some of his friends, however, he learned that the signature was not authentic. Does Clarissa have a cause of action against eBay for not verifying the authenticity of the football? Cal. Civ. Code §1739.7.

15.4.   Clarissa Janeway has a longstanding hobby of collecting flutes. Years ago, she purchased several of them on eBay. At some point, she decided to sell some of the less desirable flutes in her collection. Before too long, she was buying and selling flutes on a regular basis on behalf of many of her colleagues at WessexCard International who shared her avocation. By 2001, Clarissa had 270 positive evaluations, no neutrals, and no negatives. When Clarissa noticed one day that a particularly valuable Haynes flute was being offered, she resolved to make sure she won it, no matter what the price. She authorized esnipe.com, an automated bidding site, to bid up to $8,500 for the Haynes flute within 3 seconds of the auction closing. The bidding had reached $5,000 with 5 seconds before the auction closed. With only 1 second remaining in the auction, eSnipe entered Clarissa's bid, the bidding went up to $8,025 and Clarissa won the auction.

The member who had bid $5,000 for the flute had instructed eBay to bid up to $8,000 for the flute, never imagining anyone would bid more than that. The disappointed bidder decided to get even with Clarissa by ruining her reputation on eBay. This member began bidding aggressively on every item Clarissa offered for sale under a variety of pseudonyms, and after making a purchase, gave Clarissa spurious negative feedback. A month after she won the flute Clarissa had 280 positive evaluations and 8 negative ones. Is there anything Clarissa can do about the negative evaluations? Is there anything she can do to stop the problem from getting worse? (You should refer to the eBay site in answering this problem. Relevant excerpts are available at the course Web site.)

15.5.   Pamela Herring just got back from a trip back home to her constituency and she got an earful from constituents who were upset about having been ripped off in online auctions. She has looked over the auction laws in her state, which closely resemble Texas law, and thinks she could make a lot of points with voters if she proposed revising existing auctioneer licensing requirements to cover online auctions as well. She has asked you to prepare a memo listing the costs and benefits of such an approach and to think about whether there is a better way to respond to her constituents' concerns. A related idea is to mandate a code of conduct that would require auction participants to follow basic rules of ethics. What will you tell her?

Assignment 16: Taxing the Internet

A basic question for all commercial transactions is who has the power to tax the transaction. As Internet commerce grows, that question has become increasingly controversial in a variety of contexts. For present purposes, two topics warrant discussion: the power of American states to impose sales or use taxes on purchases of goods from Internet merchants or on purchases of Internet access from ISPs; and the power of countries to impose a tax on the profits of businesses that make Internet sales.

A. Taxation by Local Jurisdictions

Since the 1930s, state and local governments in the United States have generated a substantial portion of their revenues by imposing sales and use taxes on transactions involving the sale of tangible personal property. As of 1998, those taxes amounted to about $200 billion, representing about 25 percent of all state and local taxes.

Sales taxes are imposed on retailers as a percentage of the sales price. Retailers are responsible for collecting these taxes from consumers and are required to pay the taxes regardless of whether they actually collect them. These taxes apply only to transactions between a seller and consumer both located in the same state. Use taxes are imposed by states on purchases by local consumers, from nonlocal retailers, for use within the state. Consumers typically are responsible for paying these taxes directly. Occasionally, retailers will collect these taxes as a convenience. Use tax statutes were first enacted in the 1930s to eliminate the price disadvantage to local businesses when consumers purchased taxable merchandise from out-of-state retailers. Until recently, they primarily applied to mail-order and home-shopping sales, which were not a substantial component of total retail sales.

That framework obviously assumes that the paradigm transaction is an over-the-counter sale of a tangible product, because many consumers are unaware of their obligation to pay use taxes and enforcement schemes for use taxes generally are lax. The Internet pressures that framework by reducing the barriers to entry in national and international markets, making it much less likely that the seller and buyer will meet in a single jurisdiction. In addition, as discussed more specifically in the context of national taxation, the Internet has the potential to remove a substantial number of transactions from the reach of taxing authorities. Thus, because states typically impose sales and use taxes only on transactions involving tangible goods, the characterization of a digital good (such as music, software, or information) as an intangible may remove transactions in those goods from the reach of the tax laws.

318

Thus, states have increased their efforts to collect use taxes and have had considerable difficulty in doing so. Some states (such as Michigan) have tried to force their residents to report such purchases to the state and pay the taxes voluntarily. Those efforts have been conspicuously unsuccessful. For obvious reasons, a more successful approach would be for the merchant seller to collect the use tax and forward it to the state. After all, if the merchant is mailing the goods to the purchaser the merchant generally knows the state in which the purchaser lives and easily could withhold and pay the tax in the same way that a retail merchant withholds and pays conventional sales taxes. The problem with that approach, however, is that it is at best constitutionally suspect. The last word on the subject is the decision of the Supreme Court in the case that follows.

Quill Corporation v. North Dakota

504 U.S. 298 (1992)

Justice STEVENS delivered the opinion of the Court.

This case . . . involves a State's attempt to require an out-of-state mail-order house that has neither outlets nor sales representatives in the State to collect and pay a use tax on goods purchased for use within the State. . . .

I

Quill is a Delaware corporation with offices and warehouses in Illinois, California, and Georgia. None of its employees work or reside in North Dakota, and its ownership of tangible property in that State is either insignificant or nonexistent. Quill sells office equipment and supplies; it solicits business through catalogs and flyers, advertisements in national periodicals, and telephone calls. Its annual national sales exceed $200 million, of which almost $1 million are made to about 3,000 customers in North Dakota. It is the sixth largest vendor of office supplies in the State. It delivers all of its merchandise to its North Dakota customers by mail or common carrier from out-of-state locations.

As a corollary to its sales tax, North Dakota imposes a use tax upon property purchased for storage, use, or consumption within the State. North Dakota requires every "retailer maintaining a place of business in" the State to collect the tax from the consumer and remit it to the State. N.D.Cent.Code §57-40.2-07. In 1987, North Dakota amended the statutory definition of the term "retailer" to include "every person who engages in regular or systematic solicitation of a consumer market in th[e] state." §57-40.2-01(6). State regulations in turn define "regular or systematic solicitation" to mean three or more advertisements within a 12-month period. N.D.Admin.Code §81-04.1-01-03.1. Thus, since 1987, mailorder companies that engage in such solicitation have been subject to the tax even if they maintain no property or personnel in North Dakota.

Quill has taken the position that North Dakota does not have the power to compel it to collect a use tax from its North Dakota customers. Consequently, the State, through its Tax Commissioner, filed this action to require Quill to pay taxes (as well as interest and penalties) on all such sales made after July 1, 1987. The trial court ruled in Quill's favor . . . specifically, it found that because the State had not shown that it had spent tax revenues for the benefit of the mail-order business, there was no "nexus to allow the state to define retailer in the manner it chose."

The North Dakota Supreme Court reversed, concluding that "wholesale changes" in both the economy and the law [justified a contrary result]. The principal economic change noted by the court was the remarkable growth of the mail-order business "from a relatively inconsequential market niche" in 1967 to a "goliath" with annual sales that reached "the staggering figure of $183.3 billion in 1989." Moreover, the court observed, advances in computer technology greatly eased the burden of compliance with a "'welter of complicated obligations'" imposed by state and local taxing authorities. . . .

Turning to the case at hand, the state court emphasized that North Dakota had created "an economic climate that fosters demand for" Quill's products, maintained a legal infrastructure that protected that market, and disposed of 24 tons of catalogs and flyers mailed by Quill into the State every year. Based on these facts, the court concluded that Quill's "economic presence" in North Dakota depended on services and benefits provided by the State and therefore generated "a constitutionally sufficient nexus to justify imposition of the purely administrative duty of collecting and remitting the use tax."

II

[Our previous cases related to this topic have] relied on both the Due Process Clause and the Commerce Clause. Although the "two claims are closely related," [National Bellas Hess, Inc. v. Department of Revenue, 386 U.S. 753, 756 (1967)], the Clauses pose distinct limits on the taxing powers of the States. Accordingly, while a State may, consistent with the Due Process Clause, have the authority to tax a particular taxpayer, imposition of the tax may nonetheless violate the Commerce Clause.

The two constitutional requirements differ fundamentally, in several ways. As discussed at greater length below, see Part IV, *infra*, the Due Process Clause and the Commerce Clause reflect different constitutional concerns. Moreover, while Congress has plenary power to regulate commerce among the States and thus may authorize state actions that burden interstate commerce, it does not similarly have the power to authorize violations of the Due Process Clause.

Thus, although we have not always been precise in distinguishing between the two, the Due Process Clause and the Commerce Clause are analytically distinct. . . .

III

The Due Process Clause requires some definite link, some minimum connection, between a state and the person, property or transaction it seeks to tax, and that the income attributed to the State for tax purposes must be rationally related to values connected with the taxing State. [Quotation marks and citations omitted.] Here, we are concerned primarily with the first of these requirements. [Our early cases] held that that requirement was satisfied in a variety of circumstances involving use taxes. For example, the presence of sales personnel in the State or the maintenance of local retail stores in the State justified the exercise of that power because the seller's local activities were "plainly accorded the protection and services of the taxing State." *Bellas Hess,* 386 U.S. at 757. The furthest extension of that power was recognized in *Scripto, Inc. v. Carson,* 362 U.S. 207 (1960), in which the Court upheld a use tax despite the fact that all of the seller's in-state solicitation was performed by independent contractors. These cases all involved some sort of physical presence within the State, and in *Bellas Hess* the Court suggested that such presence was not only sufficient for jurisdiction under the Due Process Clause, but also necessary. We expressly declined to obliterate the "sharp distinction . . . between mail-order sellers with retail outlets, solicitors, or property within a State, and those who do no more than communicate with customers in the State by mail or common carrier as a part of a general interstate business." 386 U.S. at 758.

Our due process jurisprudence has evolved substantially in the 25 years since *Bellas Hess,* particularly in the area of judicial jurisdiction. Building on the seminal case of *International Shoe Co. v. Washington,* 326 U.S. 310 (1945), we have framed the relevant inquiry as whether a defendant had minimum contacts with the jurisdiction "such that the maintenance of the suit does not offend traditional notions of fair play and substantial justice." *Id.* at 316. In that spirit, we have abandoned more formalistic tests that focused on a defendant's "presence" within a State in favor of a more flexible inquiry into whether a defendant's contacts with the forum made it reasonable, in the context of our federal system of Government, to require it to defend the suit in that State. In *Shaffer v. Heitner,* 433 U.S. 186, 212 (1977), the Court extended the flexible approach that *International Shoe* had prescribed for purposes of *in personam* jurisdiction to *in rem* jurisdiction, concluding that "all assertions of state-court jurisdiction must be evaluated according to the standards set forth in *International Shoe* and its progeny."

Applying these principles, we have held that if a foreign corporation purposefully avails itself of the benefits of an economic market in the forum State, it may subject itself to the State's *in personam* jurisdiction even if it has no physical presence in the State. As we explained in *Burger King Corp. v. Rudzewicz,* 471 U.S. 462 (1985):

> Jurisdiction in these circumstances may not be avoided merely because the defendant did not *physically* enter the forum State. Although territorial presence frequently will enhance a potential defendant's affiliation with a State and reinforce the reasonable foreseeability of suit there, it is an inescapable fact of modern commercial life that a substantial amount of business is transacted solely by mail and wire communications across state lines, thus obviating the need for physical presence within a State in which business is conducted. So long as a commercial actor's efforts are 'purposefully directed' toward residents of another State, we have consistently rejected the notion that an absence of physical contacts can defeat personal jurisdiction there. Id. at 476. [Emphasis of *Buerger King* Court.]

Comparable reasoning justifies the imposition of the collection duty on a mail-order house that is engaged in continuous and widespread solicitation of business within a State. Such a corporation clearly has "fair warning that [its] activity may subject [it] to the jurisdiction of a foreign sovereign." *Shaffer v. Heitner,* 433 U.S. at 218 (STEVENS, J., concurring in judgment). In "modern commercial life" it matters little that such solicitation is accomplished by a deluge of catalogs rather than a phalanx of drummers: The requirements of due process are met irrespective of a corporation's lack of physical presence in the taxing State. Thus, to the extent that our decisions have indicated that the Due Process Clause requires physical presence in a State for the imposition of duty to collect a use tax, we overrule those holdings as superseded by developments in the law of due process.

In this case, there is no question that Quill has purposefully directed its activities at North Dakota residents, that the magnitude of those contacts is more than sufficient for due process purposes, and that the use tax is related to the benefits Quill receives from access to the State. We therefore agree with the North Dakota Supreme Court's conclusion that the Due Process Clause does not bar enforcement of that State's use tax against Quill.

IV

Article I, §8, cl. 3, of the Constitution expressly authorizes Congress to "regulate Commerce with foreign Nations, and among the several States." It says nothing about the protection of interstate commerce in the absence of any action by Congress. Nevertheless, as Justice Johnson suggested in his concurring opinion in *Gibbons v. Ogden*, 9 Wheat. 1, 231-232, 239 (1824), the Commerce Clause is more than an affirmative grant of power; it has a negative sweep as well. The Clause, in Justice Stone's phrasing, "by its own force" prohibits certain state actions that interfere with interstate commerce. *South Carolina State Highway Dept. v. Barnwell Brothers, Inc.,* 303 U.S. 177, 185 (1938).

Our interpretation of the "negative" or "dormant" Commerce Clause has evolved substantially over the years, particularly as that Clause concerns limitations on state taxation powers. Our early cases . . . swept broadly, and [indeed at one point] we declared that "no State has the right to lay a tax on interstate commerce in any form." We later narrowed that rule and distinguished between direct burdens on interstate commerce, which were prohibited, and indirect burdens, which generally were not. [Decisions beginning in the 1930s] rejected this formal, categorical analysis and adopted a "multiple-taxation doctrine" that focused not on whether a tax was "direct" or "indirect" but rather on whether a tax subjected interstate commerce to a risk of multiple taxation. [Decisions since that time have adopted a variety of approaches, including both an occasional relapse into formal distinctions between "direct" and "indirect" taxation and the more pragmatic approach of modern cases such as *Complete Auto Transit, Inc. v. Brady,* 430 U.S. 274 (1977).] . . .

While contemporary Commerce Clause jurisprudence might not dictate the same result were the issue to arise for the first time today, *Bellas Hess* [invalidating imposition of a use tax on nonresident retailers] is not inconsistent with *Complete Auto* and our recent cases. Under *Complete Auto's* four-part test, we will sustain a tax against a Commerce Clause challenge so long as the "tax [1] is applied to an activity with a substantial nexus with the taxing State, [2] is fairly apportioned, [3] does not discriminate against interstate commerce, and [4] is fairly related to the services provided by the State." 430 U.S. at 279. *Bellas Hess* concerns the first of these tests and stands for the proposition that a vendor whose only contacts with the taxing State are by mail or common carrier lacks the "substantial nexus" required by the Commerce Clause. . . .

The State of North Dakota relies less on *Complete Auto* and more on the evolution of our due process jurisprudence. The State contends that the nexus requirements imposed by the Due Process and Commerce Clauses are equivalent and that if, as we concluded above, a mail-order house that lacks a physical presence in the taxing State nonetheless satisfies the due process "minimum contacts" test, then that corporation also meets the Commerce Clause "substantial nexus" test. We disagree. Despite the similarity in phrasing, the nexus requirements of the Due Process and Commerce Clauses are not identical. The two standards are animated by different constitutional concerns and policies.

Due process centrally concerns the fundamental fairness of governmental activity. Thus, at the most general level, the due process nexus analysis requires that we ask whether an individual' s connections with a State are substantial enough to legitimate the State' s exercise of power over him. We have, therefore, often identified "notice" or "fair warning" as the analytic touchstone of due process nexus analysis. In contrast, the Commerce Clause and its nexus requirement are informed not so much by concerns about fairness for the individual defendant as by structural concerns about the effects of state regulation on the national economy. Under the Articles of Confederation, state taxes and duties hindered and suppressed interstate commerce; the Framers intended the Commerce Clause as a cure for these structural ills. It is in this light that we have interpreted the negative implication of the Commerce Clause. Accordingly, we have ruled that that Clause prohibits discrimination against interstate commerce, and bars state regulations that unduly burden interstate commerce.

The *Complete Auto* analysis reflects these concerns about the national economy. The second and third parts of that analysis, which require fair apportionment and non-discrimination, prohibit taxes that pass an unfair share of the tax burden onto interstate commerce. The first and fourth prongs, which require a substantial nexus and a relationship between the tax and state-provided services, limit the reach of state taxing authority so as to ensure that state taxation does not unduly burden interstate commerce. Thus, the "substantial nexus" requirement is not, like due process' "minimum contacts" requirement, a proxy for notice, but rather a means for limiting state burdens on interstate commerce. Accordingly, contrary to the State's suggestion, a corporation may have the "minimum contacts" with a taxing State as required by the Due Process Clause, and yet lack the "substantial nexus" with that State as required by the Commerce Clause. . . .

Complete Auto, it is true, renounced [our earlier cases] as "formalistic." But not all formalism is alike. [The] formal distinction between taxes on the "privilege of doing business" and all other taxes served no purpose within our Commerce Clause jurisprudence, but stood "only as a trap for the unwary draftsman." *Complete Auto*, 430 U.S. at 279. In contrast, the bright-line rule [we accept today] furthers the ends of the dormant Commerce Clause. Undue burdens on interstate commerce may be avoided not only by a case-by-case evaluation of the actual burdens imposed by particular regulations or taxes, but also, in some situations, by the demarcation of a discrete realm of commercial activity that is free from interstate taxation. *Bellas Hess* followed the latter approach and created a safe harbor for vendors "whose only connection with customers in the [taxing] State is by common carrier or the United States mail." Under Bellas Hess, such vendors are free from state-imposed duties to collect sales and use taxes.

Like other bright-line tests, the *Bellas Hess* rule appears artificial at its edges: Whether or not a State may compel a vendor to collect a sales or use tax may turn on the presence in the taxing State of a small sales force, plant, or office. This artificiality, however, is more than offset by the benefits of a clear rule. Such a rule firmly establishes the boundaries of legitimate state authority to impose a duty to collect sales and use taxes and reduces litigation concerning those taxes. This benefit is important, for as we have so frequently noted, our law in this area is something of a "quagmire" and the "application of constitutional principles to specific state statutes leaves much room for controversy and confusion and little in the way of precise guides to the States in the exercise of their indispensable power of taxation." [Citation omitted.]

Moreover, a bright-line rule in the area of sales and use taxes also encourages settled expectations and, in doing so, fosters investment by businesses and individuals. Indeed, it is not unlikely that the mail-order industry's dramatic growth over the last quarter century is due in part to the bright-line exemption from state taxation created in *Bellas Hess*. . . .

This aspect of our decision is made easier by the fact that the underlying issue is not only one that Congress may be better qualified to resolve, but also one that Congress has the ultimate power to resolve. No matter how we evaluate the burdens that use taxes impose on interstate commerce, Congress remains free to disagree with our conclusions. Indeed, in recent years Congress has considered legislation that would "overrule" the *Bellas Hess* rule. Its decision not to take action in this direction may, of course, have been dictated by respect for our holding in Bellas Hess that the Due Process Clause prohibits States from imposing such taxes, but today we have put that problem to rest. Accordingly, Congress is now free to decide whether, when, and to what extent the States may burden interstate mail-order concerns with a duty to collect use taxes.

Indeed, even if we were convinced that *Bellas Hess* was inconsistent with our Commerce Clause jurisprudence, "this very fact [might] giv[e us] pause and counse[l] withholding our hand, at least for now. Congress has the power to protect interstate commerce from intolerable or even undesirable burdens." *Commonwealth Edison Co. v. Montana*, 453 U.S. [609, 637 (1981)] (WHITE, J., concurring). In this situation, it may be that "the better part of both wisdom and valor is to respect the judgment of the other branches of the Government." *Id.* at 638.

The judgment of the Supreme Court of North Dakota is reversed, and the case is remanded for further proceedings not inconsistent with this opinion.

You should notice that the decision in *Quill* does not give Internet retailers an automatic exemption from tax, because it permits taxation whenever the merchant maintains a physical presence in the jurisdiction. Many retailers might maintain such a presence, either in the form of a warehouse or a service facility. Those retailers will be subject under *Quill* to taxation in all of the jurisdictions in which they have such establishments. Still, *Quill* does afford an exemption to retailers that do not maintain a presence in the state into which the goods are being shipped.

Because the decision in *Quill* rests on the Constitution's allocation to Congress of the power to regulate interstate commerce, it would be easy for Congress to reject the result in *Quill* and grant states the power to tax Internet transactions. Congress, however, has shown a greater inclination to ensure that Internet transactions remain free from tax.

In October 1998, Congress enacted the Internet Tax Freedom Act (ITFA). The ITFA set a three-year moratorium on the imposition by states and local governments of "taxes on Internet access" and "multiple or discriminatory taxes on electronic commerce." ITFA §1101(a). Taxes on Internet access imposed and actually enforced prior to October 1, 1998 were grandfathered under the statute. On October 21, 2001, the federal Internet tax moratorium expired. On November 28, 2001, Congress and the President extended the moratorium to November 1, 2003. That moratorium expired on November 1, 2003, and efforts to extend it further have been unsuccessful (although they continue even as this book goes to press).

The ITFA also created a 19-member Advisory Commission on Electronic Commerce (ACEC), which it directed to "conduct a thorough study of Federal, State and local, and international taxation and tariff treatment of transactions using the Internet and Internet access and other comparable intrastate, interstate or international sales activities." ITFA §1102. Although the Commission failed to produce the two-thirds support required to make a formal recommendation to Congress on the sales and use tax issues, it did produce a lucid report in April 2000 that contained "proposals" on those issues. First, with respect to Internet access, a divided Commission recommended that the current moratorium on taxes on Internet access be made permanent. With respect to sales and use taxes, a divided Commission recommended that the moratorium be extended five years, to give NCCUSL an opportunity to draft and promulgate a uniform sales and use tax act; the Commission contemplated that Congress would consider at the end of the five-year period whether those states that adopted the uniform statute should be permitted to impose taxes on all remote sales.

NCCUSL has not undertaken to draft such a statute, but the states have joined in a major effort to simplify and modernize the collection of sales taxes, known as the Streamlined Sales Tax Project (SSTP), *www.streamlinedsalestax.org*). Forty-two of the 45 states that impose a sales tax are participating. The ultimate goal is to provide a framework that would make compliance much simpler for multistate businesses while leaving ample discretion to individual jurisdictions to pursue local policies. So, for example, the project would create a set of uniform definitions of the categories into which products are divided — so that all products would have the same category designation nationwide — but would permit jurisdictions to decide for themselves which products would and would not be taxable. Similarly, the proposal would simplify rates so that each state jurisdiction could have at most two rates of sales tax, and each local jurisdiction could have only one additional rate. Most importantly, all jurisdictions would adopt uniform sourcing rules and procedures for unified audits, to minimize the exposure of merchants to disputes with multiple jurisdictions attempting to tax the same transactions. The provisions were adopted as an Interstate compact in 2002. By the middle of 2004, 20 states already had adopted conforming legislation and the project's administrators were beginning the process of certifying states as in compliance with the project.

It is important to understand that neither the decision in *Quill* nor the ITFA prevented states from imposing nondiscriminatory taxes on transactions over the Internet that have an adequate nexus with their jurisdiction. Indeed, several states have taken aggressive steps to tax Internet transactions. Pure-play

Internet firms like Amazon.com and eBay can avoid that pressure in the states in which they have no substantial nexus. Multichannel firms — those with combined Internet and brick-and-mortar operations, however, have been much less successful in avoiding taxation. And as the share of Internet commerce garnered by pure-play firms dwindles, strategies for collecting taxes from the multichannel firms becomes ever more important.

For example, several prominent book retailers, faced with substantial competitive pressure from Amazon.com, attempted to structure their Internet operations as separate legal entities so that they could take the position that they did not have physical operations in each of the 50 states. California rebuffed those attempts in two notable cases. In The Petition for Redetermination of Borders Online, Inc., No. 56270 (Sept. 26, 2001), the California Board of Equalization ruled that Borders Online, which had no direct physical presence within California, was required to collect taxes on sales to California customers because its affiliate, Borders, Inc., had agreed to have its brick-and-mortar stores accept returns of merchandise purchased online in exchange for either cash or store credit. Similarly, in The Petition for Redetermination of Barnes & Noble.com, No. 89872 (Sept. 12, 2002), the California Board of Equalization ruled that Barnes & Noble.com, which had no independent physical presence in California, nevertheless had to collect taxes on sales to California customers because it was selling items in California with the help of an in-state representative, Barnes & Noble Booksellers, which operates several brick-and-mortar stores within California. That help consisted of joint marketing efforts, in which Barnes & Noble.com arranged to have Barnes & Noble Booksellers place $5 Barnes & Noble.com coupons in promotional shopping bags that had the "Barnes & Noble" logo printed on one side and the "bn.com" logo printed on the other side. Barnes & Noble Booksellers distributed the bags to customers that made purchases in Barnes & Noble Bookseller's California stores.

The pressure of those efforts by states ultimately forced most of the major multichannel e-tailers — Target, Wal-Mart, and Toys 'R Us, among others — to enter into an amnesty agreement with the major taxing jurisdictions participating in the SSTP. Under the amnesty, those firms began collecting sales tax in 2003, in return for amnesty for any obligation to pay taxes on past transactions. Among retailers, the major holdouts from that arrangement are pure-play companies like Amazon.com and eBay — with no major retail operations that expose them to the risk of that liability under the reasoning of Quill. Among taxing jurisdictions, New York, Illinois, and California did not participate; Illinois already has brought suit against 62 online retailers seeking back taxes. The only thing that is clear about this area at the present time is that further developments will be forthcoming.

Another problem electronic commerce raises for jurisdictions that rely on sales taxes is that those taxes traditionally have reached only tangible goods. The shift to electronic commerce and to digital delivery of goods like software and music has raised challenging definitional problems. To date, those issues have been resolved for the most part on a case-by-case basis, through letter rulings and the like. To the extent generalization is appropriate, jurisdictions often try to distinguish between custom software (which looks more like a service and thus might be nontaxable) and prepackaged software (which looks more like a good and thus should be taxable).

B. Taxation by National Jurisdictions

Allocating taxation authority among nations is considerably more difficult, if only because there is no supra-national sovereign that can enforce a standard code of behavior in the way that the Supreme Court and Congress can. The WTO has taken the lead in some areas, but as discussed below its efforts in the area of taxation have not garnered widespread respect. Still, the leading commercial nations, often coordinating their activities through the Organization for Economic Cooperation and Development (OECD), have developed consistent approaches for resolving similar issues in the past, so there is good reason to hope that a consensus approach can be developed in this area as well.

Although taxation of cross-border trade raises a number of difficult problems, one of the most important issues is to ensure that all trade is taxed once, and only once. When businesses operate in multiple countries, one common problem that arises is whether their transactions should be taxed by the country in which the business resides (the residence country) or the country in which the transaction occurs (the source country). Countries that tend to export capital and products (developed countries, like the United States) prefer residence-based taxation, because it tends to broaden their tax base to include foreign transactions. Conversely, countries that tend to import capital (developing countries, or large countries like mainland China) prefer source-based taxation, because it tends to strengthen their ability to tax transactions that arguably occur within their borders.

The traditional resolution of that question — a compromise dating to the 1920s — turns on the existence of a "permanent establishment." Specifically, if the business maintains a permanent establishment in the source country, then the source country will tax the profits from the transaction, and the residence country will take responsibility for preventing double taxation, either by exempting the transaction from tax or by granting a credit for the tax paid to the source country. That resolution has been carried forward as standard language in an imposing number of bilateral tax treaties: tax treaties adopted on a pair-by-pair basis among the leading commercial countries. Its most common formulation appears in a commonly used model treaty promulgated by the OECD:

> The profits of an enterprise of a Contracting State shall be taxable only in that State unless the enterprise carries on business in the other Contracting State through a permanent establishment situated therein. If the enterprise carries on business as aforesaid, the profits of the enterprise may be taxed in the other State but only so much of them as is attributable to that permanent establishment.

Article 7, ¶1, OECD Model Convention on Taxes on Income and on Capital, available at *http://www.oecd.org/dataoecd/52/34/1914467.pdf*; see Article 5 (defining permanent establishment).

To understand the issues, consider a sale from a French corporation's Rio de Janeiro office to a Brazilian resident. Under a "residence" approach, the profit from that transaction would be taxed only at the residence of the seller, in this case France. Under a "source" approach, the profit would be taxed only by the jurisdiction in which the transaction occurred (in this case Brazil). Under the compromise "permanent-establishment" approach, the transaction would be taxed where it occurred, because in this case the seller had a permanent establishment in that country (the office in Rio). Conversely, if the sale was made by mail order — without any "permanent establishment" in Brazil — the transaction would be taxed only by the country of the seller's residence, France.

Resolution of such issues is particularly difficult for electronic commerce, because of the difficulty of applying concepts like "residency" and "permanent establishment." Most obviously, it is as a threshold matter hard to determine where a Web site is located for purposes of determining the taxing jurisdiction. The first intuition would be to say that the Web site is located wherever the server is located. But the location of a server can be easily manipulated. For example, the server might be moved every few hours, so that it is never in any single jurisdiction for a protracted period of time. Or it might be located intentionally in a "tax haven," that provides particularly favorable tax treatment. Because it is so much easier to move the location of a Web server than it is to move the location of physical assets (like a sales office), this problem is much more challenging for regulators of electronic commerce than for those that regulate conventional cross-border trade.

Responding to that concern, the OECD in 2000 issued a formal "clarification" of the commentary on the definition of permanent establishment in Article 5 of its model tax convention, aiming to establish a uniform practice on taxing Internet-based businesses. Generally, those changes reflect a conservative approach, treating purely electronic presence as inadequate to create a permanent establishment. For example, the clarification explains that a Web site itself is not a permanent establishment, and that a Web site hosting arrangement does not constitute a permanent establishment for the business carrying on business through the Web site. At the same time, the clarification rejected the bright-line rule that all permanent establishments must have human personnel on site, leaving open the possibility of some types of computerized operations amounting to a permanent establishment. With respect to online retailers, for example, the clarification explains that a permanent establishment exists if the "typical functions related to a sale are performed at that location," such as "the conclusion of the contract with the customer, the processing of the payment and the delivery of the products." Thus, an operation that performed those activities automatically would amount to a permanent establishment even if there were no on-site employees.

Recognizing the delicacy of the subject, the WTO for several years promulgated a "moratorium" on taxes directly affecting Internet commerce (parallel to the ITFA). Although the moratorium eventually expired, most countries voluntarily continued to refrain from taking aggressive action. The European Union, however, in 2002 created a significant controversy by imposing its value-added tax (VAT) on certain products delivered over the Internet. Generally, the VAT is a consumption tax levied on the sale of goods and services. (The difference from a conventional sales tax is that a VAT is levied on each business as a fraction of the price of each sale they make, but each business in turn is reimbursed VAT on their purchases. Hence, the tax is applied to the value of the goods that have been added, and ultimately is borne by the consumer.) A common VAT system is compulsory for members of the European Union, under Directive 77/388/EEC (commonly called the "Sixth VAT Directive"). That Directive specifies a minimum rate of 15 percent, although different rates apply in the various member states (ranging as high as 25 percent). Article 8 specifies that the place of supply of a good for taxing purposes is the place from which the shipment is made. Article 9 says that the place of supply of a service is the place where the supplier is established. These rules are sometimes referred to as the "country of origin" rule. These rules exempt Internet transactions in goods or services that originate from the United States or any other nation outside the European Union.

As discussed above, however, it is not clear that the supply of a digital product (such as music or software) can be characterized as a good or a service. Thus, following changes adopted by the EU Council of Ministers on February 12, 2002 and introduced on July 1, 2003 (under Directive 2002/38/EC), non-EU businesses providing digital electronic commerce and entertainment products and services to *consumers* in EU countries now must register with the European tax authorities and collect VAT on their sales at the appropriate rate according to the location of the purchaser. (Sales between businesses are not covered by the Directive.) The Directive provides an illustrative list of "electronically supplied services," which includes: Web-site supply, Web-hosting, distance maintenance of programs and equipment; supply of software and updating thereof; supply of images, text and information, and making databases available; supply of music, films and games, including games of chance and gambling games, and of political, cultural, artistic, sporting, scientific and entertainment broadcasts and events; and supply of distance teaching. The most administratively complex area of the new rules is that the rate of VAT that non-EU sellers must charge varies depending upon the EU member state in which a given EU consumer is resident. So, a U.S. supplier of music downloads would have to charge VAT at a rate of 19.6 percent on sales to French consumers, 17.5 percent on sales to UK consumers, and 25 percent on sales to Swedish consumers. In some cases, U.S. online retailers may have sufficient incentive to establish a presence in an EU member state, so that the Directive will not apply.

The Directive makes sense from an internal EU perspective, because it levels the playing field for European suppliers of electronically provided goods (which already were paying VAT on such transactions). Still, it has been roundly criticized for "jumping the gun" before global consensus is reached on taxation of Internet commerce. As with the rules for state and local taxation discussed in the first part of this assignment, resolution of the international conflicts is a developing problem. We present the discussion here only to highlight issues that are likely to be prominent for years to come.

Relevant Glossary Entries

Use Tax
Web Server

Problem Set 16

16.1. Your state legislator is unhappy because the largest local bookstore in the state has closed, driven out of business (he believes) by competition from Amazon.com. The state's sales tax traditionally has imposed a lower rate on the sale of books (5 percent) than on the sale of most other items (6 percent). In an effort to get back at Amazon.com, he proposes to raise the tax to 6 percent on books. Because there are no longer any significant locally owned bookstores, his view is that the tax will harm Amazon.com and other out-of-state bookstore owners. Setting to one side the plausibility of the legislator's reasoning, and assuming that Congress reenacts the ITFA, would the tax be lawful as applied to the sale of books by Amazon.com? ITFA §§1101, 1104. (You should assume that Amazon.com has a significant warehouse facility in the state and that the state has in place a typical sales and use tax system that applies to nonnecessary goods but not services.)

16.2.   Same facts as Problem 16.1, but suppose that to enhance enforcement of the tax, the statute provides that the sales tax must be collected by the Internet service provider over whose service the transaction was concluded. The legislative staff justifies the statute on the premise that the Internet service provider is acting as an agent for the retailer by displaying the retailer's Web site to customers located in the state. (This is attractive for the state, because a relatively small number of Internet service providers handle substantially all consumer Internet service within the state.) Would that provision be lawful if the ITFA were reenacted? ITFA §§1101, 1104.

16.3.   Dell Computers is based in Austin, Texas. At their facility on the north side of Austin, Dell manufactures most of the computers that it sells through its Web site and telephone-order businesses. Assuming that Texas has had a generally applicable tax on the sale of personal computers in place since before 1998, must Dell pay sales tax to the state of Texas on computers that it sells to Texas residents from the Web site? Does it matter that the manufacturing facility is entirely separate from the order-processing facility and that the order-processing facility and related warehouses are not located within Texas? What if they are owned by separate corporations?

16.4.   In connection with its deliberations on the ITFA, Congress is considering a statute that would permit states to impose a sales tax on Internet access. Specifically, the statute would authorize each state to impose a tax of up to 8 percent on the price of Internet access sold to any resident of the state, with the tax to be collected by the provider, wherever located. Would such a statute be constitutional?

16.5.   Assume that the United States has entered into bilateral tax treaties with both Japan and Romania, in each case on terms that are substantively identical to the model OECD treaty discussed in the text of the assignment above. Which jurisdiction would be entitled to tax profits from the following transactions?

(a)   Kinokuniya is a Japan-based book retailer. It has a store in New York City, from which it sells a book to an American citizen who resides in the United States.

(b)   Amazon.com is an Internet retailer based in the United States. It receives an order at its Web site from a Romanian citizen who resides in Romania. At the time of the sale, Amazon.com has no warehouses or other facilities in Romania. It is incorporated in the United States, its executive offices and all of its warehouses are in the United States, and its Web site resides on a server in the United States. How would your answer change if the relevant server was in Romania? If the product was shipped from a small, wholly automated warehouse in Romania?

Section B. B2B Transactions

The preceding assignments discuss developments that generally affect the sale of goods, particularly by Internet-based retailers. Transactions between businesses have been affected in much more intricate ways, largely because the amounts involved in those transactions present an opportunity for cost savings that justify large investments in technology. The four assignments in this section discuss some of the most prominent technological developments. The section starts with the now-venerable practice of electronic data interchange (EDI), which facilitated electronic contracting between repeat-contracting parties long before the Internet. The second and third assignments discuss two recent technological developments (digital signatures and B2B exchanges) that have not gained the broad usage that would justify the hype that greeted their invention in the early years of the commercial Internet. The last assignment looks more broadly to international trade, focusing on developments designed to facilitate an entirely electronic infrastructure for cross-border sales between businesses.

Assignment 17: Electronic Data Interchange and Trading-Partner Agreements

Before the Internet became the medium of choice for electronic commerce, businesses that wanted to improve the efficiency of their internal operations and their relationships could form contracts with their trading partners through the technology of "electronic data interchange" (EDI). Like any sophisticated new technology, the early adopters of EDI were plagued by formidable technological and administrative obstacles, mostly because of the lack of standardized information technology, accounting, and management systems. Without standardization, it was difficult for computers on the opposite sides of a transaction to exchange information and act on it without human intervention. Through the years, those problems have faded as the outmoded legacy computer systems have been replaced by modern computer networks and as formal standards-setting organizations have promulgated standards on an industry-by-industry basis to facilitate EDI in ever broader sectors of our economy.

At the outset, it is important to emphasize the limitations of EDI. Because EDI depends on advance arrangements between the parties, it cannot accommodate the spontaneous decisions or chance encounters that characterize modern Internet interactions. Nevertheless, the slow growth of EDI through the years before the Internet was even available to businesses has given it a commanding role in online business transactions. For example, a 2001 study of the United States Department of Commerce indicated that EDI accounted for 59 percent of all e-commerce transactions. Manufacturing led all sectors with e-commerce accounting for 12 percent ($485 billion) of shipments. Merchant wholesalers were second at 5.3 percent ($134 billion). The selected service industries that were studied conducted only 0.6 percent ($25 billion) of their transactions via e-commerce. Only a minuscule 0.5 percent ($15 billion) of retail trade was conducted online. Thus, a reasonable estimate of the total volume of EDI transactions in the U.S. economy (including more than the four sectors in the study) would be hundreds of billions of dollars a year already by the turn of the millennium. The volume now is doubtless much greater.

In sum, EDI is the workhorse of American electronic commerce today (at least if you include successor forms of transactions that rely on the XML technology discussed in the next assignment). As the assignments that follow should make clear, it is likely to remain so for years (if not decades) to come. Accordingly, a basic understanding of EDI is — for all relevant purposes — a basic understanding of electronic business contracting as it now exists. This assignment discusses EDI from two perspectives: Part A provides an overview of the technology and mechanics of EDI; Part B discusses the uses of a transactional perspective to discuss the trading-partner agreements that businesses use to implement their EDI contracting.

A.   The Basics of EDI

1.   The History of EDI

Although the first tentative steps toward establishing computer-to-computer links between businesses were taken during the 1960s, it was not until the 1970s that businesses became seriously interested in using computer communications to replace telex, telephone, or postal communications. The first important use occurred in the late 1970s, when some businesses in the transportation industry began experimenting with the use of electronic messages instead of paper communications. Soon after that, formal standard-setting efforts began to analyze routine business communications, so that computers could be programmed to read and process the information contained in those communications without human intervention. Those efforts produced the EDI transaction-processing systems used today by more than 100,000 businesses around the world.

The basic point of EDI is to permit businesses to exchange transaction information in a standardized, computer-readable form. Thus, before a business can send and receive EDI messages, it must agree with its trading partners on the format in which messages will be sent. Once both businesses have "reengineered" their procedures and operations to make them compatible with the appropriate EDI format, they can send and receive standard electronic versions of basic forms of business communications, such as purchase orders, invoices, delivery advices, or remittance advices. Ideally, a trading partner that receives an EDI message should be able to receive the information directly into its computer system, analyze it, and act upon it without the need for any human oversight or review.

Although that may seem like a technical detail, the efficiencies that it permits have driven some of the most prominent business trends of the last two decades. For example, Wal-Mart's early and pervasive use of EDI technologies has been a major factor contributing to its success in trouncing older, better-known competitors. Such early successes led many observers to expect that EDI rapidly would revolutionize business processes everywhere.

By the mid 1990s, however, it became clear that the impact of EDI in its then-current form would be much slower and less complete than had been predicted. Perhaps only one in ten businesses that might profitably adopt EDI had done so. Many businesses that made limited use of EDI did not enjoy any significant efficiency gains as a result, usually because they had not done any significant "reengineering" work when they started using EDI. Thus, EDI was facing a classic problem common to all network technologies: Unless a critical mass of businesses adopted it, those who invested in it could not reap the full value of the technology. But the high up-front cost of implementing EDI, combined with uncertainty about how long it might take for a business to recapture its investment in EDI through improved efficiency, made it difficult for many businesses to justify investing in EDI technology.

The chicken-and-egg problem could be solved in markets where major players (such as Wal-Mart or the Big Three automobile manufacturers) had the market power simply to demand that their smaller trading partners adopt

EDI. In addition, EDI might be widely adopted in industries with only a few players, where the terms of transactions would be easy to standardize. The relatively low costs of developing and implementing EDI standards made it easier for those industries to see net gains from rapid adoption of EDI.

Then, about the time that the complexities of adopting EDI became apparent, the availability of the Internet as a potential medium for commercial communication gave further reason for businesses to delay implementation of EDI. EDI was difficult for many businesses to adopt precisely because it required a complete reengineering of the internal administrative processes of the business to be successful. By contrast, establishing a commercial Web presence *seemed* as easy as falling off a log. Many small and medium-sized businesses that could not justify investing in EDI quickly embraced the Internet. Businesses could hire freelance Web designers to create their Web sites and find inexpensive Internet service providers to host them. The Internet seemed to be the "killer app" that finally persuaded businesses of all types that "electronic commerce" was the way to go, but at the same time it made them wonder whether they should bypass EDI, moving directly to a more sophisticated and (they thought) simpler Internet presence without the adoption of EDI.

It is important to understand the competitive landscape between the novelty of mid-1990s Internet commerce and EDI electronic commerce at the same time. Although the process of implementing EDI was normally time-consuming and expensive, a successful program often brought a decisive competitive advantage to a business by lowering overhead costs and improving management processes. By contrast, Internet commerce was cheap to set up but in most cases brought little concrete benefit to the business. For one thing, the first iterations of Web-enabled electronic commerce generally consisted of "brochureware" with little or no interactivity. Whatever businesses might have expected about the potential for that brochureware to provide access to new customers, businesses quickly realized that it was in reality only a new marketing medium; sites of that type could have no effect on the underlying costs of transacting business, which — absent the adoption of EDI — would continue to proceed "offline" in a traditionally cumbersome paper-based format. Thus, in hindsight it is fair to say that most businesses that threw together Web sites and put them up on the Internet without a clearly articulated business plan quickly discovered that Web-site development and maintenance could generate huge overhead expenses without increasing revenues or lowering transaction costs.

The problem is inherent in the standard language of textual display that defines the World Wide Web. Specifically the Hypertext Markup Language (HTML) standard is designed for publishing, not for transaction processing. Among other difficulties, it permits variations in how information is displayed, but (unlike EDI standards) it does not organize or differentiate Web-situated information based on meaning.

As Assignment 18 discusses, Web sites now can use a new standard for Web-site design, eXtensible Markup Language (XML), which permits graphical user interfaces to be coded with tags that do provide that kind of differentiation. In the early days of the Internet, however, when businesses tried to advance their Internet operations from mere marketing to transaction processing, they immediately faced the same problems that they had faced when they tried to implement EDI a decade earlier. If a business had existing "legacy" computer systems that had been designed and built years or even decades before Internet commerce was popular, and if the business was unwilling or unable to replace those legacy systems, then that business would have to develop an ad-hoc interface to permit the legacy applications to communicate with the Web-commerce applications and vice versa. If the interface was not designed with care, then the Web site would function poorly. As a result, it might transmit information that could not be processed properly by the legacy systems, or perhaps even display incorrect information to customers. The basic problem remains to this day: Until businesses that rely on legacy systems replace them with newer Web-enabled systems, those businesses will have problems offering more sophisticated marketing or transaction-processing services over the Internet.

Another obstacle to achieving greater efficiency with Internet commerce is the continued reliance on interfaces designed on the assumption that one of the contracting parties is a human being — which means that the interfaces must be designed with sufficient detail and legibility to ensure that an ordinary person can interpret a Web interface and make decisions spontaneously. The lesson of EDI, however, is that Internet commerce cannot achieve the same advances in efficiency that were possible with traditional EDI systems until it abandons the presumption that one party to the contract is a human being reacting spontaneously to a graphical user interface. The only way that Internet commerce can achieve those efficiencies will be for individual consumers to give way to shopping bots that search the Internet to identify possible transactions meeting pre-defined criteria. Merchants engaged in business-to-consumer Internet commerce then would provide interfaces parallel to the EDI invoice reprinted below — with an emphasis on standardization of the kind useful for a machine, rather than legibility to facilitate human intervention.

Given those problems, it is no surprise that many of the great success stories of Internet commerce tend to be found among businesses that have been most vigorous in their efforts to implement EDI or similar technologies. For example, Amazon.com began operations in 1995 as little more than a Web front-end to electronic fulfillment systems maintained by the nation's largest book wholesaler, Ingram Book Company. Amazon.com was established in Seattle to be near the main Ingram warehouse in Oregon. When it began operations, it did little more than receive orders for books that were available from Ingram, repackage them in Amazon boxes, and ship them out. Book wholesalers had already made the marketing and distribution of books an efficient, highly automated business process before Amazon.com gave the book buying public a window into the efficiencies of that process.

For other businesses using the Internet for commercial transactions to achieve the kind of efficiency gains that are possible when electronic commerce technologies are used effectively, something like traditional EDI standards will have to be developed and widely adopted. The Internet version of EDI standards may be nothing more than a revised version of existing standards developed in the 1980s and 1990s, or it may be based on a newer technology that merges the structures for message contents developed for EDI with the open environment and distributed processing characteristic of the Internet. Much of the current interest in XML rests on the perception that it may provide a way to bridge the gap between EDI standards and World Wide Web standards.

2. EDI Technology

Although the details of the technology may be irrelevant to most lawyers, it is important to understand the basics of the technology. Generally, two sets of technical standards govern the format of EDI messages: one developed by the American National Standards Institute (ANSI) accredited standards committee X12 (ASC X12), and the other by the United Nations Electronic Data Interchange for Administration, Commerce and Transport (UN EDIFACT). ANSI coordinates the voluntary technical standard–setting process in the United States and represents this country in such international technical standard–setting organizations as the International Organization for Standards (generally known as ISO, from the Greek for "equal"). (ISO's Web site is at *www.iso.org*.) EDIFACT performs a function similar to ANSI, but at the level of multilateral cooperation under the aegis of the United Nations. Thus, although ASC X12 standards dominate EDI technologies used in the United States, the UN EDIFACT standards are more widely used in other countries. The disparity predictably has led to ongoing efforts (not yet successful) to harmonize the two sets of standards.

The ANSI process is designed to provide an open forum where interested parties can meet and debate the need for standards and agree on the content of standards. When ANSI approves a standard, it becomes an "American National Standard." As such, it should reflect the consensus of those most directly and materially affected by the standard. The process thus starts with a request from industry or other interested parties, in response to which ANSI charters an "accredited standards committee" with a formal mandate to develop specific standards. As relevant here, the mandate of the X12 committee is to develop standards to facilitate electronic interchange relating to such business transactions as order placement and processing, shipping and receiving, invoicing, and payment associated with the provision of goods and services. The X12 committee has hundreds of members who participate in subcommittees, help draft proposed standards, and vote on proposals.

Although X12 has a number of subcommittees that study technical issues common to EDI transactions in all industries, much of the work involves the development of separate standards on an industry-by-industry basis. Thus, if businesses within an industry believe that they would benefit from the development of an X12 standard, they can apply to the X12 committee to set up a subcommittee. Industry members meet on a regular basis, often for several years, as issues are identified and proposed solutions are hammered out. The standards are based on a careful analysis of the paper documents businesses within an industry are already using and the information normally contained within those documents. The standards ideally should balance various objectives. On the one hand, the standard should not require the standardization of too much information, which would make implementation of EDI unnecessarily expensive. On the other hand, if the standard does not contain enough information to complete transactions, then different applications that conform to the standard will not be interoperable. That lack of interoperability will defeat the purpose of developing the standard in the first place. Among the industries for which such standards have been developed are automotive, chemical, electrical, electronic, grocery, metals, office products, paper, petroleum, retail, transportation, and warehousing.

The process of converting a paper form and its contents to an EDI standard can be illustrated using the example of an invoice, first in traditional paper form then in EDI form.

Figure 17.1
Traditional Paper Invoice

Invoice No. 1001

Riverfront Tools, Inc.

3814 San Jacinto Boulevard

Pasadena, Texas 76543

Tel: (713) 765-4321 Fax: (713) 765-4322

Invoice Date: 7/22/01 **Sales Person:** HSK

Charge to:	Ship to:
Ricky's Building Wreckers	same
5407 East Galveston Road	
Pasadena, Texas 76543	

Your Order No.	Customer Ref. No.	Order Date	Terms
781-AF473	99-88-341-TDB	7/8/01	2 percent 10 days

Quantity	Unit	Number	Description	Unit Price	Total Price
1	ea	4147S	Compressor	499.99	499.99
5	case	5799W	Adaptor	129.99	649.95

Please direct correspondence to:
P. Charles, tel: (713) 765-4330 direct

PLEASE PAY THIS AMOUNT 1,249.94

Date Shipped: 7/21/01 **Shipped via:** Acme Trucking

EDI Invoice

ST*810*001N/L

BIG*20010722*1001*20010701*99-88-341-TDBN/L

N1*BT* Ricky's Building WreckersN/L

N3*5407 East Galveston RoadN/L

N4* Pasadena, Texas 76543N/L

N1*ST* Ricky's Building WreckersN/L

N3*5407 East Galveston RoadN/L

N4* Pasadena, Texas 76543N/L

PER*P.Charles*TE*7137654330N/L

ITD*01*3**10N/L

ITI**1*ea*499.99**VC*4147SN/L

ITI**5*CA*129.99**VC*5799WN/L

TDS*1249.94N/L

CAD*M****Acme TruckingN/L

The conversion of routine communications with trading partners to EDI formats should offer several types of cost savings. Among other things, the business should be able to reduce overheads associated with handling paper forms, respond to queries from trading partners more quickly and reliably, and provide managers with a more timely, accurate, and complete picture of how the company is using its resources. Once one party has entered data, the data will never need to be entered again — even by the trading partner. Thus, data-entry costs should fall, as well as the total number (and consequent costs) of data-entry errors. Moreover, remaining errors often can be detected more quickly because of the verification procedures used in EDI processing. Similarly, transaction data can be stored and retrieved more readily when it is electronic from inception. Finally, transaction cycles can be compressed with the elimination of the human intervention necessary to process traditional communications such as fax or postal mail.

3.   EDI Applications

Manufacturing industries illustrate some of the most successful applications of EDI technology. To understand the technology in action, consider the following outline of the flow of goods, services, and information in a manufacturing industry engaged in transactions without EDI. The example is a single, simple finished manufactured product, such as a plastic drinking cup sold at a retail store in summer. In the era of global commerce, that cup will be the product of a long chain of supply and production processes linked by distribution and information systems. The raw material that ultimately becomes the cup has its origins in the oil industry. After the oil has been pumped and transported to a refinery, it is converted into the chemical compounds that make up plastic. A chemical company acquires those chemicals from the refinery and produces the raw plastic pellets used by the cup manufacturer. The manufacturer has injection mold machines that convert the melted plastic into cups, which are then packaged and turned over to a shipper. The shipper might deliver the cups to a wholesaler, or if the retail store has dealings directly with the manufacturer, to the retailer's distribution center. After the store places an order for the product, it is delivered directly to the retail outlet where the stock clerks place the cups on shelves for sale to consumers.

Before EDI, a traditional retailer might place orders for such goods based on estimates drawn from prior years' experience. If the cup is a seasonal item, the retailer would need to estimate what demand during the summer season would be; the orders often would be placed many months before the product would be made available to customers. If it is offered year round, then the stock clerks of the retailer might need to perform periodic stock checks, noting the number and variety of various items remaining on the store shelves and placing orders to replace those that have sold. The orders would be placed with the wholesaler or regional distribution center, which in turn would aggregate orders and send them to the manufacturer. The manufacturer would evaluate the orders in light of its own inventory of raw plastic and if necessary order additional materials to fill the orders. The cup manufacturer might find that its own supplier of raw materials was out of stock of the materials it needed, in which case it could try to obtain those materials from other sources or simply delay the production run until its normal supplier could meet its needs.

At each step of this "supply chain," the process of ordering goods would begin with a purchase order. The order would be prepared on the purchaser's own paper form, following the purchaser's own internal procedures. The purchaser might describe the ordered goods in terms of its own internal inventory control number, or it might use a stock-keeping unit number (SKU, pronounced "skew") established by the vendor, or possibly a universal product code (UPC). (UPCs are established by the Uniform Code Council and assign a globally unique bar code to a product.) The purchase order also might include delivery instructions. The purchase order might be sent by postal mail or fax, or even telex. After it is received, an employee of the vendor manually enters the order into the vendor's computer system. If the vendor can fill the order, it sends an acknowledgment to the purchaser confirming the terms of the transaction, such as price, quantity, description of the goods, and an estimated delivery date. This confirmation is prepared on the vendor's own paper form and sent by postal mail, fax, or telex.

When the goods are available, the vendor sends a delivery advice to confirm the contents of the shipment and the delivery terms and to ensure that the purchaser will keep an eye out for the shipment. The vendor also issues an invoice, which probably includes a summary description of the shipment. The accounts payable department of the purchaser matches up the delivery advice and the invoice and then waits for a record of receipt of the shipment to come from the purchaser's receiving area. In the receiving area, the purchaser's staff gives the shipper a receipt and enters into the purchaser's computer a description of what has been received.

At that point, the accounts payable department matches up the receipt record with the information in the invoice from the vendor and authorizes payment, probably by check or electronic funds transfer. It also sends a remittance advice to the vendor, either in the envelope with the check, or separately by mail (if the payment is by electronic funds transfer). If there is a discrepancy between the amount of the invoice and the amount of the payment, the remittance advice will explain the difference. The variation in amount may be due to any of a number of reasons, including some of the shipped goods being declined and returned to the vendor, some of the goods described in the delivery advice not actually being received by the purchaser, or a discount authorized by the vendor for its customers that make prompt cash payments. When the vendor receives the payment, its accounts receivable department reconciles the information in the remittance advice with the vendor's own records of the shipment.

Your reaction as a businessperson confronted with that summary should focus on the number of different pieces of paper and the number of actions that human individuals must take with respect to information on those pieces of paper. EDI communications vastly simplify and accelerate this information flow. If the purchaser and vendor have fully implemented EDI, a "reengineered" supply chain might take the following form. As the retailer's customer makes a purchase, the retailer's cashier scans a bar code on the product. This not only allows the cashier to access the price information from the retailer's database, it updates the retailer's own inventory control system and generates an order for a replacement product. That order is sent automatically to the wholesaler's computer system. The wholesaler's computer system ordinarily will be programmed automatically to accept typical purchase orders from retailers, at least if the orders are within specified volume limits or are covered by inventory on hand when the order is received. In the latter case, the inventory is applied to the order automatically, and no longer will show as available in the wholesaler's computer system. At the same time, the wholesaler's computer system can generate an order for the manufacturer, if the wholesaler finds that its own inventory levels have fallen to pre-determined levels. The same process of automatically processing orders and generating new orders to replenish vendor stocks can be repeated all the way up the supply chain to the original processors of raw materials.

In "just in time" (JIT) inventory control systems, manufacturers eliminate their own inventory of parts and instead require their suppliers to be able to send the parts they need on a very rapid schedule (often on just a few hours notice). Before JIT systems, it was common for manufacturers to carry an inventory of parts adequate for three to six months of production, to protect against production interruptions caused by short-term fluctuations in the availability of parts. The capital costs of purchasing and holding large inventories of parts substantially increased the overhead of manufacturers. In addition, because the stockpiles were created based on historical experience, many stockpiled parts would never be used at all due to changes in demand or deteriorated in quality while stockpiled, so that they become unusable before they are finally needed.

The technological sophistication of those processes soon may become even more sophisticated, with the advent of radio-frequency ID (RFID) tags — pea-sized devices that can be included in each shipping container to automatically provide information as products enter and leave a warehouse, factory, or store. Those devices present an advance over bar codes in two important features. First, because the RFID tags each include a tiny antenna, they permit scanners to receive the information for products automatically as they travel — without any need for opening or examining the individual items in a shipping container. Second, they can hold enough information to provide a unique identifier for each product, not just each class of product. Thus, Wal-Mart can track every single humidifier in its supply chain separately. This is useful for a variety of reasons, such as monitoring the age of inventory, identifying the source of defective product, and the like. To get a sense for the value of this technology, industry analysts expect Wal-Mart to save $8 *billion* in 2005 from the implementation of RFID technology.

Modern manufacturers — at least those that are profitable — enter into EDI trading-partner relationships with their suppliers and transmit their requirements for parts on an hourly or daily basis. Suppliers are expected to have the appropriate inventory on hand to meet the needs of the manufacturer immediately, and to have access to fast and efficient transportation systems to get the parts where they are needed without delay. Because suppliers are unwilling to bear the costs associated with building their own stockpiles of inventory in anticipation of possible requests from manufacturers, manufacturers and suppliers have developed systems for coordinating the type and quantity of parts the supplier produces. The manufacturer may send to the supplier before the end of each month a forecast of its requirements for the following month. By the middle of each week, it may send a more specific estimate of its requirements for the next week. The specific requirements for each day's production might be sent the night before, so that the necessary parts arrive only a few hours before they are assembled into a finished product.

When the wholesaler puts replacement product in a shipment to the retailer, it can place a bar code with a unique ID number on the box containing the product. If the delivery advice sent to the retailer includes the bar-coded number, the retailer's receiving area can simply scan the box on receipt, confirming acceptance of the order and entering the description of the shipment from the delivery order into the retailer's own inventory-control system. The retailer may then "self-bill" or calculate the information that would have appeared in the wholesaler's invoice, using prices and payment terms that the wholesaler has placed in the retailer's computer system. If it is lucky enough to have one of the few banks that already provide that service, the retailer can even remit payment to the wholesaler using "financial EDI" (FEDI). FEDI permits the remittance advice information to be sent as an electronic attachment to the electronic funds transfer instruction sent by the retailer's bank to the wholesaler's bank. When the wholesaler's bank notifies the wholesaler that the bank has received the retailer's payment, the bank can send the remittance advice electronically at the same time, so that the wholesaler can download that information directly into its own accounts receivable system.

EDI reduces the number of errors that occur in processing orders by all the various participants in the supply chain, because a description of the product entered in one computer system is transmitted to other systems automatically. For this to work, trading partners have to agree on a common (typically alphanumerical) description of the products they trade in. This number might be provided from an outside source, such as a SKU or UPC number, or it might be a purchaser's product number or a vendor's catalog number. What is important is not which description of the item is chosen, but that all the relevant participants in the supply chain can recognize and process the standardized description. If businesses are forced to receive messages containing product descriptions in a new form, the business can either reorganize its own internal description system, or develop software to convert the standard description used up and down the supply chain into a description that its own computer system can process. If that kind of translation software is not feasible, then the business will have to reorganize its system of describing the products it handles.

Before EDI, the adjustments required to accommodate multiple, inconsistent product descriptions might have been made by employees of participants in a particular supply chain. EDI removes that form of human mediation — which might work most of the time but nevertheless contributes to a significant number of errors in processing orders. It replaces it with a much more accurate but inflexible system that can run without any human intervention. Businesses unwilling to implement EDI in such a rigorous manner can develop software that converts machine-readable EDI messages into a human-readable format and prints them out, creating the equivalent of the old mailed, telexed, or faxed paper forms.

Of course, however much EDI systems can improve transaction processing, even the most sophisticated EDI system cannot protect against errors by the humans involved in the process. The difficulties that afflicted Cisco Systems in 2000 provide an illustrative cautionary tale. Early that year, Cisco Systems received considerable acclaim for its ability to achieve a "virtual close" for its accounting books on a daily basis. After years of major reengineering efforts, Cisco Systems had the enviable ability to generate consolidated financial statements on a daily basis. But shortly after announcing that breakthrough, Cisco suffered a serious setback caused by a huge backlog of inventory and a sudden decline in orders. As it turns out, the vaunted Cisco accounting system was unable to distinguish between genuine EDI orders placed by its customers and duplicate orders placed by the same customers through different channels in an effort to ensure that shipments were delivered as quickly as possible. Furthermore, Cisco's top management intentionally ignored transaction information that might have led managers in other industries or companies to cut back on production. Cisco had taken the same approach in previous economic downturns — increasing productive capacity to give itself a competitive advantage if the downturn happened to be brief. In 2001, however, Cisco found itself in the midst of a major slowdown of the entire telecommunications and networking sector of the economy. Cisco's twin failures in misunderstanding its transaction volume and in responding to a decline in that volume left Cisco severely pressed.

B.   Trading-Partner Agreements

In 1979, ANSI authorized the creation of ASC X12; in 1983, it published its first EDI standards. By the mid-1980s, businesses were asking their lawyers what their rights and obligations would be under contracts formed using EDI technology. In 1990, the American Bar Association published the Model Electronic Data Interchange Trading-Partner Agreement and Commentary (MTPAC), which gave lawyers a toolkit they could use to identify their clients' needs and craft adequate solutions for them. Generally, MTPAC contemplated a "trading-partner agreement" between each pair of contracting parties that would provide a set of master rules to govern the specific contracts into which those parties entered in particular purchase transactions.

Although the MTPAC was widely used as a basis for trading-partner agreements, many businesses implemented EDI and began entering EDI-based contracts without any form of trading-partner agreement. The major legal issues that such a relationship raises (the topic of the rest of this assignment) might suggest that it was rash or imprudent for companies to fail to use such agreements. But it is a startling fact that there has not yet been a single reported legal opinion issued in the United States arising out of a dispute between EDI trading partners. Even considering that only a small percentage of conventional paper-based contracts result in litigation, the absence of significant litigation involving EDI is notable. Perhaps the ability of EDI to reduce errors limits the instances of disputes that arise when errors must be resolved. Perhaps the nature of the transactions for which EDI is useful — those that involve significantly repetitive transactions between the same parties — makes it less likely that people will react to small difficulties by threatening litigation. But whatever the reason, the apparent ability of EDI contracting parties to resolve their problems amicably — despite the large-scale absence of basic trading-partner agreements — certainly says something positive about the process.

Despite that rosy picture, it is not typical for business lawyers considering transactions holding significant potential for disagreement to advise their clients that they should skip over the process of contracting because they should be able to resolve amicably any disputes that arise later. Accordingly, it is well worth the time to consider the legal problems that would be addressed in a basic trading-partner agreement.

1.   Writings and Records

Because EDI contracts deal with transactions in goods, the need for a signed writing under the Statute of Frauds is an easy issue to spot. Opinion was divided with regard to whether law reform was necessary for EDI contracting to achieve widespread adoption. Some felt that the common law of contracts was sufficiently flexible to accommodate EDI; others disagreed. Those willing to rely on the adaptability of the common law noted that businesses have been substituting electronic media for paper media since the middle of the nineteenth century, and that courts generally had succeeded in applying existing law to the evolving business practices. The optimists certainly were correct in arguing that courts have been flexible in interpreting signature and writing requirements for contract formation. For example, in one of the first reported opinions dealing with "electronic commerce," the New Hampshire Supreme Court held that a telegraph could constitute a signed writing. The court explained that "it makes no difference whether the operator writes the offer or acceptance . . . with a steel pen an inch long attached to an ordinary penholder, or whether his pen be a copper wire a thousand miles long. In either case the thought is communicated to the paper by the use of the finger." Howley v. Whipple, 48 N.H. 487, 488 (1869).

But that approach is not universal. Over 100 years later, the Georgia Court of Appeals held that a fax could not satisfy a statutory requirement that a government department be notified of a tort claim by certified mail, and went on to observe:

> It may also be added that a facsimile transmission does not satisfy the statutory requirement that notice be "given in writing." Such a transmission is an audio signal via a telephone line containing information from which a writing may be accurately duplicated, but the transmission of beeps and chirps along a telephone line is not a writing, as that term is customarily used.

Department of Transportation v. Norris, 474 S.E.2d 216, 218 (Ga. Ct. App. 1996). On the narrow issue of interpreting the requirements of the Georgia statute in question, the supreme court of Georgia reversed the judgment and held that a fax was adequate. Norris v. Department of Transportation, 486 S.E.2d 826 (Ga. 1997). Even then, a dissenting opinion doggedly pointed out that the statute clearly required certified mail, which the appellant had not used.

Despite the reversal by the Georgia supreme court, the "chirps and beeps" rhetorical flourish caused the 1996 opinion to become notorious among attorneys trying to advise clients regarding how flexible and adaptable courts would be in dealing with electronic contracting practices. As that case illustrates, one problem is that the Statute of Frauds requirement arises by statute — for example, Old UCC §2-201 — which significantly constrained the ability of courts to use common-law principles to find electronic messages to constitute "writings" that satisfy the Statute of Frauds. Accordingly, prudent attorneys generally advised clients that they could not rely on courts to accept EDI messages as writings. Thus, they recommended that their clients execute trading-partner agreements to resolve the problem. For example, it would be easy to see the signed trading-partner agreement that defined the significance of the later EDI messages as the writing that satisfies the Statute of Frauds requirement. Moreover, parties to a trading-partner agreement ordinarily would agree not to assert any Statute of Frauds defense in case of litigation. Although neither of those drafting solutions gained universal acceptance, it is important to notice that the issue was never litigated. As the previous assignments suggest, the enactment of E-SIGN and UETA has made the issue irrelevant for future transactions.

2. The Interchange of Documents

The first two assignments of this chapter underscore the likelihood that the ambiguities in the interaction between a human and a graphical user interface will lead to uncertainty about the intent to form a contract. That problem is only the latest manifestation of the classic battle of forms that has plagued remote contracting for decades. EDI transactions for the most part avoid that problem through their use of custom-designed processes in which specified actions are adequate to trigger obligation and responsibility. For example, §1.1 of MTPAC provides that parties may communicate through a set of agreed "transaction sets" that are the sole source of obligation between the parties:

> Each party may electronically transmit to or receive from the other party any of the transaction sets listed in the Appendix, [transaction sets which the parties regularly transmit] and transaction sets which the parties by written agreement add to the Appendix (collectively "Documents"). Any transmission of data which is not a Document shall have no force or effect between the parties unless justifiably relied upon by the receiving party.

Another way that EDI reduces conflicts about communications is through the use of a "functional acknowledgment," which automatically verifies receipt of another message. Although a functional acknowledgment does not constitute a substantive response to the message received, it does create an audit trail establishing that the primary message in fact was received. Furthermore, the absence of an expected functional acknowledgment puts the party sending the primary message on notice that the primary message probably was not delivered. Section 2.2 of MTPAC provides:

> Upon proper receipt of any Document, the receiving party shall promptly and properly transmit a functional acknowledgment in return, unless otherwise specified in the Appendix. A functional acknowledgment shall constitute conclusive evidence a Document has been properly received.

A similar provision in MTPAC §2.4 precludes post hoc claims of garbling during transmission:

> If any transmitted Document is received in an unintelligible or garbled form, the receiving party shall promptly notify the originating party (if identifiable from the received Document) in a reasonable manner. In the absence of such a notice, the originating party's records of the contents of such Document shall control.

To understand the legal implications of functional acknowledgments, consider Corinthian Pharmaceutical Systems v. Lederle Laboratories, 724 F. Supp. 605 (S.D. Ind. 1989). That case did not involve EDI messages directly, but rather a functional acknowledgment sent by an interactive telephone ordering system. Lederle Laboratories permitted customers to enter orders using touch-tone telephones by keying in their orders in response to voice prompts. The case arose when Corinthian Pharmaceutical, a pharmaceutical wholesaler, learned that Lederle planned to triple the price of one of its vaccines on the next day. Corinthian immediately dialed into Lederle's telephone order system and placed an order for 1,000 vials of the vaccine. Lederle's system automatically responded to Corinthian by giving it a tracking number for the order. Some days later, however, Lederle refused to fill the order. Corinthian sued, claiming breach of contract.

The court held that there was no contract. It reasoned that the Corinthian order was an offer to buy, which Lederle had not accepted. Although Corinthian argued that the issuance of the tracking number reflected an acceptance, the court rejected this argument, properly reasoning that the number was just an administrative message, not an acceptance. For present purposes, the order tracking number is analogous to an EDI functional acknowledgment — evidence of receipt of a message, but not a substantive response to the message. The court also observed that Lederle previously had sent to Corinthian terms and conditions making it clear that no order was effective until actually accepted by Lederle. The lesson for EDI trading partners is that the trading-partner agreement should include a clear delineation of the types of actions that would constitute acceptance of an order: If the purchaser wants to rely on the functional acknowledgment as evidence of a binding contract, it needs to have that expectation spelled out in the trading-partner agreement. If the seller does not want the functional acknowledgment to operate as an acceptance, it should be explicit on that point as well.

3. Security Procedures and Message Authentication

EDI contracts are normally formed using "closed" electronic communication systems that exchange messages only among parties that have a pre-existing trading-partner relationship. The likelihood of false messages over such closed systems obviously is much less than it is in an open system like the Internet. Still, trading partners need some assurance that a message in fact comes from the purported sender. Ordinarily, EDI trading partners will use digital signatures (discussed in Assignment 18) or user IDs and password logons that attempt to restrict access to authorized parties.

Because there is no law that specifically allocates the risk of false messages, losses from such messages typically will be allocated based on the contracts between the parties. Because EDI contracts typically are formed in a business-to-business context between sophisticated parties, there is some reason to expect that sophisticated parties would agree to the same allocation of risks as the allocation the UCC sets out in Article 4A (which governs large-dollar wire-transfer transactions, the closest thing to large business-to-business electronic contracts in the UCC). Essentially, UCC Article 4A sets up a framework that makes each party to a transaction responsible for any unauthorized instructions issued using technology under its control. Specifically, if a party agrees to send messages using a particular security procedure, the other party is entitled to rely on the authenticity of messages sent using that security procedure. See UCC §§4A-201 to 4A-203. The relevant MTPAC provision (§3.3.2 and 3.3.4) follows:

3.3.2. Any Document properly transmitted pursuant to this Agreement . . . when containing, or to which there is affixed, a Signature ("Signed Documents") shall be deemed for all purposes (a) to have been "signed" and (b) to constitute an "original" when printed from electronic files established and maintained in the normal course of business.

3.3.4.   The parties agree not to contest the validity or enforceability of Signed Documents under the provisions of any applicable law relating to whether certain agreements are to be in writing or signed by the party to be bound thereby.

4.   Terms and Conditions

The most difficult problem that faces trading partners switching from paper documents to EDI messages is likely to be the realization that they never in fact have agreed on many of the terms of the transactions in which they have routinely been engaging. That problem often arises because the business issuing the purchase order prints its standard terms and conditions on its form, noting that acceptance of the purchase order constitutes agreement to these terms and conditions. The vendor, on the other hand, is likely to issue a confirmation that purports to bind the purchaser to the vendor's terms and conditions.

The "battle of the forms" problem has vexed contract law scholars and practitioners for some time, and has steadfastly resisted resolution. Old UCC §2-207 addressed that problem with a complex rule that tries to reconcile the interests of the parties with the manifest lack of assent to the fine print appearing on each party's forms. The widespread consensus that §2-207 has failed to work in practice led the committee revising Article 2 to sidestep the problem. The amended version of UCC §2-207 now simply provides that terms are included in a contract if they appear in the records of both (such as a purchase order and an invoice), or if both parties have agreed to the term even if it is not contained in a record. That provision would leave it to courts to evaluate the circumstances under which a contract has been formed in deciding whether a term should be treated as part of the parties' agreement. If the parties had not agreed on a term for a particular topic, then the provisions of Article 2 would govern the parties' contract by default.

When parties write a trading-partner agreement, however, they have a considerable incentive to address the problem specifically. It seems likely that many parties ignore the problem at that step as well, but at least some trading-partner agreements lead to a negotiated resolution of the provisions that commonly differ in traditional paper purchase orders and confirmations. A common solution is for the parties to agree that the standard terms prepared by one party will govern the trading-partner relationship, with a copy of a printed paper form containing those terms attached to the trading-partner agreement as an annex.

Relevant Glossary Entries

American National Standards Institute (ANSI)
Application Service Provider (ASP)
Brochureware
Business to Business

Business to Consumer
Digital Signature
EXtensible Markup Language (XML)
Financial EDI (FEDI)
Functional Acknowledgment
Graphical User Interface (GUI)
Hypertext
Hypertext Markup Language (HTML)
Java Applets
Killer App
Outsource
Remittance Advice Information
Secure Sockets Layer (SSL)
Shopping Bot or Shopbot
Spoof
Stock-Keeping Unit (SKU)
Supply Chain
Supply Chain Reengineering
Trading-Partner Agreement
Uniform Resource Locator (URL)
United Nations Electronic Data Interchange for Administration, Commerce,
   and Transport
Universal Product Code (UPC)
Value Chain

Problem Set 17

17.1. Wonderful Wares is a distributor of high-end housewares and out-door furniture. Aemilia Marcus, the company's founder, comes to you for advice. She explains that she has set up an EDI trading-partner relationship with a supplier called Tampa Trading. She explains that she set up this relationship herself with some inexpensive shareware that she found on the Internet and sent to Tampa Trading. The relationship had been running without incident for about a year when a dispute suddenly arose a few days ago. Employees of the Wonderful Wares receiving department opened crates from Tampa Trading that should have contained 50 teak gliders, but found instead that they contained 50 cedar gliders. Each glider costs $599. Tampa Trading has refused to exchange the gliders or to permit Wonderful Wares to return them. Aemilia wants to know if she really has to pay the listed price for gliders that she did not order and does not need. What do you advise her? Is there anything that you would like her to find out for you? Compare MTPAC §§1.1, 2.2-2.4.

17.2. Several months later, Aemilia Marcus of Wonderful Wares calls you again. The company now has become engaged in an EDI trading-partner relationship with mega-retailer GigaMart. Wonderful Wares shipped 1,000 crystal vases (at a price of $400 each) to Wichita, Kansas in response to an order it received from GigaMart. Two months later, GigaMart is refusing to pay, saying that the shipment should have gone to Ouachita, Oklahoma and that in any event the Wichita office had returned the 1,000 vases to Wonderful Wares. Aemilia explains that Wonderful Wares has received neither the vases nor any notice from the Wichita office indicating that it had refused or returned the shipment. She wants to know who will pay for the missing vases. What do you tell her? UCC §2-602(1). Compare MTPAC §§2.1 and 2.2.

17.3.   Before long, Aemilia Marcus of Wonderful Wares calls you back yet again. The company has entered an EDI trading-partner relationship with Garden Market. Wonderful Wares recently shipped 500 canvas umbrellas to Garden Market, but (as seems typical of its EDI-related transactions) Garden Market is refusing to pay for them. It says that it never ordered, nor received the umbrellas. Aemilia's staff has managed to track down the source of the confusion. Apparently, a hacker sent a phony EDI order to Wonderful Wares, spoofing Garden Market. The hacker even managed to intercept the EDI confirmation notice that Wonderful Wares sent in response and send a functional acknowledgment of that confirmation notice. In addition, it turns out that the shipping address is a storage facility completely unassociated with Garden Market. Again, Aemilia wants to know who will pay for the missing umbrellas. Compare MTPAC §§1.2, 1.3 and 1.4.

17.4.   Wonderful Wares shipped 200 cedar swings to Garden Market to fulfill an order placed by Garden Market using an EDI message. Garden Market sold the swings through its retail stores, providing its standard two-year warranty on them to its customers. After 18 months, customers begin returning the swings, complaining that they had faded to an undesirable color. Garden Market demands that Wonderful Wares accept the returns, claiming that all Garden Market's EDI contracts are subject to Garden Market's standard terms and conditions, which require vendors to provide a two-year warranty on all goods. Wonderful Wares replies that its standard terms and conditions provide for only a one-year warranty. Must Wonderful Wares accept the returned swings from Garden Market? UCC §2-314. Compare MTPAC §3.1B.

17.5.   The state of Columbia is considering requiring all bids for government contracts to be formed using EDI. What would be the practical consequences for local businesses wishing to bid on government contracts of implementing such a mandate?

Assignment 18: Digital Signatures

EDI transactions are designed to lower the transaction costs of repeated entry of data at numerous points in a single transaction. They are not designed, however, to facilitate remote transacting, over the Internet or otherwise. Thus, the basic design of EDI contributes nothing to electronic contracting, that is, contracting in which some electronic impulse serves to identify and bind a party to the transaction.

Electronic contracting is not easily accomplished simply by shifting transactions to the Internet. The ease with which individuals can send information over the Internet offers great opportunities, but at the same time presents tremendous risks in the execution of actual transactions. At the core of the problem is the difficulty of being sure that any piece of information received over the Internet has been transmitted from a particular individual.

As it happens, that problem is not technologically insoluble. Rather, since the late 1980s, the technology of digital signatures has offered a solution. Digital signatures can tie an individual's real-world identity to a particular online communication in a way that can establish not only who sent the message but also that the message has not been altered since it was sent. Given the great potential of the technology, early proponents expected the technology to sweep the Internet rapidly as a universal vehicle for identification and authentication of individual actors. For a variety of reasons, however, commercial uses of the technology have developed slowly. The technology is now used in a variety of business contexts, primarily to authenticate transmissions of data and to identify individuals within closed networks. Even by the summer of 2004 (as this material is written), however, the use of digital signatures to authenticate identities in open networks is not yet common.

Still, the importance that digital signatures already play in some business contexts, and the likelihood that digital signatures — or some related technology — will be important in the years to come warrant a brief discussion of the technology, its use in commerce, and the legislation passed to facilitate and regulate it.

A. What is a Digital Signature?

The first point is a purely terminological one: the distinction between an "electronic signature" (the object of UETA, E-SIGN, and Assignment 14) and a "digital signature" (the object of this assignment). In the normal parlance of Internet commerce, the term "digital signature" refers to a specific technology: an electronic authentication that uses asymmetric cryptography (discussed in the pages that follow). "Electronic signature" is a broader, more generic term that can describe any system for electronic authentication. For example, the term electronic signatures can cover a name in the "From"

Figure 18.1
Conventional Cryptography

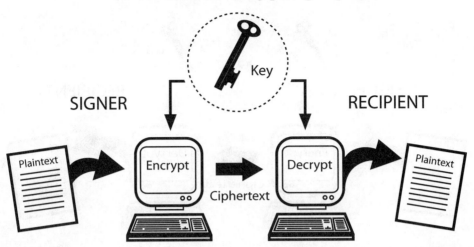

header in an electronic mail message, the digitized handwritten signature used by retail electronic point-of-sale payment systems, or a typed electronic version of a paper-based holographic signature such as "/s/ Aemilia Mann." None of those, however, would be considered a "digital" signature as that term ordinarily is used.

1. Symmetric and Asymmetric Cryptography

Various forms of encryption have been used for thousands of years. Encryption involves transforming the text to be protected into a form that is difficult to decipher without a copy of the key that was used to modify the original text. Simple cryptographic systems operate on the same principle as Captain Midnight decoder rings: A "cipher" is established to transform text into a secure form. The original text is called the "plaintext," and the transformed text is known as the "ciphertext." For example, if the cipher is the alphabet in reverse order, then the plaintext "Captain Midnight" becomes the ciphertext "Xzkgzrm Nrwmrtsg."

The process of converting plaintext to ciphertext is determined by the particular "encryption algorithm" that is used. In modern cryptography, encryption algorithms are complex mathematical functions incorporated into software that combines the plaintext with a "key" to produce the ciphertext. The key is a long, seemingly random number, the size of which is measured in bits. The unique value of the key causes the encryption algorithm to produce a unique ciphertext; if the plaintext is modified in any respect, the ciphertext will vary. The better a cryptosystem can resist attacks, the more secure it is. Keys in commercial encryption software use 40-bit, 48-bit, 56-bit, 64-bit, and 128-bit keys; the more bits, the stronger the encryption.

In conventional or symmetric cryptography (illustrated in Figure 18.1), the *same key* both encrypts and decrypts the message. The great weakness of conventional cryptography is that the key must be shared between the two parties and yet be kept secret from all others — once the shared key becomes

Figure 18.2
Asymmetric Cryptography

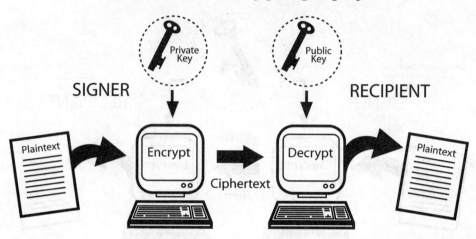

public then the system ceases to be useful. Unless the sender and recipient of the message are in direct personal contact, it is logistically challenging to find an entirely secure system for distributing the keys. That problem is compounded because the system must be refreshed periodically: Operators typically cancel old keys and issue new ones to replace them at regular intervals to reduce the chances that the key will fall into the hands of someone who is not entitled to use it.

Symmetric-key systems were commonly used during the Cold War by the United States government to protect the confidentiality of military communications. The government distributed the keys using couriers that were handcuffed to locked briefcases containing the keys. The couriers had neither the keys to the handcuffs nor the keys to the briefcases. The keys would not be used unless the courier arrived and turned over the contents of the briefcase intact. Such a system is hardly practical, however, for most commercial applications. A system that uses a single key for each pair of individuals or organizations that wish to communicate securely would require the generation and distribution of an enormous number of keys. Thus, in most cases symmetric-key cryptography is used in relatively limited environments that do not contemplate a large number of users.

Still, there are some large-scale commercial applications for symmetric-key cryptography. The first was the system of "tested telexes" that banks and their customers have been using to send messages for several decades, which is still occasionally used today for transferring funds and for sending information related to letters of credit. Telex was in widespread use around the world from the 1930s to the 1990s, but it has largely been superseded by faxes and computerized electronic communication networks. Operators typed messages into telex terminals and then transmitted them over dedicated telephone lines. A telex message would be encrypted using "symmetric key" encryption that originally required the operator to insert a tangible physical key into the telex machine. Banks shared copies of their encryption keys with other banks that kept them stored within secure locations in their funds-transfer departments. A better known and more popular application for symmetric-key encryption

Figure 18.3
Message Digest

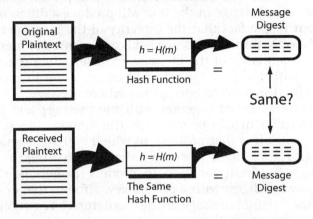

is found in the network of ATM machines today. Each terminal contains within it a symmetric key that identifies the machine to the network.

2. *Digital Signatures*

Asymmetric cryptography (illustrated in Figure 18.2) uses **two different but mathematically related keys**. One key is the "public key," which is distributed widely without regard to confidentiality; the other is the "private key," which must be kept confidential and carefully secured. (Some examples of public keys appear on the Web site for this book.) The public key may be used to encrypt information that can be decrypted only by the private key; the private key may be used to encrypt information that can be decrypted only by the public key. The key to the system is the computational oddity that, despite the mathematical relation between the two keys, it is not practicable to determine the private key from the public key.

Encryption with a public key is useful to send a confidential message to the holder of the related private key, because such a message can be decrypted and read only by a person that has the private key. Conversely, encryption with a private key is useful to send a verifiable message from the holder of the private key. Because only one person is supposed to be in control of the private key, the recipient of any message that can be decrypted with a public key should feel assured that it was sent by somebody that has the related private key.

One problem with public-key cryptography is that it often is more computationally demanding than conventional (symmetric-key) cryptography. The reason is that the mathematics of public-key cryptography are more complex than the mathematics of the typical symmetric-key cryptography system. That can make it impractical to use public-key cryptography to encrypt large files. A typical response is to reserve the use of public-key cryptography for the contexts where it is uniquely useful: Symmetric-key cryptography can be used whenever confidentiality is needed, but asymmetric-key cryptography can be used to verify the source of a document.

Message digests (illustrated in Figure 18.3) also help solve the practical problems associated with encrypting entire messages. To create a message digest, the signer runs the plain original text of the document through a program — a "one-way hash function," so-called because it makes a "hash" of the message. The result is a unique mathematical digest of an entire data file. Identical texts run through the hash function will produce the same digest, but even the smallest change in the text will produce a different digest, alerting the recipient to the fact that the integrity of the message has been compromised. If the only thing that is needed is a guarantee of message integrity, rather than confidentiality of the message text itself, then sending a message digest together with the message text will be adequate to meet the parties' needs, eliminating the need to encrypt the whole message.

Sending a message digest together with the message text is only useful, however, if the recipient can be sure that the message digest itself has not been tampered with. It is that problem to which a digital signature responds (as illustrated in Figure 18.4). To create a digital signature, the user runs the message through the hash function to produce a message digest. It then encrypts the message digest with a private key, affixing that encrypted digest to the text of the original message as the "signature." The receiving party, in turn, checks the message in three steps: (1) it produces its own message digest from the message that it has received, (2) it decrypts the encrypted message digest it received using the public key of the purported sender, and (3) it then compares the two digests. If the two-message digests match, the receiving party can be sure that the message has not been altered since it was sent. In addition, because the public key of the purported sender worked to decrypt the digest sent together with the message, the recipient also can be assured that the message was sent from somebody who has the related private key.

For a "digital signature" to function as the equivalent of a traditional manual signature, however, several additional steps are required. Most obviously, the recipient will need to have the sender's public key before it can start examining the message that it has received. Systems address that practicality through a "public key infrastructure" (discussed below), which would distribute public keys to interested parties. Second, the system for controlling access to private keys must be reliable and secure, so that only the authorized signer can use the private key to "sign" messages. That problem is largely a matter of software and hardware development, but also requires some consciousness-raising for users of the system so that they will understand the importance of security for the private keys. Finally, there must be some way to be sure that the sender does not digitally "sign" a message unless it intends to "sign" the message. As discussed in Assignment 14, a mere intention to send a message does not necessarily evidence an intent to sign the communication in a legally binding way. Thus, if software automatically affixes a digital signature to all outgoing communications from a particular computer, then the fact that a message is digitally signed may indicate nothing about the actual intent of the sender of the message.

3.   *Public-Key Infrastructure and Certification Authorities*

Systems developed to manage public keys are referred to as public-key infrastructures (PKIs). Those systems must do a variety of things, the most important of which are distributing public keys reliably and providing a reliable source of information when the security of a private key has been

Figure 18.4

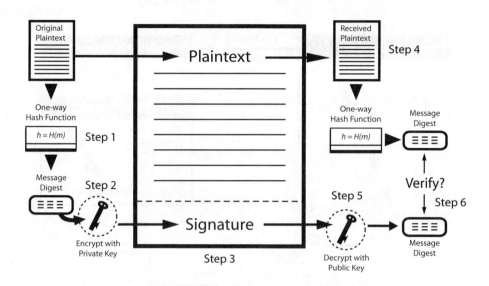

Step 1: Signer uses one-way hash function to create message digest from plaintext.

Step 2: Signer encrypts message digest with private key to create signature.

Step 3: Signer sends plaintext and signature to recipient.

Step 4: Recipient uses one-way hash function to create message digest from plaintext.

Step 5: Recipient decrypts signature with public key to create message digest.

Step 6: Recipient compares message digest generated by one-way hash function to message digest generated by public key.

compromised. The typical solution is to find a trusted third party that can take responsibility for binding an individual with a public key. The most widely discussed system involves a certification authority (CA), as illustrated in Figure 18.5. After determining that a particular individual is appropriately using a digital signature, the CA issues a "certificate," signed by the CA's private key, that contains a copy of the public key of the verified individual (the subscriber). Then anyone who wishes to verify the digital signature of the subscriber (a "relying party") may use the public key of the subscriber that appears in the certificate. A CA generally establishes policies that describe the circumstances under which it issues certificates; these policies are then published in a "certification practice statement" (CPS) or "certificate policy" that discloses those policies to any potential subscribers or relying parties.

Figure 18.5
Certification Authority

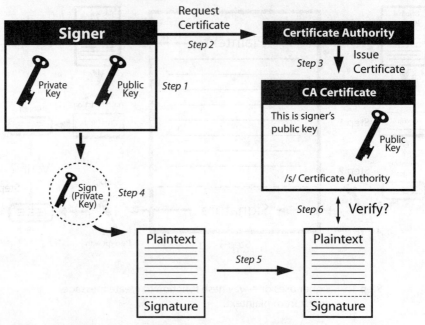

Step 1: Signer creates its own public key and private key.

Step 2: Signer requests certificate from certification
authority (CA).

Step 3: CA issues a certificate of signer's public key, signed by CA's private
key.

Step 4: Signer uses one-way hash function to create message digest from
plaintext (Step 1 from Figure 18.4) and encrypts message digest with
private key to create signature (Step 2 from Figure 18.4).

Step 5: Signer sends plaintext and signature to recipient (Step 3 from Figure
18.4).

Step 6: Recipient uses one-way hash function to create message digest from
plaintext (Step4 from Figure 18.4), decrypts signature with public key
to create message digest (Step 5 from Figure 18.4), and compares the
two message digests (Step 6 from Figure 18.4).

Subscribers and relying parties can examine those documents to assess the
reliability of certificates that the CA issues.

For a certificate issued by a particular CA to be acceptable to a prospective
relying party, the CA must establish its own trustworthiness in some way.
That trustworthiness may depend on its reputation in traditional business
transactions. Alternately, the CA may in turn be a subscriber of a higher CA
and use the certificate of the higher CA to reassure subscribers and relying
parties of its integrity. The CA at the pinnacle of the CA hierarchy is known
as a "root" CA in such a system. For example, the American Bankers
Association, the primary trade association for U.S. banks, has offered to serve

as the root CA for the financial services industry in the United States. If banks agreed to use this service, each bank would obtain a digital-signature certificate from the American Bankers Association. Each bank in turn might offer a certification service to its customers. A relying party that agreed to accept a digital signature certified by the subscriber's bank could check to make sure the bank was not a rogue CA by confirming that the bank's digital signature on the subscriber's bank-customer certificate in fact had been certified by the American Bankers Association. In the USPS NetPost service, the USPS would act as CA, individuals would have private keys stored on smart cards, and individual post offices would act as local registration agents following the same procedures used to issue U.S. passports.

The other fundamental key-management issue is how to revoke or terminate keys that have been widely distributed. A key owner may wish to revoke a public key if the security of the private key has been compromised or may have a protective policy of retiring keys after a certain period of time. In addition, the CA may wish to cancel a certificate if it becomes aware of improprieties in its issuance or at the request of the subscriber. Thus, a relying party needs to investigate the current status of a certificate before relying on it. If the CA's practice statement limits its review to the time of issuance, then there is no ongoing monitoring by the CA of the subscriber's status, which often might be problematic.

To offer a more appealing service to prospective relying parties, CAs maintain a certificate revocation list (CRL), where notices from subscribers are posted as soon as received. A prospective relying party could check that list before verifying a digital signature. Although the concept of a CRL is simple enough, the practical obstacles to implementing one that meets the needs of Internet merchants have proved to be daunting. For online commerce, it would be reasonable to expect merchants to check a CRL before completing a transaction to verify that a digital-signature certificate had not been cancelled. But the infrastructure for permitting a large number of Internet merchants to do a large number of online, realtime checks of the status of certificates is daunting — about the size of the transaction processing system they must use already for credit-card processing.

One final problem is that a CA may have a single national or even global base of operations, which makes it difficult for a single CA to have a member of its staff personally review the proof of identity proffered by an applicant seeking a digital-signature certificate. As a result, the CA may delegate the process of reviewing applications from prospective subscribers to a "local registration agent." The most effective local registration agents are likely to be those with personal knowledge of the applicant's identity, such as the applicant's employer. The need for that extra layer of interaction, however, can decrease even further the reliability of the CA's certifications.

B.   Digital Signatures in Electronic Commerce

There are many different ways to integrate digital-signature technology into electronic commerce. The simplest model does not involve commercial transactions at all. Rather, many large corporations use digital-signature technology to enhance the security of internal communications — with no intention to create legally binding contracts through those communications. When it comes to using digital signatures to create legal obligations, applications generally are classified as either "closed systems" or "open systems." A closed system limits participation to selected individuals who have been pre-screened and who have made binding commitments about their use of the signature technology. Open systems, on the other hand, facilitate the verification of digital signatures between strangers over the Internet; these are usually called "open PKI" systems.

1.   Authentication of Network Users

Many electronic commerce applications control access to resources and operations by requiring users to log on to a network with a user ID and password. After a user has logged onto a network, the security architecture of the network should ensure that the user has access to any resources that are appropriate and relevant to that user and does not have access to those in which the user has no legitimate interest. Thus, access control that employs a user ID and network password can associate an individual with particular online activities undertaken during a session while that user is logged in, but it does not create a "signature" for that user that is affixed to any particular record the user might create while accessing the network. For example, Covisint, a business-to-business exchange for the global automobile industry (discussed in detail in the next assignment), does not require members to use digital signatures either to authenticate identities or to sign documents, but instead asks for a user name and password to be entered into a graphical Web interface. Perhaps at some point in the future, Covisint will switch from the user ID and password authentication system to digital signatures, which would be more secure.

Many businesses, however, already have switched from user IDs and passwords to digital signatures as a form of network-access control. This is particularly true in the military; the U.S. military's Common Access Card represents one of the largest early adoptions of digital signature technology. If the user's private key is kept in a secure location (perhaps, as in the case of the U.S. military, stored on a smart card that can be inserted into a card reader), then digital signatures may provide a highly secure form of network-access controls. The military, for example, uses its Common Access Card both to control physical access to facilities and to control online access to secure intranets. If businesses switch from secret passwords to digital signatures as a form of network-access controls, it is not a large step to require the use of digital signatures on particular records as a substitute for manual signatures of pieces of paper.

2.   Communications Security Protocols

One of the great commercial successes of digital signatures today is the Secure Sockets Layer (SSL) communication security protocol (illustrated in Figure 18.6), commonly used to secure communications between Web sites and consumers. (Netscape originally developed this standard, but in 1999 it was modified and reissued as the "Transport Layer Security" protocol by the Internet Engineering Task Force.) Part of the key to the success of SSL in the

Figure 18.6
Secure Sockets Layer

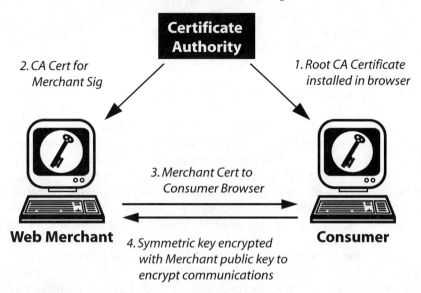

Certificate Authority

2. CA Cert for
   Merchant Sig

1. Root CA Certificate
   installed in browser

3. Merchant Cert to
   Consumer Browser

Web Merchant   4. Symmetric key encrypted
   with Merchant public key to
   encrypt communications

Consumer

marketplace seems to be that it does not perform any functions analogous to a "signature." It merely permits communications between a browser running on a personal computer and a server to be encrypted in transit, guaranteeing the confidentiality of the communications between the personal computer and the server. Thus, SSL provides some assurance to individuals visiting Web sites on the Internet that the sites are genuine merchant sites, not operated by a mere hacker masquerading as a legitimate business. The SSL service also provides assurance that transfers of information between the local computer of the customer (or "client") and the server computer of the Web site are confidential and are received intact.

Web-server applications that support electronic commerce come with software that manages the keys and the encryption processes that SSL uses in a way that is "transparent" to the visitor to the Web site. In Netscape Navigator or Microsoft Explorer, for example, the local user is alerted to the encryption only when an icon such as a key or a padlock changes or when a dialog box pops up to inform the user that a secure session will be initiated.

The SSL process runs in two separate tracks. First, an SSL certificate is placed in the browser on the user's computer, usually when the browser is first installed on the user's computer. Then the merchant site obtains a digital-signature certificate from the CA. When an SSL-enabled user contacts an SSL-enabled Web site, the server for the Web site first sends a signed copy of the server's digital-signature certificate, which the user's computer verifies. The user's computer then generates a session key that it encrypts with the Web site's public key and sends back to the server. The Web site can decrypt that key with its own private key, which then puts the Web site and the consumer in a position to use that same key to encrypt all subsequent messages sent between the local user and the Web site. Thus, the system temporarily sets up a secure channel for communication between the browser and Web site, so that credit-card information or other sensitive information cannot be misappropriated even in the unlikely event that it is intercepted. SSL uses both symmetric encryption — the merchant and the consumer are using the same key — to safeguard messages in transit, and asymmetric encryption — the merchant using the CA's public key to verify that the certificate was issued with the CA's private key — to safeguard the symmetric key while it is being exchanged.

3.   Open-Network Applications

When the commercial potential of the Internet became obvious in the early 1990s, there was tremendous optimism that a system of reliable online identities could be created for Internet commerce without the labor and delay required to build a "closed" system. It seemed easy to see that digital signatures would be the silver bullet that would permit Internet commerce to leap over earlier systems (like EDI) that used computers to process commercial transactions.

As discussed above, digital-signature technology now has a significant penetration within businesses in many industries, as a vehicle for authentication within the business's physical and network facilities. The basic problem in transacting business using digital-signature certificates to verify identity and authentication is for the two contracting partners to have a common or joint digital-signature policy. If a single market standard could gain approval by a large number of businesses — or even a critical mass of businesses in a single industry — then it would be easy for businesses to form contracts with each other by relying on each other's electronic signatures. Another possibility, at least for businesses that anticipate large numbers of contracts, would be cross-certification, in which each business would review the digital-signature policies of the other, determine that they are satisfactory, and agree to accept signatures from the other company. The difficulties of that process, however, have led all proponents of the technology to press for standardization, hoping that at some point a critical mass of businesses will coalesce around a single standard.

At one point, it seemed likely that Verisign would provide the industry standard. In the mid-1990s, Verisign was the first company to market digital-signature certificates on a large basis. An individual could submit a public key to Verisign together with the individual's name and receive from Verisign a digital-signature certificate in any of several classes (depending on the quality of the assurance of the individual's identity). Verisign's lax practices in identifying those to whom it issued certificates, however, gave it a poor reputation for reliability, which it has not yet overcome.

The most prominent recent effort is by Identrus, a venture founded in 1999 by a number of large banks from several countries: ABN AMRO, Bank of America, Bankers Trust, Barclays, Chase Manhattan, Citigroup, Deutsche Bank, and HypoVereinsbank. Identrus's core project is to facilitate reliable cross-border transactions, first among financial institutions, and ultimately more broadly among their customers. Financial institutions can avoid the problem of poor identification that plagued Verisign both because of their branch networks (which make it easy to provide physical interaction at the point at which the certificate is issued) and because of know-your-customer laws that have been strengthened since September 11. Under that system, each bank can serve as a certification authority for its customers. Wells Fargo is serving as a general certification authority for smaller banks that do not wish to establish their own certificate authorities. Identrus serves as the root certification authority for all entities in its system.

As you would expect given the discussion above, Identrus has grown slowly even with its impressive backing. Still, it does at least appear to be having a significant impact in the market. Its first major product is a system called "SimpleSign," developed with Adobe Systems, which is designed to facilitate the wholly electronic closing of financial transactions. Users can install the software on their computers, use it to obtain digital signatures, execute the relevant documents electronically, and transmit them by e-mail to other banks or businesses that use the same system. This might not be the ultimate product, but it seems quite likely that something like it will gain widespread use in the short-term future.

C. Digital-Signature Legislation

1. In the United States

The focus of this assignment is on the question of authentication, and its flip-side, the principle of non-repudiation: When has a person signed a document in such a way that a contracting partner can rely on the signature as binding, so that the purported signer cannot later repudiate the document? You will recall from Assignment 14 that neither E-SIGN nor UETA address that question. Thus, §9(b) of UETA indicates that "[t]he effect of an . . . electronic signature . . . is determined from the context and surrounding circumstances at the time of its . . . execution. . . . " The adoption of that provision in UETA (and in E-SIGN) reflected a considered — and heavily debated — determination that it was not yet practical at the time to define *any* standard of signing that would justify a bright-line rule of non-repudiation.

The promise of digital-signature technology, however, is to provide just that sort of bright-line, ironclad guarantee of authentication. Responding to the promise of the technology, an early ABA project produced the ABA Digital Signature Guidelines, which were the bases for the 1995 adoption of the Utah Digital Signature Act (DSA) and later similar statutes in Minnesota, Nevada, and Washington. Those statutes — which pre-dated UETA and E-SIGN — generally validate signatures created by digital-signature technology. Utah DSA §401 (validating only a "digital signature . . . verified by reference to the public key listed in a valid certificate issued by a licensed certification authority"). A second set of statutes, most prominently Illinois's Electronic Commerce Security Act (ECSA) and a special California statute for transactions with government agencies take a more technology-neutral approach, recognizing a class of "secure electronic signature[s]," which might or might not be created with digital-signature technology. Illinois ECSA §10-110.

The digital-signature statutes also include a substantial amount of regulation of the certification authorities (CAs) necessary for the systems to operate. For example, the statutes establish a procedure for licensing CAs. Illinois ECSA §15-115; Utah DSA §201. The statutes specify a CA's warranty of accuracy with regard to the contents of a digital-signature certificate. Illinois ECSA §15-315; Utah DSA §§302 and 303. Most importantly, the statutes generally limit the liability of the CA to a "reliance limit" that the CA specifies in the certificate in question. Utah DSA §3-309; see Illinois ECSA §15-201 (specifying that reliance on a certificate is reasonable "within any limits specified in such certificate").

The relation between those statutes and the later enactments of UETA and E-SIGN is unclear. As discussed in Assignment 14, E-SIGN §102(a)(1) excepts from preemption any state enactment of UETA. E-SIGN §102(a)(2) also excepts from preemption any state statute that

> specifies the alternative procedures or requirements for the use or acceptance (or both) of electronic records or electronic signatures . . . if . . . such alternative procedures or requirements are consistent with this [statute] . . . [and] such alternative procedures or requirements do not require, or accord greater legal status or effect to, the implementation or application of a specific technology or technical specification for . . . authenticating electronic records or electronic signatures.

It is difficult to believe that this does not preempt the Utah statute's limitation of authentication to the digital signature. (Utah, as it happens, subsequently adopted the UETA.) It is not so clear, however, that it preempts the criteria-based statutes like the Illinois ECSA, which define a relatively technology-neutral category of "secure" electronic signatures and accord more weight to them than to simple electronic signatures that are not secure. More broadly, there is no reason to think that E-SIGN would preempt the provisions of those statutes that provide for the licensing and regulation of CAs.

3. *The EU Electronic Signatures Directive*

In the European Union, some member states such as Germany and Italy enacted comprehensive, highly technical laws regulating digital signatures in much the same format as the Utah Digital Signature Act. Other member states, such as the United Kingdom, moved forward with a less invasive, more technologically neutral approach to the question of electronic-signature laws. To harmonize the law in this area and to prevent barriers to electronic commerce emerging among the member states, the EU Commission accordingly proposed a Directive, which was enacted in 1999 as the Electronic Signatures Directive (ES Directive); the provisions of the Directive were to be transposed into member state laws by July 2001. As a threshold matter, the ES Directive does not apply to electronic signatures used exclusively within closed systems, such as internal corporate networks or those whose participants are all drawn from a single industry or trade association. In that context, private agreements among the interested parties appear to provide an adequate legal framework. ES Directive recital 16.

The ES Directive is an experiment by the Commission in electronic-commerce regulation "lite." Contrary to what Americans would expect based on their perspective that the European Union is too quick to regulate and unduly skeptical of the free market, the Directive prohibits member states from imposing CA licensing requirements. The ES Directive chooses instead to encourage the development of voluntary accreditation standards and other forms of self-regulation. ES Directive art. 3. As a substantive matter, the ES Directive works much like the more modern "criteria-based" statute from Illinois. First, it provides that "advanced electronic signatures" based on "qualified certificates" and created by "secure-signature-creation devices" will be treated as equivalent to traditional signatures for legal purposes. ES Directive art. 5(1)(a). Second, following the principles of the Model Law on Electronic Commerce (the source of UETA in this country), it prohibits any member state from denying legal effect to any form of electronic signature merely because it is not an advanced electronic signature. ES Directive art. 5(2). Four annexes to the Directive provide checklists of general requirements that certificates, certification authorities, secure-signature-creation devices, and secure signature-verification must meet in order to create an advanced electronic signature. Member states are permitted to set up regulatory procedures for reviewing whether particular service providers or technologies meet the requirements sketched out in the annexes. ES Directive, art. 3(4).

The ES Directive reflects a basic element of EU electronic-commerce policy that is quite alien to the American context: a belief that consumers will refrain from participating in online markets if they do not feel confident they will be treated fairly. Thus, a major objective of the ES Directive is protection of consumers who use electronic signatures in online commerce. For example, Annex III ¶1(c) provides that a "secure-signature-creation device" must be capable of being reliably protected by the legitimate signer against the use of others. Therefore, if a signature-creation device requires the use of a private key stored on a hard drive, and member state regulators were not convinced that such a system met the requirement of reliable protection against unauthorized use by others, then signatures created using that technology would not qualify as "advanced electronic signatures" and could not be granted enhanced legal recognition. The ES Directive requires member states to enact laws making CAs liable for the accuracy of the contents of certificates they issue, although a CA may avoid liability by proving it did not act negligently in issuing a certificate. ES Directive art. 6.

Relevant Glossary Entries

Asymmetric Cryptography
Authentication System
CA Root
Certification Authority (CA)
Certification Practice Statement
Certificate Revocation List (CRL)
Cypher
Cyphertext
Closed PKI
Cryptography
Cryptosystem
Decryption
Digital Signature
Electronic Signature

Encryption
Encryption Algorithm
E-SIGN
eXtensible Markup Language (XML)
Hash Function
Key
Local Registration Agent (LRA)
Message Digest
Open PKI
Plaintext
Protocol
Public Key Infrastructure (PKI)
Secure Socket Layer (SSL)
Self-Regulation
Symmetric Cryptography
Transport Layer Security (TLS)

Problem Set 18

18.1.   Your friend Tom Taylor at tooldepot.com calls you to explain that he recently sold 200 drill bit sets to World Tool Market (WTM), using WTM's Internet interface to negotiate and execute the contract. After concluding the deal, tooldepot.com shipped 200 drill bit sets. WTM, however, refuses to pay, saying it never entered into the contract. Tom says he saved to the hard drive of his computer an electronic record that seems to be a contract signed by what appears to be WTM's digital signature. What purports to be WTM's digital signature was certified by Quick'n'Dirty Certification Authority (QND). The default settings of the browser software on the tooldepot.com computers include "Accept digital signatures certified by QND." (Mogul Software, developer of the browser used by tooldepot.com, has stock in QND.)

Before calling you, Tom went to QND's Web site and read for the first time QND's certificate practice statement. Tom was shocked to learn that QND will issue a digital-signature certificate to anyone who completes an application form and pays it $100, unless a law-enforcement agency notifies QND that the applicant is a criminal organization. QND's certificate practice statement expressly disclaims any liability to parties who rely on certificates containing inaccurate or misleading information. (Answer the questions that follow under Illinois law, Utah law, the law of a jurisdiction that has enacted the UETA but no digital-signature legislation, and under the EU Electronic Signatures Directive.)

(a)   Does tooldepot.com have a cause of action against WTM? Illinois ECSA §§5-120, 10-110, 10-115, 10-120, 10-130; Utah DSA §§401, 406; EU ES Directive art. 5; E-SIGN §102(a).

(b)   QND? Restatement (2d) of Torts §552; Illinois ECSA §§15-201, 15-310, 15-315; Utah DSA §§302, 303, 309; EU ES Directive art. 6.

(c)   The person who got a digital-signature certificate from QND impersonating WTM? Illinois ECSA §§15-210, 15-220.

(d)   How would your answers to question (a) change if the document had not been signed with an electronic signature by an impostor, but instead was an ordinary e-mail sent by an employee of WTM authorized to enter into such transactions, with a standard e-mail signature at the bottom of the message indicating the employee's name and contact information?

18.2.   Carl Eben at RFT has a number of long-standing EDI relationships with his suppliers. The major suppliers are spread throughout the United States. He recently received a proposal from Verisign offering to help establish a network of digital signatures for RFT, California Pneumatic Tools (Carl's main competitor), and their major suppliers. Carl wants to know what benefits this proposal might bring to him and what the major legal risks are that he should investigate. Can you explain to him how the process would work in practice? In addition, are there any documents that you would like to review? What would you look for in them?

18.3.   You get a call this week from Stacy Vye, your friend at Wessex Bank. Wessex Bank is setting up a digital-certificate network for its clients and will serve as its own certification authority. Stacy believes that she has an adequate form supplied by Identrus for the certification practice statement (CPS). To protect the Bank, she plans to include in the CPS a variety of detailed provisions that limit the rights of users and third parties to sue the bank. She plans to have her customers expressly agree to the CPS when they accept a certificate. She is not as sure, however, how to bind third parties. She thinks that third parties implicitly should be bound by the CPS if she posts it on the Internet and they use certificates issued after she has posted the CPS. Do you have any advice?

Assignment 19: B2B on the Internet

EDI transactions use information technology to save the costs of repeated data entry during the course of the same transaction (or set of transactions) as an asset travels through the supply chain. Digital signatures offer the potential for implementing those transactions with a reliable authentication that is electronic. Even taken together, however, those technologies still rely upon a human interaction and decision for each transaction. The combination of two new technologies offers the potential for wholly electronic transactions in which goods are bought and sold through the interaction of electronic agents on the Internet. The two intertwined technologies are the business concept of the B2B Internet exchange, a type of Web site at which one or more businesses offer to buy or sell goods or services, and XML, a sophisticated Web-based language that facilitates automated interactions between businesses.

Although business-to-consumer (B2C) Internet commerce attracted a great deal of attention in the late 1990s, most analysts studying the potential for electronic-commerce applications and technologies concluded that business-to-business Internet commerce systems would dwarf retail applications in volume of transactions. One business-to-business (B2B) Internet commerce application that seemed to have tremendous promise was an Internet marketplace or exchange that would permit all the members of an industry or sector of the economy to do business with each other more efficiently and quickly. That application could provide the same kind of advantages merchants get from a brick-and-mortar exchange, such as the exchanges typical of industries for commodities like cotton or wheat. However, a B2B Internet exchange also should be able to deliver the productivity gains from using EDI and the mass participation possible with the Internet. Businesses wishing to improve their efficiency and competitiveness could gain access to new procurement and marketing opportunities at the same time. Although price competition might intensify among vendors because purchasers could compare terms effortlessly, greater sales volumes could offset narrower profit margins, at least for the most competitive merchants.

In 1999, B2B exchanges enjoyed a brief burst of popularity with investors who assumed that markets previously untouched by electronic commerce would migrate en masse to new Internet venues. Many of the startup B2B exchanges failed almost immediately, however, in connection with the collapse of the stock market in 2001. Similarly, most of the well-capitalized and prominent exchanges of the early days have now failed. For example, Covisint was a B2B exchange started in 2000 to great acclaim by the Big Three U.S. automakers, DaimlerChrysler, Ford, and GM. Although Covisint did manage to commence operations, it ultimately was unable to justify the approximately $500 million invested in it by its founders. Covisint was sold in the summer of 2004 to Compuware for only $7 million. Similarly, EnronOnline, an Internet market created by the energy conglomerate Enron Corporation to facilitate trading in natural gas and petroleum products, was once the shining success story of B2B electronic commerce. In 2000, the first year of the site's operations, trading volume averaged $1 billion a day; by early 2001, the volume was up to $4 billion a day. Because of the accounting irregularities at the center of Enron's failure, it is difficult to be sure exactly how profitable the site was even during its heyday. It is plain, though, that the site would not have been as successful if the market had understood the true state of the financial position of that operation and of Enron itself.

But the intervening years and the potential profits from Internet transacting have seen a slow resurgence of a much larger group of smaller and more stable businesses. There now are literally thousands of businesses with some sort of B2B presence. Relatively small businesses often now use standard software packages from companies like IBM, SAP, Oracle, and Commerce One. For example, *www.Legfind.com* is a small company started by a single individual, dedicated to matching charter airplanes with businesspeople that need transportation. That small niche generated more than $20 million in revenues in 2003. At the other end of the spectrum are large and complex industry-wide exchanges like GlobalNetExchange (GNX) and WorldWideRetailExchange (WWRE). The sections that follow discuss first the various structures such an operation might take and then the legal issues that arise in drafting the necessary agreements.

A.   Structure of B2B Sites

1.   Market Models

The structure of Internet B2B sites has not settled into any simple pattern. Rather, business sites proliferate just as markets proliferate in the brick-and-mortar world. The simplest sites are "hubs" at which a single company manages its relations with its trading partners. In many of the largest cases, these involve only purchases by the hub operator. The most successful example of this model surely is Wal-Mart's Retail Link. Volkswagen — which did not join Covisint — also started a prominent market at its Electronic Supplier Link. The business proposition for those sites is the simple one that they allow the owner of the hub to manage its supply chain at a lower cost. The lower cost comes not only from the transaction cost savings of the information technology, but also because of the potential to make purchases through electronic auctions, forcing suppliers to compete directly against each other on price.

As a technological matter, however, the more ambitious sites aggregate large numbers of related purchasers and sellers in a particular area of commerce. The most common method of categorizing the different kinds of exchanges is as "vertical" or "horizontal" marketplaces. A vertical marketplace provides a venue for participants located at different points in the supply chain for a particular industry to work together. The advantage of that kind of exchange is the ability to lower the transaction costs as a particular object passes through the various stages of manufacture and distribution.

Many of the most prominent early vertical marketplaces — Covisint for the automobile industry and Chemdex for the chemical industry — have failed, but others have survived. For example, *www.wrenchead.com* provides a market for aftermarket automobile parts. It always has had a much lower profile than Covisint, but at this point in time has outlasted it. Some of the largest vertical exchanges are in the retail industry. For example, WorldWideRetailExchange is led by a consortium of 23 major retailers such as Kmart, Walgreens, Target, Tesco, and Auchan. GlobalNetExchange (GNX) is another large vertical exchange founded by Sears, Carrefour, and Oracle.

A "horizontal" market is one that provides a forum for buyers and sellers of a particular type of product or service that is used in many different vertical industries. The advantage of that type of exchange is the ability to provide a single purchasing interface across a variety of product categories. MRO.com and FindMRO.com are long-time horizontal B2B exchanges in the maintenance, repair, and operating supplies market. Alibaba.com is another prominent and successful site at which Chinese companies advertise their goods for sale. And of course eBay has moved aggressively into this area with a variety of B2B marketplaces at its site.

In either case, transactions can be implemented in a variety of ways. Some Web sites provide electronic catalogs of the goods offered for sale — often "metacatalogs" that aggregate the products of numerous different suppliers, facilitating easy comparison by potential purchasers. Others provide a vehicle for auctions at which potential purchasers or buyers can bid to provide the most favorable terms. Still others simply provide a forum for case-by-case negotiations among parties that locate each other through information available on the Web site.

2.   *Technology of a B2B Internet Exchange*

To deliver the enhanced searching, marketing, negotiating, and transaction-processing services that its members hope to receive, a B2B exchange must seamlessly incorporate many separate electronic-commerce technologies. For prospective customers to search for products, the exchange must maintain databases or grant prospective customers direct access to databases that suppliers maintain. For customers to be able to locate specific products, the description of products must be standardized just as in the EDI trading-partner relationships that Assignment 17 discusses. Robust security is necessary to prevent strangers or competitors from accessing sensitive data that suppliers are willing to display only to customers and prospective customers. Access controls are necessary to prevent unauthorized orders or modification of product information.

Some early B2B exchanges relied solely on EDI technology to streamline marketing and procurement systems. EDI standards could be combined with Internet communication systems with relatively little effort to facilitate the kind of online auctions that ESL set up among Volkswagen suppliers. Exchanges that go that route, however, can cater only to those businesses that have already gone through the painful process of reengineering their operations to accommodate that technology.

To interact with the expansive group of large and small companies that never adopted EDI, it is necessary to use newer Web-based technologies that allow companies to access information directly without the pre-arranged formatting conformities on which EDI rests. The primary technology that permits that kind of interaction is eXtensible Markup Language (XML). XML is a successor to HTML, the standard used to create Web pages. The key advance of XML is that it permits the information exchanged in Internet transactions to be organized according to the business objectives of the parties. Instead of labeling text "title" or "paragraph" as is possible with HTML, XML labels can identify blocks of text as "price" or "quantity" information. (The labels that indicate the meaning of text are called "tags" and a complete set of tags is known as a "schema." For example, the title of an HTML document is indicated by putting the tag <title> before the first word of the title and the tag </title> after the last word; the price of a product in an XML document might be indicated by putting the tag <price> before the price and the tag </price> after it.)

Once browser software implements a particular XML schema, it can recognize the difference between different terms, helping end users to organize information and generate responses. Thus, among other things, XML permits greater use of electronic searching technologies to identify potential trading partners, greater use of automated processes in negotiating the terms of transactions, and greater automation in tracking the fulfillment of transactions after deals are struck.

XML is much more flexible than EDI as a system for organizing transaction information. For an EDI message to be processed correctly, specific data fields must appear in a pre-determined order and contain no more than the allowed number of characters for a given field. For example, in a typical document it might be required that the name of the purchaser precede the street address, the street address precede the city, state, and zip code, and that no piece of address information may exceed 100 characters. By contrast, if an XML tag identifies a piece of information as "street address," then other computer systems can recognize and process the information as a street address without regard to where it appears in the document or how many characters it contains. If the musical-instrument industry develops its own standards for XML tags and agrees that <street address> </street address> will identify street addresses, then everyone in the musical-instrument industry can program their electronic-commerce software accordingly. All the individual XML tags agreed upon by the musical-instrument industry become elements in an XML schema that programmers refer to as they develop content for XML-enabled electronic-commerce applications.

To be sure, different businesses operating within the same markets still must collaborate on the definition of XML standards. The advantage over EDI is that businesses can communicate with other businesses even in the absence of a formal trading-partner relationship, something that is difficult if not impossible to accomplish in conventional EDI relationships. The implications of that are that tremendous gains are available from the broadening of consistent XML schemata. For example, suppose that some companies manufacture not only musical instruments but also medical instruments, and that the medical-instruments industry is developing XML tags independently of the musical-instruments industry effort. For example, if the medical-instruments industry agrees that <str add> </str add> tags will identify street addresses, then the company doing business in both the musical- and medical-instruments industries will have to develop a system for knowing which schema to use in coding a document and for correctly recognizing information coded using either industry's XML schema. In order to ensure that XML standards are not needlessly fragmented and that XML technologies do not become inordinately complex to implement, efforts are now being made to standardize XML schemas across industry groups. The leading initiative on that front is the Electronic Business XML (ebXML) initiative, jointly operated by the United Nations Center for Trade Facilitation and Electronic Business (UN/CEFACT) and the Organization for the Advancement of Structured Information Standards (OASIS), a technical standard–setting organization. As software companies develop specific applications, they obtain ebXML certifications, indicating that they are compatible with ebXML standards, so that companies implementing those applications can be sure that their sites will be accessible to other companies using ebXML technology in their applications.

Coupling XML technology with the RFID technology mentioned briefly in Assignment 17 creates the potential for complete end-to-end automation of business transactions, using technology that all but the smallest businesses can obtain off the shelf. As explained above, the interaction of an electronic agent of a supplier's Web site with a customer's Web site could result in an electronic purchase order from the customer. The supplier's network might transmit the information describing the products and their destination to a warehouse, where automated machinery can package the goods for shipment. If RFID tags are attached to the individual items, the shipment of the items will be noted electronically as they leave the factory and as they enter the receiving dock of the customer. The computer network of the customer, in turn, noting the data from the RFID tags, could add the products to its inventory, route them to the appropriate location, and authorize payment to the supplier.

3.   B2B Structure: Industry Operated or Third-Party Operated

The business model for a site that is a hub is an obvious one. The owner typically anticipates recapturing the cost of developing and operating the site in lower overheads for procurement or marketing, through lower prices for purchases, or through greater volumes for sales. By allowing their owners to focus on cost savings instead of fee generation, hubs have proven to be a surprisingly successful strategy for developing B2B markets. Essentially, that market allows the buyer to internalize all of the benefits of the exchange in a way that is more difficult for an exchange that contemplates a large number of unrelated buyers as customers of the exchange.

The business model for an exchange, however, is more difficult (one reason why so many of the largest exchanges have failed). The key question is whether the exchange will be organized by a consortia of industry members for their own benefit or as a neutral forum owned and operated by some third party that specializes in providing the relevant technology.

In either case, the central problem in organizing a B2B exchange is finding a way to balance the interests of its participants in an unbiased, trustworthy marketplace against the need of the exchange sponsors to recover their investment in developing and operating the exchange. The need to finance the exchange's operations creates a potential conflict of interest between those using the marketplace and those running it. That conflict is exacerbated if those running it are competitors of those using it. Several years ago, most commentators expected neutral third-party sites to be the most successful B2B exchange business models because they could avoid that conflict of interest.

But the third-party sites generally have had great difficulty, which suggests that the conflict of interest is not the most serious obstacle to a profitable B2B exchange. To be sure, the third party can offer transaction-processing technology and a centralized location to prospective members. To succeed, however, it must enroll a critical mass of buyers and sellers, who in turn would have to agree to terms under which they would pay fees adequate to finance the operations of the exchange and provide a healthy return on equity to its investors. As it turned out, prospective sellers found it easy to avoid marketplaces in which they would both pay a fee to the exchange and face significant competitive pressures to lower the prices they charge to their existing customers. Without a significant number of sellers on hand, buyers had no reason to join either. Thus, in a classic example of negative network effects, most independent exchanges were never able to give buyers and sellers an adequate reason to join the exchange.

Still, the problem of conflicts of interest is not a trivial one. Competitors naturally may be skeptical of the ability of their rivals to operate an exchange fairly. For example, General Motors, Ford, DaimlerChrysler, Nissan, and Renault all joined to create Covisint in 2000; Citroen/Peugeot joined them in 2001. Other Asian and European automakers declined to participate, however, in large part because they believe the operation of Covisint will tend to favor its original sponsors, the Big Three American automakers. That concern about potential bias is particularly compelling in the case of Covisint because one of its stated objectives is to promote online collaboration during product development cycles. During the design process, proprietary information would be sent out using a computer network controlled by competitors, so a breach of computer security might permit some members to have unauthorized access to trade secrets of their competitors. Covisint, of course, ultimately failed.

4.   Antitrust Considerations

The ink had not yet dried on the February 2000 press releases announcing the intention of General Motors, Ford, and DaimlerChrysler to create Covisint when the U.S. Federal Trade Commission announced its intention to investigate the project for possible violations of the antitrust laws. After six months of review, the FTC announced that it would suspend its investigation, reserving a right to reopen it in the future if it had reason to suspect that the operation of Covisint violated the antitrust laws. The decision to close the investigation rested in large part on the early status of the project, which made it difficult to say whether its operations would comply with the requirements of antitrust law.

The basic problem is that, although there is nothing unlawful per se about a B2B exchange, it is easy to see that the cooperative discussions incident to the operation of such an exchange could facilitate activities that violate the antitrust laws. A major FTC report on the subject identifies four main concerns. The first is the concern that an overly successful exchange could create excessive market power by buyers that would amount to an unlawful "monopsony." (A monopoly is a market with a single seller; a monopsony is a market with a single buyer.) For example, policymakers justifiably might be concerned when all three of America's largest car manufacturers formed an exchange that they might use the exchange to gain undue power over the prices their suppliers might charge. The second problem is the possibility that a decision to exclude a firm from a successful exchange might amount to an unlawful group boycott. That problem is likely to cause most large B2Bs to maintain open and equal membership policies. The third problem is the possibility of information sharing and collusion. For example, two vendors on a B2B exchange might share information about the prices that they would charge and agree upon fixed minimum prices that they would maintain. The final problem is exclusivity agreements. The flip-side of exclusionary agreements, these would be agreements designed to make it hard for a member to leave an exchange by committing members to significant up-front fees or the like. Those agreements cause a concern because they make it difficult for competing exchanges to gain ground.

Competitors that join as members of B2B exchanges must develop internal policies and procedures to ensure that their employees do not engage in unlawful conduct. Among other things, they need to ensure that members exercise independent judgment in setting prices and other terms for transactions. That may be more difficult than it sounds, given the importance of cooperative standard-setting efforts to the success of a process as complex as building and operating a B2B exchange. Most standard-setting organizations employ antitrust counsel to monitor discussions precisely because the dividing line between legitimate and illegitimate information sharing in this area is so difficult for engineers and managers to discern.

Most of the larger sites have formal policies to deal with this issue. For example, consider the following excerpt from the GNX site (a portion of an agreement to which all participants are bound):

> It is the policy of GNX that the GNX Exchange not be used by any company to further any anti-competitive or collusive conduct, or to engage in other activities that could violate any antitrust or competition law, regulation, rule or directives of any country (collectively "Antitrust Laws") or otherwise impair full and fair competition.
>
> It is also the policy of GNX to provide access to the GNX Exchange to all participants in the retail industry who meet the terms and conditions for access. Those terms and conditions for access are objective, reasonable, and designed to encourage and preserve the ability of all participants in the retail industry to compete vigorously and pursue their individual competitive advantages on such matters as quality, service and price.
>
> Company acknowledges that its participation in the GNX Exchange is subject to the Antitrust Laws and Company agrees to comply fully with the Antitrust Laws. Company agrees that it will not use the GNX Exchange, directly or indirectly, to

reach or attempt to reach agreements or understandings with one or more of its competitors to: (a) set or establish minimum or maximum prices, or standardize the method by which prices are calculated; (b) allocate any market by geography, customer, product or any other means; (c) reduce output, production rates, product development or innovation in any market; (d) engage in a group boycott of one or more customers, suppliers or buyers for any reason; or (e) further or attempt to further any anti-competitive conduct.

B.   Terms and Conditions of Exchange Transactions

The technological and business complexities of a B2B site are implemented by agreements among the parties that agree to participate. The sections that follow discuss some of the most important issues in drafting such an agreement.

1.   Role of the Exchange and Its Members

From the perspective of the exchange, perhaps the most important thing in the agreement is to clarify the role of the exchange. Just as eBay in its agreements distances itself from the conduct of underlying parties to the transactions it facilitates, the typical exchange agreement includes a disclaimer like the following excerpt from the WWRE Usage Agreement:

> WWRE is a venue through which users can transact. Users decide in their individual capacities with whom to do business. WWRE is not a party to any transaction entered into upon the Site. WWRE does not set nor endorse the price, contract terms, quality, safety, conformance or legality of the products advertised or offered for sale, the ability of sellers to sell products or the ability of buyers to buy products. WWRE cannot and does not control whether sellers will complete the sale of products they offer. WWRE is not responsible with respect to payment or collection for orders made and bids placed on the Site.

Similarly, a typical site will include a detailed disclaimer of liability on the part of the exchange. The following disclaimer is from the WWRE site. (The all-capitals typeface reflects state laws under which certain disclaimers are effective only if they are set out in a contrasting typeface.)

> IN NO EVENT SHALL THE WWRE, NOR ANY OFFICER, AFFILIATE, DIRECTOR, SHAREHOLDER, AGENT, SUBCONTRACTOR (INCLUDING WITHOUT LIMITATION TECHNOLOGY PROVIDERS AND SUPPLIERS) ACTING IN ITS CAPACITY OF PROVIDING SERVICES TO WWRE, OR EMPLOYEE BE LIABLE TO ANY USER OR ANY THIRD PARTY FOR ANY DIRECT, INDIRECT, INCIDENTAL, SPECIAL, PUNITIVE, OR CONSEQUENTIAL DAMAGES, OR LOST PROFITS, EARNINGS, OR BUSINESS OPPORTUNITIES, OR EXPENSES OR COSTS, EVEN IF ADVISED OF THE POSSIBILITY THEREOF, RESULTING DIRECTLY OR INDIRECTLY FROM, OR OTHERWISE ARISING (HOWEVER ARISING, INCLUDING NEGLIGENCE) OUT OF: THE USE OF THE SITE BY THE USER, INCLUDING, BUT NOT LIMITED TO, DAMAGES RESULTING FROM OR ARISING OUT OF SUCH USER'S RELIANCE ON

THE SITE AND/OR THE EXCHANGE, OR THE MISTAKES, OMISSIONS, INTER-RUPTIONS, ERRORS, DEFECTS, DELAYS IN OPERATION, NON-DELIVERIES, MISDELIVERIES, TRANSMISSIONS, EAVESDROPPING BY THIRD PARTIES, OR ANY FAILURE OF PERFORMANCE OF THE SITE AND/OR THE EXCHANGE; ANY AGREEMENT ENTERED INTO BETWEEN ANY USER AND ANY THIRD PARTY (OR THE NEGOTIATIONS OR DISCUSSIONS CONDUCTED IN ANTICIPATION OF ANY SUCH AGREEMENT), WHETHER OR NOT SUCH THIRD PARTY IS A THIRD PARTY PROVIDER AS DEFINED IN THIS USAGE AGREEMENT; THE TERMINA-TION OR SUSPENSION OF A USER'S ID AND PASSWORD BY THE WWRE PUR-SUANT TO THE TERMS AND CONDITIONS; THE FAILURE, OR ALLEGED FAILURE, OF ANY PRODUCT OR SERVICE PURCHASED OR TRANSFERRED PUR-SUANT TO THE EXCHANGE TO CONFORM TO ANY SPECIFICATIONS OR TERMS, WHETHER PUBLISHED ON THE EXCHANGE OR NOT; THE BREACH, OR ALLEGED BREACH, OF ANY WARRANTY, EXPRESS OR IMPLIED, RELATING TO ANY SUCH PRODUCT, SERVICE OR SHIPMENT; OR GOVERNMENT RESTRIC-TIONS, STRIKES, WAR, ANY NATURAL DISASTER OR FORCE MAJEURE, OR ANY OTHER CONDITION BEYOND THE WWRE'S REASONABLE CONTROL. WWRE'S LIABILITY TO ANY USER OR ANY THIRD PARTY IN ANY CIRCUMSTANCES IS LIMITED TO THE GREATER OF (A) THE AMOUNT OF TRANSACTION FEES PAID BY SAID USER OR PARTY IN THE ONE MONTH PERIOD PRIOR TO THE ACTION GIVING RISE TO LIABILITY, OR (B) $1000. Some states do not allow the limita-tion of liability for consequential or incidental damages, so the foregoing limita-tion may not apply to you.

2.   Terms and Conditions

Just as with EDI trading-partner relationships, there is a possible "battle of the forms" problem if B2B exchanges do not require all members to agree to a stan-dard set of terms and conditions governing transactions. The exchange might be silent as to the terms and conditions of individual transactions, leaving the parties to form their own agreements; it might provide default terms that apply in the absence of a contrary agreement; or it might impose mandatory terms. The WWRE site, for example, simply states: "The specific terms and conditions of each transaction (such as pricing, warranties, delivery, etc.) entered into through the Exchange are established between the buyer and seller."

Other sites, however, include detailed terms. The GNX site, for example, includes detailed terms for auction transactions, sales of services, and sales of perishables. Similarly, the FindMRO.com "Terms of Sale" include standard, mandatory provisions for all transactions executed using its exchange. The contract includes shipping terms that allocate responsibility for the costs of shipment as well as the risk of loss of goods during transit (with a consequent duty to secure insurance for the goods in transit). The contract also specifies a set of standard payment options — including credit cards for businesses that have not already been pre-approved to receive 30 days' credit.

3.   Authentication

B2B exchanges are a common use of the digital-signature technology dis-cussed in Assignment 18. They also, however, often still rely on simpler user ID/password authentication. In either event, the agreements are likely to include provisions that allocate the risk of loss from forged orders. The typical rule, as you might expect, is that each party is responsible for losses from orders issued using its logon information:

> User IDs and passwords are confidential and proprietary. It is a violation of the Terms and Conditions for a User to disclose its password or share its ID or password with any unauthorized third parties, or to use its ID or password for any unauthorized purpose. Each User, and not WWRE, is solely responsible for any unauthorized use of User's ID or password.

4.   *Payment*

The logic of speed and efficiency that underlies the B2B exchange model would seem to require that the exchange would process not only orders for goods and services but also payments for them. Surprisingly, this is quite unlikely. Rather, most agreements disclaim any responsibility for payment and at most obligate the parties to pay each other for transactions at the site. The reason is that it remains surprisingly difficult to integrate business purchasing systems and business payment systems. Even though business-process reengineering is supposed to result in breaking down "silos" within which different administrative units of a corporation operate as distinct and insular entities, it has not yet proved possible to break down the barriers that separate procurement from payment. As a practical matter, the principal difficulty seems to be that the information technologies that process electronic payments antedate the information technologies that process purchase orders. Because different groups of companies developed them at different times, those technologies generally involve different software or hardware applications that are not compatible.

A technical standard known as financial EDI (FEDI) has been developed to help businesses integrate their automated accounts payable and receivable functions with electronic funds-transfer functions, but this standard has not yet been widely adopted in the United States (or elsewhere). FEDI consists of adding a text attachment to an electronic funds-transfer message that is being processed through "automated clearing houses" (an ACH payment). (You will hear more about ACH payments in Assignment 27; for present purposes, it is enough to know that it is a method of making electronic payments, most familiar for its use to make direct deposits and to debit payments automatically.) This is similar to the process of attaching files to e-mail messages. Here, the payment message (which actually moves the money from the payor's bank to the payee's bank), is like the e-mail message, and the attachment (the remittance advice explaining the payment), is the attached document. After the payee's bank credits its customer's account, it forwards the remittance advice message on to the customer. Part of the resistance to using FEDI has come from financial institutions' unwillingness to upgrade their electronic funds-transfer systems to support FEDI transactions. Part is attributable to the inability of most businesses to process automatically remittance information provided in electronic form by their trading partners. As discussed more extensively in Assignments 26 and 27 the result of the lack of uniformity in methods of processing payment information is that paper checks are still used to make most business-to-business payments in the United States. Surprisingly, that remains true whether the transaction takes place on a B2B exchange or not.

5. Information Practices

To gain the confidence of prospective members, a B2B exchange must have a clear policy governing what data it will collect, how it will use that data, and how members can force the exchange to comply with that policy. There is an inherent conflict of interest between the sponsor of a B2B exchange and its members with regard to what data is collected and how that data is used. That conflict mirrors the conflicts of interest discussed above with regard to the legal form of the exchange. In this context, the sponsor of the exchange would like to collect as much information as possible (e.g., what information members browsed, both with and without completing a transaction; what information members browsed before making changes to the terms under which they offered goods or services to prospective purchasers on the site; and what changes in traffic on the site result from modifications to vendor information). By contrast, members of the exchange would like to have the exchange collect as little information as possible about their own activities on the site, while leaving the members free to collect as much data as is feasible. Any exchange that expects to gain the trust of its members must impose some credible limits both on its own data use and collection and on that of its members.

A related problem arises from the potential access to information that users gain from the site. Given the obvious potential for anti-competitive activity related to an exchange, it is important that the agreement contain firm provisions barring uses that would raise antitrust concerns.

GNX's policy is representative:

> Confidential Information; Use of Content. Company's "Confidential Information" shall include all information that is treated by Company as confidential, including without limitation, all: (a) content, pricing information and other materials which Company or any of Company's Authorized Users supply, post or otherwise provide to GNX in connection with this Agreement and (b) information which Company or any of Company's Authorized Users provide to other users to facilitate transactions occurring on the GNX Exchange. GNX "Confidential Information" shall include all information that is treated as confidential by GNX, including without limitation, all: (a) technology (including hardware and software) used to operate the GNX Exchange; and (b) technical information (including, without limitation, results of any operational or performance testing of the GNX Exchange whether conducted by GNX or Company), non-public training materials and operational, business, pricing and financial information of GNX. Confidential Information of a party shall not include any information that: (a) is known to the party receiving such information at the time of disclosure; (b) is or becomes generally known to the public other than through a breach of this Agreement; (c) is independently developed by the party receiving such information without reliance on or use of such information; or (d) is rightfully provided to the party receiving such information by a third party not subject to an obligation of confidentiality.

Each party shall take commercially reasonable precautions to safeguard the confidentiality of the other party's Confidential Information and shall not use or disclose such Confidential Information except as may be provided in this Agreement. Each party may disclose Confidential Information of another party to its employees, contractors and agents who have a need to know such information in connection with the conduct of business on the GNX Exchange, provided that each such employee, contractor or agent has agreed to be bound by confidentiality obligations similar to those contained in this Agreement. Each party acknowledges that any unauthorized use or disclosure of Confidential Information of the other party may cause irreparable damage to the other party or others. If an unauthorized use or disclosure of Confidential Information occurs, the party making the unauthorized disclosure or use shall immediately notify the other party and any other affected parties, and shall, at its own expense, take commercially reasonable steps to recover such Confidential Information and prevent subsequent unauthorized use or disclosure thereof. If Confidential Information is required to be disclosed under any law, statute, rule, regulation or policy of any country, or any instrumentality or political subdivision thereof (collectively, "Laws"), the party who is requested to disclose such information shall notify the other party which provided such information prior to disclosure and shall reasonably cooperate with the other party at the other party's expense to obtain an appropriate protective order or other assurance that confidential treatment will continue to be accorded such information.

GNX may disclose Confidential Information and other information and materials provided by a company ("Content") to other companies using the GNX Exchange who are designated through use of the GNX Exchange to be provided access to such Content. Company and other companies using the GNX Exchange receiving Content from others shall maintain the confidentiality of any confidential information provided and agree to use the Content solely for the purpose for which it was provided. GNX is not responsible for any confidentiality breach committed by a company using the GNX Exchange. GNX may extract information, in aggregated form only and in a form which does not specifically identify a company or a specific transaction (or enable this information to be derived when combined with other data) ("Aggregated Data"), from Content and other data collected through use of the GNX Exchange. GNX may only provide Aggregated Data to others for the purpose of increasing market awareness, adoption and utilization of GNX services. GNX may publish certain registration information (including company name and contact information) in a trading partner directory available only to other users of the GNX Exchange. GNX will not disclose a company's registration information to third parties for sales and marketing purposes without the company's consent.

Relevant Glossary Entries

Automated Clearing House (ACH)
Bandwidth
Biztalk
Business to Business
Business to Consumer
Clickwrap Terms
ebXML
Electronic Data Interchange (EDI)
End user

eXtensible Markup Language (XML)
Financial EDI (FEDI)
Horizontal Exchange
IP Address
Maintenance, Repair, and Operations (MRO)
Network Effect
Organization for the Advancement of Structured Information Standards
   (OASIS)
Schema
Silo
Supply Chain
Trading-Partner Agreement
United Nations Center for Trade Facilitation and Electronic Business
Vertical Exchange
Web Server

Problem Set 19

19.1.   Several leading manufacturers of textiles recently decided to set up
a B2B Internet exchange for the textile fashion market. They have agreed to
call this exchange "Textrade.com." They hope to offer an integrated "supply-
chain-management" service to members of the exchange, permitting them to
adopt "just-in-time" inventory systems to streamline their production
processes. In addition, they hope to offer global marketing and customer support systems to buyers and sellers. The organizers have asked you for advice
as to the major legal issues that the exchange needs to consider as they decide
how to organize this new exchange. What do you say?

19.2.   In connection with the preparation of a usage agreement for
Textrade.com, the client asks if the usage agreement should specify the terms
of the underlying agreements of purchase and sale (items like warranties, disclaimers of liability, insurance requirements, and similar "boilerplate" issues).
Your client suggests to you that "it sounds like a good idea to save everybody
the wasted energy of agreeing on those things. Wouldn't it just save legal fees
for everybody if we included those terms for the businesses that use our site?"
What do you say? Would your answer differ if your client was designing a hub
rather than an exchange through which it would not itself be purchasing and
selling goods?

19.3.   After Textrade.com was established, it rapidly gained members.
Soon many major U.S. buyers and sellers of textiles and textile inputs became
members of the exchange. One day when he was browsing different product
offerings posted on Textrade.com, Ned Nickerson, president of Ned's
Neckwear Co., located in Clear Lake, Texas, discovered Simply Silk, a supplier
located nearby in Pasadena, Texas. Ned hopped into his pickup truck right
away, and drove over to Pasadena to introduce himself to Ian Anderson, president of Simply Silk. Ned and Ian became acquainted over a glass of iced tea
on the veranda behind the Simply Silk plant, and Ned signed a large supply
contract on the spot. Does Textrade.com have a right to complain that the
agreement was executed off the exchange? Does your answer depend on the

way that Textrade.com generates revenues to cover its costs? Consider §§6 and 7 of the WWRE Agreement (available at the Web site for the text).

19.4. ABC Industries, a clothing manufacturer, purchased 25,000 yards of velvet fabrics from Finished Fabrics, a Scottish textile converter. The president of ABC Industries had been looking for a supplier of velvet for some time through conventional means. Unable to find a supplier at a suitable price, he allowed his IT department to set up an electronic agent, which quickly located a posting at Textrade.com from Finished Fabric's New Jersey subsidiary, at a price about 20 percent of the typical prices listed in Scotland (about € 5). Months later, when the fabric had not arrived, ABC Industries complained. Finished Fabrics at that point explained that the posting had been a typographical error, that the actual price was € 25 a yard, that no human employee of either party would have taken the posting seriously, and that Finished Fabrics would be happy to honor the contract at the actual price of € 25 a yard. The president of ABC Industries admits that he was surprised at the low price, but explains that he did not personally review the contract until some time later and relied on the IT department's planning in the electronic indication that the fabric would be forthcoming. He thinks a contract is a contract and wants you to enforce the contract. Can you enforce the contract? UCC §2-204.

19.5. A hacker steals the user ID and password of Simply Silk from the TexTrade Web site and uses it to engage in transactions selling raw silk to Finished Fabrics. After Finished Fabrics pays the impostor, it becomes disgruntled when Simply Silk does not ship the fabric. Does Simply Silk have to ship the raw silk? If so, is Textrade.com liable? (Consider the relevant provisions at the GNX and WWRE sites.)

19.6. Shortly after Ned's Neckwear joined Textrade.com in 2000, it noticed a small but significant increase in its sales volume. In 2001, however, Ned's Neckwear noticed a decrease in sales volume that more than offset the earlier gains it had enjoyed. Ned's Neckwear suspected that the decrease was not related to the general level of demand for ties, but rather was caused by something happening at the Textrade.com site. Ned's Neckwear hired Keith Mitchell, a former computer hacker who now works as a computer security consultant (following his release from prison where he served several years for computer crimes). Keith quickly discovers that Tim's Ties, a major competitor of Ned's Neckwear, appears to have devised a system to monitor all traffic on the exchange. Tim's Ties analyzes traffic on the Textrade.com site, identifies the terms at which its competitors are making offers, and then modifies its own terms to make sure it undercuts competitors on the exchange. What should Ned do? How is this issue dealt with in the agreements for WWRE and GNX? Is the exchange responsible? Should it be?

Section C.   Sales of Intangibles

Assignment 20:   Transactions in Information

Although "information" has many different meanings and is used in many different contexts, its importance for this discussion is that it often is compiled into large databases, which are the subject of various types of transactions. Those transactions are difficult under U.S. law, because the United States does not recognize any substantial ownership right in a collection of data. That is not always the case in other countries. In Europe, for example, the European Union's 1996 directive required its member states to create a new "sui generis" intellectual property right in databases. Opponents in the United States, however, successfully argued that a new intellectual-property right in data would give too much power to the collectors of information.

Thus, at least for the time being, U.S. businesses with significant investments in data have a limited ability to exploit the value in their databases. To be sure, there is nothing to prevent them from granting third parties a right to use the data, usually through some form of license. However, the rights of a licensor of information are considerably less than the rights of a property owner, largely because of the licensor's inability to enforce claims to the data against third parties. Among other things, the limited protections under the law lead to an increased emphasis on safeguarding the physical security of the data and increased concern about the reliability of those to whom they license information.

A.   Special Characteristics of Information

As a matter of economic theory, information differs in several ways from most other forms of property.

- Information is often characterized as a "public" good, because it is "nonrivalrous" (it can be consumed by one person without leaving any less for anyone else) and "nonexcludable" (one user cannot necessarily exclude other users). One way to deal with what would otherwise be public goods, such as new ideas, is to grant intellectual-property rights in them that make it possible to exclude others.
- Information is also an experience good, which means that it must be consumed in order for a consumer to know what it is. The difficulty that feature raises for business transactions is that the value of information often can be displayed only by releasing the information, at which point there is nothing left to sell. (That characteristic often is described as "Arrow's Paradox.")

- Although information often is expensive to create or collect, it is almost costless to copy and distribute it (at least if it is stored in digital form).

- Information markets often are characterized by strong "network effects," the most important of which is that each person that joins the network bestows a benefit on others by increasing the value of the network to other users. For example, e-mail programs became much more valuable in the late 1990s because each person that started using them made them more valuable for those already using them and for others who had not yet begun using them.

- Information plays a central role in sustaining economic, social, and political institutions, which means that its circulation often implicates laws and values unrelated to commerce (the most obvious of which is the First Amendment).

Collectively, this means that many of the conventions and norms that regularly apply to other commercial assets do not apply to database assets. As a result, commercial doctrines that facilitate trade in more conventional business assets often do not apply readily to information assets.

B.   Information in Internet Commerce

Collections of information were important to commerce long before the invention of the computer. But computerization has increased the volume and scope of such collections, as well as the business uses for them. Moreover, recent years have witnessed great advances in the technology for building databases and analyzing the data that they contain. The consequent ease of collecting and analyzing data has led, most prominently, to a controversial and highly visible increase in various types of data mining and customer profiling, as discussed in Chapter 3.

Not surprisingly, the increased use and visibility of databases has resulted in frequent disputes regarding the rights and obligations of those in control of databases.

For example, one major conflict involved the "WHOIS" database, which Network Solutions, Inc. (NSI) created while it had the exclusive right to register Internet domain names. When a new Internet governance structure was created, legislators, businesses, and the public asserted widely divergent views as to the legal status of data NSI had collected in the process of registering domain names. After intense negotiations among NSI, the nascent ICANN, and the U.S. Department of Commerce, NSI managed to retain control over the WHOIS database. The Internet activist community has decried that resolution of the dispute, believing that the WHOIS database belongs to the public and should not be treated as NSI's private property.

Probably the most visible single conflict arose after the bankruptcy of Internet toy store Toysmart.com. Shortly after its bankruptcy filing, Toysmart.com began selling off its assets, including its customer data. A firestorm of controversy erupted, because Toysmart.com's privacy policy had asserted that "[p]ersonal information voluntarily submitted by visitors to our site . . . is never shared with a third party." The Federal Trade Commission and dozens of state attorneys general intervened in the bankruptcy proceeding to prevent the customer data from being sold in contravention of that policy. In the end, Disney (a shareholder of Toysmart.com) bought the database and destroyed it. That outcome protected the privacy rights in that case, but it left open the question of what might happen to customer data collected by failed dot-com companies that had less restrictive privacy policies posted on their Web sites (or that had less well-capitalized and reputationally motivated shareholders).

C. Legal Protections for Information

Although the primary use of many databases is to facilitate the internal operations of a business, businesses also often seek to exploit a collection of data by permitting third parties to use the data. The sections that follow explore a variety of legal claims that the database proprietor could advance. As they suggest, it would be an exaggeration to say that there is no possibility of legal recourse, but there certainly is not much of one.

1. Copyright

U.S. copyright law protects various types of work of original authorship, one of which is "compilations." 17 U.S.C. §103. A "compilation" results from a process of selecting and arranging preexisting material of all kinds, without regard to whether the individual items in the collection could have been copyrighted. Copyright protection, however, extends only to the author's contribution of something original in the selection and arrangement of the material. It emphatically does not extend to the preexisting material itself, which is to say, the information in the database. For example, the Supreme Court held in Feist Publications, Inc. v. Rural Tele. Serv. Co., 499 U.S. 340, 344 (1991) that copyright protection did not protect a White Pages telephone book — an alphabetical database of names, addresses, and phone numbers of persons living in a defined geographic area. Thus, a competing publisher was free to create a new telephone book by using information from the plaintiff's work. In the course of its opinion, the Court firmly rejected the notion that copyright protection gave any weight to the "sweat of the brow" theory theretofore embraced by several lower courts.

Notwithstanding *Feist*, there is some "thin" protection for the creators of such works, to the extent that the creator of a database can show that it has made an expressive contribution in the way that the data is selected, arranged, or organized. Thus, even under *Feist* it is unlawful to copy an entire database. That "thin" protection, however, does not extend to the data itself. Thus, it ordinarily is perfectly permissible for a third party to take data from a database and use the data for its own purposes. Indeed, it ordinarily is lawful even to resell the data to third parties, assuming that the data reseller has repackaged the data in a way that removes any of the expressive aspects of the original selection and arrangement of data. For example, the Second Circuit has held that Matthew Bender did not violate West's copyright when it extracted cases from West's database. See Matthew Bender & Co. v. West Publishing Co., 158 F.3d 696 (2d Cir. 1998).

2. Trade Secret

At first glance, trade-secret law appears a promising tool for the proprietor of a commercial database, because it generally protects "information." The difficulty is that it protects information only if it is kept secret. Specifically, the Uniform Trade Secrets Act (UTSA) (adopted in more than 40 states) defines a "trade secret" as:

information, including a formula, pattern, compilation, device, method, technique, or process, that:

(i) derives independent economic value, actual or potential, from not being generally known to, and not being readily ascertainable by proper means by, other persons who can obtain economic value from its disclosure or use, and

(ii) is the subject of efforts that are reasonable under the circumstances to maintain its secrecy.

UTSA §1(4). Under that definition, the owner that licenses a database to a third party often would be unable to claim that it had used adequate efforts to keep the data secret. Even if the licensor released the data to the third-party licensee in an encrypted form or otherwise hindered access of third parties, it would be difficult for the licensor to claim trade-secret protection if a third party obtained the data from the licensee.

3. Misappropriation

A third possibility is the developing common-law tort of misappropriation. The boundaries of that tort remain quite unclear, but the following case illustrates its potential in this context.

National Basketball Association v. Motorola, Inc.

105 F.3d 841 (2nd Cir. 1997)

WINTER, Circuit Judge:

Motorola, Inc. and Sports Team Analysis and Tracking Systems ("STATS") appeal from a permanent injunction. . . . The injunction concerns a handheld pager sold by Motorola and marketed under the name "SportsTrax," which displays updated information of professional basketball games in progress. The injunction prohibits appellants, absent authorization from the National Basketball Association and NBA Properties, Inc. (collectively the "NBA"), from transmitting scores or other data about NBA games in progress via the pagers, STATS's site on America On-Line's computer dial-up service, or "any equivalent means."

The crux of the dispute concerns the extent to which a state law "hot-news" misappropriation claim based on International News Service v. Associated Press, 248 U.S. 215, (1918) ("INS"), survives preemption by the federal Copyright Act and whether the NBA's claim fits within the surviving INS-type claims. We hold that a narrow "hot-news" exception does survive preemption. However, we also hold that appellants' transmission of "real-time" NBA game scores and information tabulated from television and radio broadcasts of games in progress does not constitute a misappropriation of "hot news" that is the property of the NBA. . . .

I. BACKGROUND

The facts are largely undisputed. Motorola manufactures and markets the SportsTrax paging device while STATS supplies the game information that is transmitted to the pagers. The product became available to the public in January 1996, at a retail price of about $ 200. SportsTrax's pager has an inch-and-a-half by inch-and-a-half screen and operates in four basic modes: "current," "statistics," "final scores" and "demonstration." It is the "current" mode that gives rise to the present dispute. In that mode, SportsTrax displays the following information on NBA games in progress: (i) the teams playing; (ii) score changes; (iii) the team in possession of the ball; (iv) whether the team is in the free-throw bonus; (v) the quarter of the game; and (vi) time remaining in the quarter. The information is updated every two to three minutes, with more frequent updates near the end of the first half and the end of the game. There is a lag of approximately two or three minutes between events in the game itself and when the information appears on the pager screen.

SportsTrax's operation relies on a "data feed" supplied by STATS reporters who watch the games on television or listen to them on the radio. The reporters key into a personal computer changes in the score and other information such as successful and missed shots, fouls, and clock updates. The information is relayed by modem to STATS's host computer, which compiles, analyzes, and formats the data for retransmission. The information is then sent to a common carrier, which then sends it via satellite to various local FM radio networks that in turn emit the signal received by the individual SportsTrax pagers. . . .

The NBA's complaint asserted [that the use of the pager was tortious misappropriation of information related to its games. The trial court found in favor of the NBA, but stayed the injunction pending appeal.] . . .

II. THE STATE LAW MISAPPROPRIATION CLAIM

. . . The issues before us are ones that have arisen in various forms over the course of this century as technology has steadily increased the speed and quantity of information transmission. Today, individuals at home, at work, or elsewhere, can use a computer, pager, or other device to obtain highly selective kinds of information virtually at will. International News Service v. Associated Press, 248 U.S. 215 (1918) ("*INS*"), was one of the first cases to address the issues raised by these technological advances, although the technology involved in that case was primitive by contemporary standards. INS involved two wire services, the Associated Press ("AP") and International News Service ("INS"), that transmitted news stories by wire to member newspapers. INS would lift factual stories from AP bulletins and send them by wire to INS papers. INS would also take factual stories from east coast AP papers and wire them to INS papers on the west coast that had yet to publish because of time differentials. The Supreme Court held that INS's conduct was a common-law misappropriation of AP's property. [Ed.: Notice that the Court decided *INS* at a time when the Court still exercised an authority to articulate a general federal common law, two decades before the decision in Erie Railroad Co. v. Tompkins, 304 U.S. 64 (1938).] . . .

[Relying on *Feist*, the court started its discussion by rejecting any claim that the information Motorola used infringed the NBA's copyrights in the television and radio broadcasts of the games. It then turned to the preemption question.] . . .

When Congress amended the Copyright Act in 1976, it provided for the preemption of state law claims that are interrelated with copyright claims in certain ways. Under [Copyright Act §301], a state law claim is preempted when: (i) the state law claim seeks to vindicate "legal or equitable rights that are equivalent" to one of the bundle of exclusive rights already protected by copyright law under [Copyright Act §106] — styled the "general scope requirement"; and (ii) the particular work to which the state law claim is being applied falls within the type of works protected by the Copyright Act under Sections 102 and 103 — styled the "subject matter requirement." . . .

We turn, therefore, to the question of the extent to which a "hot-news" misappropriation claim based on INS involves extra elements and is not the equivalent of exclusive rights under a copyright. [Ed.: A claim that involves extra elements is not preempted because it is not covered by the general scope requirement described above.] Courts are generally agreed that some form of such a claim survives preemption. . . .

. . . The crucial question, therefore, is the breadth of the "hot-news" claim that survives preemption.

In INS, the plaintiff AP and defendant INS were "wire services" that sold news items to client newspapers. AP brought suit to prevent INS from selling facts and information lifted from AP sources to INS-affiliated newspapers. One method by which INS was able to use AP's news was to lift facts from AP news bulletins. Another method was to sell facts taken from just-published east coast AP newspapers to west coast INS newspapers whose editions had yet to appear. . . . [The Supreme Court in *INS*] characterized INS's conduct as amounting to an unauthorized interference with the normal operation of complainant's legitimate business precisely at the point where the profit is to be reaped, in order to divert a material portion of the profit from those who have earned it to those who have not; with special advantage to defendant in the competition because of the fact that it is not burdened with any part of the expense of gathering the news. . . .

In our view, the elements central to an *INS* claim are: (i) the plaintiff generates or collects information at some cost or expense; (ii) the value of the information is highly time-sensitive; (iii) the defendant's use of the information constitutes free-riding on the plaintiff's costly efforts to generate or collect it; (iv) the defendant's use of the information is in direct competition with a product or service offered by the plaintiff; (v) the ability of other parties to free-ride on the efforts of the plaintiff would so reduce the incentive to produce the product or service that its existence or quality would be substantially threatened.

INS is not about ethics; it is about the protection of property rights in time-sensitive information so that the information will be made available to the public by profit-seeking entrepreneurs. If services like AP were not assured of property rights in the news they pay to collect, they would cease to collect it. The ability of their competitors to appropriate their product at only nominal cost and thereby to disseminate a competing product at a lower price would destroy the incentive to collect news in the first place. The newspaper-reading public would suffer because no one would have an incentive to collect "hot news."

We therefore find the extra elements — those in addition to the elements of copyright infringement — that allow a "hot-news" claim to survive preemption are: (i) the time-sensitive value of factual information, (ii) the free-riding by a defendant, and (iii) the threat to the very existence of the product or service provided by the plaintiff. . . .

With regard to the NBA's primary products — producing basketball games with live attendance and licensing copyrighted broadcasts of those games — there is no evidence that anyone regards SportsTrax or the AOL site as a substitute for attending NBA games or watching them on television. In fact, Motorola markets SportsTrax as being designed "for those times when you cannot be at the arena, watch the game on TV, or listen to the radio. . . ."

. . . [T]he NBA has not shown any damage to any of its products based on free-riding by Motorola and STATS[. Accordingly,] the NBA's misappropriation claim . . . is preempted.

---

4. Contract

Because the primary legal protection licensors have against unauthorized use of their databases is the license agreement itself, an enforceable license agreement is a crucial element in any database-licensing business. The enforceability of just such an agreement was upheld by the Seventh Circuit in a notable opinion by Judge Easterbrook in ProCD, Inc. v. Zeidenberg, 86 F.3d 1447 (1996). That case involved a CD-ROM mega-phonebook compiled by ProCD, Inc. from more than 3,000 telephone directories over a two-year period at a cost of approximately $10 million. The outside of the package included a notice stating that a license was enclosed inside. The license restrictions also were set out in the user's manual that accompanied the software and appeared on the computer screen each time the end user used the software. A Wisconsin computer science student, Matthew Zeidenberg, purchased the ProCD database, extracted the directory information from the CD, and combined it with his own software to search and retrieve phone numbers. He then provided access to the data over the Internet and charged users a fee to access it. As you will recall from Assignment 13, there is considerable controversy about Judge Easterbrook's reasoning in that case. That controversy does not (for most scholars) extend to the actual decision, which denounced plainly wrongful behavior by Zeidenberg. Thus, despite the controversial reasoning in that case, the decision does suggest that such agreements will be enforceable.

5.   *Trespass to Chattels*

As you will recall from Assignment 6, courts have allowed database owners to protect themselves under the developing doctrine of trespass to chattels. Like the tort of misappropriation and the contractual claims mentioned in the preceding sections, that doctrine remains controversial. Still, its potential encourages businesses with data accessible on the Internet to use site licenses that plainly forbid access and reuse of the data, so that the database proprietor can establish the elements of a trespass to chattels in those jurisdictions that recognize such a claim.

D.   EU Sui Generis Right in Databases

Since *Feist*, the United States Congress has repeatedly considered, but never passed, a statute that would overturn the result in that case and grant some form of intellectual-property protection for databases. See, e.g., Database and Collections of Information Misappropriation Act, H.R. 3261, 108th Cong. The story has unfolded differently, however, in Europe, since the 1996 enactment by the European Union of a directive requiring member states to pass laws recognizing a sui generis right in databases. Database Directive, Directive 96/9/EC. As illustrated by the following case — the first reported opinion in England applying the English law that implements the Directive — the EU sui generis right provides database owners much greater protection against unauthorized copying of their data than database owners in the United States enjoy today.

British Horseracing Board Ltd. v. William Hill Organisation Ltd.

English Chancery Division, 23 February 2001

LADDIE J:

Introduction

1.   This is a case about a new type of intellectual property called database right. It was introduced into our law by means of the Copyright and Rights in Databases Regulations 1997 (SI 1997/3032). This implements European Parliament and Council Directive 96/9/EC of 11 March 1996 on the Legal Protection of Databases ("the Directive"). The parties agreed that the Regulations have to be construed consistently with the Directive and, for the purpose of these proceedings, attention was only paid to the provisions of the latter. . . .

The British Horseracing Board Limited ("BHB") and its Database

3.   . . . BHB is the governing authority for the British racing industry. . . .
6.   In support of its functions, BHB maintains a computerised collection of information (which the parties called the "BHB Database") which is constantly being

updated with the latest information. Computerisation began in 1964 when the Jockey Club had the functions now controlled by BHB. The scale and complexity of the data kept by BHB has grown with time. According to the particulars of claim:

> The establishment of the BHB Database has involved, and its maintenance and development continues to involve, extensive work, including the collection of raw data, the design of the database, the selection and verification of data for inclusion in the database and the insertion and arrangement of selected data in the database. The cost of establishing the BHB Database was considerable. The cost of continuing to obtain, verify and present its contents is approximately £ 4 million per annum and involves approximately 80 employees and extensive computer software and hardware.

. . . 10.   . . . The cost of running the BHB Database [is about £ 3.75 million per year] . . . [Database licensing fee revenues] currently yield an income of just over £ 1M annually, thereby meeting somewhere in the region of 25 percent of BHB's costs of maintaining the BHB Database. . . .

11.   The information, or selected parts of it, is also supplied to other interested parties, including bookmakers. . . . [D]ata are supplied to a company, Satellite Information Services Limited ("SIS"), which is allowed to use data from it for certain purposes including for onward transmission to, and use by, its own subscribers. The supply from SIS to its own subscribers takes the form of what is called a raw data feed ("RDF").

William Hill

. . . 13.   The William Hill business is one of the leading providers of off-track bookmaking services in the United Kingdom and elsewhere, to both UK and international customers. It and its subsidiaries offer odds on a large number of events at any given time, providing betting services to their customers through two principal channels: (a) a nationwide network of Licensed Betting Offices ("LBOs") and (b) telephone betting operations. In 1999 William Hill earned profits of £ 78.9 million. William Hill's principal product is the taking of fixed-odds bets on sporting and other events. The most popular event on which William Hill offers odds is horse racing. William Hill is one of the UK's largest LBO operators with currently 1,526 trading units. LBOs provide customers with comprehensive sports information and betting services including horse racing, greyhound racing and other significant sporting events. . . .

15.   It will be appreciated that a very great deal of the information displayed or used by William Hill in the horse-racing related business referred to above comes, directly or indirectly, from the BHB Database. No objection is taken to any of such use. In respect of all of it BHB takes the view that such data are all taken with its express or implied consent and for all of it BHB receives, directly or indirectly, financial compensation. . . .

The Current Dispute

16.   This action is concerned with a form of business which has recently been commenced by William Hill and a number of its competitors. It takes the form of providing betting services over the Internet. At the moment it is a minor part of the defendant's business. . . . William Hill established its first Internet site in June

1996 to promote its telephone betting business. In May 1999 it started betting on horseracing, limited initially to a small number of selected races each day on which William Hill had produced its own odds. It developed this into a comprehensive service covering the majority of horse racing, with real time changes in the odds being offered. This enhanced service was launched on two internet sites; the "International Site" on 3 February 2000 and . . . the "UK Site" on 13 March 2000. Members of the public can access these sites over the internet, see what horses are running in which races at which racecourses and what are the odds offered by William Hill. If they want, they can place bets electronically. . . .

18.   Between May 1999 and February 2000, William Hill offered Internet betting on only selected races. . . . It is since February 2000 that William Hill has offered Internet betting on all mainstream horseracing in the UK. The relevant data for all races . . . taking place that day are derived from the RDF supplied to it by SIS and published between 5.00 am and 7.00 am . . . By the time William Hill publishes this data on its Internet sites, it has been available from sources other than SIS since the previous morning. For example it will have been published in the press and on various teletext services.

19.   It is not disputed that the information displayed on William Hill's internet sites, that is to say the identity of all the horses in the race, the date and time of the race and the identity of the racecourse where the race will be held, is to be found in and comes from the RDF feed received by it from SIS. It is also not in dispute that the same information is supplied to SIS from the data stored on BHB's computer. It is information [that can be obtained from other licensees of BHB]. . . . It is not in dispute that SIS has no right to sublicense William Hill to use any of BHB's data on its internet site and has not purported to do so. . . .

20.   BHB's case is that it owns database right in the BHB Database and that William Hill is making unlicensed use of that data in its internet business. It says that what William Hill takes from the SIS RDF is derived by SIS from the BHB Database. It says that William Hill's activities constitute breaches of BHB's database right in two ways. First it says that each day's use by William Hill of data taken from the SIS RDF is an extraction or re-utilization of a substantial part of the contents of its database contrary to art 7(1) of the Directive. Second, it says that, even if the individual extracts are not substantial, nevertheless the totality of William Hill's actions amount to repeated and systematic extraction or re-utilization of insubstantial parts of the contents of the database contrary to art 7(5). . . .

An Overview of Database Right

22.   The reason for introducing a new database right into the domestic law of the Member States of the European Union is largely explained in the recitals to the Directive. Databases used to be protected by copyright in all or most states. Unfortunately there existed major differences between the relevant national laws. A collection of data which could be protected in one State might not be protected at all in another, or the scope of protection might be different. In an attempt to resolve some of the difficulties created by this lack of uniformity in national laws, the Directive does two things. First it requires Member States to implement certain common features in their national copyright law insofar as they deal with databases. These are set out primarily in arts 3 to 6 inclusive. Second, it creates an entirely new kind of right, which it refers to as "sui generis". This is dealt with primarily in arts 7 to 11 inclusive. This is the database right. It is independent of any

copyright or other intellectual property rights which may exist in the database or in any of the individual pieces of data or information collected together within the database. In this case BHB say that it may well be entitled to copyright protection as well as database right, but it is content to sue solely on the latter and the proceedings are limited accordingly.

24. The fact that database right and copyright in databases can exist side by side and that the former is described as sui generis is important. Although it is apparent that there are some features of the database right which are similar to features of copyright, it must not be assumed that the former is based upon or is to be construed as a mere continuation or development of the latter and, in particular, that it is a mere variation of United Kingdom copyright law. There may be a natural tendency, particularly for those familiar with copyright, to look at database through copyright eyes, but there are significant differences between the two rights. . . .

The Nature and Effect of Database Right

(a) What is a Database? . . .

25. . . . [T]he expression "database" is defined in art 1 as follows:

1. This Directive concerns the legal protection of databases in any form.
2. For the purposes of this Directive, "database" shall mean a collection of independent works, data or other materials arranged in a systematic or methodical way and individually accessible by electronic or other means.

. . . 27. This is very broad. Any two or more pieces of data put side by side could be said to be a collection and, therefore, a database. . . . However not all databases are protected by copyright or database right. In relation to copyright, this can be seen in Recitals 15 and 16;

(15) Whereas the criteria used to determine whether a database should be protected by copyright should be defined to the fact that the selection or the arrangement of the contents of the database is the author's own intellectual creation; whereas such protection should cover the structure of the database;
(16) Whereas no criterion other than originality in the sense of the author's intellectual creation should be applied to determine the eligibility of the database for copyright protection, and in particular no aesthetic or qualitative criteria should be applied;

28. Therefore, for copyright to subsist, it must be shown not only that there is a relevant collection of information but that it is also original. Although there is no requirement to demonstrate aesthetic or qualitative criteria, there must be a quantitative baseline of originality before protection is acquired. . . .

29. . . . There is another feature of the definition of database which needs to be considered in view of some of the arguments advanced in this case. Art 1 refers to collections in which the materials are "arranged in a systematic or methodical way and individually accessible". This might be thought to mean that for all purposes a database must be arranged systematically or methodically. However, if

that were right it might exclude many computerised databases. Recital 21 shows that this cannot be what was intended;

> (21) Whereas the protection provided for in this Directive relates to databases in which works, data or other materials have been arranged systematically or methodically; whereas it is not necessary for those materials to have been physically stored in an organized manner;

30.   It seems, therefore, that the expression "database" has a very wide meaning covering virtually all collections of data in searchable form. On any view, the BHB Database at a particular point in time, say 12.20 pm on 13 March 2000, is a "database" within art 1. Whether a database qualifies for protection by copyright, database right or both depends upon how the database was made, that is to say whether sufficient relevant effort was put into its creation. To determine this involves understanding what is the purpose of the intellectual property rights granted in a database.

(b)   The Objective Behind the Creation of Database Right

31.   Understanding the objective behind the creation of database right is important because, as both parties agree, correctly in my view, the purpose throws light on what types of activity amount to breaches. The Directive repeatedly refers to protecting and encouraging investment in database creation. . . . Further it is apparent what type of investment is considered worthy of protection. Recital 40 and art 7(1) respectively provide:

> (40) Whereas the object of this sui generis right is to ensure protection of any investment in obtaining, verifying or presenting the contents of a database for the limited duration of the right; whereas such investment may consist in the deployment of financial resources and/or the expending of time, effort and energy;

And:

> 7. Object of protection
>
>   1. Member States shall provide for a right for the maker of a database which shows that there has been qualitatively and/or quantitatively a substantial investment in either the obtaining, verification or presentation of the contents to prevent extraction and/or re-utilization of the whole or of a substantial part, evaluated qualitatively and/or quantitatively, of the contents of that database.

32.   In the light of this it appears that for database right to exist, there must be investment in its creation and, in particular, that investment must be directed at obtaining, verifying or presenting the contents. As is apparent from art 7(1), the investment must be substantial enough to justify protection. However the terms of Recital 19 . . . indicate that the qualifying level of investment is fairly low. In any event, whatever the level, it is not suggested that the investment in the BHB Database falls below it.

33.   Of more significance to this dispute is the type of investment involved. As one would expect, effort put into creating the actual data which is subsequently collected together in the database is irrelevant. . . .

34.   For this reason, the costs and effort involved in BHB fixing the date of a racing fixture does not count towards the relevant investment to which database right is directed. On the other hand, the efforts which go into gathering all the data together, including the dates of fixtures, is relevant. Such activities constitute "obtaining" the data, one of the types of investment referred to in art 7(1) and Recital 40. In practice where one person both creates the underlying data and gathers it together, as BHB does, it may be difficult to draw a sharp dividing line between the two activities.

35.   Investment in "verification" is also relevant to the subsistence and protection of database right. Verification consists of ensuring the accuracy of a collection of data. Thus even if the content or form of the collection of data are substantially unchanged, effort put into ensuring its accuracy, or continuing accuracy, is relevant and is to be protected. This point is reinforced by Recital 55:

> (55) Whereas a substantial new investment involving a new term of protection may include a substantial verification of the contents of the database.

36.   The latter Recital indicates that even if the contents of a database do not change substantially, if sufficient investment is put into ensuring that it is up to date and accurate, it is protected by the new right. . . .

(c)   Breach of Database Rights . . .

Infringement by extraction or re-utilization of a substantial part

42.   Article 7(1) provides that one of the purpose of database right is "to prevent extraction and/or re-utilization of the whole or of a substantial part, evaluated qualitatively and/or quantitatively, of the contents of" the database. BHB argues that William Hill's activities breach these rights in that the information they have taken via the RDF represents a substantial part of the contents of the BHB Database. It is, if anything, the most vital information. Although the BHB Database contains much more, the identities of which horses are racing in which races at what time at which racecourses are the core data to which everything else is secondary. Furthermore it is BHB's investment in ensuring that this information is up to date and accurate which William Hill is using for the purpose of its new commercial operation. William Hill wants to ensure that its customers can be confident that they are betting on horses which are racing at identified races. Accuracy is what they want and this is ensured by taking data which originates from the only definitive source, BHB.

43.   Although [Hill's] arguments are interrelated, they may be grouped under four headings. (1) What . . . Hill has used is not a part, in the relevant sense, of the BHB Database, (2) even if it is a part, it is not a substantial part, (3) the use does not amount to an "extraction" from the BHB Database and (4) it is not a "re-utilization" of that Database. It is the first of these which is the most fundamental submission and it goes to the very heart of what is protected by the new right.

44.   [Hill] says that one must distinguish between the data or information within a database and the characteristics which give rise to the new type of protection [and goes on to assert that the database right only protects the manner in which the data is arranged.] . . .

47.   However, in my view . . . the Recitals to the Directive are quite explicit that the form of a database is what is protected by copyright not by the sui generis right . . .

48.   Th[e] recitals make it clear that infringement of the new right is not avoided by taking the contents and rearranging them. . . . In such a case, the infringer takes advantage of the relevant investment if he makes use of the accuracy of the data in the database, not because he takes it in a particular form. . . .

50.   This leads to the next issue, substantiality. . . . [Hill] says that the information [it] used . . . cannot be regarded as substantial [based on either the quantity or quality of data used.] As far as quantity is concerned, [it] points to the fact that there is a vast amount of information in the BHB Database . . . [and] . . . if one compares the totality of the important data held on the BHB Database with what is on the William Hill internet site it can be seen that the latter contains very little but the names of a few horses. . . .

53.   Article 7(1) provides that substantiality is to be assessed by looking at the quantity and quality of what is taken[.] . . . Here what the defendant is doing is making use of the most recent and core information in the BHB Database relating to racing. William Hill is relying on and taking advantage of the completeness and accuracy of the information taken from the RDF, in other words the product of BHB's investment in obtaining and verifying that data. This is a substantial part of the contents. . . .

54.   However this finding does not dispose of the dispute. William Hill only breaches BHB's database right if its activities amount to an "extraction" or "re-utilization" of a substantial part. These two words are defined in art 7(2) as follows:

> (a) "extraction" shall mean the permanent or temporary transfer of all or a substantial part of the contents of a database to another medium by any means or in any form;
> (b) "re-utilization" shall mean any form of making available to the public all or a substantial part of the contents of a database by the distribution of copies, by renting, by on-line or other forms of transmission. The first sale of a copy of a database within the Community by the right holder or with his consent shall exhaust the right to control resale of that copy within the Community; Public lending is not an act of extraction or re-utilization.

. . . 57.   . . . The Directive does not require that extraction should be direct rather than indirect, nor does the definition involve the concept of taking away. All that is required is that a substantial part of the contents be transferred to a new medium. Thus the definition refers to "transfer . . . to another medium". It says nothing about the resultant state of the database from which the transfer has been made. If someone takes a copy of the contents of a database and loads it onto a new medium, it is no less transferred to the new medium because the same data are left on the original database. . . . The only qualification to be noted is the requirement that there be transfer "to another medium". A hacker who accesses a database without a licence, looks at the data and memorises it may well not be guilty of extraction if his actions do not involve the making of a copy of the data in material form. . . .

59.   . . . What [reutilization] is concerned with is the unlicensed use of data derived without permission from a database. Private use of such data are not treated as re-utilization but any use which transmits or makes available the extracted information to the public is covered by database right and can be restrained. If one asks the question, "is the information on the William Hill website being made available to the public by . . . on-line or other forms of transmission?"

The answer must be in the affirmative. The fact that some or all of the data are available to the public from another source is irrelevant. There is no reason why information cannot be made available to the public from more than one source. . . .

60. It follows that William Hill's actions of taking information from the RDF and loading it onto its own computers for the purpose of making it available on its website is an unlicensed act of extracting a substantial part of the BHB Database and the subsequent transmission of that data onto its website for access by members of the public is a reutilization. The defendant infringes BHB's rights in both ways.

Relevant Glossary Entries

Database
Data Mining
End User
Internet Corporation for Assigned Names and Numbers (ICANN)
Network Effect
Personal Digital Assistant (PDA)
Robot Exclusion Header
Shopping Bot or ShopBot
Site License

Problem Set 20

20.1. You have a new client today, *www.bluepages.biz*. BluePages has a Web-based directory of telephone numbers, mailing addresses, and e-mail addresses for businesses organized by type of business (much like the conventional Yellow Pages organization). BluePages has just discovered that a competitor (*www.greenpages.biz*) for the last several months has been building up its own directory by systematically searching and downloading information from the Web site at *www.bluepages.biz*. Does the activity of GreenPages violate any rights of BluePages? Is there anything further you might like to know that would help you answer the question?

20.2. Tennis Tales, a popular online magazine for tennis devotees, has a customer database that includes its customers' names, mailing addresses, and other personal information it has acquired from voluntary responses to special promotions and member surveys. Tennis Tales has a restrictive policy regarding the "rental" of its subscriber list. Under that policy, it shares its subscriber list only with merchants or not-for-profit organizations that it believes offer goods or services that are of interest to a majority of its subscribers, and that do not compete with Tennis Tales or any of its affiliates or partners in any way.

Consistent with that policy, Tennis Tales "rented" its subscriber list to Sports Station, a specialty retailer in the United States selling sports-related goods and equipment of various kinds. The agreement with Sports Station barred any transfer of the list to any third party. Weeks later, Sports Station filed for bankruptcy (in the United States). The trustee in bankruptcy promptly sold the Tennis Tales subscriber list to Tennis Online (its primary competitor). When loyal Tennis Tales' readers alerted the magazine to the fact that they were receiving targeted mailings from Tennis Online, Tennis Tales sued Tennis Online for infringing its rights in its subscriber list. Is Tennis Tales likely to obtain damages or an injunction against further mailings to its subscribers? Bankruptcy Code §365(a).

20.3. Boatdepot.com, a business-to-business Internet market for the U.S. boating community, requires participants to agree to its standard "market members agreement." The agreement requires each participant to agree to limit its data-collection practices to transactions to which the member is a party. Boatdepot.com undertakes to monitor all queries and transactions executed using its Internet market and to release a monthly report that provides summaries of all communications in a form that does not identify the parties to the communications. The monthly report groups queries and transactions according to product, quantity, and price. One of the members of Boatdepot.com is Jetboatjunction.com. Jetboatjunction.com has developed (and now is using) software that captures information about other market members that send it queries or execute transactions with it. The software works by extracting from any browser that visits the Boatdepot.com page information about all of the transactions and queries in which those visitors have been involved at Boatdepot.com (that is, information about matters that involve Jetboatjunction.com and information about matters between the visitors and unrelated third-party members of Boatdepot.com). Can the other members of Boatdepot.com complain about Jetboatjunction.com's collection of information about their activities?

20.4. As you will recall most recently from Problem Set 6, the League of Net Consumers (LNC) is a not-for-profit organization supported largely by dues paid by its members. LNC created a "shopping bot" software program that its subscribers can download from its Web site without charge. LNC subscribers using the shopping bot software can search the Internet for price and availability information on major consumer items. Consumers using the bot enter the description of the item they are looking for; the bot then trawls the Internet, identifying for the consumer every retail Web site offering that product, together with price and availability information. The LNC shopping bot disregards any "robot exclusion headers" that it might encounter. (Robot exclusion headers are features of a Web site that customarily indicate to robots that they are not welcome to search for information on the site in question.) Monster Mart, a major brick-and-mortar retailer with an online store at MonsterMart.com, files suit against LNC, complaining that LNC's software facilitates copying that violates the MonsterMart.com site license. Your firm has agreed to take on this matter as a pro bono project. What is your advice? Would the outcome be different if the dispute involved LNC's English affiliate and MonsterMart.com's UK subsidiary? EU Database Directive art. 7(1).

20.5. Congresswoman Pamela Herring has called asking your advice on a bill presented to her by lobbyists for large information companies. The draft legislation would create a sui generis database right similar to the EU sui generis database right. The lobbyists have pointed out to Congresswoman Herring that the EU will grant sui generis database rights to owners of American databases only if their national legal systems grant equivalent sui generis rights to EU database owners. Would Congresswoman Herring risk antagonizing any major constituencies if she supported such legislation? Are the public policy grounds for supporting such legislation so strong that she should be prepared to take the political heat?

Assignment 21: Music

The digitization of such traditional tangible goods as books, movies, magazines, newspapers, and videogames presents great potential for Internet commerce, because transactions in these goods can occur entirely through electronic means. Now, however, the most significant works distributed online are in the music industry. Although online music retailing is still in its infancy, controversy about transmission of music over the Internet has been one of the most salient problems in the development of electronic commerce.

A. Musical Works and Sound Recordings

Ownership in music comes from the federal Copyright Act, which draws a fundamental distinction between musical works and sound recordings. The musical work is the sequence of notes, words, and instruments devised by the composer, while the sound recording is a fixation of the sounds of a particular performance of the musical work. Thus, when Eric Clapton or the Rolling Stones release recordings of "Love in Vain," copyright law recognizes two different ownership interests. As the author of that song, Robert Johnson owns the musical work, while Eric Clapton and the Rolling Stones each have an interest in their respective sound recordings. The significance of being a copyright owner is that the Copyright Act grants copyright owners a series of exclusive rights to exploit the work, set out in Section 106 of the Copyright Act. The two most relevant to music are the right to reproduce the work and the right to perform the work.

1. The Exclusive Right to Reproduce

First, Section 106(1) grants an exclusive right to reproduce a work in "copies" or "phonorecords." Sheet music, for example, is a "copy" of the musical work. Because printing sheet music reproduces a musical work in copies, the owner of a musical work has the exclusive right to print sheet music of the work. Of more relevance to our topic, "phonorecords" are "material objects in which sounds . . . are fixed . . . and from which the sounds can be perceived, reproduced, or otherwise communicated, either directly or with the aid of a machine or device." Thus, a phonorecord of the Robert Johnson song would be an old-style LP record, a compact disc, or the hard drive of an MP3 player that includes a digital file of a performance of the song. The owner of the sound recording has the exclusive right to reproduce the sound recording in any of those formats.

Section 115 imposes a significant limit on the exclusive right to reproduce a musical work by creating a compulsory license to make phonorecords of a musical work. (This often is called the "mechanical" license for historical reasons.) Generally, this permits a recording artist to produce a "cover" of a famous song. Thus, if a musical artist wishes to include on its album a recording of a musical work previously authored by a different group, it need not obtain permission from the author. Rather, it may simply record the work, include the work on its album, and pay the statutorily prescribed royalty (currently about 7.55 cents per copy). In most cases, artists do not rely directly on the statute, but instead obtain a formal license from the Harry Fox Agency (*www.harryfox.com*), which acts as an agent for most of the owners of musical works in the United States. Notice that the mechanical license applies only to musical works, not sound recordings: It grants a right to produce and distribute your own sound recordings, it does not grant a right to copy and distribute the sound recordings of others.

Section 115(d) has a separate provision dealing with the distribution of cover songs through a "digital phonorecord delivery." This is designed, among other things, to permit a Web site to use rights under the mechanical license to sell sound recordings. Generally, it would permit an artist that has recorded a version of a song by a third party, to transmit that sound recording to third parties over the Internet, assuming that the artist (or the site) pays the statutory license fee to the owner of the musical work. Again, because the right extends only to the musical work, it does not authorize distribution of the recordings of a third party.

2. The Exclusive Right to Perform

The other exclusive right important to the music industry is the exclusive right to perform a copyrighted work publicly. Copyright Act §106(4). A musical work is performed, among other things, when it is sung or played on a musical instrument live, or when a recording is played, as long as those activities take place "publicly." Because Section 101 of the statute defines both of those terms broadly, the reach of the right is quite startling: It was not implausible for the Recording Industry Association of America to assert that the singing of campfire songs by Girl Scouts amounts to a public performance that infringes the rights of the owners of the songs in question. Crucially, the exclusive right to perform extends only to the musical work, not to the sound recording. Thus, the only permission that is necessary to play a song on the radio is the permission of the copyright owner (Robert Johnson) not the performer on the sound recording (Eric Clapton).

In practice, those who use music publicly do not negotiate individually with each owner of a musical work. Rather, they negotiate for blanket licenses with one of several collective societies that represent the owners of musical works. The most prominent of those societies are ASCAP (American Society of Composers, Artists, and Publishers), BMI (Broadcast Music, Inc.), and SESAC (Society of European State Authors and Composers).

B. Digital Performances

The framework discussed above grants relatively limited rights to the owners of sound recordings, because those who record music are not entitled to compensation when their recordings are played publicly, unless they also are the authors of the works that they have recorded. This reflects the relatively recent invention (in the days of Thomas Edison) of the technology that permits sound recordings of music. Indeed, sound recordings were not protected at all in the Copyright Act of 1909. The first significant federal protection came in the Copyright Act of 1976.

Recognizing the potential for abuse with the rise of online music sites, Congress in 1995 granted the owners of sound recordings a new exclusive right, an exclusive right to perform a sound recording publicly by "digital audio transmission." Copyright Act §106(6). Standing alone, that provision would prohibit any performance of a musical work online — any "streaming" transmission of the song, for example — without consent of the owner of the sound recording.

To accommodate Internet transmissions of radio stations (and Internet analogues to ground-based stations), Section 114 of the Copyright Act includes several important restrictions on the digital performance right. The following excerpt aptly summarizes those limitations:

R. Anthony Reese, *Copyright and Internet Music Transmissions: Existing Law, Major Controversies, Possible Solutions*

55 U. Miami L. Rev. 237 (2001)

The scope of the copyright owner's right varies with the type of digital transmission. There are four basic types. The first is a transmission made by an "interactive service" that either transmits a particular sound recording requested by the recipient or transmits a program specially created for the recipient. Several kinds of transmissions are interactive. The archetypal interactive service is the much-prophesied "celestial jukebox," an on-demand service that allows a recipient (who pays a monthly subscription fee or a per-use charge) to connect to a repository of sound recordings and select a particular recording that is immediately transmitted to the recipient's speakers. MusicBank.com has entered into agreements with all of the major record labels to provide, by subscription, on- demand streaming access to all of the recordings in the labels' catalogs. MusicBank will be offering an interactive service, because the subscriber will receive, on request, the transmission of a particular sound recording that she selected. Transmissions by an interactive service are subject to the sound recording copyright owner's digital transmission performance right, so the transmitter needs the permission of the copyright owner prior to making transmissions of the subject recording. The sound recording copyright owner is entitled to charge any price for such permission or to deny permission entirely.

Noninteractive service transmissions basically fall into three categories. First, there are nonsubscription broadcast transmissions. Such transmissions are entirely exempt from a copyright owner's digital transmission performance right, so obtaining permission from the sound recording copyright owner is not necessary. {§114(d)(1)(A).} Permission for the public performance of any musical work would be required, though. {§114(d)(4)(B)(i).} Many radio stations, in addition to broadcasting over the radio airwaves, now have Web sites where they simultaneously transmit identical programming in streaming audio format. For example, public radio station KUT in Austin, Texas, has a Web site (*www.kut.org*) that allows users to hear in real time the programming that KUT is broadcasting over the airwaves to central Texas. Despite this trend, a dispute currently exists over whether the exemption for "nonsubscription broadcast transmissions" includes a transmission over the Internet of an AM or FM radio station's over-the-air programming. In response to a petition by the Recording Industry Association of America ("RIAA"), the trade association for the major recording labels, the Copyright Office recently amended its regulations to provide that an Internet simulcast by a licensed AM or FM broadcaster is not within the "nonsubscription broadcast transmission" exemption from the digital transmission performance right. The National Association of Broadcasters has filed a suit challenging the regulation. [Ed: The Third Circuit in 2003 affirmed the district court's grant of summary judgment for the government. Bonneville International Corp. v. Peters, 347 F.3d 485 (3rd Cir. 2003).]

Second, certain noninteractive transmissions other than broadcast transmissions, although not exempt from the digital transmission performance right, are eligible for a compulsory license of the digital transmission performance right. {§114(d)(2).} For example, a hypothetical Web site, WebJazz, that runs a jazz "Web radio station" and streams jazz music to those who visit the site, just as a radio station would broadcast jazz music over the airwaves, would be eligible for such a license.[38] The transmissions are not interactive because WebJazz's programmers, not the site's listeners, select which songs are played. A noninteractive transmitter like WebJazz must adhere to a long list of detailed conditions to qualify for the compulsory license. {§114(d)(2)(A), (C).} Those conditions seek to limit the license to those transmissions thought least likely to substitute for the sale of records. Therefore, the conditions attempt to prevent listeners from getting advance notice of which songs are to be transmitted so that they could record them or listen to them "on demand." Some conditions concern the programming that is transmitted. For example, WebJazz cannot transmit, during any three-hour period, more than three different tracks from any one compact disc or more than four different tracks by the same recording artist.[41] Other conditions govern the technology and interfaces used for the transmission. If WebJazz meets all the

---

38. Both subscription and nonsubscription transmissions are eligible for the license, so the site might support itself either by limiting access to subscribers or by transmitting advertising to its listeners. *See id.* §§114(j)(9), (14). If the transmission is nonsubscription, it must, in order to qualify for the statutory license, be part of a service whose "primary purpose" is to provide audio or entertainment programming to the public and not to sell or promote particular products or services. *Id.* §114(j)(6).

41. 17 U.S.C. §§114(d)(2)(C)(i) and 114(j)(13). Other programming-related conditions include a ban on advance publication of program schedules or specific titles to be played, 114(d)(2)(C)(ii), minimum time limits for the program of which a transmission of a sound recording is a part, §114(d)(2)(C)(iii), a requirement to transmit sound recordings from lawfully made phonorecords and not from bootleg recordings, §114(d)(2)(C)(vii), and a bar on transmitting visual images along with the audio transmission in a way likely to confuse recipients as to the endorsement or affiliation of the recording artist or copyright owner, §114(d)(2)(C)(iv).

conditions, then it can obtain a compulsory license to transmit any sound recording by complying with Copyright Office procedures and paying the license fee. As with the compulsory mechanical license for [digital phonorecord deliveries or] DPDs, the license fee is to be determined every two years by voluntary negotiations among the parties to establish an industry-wide consensus on rates that would then be adopted by the Copyright Office. Failing that, rates would be set by an arbitration proceeding in the Copyright Office. . . . The compulsory license, like the broadcast exemption, applies only to the digital transmission performance right in sound recordings and not to the public performance right in musical works. A transmitter that qualifies for the compulsory license will therefore still need to obtain musical work performance licenses, usually from ASCAP, BMI, and SESAC.

Third, noninteractive transmissions that are not broadcast transmissions and that do not meet the conditions for the compulsory license are fully subject to the digital transmission performance right. Persons making such transmissions must generally obtain the permission of the copyright owner. If WebJazz wanted to program "all Ella Fitzgerald, all the time," it would not be able to comply with the limit of four tracks by one artist in three hours. Thus, it would not qualify for the compulsory license. WebJazz would therefore need permission for its digital transmission of each sound recording from the copyright owners.

C. P2P Trading

Playing music over the Internet does not change the music industry in any substantial way, because at most it substitutes Internet-based radio stations for terrestrial stations. But distribution of music over the Internet has the potential to change the music industry fundamentally, because it calls into question the continuing relevance of the extensive brick-and-mortar distribution system of record stores. Indeed, brick-and-mortar stores already are losing ground even in the market for distribution of music in conventional CD format, because of the competition of online retailers like Amazon.com and Barnes & Noble.

The biggest challenge, however, comes from wholly digital distribution of music. Industry enthusiasts for years have awaited the arrival of online stores at which consumers could purchase music and download it directly to their computers, for playing on their computer or associated portable devices such as MP3 players (or their successors). Only in 2004 did the first full-range Internet music store (Apple's iTunes) appear.

Many causes can explain the slow pace at which authorized online distribution of music has developed. One is a general reluctance of the main content owners (the large record companies that are members of the RIAA) to embrace digital technology. Another is their view that content should be distributed only under rigorous digital rights management (DRM) schemes that would limit the ability of users to copy the music or play it on multiple devices. Yet another is the industry's general view that pricing of music distributed online should not fall substantially from the pricing of conventional CD recordings, despite the obvious cost savings of online rather than physical distribution.

But the most important reason by far has been the general availability of music without charge through Napster and its successors. Because of the difficulty of suing individual users, the RIAA has instituted a number of notable actions against software companies that facilitate in some way the P2P networks through which users share music. The two opinions that follow explain the technology and the dispute in considerable detail. As you read the two opinions that follow, you should focus on the principal legal issues that the dispute raises. It is relatively plain that the activity involves copying that is covered by Copyright Act Section 106(1). Thus, the principal questions are whether the activity is a fair use (under Copyright Act Section 107) and whether the defendant's role in the copying is sufficient to support the copyright owners' claims of infringement.

A&M Records, Inc. v. Napster, Inc.

239 F.3d 1004 (9th Cir. 2001)

Before: SCHROEDER, Chief Judge, BEEZER and PAEZ, Circuit Judges.
BEEZER, Circuit Judge:

Plaintiffs are engaged in the commercial recording, distribution and sale of copyrighted musical compositions and sound recordings. The complaint alleges that Napster, Inc. ("Napster") is a contributory and vicarious copyright infringer. On July 26, 2000, the district court granted plaintiffs' motion for a preliminary injunction. . . . The district court preliminarily enjoined Napster "from engaging in, or facilitating others in copying, downloading, uploading, transmitting, or distributing plaintiffs' copyrighted musical compositions and sound recordings, protected by either federal or state law, without express permission of the rights owner." Federal Rule of Civil Procedure 65(c) requires successful plaintiffs to post a bond for damages incurred by the enjoined party in the event that the injunction was wrongfully issued. The district court set bond in this case at $5 million.

We entered a temporary stay of the preliminary injunction pending resolution of this appeal. We have jurisdiction pursuant to 28 U.S.C. §1292(a)(1). We affirm in part, reverse in part and remand.

I

We have examined the papers submitted in support of and in response to the injunction application and it appears that Napster has designed and operates a system which permits the transmission and retention of sound recordings employing digital technology.

In 1987, the Moving Picture Experts Group set a standard file format for the storage of audio recordings in a digital format called MPEG-3, abbreviated as "MP3." Digital MP3 files are created through a process colloquially called "ripping." Ripping software allows a computer owner to copy an audio compact disk ("audio CD") directly onto a computer's hard drive by compressing the audio information on the CD into the MP3 format. The MP3's compressed format allows for rapid transmission of digital audio files from one computer to another by electronic mail or any other file transfer protocol.

Napster facilitates the transmission of MP3 files between and among its users. Through a process commonly called "peer-to-peer" file sharing, Napster allows its users to: (1) make MP3 music files stored on individual computer hard drives available for copying by other Napster users; (2) search for MP3 music files stored on other users' computers; and (3) transfer exact copies of the contents of other users' MP3 files from one computer to another via the Internet. These functions are made possible by Napster's MusicShare software, available free of charge from Napster's Internet site, and Napster's network servers and server-side software. Napster provides technical support for the indexing and searching of MP3 files, as well as for its other functions, including a "chat room," where users can meet to discuss music, and a directory where participating artists can provide information about their music.

A. Accessing the System

In order to copy MP3 files through the Napster system, a user must first access Napster's Internet site and download the MusicShare software to his individual computer. Once the software is installed, the user can access the Napster system. A first-time user is required to register with the Napster system by creating a "user name" and password.

B. Listing Available Files

If a registered user wants to list available files stored in his computer's hard drive on Napster for others to access, he must first create a "user library" directory on his computer's hard drive. The user then saves his MP3 files in the library directory, using self-designated file names. He next must log into the Napster system using his user name and password. His MusicShare software then searches his user library and verifies that the available files are properly formatted. If in the correct MP3 format, the names of the MP3 files will be uploaded from the user's computer to the Napster servers. The content of the MP3 files remains stored in the user's computer.

Once uploaded to the Napster servers, the user's MP3 file names are stored in a server-side "library" under the user's name and become part of a "collective directory" of files available for transfer during the time the user is logged onto the Napster system. The collective directory is fluid; it tracks users who are connected in real time, displaying only file names that are immediately accessible.

C. Searching for Available Files

Napster allows a user to locate other users' MP3 files in two ways: through Napster's search function and through its "hotlist" function.

Software located on the Napster servers maintains a "search index" of Napster's collective directory. To search the files available from Napster users currently connected to the network servers, the individual user accesses a form in the MusicShare software stored in his computer and enters either the name of a song or an artist as the object of the search. The form is then transmitted to a Napster server and automatically compared to the MP3 file names listed in the server's search index. Napster's server compiles a list of all MP3 file names pulled from the search index which include the same search terms entered on the search form and transmits the list to the searching user. . . .

To use the "hotlist" function, the Napster user creates a list of other users' names from whom he has obtained MP3 files in the past. When logged onto Napster's servers, the system alerts the user if any user on his list (a "hotlisted user") is also logged onto the system. If so, the user can access an index of all MP3 file names in a particular hotlisted user's library and request a file in the library by selecting the file name. The contents of the hotlisted user's MP3 file are not stored on the Napster system.

D. Transferring Copies of an MP3 file

To transfer a copy of the contents of a requested MP3 file, the Napster server software obtains the Internet address of the requesting user and the Internet address of the "host user" (the user with the available files). The Napster servers then communicate the host user's Internet address to the requesting user. The requesting user's computer uses this information to establish a connection with the host user and downloads a copy of the contents of the MP3 file from one computer to the other over the Internet, "peer-to-peer." A downloaded MP3 file can be played directly from the user's hard drive using Napster's MusicShare program or other software. The file may also be transferred back onto an audio CD if the user has access to equipment designed for that purpose. In both cases, the quality of the original sound recording is slightly diminished by transfer to the MP3 format.

This architecture is described in some detail to promote an understanding of transmission mechanics as opposed to the content of the transmissions. The content is the subject of our copyright infringement analysis. . . .

III

Plaintiffs claim Napster users are engaged in the wholesale reproduction and distribution of copyrighted works, all constituting direct infringement. The district court agreed. We note that the district court's conclusion that plaintiffs have presented a prima facie case of direct infringement by Napster users is not presently appealed by Napster. We only need briefly address the threshold requirements.

A. Infringement

[The court explained that] Napster users infringe at least two of the copyright holders' exclusive rights: the rights of reproduction, §106(1); and distribution, §106(3). Napster users who upload file names to the search index for others to copy violate plaintiffs' distribution rights. Napster users who download files containing copyrighted music violate plaintiffs' reproduction rights.

Napster asserts an affirmative defense to the charge that its users directly infringe plaintiffs' copyrighted musical compositions and sound recordings.

B. FAIR USE

Napster contends that its users do not directly infringe plaintiffs' copyrights because the users are engaged in fair use of the material. *See* 17 U.S.C. §107 ("[T]he fair use of a copyrighted work . . . is not an infringement of copyright."). Napster identifies three specific alleged fair uses: sampling, where users make temporary copies of a work before purchasing; space-shifting, where users access a sound recording through the Napster system that they already own in audio CD format; and permissive distribution of recordings by both new and established artists. . . .

We conclude that . . . the record supports the district court's conclusion that Napster users do not engage in fair use of the copyrighted materials.

1.   Purpose and Character of the Use

This factor focuses on whether the new work merely replaces the object of the original creation or instead adds a further purpose or different character. In other words, this factor asks "whether and to what extent the new work is 'transformative.'" *See Campbell v. Acuff-Rose Music, Inc.*, 510 U.S. 569, 579 (1994).

The district court first concluded that downloading MP3 files does not transform the copyrighted work. This conclusion is supportable. Courts have been reluctant to find fair use when an original work is merely retransmitted in a different medium. [Citing cases.]

This "purpose and character" element also requires the district court to determine whether the allegedly infringing use is commercial or noncommercial. A commercial use weighs against a finding of fair use but is not conclusive on the issue. The district court determined that Napster users engage in commercial use of the copyrighted materials largely because (1) "a host user sending a file cannot be said to engage in a personal use when distributing that file to an anonymous requester" and (2) "Napster users get for free something they would ordinarily have to buy." The district court's findings are not clearly erroneous.

Direct economic benefit is not required to demonstrate a commercial use. Rather, repeated and exploitative copying of copyrighted works, even if the copies are not offered for sale, may constitute a commercial use. In the record before us, commercial use is demonstrated by a showing that repeated and exploitative unauthorized copies of copyrighted works were made to save the expense of purchasing authorized copies. Plaintiffs made such a showing before the district court.

We also note that the definition of a financially motivated transaction for the purposes of criminal copyright actions includes trading infringing copies of a work for other items, "including the receipt of other copyrighted works." *See* 18 U.S.C. §101 (defining "Financial Gain").

2.   The Nature of the Use

Works that are creative in nature are "closer to the core of intended copyright protection" than are more fact-based works. *See Campbell*, 510 U.S. at 586. The district court determined that plaintiffs' "copyrighted musical compositions and sound recordings are creative in nature . . . which cuts against a finding of fair use under the second factor." We find no error in the district court's conclusion.

3.   The Portion Used

. . . The district court determined that Napster users engage in "wholesale copying" of copyrighted work because file transfer necessarily "involves copying the entirety of the copyrighted work." We agree. We note, however, that under certain circumstances, a court will conclude that a use is fair even when the protected work is copied in its entirety. *See, e.g., Sony Corp. v. Universal City Studios, Inc.*, 464 U.S. 417, 449-50 (1984) (acknowledging that fair use of time-shifting necessarily involved making a full copy of a protected work).

4.   Effect of Use on Market

"Fair use, when properly applied, is limited to copying by others which does not materially impair the marketability of the work which is copied." *Harper & Row Publishers, Inc. v. Nation Enters.*, 471 U.S. 539, 566-67 (1985). "[T]he importance of this [fourth] factor will vary, not only with the amount of harm, but also with the relative strength of the showing on the other factors." *Campbell*, 510 U.S. at 591 n.21.   The proof required to demonstrate present or future market harm varies with the purpose and character of the use:

A challenge to a noncommercial use of a copyrighted work requires proof either that the particular use is harmful, or that if it should become widespread, it would adversely affect the potential market for the copyrighted work. . . . *If the intended use is for commercial gain, that likelihood [of market harm] may be presumed. But if it is for a noncommercial purpose, the likelihood must be demonstrated.*

Sony, 464 U.S. at 451 (emphases added [by *Napster* court]).

Addressing this factor, the district court concluded that Napster harms the market in "at least" two ways: it reduces audio CD sales among college students and it "raises barriers to plaintiffs' entry into the market for the digital downloading of music." The district court relied on evidence plaintiffs submitted to show that Napster use harms the market for their copyrighted musical compositions and sound recordings. [The court summarized the various expert reports on that question and the district court's evaluation of them and concluded that] [d]efendant has failed to show any basis for disturbing the district court's findings.

We, therefore, conclude that the district court made sound findings related to Napster's deleterious effect on the present and future digital download market. Moreover, lack of harm to an established market cannot deprive the copyright holder of the right to develop alternative markets for the works. Here, . . . , the record supports the district court's finding that the "record company plaintiffs have already expended considerable funds and effort to commence Internet sales and licensing for digital downloads." Having digital downloads available for free on the Napster system necessarily harms the copyright holders' attempts to charge for the same downloads.

Judge Patel did not abuse her discretion in reaching the above fair use conclusions, nor were the findings of fact with respect to fair use considerations clearly erroneous. We next address Napster's identified uses of sampling and space-shifting.

5.   Identified Uses

Napster maintains that its identified uses of sampling and space-shifting were wrongly excluded as fair uses by the district court.

a.   *Sampling*

Napster contends that its users download MP3 files to "sample" the music in order to decide whether to purchase the recording. Napster argues that the district court: (1) erred in concluding that sampling is a commercial use because it conflated a noncommercial use with a personal use; (2) erred in determining that sampling adversely affects the market for plaintiffs' copyrighted music, a requirement if the use is noncommercial; and (3) erroneously concluded that sampling is not a fair use because it determined that samplers may also engage in other infringing activity.

The district court determined that sampling remains a commercial use even if some users eventually purchase the music. We find no error in the district court's determination. Plaintiffs have established that they are likely to succeed in proving that even authorized temporary downloading of individual songs for sampling purposes is commercial in nature. The record supports a finding that free promotional downloads are highly regulated by the record company plaintiffs and that the companies collect royalties for song samples available on retail Internet sites. Evidence relied on by the district court demonstrates that the free downloads provided by the record companies consist of thirty-to-sixty second samples or are full songs programmed to "time out," that is, exist only for a short time on the downloader's computer. In comparison, Napster users download a full, free and permanent copy of the recording. The determination by the district court as to the commercial purpose and character of sampling is not clearly erroneous.

The district court further found that both the market for audio CDs and market for online distribution are adversely affected by Napster's service. As stated in our discussion of the district court's general fair use analysis: the court did not abuse its discretion when it found that, overall, Napster has an adverse impact on the audio CD and digital download markets. Contrary to Napster's assertion that the district court failed to specifically address the market impact of sampling, the district court determined that "[e]ven if the type of sampling supposedly done on Napster were a non-commercial use, plaintiffs have demonstrated a substantial likelihood that it would adversely affect the potential market for their copyrighted works if it became widespread." The record supports the district court's preliminary determinations that: (1) the more music that sampling users download, the less likely they are to eventually purchase the recordings on audio CD; and (2) even if the audio CD market is not harmed, Napster has adverse effects on the developing digital download market.

Napster further argues that the district court erred in rejecting its evidence that the users' downloading of "samples" increases or tends to increase audio CD sales. The district court, however, correctly noted that "any potential enhancement of plaintiffs' sales . . . would not tip the fair use analysis conclusively in favor of defendant." We agree that increased sales of copyrighted material attributable to unauthorized use should not deprive the copyright holder of the right to license the material. *See Campbell*, 510 U.S. at 591 n.21 ("Even favorable evidence, without more, is no guarantee of fairness. Judge Leval gives the example of the film producer's appropriation of a composer's previously unknown song that turns the song into a commercial success; the boon to the song does not make the film's simple copying fair."). Nor does positive impact in one market, here the audio CD market, deprive the copyright holder of the right to develop identified alternative markets, here the digital download market.

We find no error in the district court's factual findings or abuse of discretion in the court's conclusion that plaintiffs will likely prevail in establishing that sampling does not constitute a fair use.

b. Space-Shifting

Napster also maintains that space-shifting is a fair use. Space-shifting occurs when a Napster user downloads MP3 music files in order to listen to music he already owns on audio CD. Napster asserts that we have already held that space-shifting of musical compositions and sound recordings is a fair use. [Relying on *RIAA v. Diamond Multimedia Systems*, 180 F.3d 1072 (9th Cir. 1999), a 9th Circuit decision about the Rio player, an early portable MP3 player]. *See also generally Sony*, 464 U.S. at 423 (holding that "time-shifting," where a video tape recorder owner records a television show for later viewing, is a fair use).

We conclude that the district court did not err when it refused to apply the "shifting" analyses of *Sony* and *Diamond*. Both *Diamond* and *Sony* are inapposite because the methods of shifting in these cases did not also simultaneously involve distribution of the copyrighted material to the general public; the time or space-shifting of copyrighted material exposed the material only to the original user. In *Diamond*, for example, the copyrighted music was transferred from the user's computer hard drive to the user's portable MP3 player. So too *Sony*, where "the majority of VCR purchasers . . . did not distribute taped television broadcasts, but merely enjoyed them at home." Conversely, it is obvious that once a user lists a copy of music he already owns on the Napster system in order to access the music from another location, the song becomes "available to millions of other individuals," not just the original CD owner. . . .

We find no error in the district court's determination that plaintiffs will likely succeed in establishing that Napster users do not have a fair use defense. Accordingly, we next address whether Napster is secondarily liable for the direct infringement under two doctrines of copyright law: contributory copyright infringement and vicarious copyright infringement.

IV

We first address plaintiffs' claim that Napster is liable for contributory copyright infringement. Traditionally, one who, with knowledge of the infringing activity, induces, causes or materially contributes to the infringing conduct of another, may be held liable as a contributory infringer. [Quotation marks and citations omitted.] Put differently, liability exists if the defendant engages in personal conduct that encourages or assists the infringement. [Quotation marks and citations omitted.]

The district court determined that plaintiffs in all likelihood would establish Napster's liability as a contributory infringer. The district court did not err; Napster, by its conduct, knowingly encourages and assists the infringement of plaintiffs' copyrights.

A. Knowledge

Contributory liability requires that the secondary infringer know or have reason to know of direct infringement. [Quotation marks and citations omitted]. The district court found that Napster had both actual and constructive knowledge that its users exchanged copyrighted music. The district court also concluded that the law does not require knowledge of "specific acts of infringement" and rejected Napster's contention that because the company cannot distinguish infringing from noninfringing files, it does not "know" of the direct infringement.

It is apparent from the record that Napster has knowledge, both actual and constructive, of direct infringement. Napster claims that it is nevertheless protected from contributory liability by the teaching of *Sony Corp. v. Universal City Studios, Inc.*, 464 U.S. 417 (1984). We disagree. We observe that Napster's actual, specific knowledge of direct infringement renders *Sony's* holding of limited assistance to Napster. We are compelled to make a clear distinction between the architecture of the Napster system and Napster's conduct in relation to the operational capacity of the system.

The *Sony* Court refused to hold the manufacturer and retailers of video tape recorders liable for contributory infringement despite evidence that such machines could be and were used to infringe plaintiffs' copyrighted television shows. *Sony* stated that if liability "is to be imposed on petitioners in this case, it must rest on the fact that *they have sold equipment with constructive knowledge of the fact that their customers may use that equipment to make unauthorized copies* of copyrighted material." (emphasis added [by *Napster* court]). The *Sony* Court declined to impute the requisite level of knowledge where the defendants made and sold equipment capable of both infringing and "substantial noninfringing uses." *Id.* at 442 (adopting a modified "staple article of commerce" doctrine from patent law).

We are bound to follow *Sony*, and will not impute the requisite level of knowledge to Napster merely because peer-to-peer file sharing technology may be used to infringe plaintiffs' copyrights. *See* 464 U.S. at 436 (rejecting argument that merely supplying the "'means' to accomplish an infringing activity" leads to imposition of liability). We depart from the reasoning of the district court that Napster failed to demonstrate that its system is capable of commercially significant noninfringing uses. The district court improperly confined the use analysis to current uses, ignoring the system's capabilities. *See generally Sony*, 464 U.S. at 442-43 (framing inquiry as whether the video tape recorder is "*capable* of commercially significant noninfringing uses") (emphasis added). Consequently, the district court placed undue weight on the proportion of current infringing use as compared to current and future noninfringing use. . . . Regardless of the number of Napster's infringing versus noninfringing uses, the evidentiary record here supported the district court's finding that plaintiffs would likely prevail in establishing that Napster knew or had reason to know of its users' infringement of plaintiffs' copyrights. . . .

We agree that if a computer system operator learns of specific infringing material available on his system and fails to purge such material from the system, the operator knows of and contributes to direct infringement. Conversely, absent any specific information which identifies infringing activity, a computer system operator cannot be liable for contributory infringement merely because the structure of the system allows for the exchange of copyrighted material. *See Sony*, 464 U.S. at 436. To enjoin simply because a computer network allows for infringing use would, in our opinion, violate *Sony* and potentially restrict activity unrelated to infringing use.

We nevertheless conclude that sufficient knowledge exists to impose contributory liability when linked to demonstrated infringing use of the Napster system. The record supports the district court's finding that Napster has *actual* knowledge that *specific* infringing material is available using its system, that it could block access to the system by suppliers of the infringing material, and that it failed to remove the material.

B.   MATERIAL CONTRIBUTION

Under the facts as found by the district court, Napster materially contributes to the infringing activity. . . . [T]he district court concluded that "[w]ithout the support services defendant provides, Napster users could not find and download the music they want with the ease of which defendant boasts." We agree that Napster provides the site and facilities for direct infringement. [Quotation marks and citation omitted.] The district court . . . properly found that Napster materially contributes to direct infringement.

We affirm the district court's conclusion that plaintiffs have demonstrated a likelihood of success on the merits of the contributory copyright infringement claim. We will address the scope of the injunction in part VIII of this opinion.

V

We turn to the question whether Napster engages in vicarious copyright infringement. Vicarious copyright liability is an outgrowth of respondeat superior. [Quotation marks and citation omitted.] In the context of copyright law, vicarious liability extends beyond an employer/employee relationship to cases in which a defendant has the right and ability to supervise the infringing activity and also has a direct financial interest in such activities. [Quotation marks and citation omitted.] . . .

A.   FINANCIAL BENEFIT

The district court determined that plaintiffs had demonstrated they would likely succeed in establishing that Napster has a direct financial interest in the infringing activity. We agree. Financial benefit exists where the availability of infringing material acts as a draw for customers. [Quotation marks and citation omitted.] Ample evidence supports the district court's finding that Napster's future revenue is directly dependent upon "increases in userbase." More users register with the Napster system as the "quality and quantity of available music increases." We conclude that the district court did not err in determining that Napster financially benefits from the availability of protected works on its system.

B.   SUPERVISION

The district court determined that Napster has the right and ability to supervise its users' conduct. We agree in part.

The ability to block infringers' access to a particular environment for any reason whatsoever is evidence of the right and ability to supervise. Here, plaintiffs have demonstrated that Napster retains the right to control access to its system.

Napster has an express reservation of rights policy, stating on its website that it expressly reserves the "right to refuse service and terminate accounts in [its] discretion, including, but not limited to, if Napster believes that user conduct violates applicable law . . . or for any reason in Napster's sole discretion, with or without cause."

To escape imposition of vicarious liability, the reserved right to police must be exercised to its fullest extent. Turning a blind eye to detectable acts of infringement for the sake of profit gives rise to liability.

The district court correctly determined that Napster had the right and ability to police its system and failed to exercise that right to prevent the exchange of copyrighted material. The district court, however, failed to recognize that the boundaries of the premises that Napster controls and patrols are limited. [Quotation marks and citation omitted.] Put differently, Napster's reserved "right and ability" to police is cabined by the system's current architecture. As shown by the record, the Napster system does not "read" the content of indexed files, other than to check that they are in the proper MP3 format.

Napster, however, has the ability to locate infringing material listed on its search indices, and the right to terminate users' access to the system. The file name indices, therefore, are within the "premises" that Napster has the ability to police. We recognize that the files are user-named and may not match copyrighted material exactly (for example, the artist or song could be spelled wrong). For Napster to function effectively, however, file names must reasonably or roughly correspond to the material contained in the files, otherwise no user could ever locate any desired music. As a practical matter, Napster, its users and the record company plaintiffs have equal access to infringing material by employing Napster's "search function."

Our review of the record requires us to accept the district court's conclusion that plaintiffs have demonstrated a likelihood of success on the merits of the vicarious copyright infringement claim. Napster's failure to police the system's "premises," combined with a showing that Napster financially benefits from the continuing availability of infringing files on its system, leads to the imposition of vicarious liability. We address the scope of the injunction in part VIII of this opinion.

VI

We next address whether Napster has asserted defenses which would preclude the entry of a preliminary injunction.

Napster alleges that two statutes insulate it from liability. First, Napster asserts that its users engage in actions protected by §1008 of the Audio Home Recording Act of 1992, 17 U.S.C. §1008. Second, Napster argues that its liability for contributory and vicarious infringement is limited by the Digital Millennium Copyright Act, 17 U.S.C. §512. We address the application of each statute in turn.

A. AUDIO HOME RECORDING ACT

The statute states in part:

No action may be brought under this title alleging infringement of copyright based on the manufacture, importation, or distribution of a digital audio recording device, a digital audio recording medium, an analog recording device, or an analog recording medium, or *based on the noncommercial use by a consumer of such a device or medium* for making digital musical recordings or analog musical recordings.

17 U.S.C. §1008 (emphases added). Napster contends that MP3 file exchange is the type of "noncommercial use" protected from infringement actions by the statute. Napster asserts it cannot be secondarily liable for users' nonactionable exchange of copyrighted musical recordings.

The district court rejected Napster's argument, stating that the Audio Home Recording Act is "irrelevant" to the action because: (1) plaintiffs did not bring claims under the Audio Home Recording Act; and (2) the Audio Home Recording Act does not cover the downloading of MP3 files.

We agree with the district court that the Audio Home Recording Act does not cover the downloading of MP3 files to computer hard drives. First, "[u]nder the plain meaning of the Act's definition of digital audio recording devices, computers (and their hard drives) are not digital audio recording devices because their 'primary purpose' is not to make digital audio copied recordings." [Quoting *Diamond*, 180 F.3d at 1078.] Second, notwithstanding Napster's claim that computers are "digital audio recording devices," computers do not make "digital music recordings" as defined by the Audio Home Recording Act. *Id.* at 1077 ("There are simply no grounds in either the plain language of the definition or in the legislative history for interpreting the term 'digital musical recording' to include songs fixed on computer hard drives.").

B.   Digital Millennium Copyright Act

Napster also interposes a statutory limitation on liability by asserting the protections of the "safe harbor" from copyright infringement suits for "Internet service providers" contained in the Digital Millennium Copyright Act, 17 U.S.C. §512. The district court did not give this statutory limitation any weight favoring a denial of temporary injunctive relief. The court concluded that Napster "has failed to persuade this court that subsection 512(d) shelters contributory infringers."

We need not accept a blanket conclusion that §512 of the Digital Millennium Copyright Act will never protect secondary infringers. [The Court left the issue for further development at trial. For guidance on the relevant questions, see the decision in *CoStar Group* in Assignment 9.] . . .

Any destruction of Napster, Inc. by a preliminary injunction is speculative compared to the statistical evidence of massive, unauthorized downloading and uploading of plaintiffs' copyrighted works-as many as 10,000 files per second by defendant's own admission. The court has every reason to believe that, without a preliminary injunction, these numbers will mushroom as Napster users, and newcomers attracted by the publicity, scramble to obtain as much free music as possible before trial.

VII

[The court rejected Napster's defenses of waiver, implied license, and copyright misuse.]

VIII

The district court correctly recognized that a preliminary injunction against Napster's participation in copyright infringement is not only warranted but required. We believe, however, that the scope of the injunction needs modification in light of our opinion. Specifically, we reiterate that contributory liability may potentially be imposed only to the extent that Napster: (1) receives reasonable knowledge of specific infringing files with copyrighted musical compositions and sound recordings; (2) knows or should know that such files are available on the Napster system; and (3) fails to act to prevent viral distribution of the works. The mere existence of the Napster system, absent actual notice and Napster's demonstrated failure to remove the offending material, is insufficient to impose contributory liability. *See Sony*, 464 U.S. at 442-43.

Conversely, Napster may be vicariously liable when it fails to affirmatively use its ability to patrol its system and preclude access to potentially infringing files listed in its search index. Napster has both the ability to use its search function to identify infringing musical recordings and the right to bar participation of users who engage in the transmission of infringing files.

The preliminary injunction which we stayed is overbroad because it places on Napster the entire burden of ensuring that no "copying, downloading, uploading, transmitting, or distributing" of plaintiffs' works occur on the system. As stated, we place the burden on plaintiffs to provide notice to Napster of copyrighted works and files containing such works available on the Napster system before Napster has the duty to disable access to the offending content. Napster, however, also bears the burden of policing the system within the limits of the system. Here, we recognize that this is not an exact science in that the files are user named. In crafting the injunction on remand, the district court should recognize that Napster's system does not currently appear to allow Napster access to users' MP3 files.

After Napster, technology predictably shifted to a model in which the role of the provider was considerably more remote. In the first major litigation against such a provider, the district court held that Grokster's role in the allegedly infringing activity was not sufficient to make it responsible.

Metro-Goldwyn-Mayer Studios, Inc. v. Grokster Ltd.

380 F.3d 1154 (9th Cir. 2004)

Before ROBERT BOOCHEVER, JOHN T. NOONAN, and SIDNEY R. THOMAS, Circuit Judges.

OPINION

THOMAS, Circuit Judge:

This appeal presents the question of whether distributors of peer-to-peer file-sharing computer networking software may be held contributorily or vicariously liable for copyright infringements by users. Under the circumstances presented by this case, we conclude that the defendants are not liable for contributory and vicarious copyright infringement and affirm the district court's partial grant of summary judgment.

I.　BACKGROUND

From the advent of the player piano, every new means of reproducing sound has struck a dissonant chord with musical copyright owners, often resulting in federal litigation. This appeal is the latest reprise of that recurring conflict, and one of a continuing series of lawsuits between the recording industry and distributors of file-sharing computer software.

The plaintiffs in the consolidated cases ("Copyright Owners") are songwriters, music publishers, and motion picture studios who, by their own description, "own or control the vast majority of copyrighted motion pictures and sound recordings in the United States." Defendants Grokster Ltd. and StreamCast Networks, Inc. ("Software Distributors") are companies that freely distribute software that allows users to share computer files with each other, including digitized music and motion pictures. The Copyright Owners allege that over 90% of the files exchanged through use of the "peer-to-peer" file-sharing software offered by the Software Distributors involves copyrighted material, 70% of which is owned by the Copyright Owners. Thus, the Copyright Owners argue, the Software Distributors are liable for vicarious and contributory copyright infringement pursuant to 17 U.S.C. §§501-13, for which the Copyright Owners are entitled to monetary and injunctive relief. The district court granted the Software Distributors partial summary judgment as to liability arising from present activities and certified the resolved questions for appeal pursuant to Fed.R.Civ.P. 54(b).

To analyze the legal issues properly, a rudimentary under-standing of the peer-to-peer file-sharing software at issue is required–particularly because peer-to-peer file sharing differs from typical internet use. In a routine internet transaction, a user will connect via the internet with a website to obtain information or transact business. In computer terms, the personal computer used by the consumer is considered the "client" and the computer that hosts the web page is the "server." The client is obtaining information from a centralized source, namely the server.

In a peer-to-peer distribution network, the information available for access does not reside on a central server. No one computer contains all of the information that is available to all of the users. Rather, each computer makes information available to every other computer in the peer-to-peer network. In other words, in a peer-to-peer network, each computer is both a server and a client.

Because the information is decentralized in a peer-to-peer network, the software must provide some method of cataloguing the available information so that users may access it. The software operates by connecting, via the internet, to other users of the same or similar software. At any given moment, the network consists of other users of similar or the same software online at that time. Thus, an index of files available for sharing is a critical component of peer-to-peer file-sharing networks.

At present, there are three different methods of indexing: (1) a centralized indexing system, maintaining a list of available files on one or more centralized servers; (2) a completely decentralized indexing system, in which each computer maintains a list of files available on that computer only; and (3) a "supernode" system, in which a select number of computers act as indexing servers.

The first Napster system employed a proprietary centralized indexing software architecture in which a collective index of available files was maintained on servers it owned and operated. A user who was seeking to obtain a digital copy of a recording would transmit a search request to the Napster server, the software would conduct a text search of the centralized index for matching files, and the search results would be transmitted to the requesting user. If the results showed that another Napster user was logged on to the Napster server and offering to share the requested recording, the requesting user could then connect directly with the offering user and download the music file.

Under a decentralized index peer-to-peer file-sharing model, each user maintains an index of only those files that the user wishes to make available to other network users. Under this model, the software broadcasts a search request to all the computers on the network and a search of the individual index files is conducted, with the collective results routed back to the requesting computer. This model is employed by the Gnutella software system and is the type of architecture now used by defendant StreamCast. Gnutella is open-source software, meaning that the source code is either in the public domain or is copyrighted and distributed under an open-source license that allows modification of the software, subject to some restrictions.

The third type of peer-to-peer file-sharing network at present is the "supernode" model, in which a number of select computers on the network are designated as indexing servers. The user initiating a file search connects with the most easily accessible supernode, which conducts the search of its index and supplies the user with the results. Any computer on the network could function as a supernode if it met the technical requirements, such as processing speed. The "supernode" architecture was developed by KaZaa BV, a Dutch company, and licensed under the name of "FastTrack" technology.

Both Grokster and StreamCast initially used the FastTrack technology. However, StreamCast had a licensing dispute with KaZaa, and now uses its own branded "Morpheus" version of the open-source Gnutella code. StreamCast users connect to other users of Gnutella-based peer-to-peer file-sharing software. Both Grokster and StreamCast distribute their separate softwares free of charge. Once downloaded onto a user's computer, the software enables the user to participate in the respective peer-to-peer file-sharing networks over the internet.

Users of the software share digital audio, video, picture, and text files. Some of the files are copyrighted and shared without authorization, others are not copyrighted (such as public domain works), and still others are copyrighted, but the copyright owners have authorized software users in peer-to-peer file-sharing networks to distribute their work. The Copyright Owners assert, without serious contest by the Software Distributors, that the vast majority of the files are exchanged illegally in violation of copyright law.

II. ANALYSIS

The question of direct copyright infringement is not at issue in this case. Rather, the Copyright Owners contend that the Software Distributors are liable for the copyright infringement of the software users. The Copyright Owners rely on the two recognized theories of secondary copyright liability: contributory copyright infringement and vicarious copyright infringement. We agree with the district court's well reasoned analysis that the Software Distributors' current activities do not give rise to liability under either theory.

A. Contributory Copyright Infringement

The three elements required to prove a defendant liable under the theory of contributory copyright infringement are: (1) direct infringement by a primary infringer, (2) knowledge of the infringement, and (3) material contribution to the infringement. *Id.* The element of direct infringement is undisputed in this case.

1. Knowledge

Any examination of contributory copyright infringement must be guided by the seminal case of *Sony Corp. of America v. Universal City Studios, Inc.,* 464 U.S. 417 (1984) ("*Sony-Betamax*"). In *Sony-Betamax,* the Supreme Court held that the sale of video tape recorders could not give rise to contributory copyright infringement liability even though the defendant knew the machines were being used to commit infringement. In analyzing the contours of contributory copyright infringement, the Supreme Court drew on the "staple article of commerce" doctrine from patent law. *Id.* at 440-42. Under that doctrine, it would be sufficient to defeat a claim of contributory copyright infringement if the defendant showed that the product was "capable of substantial" or "commercially significant noninfringing uses." In applying this doctrine, the Court found that because Sony's Betamax video tape recorder was capable of commercially significant noninfringing uses, constructive knowledge of the infringing activity could not be imputed from the fact that Sony knew the recorders, as a general matter, could be used for infringement. *Id.* at 442.

In *Napster I* [, 239 F.3d 1004 (9th Cir. 2001)], we construed *Sony-Betamax* to apply to the knowledge element of contributory copyright infringement. *Napster I* held that if a defendant could show that its product was capable of substantial or commercially significant noninfringing uses, then constructive knowledge of the infringement could not be imputed. Rather, if substantial noninfringing use was shown, the copyright owner would be required to show that the defendant had reasonable knowledge of specific infringing files. *Napster I,* 239 F.3d at 1027; *see also A & M Records v. Napster,* 284 F.3d 1091, 1095-96 (9th Cir.2002) ("*Napster II* ").

Thus, in order to analyze the required element of knowledge of infringement, we must first determine what level of knowledge to require. If the product at issue is not capable of substantial or commercially significant noninfringing uses, then the copyright owner need only show that the defendant had constructive knowledge of the infringement. On the other hand, if the product at issue *is* capable of substantial or commercially significant noninfringing uses, then the copyright owner must demonstrate that the defendant had reasonable knowledge of specific infringing files and failed to act on that knowledge to prevent infringement. *See Napster I,* 239 F.3d at 1027.

In this case, the district court found it undisputed that the software distributed by each defendant was capable of substantial noninfringing uses. A careful examination of the record indicates that there is no genuine issue of material fact as to noninfringing use. Indeed, the Software Distributors submitted numerous declarations by persons who permit their work to be distributed via the software, or who use the software to distribute public domain works. *See id.* One striking example provided by the Software Distributors is the popular band Wilco, whose record company had declined to release one of its albums on the basis that it had no commercial potential. Wilco repurchased the work from the record company and made the album available for free downloading, both from its own website and through the software user networks. The result sparked widespread interest and, as a result, Wilco received another recording contract. Other recording artists have debuted their works through the user networks. Indeed, the record indicates that thousands of other musical groups have authorized free distribution of their music through the internet. In addition to music, the software has been used to share thousands of public domain literary works made available through Project Gutenberg as well as historic public domain films released by the Prelinger Archive. In short, from the evidence presented, the district court quite correctly concluded that the software was capable of substantial noninfringing uses and, therefore, that the *Sony-Betamax* doctrine applied.

The Copyright Owners submitted no evidence that could contradict these declarations. Rather, the Copyright Owners argue that the evidence establishes that the vast majority of the software use is for copyright infringement. This argument misapprehends the *Sony* standard as construed in *Napster I,* which emphasized that in order for limitations imposed by *Sony* to apply, a product need only be *capable* of substantial noninfringing uses. *Napster I,* 239 F.3d at 1021.[9]

In this case, the Software Distributors have not only shown that their products are capable of substantial noninfringing uses, but that the uses have commercial viability. Thus, applying *Napster I, Napster II,* and *Sony-Betamax* to the record, the district court correctly concluded that the Software Distributors had established that their products were capable of substantial or commercially significant noninfringing uses. Therefore, the district correctly reasoned, the Software Distributors could not be held liable for constructive knowledge of infringement, and the Copyright Owners were required to show that the Software Distributors had reasonable knowledge of specific infringement to satisfy the threshold knowledge requirement.

Having determined that the "reasonable knowledge of specific infringement" requirement applies here, we must then decide whether the Copyright Owners have raised sufficient genuine issues of material fact to satisfy that higher standard. As the district court correctly concluded, the time at which such knowledge is obtained is significant. Because contributory copyright infringement requires knowledge *and* material contribution, the Copyright Owners were required to establish that the Software Distributors had "specific knowledge of infringement at a time at which they contribute[d] to the infringement, and [ ] fail[ed] to act upon that information." [Quoting the district court opinion.] As the district court correctly observed, and as we explain further in our discussion of material contribution, "Plaintiffs' notices of infringing conduct are irrelevant," because "they arrive when Defendants do nothing to facilitate, and cannot do anything to stop, the alleged infringement" of specific copyrighted © ontent. *See Napster II,* 284 F.3d at 1096 ("[P]laintiffs bear the burden to provide notice to Napster of copyrighted works and files containing such works available on the Napster system *before* Napster has the duty to disable access *to the offending content.*") (internal quotation marks omitted) (emphasis added).

In the context of this case, the software design is of great import. As we have discussed, the software at issue in *Napster I* and *Napster II* employed a centralized set of servers that maintained an index of available files. In contrast, under both StreamCast's decentralized, Gnutella-type network and Grokster's quasi-decentralized, supernode, KaZaa-type network, no central index is maintained. Indeed, at present, neither StreamCast nor Grokster maintains control over index files. As the district court observed, even if the Software Distributors "closed their doors and deactivated all computers within their control, users of their products could continue sharing files with little or no interruption."

Therefore, we agree with the district court that the Software Distributors were entitled to partial summary judgment on the element of knowledge.

2.   Material Contribution

We also agree with the district court that with respect to their current software distribution and related activities, defendants do not materially contribute to copyright infringement.

In *Napster I,* we found material contribution after reciting the district court's factual finding that "Napster is an integrated service." 239 F.3d at 1022. We "agree[d] that Napster provides the site and facilities for direct infringement." *Id.* (internal quotation marks omitted). We further cited the holding of *Netcom,* which found "substantial participation" based on Netcom's "failure to cancel [a user's] infringing message and thereby stop an infringing copy from being distributed worldwide." *Id.* (quoting *Religious Tech. Ctr. v. Netcom On-Line Communication Servs.,* 907 F. Supp. 1361, 1372 (N.D. Cal. 1995)) (alteration in original). We have also found material contribution where a defendant operated a swap meet at which infringing products were sold and provided utilities, parking, and advertising. *Fonovisa, Inc. v. Cherry Auction, Inc.,* 76 F.3d 259, 261, 264 (9th Cir. 1996).

As indicated by the record, the Software Distributors do not provide the "site and facilities" for infringement, and do not otherwise materially contribute to direct infringement. Infringing messages or file indices do not reside on defendants' computers, nor do defendants have the ability to suspend user accounts.

While material contribution can be established through provision of site and facilities for infringement, followed by a failure to stop specific instances of infringement once knowledge of those infringements is acquired, the Software Distributors have not provided the site and facilities for infringement in the first place. If the Software Distributors were true access providers, failure to disable that access after acquiring specific knowledge of a user's infringement might be material contribution. Or, if the Software Distributors stored files or indices, failure to delete the offending files or offending index listings might be material contribution. However, the Software Distributors here are not access providers, and they do not provide file storage and index maintenance. Rather, it is the users of the software who, by connecting to each other over the internet, create the network and provide the access. "Failure" to alter software located on another's computer is simply not akin to the failure to delete a filename from one's own computer, to the failure to cancel the registration name and password of a particular user from one's user list, or to the failure to make modifications to software on one's own computer.

The Copyright Owners have not provided evidence that defendants materially contribute in any other manner. StreamCast maintains an XML file from which user software periodically retrieves parameters. These values may include the addresses of websites where lists of active users are maintained. The owner of the FastTrack software, Sharman, maintains root nodes containing lists of currently active supernodes to which users can connect. Both defendants also communicate with users incidentally, but not to facilitate infringement. All of these activities are too incidental to any direct copyright infringement to constitute material contribution. No infringing files or lists of infringing files are hosted by defendants, and the defendants do not regulate or provide access.

While Grokster and StreamCast in particular may seek to be the "next Napster," the peer-to-peer file-sharing technology at issue is not simply a tool engineered to get around the holdings of *Napster I* and *Napster II*. The technology has numerous other uses, significantly reducing the distribution costs of public domain and permissively shared art and speech, as well as reducing the centralized control of that distribution. Especially in light of the fact that liability for contributory copyright infringement does not require proof of any direct financial gain from the infringement, we decline to expand contributory copyright liability in the manner that the Copyright Owners request.

B.   Vicarious Copyright Infringement

Three elements are required to prove a defendant vicariously liable for copyright infringement: (1) direct infringement by a primary party, (2) a direct financial benefit to the defendant, and (3) the right and ability to supervise the infringers. *Napster I*, 239 F.3d at 1022. "Vicarious copyright liability is an 'outgrowth' of respondeat superior," imposing liability on those with a sufficiently supervisory relationship to the direct infringer. *Id.* (citing *Cherry Auction*, 76 F.3d at 262). In *Napster I*, we held that *Sony-Betamax* "has no application to . . . vicarious copyright infringement" because the issue of vicarious liability was "not before the Supreme Court" in that case. *Id.*

The elements of direct infringement and a direct financial benefit, via advertising revenue, are undisputed in this case.

1.   Right and Ability To Supervise

We agree with the district court that there is no issue of material fact as to whether defendants have the right and ability to supervise the direct infringers in this case. Allocation of liability in vicarious copyright liability cases has developed from a historical distinction between the paradigmatic "dance hall operator" and "landlord" defendants. *Cherry Auction*, 76 F.3d at 262. The dance hall operator is liable, while the landlord escapes liability, because the dance hall operator has the right and ability to supervise infringing conduct while the landlord does not. *Id.* Thus, the "right and ability to supervise" describes a relationship between the defendant and the direct infringer.

A salient characteristic of that relationship often, though not always, is a formal licensing agreement between the defendant and the direct infringer. *See, e.g., Napster I*, 239 F.3d at 1023; *Cherry Auction*, 76 F.3d at 261; *Shapiro, Bernstein & Co. v. H.L. Green Co.*, 316 F.2d 304, 306 (2d Cir.1963) (cited as the landmark case in *Cherry Auction*, 76 F.3d at 262). Indeed, *Napster I* found especially important the fact that Napster had an express policy reserving the right to block infringers' access for any reason. 239 F.3d at 1023 ("[A]bility to block infringers' access to a particular environment for any reason whatsoever is evidence of the right and ability to supervise.").

In *Cherry Auction,* we held that the right and ability to supervise existed where a swap meet operator reserved the right to terminate vendors for any reason, promoted the swap meet, controlled access by customers, patrolled the meet, and could control direct infringers through its rules and regulations. 76 F.3d at 262-63.

Similarly in *Napster I,* we found Napster had the right and ability to supervise Napster users because it controlled the central indices of files, users were required to register with Napster, and access to the system depended on the validity of a user's registration.

It does not appear from any of the evidence in the record that either of the defendants has the ability to block access to individual users. Grokster nominally reserves the right to terminate access, while StreamCast does not maintain a licensing agreement with persons who download Morpheus. However, given the lack of a registration and log-in process, even Grokster has no ability to actually terminate access to filesharing functions, absent a mandatory software upgrade to all users that the particular user refuses, or IP address-blocking attempts. It is also clear that none of the communication between defendants and users provides a point of access for filtering or searching for infringing files, since infringing material and index information do not pass through defendants' computers.

In the case of StreamCast, shutting down its XML file altogether would not prevent anyone from using the Gnutella network. In the case of Grokster, its licensing agreement with KaZaa/Sharman does not give it the ability to mandate that root nodes be shut down. Moreover, the alleged ability to shut down operations altogether is more akin to the ability to close down an entire swap meet or stop distributing software altogether, rather than the ability to exclude individual participants, a practice of policing aisles, an ability to block individual users directly at the point of log-in, or an ability to delete individual filenames from one's own computer. The sort of monitoring and supervisory relationship that has supported vicarious liability in the past is completely absent in this case.

The district court here found that unlike Napster, Grokster and StreamCast do not operate and design an "integrated service" which they monitor and control. We agree. The nature of the relationship between Grokster and StreamCast and their users is significantly different from the nature of the relationship between a swap meet operator and its participants, or prior versions of Napster and its users, since Grokster and StreamCast are more truly decentralized, peer-to-peer file-sharing networks.

The district court correctly characterized the Copyright Owners' evidence of the right and ability to supervise as little more than a contention that "the software itself could be altered to prevent users from sharing copyrighted files." In arguing that this ability constitutes evidence of the right and ability to supervise, the Copyright Owners confuse the right and ability to supervise with the strong duty imposed on entities that have already been determined to be liable for vicarious copyright infringement; such entities have an obligation to exercise their policing powers to the fullest extent, which in Napster's case included implementation of new filtering mechanisms. *Napster II,* 284 F.3d at 1098 ("The tolerance standard announced *applies only to copyrighted works which Plaintiffs have properly noticed* as required by the modified preliminary injunction. That is, Napster must do everything feasible to block files from its system which contain noticed copyrighted works.") (emphasis added). But the potential duty a district court may place on a vicariously liable defendant is not the same as the "ability" contemplated by the "right and ability to supervise" test. Moreover, a duty to alter software and files located on one's own computer system is quite different in kind from a duty to alter software located on another person's computer. We agree with the district court that possibilities for upgrading software located on another person's computer are irrelevant to determining whether vicarious liability exists.

C.   Turning a "Blind Eye" to Infringement

The Copyright Owners finally argue that Grokster and StreamCast should not be able to escape vicarious liability by turning a "blind eye" to the infringement of their users, and that "[t]urning a blind eye to detectable acts of infringement for the sake of profit gives rise to liability." *Napster I*, 239 F.3d at 1023. If the Software Distributors had a right and ability to control and supervise that they proactively refused to exercise, such refusal would not absolve them of liability. However, although that rhetoric has occasionally been employed in describing vicarious copyright infringement, there is no separate "blind eye" theory or element of vicarious liability that exists independently of the traditional elements of liability. Thus, this theory is subsumed into the Copyright Owners' claim for vicarious copyright infringement and necessarily fails for the same reasons.

III.

Resolution of these issues does not end the case. As the district court clearly stated, its decision was limited to the specific software in use at the time of the district court decision. The Copyright Owners have also sought relief based on previous versions of the software, which contain significant – and perhaps crucial–differences from the software at issue. We express no opinion as to those issues.

As to the question at hand, the district court's grant of partial summary judgment to the Software Distributors is clearly dictated by applicable precedent. The Copyright Owners urge a re-examination of the law in the light of what they believe to be proper public policy, expanding exponentially the reach of the doctrines of contributory and vicarious copyright infringement. Not only would such a renovation conflict with binding precedent, it would be unwise. Doubtless, taking that step would satisfy the Copyright Owners' immediate economic aims. However, it would also alter general copyright law in profound ways with unknown ultimate consequences outside the present context.

Further, as we have observed, we live in a quicksilver technological environment with courts ill-suited to fix the flow of internet innovation. The introduction of new technology is always disruptive to old markets, and particularly to those copyright owners whose works are sold through well-established distribution mechanisms. Yet, history has shown that time and market forces often provide equilibrium in balancing interests, whether the new technology be a player piano, a copier, a tape recorder, a video recorder, a personal computer, a karaoke machine, or an MP3 player. Thus, it is prudent for courts to exercise caution before restructuring liability theories for the purpose of addressing specific market abuses, despite their apparent present magnitude.

Indeed, the Supreme Court has admonished us to leave such matters to Congress. In *Sony-Betamax*, the Court spoke quite clearly about the role of Congress in applying copyright law to new technologies. As the Supreme Court stated in that case, "The direction of Art. I is that *Congress* shall have the power to promote the progress of science and the useful arts. When, as here, the Constitution is permissive, the sign of how far Congress has chosen to go can come only from Congress." 464 U.S. at 456 (quoting *Deepsouth Packing Co. v. Laitram Corp.*, 406 U.S. 518, 530 (1972)).

In this case, the district court correctly applied applicable law and properly declined the invitation to alter it. We affirm the district court, and remand for resolution of the remaining issues.

The RIAA's appeal was argued before the Ninth Circuit in February 2004, but the case has not been decided as the second edition of this book goes to print.

The defeat in *Grokster* did not, however, stop litigation by the RIAA. Rather, it commenced a campaign of thousands of lawsuits against individual users engaged in file sharing. Because those lawsuits do not involve the complex questions of attribution of responsibility at issue in *Napster* and *Grokster*, they have resulted in easy victories (usually settlements) for the record companies. It is less clear, however, that they have had any impact on the pace of file sharing.

Given the crosscutting policy implications of the debate, it should be no surprise that academics have proposed a number of legislative solutions to dissipate the tension in the industry. For example, Professors Neil Netanel and Terry Fisher separately have proposed a noncommercial use levy, in which a tax would be collected on each sale of software or hardware likely to be used in the infringing activity, the proceeds of which would be delivered to content owners in compensation for the unlawful infringing use. (A similar system is already in place to tax blank digital audio tapes and digital audio recorders. 17 U.S.C. §§1004-1007.) Taking another approach, Professors Mark Lemley and Tony Reese have proposed a stripped-down enforcement system in which copyright owners could take advantage of a summary administrative procedure to obtain recourse against flagrant file-sharers, which they tentatively define as those who upload 50 or more different songs in a 30-day period.

Relevant Glossary Entries

P2P File-Sharing
Uniform Resource Locator (URL)
Web Server

Problem Set 21

21.1. You are retained by Pacific Records, a large conglomerate that owns a variety of musical works. Among other things, it owns the entire back catalogue for the Who, including the album "Quadrophenia." Pete Townshend personally owns the musical works (which he composed for the most part), but Pacific owns the sound recordings. In combing through their records, they notice that the Who (and Pete Townshend) subsequently made a movie based on the album. For the movie, the Who returned to the studio with the same personnel as they had on the original album. They recorded substantially all of the same songs that they had recorded on the original album, for the most part recording them in a manner that so closely followed the original recordings that only the most careful listener could detect the differences. Pacific did not consent to this recording. Is there any way that the recordings could have been lawful if they were made and distributed without Pacific's consent? Copyright Act §§106 and 114.

21.2. One of your associates has been reading newspaper stories about Napster, P2P file-sharing, and unlawful copying. He has just discovered that his teenage daughter has a made an extensive collection of digital audiotapes from the associates' collection of Willie Nelson records — more than 50 altogether. He wants to know if this activity is unlawful. What do you say? Copyright Act §§106 and 1008.

21.3. One of your law-school classmates is in the process of forming a network of Internet sites that would specialize in the distribution of music targeting specialized audiences. He has a variety of different sites planned and wants your advice on which sites would be lawful under Copyright Act §§106 and 114. Please give him your views on each of the following possible models, not only their legality, but the parties from whom he will need to obtain copyright licenses. He emphasizes that everything is still in the planning stages, so feel free to suggest minor alterations in the models if that would be useful.

(a) In some cases, he will provide technology that will permit an existing terrestrial radio station to rebroadcast its programming, in its entirety over the Internet. For example, he plans to rebroadcast all of the programming of KCFX, an existing Kansas City radio station.

(b) He has obtained the trademarks of the early Internet station Deadradio.com. This service plays only music of the Grateful Dead. It has a link on the site that provides an advance program listing of the sound recordings that it will play. Most of the music is from commercially available recordings, although on Saturday nights he plans a special that plays tapes recorded at the "taping section" of one of the Grateful Dead's concerts.

(c) Bluesradio.com. This service would function as an Internet blues radio station. It would be available only to subscribers, but would not announce in advance the songs that it will play. It plans to play music from a wide variety of blues artists of all periods and genres.

(d) Celestial Jukebox. This service, his personal favorite, charges a monthly fee of $9.95. The user fills out a form describing the user's favorite artists and music preferences. The service then sends a randomly selected Internet signal to the user that includes selections designed to indulge the user's preferences.

21.4. You are the law clerk for a Justice on the United States Supreme Court, reviewing a petition for a writ of certiorari challenging the decision in *Grokster*. The Justice wants your views on how to analyze the case. Do you think the Justice should vote to affirm or reverse? Why?

Section D.   Software Licensing

The previous sections of this chapter cover the law and practice of transactions involving tangible property or its digital equivalent. Transactions that involve software do not fit well within the same framework, primarily because federal intellectual property laws heavily influence these transactions. Even in the music context, discussed above, the primary significance of copyright protection is that it gives the owner the unconditional right to control copying. In the software context, the role of IP is much more complex. As Assignment 23 explains, licenses are used not only to foster collaborative uses of software technologies, but also to constrain the activities of the end users of both commercial and consumer software programs. As Assignment 22 explains, those different (and arguably conflicting) purposes for using software licenses create substantial tensions between freedom of contract principles on the one hand and the benefits and constraints that IP law poses on the other.

To introduce the problem, it is important to recognize that software often is protected both by patent and by copyright. For example, a patent might cover a particular technique for designing a Web site. Similarly, copyright law generally protects the lines of code of which computer programs consist. Under basic principles of the law of intellectual property, a business that wishes to use material protected by copyright or patent lawfully — that is, a business that does not want to infringe — ordinarily must obtain the consent of the copyright owner or patentee. For a variety of reasons, part historical and part practical, the copyright owner or patentee ordinarily does not transfer ownership of the copyright or patent to the user. Rather, such a transaction is structured as a license: The transferor might sell some particular tangible object (a floppy disk, for example), but it normally grants only a license of the intellectual property. Thus, for example, when you purchase a computer for your home, you do not technically "buy" the software that goes on the computer; you receive a license to use the software. In the common situation where the owner will license the same software to multiple parties (think of the common Windows applications), the license is a "nonexclusive" license. If the licensor will have only one customer for the product in question, the license would be an "exclusive license."

The characteristics of the transactions can give the impression that the distinction between a sale and a license is purely technical — the user in each case goes to a store (a physical brick-and-mortar location or Internet retailer), selects a product, pays for the product, and then receives the product. However, as a legal and practical matter the two transactions are distinct in important ways. For example, as you will see in the pages that follow, a party that licenses intellectual property is much more likely to be able to control the activity of subsequent parties than a party that sells something. That is particularly important in the software industry, where similar products may be sold for significantly different prices to different sorts of customers. The pricing of a Microsoft operating system, for example, is justifiably quite different for a large thousand-seat corporate license than it is for a single consumer buying at retail. Thus, Microsoft wants to be sure that the copies of a software program that are distributed cheaply are not transferred so as to compete against products that are being distributed in other markets at higher cost.

Assignment 22:   The Basic Framework

The most important conceptual point about a license is that it does not result in the transfer of ownership of the software to the licensee. Rather, the licensee is granted the right to use the product in accordance with the terms of the license agreement. In other words, it is a release by the licensor of a right to sue the licensee for actions that otherwise would constitute infringement of the relevant patent or copyright. Accordingly, any license transaction presents the possibility of two completely distinct types of liability. The first is liability for breach of the license, which generally involves standard issues of contractual interpretation. The second is liability for infringement of the intellectual property rights of the licensor, based on claims that the licensee's conduct exceeds the grant of the license. That form of liability generally presents issues of copyright or patent law, depending on the type of intellectual property that is implicated by the allegedly infringing activity. Before turning to the terms of a license in the next assignment, it is important first to explore the interaction between those two sources of obligation.

A.   The License as a Contract

In interpreting a contract by which a user obtains rights to run a software program, the first and most basic question will be whether the contract in fact is a license or a sale. As you will see below, certain provisions of copyright law give the software developer strong reasons to prefer a "license" to a "sale." Among other things, copyright law grants certain defenses to a person that obtains a copy of a work by sale, defenses that are not available to a person that is only a licensee.

Courts attempting to apply a license also must address the basic question of what body of law applies to the contract — either Article 2 of the Uniform Commercial Code or the common law of contracts. In the purest case — the download of a software program from the Internet that involves no tangible goods of any kind — Article 2 of the Uniform Commercial Code does not apply, at least directly. UCC §2-102. On the other hand, in most custom software transactions, the "deliverables" will include substantial tangible property in the form of the disks on which the software is delivered, as well as associated documentation and hardware. In those cases, courts regularly apply Article 2 on the theory that the predominant purpose of the transaction was for the "sale" of "goods." See UCC §§2-105(1) (defining "goods" to mean "things . . . which are movable at the time of identification to the contract"), 2-106(1) (defining "sale" to "consis[t] in the passing of title from the seller to the buyer for a price"). Even if there is no such justification for a

425

direct application of Article 2, courts often apply Article 2 by analogy, reasoning that its wide adoption makes it reasonably foreseeable to contracting parties that rules in Article 2 might be applied to resolve a commercial dispute even if goods are not directly involved.

Having said that, the practical differences between a typical sale of goods and a typical software license make it problematic for courts (or parties) blindly to import principles from Article 2 directly into transactions that involve software. Thus, to offer the most obvious example, as you will see in the next assignment, the warranties that make sense in one context are likely to be excessive, irrelevant, or inadequate in the other. Thus, Article 2 generally provides relatively generous warranties and other protections for buyers, which will apply unless the seller takes adequate steps to disclaim the warranties and contract around other rules that the seller finds unsuitable. In the context of software, by contrast, the types of warranties that would make sense are quite different, particularly in the commercial context where (as you will see in the next assignment) the warranties are likely to focus on specific commitments about product functionality rather than general principles about "merchantability" and "fitness for a particular purpose."

Aside from the common law of contracts and Article 2 of the UCC, another potential source of law for licensing transactions is the Uniform Computer Information Transactions Act (UCITA). As mentioned previously, UCITA was a major — albeit unsuccessful — legislative project that covered a broad spectrum of issues affecting licenses of software and computer information, including the formation, interpretation, performance, and enforcement of such contracts in electronic-commerce contexts. Although NCCUSL has now withdrawn support for it, it was adopted in Virginia and Delaware, and it did present the culmination of more than a decade of work by a sophisticated drafting committee and advisers. Accordingly, on occasion it might be useful to turn to UCITA for guidance as to potential solutions to problems that arise in the area.

In sum, the software developer aims for a "license" of "software" — governed by the common law of contracts — while the user would prefer a "sale" of "goods" — governed by the UCC and carrying with it the rights copyright law affords purchasers.

B.   Licenses and Intellectual Property

1.   *Two Paradigms*

Our legal system is committed to the idea that private parties may structure their affairs through voluntary arrangements, and courts will enforce these arrangements without passing on their substance. This idea often is referred to as the "freedom of contract" principle, which many scholars justify on efficiency or autonomy grounds. Sometimes, however, a court will decide that the interest in freedom of contract is offset by some paramount interest of society and will refuse to enforce a contract on public policy grounds. The exceptions to the freedom of contract principle may relate the substance of the agreement (e.g., illegal subject matter, restraint of trade, impairment of familial relations) or to the process by which the agreement has been made (e.g., duress, mistake, unconscionability).

Software licenses, however, bring contract law squarely into a confrontation with the entirely different legal tradition of the law of intellectual property. The law of intellectual property is almost entirely federal, based (with respect to patent and copyright at least) in the Constitution itself. It generally affords only a limited respect for freedom of contract, reflecting a pervasive intervention into the arrangements that allocate control of aesthetic and utilitarian creations. That intervention rests on the view that the ultimate purpose of those laws is a public one: Copyright law should foster a rich and vibrant diffusion of cultural artifacts, while patent law should induce innovation in technology.

As discussed at the beginning of this section, software often is protected both by patent and copyright. For reasons that are not entirely clear, rules related to patents have not been central to licensing practice. That might be because software patents were difficult to obtain until recently, while copyright protection has been available for decades. It also might be because the relative difficulty of enforcing patent claims makes copyright enforcement preferable in cases that involve the direct use of a completed product. In any event, it is plain that copyright doctrine has produced most of the prominent legal difficulties in licensing. Some of the difficulties relate to default rules that often might conflict with commercial expectations. For example, as Assignment 5 discusses, it is crucial that a document regarding a software program deal with the question of ownership, because copyright law will provide background rules that might not match the intentions of the parties.

In the copyright context, the most important tension comes from the concern that works ultimately should pass into the "public domain," where they are free for all to use as the building blocks for their new creations. Technically, works do not pass into the public domain until the conclusion of the (now very lengthy) term of the copyright — 70 years from the death of the author if the author is an individual. Copyright Act §302. But copyright law includes a variety of rules designed to ensure that even during the term of the copyright there is adequate opportunity for potential authors to use existing works. The two doctrines that best illustrate that point are the first-sale doctrine and the defense of fair use.

(a) First-Sale Doctrine

The first-sale doctrine holds that the distribution rights of a copyright owner in a copy of software are exhausted upon the first sale of that copy. (Thus, it is one of a class of IP doctrines referred to as rules of "exhaustion.") As codified in Copyright Act §109(a), the doctrine generally provides that the "owner" of a copy of a copyrighted work "is entitled, without the authority of the copyright owner, to sell or otherwise dispose of the possession of that copy." Thus, the provision is an exception to the general rule that the copyright owner has the exclusive right to "distribute copies . . . of the copyrighted work to the public by sale or other transfer of ownership, or by rental, lease, or lending." Copyright Act §106(3). Similarly, Section 117 grants a variety of rights to the "owner" of a computer program to make copies necessary for normal use of the program, or for maintenance or repair of the machine.

(b) Fair Use

The most prominent reflection of the public-domain policy in copyright law appears in the protection of fair use. Section 106 grants copyright owners broad exclusive rights to most significant forms of exploitation of copyrightable works. But Section 107 balances those broad rights against a vague and indeterminate protection of any use that is "fair." The section does not specify precisely what is fair, but simply outlines a number of factors to be included in the determination of whether any particular use is fair:

(1)   the purpose and character of the use, including whether such use is of a commercial nature or is for nonprofit educational purposes;
(2)   the nature of the copyrighted work;
(3)   the amount and substantiality of the portion used in relation to the copyrighted work as a whole; and
(4)   the effect of the use upon the potential market for or value of the copyrighted work.

Although it is difficult to generalize about an inquiry that is so intensely fact-specific, the trend in modern cases is to condemn commercial uses unless they are "transformative" in some way (such as use in a parody or in the course of reverse engineering). For example, one leading case held that it was fair use for a video-game developer to use copyrighted software code contained in the Sega Genesis console to develop video-game cartridges compatible with that console. Sega Enterprises, Ltd. v. Accolade, Inc., 977 F.2d 1510 (CA9 1992).

For present purposes, it is important to notice that a significant amount of the use of copyrighted materials in everyday life is governed not by contracts with the copyright owner, but by the first-sale and fair-use doctrines. When we resell books to a used bookstore, when we copy materials for classroom use, even when we record music onto cassettes or compact discs, our activities are lawful (if at all) only because of those doctrines.

2.   Efforts to Enhance Control

Copyright owners naturally would prefer to have broader, more exclusive, and more definitive control over their works than they receive from the regime of incomplete and vaguely defined control that the Copyright Act erects. There are good economic reasons for their concern. Most obviously, software is a product that is quite susceptible of free-riding, in the sense that it costs much more to design and develop it than it does to copy it. That is true even if, as is often the case, the copying is not so literal as to amount to direct copyright infringement. Because copyright protects only the literal code — not the ideas reflected in that code (for which patent protection is the only source of protection) — software developers often find existing protections woefully inadequate.

It may be that the reason for licensing of software in the earliest days was the blunt reason that contract was the *only* way to protect software at a time when it was not clear that *either* patents or copyright would protect it. But now, even though copyright protection is formally available, developers seeking more robust control of their products have proceeded on two broad parallel fronts to gain that control: through technological access controls and through terms of their license agreements.

(a)   *Technological Restrictions*

The first avenue is largely technological: through the development of more sophisticated access controls that limit the ability of third parties to use software without the consent of the copyright owner. Rights of fair use and first sale do not concern the copyright author so much if the copyright author can place a technological barrier around the product that prevents the exercise of those rights. Those technological efforts have become much more controversial in the last few years, because the Digital Millennium Copyright Act includes a broad prohibition on circumvention technology that a copyright owner uses to protect its content. Among other things, Copyright Act Section 1201(a) makes it a federal offense to "circumvent a technological measure that effectively controls access to a work protected under [the Copyright Act]."

The first case interpreting that provision involved a suit by the motion-picture industry against the designers of a software program called DeCSS, which allows users to crack the "CSS" software that the motion-picture industry uses to encrypt DVDs. The trial court rejected a number of claims by the software designers. The most important conclusion for present purposes is that the statute bars circumvention even if the circumvention is designed to permit a party to exercise a right to fair use. Universal City Studios, Inc. v. Reimerdes, 82 F. Supp. 2d 211 (S.D.N.Y. 2000). If that case is correct, and it arguably does follow the natural reading of the language of the statute, then a copyright owner that can create an "effective" access control can destroy all rights of fair use and any exercise of rights under the first-sale doctrine. Although that result might seem to implicate significant First Amendment concerns, the Second Circuit rejected such claims on appeal from the *Reimerdes* opinion. Universal City Studios, Inc v. Corley, 273 F.3d 429 (2nd Cir. 2001).

Congress included one potential safety valve in the legislation by requiring the Librarian of Congress to conduct a rulemaking proceeding every three years to formulate exceptions whenever the broad statutory ban would adversely affect legitimate noninfringing users. To date, however, the Librarian of Congress has been quite chary in recognizing exceptions. The 2000 rulemaking recognized exceptions only for Web sites blocked by filtering software and works protected by malfunctioning access control systems. That is to say: It is not a crime to circumvent filtering software so as to view a site posted on the Internet or to "break into" a product if the access control is preventing your access because of a malfunction. The 2003 rulemaking (effective through 2006) added only two new categories: out-of-print software that cannot be accessed without the original media and e-books that do not have a "read-aloud" function. From the perspective of this assignment, it is conspicuous that nothing in that list permits access to reverse-engineer software or makes personal use of software that otherwise might be "fair" under Copyright Act Section 107.

That broad grant of power to content providers has been highly controversial. The premise of enactment sounded plausible at the time: You could not expect content providers to put their closely guarded content up on the Internet if they could not be sure they could protect it against copying. But the broad application of the statute has generated substantial concern. Among other things, Professor Jessica Litman has discussed how the statute's general affirmation of private power (through the public enforcement of privately designed technological controls) suggests an increasing ascendancy in Congress of a freedom-of-contract paradigm for copyright law. As suggested above, that paradigm formerly was more characteristic of state commercial law than of federal intellectual-property law. It remains to be seen whether the courts will interpret the statute as broadly as the early indications suggest, or whether Congress will narrow the statute when its broad implications become clear.

(b) Restrictions by Transactional Design

The second avenue is transactional: through contractual restrictions on the exercise of rights users otherwise might have under the Copyright Act. Because efforts to create enforceable restrictions rely on state-law enforcement of the underlying contracts, they bring the freedom-of-contract paradigm of state law directly into conflict with the traditional public-domain paradigm of the copyright law. Those cases typically present three related questions. First, because the transactions often involve remote electronic interactions, there often is a substantial question whether there is a contract at all. Because Assignment 13 discusses that question, it is not discussed further here. Second, is the transaction a license or a sale? If it is a "true" license rather than a sale, the party that takes under the license may not be the "owner" of a copy. That is the principal issue in the *DSC Communications* and *Softman* cases that follow. Third, when does copyright law preempt the enforcement of contractual provisions that prohibit uses by the licensee that copyright law would permit? That is the issue in the *Bowers* case that closes this section of the assignment.

(I) Is a Licensee an "Owner"?   The most fundamental tactic to limit the rights that copyright law grants users focuses on the statutory language in Sections 109 and 117 that grants rights to the "owner" of a particular copy of a copyrighted work. If the copyright owner structures the transaction so that the user is not an "owner" (i.e., in the form of a license), then the user cannot take advantage of the exhaustion doctrines contained in those provisions. An entirely deferential approach would accept the label that the parties placed on a transaction and hold that rights under those sections of the copyright laws are not available to any party that acquires its interest in a transaction characterized as a license. Although the courts have not been

uniformly receptive to such a deferential approach, their efforts to develop more functional definitions of the term "owner" seem unlikely to constrain licensors significantly.

DSC Communications Corp. v. Pulse Communications, Inc.

170 F.3d 1354 (Fed. Cir. 1999)

Before MAYER, Chief Judge, FRIEDMAN, Senior Circuit Judge, and BRYSON, Circuit Judge.

BRYSON, Circuit Judge.

DSC Communications Corporation (DSC) and Pulse Communications, Inc., (Pulsecom) make products for the telephone industry and compete for the business of the Regional Bell Operating Companies, more commonly known as the "RBOCs." Competition between the two parties led to this litigation over certain products that the two produce for use in commercial telephone systems.

DSC struck first, filing an action in the United States District Court for the Eastern District of Virginia in which it alleged that Pulsecom had committed various federal and state law violations, including . . . infringement of DSC's copyright in [certain] software. . . . Pulsecom then counterclaimed, charging that DSC had infringed Pulsecom's U.S. Patent No. 5,263,081 (the '081 patent).

The parties went to trial on DSC's claims, and at the close of DSC's case-in-chief, Pulsecom moved for judgment as a matter of law. The court granted the motion and dismissed . . . DSC's claims. [After further proceedings, the court also dismissed Pulsecom's patent claim against DSC.]

I

This case involves certain components of digital loop carrier systems (DLCs), electronic devices that allow telephone companies to serve large numbers of subscribers efficiently. Before the advent of DLCs, telephone companies had to run copper wire from their central offices to the telephones of each of their subscribers. DLCs allow the individual copper lines to be run over much shorter distances, resulting in large savings for telephone companies. Typically, a DLC is placed in a location central to a number of subscribers, and copper lines are run over the relatively short distances from the DLC to the subscribers.

The DLC acts as an analog-to-digital converter and as a signal modulator-demodulator. The electrical signals that travel over the copper lines between the DLC and the subscribers are voice-frequency analog signals, but the signals that travel between the DLC and the central telephone office are digital signals that travel over a high-bandwidth (*e.g.,* fiber optic) digital channel. The DLC converts the various analog signals it receives from individual subscribers to a digital format and modulates those digital signals into a high-bandwidth composite signal that is sent to the central office through the digital channel. The DLC performs the reverse process on signals traveling from the central office to individual subscribers.

The devices at the heart of the dispute in this case are the "Litespan 2000" DLC, which is manufactured by DSC, and the interface cards, which DSC and Pulsecom designed to work with the Litespan. The Litespan has a backplane connecting 500 interface card slots, through interface circuitry, to a microprocessor. The back-plane is controlled by an application-specific integrated circuit that uses a partic-ular signaling protocol. The purpose of the interface cards is to comport with the backplane protocol while providing a particular type of service to subscribers. For example, a single Litespan might have some interface cards providing POTS (plain old telephone service) service and other interface cards providing PBX (private branch exchange) service. The analog signals traveling between the subscribers and the two types of interface cards may be quite different, but the interface cards process the signals so that they are compatible with the Litespan's backplane protocol.

Litespans and individual interface cards each have their own microprocessors and interface circuitry, which require software to operate. Two software packages are at issue here. The first is the Litespan System software, which includes both the Litespan operating system software and various Litespan utility programs. The sec-ond is the POTS-DI (download image) software, which DSC developed to operate its POTS interface cards. Both the Litespan System software and the POTS-DI soft-ware normally reside in nonvolatile storage within Litespan systems. When a DSC POTS card is inserted into a Litespan and powered up, a copy of the POTS-DI soft-ware is downloaded into volatile memory on the POTS card. When the POTS card is powered down, its copy of the POTS-DI software ceases to exist. This design allows changes to be made to the POTS-DI software in a central location (*i.e.,* in the Litespan system) with no need to update software in the individual POTS cards.

DSC designed the Litespan to be used in the telephone networks of the RBOCs, and it transferred the Litespan technology to the RBOCs through a series of com-prehensive agreements. . . . The agreements all contain provisions that license, under a variety of restrictions, the Litespan System software and POTS-DI software to the RBOCs.

Pulsecom has developed a Litespan-compatible POTS card to compete with DSC's POTS card. Pulsecom decided not to develop the software necessary to operate its POTS card, but rather to design the card so that — like DSC's POTS card — it downloads the POTS-DI software from the host Litespan into its resident memory upon power-up. Pulsecom's design has the obvious advantage of allow-ing Pulsecom's POTS cards to remain compatible with the Litespan system if DSC modifies its Litespan System software and POTS-DI software.

II

A

Although DSC's complaint alleged only copyright and state law claims, we have jurisdiction over this appeal under 28 U.S.C. §1295(a)(1) because Pulsecom filed a counterclaim that raised a nonfrivolous claim of patent infringement. . . .

DSC's principal contention on appeal is that the district court improperly granted judgment to Pulsecom on DSC's contributory copyright infringement claim at the close of DSC's case. On that issue, as on the other copyright and state law issues before us, we follow the law of the circuit from which this appeal is taken. With respect to the issues raised in DSC's appeal, our task is therefore to determine how the Fourth Circuit would decide those issues.

DSC's theory of contributory infringement is that each time an RBOC powers up a Pulsecom POTS card in one of its Litespan systems, [the RBOC] directly infringes DSC's POTS-DI software copyright by copying the POTS-DI software from the Litespan into the resident memory of a Pulsecom POTS card. [Because DSC's theory is that Pulsecom is responsible for contributing to that act of infringement by the RBOC, DSC can prevail only if that copying infringes on DSC's copyright. The district court rejected DSC's claim because it did not believe that the RBOC copying infringed DSC's copyright in the software.]

Pivotal to the proper resolution of DSC's copyright infringement claim is the interpretation and application of section 117 of the Copyright Act, 17 U.S.C. §117. . . .

Section 117 provides a limitation on the exclusive rights of the owner of the copyright in a piece of software. It provides, in pertinent part:

> [I]t is not an infringement for the owner of a copy of a computer program to make or authorize the making of another copy or adaptation of that computer program provided: (1) that such a new copy or adaptation is created as an essential step in the utilization of the computer program in conjunction with a machine and that it is used in no other manner. . . .

17 U.S.C. §117.

The district court concluded that making copies of the POTS-DI software (in the resident memory of POTS cards) was an "essential step in the utilization" of the POTS-DI software and that there was no evidence that the RBOCs used the software in any other manner that would constitute infringement. Accordingly, under the district court's theory of the case there was no [infringement] if the RBOCs were section 117 "owners" of copies of the POTS-DI software.

The district court then held that the RBOCs were "owners" of copies of the POTS-DI software because they obtained the software by making a single payment and obtaining a right to possession of the software for an unlimited period. Those attributes of the transaction, the court concluded, made the transaction a "sale."

DSC challenges the district court's conclusion that, based on the terms of the purchase transactions between DSC and the RBOCs, the RBOCs were "owners" of copies of the POTS-DI software. In order to resolve that issue, we must determine what attributes are necessary to constitute ownership of copies of software in this context.

Unfortunately, ownership is an imprecise concept, and the Copyright Act does not define the term. Nor is there much useful guidance to be obtained from either the legislative history of the statute or the cases that have construed it. The National Commission on New Technological Uses of Copyrighted Works ("CONTU") was created by Congress to recommend changes in the Copyright Act to accommodate advances in computer technology. In its final report, CONTU proposed a version of section 117 that is identical to the one that was ultimately enacted, except for a single change. The proposed CONTU version provided that "it is not an infringement for the *rightful possessor of a copy* of a computer program to make or authorize the making of another copy or adaptation of that program. . . . " *Final Report of the National Commission on New Technological Uses of Copyrighted Works,* U.S. Dept. of Commerce, PB-282141, at 30 (July 31, 1978) (emphasis added). Congress, however, substituted the words "owner of a copy" in place of the words "rightful possessor of a copy." *See* Pub.L. No. 96-517, 96th Cong., 2d Sess. (1980). The legislative history does not explain the reason for the change, *see* H.R.Rep. No. 96-1307, 96th Cong., 2d Sess., pt. 1, at 23 (1980), but it is clear from the fact of the substitution of the term "owner" for "rightful possessor" that Congress must have meant to require more than "rightful possession" to trigger the section 117 defense.

In the leading case on section 117 ownership, the Ninth Circuit considered an agreement in which MAI, the owner of a software copyright, transferred copies of the copyrighted software to Peak under an agreement that imposed severe restrictions on Peak's rights with respect to those copies. *See MAI Sys. Corp. v. Peak Computer, Inc.,* 991 F.2d 511, 26 USPQ2d 1458, 1462 (9th Cir. 1995). The court held that Peak was not an "owner" of the copies of the software for purposes of section 117 and thus did not enjoy the right to copy conferred on owners by that statute. The Ninth Circuit stated that it reached the conclusion that Peak was not an owner because Peak had licensed the software from MAI. *See id.* at 518 n. 5. That explanation of the court's decision has been criticized for failing to recognize the distinction between ownership of a copyright, which can be licensed, and ownership of copies of the copyrighted software. *See, e.g.,* 2 Melville B. Nimmer, *Nimmer on Copyright* §8.08[B][1], at 8-119 to 8-121 (3d ed.1997). Plainly, a party who purchases copies of software from the copyright owner can hold a license under a copyright while still being an "owner" of a copy of the copyrighted software for purposes of section 117. We therefore do not adopt the Ninth Circuit's characterization of all licensees as non-owners. Nonetheless, the *MAI* case is instructive, because the agreement between MAI and Peak, like the agreements at issue in this case, imposed more severe restrictions on Peak's rights with respect to the software than would be imposed on a party who owned copies of software subject only to the rights of the copyright holder under the Copyright Act. And for that reason, it was proper to hold that Peak was not an "owner" of copies of the copyrighted software for purposes of section 117. *See also Advanced Computer Servs. of Mich. v. MAI Sys. Corp.,* 845 F.Supp. 356, 367, 30 USPQ2d 1443, 1452 (E.D.Va.1994) ("MAI customers are not 'owners' of the copyrighted software; they possess only the limited rights set forth in their licensing agreements"). We therefore turn to the agreements between DSC and the RBOCs to determine whether those agreements establish that the RBOCs are section 117 "owners" of copies of the copyrighted POTS-DI software.

Each of the DSC-RBOC agreements contains a provision that is similar in effect to the following, taken from the DSC-BellSouth agreement: "All rights, title and interest in the Software are and shall remain with seller, subject, however, to a license to Buyer to use the Software solely in conjunction with the Material [*i.e.,* the Litespan-2000 and related equipment] during the useful life of the Material." Two of the agreements also contain clauses that provide for the passage of title to all the material transferred from DSC to the RBOCs, except for the software. The language and the context of those clauses makes it clear that the clauses refer to DSC's rights to the copies of the software in the RBOCs' possession, not DSC's copyright interest in the software. There was no need for a contract clause making clear that DSC was not selling its copyrights in its software to its customers, as it was obvious that DSC did not intend to convey any ownership rights in its copyright as part of the licensing agreements with the RBOCs. The question of ownership of the copies of the software, by contrast, was a matter that needed to be addressed in the contracts.

Not only do the agreements characterize the RBOCs as non-owners of copies of the software, but the restrictions imposed on the RBOCs' rights with respect to the software are consistent with that characterization. In particular, the licensing agreements severely limit the rights of the RBOCs with respect to the POTS-DI software in ways that are inconsistent with the rights normally enjoyed by owners of copies of software.

Section 106 of the Copyright Act, 17 U.S.C. §106, reserves for a copyright owner the following exclusive rights in the copyrighted work: the right to reproduce the work; the right to prepare derivative works; the right to distribute copies of the work; the right to perform the work publicly; and the right to display the work publicly. Those rights are expressly limited, however, by sections 107 through 120 of the Act. Of particular importance are the limitations of sections 109 and 117. As we have seen, section 117 limits the copyright owner's exclusive rights by allowing an owner of a copy of a computer program to reproduce or adapt the program if reproduction or adaptation is necessary for the program to be used in conjunction with a machine. Section 109, which embodies the "first sale" doctrine, limits the copyright owner's otherwise exclusive right of distribution by providing, in relevant part, that

> the owner of a particular copy . . . is entitled, without the authority of the copyright owner, to sell or otherwise dispose of the possession of that copy. . . .
>
> Notwithstanding [the above], unless authorized by . . . the owner of copyright in a computer program . . . [no] person in possession of a particular copy of a computer program . . . may, for the purposes of direct or indirect commercial advantage, dispose of, or authorize the disposal of, the possession of that . . . computer program . . . by rental, lease, or lending. . . .

17 U.S.C. §109.

Each of the DSC-RBOC agreements limits the contracting RBOC's right to transfer copies of the POTS-DI software or to disclose the details of the software to third parties. For example, the DSC-Ameritech agreement provides that Ameritech shall "not provide, disclose or make the Software or any portions or aspects thereof available to any person except its employees on a 'need to know' basis without the prior written consent of [DSC]." Such a restriction is plainly at odds with the section 109 right to transfer owned copies of software to third parties. The agreements also prohibit the RBOCs from using the software on hardware other than that provided by DSC. If the RBOCs were "owners of copies" of the software, section 117 would allow them to use the software on any hardware, regardless of origin. Because the DSC-RBOC agreements substantially limit the rights of the RBOCs compared to the rights they would enjoy as "owners of copies" of the POTS-DI software under the Copyright Act, the contents of the agreements support the characterization of the RBOCs as non-owners of the copies of the POTS-DI software.

In finding that the RBOCs were owners of copies of the POTS-DI software, the district court relied heavily on its finding that the RBOCs obtained their interests in the copies of the software through a single payment and for an unlimited period of time. It is true that the transfer of rights to the POTS-DI software in each of the agreements did not take the form of a lease, and that the transfer in each case was in exchange for a single payment and was for a term that was either unlimited or nearly so. One commentator has argued that when a copy of a software program is transferred for a single payment and for an unlimited term, the transferee should be considered an "owner" of the copy of the software program regardless of other restrictions on his use of the software. *See* Raymond T. Nimmer, *The Law of Computer Technology* §1.24[1], at 1-143 to 1-144 (3d ed.1997). That view has not been accepted by other courts, however, and we think it overly simplistic. The concept of ownership of a copy entails a variety of rights and interests. The fact that the right of possession is perpetual, or that the possessor's rights were obtained through a single payment, is certainly relevant to whether the possessor is an owner, but those factors are not necessarily dispositive if the possessor's right to use the software is heavily encumbered by other restrictions that are inconsistent with the status of owner. . . .

In light of the restrictions on the RBOCs' rights in the copies of the POTS-DI software, we hold that it was improper for the court to conclude, as a matter of law, that the RBOCs were "owners" under section 117 of the copies of DSC's software that were in their possession. The court was therefore incorrect to rule, at the close of DSC's case, that section 117 of the Copyright Act gave the RBOCs the right to copy the POTS-DI software when using Pulsecom's POTS cards without violating DSC's copyright in the software. Accordingly, we reverse the district court's order granting judgment for Pulsecom on DSC's contributory infringement claim.

Softman Products Co. v. Adobe Systems Inc.

171 F. Supp. 2d 1075 (C.D. Cal. 2001)

PREGERSON, District Judge.

This matter comes before the Court on the counter-claimant Adobe's application for a preliminary injunction. After reviewing and considering the materials submitted by the parties, and hearing oral argument, the Court adopts the following order.

I. BACKGROUND

The counter-claimant Adobe Systems Inc. ("Adobe") is a leading software development and publishing company. The counter-defendant SoftMan Products Company ("SoftMan") is a Los Angeles-based company that distributes computer software products primarily through its website, www.buycheapsoftware.com. Adobe alleges that since at least November 1997, SoftMan has distributed unauthorized Adobe software, including Adobe Educational software and unbundled Adobe "Collections."[2] By distributing the individual pieces of Adobe Collections,

---

2. "Collections" are sets of individual Adobe products, such as Adobe Photoshop or Illustrator on separate CD's, that are sold together in a larger Adobe Retail Box. These Collections are offered by Adobe at a discount from the individual retail products comprising the Collection. "An example of an Adobe Collection is the Adobe Publishing Collection, comprised of Adobe PageMaker, Acrobat, Photoshop and Illustrator, for $999. Separately, these products retails as follows: Pagemaker — $499, Acrobat — $249, Photoshop — $609 and Illustrator — $399."

Adobe contends that SoftMan is infringing Adobe's copyright in these products and violating the terms of Adobe's licenses. While SoftMan agrees that it is breaking apart various Adobe Collections and distributing the individual pieces of them as single products, SoftMan claims that it is entitled to distribute Adobe software in this manner. There is no direct contractual relationship between Adobe and SoftMan.

Adobe distributes its products through "licensing" agreements with distributors. Each piece of Adobe software is also accompanied by an End User License Agreement ("EULA"), which sets forth the terms of the license between Adobe and the end user for that specific Adobe product. The EULA is electronically recorded on the computer disk and customers are asked to agree to its terms when they attempt to install the software. . . .

III.   DISCUSSION

A.   COPYRIGHT INFRINGEMENT CLAIM

. . . Copyright infringement exists when any of the rights granted under 17 U.S.C. §106 are violated. Title 17 U.S.C. §106(3) grants a copyright holder the exclusive right to distribute, and to authorize distribution of, its copyrighted work. Adobe chooses to distribute copies of its products through licensing agreements with various distributors and dealers. It is not disputed that SoftMan has no licensing agreement with Adobe.

Most computer program and database product copies are distributed with standard form terms in a document characterized as a "license". The standard terms purport, among other things: to specify permitted uses of a copy, e.g., consumer or personal versus commercial; to prohibit certain uses of a computer program copy, e.g., reverse engineering of the computer program code; to forbid any use that is not expressly authorized, e.g., commercial processing of third party data or business records; and to bar transfer of a copy and the "license" to another person.

In addition, each piece of Adobe software is accompanied by the EULA.[6] Once the products are distributed to the end-user, the EULA prohibits the individual distribution of software that was originally distributed as part of a Collection. Specifically, the Adobe EULA provides that the end user may "transfer all [his] rights to the Use of the Software to another person or legal entity provided that (a) [he] also transfer this Agreement, the Software and all other software or hardware bundled or pre-installed with the Software."

In this case, Adobe alleges that by distributing unbundled Collections, SoftMan has exceeded the scope of the EULA and has infringed Adobe's copyrights, specifically Adobe's §106 right to distribute and control distribution. SoftMan contends that the first sale doctrine allows for the resale of Adobe's Collection software.

---

6. The EULA states in part: "The receiving party accepts the terms and conditions of this Agreement (EULA) and any other terms and conditions upon which [the end user] legally purchased a license to the Software." Adobe EULA ¶ 4. Adobe's EULA permits an end user, subject to certain restrictions, to transfer the software, media, and documentation to another end user. The restrictions relating to an end user's ability to transfer include that the EULA must also be transferred and that "[t]he Software and all other software or hardware bundled or pre-installed with the Software, including all copies, Updates, and prior version, and all copies of font software converted into other formats."

(1)   First Sale Doctrine

The "first sale" doctrine was first analyzed by the United States Supreme Court in Bobbs-Merrill Co. v. Straus, 210 U.S. 339 (1908). The Court held that the exclusive right to "vend" under the copyright statute applied only to the first sale of the copyrighted work. The doctrine has been codified at 17 U.S.C. §109(a). It states in relevant part: "the owner of a particular copy . . . lawfully made under this title . . . is entitled, without the authority of the copyright owner, to sell or otherwise dispose of the possession of that copy." 17 U.S.C. §109(a). One significant effect of §109(a) is to limit the exclusive right to distribute copies to their first voluntary disposition, and thus negate copyright owner control over further or "downstream" transfer to a third party. The first sale doctrine vests the copy owner with statutory privileges under the Act which operate as limits on the exclusive rights of the copyright owners.

Adobe argues that the first sale doctrine does not apply because Adobe does not sell or authorize any sale of its software. Adobe characterizes each transaction throughout the entire stream of commerce as a license. Adobe asserts that its license defines the relationship between Adobe and any third-party such that a breach of the license constitutes copyright infringement. This assertion is not accurate because copyright law in fact provides certain rights to owners of a particular copy. This grant of rights is independent from any purported grant of rights from Adobe. The Adobe license compels third-parties to relinquish rights that the third-parties enjoy under copyright law.

In short, the terms of the Adobe EULA at issue prohibit licensees from transferring or assigning any individual Adobe product that was originally distributed as part of a Collection unless it is transferred with all the software in the original Collection. This license provision conflicts with the first sale doctrine in copyright law, which gives the owner of a particular copy of a copyrighted work the right to dispose of that copy without the permission of the copyright owner.

(2)   Sale v. License . . .

(b)   Adobe Sells its Software

A number of courts have held that the sale of software is the sale of a good within the meaning of Uniform Commercial Code. It is well-settled that in determining whether a transaction is a sale, a lease, or a license, courts look to the economic realities of the exchange. Microsoft Corp. v. DAK Indus., 66 F.3d 1091 (9th Cir. 1995). In *DAK*, Microsoft and DAK entered into a license agreement granting DAK certain nonexclusive license rights to Microsoft's computer software. The agreement provided that DAK would pay a royalty rate per copy of computer software that it distributed. Subsequently, DAK filed a petition for bankruptcy, and failed to pay the final two out of a total of five installments. Microsoft filed a motion for the payment of an administrative expense, claiming that it should be compensated for DAK's post-bankruptcy petition use of the license agreement. On appeal, the Ninth Circuit held that the economic realities of the agreement indicated that it was a sale, not a license to use. Thus, Microsoft simply held an unsecured claim and not an administrative expense. The court found that the agreement was best characterized as a lump sum sale of software units to DAK, rather than a grant of permission to use an intellectual property. . . .

Adobe frames the issue as a dispute about the ownership of intellectual property. In fact, it is a dispute about the ownership of individual pieces of Adobe software. Section 202 of the Copyright Act recognizes a distinction between tangible property rights in copies of the work and intangible property rights in the creation itself. In this case, no claim is made that transfer of the copy involves transfer of the ownership of the intellectual property within. What is at stake here is the right of the purchaser to dispose of that purchaser's particular copy of the software.

The Court finds that the circumstances surrounding the transaction strongly suggests that the transaction is in fact a sale rather than a license. For example, the purchaser commonly obtains a single copy of the software, with documentation, for a single price, which the purchaser pays at the time of the transaction, and which constitutes the entire payment for the "license. " The license runs for an indefinite term without provisions for renewal. In light of these indicia, many courts and commentators conclude that a "shrinkwrap license" transaction is a sale of goods rather than a license.

The reality of the business environment also suggests that Adobe sells its software to distributors. Adobe transfers large amounts of merchandise to distributors. The distributors pay full value for the merchandise and accept the risk that the software may be damaged or lost. The distributors also accept the risk that they will be unable to resell the product. The distributors then resell the product to other distributors in the secondary market. The secondary market and the ultimate consumer also pay full value for the product, and accept the risk that the product may be lost or damaged. This evidence suggests a transfer of title in the good. The transfer of a product for consideration with a transfer of title and risk of loss generally constitutes a sale. Professor Raymond Nimmer writes:

> Ownership of a copy should be determined based on the actual character, rather than the label, of the transaction by which the user obtained possession. Merely labeling a transaction as a lease or license does not control. If a transaction involves a single payment giving the buyer an unlimited period in which it has a right to possession, the transaction is a sale. In this situation, the buyer owns the copy regardless of the label the parties use for the contract. Course of dealing and trade usage may be relevant, since they establish the expectations and intent of the parties. The pertinent issue is whether, as in a lease, the user may be required to return the copy to the vendor after the expiration of a particular period. If not, the transaction conveyed not only possession, but also transferred ownership of the copy.

Raymond Nimmer, The Law of Computer Technology §1.18[1] p. 1-103 (1992). The Court agrees that a single payment for a perpetual transfer of possession is, in reality, a sale of personal property and therefore transfers ownership of that property, the copy of the software.

Other commentators have urged courts to look at the substance rather than the form of licensing agreements. See, e.g., David A. Rice, *Licensing the Use of Computer Program Copies and the Copyright Act First Sale Doctrine*, 30 JURIMETRICS J. 157 (1990). In particular, the following factors require a finding that distributing software under licenses transfers individual copy ownership: temporally unlimited possession, absence of time limits on copy possession, pricing and payment schemes that are unitary not serial, licenses under which subsequent transfer is neither prohibited nor conditioned on obtaining the licensor's prior approval (only subject to a prohibition against rental and a requirement that any transfer be of the entity), and licenses under which the use restriction's principal purpose is to protect intangible copyrightable subject matter, and not to preserve property interests in individual program copies. . . .

(c)   EULA Terms

Adobe argues that the EULA requires construction of the transaction as a license rather than a sale. The Court finds that SoftMan is not bound by the EULA because there was no assent to its terms.

i)   Assent

Adobe contends that the EULA limits the consumer's ability to transfer the software after buying it. According to SoftMan, a hard copy of the EULA agreement is not enclosed with the individual Adobe software disk. Instead, consumers are asked to agree to its terms as part of the installation process. . . .

In the instant case, the Court finds that there is only assent on the part of the consumer, if at all, when the consumer loads the Adobe program and begins the installation process. It is undisputed that SoftMan has never attempted to load the software that it sells. Consequently, the Court finds that SoftMan is not subject to the Adobe EULA.

Adobe fails to offer a compelling rationale for how SoftMan becomes subject to Adobe's licenses if SoftMan never loads the software onto computers. Adobe claims that the EULA is enforceable against SoftMan because the boxes containing Adobe software (including Collections) clearly indicate that use is subject to the consumer's agreement to the terms contained in EULA inside. Like the CD boxes in ProCD, Adobe's EULAs state that the product can be returned if the terms are not agreed to by the end user. The Adobe Collections boxes state: "NOTICE TO USERS: This product is offered subject to the license agreement included with the media." However, the existence of this notice on the box cannot bind SoftMan. Reading a notice on a box is not equivalent to the degree of assent that occurs when the software is loaded onto the computer and the consumer is asked to agree to the terms of the license.

Adobe further asserts that whether SoftMan is characterized as a distributor or reseller, SoftMan would be bound by the terms of these license agreements, which state that Adobe retains ownership of its software products, as well as the media upon which these software products are distributed. It is undisputed that SoftMan is not a signatory to any licensing agreements. Yet Adobe claims that although SoftMan has never signed an agreement with Adobe, the terms of Adobe's distribution agreements all apply to SoftMan. . . .

The Court finds that Adobe's EULA cannot be valid without assent. Therefore, SoftMan is not bound by the EULA because it has never loaded the software, and therefore never assented to its terms of use. . . .

In short, the transfer of copies of Adobe software making up the distribution chain from Adobe to SoftMan are sales of the particular copies, but not of Adobe's intellectual rights in the computer program itself, which is protected by Adobe's copyright. SoftMan is an "owner" of the copy and is entitled to the use and enjoyment of the software, with the rights that are consistent with copyright law. The Court rejects Adobe's argument that the EULA gives to purchasers only a license to use the software. The Court finds that SoftMan has not assented to the EULA and therefore cannot be bound by its terms. Therefore, the Court finds that

Adobe has not demonstrated a likelihood of success on the merits of its copyright infringement claim.

––––––––––

(II)   Can the License Retain Greater Rights for the Licensor?   Software licensors also attempt to limit the rights of users more directly, by including provisions in licenses that prohibit acts by the licensee that the Copyright Act would permit. Those provisions raise the issue whether the federal Copyright Act preempts state contract law that might restrict the exercise of rights granted by federal law. In recent cases, of course, software licensors (subject to the concerns discussed in Assignments 13 and 14) are capable of obtaining consent in fully enforceable contracts. The most prominent debate has related to reverse engineering. As you will recall from the discussion above, reverse engineering often is considered a fair use, largely because reverse engineering can have the pro-competitive effect of creating improved and compatible products. On the other hand, licensors often feel that reverse engineering amounts to theft, in the sense that it permits competitors to use their technology to develop products that compete against their own. This is particularly true in cases in which the technology is protected by patents. (The remedy of an action for patent infringement might seem to protect that interest adequately, but in practice it is quite a weak remedy from the licensor's perspective. For one thing, in many contexts it is quite difficult to detect copyright infringement with respect to software: If the copyright holder cannot obtain the source code of the offending program it might be unable to prove that the offending program actually infringes. For another, even if the infringement is plain, it will remain difficult and expensive to prevail in litigation alleging patent infringement.) The case that follows provides the latest word on the question whether copyright law preempts a contractual prohibition on reverse engineering.

Bowers v. Baystate Technologies, Inc.

302 F.3d 1334 (Fed. Cir. 2003)

Before CLEVENGER, RADER, and DYK, Circuit Judges.
RADER, Circuit Judge.

Following trial in the United States District Court for the District of Massachusetts, the jury returned a verdict for Harold L. Bowers on his patent infringement, copyright infringement, and breach of contract claims. . . . Because substantial evidence supports the jury's verdict that Baystate breached the contract, this court affirms that verdict. . . .

I.

Harold L. Bowers (Bowers) created a template to improve computer aided design (CAD) software, such as the CADKEY tool of Cadkey, Inc. Mr. Bowers filed a patent application for his template on February 27, 1989. On June 12, 1990, United States Patent No. 4,933,514 ('514 patent) issued from that application.

Generally, a CAD software program has many commands that the software presents to the user in nested menus many layers deep. The layering often makes it difficult for a user to find quickly a desired command. To address this problem, the claimed template works with a CAD system[, which lies on top of the digitizing tablet of a CAD computer. The user selects data from the template with a pointing device. The template places the many CAD commands in a claimed visual and logical order.

Mr. Bowers commercialized the '514 patent template as Cadjet for use with CADKEY. . . .

Since the early 1980s, CAD programs have assisted engineers to draft and design on a computer screen. George W. Ford, III, a development engineer and supervisor of quality control at Heinemann Electric, envisioned a way to improve Mr. Bowers' template and CAD software. Specifically, Mr. Ford designed Geodraft, a DOS-based add-on program to operate with CAD. Geodraft allows an engineer to insert technical tolerances for features of the computer-generated design. These tolerances comply with the geometric dimensioning and tolerancing (GD & T) requirements in ANSI Y14.5M, a standard promulgated by the American National Standards Institute (ANSI). Geodraft works in conjunction with the CAD system to ensure that the design complies with ANSI Y14.5M — a task previously error-prone due to the standard's complexity. Geodraft automatically includes symbols specifying the correct GD & T parameters. Mr. Ford obtained a registered copyright, TX 2-939-672, covering Geodraft.

In 1989, Mr. Ford offered Mr. Bowers an exclusive license to his Geodraft software. Mr. Bowers accepted that offer and bundled Geodraft and Cadjet together as the Designer's Toolkit. Mr. Bowers sold the Designer's Toolkit with a shrink-wrap license that, *inter alia,* prohibited any reverse engineering.

In 1989, Baystate also developed and marketed other tools for CADKEY. One of those tools, Draft-Pak version 1 and 2, featured a template and GD & T software. In 1988 and 1989, Mr. Bowers offered to establish a formal relationship with Baystate, including bundling his template with Draft-Pak. Baystate rejected that offer, however, telling Mr. Bowers that it believed it had "the in-house capability to develop the type of products you have proposed."

In 1990, Mr. Bowers released Designer's Toolkit. By January 1991, Baystate had obtained copies of that product. Three months later, Baystate introduced the substantially revised Draft-Pak version 3, incorporating many of the features of Designer's Toolkit. Although Draft-Pak version 3 operated in the DOS environment, Baystate later upgraded it to operate with Microsoft Windows®.

Baystate's introduction of Draft-Pak version 3 induced intense price competition between Mr. Bowers and Baystate. To gain market share over Baystate, Mr. Bowers negotiated with Cadkey, Inc., to provide the Designer's Toolkit free with CADKEY. Mr. Bowers planned to recoup his profits by selling software upgrades to the users that he hoped to lure to his products. Following pressure from Baystate, however, Cadkey, Inc., repudiated its distribution agreement with Mr. Bowers. Eventually, Baystate purchased Cadkey, Inc., and eliminated Mr. Bowers from the CADKEY network — effectively preventing him from developing and marketing the Designer's Toolkit for that program.

On May 16, 1991, Baystate sued Mr. Bowers for declaratory judgment that 1) Baystate's products do not infringe the '514 patent, 2) the '514 patent is invalid, and 3) the '514 patent is unenforceable. Mr. Bowers filed counterclaims for copyright infringement, patent infringement, and breach of contract.

Following trial, the jury found for Mr. Bowers and awarded $1,948,869 for copyright infringement, $3,831,025 for breach of contract, and $232,977 for patent infringement. The district court, however, set aside the copyright damages as duplicative of the contract damages and entered judgment for $5,270,142 (including pre-judgment interest). Baystate filed timely motions for judgment as a matter of law (JMOL), or for a new trial, on all of Mr. Bowers' claims. Baystate appeals the district court's denial of its motions for JMOL or a new trial. . . .

II.

Baystate raises a number of issues that are not unique to the jurisdiction of this court. On those issues, this court applies the law of the circuit from which the appeal is taken, here the First Circuit. . . .

A.

Baystate contends that the Copyright Act preempts the prohibition of reverse engineering embodied in Mr. Bowers' shrink-wrap license agreements. Swayed by this argument, the district court considered Mr. Bowers' contract and copyright claims coextensive. The district court instructed the jury that "reverse engineering violates the license agreement only if Baystate's product that resulted from reverse engineering infringes Bowers' copyright because it copies protectable expression." Mr. Bowers lodged a timely objection to this instruction. This court holds that, under First Circuit law, the Copyright Act does not preempt or narrow the scope of Mr. Bowers' contract claim.

Courts respect freedom of contract and do not lightly set aside freely-entered agreements. Nevertheless, at times, federal regulation may preempt private contract. The Copyright Act provides that "all legal or equitable rights that are equivalent to any of the exclusive rights within the general scope of copyright . . . are governed exclusively by this title." 17 U.S.C. §301(a). The First Circuit does not interpret this language to require preemption as long as "a state cause of action requires an extra element, beyond mere copying, preparation of derivative works, performance, distribution or display." *Data Gen. Corp. v. Grumman Sys. Support Corp.,* 36 F.3d 1147, 1164 (1st Cir. 1994); *see also Computer Assoc. Int'l, Inc. v. Altai, Inc.,* 982 F.2d 693, 716 (2d Cir. 1992) ("But if an 'extra element' is 'required instead of or in addition to the acts of reproduction, performance, distribution or display, in order to constitute a state-created cause of action, then the right does not lie "within the general scope of copyright," and there is no preemption.'") (quoting 1 Nimmer on Copyright §1.01[B] at 1-15). Nevertheless, "[n]ot every 'extra element' of a state law claim will establish a qualitative variance between the rights protected by federal copyright law and those protected by state law." *Id.*

In *Data General,* Data General alleged that Grumman misappropriated its trade secret software. 36 F.3d at 1155. Grumman obtained that software from Data General's customers and former employees who were bound by confidentiality agreements to refrain from disclosing the software. *Id.* at 1154-55. In defense, Grumman argued that the Copyright Act preempted Data General's trade secret claim. *Id.* at 1158, 1165. The First Circuit held that the Copyright Act did not preempt the state law trade secret claim. *Id.* at 1165. Beyond mere copying, that state law claim required proof of a trade secret and breach of a duty of confidentiality. *Id.* These additional elements of proof, according to the First Circuit, made the trade secret claim qualitatively different from a copyright claim. *Id.* In contrast, the First Circuit noted that claims might be preempted whose extra elements are illusory, being "mere label[s] attached to the same odious business conduct." *Id.* at 1165. For example, the First Circuit observed that "a state law misappropriation claim will not escape preemption . . . simply because a plaintiff must prove that copying was not only unauthorized but also commercially immoral." *Id.*

The First Circuit has not addressed expressly whether the Copyright Act preempts a state law contract claim that restrains copying. This court perceives, however, that *Data General's* rationale would lead to a judgment that the Copyright Act does not preempt the state contract action in this case. Indeed, most courts to examine this issue have found that the Copyright Act does not preempt contractual constraints on copyrighted articles. *See, e.g .*, *ProCD, Inc. v. Zeidenberg,* 86 F.3d 1447 (7th Cir. 1996) (holding that a shrink-wrap license was not preempted by federal copyright law).

In *ProCD,* for example, the court found that the mutual assent and consideration required by a contract claim render that claim qualitatively different from copyright infringement. 86 F.3d at 1454. Consistent with *Data General's* reliance on a contract element, the court in *ProCD* reasoned: "A copyright is a right against the world. Contracts, by contrast, generally affect only their parties; strangers may do as they please, so contracts do not create 'exclusive rights.'" *Id.* Indeed, the Supreme Court recently noted "[i]t goes without saying that a contract cannot bind a nonparty." *EEOC v. Waffle House, Inc.,* 534 U.S. 279 (2002). This court believes that the First Circuit would follow the reasoning of *ProCD* and the majority of other courts to consider this issue. This court, therefore, holds that the Copyright Act does not preempt Mr. Bowers' contract claims.

In making this determination, this court has left untouched the conclusions reached in *Atari Games v. Nintendo* regarding reverse engineering as a statutory fair use exception to copyright infringement. *Atari Games Corp. v. Nintendo of America, Inc.,* 975 F.2d 832 (Fed. Cir. 1992). In *Atari,* this court stated that, with respect to 17 U.S.C. §107 (fair use section of the Copyright Act), "[t]he legislative history of section 107 suggests that courts should adapt the fair use exception to accommodate new technological innovations." *Atari,* 975 F.2d at 843. This court noted "[a] prohibition on all copying whatsoever would stifle the free flow of ideas without serving any legitimate interest of the copyright holder." *Id.* Therefore, this court held "reverse engineering object code to discern the unprotectable ideas in a computer program is a fair use." *Id.* Application of the First Circuit's view distinguishing a state law contract claim having additional elements of proof from a copyright claim does not alter the findings of *Atari.* Likewise, this claim distinction does not conflict with the expressly defined circumstances in which reverse engineering is not copyright infringement under 17 U.S.C. §1201(f) (section of the Digital Millennium Copyright Act) and 17 U.S .C. §906 (section directed to mask works).

Moreover, while the Fifth Circuit has held a state law prohibiting all copying of a computer program is preempted by the federal Copyright Act, *Vault Corp. v. Quaid Software, Ltd.,* 847 F.2d 1488 (5th Cir. 1988), no evidence suggests the First Circuit would extend this concept to include private contractual agreements supported by mutual assent and consideration. The First Circuit recognizes contractual waiver of affirmative defenses and statutory rights. Thus, case law indicates the First Circuit would find that private parties are free to contractually forego the limited ability to reverse engineer a software product under the exemptions of the Copyright Act. Of course, a party bound by such a contract may elect to efficiently breach the agreement in order to ascertain ideas in a computer program unprotected by copyright law. Under such circumstances, the breaching party must weigh the benefits of breach against the arguably de minim[i]s damages arising from merely discerning non-protected code.

This court now considers the scope of Mr. Bowers' contract protection. . . .

In this case, the contract unambiguously prohibits "reverse engineering." That term means ordinarily "to study or analyze (a device, as a microchip for computers) in order to learn details of design, construction, and operation, perhaps to produce a copy or an improved version." *Random House Unabridged Dictionary* (1993). Thus, the contract in this case broadly prohibits any "reverse engineering" of the subject matter covered by the shrink-wrap agreement.

The record amply supports the jury's finding of a breach of that agreement. . . .

The record indicates, for example, that Baystate scheduled two weeks in Draft-Pak's development schedule to analyze the Designer's Toolkit. Indeed, Robert Bean, Baystate's president and CEO, testified that Baystate generally analyzed competitor's products to duplicate their functionality.

The record also contains evidence of extensive and unusual similarities between Geodraft and the accused Draft-Pak — further evidence of reverse engineering. James Spencer, head of mechanical engineering and integration at the Space and Naval Warfare Systems Center, testified that he examined the relevant software programs to determine "the overall structure of the operating program" such as "how the operating programs actually executed the task of walking a user through creating a [GD & T] symbol." Mr. Spencer concluded: "In the process of taking the [ANSI Y14.5M] standard and breaking it down into its component parts to actually create a step-by-step process for a user using the software, both Geodraft and Draft-Pak [for DOS] use almost the identical process of breaking down that task into its individual pieces, and it's organized essentially identically." This evidence supports the jury's verdict of a contract breach based on reverse engineering.

Mr. Ford also testified that he had compared Geodraft and Draft-Pak. When asked to describe the Draft-Pak interface, Mr. Ford responded: "It looked like I was looking at my own program [i.e., Geodraft]." Both Mr. Spencer and Mr. Ford explained in detail similarities between Geodraft and the accused Draft-Pak. Those similarities included the interrelationships between program screens, the manner in which parameter selection causes program branching, and the manner in which the GD & T symbols are drawn.

Both witnesses also testified that those similarities extended beyond structure and design to include many idiosyncratic design choices and inadvertent design flaws. For example, both Geodraft and Draft-Pak offer "straightness tolerance" menu choices of "flat" and "cylindric," unusual in view of the use by ANSI Y14.5M of the terms "linear" and "circular," respectively. As another example, neither program requires the user to provide "angularity tolerance" secondary datum to create a feature control frame — a technical oversight that causes creation of an incomplete symbol. In sum, Mr. Spencer testified: "Based on my summary analysis of how the programs function, their errors from the standard and their similar nomenclatures reflecting nonstandard items, I would say that the Draft-Pak [for DOS] is a derivative copy of a Geodraft product."

Mr. Ford and others also demonstrated to the jury the operation of Geodraft and both the DOS and Windows versions of the accused Draft-Pak. Those software demonstrations undoubtedly conveyed information to the jury that the paper record on appeal cannot easily replicate. This court, therefore, is especially reluctant to substitute its judgment for that of the jury on the sufficiency and interpretation of that evidence. In any event, the record fully supports the jury's verdict that Baystate breached its contract with Mr. Bowers. . . .

Dᴦᴋ, Circuit Judge, concurring in part and dissenting in part.

I join the majority opinion except insofar as it holds that the contract claim is not preempted by federal law. . . . The majority's approach permits state law to eviscerate an important federal copyright policy reflected in the fair use defense, and the majority's logic threatens other federal copyright policies as well. I respectfully dissent.

I

Congress has made the Copyright Act the exclusive means for protecting copyright. The Act provides that "all legal or equitable rights that are equivalent to any of the exclusive rights within the general scope of copyright . . . are governed exclusively by this title." 17 U.S.C. §301(a). All other laws, including the common law, are preempted. "[N]o person is entitled to any such right or equivalent right in any such work under the common law or statutes of any State." *Id.*

The test for preemption by copyright law, like the test for patent law preemption, should be whether the state law "substantially impedes the public use of the otherwise unprotected" material. *Bonito Boats, Inc. v. Thunder Craft Boats, Inc.,* 489 U.S. 141, 157, 167 (1989) (state law at issue was preempted because it "substantially restrict[ed] the public's ability to exploit ideas that the patent system mandates shall be free for all to use."); *Sears, Roebuck & Co. v. Stiffel Co.,* 376 U.S. 225, 231-32 (1964).

II

The fair use defense is an important limitation on copyright. Indeed, the Supreme Court has said that "[f]rom the infancy of copyright protection, some opportunity for fair use of copyrighted materials has been thought necessary to fulfill copyright's very purpose, '[t]o promote the Progress of Science and useful Arts. . . . ' U.S. Const., Art. I, §8, cl.8." *Campbell v. Acuff-Rose Music, Inc.,* 510 U.S. 569, 575 (1994). . . .

We correctly held in *Atari Games Corp. v. Nintendo of America, Inc.,* 975 F.2d 832, 843 (Fed. Cir. 1992), that reverse engineering constitutes a fair use under the Copyright Act. The Ninth and Eleventh Circuits have also ruled that reverse engineering constitutes fair use. *Bateman v. Mnemonics, Inc.,* 79 F.3d 1532, 1539 n.18 (11th Cir. 1996); *Sega Enters. Ltd. v. Accolade, Inc.,* 977 F.2d 1510, 1527-28 (9th Cir. 1992). No other federal court of appeals has disagreed.

We emphasized in *Atari* that an author cannot achieve protection for an idea simply by embodying it in a computer program. "An author cannot acquire patent-like protection by putting an idea, process, or method of operation in an unintelligible format and asserting copyright infringement against those who try to understand that idea, process, or method of operation." 975 F.2d at 842. Thus, the fair use defense for reverse engineering is necessary so that copyright protection does not "extend to any idea, procedure, process, system, method of operation, concept, principle, or discovery, regardless of the form in which it is described, explained, illustrated, or embodied in such work," as proscribed by the Copyright Act. 17 U.S.C. §102(b).

III

A state is not free to eliminate the fair use defense. Enforcement of a total ban on reverse engineering would conflict with the Copyright Act itself by protecting otherwise unprotectable material. If state law provided that a copyright holder could bar fair use of the copyrighted material by placing a black dot on each copy of the work offered for sale, there would be no question but that the state law would be preempted. A state law that allowed a copyright holder to simply label its products so as to eliminate a fair use defense would "substantially impede" the public's right to fair use and allow the copyright holder, through state law, to protect material that the Congress has determined must be free to all under the Copyright Act. *See Bonito Boats,* 489 U.S. at 157.

I nonetheless agree with the majority opinion that a state can permit parties to contract away a fair use defense or to agree not to engage in uses of copyrighted material that are permitted by the copyright law, if the contract is freely negotiated. A freely negotiated agreement represents the "extra element" that prevents preemption of a state law claim that would otherwise be identical to the infringement claim barred by the fair use defense of reverse engineering. *See Data Gen.,* 36 F.3d at 1164-65.

However, state law giving effect to shrinkwrap licenses is no different in substance from a hypothetical black dot law. Like any other contract of adhesion, the only choice offered to the purchaser is to avoid making the purchase in the first place. *See Fuentes v. Shevin,* 407 U.S. 67, 95 (1972). State law thus gives the copyright holder the ability to eliminate the fair use defense in each and every instance at its option. In doing so, as the majority concedes, it authorizes "shrinkwrap agreements . . . [that] are far broader than the protection afforded by copyright law."

IV

There is, moreover, no logical stopping point to the majority's reasoning. The amici rightly question whether under our original opinion the first sale doctrine and a host of other limitations on copyright protection might be eliminated by shrinkwrap licenses in just this fashion. If by printing a few words on the outside of its product a party can eliminate the fair use defense, then it can also, by the same means, restrict a purchaser from asserting the "first sale" defense, embodied in 17 U.S.C. §109(a), or any other of the protections Congress has afforded the public in the Copyright Act. That means that, under the majority's reasoning, state law could extensively undermine the protections of the Copyright Act.

V

The Fifth Circuit's decision in *Vault* directly supports preemption of the shrinkwrap limitation. The majority states that *Vault* held that "a state law prohibiting all copying of a computer program is preempted by the federal Copyright Act" and then states that "no evidence suggests the First Circuit would extend this concept to include private contractual agreements supported by mutual assent and consideration." But, in fact, the Fifth Circuit held that the specific provision of state law that authorized contracts prohibiting reverse engineering, decompilation, or disassembly of computer programs was preempted by federal law because it conflicted with a portion of the Copyright Act and because it " 'touche[d] upon an area' of federal copyright law." 847 F.2d at 269-70 (quoting *Sears, Roebuck,* 376 U.S. at 229). From a preemption standpoint, there is no distinction between a state law that explicitly validates a contract that restricts reverse engineering (*Vault*) and general common law that permits such a restriction (as here). On the contrary, the preemption clause of the Copyright Act makes clear that it covers "any such right or equivalent right in any such work *under the common law or statutes of any State."* 17 U.S.C. §301(a) (emphasis added).

I do not read *ProCD, Inc. v. Zeidenberg,* 86 F.3d 1447 (7th Cir. 1996), the only other court of appeals shrinkwrap case, as being to the contrary, even though it contains broad language stating that "a simple two-party contract is not 'equivalent to any of the exclusive rights within the general scope of copyright.'" *Id.* at 1455. In *ProCD,* the Seventh Circuit validated a shrinkwrap license that restricted the use of a CD-ROM to non-commercial purposes, which the defendant had violated by charging users a fee to access the CD-ROM over the Internet. The court held that the restriction to non-commercial use of the program was not equivalent to any rights protected by the Copyright Act. Rather, the "contract reflect[ed] private ordering, essential to efficient functioning of markets." *Id.* at 1455. The court saw the licensor as legitimately seeking to distinguish between personal and commercial use. "ProCD offers software and data for two prices: one for personal use, a higher prices for commercial use," the court said. The defendant "wants to use the data without paying the seller's price." *Id.* at 1454. The court also emphasized that the license "would not withdraw any information from the public domain" because all of the information on the CD-ROM was publicly available. *Id.* at 1455.

The case before us is different from *ProCD.* The Copyright Act does not confer a right to pay the same amount for commercial and personal use. It does, however, confer a right to fair use, 17 U.S.C. §107, which we have held encompasses reverse engineering.

ProCD and the other contract cases are also careful not to create a blanket rule that all contracts will escape preemption. The court in that case emphasized that "we think it prudent to refrain from adopting a rule that anything with the label 'contract' is necessarily outside the preemption clause." 86 F.3d at 1455. It also noted with approval another court's "recogni[tion of] the possibility that some applications of the law of contract could interfere with the attainment of national objectives and therefore come within the domain" of the Copyright Act. *Id.* The Eighth Circuit too cautioned in *National Car Rental* that a contractual restriction could impermissibly "protect rights equivalent to the exclusive copyright rights." 991 F.2d at 432.

I conclude that *Vault* states the correct rule; that state law authorizing shrinkwrap licenses that prohibit reverse engineering is preempted; and that the

First Circuit would so hold because the extra element here "merely concerns *the extent to which* authors and their licensees can prohibit unauthorized copying by third parties." *Data Gen.,* 36 F.3d at 1165 (emphasis in original). I respectfully dissent.

(c)   Can the Licensor Prohibit Assignment by the Licensee?

The different baseline assumptions of the copyright and commercial law systems perhaps are best illustrated by the rules regarding the ability of a licensee to assign its interest under a license. State law assumes that all assets are freely assignable, including contract rights such as interests under licenses. Thus, for example, in the absence of an agreement, rights under a contract governed by Article 2 can be assigned unless it would "materially" burden the other party. Indeed, in the context of lending transactions, assignment is permitted notwithstanding anything to the contrary in the contract. Thus, a party that wished to grant a security interest in its rights under a contract could grant that interest even if the contract itself forbad any assignment or grant of a security interest. See UCC §9-408 (discussed in considerable detail in Assignment 36). Federal bankruptcy generally incorporates the same rights for the bankruptcy trustee as state law grants lenders. Thus, a trustee in bankruptcy ordinarily can assume the contract positions of the failed debtor notwithstanding any contrary clauses in the relevant contracts. See Bankruptcy Code §365(c)(1).

In the federal context, however, the presumption, at least with respect to nonexclusive licenses, is that a licensee's interest is not assignable. Thus, even if the license fails to address the question, the licensee generally will be held barred from assigning its interest to a third party. The leading case (which involves a nonexclusive license of a patent) explained its reasoning as follows:

> [E]very licensee would become a potential competitor with the licensor-patent holder in the market for licenses under the patents. And while the patent holder could presumably control the absolute number of licenses in existence under a free-assignability regime, it would lose the very important ability to control the identity of its licensees. Thus, any license a patent holder granted — even to the smallest firm in the product market most remote from its own — would be fraught with the danger that the licensee would assign it to the patent holder's most serious competitors, a party whom the patent holder itself might be absolutely unwilling to license.

In re CFLC, Inc. (Everex Systems, Inc. v. Cadtrak Corp.), 89 F.3d 673, 679 (9th Cir. 1996). The cases to date that involve copyright licenses apply the same reasoning.

The result is startling. A provision stating that a licensee of software cannot grant a security interest in its rights to the software is one of the very few provisions that state law would reject. At the same time, it is one of the few limitations on licensee activity that federal courts would imply into a license as a matter of nonstatutory federal policy. Indeed, as the location of the *Everex* dispute in the bankruptcy courts illustrates, the effect of the rule is to make nonexclusive licenses of patents and copyrights about the only assets in a bankruptcy estate that cannot freely be assigned in connection with the bankruptcy. See In re Catapult Entertainment, Inc. (Perlman v. Catapult Entertainment, Inc.), 165 F.3d 747 (9th Cir. 1999) (preventing a bankruptcy trustee from assuming a software license when the software licensee filed for bankruptcy).

Relevant Glossary Entries

Bandwidth
Fair Use
First-Sale Doctrine
National Commission on New Technological Uses of Copyrighted Works (CONTU)
Protocol
Reverse Engineering

Problem Set 22

22.1. When you buy your books next semester, suppose that one of your classes has the books in a new E-book format. You download the books to a portable book-shaped reader that can hold all of a semester's books in one container. To get the book, however, you have to agree to a click-wrap license that includes the following language:

> THIS BOOK IS LICENSED EXCLUSIVELY FOR USE BY LICENSEE. ACCORDINGLY, LICENSEE HEREBY AGREES THAT LICENSEE SHALL HAVE NO RIGHT TO TRANSFER THE BOOK IN ANY WAY (WHETHER BY SALE, LEASE, LICENSE, SUBLICENSE, LENDING, OR OTHERWISE) TO ANY OTHER PARTY.

When the semester comes to an end, is it lawful for you to sell the book back to a Web site that buys and resells used electronic books? (Assume for now that you can transmit the file to that Web site without copying the file.) Copyright Act §109(a).

22.2. Same facts as in Problem 22.1, but you represent the licensor. Is there anything you might do in the terms of the license to enhance the likelihood that the restriction on transfer would be enforceable?

22.3. Same facts as in Problem 22.1, but assume that the license says nothing about transfer. Instead, the software and the reader are designed with a tamper-proof feature that makes it impossible for you to copy the software or transfer it to another reader. Moreover, the software is designed to terminate your access to the book after 12 months. Is it permissible for you to hire a software engineer to free the book from those constraints? Copyright Act §1201.

22.4. Your friend Rob Sears from Ecliptic Systems comes to see you again today. His company designs software to make Web pages more compatible with mobile Internet devices such as cellphones and Palm pilots. It is of crucial importance to him that his product be perfectly compatible with

Microsoft Explorer and Microsoft FrontPage (a program used to create Web pages). In order to ensure that his product works perfectly, he does not need to rewrite any code from the Microsoft program, but he does need to study carefully the "interface" that Explorer and FrontPage present to other programs. Because he has been unable to obtain that information directly from Microsoft, he wants to "reverse engineer" the interface. Specifically, by analyzing the Microsoft program he can learn what he needs to know. The only problem is that the reverse engineering process involves making a copy of the Microsoft program. His copies of the programs came with his computer. They include an End User License Agreement, to which he consented in a typical click-wrap fashion when he first started up his computer. Among other things, the license includes the following paragraph:

> **Limitations on Reverse Engineering, Decompilation, and Disassembly**. You may not reverse engineer, decompile, or disassemble the Software, except and only to the extent that such activity is expressly permitted by applicable law notwithstanding this limitation.

Is that provision effective to prohibit the activity in which Rob wishes to engage? Copyright Act §§106, 107, 117, 301.

    22.5.   Same facts as in Problem 22.4, but now assume that Rob did not acquire his Microsoft products through a license transaction, but instead downloaded it from a "shareware" site where it was available without the necessity for any license. (You should assume that whoever posted the software to the shareware site has flagrantly violated the terms of their license from Microsoft.) How does that change your answer?

Assignment 23: The Proprietary Software License

A. Types of Licenses

Because software is used in so many different contexts, there are many different types of licenses. One fundamental distinction in licensing is between an exclusive license and a nonexclusive license. An exclusive license is relatively uncommon in the software context, because it would preclude the licensor from selling the product (or parts of the product) to other customers. Thus, an inventor might grant an exclusive license of a patent to a business that has the resources to exploit the patent. However, a vendor selling a program to a customer is likely to sell the same program (or parts of the same program) to many customers. Thus, it will use a nonexclusive license.

There also is a distinction between a negotiated commercial license for the acquisition of a custom software program and a non-negotiated mass-market license for a commodity software product. Those licenses often are called end-user license agreements (EULAs). A current Microsoft end-user license agreement appears as an appendix to this assignment. (References in this assignment to the Microsoft EULA are to that document.)

Within the category of commercial licenses there also are important distinctions. For example, important parts of the software community use "open-source" licenses, covering software in which the source code will not be kept confidential. Those licenses are discussed in Assignment 25 and will not be discussed further here. The major topic of this assignment is the proprietary software license, used by a business to acquire software. Even within that context, there are important distinctions among the transactions that a business might use. For example, it is increasingly common to "outsource" the software process — so that a third-party provider manages the selection, installation, implementation, and operation of a firm's software products. In other cases, software might be provided by an application service provider, so that employees of the firm access important applications at an Internet site maintained by the provider.

Still, any specific discussion requires consideration of a particular context. The discussion here addresses a conventional license of software that a business acquires for use in its own computer network. The remainder of this assignment discusses the major terms of such a license. An example of such a license appears as an appendix to this assignment. (References to the Model Software License are to that document.)

B. The Major Terms of a License

1. Scope

In a sale of goods, the subject of the grant is usually quite easy to understand: complete ownership of a particular physical object. In a license transaction, however, things are rarely so simple. On the contrary, a major point of negotiation — and a common point of after-the-fact disputes — is the determination of precisely what the licensee has received. The licensee is motivated to ensure that the license adequately describes the operating environment in which the software will be used. Similarly, if the licensee plans to integrate the software with other products, the licensee will need adequate rights to modify the software without violating the licensor's exclusive rights to create derivative works.

Conversely, the licensor will wish to ensure that the licensee is prohibited from activities that injure the licensor's proprietary position. Thus, the license typically includes very specific limitations on forbidden uses, such as the reverse engineering prohibition at issue in the *Bowers* case in Assignment 22. Perhaps the most difficult negotiations arise in cases in which the licensee plans to redistribute products that include software code covered by the license. That raises additional issues related to ensuring that the code is distributed in a way that is not prejudicial to the original licensor.

To get a sense for how those problems can be resolved, compare the provisions set out below from the Microsoft EULA to the parallel provisions from the Model Software License.

MICROSOFT EULA

1. GRANT OF LICENSE. Microsoft grants you the following rights provided that you comply with all terms and conditions of this EULA:

> * Installation and use. You may install, use, access, display and run one copy of the Product on a single computer, such as a workstation, terminal or other device ("Workstation Computer"). A "License Pack" allows you to install, use, access, display and run additional copies of the Product up to the number of "Licensed Copies" specified above. The Product may not be used by more than two (2) processors at any one time on any single Workstation Computer. You may permit a maximum of ten (10) computers or other electronic devices (each a "Device") to connect to the Workstation Computer to utilize the services of the Product solely for file and print services, internet information services, and remote access (including connection sharing and telephony services). The ten connection maximum includes any indirect connections made through "multiplexing" or other software or hardware which pools or aggregates connections. You may not use the Product to permit any Device to use, access, display or run other executable software residing on the Workstation Computer, nor may you permit any Device to display the Product's user interface, unless the Device has a separate license for the Product.
> * Storage/Network Use. You may also store or install a copy of the Product on a storage device, such as a network server, used only to install or run the Product on your other Workstation Computers over an internal network; however, you must

acquire and dedicate an additional license for each separate Workstation Computer on or from which the Product is installed, used, accessed, displayed or run. A license for the Product may not be shared or used concurrently on different Workstation Computers.

    * Reservation of Rights. Microsoft reserves all rights not expressly granted to you in this EULA. . . .

    4. TRANSFER-Internal. You may move the Product to a different Workstation Computer. Transfer to Third Party. The initial user of the Product may make a one-time transfer of the Product to another end user. The transfer has to include all component parts, media, printed materials, this EULA, and if applicable, the Certificate of Authenticity. The transfer may not be an indirect transfer, such as a consignment. Prior to the transfer, the end user receiving the transferred Product must agree to all the EULA terms. No Rental. You may not rent, lease, or lend the Product.

    5. LIMITATION ON REVERSE ENGINEERING, DECOMPILATION, AND DISASSEMBLY. You may not reverse engineer, decompile, or disassemble the Product, except and only to the extent that it is expressly permitted by applicable law notwithstanding this limitation.

MODEL SOFTWARE LICENSE

1. LICENSE GRANT.

(A) Vendor grants to client a non-exclusive perpetual license to use the Licensed Products indicated in the Attachments A which may be executed from time to time by the parties, and to use the Modifications and Client Modifications, as follows:

    (i) only on the Designated Processor(s), at the Designated Site(s), and only by the Licensed Users, as applicable, identified in Attachments A attendant to this Agreement;

    (ii) in the case of the _____ version of the Licensed Products, to also utilize the Licensed Products on personal computers used as clients in conjunction with the Designated Processor;

    (iii) to create or procure Client Modifications to enhance Client's use of the Licensed Products solely in the manner contemplated by this Agreement and not for any independent efforts to generate revenues of any kind solely from the sale, license, sublicense or distribution of the Licensed Products and/or Client Modifications;

    (iv) only by Client and not for the benefit of any third party (in the interest of clarity, this shall not include Affiliates and parties for which Client is providing transition services under Article II, Section 6 below), including without limitation, commercial timesharing or service bureau or other rental or sharing arrangements, data processing or management information or services;

    (v) only in North America and any United States territories and may only be moved to another country with the prior written permission of Vendor, which shall not be unreasonably withheld, delayed or conditioned; and,

    (vi) copy the Licensed Products, Modifications, or Client Modifications for training, archival or backup purposes only, provided Client will pay any additional third party license fees required by Vendor's licensors for such copies, so long as all titles, trademark, copyright, and restriction notices are reproduced.

    No other uses are granted hereunder.

(B) Client may not:

(i) reverse engineer, disassemble, or decompile any part of the Licensed Products or Modifications, except to the extent required to obtain interoperability with other independently created or procured software or as specified by law;

(ii) distribute, sell or otherwise transfer (except as set forth in Article II, Section 6 or Article V, Section 10 (D) below) any part of the Licensed Products, Modifications, or Client Modifications; or

(iii) remove the patent, copyright, trade secret or other propriety protection legends or notices that appear on or in the Licensed Products.

2. Confidential Information

One of the most important concerns of the licensor will be what the licensee does with the information the licensee receives under the license. This is particularly true in cases (as in the Model Software License) in which the licensee has rights to modify the software, because the licensee in that case is likely to have access to the source code for the licensed software. Notice, for example, in the case of the Model Software License that the definition of "Licensed Products" includes the source code for many of the components. The licensor, in turn, will want to ensure that the source code provided to the licensee will not be distributed any further. The licensee will have identical concerns in situations in which the parties contemplate that the licensor will modify or enhance its products to ensure compatibility with existing software of the licensee. The licensee also might be concerned about the confidentiality of data (including customer information) that might come into the possession of the licensor during the course of the licensor's activities. (Indeed, in the context of the Microsoft EULA that concern is reflected in a specific grant to Microsoft of the right to use any data Microsoft collects in the provision of support services. Microsoft EULA §7.) In the commercial context, those provisions typically are drafted in a reciprocal fashion, so that each party has the same duty with respect to information it receives from the other. The provisions of the Model Software License on that point are as follows:

1.   Mutual Nondisclosure

(A) Pursuant to this Agreement, each party may, from time to time, furnish the other party with certain Confidential Information. The parties agree to hold each other's Confidential Information in confidence. Each party agrees to take commercially reasonable steps to ensure that Confidential Information is not disclosed or distributed by its employees or agents in violation of this Agreement. The disclosure of Discloser's Confidential Information does not grant to the Recipient any license or rights to any trade secrets or under any patents or copyrights, except as expressly provided by the licenses granted in this Agreement.

(B) The obligations of Recipient with respect to any particular portion of Confidential Information shall terminate or shall not attach, as the case may be, when such information:

(i) was in the public domain at the time of Discloser's communication thereof to Recipient;

(ii) entered the public domain through no fault of Recipient subsequent to the time of Discloser's communication thereof to Recipient;

(iii) was in Recipient's possession free of any obligation of confidence at the time of Discloser's communication thereof to Recipient;

(iv) was independently developed by Recipient as demonstrated by written records; or,

(v) is required to be disclosed by court or government order and Discloser has been given notice of such order.

(C) Discloser understands that Recipient may develop information internally, or receive information from other parties, that may be similar to Discloser's information. Accordingly, nothing in this Agreement shall be construed as a representation or inference that Recipient will not independently develop products, for itself or for others, that compete with the products or systems contemplated by Discloser's information. The parties agree that a breach of the confidentiality obligations by Recipient shall cause immediate and irreparable monetary damage to Discloser and shall entitle Discloser to injunctive relief in addition to all other remedies.

3. *Warranties and Other Obligations of the Seller*

As with many commercial transactions, provisions about warranties and other obligations of the seller present some of the most challenging issues. In a typical mass-market EULA, those provisions are likely to be quite limited, including a specific disclaimer of responsibility for any occurrence other than a failure of the software to perform in accordance with its specifications, and a disclaimer in that event of damages that exceed the cost of the product:

11. LIMITED WARRANTY FOR SOFTWARE PRODUCTS ACQUIRED IN THE US AND CANADA. Microsoft warrants that the Product will perform substantially in accordance with the accompanying materials for a period of ninety days from the date of receipt. If an implied warranty or condition is created by your state/jurisdiction and federal or state/provincial law prohibits disclaimer of it, you also have an implied warranty or condition, BUT ONLY AS TO DEFECTS DISCOVERED DURING THE PERIOD OF THIS LIMITED WARRANTY (NINETY DAYS). AS TO ANY DEFECTS DISCOVERED AFTER THE NINETY (90) DAY PERIOD, THERE IS NO WARRANTY OR CONDITION OF ANY KIND. Some states/jurisdictions do not allow limitations on how long an implied warranty or condition lasts, so the above limitation may not apply to you. Any supplements or updates to the Product, including without limitation, any (if any) service packs or hot fixes provided to you after the expiration of the ninety day Limited Warranty period are not covered by any warranty or condition, express, implied or statutory. LIMITATION ON REMEDIES; NO CONSEQUENTIAL OR OTHER DAMAGES. Your exclusive remedy for any breach of this Limited Warranty is as set forth below. Except for any refund elected by Microsoft, YOU ARE NOT ENTITLED TO ANY DAMAGES, INCLUDING BUT NOT LIMITED TO CONSEQUENTIAL DAMAGES, if the Product does not meet Microsoft's Limited Warranty, and, to the maximum extent allowed by applicable law, even if any remedy fails of its essential purpose. The terms of Section 13 below ("Exclusion of Incidental, Consequential and Certain Other Damages") are also incorporated into this Limited Warranty. Some states/jurisdictions do not allow the exclusion or limitation of incidental or consequential damages, so the above limitation or exclusion

may not apply to you. This Limited Warranty gives you specific legal rights. You may have others which vary from state/jurisdiction to state/jurisdiction. YOUR EXCLUSIVE REMEDY. Microsoft's and its suppliers' entire liability and your exclusive remedy shall be, at Microsoft's option from time to time exercised subject to applicable law, (a) return of the price paid (if any) for the Product, or (b) repair or replacement of the Product, that does not meet this Limited Warranty and that is returned to Microsoft with a copy of your receipt. You will receive the remedy elected by Microsoft without charge, except that you are responsible for any expenses you may incur (e.g. cost of shipping the Product to Microsoft). This Limited Warranty is void if failure of the Product has resulted from accident, abuse, misapplication, abnormal use or a virus. Any replacement Product will be warranted for the remainder of the original warranty period or thirty (30) days, whichever is longer. Outside the United States or Canada, neither these remedies nor any product support services offered by Microsoft are available without proof of purchase from an authorized international source. To exercise your remedy, contact: Microsoft, Attn. Microsoft Sales Information Center/One Microsoft Way/Redmond, WA 98052-6399, or the Microsoft subsidiary serving your country.

In many contexts, however, it will be difficult to persuade a commercial customer to accept such limited responsibility. For one thing, many commercial licensees will seek a broader commitment to performance. One of the key issues will be whether the warranty of performance will be limited to a commitment that the software will comply with the documentation (as in the EULA example above) or whether there will be some broader and more subjective commitment of operability. On that point, compare the following provisions from the Model Software License to an alternative provision that is more favorable to the licensee:

MODEL SOFTWARE LICENSE

2. WARRANTIES.   Vendor warrants that it possesses all rights and interests necessary to enter into this Agreement. In addition, Vendor extends the following warranties:

(A) LICENSED PRODUCTS. For a period of one (1) year following implementation of the Licensed Products at each Designated Site, Vendor warrants that the Licensed Products will materially perform the functions described in the Published Product Specifications. Vendor warrants that the Licensed Products: (i) will completely and accurately address, present, produce, store and calculate data involving dates beginning with January 1, 2000, and will not produce abnormally ending or incorrect results involving such dates as used in any forward or regression date based functions; and (ii) will provide that all "date"-related functionalities and data fields include the indication of century and millennium and will perform calculations which involve a four-digit year field.

(B) SERVICES. For a period of ninety (90) days following the date of performance of the last portion of the Services related to each project, Vendor warrants that the Services supplied hereunder shall be performed consistent with generally accepted industry standards.

(C) CUSTOMER SUPPORT AND SOFTWARE ENHANCEMENTS. During the Subscription Period, Vendor warrants that the Licensed Products will materially perform at least the functions described in the Published Product Specifications as they existed at the time of Client's acquisition of the License for such License Products. Vendor shall regression test all corrections, Software Enhancements and Software Updates in Client's environment (including any Modifications) prior to providing same to Client.

(D) WARRANTY EXCLUSIONS. EXCEPT AS EXPRESSLY SET FORTH IN THIS AGREEMENT, THERE ARE NO WARRANTIES, EXPRESSED OR IMPLIED, INCLUD-ING, BUT NOT LIMITED TO, THE IMPLIED WARRANTIES OF MERCHANTABILITY OR FITNESS FOR A PARTICULAR PURPOSE. Vendor makes no warranty with respect to and shall have no responsibility or liability whatsoever for the Client Modifications. Vendor makes no warranty with respect to and shall have no responsibility or liability whatsoever for the Client Modifications. All Client Modifications, if made, shall be made at the sole risk and expense of Client and shall void any warranties of the Licensed Products to the extent such Client Modifications cause a breach of the warranties.

3. EXCLUSIVE REMEDIES. For any breach of warranties contained in Section 2 of this Article, Client's exclusive remedy and Vendor entire liability shall be as follows:

(A) LICENSED PRODUCTS. The correction of errors in the Licensed Products that cause breach of warranty, or if Vendor is unable to provide such correction, Client shall be entitled to terminate this Agreement as it relates to the non-conforming Licensed Products and receive a refund of the License Fees paid for the non-conforming Licensed Products. If Client determines in its reasonable dis-cretion that the non-conforming Licensed Products are so integrally related to the other Licensed Products as to substantially remove the business purpose of the installation at the Designated Sites, such refund shall include a refund of the License Fees and support fees for the remaining Subscription Period for the other Licensed Products, which license will then be terminated.

(B) SERVICES. The reperformance of the Services, or if Vendor is unable to per-form the Services as warranted, Client shall be entitled to recover the fees paid to Vendor for the unsatisfactory Services. If Client determines in its reasonable dis-cretion that the non-conforming Services are so integral to the ability to use the Licensed Products as to substantially remove the business purpose of the installa-tion at the Designated Sites, such refund shall include a refund of the License Fees for the Licensed Products, which license will then be terminated.

(C) CUSTOMER SUPPORT AND SOFTWARE ENHANCEMENTS. The correction of errors in the Licensed Products that cause breach of warranty, or if Vendor is unable to provide such correction, Client shall be entitled to terminate this Agreement as it relates to the non-conforming Licensed Products and receive a refund of the Customer Support and/or Software Enhancements Fees paid for the non-conforming Licensed Products for the then-current Subscription Period.

LICENSEE-FAVORABLE PROVISION

Performance. Licensor warrants that the Licensed Software will operate without errors or interruptions and fully in accordance with all functional requirements of Licensee and all technical specifications, user manuals, and all other documenta-tion relating to the Licensed Software prepared or published by Licensor. Without limiting any other remedies available to Licensee for breach of this warranty, Licensor will, at no charge to Licensee, promptly correct any error in the Licensed Software reported to Licensor by providing to Licensee either (a) a new version of the Licensed Software in which the error has been corrected, or (b) additional software code that, when installed in accordance with Licensor's instructions, will correct the error. In addition, Licensor will immediately provide to Licensee any known methods of operating the Licensed Software in a manner that eliminates the practical effects of the error. If Licensor is unable to correct the error as provided above within a reasonable period of time not to exceed thirty (30) days, Licensor will refund to Licensee all fees paid for the Licensed Software (in addition to any other rights and remedies Licensee may have).

Unlike goods that typically are delivered at one time by a seller to a buyer, a software product's quality depends in large part on periodic service and enhancements that the licensor provides over the term during which the licensee uses the software. The licensor's obligations on those issues are more difficult to specify, but the license typically describes them in general terms, if only because the parties at the time of the initial license are likely to form a shared understanding of how those services will be provided.

ARTICLE III.   SERVICES

1. SERVICES PROVISION.   Vendor will provide Services from time to time at Client's request and under the terms and conditions of this Agreement.

2. MODIFICATIONS.   As a part of Services, Vendor will also provide Modifications at Client's request, as documented by a Detailed Design Specification or similar mutually agreed upon instrument. Client and Vendor agree that the Modifications provided to Client shall not be a "work made for hire". Client shall receive a source code, irrevocable, transferable, worldwide, sublicensable, non-exclusive license to the Modifications with the right to copy, modify, perform derivative works, market, sell, lease and distribute such Modifications as Client shall choose in its sole discretion.

3. SERVICES TERMINATION.   Client may, at its election and upon thirty (30) days prior written notice, terminate the Services to be provided hereunder. However, such termination shall not affect any right or claim of either party incurred or accruing prior to the date of termination including without limitation, any right or claim of Vendor for services rendered or reimbursable expenses incurred prior to such termination date. Vendor agrees that upon receipt of notice of termination it shall use commercially reasonable efforts to cease all work and reduce all expenses to the extent possible.

ARTICLE IV.   CUSTOMER SUPPORT AND SOFTWARE ENHANCEMENTS

1. CUSTOMER SUPPORT AND SOFTWARE ENHANCEMENTS.   Customer Support and Software Enhancements shall be provided in accordance with Vendor's Worldwide Customer Support and Software Enhancements policies as they may exist at the beginning of each annual Subscription Period, provided that any changes shall be effective only after Client receives written notice thereof. Subscriptions to Customer Support and/or Software Enhancements are offered for only the Licensed Products and Client may not elect to exclude any of the Licensed Products or any of the Designated Site(s) from Vendor's Customer Support and Software Enhancements subscriptions during the Subscription Period. Upon Client's request, Vendor shall provide support for any Modifications at a mutually agreeable cost.

2. SUBSCRIPTION PERIOD.   The Subscription Period begins upon execution of an Attachment B attendant to this Agreement. At least thirty (30) days prior to expiration of a Subscription Period, Vendor shall notify Client of the applicable Customer Support and/or Software Enhancements Fees for the succeeding year. Whereupon, unless Client notifies Vendor in writing of its desire to terminate its current subscription (s) upon the expiration date for that Subscription Period, Client's subscription(s) to Customer Support and/or Software Enhancements shall be extended and renewed for an additional period of one (1) year at the then-current subscription fees specified by Vendor. Customer Support and/or Software Enhancement Fees shall not increase by more than _____ (___%) per year.

In cases where support is crucial, the licensee might seek specific provisions about the support that will be provided, as in the following example:

> VENDOR will provide to Licensee technical support via email and over a toll free 800 number in accordance with the following service guarantees. Technical support will include assisting Licensee with understanding the nature of any errors or problems associated with the use of the Software and providing commercially reasonable efforts to identify appropriate remedies. VENDOR will use commercially reasonable efforts to develop a patch, fix or work-around for the Software as soon as reasonably practicable.

SERVICE GUARANTEES

> 1. Problems are High priority when the system is down or unusable, purchasing orders cannot be generated, the nightly batch job cannot continue running, or the software is otherwise severely impacted. The initial response from the support representative will occur with in one (1) hour of notification during business hours and one (1) hour outside of business hours. The status of the problem will be updated at least two (2) times per day until the problem is resolved.
>
> 2. Problems are Medium priority when the system is working and there is a work-around for the issue encountered or some other degradation in the performance of the Software is perceivable by a user of the Software. The initial response from the support representative will occur within two (2) hours of notification. The status of the problem will be updated every two (2) business days until the problem is resolved.
>
> 3. Problems are Low priority when there is a cosmetic issue with the system, when a functionality question or clarification requested, or when a malfunction of the Software is limited to back-end processes or data exchange and not perceived by the user of a Software. The initial response from the support representative will occur within one (1) business day after notification. The status of the problem updated with the release notes or plan for next release. Updated status reports on low priority problems are provided during regularly scheduled customer status calls.

The commercial license also will include some commitment with respect to claims that the licensed software infringes the IP rights of third parties. That topic is much more important in a software transaction than in a transaction involving tangible goods. Thus, a merchant selling goods generally warrants that "the goods shall be delivered free of the rightful claim of any third person by way of infringement or the like." UCC §2-312(2). Because it is unlikely that the seller in a sale of goods transaction under UCC Article 2 would be unaware that the goods infringed the intellectual property of a third party, that warranty seems to be a reasonable resolution of an issue that arises infrequently.

In transactions that involve intellectual property, however, such a warranty would involve considerable risk. That is particularly true with respect to claims of patent infringement. Copyright infringement occurs only in cases of actual copying, so a licensed software program will infringe only if portions of the program were copied from copyrighted work of a third party. Absent employee misconduct, substantial licensors typically can avoid such claims. Patent infringement, however, occurs whenever the licensed software uses a patented method or process, even if the software developer did not know of the patent. Given the large number of patents on software products, the risk that any particular product might infringe is significant.

In the end, the risks in that context typically result in some limitation on the licensor's commitment. For example, the licensor might decline to provide a warranty of noninfringement, but agree that it will indemnify the licensee from any claims of infringement by third parties. In that arrangement, the licensee would not be responsible to a third party for infringement, but it also would not be able to recover from the licensor for any damages it might suffer from loss of the license, whether in the form of lost profits or in the nature of some less direct consequential or incidental damages.

For illustrative purposes, consider the provisions that follow from the Model Software License:

> **4. INDEMNITIES.** Vendor, at its sole expense, agrees to hold harmless, defend and indemnify Client against any claim that the Services, Licensed Products or Modifications infringe a copyright, patent, or other intellectual property right, provided that: (i) Client notifies Vendor in writing within thirty (30) days of Client's management's notice of the claim; (ii) Vendor has sole control of the defense and all related settlement negotiations; and (iii) Client provides Vendor with the information, assistance and authority reasonably required to enable Vendor to perform Vendor's obligations under this paragraph. However, Vendor shall have no liability for any claims of infringement to the extent that such claims result from the use of the Licensed Products in conjunction with non-Vendor software or other non-Vendor products (other than the operating systems and equipment specified by Vendor) or upon a use of the Licensed Products in a manner not disclosed to Vendor, which would give rise to a claim, suit, proceeding, finding or conclusion solely for contributory infringement or inducement of infringement. Nothing in this provision shall be construed as a limitation on Client's ability to retain legal counsel at its own expense to monitor the proceedings.
>
> Vendor further agrees that if Client is prevented from using the Licensed Product(s) due to an actual or claimed infringement of any patent, copyright or other intellectual property right, then at Vendor's option and as its entire obligation to Client with respect to such claims, Vendor shall promptly either:

(i) procure for Client, at Vendor's expense, the right to continue to use the Licensed Product(s);

(ii) replace or modify the Licensed Product(s) at Vendor's expense so that the Licensed Product(s) become non-infringing, but substantially equivalent in functionality; or

(iii) in the event that neither (i) or (ii) are reasonably feasible, terminate the Agreement as to the infringing Licensed Products and return Client's License Fees for the infringing Licensed Product(s) and the fees for the remaining portion of the Subscription Period for such Licensed Product(s). If Client determines in its reasonable discretion that the terminated Licensed Products are so integrally related to the other Licensed Products as to substantially remove the business purpose of the installation at the Designated Sites, such refund shall include a refund of the License Fees and support fees for the other Licensed Products, which license will then be terminated.

C.   Termination and Remedies

One of the most controversial issues related to licensing has been the question of the remedies that are appropriate responses to default by the parties.

1.   *Licensor Default*

The most visible problem has related to default by a licensor, which could happen in two ways: the licensor might fail to satisfy ongoing obligations to maintain, upgrade, or support the software; or the licensor might become insolvent and thus attempt to terminate the license. In either case, the perspective of the licensee is likely to be that monetary damages are not an adequate remedy. That is particularly true in cases in which the licensee has integrated the software into its business, so that the costs of removing the software and ceasing use of it would exceed by far the amount paid (or to be paid) for the software. Rather, the licensee's goal is to determine a way to continue to use the software despite the breach by the licensor. Compare UCITA §813 (licensee has right to continue use of software upon breach of contract by a licensor).

One common contractual approach involves a "source-code escrow." That remedy is particularly common in cases in which a large company purchases a software component from a much smaller (and less financially reliable) trading partner. A source-code escrow obligates the (smaller) licensor to deposit a copy of the underlying source code for the software program with a responsible third party. See Model Software License art. II, §4. Typically, the licensor will be obligated to make periodic deposits to reflect changes and improvements in the software. The information also might include details regarding the particular individuals that are familiar with particular portions of the program. Then, the agreement provides, the escrow agent will deliver to the licensee the source code and related information in the event of a failure of the licensor to conform to its ongoing obligations. At that point, the licensee can use that information to perform the activities that the licensor failed to perform. That arrangement protects the licensee by ensuring that, in the event of a default by the licensor, the licensee will be in a position to understand the software well enough to have it maintained on an ongoing basis.

A more contentious problem relates to the effect on a license of the bankruptcy of the licensor. Under Bankruptcy Code §365(a), a debtor in bankruptcy generally is entitled to reject (that is, terminate) any ongoing contracts, subject only to an obligation to pay damages related to the rejection in the same way that the debtor might pay damages to any other contract claimant. As a practical matter, in the typical bankruptcy in which unsecured creditors receive little or nothing on their claims, that means that the debtor can reject a contract with impunity, leaving the creditor with no serious expectation that it will recover damages for the breach of contract.

The possibility that a licensor might use Section 365 to invalidate a license became a reality in 1985 with the decision of the Fourth Circuit in Lubrizol Enterprises, Inc. v. Richmond Metal Finishers, Inc., 756 F.2d 1043. That case arose out of a license Lubrizol had obtained to use a patented metal-coating process. When the licensor filed for bankruptcy, the licensor attempted to reject the license and terminate Lubrizol's rights to use the process. Although the district court did not permit the debtor to terminate the license, the Court of Appeals reversed and concluded that Lubrizol had no continuing right to the technology.

Licensees responded with such an outcry that Congress amended the statute to provide special rules for rejection of patent and copyright licenses. Those rules (which appear in Bankruptcy Code §365(n)) sharply limit the ability of the licensor to reject the license. Specifically, they authorize a licensee to ignore such a rejection and retain the rights to use the intellectual property that the license granted. Bankruptcy Code §365(n)(1)(B). The major twist is that the licensee that takes advantage of that provision must continue making all payments due under the purportedly rejected license, even if the licensor is not performing the duties it accepted in the license. Bankruptcy Code §365(n)(2)(B).

2. *Licensee Default*

In many commercial contexts, the likelihood of default by the licensee is much greater than the likelihood of default by the licensor: the licensor often will be a large well-capitalized company that may have relatively limited ongoing obligations, while the licensee might be a small business or individual using the software in question. The basic problem in that context is that the intangible nature of the collateral makes it practical for the licensor to take advantage of a variety of remedies that would not be available in transactions involving tangible goods.

The most visible default is that the licensee fails to make a payment due to the licensor. Although the licensor might respond with a lawsuit to collect the funds that are owed under the license, a more effective remedy often would be to terminate the licensee's ability to use the software. Thus, for example, the basic remedies that UCITA would have granted to a licensor included the rights "(1) to possession of all copies of the [software] . . . and (2) to prevent the continued exercise of . . . rights . . . under the license." UCITA §815(a).

Acting by analogy to tangible goods, the licensor could implement that remedy through cooperation with the licensee: The licensee might uninstall all of the software from its computers, download any data files to diskettes, and collect them all in a single location for the licensor to collect. In that case, the licensor can take the goods away without legal action. See UCITA §815(b) (permitting a licensor to exercise its right to prevent further use if it can do so "without a breach of the peace" and "without a foreseeable risk of personal injury or significant physical damage"). But that is just as likely as it is that a breaching buyer will collect the purchased goods and make them available for the seller to take away — it might happen some times, but sellers as a group are not willing to design their transactions on the assumption that the typical defaulting buyer will be so cooperative.

Accordingly, the licensor may seek some more aggressive remedy. For intangible goods like software, there are several ways to terminate use of the software without the cooperation of the licensee. For example, the software might be designed to work only with a code to be supplied from time to time by the licensor. If the codes are valid only for a limited period of time (30 days, for example), then the licensor effectively could terminate use for non-payment by declining to supply the codes necessary to permit continued operation. Alternatively, if the licensor functions as an application service provider — so that the software resides on the licensor's Web site rather than the licensee's computers — the licensor can simply stop providing service to the licensee.

More aggressively, even if the software resides on the licensee's computers, the licensor might contact the software from a remote location and disable it (using an Internet connection, for example, which might even be wireless). From the licensor's perspective, such a remedy is highly effective. For one thing, it is likely to be quite inexpensive: It costs much less to disable the software than it would to hire a lawyer to institute litigation or pay a sheriff to go out to take away goods. For another, it is most effective: The disabling of the software is likely to succeed almost every time; legal remedies are considerably less predictable.

From the licensee's perspective, such a remedy appears quite onerous. As mentioned above, a licensee that has purchased software often has integrated the software into its business so that loss of the use of the software could be catastrophic, causing damages far beyond the cost of the software. If that is so, the licensor's threat to terminate the software can have an extortionate leverage over the licensee. Another problem is the possibility of a sincerely mistaken application of the remedy: where the licensor, for example, misapplies or misplaces a payment from the licensee and uses the remedy against an innocent licensee. The serious consequences of such an error make the remedy troubling.

As a legal matter, the propriety of such a remedy is unclear. It is quite similar to the self-help remedy that generally is permitted by Article 9 of the UCC. See UCC §9-609. But that remedy often is criticized as unduly harsh, especially by consumers and businesses from other countries (which have different norms of enforcement). The only reported case addressing the use of electronic self-help concluded that the remedy was appropriate. American

Computer Trust Leasing v. Jack Farrell Implement Co., 763 F. Supp. 1473, 1492-1493 (D. Minn. 1991). That case, however, is not likely to be considered authoritative. The analysis in that case was a relatively cursory part of a lengthy trial court opinion largely devoted to other topics, and it does not directly involve a claim for breach of contract.

The only statute to address the point is UCITA, which would have validated what it termed "electronic self-help" in a guarded way. Specifically, UCITA permits electronic self-help only if (a) the licensee separately agrees (that is, agrees with a separate signature or other manifestation of assent) to a term of the license authorizing electronic self-help; and (b) the licensor gives 15 days advance notice of its intent to exercise the remedy. UCITA §816(c) and (d). Even if those conditions are satisfied, electronic self-help is prohibited if the licensor "has reason to know that its use will result in substantial injury or harm to the public health or safety or grave harm to the public interest." UCITA §816(f). Thus, for example, that provision probably would bar a licensor from shutting down software that would disable a hospital from providing services to its patients. Even with those limitations, the provision has come in for heated criticism. Before NCCUSL withdrew its support for UCITA, the UCITA Standby Committee recommended limiting the provision so that it generally would have permitted self-help only in the form of taking possession of the disks (or other storage media) on which the program is stored.

Relevant Glossary Entries

Deliverables
End User
Source Code
Source Code Escrow

Problem Set 23

23.1.   Referring back to Assignments 13 and 22, is the Microsoft EULA binding on users who purchase computers that it covers? Will the terms of the license (such as §5) bind subsequent purchasers of the computer?

23.2.   You represent a potential licensee who has been presented with the Model Software License by Dodona Software, the maker of a successful database software product. Your client plans to take the Dodona database software, modify it and incorporate it into a product that she is developing, and then license the resulting product to customers. Your client assures you that this is all "just fine" with the licensor. What revisions would you suggest to the Model Software License to accommodate your client's plans?

23.3.   Same facts as in Problem 23.2, one year later. You have received a demand letter from one of your customers, to whom you licensed your product under the Model Software License. The customer has been sued based on a claim by Junipero Serra Operations (JSO) that the software infringes copyright and patent rights of JSO. On investigation, it appears that the challenged portion of the software is code taken without alteration from the Dodona software described in Problem 23.2. Does the customer have a claim against you? Do you have a claim against Dodona? Model Software License art. V, §§2, 4, 10.

23.4. Same facts as in Problem 23.3, but now you receive a demand letter from JSO, challenging your use of the Dodona product. Relying on Article V, §4 of the Model Software License, you called on Dodona Software to handle the litigation. Dodona recently learned that you are now using the Dodona software on Dell servers, rather than the Sun servers that you were using at the time of the license. Dodona claims that because of the switch to Dell you have no claim against Dodona under the indemnity. You are puzzled, because the claim of infringement has nothing to do with the computer on which the software is operated. What do you tell your client? Model Software License art. V, §4.

23.5. Stacy Vye (your client from Wessex Bank) calls to ask for help on an upcoming transaction in which Wessex Bank plans to sell its highly successful credit-card processing subsidiary to Second Data Corporation. The subsidiary processes transactions using software that it has obtained on terms identical to those in the Model Software License. Second Data plans to keep the subsidiary as a separate entity, but to use the subsidiary to process all of Second Data's transactions. Do you foresee any difficulty? Model Software License art. II, §6, art. V, §10(D).

23.6. Stacy Vye calls back a few weeks later concerned about another matter. Her bank last year purchased a file management system that it uses to store, update, and analyze all information related to its customers' accounts. The system is integrated with the bank's check-processing center so that information from checks that pass through the readers at that center is added automatically in real time to the accounts. The bank pays a monthly license fee for the software of $200,000. It also pays a monthly maintenance and upgrade fee of $50,000.

The bank has been very happy with the software. The problem is that the licensor filed for bankruptcy last month. Earlier this week, Stacy received a letter from the debtor (still in bankruptcy) explaining that all of its fees would double next month, and then again next year. The letter explained that if the bank chooses not to pay the increased fees the bankruptcy will cancel the license and the associated maintenance agreement. Stacy is appalled, but does not know what to do. She desperately needs the software — her bank has spent hundreds of thousands of dollars transferring all of its account data into the software. And she also needs the maintenance and upgrade service — without which the software would swiftly become useless to her — for which there is no other provider. She cannot believe, however, that the licensor can just unilaterally increase the charges after a contract has been signed. Must she pay the increased fees? Bankruptcy Code §365(a), (b) and (n).

23.7. Just as you are leaving the office, you get an e-mail from Mark Kelp at GenenText. He is trying to close the first big license of his genetic-code analyzing software, to the research lab of a major pharmaceutical company (Pheazer Pharmaceuticals). He expects that the monthly revenue from this one license will keep his company solvent for years to come. At the same time, he is worried that Pheazer has a reputation for sharp dealing, and worries that it might try to avoid paying for the software in the years to come. Accordingly, Mark wants to do everything he can to make sure that the revenue stream is secure. He read recently in an industry periodical about electronic self-help. Given the way that his software works, it would be easy for him to design the software in a way that would permit him to enter Pheazer's computers remotely and disable the software. Mark wants your advice. Should he do that? If so, is there anything special that you should put in the license? Would the provisions in the license be enforceable if you included them? UCITA §§815 and 816.

END-USER LICENSE AGREEMENT

IMPORTANT-READ CAREFULLY: This End-User License Agreement ("EULA") is a legal agreement between you (either an individual or a single entity) and Microsoft Corporation for the Microsoft software product identified above, which includes computer software and may include associated media, printed materials, and "online" or electronic documentation ("Product"). An amendment or addendum to this EULA may accompany the Product. YOU AGREE TO BE BOUND BY THE TERMS OF THIS EULA BY INSTALLING, COPYING, OR OTHERWISE USING THE PRODUCT. IF YOU DO NOT AGREE, DO NOT INSTALL OR USE THE PRODUCT; YOU MAY RETURN IT TO YOUR PLACE OF PURCHASE FOR A FULL REFUND.

1. GRANT OF LICENSE. Microsoft grants you the following rights provided that you comply with all terms and conditions of this EULA:

* Installation and use. You may install, use, access, display and run one copy of the Product on a single computer, such as a workstation, terminal or other device ("Workstation Computer"). A "License Pack" allows you to install, use, access, display and run additional copies of the Product up to the number of "Licensed Copies" specified above. The Product may not be used by more than two (2) processors at any one time on any single Workstation Computer. You may permit a maximum of ten (10) computers or other electronic devices (each a "Device") to connect to the Workstation Computer to utilize the services of the Product solely for file and print services, internet information services, and remote access (including connection sharing and telephony services). The ten connection maximum includes any indirect connections made through "multiplexing" or other software or hardware which pools or aggregates connections. You may not use the Product to permit any Device to use, access, display or run other executable software residing on the Workstation Computer, nor may you permit any Device to display the Product's user interface, unless the Device has a separate license for the Product.

* Storage/Network Use. You may also store or install a copy of the Product on a storage device, such as a network server, used only to install or run the Product on your other Workstation Computers over an internal network; however, you must acquire and dedicate an additional license for each separate Workstation Computer on or from which the Product is installed, used, accessed, displayed or run. A license for the Product may not be shared or used concurrently on different Workstation Computers.

* Reservation of Rights. Microsoft reserves all rights not expressly granted to you in this EULA.

2. UPGRADES. To use a Product identified as an upgrade, you must first be licensed for the product identified by Microsoft as eligible for the upgrade. After upgrading, you may no longer use the product that formed the basis for your upgrade eligibility.

3. ADDITIONAL SOFTWARE. This EULA applies to updates or supplements to the original Product provided by Microsoft, unless we provide other terms along with the update or supplement.

4. TRANSFER-Internal. You may move the Product to a different Workstation Computer. Transfer to Third Party. The initial user of the Product may make a one-time transfer of the Product to another end user. The transfer has to include all component parts, media, printed materials, this EULA, and if applicable, the Certificate of Authenticity. The transfer may not be an indirect transfer, such as a consignment. Prior to the transfer, the end user receiving the transferred Product must agree to all the EULA terms. No Rental. You may not rent, lease, or lend the Product.

5. LIMITATION ON REVERSE ENGINEERING, DECOMPILATION, AND DISAS-SEMBLY. You may not reverse engineer, decompile, or disassemble the Product, except and only to the extent that it is expressly permitted by applicable law notwithstanding this limitation.

6. TERMINATION. Without prejudice to any other rights, Microsoft may cancel this EULA if you do not abide by the terms and conditions of this EULA, in which case you must destroy all copies of the Product and all of its component parts.

7. CONSENT TO USE OF DATA. You agree that Microsoft and its affiliates may collect and use technical information you provide as a part of support services related to the Product. Microsoft agrees not to use this information in a form that personally identifies you.

8. NOT FOR RESALE SOFTWARE. Product identified as "Not for Resale" or "NFR," may not be resold, transferred or used for any purpose other than demonstration, test or evaluation.

9. ACADEMIC EDITION SOFTWARE. To use Product identified as "Academic Edition" or "AE," you must be a "Qualified Educational User." For qualification-related questions, please contact the Microsoft Sales Information Center/One Microsoft Way/Redmond, WA 98052-6399 or the Microsoft subsidiary serving your country.

10. EXPORT RESTRICTIONS. Export-Restricted Encryption. If the Product is identified as "North America Only Version," the following terms apply: The Product contains strong encryption and cannot be exported outside of the United States (including Puerto Rico, Guam and all other territories, dependencies and possessions of the United States) or Canada without a U.S. Commerce Department export license or an applicable license exception. You agree that you will not directly or indirectly export or re-export the Product (or portions thereof), other than to Canada, without first obtaining an export license or determining that a license exception is applicable. For additional information see <http://www.microsoft.com/exporting/>.

Exportable Encryption. If the Product is not identified as "North America Only Version," the following terms apply: You agree that you will not export or re-export the Product (or portions thereof) to any country, person or entity subject to U.S. export restrictions. You specifically agree not to export or re-export the Product (or portions thereof): (i) to any country subject to a U.S. embargo or trade restriction; (ii) to any person or entity who you know or have reason to know will utilize the Product (or portions thereof) in the production of nuclear, chemical or biological weapons; or (iii) to any person or entity who has been denied export privileges by the U.S. government. For additional information see <http://www.microsoft.com/exporting/>.

11. LIMITED WARRANTY FOR SOFTWARE PRODUCTS ACQUIRED IN THE US AND CANADA. Microsoft warrants that the Product will perform substantially in accordance with the accompanying materials for a period of ninety days from the date of receipt. If an implied warranty or condition is created by your state/jurisdiction and federal or state/provincial law prohibits disclaimer of it, you also have an implied warranty or condition, BUT ONLY AS TO DEFECTS DISCOVERED DURING THE PERIOD OF THIS LIMITED WARRANTY (NINETY DAYS). AS TO ANY DEFECTS DISCOVERED AFTER THE NINETY (90) DAY PERIOD, THERE IS NO WARRANTY OR CONDITION OF ANY KIND. Some states/jurisdictions do not allow limitations on how long an implied warranty or condition lasts, so the above limitation may not apply to you. Any supplements or updates to the Product, including without limitation, any (if any) service packs or hot fixes provided to you after the expiration of the ninety day Limited Warranty period are not covered by any warranty or condition, express, implied or statutory. LIMITATION ON REMEDIES; NO CONSEQUENTIAL OR OTHER DAMAGES. Your exclusive remedy for any breach of this Limited Warranty is as set forth below. Except for any refund elected by Microsoft, YOU ARE NOT ENTITLED TO ANY DAMAGES, INCLUDING BUT NOT LIMITED TO CONSEQUENTIAL DAMAGES, if the Product does not meet Microsoft's Limited Warranty, and, to the maximum extent allowed by applicable law, even if any remedy fails of its essential purpose. The terms of Section 13 below ("Exclusion of Incidental, Consequential and Certain Other Damages") are also incorporated into this Limited Warranty. Some states/jurisdictions do not allow the exclusion or limitation of incidental or consequential damages, so the above limitation or exclusion may not apply to you. This Limited Warranty gives you specific legal rights. You may have others which vary from state/jurisdiction to state/jurisdiction. YOUR EXCLUSIVE REMEDY. Microsoft's and its suppliers' entire liability and your exclusive remedy shall be, at Microsoft's option from time to time exercised subject to applicable law, (a) return of the price paid (if any) for the Product, or (b) repair or replacement of the Product, that does not meet this Limited Warranty and that is returned to Microsoft with a copy of your receipt. You will receive the remedy elected by Microsoft without charge, except that you are responsible for any expenses you may incur (e.g. cost of shipping the Product to Microsoft). This Limited Warranty is void if failure of the Product has resulted from accident, abuse, misapplication, abnormal use or a virus. Any replacement Product will be warranted for the remainder of the original warranty period or thirty (30) days, whichever is longer. Outside the United States or Canada, neither these remedies nor any product support services offered by Microsoft are available without proof of purchase from an authorized international source. To exercise your remedy, contact: Microsoft, Attn. Microsoft Sales Information Center/One Microsoft Way/Redmond, WA 98052-6399, or the Microsoft subsidiary serving your country.

LIMITED WARRANTY FOR SOFTWARE PRODUCTS ACQUIRED OUTSIDE THE US AND CANADA. FOR THE LIMITED WARRANTIES AND SPECIAL PROVISIONS PERTAINING TO YOUR PARTICULAR JURISDICTION, PLEASE REFER TO YOUR WARRANTY BOOKLET INCLUDED WITH THIS PACKAGE OR PROVIDED WITH THE SOFTWARE PRODUCT PRINTED MATERIALS.

12. DISCLAIMER OF WARRANTIES. The Limited Warranty that appears above is the only express warranty made to you and is provided in lieu of any other express warranties (if any) created by any documentation or packaging. Except for the Limited Warranty and to the maximum extent permitted by applicable law,

Microsoft and its suppliers provide the Product and support services (if any) AS IS AND WITH ALL FAULTS, and hereby disclaim all other warranties and conditions, either express, implied or statutory, including, but not limited to, any (if any) implied warranties, duties or conditions of merchantability, of fitness for a particular purpose, of accuracy or completeness of responses, of results, of workmanlike effort, of lack of viruses, and of lack of negligence, all with regard to the Product, and the provision of or failure to provide support services. ALSO, THERE IS NO WARRANTY OR CONDITION OF TITLE, QUIET ENJOYMENT, QUIET POSSESSION, CORRESPONDENCE TO DESCRIPTION OR NON-INFRINGEMENT WITH REGARD TO THE PRODUCT.

13. EXCLUSION OF INCIDENTAL, CONSEQUENTIAL AND CERTAIN OTHER DAMAGES. TO THE MAXIMUM EXTENT PERMITTED BY APPLICABLE LAW, IN NO EVENT SHALL MICROSOFT OR ITS SUPPLIERS BE LIABLE FOR ANY SPECIAL, INCIDENTAL, INDIRECT, OR CONSEQUENTIAL DAMAGES WHATSOEVER (INCLUDING, BUT NOT LIMITED TO, DAMAGES FOR LOSS OF PROFITS OR CONFIDENTIAL OR OTHER INFORMATION, FOR BUSINESS INTERRUPTION, FOR PERSONAL INJURY, FOR LOSS OF PRIVACY, FOR FAILURE TO MEET ANY DUTY INCLUDING OF GOOD FAITH OR OF REASONABLE CARE, FOR NEGLIGENCE, AND FOR ANY OTHER PECUNIARY OR OTHER LOSS WHATSOEVER) ARISING OUT OF OR IN ANY WAY RELATED TO THE USE OF OR INABILITY TO USE THE PRODUCT, THE PROVISION OF OR FAILURE TO PROVIDE SUPPORT SERVICES, OR OTHERWISE UNDER OR IN CONNECTION WITH ANY PROVISION OF THIS EULA, EVEN IN THE EVENT OF THE FAULT, TORT (INCLUDING NEGLIGENCE), STRICT LIABILITY, BREACH OF CONTRACT OR BREACH OF WARRANTY OF MICROSOFT OR ANY SUPPLIER, AND EVEN IF MICROSOFT OR ANY SUPPLIER HAS BEEN ADVISED OF THE POSSIBILITY OF SUCH DAMAGES.

14. LIMITATION OF LIABILITY AND REMEDIES. Notwithstanding any damages that you might incur for any reason whatsoever (including, without limitation, all damages referenced above and all direct or general damages), the entire liability of Microsoft and any of its suppliers under any provision of this EULA and your exclusive remedy for all of the foregoing (except for any remedy of repair or replacement elected by Microsoft with respect to any breach of the Limited Warranty) shall be limited to the greater of the amount actually paid by you for the Product or U.S.$5.00. The foregoing limitations, exclusions and disclaimers (including Sections 11, 12 and 13 above) shall apply to the maximum extent permitted by applicable law, even if any remedy fails its essential purpose.

15. NOTE ON JAVA SUPPORT. THE PRODUCT MAY CONTAIN SUPPORT FOR PROGRAMS WRITTEN IN JAVA. JAVA TECHNOLOGY IS NOT FAULT TOLERANT AND IS NOT DESIGNED,MANUFACTURED, OR INTENDED FOR USE OR RESALE AS ONLINE CONTROL EQUIPMENT IN HAZARDOUS ENVIRONMENTS REQUIRING FAIL-SAFE PERFORMANCE, SUCH AS IN THE OPERATION OF NUCLEAR FACILITIES, AIRCRAFT NAVIGATION OR COMMUNICATION SYSTEMS, AIR TRAFFIC CONTROL, DIRECT LIFE SUPPORT MACHINES, OR WEAPONS SYSTEMS, IN WHICH THE FAILURE OF JAVA TECHNOLOGY COULD LEAD DIRECTLY TO DEATH, PERSONAL INJURY, OR SEVERE PHYSICAL OR ENVIRONMENTAL DAMAGE. Sun Microsystems, Inc. has contractually obligated Microsoft to make this disclaimer.

16. U.S. GOVERNMENT LICENSE RIGHTS. All Product provided to the U.S. Government pursuant to solicitations issued on or after December 1, 1995 is provided with the commercial license rights and restrictions described elsewhere

herein. All Product provided to the U.S. Government pursuant to solicitations issued prior to December 1, 1995 is provided with "Restricted Rights" as provided for in FAR, 48 CFR 52.227-14 (JUNE 1987) or DFAR, 48 CFR 252.227-7013 (OCT 1988), as applicable.

17. APPLICABLE LAW. If you acquired this Product in the United States, this EULA is governed by the laws of the State of Washington. If you acquired this Product in Canada, unless expressly prohibited by local law, this EULA is governed by the laws in force in the Province of Ontario, Canada; and, in respect of any dispute which may arise hereunder, you consent to the jurisdiction of the federal and provincial courts sitting in Toronto, Ontario. If this Product was acquired outside the United States, then local law may apply.

18. ENTIRE AGREEMENT. This EULA (including any addendum or amendment to this EULA which is included with the Product) are the entire agreement between you and Microsoft relating to the Product and the support services (if any) and they supersede all prior or contemporaneous oral or written communications, proposals and representations with respect to the Product or any other subject matter covered by this EULA. To the extent the terms of any Microsoft policies or programs for support services conflict with the terms of this EULA, the terms of this EULA shall control.

19. The Product is protected by copyright and other intellectual property laws and treaties. Microsoft or its suppliers own the title, copyright, and other intellectual property rights in the Product. The Product is licensed, not sold.

SOFTWARE LICENSE, SERVICES, SUPPORT AND
ENHANCEMENTS AGREEMENT ("AGREEMENT")

Client _____

Address _____

_____

Vendor, a _____ corporation, ("_____") markets and supports certain software applications licensed hereunder as "Licensed Products" and Client is a(n) _____ corporation or _____ having a principal place of business as noted above and Client is desirous of obtaining a license to use the Licensed Products, subject to the terms and conditions of this Agreement.

NOW THEREFORE, in consideration of the background, the covenants herein contained, and intending to be legally bound hereby, the parties agree as follows:

ARTICLE I. DEFINITIONS

For purposes of this Agreement, the following terms shall mean:

Affiliate(s)
With respect to any party at any time, any other person that Controls, is Controlled by, or is under common Control with the first mentioned party.

Client Modifications
Any enhancements, modifications, derivations, or substitutions to the Licensed Products made by or at the direction of Client and not made by Vendor.

Confidential Information
Certain confidential technical and business information, including without limitation, business plans and interests, the Licensed Products and associated user documentation and the pricing terms of this Agreement.

Control
As to any person, the ownership, directly or indirectly, of at least a majority of the common stock, voting securities, or other voting interests of such person. "Controlling" and Controlled" have the meaning correlative thereto.

Customer Support
Services provided by Vendor pursuant to this Agreement, for which Client has elected to subscribe, and related to technical support on Licensed Products. Software Updates for Licensed Products are included as a part of a Customer Support subscription.

Customer Support and Software Enhancements Fees
The fee(s) defined in Article V, Section 5(C).

Designated Processor
The hardware server identified in any Attachment to this Agreement or a written notification as described in Article II, Section 1(C). In the case of non-server based software, the personal computers on which the Licensed Products are resident.

Designated Site
The physical location(s) where (a) the Licensed Products are installed upon the Designated Processor(s); or (b) are otherwise utilized; and which are specifically identified in any Attachment to this Agreement or a written notification as described in Article II, Section 1(C).

Discloser
The party disclosing Confidential Information.

Implementation Period
The time period until all Licensed Products have been implemented at all of the Designated Sites.

Licensed Fee
The fee(s) defined in Article V, Section 5(A).

Licensed Product(s)
The computer programming source and object code for the Licensed Products identified in each Attachment A to this Agreement, any Software Enhancements, any Software Updates, the media in which the Licensed Products are delivered, and the associated documentation. Certain security operational controls [and programs] are provided in object code only.

Licensed User(s)

Any individual which currently has access to the Licensed Products. Licensed Users are counted concurrently and the total number of Licensed Users simultaneously using the Licensed Products at any one time may not exceed the total number for which License Fees have been paid, subject to the True-Up Provisions of Article II, Section 1 (D).

Modifications

Any mutually agreed upon enhancements, modifications, or substitutions to the Licensed Products made by or at the direction of Vendor.

Published Product Specifications

The User Guides and the Implementation Guides (in whatever media) associated with the Licensed Products, as they may exist at the time Client receives the relevant version of the Licensed Products.

Recipient

The party receiving Confidential Information.

Services

Professional services provided to Client by Vendor pursuant to Article III of this Agreement and related to the Licensed Products, including programming, consulting, analysis, and training.

Software Enhancements

Subsequent versions and releases of the Licensed Products which Vendor makes generally available without payment of additional License Fees during the Subscription Period. Software Updates for Licensed Products are included as a part of a Software Enhancements subscription. Vendor agrees that any software product that provides substantially the same functionality as the Licensed Products, even if on a different platform or operating system, shall be included within the definition of Software Enhancements and shall be available to Client as a part of a Software Enhancements subscription.

Software Updates

Corrections to Client's current version of the Licensed Products.

Subscription Periods

The time periods in annual increments during which Customer Support and/or Software Enhancements are available under this Agreement. Vendor shall provide Client calendar year subscription periods through prorating all Designated Sites' Customer Support and Software Enhancement Subscription Periods from the date such site is implemented.

ARTICLE II. SOFTWARE LICENSE ("LICENSE")

1. LICENSE GRANT.

(A) Vendor grants to client a non-exclusive perpetual license to use the Licensed Products indicated in the Attachments A which may be executed from time to time by the parties, and to use the Modifications and Client Modifications, as follows:

(i) only on the Designated Processor(s), at the Designated Site(s), and only by the Licensed Users, as applicable, identified in Attachments A attendant to this Agreement;

(ii) in the case of the _____ version of the Licensed Products, to also utilize the Licensed Products on personal computers used as clients in conjunction with the Designated Processor;

(iii) to create or procure Client Modifications to enhance Client's use of the Licensed Products solely in the manner contemplated by this Agreement and not for any independent efforts to generate revenues of any kind solely from the sale, license, sublicense or distribution of the Licensed Products and/or Client Modifications;

(iv) only by Client and not for the benefit of any third party (in the interest of clarity, this shall not include Affiliates and parties for which Client is providing transition services under Article II, Section 6 below), including without limitation, commercial timesharing or service bureau or other rental or sharing arrangements, data processing or management information or services;

(v) only in North America and any United States territories and may only be moved to another country with the prior written permission of Vendor, which shall not be unreasonably withheld, delayed or conditioned; and,

(vi) copy the Licensed Products, Modifications, or Client Modifications for training, archival or backup purposes only, provided Client will pay any additional third party license fees required by Vendor's licensors for such copies, so long as all titles, trademark, copyright, and restriction notices are reproduced. No other uses are granted hereunder.

(B) Client may not:

(i) reverse engineer, disassemble, or decompile any part of the Licensed Products or Modifications, except to the extent required to obtain interoperability with other independently created or procured software or as specified by law;

(ii) distribute, sell or otherwise transfer (except as set forth in Article II, Section 6 or Article V, Section 10 (D) below) any part of the Licensed Products, Modifications, or Client Modifications; or

(iii) remove the patent, copyright, trade secret or other propriety protection legends or notices that appear on or in the Licensed Products.

(C) Within thirty (30) days after receipt of a written request, from Vendor, Client shall provide Vendor with a written list of any model change to a Designated Processor(s), change in Designated Site(s) within the same country, or any reallocation of Licensed Users among the various Designated Site(s). Vendor shall not request such report more than twice each year. Client shall not responsible for any additional fees related to such re allocations of Licensed Users, changes of Designated Processor(s), or changes of Designated Site(s) within North America and any United States territories.

2. OWNERSHIP.   Vendor retains all title, copyright and other proprietary rights in the Licensed Products, Modifications, and Client Modifications, and all versions of each. Client does not acquire any rights, express or implied, other than those specified in this Agreement. Client agrees to use commercially reasonable efforts to secure and protect the Licensed Products, Modifications, and Client Modifications within Client's custody and control in a manner consistent with maintaining Vendor's rights therein. Client shall provide notice to its Licensed Users that the use of the Licensed Products is subject to the terms of this Agreement. In the event of a violation of Vendor's intellectual property rights by Client or its Licensed User(s), either party having notice of such event shall provide the other party with written notice thereof. Upon receipt of such written notice, Client shall take commercially reasonable efforts to resolve the related issue, including the payment of any fees due under Article II, Section 5, and Vendor agrees that Client shall have thirty (30) days to implement such actions. If Client does not reasonably resolve the issue within such time period, Vendor shall have the right to terminate this Agreement without further notice, which termination shall be in addition to and not in lieu of any equitable remedies available to Vendor. At Vendor's written request and sole expense, Vendor may audit Client's use of the Licensed Products, Modifications, or Client Modifications, at Vendor's expense, but not more frequently than annually. Such audit shall not unreasonably interfere with Client's business activities. If an audit reveals that Client has underpaid fees to Vendor, Client shall promptly pay any such underpaid fees, which payment shall be Vendor's sole remedy.

3. WRONGFUL POSSESSION OR ACCESS. Upon knowledge by the senior management of Client of any unauthorized possession, use of, or access to, any Licensed Products, Modifications, or Client Modifications by or through Client, Client shall promptly notify Vendor and furnish Vendor with full details of such knowledge, assist in preventing any recurrence thereof, and reasonably cooperate at Vendor's expense in any litigation or other proceedings reasonably necessary to protect the rights of Vendor.

4. SOURCE CODE ESCROW. By executing an Attachment C attendant to this Agreement, Client elects to have the remaining source code of the License Products which it does not receive placed on deposit in Vendor's master escrow account, which source code shall be released upon the conditions outlined in said Attachment. Upon making such election, Client agrees to pay to Vendor the then-current annual fee associated with being a beneficiary of such account. Further, Client will receive written confirmation from the escrow agent of Client's registration. At least thirty (30) days prior to expiration of Client's annual subscription to Source Code Escrow, Vendor shall notify Client of the applicable escrow fees for the succeeding year, whereupon, unless Client notifies Vendor in writing of its desire to terminate its escrow subscription upon such expiration date, Client's subscription to Source Code Escrow shall be extended and renewed for an additional period of one (1) year at the then-current fees specified by Vendor. If Client fails to remit escrow fees pursuant to the terms hereof, Vendor will have no duty to include Client as a beneficiary of account. Vendor agrees that any increase in the escrow fees shall not exceed the amount of increase charged by the third party escrow agent.

5. TRUE-UP REPORTS. Client shall provide Vendor with a list of all Designated Processor(s), Designated Site(s) and the number of Licensed User(s) within thirty (30) days after the end of each calendar year. If Client has increased its use of the Licensed Product(s) such that additional fees are due Vendor for Licensed User(s), Designated Processor(s) or Designated Site(s), Client shall pay such amount within forty-five (45) days after the end of the calendar year at the rate set forth on Attachment A. Client's payment shall be Vendor's sole remedy for such use.

6. DIVESTED AFFILIATE.   Notwithstanding anything herein to the contrary, (a) in the event that Client or an Affiliate divests an Affiliate, and for whose benefit the Client was using the Licensed Products at the time of such divestiture ("Divested Entity"), and (b) Client is current with all fees hereunder and in all other agreements with Vendor, Client may continue to use the Licensed Products for the benefit of such Divested Entity pursuant to all terms of this Agreement and the following additional terms:

(A) Any such use must be to process only that business and data that had previously been processed on behalf of said Divested Entity in the ordinary course immediately prior to such divestiture. No business of the new parent or any of its subsidiaries or affiliates may be processed using the Licensed Products without the prior written permission of Vendor, and without payment of an additional fee.

(B) Such Use shall be at no additional charge for up to one (1) year following such divestiture.

(C) No additional fee shall apply in the event that the acquiring entity (the Divested Entity's new parent) is already a Vendor Client for the same Licensed Products, the license agreement between Vendor and such acquiring entity allows for the processing of business from an acquired entity, and the acquiring entity is fully up to date with all fees owed to Vendor.

(D) All Customer Services and Software Enhancements shall be provided to the Divested Entity through Client and its contacts. Vendor shall have no obligation to respond directly to any calls or requests made by the Divested Entity.

(E) Under no circumstances shall Client continue to process the business or data of the Divested Entity for any period of time longer than twelve (12) months following such divestiture without the prior written permission of Vendor.

ARTICLE III.   SERVICES

1. SERVICES PROVISION.   Vendor will provide Services from time to time at Client's request and under the terms and conditions of this Agreement.

2. MODIFICATIONS.   As a part of Services, Vendor will also provide Modifications at Client's request, as documented by a Detailed Design Specification or similar mutually agreed upon instrument. Client and Vendor agree that the Modifications provided to Client shall not be a "work made for hire". Client shall receive a source code, irrevocable, transferable, worldwide, sublicensable, non-exclusive license to the Modifications with the right to copy, modify, perform derivative works, market, sell, lease and distribute such Modifications as Client shall choose in its sole discretion.

3. SERVICES TERMINATION.   Client may, at its election and upon thirty (30) days prior written notice, terminate the Services to be provided hereunder. However, such termination shall not affect any right or claim of either party incurred or accruing prior to the date of termination including without limitation, any right or claim of Vendor for services rendered or reimbursable expenses incurred prior to such termination date. Vendor agrees that upon receipt of notice of termination it shall use commercially reasonable efforts to cease all work and reduce all expenses to the extent possible.

ARTICLE IV.   CUSTOMER SUPPORT AND SOFTWARE
ENHANCEMENTS

1. CUSTOMER SUPPORT AND SOFTWARE ENHANCEMENTS. Customer Support and Software Enhancements shall be provided in accordance with Vendor's Worldwide Customer Support and Software Enhancements policies as they may exist at the beginning of each annual Subscription Period, provided that any changes shall be effective only after Client receives written notice thereof. Subscriptions to Customer Support and/or Software Enhancements are offered for only the Licensed Products and Client may not elect to exclude any of the Licensed Products or any of the Designated Site(s) from Vendor's Customer Support and Software Enhancements subscriptions during the Subscription Period. Upon Client's request, Vendor shall provide support for any Modifications at a mutually agreeable cost.

2. SUBSCRIPTION PERIOD.   The Subscription Period begins upon execution of an Attachment B attendant to this Agreement. At least thirty (30) days prior to expiration of a Subscription Period, Vendor shall notify Client of the applicable Customer Support and/or Software Enhancements Fees for the succeeding year. Whereupon, unless Client notifies Vendor in writing of its desire to terminate its current subscription (s) upon the expiration date for that Subscription Period, Client's subscription(s) to Customer Support and/or Software Enhancements shall be extended and renewed for an additional period of one (1) year at the then-current subscription fees specified by Vendor. Customer Support and/or Software Enhancement Fees shall not increase by more than _____ (___%) per year.

ARTICLE V.   GENERAL

1. MUTUAL NONDISCLOSURE.

(A) Pursuant to this Agreement, each party may, from time to time, furnish the other party with certain Confidential Information. The parties agree to hold each other's Confidential Information in confidence. Each party agrees to take commercially reasonable steps to ensure that Confidential Information is not disclosed or distributed by its employees or agents in violation of this Agreement. The disclosure of Discloser's Confidential Information does not grant to the Recipient any license or rights to any trade secrets or under any patents or copyrights, except as expressly provided by the licenses granted in this Agreement.

(B) The obligations of Recipient with respect to any particular portion of Confidential Information shall terminate or shall not attach, as the case may be, when such information:

(i) was in the public domain at the time of Discloser's communication thereof to Recipient;

(ii) entered the public domain through no fault of Recipient subsequent to the time of Discloser's communication thereof to Recipient;

(iii) was in Recipient's possession free of any obligation of confidence at the time of Discloser's communication thereof to Recipient;

(iv) was independently developed by Recipient as demonstrated by written records; or,

(v) is required to be disclosed by court or government order and Discloser has been given notice of such order.

(C) Discloser understands that Recipient may develop information internally, or receive information from other parties, that may be similar to Discloser's information. Accordingly, nothing in this Agreement shall be construed as a representation or inference that Recipient will not independently develop products, for itself or for others, that compete with the products or systems contemplated by Discloser's information. The parties agree that a breach of the confidentiality obligations by Recipient shall cause immediate and irreparable monetary damage to Discloser and shall entitle Discloser to injunctive relief in addition to all other remedies.

2. WARRANTIES. Vendor warrants that it possesses all rights and interests necessary to enter into this Agreement. In addition, Vendor extends the following warranties:

(A) LICENSED PRODUCTS. For a period of one (1) year following implementation of the Licensed Products at each Designated Site, Vendor warrants that the Licensed Products will materially perform the functions described in the Published Product Specifications. Vendor warrants that the Licensed Products: (i) will completely and accurately address, present, produce, store and calculate data involving dates beginning with January 1, 2000, and will not produce abnormally ending or incorrect results involving such dates as used in any forward or regression date based functions; and (ii) will provide that all "date"-related functionalities and data fields include the indication of century and millennium and will perform calculations which involve a four-digit year field.

(B) SERVICES. For a period of ninety (90) days following the date of performance of the last portion of the Services related to each project, Vendor warrants that the Services supplied hereunder shall be performed consistent with generally accepted industry standards.

(C) CUSTOMER SUPPORT AND SOFTWARE ENHANCEMENTS. During the Subscription Period, Vendor warrants that the Licensed Products will materially perform at least the functions described in the Published Product Specifications as they existed at the time of Client's acquisition of the License for such License Products. Vendor shall regression test all corrections, Software Enhancements and Software Updates in Client's environment (including any Modifications) prior to providing same to Client.

(D) WARRANTY EXCLUSIONS. EXCEPT AS EXPRESSLY SET FORTH IN THIS AGREEMENT, THERE ARE NO WARRANTIES, EXPRESSED OR IMPLIED, INCLUDING, BUT NOT LIMITED TO, THE IMPLIED WARRANTIES OF MERCHANTABILITY OR FITNESS FOR A PARTICULAR PURPOSE. Vendor makes no warranty with respect to and shall have no responsibility or liability whatsoever for the Client Modifications. Vendor makes no warranty with respect to and shall have no responsibility or liability whatsoever for the Client Modifications. All Client Modifications, if made, shall be made at the sole risk and expense of Client and shall void any warranties of the Licensed Products to the extent such Client Modifications cause a breach of the warranties.

3. EXCLUSIVE REMEDIES.   For any breach of warranties contained in Section 2 of this Article, Client's exclusive remedy and Vendor entire liability shall be as follows:

(A) LICENSED PRODUCTS. The correction of errors in the Licensed Products that cause breach of warranty, or if Vendor is unable to provide such correction, Client shall be entitled to terminate this Agreement as it relates to the non-conforming Licensed Products and receive a refund of the License Fees paid for the non-conforming Licensed Products. If Client determines in its reasonable discretion that the non-conforming Licensed Products are so integrally related to the other Licensed Products as to substantially remove the business purpose of the installation at the Designated Sites, such refund shall include a refund of the License Fees and support fees for the remaining Subscription Period for the other Licensed Products, which license will then be terminated.

(B) SERVICES. The reperformance of the Services, or if Vendor is unable to perform the Services as warranted, Client shall be entitled to recover the fees paid to Vendor for the unsatisfactory Services. If Client determines in its reasonable discretion that the non-conforming Services are so integral to the ability to use the Licensed Products as to substantially remove the business purpose of the installation at the Designated Sites, such refund shall include a refund of the License Fees for the Licensed Products, which license will then be terminated.

(C) CUSTOMER SUPPORT AND SOFTWARE ENHANCEMENTS. The correction of errors in the Licensed Products that cause breach of warranty, or if Vendor is unable to provide such correction, Client shall be entitled to terminate this Agreement as it relates to the non-conforming Licensed Products and receive a refund of the Customer Support and/or Software Enhancements Fees paid for the non-conforming Licensed Products for the then-current Subscription Period.

4. INDEMNITIES.   Vendor, at its sole expense, agrees to hold harmless, defend and indemnify Client against any claim that the Services, Licensed Products or Modifications infringe a copyright, patent, or other intellectual property right, provided that: (i) Client notifies Vendor in writing within thirty (30) days of Client's management's notice of the claim; (ii) Vendor has sole control of the defense and all related settlement negotiations; and (iii) Client provides Vendor with the information, assistance and authority reasonably required to enable Vendor to perform Vendor's obligations under this paragraph. However, Vendor shall have no liability for any claims of infringement to the extent that such claims result from the use of the Licensed Products in conjunction with non-Vendor software or other non-Vendor products (other than the operating systems and equipment specified by Vendor) or upon a use of the Licensed Products in a manner not disclosed to Vendor, which would give rise to a claim, suit, proceeding, finding or conclusion solely for contributory infringement or inducement of infringement. Nothing in this provision shall be construed as a limitation on Client's ability to retain legal counsel at its own expense to monitor the proceedings.

Vendor further agrees that if Client is prevented from using the Licensed Product(s) due to an actual or claimed infringement of any patent, copyright or other intellectual property right, then at Vendor's option and as its entire obligation to Client with respect to such claims, Vendor shall promptly either:

(i) procure for Client, at Vendor's expense, the right to continue to use the Licensed Product(s);

(ii) replace or modify the Licensed Product(s) at Vendor's expense so that the Licensed Product(s) become non-infringing, but substantially equivalent in functionality; or

(iii) in the event that neither (i) or (ii) are reasonably feasible, terminate the Agreement as to the infringing Licensed Products and return Client's License Fees for the infringing Licensed Product(s) and the fees for the remaining portion of the Subscription Period for such Licensed Product(s). If Client determines in its reasonable discretion that the terminated Licensed Products are so integrally related to the other Licensed Products as to substantially remove the business purpose of the installation at the Designated Sites, such refund shall include a refund of the License Fees and support fees for the other Licensed Products, which license will then be terminated.

5. PAYMENT.

(A) LICENSE FEES. In consideration for the License granted in Article 11, Client agrees to pay to Vendor the License Fees designated on any Attachment A attendant to this Agreement upon the execution of this Agreement and any Attachment A attendant to this Agreement.

(B) SERVICES FEES / EXPENSES. As compensation for performing Services, Client agrees to pay Vendor on a time and materials basis which shall be billed at Vendor's then-current list prices, which shall not increase during the term of the Implementation Period. Training shall be billed at Vendor's then-current list prices, which shall not increase during the term of the Implementation Period. Vendor will invoice Client every two (2) weeks while Services are being performed. Client agrees to reimburse Vendor for all reasonable out-of-pocket expenses Vendor incurs in providing Services. If uncontested amounts remain unpaid for thirty (30) days or more, Vendor may, at its option, refuse to perform additional Services under this Agreement until such amounts are paid.

(C) CUSTOMER SUPPORT AND SOFTWARE ENHANCEMENTS FEES. In consideration for the Customer Support and/or Software Enhancements to be provided hereunder and for which Client elects to subscribe, Client shall pay Customer Support and/or Software Enhancements Fees in accordance with any Attachment B attendant to this Agreement and subsequently as an annual charge. The first payment shall be due upon execution of any Attachment B attendant to this Agreement. During the Subscription Period, Client may be billed additional Customer Support and Software Enhancements Fees resulting from additional Designated Sites, additional Licensed Products, additional Licensed Users, or from the upgrade of service level. If Client fails to remit Customer Support and/or Software Enhancements Fees pursuant to the terms hereof, Vendor will have no duty to provide Customer Support and Software Enhancements as specified under Article IV.

(D) TAXES. The fees listed in this Agreement do not include taxes. If Vendor is required to pay any sales, use, property, excise, value added, gross receipts, or other taxes levied on the Licensed Products or Services under this Agreement or on Client's use thereof, then such taxes shall be billed to and paid by Client. This Section does not apply to taxes based on 's net income or 's employer contributions and taxes.

(E) INVOICES. Client agrees to pay for all amounts due under this Agreement upon receipt of invoice. Such amounts which remain unpaid for thirty (30) days after invoice date will bear interest from the invoice date of _____ percent (___%) per month or the highest rate permitted by law, if less. Time is of the essence for all payments due under this Agreement, and in the event any payment due to is collected at law, through an attorney-at-law or a collection agency, Client agrees to pay all costs of collection, including without limitation, all court costs and reasonable attorney's fees.

(F) All payments made hereunder are nonrefundable, except as specifically provided otherwise in this Agreement.

6. LIMITED LIABILITY.   EXCEPT FOR a) A MATERIAL AND WILLFUL VIOLATION OF VENDOR'S PROPRIETARY RIGHTS WHICH ARE NOT COMPENSABLE BY PAYMENT OF LICENSE FEES IN THE TRUE-UP REPORTING PROCESS, b) FAILURE TO COMPLY WITH THE MUTUAL NONDISCLOSURE PROVISION, OR c) THE INFRINGEMENT INDEMNITY PROVISIONS CONTAINED HEREIN:

(A) IN NO EVENT SHALL EITHER PARTY BE LIABLE TO THE OTHER PARTY FOR A MONETARY AMOUNT GREATER THAN THE AMOUNTS PAID OR DUE PURSUANT TO THIS AGREEMENT, AND

(B) IN NO EVENT SHALL EITHER PARTY BE LIABLE TO THE OTHER PARTY FOR ANY LOSS OR INJURIES TO EARNINGS, PROFITS OR GOODWILL, OR FOR ANY INCIDENTAL, SPECIAL, PUNITIVE OR CONSEQUENTIAL DAMAGES OF ANY PERSON OR ENTITY WHETHER ARISING IN CONTRACT, TORT OR OTHERWISE, EVEN 1F EITHER PARTY HAS BEEN ADVISED OF THE POSSIBILITY OF SUCH DAMAGES.

THE LIMITATIONS SET FORTH IN THIS SECTION SHALL APPLY EVEN IF ANY OTHER REMEDIES FAIL OF THEIR ESSENTIAL PURPOSE. The provisions of this Agreement allocate the risks between Vendor and Client. Vendor's pricing reflects this allocation of risk and the limitation of liability specified herein.

7. EMPLOYEE RECRUITING.   Each party acknowledges that the other party's employees are critical to the servicing of its customers. Therefore, Client agrees not to knowingly solicit, employ or otherwise engage Vendor's employees without Vendor's prior written consent for a period of twelve (12) months following that employee's last date of employment by Manhattan and agrees not to knowingly solicit, employ or otherwise engage Client's employees involved in the services contemplated by this Agreement without Client's prior written consent for a period of twelve (12) months following that employee's last date of employment by Client. Should either party violate this provision, the violating party agrees to pay the other party an amount equal to ____% of the former employee's annual salary. The parties further agree that in the event of any actual or threatened breach of any of the provisions of this section, the non-breaching party shall be entitled (in addition to any and all other rights and remedies at law or in equity for damages or otherwise, which rights and remedies are and shall be cumulative) to specific performance, a temporary restraining order, or an injunction to prevent such breach or contemplated breach. Further, such payment and additional relief does not restrict the non-breaching party's rights or remedies as they relate to such former employee.

8. TERMINATION.   If either party materially breaches this Agreement, the other party may give written notice of its desire to terminate and the specific grounds for termination and, if such default is capable of cure and the party in default fails to cure the default within thirty (30) days of the notice, the other party may terminate this Agreement. If a party reasonably determines that a default is incapable of cure, the party shall inform the other party of such determination and if both parties are in reasonable agreement, such party may terminate this Agreement immediately upon thirty (30) days written notice of its desire to terminate. Upon termination by Vendor for Client's non-payment or Client's violation of Article II, Section 1, the License to use the Licensed Products shall be immediately revoked and all Licensed Products and supporting materials will be returned to Vendor or destroyed and documentation supplied to Vendor certifying destruction. Confidentiality obligations shall survive this Agreement for a term of five (5) years, except as to the source code of the Licensed Products which shall survive in perpetuity.

9. EXPORT ADMINISTRATION.   Client agrees to comply fully with all relevant export laws and regulations of the United States ("Export Laws") to assure that neither the Licensed Products nor any direct product thereof are (A) exported, directly or indirectly, in violation of Export Laws; or (B) are intended to be used for any purposes prohibited by Export Laws. Client will indemnify Vendor for any losses, costs, liability, and damages, including reasonable legal fees, incurred by Vendor as a result of failure by Client to comply with this Section. Vendor may, from time to time, deny Client the right to license in certain countries in order to protect Vendor's interests.

10. GENERAL.

(A) WAIVER. The waiver of one breach hereunder shall not constitute the waiver of any other or subsequent breach. No amendments, modifications or supplements to this Agreement shall be binding unless in writing and signed by the parties.

(B) NOTICES. All notices shall be in writing and shall be sufficiently given if: (i) delivered by hand; (ii) delivered by courier with a signed receipt; (iii) sent by facsimile transmission, but only if original documents are delivered as of the fifth (5th) working day thereafter; or (iv) sent by registered mail or certified mail, postage prepaid to the respective addresses of the parties noted herein or such other address as shall be furnished from time to time in writing by either party. To expedite order processing, Client agrees that Vendor may treat documents faxed by Client to Vendor as original documents. However, either party may require the other to exchange original signed documents.

(C) GOVERNING LAW. The laws of the State of Georgia shall govern this Agreement, and all matters arising out of or related to this Agreement, except actions arising under the patent and copyright provisions of the U.S. Code. The parties agree that this Agreement is not subject to and shall not be interpreted by the United Nations Convention on Contracts for the International Sale of Goods. No action arising out of this Agreement, regardless of form, may be brought more than one (1) year after the claiming party knew or should have known of the cause of action.

(D) ASSIGNMENT. Except as specifically provided herein, this Agreement may not be assigned by Client without Vendor's prior written consent, which shall not be unreasonably withheld, delayed or conditioned. Client shall be entitled to assign this Agreement to any of its Affiliates and shall further have the right to assign the individual License to Licensed Product(s) installed at any Designated Site to any purchaser of all or substantially all of the assets of such Designated Site or Affiliate that owns such Designated Site. Any assignee or successor shall execute a written agreement for Vendor's benefit acknowledging their agreement to comply with the terms and provisions of this Agreement. Client and Vendor will work in good faith to designate the proper Licensed Products, Designated Processors and number of Licensed Users for each such transaction. Any attempted assignment which does not adhere to these provisions shall be void.

(E) PUBLICITY RIGHTS. Vendor may include Client's name and logo among its list of customers and may include a brief description of counterpart shall govern all disputes, performances and interpretations, and the counterpart in another language shall be for convenience only and shall not affect the performance or interpretation of this Agreement.

(G) CURRENCY. All amounts stated in and payable under this Agreement shall be denominated and payable in United States Dollars.

(H) SEVERABILITY. If any provision or portion thereof of this Agreement is held to be invalid or unenforceable, the remaining provisions will remain in full force.

(I) THIRD PARTY SOFTWARE. Third party software which is licensed by the third party to Vendor ("Software"), is hereby sublicensed or assigned by Vendor to Client on a nonexclusive, nontransferable basis to be used exclusively with the Licensed Products to which it relates. This third party software license will terminate when this agreement terminates or when the Licensed Products are no longer being used by Client. Client shall not reverse engineer, modify, copy, distribute or otherwise disclose the Software. EXCEPT FOR ANY LIABILITY ARISING DUE TO AN INFRINGEMENT OF A THIRD PARTY'S INTELLECTUAL PROPERTY RIGHTS OR FROM THE NEGLIGENT PERFORMANCE OF SERVICES BY VENDOR: IN NO EVENT WILL THE THIRD PARTY SOFTWARE MANUFACTURER BE LIABLE FOR ANY SPECIAL, INCIDENTAL OR CONSEQUENTIAL LOSS OR DAMAGE, INCLUDING WITHOUT LIMITATION, ANY LOST PROFITS OR SAVINGS, AND ANY LOSS OR DAMAGE CAUSED BY THE LOSS OF USE OF ANY DATA OR INFORMATION OR ANY INACCURATE DATA OR INFORMATION.

(J) The License granted herein shall be deemed to be, for purposes of Section 365(n) of the U.S. Bankruptcy Code (the "Bankruptcy Code"), licenses to rights in "intellectual property" as defined in Section 101 of the Bankruptcy Code ("Section 101"). The parties agree that each party shall retain any may fully exercise all of its rights and elections under the Bankruptcy Code. In the event that a bankruptcy proceeding under the Bankruptcy Code is commenced by or against either party, the other party shall be entitled, at its option, retain all of its rights under this Agreement pursuant to Section 365(n) of the Bankruptcy Code or receive a complete duplicate of, or complete access to, all the existing intellectual property rights that are the subject to the license provisions hereunder, to the extent that such materials constitute "intellectual property" under Section 101. If such materials are not already in the party's possession, they shall be promptly delivered upon the party's written request (i) upon any such commencement of a bankruptcy proceeding, unless the bankrupt party elects to continue to perform all of its obligations under this Agreement; or (ii) upon the rejection of this Agreement by the bankrupt party.

This Agreement, including its terms and conditions and its attachments and amendments, is a complete and exclusive statement of the agreement between the parties, which supersedes all prior or concurrent proposals and understanding, whether oral or written, and all other communications between the parties relating to the subject matter of this Agreement. This Agreement, and any amendments, Attachments, modifications or supplements thereto, shall not be effective until executed by Client and accepted and executed by the Chief Financial Officer, Chief Legal Officer or Chief Executive Officer of Vendor.

Assignment 24: Antitrust Issues in Licensing Transactions

A. The Basics of Antitrust Law

Notwithstanding the major advances in economic analysis of competition, the fundamental structure that regulates competitive behavior in our economy still rests on a statute enacted in 1890, the Sherman Act. The basic provisions of the Sherman Act state:

Section 1. Every contract, combination in the form of trust or otherwise, or conspiracy, in restraint of trade or commerce among the several States, or with a foreign nation, is declared to be illegal. . . .

Section 2. Every person who shall monopolize, or attempt to monopolize, or combine or conspire with any other person or persons, to monopolize any part of the trade or commerce among the several States, or with foreign nations, shall be deemed guilty of a felony.

Although Congress has passed several other antitrust statutes of importance (most prominently, the Clayton Act and the Hart-Scott-Rodino Act), the basic antitrust rules relevant to licensing transactions come from those two sections of the Sherman Act.

1. Unreasonable Restraints of Trade

The broad and simple sweep of those provisions is quite misleading, because neither of those provisions is interpreted in a manner that draws in any meaningful way on the language of the statute. For example, Section 1 broadly prohibits "[e]very contract . . . in restraint of trade." Read literally, that would prohibit a broad range of contracts that are not in the least bit objectionable. Accordingly, the Supreme Court decided promptly after the statute was enacted that it prevents only unreasonable restraints of trade. Much of antitrust law is devoted to the task of determining whether any particular arrangement is or is not sufficiently unreasonable to be sanctioned under Section 1 of the Sherman Act.

Courts traditionally analyze restraints as either "horizontal" or "vertical." A horizontal restraint is a restraint among parties that compete with each other, such as an agreement among all of the parties that sell gasoline in the United States. Horizontal restraints tend to be subject to relatively severe scrutiny. Indeed, for many years most horizontal restraints were held "per se" unlawful. A few restraints are still subject to that treatment — such as agreements to fix prices or divide territories. In recent years, however, the Supreme Court has advocated a more nuanced approach, under which many types of horizontal restraints are tested under a "rule of reason." The rule of reason requires a court to conduct a far-ranging inquiry into all relevant economic considerations, with a view to determining whether the net effect of the arrangement benefits or burdens competition.

The Court tends to be much more generous to vertical restraints — agreements between a petroleum refinery and a gas station that purchases from the refinery — largely because of the view that such restraints often serve bona fide procompetitive purposes. For example, a contract under which a licensee can use software only for specified purposes or in specified geographical areas has the potential to benefit competition by allowing particular licensees to specialize in particular uses of the software in different markets. Thus, such a restraint probably would be evaluated under the rule of reason. Indeed, in modern jurisprudence most vertical restraints are judged under the rule of reason.

2. Monopolization

Section 2 purports to bar any monopoly in any part of American business. Yet in many industries (particularly the technology industries in which licensing transactions occur) economic factors such as economies of scale or network effects often tend ineluctably toward monopoly for the most successful competitor. Accordingly, the Supreme Court has limited the statute so that there is nothing unlawful about having a monopoly *per se*. The statute prohibits only the use of anticompetitive conduct to obtain (or maintain) the monopoly.

Under that framework, a competitor acts unlawfully only if it both has "market power" and uses the power in an illegitimate way (typically by raising prices or excluding competitors in some way). Thus, cases under Section 2 start with a threshold determination of the boundaries of the relevant market. Once the relevant market has been identified, the court proceeds to consider whether the defendant has market power in that market. Finally, the court examines the defendant's conduct to determine if the conduct is anticompetitive.

B. The Players

To understand antitrust law, it is important to understand the roles of the various participants in the system. The most important player is the judiciary. Although antitrust law is governed by statute, the Supreme Court's interpretation of the broad statutory provisions has been driven by the view that the Sherman Act is a general direction to the federal judiciary to articulate a federal law of competition policy. The fundamental nature of that policy has been controversial at times. Some Justices and academics have advocated an emphasis on limiting the size and power of big businesses, on the premise that the populist impulse of the 1890s was opposed to big companies simply because of the power intrinsic in their size. Similarly, some have seen in the antitrust laws a device for sheltering small "mom and pop" businesses from efforts by large companies to "squeeze out" local businesses. But whatever the historical impulse behind the statute, the modern Supreme Court holds firmly to the view that the purpose of the antitrust laws is to promote social welfare through the development of efficiently functioning markets. Thus, modern doctrine focuses almost exclusively on the tendency of challenged conduct to benefit or burden the competitive process. There is no significant continuing concern about excessive concentration of industries or about the exclusion of small businesses by vigorous competition from larger rivals.

The executive branch of the federal government also plays an important role. Two separate federal agencies — the Federal Trade Commission (FTC) and the Antitrust Division in the Department of Justice — have parallel and overlapping responsibility to enforce the antitrust laws. Accordingly, it is common for conduct to be challenged by either civil or criminal enforcement actions brought either by the FTC or the Department. Similarly, some types of activity (such as a merger of large companies) require advance approval from the FTC and the Department. For example, the Department of Justice in the spring of 2004 refused to approve Oracle's proposed hostile acquisition of PeopleSoft. When Oracle nevertheless decided to press ahead, the result was litigation in the federal courts (ongoing as this book goes to print).

Finally, the antitrust laws generally permit enforcement by private parties and by the states (acting on behalf of their citizens). Thus, private parties that find themselves injured by conduct that violates the antitrust laws can seek relief in federal court, with the attractive possibility of relief that includes treble damages. In the Microsoft litigation with the Justice Department (discussed below), for example, numerous states brought parallel enforcement actions, several of which were settled separately from the litigation with the Department.

More broadly, all developed countries have some form of competition policy. Those laws are especially problematic in light of the jurisdictional rules discussed in Assignment 1, which make it clear that any jurisdiction in which a product has substantial effects has a plausible claim of regulatory authority. That makes it quite likely that many technology companies will be subject to the laws of multiple jurisdictions. For example, even though Microsoft's conduct with respect to its operating system has not produced severe sanctions in this country, it remains subject to ongoing litigation on that subject with the European Union. Because its business is inherently global, restrictions that force it to alter its products there will have substantial repercussions in the United States as well. For reasons of space, the coverage here focuses solely on the competition policy of the United States.

C. Antitrust and Intellectual Property

The intersection between antitrust law and intellectual property presents one of the most contentious legal problems for technology industries. As discussed above, antitrust laws articulate a competition policy largely predicated on a suspicion of monopoly power, implemented by scrutiny of the mechanisms that monopolists use to profit from that power. At a basic level, intellectual property laws seem directly inconsistent with antitrust law, because they use a directly contrary mechanism: The fundamental premise of intellectual property law is to grant monopoly power to an innovator (the inventor that earns a patent or the author of a copyright work), with the view that the profits the innovator expects to earn from such a monopoly will enhance the innovator's incentive to produce the work or invention in question.

At a more general level, however, the intellectual property laws and the antitrust laws can be seen as two different tools to further a single policy of promoting a marketplace that has efficient levels of competition and innovation in the long run. We would not think it notable, for example, if a court held that a private party violated the antitrust laws by using tangible property in ways designed to have anticompetitive effects. Indeed, there is an "essential facilities" doctrine that requires parties with assets necessary for competition to grant competitors reasonable access to those facilities. In the leading case, for example, the Supreme Court held that the owner of a particularly popular ski slope in Aspen was obligated to join with competitors in a joint lift ticket that permitted skiers to use all slopes. Aspen Skiing Co. v. Aspen Highlands Skiing Corp., 472 U.S. 585 (1985). Rules that limit the right to enforcement of intellectual property should not necessarily be different.

However that theoretical conflict is resolved, the antitrust laws must be reconciled with the federal policies reflected in the patent and copyright statutes. Responding to that concern, the Department of Justice and the FTC have jointly promulgated a set of *Antitrust Guidelines for the Licensing of Intellectual Property*, which reflect the enforcement policies of the Department of Justice and the FTC. Analysis of those *Guidelines* and the actions of the courts in the area gives a good sense for how the law constrains software licensing in practice.

1. Monopolization

Perhaps the most basic thing that the *Guidelines* do is reject the simplistic idea that the "monopoly" granted by the patent and copyright laws is sufficient to constitute "market power" that is cognizable under the antitrust laws. *Guidelines* §2.0(b). Rather, the *Guidelines* contemplate a careful case-by-case analysis of the circumstances of a particular market, a particular actor in that market, and the conduct in question.

The first question, as discussed above, is how the relevant market is to be defined. Because of the fluid nature of software markets, this has been a controversial question. In the litigation with Microsoft discussed below, for example, Microsoft argued that various distant competitors kept it from having monopoly power in the market for operating systems. Similarly, in the Oracle/Peoplesoft Litigation, one of the main questions is whether the market for enterprise-resource software is a narrow one dominated by Oracle, SAP, and PeopleSoft (in which case the merger would seem highly suspect) or a much broader one that included competitors like IBM and Microsoft (in which case the merger would seem more palatable).

Once a market has been defined and it has been determined whether somebody has monopoly power in that market, the next question is to consider whether the conduct in question is permitted. Mere enforcement of a patent or copyright obviously is not wrongful. Nor is there any general problem with licensing. As the *Guidelines* expressly recognize, "intellectual property licensing allows firms to combine complementary factors of production and is generally procompetitive." *Guidelines* §2.0(c).

Part 5 of the *Guidelines* provides detailed analysis of a number of specific restraints, but it is fair to say as a general matter that the recognition of the procompetitive characteristics of licensing counsels against *per se* condemnation of vertical restraints in licensing arrangements and in favor of the more lenient analysis provided by the rule of reason. This of course does not mean that all conduct is permitted. Perhaps the strongest case for the owner of intellectual property is the case closest to the core of the intellectual-property right, the case where the challenged activity is a simple refusal to allow third parties to exploit the protected technology. Even here, as you will see, courts have been unwilling to give licensors a *completely* free hand.

Image Technical Services, Inc. v. Eastman Kodak Co.

125 F.3d 1195 (9th Cir. 1997)

Before: BEEZER and THOMPSON, Circuit Judges, GILLMOR, District Judge.
BEEZER, Circuit Judge:

Plaintiffs-Appellees Image Technical Services, and ten other independent service organizations ("ISOs") that service Kodak photocopiers and micrographic equipment sued the Eastman Kodak Co. ("Kodak") for violations of the Sherman Act. The ISOs alleged that Kodak used its monopoly in the market for Kodak photocopier and micrographic parts to create a second monopoly in the equipment service markets. A jury verdict awarded treble damages totaling $71.8 million. [Kodak appealed.] . . .

I

Kodak manufactures, sells and services high volume photocopiers and micrographic (or microfilm) equipment. Competition in these markets is strong. In the photocopier market Kodak's competitors include Xerox, IBM and Canon. Kodak's competitors in the micrographics market include Minolta, Bell & Howell and 3M. Despite comparable products in these markets, Kodak's equipment is distinctive. Although Kodak equipment may perform similar functions to that of its competitors, Kodak's parts are not interchangeable with parts used in other manufacturers' equipment.

Kodak sells and installs replacement parts for its equipment. Kodak competes with ISOs in these markets. Kodak has ready access to all parts necessary for repair services because it manufactures many of the parts used in its equipment and purchases the remaining necessary parts from independent original-equipment manufacturers. In the service market, Kodak repairs at least 80% of the machines it manufactures. ISOs began servicing Kodak equipment in the early 1980's, and have provided cheaper and better service at times, according to some customers. ISOs obtain parts for repair service from a variety of sources, including, at one time, Kodak.

As ISOs grew more competitive, Kodak began restricting access to its photocopier and micrographic parts. In 1985, Kodak stopped selling copier parts to ISOs, and in 1986, Kodak halted sales of micrographic parts to ISOs. Additionally, Kodak secured agreements from their contracted original-equipment manufacturers not to sell parts to ISOs. These parts restrictions limited the ISOs' ability to compete in the service market for Kodak machines. Competition in the service market requires that service providers have ready access to all parts.

Kodak offers annual or multi-year service contracts to its customers. Service providers generally contract with equipment owners through multi-year service contracts. ISOs claim that they were unable to provide similar contracts because they lack a reliable supply of parts. Some ISOs contend that the parts shortage forced them out of business.

In 1987, the ISOs filed this action against Kodak, seeking damages and injunctive relief for violations of the Sherman Act. The ISOs claimed that Kodak both: (1) unlawfully tied the sale of service for Kodak machines with the sale of parts in violation of §1 of the Sherman Act, and (2) monopolized or attempted to monopolize the sale of service for Kodak machines in violation of §2 of the Sherman Act.

[The district court granted summary judgment for Kodak. The court of appeals reversed the grant of summary judgment. The Supreme Court affirmed the decision of the court of appeals and remanded the case for trial.] *Eastman Kodak Co. v. Image Technical Serv., Inc.,* 504 U.S. 451 (1992). . . .

[The trial resulted in a $72 million verdict and a ten-year injunction against Kodak.]

II

[The court determined that Kodak had monopoly power in the relevant market and used that power to exclude its rivals.]

III

Our conclusion that the ISOs have shown that Kodak has both attained monopoly power and exercised exclusionary conduct does not end our inquiry. Kodak's conduct may not be actionable if supported by a legitimate business justification. When a legitimate business justification supports a monopolist's exclusionary conduct, that conduct does not violate §2 of the Sherman Act. A plaintiff may rebut an asserted business justification by demonstrating either that the justification does not legitimately promote competition or that the justification is pretextual. Kodak asserts that the protection of its patented and copyrighted parts is a valid business justification for its anticompetitive conduct and argues that the district court's erroneous jury instructions made it impossible for the jury to properly consider this justification. . . .

B.   INTELLECTUAL PROPERTY RIGHTS

. . . Kodak argues that the court failed to instruct the jury that Kodak's numerous patents and copyrights provide a legitimate business justification for Kodak's alleged exclusionary conduct. Kodak holds 220 valid United States patents covering 65 parts for its high volume photocopiers and micrographics equipment, and all Kodak diagnostic software and service software are copyrighted. . . .

Kodak's challenge raises unresolved questions concerning the relationship between federal antitrust, copyright and patent laws. In particular we must determine the significance of a monopolist's unilateral refusal to sell or license a patented or copyrighted product in the context of a §2 monopolization claim based upon monopoly leveraging. This is a question of first impression.

1.

We first identify the general principles of antitrust, copyright and patent law as we must ultimately harmonize these statutory schemes in responding to Kodak's challenge.

Antitrust law seeks to promote and protect a competitive marketplace for the benefit of the public. The Sherman Act, the relevant antitrust law here, prohibits efforts both to restrain trade by combination or conspiracy and the acquisition or maintenance of a monopoly by exclusionary conduct. 15 U.S.C. §§1, 2.

Patent law seeks to protect inventions, while inducing their introduction into the market for public benefit. Patent laws reward the inventor with the power to exclude others from making, using or selling [a patented] invention throughout the United States. Meanwhile, the public benefits both from the faster introduction of inventions, and the resulting increase in market competition. Legally, a patent amounts to a permissible monopoly over the protected work. Patent laws "are in *pari materia* with the antitrust laws and modify them *pro tanto* (as far as the patent laws go)." *Simpson v. Union Oil Co.,* 377 U.S. 13, 24 (1964).

Federal copyright law "secure[s] a fair return for an author's creative labor" in the short run, while ultimately seeking "to stimulate artistic creativity for the general public good." *Twentieth Century Music Corp. v. Aiken,* 422 U.S. 151, 156 (1975) (internal quotations omitted). The Copyright Act grants to the copyright owner the exclusive right to distribute the protected work. 17 U.S.C. §106. This right encompasses the right to refrain from vending or licensing, as the owner may content [itself] with simply exercising the right to exclude others from using [its] property. *[S]ee Stewart v. Abend,* 495 U.S. 207, 228-29 (1990) ("nothing in the copyright statutes would prevent an author from hoarding all of his works during the term of the copyright.").

Clearly the antitrust, copyright and patent laws both overlap and, in certain situations, seem to conflict. This is not a new revelation. . . . Similarly, tension exists between the antitrust and copyright laws.

Two principles have emerged regarding the interplay between these laws: (1) neither patent nor copyright holders are immune from antitrust liability, and (2) patent and copyright holders may refuse to sell or license protected work. First, as to antitrust liability, . . . a holder of a patent or copyright violates the antitrust laws by concerted and contractual behavior that threatens competition. In *Kodak,* the Supreme Court noted:

> [we have] held many times that power gained through some natural advantage such as a patent, copyright, or business acumen can give rise to liability if 'a seller exploits his dominant position in one market to expand his empire into the next.'

504 U.S. at 479 n.29.

2.

Next we lay out the problem presented here. The Supreme Court touched on this question in *Kodak,* i.e., the effect to be given a monopolist's unilateral refusal to sell or license a patented or copyrighted product in the context of a §2 monopoly leveraging claim. In footnote 29, previously discussed, the Supreme Court in *Kodak* refutes the argument that the possession by a manufacturer of "inherent power" in the market for its parts "should immunize [that manufacturer] from the antitrust laws in another market." 504 U.S. at 479 n.29. The Court stated that a monopolist who acquires a dominant position in one market through patents and copyrights may violate §2 if the monopolist exploits that dominant position to enhance a monopoly in another market. . . . By responding in this fashion, the Court in *Kodak* supposed that intellectual property rights do not confer an absolute immunity from antitrust claims.

The *Kodak* Court, however, did not specifically address the question of antitrust liability based upon a unilateral refusal to deal in a patented or copyrighted product. Kodak and its amicus correctly indicate that the right of exclusive dealing is reserved from antitrust liability. We find no reported case in which a court has imposed antitrust liability for a unilateral refusal to sell or license a patent or copyright. Courts do not generally view a monopolist's unilateral refusal to license a patent as exclusionary conduct.

This basic right of exclusion does have limits. For example, a patent offers no protection if it was unlawfully acquired. Nor does the right of exclusion protect an attempt to extend a lawful monopoly beyond the grant of a patent. Section 2 of the Sherman Act condemns exclusionary conduct that extends natural monopolies into separate markets. Much depends, therefore, on the definition of the patent grant and the relevant market.

The relevant market for determining the patent or copyright grant is determined under patent or copyright law. The relevant markets for antitrust purposes are determined by examining economic conditions. . . .

Parts and service here have been proven separate markets in the antitrust context, but this does not resolve the question whether the service market falls reasonably within the patent [or copyright] grant for the purpose of determining the extent of the exclusive rights conveyed. These are separate questions, which may result in contrary answers. At the border of intellectual property monopolies and antitrust markets lies a field of dissonance yet to be harmonized by statute or the Supreme Court. . . .

The effect of claims based upon unilateral conduct on the value of intellectual property rights is a cause for serious concern. Unilateral conduct is the most common conduct in the economy. After *Kodak,* unilateral conduct by a manufacturer in its own aftermarkets may give rise to liability and, in one-brand markets, monopoly power created by patents and copyrights will frequently be found. Under current law the defense of monopolization claims will rest largely on the legitimacy of the asserted business justifications. . . .

Without bounds, claims based on unilateral conduct will proliferate. The history of this case demonstrates that such claims rest on highly disputed factual questions regarding market definition. Particularly where treble damages are possible, such claims will detract from the advantages lawfully granted to the holders of patents or copyrights by subjecting them to the cost and risk of lawsuits based upon the effect, on an arguably separate market, of their refusal to sell or license.

The cost of such suits will reduce a patent holder's "incentive . . . to risk the often enormous costs in terms of time, research, and development." *Kewanee Oil Co. v. Bicron Corp.,* 416 U.S. 470, 480 (1974). Such an effect on patent and copyright holders is contrary to the fundamental and complementary purposes of both the intellectual property and antitrust laws, which aim to encourag[e] innovation, industry and competition.

3.

We now resolve the question detailed above. . . . [S]ome measure must guarantee that the jury account for the procompetitive effects and statutory rights extended by the intellectual property laws. To assure such consideration, we adopt a modified version of the rebuttable presumption created by the First Circuit in [*Data General v. Grumman Systems Support,* 36 F.3d 1147 (1994)], and hold that "while exclusionary conduct can include a monopolist's unilateral refusal to license a [patent or] copyright," or to sell its patented or copyrighted work, a monopolist's "desire to exclude others from its [protected] work is a presumptively valid business justification for any immediate harm to consumers." *Data General,* 36 F.3d at 1187.

This presumption does not "rest on formalistic distinctions" which "are generally disfavored in antitrust laws;" rather it is based on "actual market realities." *Kodak,* 504 U.S. at 466-67. This presumption harmonizes the goals of the relevant statutes and takes into account the long term effects of regulation on these purposes. The presumption should act to focus the factfinder on the primary interest of both intellectual property and antitrust laws: public interest.

Given this presumption, the district court's failure to give any weight to Kodak's intellectual property rights in the jury instructions constitutes an abuse of discretion. . . .

The more interesting questions for the transactional lawyer obviously involve antitrust constraints on the types of provisions that are included in licenses. On that point, there is no better example than the D.C. Circuit's analysis of Microsoft's conduct with respect to licenses of Microsoft's operating system.

United States v. Microsoft Corporation
253 F.3d 34 (D.C. Cir. 2001) (en banc)

PER CURIAM:
Microsoft Corporation appeals from judgments of the District Court finding the company in violation of §§1 and 2 of the Sherman Act and ordering various remedies. [The court of appeals heard the case en banc in the first instance. After concluding that Microsoft had monopoly power in the relevant market, the court had this to say about the lawfulness of Microsoft's conduct in licensing its software.]

As discussed above, having a monopoly does not by itself violate §2. A firm violates §2 only when it acquires or maintains, or attempts to acquire or maintain, a monopoly by engaging in exclusionary conduct "as distinguished from growth or development as a consequence of a superior product, business acumen, or historic accident." [*United States v. Grinnell Corp.*, 384 U.S. 563, 571 (1966)]; *see also United States v. Aluminum Co. of Am.*, 148 F.2d 416, 430 (2d Cir.1945) (Hand, J.) ("The successful competitor, having been urged to compete, must not be turned upon when he wins.").

In this case, after concluding that Microsoft had monopoly power, the District Court held that Microsoft had violated §2 by engaging in a variety of exclusionary acts (not including predatory pricing), to maintain its monopoly by preventing the effective distribution and use of products that might threaten that monopoly. Specifically, the District Court held Microsoft liable for: (1) the way in which it integrated IE into Windows; (2) its various dealings with Original Equipment Manufacturers ("OEMs"), Internet Access Providers ("IAPs"), Internet Content Providers ("ICPs"), Independent Software Vendors ("ISVs"), and Apple Computer; (3) its efforts to contain and to subvert Java technologies; and (4) its course of conduct as a whole. Upon appeal, Microsoft argues that it did not engage in any exclusionary conduct.

Whether any particular act of a monopolist is exclusionary, rather than merely a form of vigorous competition, can be difficult to discern: the means of illicit exclusion, like the means of legitimate competition, are myriad. The challenge for an antitrust court lies in stating a general rule for distinguishing between exclusionary acts, which reduce social welfare, and competitive acts, which increase it.

From a century of case law on monopolization under §2, however, several principles do emerge. First, to be condemned as exclusionary, a monopolist's act must have an "anticompetitive effect." That is, it must harm the competitive *process* and thereby harm consumers. In contrast, harm to one or more *competitors* will not suffice. . . .

Second, the plaintiff, on whom the burden of proof of course rests, must demonstrate that the monopolist's conduct indeed has the requisite anticompetitive effect. . . .

Third, if a plaintiff successfully establishes a *prima facie* case under §2 by demonstrating anticompetitive effect, then the monopolist may proffer a "procompetitive justification" for its conduct. If the monopolist asserts a procompetitive justification — a nonpretextual claim that its conduct is indeed a form of competition on the merits because it involves, for example, greater efficiency or enhanced consumer appeal — then the burden shifts back to the plaintiff to rebut that claim.

Fourth, if the monopolist's procompetitive justification stands unrebutted, then the plaintiff must demonstrate that the anticompetitive harm of the conduct outweighs the procompetitive benefit. In cases arising under §1 of the Sherman Act, the courts routinely apply a similar balancing approach under the rubric of the "rule of reason.". . .

Finally, in considering whether the monopolist's conduct on balance harms competition and is therefore condemned as exclusionary for purposes of §2, our focus is upon the effect of that conduct, not upon the intent behind it. Evidence of the intent behind the conduct of a monopolist is relevant only to the extent it helps us understand the likely effect of the monopolist's conduct.

With these principles in mind, we now consider Microsoft's objections to the District Court's holding that Microsoft violated §2 of the Sherman Act in a variety of ways.

1. LICENSES ISSUED TO ORIGINAL EQUIPMENT MANUFACTURERS

The District Court condemned a number of provisions in Microsoft's agreements licensing Windows to OEMs, because it found that Microsoft's imposition of those provisions (like many of Microsoft's other actions at issue in this case) serves to reduce usage share of Netscape's browser and, hence, protect Microsoft's operating system monopoly. The reason market share in the browser market affects market power in the operating system market is complex, and warrants some explanation.

Browser usage share is important because . . . a browser (or any middleware product, for that matter) must have a critical mass of users in order to attract software developers to write applications relying upon the [application programming interface (API) that] it exposes, and away from the APIs exposed by Windows. Applications written to a particular browser's APIs, however, would run on any computer with that browser, regardless of the underlying operating system. . . . If a consumer could have access to the applications he desired — regardless of the operating system he uses — simply by installing a particular browser on his computer, then he would no longer feel compelled to select Windows in order to have access to those applications; he could select an operating system other than Windows based solely upon its quality and price. In other words, the market for operating systems would be competitive.

Therefore, Microsoft's efforts to gain market share in one market (browsers) served to meet the threat to Microsoft's monopoly in another market (operating systems) by keeping rival browsers from gaining the critical mass of users necessary to attract developer attention away from Windows as the platform for software development. Plaintiffs also argue that Microsoft's actions injured competition in the browser market — an argument we will examine below in relation to their specific claims that Microsoft attempted to monopolize the browser market and unlawfully tied its browser to its operating system so as to foreclose competition in the browser market. In evaluating the §2 monopoly maintenance claim, however, our immediate concern is with the anticompetitive effect of Microsoft's conduct in preserving its monopoly in the operating system market.

In evaluating the restrictions in Microsoft's agreements licensing Windows to OEMs, we first consider whether plaintiffs have made out a *prima facie* case by demonstrating that the restrictions have an anticompetitive effect. In the next subsection, we conclude that plaintiffs have met this burden as to all the restrictions. We then consider Microsoft's proffered justifications for the restrictions and, for the most part, hold those justifications insufficient.

a.   Anticompetitive Effect of the License Restrictions

The restrictions Microsoft places upon Original Equipment Manufacturers are of particular importance in determining browser usage share because having an OEM pre-install a browser on a computer is one of the two most cost-effective methods by far of distributing browsing software. (The other is bundling the browser with internet access software distributed by an IAP.) The District Court found that the restrictions Microsoft imposed in licensing Windows to OEMs prevented many OEMs from distributing browsers other than IE. In particular, the District Court condemned the license provisions prohibiting the OEMs from: (1) removing any desktop icons, folders, or "Start" menu entries; (2) altering the initial boot sequence; and (3) otherwise altering the appearance of the Windows desktop.

The District Court concluded that the first license restriction — the prohibition upon the removal of desktop icons, folders, and Start menu entries — thwarts the distribution of a rival browser by preventing OEMs from removing visible means of user access to IE. The OEMs cannot practically install a second browser in addition to IE, the court found, in part because "[p]re-installing more than one product in a given category . . . can significantly increase an OEM's support costs, for the redundancy can lead to confusion among novice users." That is, a certain number of novice computer users, seeing two browser icons, will wonder which to use when and will call the OEM's support line. Support calls are extremely expensive and, in the highly competitive original equipment market, firms have a strong incentive to minimize costs. . . .

As noted above, the OEM channel is one of the two primary channels for distribution of browsers. By preventing OEMs from removing visible means of user access to IE, the license restriction prevents many OEMs from pre-installing a rival browser and, therefore, protects Microsoft's monopoly from the competition that middleware might otherwise present. Therefore, we conclude that the license restriction at issue is anticompetitive. We defer for the moment the question whether that anticompetitive effect is outweighed by Microsoft's proffered justifications.

The second license provision at issue prohibits OEMs from modifying the initial boot sequence — the process that occurs the first time a consumer turns on the computer. Prior to the imposition of that restriction, among the programs that many OEMs inserted into the boot sequence were Internet sign-up procedures that encouraged users to choose from a list of IAPs assembled by the OEM. [Quotation marks omitted.] Microsoft's prohibition on any alteration of the boot sequence thus prevents OEMs from using that process to promote the services of IAPs, many of which — at least at the time Microsoft imposed the restriction — used Navigator rather than IE in their internet access software. Microsoft does not deny that the prohibition on modifying the boot sequence has the effect of decreasing competition against IE by preventing OEMs from promoting rivals' browsers. Because this prohibition has a substantial effect in protecting Microsoft's market power, and does so through a means other than competition on the merits, it is anticompetitive. Again the question whether the provision is nonetheless justified awaits later treatment.

Finally, Microsoft imposes several additional provisions that, like the prohibition on removal of icons, prevent OEMs from making various alterations to the desktop: Microsoft prohibits OEMs from causing any user interface other than the Windows desktop to launch automatically, from adding icons or folders different in size or shape from those supplied by Microsoft, and from using the "Active Desktop" feature to promote third-party brands. These restrictions impose significant costs upon the OEMs; prior to Microsoft's prohibiting the practice, many OEMs would change the appearance of the desktop in ways they found beneficial.

The dissatisfaction of the OEM customers does not, of course, mean the restrictions are anticompetitive. The anticompetitive effect of the license restrictions is, as Microsoft itself recognizes, that OEMs are not able to promote rival browsers, which keeps developers focused upon the APIs in Windows. This kind of promotion is not a zero-sum game; but for the restrictions in their licenses to use

Windows, OEMs could promote multiple IAPs and browsers. By preventing the OEMs from doing so, this type of license restriction, like the first two restrictions, is anticompetitive: Microsoft reduced rival browsers' usage share not by improving its own product but, rather, by preventing OEMs from taking actions that could increase rivals' share of usage.

b.   Microsoft's Justifications for the License Restrictions

Microsoft argues that the license restrictions are legally justified because, in imposing them, Microsoft is simply "exercising its rights as the holder of valid copyrights.". . .

Microsoft's primary copyright argument borders upon the frivolous. The company claims an absolute and unfettered right to use its intellectual property as it wishes: "[I]f intellectual property rights have been lawfully acquired," it says, then "their subsequent exercise cannot give rise to antitrust liability." Appellant's Opening Br. at 105. That is no more correct than the proposition that use of one's personal property, such as a baseball bat, cannot give rise to tort liability. As the Federal Circuit succinctly stated: "Intellectual property rights do not confer a privilege to violate the antitrust laws." *In re Indep. Serv. Orgs. Antitrust Litig.*, 203 F.3d 1322, 1325 (Fed. Cir. 2000).

Although Microsoft never overtly retreats from its bold and incorrect position on the law, it also makes two arguments to the effect that it is not exercising its copyright in an unreasonable manner, despite the anticompetitive consequences of the license restrictions discussed above. In the first variation upon its unqualified copyright defense, Microsoft [argues] that a copyright holder may limit a licensee's ability to engage in significant and deleterious alterations of a copyrighted work. . . .

The only license restriction Microsoft seriously defends as necessary to prevent a "substantial alteration" of its copyrighted work is the prohibition on OEMs automatically launching a substitute user interface upon completion of the boot process. We agree that a shell that automatically prevents the Windows desktop from ever being seen by the user is a drastic alteration of Microsoft's copyrighted work, and outweighs the marginal anticompetitive effect of prohibiting the OEMs from substituting a different interface automatically upon completion of the initial boot process. We therefore hold that this particular restriction is not an exclusionary practice that violates §2 of the Sherman Act. . . .

2.   Integration of IE and Windows

Although Microsoft's license restrictions have a significant effect in closing rival browsers out of one of the two primary channels of distribution, the District Court found that "Microsoft's executives believed . . . its contractual restrictions placed on OEMs would not be sufficient in themselves to reverse the direction of Navigator's usage share. Consequently, in late 1995 or early 1996, Microsoft set out to bind [IE] more tightly to Windows 95 as a technical matter."

Technologically binding IE to Windows, the District Court found, both prevented OEMs from pre-installing other browsers and deterred consumers from using them. In particular, having the IE software code as an irremovable part of Windows meant that pre-installing a second browser would increase an OEM's product testing costs, because an OEM must test and train its support staff to answer calls related to every software product preinstalled on the machine; moreover, pre-installing a browser in addition to IE would to many OEMs be a questionable use of the scarce and valuable space on a PC's hard drive. [Quotation marks omitted.]

[The District Court's] findings of fact . . . center upon three specific actions Microsoft took to weld IE to Windows: excluding IE from the "Add/Remove Programs" utility; designing Windows so as in certain circumstances to override the user's choice of a default browser other than IE; and commingling code related to browsing and other code in the same files, so that any attempt to delete the files containing IE would, at the same time, cripple the operating system. As with the license restrictions, we consider first whether the suspect actions had an anticompetitive effect, and then whether Microsoft has provided a procompetitive justification for them.

a.   Anticompetitive Effect of Integration

As a general rule, courts are properly very skeptical about claims that competition has been harmed by a dominant firm's product design changes. In a competitive market, firms routinely innovate in the hope of appealing to consumers, sometimes in the process making their products incompatible with those of rivals; the imposition of liability when a monopolist does the same thing will inevitably deter a certain amount of innovation. This is all the more true in a market, such as this one, in which the product itself is rapidly changing. Judicial deference to product innovation, however, does not mean that a monopolist's product design decisions are per se lawful.

The District Court first condemned as anticompetitive Microsoft's decision to exclude IE from the "Add/Remove Programs" utility in Windows 98. Microsoft had included IE in the Add/Remove Programs utility in Windows 95, but when it modified Windows 95 to produce Windows 98, it took IE out of the Add/Remove Programs utility. This change reduces the usage share of rival browsers not by making Microsoft's own browser more attractive to consumers but, rather, by discouraging OEMs from distributing rival products. Because Microsoft's conduct, through something other than competition on the merits, has the effect of significantly reducing usage of rivals' products and hence protecting its own operating system monopoly, it is anticompetitive; we defer for the moment the question whether it is nonetheless justified.

Second, the District Court found that Microsoft designed Windows 98 "so that using Navigator on Windows 98 would have unpleasant consequences for users" by, in some circumstances, overriding the user's choice of a browser other than IE as his or her default browser. Plaintiffs argue that this override harms the competitive process by deterring consumers from using a browser other than IE even though they might prefer to do so, thereby reducing rival browsers' usage share and, hence, the ability of rival browsers to draw developer attention away from the APIs exposed by Windows. Microsoft does not deny, of course, that overriding the user's preference prevents some people from using other browsers. Because the override reduces rivals' usage share and protects Microsoft's monopoly, it too is anticompetitive.

Finally, the District Court condemned Microsoft's decision to bind IE to Windows 98 "by placing code specific to Web browsing in the same files as code that provided operating system functions." Putting code supplying browsing functionality into a file with code supplying operating system functionality "ensure[s] that the deletion of any file containing browsing-specific routines would also delete vital operating system routines and thus cripple Windows. . . ." As noted above, preventing an OEM from removing IE deters it from installing a second browser because doing so increases the OEM's product testing and support costs; by contrast, had OEMs been able to remove IE, they might have chosen to pre-install Navigator alone.

Microsoft denies, as a factual matter, that it commingled browsing and non-browsing code, and it maintains the District Court's findings to the contrary are clearly erroneous. [The court of appeals concluded, however, that the District Court's findings were supported by the record.]

. . . [W]e conclude that such commingling has an anticompetitive effect; as noted above, the commingling deters OEMs from pre-installing rival browsers, thereby reducing the rivals' usage share and, hence, developers' interest in rivals' APIs as an alternative to the API set exposed by Microsoft's operating system.

b. Microsoft's Justifications for Integration

Microsoft proffers no justification for two of the three challenged actions that it took in integrating IE into Windows — excluding IE from the Add/Remove Programs utility and commingling browser and operating system code. . . . Accordingly, we hold that Microsoft's exclusion of IE from the Add/Remove Programs utility and its commingling of browser and operating system code constitute exclusionary conduct, in violation of §2.

As for the other challenged act that Microsoft took in integrating IE into Windows — causing Windows to override the user's choice of a default browser in certain circumstances — [the court accepted Microsoft's claim of "valid technical reasons" for the design.] Accordingly, Microsoft may not be held liable for this aspect of its product design.

3. AGREEMENTS WITH INTERNET ACCESS PROVIDERS

The District Court also condemned as exclusionary Microsoft's agreements with various IAPs. The IAPs include both Internet Service Providers, which offer consumers internet access, and Online Services ("OLSs") such as America Online ("AOL"), which offer proprietary content in addition to internet access and other services. . . .

The District Court condemned Microsoft's actions in (1) offering IE free of charge to IAPs and (2) offering IAPs a bounty for each customer the IAP signs up for service using the IE browser. In effect, the court concluded that Microsoft is acting to preserve its monopoly by offering IE to IAPs at an attractive price. Similarly, the District Court held Microsoft liable for (3) developing the IE Access Kit ("IEAK"), a software package that allows an IAP to create a distinctive identity for its service in as little as a few hours by customizing the [IE] title bar, icon, start and search pages, and (4) offering the IEAK to IAPs free of charge, on the ground that those acts, too, helped Microsoft preserve its monopoly. [Quotation marks omitted.] Finally, the District Court found that (5) Microsoft agreed to provide easy access to IAPs' services from the Windows desktop in return for the IAPs' agreement to promote IE exclusively and to keep shipments of internet access software using Navigator under a specific percentage, typically 25%. We address the first four items — Microsoft's inducements — and then its exclusive agreements with IAPs.

Although offering a customer an attractive deal is the hallmark of competition, the Supreme Court has indicated that in very rare circumstances a price may be unlawfully low, or "predatory." Plaintiffs argued before the District Court that Microsoft's pricing was indeed predatory; but instead of making the usual predatory pricing argument — that the predator would drive out its rivals by pricing below cost on a particular product and then, sometime in the future, raise its prices on that product above the competitive level in order to recoup its earlier losses — plaintiffs argued that by pricing below cost on IE (indeed, even paying people to take it), Microsoft was able simultaneously to preserve its stream of monopoly profits on Windows, thereby more than recouping its investment in below-cost pricing on IE. The District Court did not assign liability for predatory pricing, however, and plaintiffs do not press this theory on appeal.

The rare case of price predation aside, the antitrust laws do not condemn even a monopolist for offering its product at an attractive price, and we therefore have no warrant to condemn Microsoft for offering either IE or the IEAK free of charge or even at a negative price. Likewise, as we said above, a monopolist does not violate the Sherman Act simply by developing an attractive product. Therefore, Microsoft's development of the IEAK does not violate the Sherman Act.

We turn now to Microsoft's deals with IAPs concerning desktop placement. . . . The most significant of the OLS deals is with AOL, which, when the deal was reached, accounted for a substantial portion of all existing Internet access subscriptions and . . . attracted a very large percentage of new IAP subscribers. [Quotation marks omitted.] Under that agreement Microsoft puts the AOL icon in the OLS folder on the Windows desktop and AOL does not promote any non-Microsoft browser, nor provide software using any non-Microsoft browser except at the customer's request, and even then AOL will not supply more than 15% of its subscribers with a browser other than IE.

The Supreme Court most recently considered an antitrust challenge to an exclusive contract in *Tampa Electric Co. v. Nashville Coal Co.*, 365 U.S. 320 (1961). That case, which involved a challenge to a requirements contract, was brought under §3 of the Clayton Act and §§1 and 2 of the Sherman Act. The Court held that an exclusive contract does not violate the Clayton Act unless its probable effect is to "foreclose competition in a substantial share of the line of commerce affected." *Id.* at 327. . . .

[E]xclusivity provisions in contracts may serve many useful purposes. Permitting an antitrust action to proceed any time a firm enters into an exclusive deal would both discourage a presumptively legitimate business practice and encourage costly antitrust actions. Because an exclusive deal affecting a small fraction of a market clearly cannot have the requisite harmful effect upon competition, the requirement of a significant degree of foreclosure serves a useful screening function.

In this case, plaintiffs challenged Microsoft's exclusive dealing arrangements with the IAPs under both §§1 and 2 of the Sherman Act. The District Court, in analyzing the §1 claim, stated, "unless the evidence demonstrates that Microsoft's agreements excluded Netscape altogether from access to roughly forty percent of the browser market, the Court should decline to find such agreements in violation of §1." The court recognized that Microsoft had substantially excluded Netscape from "the most efficient channels for Navigator to achieve browser usage share," and had relegated it to more costly and less effective methods (such as mass mailing its browser on a disk or offering it for download over the internet); but because Microsoft has not "completely excluded Netscape" from reaching any potential user by some means of distribution, however ineffective, the court concluded the agreements do not violate §1. Plaintiffs did not cross-appeal this holding.

Turning to §2, the court stated: "the fact that Microsoft's arrangements with various [IAPs and other] firms did not foreclose enough of the relevant market to constitute a §1 violation in no way detracts from the Court's assignment of liability for the same arrangements under §2 . . . [A]ll of Microsoft's agreements, including the non-exclusive ones, severely restricted Netscape's access to those distribution channels leading most efficiently to the acquisition of browser usage share.". . .

In this case, plaintiffs allege that, by closing to rivals a substantial percentage of the available opportunities for browser distribution, Microsoft managed to preserve its monopoly in the market for operating systems. The IAPs constitute one of the two major channels by which browsers can be distributed. Microsoft has exclusive deals with fourteen of the top fifteen access providers in North America[, which] account for a large majority of all Internet access subscriptions in this part of the world. [Quotation marks omitted.] By ensuring that the "majority" of all IAP subscribers are offered IE either as the default browser or as the only browser, Microsoft's deals with the IAPs clearly have a significant effect in preserving its monopoly; they help keep usage of Navigator below the critical level necessary for Navigator or any other rival to pose a real threat to Microsoft's monopoly.

Plaintiffs having demonstrated a harm to competition, the burden falls upon Microsoft to defend its exclusive dealing contracts with IAPs by providing a pro-competitive justification for them. Significantly, Microsoft's only explanation for its exclusive dealing is that it wants to keep developers focused upon its APIs — which is to say, it wants to preserve its power in the operating system market. That is not an unlawful end, but neither is it a procompetitive justification for the specific means here in question, namely exclusive dealing contracts with IAPs. Accordingly, we affirm the District Court's decision holding that Microsoft's exclusive contracts with IAPs are exclusionary devices, in violation of §2 of the Sherman Act.

4. Dealings with Internet Content Providers, Independent Software Vendors, and Apple Computer

The District Court held that Microsoft engages in exclusionary conduct in its dealings with ICPs, which develop websites; ISVs, which develop software; and Apple, which is both an OEM and a software developer. The District Court condemned Microsoft's deals with ICPs and ISVs, stating: "By granting ICPs and ISVs free licenses to bundle [IE] with their offerings, and by exchanging other valuable inducements for their agreement to distribute, promote[,] and rely on [IE] rather than Navigator, Microsoft directly induced developers to focus on its own APIs rather than ones exposed by Navigator."

With respect to the deals with ICPs, the District Court's findings do not support liability. After reviewing the ICP agreements, the District Court specifically stated that "there is not sufficient evidence to support a finding that Microsoft's promotional restrictions actually had a substantial, deleterious impact on Navigator's usage share." Because plaintiffs failed to demonstrate that Microsoft's deals with the ICPs have a substantial effect upon competition, they have not proved the violation of the Sherman Act.

As for Microsoft's ISV agreements, however, the District Court did not enter a similar finding of no substantial effect. The District Court described Microsoft's deals with ISVs as follows:

> In dozens of "First Wave" agreements signed between the fall of 1997 and the spring of 1998, Microsoft has promised to give preferential support, in the form of early Windows 98 and Windows NT betas, other technical information, and the right to use certain Microsoft seals of approval, to important ISVs that agree to certain conditions. One of these conditions is that the ISVs use Internet Explorer as the default browsing software for any software they develop with a hypertext-based user interface. Another condition is that the ISVs use Microsoft's "HTML Help," which is accessible only with Internet Explorer, to implement their applications' help systems.

. . . The District Court did not specifically identify what share of the market for browser distribution the exclusive deals with the ISVs foreclose. Although the ISVs are a relatively small channel for browser distribution, they take on greater significance because, as discussed above, Microsoft had largely foreclosed the two primary channels to its rivals. In that light, one can tell from the record that by affecting the applications used by "millions" of consumers, Microsoft's exclusive deals with the ISVs had a substantial effect in further foreclosing rival browsers from the market. . . . Because, by keeping rival browsers from gaining widespread distribution (and potentially attracting the attention of developers away from the APIs in Windows), the deals have a substantial effect in preserving Microsoft's monopoly, we hold that plaintiffs have made a *prima facie* showing that the deals have an anticompetitive effect.

Of course, that Microsoft's exclusive deals have the anticompetitive effect of preserving Microsoft's monopoly does not, in itself, make them unlawful. A monopolist, like a competitive firm, may have a perfectly legitimate reason for wanting an exclusive arrangement with its distributors. Accordingly, Microsoft had an opportunity to, but did not, present the District Court with evidence demonstrating that the exclusivity provisions have some such procompetitive justification. On appeal Microsoft likewise does not claim that the exclusivity required by the deals serves any legitimate purpose; instead, it states only that its ISV agreements reflect an attempt "to persuade ISVs to utilize Internet-related system services in Windows rather than Navigator." As we explained before, however, keeping developers focused upon Windows — that is, preserving the Windows monopoly — is a competitively neutral goal. Microsoft having offered no procompetitive justification for its exclusive dealing arrangements with the ISVs, we hold that those arrangements violate §2 of the Sherman Act.

Finally, the District Court held that Microsoft's dealings with Apple violated the Sherman Act. Apple is vertically integrated: it makes both software (including an operating system, Mac OS), and hardware (the Macintosh line of computers). Microsoft primarily makes software, including, in addition to its operating system, a number of popular applications. One, called "Office," is a suite of business productivity applications that Microsoft has ported to Mac OS. The District Court found that "ninety percent of Mac OS users running a suite of office productivity applications [use] Microsoft's Mac Office." Further, the District Court found that:

> In 1997, Apple's business was in steep decline, and many doubted that the company would survive much longer. . . . [M]any ISVs questioned the wisdom of continuing to spend time and money developing applications for the Mac OS. Had Microsoft announced in the midst of this atmosphere that it was ceasing to develop new versions of Mac Office, a great number of ISVs, customers, developers, and investors would have interpreted the announcement as Apple's death notice.

. . . [Microsoft and Apple entered into an agreement under which Microsoft would continue for at least five years to produce up-to-date versions of Mac Office and Apple would make the most current version of IE the default browser on its computers.]

This exclusive deal between Microsoft and Apple has a substantial effect upon the distribution of rival browsers. If a browser developer ports its product to a second operating system, such as the Mac OS, it can continue to display a common set of APIs. Thus, usage share, not the underlying operating system, is the primary determinant of the platform challenge a browser may pose. Pre-installation of a browser (which can be accomplished either by including the browser with the operating system or by the OEM installing the browser) is one of the two most important methods of browser distribution, and Apple had a not insignificant share of worldwide sales of operating systems. Because Microsoft's exclusive contract with Apple has a substantial effect in restricting distribution of rival browsers, and because (as we have described several times above) reducing usage share of rival browsers serves to protect Microsoft's monopoly, its deal with Apple must be regarded as anticompetitive.

Microsoft offers no procompetitive justification for the exclusive dealing arrangement. . . . Accordingly, we hold that the exclusive deal with Apple is exclusionary, in violation of §2 of the Sherman Act.

5.   Java

Java, a set of technologies developed by Sun Microsystems, is another type of middleware posing a potential threat to Windows' position as the ubiquitous platform for software development. The Java technologies include: (1) a programming language; (2) a set of programs written in that language, called the "Java class libraries," which expose APIs; (3) a compiler, which translates code written by a developer into "bytecode"; and (4) a Java Virtual Machine ("JVM"), which translates bytecode into instructions to the operating system. Programs calling upon the Java APIs will run on any machine with a "Java runtime environment," that is, Java class libraries and a JVM.

In May 1995 Netscape agreed with Sun to distribute a copy of the Java runtime environment with every copy of Navigator, and Navigator quickly became the principal vehicle by which Sun placed copies of its Java runtime environment on the PC systems of Windows users. [Quotation marks omitted.] Microsoft, too, agreed to promote the Java technologies — or so it seemed. For at the same time, Microsoft took steps to maximize the difficulty with which applications written in Java could be ported from Windows to other platforms, and vice versa. [Quotation marks omitted.] Specifically, the District Court found that Microsoft took four steps to exclude Java from developing as a viable cross-platform threat: (a) designing a JVM incompatible with the one developed by Sun; (b) entering into contracts, the so-called "First Wave Agreements," requiring major ISVs to promote Microsoft's JVM exclusively; (c) deceiving Java developers about the Windows-specific nature of the tools it distributed to them; and (d) coercing Intel to stop aiding Sun in improving the Java technologies.

a. The Incompatible JVM

The District Court held that Microsoft engaged in exclusionary conduct by developing and promoting its own JVM. Sun had already developed a JVM for the Windows operating system when Microsoft began work on its version. The JVM developed by Microsoft allows Java applications to run faster on Windows than does Sun's JVM, but a Java application designed to work with Microsoft's JVM does not work with Sun's JVM and vice versa. . . . As explained above, however, a monopolist does not violate the antitrust laws simply by developing a product that is incompatible with those of its rivals. In order to violate the antitrust laws, the incompatible product must have an anticompetitive effect that outweighs any pro-competitive justification for the design. Microsoft's JVM is not only incompatible with Sun's, it allows Java applications to run faster on Windows than does Sun's JVM. Microsoft's faster JVM lured Java developers into using Microsoft's developer tools, and Microsoft offered those tools deceptively, as we discuss below. The JVM, however, does allow applications to run more swiftly and does not itself have any anticompetitive effect. Therefore, we reverse the District Court's imposition of liability for Microsoft's development and promotion of its JVM.

b. The First Wave Agreements

The District Court also found that Microsoft entered into First Wave Agreements with dozens of ISVs to use Microsoft's JVM. Again, we reject the District Court's condemnation of low but non-predatory pricing by Microsoft.

To the extent Microsoft's First Wave Agreements with the ISVs conditioned receipt of Windows technical information upon the ISVs' agreement to promote Microsoft's JVM exclusively, they raise a different competitive concern. The District Court found that, although not literally exclusive, the deals were exclusive in practice because they required developers to make Microsoft's JVM the default in the software they developed.

While the District Court did not enter precise findings as to the effect of the First Wave Agreements upon the overall distribution of rival JVMs, the record indicates that Microsoft's deals with the major ISVs had a significant effect upon JVM promotion. As discussed above, the products of First Wave ISVs reached millions of consumers. . . . Because Microsoft's agreements foreclosed a substantial portion of the field for JVM distribution and because, in so doing, they protected Microsoft's monopoly from a middleware threat, they are anticompetitive.

Microsoft offered no procompetitive justification for the default clause that made the First Wave Agreements exclusive as a practical matter. Because the cumulative effect of the deals is anticompetitive and because Microsoft has no procompetitive justification for them, we hold that the provisions in the First Wave Agreements requiring use of Microsoft's JVM as the default are exclusionary, in violation of the Sherman Act.

c.   Deception of Java Developers

Microsoft's "Java implementation" included, in addition to a JVM, a set of soft-ware development tools it created to assist ISVs in designing Java applications. The District Court found that, not only were these tools incompatible with Sun's cross-platform aspirations for Java — no violation, to be sure — but Microsoft deceived Java developers regarding the Windows-specific nature of the tools. Microsoft's tools included certain 'keywords' and 'compiler directives' that could only be exe-cuted properly by Microsoft's version of the Java runtime environment for Windows. [Quotation marks omitted.] As a result, even Java developers who were opting for portability over performance . . . unwittingly [wrote] Java applications that [ran] only on Windows." That is, developers who relied upon Microsoft's public commitment to cooperate with Sun and who used Microsoft's tools to develop what Microsoft led them to believe were cross-platform applications ended up producing applications that would run only on the Windows operating system. . . .

Microsoft's conduct related to its Java developer tools served to protect its monopoly of the operating system in a manner not attributable either to the supe-riority of the operating system or to the acumen of its makers, and therefore was anticompetitive. Unsurprisingly, Microsoft offers no procompetitive explanation for its campaign to deceive developers. Accordingly, we conclude this conduct is exclusionary, in violation of §2 of the Sherman Act.

d.   The Threat to Intel

The District Court held that Microsoft also acted unlawfully with respect to Java by using its "monopoly power to prevent firms such as Intel from aiding in the creation of cross-platform interfaces." In 1995 Intel was in the process of devel-oping a high-performance, Windows-compatible JVM. Microsoft wanted Intel to abandon that effort because a fast, cross-platform JVM would threaten Microsoft's monopoly in the operating system market. . . .

Intel finally capitulated in 1997. . . .

Microsoft does not . . . offer any procompetitive justification for pressuring Intel not to support cross-platform Java. . . . Therefore we affirm the conclusion that Microsoft's threats to Intel were exclusionary, in violation of §2 of the Sherman Act.

———————

Comparing the two opinions you have just read, consider why the license restrictions that the *Microsoft* court considers are different from the conduct validated in *Image Technical Services*. If Microsoft would have been free to deny licenses to the OEMs altogether, why should it not be permitted to insist that the licenses that it does grant include the restrictive provisions in question?

2.   Unreasonable Restraints of Trade

In litigation under Section 1 of the Sherman Act, plaintiffs claim more broadly that agreements constitute unreasonable restraints of trade — an allegation that can be made even if the defendant is not a monopolist. Again, the *Guidelines* generally explain that software licensing is not unreasonable. Rules that prohibited licensing or constrained the terms of licensing unduly plainly would undermine both competition and innovation:

2.3   PROCOMPETITIVE BENEFITS OF LICENSING

Intellectual property typically is one component among many in a production process and derives value from its combination with complementary factors. Complementary factors of production include manufacturing and distribution facilities, workforces, and other items of intellectual property. The owner of intellectual property has to arrange for its combination with other necessary factors to realize its commercial value. Often, the owner finds it most efficient to contract with others for these factors, to sell rights to the intellectual property, or to enter into a joint venture arrangement for its development, rather than supplying these complementary factors itself.

Licensing, cross-licensing, or otherwise transferring intellectual property (hereinafter "licensing") can facilitate integration of the licensed property with complementary factors of production. This integration can lead to more efficient exploitation of the intellectual property, benefiting consumers through the reduction of costs and the introduction of new products. Such arrangements increase the value of intellectual property to consumers and to the developers of the technology. By potentially increasing the expected returns from intellectual property, licensing also can increase the incentive for its creation and thus promote greater investment in research and development.

Sometimes the use of one item of intellectual property requires access to another. An item of intellectual property "blocks" another when the second cannot be practiced without using the first. For example, an improvement on a patented machine can be blocked by the patent on the machine. Licensing may promote the coordinated development of technologies that are in a blocking relationship.

Field-of-use, territorial, and other limitations on intellectual property licenses may serve procompetitive ends by allowing the licensor to exploit its property as efficiently and effectively as possible. These various forms of exclusivity can be used to give a licensee an incentive to invest in the commercialization and distribution of products embodying the licensed intellectual property and to develop additional applications for the licensed property. The restrictions may do so, for example, by protecting the licensee against free-riding on the licensee's investments by other licensees or by the licensor. They may also increase the licensor's incentive to license, for example, by protecting the licensor from competition in the licensor's own technology in a market niche that it prefers to keep to itself. These benefits of licensing restrictions apply to patent, copyright, and trade secret licenses, and to know-how agreements.

EXAMPLE 1

Situation:

ComputerCo develops a new, copyrighted software program for inventory management. The program has wide application in the health field. ComputerCo licenses the program in an arrangement that imposes both field of use and territorial limitations. Some of ComputerCo's licenses permit use only in hospitals; others permit use only in group medical practices. ComputerCo charges different royalties for the different uses. All of ComputerCo's licenses permit use only in specified portions of the United States and in specified foreign countries. The licenses contain no provisions that would prevent or discourage licensees from developing, using, or selling any other program, or from competing in any other good or service other than in the use of the licensed program. None of the licensees are actual or likely potential competitors of ComputerCo in the sale of inventory management programs.

Discussion:

The key competitive issue raised by the licensing arrangement is whether it harms competition among entities that would have been actual or likely potential competitors in the absence of the arrangement. Such harm could occur if, for example, the licenses anticompetitively foreclose access to competing technologies (in this case, most likely competing computer programs), prevent licensees from developing their own competing technologies (again, in this case, most likely computer programs), or facilitate market allocation or price-fixing for any product or service supplied by the licensees. If the license agreements contained such provisions, the Agency evaluating the arrangement would analyze its likely competitive effects. . . . In this hypothetical, there are no such provisions and thus the arrangement is merely a subdivision of the licensor's intellectual property among different fields of use and territories. The licensing arrangement does not appear likely to harm competition among entities that would have been actual or likely potential competitors if ComputerCo had chosen not to license the software program. The Agency therefore would be unlikely to object to this arrangement. Based on these facts, the result of the antitrust analysis would be the same whether the technology was protected by patent, copyright, or trade secret. The Agency's conclusion as to likely competitive effects could differ if, for example, the license barred licensees from using any other inventory management program.

To get a good sense for the types of concerns that licenses might raise, consider the following excerpt from the next section of the *Guidelines*:

3.1   NATURE OF THE CONCERNS

While intellectual property licensing arrangements are typically welfare-enhancing and procompetitive, antitrust concerns may nonetheless arise. For example, a licensing arrangement could include restraints that adversely affect competition in goods markets by dividing the markets among firms that would have competed using different technologies. . . . An arrangement that effectively merges the research and development activities of two of only a few entities that could plausibly engage in research and development in the relevant field might harm competition for development of new goods and services. An acquisition of intellectual property may lessen competition in a relevant antitrust market. The Agencies will focus on the actual effects of an arrangement, not on its formal terms.

The Agencies will not require the owner of intellectual property to create competition in its own technology. However, antitrust concerns may arise when a licensing arrangement harms competition among entities that would have been actual or likely potential competitors in a relevant market in the absence of the license (entities in a "horizontal relationship"). A restraint in a licensing arrangement may harm such competition, for example, if it facilitates market division or price-fixing. In addition, license restrictions with respect to one market may harm such competition in another market by anticompetitively foreclosing access to, or significantly raising the price of, an important input, or by facilitating coordination to increase price or reduce output. When it appears that such competition may be adversely affected, the Agencies will follow the analysis set forth below.

One of the most common claims in this context is a "tying" claim — a claim that a competitor with market power in one market requires customers that wish to purchase that product (the "tying" product) also to purchase a related product (the "tied" product) in a market in which the competitor wishes to obtain market power. Again, the D.C. Circuit's analysis of the tying claim in the *Microsoft* litigation is the most definitive treatment of the subject.

United States v. Microsoft Corporation

253 F.3d 34 (D.C. Cir. 2001) (en banc)

. . . IV.   TYING

Microsoft also contests the District Court's determination of liability under §1 of the Sherman Act. The District Court concluded that Microsoft's contractual and technological bundling of the IE web browser (the "tied" product) with its Windows operating system ("OS") (the "tying" product) resulted in a tying arrangement that was per se unlawful. We hold that the rule of reason, rather than per se analysis, should govern the legality of tying arrangements involving platform software products. . . . While every "business relationship" will in some sense have unique features, some represent entire, novel categories of dealings. As we shall explain, the arrangement before us is an example of the latter, offering the first up-close look at the technological integration of added functionality into software that serves as a platform for third-party applications. There being no close parallel in prior antitrust cases, simplistic application of per se tying rules carries a serious risk of harm. Accordingly, we vacate the District Court's finding of a per se tying violation and remand the case. Plaintiffs may on remand pursue their tying claim under the rule of reason.

The facts underlying the tying allegation substantially overlap with those set forth in . . . connection with the §2 monopoly maintenance claim. The key District Court findings are that (1) Microsoft required licensees of Windows 95 and 98 also to license IE as a bundle at a single price; (2) Microsoft refused to allow OEMs to uninstall or remove IE from the Windows desktop; (3) Microsoft designed Windows 98 in a way that withheld from consumers the ability to remove IE by use of the Add/Remove Programs utility; and (4) Microsoft designed Windows 98 to override the user's choice of default web browser in certain circumstances. The court found that these acts constituted a per se tying violation. Although the District Court also found that Microsoft commingled operating system-only and browser-only routines in the same library files, it did not include this as a basis for tying liability despite plaintiffs' request that it do so.

There are four elements to a per se tying violation: (1) the tying and tied goods are two separate products; (2) the defendant has market power in the tying product market; (3) the defendant affords consumers no choice but to purchase the tied product from it; and (4) the tying arrangement forecloses a substantial volume of commerce.

Microsoft does not dispute that it bound Windows and IE in the four ways the District Court cited. Instead it argues that Windows (the tying good) and IE browsers (the tied good) are not "separate products," and that it did not substantially foreclose competing browsers from the tied product market. . . .

We first address the separate-products inquiry, a source of much argument between the parties and of confusion in the cases. Our purpose is to highlight the poor fit between the separate-products test and the facts of this case. We then offer further reasons for carving an exception to the per se rule when the tying product is platform software. In the final section we discuss the District Court's inquiry if plaintiffs pursue a rule of reason claim on remand.

A.   SEPARATE-PRODUCTS INQUIRY UNDER THE PER SE TEST

The requirement that a practice involve two separate products before being condemned as an illegal tie started as a purely linguistic requirement: unless products are separate, one cannot be "tied" to the other. . . .

[The court discussed Supreme Court cases articulating a test under which no tying arrangement can exist unless there is a sufficient demand for the purchase of the tied product separate from the tying product to identify a distinct product market in which it is efficient to offer the tied product separately from the tying product.]

To understand the logic behind the Court's consumer demand test, consider first the postulated harms from tying. The core concern is that tying prevents goods from competing directly for consumer choice on their merits, *i.e.,* being selected as a result of buyers' independent judgment. [Quotation marks omitted.] . . . Direct competition on the merits of the tied product is foreclosed when the tying product either is sold only in a bundle with the tied product or, though offered separately, is sold at a bundled price, so that the buyer pays the same price whether he takes the tied product or not. In both cases, a consumer buying the tying product becomes entitled to the tied product; he will therefore likely be unwilling to buy a competitor's version of the tied product even if, making his own price/quality assessment, that is what he would prefer.

But not all ties are bad. Bundling obviously saves distribution and consumer transaction costs. This is likely to be true, to take some examples from the computer industry, with the integration of math co-processors and memory into microprocessor chips and the inclusion of spell checkers in word processors. Bundling can also capitalize on certain economies of scope. A possible example is the "shared" library files that perform OS and browser functions with the very same lines of code and thus may save drive space from the clutter of redundant routines and memory when consumers use both the OS and browser simultaneously.

Indeed, if there were no efficiencies from a tie (including economizing on consumer transaction costs such as the time and effort involved in choice), we would expect distinct consumer demand for each individual component of every good. In a competitive market with zero transaction costs, the computers on which this opinion was written would only be sold piecemeal — keyboard monitor, mouse, central processing unit, disk drive, and memory all sold in separate transactions and likely by different manufacturers.

Recognizing the potential benefits from tying, the Court [has] forged a separate-products test that, like those of market power and substantial foreclosure, attempts to screen out false positives under per se analysis. The consumer demand test is a rough proxy for whether a tying arrangement may, on balance, be welfare-enhancing, and unsuited to per se condemnation. In the abstract, of course, there is always direct separate demand for products: assuming choice is available at zero cost, consumers will prefer it to no choice. Only when the efficiencies from bundling are dominated by the benefits to choice for enough consumers, however, will we actually observe consumers making independent purchases. In other words, perceptible separate demand is inversely proportional to net efficiencies. On the supply side, firms without market power will bundle two goods only when the cost savings from joint sale outweigh the value consumers place on separate choice. So bundling by all competitive firms implies strong net efficiencies. If a court finds either that there is no noticeable separate demand for the tied product or, there being no convincing direct evidence of separate demand, that the entire competitive fringe engages in the same behavior as the defendant, then the tying and tied products should be declared one product and per se liability should be rejected. [Quotation marks omitted.]

Before concluding our exegesis of [the Court's] separate-products test, we should clarify two things. First, [the Court] does not endorse a direct inquiry into the efficiencies of a bundle. Rather, it proposes easy-to-administer proxies for net efficiency. In describing the separate-products test we discuss efficiencies only to explain the rationale behind the consumer demand inquiry. To allow the separate-products test to become a detailed inquiry into possible welfare consequences would turn a screening test into the very process it is expected to render unnecessary.

Second, the separate-products test is not a one-sided inquiry into the cost savings from a bundle. . . .

With this background, we now turn to the separate-products inquiry before us. The District Court found that many consumers, if given the option, would choose their browser separately from the OS. Turning to industry custom, the court found that, although all major OS vendors bundled browsers with their OSs, these companies either sold versions without a browser, or allowed OEMs or end-users either not to install the bundled browser or in any event to "uninstall" it. . . .

Microsoft does not dispute that many consumers demand alternative browsers. But on industry custom Microsoft contends that no other firm requires non-removal because no other firm has invested the resources to integrate web browsing as deeply into its OS as Microsoft has. (We here use the term "integrate" in the rather simple sense of converting individual goods into components of a single physical object (*e.g.*, a computer as it leaves the OEM, or a disk or sets of disks), without any normative implication that such integration is desirable or achieves special advantages.) Microsoft contends not only that its integration of IE into Windows is innovative and beneficial but also that it requires non-removal of IE. In our discussion of monopoly maintenance we find that these claims fail the efficiency balancing applicable in that context. But the separate-products analysis is supposed to perform its function as a proxy *without* embarking on any direct analysis of efficiency. Accordingly, Microsoft's implicit argument — that in this case looking to a competitive fringe is inadequate to evaluate fully its potentially innovative technological integration, that such a comparison is between apples and oranges — poses a legitimate objection to the operation of . . . the separate-products test for [application of] the per se rule [against tying].

. . . The per se rule's direct consumer demand and indirect industry custom inquiries are, as a general matter, backward-looking and therefore systematically poor proxies for overall efficiency in the presence of new and innovative integration. The direct consumer demand test focuses on historic consumer behavior, likely before integration, and the indirect industry custom test looks at firms that, unlike the defendant, may not have integrated the tying and tied goods. Both tests compare incomparables — the defendant's decision to bundle in the presence of integration, on the one hand, and consumer and competitor calculations in its absence, on the other. If integration has efficiency benefits, these may be ignored by the . . . proxies. Because one cannot be sure beneficial integration will be protected by the other elements of the per se rule, simple application of that rule's separate-products test may make consumers worse off.

In light of the monopoly maintenance section, obviously, we do not find that Microsoft's integration is welfare-enhancing or that it should be absolved of tying liability. Rather, we heed Microsoft's warning that the separate-products element of the per se rule may not give newly integrated products a fair shake.

B.   Per Se Analysis Inappropriate for this Case

We now address directly the larger question as we see it: whether standard per se analysis should be applied "off the shelf" to evaluate the defendant's tying arrangement, one which involves software that serves as a platform for third-party applications. There is no doubt that [some tying arrangements are unreasonable *per se*]. But there are strong reasons to doubt that the integration of additional software functionality into an OS falls among these arrangements. Applying per se analysis to such an amalgamation creates undue risks of error and of deterring welfare-enhancing innovation. . . .

In none of the [Supreme Court's existing tying] cases was the tied good physically and technologically integrated with the tying good. Nor did the defendants ever argue that their tie improved the value of the tying product to users *and* to makers of complementary goods. In those cases where the defendant claimed that use of the tied good made the tying good more valuable to users, the Court ruled that the same result could be achieved via quality standards for substitutes of the tied good. Here Microsoft argues that IE and Windows are an integrated physical product and that the bundling of IE APIs with Windows makes the latter a better applications platform for third-party software. It is unclear how the benefits from IE APIs could be achieved by quality standards for different browser manufacturers. We do not pass judgment on Microsoft's claims regarding the benefits from integration of its APIs. We merely note that these and other novel, purported efficiencies suggest that judicial experience provides little basis for believing that, because of their pernicious effect on competition and lack of *any* redeeming virtue, a software firm's decisions to sell multiple functionalities as a package should be conclusively presumed to be unreasonable and therefore illegal without elaborate inquiry as to the precise harm they have caused or the business excuse for their use. [Quotation marks omitted.]. . .

While the paucity of cases examining software bundling suggests a high risk that per se analysis may produce inaccurate results, the nature of the platform software market affirmatively suggests that per se rules might stunt valuable innovation. We have in mind two reasons.

First, as we explained in the previous section, the separate-products test is a poor proxy for net efficiency from newly integrated products. Under per se analysis the first firm to merge previously distinct functionalities (*e.g.,* the inclusion of starter motors in automobiles) or to eliminate entirely the need for a second function (*e.g.,* the invention of the stain-resistant carpet) risks being condemned as having tied two separate products because at the moment of integration there will appear to be a robust "distinct" market for the tied product. Rule of reason analysis, however, affords the first mover an opportunity to demonstrate that an efficiency gain from its "tie" adequately offsets any distortion of consumer choice.

The failure of the separate-products test to screen out certain cases of productive integration is particularly troubling in platform software markets such as that in which the defendant competes. Not only is integration common in such markets, but it is common among firms without market power. We have already reviewed evidence that nearly all competitive OS vendors also bundle browsers. Moreover, plaintiffs do not dispute that OS vendors can and do incorporate basic internet plumbing and other useful functionality into their OSs. Firms without market power have no incentive to package different pieces of software together unless there are efficiency gains from doing so. The ubiquity of bundling in competitive platform software markets should give courts reason to pause before condemning such behavior in less competitive markets.

Second, because of the pervasively innovative character of platform software markets, tying in such markets may produce efficiencies that courts have not previously encountered and thus the Supreme Court had not factored into the per se rule as originally conceived. For example, the bundling of a browser with OSs enables an independent software developer to count on the presence of the browser's APIs, if any, on consumers' machines and thus to omit them from its own package. It is true that software developers can bundle the browser APIs they need with their own products, but that may force consumers to pay twice for the same API if it is bundled with two different software programs. It is also true that OEMs can include APIs with the computers they sell, but diffusion of uniform APIs by that route may be inferior. First, many OEMs serve special subsets of Windows consumers, such as home or corporate or academic users. If just one of these OEMs decides not to bundle an API because it does not benefit enough of its clients, ISVs that use that API might have to bundle it with every copy of their program. Second, there may be a substantial lag before all OEMs bundle the same set of APIs — a lag inevitably aggravated by the first phenomenon. In a field where programs change very rapidly, delays in the spread of a necessary element (here, the APIs) may be very costly. Of course, these arguments may not justify Microsoft's decision to bundle APIs in this case, particularly because Microsoft did not merely bundle with Windows the APIs from IE, but an entire browser application. . . . . A justification for bundling a component of software may not be one for bundling the entire software package, especially given the malleability of software code. . . .

. . . We do not have enough empirical evidence regarding the effect of Microsoft's practice on the amount of consumer surplus created or consumer choice foreclosed by the integration of added functionality into platform software to exercise sensible judgment regarding that entire class of behavior. . . . We remand the case for evaluation of Microsoft's tying arrangements under the rule of reason. That rule more freely permits consideration of the benefits of bundling in software markets, particularly those for OSs, and a balancing of these benefits against the costs to consumers whose ability to make direct price/quality tradeoffs in the tied market may have been impaired.

Our judgment regarding the comparative merits of the per se rule and the rule of reason is confined to the tying arrangement before us, where the tying product is software whose major purpose is to serve as a platform for third-party applications and the tied product is complementary software functionality. While our reasoning may at times appear to have broader force, we do not have the confidence to speak to facts outside the record, which contains scant discussion of software integration generally. Microsoft's primary justification for bundling IE APIs is that their inclusion with Windows increases the value of third-party software (and Windows) to consumers. Because this claim applies with distinct force when the tying product is *platform* software, we have no present basis for finding the per se rule inapplicable to software markets generally. Nor should we be interpreted as setting a precedent for switching to the rule of reason every time a court identifies an efficiency justification for a tying arrangement. Our reading of the record suggests merely that integration of new functionality into platform software is a common practice and that wooden application of per se rules in this litigation may cast a cloud over platform innovation in the market for PCs, network computers and information appliances.

C. On Remand

Should plaintiffs choose to pursue a tying claim under the rule of reason, we note the following for the benefit of the trial court:

[O]n remand, plaintiffs must show that Microsoft's conduct unreasonably restrained competition. Meeting that burden involves an inquiry into the actual effect of Microsoft's conduct on competition in the tied good market, the putative market for browsers. [Quotation marks omitted.] To the extent that certain aspects of tying injury may depend on a careful definition of the tied good market and a showing of barriers to entry other than the tying arrangement itself, plaintiffs would have to establish these points. But plaintiffs were required — and had every incentive — to provide both a definition of the browser market and barriers to entry to that market as part of their §2 attempted monopolization claim; yet they failed to do so. Accordingly, on remand of the §1 tying claim, plaintiffs will be precluded from arguing any theory of harm that depends on a precise definition of browsers or barriers to entry (for example, network effects from Internet protocols and extensions embedded in a browser) other than what may be implicit in Microsoft's tying arrangement.

Of the harms left, plaintiffs must show that Microsoft's conduct was, on balance, anticompetitive. Microsoft may of course offer procompetitive justifications, and it is plaintiffs' burden to show that the anticompetitive effect of the conduct outweighs its benefit. . . .

On remand, Microsoft promptly settled with the Justice Department and most of the states that were plaintiffs. In the summer of 2004, the D.C. Circuit rejected appeals from the states that had not accepted the settlement. However, Microsoft's antitrust troubles are not over. At about the same time as the U.S. antitrust litigation came to a conclusion, the European Commission issued an order finding that Microsoft's conduct with respect to its Windows Media Player violated European antitrust laws and ordering Microsoft to make changes that would facilitate competition with the Windows product. Appeals of that order are likely to be continuing for years to come.

Relevant Glossary Entries

Grantback Provision
Network Effect

Problem Set 24

24.1. Your client operates a Web site that sells books. It has a patent on software for a "one-click" purchasing system. The software stores information about visitors to the site so that when they wish to purchase a book they can complete the purchase transaction by clicking on a single button. A competing Internet retailer has recently introduced a one-button system, which appears to infringe the patent. Your client was just about to sue the competitor, but stopped, worried about antitrust concerns. The client explains that its patent gives it a "monopoly" on the one-click purchasing system, and that the sole purpose of the suit is to prevent the competitor from competing with that product. Does this raise a concern for you? What kinds of things would you like to know about your client's business to help you provide an informed response? Sherman Act §2.

24.2. Same facts as in Problem 24.1, but now assume that your client sells 80 percent of the new books sold over the Internet and that, as a practical matter, competitors are unable to compete in that market without access to the one-click technology. That might be true because, among other things, convenience of the purchase process is one of the most important factors driving Web-site success. Given those facts, would you be concerned if your client adopted an across-the-board policy refusing to license the technology to any of its competitors, for the admitted purpose of hindering their ability to compete with your client? Sherman Act §2.

24.3. Suppose that Red Hat (which sells an operating system that competes with Microsoft) has its own instant-messaging (IM) product. Is it lawful for Red Hat to enter into a contract with a third-party Internet service provider (ISP) under which Red Hat produces a special version of its software with a desktop icon for the ISP, if the provider agrees that it will not distribute any IM service to its customers other than the Red Hat product?

24.4. Your Congresswoman Pamela Herring has before her a bill, supported by America Online and TimeWarner, which would remove entirely any special antitrust treatment for intellectual property. The proposed bill adds a new section to the Sherman Act, which would state:

> Notwithstanding anything to the contrary in [the Patent Act] or [the Copyright Act], any conduct that involves a restraint of trade in, or the exercise of monopoly power with respect to, any device or work that is protected by [the Patent Act] or [the Copyright Act] shall be subject to the same scrutiny under Sections 1 and 2 of this Act as the scrutiny to which it would be subject without regard to any such protection.

Congresswoman Herring would like your advice. Should she support such a bill?

Assignment 25:   Open-Source Software

A.   Software Development: Source and Object Code

The actual text of a software program normally uses what is known as "source" code. Source code is written in a computer programming language such as BASIC, FORTRAN, COBOL, PASCAL, or C. The defining characteristic of source code is that it can be read and understood by people trained in programming, but for the most part it is not directly usable by computers. For the computer to use the software code, the source code must be converted into "object" code, which consists of bits — often represented by the digits 1 or 0 to correspond to on and off states in the electric circuits that make up the computer's processing units. The normal process of conversion to object code uses a special type of software program called a compiler.

Although it usually is not difficult to convert source code to object code, it is often difficult if not impossible to convert object code back into source code. Thus, access to source code and object code is an important issue in the drafting of software licenses. Free access to the object code may be adequate for most of the licensee's purposes. If the software needs to be upgraded or modified, however, the licensee will have to make changes to the source code. Thus, in the proprietary software context on which the preceding assignments have focused, software developers attempt to prevent outsiders from gaining access to their source code, so that only the licensor can add features or correct defects. (As discussed in Assignment 23, a license to use proprietary software generally prohibits the copying, modification, or redistribution of the software to other users.) Given the rapid pace of technological development in the commercial-software industry, this strategy creates a "lock-in" effect, where the user is forced to purchase upgrades from the proprietary developer or abandon the product entirely. The open-source development model, which is the topic of this assignment, is a response to the proprietary, closed-source model.

B.   The Open-Source Movement

In the last five years, the open-source movement has transformed from an oddity that could be dismissed as a relic of the hacker-dominated days of the early Internet to a major business model that cannot be ignored by any business or informed lawyer. The rise of GNU/Linux as a serious competitor to the Microsoft operating system (particularly in Europe) has shown to all the power of the movement.

The open-source movement is difficult to characterize, because it is in some ways a populist political movement — its rhetoric sounds like nothing so much as the rhetoric of William Jennings Bryan decrying the power of large eastern seaboard interests — but it also includes a strong business aspect: Its proponents believe that open-source development produces software of higher quality than proprietary development. The excerpt below gives a good overview of the movement.

Jonathan Zittrain, Normative Principles for Evaluating Free and Proprietary Software

71 U. Chi. L. Rev. 265 (2004)

I.   DEFINING FREE AND PROPRIETARY SOFTWARE ALONG THREE DIMENSIONS

A.   Legal Differences between Free and Proprietary Software

In 1984 Richard Stallman quit his job at the MIT artificial intelligence lab to develop what he called "free" software — software that others could copy and change as they pleased. He found this type of sharing ethically important and endeavored to rewrite the proprietary Unix operating system from scratch so that his version would be substitutable for Unix without infringing any copyrights in the existing Unix code. He named his project GNU, for "GNU's Not Unix." GNU culminated in 1992 after the contribution of a small but crucial piece of code captained by computer science student Linus Torvalds. Torvalds's addition of the "Linux kernel" made GNU (now called GNU/Linux, or, confusingly, just Linux) complete.

Stallman's own vision of free software evolved from that of software released without authorial restrictions on copying or derivation — a notion that could be accomplished by simply releasing one's work into the public domain — into software governed by a licensing scheme that would prohibit authors of derivations from placing restrictions on the distribution of their derived works that had not been placed on the distribution of the original code. Preventing the "proprietization" of derivative software lies at the heart of Stallman's "copyleft" General Public License (GPL), under which GNU/Linux and a great deal of other free software are now distributed. Copyleft was styled as a form of legal jujitsu — a use of copyright (and the availability of accompanying licensing terms) to "protect" free software from being more restrictively copyrighted by those who added their own code to the existing software and redistributed the end product. Indeed, copyleft's restrictions may kick in even before a later work incorporates sufficient code from a copylefted program to be considered a derivative work; Stallman's license is written to cover any work "that in whole or in part contains or is derived from the Program or any part thereof."

Stallman's flagship GPL has been joined by a flotilla of other similar licenses by other authors, all with their own variations. Beyond the universal trait of allowing others to build upon the base code and release the result, some, such as the license for a variant of Unix called BSD, allow others to build upon the underlying software without passing on the accompanying "copyleft" restrictions. The BSD license materially differs from a wholly public domain release only in that it requires a particular kind of credit or attribution for the original author on whose work the new program is based. Such works are usually called "open" rather than "free," or if "free" are qualified as "but not copyleft." Other licenses allow new derivative works only under some form of copyleft restriction, but vary on whether "nearby works" (that is, works bundled on the same CD-ROM or linked to, but not literally incorporated into, the licensed code) must themselves be copylefted.

Proprietary software in mass distribution almost uniformly reserves all rights to the author except a license to "run" the software on the purchaser's computer. For many users this restriction does not bar desired activity; non-programmers will evaluate a software purchase on the basis of the program's functionality rather than on its use as a base in producing other software. The most popular software includes tools that allow a user to adjust how the software operates in fine detail. Far beyond checking a box in a "Preferences" window, powerful "macro" languages are often built in to allow skilled users to alter the way in which their proprietary software operates, essentially writing software that is run by their own software. There has been no suggestion that macros written by users cannot themselves be transferred, copied, or licensed however the users desire, without claim of right by the proprietary software maker. (The absence of any claim to users' macros may be more a market decision than a presumption that such a claim would not be sustained.)

For proprietary software not in the mass market, any number of arrangements might be agreed upon between the vendor and the consumer. The user might be permitted, for example, to see the source code and make changes, but not to distribute those changes to others. (Without such permission, consumer changes, if substantial enough, would comprise derivative works — the creation of which is a right reserved to the original author.) Most recently, in an apparent response to the successes of the free software movement, certain proprietary software makers have attempted to allow approved users some measure of ability to adapt proprietary software to their own uses by accessing and altering the software's source code. Microsoft's "Shared Source Initiative" (SSI) is one such example. Through it, certain users can adapt Microsoft code to their own special needs, so long as they promise not to further share or sell that code to others. It is too early in the deployment of SSI to gauge how central it is to Microsoft's software marketing efforts. While the company has not released systematic data on its adoption, Microsoft's manager of the SSI reports that over 650,000 developers are using shared source code from the company.

B. TECHNICAL DIFFERENCES BETWEEN FREE AND PROPRIETARY SOFTWARE

As suggested by the use of the term "recipe" for the code underlying functioning software, a given piece of software typically exists in two related components: source code and object code. Source code is what programmers write; object code is what computers run. Software developers produce object code from source code through the use of a compiler. Object code without source code is useful for running a program, but not for easily learning how it works or was written. An attempt to "decompile" object code back into source code yields instructions that bear little resemblance to the original recipe for the program, even if they are functionally equivalent. To analogize, imagine a "decompiled" recipe that calls for adding 3/4 teaspoon of sugar, mixing, and then removing

1/4 teaspoon of sugar. This is perhaps functionally equivalent to the original recipe that calls for adding 1/2 teaspoon of sugar, but would be a much more frustrating, though to be sure not impossible, task.

Free software — at least as defined by Richard Stallman — is not free if the source code is not also included with the object code. Stallman has famously stated that the "free" in "free software" is more like free speech than free beer. One can charge for a particular copy of free software so long as the source is provided and a specific bundle of rights is delivered with the software — such as the right to further copy it. On the other hand, one can give away proprietary software, like the Internet Explorer Web browser, without charge, and it still isn't "free." The GPL requires that any release of a covered program (for example, one whose author drew upon someone else's GPL'd code to write it) must also readily make available the program's corresponding source code.

Releasing the object code without the source code has been a hallmark of proprietary software, complementing the creator's exercise of a legal right to prevent the use of source code in new works with a technical barrier to unauthorized use. Still, these legal and technical facts are analytically independent of one another. Some proprietary programming code happens not to be compiled, so the "executable" and source are one and the same thing. For example, the code by which Web pages are rendered is typically this way; anyone viewing a Web page can, in most browsers, ask to "view source" and will promptly be shown the code by which the page came about. To copy such code and use it for purposes other than viewing the Web page in question might well infringe the copyright of the code's author. Apart from the more typical instances in which the technical nature of coding permits object code to be given to users without easily revealing to them its ancestral source, phenomena like Microsoft's SSI illustrate that vendors might willingly forgo the technical protections of releasing object code without source code, while still asserting strong legal protection over the uses of that released source code.

Conversely, one might imagine a software author releasing, for whatever reason, only object code into the public domain. Such a release would leave no legal rights vested in the author, but the author might still be in an advantageous position to further exploit the software in new works, since only the author would have access to the clean source code for the program.

Thus, the legal and technical protections afforded respectively by copyright in a program and the selective release of its object but not source code are by no means coextensive. In the technical realm, one can only make the general observation that there currently exists a spectrum — from public domain, through free, on to shared and then "fully" proprietary — and that along that spectrum one tends to see increasing legal and technical restrictions on code's use.

C.   DEVELOPMENTAL DIFFERENCES BETWEEN FREE AND PROPRIETARY SOFTWARE

A third analytically independent difference along the spectrum from free to proprietary is the manner in which the software is typically developed. As most famously chronicled in Eric Raymond's essay *The Cathedral and the Bazaar*, at least two prevailing models of software development exist, roughly grouped around notions of free and proprietary software. The former "open" mode of development grows out of venerable academic computer science and amateur tinkering circles (amateur not in the sense of dilettante, but rather in the sense of one who undertakes something more out of love or fascination than professional duty). Open development emphasizes collaborative work even among strangers and across or even entirely outside of the boundaries of firms, with users of a piece of software themselves contributing changes and improvements to the larger project over time. These improvements are often not made in response to others' requests, but rather in order to make the software more usable to the person making the changes. The perceived absence of legal or technical constraints on the use and modification of a program's code can, under the right circumstances, spawn hundreds of variants among myriad developers. For example, the operating system Unix counts dozens of variants in its line, some licensed from an upstream claimant to proprietary rights. Some versions of Unix available in source code to the tinkering public (such as FreeBSD and the self-consciously intended-as-free GNU/Linux) have been thought by those working on them to be free of practically all legal restrictions.

The tremors of the SCO v IBM lawsuit — in which a single company has claimed rights to pieces of Unix that are claimed to have been incorporated into GNU/Linux — are significant precisely because they undermine the collaborative development model. Verifying the "legality" of code offered by a contributor to a project is both superfluous to its technical merit — and thus possibly only of peripheral interest to project leaders — and nearly impossible to do with any thoroughness, since the proprietary code that is, by hypothesis, the source of pilfered free code is not accessible to project leaders assembling the free code from willing sources purporting to have the right to offer it. Any doubt as to the legal character of the result of the collaborative development process, if taken seriously, could impel software developers to work only on code that they themselves originated, or for which ownership interests are as clear as possible, with clarity achieved through certification procedures among contributors that circumscribe the number of participants and the pace of their contributions.

The typical mode of development for proprietary software, by contrast, revolves around a firm and those software developers or other firms in specific privity to it. Software is conceived of, written, and tested in-house, and the firm takes some responsibility for user support and upgrades, all typically in response to market pressures and influences. More important for legal purposes, a proprietary firm can stand behind the pedigree of its code, both because it presumably originated in controlled and known circumstances and because the absence of accompanying source code makes the firm's offerings difficult to examine for evidence of theft, whether from competing proprietary companies or from copylefted, publicly available software.

———————————

Professor Zittrain emphasizes three major distinctions between proprietary and open-source software. He does not, however, emphasize one growing similarity between the two: the use of both forms of development in profit-oriented business models. The day has long since passed when open-source software was a hobby for hackers with no interest in profit. Many large technology companies — IBM, HP, and Sun — have contributed in substantial ways to open-source projects in an effort to enhance their profits. The key factor in all of those cases is the ability to take advantage of the benefits of open-source development, while retaining a competitive edge through proprietary control over some other aspect of the software, the provision of services, or bundling with a hardware product. Among other things, the need for interoperability in the industry makes the collaborative aspects of open-source development particularly attractive. Still, firms must retain some way to protect the differentiating aspects of their own contributions to a project. Managing those conflicting impulses requires considerable forethought.

Therefore, to offer an example, a hardware firm might use open-source software as part of a project in which it plans to profit from the sale of hardware. If the hardware firm improves the software and tailors it specifically to its hardware, the hardware firm might be willing to distribute the product through an open-source licensing model. On the other hand, if the project is likely to involve extensive resources and development, even a hardware firm might be reluctant to release the product entirely. In that case, it could license the product under a "hybrid" form of license that advertises itself as "open-source," but retains ultimate rights to commercialize the technology in the hands of the developer. Thus, for example, Sun's Community Source License freely grants access to source code to developers and researchers, but its limitations on modification and deployment of the technology cause the license to look in practice more like a standard proprietary license than anything typical of the open-source movement.

The business model for a firm with its core competence in the software area, by contrast, is more complex. Such a firm might want to retain control of any "bells and whistles" that it adds to an underlying core of open-source software. One approach in that context would be to profit from service plans sold with a particular distribution of an open-source program. Red Hat, for example, primarily profits from services and support provided to customers that use Red Hat's open-source products (primarily its version of the GNU/Linux operating system). A more difficult strategy involves selling a proprietary product on top of an open-source product. For example, Gluecode and MySQL sell server and database software that builds on the highly successful Apache open-source program. Programs such as those must take particular care that they do not transgress the requirements of the licenses on which their products are based. To illuminate the centrality of licensing terms — lawyering — to the convergence of the open-source and proprietary software-development models, the next section of the assignment discusses some of the most important terms of open-source licenses.

C. Open-Source Licenses

Although press accounts describe the open-source movement as a monolithic opposition to proprietary software companies, the open-source nature of any particular software program depends on the particular license used to open the source code of the program in question. Because the specific terms of the major licenses differ in important ways, it is difficult to generalize. The following excerpt discusses some of the common principles shared by most open-source licenses, drawing on the Open Source Definition, promulgated by the Open Source Initiative at *www.opensource.org*.

Robert W. Gomulkiewicz, How Copyleft Uses License Rights to Succeed in the Open Source Software Revolution and the Implications for Article 2B
36 Houston L. Rev. 179 (1999)

III.   LICENSING: THE UNNOTICED FORCE BEHIND OPEN SOURCE

The terms "free software" and "open source software" might lead observers of the open source revolution to conclude that hackers make software free or open by placing their code into the public domain; however, hackers employ a different approach. The proponents of open source software rely on owning the copyright in the code and then licensing it according to a very particular mass-market licensing model. Below, this Article describes why hackers use this model, known as copyleft, and the licensing principles embodied in copyleft licensing.

A.   WHY DO HACKERS USE LICENSES?

Hackers license software, rather than place it in the public domain, because they want to control what is done with their code. Licensing allows hackers to perpetuate their particular software development and distribution model. Without licensing, the open source software development model would be nothing more than an honor system.

Most software publishers choose licensing as a transaction model for the same reasons. The distinction between open source software and typical commercial software is not one based on the absence of a license in one case and the presence of a license in the other case, but instead is based on the presence or absence of certain license terms. The principal terms that characterize open source licensing are explained below.

B.   PRINCIPLES OF OPEN SOURCE LICENSING

Open source licensing is based on several key principles. These principles are embodied in The Open Source Definition, published by the Open Source Initiative, and in sample licenses published by the Free Software Foundation and others, such as the GNU General Public License, the GNU Library General Public License, the Artistic License, and the Berkeley Software Design-style license. If a license does not comply with these principles, the software cannot (at least according to the open source community) be labeled "open source."

1. Unencumbered Redistribution. The license may not restrict any party from either selling or giving away open source software. According to Mr. Stallman: "Since 'free' refers to freedom, not to price, there is no contradiction between selling copies and free software." This license condition protects the freedom to chose to redistribute either gratis or for a fee.

Why would anyone pay for free software? Fees may cover the cost of media or duplication. Fees are also earned by including additional software with the free software or by providing training or services. Moreover, fees might be attributable to the benefits associated with acquiring from a trusted distributor with a well-known brand name, such as Red Hat's version of Linux.

2. Source Code Form. The license agreement must license the software in source code form. The source code provided under the license must be in the preferred form a programmer would need to modify the program. To quote the Open Source Initiative: "We require access to un-obfuscated source code because you can't evolve programs without modifying them. Since our purpose is to make evolution easy, we require that modification be made easy."

3. Derivative Works. The license agreement must grant the licensee the right to create modifications and derivative works. The license must explicitly permit distribution of software built from modified or derivative source code.

4. The Author's Attribution and Integrity. Open source licensing requires that the author of a particular piece of code be acknowledged. This requirement is often satisfied by retaining the author's copyright notice on the code he or she creates as the code is passed on and modified further. As described by open source pioneer Eric S. Raymond, this credit-giving is fundamental to perpetuating open source software. Mr. Raymond postulates that hackers contribute many hours of volunteer labor to a development project because they highly value the reputation it gives them within the hacker community. Without this incentive, the open source movement would not exist on any significant scale.

Hackers may also believe that those who contribute code to an open source development may not want to have their reputation soiled if their code is grafted to shoddy code. Therefore, a license may require that derivative works be labeled with a different version number, or that their source code be distributed unmodified along with a mechanism that combines this code with modifications and derivatives when the software is actually compiled into binary or executable form for use by the computer. In addition, certain open source licenses prohibit the use of the name of the author of a given piece of code to endorse or promote products derived from that code.

5. No Warranties. The license agreement must provide the software "as is," with no warranties either as to product performance or non-infringement of third-party intellectual property rights. The purpose of this term is straightforward: shift risk away from the code developer.

6. Self-Perpetuating License Terms. The rights attached to the software must apply to everyone to whom the software is redistributed. In other words, the licensee must agree to pass the open source license terms on to its licensees, and require those licensees to pass the terms on to all subsequent licensees. For example, the right to create derivatives must follow the software throughout the chain of distribution. Warranty disclaimers must also be passed on.

7. Non-Discriminatory. The license must not discriminate against any individual or group. In addition, the license must not restrict the use of the software in a particular field or endeavor. For example, the license may not restrict use of the software for business purposes or use in a controversial field of research, such as genetic engineering.

8. Non-Contamination. The license must not place restrictions on other software distributed along with it. "For example, the license must not insist that all other programs distributed on the same medium be open source software."*

---

*[Professor Gomulkiewicz notes that this condition is not consistent with the GPL. As he puts it, this provision "fixes a bug in the GNU General Public License."]

As this book goes to press, the Open Source Initiative has approved and certified 54 licenses, with many more under review. However, to give some context to Professor Gomulkiewicz's comments, consider the provisions of the GPL and the BSD that set forth the conditions on which a user can modify and redistribute programs covered by the GPL. In general, as shown below, the GPL licensing model tends to favor rigid adherence to the basic principles of the open-source movement and the BSD model provides greater rights for the licensee.

First the GPL:

1. You may copy and distribute verbatim copies of the Program's source code as you receive it, in any medium, provided that you conspicuously and appropriately publish on each copy an appropriate copyright notice and disclaimer of warranty; keep intact all the notices that refer to this License and to the absence of any warranty; and give any other recipients of the Program a copy of this License along with the Program.

You may charge a fee for the physical act of transferring a copy, and you may at your option offer warranty protection in exchange for a fee.

2. You may modify your copy or copies of the Program or any portion of it, thus forming a work based on the Program, and copy and distribute such modifications or work under the terms of Section 1 above, provided that you also meet all of these conditions:

a) You must cause the modified files to carry prominent notices stating that you changed the files and the date of any change.

b) You must cause any work that you distribute or publish, that in whole or in part contains or is derived from the Program or any part thereof, to be licensed as a whole at no charge to all third parties under the terms of this License.

c) If the modified program normally reads commands interactively when run, you must cause it, when started running for such interactive use in the most ordinary way, to print or display an announcement including an appropriate copyright notice and a notice that there is no warranty (or else, saying that you provide a warranty) and that users may redistribute the program under these conditions, and telling the user how to view a copy of this License. (Exception: if the Program itself is interactive but does not normally print such an announcement, your work based on the Program is not required to print an announcement.)

These requirements apply to the modified work as a whole. If identifiable sections of that work are not derived from the Program, and can be reasonably considered independent and separate works in themselves, then this License, and its terms, do not apply to those sections when you distribute them as separate works. But when you distribute the same sections as part of a whole which is a work based on the Program, the distribution of the whole must be on the terms of this License, whose permissions for other licensees extend to the entire whole, and thus to each and every part regardless of who wrote it.

Thus, it is not the intent of this section to claim rights or contest your rights to work written entirely by you; rather, the intent is to exercise the right to control the distribution of derivative or collective works based on the Program.

In addition, mere aggregation of another work not based on the Program with the Program (or with a work based on the Program) on a volume of a storage or distribution medium does not bring the other work under the scope of this License.

The BSD, by contrast, is much less restrictive, omitting any requirement that subsequent works comply with the open-source license:

Redistribution and use in source and binary forms, with or without modification, are permitted provided that the following conditions are met:

- Redistributions of source code must retain the above copyright notice, this list of conditions and the following disclaimer.
- Redistributions in binary form must reproduce the above copyright notice, this list of conditions and the following disclaimer in the documentation and/or other materials provided with the distribution.
- Neither the name of the <ORGANIZATION> nor the names of its contributors may be used to endorse or promote products derived from this software without specific prior written permission.

As discussed above, it is central to the open-source development model that software be distributed without any warranties, whether of quality, non-infringement, or anything else, the general intent being to shift all risks from the software developer to the user. The provisions that implement that approach warrant careful attention because they are central to any effort to make use of open-source software as part of a proprietary business model.

The GPL provision provides as follows:

NO WARRANTY

11.   BECAUSE THE PROGRAM IS LICENSED FREE OF CHARGE, THERE IS NO WARRANTY FOR THE PROGRAM, TO THE EXTENT PERMITTED BY APPLICABLE LAW. EXCEPT WHEN OTHERWISE STATED IN WRITING THE COPYRIGHT HOLDERS AND/OR OTHER PARTIES PROVIDE THE PROGRAM "AS IS" WITHOUT WARRANTY OF ANY KIND, EITHER EXPRESSED OR IMPLIED, INCLUDING, BUT NOT LIMITED TO, THE IMPLIED WARRANTIES OF MERCHANTABILITY AND FITNESS FOR A PARTICULAR PURPOSE. THE ENTIRE RISK AS TO THE QUALITY AND PERFORMANCE OF THE PROGRAM IS WITH YOU. SHOULD THE PROGRAM PROVE DEFECTIVE, YOU ASSUME THE COST OF ALL NECESSARY SERVICING, REPAIR OR CORRECTION.

12.   IN NO EVENT UNLESS REQUIRED BY APPLICABLE LAW OR AGREED TO IN WRITING WILL ANY COPYRIGHT HOLDER, OR ANY OTHER PARTY WHO MAY MODIFY AND/OR REDISTRIBUTE THE PROGRAM AS PERMITTED ABOVE, BE LIABLE TO YOU FOR DAMAGES, INCLUDING ANY GENERAL, SPECIAL, INCIDENTAL OR CONSEQUENTIAL DAMAGES ARISING OUT OF THE USE OR INABILITY TO USE THE PROGRAM (INCLUDING BUT NOT LIMITED TO LOSS OF DATA OR DATA BEING RENDERED INACCURATE OR LOSSES SUSTAINED BY YOU OR THIRD PARTIES OR A FAILURE OF THE PROGRAM TO OPERATE WITH ANY OTHER PROGRAMS), EVEN IF SUCH HOLDER OR OTHER PARTY HAS BEEN ADVISED OF THE POSSIBILITY OF SUCH DAMAGES.

The BSD provision is simpler, but to the same effect:

THIS SOFTWARE IS PROVIDED BY THE COPYRIGHT HOLDERS AND CONTRIBUTORS "AS IS" AND ANY EXPRESS OR IMPLIED WARRANTIES, INCLUDING, BUT NOT LIMITED TO, THE IMPLIED WARRANTIES OF MERCHANTABILITY AND

FITNESS FOR A PARTICULAR PURPOSE ARE DISCLAIMED. IN NO EVENT SHALL THE COPYRIGHT OWNER OR CONTRIBUTORS BE LIABLE FOR ANY DIRECT, INDIRECT, INCIDENTAL, SPECIAL, EXEMPLARY, OR CONSEQUENTIAL DAMAGES (INCLUDING, BUT NOT LIMITED TO, PROCUREMENT OF SUBSTITUTE GOODS OR SERVICES; LOSS OF USE, DATA, OR PROFITS; OR BUSINESS INTERRUPTION) HOWEVER CAUSED AND ON ANY THEORY OF LIABILITY, WHETHER IN CONTRACT, STRICT LIABILITY, OR TORT (INCLUDING NEGLIGENCE OR OTHERWISE) ARISING IN ANY WAY OUT OF THE USE OF THIS SOFTWARE, EVEN IF ADVISED OF THE POSSIBILITY OF SUCH DAMAGE.

As more hybrid firms use the open-source development model, the variety in the types of licenses is likely to increase even further. That is particularly true in cases in which firms would like to take advantage of the PR punch of a generous "open-source" program, but wish to retain in the details of their licenses continuing levels of control that would be offensive to traditional open-source principles. The ultimate outcome is a spectrum of licenses, ranging from the traditional proprietary licenses discussed in Assignment 23 (in which no access to source code is permitted), to the more modern licenses discussed in that assignment (in which access is granted, but further distribution is prohibited) through a further range of carefully delineated permissible activities culminating in the pristine open-source license that absolutely bars any future constraints on alteration or distribution of the source code.

D. Open-Source and Intellectual Property

The open-source development model interacts in crucial ways with the law of intellectual property. First, as the excerpts above make clear, open-source programs rely on copyright law as a vehicle for imposing constraints that bind subsequent users. As you will recall from the opening sections of this chapter, only a license transaction can ensure that constraints on the use of copyrighted material will be binding on future parties that come into possession of the material. In this case, the enforceability of a license transaction is central to the goal of ensuring that code that is once made free will always be kept free.

The law of patents also plays a central role in the structure of the open-source model. Because the open-source movement depends on fragmented creation by parties without financial responsibility, it could not go forward if users of the software relied in any substantial way on an ability to sue those who had written the software. For copyright claims, this is not a significant problem, because a copyright claim can have merit only if the code actually is copied from another program. Thus, there always is the possibility that somebody will contribute code that it has stolen from a third party — as discussed below, SCO has claimed that IBM contributed code owned by SCO to the GNU/Linux project, but those claims seem relatively manageable.

Claims of patent infringement, which does not depend on direct copying, are more difficult to resolve. Thus, for example, if Microsoft holds patents on advances in the technology of an operating system (which it does), and if the open-source contributors to GNU/Linux devise the same methods of improving their own operating system, then a GNU/Linux operating system that included those improvements would violate the Microsoft patents *even if it was invented entirely independently, innocently, and with no knowledge of the Microsoft patents or technology*. That circumstance makes the existence of patents on software a substantial problem for the open-source movement.

That problem is exacerbated by a substantial change in the law of patents over the last quarter century that has made patents on software available for the first time. At one time, early in the days of the software industry, the Supreme Court suggested quite broadly that patents on software would not be available, based on the idea that software essentially is an algorithm that is equivalent to a law of nature that cannot be patented. Gottschalk v. Benson, 409 U.S. 63 (1972). Since that time, however, the Supreme Court repeatedly has backed away from decisions that have imposed limits on the patentable subject matter. Thus, for example, in Diamond v. Diehr, 450 U.S. 175 (1981), the Court validated a patent on a computerized process that relied on a software program to modulate the time and temperature used for molding synthetic rubber. More recently, the U.S. Court of Appeals for the Federal Circuit has issued a string of decisions culminating in the 1994 decision of In re Alappat, 33 F.3d 1526 (1994), which generally have made it possible for a firm to obtain a patent on any advance in software that meets the standard requirements of patentability (utility, novelty, and nonobviousness). The demise of any limits on patentability was underscored by the Federal Circuit's decision four years later in State Street v. Signature Financial Group, 149 F.3d 1368 (1998), which generally approved patents on business methods. Although many businesses and academics have criticized those decisions, it is relatively clear that they follow the lead set by the Supreme Court in decisions like Diamond v. Chakrabarty, 447 U.S. 303 (1980) (upholding a patent on a human-made microorganism), which emphasize that Section 101 of the Patent Act itself imposes no substantial constraints on patentable subject matter. Thus, if there is to be any limitation on patentability in this area, it is much more likely to come from Congress than from the Supreme Court.

Absent such a limitation, the potential for patent infringement is likely to pose a problem of increasing severity for the open-source development model. That problem came clearly into focus in 2003 in litigation between Santa Cruz Operations (SCO) and IBM. SCO currently holds a variety of IP rights related to the original Unix operating system out of which the GNU/Linux system was developed. Although the original GNU/Linux system was modeled on Unix in many ways, it was written with "fresh" code to avoid the possibility of copyright infringement. The problem arose in the late 1990s, when a variety of firms contributed code to the GNU/Linux project. IBM had access to Unix code through, among other things, a license from SCO. SCO's lawsuit claims that IBM improperly contributed to the GNU/Linux project code derived from Unix that is either a trade secret of SCO or material for which SCO holds the copyright. SCO has sought literally billions of dollars in damage from IBM and, more chillingly, has begun to pursue claims against ordinary corporate GNU/Linux users, contending that their use of the program infringes SCO's rights in the code contributed by IBM. Those claims have numerous difficulties, including the fact that SCO itself appears to have distributed the GNU/Linux program since the date of the additions in question, an action that may result in a waiver of any IP claim by SCO related to the offending code.

Whatever the outcome in that case, however, it is plain that the world of open source will get a reality check moving it away from its relatively cavalier attitude to intellectual property claims. Licenses in the area already recognize that problem, typically by including clauses that waive any right to patent enforcement by people participating in the open-source process. A typical clause is the one below, from the Apache license:

> Grant of Patent License. Subject to the terms and conditions of this License, each Contributor hereby grants to You a perpetual, worldwide, non-exclusive, no-charge, royalty-free, irrevocable (except as stated in this section) patent license to make, have made, use, offer to sell, sell, import, and otherwise transfer the Work, where such license applies only to those patent claims licensable by such Contributor that are necessarily infringed by their Contribution(s) alone or by combination of their Contribution(s) with the Work to which such Contribution(s) was submitted. If You institute patent litigation against any entity (including a cross-claim or counterclaim in a lawsuit) alleging that the Work or a Contribution incorporated within the Work constitutes direct or contributory patent infringement, then any patent licenses granted to You under this License for that Work shall terminate as of the date such litigation is filed.

Clauses like that one might be effective to limit the rights of a business like SCO that participated for some time in the open-source movement before trying to claim IP rights in the GNU/Linux project, but it would have no effect on a patent claim by a wholly proprietary company like Microsoft, which is unlikely ever to have distributed software under such a license.

Relevant Glossary Entries

Compiler
Object Code

Problem Set 25

25.1. Your friend Rob Sears has discovered an open-source software program that responds well to one of the common problems of his customers. The program automatically adjusts the size of incoming Web pages to match the screen size of the device on which the page is being received. Rob would like to sell the program to his customers. Although they could download it for free from a site in Europe, he plans to sell a nice package that includes a cd-rom with the software and a user's manual. He also plans to provide online and telephone support for purchasers. Does the open-source license under which he has obtained the source code for this product permit him to do this? Consider the question under the General Public License, under the BSD License, and under the Sun Community Source License (all available on the Web site for this text). GPL flfl 1, 2; BSD License, SCSL art. III(A)(1).

25.2. A few months later, Rob calls back angry. Somebody has been copying the open-source program from the materials that he sells and is reselling the program at a rate far below the rate he is charging. Does Rob have any remedy? Does it help if he can prove that the competitor is copying the software from Rob's materials rather than obtaining it from some independent source?

25.3. Suppose that Rob instead wants to incorporate the open-source software program directly into his product.

(a) Would that cause him any difficulties? If so, are there any particular strategies that he might follow to make his program and the open-source program available to his customers at the same time? GPL § 2, BSD License.

(b) What approach should Rob take in the license with respect to warranties related to the open-source components of his product?

25.4. Consider the products of Gluecode (discussed at *www.gluecode.com*). You should assume that those products are based on the Apache open-source project and include a substantial amount of the Apache source code. When Gluecode sells those products to customers, it licenses them on terms that permit the customers to "customize and extend the code according to [their] requirements, but [they] may not embed, distribute, sub-license, or resell the product to third parties." Would that licensing program be permissible if the Apache program were licensed under the GPL? Compare Apache Software License with GPL §1.

25.5. A few months later, Rob returns. He has for some time been using a widely disseminated open-source program to operate the main server on which his Web site resides. He has just received a demand letter contending that the program infringes copyright and patent interests held by the company (Junipero Serra Operations, or JSO). He wants to know how this claim can be plausible. He reminds you that you had told him that all code used in open-source software is contributed free of copyright and patent claims by those that contribute it. What do you say? Is there any practical way to protect himself against similar claims in the future?

THE CAMFORD BOOKS PROBLEM

(PART IV)

Your friends at Camford Books are back. They have spent a lot of time and resources developing some specific plans for the products they wish to sell at their site and seek advice from you about some general issues.

1. Their Web site has a variety of provisions (privacy policies, terms of use, and the like) to which they would like to bind their customers. Do you have any specific advice about how those terms should be presented in a way that would make them binding?

2. They would like to include an auction feature at which their customers can resell used books, relying on the reviews that Camford itself posts and also on reviews that customers post. What legal considerations should predominate in their evaluation of that project?

3. Will they need to collect sales tax? The European VAT? Their main facility is located in England, but they expect to have an automated warehouse — though no employees — in each of the countries in which they sell books. Initially that will include only the United States and countries in the European Union.

4. They have been approached by several of the large publishing companies about integrating their purchasing operations with a Web site that those companies are establishing at *www.PublishersOnline.com*. What benefits might Camford Books gain from such an endeavor? What risks do you foresee? Is there anything you can do as a lawyer to evaluate or mitigate those risks?

5. Camford Books currently has an enviable catalog of information about classical texts available from publishers around the world. They have planned to sell this catalog by download from their Web site. Do you have any concerns about this?

6. Camford Books initially uses an open-source search engine for its Web site. But after a few months, one of its employees comes up with some modifications that substantially improve the search engine. Because the resulting engine is much better than anything currently available on the market, Camford Books now wants to license the resulting engine to other retail book and music sites. Do you foresee any problems?

Chapter 5.   Electronic Payments

For several reasons, it is harder to discuss electronic payments than many of the topics you have studied earlier in the book. First, information technology has had an almost pervasive influence on payment systems. It is, therefore, difficult to discuss almost any aspect of payments law without considering the influence of information technology. Still, few of the truly new electronic payment systems have succeeded in the market, which makes it difficult to provide a "hands-on" description of how those systems function. They are still changing month-by-month as they struggle to attract merchants, consumers, and financial institutions. Hence, you may find much of the discussion sketchy.

Another problem, related to the first, is that many of the developments have been in the form of incremental changes to existing systems. Thus, to discuss those developments in detail, it would be necessary to describe the existing systems. However, those issues are covered in separate courses in many law schools, such as Payment Systems, Negotiable Instruments, or Commercial Paper. Moreover, those courses often focus on older systems instead of the modern systems that are central to current commercial practice, so even if you had taken one of those courses you might have insufficient background to understand fully the systems discussed in this chapter. Accordingly, the assignments that follow try to provide summary descriptions of the major features of the check-collection and electronic fund–transfer systems, without attention to all of the details you would learn in other courses.

Finally, the bodies of law that govern payment systems — such as UCC Article 3 for negotiable instruments, UCC Article 4 for checks, and the federal Electronic Funds Transfer Act for various consumer electronic-payment systems — have not changed in any significant way to accommodate the rapid pace of innovation. Thus, the legal rules that govern electronic payments tend to fit poorly with the emerging issues raised by electronic payments. Those rules were designed to deal with old paper-based transactions or legacy computer systems that are fading from use. On the other hand, until any of the new electronic payment systems move from the realm of novelty to the mainstream of commercial transactions, it is difficult to decide exactly what changes would be appropriate.

Section A.   Electronic Technology and the Checking System

Recognizing the difficulty of the task, the discussion begins with checks. The check is the dominant non-cash consumer payment system in the United States. As of 2001, Americans wrote about 43 billion checks a year. Individuals used about 15 billion of those checks to make payments to businesses for goods and services worth a total of about $5 trillion.

The check, of course, is a piece of paper, a tangible object. And so the procedures for paying with and collecting on checks center on the tangible object. By comparison to procedures that manage information electronically, the existing procedures are quite costly, perhaps in the range of $2 to $3 per check (including the costs of handling the item by the payor, the payee, and the various banks that process it). The procedures also are quite slow, typically requiring a period of days to determine whether a check ultimately will be paid by the bank on which it is drawn. The delays required by such procedures pose a direct and obvious hindrance to the efficiency of the system. Less obviously but just as seriously, they also raise costs by increasing the potential for fraud: The long period between the time of deposit and the time at which the bank of deposit discovers whether the check will be honored presents an opportunity for a variety of creative schemes to steal money from the depositary bank. Accordingly, it should be no surprise that the banking industry has supported various efforts to foster the use of electronic technology as a means for controlling costs in the checking system.

At the same time, despite the obvious costs of the checking system, American consumers and businesses have been quite resistant to change. However inefficient the checking system is — and it is strikingly inefficient — businesses and individuals are accustomed to it and have organized their lives and affairs around the way it works. One thing it offers is a relatively complete and specific set of rules for allocating losses among the parties that participate in the system. That set of rules is important because the rules for all of the other systems, to one degree or another, develop as exceptions from the basic rules that have governed checks for decades.

For whatever reason, although a number of competitors and purported substitutes have appeared, there is no clear successor to the checking system. Thus, it is difficult to get merchants to invest in changing their affairs to accommodate non-check payments. Similarly, consumers resist trying new methods of payment when they are comfortable with the system they normally use. Americans are "locked in" to the checking system: probably inefficient as an ending position, but probably (for now at least) more expensive to change out of it than to live with it.

This section of the book discusses the efforts to improve the checking system or move beyond it. The first assignment discusses check truncation: transactions in which a check is written, but in which electronic systems eliminate the need to transport the paper check through the normal check-collection process. The second assignment discusses ACH transfers and electronic checks: transactions in which electronic substitutes for checks entirely obviate the need for the paper check.

Assignment 26: The Road to Truncation

A. The Basics of Check Collection

To explain how truncation of check processing affects the checking system, it is useful to start with a brief summary of the regular, nontruncated system by which checks are processed. The process starts when a person making a payment (the "payor") delivers the check to the person to be paid (the "payee"). The check in essence is an instruction from the payor to a bank at which the payor has an account (the "payor bank"); the name of that bank is indicated on the face of the check. Because the check is a type of "draft" (see UCC §3-104(e) and (f)), we also can say that the payor "draws" the check on the payor bank. Hence, the payor also is known as the "drawer" and the payor bank as the "drawee." The substance of the check is an instruction to the payor bank to pay the indicated amount of money to the indicated payee (or to some other party, if the payee so orders).

1. Direct Presentment

Conceptually, the simplest way for the payee to obtain payment for the check is to take it directly to the payor bank and cash it. In that case, illustrated in Figure 26.1, the payor bank removes funds from the drawer's account in an amount equal to the amount of cash disbursed to the payee. Similarly, if the payee happens to have an account at the payor bank, the payee could deposit the check into an account at the payor bank. In that case, the payor bank transfers funds from the drawer's account to the payee's account, in an amount equal to the amount of the check.

2. Indirect Collection

As it happens, however, most payees of checks do not find it convenient to cash a check at the payor bank or deposit it into an account at a payor bank. Rather, the typical payee deposits the check into an account at a different bank (the "depositary bank"). Alternatively, but much the same for present purposes, the payee might cash the check at a nonbank that deposits the check into its at a depositary bank that is not the payor bank. In either case, the depositary bank will have no relation with the drawer of the check. Accordingly, the depositary bank must communicate with the payor bank to find out if the check is good and to obtain the funds that the check represents. Surprisingly, even in the twenty-first century, those tasks ordinarily

Figure 26.1
Direct Presentment

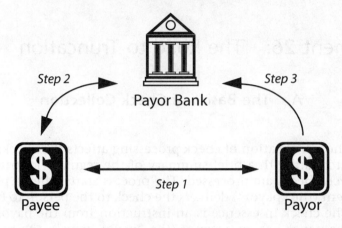

Step 2 → **Payor Bank** ← Step 3

$ **Payee** ←——— Step 1 ———→ $ **Payor**

Step 1   Payee provides goods and services to payor; payor gives check to payee.

Step 2   Payee presents check to payor bank; payor bank gives cash to payee.

Step 3   Payor bank removes funds from payor's account.

are accomplished not by telephone, telecopy, e-mail, or some other electronic communication system, but by the tedious exercise of transporting the check physically from the depositary bank to the payor bank. The depositary bank usually does this in one of three ways: through a clearinghouse, through a direct arrangement with the payor bank, or through the Federal Reserve system.

a.   Clearinghouse Collection

If the bank is located in a large metropolitan area, many local checks can be processed through a clearinghouse that handles checks for large banks in the region. If a bank that receives checks for deposit is a member of a clearinghouse, it collects each day the checks drawn on other members of the clearinghouse and sends them to the clearinghouse — you should imagine large trucks filled with large (and heavy) canvas bags of checks. The clearinghouse acts on the assumption — which turns out to be true more than 99 percent of the time — that the checks will be honored. Thus, it credits each bank each day for all of the checks that the bank sends to the clearinghouse. The clearinghouse then sorts the checks and sends to each member bank the checks received that day that are drawn on that bank. Again, acting on the assumption that the checks will be honored, the clearinghouse debits each bank for all of the checks that the clearinghouse

Figure 26.2
Clearinghouse Collection

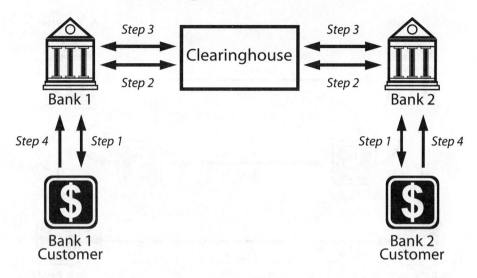

Step 1   Customers deposit checks at their banks. Their banks credit their
          accounts.

Step 2   Banks send to the clearinghouse checks they have received for
          deposit. Clearinghouse credits banks for those checks.

Step 3   Clearinghouse sends to banks checks drawn on them.
          Clearinghouse debits banks for those checks.

Step 4   Banks debit customer accounts for checks received from
          clearinghouse.

sends to that bank each day. Mechanically, the clearinghouse applies a single net credit or debit to a designated account of each bank (often an account at the local Federal Reserve bank). When the checks reach the payor banks, those banks charge the accounts of their customers for the checks written on their accounts. Figure 26.2 illustrates this process.

b. Direct-Send Collection

Second, if the depositary bank is a large bank, it often will have agreements with large nonlocal banks whose checks it frequently receives for deposit. For example, Wells Fargo in San Francisco might have such an arrangement (a "direct-send" agreement) with CitiBank in New York. If so, Wells Fargo each day would collect the checks deposited by its customers drawn on CitiBank and would send them directly east to CitiBank, normally by airplane, again in

Figure 26.3
Direct-Send Collection

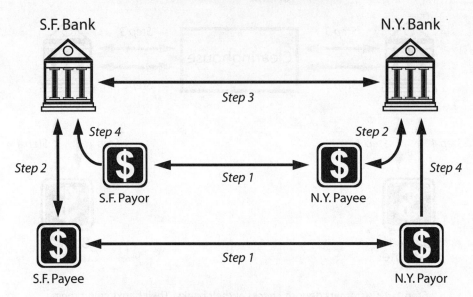

Step 1   Payees provide goods and services to payors. Payors give checks to
          payees. Because the process proceeds simultaneously on checks in
          each city, it can apply when a New York payor sends a check to a San
          Francisco payee and also when a San Francisco payor sends a check
          to a New York payee.

Step 2   Payees deposit checks (one in San Francisco and one in New York).
          Their banks credit their accounts.

Step 3   Each bank sends to the other the checks the first bank has received
          that are drawn on the other. Specifically, the San Francisco bank
          sends to New York the checks that the San Francisco bank has
          received that are drawn on the New York bank; the New York bank
          sends to San Francisco the checks that the New York bank has
          received that are drawn on the San Francisco bank. Funds are
          transferred to settle the difference in amount.

Step 4   Both banks remove funds from the payors' accounts: the San
          Francisco bank from its customers and the New York bank from its
          customers.

large canvas bags. At the other end, CitiBank does the same thing in New York
and sends a similar set of bags flying west to Wells Fargo in San Francisco.
Operating (as above) on the assumption that all checks will be honored, the
banks would transfer funds between themselves to settle the net difference
between the checks sent between the two banks. Each bank then removes
from its customers' accounts funds equal to the amounts of the checks they
have received for payment from those accounts. Figure 26.3 illustrates this
process.

Figure 26.4
Federal-Reserve Collection

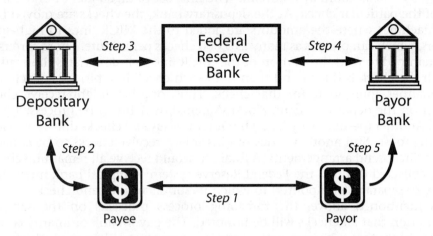

Step 1   Payee provides goods and services to payors; payor gives check to payee.

Step 2   Payee deposits check. Depositary bank credits payee's account.

Step 3   Depositary bank sends check to the Federal Reserve bank. The Federal Reserve Bank credits the depositary bank for the check.

Step 4   The Federal Reserve bank sends the check to the payor bank and debits it for the check.

Step 5   The payor bank debits the payor for the check.

c.   *Federal-Reserve Collection*

Finally, for checks that can be cleared neither through the clearinghouse nor through a direct-send arrangement, the depositary bank can rely upon the services of the Federal Reserve. Hence, the remaining checks generally are sent to the local Federal Reserve bank for processing. The Federal Reserve bank forwards the checks to the payor bank directly (if the payor bank is in the same region) or indirectly through a remote Federal Reserve bank (if the payor bank is in a different Federal Reserve region). Figure 26.4 illustrates this process.

The process of sorting the checks and delivering them to the appropriate collection points is already highly mechanized. In a typical process, the depositary bank transports checks from all points of deposit (that is, all branches and all ATMs) to a single operations center. At the operations center, the checks are run one by one through feeders that present each check to a keyboard operator. The operator determines the amount of the check and types that amount in magnetic ink onto the right-hand side of the bottom of the check, just to the right of the line of magnetic characters that appear on the check at the time of issue.

The preprinted portion of the "MICR" line (pronounced "miker" to rhyme with "biker") includes three series of digits. The first series of nine digits is a routing number assigned by the American Bankers Association, which identifies the specific bank on which the check is drawn. The second series of digits identifies a specific account at that bank. The final set of digits identifies the number of the particular check. At the depository bank, the checks are moved from the machines where the amounts are added to the MICR lines to high-speed sorters, which can process as many as 1,000 checks per minute. Those sorters are programmed to read the portion of the MICR line that designates the bank on which the check is drawn and then send each check to a bin for collection in the manner appropriate for that check. Thus, one bin might receive checks drawn on the depository bank ("on-us" items), which can be processed internally. Another (perhaps very large) bin might receive all checks drawn on a local clearinghouse. Still another series of bins might receive checks to be collected under direct-send arrangements. A final bin would receive all remaining checks, to be collected through the Federal Reserve system. A typical bank might have about 20 separate "end points" to which its sorters would send checks.

As mentioned above, the foregoing process proceeds on the sanguine assumption that all checks will be honored. The payor bank ordinarily collects all the checks that it honors, sorts them by account, and then mails them to its customers each month with their monthly statements. Of course, a significant number of checks are not paid, but instead are dishonored. If a payor bank decides to dishonor a check, it returns the check through the system, normally using the same route by which the check was sent to it. For example, a check received from a clearinghouse normally would be returned to the clearinghouse the next day; the payor bank would receive a credit for the check when it sent the check to the clearinghouse. The clearinghouse then would return the check to the depository bank; the clearinghouse would charge the depository bank for the check. The depository bank then would have an opportunity to charge the depositing customer for the bounced check.

B.   Allocation of Loss in the Checking System

To understand the way check processing works in practice, it also is necessary to understand the rules that allocate losses from the fraud and error that inevitably plague the relatively insecure paper-based checking system. Those rules appear in Articles 3 and 4 of the Uniform Commercial Code. Scattered through those two articles, the system has two sets of rules: the first set consists of three general rules of liability to deal with the three principal events that can interfere with the proper collection of a check, the second set is a series of special rules that apply when one party has acted in some particular way condemned by the statute.

1.   The General Rules

First, if a payor bank pays a check that in fact is not authorized (because the purported drawer did not in fact sign the check), the payor bank bears that loss except in the rare case in which it can locate the malefactor. The general premise of the rule is that the payor bank is charged with the duty of recognizing the signature of its customer (the purported drawer) or otherwise verifying the validity of the item. If the purported drawer in fact has not authorized the check, the payor bank cannot charge the drawer's account for the check and it cannot recover from other innocent parties that took the check from the malefactor or participated in the process of collecting the check. UCC §§4-208 and 4-401.

Second, if a payor bank pays a check that is in fact authorized, but pays it to the wrong party (ordinarily because the check has been stolen at some point between the time it was written and the time it is presented to the payor bank), the payor bank cannot charge the account of the drawer. Instead, it can recover from any party that participated in the course of collection after the theft: the malefactor that stole the check, any party that took the check from the malefactor, the bank into which the check was deposited, and any other bank that participated in the collection of the check. The general intent of those rules is to leave the loss on the party that dealt with the malefactor. UCC §§4-208 and 4-401.

Finally, if the payor bank declines to pay a check, the party holding the check has no rights against the payor bank. Rather, its remedy is against the party from whom it took the check (assuming that the party that has the check is no longer the original payee) or against the original drawer of the check. UCC §§3-408, 3-414, 3-415.

2.   Special Liability Rules (Negligence and the Like)

The rules discussed above are general principles, which apply without regard to the circumstances of any particular situation. Thus, those rules allocate losses in the cases where all of the responsible parties are innocent, victimized by an absent (or insolvent) wrongdoer. Often, however, one of the responsible parties will have been negligent. Article 3 includes a general rule that makes a party whose negligence contributes to a forged signature or indorsement on a check responsible for losses caused by the forgery. UCC §3-406. It also includes a number of specific applications of that principle, which hold particular parties responsible (without the need to prove negligence) in situations where they were in a position to prevent particular losses. Under those rules, a party tricked into giving an instrument to an impostor cannot complain about the actions of the impostor (UCC §3-404), an employer cannot complain about certain actions by its responsible employees (UCC §3-405), and customers cannot complain about losses attributable to their failure to review their bank statements in a timely manner (UCC §4-406). Under each of those provisions, proof of negligence by both the bank and the customer leads to a comparative-negligence regime, in which losses are allocated based on the relative fault. See UCC §§3-404(d), 3-405(b), 3-406(b), 4-406(e).

C.   Payor-Bank Truncation

From the perspective of the banking industry, the process of transporting and sorting checks and delivering them to their customers each month is a wasteful expenditure of resources. Thus, the banking industry for decades has tried to develop procedures that limit its need to transport checks and return them to those who wrote them. Those procedures generally are designed to "truncate" the check-transportation process and thus customarily are referred to as check truncation.

The simplest way in which truncation can occur is at the payor bank: When the checks reach the payor bank, the bank does not sort the checks and return them to its customers. Instead, it retains the checks (or destroys them) and provides the customer a statement that either includes images of the items or describes the items in some detail. Unfortunately for banks, consumer advocates have interposed trenchant objections to all efforts by banks to implement check truncation. Those objections rest on the perception by consumer advocates that it is important to consumers that their checks are returned to them. The idea is that consumers need to receive the actual checks both to assess the propriety of charges to their accounts and to prove payment of the items for which the checks were written. That attitude is particularly ironic given the history of the process: Banks originally began returning checks to their customers to avoid the costs of internal storage of the items. Therefore, what started as a convenience to the banks has now become a burdensome obligation for banks and a coveted privilege of accountholders.

The legal status of payor-bank truncation differs from state to state and at the same time is in flux. Forty-eight states have adopted the version of UCC §4-406(a) included in the 1990 revisions to Article 4. That provision describes the items a bank must provide in periodic statements it sends to consumers:

> [The] bank . . . shall either return or make available to the customer the items paid or provide information in the statement of account sufficient to allow the customer reasonably to identify the items paid. The statement of account provides sufficient information if the item is described by item number, amount, and date of payment.

Because that provision permits the bank to provide *either* the items *or* the requisite information, it fully authorizes payor-bank truncation. Hence, that provision authorizes payor-bank truncation in all of the states except for New York and South Carolina (the two states that have not adopted the 1990 version of UCC Article 4), at least if the bank provides a statement that includes the three items required by the safe harbor included in the last sentence of the provision.

As a practical matter, that provision has led to truncation for a large share of bank customers in this country. Consumer advocates have criticized not only the general process of truncation, but also the specific method permitted by the statute. For example, one complaint is that the information required by UCC §4-406 does not include the identity of the payee of the check (information that consumers ordinarily receive on credit-card

Figure 26.5
MICR Line

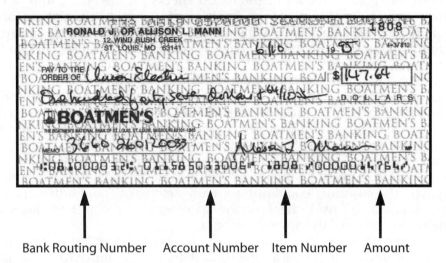

Bank Routing Number   Account Number   Item Number   Amount

statements). The reason for the limited information permitted by the safe harbor is that banks rely on the MICR line for the information they put in bank statements. The MICR line of a processed check — designed for easy reading by automated machines — includes all of the information required by the safe harbor. (See Figure 26.5.) Hence, banks can use automated processing to produce statements including the safe-harbor information. A requirement that payor banks include the name of the payee in statements sent to their customers would require a more costly process of item-by-item examination to determine the name of the payee from a line on the check that commonly is handwritten (perhaps illegibly).

As noted, New York and South Carolina have not adopted the 1990 version of Article 4. The dissatisfaction of consumer advocates with the limited-information statements that the provision permits is one of the principal reasons for New York's unwillingness to adopt that statute.

The banking industry has been critical of that argument, on the theory that the potential harm to consumers is quite limited and certainly insubstantial when compared to the cost of paper-based processing. For one thing, the absence of information from bank statements permitted by Section 4-406(a) is not likely to seriously prejudice consumers attempting to review their bank statements, at least with respect to their relationship with their bank. The main legal consequence to a consumer of receiving a bank statement is that Section 4-406(d) punishes consumers that fail to detect unauthorized charges to their accounts by limiting their ability to complain about those charges if they do not promptly notify their bank after the bank sends the relevant statement. But that provision applies only if the customer "should reasonably have discovered the unauthorized payment" based on the information that the bank chooses to include in the statement, Section 4-406(c).

If the unauthorized payment results from a wholly unauthorized check, consumers should be able to identify the unauthorized payment by noticing that a check was charged to their account that they had never written.

Information identifying the payee ordinarily should not be necessary for a consumer to notice that type of problem. See UCC §4-406 comment 1 ("If the customer made a record of the issued checks on the check stub or carbonized copies furnished by the bank in the checkbook, the customer should usually be able to verify the paid items shown on the statement of account and discover any unauthorized . . . checks."). On the other hand, if the unauthorized payment resulted from the theft of a check the consumer wrote, the absence of payee information would make it difficult for the customer to discover the theft by review of the statement. Thus, a bank that sends a statement that does not include the items (or identify the payee) could not plausibly claim that the customer "should reasonably have discovered the unauthorized payment," Section 4-406(c). Hence, truncating payor banks often would end up bearing losses from such problems. See UCC §4-406 comment 1 ("[I]f a check is altered by changing the name of the payee, the customer could not normally detect the fraud unless the customer is given the paid check or the statement of account discloses the name of the payee of the altered check.").

Consumer advocates also express concerns about the ability of consumers that do not receive checks with their bank statements to prove that they have made the payments in question. That problem is difficult to resolve because it is more practical than legal. There is no general legal rule that requires a person to present an original check to prove that a payment has been made. There does, however, appear to be a cultural practice in some parts of our society (or, at least, a perception of such a practice) that treats the ability to display a cancelled check as the most persuasive method of proving that a payment has been made. To the extent such a practice exists, bank statements that do not return paid items to consumers cause problems for the consumers that receive them.

Because of the large cost savings available to banks that do not have to return paid items with the statements that they send to their customers, recent years have seen continuing efforts to reach a compromise acceptable to all parties that would allow banks to proceed with summary item-less statements. Those efforts include both continuing progress toward agreement on a revised version of Section 4-406 that could be adopted by New York and, more broadly, a failed attempt by NCCUSL and the ALI to produce a revised version of Section 4-406 that would respond to those concerns in a way that could be adopted uniformly throughout the country. Three types of provisions are typical of those efforts at compromise.

First, responding to the problems discussed above with statements that do not identify the payee, reformers in New York have proposed a rule to enhance the protection for consumers that receive safe-harbor statements without payee information. Under that rule, those consumers would be precluded from complaining about a payment based on the alteration of the payee's name only if the consumer had actual knowledge of the unauthorized payment. That knowledge could come, for example, from a complaint of the intended payee about the failure of payment. That rule differs from the current UCC rule discussed above, because under the current UCC rule customers are responsible if they reasonably should have discovered the unauthorized payment, even if they in fact did not discover it. Thus, the revision would help to diminish concerns that consumers receiving summary statements would be held responsible for losses related to stolen items.

The second set of provisions addresses the proof-of-payment concern directly, by adding specific statutory reassurance regarding the ability of consumers to prove payment. For example, the Drafting Committee that recently proposed amendments to Article 4 gave serious attention to a provision stating that any image a customer receives with its statement should have the same value in proving payment as the item itself. Because the need for the actual items comes not from any legal rule but rather from a practical view that the actual item is the most reliable form of proof, it was not clear that such a provision would have any significant effect on the problem. Indeed, the acceptance of such images is likely to turn less on any formal legal "blessing" of the validity of such images than on such practical considerations as whether banks deliver the images in a form that makes them appear more official — printing them on thicker document-style paper, for example. On that point, reports of a Federal Reserve truncation pilot project in Montana suggest that efforts to give the images a more official appearance substantially enhance customer satisfaction with the images as a substitute for the originals. Similarly, customers surely will be more receptive to images when it becomes common practice for the image to include both sides of the check (instead of the front only, as is the general practice currently). In any event, the drive to prepare a new version of Section 4-406 failed because of industry opposition to any alterations of Section 4-406.

Finally, various states (including California, Colorado, and Texas) have adopted statutes that obligate banks that do not provide items with the statements to provide a small number of items to their customers free of charge. Massachusetts goes even further, requiring the bank to return any original check on request without charge. Those provisions attempt to mitigate consumer concerns by making it practical for them to obtain copies when they want them.

D. Depository-Bank Truncation and the Check 21 Act

A more significant step toward truncation is the effort to develop systems for truncating check processing at the depositary bank. The depositary bank retains the check (or an image of the check) in storage and collects the check by sending (presenting) electronic information to the payor bank. Hence, the process often is called electronic check presentment (ECP). Because imaging technology remains relatively expensive, that process currently tends to rely on the information from the MICR line of the check, which depositary banks easily can capture and transmit to payor banks. In those systems as they currently operate, the depositary bank often must forward the actual check later by conventional methods; the principal benefit of ECP is that it gets the information to the payor bank sooner, which provides the depositary bank substantial protection against fraud losses.

To obtain the cost savings of truncation, banks must develop arrangements in which they do not forward the paper check, but instead send only the MICR-line information or an image of the check. In those more advanced arrangements, the check can be retained in storage at the depositary bank; the check itself is never sent to the payor bank and is destroyed in due course (usually in about 90 days). Then, the payor bank can rely on the MICR-line information or the image of the check itself to determine whether it will honor the check.

Although systems for ECP are growing rapidly, they still control a relatively small portion of the check market, perhaps one-tenth of the volume in the United States. The immense size of that market, however, makes even a small share quite significant (about 6 billion checks in 1999). And the share seems to be growing rapidly.

The biggest problem in getting check-truncation systems into place arises from this country's highly dispersed check-collection system. If our country had a single entity on which all checks were drawn, electronic processing could be implemented easily enough, whenever that bank chose to accept electronic information in lieu of the paper checks. As it happens, however, checks are drawn on literally thousands of banks. No single payor bank can implement a full system for electronic processing of checks that its customers deposit until each and every one of the thousands of payor banks is in a position to accept and process electronic information. In a country with so many payor banks, that cannot happen until there is considerable standardization of the technology for processing checks electronically.

Another problem is the continuing reluctance of the users of the system (those that write and receive checks) to rely on entirely electronic information. Thus, people who write checks still have a significant desire for a paper document to evidence the transaction. Similarly, people who receive checks that are dishonored will need some paper document to evidence the check that has failed to clear. Such documents are unlikely to be necessary in the great majority of cases; far more than 99 percent of checks clear when first presented, and it seems unlikely that creditors disavow their receipt of payment in any significant percentage of checking transactions. Thus, because one of the major goals of truncation is to eliminate the costs of transporting the original paper from place to place, it would be ideal if the users of the system would accept an image as a substitute for the original check.

One final complicating factor is the likelihood — at least in the short run — that despite the best efforts of system designers and statutory drafters, consumer advocates will be unsatisfied with substitute checks and will insist upon provisions for the return of the original checks. Obviously, it would be a relatively expensive proposition for banks to retain the original checks and to locate, retrieve, and deliver the original on demand. Still, at least in the short run there are plausible reasons why consumers might want the original checks. For example, in a dispute about the authenticity of a check, examination of the original might provide information about the signature (the traces of the actual physical impression made at the time of signing) that currently is not included in the image or the substitute check.

In an attempt to facilitate check truncation, the Board of Governors of the Federal Reserve sponsored legislation that resulted in the Check Clearing in the 21st Century Act of 2003 (commonly known as Check 21), enacted in October of 2003 with an effective date of October 2004, 12 U.S.C. §§5001-5018. The most important thing to understand about Check 21 is its limited scope. The purpose of the statute is to make a "substitute check" the legal equivalent of the original check. Check 21 does not authorize electronic check processing: A bank can collect or present an electronic check only by means of a contractual agreement with the bank to which the check

Figure 26.6
Check Processing Under Check 21

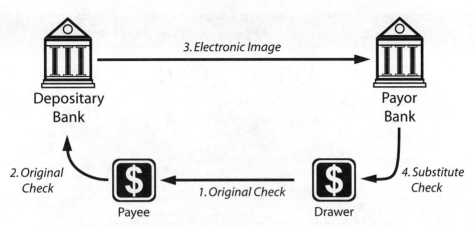

is being transferred or presented. Similarly, because Check 21 does not require banks to accept electronic images, it imposes no obligations on those that create them. Nor does Check 21 even alter whatever rights customers currently have to the return of their original checks. Rather, all of the provisions of the Act relate to the intermediate practical questions described above: facilitating truncation by depositary banks through the creation of reliable mechanisms for making an acceptable substitute of the original check in the few cases in which a substitute is necessary. Thus, the process contemplated by Check 21 is that banks will agree among themselves to present and accept electronic images of checks; the statute will facilitate the reconversion of those images to paper documents. Figure 26.6 illustrates that process.

The centerpiece of the statute is the concept of the substitute check, defined in §3(16) as follows:

The term "substitute check" means a paper reproduction of the original check that—

   (A) contains an image of the front and back of the original check;

   (B) bears a MICR line containing all the information appearing on the MICR line of the original check, except as provided under generally applicable industry standards for substitute checks to facilitate the processing of substitute checks;

   (C) conforms, in paper stock, dimension, and otherwise, with generally applicable industry standards for substitute checks; and

   (D) is suitable for automated processing in the same manner as the original check.

Among other things, that provision makes it clear that a typical American-Express style "image statement" — reduced photocopies of checks sent perhaps six to the page — will *not* qualify as a substitute check. Rather, the document will need to include a MICR line and otherwise be of a size and texture suitable for automated processing. To give that definition some content, consider Figure 26.7, which shows the current ANSI standard for what such a document would look like.

Figure 26.7
Substitute Check

To help foster public acceptance, the statute requires that banks provide customers with a plain-English statement — evident in Figure 26.7 — that states: "This is a legal copy of your check. You can use it the same way you would use the original check." If a substitute check includes that legend and accurately represents the information on the original check, it is the legal equivalent of the check for all purposes. Check 21 §4(b). Similarly, although the statute does nothing directly to authorize the processing of electronic checks, it does provide that a person can deposit, present, or send a substitute check without consent of the party to whom it is sent. Check 21 §4(a).

To implement those rules, Check 21 creates a new series of warranties and indemnities. Those rules generally deal with three problems. The first is the problem that the image might not accurately reflect the original check. On that point, Section 5(1) obligates the reconverting bank to warrant that the substitute check meets the requirements for legal equivalence in Section 4(b) — which means, among other things, that the reconverting bank must warrant that the substitute check (made from an image that the reconverting bank has received from the converting bank) accurately represents the check still in the possession of the converting bank.

The second is the problem that despite the presentment of a check electronically the original paper check somehow might find its way into the check-collection process and be presented for payment in the future. To avoid losses from that scenario, the reconverting bank must warrant that no party will be called upon to pay either the original item or a subsequent substitute check made from that item. Check 21 §5(2).

The third problem is that the substitute check in some way might be an inadequate substitute for the original check. On that point, Section 6 obligates the reconverting bank and subsequent banks that process the substitute check to indemnify parties that suffer a loss because of the receipt of a substitute check instead of the original. If the substitute check complied with the statute, the indemnity is limited to the amount of the check, plus interest and expenses. Check 21 §6(b). If the check did *not* comply with the statute, the reconverting bank is liable for the entire loss proximately caused by the breach. Check 21 §6(b). To make it clear that banks can protect themselves by providing the original when it is necessary, liability on that indemnity is limited to losses that are incurred before the original check (or a copy that remedies a defect in the substitute check) is provided. Check 21 §6(d).

Finally, the most controversial provision of the statute is an expedited recredit right for consumers, set forth in Check 21 §7. Under that provision, a consumer can claim a recredit if the consumer asserts that an item is not properly payable or that there has been a breach of one of the warranties in Section 5. Check 21 §7(1). The consumer must make the claim within 40 days of the date that the bank has delivered to the customer the substitute check and the relevant bank statement. Check 21 §7(2). The bank then must provide the recredit if it cannot "demonstrate[e] to the consumer that the substitute check was properly charged to the consumer account." Check 21 §7(c)(1). The recredit must be made no later than the end of the business day following the business day on which the bank determines the claim is valid. Check 21 §7(c)(2). Pending investigation, the recredit must be made before the end of the tenth business day after the submission of the claim. (If the item is for more than $2,500, the bank can delay recrediting the excess over $2,500 until the forty-fifth calendar day after the claim.) To protect the payor bank responding to such a claim, Section 8 includes a parallel expedited recredit right that permits the payor bank to recover funds from the bank from which it received the item in question.

Problem Set 26

26.1. One Friday afternoon your client Bertie Wooster comes to see you. He tells you that he has a dispute with Roderick Spode regarding an antique silver cow creamer that Bertie recently purchased for $18,000. Bertie explains that he bought the item based on an Internet ad and mailed Spode a check as soon as he received the creamer. Spode has been hounding Bertie, claiming that Bertie has never paid for the item.

Bertie is certain that he did, both because he remembers mailing the check and, more importantly, because he received an image of the original check with his statement this month. (Bertie receives "image statements" that have a photocopy of the front of six checks on each page.) The image shows a signature on the back that appears to be the grandiose signature of Roderick Spode (with which Bertie is familiar). Bertie faxed the image to Spode, who claims that it is a forgery, that he never received the check, and that he will sue Bertie immediately if Bertie does not pay. "If you really paid, then you should be able to show me an original cancelled check," Spode says. At his wit's end, Bertie is worried that a suit against Spode would harm his reputation in the antiques industry, making it hard for him to acquire future items. But he can't believe he should have to pay twice. What do you advise?

26.2. If the facts of Problem 26.1 eventually lead to a point where Bertie needs the original check, must his bank provide it to him? What if it is willing to provide the original check, but will charge $10 to do so? UCC §4-406(b) and comments 1 and 3.

26.3. Same facts as in Problem 26.2, but now assume that the image was a substitute check that complied with Check 21.

(a) Does that impose any new obligations on his bank? Check 21 §7.

(b) What if Bertie claims that pen-impression data (expert evidence about the way in which the pen was pressed onto the paper) could have proven that Spode in fact signed the check, and that he cannot obtain that evidence because the substitute check does not include that data and the original has been destroyed? Check 21 §6.

26.4. The next morning your old friend Carl Eben comes to see you. He has just discovered that a thief has been stealing money from him for several months. The thief has been stealing from Carl's mailbox on a regular basis and managed to steal an incoming package with some blank checks as well as several outgoing envelopes with payments to Carl's suppliers. The thief then wrote several checks payable to himself, which he cashed. On the checks to Carl's suppliers, he forged the name of the suppliers and then cashed the checks. Carl discovered the problem when a number of suppliers complained about his late payments.

When you asked Carl why he did not notice this on his bank statement, he admitted that he has been very busy lately and has simply failed to reconcile his bank statement for the last six months. Carl's bank admits that Carl ordinarily would not be responsible for any of the checks cashed by the thief. (Carl says that the officer said something about the checks not being "properly payable" under UCC §4-401.) The bank has, however, told Carl that Carl is liable for all of the unauthorized checks because of his failure to notify the bank about the problems when they sent him statements showing the charges for the forged checks. Carl has brought the statements with him. They are summary statements that show only the item number, amount, and date of payment. Is the bank right? UCC §4-406(a), (c), (d), and comment 1.

26.5. Thursday morning you come into the office to find your old friend from college Mike McLaughlin waiting for you. Mike operates a computer services business. He wants to talk to you about a check for $20,000 that he recently received from one of his customers in payment of an invoice. When he deposited the check, it bounced. His bank did not, however, return the original check to him. Instead, it returned the image. He wants to know if this will hinder him in trying to collect the funds from the customer. (You should assume for purposes of the question that Mike would have been a person entitled to enforce the check if the check had been returned to him. The issue on which you should focus is whether he will be hindered by having an image of the check instead of the original.)

(a) What if the image is a simple photocopy? UCC §§1-201(20), 3-104(f), 3-301, 3-309, 3-310(b)(1), and 3-414(b).

(b) What if the image is a substitute check that complies with Check 21? Check 21 §4(b).

(c) What if the image is a substitute check that complies with Check 21 except that it omits the legend? In answering that question, assume that the check was reconverted by Mike's bank and that it inadvertently omitted the legend. Check 21 Act §§4(b), 5, and 7; Proposed Regulation CC 12 C.F.R. 229.2(bbb).

26.6. Stacy Vye (a longtime client and banker at Wessex Bank) comes to you for advice. She is about to enter into a major electronic-check presentation agreement with Wells Fargo, in which she agrees to accept electronic images from Wells Fargo in lieu of original checks. Can you think of any particular provisions she might need to include in such an agreement to protect herself from liability under Check 21? Check 21 §§5, 6, and 7.

26.7. A few months later, Stacy calls you back. She has had major difficulties with recredit claims under the statute. Apparently, a small but determined number of people are submitting large numbers of fraudulent claims. When she provides the recredited funds, the people remove it from their accounts. When Stacy is unable to recover the funds from the bank from which she received the item, she discovers that the customer and the funds are gone. Does Check 21 provide any help for her? Does it protect her adequately? Check 21 §7(d)(2).

Assignment 27: Electronic Checks and ACH Transfers

The previous assignment discusses ways in which electronic technology enhances the processing of paper checks. This assignment takes that topic to the next level, discussing the possibility of "true" electronic checks — paperless instructions processed through the checking system — and then the development of electronic transfers to and from bank accounts through the ACH system.

A. True Electronic Checks

The ultimate goal of technologists in this context is a product that has not yet come into existence: a true electronic check that would clear through the same processes as paper checks but work and move without the need for a paper check. If such a product was able to retain many of the features that make paper checks so attractive to consumers, that product could be quite successful. The great virtue of checks is that they are (at least in the United States) as close as we can get to a functionally universal person-to-person payment system. Unlike credit cards and most other competing payment systems, a check can be given to anybody. To send the check, you need know only the address to which you wish to send the check (mailing address for paper check; e-mail address for electronic check). To collect the check, the person who receives it need only have a bank account: They do not have to be a merchant approved by a credit-card network, or a member of the ACH network or some other collection system. To be sure, quite a number of people do not have bank accounts, which makes it somewhat harder to collect a check, particularly if it is written by an individual rather than a business. (Check-cashing services may be reluctant to pay for a non-business check.) But the key point is that checks are much more universal than their competitors. Credit-card payments, for example, can be made only to merchants who have contracts with members of the applicable credit-card network.

It also is significant, especially to lawyers, that the checking system comes with a full range of legal rules that provide the consumer considerable protection against fraud and negligent conduct by other parties to the transaction. There is no similar framework in the new and developing systems. And last, but certainly not least, the checking system is relatively inexpensive for both the payor and the payee. Indeed, because consumer accounts normally do not impose per-check fees, the actual costs are relatively obscure, because they appear in the lower-than-normal (or nonexistent) interest rates that banks pay customers for the funds the customers have on deposit. The indirect nature of those charges may make the system appear totally free to the user. Thus, despite the inefficiencies of the paper-based collection process, consumers have a strong preference for the check system. An electronic system that can replicate those features has a good chance of being successful with consumers.

The closest thing to such a product to date was the patented eCheck™ developed by the Financial Services Technology Consortium (FSTC), a group of large American banks. From the perspective of the payor and the payee, that product was designed to work much like the ACH checks described above. The payor would "write" the eCheck on a software product that displayed an image of a check with blanks for the information customarily written on a check. The payor then would deliver the eCheck to the payee (perhaps by e-mail). The payee then could deposit the eCheck with its bank. As originally designed, the depository bank would have cleared the check in the same way that it would clear an ordinary check. The advantage, however, is that it was expected that the paperless process would be considerably less expensive for the banks and at the same time much faster.

That process could have had a number of other operational benefits. Most obviously, designers hoped that the process would increase the speed with which funds were made available to the payee and thus aid substantially in limiting losses from fraud in check transactions. More directly, because the ability to issue eChecks would be PIN-protected (like debit cards), the opportunities for fraudulent issuance would have been reduced quite significantly. Also, the potential for fraud based on interception and alteration would have been significantly lower than it is for conventional checks. Given the roughly $15 billion of check fraud per year (about 70 cents per $100), there is a lot of room for value to be gained by reduction in fraud losses.

In practice, however, the "true" electronic check seems to have been overtaken by the rapid success of the ACH products discussed below. One obvious reason for that success lies in the product's use of the traditional check-clearing system. An electronic check designed to clear through the ordinary check-clearing system must face the problem that the rules for check collection — which provide clear legal relations among all parties to a check-payment transactions — are limited to instruments that qualify as a "check" as defined in UCC §3-104(f), which includes only "a draft . . . drawn on a bank." Under UCC §3-104 (e), an instrument can be a draft only if it is an "order" for purposes of UCC §3-103(a)(6). And under that provision, an order must be "a written instruction." Thus, under current law, the eCheck cannot be governed by Article 4. That continues to be true notwithstanding the series of recent enactments generally tolerating electronic records as substitutes for paper documents. For example, although UETA generally validates electronic records as substitutes for paper documents, it specifically excludes issues related to UCC Articles 3 and 4. See UETA §3(b)(2). The federal E-SIGN Act includes a similar exception for Articles 3 and 4. See E-SIGN §103(a)(3).

To be sure, banks that decide to offer the eCheck product to their customers and that accept eChecks for deposit by their customers can agree that the transactions will be governed by Article 4. And they can even cause their customers to sign account agreements providing for treatment as if the transactions were governed by Article 4. But if the instruments are to be as flexible as checks, then they will come into the control of parties other than those that have dealt directly with the banks. For example, a payee whose bank does not accept such checks might receive one and assign it to a friend who can deposit it at her bank, just as a consumer might indorse a check to a friend. In that case, the payee would not have entered into any agreement regarding UCC coverage, so the Article 4 rules would not govern the rights of the payee.

It appears that the basic problem of UCC coverage is a sufficiently serious obstacle that the product will not be broadly introduced until the UCC can be generally amended to provide for Article 4 coverage of electronic checks. The Drafting Committee that recently promulgated amendments to Articles 3 and 4 considered, but declined to adopt, provisions that would have facilitated electronic checks. Thus, it seems unlikely that any such amendments will be generally promulgated and adopted in the foreseeable future.

Even if the laws are revised to support electronic checks, it is difficult to predict whether they would succeed. The electronic check would have to overcome numerous obstacles: getting the appropriate software and hardware into the hands of consumers; making the software sufficiently simple that the computers of ordinary people can run it without crashing or slowing to a crawl; making the system sufficiently simple and fast that consumers will use it; and, finally, convincing consumers that it is worth their effort to consider using the system at all. As you will see in the pages that follow, ACH transfers and newer P2P systems already may be providing much of the functionality that a hypothetical electronic check would have provided.

B.   ACH Transfers

1.   The Basics of ACH Transfers

To put the developments discussed above in context, it is important to recognize that banks have been making electronic transfers to and from consumer accounts for years. With respect to commercial accounts, those transfers normally are made through specialized systems covered by Article 4A, and not discussed in this course. See UCC §4A-108 and comment (explaining that Article 4A does not apply to transactions that involve transfers to consumer accounts). With respect to consumer accounts, those payments frequently are made through a separate network, known as the Automated Clearing House (ACH) network. Although the ACH payment is not a widely known device, it is in fact quite common. During 2003, for example, the ACH network cleared 10 billion payments worth a total of about $27 trillion. (ACH transactions closely resemble the bank transfers and "giro" transactions that are common in Japan and those parts of Europe where checks are used less frequently than they are here.)

The ACH network is a nationwide computerized counterpart to the checking system, parallel to (but separate from) the networks used for transactions on credit cards or on debit (and ATM) cards. The network is used for electronic transfers between accounts at American financial institutions — most commonly for automated deposits of salaries and for automated payments of recurring bills (mortgages, car payments, and the like).

The network generally is governed by the Operating Rules issued by NACHA (formerly known as the National Automated Clearing House Association), a not-for-profit association of 36 regional clearinghouse associations. Those associations, in turn, are composed of the roughly 13,000 depositary institutions that participate in the network. The network also is closely associated with the Federal Reserve system, if only because (as described in more detail below) ACH payments generally are cleared through accounts at Federal Reserve banks and because communications to make payments on the ACH network are made over the communication system of the Federal Reserve. The financial institutions that participate in the network agree to those rules as a condition of their ability to send or receive entries on that network.

The other important source of law is the Electronic Fund Transfers Act (commonly known as the EFTA). Because the EFTA is codified as Title IX of the Consumer Credit Protection Act, 15 U.S.C. §1693-1693r, it typically is referred to by the section numbers of the Consumer Credit Protection Act (§§902 through 920). The EFTA is supplemented and explained in important ways by Regulation E (12 CFR Part 205), which the Federal Reserve has promulgated pursuant to its authority to administer and interpret the EFTA.

The statute generally applies to "electronic fund transfers," which EFTA §903(6) defines to mean "any transfer of funds, other than a transaction originated by check, . . . which is initiated through an electronic terminal, telephonic instrument, or computer so as to order, instruct, or authorize a financial institution to debit or credit an account." Because all ACH transfers involve such a transfer, all ACH transfers are covered by the EFTA.

When the EFTA applies, it provides a variety of protections for consumers. First, it requires the merchant to provide a written receipt for each transaction (presumably satisfied here by the check the merchant hands back to the customer). EFTA §906(a); Regulation E §205.9. More importantly, as discussed in more detail below, the EFTA provides strong protection against unauthorized transactions.

The EFTA also includes a mandatory dispute-resolution mechanism. If a consumer notifies the bank that the consumer believes that the bank has charged an account for a transaction that the consumer did not authorize, the bank must within 10 business days either recredit the consumer's account or investigate the alleged error and provide the customer a written explanation of the results of that investigation. EFTA §909(a); Regulation E §205.11.

One last benefit of EFTA coverage is that the bank statement that the customer receives must identify the party to whom funds are paid. EFTA §906(c); Regulation E §205.9(b)(1)(v). As explained in the previous assignment, consumer advocates value that information highly, but banks are not obligated to provide it in conventional check transactions (if they do not return the customer's cancelled checks).

To understand how those payments work, four topics are useful points of discussion: the basic terminology of ACH transfers, the mechanics of ACH entries, the various types of ACH entries, and issues related to finality, errors, and fraud.

a. The Basic Terminology

The ACH network is quite flexible, contemplating transactions in which the initial instruction can come either from the payor or from the payee. That instruction — an "entry" in NACHA terminology, NACHA Rules §13.1.20 — can be either a credit entry initiated by the payor (asking the payor's institution to credit the account of the recipient) or a debit entry initiated by the payee (asking the payee's institution to debit the account of the recipient).

In the terminology of the NACHA rules, each ACH transfer involves (at least) five participants, as follows:

- *Originator:* The party that makes the entry (or communication) that initiates the transaction. NACHA Rules §13.1.33. In a credit transfer that is the payor; in a debit transfer that is the payee.
- *Originating Depository Financial Institution (or ODFI):* The financial institution of the Originator. NACHA Rules §13.1.31. Normally this is the location of the account from which payment is to be made in a credit entry, or the account to which payment is to be made in a debit entry.
- *Automated Clearing House Operator or ACH Operator:* The party that carries communications (and funds) from the ODFI to the RDFI (described below). NACHA Rules §13.1.1. Except in the New York Federal Reserve District, this normally is the local Federal Reserve bank. In transfers between different Federal Reserve districts, there will be an Originating ACH Operator (normally the Federal Reserve bank in the district in which the ODFI is located) and a Receiving ACH Operator (normally the Federal Reserve bank in the district in which the RDFI is located).
- *Receiving Depository Financial Institution (or RDFI):* The financial institution of the Recipient. NACHA Rules §13.1.45. Normally this is the location of the account to which payment is to be made in a credit entry, or the account from which payment is to be made in a debit entry.
- *Receiver:* The party to which the entry is directed. NACHA Rules §13.1.43. In a credit transfer, that is the payee; in a debit transfer, that is the payor.

b.   The Mechanics

The ACH network is a computerized alternative to the checking system. Thus, it relies entirely on electronic messages to convey the information that paper checks convey in the conventional checking system. The process of an ACH transfer starts with a message from the Originator to the ODFI. That message — an entry for each transaction — is likely to be sent to the ODFI as part of a large volume of messages (a "batch"), which the ODFI will process in due course. (The use of "batch" processing — as opposed to real-time processing of each transaction that the ODFI creates — is a relic of the relatively primitive state of computer technology at the time the ACH network was designed.) Each entry is in a standardized format that defines the type of entry and includes the specific information necessary for the ODFI to process the particular type of entry. (The next section of this assignment includes more information about the various types of specialized entries that are possible.)

When the ODFI receives a batch of data, it examines the data to ensure that all of the data is in a comprehensible format so that the ODFI can process the requested transactions. It directly processes entries for which it is the RDFI ("on-us" entries). It then merges the remaining valid entries with data from

Figure 27.1
ACH Entries

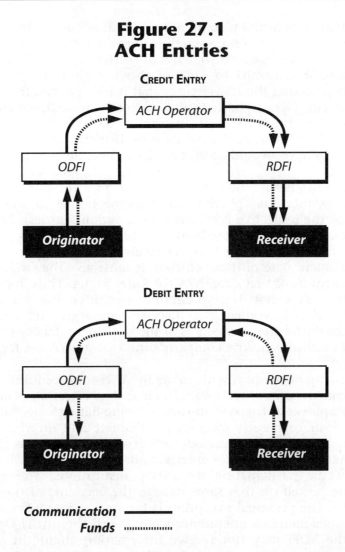

CREDIT ENTRY

DEBIT ENTRY

Communication ─────
Funds ···············

other originators and transmits the data to its ACH Operator. When it transmits the data to the ACH Operator, it binds itself to pay the ACH Operator for all credit transfers included in the data (with the actual funds to be taken from the Federal Reserve account of the ODFI; NACHA Rules §6.2). So, for example, if an employer processed the direct-deposit portion of its payroll through the ACH system, the employer (as Originator) would send a file of credit entries to its bank (the ODFI). That bank would charge the employer's account for the total amount of the payroll, keep data for employees that were its own customers, and send the remaining data on to the local Federal Reserve bank (as the ACH Operator).

The ACH Operator engages in a similar process. It then sorts the transactions by region (to determine the appropriate Receiving ACH Operator). It retains transactions for which it is the Receiving ACH Operator, but transmits to the appropriate entity all transactions from other regions (for which some other entity would be the Receiving ACH Operator). At the same time, it is receiving transactions from other ACH Operators for which it is the

Receiving ACH Operator. It sorts all of those transactions — that is, both the intra-region and inter-region transactions for which it is the Receiving ACH Operator — to produce separate batches of entries for each of the local institutions. Then, it transmits to each of those institutions (the respective RDFIs) a file reflecting the transactions that it has received for that institution. In our employer hypothetical, the Receiving ACH Operator would send back to all of the banks in its district the data for all of the employees that use a bank in the same Federal Reserve district as their employer. Data for remote employees would be sent to the Federal Reserve bank in the relevant district.

Finally, the RDFIs sort the data by account, post the transactions to the respective accounts, and provide the relevant notice to the holders of the accounts (the respective Receivers for the various entries). Thus, continuing our example, each of those banks would credit the employees with the appropriate funds. When the Receiver receives the funds for credit entries (on the settlement date of those entries), it must give the Originator credit for the payment as of that date. NACHA Rules §4.4.4. Thus, for example, if an Originator makes an ACH payment to its electric company to pay its electric bill, the electric company as Receiver must give its customer, the Originator, credit for the payment as of the settlement date of the payment, without regard to the electric company's internal procedures for processing payments.

Because many of the payments made by ACH transfer fulfill obligations to make payments on a specific date (such as the obligation of an employer to pay its employees), the system uses a "value-dating" mechanism. With that mechanism, each entry specifies a settlement date, on which the funds are to be transferred among the relevant accounts. The funds transfers are made on that date through net entries on designated Federal Reserve bank accounts of the participating depository institutions. The entries also normally are posted on that same date to the accounts of the Originator and Receiver. The principal exception is for smaller institutions that have less expeditious methods of communicating with their ACH Operators; in that case the RDFI may not receive information about the transaction in time to credit the account of the Receiver until a few days after the settlement date.

A final question is how far in advance a payment can be entered. Under rules promulgated by the Federal Reserve, a debit entry must be transmitted by the ODFI the day before the settlement date; a credit transaction typically can be transmitted either on the day before the settlement date or two days before the settlement date. That rule has several ramifications. For one thing, it means that financial institutions cannot send entries long periods in advance and expect the receiving ACH Operators and financial institutions to hold onto them and process them on the appropriate day. More importantly, it effectively means that ACH entries cannot (like debit cards) be used to provide immediate payment in retail transactions (which might be desirable for POP or WEB entries, both discussed below), because a transaction will not in any event settle until the business day after the date on which it is transmitted. As NACHA continues in its efforts to make ACH a payment system of general desirability, there may be pressure to move to systems that permit more contemporaneous payment.

c. Types of ACH Entries

Although ACH transfers are used in contexts that involve only businesses, the focus here is on their use for payments to or from consumers. In that context, the typical and most common ACH transfer is a credit entry sending payment from an employer to an employee (a "direct deposit" in common parlance). Probably the second most common ACH transfer is a preauthorized debit entry, in which a consumer agrees that a payee periodically can deduct funds to pay a bill. For example, it is common for mortgage payments to be made by a pre-authorized ACH transaction in which the lender is the Originator and the homeowner is the Receiver.

There also are a variety of specialized types of ACH entries used in particular contexts. Most of these have been created recently, as NACHA struggles to come up with products that allow it to retain (or increase) its market share in a vigorous competition against checks, credit cards, and debit cards. For example, several of the new products are designed to remedy a variety of common problems in the check-collection process. For example, if a check is lost in the course of processing, it often is possible for the depositary bank to collect the check by sending a "destroyed check entry" (an XCK entry in the terminology of the NACHA Rules) to the payor bank. NACHA Rules §§2.7.1 and 13.1.60. Similarly, if a check bounces, a depositary bank that wants to make a second attempt at collection can do so by the expeditious method of submitting an ACH entry called an RCK entry (instead of sending the physical check a second time through the normal channels for check processing). NACHA Rules §§2.8 and 13.1.41 (discussing those entries). You will notice that in the limited context of those problems, the NACHA Rules permit debit entries against consumer accounts without the prior consent of the Receiver. NACHA Rules §2.1.3.

Later sections of this assignment and the one that follows discuss three of the most successful new entries: POP entries (for point-of-purchase check conversion), TEL entries (for telephone transactions), and WEB entries (for Internet transactions).

d. Finality, Error, and Fraud in ACH Transfers

Because ACH transfers are governed by NACHA Rules, the obligations of the parties to those transactions are generally determined by those rules. Given the close parallel between those transactions and payments made by check, you should consider as you study those obligations the extent to which the privately designed NACHA Rules depart from the legislative rules that the UCC establishes for check transactions.

The first topic is finality: the possibility that an entry sent forth by the Originator in fact will not result in payment. With respect to credit entries, finality has two aspects: the point at which the RDFI loses its right to return the item (the analogue to final payment of a check) and the point at which the Originator and ODFI lose their right to retract the item (the analogue to losing the right to stop payment on a check). On the first point, the ACH system (like the checking system) imposes no general substantive constraint on the right of the RDFI to reject any entry. See NACHA Rules §5.1.1 (permitting return "for any reason"). The most important constraint (parallel to the midnight deadline in Article 4) is that the return must be made in time to be received by the ODFI by the opening of business on the second banking day following the settlement date. NACHA Rules §5.1.2; see NACHA Rules §13.1.11 (defining banking day). Thus, if the RDFI wishes to return a credit entry that was to be paid on Wednesday March 31, it must get the return back to the ODFI by Friday April 2. As long as it returns the entry within that time period, it need not have any particular reason for the return.

Of course, it is not as easy to see why an RDFI would reject ACH entries as frequently as payor banks would reject checks drawn on them. For one thing, credit entries are transmissions of funds to the RDFI, not requests that the RDFI disburse funds. Accordingly, the customers of the RDFI have little reason to complain of those entries. Only if the entries are debit entries is there a possibility of rejection for insufficient funds. The rules above permit such a rejection easily. What they do not permit, however — and here they differ, for example, from the credit-card system discussed in the next assignment — is any later rejection for reasons such as dissatisfaction with the underlying performance by the Originator of a debit entry.

From the other side, the ACH system has a much more limited right of retraction and stopping payment than other systems. Specifically, except for the narrow rules discussed below related to errors, neither the Originator nor the ODFI has any right to stop or recall an entry once it has been received by the Originating ACH Operator. NACHA Rules §7.1.

With respect to debit entries, the right to stop payment is much different, generally resembling the rules in Article 4 for stopping payment on checks. Thus, the Receiver of a debit entry can stop payment on the entry by providing notice to the RDFI "at such time and in such manner as to allow the RDFI a reasonable opportunity to act upon the stop payment order before acting on the debit entry." NACHA Rules §7.5; compare UCC §4-403(a) (similar rule for stopping payment on a check). Debit entries against consumer accounts are treated slightly differently. Specifically, although the same rule applies to a variety of specialized debit entries (RCK, PPD, POP, WEB, and TEL entries, all discussed above), a consumer who wants to stop payment on a "normal" entry must provide notice to the RDFI three banking days before the scheduled transfer date. NACHA Rules §7.4. The only substantial right to stop payment is a right granted to a consumer who owns an account against which a debit entry is being made. That consumer can stop payment by providing notice to the RDFI three banking days before the date on which the entry is to be executed against the consumer's account. NACHA Rules §7.4.

Although the NACHA Rules discussed above create a payment that is final in a relatively firm way, they do include a variety of procedures to deal with innocent or fraudulent mistakes in ACH entries. The simplest preventative is a procedure that allows the Originator to test the efficacy of an ACH entry before actually sending the entry. To use that procedure, the Originator sends a "pre-notification" through the ODFI to the RDFI, describing the entries that the Originator plans to initiate with regard to a Receiver's account. After sending a pre-notification, the Originator must wait six banking days before it can initiate entries to the Receiver's account. During that period, the RDFI has an opportunity to transmit a "Notification of Change" (NOC). If the ODFI receives an NOC, it can initiate the entries in question only if it complies with the NOC. NACHA Rules §§2.3 and 5.3.

The NACHA Rules recognize that one of the most typical problems of all electronic systems is the problem of duplicate files or entries — correct transmissions that are sent more than once. The NACHA Rules include specific rules that permit the ODFI to reverse such transactions, whether they are whole files (batches of entries) or individual entries. Under the NACHA Rules, the ODFI can reverse an entire file if it acts within five banking days of the settlement date of the file in question, but no later than 24 hours after discovery of the duplication or other error. NACHA Rules §2.4.2. Any such request obligates the reversing ODFI to indemnify all participating financial institutions and ACH Operators for all losses related to their compliance with either the original or reversing instructions. NACHA Rules §2.4.5.

By contrast, if an Originator wishes to reverse a single entry (rather than an entire file of entries), the Originator must notify the Receiver not later than the settlement date for the entry claimed to be erroneous. NACHA Rules §2.5.1. Thus, the Originator has no general right to retract an entry once the settlement date has passed. Moreover, even if it acts by the settlement date, it must, as in the case of reversing an entire file, provide a broad indemnity to the relevant financial institutions and ACH Operators. NACHA Rules §2.5.2.

The biggest problem for erroneous or fraudulent transmissions is not an erroneous credit entry — in which an Originator mistakenly sends funds to a third party — if only because the party most likely to be inconvenienced is the party that has erroneously sent the transmissions. The more serious problem occurs when a debit entry is sent that withdraws funds from the account of a Receiver that has not authorized such a transaction. In that context, the NACHA Rules grant consumers a specific right to have their account recredited. The Receiver that wants to get the funds back from an allegedly erroneous debit entry must act within 15 calendar days of the date that the RDFI sends a statement showing the debit, and must provide an affidavit "in the form required by the RDFI" declaring that the entry was not in fact authorized. NACHA Rules §§7.6.1 and 7.6.2. When the consumer Receiver complies with those requirements, the RDFI must credit the consumer's account "promptly." NACHA Rules §7.6.1. See also NACHA Rules §§7.6.2 and 7.6.3 (requiring an RDFI to recredit a consumer's account promptly if the RDFI honors an RCK or PPD entry despite a proper stop-payment request from the consumer).

Those rules reflect rules in the EFTA that limit the consumer's responsibility for those transactions. Specifically, the bank normally cannot hold the consumer responsible for more than $50 for any series of unauthorized transactions unless the consumer fails to identify the unauthorized transaction to the bank within 60 days of the relevant monthly statement. EFTA §908(a); Regulation E §205.6. There also is a rule that permits the bank to hold the customer responsible for up to $500 of transactions if the consumer fails to notify the bank within two days after discovering that the consumer has lost the "access device" with which the consumer makes transfers. EFTA §909(a); Regulation E §205.6(b)(2).

2. POS Conversion

As originally designed, ACH transfers were a useful substitute for transactions in which consumers previously might have sent checks through the mail: An

ACH debit entry substitutes for the monthly mortgage check. More recently, NACHA has developed entries that substitute for conventional retail payments. The most successful of those transactions to date is the conversion at the point of sale of a check to an electronic-payment transaction. Confusingly enough, this normally is referred to as a POS conversion, although the NACHA entry is called a POP entry (for point of purchase). Although that transaction in legal contemplation is an electronic funds transfer, it works from the consumer's perspective much like a conventional check transaction. The consumer writes a check and hands it to the retail clerk (at a grocery store, for example). The clerk takes information from the check's MICR line (ordinarily by passing the check through a reader designed to collect that information), marks the check as void, and then hands the check back to the consumer. The merchant then sends that information to its bank, which uses it to process an ACH transaction taking money for the transaction from the consumer's account at its own bank (as illustrated in Figure 27.2). The consumer sees the charge for the check on the consumer's next monthly bank statement. In any event, POS conversion to automated-clearinghouse transactions has been highly successful. In 2003, it was used for more than 200 million checks, with an average amount of about $70.

The most significant concern for consumers in POS conversions relates to the speed of the transactions. Because the transactions are cleared electronically, the funds are likely to be removed from the consumer's account on the next business day if the transaction involves conversion to an ACH transaction. If the consumer had paid with a conventional check, the consumer might have relied on the "float," expecting the check not to clear for a number of days.

For several reasons, that problem probably will not be a major obstacle for POS conversion. First, as a practical matter, consumers at the check-out counter are not likely to object in any significant way to the conversion process based on the speed of clearing: After all, they can't really object if the merchant is simply trying to get paid sooner for goods that the consumer already has taken from the merchant's store. For another thing, although it has not always been true, it now is the case that checks a consumer writes locally are likely to be collected by the next business day anyway. If the great majority of retail checks that consumers write are written to merchants in the same metropolitan area as the consumer's bank, then the substitution of POS conversion for conventional checks will not significantly alter the float available to consumers. More generally, consumers are unlikely to object because they are unlikely to understand the nature of the transaction (i.e., the difference from a conventional check) and the legal rules that govern the transaction.

A similar issue relates to the consumer's right to stop payment. Under UCC Article 4, a check-writer has the right to stop payment by giving notice to the bank on which the check is drawn, if the notice arrives in time to permit the bank on which the check is drawn to refuse to pay the check. UCC §§4-303 and 4-403. As discussed above, NACHA Rules ordinarily require any stop-payment order to be sent at least three days before the payment is to be made. NACHA Rules §7.4. Because that would bar any stop-payment right in POS conversions, NACHA has adopted a special rule for POS conversions, which tracks UCC §4-303 in permitting the customer to stop payment if the consumer sends notice at a time that allows the bank a reasonable opportunity to act before it becomes obligated on the item. NACHA Rules §7.4. Because the transactions are cleared

Figure 27.2
POS Conversion

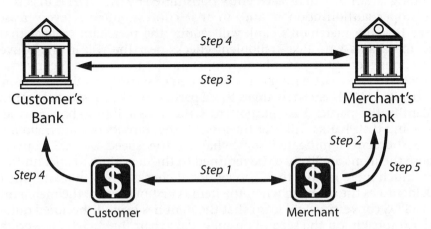

Step 1   The Customer gives a check to the Merchant. The Merchant runs the check through a reader (capturing the information on the MICR line of the check) and returns the paper check to the Customer.

Step 2   The Merchant sends to its bank a message including both the amount of the transaction and the data from the check about the Customer's bank account.

Step 3   The Merchant's Bank sends an ACH debit entry to the Customer's Bank.

Step 4   The Customer's Bank responds to that entry by removing funds from the Customer's account and sending them to the Merchant's Bank (through the ACH network).

Step 5   The Merchant's Bank credits the Merchant's account.

electronically, even that right will last only a short time, certainly less than one business day. Again, however, because the relevant universe is local retail payments, that rule does not put the customer at a significant disadvantage compared to conventional check transactions. Those transactions also tend to clear very quickly, so the customer normally has less than a full business day to stop payment in those transactions as well.

The most important difference for the parties to a POS conversion is the risk of fraud. For conventional check transactions, the payor bank ordinarily bears the risk of loss if it pays an item that is unauthorized (not signed by the purported drawer). See UCC §4-208(a)(3) (permitting a payor bank to recover for an unauthorized item only if the depositary bank knew that the purported customer had not authorized the item). (As you might recall from Assignment 26, the depositary bank will bear the loss if the item was authorized, but bore a forged indorsement.) Thus, with a check, the merchant bears the loss if the check bounces, but the payor bank bears the loss if the fraud is sufficiently skillful to trick the payor bank into honoring the fraudulent item.

Under NACHA Rules, however, the bank that originates an ACH transaction (normally the merchant's bank) bears that responsibility. NACHA Rules §2.2.1.1 (including a warranty that "each entry transmitted by the ODFI is in accordance with proper authorization"). And, in that context, there is every reason to believe that the merchant's bank will require the merchant to bear that risk. Thus, merchants who take fraudulent checks bear the risk in the conversion transactions even if the payor bank honors the item. Hence, POS conversions to ACH transactions place a much greater burden of security on the merchants and their banks. NACHA strongly urges those parties to take substantial precautions to identify the parties that purport to send transactions — because the merchants and their banks will bear the losses if the transactions are fraudulent.

That burden is mitigated somewhat by the speed of POS conversions, because the items are likely to be returned to the depositary bank and the merchant much more rapidly than conventional checks. Thus, at least if the payor bank identifies the problem when the item is first processed, the merchant who takes a POS conversion will learn that the item has been dishonored quite a bit sooner (probably on the second business day) than the merchant who takes a paper check. Experience suggests several reasons why losses from bad checks are mitigated significantly as the speed of response increases: because the customer will have less time to stop payment on the check; because of the greater likelihood that funds will remain in the account if the check is processed more promptly; and because the merchant will have greater success at collecting the bounced check if it starts its efforts more promptly. Of course, those advantages will not help the merchant if the payor bank fails to notice the problem at the time — because the return will come much later, at the end of the month when the purported drawer challenges the item on its monthly statement.

C.   Telephone-Initiated Payments

The final subject of this assignment is the telephone-initiated payment, which has become controversial in recent years because of its frequent use to defraud consumers. The situation arises when a payee obtains consent for a transaction completed over the telephone. If the payee wants to use a telephone check to obtain payment, it will induce the customer (the drawer of the check) to recite (from the bottom of one of the customer's conventional checks) the routing number for the customer's bank and the account number of the customer. The payee (typically a bill-collection service or a telemarketer) then will use that information in one of two ways. A few years ago, the most common approach would be, using software readily available on the Internet, to print a check drawn on the customer's account. The check of course would not include a manual signature by the customer but would suggest in some way that a signature is not required (for example, by a stamp that might say "AUTHORIZED BY DRAWER" or (with less sincerity) "SIGNATURE ON FILE"). More recently, using an ACH TEL entry (a new service offered by NACHA about the same time as the WEB entry discussed above), the payee might use the bank account information to initiate an ACH entry. NACHA reports that it processed 170 TEL entries in 2003, for an average amount of $374.

Under applicable FTC regulations, the payee must retain a "verifiable authorization" of the transaction for 24 months. 16 CFR §310.5(a)(5). That authorization could be in writing, or it could be a tape recording of an oral authorization. 16 CFR §310.3(a)(3). Given the purpose of the system — to allow payees to obtain payment without waiting for the payor to transmit a written check — it is not surprising that the companies that have designed telephone-check software recommend that their customers rely on oral authorizations.

As the existence of the FTC regulation suggests, some of the businesses that use telephone checks have come under fire for processing checks that have not been authorized by their customers (or, in some cases, checks in amounts larger than the amounts authorized by their customers). Canada, indeed, has gone so far as to ban all telephonically initiated checks. No legislature in this country has yet gone so far, but several states (including California and Texas) have adopted non-uniform UCC provisions addressing the problem. Responding to those provisions, recently approved amendments to UCC Articles 3 and 4 have altered the warranty rules for such items. Specifically, those amendments add a new subsection to each of the warranty provisions under which each transferor makes a transfer warranty and a presentment warranty that the purported drawer has authorized the item in the amount in which the item has been issued. See UCC §§3-416(a)(6), 3-417(a)(4), 4-207(a)(6), and 4-208(a)(4).

The premise of those provisions is that in that context at least the possibility of fraud is better policed by action on the part of the depositary bank. For example, depositary banks that accept deposits of telephone checks might be induced to monitor the activities of those customers or require them to provide financial assurances of the authenticity of the items, lest the depositary bank be left holding the bag on warranty claims for unauthorized items.

Those provisions do not apply to TEL entries, of course, which do not involve checks governed by Article 4. Thus, when the telemarketer uses a TEL entry, the transaction is governed by the EFTA and by the standard NACHA Rules discussed above, which place responsibility for fraud and error on the bank that accepted the incorrect or fraudulent entry. EFTA protections are not available for telephone-initiated check transactions, because the Federal Reserve has concluded that those do not constitute electronic fund transfers under the applicable statutory provisions. Commentary to Regulation E §205.3(c)(6).

Relevant Glossary Entry

Automated Clearing House (ACH)

Problem Set 27

27.1. A few weeks ago (in a hypothetical state in which Article 4 applies to wholly electronic checks), your old friend Cliff Janeway calls you, quite flustered. Because his rare-book business requires him to buy so many books from remote suppliers, he recently started using his bank's eCheck product.

The first month he got his statement, he saw literally hundreds of checks on his account that he had not written, depleting his entire business account and using several thousand dollars of the overdraft facility that he has with his bank. What should he do? EFTA §§903(5), 903(6), 908, and 909; UCC §4-401.

27.2. One Monday morning you have a meeting with your client Stacy Vye from Wessex Bank. She tells you that her bank (operating in the same hypothetical state as you considered in the previous problem) recently has become involved in eChecks and that she generally is in charge of all issues arising out of deposited eChecks. The program seems to be quite successful; hundreds of eChecks are being deposited each week. Still, by this point several dozen of those checks have bounced. She explains that her first response is to try to recover the funds from her depositors' accounts. If that does not work, she normally hands bounced checks over to collection attorneys. She instructs them to sue either (a) her depositors; (b) the issuers of the checks; or (c) if some other party has indorsed the check, the indorsing party. She is not sure what to do here, where there is nothing to "hand over" to her collection attorneys. What, she asks, do you advise? UCC §§1-201(b)(21), 3-204, 3-301, 3-412, 3-414, 3-415, 4-214(a), (c) and (d), and 9-105.

27.3. Suppose that your bill for Internet service at your home each month is paid by an automatic deduction from your bank account. You agreed to this when you signed up for Internet service with your Internet service provider (ISP), and at that time provided to your ISP information about your bank so that the ISP could arrange for the payments.

(a) Determine what type of ACH entry (credit entry or debit entry) is most likely to be involved. NACHA Rules §13.1.20.

(b) Assuming that you reside in Chicago and that the ISP is located in Washington state (near the Seattle Federal Reserve bank), identify the most likely parties to the transaction and the roles they would play under applicable NACHA Rules. NACHA Rules §§13.1.30, 13.1.31, 13.1.33, 13.1.43, 13.1.44, and 13.1.45.

(c) Assuming that the next payment is due on Monday April 1, what would you need to do to cancel that payment and what is the latest date on which you could act to do so in a timely manner? NACHA Rules §§7.4, and 13.1.11

27.4. Suppose that you pay your credit-card bill through an Internet bill-payment service offered by your bank, through which you can direct your financial institution to pay bills using ACH transfers. Using that service, you direct a transfer to pay a $7,000 credit-card bill in its entirety. Suppose that you change your mind the next day. Is there anything that you can do to prevent the payment from being made? NACHA Rules §§2.5, 7.1, and 7.3

27.5. Your bank mistakenly honors a check that is not properly payable from your bank account, which has the effect of depleting the funds in your account. As a result, the regularly scheduled debit entry to pay your car payment is returned unpaid by your bank. The car lender at that point repossesses your car, which causes you to incur a variety of expenses. Is your bank liable for those losses? UCC §§4-402, 4-104(a)(9), and 3-103; NACHA Rules §§5.1 and 13.1.20.

27.6. Your old friend Cliff Janeway mentions a small problem to you over lunch one day. He explains that he customarily pays for his groceries with checks. Starting last month, his grocery store has a new system under which it marks his checks void and hands them back to him at the register. Although he was worried at first that the grocery store was making a mistake and would not be paid (because the check was marked void), the clerks assured him that the charges would show up on his monthly statement. To his surprise, the charges did show up. Indeed, he was charged twice for one of them — his statement showed two transactions at Kroger's on February 14, each at the same time and each for $92.36. Cliff understandably thinks he should pay only once.

(a)   What should he do? EFTA §§908(a) and 909; Regulation E, §205.11.

(b)   What if the transaction resulted from a telephone conversation between Cliff and a telemarketer, in which he ultimately declined to make a purchase, but the telemarketer still created a paper check to draw funds from Cliff's account? EFTA §909, UCC §§4-207, 4-208, and 4-401.

(c)   Same facts as (b), but assume that the telemarketer used a TEL entry. EFTA §909, NACHA Rule §2.2.1.1.

(d)   Who will bear the loss in each of those transactions? NACHA Rule §2.2.1.1; EFTA §909; UCC §§4-207, 4-208, and 4-401.

Section B.   Internet Payments and Emerging Payment Systems

As Chapter 4 illustrates, the Internet has provided an immense new market opportunity, with new retailers, new products, and new methods of delivering those products. The three assignments that follow discuss some of the important practical and legal developments in paying for products that are for sale on the Internet. In this discussion, you should think about the material in the two excerpts that follow, which underscore two fundamental problems for payments on the Internet. The first is a practical one: The markets began with strongly established networks for existing participants in the form of Visa and MasterCard. The second is a policy one: The legal distinctions developed for payment transactions in conventional face-to-face retailing do not apply coherently to the new payment transactions developing on the Internet.

Mark A. Lemley & David McGowan, Legal Implications of Network Economic Effects

86 Cal. L. Rev. 479 (1998)

Many things may increase in value as the number of users increases. The term network effects therefore must be used with great care, for it has been used to describe a number of distinct conditions in which value may increase with consumption. The state of both theoretical development and empirical research varies, and the confidence with which the law uses network theory as a basis for modifying or extending existing doctrine should be calibrated accordingly. Following Katz and Shapiro, we view network markets as falling on a continuum that may roughly be divided into actual networks, virtual networks, and simple positive feedback phenomena. The essential criterion for locating a good along this continuum is the degree to which the good provides inherent value to a consumer apart from any network characteristics. The greater the inherent value of the good relative to any value added by additional consumers, the less significant the network effect.

A.   ACTUAL NETWORKS

The archetypal examples of network markets involve products whose entire value lies in facilitating interactions between a consumer and others who own the product. The benefit to a purchaser, in other words, is access to other purchasers. Telephones and fax machines are classic examples of actual network goods; owning the only telephone or fax machine in the world would be of little benefit because it could not be used to communicate with anyone. The value of the telephone or fax machine one has already purchased increases with each additional purchaser, so long as all machines operate on the same standards and the network infrastructure is capable of processing all member communications reliably. In this relatively strict sense, actual networks are effectively limited to communications markets. The principal characteristics distinguishing such products from others discussed below are the absence of material inherent value and the necessity for common standards among goods incorporated into the network. . . .

Property rights (most importantly, the right to exclude others from a network) play a crucial role in network markets. In many potential networks, property rights created by legal rules, rather than physical laws, set the boundary conditions for the network. Actual networks such as telephone lines require capital investments in physical infrastructure. Such networks therefore may be owned: there are tangible assets to which property rights may be attached. Even where the capital investment in a network is negligible, the law can establish ownership rights by fiat (in this case by awarding exclusive rights in "intellectual property"). Where the law establishes a right to exclude others from the use of a thing — as with intellectual property — it constrains the ability of consumers to move between network standards, and it gives control over access and pricing to the owner of the intellectual property embodied in the standard. . . .

B. VIRTUAL NETWORKS

Goods constitute virtual networks when they provide inherent value to consumers that increases with the number of additional users of identical and/or interoperable goods. Virtual network goods need not be linked to a common system as are the constituents of a communications network; very strong positive feedback effects tied to functional compatibility are sufficient. Computer software is the paradigm example. Unlike telephones and fax machines, an operating system or application program will allow even a single user to perform a variety of tasks regardless whether even a single other consumer owns the software. At the same time, the value of a given program grows considerably as the number of additional purchasers increases. As more consumers adopted WordPerfect, for example, it became easier for each previous user to share files without the need for a conversion program and easier for employees to switch jobs without retraining. And as Microsoft Word has replaced WordPerfect as the word processing program of choice, it in turn gained the benefits of widespread adoption. Data sharing in this sense requires direct horizontal technological compatibility akin to that required for telephones and fax machines to work together, but it does not require the actual connections that communications networks do. Further, the existence of conversion software may expand the network beyond a single, proprietary product.

In addition to horizontal technological compatibility, software may be subject to "increasing returns" based on positive feedback from the market in the form of complementary goods. Software developers will write more applications programs for an operating system with two-thirds of the market than for a system with one-third because the operating system with the larger share will provide the biggest market for applications programs. The availability of a broader array of application programs will reinforce the popularity of an operating system, which in turn will make investment in application programs compatible with that system more desirable than investment in programs compatible with less popular systems. Similarly, firms that adopt relatively popular software will likely incur lower costs to train employees and will find it easier to hire productive temporary help than will firms with unpopular software. Importantly, the strength of network effects will vary depending on the type of software in question. Network effects will be materially greater for operating systems software than for applications programs, for example, and a proper legal analysis of network effects in software markets must account for this difference.

Of course, technology comprises only one element of virtual networks. Like actual networks, virtual networks are likely to require intricate webs of both formal and informal contracts to create the value the network delivers. Bank-issued credit cards provide a good example. Although they might confer some utility on their own (particularly in their credit aspect), credit cards exhibit network effects because their utility increases dramatically as a network develops. As the number of merchants willing to accept a card grows, the utility of the card to consumers increases, thus likely increasing the number of consumers who will want to own the card, which in turn provides incentive for more merchants to accept the card, and so on. With innovation in computer and telephone technology yielding such benefits as real-time transaction processing, including such features as fraud detection and verification of available credit, transactions involving bank-issued credit cards have come to resemble interactions on an actual network.

But the technological links and potential for positive returns to scale in the credit card industry cannot themselves create value without a sophisticated system of contracts, including agreement on the compensation card issuers will receive and the rules governing their conduct relative to the network. Thus, merchants will have a contractual relationship with a bank, which will to some extent be subject to the bank's contractual relationship with the credit card entity. If the merchant's bank did not issue the consumer's credit card, it in turn will have a contractual relationship with the issuing bank pursuant to which transactions may be cleared. The issuing bank will of course have a contractual relationship with the consumer. These contracts are as vital to the functioning of the credit card network as are the electronic links that facilitate transactions.

Many of these contracts are standardized by the rules of the Visa and MasterCard joint ventures. Those rules govern general network membership, such as the manner in which member banks may use the Visa and MasterCard marks, communication among member banks, and fees charged by member banks for processing transactions with one another. The rules do not specify standard terms, however, for contracts between merchants and their banks or between consumers and their banks. Therefore, the degree to which network theory plays a role in the legal analysis of credit card networks depends in significant part upon the legal and economic analysis of contract law, including the relative efficiency of standard contract terms versus either a joint venture or horizontal integration, and limitations on the ability to contract (such as those imposed by antitrust law). . . .

C.   POSITIVE FEEDBACK EFFECTS

Lastly, goods may increase in value as consumption increases even where the goods are not themselves connections to a network and do not interoperate with like (or "compatible") goods. Such goods reflect little more than the need for a given degree of demand to sustain production of the good and complementary goods and services. Where production of goods involves both fixed and marginal costs, the average fixed costs will decline as demand for the good increases, and the fixed costs are spread over a larger number of units. This is a common economic phenomenon—economies of scale. In some cases, a large population may be necessary to justify any production at all. We would intuitively expect exotic car repair shops to be more prevalent in large cities than rural towns because a minimum concentration of car owners is required to generate sufficient demand to sustain a shop.

Unlike actual or virtual networks, no technological compatibility, interoperability, or even contractual relationships are necessary to sustain this "network." Strictly speaking, it is not a network at all. Network effects are demand-side effects — they result from the value that consumers place on owning what other consumers already own. By contrast, economies of scale are supply-side effects — they are a function of the cost of making the goods and exist (at least conceptually) regardless of positive utility payoffs among consumers. Markets characterized by economies of scale are, of course, potentially subject to material diseconomies of scale as well. If too many consumers purchase the same exotic car, it may become difficult to schedule repairs, obtain parts, and the like. Similarly, once a steel plant is used to its full capacity, expanding supply will require building a whole new plant, raising the average cost. Thus, there are definite limits in most markets to the "value" to consumers of buying whatever other consumers want. By definition, those markets do not exhibit network effects.

D. WHY WE SHOULD CARE: THE POSSIBLE "EFFECTS" OF NETWORKS

. . . [M]any of the concerns surrounding network markets are based on the presumption that such markets offer increasing returns over a very large portion of the demand curve. Outside the realm of natural monopoly, by contrast, neo-classical economics generally posits declining returns to scale and thus offers few conceptual tools to address the problems that arise when returns increase over a very large portion or even all of the demand curve. Thus, arguments based on network effects may suggest that the law must rethink the rationality of behavior considered unlikely under neoclassical theory, such as predation in antitrust jurisprudence, and address new risks not considered under models based on declining returns.

With respect to the behavioral issues, network markets by definition offer potentially lucrative returns to firms that can establish their own products as standards on which competition in the market, or in aftermarkets for complementary goods, will be based. This fact presents the possibility of material first-mover advantages: being the first seller in a market may confer an important advantage over later entrants. Because the returns to the standards winner will be higher than in "normal" markets, relatively risky strategies, such as predation or, at a minimum, penetration pricing, might be rational in a networks market.

Increasing returns also raise questions about the possibility of effectively leveraging a monopoly from one market to another, an argument most commonly associated with antitrust tying claims. Chicago-school analysts have argued that leveraging is unlikely because a given amount of monopoly power can extract only a given amount of revenue from consumers, whether taken all in the monopolist's primary market or split between that market and some other. This view has been challenged even without regard to network theory, but the possibility of leveraging from a non-network market into a network market poses an important new challenge. Recent activity in the software industry also raises the possibility that markets for products that would be considered distinct under traditional antitrust analysis, such as Web browsers, might simply be absorbed into a network market through bundling with a strong network product, such as an operating system. One might also rethink unfair competition law in light of the arguably greater sensitivity of network markets to public pronouncements: in a market in which the standard product is preferred, statements about such products might carry greater weight than in other markets.

These arguments are closely related to the idea of "tipping," a concept Katz and Shapiro summarize as being based on

> [a] natural tendency toward de facto standardization, which means everyone using the same system. Because of the strong positive-feedback elements, systems markets are especially prone to 'tipping,' which is the tendency of one system to pull away from its rivals in popularity once it has gained an initial edge. Tipping is neither inherently good nor bad. If the economics of a particular market dictate that having one standard is more efficient than competition among standards, then "tipping" to one standard is in theory inevitable, absent significant transaction costs or some form of regulation. In such circumstances a "tipped" market would be efficient and therefore desirable; efforts to forestall tipping would result in suboptimal heterogeneity among systems and losses in terms of unrealized efficiencies. That a market is best served by a single standard, however, does not always imply that the standard should be owned by a single firm, or even that the standard should be owned at all.

Even in markets best served by a single standard or system, however, there is at least a theoretical risk that the "wrong" standard will be adopted or that a standard that was efficient when adopted will become relatively inefficient over time. The conclusion that a standard adopted by consumers is suboptimal should be approached with caution. Setting aside for the moment the very difficult question of deriving determinative criteria for defining "suboptimality," consumers might have difficulty moving to a new standard — even if they all agreed that the adopted standard was suboptimal — because of collective action problems. The value of any alternative system would depend on the number of users adopting it; the rational consumer might well choose to wait until an alternative had been adopted by others who incurred the costs of shifting to the new standard but reaped fewer benefits relative to later adopters.

From the standpoint of legal adaptation of network theory, each of these arguments is to some degree problematic. The presumed increasing returns of network markets are not guaranteed; networks will suffer net diseconomies of scale if the volume of interactions exceeds network capacity and causes delays or failure. Positive returns to some level of scale are in any event quite common, if not ubiquitous. Further, network effects might not be the only effects at work. A user might prefer Lexis to Westlaw, but only up to a certain point. If the information she needs is available only on Westlaw, she may start using that service, whatever the cost in terms of lost convenience. At a minimum, common sense tells us that there likely are differences material to most areas of the law between a network of telephones or fax machines and a "network" of Ferrari owners. It is thus important to analyze markets to determine the source of increasing returns — whether from actual or virtual networks — and to distinguish among markets displaying merely positive returns to scale, markets displaying network effects only up to a relatively low point on the demand curve, and markets displaying increasing returns over most or all of the demand curve. The ratio of inherent value to network value is of similar importance.

One final feature of network theory bears significant emphasis. Network effects tend to have conflicting implications that are very difficult to interpret. To take corporate governance as an example, some have argued that a given corporate governance term might display network effects by gaining greater clarity of meaning over time and through repeated interpretation by courts. If one observes that firms all use that term, however, does that reflect maximization of positive interpretive network effects or does it reflect suboptimal tipping? Or is the term inherently the best one? If firms use a variety of different terms on a given point, does that reflect the optimal convergence of heterogeneous firms with heterogeneous governance provisions or does it reflect opportunity costs of not using a standard term? In many cases, the observable data can lead to diametrically opposed conclusions, making the task of judicial adaptation extremely difficult.

Ronald J. Mann, Making Sense of Payments Policy in the Information Age

93 Geo. L.J. (forthcoming 2004)

Two events at the close of the twentieth century have underscored the need to think more clearly about payments policy. The first is the proliferation of markets in which credit and debit cards are used. What once was a niche product designed for the payment of expenses by business travelers has now come into widespread use in a wide variety of contexts that raise differing policy concerns. The second, related to the first, is the substantial shift in the locus of retail payment transactions from retail, face-to-face payments in brick-and-mortar stores to remote payments for Internet purchases. Collectively, those changes have destabilized the system for which existing payments rules were designed.

. . . [I]t would be remiss to discuss harmonization of rules for payment cards without some general consideration of the propriety of uniformity in the law of payment systems. I am of course not the first to come upon that problem. The [Uniform New Payments Code], for example, rested on the basic premise that the law governing issues common to multiple payments should be as uniform as possible. As the Reporter explained in his memorandum justifying the project, the goal is "to arrive at a set of comprehensive rules applicable in some respects to all payment systems." Conversely, Peter Alces's perceptive analysis of that project argues that the UNPC goes too far by ignoring important differences between payment systems that justify differing rules for devices (primarily credit cards) that provide for the extension of credit. More recently, Clay Gillette has presented a particularizing argument about rules for unauthorized transactions, contending that those rules should turn on the relative ability of courts and legislatures to identify optimal risk-bearers.

Looking back from the vantage point of the 21st century, it seems clear that the basic problem with the earlier proposals is not that they are excessively uniform or excessively particularizing. The problem is that they have not undertaken to consider why it might be useful to have uniform or particularized rules on particular subjects. I attribute that blind spot in the existing literature to the historical accident of the structure of the modern commercial-law curriculum.

Even with the law of payments itself, work that attempts to address broader policy concerns is hampered by the balkanized nature of the existing regulatory apparatus. The UCC itself is promulgated by the ALI and NCCUSL for adoption by the various state legislatures. The Federal Reserve — motivated primarily by concerns about stability and to a lesser degree by concerns about cost-effectiveness — implements most of the relevant provisions of the EFAA, TILA, and the EFTA. Even the Federal Trade Commission has a minor role, with some frankly protective regulations related to holder-in-due-course status.

The basic problem is that payments policy needs to attend more consciously to the contexts of the transactions in which payments are made. Existing law articulates rules that are bounded almost entirely by the nature of the technology with which the payment is made. Thus, we have separate rules for wire transfers, letters of credit, checks, electronic transfers, and the like. That type of boundary makes sense only for issues driven by the nature of the technology. It makes no sense, however, for issues that should be resolved by reference to the nature of the underlying transaction in which the payment is made.

At its heart, payments law must resolve four fundamental questions: who bears the risk of unauthorized payments, what must be done about claims of error, when are payments completed (so that they discharge the underlying liability), and when can they be reversed. The first three questions are categorically different from the last, because they often should be resolved based on the nature of the underlying technology. Thus, for example, with respect to the risk of unauthorized payments, the fundamental question is how to design a system that gives adequate incentive to the user to avoid and mitigate losses from unauthorized transactions, while giving adequate incentive to the system operator to make advances in technology and system design that can avoid and mitigate those losses. In our legal system, we have taken the view for most high-technology payments that an almost complete allocation of the risk of those losses to the system operator is appropriate.

The premise of those rules (admittedly unspoken) is that even a complete allocation of loss to the network operator will leave the consumer a sufficient incentive to attend to these problems. That could be true because of the hassle of reversing unauthorized charges, because of doubts that financial institutions readily will fulfill their obligations in such a situation, or even because of ignorance of the legal protections for unauthorized transactions. At the same time, the rules reflect the implicit premise that losses in technology-driven systems are most effectively reduced by technological and system-design initiatives that are exclusively within the control of the system operator. Thus, we are not surprised to see major investments in fraud-prevention technology in the credit-card and debit-card sectors. Because the justifications for those rules relate to the nature of the technology, it is plausible for federal law to prescribe such a rule for all electronic transfers from consumer accounts. It is less plausible to include a similar rule for credit card transactions based on the availability of credit in the transaction. It would be more sensible, surely, for that rule to be justified by the fact that the transactions are processed and cleared in an electronic way, which justifies rules like those discussed above.

Rules related to error are similar. The types of events that are likely to lead to an error, as well as the mechanisms for detecting, confirming, and responding to an error are likely to depend on the technology that is used to clear and process payments. Thus, it makes some sense that the rule for transactions processed electronically (covered by the EFTA) would differ from the rule for transactions processed entirely by paper (conventional check transactions governed by Article 4). At the same time, the continuing shift of check transactions from paper to electronic processing (probably to be accelerated by the Check 21 Act) might undermine that distinction.

Rules that determine when a payment is made are similar, in that they are for the most part made based on the practicalities of a particular system. Thus, in the wire-transfer system, we say that the payment is complete when the beneficiary's bank becomes obligated to pay the beneficiary. In the checking system, we say that the payment is not complete with respect to an ordinary check until the check is paid, but that it occurs with respect to a cashier's check when the payee accepts the instrument.

Rules related to reversibility however, are completely different. Rules related to reversibility should depend on the dynamics of the underlying transaction in which the payment is made. In the simplest cases, payment systems are specialized for use in particular situations. Thus, for example, in business transactions, parties often choose to make payments with letters of credit or wire transfers. Those systems include particular rules designed for the particular transactions in which they are used, which determine the timing and circumstances in which payments can be recovered or stopped once the process has been initiated. Because those systems are quite specialized, the system-specific rules work well for them.

It is important to see that the rules make sense because of the underlying transaction, not because of anything about the payment instrument itself. For example, there is nothing inherent in the use of a bank's written commitment to pay that calls for the formalistic emphasis on both an absolute obligation of payment upon presentation of conforming documents and at the same time an utterly unconstrained right to refuse payment upon presentation of nonconforming documents. On the contrary, that structure has grown up solely as an adjunct to the particular sales transaction for which the instrument is commonly used. If the law of letters of credit makes sense — and for the most part I think it does — it makes sense only in the light of a practical assessment of the realities of the sales transactions in which that law is brought to bear.

The law of wire transfers is animated by an even more conclusive rejection of reversibility. From the perspective articulated here, that emphasis reflects a desire to create an entirely "pure" payment system, entirely divorced from any transaction: the wire transfer is suitable for cases in which the party making the payment is willing to forgo any payment-related right of recovery at all. Once the payment is made by wire transfer, there is no substantial recourse inside the system. That makes sense in context, because wire transfers are used typically by reasonably informed businesses that select such a pure system in contexts in which the most important aspect of the transaction is to provide reliably final payment as promptly as possible.

When we turn to less specialized payment systems, however, the issues become considerably more difficult. Historically (if not in current practice), the most prominent is the negotiable instrument. The most distinctive feature of the negotiable instrument is the ability of those that acquire the instrument to obtain holder-in-due-course status. As a practical matter, that status involves an ability to separate the instrument from the transaction as much as possible and thus make the obligation to pay irreversible at an early point, at least as regards claims related to the underlying transaction.

The complicating features of negotiable instruments law, however, largely operate to render that separation irrevocably permeable. For present purposes, what is most important is that the policy justifications for those complicating features uniformly relate to concerns about the balance of power in the underlying transaction for which the instrument was issued. For example, a series of arbitrary formalities limit the use of the negotiable instrument to cases in which the parties are sufficiently sophisticated and focused to ensure that the payment instrument is drafted in a stripped-down form that includes the requisite formal language and omits any substantial discussion of the underlying transaction. Similarly, even if the instrument is issued in a proper form and transferred in the appropriate way, certain defenses will remain valid against the purchaser. These defenses — the so-called real defenses — address such matters as contracts with minors or contracts procured by fraud; they plainly are designed to protect fundamental concerns about fairness in the underlying transaction. Finally, in nonmortgage credit transactions that involve consumers, holder-in-due-course status is generally prohibited as a matter of supervening federal law.

The negotiable instrument, of course, has been superseded for the most part by its main surviving descendant, the check, an instrument for which the classic rules of negotiability have little continuing significance. Because the check is less specialized than the letter of credit or the wire transfer (or the negotiable instrument in its heyday), its rules do not reflect the close accommodation to the balance of the underlying transaction that typifies the law of those earlier, primarily business-related payment systems. Thus, many of the most important rules in the checking system reflect issues discussed above, allocating losses from unauthorized transactions and risks of errors related to the payment device that have little or nothing to do with problems in any underlying transaction. Of course, the focus of modern check law on such questions, to the exclusion of any substantial concern for the consumers that use them, is the basis of much of the most forceful criticisms of Articles 3 and 4 as they now appear in the UCC. But even the checking system includes rules that address the basic problem at the intersection of every payment system and the transactions for which it is used: the consequences of the payee's failure to perform. On that point, the UCC frankly grants the check-writer a right to stop payment, without any assessment of the validity of the claim.

The check, however, is now outdated. As we now know, it has been declining in use for some time. The pressure to revise rules related to the check thus will continue to decrease. At the same time, consumer use of credit and debit cards is increasing rapidly. Moreover, of importance for our purposes, credit and debit cards over the last decade have come into dominance in areas in which they were not frequently used. Thus, credit cards have come to dominate payments in remote purchase transactions, especially on the Internet. Debit cards, reaching broad use in this country only in the last decade, are now commonly used in face-to-face transactions and perhaps soon will be a major option for remote transactions as well.

Thus, if there is an area of payments law that is both important and currently contestable, it is the law that addresses card-based payment transactions.

———————————

Assignment 28:   Paying for Retail Internet Purchases

It certainly would come as a surprise to those who watched the Internet in its infancy, but consumers still pay for the overwhelming majority of retail Internet purchases with credit cards. There has been some shift to debit cards processed by Visa and MasterCard (which take advantage of their existing networks) and a more recent shift in favor of ACH transfers, but at least for now, those three products are the principal vehicles for making retail Internet payments.

A.   Credit Cards

Because there are no official or comprehensive statistics regarding payment methods at Internet sites, estimates of the percentages of payments made by various methods vary considerably. Still, it seems clear that credit cards are used for at least 90 percent of the transactions in which payments are made online. The fundamental reason for the dominant position of the credit card is not difficult to understand. Putting debit cards to the side for the moment, credit cards are the only payment system readily available to consumers in the United States that can provide the merchant a substantially contemporaneous commitment to pay in a remote payment transaction such as an Internet purchase. This section of the assignment provides some background material on the basics of credit cards, and then discusses how they have come to be used on the Internet.

1.   The Basics of Credit Cards

a.   The Issuer-Cardholder Relationship

Credit-card transactions generally involve four participants: a purchaser who holds a credit card, the issuer that issues the credit card, a merchant who makes a sale, and an acquirer that collects payment for the merchant. ("The acquirer is so named because it "acquires" the transaction from the merchant and then processes it to obtain payment from the issuer.) In some cases (American Express and Discover, for example), the same entity issues the card and acquires the transaction, but that arrangement is less common. Although those four parties are the nominal parties to the transaction, lurking behind them in most cases is the network under which the card has been issued (usually Visa or MasterCard). The networks (associations of member banks that issue Visa or MasterCard branded cards) provide information and transaction-processing services with respect to the transaction between the acquirer and the issuer and (more importantly) establish and enforce rules and standards surrounding the use of cards carrying their brands. These rules govern the contract between the acquirer and the issuer.

Because there is no UCC Article generally applicable to credit-card transactions, state law has a much less pervasive influence on the credit-card system than it has on the checking system. Thus, the principal legal regulation of the credit-card system comes from the federal Truth in Lending Act (TILA) and Regulation Z (12 C.F.R. Part 226), promulgated by the Federal Reserve under TILA. TILA is codified at 15 U.S.C. §§1601 through 1667e, as Title I of the Consumer Credit Protection Act. Hence, it is not surprising that TILA applies only to credit that is extended to individuals, and does not apply to credit extended "primarily for business, commercial, or agricultural purposes," TILA §104(1), or to transactions involving more than $25,000, TILA, §104(3). (The provisions of the EFTA and Regulation E discussed in the preceding assignment do not apply to credit cards. Because credit cards do not draw directly on a bank account, the credit-card account is not an "account" as defined in those provisions. EFTA §903(2); Regulation E, §205.2(b)(1).)

The key to any credit-card transaction is the relationship between the cardholder and the card issuer. The typical relationship is familiar to you: The issuer commits to pay for purchases made with the card, in return for the cardholder's promise to reimburse the issuer over time. That relationship is exactly the opposite of the common checking relationship, where the customer normally must deposit funds *before* the bank will pay checks.

The buy-first, pay-later aspect of most credit-card relationships alters the underlying economics of the system. Banks that provide checking accounts can earn profits by investing the funds that customers have placed in their accounts. A credit-card issuer does not have that option because most cardholders do not deposit funds before they make purchases on their cards. The profit for the typical card issuer comes predominantly from the interest income that the issuer earns on the balances that its cardholders carry on their cards from month to month. The dependence on interest revenues produces an important irony. The consumers who pay their credit-card balances every month—so-called convenience users—generally are the most creditworthy individuals in the system, but are definitely bad customers for the issuers, for whom interest is such an important part of the income stream. Partially in response to that problem, issuers in recent years have substantially increased other fees they charge (especially fees for late payments or overlimit transactions), attempting to ensure that they can collect fees even from those customers who do not pay substantial amounts of interest.

b. Processing Credit-Card Transactions

Conventional credit-card transactions are successful primarily because they are fast and convenient. But the convenience to the customer hides a complex authorization and collection process. As the credit card is swiped at the merchant's counter, the terminal captures the information on the magnetic stripe on the back of the card and transmits that information through the issuer's network. The issuer (or, more commonly, an agent processing transactions on behalf of the issuer) examines that information to determine if the transaction is within the cardholder's limit and also to assess the likelihood that the card is legitimate (rather than a forgery) and that the transaction is being conducted by the cardholder (rather than a thief). If the issuer's computer approves the transaction, it sends back an authorization message a few seconds after the merchant's terminal contacts it.

After the cardholder leaves the merchant, the merchant collects payments by transferring the data for its transactions (usually at least once a day) to the acquirer that processes its transactions for the appropriate network. A merchant cannot accept a card for any network unless it has an agreement with an entity that acquires transactions for that network. Thus, a merchant cannot accept Visa cards unless it has an agreement with an entity that is a member of the Visa network and thus can collect from the issuer for the merchant's Visa transactions. When the merchant sends the transaction data to the acquirer, the acquirer credits the merchant for the total amount of the transactions, reduced by a "discount," which the acquirer charges for the service of collecting the transactions. The amount of that discount varies widely based on the type of transaction (the fee is higher for transactions in which a card is not swiped), network (American Express and Discover charge more than Visa and MasterCard) and the characteristics of the merchant (high-volume and creditworthy merchants pay less), but in the United States it is rarely less than 1 percent and for conventional brick-and-mortar merchants not often more than 3 percent.

The acquirer, in turn, processes the transactions by sending to each issuer the transactions that involve that issuer's cards. Each issuer pays each acquirer the total amount of the transactions the acquirer has sent, reduced by an "interchange fee" in an amount set by the network. Because the interchange fee is set for the entire network, it is not negotiable on a case-by-case basis. Fees for most classes of Visa and MasterCard transactions currently are between 1 and 2 percent, with fees for American Express and Discover somewhat higher. For acquirers to be profitable, the discount fees that they charge merchants (discussed above) generally must be slightly higher than the interchange fees acquirers must pay issuers. (If the joint fixing of the interchange fees sounds suspiciously like price-fixing, you will be interested to know that antitrust litigation challenging the joint setting of that fee has not been successful.)

The issuers, in turn, sort the transactions reported to them, post them to the separate accounts, and bill their cardholders on a monthly basis. When the process is complete, the cardholder has been charged for the total amount of the transaction. The issuer has a receivable for the entire amount of the transaction, but has paid approximately 98.5 percent of the value of that transaction to the acquirer. From the 1.5 percent "spread," (together with interest and other fee income), the issuer must cover the costs of its operations and losses from cardholders that do not pay their bills in a timely manner. The acquirer has received about 98.5 percent of the transaction and has paid the merchant about 98 percent of the value of the transaction; its spread must cover the costs of its operations. The merchant has received about 98 percent of the value of the transaction and has sold the good to the customer; it must be able to make a profit at that price.

One of the most distinctive features of the credit-card system is that it gives the consumer a right to cancel payment that is much broader than the consumer's rights in any of the competing systems. Specifically, TILA §170(a) grants a cardholder the right to withhold payment on the basis of any defense that the cardholder could assert against the original merchant. Thus, for example, suppose that Cliff Janeway uses a credit card to purchase some books as a gift for a friend, relying on the merchant's assurance that the books are rare first editions. If Cliff later discovers that the books in fact are not first editions, TILA §170(a) allows Cliff to refuse to pay the charge on his credit-card account.

Standing alone, that provision would wreak havoc with credit cards as a payment system, because it would leave issuers in a position of dealing with complaints against often distant merchants. The card-issuing networks solve that problem by the simple expedient of adopting rules that pass those losses ("chargebacks") back to the merchants. Thus, when a cardholder raises a defense against the issuer under Section 170(a), the issuer can charge the transaction back to the acquirer. This is done by notifying the acquirer of the claim and withholding funds equal to the claim from the daily transmission of funds paying the acquirer for the day's transactions. The acquirer, in turn, charges the transaction back to the merchant by withholding payment from the merchant equal to the claim. Visa and MasterCard also impose fees (generally about $25) for each chargeback processed through their networks. Merchants that have too many chargebacks eventually are evicted from the networks.

c. Fraud and Error in Credit-Card Transactions

In addition to the right to withhold payment in TILA §170, TILA also includes consumer-protection rules for fraud and error in credit-card transactions. First, TILA §161 sets out detailed provisions for resolving alleged billing errors related to credit cards. See also Regulation Z, §226.13 (details on those procedures). Generally, the cardholder must provide written notice within 60 days after the creditor sent the relevant statement to the cardholder. TILA §161(a). If the cardholder sends the proper notice, the creditor must resolve the claim within two billing cycles.

The definition of billing error is quite broad, extending not only to claims that the cardholder did not conduct the transaction in question or that the charge is duplicative, but also to claims that the merchant failed to deliver the goods and services covered by the charge in question. TILA §161(b). If the cardholder presents such a claim, the creditor cannot reject the claim without first "conduct[ing] a reasonable investigation and determin[ing] that the property or services were actually delivered . . . as agreed." TILA §161(a)(B)(ii); Regulation Z, §226.13(f) n.31. If the issuer rejects the cardholder's claim, it must (within the two billing cycles) give the cardholder a written explanation of the issuer's reason for not correcting the charge. TILA §161(a); Regulation Z, §226.13(c)(2), (f). Most importantly, the creditor cannot close or restrict the cardholder's account for failure to pay the disputed amount during the pendency of the dispute, although it can accrue a finance charge that would be due if the dispute is resolved against the cardholder. TILA §161(d), Regulation Z, §226.13(d), (g).

TILA also includes strong protection against unauthorized charges, similar (though slightly broader) than the EFTA provisions discussed in the preceding assignment. TILA §133(a)(1)(B) limits the cardholder's liability for unauthorized charges to a maximum of $50. That $50 limit is absolute, even if the cardholder knows that its card has been stolen and does not bother to notify the issuer of the theft. Regulation Z, §226.12(b)(1). Thus, the issuer generally cannot shift losses from unauthorized transactions to the cardholder. Moreover, within the network, credit-card issuers retain the risk of unauthorized transactions. Thus, although merchants bear responsibility when customers complain about the quality of goods and services that they have sold, the issuer bears the loss when the cardholder contends that it did not in fact engage in the transaction. As a matter of incentives, that leaves the issuer with the responsibility to develop technologies that minimize the risk of loss from unauthorized transactions.

2.   Credit Cards on the Internet

With the rise of Internet retailing, the advantages of the credit card as a payment system are obvious. The preexisting Visa and MasterCard networks, and the widespread distribution of cards to consumers in the United States, gave credit-card issuers a built-in nationwide payment network available when Internet commerce began. Other payment systems that existed at the time were not as easily transferred to the Internet setting. For example, cash is entirely impractical in a remote transaction unless the consumer has some reliable way to send the cash to the merchant; and even if some hypothetical consumer were willing to mail cash for an Internet purchase, the merchant would not receive the cash for several days until it came in the mail. Similarly, a commitment to pay by check gives the merchant nothing for several days while the merchant waits for the check (except a promise that "the check is in the mail"). Finally, when commerce on the Internet began, there was no system by which online retailers could accept ACH transfers. That is changing—as you will see in the discussion below—but the change is slow and is happening only after the system is to some degree "locked in" to reliance on credit-card payments.

a.   Processing the Transactions

Although some merchants (and third-party security providers) are developing creative ways to enhance the authenticity of their online credit-card transactions, the typical process requires nothing more than that the consumer enter a credit-card number and billing address on the merchant's checkout page. Indeed, if the consumer uses an electronic-wallet product, the information might be entered automatically (a possibility that would be more likely if those products become more functional and less cumbersome). As discussed below, a merchant concerned about fraud might request some additional information, but the need for that information is unlikely to delay the completion of the transaction more than a few seconds beyond the time necessary to provide the information to the merchant's checkout software.

With respect to unauthorized transactions, the cardholder that purchases on the Internet often is not responsible even for $50. The relevant provision of TILA conditions the cardholder's responsibility for $50 on the issuer's having provided some method for the cardholder to identify itself as the authorized user of the card (such as a signature, photograph on the card, or the like). TILA §133(a)(1)(F); Regulation Z, §226.12(b)(3). At least in the view of the Federal Reserve staff, an Internet transaction that verifies the customer's identity solely by asking for the card number and billing address has not identified the customer adequately. Accordingly, the Federal Reserve has concluded in its commentary to Regulation Z, cardholders have no responsibility at all in unauthorized transactions that are conducted based solely on card numbers. Regulation Z Official Staff Commentary to §226.12(b)(2)(iii). In any event, the ability to impose the $50 on cardholders has diminishing practical relevance, because both Visa and MasterCard generally waive the $50 of liability that the statute permits, at least if the cardholder notifies the issuer promptly after discovering the loss of control of the card (or its number).

b. Problems

Despite its current dominance, the credit card faces a number of problems as a long-term vehicle for Internet purchases. Thus, it remains to be seen whether it can retain its first-mover advantage in the long run. The following sections discuss the three most salient obstacles to continued use of credit cards as the dominant Internet payment system: fraud, privacy, and the need to facilitate micropayments.

Fraud The most obvious problem is the astonishing rate of fraud perpetrated through the relatively insecure system of credit-card authorization as it currently exists for Internet transactions. In a face-to-face credit-card transaction, the merchant can swipe the card. When that is done, the terminal on which the card is swiped transmits to the card issuer (or its agent) data on the back of the card (unknown to the cardholder) that allows the issuer to verify that the card in fact is physically present. Although it is possible to forge a card, it is relatively difficult. Thus, because of the costs of the technology necessary to collect that data and apply it to forged cards, only sophisticated and professional criminals will be able to produce such cards.

By contrast, in an Internet transaction (included in the industry within the category known as card-not-present transactions), the merchant often will proceed with no information other than the card number and the billing address (the idea being that it is harder for a malefactor to obtain a billing address than it is to obtain a card number). As it happens, it is not difficult for malefactors to obtain the credit-card number, either from a credit-card slip used in a face-to-face transaction or by hacking into the records of Internet merchants from whom cardholders have made purchases. The billing address of course ordinarily can be obtained from public records (such as a telephone book or Internet database). The ease of obtaining that information has led to a rash of so-called "identity thefts," in which malefactors masquerade for a considerable period of time as another individual, often even obtaining new credit cards in the name of other individuals. Those thefts have been a particular problem on the Internet (where, of course, the risk of being caught is relatively small); they were one of the main causes of the failure in late 2001 of NextBank.

The problem is exacerbated by the ease with which a cardholder can disavow an Internet transaction in which it in fact did participate. That seems to be particularly common for merchants that sell information that is delivered over the Internet. (It is harder for cardholders to disavow transactions in which tangible goods were delivered to their home or office.) Online merchants try to counter that activity through a variety of responses, which collectively consume 1 to 2 percent of their revenues. About half of online merchants now require the "card verification code," a three-digit code that is not part of the card number and not embossed on the card, but included in the string of digits encoded on the magnetic stripe and visible on the signature strip on the back of the card. About 45 percent of merchants currently use some form of a "hot list," which identifies card numbers known to be stolen. Others use sophisticated analysis of transaction information to identify transactions that match profiles of fraudulent behavior. Finally, the newest response is geolocation technology, which examines the ISP through which the purchaser is connecting to assess the likelihood that the purchaser would be contacting the merchant from that location. But even with those products, the costs of fraud are high. Fraud in the early days of the commercial Internet ranged as high as 5 to 15 percent of all transactions, but persistent technological advances have brought the rate down to about 33 basis points (one-third of 1 percent), about five times the rate for face-to-face transactions.

For legal and historical reasons, losses from unauthorized transactions on the Internet are not treated the same way as losses from unauthorized transactions in conventional face-to-face retail transactions. As discussed above, issuers absorb losses from unauthorized transactions in the conventional face-to-face setting. Because the risk of fraud in transactions where the card is not present is so high, for many years the major credit-card networks excluded mail-order and telephone-order (MOTO) transactions from their networks. With the rise of the credit card as a major payment device of the American consumer, it became increasingly important to mail-order and telephone-order merchants that they be permitted to accept credit cards. So, after discussions with the credit-card networks, MOTO merchants began conducting card-not-present transactions, but they agreed to accept the risk that those transactions would be unauthorized. When Internet merchants began accepting credit cards, they became subject to the same card-not-present rules developed for MOTO transactions.

Still, even though Internet merchants bear the losses from fraud, credit-card issuers have a strong incentive to respond to fraud losses: If fraud losses remain as high as they have been to date, Internet merchants will have a powerful incentive to encourage their customers to use other payment systems that are more secure. The simplest possibility for the credit-card issuers would be to disseminate some PIN-like password authentication system. This is an almost revolutionary step, because for years only the debit-card system has relied on personal identification numbers (PINs); the credit-card system (as well as the debit-card systems promulgated by Visa and MasterCard) have stubbornly relied on the signature and account number alone as adequate for authentication. Finally, though, Visa and MasterCard introduced such products in the fall of 2001. The first step in getting those products deployed was to persuade individual issuing banks to implement systems to issue and check passwords. That process has been successful; more than 90 percent of Visa issuers, for example, participate in the "Verified by Visa" program. MasterCard's parallel program is called SecureCode.

The second step is to persuade merchants to modify their check-out software to require the consumer to enter the password. Merchants obviously have an incentive to keep their check-out procedures as simple as possible — data indicate that a substantial number of Internet purchases are lost from consumer frustration caused by lengthy check-out procedures. Nevertheless, to date merchants have been cooperative, at least in making the systems available to their customers. The incentive has been the willingness of the major networks to consider transactions authorized through the new PIN systems as card-present transactions: The issuers of the cards accept the risk of loss on those transactions. (The experience with debit-card transactions in the offline world suggests that fraud in those transactions will be quite low. Retail fraud on PIN-based cards is about one-twentieth the rate of fraud on signature-authorized cards.)

The problem, however, has been to persuade customers to sign on to those systems. The consumer is not liable in either event, so the consumer has little incentive to go to the trouble of collecting a PIN from the consumer's issuer for credit-card transactions. Thus, unless the issuer or the merchant *forbid* Internet transactions without a PIN (which no merchant or issuer has done to date), it is not at all obvious why any consumer would use the system.

A more dramatic possibility is that credit-card issuers could deploy "smart" cards. In this context, "smart" cards or "chip" cards refer to credit cards enhanced with an integrated-circuit chip. That chip includes a microprocessor and storage device which allows the card to perform a variety of functions, including — crucially for security reasons — a card-authentication function. When the cardholder first received the card, it would insert the card into a card-reader attached to a personal computer and enter a PIN.

Thereafter, to use the card in a card-not-present credit-card transaction, the cardholder would have to enter the card in the reader and enter the correct PIN. If the card and PIN are entered properly, the issuer can verify with considerable certainty that the card in fact is present and that the proper PIN has been entered. If the card and PIN were not properly entered, the issuer would decline the transaction. It is expected that those precautions would lower the fraud rate to something approaching the rate for PIN-protected transactions in the current environment.

The biggest obstacle to that solution is in getting the cards and readers disseminated to cardholders. Credit-card issuers have been looking for ways to use smart-card technology for years, without success. Several times in the last decade major American issuers have initiated widely advertised programs to issue general-purpose credit cards enhanced with such a chip; American Express's Blue card being the most prominent. No issuer, however, has yet succeeded in shifting a substantial portion of its Internet purchases to that technology.

Deployment of smart cards has been much more successful in other countries, but the driving force in most cases (as in the UK "Chip-and-PIN" program) has been brick-and-mortar fraud, not Internet transactions, which are much less important to overseas issuers than they are to American issuers. Thus, even in those countries in which consumers have chip-enhanced smart cards, they do not appear to use them commonly to make Internet purchases.

Looking even farther ahead, the "holy grail" of fraud prevention would be some form of "biometric" identification, which would authenticate transactions based on verification that certain physical characteristics (retina, fingerprint, or the like) of the individual presenting the card match the previously recorded physical characteristics of the person to whom the card was issued. For example, a smart card might store a record of the cardholder's fingerprint and prevent use of the card without entry of a matching fingerprint into a fingerprint pad connected to the computer through which the card was being used. Biometric technology has struggled for a variety of reasons, including not only technical difficulties but also consumer resistance. That technology has received a big boost in recent years from government initiatives that have forced the development of technology for use in, among other things, passports of foreign nationals entering this country. There is some possibility that the improvement in that technology might lead to its use in the credit-card market in the coming decade, but it remains quite a speculative subject.

Privacy   Even if the fraud problems are resolved, credit cards still face other serious issues, which continue to undermine the use of credit cards for Internet purchases. The most important of those issues surely is the privacy problem, which should be familiar to you from Chapter 3. For this context, the privacy problem has two manifestations. The first is the prospect, mentioned above, that interlopers will steal data from Internet merchants. In several widely publicized incidents, malefactors have succeeded in stealing large volumes of consumer data from prominent Internet merchants. The prospect that their transaction data will be compromised is likely to trouble some consumers even apart from the burden they will face in convincing their issuers to credit them for any unauthorized transactions that may result.

A more serious problem for consumers is the likelihood that the merchants and issuers themselves will make use of the data for reasons that trouble consumers. As a greater share of consumer purchases drift into online venues, the possibility continuously grows of aggregating individual consumer profiles at greater levels of detail. Consumers find it chilling to contemplate a database in the hands of direct marketers (or investigative reporters) that describes in detail the kinds of books, music, videotapes, clothes, and information they tend to purchase.

It is difficult to assess the seriousness of that problem. For many years, privacy concerns were thought to be a substantial obstacle that would keep consumers from using credit cards on the Internet and foster the development of more anonymous payment systems, such as so-called "electronic-money" systems. But the rapid growth of Internet retail transactions and the dominance of credit cards in those transactions suggest that the privacy issue may trouble consumers less than many observers expected.

The industry also has developed a technological response in the form of disposable credit-card numbers that inhibit the aggregation of payment information. Those systems (pioneered by Orbiscom, but now widely available) provide software to the purchaser's personal computer. The software generates a new credit-card number for each transaction. When the merchant sends the number through to the issuer, the number is valid only for that transaction. Thus, the merchant is no longer in a position to aggregate information based on the credit-card number (which will differ in each transaction). The only party in a position to aggregate information is the issuer (or, depending on the structure of the system, a third party generating the disposable numbers).

Thus, at least for the time being, it seems unlikely that privacy concerns will pose a substantial obstacle to the continued primacy of credit cards as a vehicle for Internet retail payments. However serious the concerns might be, the available technological solutions should solve the problem without significant disruption.

Micropayments   Another problem that confronts credit cards is that of micropayments. Because of their relatively high fixed costs, merchants generally have found credit cards unsuitable for transactions much below $10 in amount. In the early days of the Internet, it was expected that much of Internet commerce would involve information merchants selling information piece by piece for very small amounts—twenty-five cents or less in the near future, perhaps even fractions of a cent in decades to come. Those transactions could not occur, however, unless merchants could find a practical way to obtain payment. If credit cards could not provide that, then some other alternative would be necessary. As with the privacy issue, observers thought that the natural solution was a purely electronic payment system.

As it happens, however, the market has developed quite robustly without such a system, relying for payment on a variety of relatively conventional devices, most but not all of which rely on credit cards or checks in some way. First, most existing information merchants (primarily newspapers and sports-information sources) do not charge piece-by-piece, but instead charge a monthly subscription fee in an amount adequate to justify conventional credit-card payment. Economists studying the issue suggest that the piece-by-piece pricing model will be useful in many fewer contexts than observers originally had expected. Generally, they reason that the development of sophisticated bundling techniques by merchants, together with customer aversion to piece-by-piece pricing plans, has lessened the importance of the issue. Of course, it is entirely possible that customer aversion was caused not by piece-by-piece pricing models, but by the "clunky" software available for such programs several years ago. Software programs available now, not surprisingly, work much more smoothly and simply, and thus might be more acceptable to consumers.

Moreover, even when merchants do charge piece-by-piece, the problem has been resolved by one of a variety of payment aggregators that have arisen. Those aggregators provide software that gathers up a large number of a consumer's small transactions and then uses a conventional payment system to charge the consumer for the transactions periodically (normally once a month). For example, a consumer might receive a single monthly bill for all Internet information purchases, which the consumer could pay with a conventional check or credit card. In other systems, such as the highly touted

Bitpass system that went online in late 2003, the consumer deposits money in advance (perhaps $20) through some conventional payment system and then replenishes the funds whenever they are consumed. The provider typically provides the consumer a PIN to help ensure authenticity of the transactions. Yet another model (used most prominently by MicroCreditCard) aggregates a number of charges and then when the aggregate amount reaches a certain point (perhaps $8 to $10), charges the aggregate amount to the customer's credit card.

A variation on that model (used by companies like NTT DoCoMo in Japan, and by iPin and Trivnet in this country and in Europe) works through an Internet or wireless service provider to obtain a reliable identification of the payor from the payor's point of access to the Internet or wireless network: The Internet service provider and wireless service provider invariably are able to identify in a reliable way the account of the person accessing their systems. (At least theoretically, that person might not be the accountholder, but that seems to be a relatively small problem under current conditions.) Relying on that identification, those systems can dispense with the PIN requirement, which makes the transactions simpler to execute. Those systems then charge for the transactions by adding the appropriate charges to the monthly bill for Internet or wireless access. Because those payments come much later (perhaps 45 days after the transaction by the time the bills are sent and collected), merchants often must wait a considerable amount of time to obtain payment. But the charges merchants incur to obtain payment through those systems are so much lower than those associated with traditional credit cards that the systems are relatively attractive.

In sum, although it is much too early to identify what response will resolve the problem definitively in the long run, the technological responses discussed above seem to have solved the micropayment problem quite adequately for the time being. They might result in the insertion of an intermediary between credit-card issuers and merchants, but it is not clear that they will result in a major shift of Internet payments away from the credit card.

B.   Debit Cards

Besides the WEB entry discussed in Assignment 27, the most important shift in Internet payments in the last few years has been an almost invisible one: the rise of the debit card. This part of the assignment provides some basic background about debit cards and then discusses their use on the Internet.

1.   The Basics of Debit Cards

a.   Payment with a Debit Card

A debit card is physically almost indistinguishable from a credit card, with a magnetic stripe that technologically is quite similar to the stripe on a credit card. The distinction is that a debit card always serves as an adjunct to a checking (or savings) account. Thus, unlike a credit card, a debit card does not reflect an independent source of funds. Rather, it is a device to facilitate the customer's ability to draw on funds that are already in its account. Because transactions with a debit card draw on that account they are governed by the EFTA and Regulation E, just like the ACH transactions discussed in the previous assignment. See EFTA §903(6) (defining electronic funds transfer to include any "transfer of funds . . . initiated through an electronic terminal so as to order . . . a financial institution to debit . . . an account").

Debit cards have two primary uses. The first is for depositing and withdrawing money from an account at an automated teller machine (ATM). For present purposes, however, the more important function is use in point-of-sale (POS) transactions. Those transactions work much like the credit-card transactions described above. The customer (or the merchant) swipes the card at a terminal, the terminal conducts an online authorization transaction to verify the authenticity of the card and the availability of funds in the account, and the transaction is completed a few seconds later.

There is, however, an important distinction between two classes of debit cards: PIN-based (online) cards and PIN-less (offline) cards. PIN-based cards require the customer to enter a PIN to complete the transaction. Those cards are issued by one of a number of regional or national networks of banks, which clear transactions in much the same way as Visa and MasterCard. The use of a PIN in those transactions lowers the risk of fraud by a factor of about 20 (about three-tenths of a cent per $100 in PIN-based transactions versus six cents per $100 in credit-card and PIN-less debit transactions). The charges to merchants for PIN-based transactions also are much lower than the charges for conventional credit-card transactions, rarely more than 35 cents per transaction.

PIN-less debit transactions are authorized just like credit-card transactions, solely by presentation of the card and the cardholder's signature. Those transactions are cleared through the Visa and MasterCard networks and cost the merchants much more than the PIN-based transactions, roughly 1 percent of the transaction amount.

The precise amounts are shifting rapidly, because of successful antitrust litigation by major retailers that recently gave retailers the right to refuse Visa and MasterCard debit cards even if they accept Visa and MasterCard credit cards. The retailers had claimed that the Visa and MasterCard "honor-all-cards" rules amounted to an illegal tying arrangement. A settlement just before trial resulted in an agreement by Visa and MasterCard to abandon that rule and substantially lower the interchange fees for their PIN-less debit products.

b.   *Error and Fraud with Debit Cards*

The EFTA includes provisions for error and fraud that are parallel to (though not identical to) the TILA provisions on the same subject. For example, EFTA §908 includes a procedure for resolving disputed charges much like the billing-error procedure in TILA §161. The definition of billing error, however, is much narrower, generally applying only to claims that the cardholder in fact did not conduct a transaction that corresponds to the charge posted to the cardholder's account. See EFTA §908(f).

Similarly, EFTA §909 includes a general rule that limits customer responsibility for unauthorized transactions to $50. Unlike the rule in TILA §133, however, the bank can hold the customer responsible for more than $50 in several circumstances: if, for example, the cardholder does not notify its bank within two days of discovering a theft of the card or if the cardholder does not report unauthorized transactions within 60 days of receiving a statement that shows the transactions. EFTA §909(a).

2. Debit Cards on the Internet

In the early days of the Internet, credit cards had an appreciable advantage over debit cards largely because debit cards were relatively uncommon at the time. Debit cards, however, have made major advances in the United States since 1999, so that they now are used almost as frequently as credit cards. Moreover, because about 20 percent of American consumers do not have a credit card (including many teens and elderly persons that might be ideal customers for Internet retailers), Internet retailers that accept both credit cards and debit cards have access to a broader customer base than those that accept only credit cards. Moreover, acceptance of PIN-less debit cards is easy, because those transactions can be processed with precisely the same interface as Visa and MasterCard credit transactions.

Several other reasons apparent from the discussion above also motivate Internet merchants to accept debit cards. First, Internet merchants also prefer debit cards because of the smaller interchange fee they pay. Second, Internet merchants should prefer the finality of debit cards. As discussed above, credit-card transactions have been plagued with chargebacks. The more limited chargeback rights of debit cards should be particularly attractive to merchants. Third, the security of the debit card makes it a good substitute for the credit card. As discussed above, many Internet merchants are losing substantial revenues to claims of unauthorized transactions. If a product based on the PIN-based debit card could provide payment with the success rate that PIN-based debit cards enjoy in the offline environment, merchants would eradicate more than 99 percent of those fraud losses.

Given those advantages, it is not surprising that online retailers prefer debit-card transactions. For example, one recent survey of the top 25 online merchants suggested that they actually receive about 5 percent of their online payments by debit card, but that they would prefer to be paid by debit card in 25 percent of their transactions.

To date debit-card transactions on the Internet overwhelmingly are conducted with signature-based debit cards (VisaCheck and MasterMoney cards). Because those cards do not require a PIN, they can be used at most major online retailers in precisely the same way consumers use credit cards. Merchants would prefer that their customers be able to use PIN-based cards, both because of the diminished risks of fraud and because the charges they would pay for the transactions would be smaller as well. As it happens, however, it has been harder than expected to develop an Internet version of the debit card that would allow consumers to make PIN-protected debit transactions from the personal computer. The most likely significant advance in the next few years will be widespread deployment of such a product. Unlike the parallel credit-card programs, banking experts expect it to be quite easy to get customers to use PINs with those cards, because customers are accustomed to using PINs with those cards at ATMs and at retail locations.

C.   ACH Transfers (WEB Entries)

The last advance in Internet payments has been the development of an ACH transfer that can be used to make retail Internet purchases. Those transactions have grown exponentially in the years since the promulgation in early 2001 of new NACHA Rules governing "Internet-Initiated Entries" — WEB entries in the NACHA terminology. In 2003, customers initiated almost 700 million of those transactions, with an average amount of $291. NACHA reports that 80 percent of the payments have been to pay bills, 18 percent to transfer funds, and about 1 percent to make purchases.

The NACHA Rules make WEB systems generally available to all banks that participate in the ACH system, which in turn should facilitate merchants in incorporating those systems into their Web sites so that consumers can use them. Because about one in five consumers in the United States lacks a credit card, the availability of this system offers merchants a way to serve those customers. Thus, although retail Internet use has a relatively small market share (about 6 percent of payments in 2003), it is expected to grow rapidly, as major merchants like Wal-Mart have recently started accepting such payments at their sites.

Those systems start with a software program that a buyer and a seller place on their respective computers. If the buyer wishes to purchase an item using one of the ACH-check systems, a check-like form appears on the buyer's screen. The buyer fills out the form, except for the signature line (which typically is marked "No Signature Required"). When the buyer confirms the information on the form, the software encrypts the information and transmits it to the service provider. The service provider then generates a WEB ACH debit entry based on the information and clears that information through the normal ACH system discussed above. That entry is processed and cleared in much the same way a typical ACH transaction is cleared. Thus, the buyer's account is debited one or two business days later, and the merchant receives the funds at that time (or perhaps a few days later, depending on the system's specific features). Figure 28.1 illustrates that process.

Those transactions functionally are quite similar to debit-card transactions: They result in a contemporaneous transfer of funds from the purchaser's bank account to the seller, and the EFTA and Regulation E govern them. The principal difference is the information that the purchaser must provide: normally

Figure 28.1
ACH "Checks"

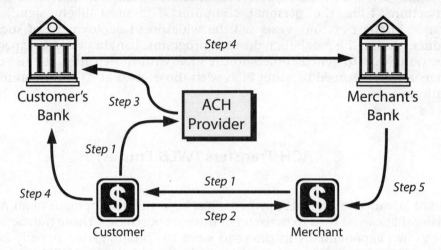

Step 1   The Customer sends payment information to the ACH Provider
          (probably through a link at the Merchant's Web site). The
          information should include the information from the MICR line
          of the Customer's check (the ABA routing number of the Customer's
          Bank and the Customer's account number at the bank).

Step 2   Based on the commitment to pay represented by that
          information, the Merchant completes the transaction. It might
          ship the goods at that time, or it might wait a few days to
          receive payment.

Step 3   The ACH Provider sends the ACH debit entry to the Customer's
          Bank.

Step 4   The Customer's Bank responds to that entry by removing funds
          from the Customer's account and sending them to the
          Merchant's Bank (through ACH network).

information that identifies the customer's bank account. Industry officials
expect considerable consumer resistance to providing that information to a
retailer; although the legal and practical risks are not in fact very different,
consumers are much more willing to provide their credit- or debit-card number to an Internet merchant than the information from the bottom of a check
that identifies their bank account.

   As with all ACH transactions, the system places fraud risks on the party
that sends the entry to the system. Thus, if a transaction is fraudulent, the
provider that is a member of the ACH system and entered the entry will bear
the loss: It will have to return the funds to the account from which they were
taken and will be left with a right to pursue the malefactor. Again, NACHA
strongly urges those providers to use robust methods of identifying parties
that enter transactions.

   When the buyers are consumers (rather than businesses), those transactions are subject to all of the protections of the EFTA. Thus, as discussed

above, the consumer ordinarily will have the right to disavow any transaction that is unauthorized. The consumer also will have the benefit of the EFTA dispute-resolution mechanism and will be able to see the identity of the payee on its monthly bank statement.

D.   Foreign and Cross-Border Payments

Because consumers in countries other than the United States use credit cards much less frequently, credit cards are not as dominant for Internet retail purchases in other countries. They are, however, the leading method of paying for Internet retail purchases. Interestingly, jurisdictions outside the United States generally have statutory protections for the users of those cards that are much less protective than those in the TILA/Z regime discussed above. There is a great deal of variety among the specific protections, but often there are no protections at all, and where protections exist, they often have more exceptions than the rules in TILA and Regulation Z. Thus, disputes about payments in those countries are much more likely to be resolved under the contracts between the issuer and the cardholder or between the issuer, the merchant, and the merchant's financial institution.

In the absence of a substitute for the credit card, one consequence has been to make it more common in other countries to pay for an Internet purchase with an offline payment method—a check sent through the mail or cash on delivery. In Japan, for example, a common model involves the retailer mailing the goods to a convenience store near the purchaser's home. The purchaser can obtain the goods by going to the convenience store and paying for them at that location. Similarly, statistics indicate that as of 2002 almost two-thirds of German online shoppers regularly used cash on delivery as a payment method. Few U.S. online shoppers have ever used that method.

In the absence of credit cards, retailers that wish to establish a presence in foreign markets have strong incentives to accept alternate forms of payment. Technology is still developing, but the most common denominator among developing alternative systems is some form of bank transfer or giro (the functional equivalent of an ACH transfer in the United States), which would result in a payment directly from the consumer's bank account to the merchant. The problem with that system is that it generally involves a separate transaction between the consumer and the consumer's financial institution, followed by a payment from the financial institution to the merchant and only at that point by shipment of the product. Given the common use of bank transfers in so many countries, it seems highly likely that an important payment product eventually will be one in which (1) a consumer can request a bank transfer directly from the merchant's site, (2) the merchant can verify the transfer in real time, and (3) shipment can be made immediately. Such a transaction would not differ in any substantial way from an online debit-card transaction in this country, except that the information entered by the consumer would be bank account information rather than a debit-card number. Such systems are not, however, widely deployed at this time.

At this time, cross-border payments are an even smaller market than for-eign payments. Because most of the major retailers operate a number of coun-try-specific sites, the great majority of Internet retailing occurs on a "national" basis. To date, transactions that occur across borders are predomi-nantly settled by Visa, MasterCard, American Express, or JCB, because those are the only major card brands with substantial cross-border clearance net-works. The law that applies to domestic purchases by the cardholder usually would govern payments in those transactions. The agreement between a card issuer and cardholder establishes the cardholder's obligations, and TILA and the EFTA limit those obligations, regardless of whether the card is used to buy something from Amazon.co.uk, from a brick-and-mortar retailer in London or Tokyo, or a restaurant in the United States. The principal difference is that the right to withhold payment under TILA §170 does not technically apply to transactions overseas. (Indeed, strictly speaking it does not apply to transac-tions more than 100 miles from, or outside the state of, the cardholder's res-idence. In practice, most issuers do not enforce any geographical limitation on rights under that section.)

The credit card is likely to face serious competition for cross-border pay-ment systems that can affect transfers directly from bank accounts. In the absence of international bank-clearance systems—something that the indus-try is only beginning to develop—those payments are not likely to be gen-erally available for some time. They do, however, have considerable potential within closely integrated economies like the member states of the European Union or NAFTA, where those kinds of clearing networks already are devel-oping.

E.   A Note on Mobile Payments

Although Internet retail transactions have been growing steadily over the last few years, the most rapid growth has been in mobile transactions—transac-tions where the purchase is made over a cellphone or other mobile electronic device. M-commerce transactions in the United States are expected to amount to $600 million in 2005. Those transactions are much more common over-seas, largely because of the greater penetration of the mobile phone: estimates are for $1.7 billion in Europe and $3.5 billion in Japan. For example, one recent press report contends that 40 percent of parking meter charges in Estonia are currently paid by use of a mobile phone with a proximity-pay-ment feature (discussed in more detail below).

Because the market is developing so rapidly, it is difficult to generalize, but a few points warrant attention. Security is the most serious issue that network operators confront. Because mobile-phone calls are notoriously insecure, it is important for payment information to be encrypted in some way that pre-vents it from being intercepted between the holder of the phone and the other party to the communication.

Generally, there are three main categories of payments. The first are so-called "in-band" or content payments, normally payments for information or content delivered directly to the telephone. For example, the most successful m-commerce application to date is the I-mode service provided by Japan's DoCoMo, which is used primarily to download "character" information. Other promising applications would deliver driving instructions, weather information, or the like. A second category is "out-of-band" payments — purchases in which a telephone is used to purchase something that cannot be delivered to the telephone. For example, industry officials hope to design systems in which pay-per-view television events can be purchased by mobile phone and charged directly to the telephone. The final category is proximity payments — when the telephone is used to make a payment by communication with a local device such as a parking meter or vending machine.

The methods of collecting for those payments are likely to develop over time, but presently two methods dominate. The first is the aggregation method discussed above for micropayments. For example, charges for i-Mode usage are simply added to the monthly mobile-phone bill; payments can be forwarded from the telephone company to the appropriate content provider. The second is for the merchant to use information sent from the telephone to conduct a contemporaneous credit- or debit-card transaction. That method makes much more sense for larger transactions, especially the out-of-band transactions discussed above. It functions in practice in just the same way as a conventional retail Internet purchase.

Relevant Glossary Entries

Identity Theft
Smart Card

Problem Set 28

28.1. Cliff Janeway (your book-dealer client) comes to see you to talk about developments in his industry. He finds that many of the people from whom he buys books now have many of the items he needs available for sale over the Internet. The three sites that he has examined so far accept both credit cards and debit cards. He has heard a lot about fraudulent transactions on the Internet, and he particularly remembers the press coverage when credit-card numbers were stolen in 2000 from CD Universe. As a result, he is worried that if he starts making such purchases he will expose himself to a significant risk. What do you tell him about his risks of being charged for unauthorized transactions on his credit card? Would it matter if the retailer from whom he made the purchase forced him to enter a PIN or the CVV from the back of his card? Would your advice be any different for his debit card? What if he made the purchase with a WEB entry? Does it make sense that those things should change the outcome? TILA §133; EFTA §§903(5), 909; Regulation E, §205.6; Regulation Z, §226.12.

28.2. Shortly after Cliff leaves, you get a call from your old friend Don Branson, who recently opened a Web site selling a variety of content useful for philosophy professors and graduate students, ranging from analytical outlines of major works, to translations of works in other languages, to sample questions for use in undergraduate philosophy courses. He had a major sale last week of $4,400 to one Quentin Lathrop (or, at least, to someone sending e-mail from quentin.lathrop@hotmail.com). As required by his bank, Don's Web page collected Lathrop's credit-card number, billing address, and telephone number. All of those items appear to match information for the holder of the card that was used for the transaction. Also as required by his bank, Don transmitted that information to the bank before completing the transaction, and waited to be sure that the bank had authorized the transaction. Don then sent the purchased information to Lathrop electronically. Don was happy to receive the money from that sale a few days later, because it was by far the largest sale he ever had done.

Things got worse after that. About three weeks later, Don got a call from the bank saying that Lathrop had repudiated the transaction, claiming that he never visited Don's Web site or purchased anything there. Don's banker called this morning to tell Don that Don had to return the money from the transaction. Don (a philosopher by trade) is most puzzled. He feels that he did everything he was supposed to do, and has already sent the purchased information to Lathrop. He does not understand what the purpose of having the bank authorize the transaction is if he's still liable if something goes wrong. What do you tell him? Would your answers differ if the purchase had been made with a PIN-based debit card? A signature-based debit card? A WEB entry?

28.3.   Would your answers to the previous questions be different if the purchaser used a cellphone to communicate with and received information from the merchant instead of an Internet connection? Would the EFTA apply? TILA? (Consider both the case where the charges are added to the cellphone bill and the case where the charges are posted to a credit-card or debit-card account.)

28.4.   Your congressional representative, Pamela Herring, asks for your help on a new bill she is developing. She has been trying to update the protections Congress has provided for consumer payment systems. Her perception is that debit cards and credit cards are more or less substitutes for each other. Thus, she wonders whether you think it would be a good idea, at least in the Internet context, to extend the right to withhold payment from TILA §170(a) to the EFTA, so that debit-card Internet purchasers would have the same right to withhold payment as credit-card purchasers do. What do you think?

Assignment 29: P2P Payments and EBPP Systems

As discussed in the preceding assignment, the rise of Internet retailers has not produced any substantial revolution in payment practices. Rather, most payments to Internet retailers are made with conventional card-based payment systems. This is not to say, however, that the Internet has not led to the development of new methods of payment. The last decade has seen the rise of two significant new payment methods. The first are person-to-person (P2P) systems like PayPal, which is used by about one in three online shoppers in the United States. In 2003, the PayPal platform was used to process payments in approximately 230 million transactions, or about 629,000 transactions per day. The second are systems for electronic bill presentment and payment (EBPP). One interesting aspect of those developments is that neither presents a "new" payment system — both rely on existing systems (credit cards, debit cards, checking accounts, and ACH transfers) to make payments. Essentially, they use the technology of the Web site to facilitate the use of conventional payment networks.

A. The Basics

The excerpt that follows discusses how those new systems work and the federal regulatory apparatus that covers their operations.

Ronald J. Mann, Regulating Internet Payment Intermediaries
82 Texas L. Rev. 681 (2004)

II. THE NEW TRANSACTIONS

A. P2P SYSTEMS

The success of eBay's auction business had the rare effect of creating a vast market for an entirely new payment product, one that would allow non-merchants (who cannot accept conventional credit-card payments) to receive payments quickly in remote transactions. Without such a system, purchasers in the early days of eBay had to use cashier's checks or money orders. Typically, sellers waited to ship products until they received the paper-based payment device in the mail. From a flood of startups offering competing products, PayPal (now owned by eBay) has emerged as the dominant player in the industry, now processing hundreds of millions of payments each year. Indeed, industry sources expect that by

2005, auction payments will account for 95% of the possibly four *billion* person-to-person payment transactions expected to be made that year. A separate (and much smaller) submarket, exemplified by CitiBank's c2it service, uses similar systems for cross-border payments.

To understand the policy ramifications of P2P payments, it is necessary to understand the relation between the P2P provider and the conventional accounts from which and to which P2P payments are made. That relation can be illustrated by a summary of the three steps that must be completed for a successful P2P transaction.

1.   Providing Funds for Payment

The purchaser that wishes to use a P2P provider to make a payment has two general ways to provide funds for payment. First, it could fund an account with the provider, normally by drawing on a deposit account or a credit-card account. Because it ensures that funds are available for an immediate transfer, that process is common for those who make frequent purchases. P2P account balances also are common for frequent eBay sellers, who receive funds into their P2P accounts from those to whom they make sales. Alternatively, the purchaser could wait until the moment that it wishes to make a purchase. Again, it could choose at the time of payment to provide the funds in question by drawing on either a deposit account or a credit-card account. As discussed below, the choice between a credit card and a deposit account as a funding source has significant legal consequences to the user.

In either case, the fee structure is likely to discourage the use of credit cards, because the P2P provider incurs higher fees when it pays the interchange owed to the bank that has issued the credit card from which funds are drawn than when it pays the fees necessary to draw funds from a deposit account through a debit entry in the ACH system. Similarly, because the P2P provider can profit by investing funds that remain in transaction accounts, some providers (including PayPal) encourage users to leave funds in those accounts by paying interest on them.

2.   Making Payments

The attraction of the P2P process, of course, is that it is quite simple to make payments. Normally, the only information that the purchaser needs to make a payment is the amount of money and the email address of the intended recipient. After entering that information into a form at the P2P provider's Web site, the purchaser clicks on a "send money" button to request execution of the transaction. If the funds are sent from a balance in an account with the P2P provider or if they are drawn from a credit card, they should arrive in a few hours. If they are drawn directly from a deposit account, arrival will be delayed by a few days (until settlement of the ACH transaction to obtain the funds from the user's bank).

3.   Collecting Payments

The final step is for the recipient (the seller if the payment is for an auction) to collect the payment. In the typical process, the recipient receives an email notifying it that the payment has arrived. If the recipient has an account with the P2P provider and is willing to leave the funds in that account, then it need do nothing further. If it does not have an account, or if it wishes to withdraw the funds, it will need to go to the provider's Web site and provide the necessary details.

Ordinarily, the recipient will pay some fee to the provider for making the payment available. Those fees vary considerably, but a typical charge at PayPal would be 25-50 cents plus 2-4 percent of the transaction amount. In addition, if the payment is made with a credit card, the recipient may be required to bear the cost of any chargeback that the payor seeks under its agreements with the provider and card issuer.

B.   EBPP SYSTEMS

EBPP systems are at a much less mature stage in their development than P2P systems. Accordingly, it is much harder to provide a clear picture of their operations. Generally, though, three different models compete within that industry. The first are products presented by the billing businesses, which send bills to consumers by email and provide a Web site at which payment can be made. The second are products of depositary institutions, which permit their customers to pay bills at a Web site operated by the institution. The third are offered by third-party intermediaries. The intermediaries operate Web sites that collect bills from various businesses, present them to consumers on behalf of the billers, and then forward payment from the consumers to the billers.

As with P2P systems, the fact that the different models compete to perform quite similar services for consumers should not obscure the significantly differing legal and policy implications of the different models. Accordingly, it is important to explain briefly how each of the three models works.

1.   Biller Web Sites

As the name suggests, the biller Web site model is quite simple: the consumer goes directly to the biller's Web site to view the bill. In many cases, the site will "push" the bill to the consumer by sending an email that includes a link to the full details of the bill. If the consumer is satisfied with the bill, it authorizes the biller to collect payment. The biller, in turn, proceeds to collect the payment (often through a third-party provider such as CheckFree). Alternatively, the biller itself could initiate an ACH transaction debiting the consumer's account.

As compared to conventional paper-based billing processes, those sites can save the substantial costs of preparing and mailing paper bills, as well as the costs of receiving and processing payments by mail. There is likely to be a substantial reduction in the costs of customer-support systems, as many inquiries can be shifted from the telephone to Web-site response systems. Those sites also can have considerable marketing advantages, by enhancing the biller's ability to provide targeted advertising and by enabling the biller to develop more sophisticated customer profiles through the collection of information about bill-paying habits. Many consumers also will view the systems as more convenient than traditional paper-based systems. The biggest problem with those systems is the inefficiency of each consumer going to a separate site to pay each bill.

In the marketplace, those sites have been moderately successful, particularly for credit-card issuers. Because the costs of the technology continue to decrease, there is good reason to think that more billers will offer such sites, as the number of customers necessary for the sites to break even falls.

2.   Internet Banking

When banks provide sites, they can overcome the biggest problem that biller Web sites face: the need for consumers to pay their bills site by site. Thus, at the typical bank site, a consumer can pay any bill necessary, by entering onto a form at the site the information that the consumer has about the payment. Smaller banks are likely to outsource all of the payment functions to a third-party provider like CheckFree. Larger banks, however, may arrange the payments themselves in whatever manner is most cost-effective. For example, if the recipient is a major biller (such as a local utility), the bank may aggregate payments in a batch and pay them with a single ACH transaction. For isolated transactions, the bank might even cut a paper cashier's check and mail it to the recipient. Those sites have been particularly successful in recent years. One possible reason is that consumers are more willing to trust the necessary financial information to a bank at which they have a depositary relationship than to a third party billing them for a payment.

Another advantage, particularly by comparison to the third-party sites discussed below, is the simplicity of operation. The bank already would be involved in the payment transaction — whatever type of site the consumer used — but use of the bank's site obviates the need for involvement of an extra party. Also, many bank sites do not undertake to present bills electronically. Rather, they simply provide an easy method for consumers to pay the bills that are delivered to them by conventional means. Thus, they avoid the complications attendant on electronic presentation of bills, which is a common feature of the two competing models. Of course, that may not be an advantage if consumers desire the functionality available from bill presentment. Thus, it is no surprise that bank sites increasingly offer bill-presentment services.

3.   Third-Party Providers

The most ambitious systems are Web sites operated by third parties at which consumers can view and pay all (or almost all) of their bills. The promise of those sites is a future of a single integrated portal, through which all bills will be sent to a consumer and at which the consumer will be able to pay all bills. The logistical problems of operating such a site are daunting. For one thing, the intermediary operating such a site (CheckFree, for example) must reach agreements with a large number of billers allowing it to present bills on their behalf and establishing a standardized data format for the information in those bills. At the same time, the intermediary must persuade enough consumers to use the site to justify the fixed costs of developing the site's technology. Without a critical mass of billers and consumers, the site cannot prosper. This is, of course, a standard problem of bandwagon effects.

When a consumer uses such a site to pay a bill, the process operates much as it does at a bank Web site. The consumer identifies the appropriate bill and authorizes payment. The intermediary, in turn, arranges for the payment to be sent to the biller, normally through an ACH debit entry from the consumer's deposit account.

For billers that do not operate their own site, these sites offer a significant benefit because of the potential for the cost savings that come from electronic presentation of bills (discussed above as a benefit of biller Web sites). But the cumbersome nature of the technology to date has made progress slow. Still, if they can overcome technical problems, they could ultimately become the dominant model.

III.   DESIGNING A SOUND REGULATORY SYSTEM

The first question in assessing the adequacy of regulatory protections for the developing Internet payment transactions is to assess the extent to which the consumer protections that apply to existing transactions extend to the new transactions. Two forms of consumer protection are relevant here: information privacy and protection from losses related to fraud or error.

The simpler of those relates to information privacy. Specifically, under Gramm-Leach-Bliley (GLB), "financial institutions" must not disclose nonpublic personal information to third parties unless they have given their customers an opportunity to opt out of any such disclosures.[53] Some might criticize the narrowness of that protection. It is much narrower, for example, than protections afforded European consumers under the EU's Data Protection Directive and the statutes that implement it. For present purposes, however, what is important is that a broad definition of "financial institution" in the applicable regulations means that the rules in GLB apply with just as much force to the new intermediaries as they do to banks and other depository institutions.[57]

It is much more complicated to assess the legal framework that protects consumers from fraud and error, because that framework plainly does not extend completely to the new payment intermediaries. . . .

B.   PROTECTIONS AGAINST FRAUD AND ERROR IN THE NEW TRANSACTIONS

Unfortunately, the legal framework protecting consumers against fraud and error has not been updated to accommodate the new transactions. Thus, that framework includes three types of problems: situations where the incoherent distinction between the TILA/Z and EFTA/E regime is replicated in the new environment, minor oversights in regulatory drafting, and more significant omissions in regulatory coverage. The sections below discuss how those rules apply to the new transactions, underscoring those problems where they arise.

1.   P2P Transactions

Current experience suggests that fraud is a serious problem in P2P transactions. One Federal Reserve researcher, for example, estimates that PayPal's fraud rate of 0.66 percent, albeit much lower than the rate of online credit-card fraud, is about four times the rate of fraud for retail credit-card transactions and more than sixty times the rate for retail debit-card transactions. The legal rules for determining whether the consumer bears the losses from that fraud, however, depend in an important way on how the consumer pays for the transaction. To see the point,

---

53. 15 U.S.C. §6802(a) (financial institutions "may not . . . disclose to any nonaffiliated third party any nonpublic personal information, unless such financial institution provides . . . notice").

57. *See* 16 C.F.R. §313.3(k)(2)(vi) ("A business that regularly wires money to and from consumers is a financial institution. . . .").

imagine an eBay auction in which a fraudulent seller never ships any goods to the buyer. If the transaction is funded from the purchaser's account with the P2P provider, it is an EFT governed by the EFTA.[83] In that event, the purchaser has no right — as against the financial institution or the P2P provider — to recover the funds for an authorized transaction solely because of a complaint about misconduct by the seller, however meritorious the complaint. The same analysis applies if the purchaser funds the transaction by authorizing a transfer directly from the purchaser's deposit account: that also leads to an EFT covered by the EFTA/E regime.

But if the buyer has the good luck (or foresight) to fund the purchase directly from a credit card, the transaction is governed instead by the TILA/Z regime. Among other things, that means that the purchaser would have the right to withhold payment if the seller in fact never supplies the goods.[85] The statute grants a broad right to the cardholder to withhold payment based on "all claims (other than tort claims) and defenses arising out of any transaction in which the credit card is used as a method of payment." [TILA §170(a).] Thus, if the transaction through PayPal is viewed as a single unified transaction in which the auction purchaser uses PayPal and the credit card to buy something from an auction seller, the TILA/Z regime protects the purchaser.[87] As discussed above, it is odd to have such an important protection turn on something that is as trivial to the transaction as the method by which the purchaser funds the transaction to the P2P provider. . . .

The other likely type of fraud is for a third party to obtain the consumer's PayPal login information and use that information to conduct an unauthorized transaction by drawing on the consumer's PayPal account. If the interloper draws directly on the P2P account, Regulation E makes the P2P intermediary directly responsible: subject to the normal exceptions, the P2P provider cannot charge the consumer's account for the transaction.[89] The same result applies under the TILA/Z regime if the interloper uses the information to draw funds from the consumer's credit card.[90]

The only ambiguity applies if the interloper uses the information to withdraw funds from the consumer's deposit account. In that event — because of an odd glitch in the regulation — it seems that neither the P2P provider nor the bank is obligated to return the funds to the consumer's deposit account. The bank apparently is not obligated, because it is entitled to treat the transaction as

---

83. Section 903(6) of the EFTA defines an "electronic fund transfer" as a "transfer of funds . . . initiated through an electronic terminal . . . so as to . . . authorize a financial institution to debit or credit an account." *See* Regulation E §205.3(b) (similar definition).

85. In the framework of the statute, the bank attempting to collect the credit-card bill would be subject to the defense that the PayPal purchaser never received the goods it purchased. [TILA §170; Regulation Z §226.12(c).]

87. The statute could be read more narrowly. American Express, for example, apparently has argued that the transaction is one in which PayPal is the seller and that PayPal has satisfied its obligation by sending money to the seller. On that understanding, American Express (or any other card issuer with the boldness to raise the argument) would have no obligation to respect the defense under [TILA §170]. Even American Express, however, receded from that position after it was challenged recently by the New York Attorney General. [The New York Attorney General subsequently succeeded in a similar confrontation with Discover.] My students' reaction to this question convinces me that the reading advanced by American Express is a plausible one. Accordingly, a revision of Regulation Z to remove that ambiguity would be useful.

89. The intermediary is a financial institution under [EFTA §903a(8) and Regulation E] §205.2(i). Because the transaction is unauthorized, the intermediary cannot remove more than $50 of funds from the account under [EFTA §909(a)]. *See also* [Regulation E] §205.6(b)(1) (limiting consumer liability for unauthorized transfers to $50 if the financial institution is timely notified of loss or theft). If the intermediary does remove more than $50, it must restore the funds within ten days of proper notice under [EFTA §908(c) and Regulation E] §205.11(c)(2)(i).

90. [Regulation Z] §226.12(b).

authorized — a transaction is authorized under the EFTA if it is executed by a party (the P2P provider in this case) to whom the consumer has given the relevant access information.[91] Because that fact makes the transaction "authorized" with respect to the account from which funds were drawn, it appears that the rules related to "unauthorized" transaction impose no obligation on the P2P provider for the loss. The most likely source of recovery for the consumer would be an action against the P2P provider's depositary institution (the entity that originated the ACH transfer) for a breach of the applicable NACHA warranties.[92] Because of the limited litigation to date in that area, it is difficult to assess the likelihood of prevailing in such an action.[93]

That problem, however, is not a serious one. Unlike the incoherent boundary between the EFTA/E and TILA/Z regimes — which is a somewhat more permanent feature of our system — this problem seems to be a simple glitch, which the Federal Reserve easily could remedy on its own volition.[94]

2.   EBPP Transactions

Because of the variety of business models, it is difficult to provide a comprehensive schema of the types of transactions that pose risks for consumers. One simplifying factor, however, is the general absence of credit-card payments from those transactions. What that means is that the legal issues focus almost entirely on the reach of the EFTA/E regime,[95] rather than its boundary with the TILA/Z regime. The simplest approach is to look separately at the risks posed by each of the three prevailing business models.

(a)   Biller Web Sites

The most likely difficulty is an unjustified payment to the biller: the biller might pay one consumer's bill from another consumer's account or it might pay itself for a bill even if the consumer in fact did not authorize payment. Interestingly enough, the EFTA/E regime would not provide protection in either case. As discussed above, the consumer cannot claim that the transactions are "unauthorized" for purposes

---

91. *See* [EFTA §§903(1)] (defining "accepted card or other means of access"), [903(11)] (defining "unauthorized electronic fund transfer"); [Regulation E §§] 205.2(a)(1) (defining "[a]ccess device"), 205.2(m) (defining "[u]nauthorized electronic fund transfer").

92. *See* NACHA Rules §2.2.1.1 (warranty of authorization by the Originator of an ACH transfer).

93. The limited cases to date suggest that all parties to the transaction arguably have a claim for breach of that warranty. *E.g., Security First Network Bank v. C.A.P.S., Inc.,* 2002 WL 485352 (N.D. Ill. 2002) (permitting suit by victim of fraud against bank that executed unauthorized ACH transfers; discussing earlier cases).

94. One simple response would be to add a new subsection 205.14(c)(3) stating as follows:

Any unauthorized transaction that results in the removal of funds from the account at the financial institution will constitute a billing error for purposes of Section 205.11(a)(1), for which the payment service provider is responsible under Section 205.14(a), if the transaction involves the use either of (A) the access device issued by the payment service provider to the customer or (B) the access device provided by the consumer to the payment service provider for the account at the financial institution.

Because Section 205.14(c)(2) plainly implements the error-resolution procedures as against the payment service provider, the proposed subsection would ensure that the provider is obligated to restore funds to the consumer's account at the consumer's bank just as quickly as the bank would have to restore funds for a traditional unauthorized transaction.

95. *See* [Regulation E Official Staff Commentary §3(b)-1(vi)] (including within the definition of electronic fund transfer "payment made by a bill payer under a bill-payment service available to a consumer via computer or other electronic means").

of the EFTA/E regime. For similar reasons, the consumer cannot claim that they amount to an "error." The statutory definition of "error," albeit vague, is directed to errors by the bank, not errors by a third party to whom the consumer has granted access.[97] Thus, the statute offers the consumer no recourse in that situation. Perhaps the situation is not unduly troublesome — given the likely solvency of the typical billing entity — but it does seem inconsistent with the general philosophy of the EFTA/E regime. . . .

(b)   Internet Banking

The framework for Internet banking is the simplest. Because there is no intermediary,[98] the financial institution takes all actions regarding the account. Accordingly, the rules in the EFTA/E regime apply directly to protect the consumer from unauthorized transactions and errors.

(c)   Third-Party Providers

As the discussion above suggests, the harshest results for consumers come from the third-party systems, where the insertion of an intermediary enhances the likelihood that the EFTA/E regime will not apply. Two general problem transactions are apparent:

(I)   Interloping and Erroneous Bills

In this scenario, a malefactor fabricates a bill and has the provider send it to the consumer. Alternatively, and less maliciously, the bill is a legitimate one that, because of an error by the intermediary, is posted and distributed to the wrong consumer. Then, suppose that the consumer pays the fraudulent or erroneous bill. For the reasons discussed above, the consumer will not be able to claim that the transaction is either unauthorized or a remediable error. Of course, in this particular transaction it is easy to fault the consumer for not detecting the spoofed bill. But in many of the existing cases of Internet fraud, a consumer of ordinary sophistication would not necessarily have recognized the problem. Imagine a bill purporting to come from your local electric utility, in a format visually identical to the electric bill you receive every month, which arrives 29 days after your last bill and is in an amount approximately equal to that bill. Your first hint of a problem is likely to come when the legitimate bill appears the next day. Given that problem (a variation on the new Internet crime called "phishing"), it is reasonable to consider whether intermediaries should bear those losses. If they were responsible for those losses, they might be better motivated to develop technology to detect such infiltrations. For present purposes, the important point is that the existing legal rule for this situation reflects pure happenstance rather than a reasoned resolution of the economic and policy issues.

(II)   Interloping Payments

In this scenario, the intermediary makes a payment based on an instruction from an interloping malefactor rather than the consumer. As with the analogous P2P transactions, the ambiguity in the regulation's coverage of unauthorized transactions leaves a substantial possibility that the consumer has no protection.

97. [EFTA §908(f).]
98. As discussed above, there might be an intermediary (such as CheckFree) between the bank and the payee, but that is irrelevant to the concerns of this paper, because there would be no intermediary between the consumer and the institution that holds the consumer's deposit account. To put it another way, it is plain that Regulation E would protect the consumer from mistakes by CheckFree operating as an intermediary between the bank and the payee.

3.   Summary

Although the discussion in the preceding sections might seem unduly detailed, the level of detail is important to show how difficult it is to design a system to govern the transactions in question. Neither the EFTA nor Regulation E is particularly old. Nor are they supervised by a regulatory agency out of touch with the developments in these transactions — many of the most informative papers in the area are written by Federal Reserve staff, particularly by members of the group studying emerging payments in its Chicago branch. The point, however, is that these transactions are developing so rapidly and with such fertile inventiveness that it is difficult to expect any regulatory system to keep pace and ensure coherent coverage as long as the system is premised on the categorical distinctions that drive the current framework.

Thus, even with a coherent response to the problems addressed above, there is every reason to expect that new problems would emerge rapidly, leaving the regulatory coverage again uncertain. The basic point is that such problems are inevitable until and unless a more functional code is adopted to govern electronic payments generally. Meanwhile, the minor change discussed above could at least make the system as coherent for these transactions as it is for conventional transactions.

IV.   ENSURING REGULATORY COMPLIANCE

Part III of this paper operates entirely within the framework of the existing regulatory apparatus. Thus, it is limited to considering the extent to which GLB and the EFTA/E and TILA/Z regimes replicate for the new transactions the regulatory environment that they impose on conventional transactions. This Part examines the regulatory system from a broader perspective. It starts by focusing on a fundamental problem implicit in the existing system: the distinction between the level of responsibility to be expected from conventional financial institutions and that to be expected from the new Internet-based intermediaries. It then discusses three types of potential regulatory approaches. Finally, it summarizes tentative recommendations for the P2P and EBPP contexts based on what we currently know about them.

A.   THE PROBLEM

The EFTA and TILA use the typical apparatus of the modern federal regulatory statute: provisions for class actions, statutory damages, attorney fees, and the like.[105] Accordingly, it would be natural to conclude that a careful analysis of the problems discussed in Part III of this paper should be enough to resolve the problem. Once the EFTA/E and TILA/Z regimes are brought up to date, we might think, the new entities would comply and all would be well.

Two general concerns, however, make that optimistic outlook seem implausible. First, it is doubtful that the kinds of civil-liability regimes at hand — which rely primarily on litigation by small and dispersed consumers — will be able to control the behavior of the large businesses at which they are directed. That is particularly

---

105. [EFTA §915; TILA §130.]

true in this context, where the facts of each unauthorized transaction and billing error often will be specific to each individual consumer.

Second, the pervasive federal regulation of banks substantially increases the likelihood that banks will comply with their obligations under the TILA/Z and EFTA/E regimes. At the most basic level, the direct purpose of much of federal banking regulation — federal supervision of capital maintenance and lending practices — is to ensure the solvency and fiscal prudence of the institutions. If that regulation is even marginally effective, it increases the likelihood that banks will have the assets necessary to comply with their obligations under those statutes. That might seem like a small thing, but the likelihood that a major Internet payment fraud could create a regulatory responsibility beyond the assets of a small dotcom P2P provider is plausible. That is particularly true given the likelihood that those providers will be targets for fraudulent activity, as PayPal has been. More generally, the persistent supervision and need to accommodate regulators on a regular basis makes it quite difficult for a bank to adopt a cavalier attitude about regulatory compliance.

The same analysis applies to privacy obligations. It does not take a hardened cynic to think that the chances of systematic noncompliance — or even lackadaisical compliance that tolerates a significant number of low-level violations — is much more likely for unregulated companies than for regulated depository institutions. In assessing that likelihood, it is important to note that GLB, unlike TILA and the EFTA, does not provide for a private cause of action.[113] Finally, it also is worth wondering whether smaller companies that are unregulated and financially constrained will be adequately motivated to expend the resources necessary to protect their consumer's information from unauthorized access by third parties.

To put the point generally, the regulatory regimes directed to the activities of the new payment intermediaries depend in part for their effectiveness on the background regulatory supervision of the banks governed by those regimes. Because nonbank payment intermediaries are not generally subject to that supervision, there is a cognizable risk that they will show less care in complying with those regimes than conventional depository institutions.

B.   State Regulation

The absence of pervasive federal regulation has not left the new payment providers entirely free from regulation. On the contrary, P2P systems in particular have drawn the attention of state regulators either because of their potential for money laundering or because of the use of the systems to make payments connected with online gambling operations. Thus, PayPal currently is registered as a money transmitter in 23 states and the District of Columbia. Money-transmitter statutes generally require businesses to obtain a state licenses, impose periodic reporting requirements, and make businesses subject to audits

---

113. *See* 15 U.S.C. §6805 (authorizing enforcement by regulatory authorities).

by state officials. They also may include minimum net worth or bond requirements or impose restrictions on permissible investments. EBPP systems, in contrast, have drawn less attention, primarily because the market is so fragmented
that no nonbank player has become large enough to warrant attention.

As the industry has become more consolidated, considerable pressure has
arisen for more uniformity in the various state regulatory schemes. That pressure in turn has led to the recent drafting and promulgation of the proposed
Uniform Money Services Act (already adopted in Iowa, Vermont, and
Washington). That statute, however, does not apply to most EBPP providers.
See UMSA §102(14) (defining "Money transmission" to mean "selling or issuing payment instruments, stored value, or receiving money or monetary
value for transmission").

C.   Foreign and Cross-Border Transfers

EBPP systems have little cross-border application, because the overwhelming
majority of bills come from the same jurisdiction as the consumer. Moreover,
they have gained even less penetration overseas than they have in the
United States.

The foreign market for P2P payments is growing rapidly. P2P payments also
increasingly are used for cross-border transactions. The cross-border market is
expected to be significant in the years to come, primarily because P2P transfers are the most effective vehicle by which individuals can transfer funds
from one country to another. Credit cards cannot be used to pay individuals,
and checks (even electronic checks) are unwieldy because of the long delays
in clearing checks sent across national borders. Thus, PayPal currently sends
funds not only in U.S. dollars, but also in Canadian Dollars, Pounds Sterling,
Euros, and Yen. PayPal transactions also are particularly well suited to cross-
border purchases in the European Union, where many purchasers do not have
a credit card. They allow a purchaser in one country to pay a seller in another
country without the concerns about cross-border bank clearing that make
cross-border debit-card transactions difficult.

Because of concerns about fraud, PayPal's seller protection policy generally
does not apply to cross-border transactions except for sales into the United
States from Canada and the United Kingdom. Using PayPal, customers with
credit cards can send payments from 45 countries (including the United
States) and can receive payments in 44 of those countries. In 22 countries,
customers can withdraw funds from their PayPal accounts to local bank
accounts. PayPal imposes fees for withdrawal and receipt of funds outside the
United States, for cross-border transactions and for currency conversion.
PayPal strongly recommends against making shipments to addresses outside
of those countries.

PayPal also is licensed under the EU Directive on Electronic Money in most
EU countries. Thus, its subsidiaries that operate in those countries are subject
to minimum capitalization requirements (Article 4), investment limitations
(Article 5), and auditing requirements (Article 6), much like the requirements
that the Uniform Money Services Act and similar statutes impose on PayPal

in jurisdictions where it has registered in the United States. There have not, however, yet been any regulations that would govern allocation of losses internal to the transactions (analogous to the TILA and EFTA rules discussed above). Thus, as with conventional credit- and debit-card transactions, the European Union has been much more deferential to the contracts established by the parties than the United States. As these transactions become more common in the European Union, of course, that might change.

Problem Set 29

29.1. Cliff Janeway comes to talk to you. It appears that he has taken to going to eBay to purchase rare books for his store. His problem relates to an auction he won yesterday for a rare and beautiful edition of Poe's *The Raven*. As he always does, Cliff paid for the purchase with his PayPal account. Unfortunately, he confused the seller at the *Raven* auction with the seller at another auction on which Cliff had bid unsuccessfully earlier in the day. The result is that Cliff inadvertently typed the wrong e-mail address in his payment request on PayPal and sent the money off to the wrong seller (someone from whom he previously had purchased a much less expensive book). When the seller of *The Raven* contacted Cliff several hours later seeking to arrange for payment of the $12,000 purchase price, Cliff tried unsuccessfully to cancel the payment. He then tried to contact the actual (but unintended) recipient by telephone, but was unable to find a working telephone number. Worried about the problem, Cliff wants your advice on what he can do. What do you say? EFTA §§903, 908, 909; TILA §§103, 104, 133, 161; Regulation E, §§205.2, 205.6, 205.11; Regulation Z, §226.13.

29.2. Cliff's next question for you arises from frustration. He buys many more things than he sells on eBay. And his common practice is to fund those purchases with transfers from his bank account. When he transfers funds from his bank account, however, the transfers do not show up in his PayPal account for several days (usually about four business days, as illustrated by the policy displayed on the PayPal Web site). Recalling earlier discussions with you about funds availability rules, he can't understand how their policy is lawful. "Isn't there some federal law that says they're obligated to give me the money quickly? I thought if it was a local transaction they had to make the money available to me in just a couple of days? How can they get away with this?" Regulation CC, §§229.2(a), 229.10(b).

29.3. The next morning you meet with Dorothea Brooke. She has started a small business buying up small, hand-made craft objects in nearby rural towns and reselling them on Internet sites. She thinks she would like to sign up with at least one prominent P2P provider. Her basic motivation is that she has been selling things only for money orders or personal checks, which means that she doesn't get paid for a week or more after the conclusion of the auction. Not surprisingly, she is attracted to the idea of getting paid almost immediately. When she went in to set up the account, however, she noticed a lot of material on the Web site about her "payment preferences." (You can review material from PayPal on that topic at the Web site for this text.) She wants to know your views on whether she should enable her system to accept payments funded by credit cards or insist on the more cashlike forms of payment. What are the risks to her of accepting the credit-card payments? Is there any reason why she nevertheless might wish to accept the credit-card payments?

29.4. You have a meeting this afternoon with a new client, Hallie Kent, who operates a P2P service called WePayNow.com. She wants to talk to you about problems that she has been having with fraudulent transactions. The specific scheme that has been most common involves people who have stolen credit-card numbers. Each person opens two WePayNow accounts in different names. They then use the stolen credit-card number to make payments from one account to the other. They promptly withdraw the money and take no further action on the accounts when the card's limit has been reached. Then, at the end of the month when the bill reaches the actual cardholder, that cardholder normally declines to pay the charges. This week Hallie received a letter from her bank explaining that it was deducting $75,000 from her account for funds that it had forwarded to a large issuer for fraudulent transactions on that issuer's cards last month. Is Hallie obligated to make that payment?

29.5. Your first meeting this week is with a new client named Chris Nelson, who runs a startup software firm. Chris set up his firm to pay all of its bills through PaySure, an Internet bill-presentment service. After just one month, he has formed a very low opinion of PaySure's reliability, based on two separate incidents arising out of their service. In the first incident, he received an e-mail message from PaySure advising him that his electric bill needed to be paid. He clicked through on the link in the e-mail to a page that seemed to indicate his electrical usage for the month and asked him to authorize payment of the bill. Because the amount seemed about right, he paid the bill. Accordingly, he was shocked when he received another message the next day purporting to enclose his electric bill. When he called the electric company, it quickly became clear that the first bill was false ("spoofed" was the term the electric company representative used). Notwithstanding the genuine appearance of the page that Nelson viewed, it appears that the first payment was sent to a thief with no relation either to the electric company or to PaySure.

The second incident was discovered when Chris (perturbed by the electric company incident) went to his bank and looked at the bank's records of all of the charges on his account. He immediately noticed that the car payment he paid on PaySure the previous week appeared to have been sent twice.

Chris came to see you because his bank was unwilling to recredit Chris's account for either of the payments. What do you tell him? Is there anything that you would like to know? EFTA §§903, 908, 909; Regulation E §§205.2, 205.6, 205.11.

29.6. The next day, Chris Nelson comes back again, with more complaints about PaySure. It now appears that the principals of PaySure have used Chris's password information to abscond with all of the funds from his bank account. Does Chris have any remedy here? EFTA §909, Regulation E §205.6.

29.7. Your representative Pamela Herring is back with more questions. She has seen statistics indicating that 10 percent of P2P payments are made either to purchase pornographic content (which often is sold by organized crime enterprises) or pay for gambling. She also read press reports about how pressure by New York officials to prevent payments from being made to online gambling venues helped lower the rate of online gambling by New York residents. She wants to know if there is any good reason why Congress should not adopt a law that forbids P2P or EBPP providers from making payments to illegal enterprises. She proposes that the Department of Commerce would be responsible for maintaining a list of enterprises that it has determined to be operating illegal businesses (including e-mail addresses and bank account information for the enterprises in question). Providers who knowingly made payments to those enterprises would be subject to sanctions. What do you think about her proposal?

Assignment 30: Electronic Money

The earlier assignments in this chapter discuss ways in which the use of electronic technology has facilitated the enhancement of existing payment systems or created new markets for existing payment systems. The obvious question is whether electronic technology can do more. In other words, what are the prospects for a payment product that is the electronic equivalent of money?

The basic story is one of alternating bouts of disappointment and renewed optimism. For years, the credit-card industry in this country has assumed that consumers soon would be using sophisticated "stored-value" cards on which consumers could store money in the form of encrypted packets of electronic information. Similarly, in the early days of the Internet, it was widely assumed that some form of electronic money soon would become the dominant method of payment for Internet purchases. By the turn of the millennium, however, those expectations had been doused by a continuing series of market disappointments for such products. Among other things, numerous high-profile tests of chip-enabled stored-value cards (in the United States and elsewhere) have been characterized by a startling inability to generate consumer acceptance. Similarly, despite the fascinating technological details of Internet-capable electronic money, the years continue to pass without the widespread deployment of such a product; the most prominent early developer (DigiCash) filed for bankruptcy. More recently, a group of companies (Beenz.com and Flooz.com being the most obvious) that tried to build forms of electronic money founded on gift certificates and loyalty points failed dismally, like so many other Internet startups in the second half of 2001.

Still, despite those failures, there is reason to believe that some form of electronic currency will have a significant role in two types of commerce in the decades to come. In the traditional retail context, a portable currency that is capable of being stored on a card or other device (such as a personal digital assistant) could have a number of useful applications; current applications in the arena of gift cards and payroll cards show particular promise. On the Internet, a wholly electronic currency offers advantages of higher security, lower costs (especially for low-value "microtransactions"), and greater user privacy. It remains to be seen whether electronic money will dominate those contexts, but it does seem certain that efforts to promote the use of electronic money will be a significant feature of commerce during the years ahead.

Ideally, of course, a truly electronic currency could be used interchangeably in both contexts. Because electronic products have not yet had great success in either market, however, the existing products in those two contexts have not begun to merge. Accordingly, it is best to consider the two contexts separately.

A. Portability: Stored-Value Cards

1. The Basics

In its most basic form, a stored-value card is a card that accesses value that the cardholder (or some third party) previously has paid to the issuer. Its most distinctive feature is that the indicator of value can (but need not be) carried directly on the card. Thus, unlike a credit card, there is no need for a contemporaneous authorization of the transaction to confirm that an account holds funds for the transaction. Rather, the transaction often can be completed entirely based on an interaction between the merchant's terminal and the card itself.

Conceptually, writers (and occasionally legislators, as discussed below) often refer to the "value" as "residing" on the card — as if value were a tangible object with a specific location. The concept of value being located in a tangible object might make some sense for currency — which passes from hand to hand without any realistic prospect of redemption. But in this context, where each transaction is likely to involve almost immediate collection of funds from the issuer of the card, it makes more sense to recognize that the "value" involved in a stored-value card is an obligation of the issuer, which does not have any specific physical location.

The most common use of stored-value cards traditionally has been as substitutes for cash in small-dollar contexts where it is inconvenient to pay cash for each transaction. For example, mass-transit farecards and copier cards long have provided two successful applications for primitive stored-value cards. The cards also can limit the risk of violent crime against cardholders because they lower the amount of cash that cardholders are carrying — at least to the extent that the thief who steals the card is unable to use the value on the card for the thief's own purposes.

The technology behind the earliest stored-value cards was quite simple. Those cards carried a simple magnetic stripe that maintained a balance of value that was reduced by each subsequent use of the card. There was no significant encryption of the cards; the value was indicated by the number of magnetic impulses on the card. Moreover, the value was easily lost if the card was placed next to an object with a strong magnetic field.

Those cards are likely to continue in contexts where the attractiveness of theft is limited either by the low value of the amounts that can be stored on the card or by the limited use to which the funds can be put (such as subway rides in a particular city or on a particular line, or gift certificates to be redeemed at a particular store). In other contexts, however, two products that have more robust protections against fraud have replaced them: prepaid cards that verify transactions contemporaneously, and chip-enhanced "smart" cards that can verify their own transactions.

Mass-market prepaid cards have grown rapidly since their 2001 introduction by MasterCard; in 2003 they amounted to $240 billion in payments. The basic concept of this product is to have the value that is to be placed on the card collected by the person that sells the card: An employee at a 7-11 might sell a $50 prepaid MasterCard, take the cash (plus the commission), and dispense the card to the customer. The most successful example of that product doubtless is the Starbucks card, debuted to wide acclaim in 2002: The card was used for 100 million transactions worth about $350 million dollars in its first year. They also increasingly are used as payroll cards — a relatively inexpensive way to pay employees that do not have bank accounts.

These cards typically include a unique card number on a magnetic stripe that can be used in an authorization transaction much like the authorization transaction for a conventional credit- or debit-card transaction. Because they contemplate contemporaneous authorization of the transactions for which they are used, the problem of fraud and forgery that plagues the older magstripe stored-value cards is avoided. The host simply tracks the amount remaining on the card, reducing it each time a transaction is authorized, or increasing it whenever the card is reloaded.

Those cards (referred to as "host-based" cards because a record for the value of the card is maintained at a host) often are marketed by third-party processors like WildCard Systems, which maintain databases for all cards issued by their clients and verify the individual transactions. Cards often can be reloaded, either at a participating merchant or by telephone or Internet (drawing on a credit card or debit card).

The more visionary product plainly is the chip-enhanced smart card. That product carries a tiny microprocessor on the card that includes an electronic record of the value on the card. Those cards interact with readers at the merchant's terminal, so that no contemporaneous authorization is necessary. In this country, they remain relatively uncommon, limited for the most part to closed environments like university and corporate campuses. For example, the most prominent deployment in recent times has been a project by the U.S. Navy to deploy smart cards on all of its vessels. In that context, the project can take advantage of the Navy's desire for its personnel to carry ID cards that have a chip carrying a digital signature. Once those cards are universally deployed it is relatively simple to add an electronic-money feature to the card.

Smart stored-value cards are much more common overseas, generally because the infrastructure for conventional telephonic authorization of credit-card transactions is much less satisfactory. In that context, there is much to be gained from a product that permits reliable authorization without the need for a contemporaneous telephonic connection. The value to be gained overseas from sophisticated local authorization is underscored by circumstances in the United Kingdom, where *all* card users are migrating in 2004 and 2005 to smart cards, generally to cure intractable problems with fraud, attributable at least in part to relatively low rates of telephonic authorization of conventional credit-card transactions.

Another benefit of that product is that the transactions are entirely anonymous: Without a host maintaining a record of each card, there is no central record from which transaction data can be compiled for individuals that use the system. As discussed below with respect to electronic money, that privacy concern has not been an important driver of payment preferences in this country, but it may be more important overseas, where these products have been more successful.

A typical product is the Octopus card widely used in Hong Kong. There are about 10 million cards in circulation (in a country with a population of about 7 million), used for 8 million transactions a day. Originally developed to simplify the process of collecting fares for mass transit, the card is now accepted widely at convenience stores, fast-food restaurants, and other outlets with low average checks. Tellingly, the Web site for the card emphasizes to users that the card is completely anonymous.

2. Legal Issues

a. EFTA

The legal framework that governs stored-value cards in this country is quite uncertain. Most importantly, it is not yet clear whether the transactions are governed by the EFTA. The Federal Reserve proposed some limited regulations in 1996, but withdrew them in the face of congressional opposition. The rapid rise of the cards, however, has made them sufficiently important that some regulatory pronouncement seems all but inevitable.

In the terms of the EFTA, the fundamental question that the cards present is whether transactions that use the card involve an "electronic fund transfer" under EFTA. To understand that question, three definitions from the statute are important. First, an electronic fund transfer is defined in §903(6) as any "transfer of funds . . . which is initiated through an electronic terminal . . . so as to order, instruct, or authorize a financial institution to debit . . . an account." An account, in turn, "means a demand deposit (checking), savings, or other consumer asset account held directly or indirectly by a financial institution." Regulation E §205.2(b)(1). Finally, the term "financial institution" is defined broadly to include "a State or National bank, a State or Federal savings and loan association . . . or any other person who, directly or indirectly, holds an account belonging to a consumer." EFTA §903(8). For a host-based card like the ones discussed above, it would be plausible to characterize an entity like WildCard Systems as a financial institution, holding a "consumer asset account" for each consumer to which it has issued a card. Then, it would be plausible to say that each transaction using the card is a transfer, initiated through an electronic terminal, instructing WildCard to debit that account (and pay the money to the appropriate merchant). That view has gained significant weight from a recent proposal by the FDIC under which banks that hold such funds would need to treat them as deposits (to which deposit insurance would apply and against which banks must hold reserves).

If the EFTA does apply, that would have several ramifications for the industry. Among other things, issuers would be responsible for unauthorized transactions and would have to refund amounts previously loaded on cards that are lost.

Many, but not all, issuers already provide such protections. Application of the EFTA would make protection universal. Also, many of the protections that apply — such as the Visa and MasterCard "zero liability" policies — have loopholes that could not continue if the statute applied. For example, MasterCard's policy does not apply if there are multiple unauthorized transactions in a single year, if the cardholder has failed to use reasonable care to safeguard the card, or if the cardholder is delinquent in payments on the account. The EFTA includes no such restrictions.

At the same time, application of the EFTA to common "smart" stored-value cards seems much more dubious. In contrast to host-based cards, the only record of value for those cards often is on the card itself. In that case, it is difficult to view use of the card as a "transfer," because there seems to be no "account" out of which funds are being transferred.

b. Other Issues

The rise of prepaid cards also has generated controversy in several other areas. For example, there has been considerable discussion of the applicability of the money-transmitter laws discussed in Assignment 29. Here, as in the discussion of P2P payments in that assignment, at least some of those laws rather clearly apply to the host of a stored-value system. See, e.g., Uniform Money Services Act §102(14) (defining "Money transmission" to include "selling or issuing . . . stored value").

Similar regulations in the European Union, issued under its Electronic Money Directive, apply to many of these products. Article 1 of that Directive defines "electronic money" to include
monetary value as represented by a claim on the issuer which is:

　　(i) stored on an electronic device;

　　(ii) issued on receipt of funds of an amount not less in value than the monetary value issued;

　　(iii) accepted as means of payment by undertakings other than the issuer.

As discussed in the opening pages of this assignment, that definition relies on the notion that the "value" involved in stored-value resides in some particular location. However difficult it might be to apply that definition in some situations — as with the host-based products common in this country — it quite naturally extends to the chip-enhanced "smart" stored-value cards that are more common in Europe. For institutions that issue those cards, the Directive imposes minimum capitalization requirements (Article 4), investment limitations (Article 5), and auditing requirements (Article 6) much like the requirements that the Uniform Money Services Act and similar statutes impose on money transmitters in the United States.

In some states, however, older statutes are being updated to ensure that they reach the variety of prepaid card models described above. Again, those laws typically do not regulate the transactions directly by protecting the user against an improper use of the funds. Rather, they focus on regulation of the host — rules to prevent the funds from disappearing through financial irresponsibility of the host before the cardholder can get an opportunity to spend them.

Another issue relates to unused funds on the cards. Many systems impose fees for inactivity or otherwise provide that the funds revert to the issuer if they are not spent within a certain time. (Starbucks, for example, initially included a $2.00 fee for inactive cards, but ultimately rescinded the fee before ever charging it.) Motivated in part by the rapid rise of prepaid cards, about 20 states now have statutes that ban such provisions, at least for gift cards. Because the statutes vary in their details — most do not apply, for example, to cards issued by financial institutions — the significance of those statutes is difficult to gauge.

The cards also raise a final set of problems related to the question whether they can be sold anonymously. For example, the USA Patriot Act requires a bank to verify its account holders against lists of known terrorists and take steps to ensure that its products are not being used to support terrorism. If the purchase of a prepaid card establishes an "account" under 31 U.S.C. §5318 (which includes "a formal . . . business relationship established to provide regular services, dealings, and other financial transactions"), then the financial institution might be subject to those obligations with respect to persons about whom it knows nothing. More broadly, even a nonbank issuer might be covered if its activities involve sufficient conduct to make it a "financial institution" under applicable definitions. See 31 U.S.C. §5312(a)(2)(R) (including "a licensed sender of money or any other person who engages as a business in the transmission of funds, including any person who engages as a business in an informal money transfer system or any network of people who engage as a business in facilitating the transfer of money domestically or internationally outside of the conventional financial institutions system"). Similar issues arise under the Bank Secrecy Act, which generally requires reports of large financial transactions conducted either through banks or through "money servicing businesses," a term defined in 31 C.F.R. §103.11 specifically to include parties that send or redeem stored value.

Those regulations reflect an intuition directly opposed to the privacy concern that has been one of the motivating forces behind electronic-money products. The problem is that if those regulations were enforced against stored-value products they would drive from the market most of the products that have been successful in recent years. To be sure, it might be easy to comply with such regulations for payroll products, but gift cards and convenience-store-purchased cards are not products for which "know-your-customer" rules work well. The payor-anonymous chip cards that have not yet succeeded in this country would, it seems, be similarly unlawful.

For years, the stored-value card industry opposed regulation, fearing that regulation would stifle developing business models. That attitude seems to be rapidly shifting, as the growth of large businesses has made the level of uncertainty in the interpretation of existing law such that clarity now seems preferable.

B.   Remote Transactions: Internet-Capable Electronic Money

Internet-capable electronic-money systems are much more difficult to implement than stored-value card systems, because they do not rely on a card to provide authentication of the transaction. Rather, all of the authenticating information must be contained in the electronic-money packets that the consumer sends to the merchant. Still, technology adequate to the task seems to have been developed, although commercialization of that technology has been much less successful to date than the stored-value card technology discussed above. Generally, the issue seems to be that there is not a problem sufficiently important to consumers to motivate widespread use of the product.

1.   Obtaining E-Money

As with any payment system, the user must start by arranging to have the stakeholder make payments on the user's behalf. Typically, the user opens an e-money account at the institution that is operating the system (the issuer) and makes an initial deposit to that account, either by wire transfer or by some more traditional method (such as mailing a check or cash). The user normally downloads software from the issuer's Web page to facilitate use of the account. That software typically would include mechanisms to make the account password-protected.

The heart of an e-money system is the electronic packet that reflects the user's deposit of value into the system. Those packets — ecoins — are created on the user's computer with the software downloaded from the issuer. Once the user creates an ecoin, the user's software contacts the issuer, which checks the validity of the ecoin and "stamps" a digital electronic signature on the exterior of the ecoin to verify the issuer's approval of it. The ecoin is actually an electronic record that contains both the serial number generated by the user's software to mint the ecoin and also the amount of it. The ecoin that the issuer returns to the user is the record with the serial number and amount, imprinted with the issuer's signature to produce the encrypted hash value for the ecoin. (Assignment 18 discusses digital signatures and the hash values that are used with them.)

Anyone with a copy of the issuer's public key easily can determine whether the ecoin is valid. First, the person would apply the e-money software to the serial number and amount contained in the text of the ecoin to generate the hash value a second time. It then would use the issuer's public key to decrypt the hash value attached to the signed ecoin. If the hash value from that ecoin matched the hash value produced by the software, then the person knows both that the ecoin was validated by the issuer and also that the ecoin has not been tampered with since the issuer signed it. If the ecoin has been tampered with, such as by increasing its nominal value, then the hash value attached to the ecoin in the signature of the issuer and the hash value created by someone thinking of accepting the ecoin as payment will not match.

After checking the ecoin and signing it, the issuer sends it back to the user and deducts funds from the user's account in an amount equal to the amount of the ecoin. When that deduction has been made, the first step of the process is complete. The user has paid to the issuer funds equal to the amount of the ecoin. The ecoin reflects the issuer's agreement to pay the amount of those funds to any party that presents an authentic ecoin.

2.   Spending E-Money

The user can spend its ecoin at any merchant that is set up to accept it. The principal difficulty for the systems has been that only a small number of merchants have been persuaded to accept any of the versions of e-money. Thus, consumers have had few places to spend it, so they have not been motivated to participate in the system. It remains to be seen whether that reluctance can be changed in the years to come. If not, e-money will remain a curious technological novelty.

If the consumer can find a merchant that will accept its e-money, the process of spending it is no more difficult than spending ordinary cash (taking account of the fact that the parties are in communication only through an Internet link). The user identifies the item that it wishes to purchase from the merchant, the merchant advises the user of the price, and the user sends the appropriate amount of currency to the merchant's site over the Internet. (Although the details are still developing, presumably the user's machine will store ecoins in small denominations so that it can send the exact amount of the transaction.) To facilitate microtransactions, designers expect that users will preset their computers to send ecoins for small transactions without requiring independent confirmation by the user. For example, a user might preset its computer to make automatic payments of any sum that a merchant requests that falls below five cents. Because the systems are entirely electronic, designers expect that their per-transaction costs will be much lower than the costs for older systems (like credit cards and checks), and thus hope to dominate the market for small "microtransactions." Again, whatever the validity of that analysis, the problem has been that the market for microtransactions has grown so slowly that there is still no significant market for electronic money as a vehicle of payment. There is an obvious chicken-and-the-egg problem here: It is not clear whether the microtransaction market has grown slowly because consumers are inherently disinterested in those products or because consumers have had no practicable way to pay merchants for those transactions.

3. Clearing and Settling E-Money Transactions

The electronic-money system rests on a commitment by the issuer to honor all unaltered ecoins that bear the issuer's electronic signature. Currently, the merchant uses an online connection to determine at the time of the payment transaction whether the issuer will honor the ecoin. The merchant uses that connection to send the ecoin to the issuer before accepting the ecoin as payment. The issuer examines the ecoin, verifies that it bears the issuer's signature, that it has not been altered, and that the ecoin has not previously been spent (discussed below). If the ecoin appears to be valid, the issuer notifies the merchant and the merchant completes the transaction by releasing the purchased items to the user.

At that point, the merchant deposits the ecoin in its account with the issuer. The issuer (which already has determined that the ecoin is valid) credits the merchant for the face amount of the ecoin, reduced by the applicable system charges, all as illustrated in Figure 30.1. Although the amounts of those charges are so unsettled as to make generalization pointless, system designers expect that the charges in a market in which e-money has a significant market share would be much lower for e-money than for credit cards and other competing systems. The question, of course, is whether such a market ever will exist.

One final twist will complicate the system if multiple entities issue electronic money. The clearing process described above assumes that each merchant that accepts e-money has an account with each bank that issues e-money. That assumption is plausible in a world where there are very few issuers in any given country, and in which most transactions occur within

Figure 30.1
Using Electronic Money

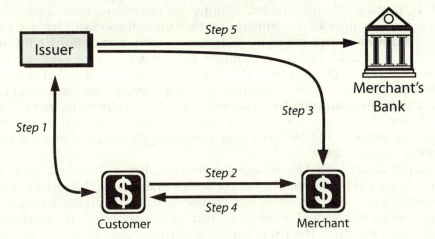

Step 1   Customer opens account and creates ecoins.

Step 2   Customer sends coins to Merchant.

Step 3   Merchant confirms authenticity of coins by
          communication with issuer.

Step 4   Merchant releases product to Customer.

Step 5   Issuer sends funds to account at Merchant's Bank.

a single country in a common currency. If numerous banks begin to issue
e-money, however, it will become desirable to allow merchants to clear those
transactions through arrangements with their own banks (merchant banks),
even if those merchant banks did not themselves issue the e-money that the
merchant has received.

Under that system, a paradigm merchant (a baseball-score provider, for
example) would send the e-money to its merchant bank; the merchant bank
would send the e-money on to the issuing bank for confirmation. If the issuer
decided to honor the e-money, the issuer would notify the merchant bank
and credit the merchant bank's account with the issuing bank; the merchant
bank would notify the merchant and credit the merchant's account at the
merchant bank; and the merchant safely could complete the sale.

4.   Problems with E-Money Systems

Notwithstanding the technological sophistication of electronic-money systems, those systems must deal with the same problems as more conventional
payment systems. The discussion here addresses three of the most significant
problems: concerns about privacy in electronic commerce; duplicate spending; and forgery.

a.   Privacy

The most difficult problem that has confronted designers of e-money systems is privacy. Despite recent slumps in electronic commerce, many observers still believe that commerce on the Internet soon will replace a substantial portion of the relatively untraceable cash transactions consumers make today. As discussed in Assignment 28, the use of a traceable payment system (like the credit card) would permit the creation of detailed consumer profiles: imagine a consumer profile that reflects every newspaper and magazine article the consumer has read, every food item the consumer has purchased, and every song to which the consumer has listened (to say nothing of less reputable activities involving pornography, controlled substances, weapons, or the like).

E-money designers have responded to that problem by developing a system for providing payments that leaves the issuer unaware of the identity of the transaction payor for any particular transaction. In the classic terminology, the system uses "blinded" ecoins to effect "payor-anonymous" transactions (transactions in which the issuer cannot determine the identity of the party that spent a particular ecoin). To create a blinded ecoin, the user's computer starts with the large random number that is the serial number for the ecoin. The user's computer then multiplies the serial number by a second random number (the "blinding factor") and creates an ecoin that includes the product of those two random numbers (the "blinded" number). The user then transmits the ecoin containing the "blinded" number to the issuer. The issuer then signs the ecoin with its private key. Because the issuer does not know the blinding factor, it cannot determine the serial number of the ecoin at the time that it signs the ecoin. The issuer knows only that the user has purchased an ecoin of a certain denomination. When the issuer returns the ecoin to the user, the user's software permits it to remove the blinding factor without disturbing the issuer's signature.

The result is an ecoin that carries the issuer's verifying signature, but has a serial number that the bank has never seen and thus cannot identify as coming from a particular user. When the merchant returns the ecoin to the issuer, the issuer recognizes its signature and thus honors the ecoin as valid. It has no way, however, of identifying the user that minted the ecoin in question. By limiting the knowledge that issuers have of the transactions in which their customers engage, the designers hope to attract consumers concerned about privacy in their Internet transactions. To date, however, that feature has not been adequate to spur significant interest in the system. More generally, as the discussion above suggests, it is not clear that regulators in this country would tolerate such an anonymous product so readily adapted to money laundering.

b.   Duplicate Spending

The second basic problem for e-money systems is duplication of ecoins. If the systems use sophisticated encryption procedures for imprinting the issuer's electronic signature, it will be quite difficult for a counterfeiter to forge completely false ecoins. It is, however, not as difficult to copy a valid ecoin. Accordingly, the issuer needs to design mechanisms that prevent double-spending of ecoins.

Without such mechanisms, a user (or thief) could obtain a single blinded ecoin, copy it dozens of times, and then spend the same money dozens of times without the bank having any opportunity to locate the culprit. The payor-anonymous feature of a blinded-coin electronic-money system exacerbates the problem by making it impossible for the issuer to identify the user that created any particular ecoin. Thus, the issuer faced with such a situation (usually referred to as "spawning") has no way of noticing that the ecoins emanating from a particular user's computer exceed the legitimately deposited funds available for the production of ecoins on that computer. The problem is analogous to the difficulty that arises in stored-value card systems, where it is much easier for the operator of a typical host-based system to detect a counterfeit card than it is for the operator of a card in which all indications of value reside on the card.

The existing response to that problem is to process the transactions online in real time — the merchant transmits the ecoin to the issuer at the time of the transaction. That allows the issuer to examine the ecoin's serial number at the time of the transaction, determine that the serial number has not previously been spent, retire the serial number so that it cannot be used in the future, and accept the ecoin, all at the time of the transaction. If anybody attempts to spend a duplicate of that ecoin in the future, the issuer will not accept it: Although the ecoin will bear a valid signature, the issuer will recognize the serial number from its records as having been used in the past. Accordingly, the issuer will reject the ecoin as a duplicate and the merchant will not complete the sale.

An online clearing system provides almost perfect protection against double-spending, but its dependency on a real-time connection to the issuer is problematic. The obvious response to *that* problem would be to design an offline clearing process that can provide the merchant a way to confirm that an ecoin tendered by the user has not previously been spent. Software designers have not yet succeeded in designing such a process, and there is some reason to think that it might be impossible. Moreover, as time goes by and the reliability of Internet connections increases, the problems associated with online clearing are likely to diminish. Hence, it seems unlikely that offline electronic money will become common in the immediate future.

c. *Forged Ecoins*

No matter how secure the system, a residual risk of counterfeiting remains. In this system (as in the stored-value card system), the stakeholders typically accept the risk of counterfeit ecoins. Thus, if the issuer agrees to accept an ecoin at the time of a sale transaction, it will pay the merchant the funds represented by the ecoin even if the issuer subsequently discovers that the ecoin was forged. Accordingly, the issuer has a considerable incentive to prevent counterfeiting.

As mentioned above, a scheme to forge ecoins ordinarily would not succeed unless the counterfeiter obtains the issuer's private key. Without that key, the counterfeiter cannot produce forged ecoins that the issuer will honor. Accordingly, the system's first response is to enhance the difficulties that a would-be counterfeiter faces in trying to obtain the issuer's private key. The primary actions are obvious: considerable security procedures at the issuer's location, which should be sufficient to prevent outsiders from entering the mint and obtaining the key directly.

Designers also have taken steps to enhance the difficulty would-be counterfeiters face in obtaining the issuer's private key through decryption of legitimately issued ecoins. As with any currently existing encryption system, it is at least theoretically possible for an outsider to determine the private key by using the public key to "hack" into the ecoin. Given the increasing processing power of computers, and the correlative increasing power of hackers, designers must continually raise the level of encryption to stay ahead of the hackers. Another tactic is to shorten the time within which a hacker's ability to break into any particular ecoin would be useful. That can be done by placing expiration dates on each ecoin and changing the issuer's private key with great frequency. When that is done, the hacker has only a short period between the first appearance of an ecoin signed with a particular key and the date on which that ecoin (and forgeries made with the key used on that ecoin) will become worthless.

To understand how dependent the system is on those precautions, it is worth considering what would happen if a counterfeiter somehow managed to obtain the issuer's private key and mint forged ecoins that the system could not identify as counterfeit. In that scenario, the issuer would be transferring funds to merchants for ecoins for which the issuer had not received funds. The difficulty of that problem is exacerbated if the system is payor-anonymous, because the issuer might pay on a large number of forged ecoins before it discovers the scheme: If it does not know the account from which any particular ecoin comes, the only sure way for the issuer to discover such a scheme is for the issuer to receive forged ecoins in amounts that exceed the total amount of legitimate ecoins in circulation.

5. Legal Issues with E-Money

Because pure electronic money has made almost no market penetration in this country, it is purely hypothetical to discuss what legal regimes might apply if it did. The basic points should be obvious from the discussion above. At a minimum, any issuer surely would be governed by conventional money-transmitter legislation. See Uniform Money Services Act §102(14) (defining "Money transmission" to include "receiving money or monetary value for transmission"). Without knowing more about the details of the transactions, it is difficult to predict whether the EFTA would apply to them. If they cleared in an offline manner, it might be thought that there was no transfer from an "account," and thus that the EFTA would not apply. As discussed above, however, that seems implausible. If the transactions involve online verification by the issuer, it seems likely that the EFTA would treat the record of deposited values against which transactions are verified as the kind of account that makes the transactions qualify for coverage under the EFTA.

The only jurisdiction in which a substantial quantity of electronic-money systems are operating is the European Union — and even there the systems are mostly in the trial stage. (Interestingly, even in the European Union all of those systems appear to operate on a "national" basis, so that there are not yet any cross-border transfers of electronic money.) Still, concern has been sufficient to motivate passage of the Electronic Money Directive discussed above. The definition of electronic money in Article 1 of that Directive (quoted above) applies directly to the kind of Internet-based electronic money at issue here. Accordingly, any institution that issues electronic money in the European Union is subject to the rules in that Directive, summarized in the discussion of stored-value cards.

Relevant Glossary Entries

Decryption
Electronic Data Interchange (EDI)
Electronic Signature
Encryption
Smart Card

Problem Set 30

30.1.   Your daughter calls home after her first day away at college. She is excited about the stored-value card she has been issued — particularly with the feature that allows her to use the Internet to retrieve money that you send her. Do you have any concerns about sending her $500 allowance to her each month for her to store on the card? (The card can hold only $50 at a time, so the "money" would remain on the university computer until she downloaded it. The general habit is to download the funds in installments every few days.) Do you want to know anything further about the details of the card system to answer that question? If so, why should the details of the technology affect the answer to such a simple and practical question?

30.2.   You have a meeting this morning with a new client, Mike McLaughlin, who runs a sporting goods store near the local university. Because many of his customers are students, he signed up to join the university's stored-value-card program (called I-Card). His problem arises from a series of transactions totaling several thousand dollars that occurred over a three-day period last week, all from students that live at a single fraternity house near his store. The first day's transactions went through fine last Tuesday night, but the second day's transactions were rejected when he tried to send them in for collection last Wednesday and Thursday night.

As best as he can understand based on his conversations with the University's I-Card office, the students at the fraternity appear to have discovered a way to create false value on their I-Cards — an amusing prank in the view of the fraternity members, but not in the view of the I-Card administrators (or, it seems, Mike). The students apparently used information one of them took from I-Card computers when he worked at the I-Card office as an intern last semester.

It appears that none of the transactions in question involved funds that actually had been deposited on the cards. The I-Card administrators haven't paid Mike for the bulk of the transactions, and have told him they may ask him to refund money from the Tuesday night transactions for which he already has been paid. He doesn't understand why this should be his problem. "It's their equipment — the terminal, the software, the cards, everything. I did everything exactly like they said, running the cards in the readers, having them type in the PINs. How can they refuse to pay?" What do you tell him? Is there anything you would like to know?

30.3. Another new client this afternoon is Kate Raven. She works for a local technology company that is trying to market a stored-value card product for corporate campuses. Largely because of what she perceives to be the attraction to users of the ability to have their transactions be anonymous, the product would not involve any host-based records of the accounts. She contemplates allowing employees to put up to $100 on the card at any given time, expecting them to spend the money at vending machines, the corporation's onsite dining facilities, and gift shops (which sell typical corporate paraphernalia). As a legal matter, do you foresee any difficulty with her plan? EFTA §§903, 909, Regulation E, §§205.3, 205.6.

30.4. Seattle's Finest Coffee introduces a new prepaid card product, competing with the Starbuck's card. The card is host-based, so that Seattle's Finest can add rewards points to the balance on the card for frequent users. After a rash of claims for lost cards, Seattle's Finest adopted a rule that it would not replace lost cards. Is this permissible? Are there any other ways that Seattle's Finest can protect itself against losses from lost cards? EFTA §§903, 909.

30.5. Your last call of the day is from Congresswoman Pamela Herring, who is interested in regulation of electronic money. Her specific concern relates to the companies that issue the money. She is considering a statute that would limit the issuance of electronic money to banks. She is interested in your views on that proposal as a matter of policy. What do you tell her?

Section C.   B2B Payments

Assignment 31:   Cross-Border Sale Transactions

International sales transactions rely heavily on the use of paper documents to reflect rights to possession of the goods and payment for the goods. Advances in information technology have fostered a number of initiatives to reduce the reliance on paper to document those transactions. This assignment starts by summarizing the existing paper-based methods for conducting those transactions and then discusses the two most salient electronic initiatives: the BOLERO project to facilitate electronic bills of lading and the International Chamber of Commerce's Uniform Customs and Practice for Documentary Credits Supplement for Electronic Presentation (the "eUCP").

A.   The Basic Transactions

In a cross-border sale of goods transaction, the buyer and seller often do not have the kind of longstanding relationship that justifies high levels of trust in each other. For example, suppose that a company in Italy (the Toy Importing Company) has contracted to buy certain toys from a company in Kansas (the Toy Manufacturing Company) for a price of $250,000. The manufacturer is reluctant to ship the goods overseas until it has been paid, but the importer is reluctant to send money off to America until it has received the goods. To resolve that problem, the parties often resort to one of several transactions, the most important of which for this discussion are a documentary draft and a letter of credit.

1.   Documentary-Draft Transactions

The "document" in a documentary-draft transaction is a document of title, a record that reflects the right to possession of certain goods. See UCC §1-201(b)(16) (defining "Document of title"). The document is issued by a person in the business of receiving goods and holding or transporting them. Once such a document is issued, the parties can transfer it to reflect a transfer of a right to possession of the goods, much as you would transfer a check to reflect a transfer of a right to receive payment. Two sources of law govern those documents: the Federal Bills of Lading Act, 49 U.S.C. §§80101 et seq. (the FBLA) and Article 7 of the Uniform Commercial Code. The FBLA preempts Article 7 where it applies, which includes any transaction that involves a shipment between American states or from one country to another country. FBLA §80102. Because the FBLA does not apply to shipments from a foreign country into the United States, Article 7 applies to those shipments. The distinction between the two bodies of law is not important, because both include rules similar to the rules under the old Uniform Bills of Lading Act.

The threshold question of importance for our discussion is what type of document is covered. Until recently, the UCC required the document to be in writing, but revisions in 2003 to UCC Articles 1 and 7 now permit an electronic record to serve as a document. See UCC §1-201(b)(31) (defining "Record"). The FBLA's definitions do not expressly require that the document be in writing (although they do refer to information "on [the] face of" the bill, FBLA §80103). In any event, the enactment of E-SIGN makes it plain that an electronic record should suffice to serve as a bill of lading under the FBLA. See E-SIGN §101(a)(1) ("[W]ith respect to any transaction in or affecting interstate or foreign commerce — a . . . record relating to such transaction may not be denied legal effect, validity, or enforceability solely because it is in electronic form.").

a. Delivering the Goods to the Carrier

To see how such a transaction works, consider the transaction described above. In that transaction, the seller would deliver the goods to a carrier (perhaps a train that will take the goods to a boat crossing the Atlantic, or perhaps a commercial airline), in return for which the seller would receive a "bill of lading," a particular type of document of title issued by a party in the business of transporting goods. See UCC §1-201(b)(6) (defining "Bill of lading"); FBLA §80103 (defining negotiable and non-negotiable bills of lading). If the document is issued in a "negotiable" form as it often is in these transactions, the carrier thereafter will release the goods only to a party that is in possession of the bill. See UCC §§7-104(1)(a) (requirements for a negotiable bill), 7-403(3) (requiring delivery of goods covered by a negotiable document to the person entitled under that document); FBLA §80110(a). Thus, the bill is a tangible reflection of the right to possession of the goods.

b. Issuing the Draft

If the seller wants to use the document to ensure payment, the seller issues a documentary draft, similar to the draft shown in Figure 31.1. The draft is addressed to — "drawn on" — the party expected to pay, the buyer in this case. It states that it is payable at "sight," to indicate that payment should be made promptly after the buyer receives it. See UCC §3-108(a) (a draft is payable on demand if it states that it is payable at sight). If the transaction contemplated delayed payment, it would be a "time" draft — specifying payment a certain number of days after sight. The draft also typically includes information about the buyer's bank (which the seller should have obtained from the buyer at the time of the contract); the seller's bank will use that information to collect payment. In this case, for example, it states that it is "payable through" a particular Italian bank. See UCC §4-106 (stating that a "payable through" draft can be "presented for payment only by or through" the identified bank).

Figure 31.1
Sight Draft for Documentary Collection

<u>At Sight</u>	<u>Any City, KS</u>	<u>May 2, 1997</u>
Pay to the order of **Seller**		
Ten thousand and no/100 U.S. Dollars		
Through <u>Banco di Roma</u>		
Buyer	Seller	
Any City, Italy		
	Exporter	

c. Processing by the Seller's Bank

Once the seller has the document of title and the draft, the seller takes the documents to its bank, together with an instruction letter detailing the terms of the transaction (identity of the buyer, identity of the buyer's bank, amount of payment, and the like). The seller then indorses the draft to its bank so that the bank becomes a holder of the draft. UCC §§1-201(b)(21) (defining "Holder"), 3-205 (describing how indorsement makes a party the holder of a draft); FBLA §80104 (procedures for making a party the holder of a bill of lading). This is analogous to indorsing a check to your bank so that your bank will attempt to collect the check for you. The only difference is that this draft is drawn on a merchant to whom you have sold goods; the check that you write is drawn on your bank. The seller also gives the bank, among other things, the bill of lading that covers the goods, adding any indorsement necessary to make the bank a holder of that bill as well. See UCC §§7-403(4) (holder is the person entitled to possession of goods covered by a negotiable document of title), 7-501 (rules for indorsement and transfer of documents of title); FBLA §80104 (procedures for transferring bills of lading).

The seller's bank often is called the remitting bank, because it is the bank that remits the draft for collection. See UCC §3-103(a)(11) (defining remitter). Once the remitting bank receives the documents, it prepares a collection document or instruction describing the terms of the transaction for the buyer's bank. Because the buyer's bank will present the draft to the buyer, the buyer's bank usually is described as the presenting bank. Among other things, the collection document ordinarily will incorporate by reference the provisions of International Chamber of Commerce Publication No. 522, *Uniform Rules for Collections* (URC). The URC provides a standardized set of procedures for documentary collections and calls for the collection document to include standardized details about the identity of the principal seeking payment (the seller), identity of the drawee from whom payment is to be obtained (the buyer), and the amount and currency of the payment to be obtained.

Most importantly, the collection document must state the terms upon which the documents are to be delivered to the buyer. Usually the collection document states that the underlying documents are to be "delivered against payment," which means that the presenting bank is not authorized to release the documents until it obtains payment from the buyer. After placing the appropriate instructions on the collection document, the remitting bank indorses the draft and the bill in blank and transmits the entire package (including the collection document, invoice and bill of lading, and the draft) to the presenting bank. See UCC §7-501(1) (after "indorsement in blank or to bearer," a bill can be negotiated "by delivery alone"); FBLA §80104(a)(1) (discussing indorsement in blank). The documents may be sent by mail or (if the seller requests faster service) by overnight courier.

d. Processing by the Buyer's Bank

When the buyer's bank receives the documents, it notifies the party indicated in the collection document. Under Article 6 of the URC, the presenting bank is obligated to "make presentation . . . without delay," which ordinarily takes no more than a few days. At that point, the buyer must make arrangements with the presenting bank to pay the amount specified in the documents to receive the goods. If the buyer has a credit line with the presenting bank, it might draw against that credit line to pay for the goods. If not, the buyer will have to obtain funds from another source. Once the buyer pays the presenting bank, the presenting bank releases the documents, including the bill of lading. At that point, the buyer can use the bill of lading to obtain the goods from the carrier. Meanwhile, the presenting bank transmits the funds it received from the buyer back to the remitting bank. The remitting bank puts those funds in the seller's account, at which point the transaction is complete.

To make that summary more concrete, refer to Figure 31.2. (It may seem complicated at first glance, but it should be helpful to take a moment to work through the various steps of the transaction.) When the presenting bank notifies Toy Importing Company that the presenting bank has the bill of lading, Toy Importing Company pays the bank for the toys. At that point, the presenting bank sends the funds back to Toy Manufacturing Company's bank to pay for the goods and gives the original bill of lading to Toy Importing Company. Notice that all of this is likely to occur while the boat transporting the goods is still in the middle of the Atlantic, long before the goods arrive in Italy or Toy Importing Company has an opportunity to inspect them. The concept is that the negotiable document (bolstered by some amount of confidence in the reliability of the seller Toy Manufacturing Company) is sufficient to convince Toy Importing Company to pay before the goods arrive. When the goods do arrive in Italy, Toy Importing Company can present the bill to the vessel. At that point the vessel releases the goods to Toy Importing Company and the transaction is complete.

2. Letter-of-Credit Transactions

The documentary draft transaction provides the seller considerable protection because, at least in the absence of some relatively egregious fraud, it prevents the buyer from obtaining custody of the goods without paying for them. It does not, however, provide any assurance that the buyer actually will pay for the goods when they arrive. If the buyer chooses not to pay (Step 5 in Figure 31.2),

Figure 31.2
Documentary-Draft Transaction

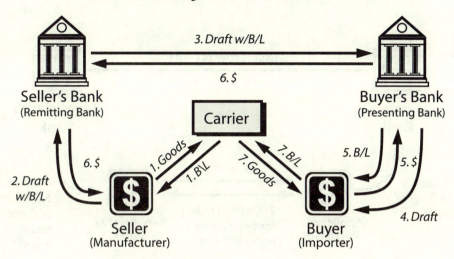

Step 1	Seller delivers the goods to Carrier; Carrier issues a bill of lading to Seller.
Step 2	Seller sends the draft and the bill of lading to Seller's bank.
Step 3	Seller's Bank sends the draft and the bill of lading to Buyer's Bank.
Step 4	Buyer's Bank presents the draft to Buyer.
Step 5	Buyer pays for the goods and receives the bill of lading.
Step 6	Buyer's Bank forwards payment to Seller's Bank and Seller's Bank forwards payment to Seller.

the only consequence will be that the buyer will not have the document of title that it needs to get the goods. The seller will be left with goods that it has shipped to a foreign country without a buyer willing to pay for them. To be sure, the seller might have a remedy against the buyer for breach of contract, but such a remedy often will be impracticably expensive to pursue when goods have been shipped overseas.

To address that concern — the credit risk — the seller can use a letter of credit. A letter of credit is a letter issued by a bank in which the bank agrees that it will pay a stated sum of money if it receives specified documents. In this context, for example, a bank might agree that it would pay the invoiced price for certain goods if it received documents indicating that the goods had been shipped, including a bill of lading from the carrier. Thus, a manufacturer concerned about the reliability of the importer to whom it is selling goods might insist that the importer provide a letter of credit from a reputable bank before the manufacturer actually ships the goods. (The manufacturer in that case would be described as the "beneficiary" of the letter of credit, because it is the party to whom payment would be made. See UCC §5-102(a)(3). The

Figure 31.3
Issuing the Letter of Credit

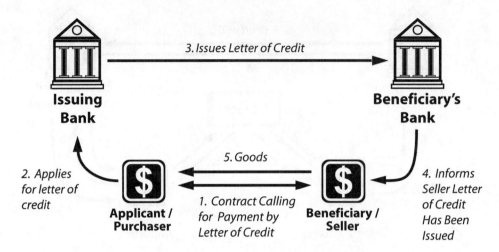

importer would be known as the "applicant," the party that applied for the letter of credit. See UCC §5-102(a)(2).) Figure 31.3 illustrates the typical process of issuing a letter of credit.

Once the manufacturer receives the letter of credit, it can ship the goods, secure in the knowledge that it can obtain payment from the importer's bank as long as it obtains the documents specified in the letter of credit. Once the manufacturer obtains those documents, the manufacturer presents them to the importer's bank (or to its own bank, which then can forward them to the importer's bank). If the documents comply, the importer's bank (known as the "issuer" of the letter of credit) pays the manufacturer (or the manufacturer's bank) the amount stated in the letter of credit. Figure 31.4 illustrates the process of obtaining payment on a letter of credit.

The rules that govern letters of credit in the United States come from two sources. The most important source is the Uniform Customs and Practice for Documentary Credits (the UCP) issued by the International Chamber of Commerce. As a matter of practice, that document is incorporated by reference in substantially all letters of credit issued by major commercial banks anywhere in the world. It includes a variety of rules governing the interpretation of the terms of letters of credit and establishes uniform procedures for processing requests for payment on letters of credit. The other main source of law is Article 5 of the Uniform Commercial Code. Article 5 for the most part tracks the rules stated in the UCP, but it also supplements them by (among other things) providing procedures for resolving disputes in American courts.

In both the UCP and Article 5, the central rule for letters of credit is the independence principle: The issuer's obligation on the letter of credit and the buyer's obligation on the underlying sales transaction are entirely independent. UCP art. 3(a); UCC §5-103(d). What that means is that the issuer's obligation is judged entirely by the documents that the beneficiary submits: if those

Figure 31.4
Payment by Letter of Credit

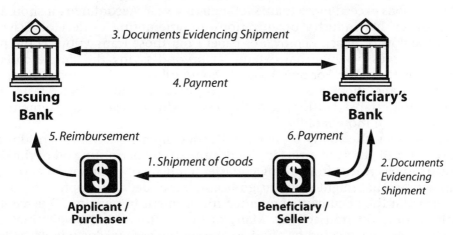

documents match the letter of credit the issuer must pay and is entitled to reimbursement from the applicant, even if it is plain in the circumstances that the applicant has not complied with the sales contract. See UCP art. 14(a) (stating duty of reimbursement); UCC §5-107(a) (same). If the documents do not match the letter of credit, the issuer is not obligated to pay, even if the defect in the documents does not in any way suggest that the beneficiary has failed to comply with the sales contract. Because the independence principle makes the applicant's compliance with the underlying contract irrelevant, in practice the bank's duty to pay is relatively objective, depending solely on the conformity of the documents that are presented to the documents described in the original letter. See UCP art. 13(c) (bank is obligated to ignore non-documentary conditions in deciding whether to honor a request for payment on a letter of credit); UCC §5-108(g) (same). The willingness of businesses to purchase letters of credit so frequently is attributable in large part to that objectivity, coupled with an industry tradition that makes a bank's reputation depend on its commitment to honoring its letters of credit — even when its customer the applicant is unsatisfied with the beneficiary's performance.

B.   Electronic Advances

The existing systems that rely on documents of title and letters of credit are among the most elegant creations of commercial law. They do confront some practical problems, and certainly can be improved with information technology. But businesses throughout the world have embraced them because they successfully put the rights to possession and payment in pieces of paper that can be transported from one place to another and transferred from person to person much more rapidly and much less expensively than the physical goods. And they do the job so well that buyers and sellers around the world, as well as their lenders, accept them without complaint.

In an electronic age, however, any transaction that generates a significant amount of paper is a target for potential cost savings. In this context, a recent United Nations study suggested that the costs of using paper in cross-border sales of goods exceed more than $400 billion a year. Accordingly, it should be no surprise that industry organizations are attempting to develop ways to limit the flow of paper. Removal of paper from those transactions could provide numerous benefits that extend far beyond saving the simple costs of processing the paper. For one thing, it should substantially increase the speed at which transactions are processed — transatlantic e-mail is a lot faster and cheaper than transatlantic Federal Express — which means that payment can be made much more rapidly.

For another, the ability to make all the documents electronic can substantially lower the costs of errors in the documents by permitting all of the documents to be created from a single master template of information about the transaction. That might seem insignificant, but under current practices, there are errors in the documents presented for payment in perhaps 70 percent of all letter-of-credit transactions. Many of those errors could be eliminated if precise consistency could be attained among the various documents (bills of lading, invoices, insurance certificates, letters of credit, etc.). Removal of those errors would improve the reliability of the letter of credit because it would limit the occasions when technical defects irrelevant to the beneficiary's actual performance would give the issuer a legitimate excuse for refusing payment.

1. *Bolero*

The most substantial effort to remove paper from cross-border sale transactions is the work of the Bills of Lading Registry Organisation (BOLERO). Although the Bolero project has received strong informal backing from the European Union, it is directly owned by a trade association of companies that insure cross-border shipments (the Through Transport Mutual Insurance Association, generally known as the TT Club) and an alliance of banks that participate in cross-border payments (the Society for Worldwide Inter-bank Financial Telecommunications, generally known as SWIFT). Companies that wish to use Bolero (importers, exporters, common carriers, or financial institutions) must join the Bolero Association and execute an agreement accepting the Bolero Rule Book for all of their Bolero transactions.

Much like the UCP, the Bolero Rule Book includes a variety of procedures for the transactions. The most important provision for our purposes, however, is a provision under which users agree that they will accept digital Bolero messages as if they were in writing and that they will not challenge the validity of a Bolero digital signature.

The focus of the Bolero process is to dispense entirely with the paper bill of lading. Thus at the point of shipment, the bill of lading would be issued in the form of an electronic message from the carrier to Bolero. That message would include all the information that typically would be found in a conventional bill of lading, such as a description of the type of cargo, its weight or volume, the identity of the party sending the goods (the seller or the shipper, not to be confused with the carrier), the party to whom the shipment is being sent, and the like. The message would be authenticated by use of a digital signature. Currently, the carrier imprints its private key with a smart card that Bolero issues to the carrier. Bolero relies quite heavily on those cards, and the signatures that they create: All parties are responsible for any signatures made with their cards, even if the signatures in fact are not authentic. See BOLERO RULE BOOK §2.2.4(1) ("Each User is responsible for all messages Signed by means of its Private Key, regardless of any failure to maintain security of its own Private Key.").

When Bolero receives the electronic bill, it verifies the digital signature of the carrier and then issues the bill according to the instructions of the carrier, ordinarily to the shipper. When the shipper wishes to transfer the bill (to its bank or to the recipient of the goods), it sends a message (signed, of course, with its digital signature) to Bolero indicating the identity of the new owner of the bill. Bolero then cancels the shipper's ownership of the bill on its registry and makes a new entry indicating the current owner of the bill. To receive the goods at the end of the voyage, the holder of the bill sends a message to Bolero surrendering the bill. Bolero, in turn, sends a message to the carrier indicating that the bill has been surrendered and identifying the company that has surrendered the bill. (It is up to the shipper to determine which individual at the port in fact represents that company!)

To accommodate the possibility that goods covered by a Bolero-generated bill will be transferred to a party that is not a member of Bolero (which certainly will be true often in the early days of Bolero), Bolero includes procedures for switching from an electronic Bolero bill to a conventional paper bill. Essentially, the current holder of the bill sends a message to Bolero advising Bolero that it wishes to terminate the Bolero registry. Bolero then advises the carrier of that message. The carrier then issues a conventional paper bill of lading, which indicates that it is issued in replacement of a Bolero bill issued on a specified date in the past. (This is analogous to the concept of a substitute check under Check 21.)

As discussed above, the Bolero process should have several benefits. Most obviously, it should be cheaper for carriers, shippers, and others to issue, process, and transfer bills. By accelerating the pace at which the bills can be transferred among remote parties, it should speed the flow of funds for the transaction, which in turn lowers the cost of the transaction. It also should lower the errors in those bills, by causing increasing amounts of information to be entered from pre-checked databases instead of by handwriting or manual typing. Perhaps most importantly, even if the signature technology is not as secure as Bolero claims, it should decrease significantly the potential for forged bills — it certainly will be much harder to forge a Bolero bill or registration than it is now to forge a conventional paper bill.

Bolero has the notable advantage that a large number of the most prominent potential users are strong supporters of the system, largely because of the cost savings that they expect. Among others, seven of the ten largest banks in the world are participating. On the other hand, it faces a number of notable obstacles. The biggest obstacle for our purposes is the basic legal problem that until Bolero is implemented by some law beyond the agreement of the parties, Bolero can bind only the parties that have agreed to it: third parties need take no notice of a Rule Book to which they have not agreed. In these transactions, there are many third parties that could raise such problems:

good-faith purchasers of goods covered by a Bolero bill, creditors that have reduced their claims to judgment and come out with the sheriff to levy on the goods covered by a Bolero bill of lading to satisfy the judgment, or a trustee in bankruptcy who may claim goods covered by a Bolero bill of lading on behalf of other creditors. Such third parties are often given the right to ignore competing claims of ownership in goods that have not been "perfected." What constitutes a perfected claim varies considerably in different contexts, but as a general rule, it is determined by reference to statutes, not to private agreements such as the Bolero Rule Book. For the rights conferred by the Bolero Rule Book to be universally recognized anywhere the goods might go, the applicable statutes would have to be revised to make a Bolero bill of lading the legal equivalent of a paper bill of lading. In the United States at least, that may occur quite soon, as the revision to UCC Article 7 promulgated in 2003 includes a definition of "Document" (discussed above) that accommodates that kind of electronic bill of lading. Unfortunately, however, most other trading countries have not yet addressed the problem.

It also appears that a number of large users already have developed their own internal electronic systems. For those users, most of the cost savings already have been achieved and a switch to Bolero would require a second round of costs. But even for those users, a switch to Bolero should bring wider acceptance of their electronic bills and, in many cases, probably greater security. A final problem is the same compatibility problem that we have seen in the assignments about EDI and B2B exchanges. The savings from Bolero technology will be realized only for businesses that can transport substantially all of their transactions to that format. But that requires something approaching an industrywide adoption of Bolero — manufacturers can transport their transactions to Bolero only if substantially all of their suppliers switch to Bolero, and the individual suppliers can switch only if substantially all of the manufacturers switch. Although some major stakeholders in relevant financial services organizations, including SWIFT, are throwing their considerable weight behind Bolero, many other major players see Bolero as a potential competitor and are standing on the sidelines, watching and waiting. The next few years should tell us much about Bolero's ability to overcome those problems.

2. The eUCP

The other major document in the cross-border sale transaction is the letter of credit. Electronic issuance and transmission of the letter of credit itself would be nothing new. For years the overwhelming majority of major commercial banks have transmitted letters of credit overseas by encrypted messages over the SWIFT network, sent from the issuing bank (the buyer's bank, typically in the country to which the goods are being sent) to the beneficiary's bank (typically in the country from which the goods are being shipped). (In letter-of-credit law, the beneficiary's bank (which receives the letter of credit from the issuing bank) will be called the "advising" bank if it merely informs the beneficiary of the credit; it will be called the "confirming" bank if it confirms the credit and accepts direct responsibility for payments due on the credit. See UCP arts. 7(a) and 9(b), UCC §5-107.) Because the UCP and the UCC expressly validate that practice, there is no doubt that it is permissible for the letter of credit to be issued electronically. UCP art. 11; UCC §5-104.

What is not at all clear, however, is whether a bank can accept an electronic presentation of the documents called for by the letter of credit. Under current practice, presentations still are made by the time-honored but cumbersome transmission of stacks of paper, moved from place to place around the world as the shipment occurs. As projects like Bolero move along, however, there is the potential for shippers to have electronic records rather than paper documents that would satisfy all of the requirements of a typical commercial letter of credit. Accordingly, the ICC has undertaken to develop a supplement to the UCP (the eUCP) that would permit documents to be presented electronically. That project has gained widespread support and was rapidly adopted by the ICC in November of 2001.

The basic concept is that a bank that is willing to accept electronic documents in a particular transaction would add a line in its letter of credit incorporating the eUCP by reference. eUCP art. e1(b). It would require presentation of electronic records, not telecopies: The purpose is to accommodate purely electronic documents (like a Bolero bill), not to encourage the scanning (and consequent degradation) of paper documents into electronic form.

The eUCP is intended to be technology neutral. Thus, it does not include a detailed description of how the electronic records are to be created; it requires only

- data created, generated, sent, communicated, received, or stored by electronic means,
- that is capable of being authenticated as to the apparent identity of a sender and the apparent source of the data contained in it, and as to whether it has remained complete and unaltered, and
- is capable of being examined for compliance with the terms and conditions of the eUCP Credit.

eUCP art. e3(b)(i) (defining "electronic record"). Similarly, an electronic signature "means a data process attached to or logically associated with a record and executed or adopted by a person in order to identify that person and to indicate that person's authentication of the electronic record." eUCP art. e3(b)(ii). To ensure that the documents are compatible with the bank's systems, the eUCP requires: "The Credit must specify the formats in which electronic records are to be presented. If the format of the electronic record is not so specified, it may be presented in any format." eUCP art. 4.

The eUCP also alters a variety of minor terms of the UCP to accommodate electronic documentation. For example, it defines the phrase "appears on its face" (used in the UCP, among other things, as part of the standard in UCP art. 13(a) for determining whether documents comply with a letter of credit), to "apply to examination of the data content of an electronic record." eUCP art. e3(a)(i). It specifies that an electronic signature is adequate in any provision that requires a document to be signed. eUCP art. e3(a)(iv). Compare, e.g., UCP art. 20 (describing requirements that documents be "signed").

Most importantly, the eUCP includes a variety of rules to be followed in electronic presentations. First, it requires that the credit specify a place for presentation of the electronic records (presumably an e-mail address).

eUCP art. e5(a)(i). The eUCP also permits presentation of documents by hyperlink — it is enough for the presentation to indicate a specific Web site at which the bank can view the document. eUCP art. e6(a). (That apparently will be the mechanism used for Bolero bills, which will be maintained at the central Bolero registry.)

3. *Future Advances*

It is too early to know how many banks will switch to electronic presentation, but the potential cost savings led most of the major issuers to participate in the drafting of the eUCP, so there is every reason to think that they will encourage their customers to rely on it. As XML technology increases the use of wholly electronic transmission of information through the supply chain, it seems inevitable that the documents that facilitate payment will become electronic as well.

The ultimate goal, of course, would be an entirely electronic process, integrated from start to finish using electronic contracting processes through the entire length of the supply chain. Such a process is probably still at least a decade in the future. Still, there are glimpses of how such a process would look, as entrepreneurs try to automate the financial supply chain in the same way EDI has begun to automate the physical supply chain. The most ambitious effort probably is the project of TradeCard, just going into operation as this book goes to press. As with Bolero, buyers and sellers that join the TradeCard system agree that all of the relevant "documents" will be submitted by sellers in an electronic form. Using an XML schema, the buyer for each individual contract enters into the TradeCard system the data for the documents that are required before payment is to be authorized.

When the goods have been shipped and the seller seeks payment it enters the data (verified, as appropriate, by digital signatures) into the TradeCard network. The TradeCard network then compares the data entered by the seller to the data previously entered as the requirements for that particular transaction. If the data do not match the contract requirements, the network notifies the parties and they determine by e-mail whether the discrepancies can be resolved.

If the documents match (or if the parties agree to waive any discrepancies), the transaction proceeds to the stage of payment. If the parties have selected Auto-Approved Payment (the equivalent of using a letter of credit), TradeCard submits a payment instruction to Thomas Cook. Thomas Cook then automatically debits a designated account of the buyer and credits a designated account of the seller. If the account does not contain adequate funds, the seller can obtain payment from a third-party insurer that guarantees payment in all TradeCard transactions.

Although TradeCard started several years after Bolero, it appears to be progressing much more rapidly. By 2004, it already was processing more than a billion dollars in transactions each year, with a number of major retailers using it for large portions of their supply chain. For example, Linens 'N Things in early 2004 moved its entire supply chain (both domestic and international) onto the TradeCard system. How it will grow in the future obviously is unclear. The only thing that is certain is that businesses will continue to work to eliminate the massive paper trails from cross-border transactions.

Relevant Glossary Entries

Bill of Lading
Bolero
Business to Business
Digital Signature
Electronic Data Interchange (EDI)
Electronic Signature
eXtensible Markup Language (XML)

Problem Set 31

31.1. You have a call today from your longstanding client Bob Puget at Puget Shipping Company. His company has just been acquired by Mitsubishi Fuso. One of the first things he discovers is that Mitsubishi is a member of Bolero and expects Bob to use it in all transactions shipped by Bolero members. Bob is puzzled. He wants you to explain to him in particular what he is supposed to do when he gets a shipment of goods. What does he give the person at the dock if he does not deliver a bill of lading? Surely he cannot reasonably expect people to give him goods on trust without getting a document, can he? What do you say?

31.2. A few weeks later, you get a call from Bob again. He wants to discuss a shipment from RiverFront Tools (RFT) in Texas that originally was sent to Brasileira Lumber (BL) in Rio de Janeiro. The goods were covered by a negotiable bill of lading issued electronically through Bolero. When the goods reached Rio, Puget released the goods to an individual representing BL, based on an e-mail from Bolero advising Puget that BL was the party in Rio that had surrendered the bill of lading. The next day Puget received an infuriated telephone call from Banco de Janeiro (BDJ), which claims it is entitled to the goods.

The officer at BDJ explains that the original bill was transferred from RFT to its bank Olympia National Bank and then transmitted to BDJ for delivery to BL if BL paid for the goods. The officer does not know how BL convinced Bolero that it in fact owned the bill of lading, but the officer is sure that BL has not paid for the goods. Based on the arrangement between BDJ and Olympia (under the URC), BDJ's release of the bill makes it obligated to pay Olympia for the goods. BDJ plans to hold Puget responsible for delivering the goods to the wrong party.

Bob promptly asked Bolero about the e-mail it sent advising him to release the goods to BL. Bolero advises that it transferred the bill of lading from BDJ to BL based on its receipt of an e-mail purporting to be from BDJ, signed digitally with the smart card that Bolero previously issued to BDJ. BDJ denies that it sent any such message.

Bob is confused. He wants to know how he possibly can be liable here. Is he liable? If not, who is likely to end up losing here? (You should assume that the information from Bolero is correct — it did receive a message with BDJ's signature — but also that BDJ did not in fact authorize any such message.) UCC §7-403; FBLA §80110.

31.3. A week later you get a call from Bob about a shipment currently in New Orleans on its way to London. It appears that the shipper is insolvent. Creditors have caused a Louisiana sheriff to levy upon the goods. Bob just received a call from the captain of the vessel. The captain is trying to persuade the sheriff that the goods cannot be surrendered to creditors because they are covered by a negotiable bill of lading. The sheriff refuses to recognize the Bolero bill, claiming that it does not qualify for those protections because it is not in writing. The sheriff has agreed to wait until tomorrow to give Bob's company a chance to resolve the problem. Bob wants you to have a firm in Louisiana go into court to enjoin the sheriff from levying on the goods. What do you tell Bob about your chances in that litigation? UCC §§1-201(b)(16), 7-403, 7-602; FBLA §§80104, 80105, 80110. Does it matter if Louisiana has not yet adopted the Revised Article 7?

31.4. Your client Vincent Maloney at Hunt Bank is enthusiastic about the eUCP. He wants to begin issuing entirely electronic letters of credit, incorporating the eUCP and the UCP by reference, contemplating entirely electronic presentations against those letters. Does New York law permit this? What about the requirement in UCC §5-108(g) that limits letters of credit to conditions that can be satisfied by "documents"?

31.5. Vincent Maloney calls you back several months later with a question. His bank began issuing letters of credit that incorporate the eUCP and the UCP by reference. He got tired, however, of long lists of documents each followed by a specification of the format in which the document would be received, with different formats for invoices from one company, insurance certificates from another company, customs certifications from the government, and the like. So now he wants to start issuing letters of credit that do not specify the format in which the documents will be received. What happens if he issues such a letter of credit and receives a document that he is unable to read? eUCP arts. e4, e6(c), e11.

31.6. While he has you on the telephone, Vincent has another question for you about an eUCP transaction. In this case, the documents came in today by e-mail. Everything appeared to be in order except the bill of lading, for which the presenting bank indicated a hyperlink to Bolero's records. When Vincent tried to examine those records, he received a message indicating that Bolero's system is down this afternoon for routine maintenance. Does the presentation conform or not? UCP art. 14(d), eUCP art. e6(a). What happens if he looks again tomorrow morning and finds the bill of lading at that time?

THE CAMFORD BOOKS PROBLEM

(Part V)

Your friends at Camford are working to streamline the processes by which they collect payments from their customers. They have several questions for you.

1. The bank that deals with their U.S. operations plans to clear all of the checks that Camford deposits electronically. It is offering Camford a substantial discount in check-processing charges if Camford will install software that converts the checks to images at the point of sale and transmit check information to the bank electronically. The main catch, as far as your friends can tell, is a requirement that Camford indemnify the bank for any losses the bank might incur under the warranties and indemnities that it gives in connection with Check 21. Should Camford be concerned about such a broad indemnity? Check 21 §§5 and 6.

2. Camford plans to accept payments by electronic check (technically, a Web entry processed through NACHA), credit card, debit card, and PayPal. In the design of the payment interface, there is an opportunity to make one of those payments the default option. Would any one of those payment mechanisms be substantially safer for Camford?

3. Camford also is considering whether to use TradeCard to pay its suppliers. Will that system protect Camford adequately against the risk that it will send payment overseas to a supplier that fails to ship products as agreed?

Chapter 6.   Lending in the Information Age

Assignment 32:   Registry Systems — Electronic Filing

Lending systems are affected just as much by developments in information technology as the systems for the underlying transactions and the payments discussed in Chapters 4 and 5. The most important effects have been on the systems used to maintain the records of the transactions that provide notice to third parties of the lender's interest in its borrower's collateral. At a high level of generality, modern commercial transactions use three distinctly different types of systems to fulfill that function. The first is a registry system, in which parties claiming an interest in an asset file a record evidencing their claim at a central location (a registry). The second is an account system, in which the owners of assets (normally intangible assets like money) deposit the assets with institutions that keep records of the deposits of each individual. The third is a token system, in which the assets are represented by reified tokens that can be passed from hand to hand as evidence of rights in the underlying asset.

Recent years have seen efforts to use electronic technology to facilitate each of those three systems. This assignment starts by providing some background on secured credit in general. It then discusses the registry systems used for filings against personal property (under UCC Article 9) and real property (under the various local statutes that apply to that topic). Assignment 33 discusses the account system developed under Articles 8 and 9 of the UCC. Assignment 34 discusses the developing systems for electronic tokens under UCC Article 9, E-SIGN, and UETA.

A.   The Basics of Secured Lending

When a lender makes a loan to a borrower, one of the most fundamental choices in the design of the transaction is whether the borrower will offer collateral to the lender. A transaction in which the borrower gives collateral is called a "secured" loan; a transaction without collateral is an "unsecured" loan. Although the dynamics of those transactions are quite complicated, the basic structure is not. Essentially, the arrangement is that the borrower grants the lender an interest (usually called a "security interest" or a "lien") in some asset or assets of the borrower (usually called the "collateral").

Although the interest usually carries with it some procedural advantages (that allow secured lenders to proceed more expeditiously than unsecured lenders), the more important advantages are substantive. First, the secured lender normally has the right to force a sale of the collateral (a "foreclosure sale") to satisfy the debt. Thus, if the borrower does not repay the loan voluntarily, the lender can take the collateral and sell it in a relatively expeditious manner. Also, the Bankruptcy Code gives priority to secured lenders, in the sense that they generally have the first claim to their collateral in a bankruptcy proceeding unless the bankrupt borrower is in a position to continue performing its obligations to the secured creditor or pay the secured creditor the value of the collateral as of the time of bankruptcy.

The rights of secured creditors can impose significant costs on other creditors, because in a time of financial distress secured creditors are likely to take all of the assets of the borrower, so that the secured loans are repaid to a considerable extent. That often leaves no assets for other, unsecured creditors, whose loans thus often go completely unpaid. That problem is exacerbated by the way in which a creditor gains that preferred position: an agreement between the borrower and the secured creditor, to which the disadvantaged unsecured creditor is not a party. As it often is said, secured credit is an agreement between the borrower and one creditor that all other creditors should take nothing.

The secured credit systems in the United States generally mitigate the unfairness to third parties through some form of notice: a mechanism by which third parties can discover the interest of the secured parties. That notice, in turn, allows the third parties (at least theoretically) to protect their own interests — perhaps by refraining from lending, perhaps by charging more for their loans, or perhaps by obtaining collateral for themselves. Generally, a lender that complies with the notice system is said to have "perfected" its interest. An "unperfected" interest — one that is not perfected — ordinarily is not valid against third parties, and thus loses most of the benefits that make secured credit attractive.

The simplest and oldest method of notice is possession. If a borrower does not have possession of collateral that is held in a bank's vault (for example, marketable securities such as stocks and bonds), a third party interested in using those securities as collateral should recognize the possibility that the bank already claims a security interest in the securities. As a legal matter, we say that the bank's possession of the securities is adequate to perfect the lender's security interest in them. UCC §9-313(a).

In most cases, however, possession is not a useful method of perfection. For example, if the collateral is inventory or equipment, the borrower would not be able to operate its business effectively if the lender retained possession of the collateral. Similarly, imagine how unsatisfying the home mortgage would be if the lender took possession of the home during the 30-year term of the mortgage. Also, of particular relevance here, many valuable assets are wholly intangible, so that the concept of possession is not useful in transactions that use those assets as collateral.

To respond to the difficulties of using possession to provide notice to third parties, most systems for secured lending include some type of filing system, in which a secured lender can place a notice of its interest. Third parties will have an opportunity to discover the lender's interest by searching those records. As discussed below, the two most common systems govern real estate and personal property. Real estate transactions are governed by state law, which varies considerably from state to state, but invariably requires filings in real estate records established for that purpose in the county (or parish) in which the land is located.

Personal property lending transactions usually are governed by the system set out in Article 9 of the Uniform Commercial Code. Article 9 in most cases contemplates a filing in the UCC records in the office of the Secretary of the State of the state in which the debtor is located. For individuals (and unincorporated businesses), that is the state in which the individuals reside; for corporations and limited partnerships, it is the state in which the entity is incorporated (or registered). UCC §§9-301(1) and 9-307.

The Article 9 filing system does not apply, however, to all assets. The most common exception covers security interests in consumer automobiles; those interests typically are perfected through notation on a certificate of title that covers the car, rather than by an Article 9 filing. More important for our purposes, however, are the central filing systems established for particular classes of assets by federal law. In many cases, such federal statutes may preempt Article 9 under the principle that federal law is superior to conflicting state law. If that is so, a federal filing is necessary for perfection and a state-law filing may be pointless. Although the question of preemption ultimately is a question of federal law (under the Supremacy Clause of the Constitution), Article 9 recognizes that problem in Section 9-311(a)(1), which states that the filing of a financing statement is neither necessary or effective to perfect a security interest in property subject to:

> (1) a statute, regulation, or treaty of the United States whose requirements for a security interest's obtaining priority over the rights of a lien creditor with respect to the property preempt [the filing requirement established in] Section 9-310(a).

The clearest example of such a statute relates to nonmilitary aircraft, for which it is well recognized that security interests must be perfected by filing in a centralized federal facility (in Oklahoma). See UCC §9-311(a) comment 2. Similar problems arise for intellectual property because federal law establishes federal filing systems for copyrights, patents, and trademarks. Surprisingly, the extent to which those systems preempt state law is not at all clear. The next chapter discusses those systems, as well as the system for trade secrets (which raises similar questions despite the absence of any federal trade secret filing system).

B.   The Basics of Secured Credit Filing Systems

As discussed above, secured lending systems typically condition the secured lender's priority on taking some action that reasonably can be expected to give notice of the secured lender's interest to competing creditors. In the major real estate and personal property systems in the United States, a central filing system provides the most common way to provide that notice.

Although it is possible for those systems to use the same filing system as ownership registries (as in the typical county real estate records), the purpose of these filing systems is distinct from the purpose of an ownership registry. Among other things, the conveyance of multiple mortgages against a single piece of land is relatively common, and in no way inherently fraudulent. In contrast, the simultaneous conveyance of ownership of a piece of land to multiple people is inherently fraudulent, and thus considerably less common. As a result, the purposes of ownership records are quite different from those of loan filing records.

A basic question about any filing system is how the records are organized. For example, the records maintained under Article 9 of the UCC are organized by borrower. That means that a lender trying to glean information from those records must provide the name of the borrower in the relevant transactions; the lender receives information about that particular borrower, rather than information about any particular asset. If the lender does not know the borrower's name, ordinarily it will be unable to obtain any useful information from the records. Conversely, the patent and copyright records discussed in Assignments 35 through 37 are organized by asset. A lender that searches those records identifies the asset in question and receives information about that asset (not information about the transactions of a particular borrower). Only recently, with the advent of electronic searching, could a search be done for *either* a particular asset *or* assets of a particular person.

The organization of the filing system has important consequences for those that use the system. A system organized by asset is ideal in sectors in which lenders commonly take an interest in large discrete assets that are easily identified and distinguished such as movies, books, or land. Conversely, a system organized by borrower is ideal in sectors in which lenders commonly take security interests in all or a large variety of the borrower's assets, because a lender can perfect in all of those assets with a single filing.

A borrower-based system also is particularly useful in a variety of specialized transactions. For example, a borrower-based system is ideal for "floating" liens — liens against pools of assets (most commonly inventory or accounts receivable) that change from time to time — because it is much simpler to file once against the borrower's inventory or accounts than it is to file from time to time against the individual assets as they come and go from the borrower's ownership. As a related point, a borrower-based system is almost necessary for transactions involving liens on after-acquired property. For example, consider the typical transaction in which the agreement is that the lender's interest will attach to any property that the borrower acquires in the future. There, it is not practicable for the lender to make a filing against those assets at the time of the loan, because the lender cannot know at that time what those assets will be.

Advances in electronics and information technology have the potential to improve filing systems significantly. The essence of a filing system is the transportation, storage, retrieval, and examination of records; all of those tasks can be accomplished more rapidly and cheaply in electronic systems than in paper-based systems.

The cost savings are much more significant than the simple savings of allowing a person to send an e-mail message with a filing (or search request) instead of driving across town to deliver the filing by hand (or perform the search). Most obviously, a system that permits filings and searches to be done electronically makes it much easier for lenders to engage in business on a national rather than a local basis. Indeed, you might say that the advantages of electronic systems favor remote national lenders, because they save much more (the costs of filing from a location perhaps thousands of miles away) than the local lender that easily can maintain a location near the filing office.

The ability of lenders to conduct their operations nationally, in turn, supports the formation of a national capital market that provides a broader sphere of competition for the transactions in any particular geographic region.

Electronic technology also offers the prospect of substantial benefits through a variety of enhancements to the filing system. Among other things, it can lessen the risk of incorrect filings, by providing for real-time electronic analysis of a filing to confirm that it correctly identifies the target of the filing. Thus, in a borrower-based system, the filing office might cross-check filings against the state's corporation records to make sure that the filing accurately identifies an existing corporation. In an asset-based system (like the one that the Patent and Trademark Office maintains), the filing office might cross-check filings to verify that the filings identify an existing patent.

The biggest potential advantages, however, are for searchers. For one thing, it is much easier to design electronic systems to protect against search errors based on incorrect names, either by searching against names that resemble the identified name in various ways or by searching against a variety of fields that might locate the transaction in question even if the name is slightly incorrect in the filing or the search request.

Modern database systems also offer a simple solution to the problem of systems that require filings and searches either by borrower or by asset, but not by both (and certainly not by other identifying characteristics such as address or lender). Modern databases ordinarily are "relational," so that a user can query the database regarding information from any of several fields. When a filing system is organized in that manner, a creditor can search for any record either by "borrower," or by "asset," or even by groups of characteristics (such as loans to a particular borrower in amounts that exceed $1,000,000).

To provide a sense for how those advantages have been realized in practice, and a sense of why the reality lags so far behind the potential, the remainder of this assignment provides a more detailed discussion of the course of electronic advances in personal property filing systems (Section C) and in real estate filing systems (Section D).

C. Updating Personal-Property Filing Systems

For loans against personal property, the dominant filing system is the filing system established under Article 9 of the Uniform Commercial Code. Unlike the better-known system for real estate filings (discussed below), the Article 9 system is designed specifically for loan transactions. Thus, it generally includes filings only for loan transactions; absent some special rules for certain intangible assets, it provides no evidence of ownership of personal property.

The central point of the Article 9 filing system is the concept of the "notice" filing. Creditors using the Article 9 system do not need to file their security agreement or any other detailed description of the transaction or the collateral. Rather, they file only a simple "financing statement," which identifies the debtor, the secured party, and the collateral. UCC §9-502(a). For the debtor, the statement must provide the name and address and, if the debtor is an organization such as a corporation, indicate the type of organization (such as "RiverFront Tools, Inc., a Texas corporation"). UCC §9-516(b)(5). For the secured party, the statement need indicate only the name and mailing address. UCC §9-516(b)(4). The description of the collateral need not be technical; the statute accepts a general description by type or category, or even a simple statement that the collateral is "all personal property" of the debtor. UCC §§9-108 and 9-504. That means that the UCC financing statement can be a simple one-page standard form. See UCC §9-521 (setting out a standard written form that filing offices must accept).

Practice at the time Article 9 originally was enacted, of course, involved written financing statements, delivered to filing offices in tangible form. Not surprisingly, the statute at least contemplated tangible documents, if it did not in specific terms require them. See, e.g., Old UCC §9-402(1) (requiring that a financing statement be "signed by the debtor") and 9-402(4) (permitting financing statements to be amended "by filing a writing signed by both the debtor and the secured party"); see also Old UCC §1-201(39) ("'Signed' includes any symbol executed or adopted by a party with present intention to authenticate a writing.") and 46 ("'Writing' or 'written' includes printing, typewriting or any other intentional reduction to tangible form.").

People interested in the UCC filing system recognized early on the advantages of updating the system to accommodate electronic filings. Accordingly, by the mid-1990s, several states (most notably Iowa, Kansas, and Texas) were accepting electronic filings under that statute. Indeed, the American National Standards Institute by that point already had created a filing standard designed to promote uniformity nationwide. That effort gained steam when the Permanent Editorial Board of the Uniform Commercial Code addressed the topic in 1996. (The Permanent Editorial Board (PEB) is a group of experienced practitioners and academics that acts under the authority of the American Law Institute and the National Conference of Commissioners on Uniform State Laws (NCCUSL) to provide commentaries on troublesome provisions of the UCC. The actual legal force of the commentaries is debatable, because they do not purport to amend the underlying statutory text adopted by the various states.)

PEB Commentary No. 15 addresses the question whether data transmitted electronically to a filing office constitute a financing statement for purposes of Article 9. The Commentary relies heavily on the mandate in UCC §1-102 that the UCC is to "be liberally construed and applied to . . . modernize the law governing commercial transactions." It also points out that nothing in Article 9 specifically requires financing statements to be in writing. Most importantly, it argues that a financing statement prepared in an electronic form can qualify as "signed" by a debtor without a manual signature if the debtor indicates its intention to authenticate the statement by some electronic symbol (such as an asterisk or the checking of a box). Accordingly, the PEB reasoned, Article 9 should be construed to permit electronic filings.

However progressive the PEB's intentions might have been, the commentary was not adequate to bring about a wholesale conversion of the UCC filing system from paper-based to electronic. The impetus for that conversion appears in the revised Article 9 (which has been adopted nationwide). Unlike its predecessor, that statute expressly contemplates electronic filings and works in numerous ways to encourage them as the customary method of filing.

On the first point, Article 9 pervasively removes references to "writings" and other terms that suggest tangible documents, generally replacing them with references to "records." See, e.g., UCC §9-516(a) (providing that a filing is made by the "communication of a record to a filing office"). The definition of record, in turn, plainly contemplates an electronic document: "'Record' . . . means information that is inscribed on a tangible medium or which is stored in an electronic or other medium and is retrievable in perceivable form." UCC §9-102(a)(69).

Similarly, the revised Article 9 also removes any requirement that a financing statement be "signed" by the debtor (or any other party, for that matter). Rather, the financing statement need only "provide" or "indicate" the relevant information. UCC §§9-502(a) and 9-516(b)(5). That might seem at first glance to be a trivial matter. But the old version of Article 9 required such a signature. Old UCC §9-402(1). For national lenders that are distant from many of their borrowers, the signature requirement posed a significant problem when the documents to be filed were not signed at the closing. The revisers of Article 9 concluded that the only important requirement is that the debtor in fact authorizes the filing of the statement. Authorization can be obtained in a variety of ways not nearly as burdensome as an actual signature on the document to be filed. Also, a requirement that a debtor "sign" an electronic financing statement would be quite difficult to implement in any robust way, given the great difficulties (discussed in Assignment 18) of deploying digital-signature technology to ordinary individuals. Finally, a signature requirement does not really enhance the level of authorization, because a secured party willing to file a statement without authorization is also likely to be willing to forge the debtor's signature. Accordingly, the final statute requires only that the financing statement be authorized by the debtor, not signed (electronically or manually). UCC §9-509(a). To give at least nominal substance to that requirement, Article 9 authorizes statutory damages in the amount of $500 as a remedy for the filing of an unauthorized financing statement. UCC §9-625(e).

Moreover, Article 9 generally abandons references to the signing of documents, calling instead for "authentication," which is defined specifically to include electronic forms of approval. UCC §9-102(a)(7) (defining "Authenticate"); see also UCC §9-203(b)(3)(A) (requiring a debtor to "authenticat[e]" a security agreement as a condition for a security interest to become enforceable against the debtor). (Those provisions are necessary because neither UETA nor E-SIGN applies to transactions governed by Article 9. UETA §3(b)(2); E-SIGN §103(a)(3).)

Having made it clear that filing offices are *permitted* to accept electronic records, the statute stops short of *requiring* filing offices to accept them. Indeed, UCC §9-516(b)(1) preserves the right of a filing office to reject a tendered filing because "the record is not communicated by a method or medium of communication authorized by the filing office." That provision is central to the technology-neutral stance of the statute, reflecting the rapidly developing state of information technology and similarly rapid changes in the technology for filing systems.

If the statute had required offices to accept any particular form of technology in existence at the time the statute was written in the late 1990s, it is likely that the technology would have been largely obsolete, if not by the time the statute went into effect, at least by the end of this decade. Accordingly, the statute rests on the premise that over time experimentation with different technological approaches by the various filing offices eventually will lead to convergence on a single effective filing practice nationwide.

The statute's neutrality on what particular form of electronic technology would work best does not mean that the drafters had any ambivalence about electronic filing. Indeed, in a variety of respects the statute takes steps that are likely as a practical matter to increase the attractiveness of electronic filing, all with a view to seeing rapid growth of electronic filings in the years to come. For example, the statute calls for filing offices to collect double fees for financing statements filed in writing rather than electronically (and quadruple fees for written financing statements that exceed two pages). UCC §9-525(a). Similarly, the basic form that the statute requires offices to accept (see UCC §9-521) is a form that was developed as part of the ANSI effort described above, tailor-made for electronic generation and reproduction.

More seriously, the statute imposes ambitious time constraints on filing offices. First, the filing office must respond to all search requests within two business days. UCC §9-523(e). Also — and perhaps more difficult — the response must include any references to filings made at least three business days before the request. UCC §9-523(c)(1). Accordingly, the filing office must place filings of record no later than five business days after a record is presented. That calls for a startling change from current practice — anecdotal evidence suggests that delays of weeks or even months are routine in the current system. The most obvious way to satisfy those deadlines, of course, is to go to a system of electronic filing and searching.

Another important step is the elimination of county-based filings. Depending on the alternative that the state chose to adopt, the old version of Article 9 contemplated county-based filings for a broad range of collateral. See Old UCC §9-401(a). Under the new statute, all filings are made at a single central state office except for filings on real estate – related collateral, which still must be filed in the county real estate records. UCC §9-501(a). That change should enhance the comparative advantage of electronic filings because it is likely to increase the size and sophistication of the typical filing office. In Texas, for example, all filings will be made in a single office in Austin instead of in the 254 county offices spread throughout the state. The size of that office and its location in the state capital makes it more likely to take advantage of economies of scale in the deployment of the information technology required to adopt a modern filing system.

Finally, one other factor likely to facilitate standardization of financing-statement forms (which in turn should promote the use of electronic filings) is the rule in UCC §9-516 that prohibits filing officers from requiring additional information not required by the statute. Specifically, UCC §9-516(b) includes an exhaustive list of reasons for which the office can reject a filing. If the office rejects a filing for a reason not on the list, the filing nevertheless generally is effective as a filed statement as against purchasers of the collateral. UCC §9-516(d). The confusion such a situation would cause is likely to discourage offices from rejecting filings for non-statutory reasons. Helping national lenders to avoid the tyranny of non-standard local filing requirements may seem minor, but it has the potential to provide significant benefits.

In sum, there is good reason to believe that we are only a few years from a transformation of the UCC system into one that largely relies on electronic filings and searches, bringing with it the advantages of speed and cost savings discussed above.

D.   Updating Real Property Filing Systems

The foregoing story of the personal property system is one of great opportunity: a recently drafted statute sensitive to efforts to support electronic filings, widely adopted, with a prospect for rapid growth in electronic filings. The story of the real estate system could hardly be more different.

1.   The Existing Mortgage Filing Systems

To understand the difficulties of bringing real estate filings into the electronic age, a few words about the real estate filing system are appropriate. First, unlike the UCC system, the real estate system provides a repository not only for records of credit transactions, but also for records about ownership and for all other interests that affect land. The statutes that govern those systems are not uniform. (NCCUSL promulgated a Uniform Land Security Interest Act in 1985, but no state adopted it.) Generally, though, the statutes provide a broader definition of documents than can be recorded. The practice is that the filing systems are treated like an "open drawer," into which filers may place anything they wish. It is left to later parties to sort out the significance, if any, of the documents that appear in the records. Given that broad reach of coverage, the operators of the real estate systems are much less concerned about the need for an efficient system of lending, because lending is only a small part of the filings that those offices process.

In addition, largely for reasons of historical practice, real estate filing systems universally contemplate the recordation of the entire document — the entire mortgage agreement between the borrower and the lender — rather than the short financing statement that the UCC system uses. What that means is that it is much harder to standardize the filings for real estate loans than it is for personal property loans. Standardization of UCC filings is relatively easy because the information in the filings is wholly descriptive. Standardization of mortgage filings is much harder because it requires standardization of the substantive terms of the transactions. The pressures for standardization in the national capital markets have made some headway on that front, particularly in the residential context, but the market for commercial mortgages still shows relatively little progress toward standardization. To those who have practiced in the industry, it is difficult to imagine the creation of a national standard-form commercial mortgage.

Two key aspects about the real estate system have made it almost impervious to efforts to foster electronic filing. The first is the difficulty of eliminating county-level filing. Even in the UCC, the elimination of county filings was a serious political problem, because it was likely to lead to the dislocation of the employees of the county-level filing offices. In the real estate system, that problem is likely to be much more serious, because the offices tend to be much larger (increasing the amount of dislocation) and much more entrenched. UCC filing is a relatively recent innovation, something that began during the lifetime of many of us. The real estate systems, in contrast, have existed for centuries. The sense of entitlement on the part of those offices is likely to receive commensurately more weight from the state legislatures.

The second difficulty comes from the non-standard documentary practice of real estate lending discussed above. Electronic filings are not that challenging in a UCC system in which filings as a practical matter were standardized before the electronic filings became feasible. An electronic filing system for lengthy and non-standard filings is much harder, because it must differ so substantially from existing practice.

One approach would be for the industry to adopt standardized filings, just as the UCC system has. As explained above, that is quite difficult in a system where the entire document is placed of record. Another approach would be to ignore any benefits from standardization and expect wholly non-standard electronic filings. Even in that system, however, the practical needs to search and index the documents would require (or, at least, strongly support) some format for providing electronic tags with the appropriate information. Because no such format currently exists, it probably would take years (if not decades) for a reasonably standardized format to be adopted by a substantial number of jurisdictions.

Still another approach would be to abandon the whole-document practice, adopting a notice-filing system much like the UCC system. The most obvious problem with that approach is the dispersed nature of the rules for real estate filings: It would be years (if not decades) before such a change could be brought into law in a substantial number of jurisdictions.

2. *E-SIGN and Electronic Mortgage Filings*

The difficulties in updating the real estate filing system are evident from the problems that system has faced arising out of the enactment of E-SIGN. As discussed in Assignment 14, Congress adopted E-SIGN in 2000 shortly after the promulgation by NCCUSL of its Uniform Electronic Transaction Act (the UETA). The core of UETA and E-SIGN is a provision that gives electronic records and signatures the same validity as paper records and the signatures on them. UETA §7, E-SIGN §101.

As Assignment 14 emphasizes, the general thrust of both UETA and E-SIGN is to facilitate the voluntary use of electronic contracting and recordkeeping. If parties decide to use electronic contracts or to maintain records in an electronic form, courts and the government generally should accord their contracts and records the same respect that they would accord written documents. Both statutes, however, also consider the status of government operations. UETA specifically considered the practice of paper filings for real estate documents and concluded that a statutory exception validating that practice was not warranted. See UETA §3 legislative note 3. Recognizing that few states have electronic filing systems in place, however, the statute included an optional provision that provides that each governmental agency "shall determine whether, and the extent to which [it] will send and accept electronic records and electronic signatures." UETA §18(a). Accordingly, because the overwhelming majority of the 46 states that have adopted UETA to date have included that section (or something like it) in their enactments, UETA in those states provides a clear signal that it is lawful for a real estate filing office to continue to insist on paper filings.

E-SIGN is less clear on this point. First, E-SIGN generally applies to any "transaction" in interstate commerce, with "transaction" defined as "an action or set of actions relating to the conduct of business, consumer, or commercial affairs between two or more persons, including . . . the sale, lease, exchange, or other disposition of any interest in real property." E-SIGN §106(13). That definition is slightly different from the UETA definition of "transaction," which refers to "an action or set of actions occurring between two or more persons relating to the conduct of business, commercial, *or governmental* affairs." UETA §2(16) (emphasis added).

Some have seized on the difference between the two definitions to argue that E-SIGN does not apply to the filing of real estate documents, on the premise that the filing is a "governmental" affair, and thus not part of a "transaction." That reading may be plausible, but it is difficult to reconcile with the precise wording of E-SIGN's operative provision, which provides that a "contract, or other record relating to [a] transaction [in or affecting interstate or foreign commerce] may not be denied legal effect, validity, or enforceability solely because it is in electronic form." E-SIGN §101(a)(1). The transactions in question are the underlying real estate transactions in which records are generated; those plainly are "commercial" affairs within the E-SIGN definition of transaction. Because the government's unwillingness to accept the document as a record has the effect of denying the document validity against third parties, Section 101(a)(1) would seem to apply. See E-SIGN §101(b)(2) ("This title does not . . . require any person to agree to . . . accept electronic records or electronic signatures, *other than a governmental agency with respect to a record other than a contract to which it is a party*.") (emphasis added). If it does apply, absent some exception in the statute, it would require state recording offices to accept electronic records for filing.

The most substantial basis for an exception is E-SIGN §104(a), which provides that "nothing in [E-SIGN] limits or supersedes any requirement by a . . . State regulatory agency that records be filed with such agency . . . in accordance with specified standards or formats." Read literally, that would provide little solace for the county recorder's office, because such an office seems unlikely to be covered by the term "State regulatory agency." The absence of any statutory definition of that term makes it hard to justify a non-literal reading.

To protect the recording offices, however, many have pointed to the broad definition of federal regulatory agency, which includes "an agency, as that term is defined in [5 U.S.C. §552(f)]," and thus reaches all arms of

the federal Executive Branch. If the statute had included a similar definition of "State regulatory agency," it would be plausible to think that a local
county recorder's office would qualify and thus would be entitled to determine the format of the records that it would accept for filing. On the other
hand, the express definition of "federal regulatory agency," coupled with
the absence of any definition of "State regulatory agency" might be taken
more naturally to suggest that only the federal term should receive a non-
literal reading.

One final point supporting an exception for state regulatory agencies is the
congressional report that accompanies E-SIGN, which states that the statute
would not impose costs on state governments that exceed $50 million. That
estimate plainly would be false if all county recorder's offices were required to
accept electronic filings.

A traditional perspective on the distinction between UETA and E-SIGN suggests that the decision of Congress to enact a statute that omits the clear
exemption for hardcopy filing in UETA reflects a considered decision to reject
UETA's view on that point. That perspective is bolstered by the persistent
effort of real estate professionals to have this issue addressed in E-SIGN. This
issue was forcefully and repeatedly brought to Congress's attention. Given
that background, it is difficult to explain the failure of the drafters of E-SIGN
to treat the problem more plainly. In the end, however, it seems unlikely that
courts will compel county recorder's offices to accept electronic filings. To be
sure, though, that view rests much less on a fair reading of the enacted text
than it does on a sense of the willingness of courts to repair patently defective statutes brought before them for interpretation. There have been no judicial decisions to date. The most authoritative pronouncement is an opinion
of the California Attorney General concluding that the refusal to record a document does not amount to a refusal to recognize a document that violates
E-SIGN §101(a)(1). Office of the Attorney General, State of California, Op. No.
02-112 (Sept. 4, 2002).

Moving forward, the potential cost savings from electronic filing have led
to a variety of grassroots efforts by local county recorders to accept electronic
recording in certain circumstances, and a notable statewide effort in
Minnesota. Currently about 35 counties are accepting some real estate documents for electronic filing, although very few (about five) appear to be accepting closing documents. (Most counties are accepting only documents that
release a mortgage, which can be easily standardized to include only a few
fields for information that identifies the mortgage to be released and the person purporting to grant the release.)

One obstacle to that effort has been a concern that in some cases state law
actually would prohibit a recorder from accepting electronic documents: The
California Attorney General opinion discussed above did not stop at a conclusion that California law did not require offices to accept electronic filings;
it went on to conclude that it directly prohibited recorders from accepting
electronic filings except in two counties for which the legislature had
enacted specific implementing statutes. To mitigate that concern, NCCUSL
has drafted a proposed Uniform Real Property Electronic Recording Act
(URPERA), which is expected to be approved for promulgation in the summer of 2004. That brief statute generally removes the ambiguity of E-SIGN,
including a specific statement that electronic real property records are to be

accepted for filing. URPERA §3(a). It contemplates that each state will appoint an electronic recording commission to establish technical standards for the documents to be recorded and help promote uniformity of standards nationwide. URPERA §5.

E.   Problems with Electronic Filing

Although electronic filing can bring great benefits to commercial transactions, a complete picture of their effects must acknowledge some problems as well, which arise from the greater vulnerability of electronic systems to external attacks. The current filing systems generally permit any party to file anything that it wants. The filing officers do little or nothing to evaluate the utility or propriety of any particular submission. That always has been the case in the real estate system (assuming that the document satisfies the relevant formal prerequisites). In the personal property system, the old version of Article 9 left some leeway for filing officers to reject filings for non-statutory reasons, but (as mentioned above), the revised Article 9 narrows that ability as much as possible. See UCC §9-516.

Naturally enough in an era characterized by creative forms of grassroots activism, the openness of the filing systems (especially the mortgage filing systems) has permitted their use as a vehicle for harassment, most prominently by the filing of so-called "public liens." A public lien is a document filed not by a lender, but by a self-styled representative of the "public," often acting under the authority of a purported "common-law court." The document is placed in the real estate records and purports to create a lien (often in quite a large amount) against the home (or other assets) of the target, normally a judge or other governmental official under attack. (A typical pattern is to target a judge that has had the misfortune to be called upon to convict a member of a local "militia.") The premise is that the alleged misconduct of the official leaves the official responsible, in the judgment of the "court," for damages in the amount stated in the lien.

In the current system, those attacks provide amusing fodder for the newspapers, rising to irritation on the part of the targets. But they do not pose any serious threat to the system, because no lender or other official would take the document seriously. It takes some effort to have the document removed from the records, ordinarily a suit in the local state court for an injunction to have the filing officer remove the filing or a suit for a declaratory judgment that the filing is invalid. And there always is the potential for a criminal action based on filing a false document in public records. However, those filings have not been common in the UCC system. In any event, they are not likely to pose any serious long-term problem for the filing office or the target.

Advances in information technology, however, can make those kinds of attacks substantially more troublesome. For one thing, it is much easier to make multiple filings on a large scale in an electronic world than in a paper-based world. Thus, the scope of such attacks can be broadened considerably, constrained only by the filing fees of the various offices. Perhaps filing offices eventually will be forced to respond to those problems with some filtering device that allows them in some way to screen out wholly malicious or unfounded filings.

Relevant Glossary Entries

American National Standards Institute (ANSI)
Digital Signature
Electronic Signature
E-SIGN

Problem Set 32

32.1. Stacy Vye at Wessex Bank is charged with the task of updating the Bank's lending procedures to take advantage of electronic technologies. Her task this week is to set up a method for closing loan transactions remotely. The transactions involve security interests in personal property, but not real estate. The principal documents are a security agreement and a financing statement. She would like to send the documents to the borrower by e-mail, have them approved by the borrower, and returned to her.

She wants to know how the borrower needs to sign the documents to conform to applicable law. Is it enough for the borrower to return an e-mail, with the documents attached, indicating that the borrower accepts the attached documents? Her concern is that she does not want to use full-blown digital signatures, because (among other things) she fears the expense and practical difficulties of getting all of her customers sufficiently conversant with the technology. What do you say? UCC §§9-102(a)(7), 9-203, 9-502, and comment 3, 9-516.

32.2. A few weeks later, Stacy calls you back. She is shocked and surprised to discover that the UCC filing office in the Secretary of State's Office in her state does not accept electronic filings and has no plans to accept them in the immediate future. She tells you that she thought federal law now required government agencies to accept electronic filings. She wants to know if there is anything that she can do to force them to take electronic filings. Is there? UCC §9-516(b); UETA §3, E-SIGN §103. How would that change if the jurisdiction had adopted URPERA?

32.3. Stacy calls you back several months later with a few new problems that have come up in the operation of her program. The first one involves a real estate transaction. The loan officer mistakenly closed that transaction with electronic documents, even though Stacy's program contemplated electronic documents only for personal property transactions. The filing office in the loan officer's county rejected the filing out of hand when it came by e-mail, explaining that it does not accept electronic filings of any kind. What should the loan officer do? What are the consequences for the transaction? UETA §18, E-SIGN §§101(a)(1), 104(a)(1), UCC §9-516(d), 9-517.

32.4. Her other problem relates to a personal property transaction in which the borrower has filed for bankruptcy. The transaction was closed with the entirely electronic documents that you recommended in your work on

Problem 32.1. Thus, Wessex has an electronically signed security agreement and a financing statement that was filed without any form of debtor signature. In an effort to avoid the secured claim of Wessex Bank, the borrower claims that the financing statement is invalid because it was not authorized. The borrower points out that UCC §9-509(a) requires the debtor's authorization for any financing statement and that nothing in the security agreement authorizes Wessex to file a financing statement and denies having authorized such a filing elsewhere. What do you tell Stacy? Did you err by writing a security agreement that does not specifically authorize the lender to file a financing statement? UCC §9-509.

32.5. Your last matter of the day relates to your client *www.GnoMania.com*. The Mouvement d'Emancipation des Nains de Jardin ("MENJ" or Movement for the Liberation of Garden Gnomes) has been engaging in a variety of activities opposed to the operations of your client. The CEO calls you today, quite angry. It appears that MENJ has attacked her by filing "public lien" claims against the CEO in the UCC records of every state in the country. Each filing states an obligation to MENJ of $5 million. The filings turned up when she recently had a credit report run in connection with a pending home purchase for which the client was seeking a mortgage loan. Shortly thereafter (apparently because the information was disseminated generally as part of her credit profile), the limits on all of her credit cards were severely truncated and the interest rates increased by 8 to 12 percent. She is very upset. What can she do? How would your answer change if the filings also had been made in the real estate records? UCC §§9-509(d), 9-510, 9-513, and comment 3; Fair Credit Reporting Act, 15 U.S.C. §1681s-2.

Assignment 33: Account Systems — Financial Assets

A. Account-Based Lending Systems

The registries described in the previous assignment typically are used in loan transactions in which the collateral is something tangible that remains in the possession of the borrower. That is important in transactions in which the borrower needs those assets for the operation of its business. It does, however, lead to significant expenses and delay in cases in which the lender seeks to liquidate the assets to repay the secured debt. The expenses and delay are mitigated by special procedural rules that give secured creditors relatively expeditious remedies, at least by comparison to the remedies available for unsecured creditors.

For intangible financial assets like money and securities, however, a different system is more common, in which the assets are placed in the hands of a third-party intermediary, who maintains an "account" that includes those assets. Once those assets are in the hands of the third party, it is a simple matter for the lender to establish a relationship with the intermediary under which the intermediary agrees to turn the assets over to the lender (or dispose of them) if the lender so requests. That system permits the lender much faster access to financial assets than it has to the tangible assets covered by the systems discussed in the preceding assignment. That is acceptable, however, largely because the assets in question tend to be so liquid that there normally will be no dispute over their value at the time of disposition.

Central to that system is a set of highly formal rules that makes the right to sue the intermediary for the asset much easier to enforce and much more reliable than a typical right to sue. As Joseph Sommer puts it:

> [W]hat is "money in the bank"? Most forms of money are mere lawsuits in embryo, a chose in action. We have a paradox. To a payment lawyer, the best kind of asset, money in the bank, is a species of the worst kind of asset — so-sue-me. This result, although analytically correct, does not comport with intuition and feels wrong or incomplete.
>
> Let us examine our intuition more closely. We do not usually view money in the bank as a right to sue the bank. We view it as somehow more real, a possessory fact, not a mere legal right. The same is true for securities holdings. We view our broker as having "our" securities in custody for us, though most

Figure 33.1
Account-Based Lending Systems

Step 1: Borrower deposits assets with Intermediary.

Step 2: Lender arranges with Intermediary to have control of assets.

Step 3: On default, Lender takes assets or directs Intermediary to dispose of them on Lender's behalf.

securities holdings are structured as financial accounts [which means, as discussed below, that the broker in fact does not have any securities in custody for us]. Of course, banks and brokerages are closely regulated and have a strong incentive to retain the public trust. But insurance companies are also regulated firms, in the business of paying claims. Most of us, however, view a claim against an insurance company with far less confidence than we view our money or securities. There is something about money (or securities) that is special.

The difference between banks (or brokerages) on the one hand, and insurance companies on the other, lies in commercial law. The commercial law governing payments (or securities transfers) assures the reliability of money and securities holdings. . . . The success of this law is apparent: we view these accounts as possessory money and securities.

Joseph H. Sommer, *A Law of Financial Accounts: Modern Payment and Securities Transfer Law*, 53 BUS. LAWYER 1181, 1193 (1998).

The account-based system could not exist without electronic technology, and it becomes more prevalent as the costs of managing information decline compared to the relatively stable costs of more traditional arrangements. For example, as the next assignment discusses, certain aspects of the system are used successfully even for real estate mortgages that still must be recorded with county recorders. The more complete use, however, is with respect to securities accounts and deposit accounts. Accordingly, the remainder of this assignment discusses the UCC rules for those systems: first the relatively detailed rules in Articles 8 and 9 for securities accounts, and then the brief rules articulated in the revised Article 9 to facilitate lending against deposit accounts.

B.   The Article 8 System

The average student (or lawyer) probably assumes that the legal rules for securities are confined to the extensive federal regime of securities regulation reflected in the Securities Act, the Securities Exchange Act, and the voluminous regulations issued by the Securities Exchange Commission (the SEC).

Although those rules obviously are crucial to a complete picture of the market for securities, they are not directly relevant to this course. For the most part, those rules address the potential for fraud or sharp dealing in the issuance and sale of securities. Thus, they require various registrations and disclosures as a condition to the issuance of certain types of securities. Similarly, they regulate securities exchanges to ensure that those exchanges provide fair venues for the purchase and sale of securities. (You will recall the brief discussion in Assignment 7 of some of the disclosure rules that affect the operation of Web sites.)

Our concern in this course, however, is not with the fairness of the market in which securities are sold, but with the way in which the mechanisms for effecting their issuance and sale can enhance their liquidity and thus their value as collateral. The primary legal rules relevant to that topic appear in the revised version of Article 8 of the UCC. Adopted by the American Law Institute in 1994, that statute has been enacted in all 50 states. Moreover, pursuant to regulations issued by the United States Treasury, the rules in Article 8 apply to United States Treasury securities. To summarize the Article 8 system, the following discussion first describes the two separate holding systems and then explains how lenders can perfect their interests in assets held in those systems.

1. The Direct Holding System

Article 8 recognizes two separate systems for holding and transferring securities. The first is the direct holding system, a traditional system in which the issuer deals directly with the purchaser of the security, typically by issuing a certificate for the security and delivering it to the owner of the security. When the owner transfers the security, it registers the transfer on the books of the owner, which then issues a new certificate to the new owner.

For many reasons, the direct holding system is no longer the principal method for holding securities. Among other things, the requirement that each sale of a security be registered on the books of the issuer caused that system to fail. It is not practical for each sale of a security to be completed by transportation of a paper certificate to the issuer, registration of the transfer by the issuer, and issuance of a new certificate to the purchaser. Indeed, during the 1960s (when that system was widely used), the major securities exchanges frequently experienced considerable disruptions of trading because of backlogs in the process of delivering certificates to settle previous trades.

To be sure, that problem could have been solved to some extent by the issuance of uncertificated securities. By abandoning the paper certificate, an issuer of uncertificated securities saves the bulk of the transaction costs contemplated by the classic paper-based system. But abandonment of certificates — dematerialization of securities — would have required each separate issuer (or some agent on its behalf) to maintain procedures for processing transfers of securities. In any event, the issuance of uncertificated securities has not been the dominant response to the inconveniences of the paper-based system.

2. The Indirect Holding System

The most common response has been a system of indirect holding of securities — immobilization — in which the overwhelming majority of securities that are in circulation are immobilized in the custody of a small number of intermediaries. Trades among the vast number of retail purchasers of securities are consummated by entries on the books of those intermediaries. The following explanation by the Reporter for the revised Article 8 is illuminating:

> If one examined the shareholder records of large corporations whose shares are publicly traded on the exchanges or in the over-the-counter market, one would find that one entity — Cede & Co. — is listed as the shareholder of record of somewhere in the range of sixty to eighty per cent of the outstanding shares of all publicly traded companies. Cede & Co. is the nominee used by The Depository Trust Company ("DTC"), a limited purpose trust company organized under New York law for the purpose of acting as a depository to hold securities for the benefit of its participants, some six hundred or so broker-dealers and banks. Essentially all the trading in publicly held companies is executed through the broker-dealers who are participants in DTC, and the great bulk of public securities — the sixty to eighty per cent figure noted above — is held by these broker-dealers and banks on behalf of their customers. If all of these broker-dealers and banks held physical certificates, then as trades were executed each day it would be necessary to deliver the certificates back and forth among these broker-dealers and banks. By handing all of their securities over to a common depository, all of these deliveries can be eliminated. Transfers can be accomplished by adjustments to the participants' DTC accounts. . . .
>
> The development of the book-entry system of settlement seems to have accomplished the objective of ensuring that the settlement system has adequate operational capacity to process current trading volumes. At the time of the "paperwork crunch" in the late 1960s, the trading volume on the New York Stock Exchange that so seriously strained the capacities of the clearance and settlement system was in the range of ten million shares per day. Today, the system can easily handle trading volume on routine days of hundreds of millions of shares. Even during the October 1987 market break, when daily trading volume reached the current record level of six hundred eight million shares, the clearance and settlement system functioned relatively smoothly.

James Steven Rogers, *Policy Perspectives on Revised U.C.C. Article 8*, 43 UCLA L. Rev. 1431, 1443-45 (1996).

a. The Basic Framework

In the indirect holding system, transfers of securities rarely require either physical delivery of a certificate or registration on the books of the issuer. On the contrary, most transfers can be made by the book-entry method, which requires nothing more than entries on the accounts of the various intermediaries at a central depository. For example, assume that Edward Casaubon has purchased 100 shares of stock in ABC Corp. Like most investors, Casaubon never received a stock certificate. He purchased the stock through his broker

Bullish Broker and monitors the transaction (and the securities that he "owns") only through the statements that Bullish periodically sends to him. In fact, it may be that Bullish also has no certificates, but instead has an account at DTC that contains 100,000 shares in ABC Corp. DTC, in turn, has certificates representing 3,000,000 shares in ABC Corp. If Casaubon sells his stock to Dorothea Brooke, nothing will happen to any of the certificates. Instead, Bullish will simply transfer some shares from its DTC account to the DTC account of Dorothea's broker, which will hold those shares on Dorothea's account. Alternatively, if Bullish also is Dorothea's broker, then Bullish need only transfer the shares from Casaubon's account to Dorothea's account. DTC need take no action. Most importantly, the issuer takes no action in either case.

Article 8 embraces the indirect holding system and includes a number of rules to facilitate transactions using that system. Working from the classic holding system, it would be possible to construct rules that would treat the retail purchasers as owning individual stock certificates, based on the intermediaries' status as agents for the retail purchasers. And Article 8 still permits that result, but only if the intermediaries register their individual purchasers' transactions with the issuer. UCC §§8-301(a)(3) and 8-301(b)(2).

For the most part, however, Article 8 dispenses with such a cumbersome framework and instead attempts to articulate functional rules that more directly reflect the true relationships of the parties. Those rules reflect the absence of any direct relationship between Casaubon and Dorothea, on the one hand, and the issuer, on the other. Instead, the only relationship that has any substance is the relationship between the retail purchaser and the intermediary with whom it deals. Part 5 of Article 8 establishes a legal framework to govern that relationship. In that framework (illustrated in Figure 33.2), Casaubon's right to the securities makes him an "entitlement holder" (defined in UCC §8-102(a)(7)). His right to the shares of ABC Corp. is a "security entitlement" (defined in UCC §8-102(a)(17)). Bullish, the party against which Casaubon holds that entitlement, is a "securities intermediary" (defined in UCC §8-102(a)(14)). The same rules apply at each tier of the holding system, so that Bullish also is an entitlement holder with a security entitlement against DTC based on the shares in Bullish's account at DTC. To illustrate the basic features of that framework, it is useful to discuss the rights of the entitlement holder against its securities intermediary and the rights of the entitlement holder against third parties.

b.   Rights Against the Intermediary

The best place to start in examining the relationship between the entitlement holder and its securities intermediary is to see how an entitlement holder can obtain an entitlement that is valid against its securities intermediary: How does Casaubon get the stock into his account at Bullish in the first place? Article 8 uses two separate, overlapping functional tests. The first test focuses on Bullish's conduct, recognizing that Casaubon has a security entitlement if Bullish agrees that Casaubon has one, that is, if Bullish "indicates by book

Figure 33.2
The Indirect Holding System

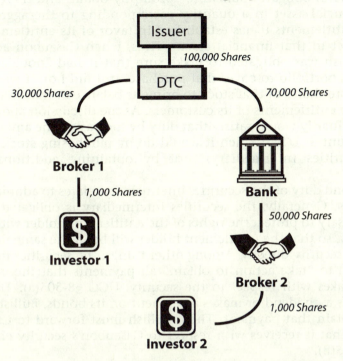

Note 1: DTC owns a "security" (UCC § 8-102(a)(15)) represented by a "security certificate" (UCC § 8-102(a)(16)) in DTC's possession. There are no other security certificates in this scenario; none of the other parties "own" securities.

Note 2: DTC is a "securities intermediary" (UCC § 8-102(a)(14)) with respect to "security entitlements" (UCC § 8-102(a)(17)) held by Broker 1 and Bank as "entitlement holders" (UCC § 8-102(a)(7)).

Note 3: Broker 1, in turn, is a securities intermediary with respect to a security entitlement held by Investor 1 as entitlement holder. In the same way, Bank is a securities intermediary with respect to a security entitlement held by Broker 2 as entitlement holder, and Broker 2 is a securities intermediary with respect to a security entitlement held by Investor 2 as entitlement holder.

entry that a financial asset has been credited to the person's securities account," UCC §8-501(b)(1). The second test focuses on actions that other parties take that should lead to the same result. If Bullish receives some securities on Casaubon's behalf, Casaubon has a security entitlement to the extent of those securities. UCC §8-501(b)(2).

Once Casaubon obtains a security entitlement, Article 8 imposes a variety of duties on Bullish with respect to that entitlement. The most important duty is a duty to maintain assets sufficient to cover the entitlement. Because Article 8 recognizes an entitlement for Casaubon immediately upon Bullish's crediting Casaubon's account, it is entirely possible for

Casaubon to acquire an entitlement against Bullish to stock of ABC Corp. without Bullish obtaining a corresponding amount of ABC Corp. stock. UCC §8-504(a) obligates Bullish to "promptly obtain and thereafter maintain a financial asset in a quantity corresponding to the aggregate of all security entitlements it has established in favor of its entitlement holders with respect to that financial asset." Thus, when Casaubon acquired the stock, Bullish was obligated to make sure that it had enough ABC Corp. stock in its portfolio to cover that purchase. If it did not, it would have to acquire more shares of that stock to bring its balance of that stock up to the level of the entitlements of its customers. As the discussion above suggests, Bullish ordinarily would satisfy that duty by increasing the amount of stock in its account at DTC (which it would do by purchasing stock from some other securities intermediary), not by obtaining additional physical certificates.

The second duty of the securities intermediary relates to administration of the security. Generally, the securities intermediary is obligated to take all steps necessary to protect the rights of the entitlement holder with respect to the security, so that the entitlement holder will be in the same position as if it held the security directly. Among other things, the securities intermediary is obligated to "take action to obtain" all payments that the issuer of the security makes with respect to the security. UCC §8-505(a). Thus, if ABC Corp. issues a dividend or makes a payment on its bonds, Bullish must take steps to obtain that payment. Then, Bullish must forward to Casaubon all payments that it receives with respect to Casaubon's security entitlements. UCC §8-505(b).

In the same way, Bullish is obligated to act for Casaubon with respect to voting rights and other rights related to the securities (such as rights to redeem securities). UCC §8-506. With respect to those matters, Bullish either can take steps necessary to allow Casaubon to vote on his own behalf (to "exercise the rights directly," UCC §8-506(1)), or it can act for Casaubon, provided that it "exercises due care in accordance with reasonable commercial standards to follow the direction of the entitlement holder," UCC §8-506(2).

Finally, the securities intermediary is obligated to follow the instructions of the entitlement holder regarding sale or other disposition of the security entitlement. UCC §§8-507(a) (obligating securities intermediary to comply with an "entitlement order"), 8-102(a)(8) (defining "entitlement order"). Because the foundation of the account-based system is the relation between the securities intermediary and the entitlement holder, the standard to which the securities intermediary is held in verifying the instructions of the entitlement holder is fundamental to the integrity of the system. The following case illustrates one court's effort to apply basic principles of commercial law to that question.

Powers v. American Express Financial Advisors, Inc.

82 F. Supp. 2d 448 (D. Md. 2000)

SMALKIN, District Judge.

This is a diversity case removed from a Maryland state court, in which Amy Lynn Powers seeks to hold the defendant, American Express Financial Advisors,

Inc. (American Express), liable under a number of theories for an alleged wrongful transfer of financial assets that she held in a joint-and-survivor account with her former boyfriend, Michael D'Ambrosia, whom American Express has sued as a third party defendant. . . .

The relevant, undisputed facts establish that Powers and D'Ambrosia started a romantic union in 1983 and jointly purchased a house in Emmitsburg, Maryland, in 1990. At that time, D'Ambrosia was an accountant for a corporation called Signal Perfection, Ltd. (Signal). Powers and D'Ambrosia had a number of joint bank accounts, and, in mid-July, 1994, they entered into a mutual fund investment relationship with American Express. Their holdings were in joint-and-survivor form, pursuant to the Investment Application they filled out when making their first investment. It is undisputed that all of the deposits were made by D'Ambrosia and none of the income or losses was reported by Powers. Apparently, this account was intended to provide some sort of reimbursement to Powers for her domestic services and was also intended, should both she and D'Ambrosia die, ultimately to go to her mother.

The ship of domestic bliss on which Powers and D'Ambrosia had been sailing struck a reef in the summer of 1997, one result of which was that American Express was given an oral request by D'Ambrosia himself to "freeze" the investments, apparently to assure Powers that the assets would remain untouched until they could agree on their disposition. On October 16, 1997, D'Ambrosia sent American Express a communication requesting redemption of the investments and wire transfer of the proceeds to a joint bank account he had with Powers in Frederick. Attached to the faxed communication — which appeared on the letterhead of Signal, and was signed "Michael" — was a letter addressed to American Express, dated September 26, 1997, and bearing what purported to be the signatures of D'Ambrosia and Powers and the notary seal and signature of one Otis K. Comstock, a notary public in and for Carroll County, Maryland, releasing the freeze and directing transfer of the proceeds to Prudential (another financial services agency). . . .

It is undisputed that Mr. Jeffrey Helms of American Express compared the signature on the September 26 letter with an exemplar of Amy Powers' signature, and verified the signature as hers. At her deposition, Powers acknowledged the fact that the signature on this instrument "resembled" her signature, but, indeed, the fly in the ointment — and what engendered this lawsuit — is that D'Ambrosia had forged Powers' signature to that document.

As one might expect, D'Ambrosia cleaned out the joint bank account after the transfer and fled with the funds, thus leaving Powers both stranded and penurious. She has now turned to American Express to seek satisfaction, at least for the financial part of her loss.

One more little fact is needed to round out the picture. Defendant raises a strong suspicion that much — if not all — of the funds in the account was money embezzled by D'Ambrosia from Signal. D'Ambrosia entered into a civil settlement with Signal, and, apparently as a result, is not now in jail, although he is said to be "on the run." (He is a third-party defendant in this lawsuit.) There is a dispute as to the extent of Powers' knowledge of her former boyfriend's malefactions, but it is not material to the disposition of the pending motions, for reasons that will appear *post*. . . .

There is agreement that this case involves "financial assets," as defined in MARYLAND COMMERCIAL LAW CODE ANN. ("U.C.C.") §8-102(a)(9). As such, this transaction is governed by [Article 8], as recently revised, which sets up a comprehensive mechanism for dealing with rights and obligations of those who own (called "entitlement holders") and those who hold financial assets for them (called "intermediaries"). Entitlement holders are entitled to give orders to their intermediaries on the transfer, disposition, etc., of financial assets. Unfortunately, there is no discernible case law anywhere under revised Article 8 of the U.C.C. . . . — and very little commentary — dealing with the question of the effect of an entitlement order that is authorized by only one of the entitlement holders on a joint account. What commentary there is, as will be seen, has been taken into account by the Court.

It is clear that both D'Ambrosia and Powers were entitlement holders, as defined in Section 8-102(a)(7), in that they were identified in the records of the securities intermediary (defendant) as having a security entitlement against the intermediary. As such, D'Ambrosia was an "appropriate person" to give an entitlement order to the defendant. See U.C.C. §8-107(a)(3). When the appropriate person gives an entitlement order, the securities intermediary has a duty to comply with the order, a duty which is satisfied if the intermediary exercises due care in accordance with reasonable commercial standards to comply with the entitlement order. U.C.C. §8- 507(a)(2). That duty requires that the intermediary will first have had a reasonable opportunity to assure itself that the entitlement order is genuine and authorized.

The problem for the defendant here is that, according to the terms of Section C of its Investment Application, under which the account was established, it is clear that *signatures* of *both* D'Ambrosia and Powers were required for any redemption request for over $50,000. Thus, for any redemption over $50,000 (and this one was for over $86,000), the defendant itself required both holders' authorizations.

Powers claims, as an entitlement holder, that American Express failed in its duty to her under Section 8-507 (which is the section that is intended to govern the liability of the securities intermediary to its entitlement holder *as such*) by following an instruction made without her authority. The Court is of the opinion, as a matter of law, that, even if American Express exercised due care in accordance with reasonable commercial standards by verifying the signature against a known Amy Powers' exemplar and by noting the presence of a notary's signature and seal on the document (but note that the document bearing the signature authorized transfer to Prudential, not to a bank), it is still liable to Powers, because the order, for which she never gave any form of authorization or ratified, was "ineffective."

As is made clear by the Official Comments to Section 8-507, an intermediary such as defendant incurs liability to an entitlement holder if it honors an order that is "ineffective." Section 8-107(b) establishes when an order is effective. Although that provision is somewhat tautological (by its reference to effective orders as those made by the "appropriate person," notwithstanding the discussion in Official Comment 4 to Section 8-507 of the purported difference between orders made by an appropriate person and ineffective orders), both the reference in Section 8-107 to principles of agency and Official Comment 4 to Section 8-507 lead to no other conclusion than that, when the intermediary has agreed that the "appropriate person" to make an order is both owners of a joint account, both owners must make the order (unless, of course, agency and ratification principles might render the order "effective" under Section 8-107(b)(2) and/or (3), which is not the case here). No facts whatever are advanced that would show that D'Ambrosia had any sort of authority to affix Powers' forged signature to the document accompanying the order or that she ever ratified it.

As noted above, the commentary found by the Court supports this conclusion. For example, it is noted in Hawkland's *Uniform Commercial Code Series,* Section 8-107:03:

> Thus, to say that . . . a direction is not effective is to say that . . . the [intermediary] is liable to the true owner . . . if it turns out that the . . . entitlement order was not actually authorized. Note too that . . . liability . . . does not depend on awareness of the lack of authority. The record keepers must, at peril of absolute liability, take steps to assure themselves that the transfer is authorized.

In this case, it may be argued that the imposition of liability on defendant is unfair. There are two answers to that argument. The first is that, whenever two relatively innocent persons are bamboozled by the same evil-doer, the loss must rest somewhere. In such cases, the loss usually rests with he who is in the better position to protect himself and does not do so. Looking at the analogous situation under the (perhaps more familiar) law of commercial paper, and particularly the warranties on presentment, in the case of a forged drawer's signature on a check, the loss rests with the paying drawee, who is in a position to verify the drawer's signature. *See Price v. Neal,* 3 Burr. 1354 (1762). That loss rests with the drawee no matter how artful the forgery, unless the drawer is precluded from asserting the forgery (as he may be by, *inter alia,* agency law, just as an entitlement holder may be under Section 8-107(b)(3)). Similarly, the ultimate loss from a forged title endorsement rests with the first taker of the check post-forgery, no matter how artful the forgery. In short, the drawee and the taker, respectively, are in better positions to protect themselves from the loss occasioned by the forgery than is the person whose signature has been forged while she was unaware she was being victimized, even though they exercised due care and followed reasonable commercial standards.

Under the facts of this particular case, it is evident that the defendant could have protected itself better against the loss in question, as it acted only on the basis of Powers' signature on a faxed transfer request; the instrument purportedly signed by Powers was not only almost three weeks older than the transfer order, but dealt with a transfer to a different entity (Prudential Securities) than did the faxed request (to a bank account in Frederick). Furthermore, the defendant did not request the original document to check it for any obvious alteration, nor did it require an acknowledged signature (which would, if the notary properly performed his duty, have required him to state that Powers had personally appeared before him). Hence, there is no unfairness in bringing the loss to rest with defendant.

It should also be noted that, as to joint accounts, it is the intermediary's own contract that has defined what constitutes an effective order. The Court's conclusion is, thus, entirely consonant with Official Comment 4 (second paragraph) to Section 8-507, which leaves to "other law" questions "such as allocation between the securities intermediary and the entitlement holder of the risk of fraudulent entitlement orders." Here, such risk, as to transfers over $50,000, has been assumed by the defendant, by a contract, which, although not specifically dealt with in Title 8 is not inconsistent therewith. *See* U.C.C. Section 1-103. The remedy to which Powers is entitled is a recredit of the account. Of course, defendant is entitled to recover its loss against D'Ambrosia under Section 8-109. Because it is clear that . . . a joint tenant is entitled to the entirety of the property held jointly, regardless of which tenant generated the property, the Court will order the entire account restored in favor of Powers. . . .

Next, the defendant claims that certain language in section J of the same application form constitutes a general release of liability in connection with wire transfers. It does not, for many reasons. First, it is so ambiguous that it cannot fairly be read as a release of liability under Title 8 of the U.C.C., and, second, it would be against public policy for such a general, form release to be given effect over the standards of care and liability established in that statutory scheme. Finally, there is no signature, no initialing, or even a check mark in the applicable space showing that section J ever was agreed to, or became part of, the application. It stands, for the purposes of the parties' agreement and their contract (*see* U.C.C. Section 1-202(3) and (11)), outside the gate.

For the reasons stated, an Order will be entered separately, granting summary judgment in favor of plaintiff, and against American Express. . . .

Another common problem arises when a third party asserts a claim to the securities reflected by the security entitlement. If the securities intermediary proceeded to sell the securities pursuant to the instructions of its customer (the entitlement holder), the third party would be likely to assert a claim against the securities intermediary contending that the intermediary should not have allowed the entitlement holder to sell the securities. To ensure liquidity of securities, UCC §8-115 bars any such claim against the securities intermediary except in three narrow cases: the creditor obtains an injunction barring transfer of the securities (UCC §8-115(1)); the intermediary "acted in collusion with the wrongdoer" (UCC §8-115(2)); or the securities intermediary has notice of a claim that the applicable security certificate constitutes stolen property (UCC §8-115(3)). (The last exception obviously could arise only in the relatively unusual case in which the securities intermediary received a stock certificate as the basis for the entitlement instead of an entry in the securities intermediary's account at a higher-level securities intermediary.)

c. Rights Against Third Parties

The indirect holding system must deal with two distinct claims that third parties can interpose against an entitlement holder: claims that third parties assert against a particular security and claims that third parties assert against the securities intermediary.

The first is a simple one, as to which the indirect holding system uses traditional rules that allow the entitlement itself to pass free of claims of third parties. Specifically, an entitlement holder that acquires a security entitlement for value and without notice of an adverse claim takes completely free of the claim. UCC §§8-502 and 8-503(e). That is true even though the entitlement holder does not obtain "control" of any particular certificate representing the security in question. The entitlement holder need only obtain a valid security entitlement. As discussed above, that only requires an entry by the securities intermediary on the account of the entitlement holder. UCC §§8-502 (providing that purchasers that become entitlement holders have control), 8-501(b)(1) (specifying how to become an entitlement holder).

The second topic is considerably more difficult. Because Article 8 recognizes security entitlements that are not necessarily backed by specific stock certificates, it is possible for a securities intermediary to incur obligations that exceed the amount of the securities that it owns. Of course, the system includes a variety of safeguards designed to limit the possibility of such losses. For one thing, most securities intermediaries are subject to considerable regulatory oversight, which substantially diminishes the risk of malfeasance that would result in such a shortage. Moreover, all brokers and dealers in securities are required to join the Securities Investor Protection Corporation (the SIPC). The SIPC provides retail purchasers insurance analogous to the deposit insurance provided by the FDIC. That insurance currently covers up to a $500,000 shortfall that a customer experiences upon a liquidation of the assets of a securities intermediary. For example, if a customer had $1,500,000 in its account, but received only $900,000 upon liquidation of the intermediary, the SIPC insurance would provide $500,000, leaving the customer short "only" $100,000.

3. Lending Against Securities Entitlements

The system for lending against securities entitlements in the revised Article 9 takes full advantage of the account-based system for indirect holdings delineated in Part 5 of Article 8. Article 9 defines a broad category of assets as "investment property," which includes, among other things, securities and securities accounts. UCC §9-102(a)(49). For the assets placed in those accounts (including the securities entitlements that are relevant here), the creditor takes and perfects a security interest by taking and perfecting a security interest in the account itself. UCC §§9-203(h) and 9-308(f).

The statute does permit perfection by filing. UCC §9-312(a) and comment 4. However, the statute recognizes the uncomfortable fit between perfection by filing — notice in a remote registry — and the immobilization of the asset in an account. Accordingly, a creditor that perfects only by filing is subordinate to creditors that perfect directly against the account. UCC §9-328.

The preferred method of perfection is tailored to the account-based system discussed above, because it involves a direct relationship between the lender and the intermediary holding the account. In Article 9 terms, the lender that seeks the highest priority perfects by taking "control" of the account. UCC §9-314(a). Control, in turn, depends upon a consensual relationship with the securities intermediary. Specifically, the lender must either become the entitlement holder itself or obtain an agreement from the securities intermediary that the securities intermediary will comply with the lender's instructions regarding disposal of the asset. UCC §§9-106(a) and 8-106(d). The statute also includes a special rule for cases in which the intermediary is the lender. Recognizing the tautology of the intermediary establishing a relationship with itself, the statute grants automatic perfection to a security interest that is granted to the intermediary. UCC §9-309(10); see also UCC §8-106(e) (granting automatic "control" to the intermediary).

UCC §9-328 sets out the priority rules for security interests in security entitlements. Absent any contrary agreement, the first priority goes to a security interest held by the securities intermediary. UCC §9-328(3). If there is no such security interest (or if the securities intermediary has subordinated it by granting control to a third-party lender), the secured party with control has first priority. UCC §9-328(1). As mentioned above, that secured party also would have priority even over entitlement holders in the event that the intermediary fails. UCC §8-511(b). In the unusual case in which multiple secured parties have control, those parties generally rank by priority of time in obtaining control. UCC §9-328(2). Finally, a security interest perfected only by filing is subordinate to those who have perfected either automatically or by control. UCC §§9-328(1), (3) and comment 3; UCC §9-312 comment 4.

C. Lending Against Deposit Accounts

Deposit accounts are more familiar to us than securities accounts, but third-party lending against them is less common. Only with the recent revisions to Article 9 has the UCC articulated a set of rules for lending against commercial deposit accounts. (Consumer accounts are excluded. UCC §9-109(d)(13).) And the UCC still includes no rules to govern the basic account relationship, although there has been some impetus to add such rules to UCC Article 4.

The lending rules in Article 9 closely resemble the account-based system discussed above for securities accounts, except that perfection of deposit accounts cannot be achieved by filing. Except for perfection under UCC §9-315 in funds that are proceeds generated by the disposition of other forms of collateral (a topic that we leave for other courses), the only method of perfection is control. UCC §§9-312(b)(1) and comment 5 and 9-314(a). As with securities accounts, the bank at which the account is located has control automatically. UCC §9-104(a)(1). Third-party lenders gain control by arrangement with the bank, either by becoming the customer on the account (UCC §9-104(a)(3)) or by obtaining from that bank an agreement "that the bank will comply with instructions originated by the secured party directing disposition of the funds in the deposit account without further consent by the debtor" (UCC §9-104(a)(2)).

It should not be surprising that UCC §9-327 grants priority in the account to the secured party with control. UCC §9-327(1). The bank at which the account is located comes behind the secured party (or parties) with control, but ahead of all other security interests (which ordinarily will be security interests in proceeds under UCC §9-315). UCC §9-327(3) and comment 4.

Problem Set 33

33.1. Edward Casaubon comes to you to ask you a question about a potential problem that he has with his broker (Bullish Broker). Casaubon tells you that he asked his contact at Bullish last week to purchase 10,000 shares of stock in Advanced Tactical Devices, Inc. (ATDI). The contact advised Casaubon that the purchase had been completed. Furthermore, Casaubon has ascertained by examining his account record from his home computer that Bullish credited Casaubon's account with the ATDI stock on the date of the purchase.

While talking to his broker this morning, Casaubon was upset by a stray comment to the effect that the broker had not yet been able to obtain the ATDI securities that Casaubon thought he had purchased last week. Casaubon wants to know if he has anything to be worried about. Does Casaubon own the securities or not? Does Bullish have any obligation to remedy the situation? UCC §§8-102(a)(7), 8-102(a)(14), 8-102(a)(17), 8-501(b), 8-503(a), 8-503(b), 8-504(a).

33.2.   Consider the *Powers* case in the assignment. Suppose that D'Ambrosia instead of having the funds sent to a bank account had the securities in the account sold to third parties (so that he could take the funds directly). Would Powers have had a claim against the third parties to which the securities were sold? UCC §§8-501, 8-502.

33.3.   You have an angry call this afternoon from Ben Darrow, your old classmate who now works at First State Bank of Matacora (FSB). It appears that Ben extended a large loan to Estacado Shipping. For collateral, he took a security interest not only in the trucks and other equipment of Estacado, but also in a large brokerage account at Fidelma Funds. Ben dutifully perfected by filing a financing statement in the office of the Secretary of State, which describes the collateral as "all investment property of the Debtor." He has been watching with concern as Estacado's operations have deteriorated over the last several months. Accordingly, when Estacado missed its payment last week, he moved quickly to take the assets from the securities account. He was horrified when he got a call back from Fidelma indicating that his claim on the account was inferior to a claim by Bulstrode Bank. He cannot understand how this could be correct. He searched the UCC records after his filing was made and saw that his filing was the only filing against Estacado. How did this happen to Ben? Does he in fact lose to Bulstrode? Would it matter if Bulstrode came along after Ben's loan, with full knowledge that Ben's loan already had been perfected against the securities? UCC §§8-106(d) and comment 4, 9-106(a), 9-102(a)(49), 9-203(h), 9-308(f), 9-312(a), 9-328 and comment 3.

33.4.   If you represented Bulstrode in Problem 33.3, would you have any concerns about your priority being defeated by yet another claimant? Is there any way that you can see to assuage any such concerns? UCC §§8-106(e), 9-106(a), 9-328(1) and (3).

33.5.   Consider again the facts of Problem 33.3 — a filing by Ben Darrow at FSB against all assets of Estacado Shipping. But instead of a contest with a competing secured creditor, assume that Estacado Shipping files for bankruptcy, and that FSB is the only secured creditor. Who will get the securities? What about Estacado's bank account? UCC §§9-312(a), (b)(1) and comments 4-5, 9-317(a)(2), 9-504(2); Bankruptcy Code §544(a).

33.6.   Stacy Vye calls you with an interesting problem. One of her clients (Diggory Venn) has invested in a Web site for fantasy baseball leagues called YourFantasyTeam.com. He has a 5 percent interest in the limited partnership that owns the site, evidenced by an ownership certificate. All transfers must be registered with the site; no interest can be transferred to any person without approval by the managing partner of the partnership. Based on the economics of the arrangement, Stacy would like to make a loan to Venn, provided she can perfect a security interest in Venn's interest in the site. How would you do that? UCC §§8-102(a)(15), 8-103(c), 9-102(a)(42) and (49), 9-102(b), 9-310(a).

Assignment 34: Token Systems — Electronic Notes

A final way for lenders to protect their collateral is to take possession of the collateral itself or something that represents it. The concept is that lenders transform some monetary obligation into a "token" that can be passed from party to party, with the token evidencing the right to receive payment on the obligation. The token traditionally has been a piece of paper — following the rules in UCC Article 3 that require negotiable instruments to be written. In recent years, however, two separate legal systems have been enacted that provide the infrastructure for intangible tokens of monetary obligations. The first is the system for transferable records included in E-SIGN and UETA. The second is the system for electronic chattel paper in the Revised UCC Article 9. Those systems are the subject of this assignment. The most important theme of the discussion is the extent to which those systems must (at least for now) rely in part on the registry and account systems described in the previous assignments.

A. Transferable Records Under E-SIGN and the UETA

The provisions of UETA and E-SIGN that preempt "writing" requirements do not apply to transactions governed by UCC Article 3. UETA §3(b)(2); E-SIGN §103(a)(3). Instead, in that context those statutes create rules for a new type of obligation, known in both statutes as a "transferable record." UETA §16; E-SIGN §201. Essentially, the transferable record is an electronic substitute for the negotiable instrument that is the subject of UCC Article 3. Indeed, both statutes define it in terms of Article 3, as an instrument (a) that would qualify as a negotiable instrument under Article 3 if the electronic record were in writing; and (b) the issuer of which has agreed that it shall be treated as a transferable record. UETA §16(a); E-SIGN §201(a). E-SIGN also limits its coverage to a note that "relates to a loan secured by real property," E-SIGN §201(a)(1)(C), but UETA includes no such subject matter limitation. Because the "supersede" provision of E-SIGN (E-SIGN §102(a)(1)) applies only to E-SIGN §101, the enactment of UETA has no effect on the applicability of the provisions in E-SIGN §201, which thus apply even in states that have enacted UETA.

1. The Basics of Negotiability

Because the major substantive requirements for transferable records come from Article 3's provisions that define the instruments that qualify for treatment as negotiable, it is useful to summarize those provisions. The basic definition is set out in UCC §3-104(a), supplemented by definitions and amplifications contained elsewhere in Part 1 of Article 3 and in Article 1. Those requirements are formal and technical, but a simple summary of them suffices for present purposes:

1. The obligation must be a promise or order. UCC §3-104(a). A "promise" is a direct commitment to pay, contained in a written document called a "note." UCC §§3-103(a)(9), 3-104(e). An "order" is an instruction to pay a third party, contained in a written document called a "draft" (the check being the most common example). UCC §§3-103(a)(6) and 3-104(e). Because the relevant provisions of UETA and E-SIGN apply only to notes, not to drafts, we need not consider drafts further in this assignment.

2. The obligation must be unconditional. UCC §3-104(a) and 3-106.

3. The obligation must require the payment of money (domestic or foreign). UCC §§3-104(a), 1-201(24), 3-107.

4. The obligation must be for a fixed amount, although it is permissible to supplement the fixed principal amount with variable interest rates or other charges, as long as they are described in the instrument. UCC §3-104(a).

5. The obligation must be payable to bearer or order. If an instrument is payable to bearer, then any person in possession of it is a holder entitled to enforce it. An instrument generally is payable to bearer if it says that it is ("Pay to Bearer") or if it fails to identify any payee ("Pay to ____" or "Pay to Cash").

    If it is payable to order, then the only person that can be a full-fledged holder of the instrument is the person identified on the instrument as the person to whom payment is to be made. An instrument is payable to order if it identifies a particular person to whose order it should be paid ("Pay to the order of Dan Keating"). UCC §§3-104(a)(1), 3-109, 1-201(20).

6. The instrument must be payable on demand (that is, immediately upon request) or at a definite time stated in the instrument. UCC §§3-104(a)(2) and 3-108.

7. The instrument must not include any extraneous non-monetary obligations. UCC §3-104(a)(3).

To summarize how those provisions interact with UETA and E-SIGN: because the "writing" requirement in Article 3 appears only in the definition of "promise" (and the definition of "order," irrelevant for present purposes), a record qualifies as a transferable record under UETA or E-SIGN only if it is a direct commitment to pay that states that it is intended to qualify as a transferable record and satisfies the second through seventh requirements above. (The writing requirement is not directly preempted by UETA or E-SIGN because neither statute applies to transactions governed by UCC Article 3. UETA §3(b)(2); E-SIGN §103(a)(3).)

The concepts of the "holder" and especially the "holder in due course" are central to the law of negotiability. The "holder" of an instrument is entitled to enforce the instrument against (among others) the person that issued it. UCC §§3-301 and 3-412. Thus, the "holder" of a check can enforce it against the person who wrote it, even if the holder had nothing to do with the original transaction.

Determining whether somebody is a holder is relatively mechanical, because it depends solely on (a) determining if the instrument is bearer paper or order paper; (b) determining who is in possession; and (c) if the paper is order paper (rather than bearer paper), determining who is entitled to receive payment (the "identified person," in the language of Article 3). (That person will be either the original named payee or some other person to whom the instrument has been indorsed. See UCC §3-205 (discussing how indorsement can change the character of the paper and the identified person).) If the instrument is bearer paper, the person in possession is the holder. If the instrument is order paper, the holder is the identified person, but only if that person possesses the paper. For example, if a check is written to Dan Keating, and indorsed by Dan to Jane Keating ("Pay to Jane Keating"), then Jane Keating would be the holder if she was in possession of the check. If the identified person is not in possession of order paper, there is no holder. UCC §1-201(20).

When a person becomes a holder of an Article 3 note in a transaction without irregularities, that person obtains the highly desirable status of a holder in due course. Specifically, the person must take the instrument for value, in good faith, and without notice of any of a series of problems with the instrument that should have undermined the person's expectation that payment would be forthcoming. UCC §3-302(a). A person that qualifies as a holder in due course takes the instrument free of most defenses to payment that the original issuer of the note would have. UCC §3-305(b). The main exceptions are defenses of incapacity, infancy, illegality, and the like, which rarely would be relevant in commercial transactions. UCC §3-305(a). What that means in practice is that an issuer that has a valid defense to payment — which would mean that the original payee (lender) could not force the issuer to pay — would be unconditionally obligated to pay a later purchaser of the note, if that purchaser managed to obtain holder-in-due-course status.

Perhaps more importantly for commerce, the holder in due course also takes the instrument free from claims to the instrument itself, without any exceptions. UCC §3-306. Thus, if the instrument passes through the hands of several parties on the way from the payee to the holder in due course, the holder in due course can be sure that no creditor of any one of those intermediate parties can assert a valid claim to the instrument, even if one of those parties files for bankruptcy. See UETA §16 comment 5 (discussing that problem).

The holder-in-due-course doctrine makes the instruments to which it applies more liquid — easier to sell — by limiting the need for a purchaser of such an instrument to investigate the likelihood that the issuer of the note has a valid defense to payment. Essentially, the doctrine reflects a policy view that, in the contexts in which the instruments are used, the benefits of transferability outweigh any harms from enforcing notes for which issuers otherwise would have defenses to payment.

Despite those benefits, in this country negotiable notes are used in limited contexts. They rarely appear in transactions among businesses, generally because the simple form that will satisfy Article 3 is often not suitable for those transactions and because the notes in those transactions are large enough and transferred with sufficient infrequency that the costs of investigating the obligation are tolerable. They rarely appear in consumer sales transactions because FTC regulations bar their use in transactions involving consumer purchases of personal property for $25,000 or less. 16 C.F.R. §433.2(a). The only major context in which they appear is the home mortgage (to which the FTC regulations do not apply). Even there, it is not clear that negotiable instruments are used in practice, because the standard form typically used for those transactions arguably fails to satisfy the Article 3 standards for negotiability.

As the discussion above suggests, negotiability has fallen out of use in the paper-based world for a number of reasons. The largest reason doubtless is the discomfort policymakers have with the holder-in-due-course doctrine, particularly as applied to consumers. As the FTC regulation mentioned above suggests, it often is thought to be unacceptable that consumers should be forced to pay for purchases that failed to conform to their contract with the seller. The same instinct underlies the right to withhold payment in TILA §170 (discussed in Chapter 5). Another practical reason is that the benefits of negotiability in most contexts actually are quite small — at least in part because valid defenses to payment on notes are uncommon — and thus do not justify any cognizable effort to ensure that the documentation complies with the technical rules of Article 3 that govern negotiability.

2.   *Negotiability Under E-SIGN and the UETA*

Because UETA and E-SIGN deal with intangible records rather than documents, they cannot import principles of negotiability wholesale, if only because it is difficult to apply the concept of "possession" — a basic requirement for holder status — to intangible records. As you might guess from the previous assignment, UETA and E-SIGN solve that problem by giving the rights of a holder to the party that gains control of the record. UETA §16(d); E-SIGN §201(d). Indeed, if the person acquires the instrument in a way that satisfies the other requirements described in UCC §3-302, the person with control also will have the rights of a holder in due course. UETA §16(d); E-SIGN §201(d).

The statutes define a person as having control when "a system employed for evidencing the transfer of interests in the transferable record reliably establishes that person as the person to which the transferable record was issued or transferred." UETA §16(b); E-SIGN §201(b). To give content to that relatively general definition, UETA and E-SIGN provide a more detailed six-prong safe harbor that focuses on the creation of an "authoritative copy" of the record, intended to be the electronic equivalent of an identifiably unique original document. Any system that satisfies all six prongs is adequate to provide "control" for purposes of the transferable-record rules. UETA §16 comment 3. The safe harbor generally requires the authoritative copy to share the functional characteristics that make paper originals useful:

- There must be a single, unique, identifiable copy.
- The copy must identify the person in control as the person to whom the note was issued or, if the note has been transferred, the person to whom it has most recently been transferred.
- The copy must be "communicated to" and "maintained" by the person in control *or* its designated custodian.
- It must not be possible to add or change an identified assignee without the consent of the person asserting control.
- Other copies of the record must be readily distinguishable from the authoritative copy.
- Any revision of the authoritative copy must be readily identifiable as authorized or unauthorized.

UETA §16(c); E-SIGN §201(c).

The requirements for obtaining control are intended to be sufficiently flexible to accommodate future technological developments, but it is apparent that the drafters anticipated that systems might satisfy those requirements in two general ways. First, in the short run, it seems relatively easy to satisfy the requirements through an account system similar to the systems discussed in the preceding assignment. The comments to UETA note that such systems already exist for security entitlements and cotton warehouse receipts. UETA §16 comment 3 ¶ 3. In a system like those, the electronic record of the transaction would be provided to a central registrar, which would maintain a listing of the holdings of each participant in the system.

(The UETA comment describes the existing systems as "third party registry" systems, but in this text they are characterized as account systems, to indicate that the assets actually are maintained on the records of the third party, where in pure registry systems like Article 9 the registrar simply maintains a "register" of the assets. As explained in the preceding assignments, the account systems are ideally suited for intangible assets, while the pure registry systems are better suited for tangible collateral.)

With advances in technology, however, the statute would accommodate a true electronic token — a digital file that could be transferred electronically from person to person, impervious to unauthorized alteration or duplication. Although such tokens would be interesting as a theoretical matter, it remains to be seen whether there is any practical need for them. The obvious success of the account-based systems discussed in the previous assignment calls into question the need for any such development.

Interestingly, because the UETA/E-SIGN rules for control limit the possibility that multiple parties could have a plausible claim to enforce a transferable record, they obviate the need for indorsement that is so central to the Article 3 system for negotiable instruments. It is important to notice, however, that the absence of indorsements also does away with the liability that indorsers have under UCC §3-415 — a liability to pay subsequent transferees if the instrument is not paid. Because indorser liability can be (and often is) waived under Article 3 (see UCC §3-415(b)), that does not have a major structural impact.

You would think, however, that market pressures would force those designing the systems to provide some assurance (whether in the form of a warranty or insurance) regarding the reliability of the system and its imperviousness to forgery. The statute does not, however, impose any such requirement.

3.   Implementation for Real Estate Notes

The transferable-record provisions of UETA and E-SIGN do permit the creation of wholly intangible promissory notes. Because the largest market in which there is any concern about negotiability is the home mortgage market, that market is the natural first place for the concept to be tested. (It is not a coincidence that mortgage notes are the only type of transferable records authorized by E-SIGN §201(a)(1).) The problem, however, as you will recall from the preceding assignment, is that local real estate recording offices are not, by and large, equipped to accept electronic mortgage filings. Thus, even if the note itself is intangible, the mortgage usually will still need to be tangible. And that means that the mortgage must be recorded physically and that each of the (numerous) transfers of the mortgage and the note should be recorded as well.

The industry is responding to that problem on two separate fronts. First, as mentioned in Assignment 32, a few counties have begun accepting electronic filings, with the result that the first few wholly electronic home mortgage transactions already are beginning to close. For many years, however, those will be the exception rather than the rule, because it will be quite a long time before county recording offices generally accept electronic filings of mortgages.

A second answer for the short run is something like the account-based systems from the preceding assignment: the Mortgage Electronic Recording System (MERS). Although MERS does not deal with transferring the note, it does limit the costs of filing a notice of a transfer of the mortgage in the county real estate records. Under MERS, all home mortgages that enter the secondary market are transferred to MERS and recorded with MERS as the lender of record. MERS assigns each mortgage a unique Mortgage Identification Number (MIN) that follows the transaction throughout the system. For example, when the documents are transferred in the secondary market, all the parties need to do with respect to the mortgage filing is send a notice of the transfer with the MIN to MERS, which can note the transfer on its central record for that particular mortgage. The records that MERS maintains are (as its name indicates) entirely electronic. The result is that, after the first filing of the mortgage, all transactions for the mortgage can be wholly electronic: The note can qualify as a UETA/E-SIGN transferable record and the mortgage can be transferred through the MERS system. Industry analysts estimate that the MERS process saves about $20 on each mortgage loan transaction (a substantial sum when you consider the number of home mortgages in the United States each year).

MERS has been accepting filings of mortgages into its registry for several years, with about 22 million filings as of 2004, and a 50 percent market share of newly originated mortgages. Its biggest problem to date has been the decision of one county recorder (in Suffolk County New York) to refuse to accept MERS filings. (The recorder found the filings unacceptable because they showed MERS as the lender even though MERS in fact was not the lender on the transactions.) But the Appellate Division of the New York Supreme Court promptly ordered a preliminary injunction requiring the recorder to accept those filings. Merscorp, Inc. v. Romaine, 743 N.Y.S.2d 562 (A.D. 2002).

As of 2004, MERS is expanding into commercial loans, with about $2 billion of those loans registered on its system. More dramatically, MERS began pilot tests in the early months of 2004 of its eNote Registry, which is expected to be fully operational by the end of 2004. At that point, not only mortgage assignments, but the mortgage notes themselves will be maintained in the registry, fulfilling the promise of the transferable record provisions in UETA and E-SIGN.

B. Electronic Chattel Paper Under Article 9

Revised Article 9 includes a similar set of provisions for instruments associated with the financing of personal property, known as electronic chattel paper. UCC §9-102(a)(31). Conventional chattel paper (defined in UCC §9-102(a)(11)) is paper that arises from the sale or lease of personal property. Specifically, it is a document that includes both a monetary obligation (to pay for the property or its use) and a security interest or a lease of the goods. For example, the contract signed on the purchase or lease of a car ordinarily is chattel paper. One other fundamental fact about chattel paper is that Article 9 applies not only to transactions in which a lender takes a security interest in chattel paper, but also to transactions in which the chattel paper is sold. UCC §9-109(a)(3). Thus, a party that purchases chattel paper risks having its interest defeated by a later party (or the trustee in bankruptcy) if it does not perfect that interest under Article 9.

A secured party (or purchaser) can perfect in chattel paper by either possession or filing. UCC §§9-312(a) and 9-313(a). Filing is not common for parties that finance the individual chattel-paper transaction, however, because (with some exceptions) a party that perfects by possession generally has priority over a party that perfects solely by filing. UCC §9-330. Perfection of a security interest in the chattel paper also perfects a security interest in the underlying lien. UCC §9-308(e). Thus, the creditor with possession of the chattel paper has both a security interest in the car purchaser's obligation to pay and a security interest in the lien on the car. That means that on foreclosure the creditor would acquire both the obligation and the underlying lien.

Because chattel paper circulates broadly in a secondary market of investors (much like the securities discussed in the preceding assignment), the drafters of the revised Article 9 wanted to accommodate the possibility that intangible records would replace the tangible chattel paper in use today. Accordingly, the drafters included provisions in the revised Article 9 that recognize a type of chattel paper that is intangible. Like the provisions for securities, they permit perfection by filing. UCC §9-312(a). But they also permit perfection by control under UCC §9-314(a), as a substitute for the perfection by possession that is permitted for tangible chattel paper under UCC §9-313(a).

The definition of control, in turn, is the same as the six-part authoritative-copy safe harbor for control from UETA and E-SIGN discussed above. Indeed, the provisions in UETA and E-SIGN were taken from the drafts of Article 9 already in existence at the time those provisions of UETA and E-SIGN were drafted. See UETA §16 comment 3. As with the UETA and E-SIGN provisions, the drafters contemplated that, for the time being, the control would come not from sophisticated tokenization of the record itself, but from the intervention of a third-party custodian. See UCC §9-105 comment 4 ("Systems that evolve for control of electronic chattel paper may or may not involve a third party custodian of the relevant records."). The fact that existing chattel-paper financers have not already turned to the use of such registries suggests, however, that they are unlikely to do so now. Rather, for now at least, they seem more likely to attempt the difficult task of developing authoritative-copy technology that creates true electronic tokens. It is not yet clear whether any such system will emerge in the foreseeable future.

The most important consequence of perfecting by control as opposed to filing is that it enhances the rights of the secured party against a party that purchases the electronic chattel paper. Under UCC §9-330(a) and (b), purchasers of chattel paper can take priority over existing security interests, but only if (among other things) they take control of the electronic chattel paper. If the secured party retains control of the electronic chattel paper, its interest cannot be defeated by the claim of any other party except a party with a filing that preceded the secured party's control.

Relevant Glossary Entry

E-SIGN

Problem Set 34

34.1. Your first meeting on Monday morning this week is with Stacy Vye from Wessex Bank. She has a large business originating home mortgage loans. She has a directive from upper management to start a program where the transactions are electronic. She wants to know if that is lawful and, if so, wants you to design the documentation. She emphasizes that her transactions are sold into the secondary market, so the documents will need to be readily transferable in electronic form. What do you tell her? UETA §16, E-SIGN §201.

34.2. Later in the day, you have a call from a new client at Goatway Computers (famous for their computers that come in boxes with pictures of goats on the sides). They sell their personal computers from their Web sites and would like to set up their transactions to use electronic notes and security agreements. Of course, they sell all the "paper" that they generate from their transactions so the electronic documents need to be freely marketable. Are there significant legal obstacles to the plan? If not, how should they proceed? UCC §§9-102(a)(11) and (31), 9-105; UETA §16; E-SIGN §201, 16 CFR 433.2(a).

34.3. You have a meeting this afternoon with Mark Kelp at GenenText. Mark operates a software "leasing" program in which he sells software to users and receives back from the users a promise to pay for the software in regularly scheduled monthly payments. He wants to set up his program to use electronic documents that he can transfer to investors in the secondary market. Is your advice for him any different from your advice for your earlier clients?

UETA §16, E-SIGN §201, UCC §§9-102(a)(11) and (31), 9-105, 9-312, 9-314, 9-330, 16 CFR 433.2(a).

34.4. Shortly after you establish a system for Goatway Computers, Tad Goatway comes to you with a problem. It appears that Goatway is not only loaning money to its own customers, but also purchasing electronic chattel paper issued by other manufacturers. He wants to talk to you about a transaction in which he purchased an electronic note for $100,000 for an industrial computer system sold by Fell Computers. Fell Computers sold the note to Goatway (together with the security interest in the computer), but when Goatway sought payment, the purchaser of the computer refused to pay, citing defects with the computers. Assuming that the claims of defects are valid, what can Goatway do? Does Goatway have any claim against Fell? UCC §§3-305, 3-412, 3-415, 3-416, UETA §16(d), E-SIGN §201(d).

34.5. Tertius Lydgate has a problem related to the note on the ultrasound machine he bought last month for his medical clinic. He signed an electronic promissory note (his state has passed UETA), happy to hear that the payments could be made electronically. This month, however, after he made the payment to his original lender, he received an e-mail from Bulstrode Bank asserting that he must pay Bulstrode. He shows you the e-mail that asserts that Bulstrode "has control of the note" and thus is entitled to payment. What should he do? UETA §16, UCC §§3-417, 3-602.

34.6. Pamela Herring comes by to talk this afternoon. She has been reading a lot about E-SIGN and UETA. She wants your advice. Was it a good idea to include the transferable records provisions? Should they be repealed? Should E-SIGN be extended to cover other types of instruments (other than real estate loans, for example)?

Chapter 7.   Financing the Technology Company

Assignment 35:   Lending Against Copyrights

One of the most prominent features of the information age has been a shift in the types of assets that are held by businesses. Real estate and tangible equipment or inventory are still important, but as a relative matter their importance has diminished considerably by comparison to intellectual property and other intangible assets. Thus, for many firms — particularly firms in sectors devoted to electronic commerce — the most important assets on their balance sheets are intangible assets, including copyrights, patents, trademarks, or trade secrets. Not surprisingly, the shift in the balance sheets has brought with it a shift in lending practices, as lenders seek to develop lending transactions that safely provide financing on the strength of the intellectual property those firms own or develop.

Unfortunately, the legal rules that govern those transactions are largely in disarray. This assignment describes the rules for loans related to copyrights. The next assignment discusses specialized transactions for financing the purchase of software. The third assignment discusses rules for loans related to patents. The final assignment discusses rules for three related assets: trade secrets, Web sites, and domain names.

A.   The Basics of Copyright

The topic of security interests in copyright has generated the most controversy. As you will recall from Chapter 2, the fundamental purpose of copyright is to grant authors an exclusive right to use their expression: Copyright permits an author to enjoin any other party from copying or distributing the author's expression, or from making derivative works based on the author's expression. Depending on the nature of the work, copyright law also often prohibits public performance and display of the work. Copyright Act §106. The requisite level of expression is quite low. Any work that contains any cognizable originality is likely to include sufficient expression to qualify. For example, one leading case found copyrightable originality in a high-quality reproduction of a Rodin sculpture because of the originality and creativity necessary to reproduce the sculpture in a smaller size than the original.

The covered types of expression are broad, including books, musical works, movies, plays, paintings, sculpture, sound recordings, photography, choreography, and architectural works. Copyright Act §102(a). Most important for our purposes, although it is not explicit in the statute, is the coverage of software. The Copyright Act provides the principal protection against unauthorized copying and distribution of software.

Just as important to understand are two major things that copyright does *not* cover: facts and ideas. Copyright Act §102(b). Facts — even newly discovered facts of great importance or value — are not protected under any form of federal intellectual property; they are protected as trade secrets if they are protected at all. Ideas are protected principally by the patent system, which provides much more limited protection: It is much harder to satisfy the novelty requirements of patent law than the originality requirements of copyright law, and the term is much shorter (20 years for patents; life of the author plus 70 years for copyright).

Another notable feature of copyright protection is that it is automatic. Copyright protection vests at the moment that a copyrightable work is "fixed in any tangible medium of expression," Copyright Act §102(a). The fixation requirement is not formal; it can be satisfied in a number of ways, including writing the work on paper, saving it on a computer, videotaping it, or photographing it.

To be sure, the Copyright Act does include provisions for various formalities associated with copyright protection. But the benefits of complying with those formalities are surprisingly trivial. For example, if a party puts a copyright notice (©) on a work, the principal benefit for the copyright owner is that alleged infringers generally cannot limit their responsibility by claims that they infringed innocently: The copyright protection attaches automatically when the work is written (or otherwise "fixed" in some tangible medium), even if the notice is omitted. Copyright Act §§102(a) and 401(d). Similarly, if an author fails to register its work with the Copyright Office, the main consequence is that Copyright Act §412 bars the author from recovering either the statutory damages available under Copyright Act §504 or the attorney's fees available under Copyright Act §505. Thus, copyright protection vests automatically at the moment of fixation without any substantial formal or procedural requirements.

B.   Perfecting Security Interests in Copyrightable Materials

Although there is no requirement that authors register their works with the Copyright Office, the Register of Copyright does maintain a recording system that facilitates verifiable transfers of interests in copyright. As a matter of property law, a seller that sells an item to a buyer cannot later sell the item to a later buyer, because the seller has no property remaining to convey to the later buyer. (As the venerable Latin maxim puts it, *nemo dat quod non habet* (nobody gives what he does not have).) In commercial settings, however, that poses a problem for a potential buyer who worries that the seller previously might have conveyed the asset to an earlier buyer. The common solution for assets that cannot be conclusively transferred by tangible possession is to provide a recording system that allows purchasers to put later parties on notice of their transactions. Then, if a later buyer attempts to purchase an asset after an earlier buyer has recorded a purchase in such a system, the later party can be said to be on "constructive notice" of the earlier sale, and thus subject to it. If a later buyer takes after a sale to an earlier buyer for which notice was not recorded in a timely manner, the later buyer's interest generally is free of the claims of the earlier buyer.

The Copyright Act includes such a system in Section 205. Section 205(c) states that recordation of a document "gives all persons constructive notice of the facts stated in the document," but only if the document reasonably identifies the work and if the work has been registered. Section 205(d) gives effect to the notice by providing that a transfer to the earlier of two buyers is valid only if it is either (a) recorded within one month after its execution (two months if it is executed outside the United States); or (b) recorded before the competing transfer. As discussed below, the limitation of the system to assets for which the copyright has been registered has significant consequences for software transactions.

Section 205(d) applies to any "transfer" of copyright. Under Section 101, that term includes "an assignment, mortgage, exclusive license, or any other conveyance, alienation, or hypothecation of a copyright or of any of the exclusive rights comprised in a copyright." Thus, the statute applies not only to a sale of the copyright, but also to an exclusive license of the copyright. It does not apply, however, to a nonexclusive license. (You should recall the distinction between exclusive and nonexclusive licenses from Assignment 22.) For present purposes, it is crucial to note that the definition of "transfer" includes the term "mortgage," so that a lender that takes a "mortgage" of a copyright interest should be able to record it in the Copyright Office and claim priority over competing transferees under Section 205(d). The fee for recording is a nominal $30.

The question, then, is whether — and to what extent — those provisions preempt the Article 9 provisions related to copyrights and copyright-related assets. The first — and by far most famous — case to consider that question is a 1990 decision written by Judge Kozinski sitting by designation in the United States District Court for the Northern District of California.

National Peregrine, Inc. v. Capitol Federal Savings & Loan Ass'n (In re Peregrine Entertainment, Ltd.)

116 B.R. 194 (C.D. Cal. 1990)

KOZINSKI, Circuit Judge.

This appeal from a decision of the bankruptcy court raises an issue never before confronted by a federal court in a published opinion: Is a security interest in a copyright perfected by an appropriate filing with the United States Copyright Office or by a UCC-1 financing statement filed with the relevant secretary of state?

I

National Peregrine, Inc. (NPI) is a Chapter 11 debtor in possession whose principal assets are a library of copyrights, distribution rights and licenses to approximately 145 films, and accounts receivable arising from the licensing of these films to various programmers. . . .

In June 1985, Capitol Federal Savings and Loan Association of Denver (Cap Fed) extended to American National Enterprises, Inc., NPI's predecessor by merger, a six million dollar line of credit secured by what is now NPI's film library. Both the security agreement and the UCC-1 financing statements filed by Cap Fed describe the collateral as "[a]ll inventory consisting of films and all accounts, contract rights, chattel paper, general intangibles, instruments, equipment, and documents related to such inventory, now owned or hereafter acquired by the Debtor." Although Cap Fed filed its UCC-1 financing statements in [the appropriate state offices], it did not record its security interest in the United States Copyright Office.

NPI filed a voluntary petition for bankruptcy on January 30, 1989. On April 6, 1989, NPI filed an amended complaint against Cap Fed, contending that the bank's security interest in the copyrights to the films in NPI's library . . . [was] unperfected because Cap Fed failed to record its security interest with the Copyright Office. . . .

The parties filed cross-motions for partial summary judgment on the question of whether Cap Fed had a valid security interest in the NPI film library. The bankruptcy court held for Cap Fed. NPI appeals.

II

A. Where to File

The Copyright Act provides that "[a]ny transfer of copyright ownership or other document pertaining to a copyright" may be recorded in the United States Copyright Office. 17 U.S.C. §205(a). A "transfer" under the Act includes any "mortgage" or "hypothecation of a copyright," whether "in whole or in part" and "by any means of conveyance or by operation of law." 17 U.S.C. §§101, 201(d)(1). The terms "mortgage" and "hypothecation" include a pledge of property as security or collateral for a debt. See Black's Law Dictionary 669 (5th ed. 1979). In addition, the Copyright Office has defined a "document pertaining to a copyright" as one that

> has a direct or indirect relationship to the existence, scope, duration, or identification of a copyright, or to the ownership, division, allocation, licensing, transfer, or exercise of rights under a copyright. That relationship may be past, present, future, or potential.

37 C.F.R. §201.4(a)(2).

It is clear from the preceding that an agreement granting a creditor a security interest in a copyright may be recorded in the Copyright Office. . . . Thus, Cap Fed's security interest could have been recorded in the Copyright Office; the parties seem to agree on this much. The question is, does the UCC provide a parallel method of perfecting a security interest in a copyright? One can answer this question by reference to either federal or state law; both inquiries lead to the same conclusion.

1. Even in the absence of express language, federal regulation will preempt state law if it is so pervasive as to indicate that Congress left no room for supplementary state regulation, or if the federal interest is so dominant that the federal system will be assumed to preclude enforcement of state laws on the same subject.

Here, the comprehensive scope of the federal Copyright Act's recording provisions, along with the unique federal interests they implicate, support the view that federal law preempts state methods of perfecting security interests in copyrights.

The federal copyright laws ensure "predictability and certainty of copyright ownership," "promote national uniformity" and "avoid the practical difficulties of determining and enforcing an author's rights under the differing laws and in the separate courts of the various States." Community for Creative Non-Violence v. Reid, 490 U.S. 730 (1989). As discussed above, section 205(a) of the Copyright Act establishes a uniform method for recording security interests in copyrights. A secured creditor need only file in the Copyright Office in order to give "all persons constructive notice of the facts stated in the recorded document." 17 U.S.C. §205(c).[7] Likewise, an interested third party need only search the indices maintained by the Copyright Office to determine whether a particular copyright is encumbered.

A recording system works by virtue of the fact that interested parties have a specific place to look in order to discover with certainty whether a particular interest has been transferred or encumbered. To the extent there are competing recordation schemes, this lessens the utility of each; when records are scattered in several filing units, potential creditors must conduct several searches before they can be sure that the property is not encumbered. It is for that reason that parallel recordation schemes for the same types of property are scarce as hens' teeth; the court is aware of no others, and the parties have cited none. No useful purposes would be served — indeed, much confusion would result — if creditors were permitted to perfect security interests by filing with either the Copyright Office or state offices.

If state methods of perfection were valid, a third party (such as a potential purchaser of the copyright) who wanted to learn of any encumbrances thereon would have to check not merely the indices of the U.S. Copyright Office, but also the indices of any relevant secretary of state. . . .

Moreover, as discussed at greater length below, the Copyright Act establishes its own scheme for determining priority between conflicting transferees, one that differs in certain respects from that of Article Nine. Under Article Nine, priority between holders of conflicting security interests in intangibles is generally determined by who perfected his interest first. [UCC §9-312(5) (old version). The same rule now appears in UCC §9-322(a)(1)]. By contrast, section 205(d) of the Copyright Act provides:

> As between two conflicting transfers, the one executed first prevails if it is recorded, in the manner required to give constructive notice under subsection (c), within one month after its execution in the United States or within two months after its execution outside the United States, or at any time before recordation in such manner of the later transfer

Thus, unlike Article Nine, the Copyright Act permits the effect of recording with the Copyright Office to relate back as far as two months.

Because the Copyright Act and Article Nine create different priority schemes, there will be occasions when different results will be reached depending on which

---

7. For a recordation under section 205 to be effective as against third parties, the copyrighted work must also have been registered pursuant to 17 U.S.C. §§408, 409, 410. See 17 U.S.C. §205(c)(2).

scheme was employed. The availability of filing under the UCC would thus undermine the priority scheme established by Congress with respect to copyrights. This type of direct interference with the operation of federal law weighs heavily in favor of preemption.

The bankruptcy court below nevertheless concluded that security interests in copyrights could be perfected by filing either with the copyright office or with the secretary of state under the UCC, making a tongue-in-cheek analogy to the use of a belt and suspenders to hold up a pair of pants. According to the bankruptcy court, because either device is equally useful, one should be free to choose which one to wear. With all due respect, this court finds the analogy inapt. There is no legitimate reason why pants should be held up in only one particular manner: Individuals and public modesty are equally served by either device, or even by a safety pin or a piece of rope; all that really matters is that the job gets done. Registration schemes are different in that the way notice is given is precisely what matters. To the extent interested parties are confused as to which system is being employed, this increases the level of uncertainty and multiplies the risk of error, exposing creditors to the possibility that they might get caught with their pants down.

A recordation scheme best serves its purpose where interested parties can obtain notice of all encumbrances by referring to a single, precisely defined recordation system. The availability of parallel state recordation systems that could put parties on constructive notice as to encumbrances on copyrights would surely interfere with the effectiveness of the federal recordation scheme. Given the virtual absence of dual recordation schemes in our legal system, Congress cannot be presumed to have contemplated such a result. The court therefore concludes that any state recordation system pertaining to interests in copyrights would be preempted by the Copyright Act.

2. State law leads to the same conclusion. [The court concluded that the so-called "stepback" provisions of the old version of UCC §9-104 withdrew Article 9 coverage from copyrightable assets. The current version of Article 9 has eliminated those provisions as of 2001, so they have only limited continuing relevance. The court viewed the filing systems as generally similar, although it does acknowledge some difficulties with the federal filing system's organization.] Except for the fact that the Copyright Office's indices are organized on the basis of the title and registration number, rather than by reference to the identity of the debtor, this system is nearly identical to that which Article Nine generally provides on a statewide basis.[10] . . .

_____

10. Moreover, the mechanics of recording in the Copyright Office are analogous to filing under the UCC. In order to record a security interest in the Copyright Office, a creditor may file either the security agreement itself or a duplicate certified to be a true copy of the original, so long as either is sufficient to place third parties on notice that the copyright is encumbered. See 17 U.S.C. §§205(a), (c); 37 C.F.R. §201.4(c)(1). Accordingly, the Copyright Act requires that the filed document "specifically identif[y] the work to which it pertains so that, after the document is indexed by the Register of Copyrights, it would be revealed by a reasonable search under the title or registration number of the work." 17 U.S.C. §205(c). That having been said, it's worth noting that filing with the Copyright Office can be much less convenient than filing under the UCC. This is because UCC filings are indexed by owner, while registration in the Copyright Office is by title or copyright registration number. See 17 U.S.C. §205(c). This means that the recording of a security interest in a film library such as that owned by NPI will involve dozens, sometimes hundreds, of individual filings. Moreover, as the contents of the film library changes, the lienholder will be required to make a separate filing for each work added to or deleted from the library. By contrast, a UCC-1 filing can provide a continuing, floating lien on assets of a particular type owned by the debtor, without the need for periodic updates. See [UCC §9-204 (old version)].

B. Effect of Failing to Record with the Copyright Office

Having concluded that Cap Fed should have, but did not, record its security interest with the Copyright Office, the court must next determine whether NPI as a debtor in possession can subordinate Cap Fed's interest and recover it for the benefit of the bankruptcy estate. As a debtor in possession, NPI has . . . the authority to set aside preferential or fraudulent transfers, as well as transfers otherwise voidable under applicable state or federal law. See 11 U.S.C. §§544, 547, 548.

Particularly relevant is the "strong arm clause" of 11 U.S.C. §544(a)(1), which, in respect to personal property in the bankruptcy estate, gives the debtor in possession every right and power state law confers upon one who has acquired a lien by legal or equitable proceedings. If, under the applicable law, a judicial lien creditor would prevail over an adverse claimant, the debtor in possession prevails; if not, not. A lien creditor generally takes priority over unperfected security interests in estate property because, under Article Nine, "an unperfected security interest is subordinate to the rights of . . . [a] person who becomes a lien creditor before the security interest is perfected." [UCC §9-301(1)(b) (old version). A similar rule appears now in UCC §9-317(a)(2).]. But, as discussed previously, the UCC does not apply to the extent a federal statute "governs the rights of parties to and third parties affected by transactions in particular types of property." [UCC §9-104 (old version). The current version, mentioned in the text that precedes this case, appears at UCC §9-311(a)(1)]. Section 205(d) of the Copyright Act is such a statute, establishing a priority scheme between conflicting transfers of interests in a copyright. . . . For the reasons discussed above, the federal priority scheme preempts the state priority scheme.

Section 205(d) does not expressly address the rights of lien creditors, speaking only in terms of competing transfers of copyright interests. To determine whether NPI, as a hypothetical lien creditor, may avoid Cap Fed's unperfected security interest, the court must therefore consider whether a judicial lien is a transfer as that term is used in the Copyright Act.

As noted above, the Copyright Act recognizes transfers of copyright ownership "in whole or in part by any means of conveyance or by operation of law." 17 U.S.C. §201(d)(1). Transfer is defined broadly to include any "assignment, mortgage, exclusive license, or any other conveyance, alienation, or hypothecation of a copyright . . . whether or not it is limited in time or place of effect." 17 U.S.C. §101. A judicial lien creditor [typically] is [an otherwise unsecured] creditor [that has obtained a judgment against the borrower and who then] has obtained a lien "by judgment, levy, sequestration, or other legal or equitable process or proceeding." 11 U.S.C. §101(32). Such a creditor typically has the power to seize and sell property held by the debtor at the time of the creation of the lien in order to satisfy the judgment or, in the case of general intangibles such as copyrights, to collect the revenues generated by the intangible as they come due.[16] Thus, while the

---

This technical shortcoming of the copyright filing system does make it a less useful device for perfecting a security interest in copyright libraries. Nevertheless, this problem is not so serious as to make the system unworkable. In any event, this is the system Congress has established and the court is not in a position to order more adequate procedures. If the mechanics of filing turn out to pose a serious burden, it can be taken up by Congress during its oversight of the Copyright Office or, conceivably, the Copyright Office might be able to ameliorate the problem through exercise of its regulatory authority. See 17 U.S.C. §702.

16. A critical issue — curiously overlooked by the parties — is whether a judicial lien may be used to encumber a copyright. If not, the debtor in possession would be unable to use 11 U.S.C. §544(a)(1) to avoid prior unperfected security interests in copyrights.

creation of a lien on a copyright may not give a creditor an immediate right to control the copyright, it amounts to a sufficient transfer of rights to come within the broad definition of transfer under the Copyright Act. . . .

. . . Cap Fed's unperfected security interest in NPI's copyrights . . . is trumped by NPI's hypothetical judicial lien. NPI may therefore avoid Cap Fed's interest. . . .

Judge Kozinski's decision has been controversial for several reasons. The most important probably has been that his discussion in footnote 10 seriously understates the difficulties of accommodating modern commercial-lending practices to the simple Copyright Office filing system. As he explains, the Copyright Office's asset-based filing system in many cases will be considerably less practical than the UCC's borrower-based filing system. However, the bigger problems are more fundamental: The federal statute simply does not reflect any attempt to address (much less resolve) the many legal questions presented by modern commercial-lending practice. To get a good understanding of what is missing from the Copyright Act, you might compare the three sentences of Section 205(c) and (d) with the 250 pages of two-column small print required to print Article 9 in the standard commercial-statutes supplement.

In the software context, which is of course one of the most important contexts for electronic commerce, those problems are complicated further by the practicalities of the registration requirement. Software designers are reluctant to deposit a copy of the code of their software with the Copyright Office, because they are concerned that some other software developer will view that code and use it to develop competing products. The Copyright Office has attempted to respond to that concern with regulations that permit developers to comply with the registration requirement by making deposits that omit large portions of the original code. Those regulations, however, still require the author to deposit a substantial part of the code. 37 C.F.R. §202.20(c)(2)(vii). Fearing the consequences of such a deposit, software developers in practice continue to resist registration of their software. As the case below illustrates, the treatment under *Peregrine* of unregistered software has been an important issue during the intervening decade.

Aerocon Engineering, Inc. v. Silicon Valley Bank (In re World Auxiliary Power Co.)

303 F.3d 1120 (9th Cir. 2002)

Before MELVIN BRUNETTI, ANDREW J. KLEINFELD and SIDNEY R. THOMAS, Circuit Judges. KLEINFELD, Circuit Judge:

In this case we decide whether federal or state law governs priority of security interests in unregistered copyrights.

To determine this, we must first look to state law, as state law generally determines the validity of liens in bankruptcy cases. [The court concludes that the typical state-law right to levy on "general intangibles" extends to copyrights, and thus that a lien creditor would be able to defeat an unperfected security interest in a copyright.]

FACTS

Basically, this is a bankruptcy contest over unregistered copyrights between a bank that got a security interest in the copyrights from the owners and perfected it under state law, and a company that bought the copyrights from the bankruptcy trustees after the copyright owners went bankrupt. These simple facts are all that matters to the outcome of this case, although the details are complex.

Three affiliated California corporations — World Auxiliary Power, World Aerotechnology, and Air Refrigeration Systems — designed and sold products for modifying airplanes. . . . The three companies owned copyrights in the drawings, technical manuals, blue-prints, and computer software used to make the modifications. . . . The companies did not register their copyrights with the United States Copyright Office.

The companies got financing from Silicon Valley Bank, one of the appellees in this case. Two of the companies borrowed the money directly, the third guaranteed the loan. The security agreement, as is common, granted the bank a security interest in a broad array of presently owned and after-acquired collateral. The security agreement covered "all goods and equipment now owned or hereafter acquired," as well as inventory, contract rights, general intangibles, blueprints, drawings, computer programs, accounts receivable, patents, cash, bank deposits, and pretty much anything else the debtor owned or might be "hereafter acquired." The security agreement and financing statement also covered "[a]ll copyright rights, copyright applications, copyright registrations, and like protections in each work of authorship and derivative work thereof, whether published or unpublished, now owned or hereafter acquired."

The bank perfected its security interest in the collateral, including the copyrights, pursuant to California's version of Article 9 of the Uniform Commercial Code, by filing UCC-1 financing statements with the California Secretary of State. The bank also took possession of the . . . copyrighted materials. But the copyrights still weren't registered with the United States Copyright Office, and the bank did not record any document showing the transfer of a security interest with the Copyright Office.

Subsequently, the three debtor companies filed simultaneous but separate bankruptcy proceedings. Their copyrights were among their major assets. Aerocon Engineering, one of their creditors (and the appellant in this case), [eventually acquired the debtor's rights in the copyrighted assets.] Once Aerocon owned the copyrights, it planned to exercise the trustees' power to avoid Silicon Valley Bank's security interest so that the venture would own the copyrights free and clear. . . .

Meanwhile, Silicon Valley Bank won relief from the bankruptcy court's automatic stay and, based on its security interest, foreclosed on the copyrights. . . .

Aerocon sued to avoid Silicon Valley Bank's security interest. . . . The bankruptcy court . . . granted summary judgment to Silicon Valley Bank on all of Aerocon's claims on the ground that the bank had perfected its security interest in the copyrights under California's version of Article 9 of the Uniform Commercial Code. [The district court affirmed.] Aerocon appeals from the district court's order.

ANALYSIS

. . . Copyright and bankruptcy law set the context for this litigation, but the legal issue is priority of security interests. The bankruptcy trustees sold Aerocon their power to avoid any security interest "that is voidable by a creditor that extends credit to the debtor at the time of the commencement of the case, and that obtains, at such time and with respect to such credit, a judicial lien." Under this "strong-arm" provision, Aerocon has the status of an "ideal creditor" who perfected his lien at the last possible moment before the bankruptcy commenced, and if this hypothetical creditor would take priority over Silicon Valley Bank's lien, then Aerocon may avoid the bank's security interest.

Whether Aerocon's hypothetical lien creditor would take priority turns on whether federal or state law governs the perfection of security interests in unregistered copyrights. The bank did everything necessary to perfect its security interest under state law, so if state law governs, the bank has priority and wins. The bank did nothing, however, to perfect its interest under federal law, so if federal law governs, Aerocon's hypothetical lien creditor arguably has priority, although the parties dispute whether Aerocon might face additional legal hurdles.

We are assisted in deciding this case by two opinions, neither of which controls, but both of which are thoughtful and scholarly. The first is the bankruptcy court's published opinion in this case, *Aerocon Engineering Inc. v. Silicon Valley Bank* (*In re World Auxiliary Power Co.*), which we affirm largely for the reasons the bankruptcy judge gave. The second is a published district court opinion, *National Peregrine, Inc. v. Capitol Federal Savings & Loan Association* (*In re Peregrine Entertainment, Ltd.*), [116 B.R. 194 (C.D. Cal. 1990) (per Kozinski, J.),] the holdings of which we adopt but, like the bankruptcy court, distinguish and limit.

Our analysis begins with the Copyright Act of 1976. Under the Act, "copyright protection subsists . . . in original works of authorship fixed in any tangible medium of expression." While an owner must register his copyright as a condition of seeking certain infringement remedies, registration is permissive, not mandatory, and is not a condition for copyright protection. Likewise, the Copyright Act's provision for recording "transfers of copyright ownership" (the Act's term that includes security interests) is permissive, not mandatory: "Any transfer of copyright ownership or other document pertaining to copyright may be recorded in the Copyright Office." The Copyright Act's use of the word "mortgage" as one definition of a "transfer" is properly read to include security interests under Article 9 of the Uniform Commercial Code.

Under the Copyright Act, "[a]s between two conflicting transfers, the one executed first prevails if it is recorded, in the manner required to give constructive notice . . . within one month after its execution . . . or at any time before recordation . . . of the later transfer. Otherwise the later transfer prevails if recorded first in such manner, and if taken in good faith, for valuable consideration . . . and without notice of the earlier transfer.

The phrase "constructive notice" refers to [Section 205(c)] providing that recording gives constructive notice

but only if —

(1) the document, or material attached to it, specifically identifies the work to which it pertains so that, after the document is indexed by the Register of Copyrights, it would be revealed by a reasonable search under the title or registration number of the work; and

(2) registration has been made for the work.

A copyrighted work only gets a "title or registration number" that would be revealed by a search if it's registered. Since an unregistered work doesn't have a title or registration number that would be "revealed by a reasonable search," recording a security interest in an unregistered copyright in the Copyright Office wouldn't give "constructive notice" under the Copyright Act, and, because it wouldn't, it couldn't preserve a creditor's priority. There just isn't any way for a secured creditor to preserve a priority in an unregistered copyright by recording anything in the Copyright Office. And the secured party can't get around this problem by registering the copyright, because the secured party isn't the owner of the copyright, and the Copyright Act states that only "the owner of copyright . . . may obtain registration of the copyright claim."

Aerocon argues that the Copyright Act's recordation and priority scheme exclusively controls perfection and priority of security interests in copyrights. First, Aerocon argues that state law, here the California U.C.C., by its own terms "steps back" and defers to the federal scheme. Second, whether or not the U.C.C. steps back, Aerocon argues that Congress has preempted the U.C.C. as it applies to copyrights. We address each argument in turn.

A. U.C.C. Step Back Provisions

Article 9 of the Uniform Commercial Code, as adopted in California, provides that unperfected creditors are subordinate to perfected, and as between perfected security interests, the first perfected interest prevails. The bank perfected first under state law by filing a financing statement with the California Secretary of State on existing and after-acquired copyrights. The U.C.C. treats copyrights as "general intangibles." Security interests in general intangibles are properly perfected under the U.C.C. by state filings such as the one made by the bank in this case.

To avoid conflict with the federal law, the U.C.C. has two "step-back provisions," by which state law steps back and out of the way of conflicting federal law. The first, more general "step-back" provision says that Article 9 "does not apply . . . [t]o a security interest subject to any statute of the United States to the extent that such statute governs the rights of parties to and third parties affected by transactions in particular types of property." As applied to copyrights, the relevant U.C.C. Official Comment [Old 9-104 comment 1] makes it clear that this stepback clause does not exclude all security interests in copyrights from U.C.C. coverage, just those for which the federal Copyright Act "governs the rights" of relevant parties:

> Although the Federal Copyright Act contains provisions permitting the mortgage of a copyright and for the recording of an assignment of a copyright such a statute would not seem to contain sufficient provisions regulating the rights of the parties and third parties to exclude security interests in copyrights from the provisions of this Article.

The second step-back provision speaks directly to perfection of security interests. It exempts from U.C.C. filing requirements security interests in property "subject to . . . [a] statute . . . of the United States which provides for a national . . . registration . . . or which specifies a place of filing different from that specified in this division for filing of the security interest." Compliance with such a statute "is equivalent to the filing of a financing statement . . . and a security interest in property subject to the statute . . . can be perfected only by compliance therewith. . . ."

Under the U.C.C.'s two step-back provisions, there can be no question that, when a copyright has been registered, a security interest can be perfected only by recording the transfer in the Copyright Office. As the district court held in *Peregrine,* the Copyright Act satisfies the broad U.C.C. step-back provision by creating a priority scheme that "governs the rights of parties to and third parties affected by transactions" in registered copyrights and satisfies the narrow step-back provision by creating a single "national registration" for security interests in registered copyrights. Thus, under these step-back provisions, if a borrower's collateral is a registered copyright, the secured party cannot perfect by filing a financing statement under the U.C.C. in the appropriate state office, or alternatively by recording a transfer in the Copyright Office. For registered copyrights, the only proper place to file is the Copyright Office. We adopt *Peregrine*'s holding to this effect.

However, the question posed by this case is whether the U.C.C. steps back as to unregistered copyrights. We, like the bankruptcy court in this case, conclude that it does not. As we've explained, there's no way for a secured creditor to perfect a security interest in unregistered copyrights by recording in the Copyright Office. The U.C.C.'s broader step-back provision says that the U.C.C. doesn't apply to a security interest "to the extent" that a federal statute governs the rights of the parties. The U.C.C. doesn't defer to the Copyright Act under this broad step-back provision because the Copyright Act doesn't provide for the rights of secured parties to unregistered copyrights; it only covers the rights of secured parties in *registered* copyrights. The U.C.C.'s narrow step-back provision says the U.C.C. doesn't apply if a federal statute "provides for a national . . . registration . . . or which specifies a place of filing different from that specified in this division for filing of the security interest." The U.C.C. doesn't defer to the Copyright Act under this narrow step-back provision because the Copyright Act doesn't provide a "national registration": unregistered copyrights don't have to be registered, and because unregistered copyrights don't have a registered name and number, under the Copyright Act there isn't any place to file anything regarding unregistered copyrights that makes any legal difference. So, as a matter of state law, the U.C.C. doesn't step back in deference to federal law, but governs perfection and priority of security interests in unregistered copyrights itself.

B.   Federal Preemption

It wouldn't matter that state law doesn't step back, however, if Congress chose to knock state law out of the way by preemption. . . .

Aerocon argues, relying on *Peregrine,* that Congress intended to occupy the field of security interests in copyrights. Aerocon also argues that the U.C.C. actually conflicts with the Copyright Act's text and purpose. . . .

The district court in *Peregrine* held that Congress had preempted state law because of "the comprehensive scope of the Copyright Act's recording provisions." As applied to registered copyrights, the Act's recording scheme is comprehensive; it doesn't exclude any registered copyright from its coverage. But as applied to unregistered copyrights, the Act doesn't have comprehensive recording provisions. Likewise, *Peregrine* notes that "[t]o the extent there are competing recordation schemes, this lessens the utility of each." This holds true for registered copyrights. But there aren't two competing filing systems for unregistered copyrights. The Copyright Act doesn't create one. Only the U.C.C. creates a filing system applicable to unregistered copyrights. *Peregrine* reasoned that creditors could get conflicting results under the U.C.C. and the Copyright Act, because each provides a different priority scheme. That's true only for registered copyrights. The Copyright Act wouldn't provide a conflicting answer as to unregistered copyrights because it wouldn't provide any answer at all. *Peregrine*'s holding applies to registered copyrights, and we adopt it, but as the bankruptcy court reasoned in the case at bar, it does not apply to unregistered copyrights.

. . . We reject [contrary lower court] opinions because they miss the point made by the bankruptcy judge in this case, and discussed above, that *Peregrine's* analysis doesn't work if it's applied to security interests in unregistered copyrights. Moreover, such extensions of *Peregrine* to unregistered copyrights would make registration of copyright a necessary prerequisite of perfecting a security interest in a copyright. The implication of requiring registration as a condition of perfection is that Congress intended to make unregistered copyrights practically useless as collateral, an inference the text and purpose of the Copyright Act do not warrant.

In the one instance where the Copyright Act conditions some action concerning a copyright on its registration — the right to sue for infringement — the Act makes that condition explicit. Nowhere does the Copyright Act explicitly condition the use of copyrights as collateral on their registration. Second, the Copyright Act contemplates that most copyrights will not be registered. Since copyright is created every time people set pen to paper, or fingers to keyboard, and affix their thoughts in a tangible medium, writers, artists, computer programmers, and web designers would have to have their hands tied down to keep them from creating unregistered copyrights all day every day. Moreover, the Copyright Act says that copyrights "may" be registered, implying that they don't have to be, and since a fee is charged and time and effort is required, the statute sets up a regime in which most copyrights won't ever be registered.

Though Congress must have contemplated that most copyrights would be unregistered, it only provided for protection of security interests in registered copyrights. There is no reason to infer from Congress's silence as to unregistered copyrights an intent to make such copyrights useless as collateral by preempting state law but not providing any federal priority scheme for unregistered copyrights. That would amount to a presumption in favor of federal preemption, but we are required to presume just the opposite. The only reasonable inference to draw is that Congress chose not to create a federal scheme for security interests in unregistered copyrights, but left the matter to States, which have traditionally governed security interests.

For similar reasons, we reject Aerocon's argument that congressional intent to preempt can be inferred from conflict between the Copyright Act and the U.C.C. There is no conflict between the statutory provisions: the Copyright Act doesn't speak to security interests in unregistered copyrights, the U.C.C. does.

Nor does the application of state law frustrate the objectives of federal copyright law. The basic objective of federal copyright law is to "promote the Progress of Science and useful Arts" by "establishing a marketable right to the use of one's expression" and supplying "the economic incentive to create and disseminate ideas." Aerocon argues that allowing perfection under state law would frustrate this objective by injecting uncertainty in secured transactions involving copyrights. Aerocon conjures up the image of a double-crossing debtor who, having gotten financing based on unregistered copyrights, registers them, thus triggering federal law, and gets financing from a second creditor, who then records its interest with the Copyright Office and takes priority. We decline to prevent this fraud by drawing the unreasonable inference that Congress intended to render copyrights useless as collateral unless registered.

Prudent creditors will always demand that debtors disclose any copyright registrations and perfect under federal law and will protect themselves against subsequent creditors gaining priority by means of covenants and policing mechanisms. The several *amici* banks and banking association in this case argue that most lenders would lend against unregistered copyrights subject to the remote risk of being "primed" by subsequent creditors; but no lender would lend against unregistered copyrights if they couldn't perfect their security interest. As we read the law, unregistered copyrights have value as collateral, discounted by the remote potential for priming. As Aerocon reads the law, they would have no value at all.

Aerocon's argument also ignores the special problem of copyrights as after-acquired collateral. To use just one example of the multi-industry need to use after-acquired (really after-created) intangible intellectual property as collateral, now that the high-tech boom of the 1990s has passed, and software companies don't attract equity financing like tulips in seventeenth century Holland, these companies will have to borrow more capital. After-acquired software is likely to serve as much of their collateral. Like liens in any other after-acquired collateral, liens in after-acquired software must attach immediately upon the creation of the software to satisfy creditors. Creditors would not tolerate a gap between the software's creation and the registration of the copyright. If software developers had to register copyrights in their software before using it as collateral, the last half hour of the day for a software company would be spent preparing and mailing utterly pointless forms to the Copyright Office to register and record security interests. Our reading of the law "promote[s] the Progress of Science and useful Arts" by preserving the collateral value of unregistered copyrights, which is to say, the vast majority of copyrights. Aerocon's reading of the law — which would force producers engaged in the ongoing creation of copyrightable material to constantly register and update the registrations of their works before obtaining credit — does not.

CONCLUSION

Regarding perfection and priority of security interests in unregistered copyrights, the California U.C.C. has not stepped back in deference to federal law, and federal law has not preempted the U .C.C. Silicon Valley Bank has a perfected security interest in the debtors' unregistered copyrights, and Aerocon, standing in the bankruptcy trustees' shoes, cannot prevail against it.

Bills have been introduced in most of the Congresses that have convened since *Peregrine*, proposing either to codify *Peregrine* (specifying that all filing for copyright lending must be done at the federal level) or overrule it (specifying that filing in the state system is effective for copyright lending). Still, notwithstanding the great lack of certainty in the law, it does not appear likely that a bill in either form will be enacted during the foreseeable future. Until that point, lenders looking for certainty can only hope that some of the cases will proceed to an appellate level so that some definitive rules can be provided.

One final issue of significance relates to the implications of *Peregrine* for transactions involving exclusive and nonexclusive licenses. As mentioned above, the "transfer" that is validated by recording in the Copyright Office specifically includes an exclusive license, but excludes a nonexclusive license. What that means is that federal recordation with respect to the interest of the licensee under an exclusive license has the same effect as it does with respect to the interest of an author or purchaser of the copyright itself. Conversely, because a nonexclusive license is not a transfer that can gain priority under Section 205(d), a federal recordation with respect to a nonexclusive license seems most unlikely to have any effect, for the reasons explained in *Aerocon* with respect to unregistered goods.

Relevant Glossary Entry

Source Code

Problem Set 35

35.1. When you arrive in the office on Monday, you find a telecopy from your old friend Karel McGeehan. Karel works for a venerable Massachusetts publisher named Small Red Books (SRB). Last month he was delighted to sign a contract to publish a new children's book by the noted author Jane Ulen. Jane and Karel signed their contract on March 1; in the contract Jane transferred the (previously registered) copyright in her book to SRB in return for SRB's commitment to pay royalties on the book out of future sales. Karel left the contract with his administrative assistant, asking him to file a notice of the transfer to SRB with the Copyright Office as soon as possible. Karel then left town on his spring vacation.

When Karel returned, he discovered a series of urgent telephone messages from Jane, the last of which (dated two weeks ago) stated that if Karel did not call Jane back immediately, Jane would change her mind and sell the book to Birch Publishing (a large New York publisher). It appears that Jane has followed through on the threat. She appears to have signed a contract selling the book to Birch Publishing on April 2, which Birch recorded at the Copyright Office in Washington, D.C. on the next day. When Karel checks his office's records, he is distressed to discover that his assistant neglected to file anything with the Copyright Office. It now is April 10.

Karel wants to know who will have priority in the book, SRB or Birch. What do you say? Copyright Act §205(d).

35.2. Same facts as in Problem 35.1, but now suppose that Birch knew of the sale to Karel and SRB at the time Birch purchased the book from Jane. Would your answer change?

35.3. Same facts as in Problem 35.1 but now suppose that Karel returned on March 25, to find that Jane had sold the book to Birch on March 15. Assuming that Birch recorded the next day and that Karel has not recorded, is there anything that Karel and SRB can do to improve their chances against Birch?

35.4. The next morning you have a meeting with Mark Kelp. Mark is managing the affairs of GenenText, Inc., a software startup company. The company's only product is a program for searching the database of the Human Genome Project. The software is designed to assist in the tedious task of locating sequences of genetic code that might be useful in efforts devoted to particular diseases. Mark's existing lender (Bulstrode Bank) is unwilling to advance any new funds at this time. Mark thinks that the company has some promising opportunities, which it could pursue if he could get some new financing.

You see from examining the file that the software has been registered with the Copyright Office, that Bulstrode has taken a security interest in the software (the only substantial asset on the balance sheet), and that Bulstrode has recorded in the state UCC records, but not at the Copyright Office. There are no precedents in your jurisdiction on the *Peregrine* question. In your judgment, does Bulstrode have a perfected security interest? UCC §9-311, Copyright Act §§101 (transfer of copyright ownership), 201, 205.

35.5. At a lunch meeting that day with Stacy Vye from Wessex Bank, you are discussing her procedures for copyright-related loans. Because your advice on many of the questions has been guarded and indeterminate, she is somewhat frustrated. Today she presents to you her new idea: "Why can't we avoid the whole problem by having our borrowers leave off the copyright notices. If they don't put copyright notices on the material, then it won't be copyrighted, so state law will apply for perfection." What do you think about that? Copyright Act §102(a).

35.6. The last file you handle for Stacy today is a loan to McCallie Concepts. This is a software development company to which Stacy wants to make a loan. All of the business and financial terms have worked out fine, but negotiations have broken down because Kate McCallie (the principal of the borrower) insists that she will not agree to register the software. "This is a cutting-edge product. There is no way I am going to put a copy of my source code — not one line of it — in some public file where my competitors can take it legally. It's hard enough to keep them from stealing it from me now without me giving it away like that." Stacy has two questions.

(a) First, as a general matter, she wants to know when the software needs to be registered. Would it need to be done at the time of the loan or can she wait until it is finished?

(b) Second, she wants to know what you really have to lose from letting the software go unregistered. Are Kate's concerns enough to justify forgoing registration?

35.7. Assume that after listening carefully to your advice in Problem 35.6, Stacy proceeded to make a loan without requiring registration of the software.

Months later, when the software was finished, Kate at that point registered the software and promptly sold it to a competitor, which promptly recorded in the Copyright Office and in the UCC Records. Stacy is worried. Does she have a prior claim over the new purchaser?

Assignment 36: Financing the Acquisition of Software

Because of its constitutive role in electronic commerce, software is of crucial importance to businesses in the information age. Accordingly, it should be no surprise that lenders have developed specialized transactions in which they advance money to fund the acquisition of software. This assignment discusses legal and practical issues raised by the two most prominent ways to structure such transactions: software "leases" and finance licenses.

A. Software Leases

The most successful method of financing the acquisition of software is the software "lease." Functionally, that transaction works much like the better-known equipment lease, from which it has developed. Indeed, many of the most prominent software-leasing financiers are related to equipment-leasing companies that have attempted to shift the focus of their business to reflect the shift of the emphasis of our economy toward software and away from hard, tangible equipment.

The transaction involves three parties. The first is a software licensor, a company that owns or controls the copyright to a valuable software program. Normally, the programs involved are complicated programs for business operations, such as a reservations system for an airline or a database system for a large corporation. The typical price for such a program would start in the low six-figure range and go up from there. The second party is a user, a business that wishes to acquire and use a copy of the program in question. The third party is a financier, an entity in the business of funding the acquisition of software.

The structure of the transaction is simple. The licensor grants the user a nonexclusive license to use the software and provides a copy of the software. (The license ordinarily is a nonexclusive license because the user is one of many entities using the software or a related version of it.) Ordinarily, the licensor also will agree to provide a variety of related services to maintain, service, and upgrade the software in the months and years to come. The financier will pay the cost of the software to the licensor (typically in a one-time payment). The user will agree to make monthly payments to the financier for the software over a period of years (three years being a common term). The payments should total an amount that repays the financier (with interest) for the cost of the purchased software.

In practice, the financier often has a close relationship with the software licensor. For a few of the largest software companies, the financier might

Figure 36.1
Software Leasing

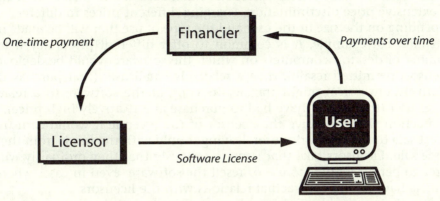

actually be an entity affiliated with or controlled by the licensor. In most cases, however, the financier is independent, but has a close relationship with the licensor. That relationship benefits the financier because it brings the financier considerable marketing exposure — the licensor directs users that need financing to the financier — as well as the opportunity to secure the licensor's consent to provisions that make the lending considerably less risky, as discussed below. The licensor benefits, on the other hand, by the availability of lenders knowledgeable about its products that can assist those that wish to purchase those products. Figure 36.1 is a simple diagram of the process.

Although the structure of the transaction is relatively simple, it presents a variety of troubling legal problems. The first relates to the financier's control of the collateral. In an ordinary secured lending transaction, a lender expects that upon default it will be able to take control of the collateral and use or dispose of the collateral as freely as if it were the original owner of the collateral. So, if a lender forecloses on an office building, it expects that it can take the building for its own use or sell the building to a third party. Similarly, if the collateral is a promissory note, the lender expects that it can take control of the promissory note, hold it and enforce it against the person obligated to pay, or sell it to a third party.

The financier's rights in a transaction financing the acquisition of software are considerably more limited. For one thing, because the software is intangible, removing it from the user's possession and control may be trickier than is typically the case for tangible assets: The financier might take the original disks on which the software was delivered, as well as the software as it exists on some central computer, but it is difficult for the financier to be sure that the user has not retained another copy in some other location.

Another problem is that the financier generally will not have the right to use the software upon a default by the user. As you will recall from Chapter 4, software licensors generally bar their customers from subsequent transfers of licensed software. Accordingly, the licensee of software, unlike the purchaser of a book, generally cannot resell the software to a third party. That is true even if that third party is a financier that paid for the acquisition of the software.

Although a variety of complicated justifications support those prohibitions in various contexts, the most general reason is the concern that such resales will undermine the licensor's price structure. Software licensors often engage in extensive price discrimination, charging different prices to different users, depending on the size of the user and the type of use that will be made of the software. For example, it is common to offer different prices keyed to the number of desktop computers on which the software would be deployed. If licensors permitted resales, then a relatively small user (that purchased at a relatively low price) might transfer its copy of the software to a relatively larger user (that would have had to purchase at a relatively high price). That transaction would deprive the licensor of the revenue it would earn from a direct sale to the high-price user, leaving it only with the funds from the low-value sale. Licensors take that issue so seriously that they ordinarily will not agree to permit lenders to use or resell the software, even in cases where the lenders have strong contractual relations with the licensors.

One obvious problem with such restrictions is that they appear to conflict with traditional principles of copyright law. Under the "first-sale" doctrine, a person that purchases a copy of a copyrighted work generally obtains the right to resell that copy of the work, without regard to any contrary contractual terms imposed by the seller of the work. Copyright Act §109(a). In the common parlance, we say that the seller's exclusive right to control distribution of the work is exhausted by the first sale of any particular copy. As discussed in Assignment 22, software licensors attempt to avoid that doctrine by avoiding any "sale" of their products: They do not sell users a copy of the work; they grant users a license to use the work. Although the industry relies heavily on those provisions, no specific statute or definitive case supports it.

In the financing context, though, some legal rules are developing that recognize the propriety of such a "license," at least in transactions involving commercial users of software. For example, UCC §9-408 implements the traditional general rule discussed above — permitting a party that owns an asset to grant a security interest in the asset notwithstanding any contrary contractual provisions related to the asset. For example, consider a construction contract between a developer and a general contractor. Because the developer ordinarily is quite concerned about the identity of the party doing the construction, it often will include in the contract a term that forbids any assignment of the contract from the contractor to a third party. Under UCC §9-408, the contractor can assign its interest in that contract (the right to receive money from the developer) to a lender as collateral for a loan to fund the contractor's work under the contract.

The text of UCC §9-408 is confusing at first glance, but in substance it provides a two-step treatment for such arrangements. The first step generally invalidates restrictive terms to the extent they prohibit parties from granting security interests. UCC §9-408(a). The second step generally enforces such terms to the extent that they prohibit the lender from exercising dominion over the collateral. UCC §9-408(d). The key to understanding the statute starts with understanding that Article 9 generally classifies software licenses (like construction contracts) as general intangibles. In Article 9 terms, the parties to a lending transaction involving a general intangible are (1) the secured party, (2) the debtor (the borrower that has a right under the contract or software license), and (3) the account debtor (the party that has an obligation

Figure 36.2
Article 9 View of General Intangibles

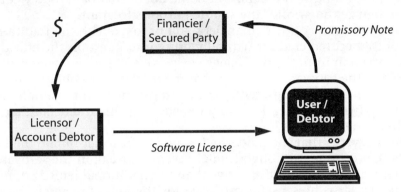

under the contract or software license). As illustrated in Figure 36.2, in a typical transaction the licensee ordinarily would be the debtor; the licensor would be the account debtor. Working with that terminology, Section 9-408(a)(1) states a general rule that provides that

> a term . . . in an agreement between an account debtor and a debtor which relates to . . . a general intangible, including a . . . license . . ., and which term prohibits . . . the assignment or transfer of . . . the . . . general intangible, is ineffective to the extent that the term
>
> (1) would impair the creation, attachment, or perfection of a security interest.

See UCC §9-408 comment 5 and example 2. Thus, in our context, Section 9-408(a)(1) bars terms impairing the creation of a security interest in any contract between a software licensor and a user/borrower.

The second step of Section 9-408 is to take away most of what the first step has given: Subsection (d) generally provides that the financier that has received a security interest under the blessing of UCC §9-408(a)(1) can do nothing with the collateral that violates the terms of the licensee's arrangement with its licensor. Among other things, the statute provides that the financier

- Cannot force the licensor to recognize any transfer of the software to the financier (which means that the licensor need not recognize the financier as the licensee for purposes of any obligations the licensor might have to provide maintenance, service, or the like). UCC §9-408(d)(1) and (3).
- Cannot use the software itself. UCC §9-408(d)(4).
- Cannot assign the debtor/user's rights to a third party. UCC §9-408(d)(4).

The general import of those provisions is to limit the effect of the security interest to a priority in bankruptcy: The lender has a formal security interest, but no rights to use or transfer the collateral itself. The only effect of the security interest is to give the lender a first claim against the value the software might have if the debtor files for bankruptcy. See UCC §9-408 comment 7.

Given the odd structure of those provisions — they are promulgated as state law, the principal purpose of which is to effect a grant of priority in a bankruptcy proceeding — there must be some doubt that bankruptcy courts freely will recognize the priority the statute purports to grant.

The strict limits on the financier's ability to exercise the traditional remedies of the secured creditor naturally bring into question the effectiveness of the transaction from the financier's perspective. If the financier cannot use or dispose of the software, what is it that makes the user's obligation to pay sufficiently credible to differentiate the transaction from simple unsecured financing (where the lender's only remedy is to sue the defaulting borrower for the money)?

The answer is that the lender relies on a right to terminate the borrower's use of the software. Although it might seem unusual, in the software context that remedy often is more effective than the traditional remedy of foreclosure and resale. First, how useful can it be for the lender to resell the software? Most business software develops so rapidly that a software product purchased even a few months ago (much less a few years ago) is likely to be significantly less functional than products currently available. Moreover, because complicated software programs depend on support from the licensor, a resale would be useful only if the financier could force the licensor to provide support to the purchaser. Often that is not practical, particularly in the common situation in which the licensor is opposed to the resale and actively has tried to prohibit it.

Conversely, a right to terminate the use of the software is a valuable remedy, particularly for the kinds of software for which software leasing is common: mission-critical business software. For example, assume that the financed software is a reservation system for an airline. If the financier terminates the user's use of the software — even for a few hours — the user might suffer catastrophic financial losses. The potential for those losses gives the financier a tremendous amount of leverage over the borrower, even if the financier has no right to repossess the software. The financiers enhance that leverage by ensuring (as part of their relationship with the vendor) that the vendor will recognize the termination of the software by the financier, and thus will not support any continued efforts by the user to make use of the software for which it has failed to pay. Also, when it is practical, the ability to terminate the software remotely (by accessing the software through an Internet connection) only makes the remedy easier to implement.

Financiers analogize their role to that of an electric company: if the borrower can pay only a small portion of its bills, it will pay the electric bill before most (if not all) others. Software financiers like to put themselves in the same position by limiting their activities to software necessary for the continued operation of the user.

Given the leverage — and consequent possibility of abuse — that the right to terminate gives the financier over the user, it is natural to wonder whether those provisions are enforceable. Again, as explained in Assignment 23, there is no case authority on the question, but the illustrative provisions of UCITA suggest that the power generally will be upheld, at least in cases in which the contract provides reasonable safeguards for the user. On the one hand, UCITA §510(a)(4) provides that the financier "may enforce a contractual right . . . to preclude the licensee's further use of the [software]." On the other hand, although UCITA generally validates a licensor's right to terminate a licensee's use remotely when the licensee breaches the license — to use "electronic self-help" in the terms of the statute — those provisions do not extend to actions by the financier. Thus, UCITA offers no guidance as to the propriety of electronic self-help by financiers. See UCITA §§815 and 816. The failure of the final statute to authorize such activity (as earlier drafts did) — coupled with the move (discussed in Assignment 23) to remove even the licensor's right to self-help — underscores the questionable legal nature of that remedy for the software lender.

The Problem of Smart Goods

One related issue involves the indirect financing of the acquisition of software as part of the acquisition of "smart" goods. It is a fact of modern commerce that ordinary tangible personal property (like automobiles) often includes within it a wide variety of software products that are not separately purchased or licensed in any way visible to the ordinary end user. The modern UCC has taken the functional view that those "smart" goods should be treated entirely as goods for purposes of the Article 9 regime. See UCC §9-102(a)(44) (defining "Goods" to include "a computer program embedded in goods . . . if . . . the program is associated with the goods in such a manner that it customarily is considered a part of the goods"). Because UCC §9-408 does not apply to goods, the benefits discussed above that UCC §9-408 specifically grants to software licensors (including the general invalidation of any rights a lender might have to enforce a security interest) do not apply to smart goods. See UCC §9-401.

The ultimate owner of the software theoretically might object to the claim by a lender foreclosing on smart goods to use the software if the lender acquired control of the goods, arguing that the rights of the lender under Article 9 could not extend to a right to use the copyrighted software (because of federal preemption of any state law rule purporting to permit a transfer contrary to the terms of the license). Such an argument seems, however, most unlikely to prevail. Remember, the original licensor of the software licensed the software to a manufacturer that embedded the software in goods sold at retail. It seems unreasonable for the licensor thereafter to complain that the software is being used in connection with the goods. It seems more likely — although there is no judicial analysis to date — that such a licensor would be held to have granted an implied license that permits all owners of the goods to use the software in connection with their use of the goods.

B.   Finance Licenses

Another well-known method for financing the acquisition of software is the finance license. The finance license involves the same three parties, but they interact in a different way. In that transaction, the licensor licenses the software to the financier. The financier then sublicenses the software to the user.

Figure 36.3
Finance Licensing

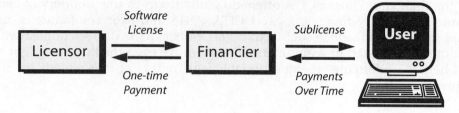

Historically, that transaction developed earlier than the modern software lease because it resembles more closely the structure of the equipment lease, from which software financing generally has developed. In that context, the owner of equipment sells it to the equipment lessor/financier, who then leases the equipment to the user in the same way that the finance licensing financier can sublicense software to the user. Figure 36.3 is a simple diagram of the process.

In recent years, many sophisticated financiers have drifted away from the finance licensing model to the software leasing model discussed above. The principal reason is concern about the financier's potential liability arising out of the sublicense model. Because the software formally passes through the control of the financier, the financier is concerned — if the software is defective or damages the user's other assets in some way — that the financier's ability to obtain repayment will be compromised or, even worse, that the financier might be exposed to tort liability based on the user's problems with the software. UCITA attempted to limit that problem in commercial transactions, by providing that it is permissible for the licensor's contract with the user to make the user's obligation to pay "irrevocable and independent [of problems with the software]." UCITA §509. But UCITA, of course, was not successful in obtaining widespread enactment. The concerns have been thought serious enough to undermine interest in the sublicense model.

Because the finance licensor puts itself into the chain of "title" of the software solely for financing purposes, with no intent to use the software itself, the licensor has less of a reason to object to a transfer of the license from the financier to the user: That transfer is the whole purpose of the transaction. The licensor might need to know the identity of the user before it transfers the software to the finance licensor — to ensure that it provides the correct version and charges a price appropriate for the user — but if the licensor has that information, there is no obvious reason that the licensor should object. Accordingly, it is not surprising that UCITA would have permitted such a transfer by the finance licensor, provided that it gives prior notice to the licensor of the proposed user and obtains the agreement of the user to the terms of the license. UCITA §508.

The rights of the finance licensor on default, however, are similar in most respects to those of the software lessor. The Article 9 analysis discussed above would not apply directly, but the actions of the finance licensor would be limited by the terms of its underlying agreement with the original licensor, which are likely to constrain redistribution of the software to transactions in which new payments are made to the licensor.

The most interesting difference is that UCITA §510 would have provided much more generous support for self-help remedies by the finance licensor than for conventional licensors. Section 510(a)(3) permits the finance licensor to exercise the right to terminate use of the software by the user and specifically permits electronic self-help. The specific limitation of that provision to finance licensors makes it clear (particularly in light of the critical comments on this point that preceded the promulgation of the statute) that the statute is intended to provide more favorable treatment to the finance licensor than it does to the software lessor. The most likely justification is that the finance licensor's formal position in the chain of "title" makes it easier to justify giving the licensor the remedies typically available to conventional licensors. But that rationale is quite weak, given the entirely formal nature of the finance licensor's role. In function that role is no different than the role of the software lessor. A rule providing more favorable benefits to one rather than the other ends up favoring one transaction over the other for no justifiable policy reason.

Problem Set 36

36.1. Mark Kelp from GenenText comes back to see you again this week. He has just landed his first major customer, who has agreed to pay him a hefty license fee of $800,000 for a three-year license of Mark's software. The only hitch for Mark is that the customer wants to finance the software with a loan from Silicon Valley Bank. The Bank sent Mark an e-mail mentioning that it needs to take a security interest in the software as a routine matter, something which (the Bank explains) should not bother Mark in any way.

Mark understands that a security interest means that the Bank might foreclose on the software and sell it to somebody else. He is very worried about losing control of the software. He does not want anybody else having access to the code, and he is particularly worried about some other customer getting the software from the Bank instead of Mark. Can he prevent this from happening? Should he worry about it? UCC §9-408, UCITA §510.

36.2. Stacy Vye from Wessex Bank calls to ask you several questions about a program that Wessex Bank is about to start in which it would "lease" software, in the sense that it would loan money to people buying large pieces of software. One concern she has is how she would perfect her interest in the software. She is happy to file UCC-1 financing statements (even if they have only limited value). What she wants to know is whether perfection also requires a filing in the Copyright Office. What do you say? Copyright Act §§101 ("transfer of copyright ownership") and 205.

36.3. Stacy also wants to know whether she needs to file at all. She understands that she will rarely be able to use or resell the software, so she wonders if she can simply forgo filing entirely. In any event, she wonders, how can the transactions really be safe for her if she can't use or resell the software? What do you say?

36.4. Stacy's last question relates to software defects. She is worried about financing software because of the possibility that she will be responsible for defects in the software or that her borrowers will try to avoid payment because of those defects. What do you tell her? Does it matter what form of transaction she uses? UCITA §509.

36.5.   You get another call the next day from Stacy. She is now negotiating a loan to SuperComp, a large electronics retailer that sells a variety of products ranging from cellphones to personal digital assistants (Palm Pilots and the like) to personal computers of various kinds (which come pre-loaded with various operating systems selected by the manufacturers). Stacy plans to take a security interest in "all inventory" of the debtor and file a financing statement covering "all inventory" in the office of the Secretary of State of Delaware (where SuperComp is incorporated). Will that financing statement be adequate to perfect a security interest in all of the collateral? UCC §9-102(a)(44) and (48).

36.6.   Your next question is from Tertius Lydgate, an old friend of yours who operates a medical clinic. He is interested in buying some office-management software, which will include in a single application the ability to make appointments, send e-mails reminding of appointments, generate and send invoices, receive payments, and produce monthly, quarterly, and annual financial statements. He plans to finance the transaction, but becomes concerned when he notices that the documents give the bank the right to turn the software off if he misses a payment. He points out that the software operates through a high-speed Internet connection, and that the bank will have the ability over that connection to turn off the software remotely, without even coming to see him. How much should he be troubled? UCITA §§510, 815, 816.

36.7.   Referring to the facts of Problems 35.6 and 35.7, assume that Stacy makes a loan to McCallie Concepts at a time when McCallie has several existing customers with licenses to use McCallie's software. Later, Stacy forecloses on McCallie. What is the relation after the foreclosure between Stacy, on the one hand, and the licensees, on the other? Copyright Act §205; UCC §9-317(d). Does your answer differ based on whether McCallie had registered the software or not? (You should assume that Stacy perfected her loan by filing in both the UCC records and, with respect to any registered software, in the Copyright Office as well, but that the licensees had recorded nothing in the Copyright Office.)

Assignment 37: Lending Against Patents

A. The Basics of Patent Law

Unlike the copyright system discussed in the preceding two assignments, which abjures any protection for the functional aspects of expressive content, the patent system squarely protects the functional aspects of inventions, so long as they fall within the broad subject matter of a "process, machine, manufacture, composition of matter, or . . . improvement thereof." Patent Act, 35 U.S.C. §101. Although for a time it was doubted that wholly intangible software could qualify for protection, you will recall from Assignment 25 that it is now well settled that software-based inventions are patentable. Similarly, traditional doubts about the availability of patent protection for business methods have dissipated, so that (at least as we write), business methods are readily patentable. Thus, all of the basic building blocks of Internet commerce are subject to protection by patent.

Another major difference from copyright protection — which is available to any but the most banal expression — patent protection is available only to serious inventions. Among other things, patentability requires proof of "novelty" (Patent Act §102) and "nonobviousness" (Patent Act §103). Both of those requirements are quite detailed, but collectively they should exclude from the patent system innovations that do not meet a substantial threshold of creative intuition.

Still another difference from copyright protection — which springs up automatically when the expression is fixed — is that patents are issued only after examination and assessment by the federal government, in this case the Patent and Trademark Office (the PTO). A person seeking patent protection must go through the laborious process of filing a complex application that includes both a detailed specification of the invention and claims about the invention. The specification is a description of what the invention does and how it works; it often includes one or more detailed diagrams. Claims are the operative legal part of the patent: a narrative description of what the inventor claims to be the new contributions of the invention, from which others will be excluded if the patent issues.

Patent protection is not only difficult to obtain, it also is much shorter than copyright protection. It runs only 20 years from the date of the application. Because the average application process takes about 2 to 3 years, and because the patent is not valid until the application is granted, the period of exclusive entitlement is typically in the range of 17 to 18 years. For complicated or contested patents, however, the examination period might be much longer, and thus the period of protection might be much shorter or (at least theoretically) no time at all. By making the date at which the patent terminates run from the date of the application, Congress puts the risk of a long examination period on the applicant, which gives the applicant a considerable incentive to push the process forward. In contrast, an earlier statute under which the date of termination ran from the date that the patent was granted often gave an applicant an incentive to delay the examination process.

Finally, although there is a presumption that any patent issued by the PTO is valid, that presumption does not carry great weight. Thus, it is common in litigation challenging alleged patent infringement for a defendant to prevail by having the patent declared invalid. To ensure that uniform standards of validity apply — lest some patents be valid in some parts of the country and invalid in others — all appellate litigation regarding patents is centralized at the United States Court of Appeals for the Federal Circuit in Washington, D.C. That produces a complicated procedural system of trial litigation in the regional district courts, with appeals to the Federal Circuit, and then (occasionally) to the Supreme Court.

B. Perfecting Security Interests in Patents

Because the government issues patents, the patent system (unlike the copyright system) does not have a mechanism for inventors to record the issuance of patents. It, however, does have a recording system in which participants can provide evidence of *transfers* of patents. Patent Act §261 establishes that system. Under that section, it is permissible to assign either a patent or an application for a patent "by an instrument in writing." To resolve disputes among multiple purported purchasers, the last paragraph of Section 261 provides: "An assignment, grant or conveyance shall be void as against any subsequent purchaser or mortgagee for a valuable consideration, without notice, unless it is recorded in the Patent and Trademark Office within three months from its date or prior to the date of such subsequent purchase or mortgage."

To implement that section, the PTO has issued regulations that permit the recordation of either "[a]ssignments of applications, patents, and registrations," or "[o]ther documents . . . affecting title to applications, patents, or registrations." 37 C.F.R. §3.11. The recording system is indexed by the number of the patent (or application). Thus, the assignment (or other document) to be recorded must indicate the number of the patent or application. 37 C.F.R. §3.21. The fee for recording is currently $40. 37 C.F.R. §1.21(h). It also bears noting, in light of the discussion in Assignment 32 that the Patent and Trademark Office is one of the leaders in developing systems for accepting electronic filings.

The key question for present purposes is the question addressed for copyright law in *Peregrine*: Does the Patent Act preempt the application of Article 9 with respect to security interests in patents or, more generally, what is the proper method for perfecting a security interest in a patent? The Ninth Circuit recently provided a comprehensive analysis of that question.

Moldo v. Matsco, Inc. (In re Cybernetic Services, Inc.)

252 F.3d 1039 (9th Cir. 2001)

Before: Harry Pregerson, Ferdinand F. Fernandez, and Susan P. Graber, Circuit Judges.

Graber, Circuit Judge:

As is often true in the field of intellectual property, we must apply an antiquated statute in a modern context. The question that we decide today is whether 35 U.S.C. §261 of the Patent Act, or Article 9 of the Uniform Commercial Code (UCC), . . . requires the holder of a security interest in a patent to record that interest with the federal Patent and Trademark Office (PTO) in order to perfect the interest as against a subsequent lien creditor. We answer "no"; neither the Patent Act nor Article 9 so requires. . . .

FACTUAL AND PROCEDURAL BACKGROUND

The parties stipulated to the relevant facts: Matsco, Inc., and Matsco Financial Corporation (Petitioners) have a security interest in a patent developed by Cybernetic Services, Inc. (Debtor). The patent is for a data recorder that is designed to capture data from a video signal regardless of the horizontal line in which the data is located. Petitioners' security interest in the patent was "properly prepared, executed by the Debtor and timely filed with the Secretary of State of the State of California," in accordance with the California Commercial Code. Petitioners did not record their interest with the PTO.

After Petitioners had recorded their security interest with the State of California, certain creditors filed an involuntary Chapter 7 petition against Debtor, and an order of relief was granted. The primary asset of Debtor's estate is the patent. Petitioners then filed a motion for relief from the automatic stay so that they could foreclose on their interest in the patent. The bankruptcy Trustee opposed the motion, arguing that Petitioners had failed to perfect their interest because they did not record it with the PTO.

The bankruptcy court ruled that Petitioners had properly perfected their security interest in the patent by following the provisions of Article 9. Furthermore, the court reasoned, because Petitioners had perfected their security interest before the filing of the bankruptcy petition, Petitioners had priority over the Trustee's claim in the patent and deserved relief from the stay. Accordingly, the bankruptcy court granted Petitioners' motion. The BAP [that is, Bankruptcy Appellate Panel] affirmed.

Petitioners then filed this timely appeal. . . .

DISCUSSION

Article 9 of the UCC . . . governs the method for perfecting a security interest in personal property. Article 9 applies to "general intangibles," a term that includes intellectual property. [Revised UCC §9-102(a)(42).] The parties do not dispute that Petitioners complied with Article 9's general filing requirements and, in the case of most types of property, would have priority over a subsequent lien creditor. The narrower question in this case is whether Petitioners' actions were sufficient to perfect their interest when the "general intangible" to which the lien attached is a patent. The parties also do not dispute that, *if* Petitioners were required to file notice of their security interest in the patent with the PTO, then the Trustee, as a hypothetical lien creditor under 11 U.S.C. §544(a)(1), has a superior right to the patent.

The Trustee makes two arguments. First, the Trustee contends that the Patent Act preempts Article 9's filing requirements. Second, the Trustee argues that Article 9 itself provides that a security interest in a patent can be perfected only by filing it with the PTO. We discuss each argument in turn.

A. PREEMPTION

1. The Analytical Framework

"[T]he Supremacy Clause, U.S. Const., Art. VI, cl. 2, invalidates state laws that 'interfere with, or are contrary to,' federal law." Hillsborough County, Fla. v. Automated Med. Labs., Inc., 471 U.S. 707, 712 (1985) (quoting Gibbons v. Ogden, 22 U.S. (9 Wheat.) 1, 92, (1824)). Congress may preempt state law in several different ways. Congress may do so expressly (express preemption). *Id.* at 713. Even in the absence of express preemptive text, Congress' intent to preempt an entire field of state law may be inferred "where the scheme of federal regulation is sufficiently comprehensive to make reasonable the inference that Congress 'left no room' for supplementary state regulation" (field preemption). *Id.* (quoting Rice v. Santa Fe Elevator Corp., 331 U.S. 218, 230, (1947)). State law also is preempted "when compliance with both state and federal law is impossible," or if the operation of state law "stands as an obstacle to the accomplishment and execution of the full purposes and objectives of Congress" (conflict preemption). Kewanee Oil Co. v. Bicron Corp., 416 U.S. 470, 479 (1974). In all cases, congressional intent to preempt state law must be clear and manifest.

The Patent Act does not contain preemptive text, so express preemption is not an issue here. . . .

The Trustee argues that the recording provision found in 35 U.S.C. §261 requires that the holder of a security interest in a patent record that interest with the PTO in order to perfect as to a subsequent lien creditor. Section 261 provides:

> . . . An assignment, grant or conveyance shall be void as against any subsequent purchaser or mortgagee for a valuable consideration, without notice, unless it is recorded in the Patent and Trademark Office within three months from its date or prior to the date of such subsequent purchase or mortgage.

[Emphasis added by court.]

If the Trustee's reading of the relevant portion of §261 is correct, then to the extent that Article 9 allows a different method of perfection, it would be preempted under either a "field" or "conflict" preemption theory. That is because recording systems increase a patent's marketability and thus play an integral role in the incentive scheme created by Congress. Recording systems provide notice and certainty to present and future parties to a transaction; they work "by virtue of the fact that interested parties have a specific place to look in order to discover with certainty whether a particular interest has been transferred." Nat'l Peregrine, Inc. v. Capitol Fed. Savs. & Loan Ass'n (In re Peregrine Entm't, Ltd.), 116 B.R. 194, 200 (C.D.Cal.1990); *see also* Littlefield v. Perry, 88 U.S. (21 Wall.) 205, 221 (1874) (noting that the Patent Act's recording system "is intended for the benefit of the public" and that "[*b*]*ona fide* purchasers look to it for their protection"). If, as the Trustee argues, the Patent Act expressly delineates the place where a party must go to acquire notice and certainty about liens on patents, then a state law that requires the public to look elsewhere unquestionably would undercut the value of the Patent Act's recording scheme. If, on the other hand, §261 does not cover liens on patents, then Article 9's filing requirements do not conflict with any policies inherent in the Patent Act's recording scheme. . . .

2. The Patent Act Requires Parties to Record with the PTO Only Ownership Interest in Patents.

As noted, the Patent Act's recording provision provides that an "assignment, grant or conveyance shall be void as against any subsequent purchaser or mortgagee for a valuable consideration, without notice, unless it is recorded in the [PTO]." 35 U.S.C. §261. In order to determine whether Congress intended for parties to record with the PTO the type of interest that is at issue in this case, we must give the words of the statute the meaning that they had in 1870, the year in which the current version of §261 was enacted.

Our task is not an easy one because security interests, and the words used to describe them, have changed significantly since the 19th Century. For example, before Article 9, a party could secure property using a pledge, an assignment, a chattel mortgage, a chattel trust, a trust deed, a factor's lien, or a conditional sale. Each type of device carried with it elaborate rules that controlled its use, and each conferred different rights and liabilities upon the contracting parties. Article 9, which was first enacted in 1962, brought the "long history of the proliferation of independent security devices . . . to an end." GRANT GILMORE, SECURITY INTERESTS IN PERSONAL PROPERTY §10.1, at 296 (1965). It did so in part by introducing a body of law that would govern a "single, 'unitary' security device": the Article 9 security interest. 4 JAMES J. WHITE & ROBERT S. SUMMERS, UNIFORM COMMERCIAL CODE §30-1, at 2 (4th ed.1995).

With that history in mind, we must determine whether Congress intended to include the kind of transaction at issue in this case within the scope of 35 U.S.C. §261. The first phrase in §261's recording provision — "assignment, grant or conveyance" — refers to different types of transactions. The neighboring clause — "shall be void as against any subsequent purchaser or mortgagee" — refers to the status of the party that receives an interest in the patent. Therefore, for the Trustee to prevail in this case, (1) Petitioners' transaction with Debtor must have been the type of "assignment, grant or conveyance" referred to in §261, and (2) the Trustee, who has the status of a hypothetical lien creditor, must be a "subsequent purchaser or mortgagee." We hold that neither condition is met.

As we will discuss next, our conclusion finds support in the text of §261, keeping in view the historical definitions of the terms used in the recording provision; the context, structure, and policy behind §261; Supreme Court precedent; and PTO regulations. We will begin by analyzing the statute's text and context, as interpreted by the Supreme Court. For the sake of clarity, we will discuss the two relevant phrases in the recording provision of §261 separately.

a. The Phrase "Assignment, Grant or Conveyance" Concerns Transfers of Ownership Interests Only

The historical meanings of the terms "assignment, grant or conveyance" all involved the transfer of an ownership interest. A patent "assignment" referred to a transaction that transferred specific rights in the patent, all involving the patent's title. *E.g.,* Oliver v. Rumford Chem. Works, 109 U.S. 75, 82-83 (1883) (noting that an "assignment" involves a transfer of a patent's title); Waterman v. MacKenzie, 138 U.S. 252, 255 (1891) (explaining that an "assignment" vests in the assignee "title in so much of the patent itself"); 2 William C. Robinson, The Law of Patents §762, at 517 (1890) ("An assignment is a transfer of the entire interest in a patented invention, or of an undivided portion of such entire interest, as to every section of the United States."); 48 C.J. *Patents* §390, at 253 (1929) ("Generally an assignment of a patent vests in the assignee a title to so much of the patent itself, and transfers to the assignee an exclusive right to do everything under the patent which the patentee himself could do.").

A "grant," historically, also referred to a transfer of an ownership interest in a patent, but only as to a specific geographic area. *See* Moore v. Marsh, 74 U.S. (7 Wall.) 515, 521 (1868) (explaining that grants "must convey the exclusive right, under the patent, to make and use, and vend to others to be used, the thing patented, within and throughout some specified district or portion of the United States, and such right must be exclusive of the patentee, as well as of all others except the grantee"); 2 Robinson §763, at 518 (noting that the "essential differ-ence" between an assignment and a grant is "the territorial area to which they relate").

Although older cases defining the term "conveyance" in the context of intan-gible property are sparse, and its historic meaning tended to vary, the common contemporaneous definition was "to transfer the legal title . . . from the present owner to another." Abendroth v. Town of Greenwich, 29 Conn. 356 (1860); *see also, e.g.,* Frame v. Bivens, 189 F. 785, 789 (C.C.E.D.Okla.1909) ("A conveyance is the transfer of the title of land from one person or class of persons to another."); 1 Bouvier's Law Dictionary 361 (14th ed. 1874) (defining "conveyance" as the "transfer of the title of land from one person or class of persons to another"); 1 Burrill's Law Dictionary 375 (2d ed. 1871) (defining "conveyance" as an "instrument in writing, by which property or the title to property is transferred from one person to another"); Black's Law Dictionary 431 (3d ed. 1933) ("In the strict legal sense, a transfer of legal title to land.").

That Congress intended to incorporate the common, contemporaneous mean-ings of the words "assignment," "grant," and "conveyance" into the Patent Act's recording provision can be seen when §261 is examined in its entirety. The first clue is the provision's title: "Ownership; assignment." By using the unambiguous words "ownership; assignment," Congress must have intended to introduce the subject that was to follow: the ownership of patents and the assignment thereof.

Continuing through §261, the second paragraph states that patents shall be assignable by an instrument in writing. That paragraph goes on to provide that the patentee or the patentee's assigns "may in like manner *grant and convey an exclusive right* under his application for patent . . . to the whole or any specified part of the United States." (Emphasis added.) The types of transactions referred to in §261's second paragraph — (1) the assignment of a patent, and (2) the grant or conveyance of an exclusive right in a patent in the whole or part of the United States — track the historical definitions of assignment, grant, and conveyance that we just discussed — transactions that all involve the transfer of an ownership inter-est in a patent.

Moreover, we presume that words used more than once in the same statute have the same meaning throughout. Here, the second paragraph of §261 uses the words "grant and convey" to signify the transfer of an "exclusive right [in a patent] . . . to the whole or any specified part of the United States." We presume, then, that when Congress used the words "grant or conveyance" two paragraphs later in the same statute, Congress still intended to refer to ownership interests only.

Supreme Court precedent supports our view that the terms "assignment, grant or conveyance" refer to ownership interests only. In *Waterman,* the Supreme Court analyzed the nature of a patent "assignment" and "mortgage." The plaintiff in *Waterman* assigned to his wife a patent for an improvement in fountain pens. The plaintiff's wife then granted back to the plaintiff a license to use the patent. That license was never recorded. The wife then assigned the patent to a third party as collateral for a debt; the document concerning this arrangement was filed with the PTO. Finally, the wife assigned the patent back to the plaintiff. The question for the Court was whether the plaintiff had standing to bring an action for infringement of the patent. The Court held that only the third party had standing. 138 U.S. at 261.

In resolving the matter, the Court noted that a patent's owner may convey, assign, or grant one of three interests:

> the whole patent, comprising the exclusive right to make, use and vend the invention throughout the United States; or [2] an undivided part or share of that exclusive right; or [3] the exclusive right under the patent within and throughout a specified part of the United States. A transfer of either of these three kinds of interests is an *assignment,* properly speaking, and vests in the assignee a *title* in so much of the patent itself, with a right to sue infringers. . . . Any assignment or transfer, short of one of these, is a *mere license,* giving the licensee no title in the patent, and no right to sue at law in his own name for an infringement.

Id. at 255 (emphasis added) (citation omitted). Whether a particular conveyance qualifies as an assignment or a license "does not depend upon the name by which it calls itself, but upon the legal effect of its provisions," *id.* at 256; that is, whether title is passed depends on the rights that were transferred by the contracting parties. Only the holder of an ownership interest in the patent had standing to sue.

Waterman contains no explicit holding that 35 U.S.C. §261 applies only to a secured transaction that effects a transfer of ownership, but it does imply as much. The Court in *Waterman* expressly differentiated between three kinds of transfers of ownership interests — all of which it labeled as versions of "assignments" — and everything else, which it referred to as "mere licenses." The Court did not discuss "grants" or "conveyances" separately, but (1) as a matter of logic, they must fall into one of the two overarching and mutually exclusive categories that the Court created: assignments (ownership interests) or licenses (less than ownership interests); and (2) the kinds of transfers of ownership interests discussed by the Court (and labeled "assignments") correspond neatly to the historical definitions of the transactions delineated in the statute. *See* [HILLMAN, DOCUMENTING SECURED TRANSACTIONS 2-19 to 2-20 (May 1998 rev.)] (observing that the Patent Act "distinguishes 'assignments' of patents (of which 'grants' and 'conveyances' are specific types) from all other transfers (which are called 'licenses')"). It is clear, then, that the transactions that the Court referred to as effecting a transfer of ownership are the same transactions that Congress referred to as an "assignment, grant or conveyance."

The Court's decision in *Littlefield* compels a similar conclusion. In *Littlefield*, a patent holder (the defendant) "granted" rights in a patent to a third party (the plaintiff), but did so through two separate contracts. The Court described the first contract as an "absolute conveyance" of the patent from the defendant to the plaintiff. In the second contract, the parties reserved some of the rights in the patent to the defendant. 88 U.S. at 219-20. The plaintiff recorded the first agreement but not the second, and eventually he sued the defendant for infringement. The defendant argued that the plaintiff could not sue him for infringement because the plaintiff held only a license. The Supreme Court disagreed.

In evaluating the claim, the Court examined the two agreements at issue. The Court noted that, in determining which party had an assignment and which had a license, it was an "important fact . . . that only one of the parts is recorded. . . . The record[ing] of the [first contract] alone . . . furnishes the strongest evidence of the intention of the parties to give effect to the two instruments as an assignment" to the plaintiff. *Id.* at 221. Therefore, under the "absolute conveyance," the plaintiff held an assignment, while the unrecorded agreement gave the defendant a "mere license."

In summary, the statute's text, context, and structure, when read in the light of Supreme Court precedent, compel the conclusion that a security interest in a patent that does not involve a transfer of the rights of ownership is a "mere license" and is not an "assignment, grantor conveyance" within the meaning of 35 U.S.C. §261. And because §261 provides that only an "assignment, grant or conveyance shall be void" as against subsequent purchasers and mortgagees, only transfers of ownership interests need to be recorded with the PTO.

In the present case, the parties do not dispute that the transaction that gave Petitioners their interest in the patent did not involve a transfer of an ownership interest in the patent. Petitioners held a "mere license," which did not have to be recorded with the PTO.

> b.   The Phrase "Subsequent Purchaser or Mortgagee"
>   Does Not Include Subsequent Lien Creditors

The Trustee's argument fails not only because a security interest that does not transfer ownership is not an "assignment, grant or conveyance," but also because he is not a subsequent "purchaser or mortgagee." Congress intended for parties to record their ownership interests in a patent so as to provide constructive notice only to subsequent holders of an ownership interest. Again, we derive our conclusion from the historical definitions of the words, from the context and structure of §261, and from Supreme Court precedent.

The historical meaning of "purchaser or mortgagee" proves that Congress intended for the recording provision to give constructive notice only to subsequent holders of an ownership interest. For the sake of convenience, we begin with the definition of "mortgagee."

Historically, a "mortgagee" was someone who obtained title to property used to secure a debt. *See* JAMES SCHOULER, PERSONAL PROPERTY §416, at 622 (5th ed.1918) (noting that "[m]ortgages of chattels, then, are to be distinguished at common law from liens and pledges in this sort of out-and-out transfer of the title conditionally which is carried by the original transaction"). A "mortgage" must be differentiated from a "pledge," a term that is absent from the Patent Act. Professor Gilmore, in his treatise, SECURITY INTERESTS IN PERSONAL PROPERTY §1.1, at 8, notes that the historical distinction between a pledge and a mortgage was that "the mortgagee got title or an estate whereas the pledgee got merely possession with a right to foreclose on default.". . .

That the Patent Act refers to securing a patent through a "mortgage" but not through a "pledge" is significant, for both were common methods of using a patent as collateral. *See* SCHOULER §395, at 589 (noting that patent rights "are constantly interchanged in our business community for the purpose of pledge"); *cf.* GILMORE §1.2, at 9-10 ("If it ever was true that only tangible chattels could be pledged, it is well over a century since that proposition had any vitality."). . . . It seems then, that by using the term "mortgagee," but not "lien" or "pledge," Congress intended in 1870 for the Patent Act's recording provision to protect only those who obtained title to a patent.

The term "purchaser" does not detract from this conclusion. Section 261 instructs that an unrecorded "assignment, grant or conveyance" shall be void as against a subsequent "purchaser . . . for a valuable consideration, without notice." The historical definition of a "purchaser for value and without notice" was a purchaser . . . who takes a conveyance purporting to pass the entire title, legal and equitable, who pays value and does not have notice of the rights of others to the property. . . .

Congress, by stating that certain transactions shall be void as against a subsequent "purchaser or mortgagee" intended for the words to be read together: A "purchaser" is one who buys an ownership interest in the patent, while a "mortgagee" is one who obtains an ownership interest in a patent as collateral for a debt.

Our previous comments about the context and structure of §261 support our conclusion that Congress intended to protect only subsequent holders of an ownership interest. As noted, the title of §261 is "Ownership; assignment," which suggests that the recording provision is concerned only with ownership interests.

Similarly, the second paragraph delineates the types of transactions that §261 covers — (1) the assignment of a patent, and (2) the grant or conveyance of an exclusive right in the patent to the whole or any specified part of the United States — each involving the transfer of an ownership interest in a patent. It follows that, when Congress referred to a "subsequent purchaser or mortgagee," it was simply describing the future recipients of those transactions. In one case the recipient bought the interest (purchaser), while in the other the recipient loaned money and received the interest as collateral (mortgagee). In either case, an ownership interest was transferred.

Precedent confirms our reading of the statute. The Supreme Court has endorsed the view that Congress intended to provide constructive notice only to subsequent recipients of an ownership interest in a patent. In *Waterman,* the Court observed, as we do, that the Patent Act refers to a "mortgage" but not to a "pledge." The Court noted that, when a party has the status of a mortgagee,

> It is not merely the possession or a special property that passes; but, both at law and in equity, *the whole title is transferred to the mortgagee, as security for the debt,* subject only to be defeated by performance of the condition . . . and the right of possession, when there is no express stipulation to the contrary, goes with the right of property.

138 U.S. at 258 (emphasis added). Moreover, with title or possession of the property came certain rights in the mortgagee. *Id.* at 258-59. But a patent right "is incorporeal property, not susceptible of actual delivery or possession." *Id.* at 260.

Therefore, when "it is provided by statute that a mortgage of personal property shall not be valid against third persons, unless the mortgage is recorded, *a recording of the mortgage is a substitute for, and . . . equivalent to, a delivery of possession, and makes the title and the possession of the mortgagee good against all the world.*" *Id.* at 260 (emphasis added).

The Court then observed that, once a mortgagee has recorded the transaction, that party is "entitled to grant licenses, to receive license fees and royalties, and to have an account of profits or an award of damages against infringers." *Id.* Because the Court had already noted that only the holder of an ownership interest in a patent could sue for damages against infringers, it is clear that the Court read the term "mortgagee" to refer to a party who held an ownership interest in the patent.

In summary, the historical definitions of the terms "purchaser or mortgagee," taken in context and read in the light of Supreme Court precedent, establish that Congress was concerned only with providing constructive notice to subsequent parties who take an ownership interest in the patent in question.

The Trustee is not a subsequent "mortgagee," as that term is used in 35 U.S.C. §261, because the holder of a patent mortgage holds title to the patent itself. *Waterman*, 138 U.S. at 258. Instead, the Trustee is a hypothetical lien creditor. The Patent Act does not require parties to record documents in order to provide constructive notice to subsequent lien creditors who do not hold title to the patent.

3.   Public Policies that Underlie Recording Provisions Cannot Override the Text of the Patent Act

The Trustee argues that requiring lien creditors to record their interests with the PTO is in line with the general policy behind recording statutes. It may be, as the Trustee argues, that a national system of filing security interests is more efficient and effective than a state-by-state system. However, there is no statutory hook upon which to hang the Trustee's policy arguments. Moreover, we are not concerned with the policy behind recording statutes generally but, rather, with the policy behind 35 U.S.C. §261 specifically.

Title 35 U.S.C. §261, as we have demonstrated and as its label suggests, is concerned with patent ownership. In that provision Congress gave patent holders the right to transfer their ownership interests, but only in specific ways. The congressional policy behind that decision was to protect the patent holder and the public for, as the Supreme Court put it,

> it was obviously not the intention of the legislature to permit several monopolies to be made out of one, and divided among different persons within the same limits. Such a division would inevitably lead to fraudulent impositions upon persons who desired to purchase the use of the improvement, and would subject a party who, under a mistake as to his rights, used the invention without authority, to be harassed by a multiplicity of suits instead of one, and to successive recoveries of damages by different persons holding different portions of the patent right in the same place.

Gayler v. Wilder, 51 U.S. (10 How.) 501, 519-20 (1850); *see also* HILLMAN at 2-19 (noting that patent law "adheres to strict concepts of title, in order to protect the ownership of new inventions"). The recording provision, if read to include ownership interests only, is perfectly aligned with that policy. By contrast, a security interest in a patent does not make "several monopolies . . . out of one, . . . divided among different persons within the same limits." *Gayler,* 51 U.S. at 519.

We must interpret §261 in the light of the purposes that Congress was seeking to serve. Congress simply was not concerned with nonownership interests in patents, and this limitation was well understood at the time. As explained in a venerable treatise on the law of patents:

> A license is not such a conveyance of an interest in the patented invention as to affect its ownership, and hence is not required to be recorded. . . . The value of the patented invention to the vendee may be impaired by such outstanding licenses, but of this he must inform himself at his own risk as best he may. The record of a license, not being legally required, is not constructive notice to any person for any purpose.

2 ROBINSON §817, at 602-03 (footnotes omitted).

The Patent Act was written long before the advent of the "unitary" Article 9 security interest. But we must interpret 35 U.S.C. §261 as Congress wrote it. The Constitution entrusts to Congress, not to the courts, the role of ensuring that statutes keep up with changes in financing practices. It is notable that Congress has revised the Patent Act numerous times since its enactment, most recently in 1999, but it has not updated the Act's recording provision. We decline the Trustee's invitation to do so in Congress' place.

4. Cases Interpreting the Copyright Act Do Not Control

The Trustee's final argument is that this court should follow *Peregrine,* in which a bankruptcy court held that the Copyright Act preempts state methods of perfecting security interests in copyrights. The court in *Peregrine* observed that the "federal copyright laws ensure predictability and certainty of copyright ownership, promote national uniformity and avoid the practical difficulties of determining and enforcing an author's rights under the differing laws and in the separate courts of the various States." 116 B.R. at 199 (internal quotation marks omitted). The court reasoned that allowing state methods to stand would conflict with those goals. *Id. But see* 4 WHITE & SUMMERS §30-12, at 86 (referring to *Peregrine* as "misguided").

Of course, *Peregrine* is not binding on this court although, in the present case, we have no occasion to pass on its correctness as an interpretation of the Copyright Act. We note, however, that the Copyright Act, by its terms, governs security interests. The Copyright Act governs any "transfer" of ownership, which is defined by statute to include any "hypothecation." 17 U.S.C. §§101, 201(d)(1). A "hypothecation" is the "pledging of something as security without delivery of title or possession." BLACK'S LAW DICTIONARY 747 (7th ed.1999).

By contrast, the Patent Act does not refer to a "hypothecation" and, as we have demonstrated, does not refer to security interests at all. The fact that one federal intellectual property statute with a recording provision expressly refers to security interests (the Copyright Act), while another does not (the Patent Act), is more evidence that security interests are *outside* the scope of 35 U.S.C. §261.

5. PTO Regulations Require Only the Recording of Documents that Transfer Ownership in a Patent

It is worthy of mention that the applicable PTO regulations parallel our interpretation of 35 U.S.C. §261. Title 37 C.F.R. §3.11(a) provides that "assignments" must be recorded in the PTO. That regulation also states that "[o]ther documents *affecting title* to applications, patents, or registrations, will be recorded at the discretion of the Commissioner" of Patents and Trademarks. (Emphasis added.) Section 313 of the Manual of Patent Examining Procedure (7th ed.1998) explains that "[o]ther documents" that may be filed include "agreements which convey a security interest. Such documents are recorded in the public interest in order to give third parties notification of equitable interests. . . ."

Title 37 C.F.R. §3.11 is illuminating because it shows that the PTO does not consider security interests to be "assignments, grants or conveyances." Under 35 U.S.C. §261, certain conveyances — those that transfer an ownership interest — *must* be recorded to be effective as against a subsequent purchaser or mortgagee. If security interests *were* "assignments, grants or conveyances," then they would *have* to be filed to provide constructive notice to a subsequent purchaser or mortgagee, consistent with the Patent Act. As a matter of law and logic, the Commissioner would not have the "discretion" to reject federal filing.

The PTO consistently has interpreted 35 U.S.C. §261 in this way. An earlier version of the regulation, 37 C.F.R. §1.331, which was originally enacted in 1959, allowed for the federal filing of "[o]ther instruments affecting title to a patent . . . *even though the recording thereof may not serve as constructive notice under 35 U.S.C. 261.*" 37 C.F.R. §1.331(a) (emphasis added). Similarly, 37 C.F.R. §7, also originally enacted in 1959, distinguished between "assignments" and "licenses," much as *Waterman* had. "Assignment[ ]" meant any "instrument which conveys to the Government only the title to a patent." 37 C.F.R. §7.2 (removed and reserved Oct. 10, 1997). "Licenses" were any instruments other than assignments. 37 C.F.R. §7.3 (removed and reserved Oct. 10, 1997).

We acknowledge that the issue in this case is a pure question of statutory construction for the courts to decide and that the PTO's interpretation is not entitled to any particular deference. Although the statute is ambiguous now, it seems not to have been in 1870. Moreover, we do not believe that 35 U.S.C. §261 contains within it a delegation of authority, either explicit or implicit, that would enable the PTO to broaden or narrow the reach of the Patent Act's recording provision. *See id.* at 844 (noting that deference is appropriate only when Congress has delegated the authority to an administrative agency to fill a statutory gap or interpret an ambiguous provision.)

However, when we must interpret an archaic statute, the historic practice of the agency that was created to help implement that statute can shed light on its meaning. Under 37 C.F.R. §3.11, Petitioners were not required to record with the PTO their security interest in order to perfect as to the Trustee.

6. There is No Conflict Between the Patent Act and Article 9 in This Case

Because the Patent Act does not cover security interests or lien creditors at all, there is no conflict between 35 U.S.C. §261 and Article 9. Petitioners did not have to file with the PTO to perfect their security interest as to a subsequent lien creditor.

B. ARTICLE 9'S STEP-BACK PROVISION

The Trustee's second major argument is that Article 9 itself requires that a creditor file notice of a secured transaction with the PTO in order to perfect a security interest. [Old UCC §9-302(3)(a)] states that the filing of a financing statement pursuant to Article 9 "is not necessary or effective to perfect a security interest in property subject to . . . [a] statute . . . which provides for a national or international registration . . . or which specifies a place of filing different from that specified in" Article 9. If §9-302(3)(a) applies, then a party *must* utilize the federal registration system in order to perfect its security interest.[9]

The question, then, is whether the Patent Act is "[a] statute . . . which provides for a national or international registration . . . or which specifies a place of filing different from that specified in" Article 9. [The Court concludes, largely for the reasons summarized above, that the Patent Act is not such a statute.]

C. Conclusion

Because 35 U.S.C. §261 concerns only transactions that effect a transfer of an ownership interest in a patent, the Patent Act does not preempt Article 9. . . . Consequently, Petitioners perfected their security interest in Debtor's patent by recording it with the California Secretary of State. They have priority over the Trustee's claim because they recorded their interest before the filing of the bankruptcy petition.

Although several other courts have considered related questions, *Cybernetic Services* is the first appellate decision on this topic. Because its analysis is generally consistent with the analysis in the earlier cases, there is good reason to believe that the rules it summarizes will be accepted for the indefinite future. If so, that would give patent financing a sense of stability that copyright financing lacks.

Problem Set 37

37.1. (a) When you first come into the office on Monday, you find a telecopy from your client Mark Kelp at GenenText, Inc. Last month he purchased a patent from one of his competitors (GenCode). GenCode signed the documents transferring the patent to GenenText on March 1. Mark left the documents with his administrative assistant, asking him to file a notice of the transfer with the PTO as soon as possible. Mark then left town for his spring vacation.

When Mark returned, he discovered a series of urgent telephone messages from GenCode. Facing serious financial difficulties, it wanted immediate cash from Mark (rather than payments over a five-year period, as previously agreed). The last of the messages (dated two weeks ago) stated that if Mark did not call back immediately, GenCode would sell the patent instead to Venter Pharmaceuticals (a large East Coast firm, flush with cash). It now appears that GenCode has followed through on this threat, signing a contract to sell the

---

9. Section 9-302(3)(a) concerns only the "where to file" question; any issues left unresolved by the federal statute (e.g., priority), are resolved by looking to Article 9. *See* [Old UCC § 9-104(a)] (instructing that Article 9 does not apply "to the extent" that federal statutes govern the rights of parties to a secured transaction).

patent to Venter dated April 2, which Venter recorded in Washington, D.C. at the PTO on the next day.

It is now April 10. Mark wants to know who has priority in the patent. What do you say? Patent Act §261.

(b) Would your answer to question (a) change if Venter instead received the patent as a charitable contribution? In that event, GenCode would have received a tax deduction but no other consideration. Patent Act §261.

37.2. Would your answer to Problem 37.1 change if the technology in question was a software program that had not been patented, and thus was protected only by copyright law? Is there any policy reason that it should? (Assume that the relevant filings described in questions (a) and (b) had been made in the Copyright Office instead of the PTO.) Copyright Act §205 (d).

37.3. This afternoon you meet with Stacy Vye from Wessex Bank. She has just agreed to make a large loan to a client (Pheazer Pharmaceuticals, a Delaware corporation with its principal place of business in St. Louis, Missouri) that is acquiring a patent which grants the exclusive right to sell a pharmaceutical thought to be useful in preventing baldness. This is a large loan, the first of its kind for her, and she wants to be careful about the procedures. She wants to know four things.

(a) In what systems should you search for competing claimants?

(b) When can she complete the transaction (that is, how long after you complete the searches that you recommend in (a) would you recommend to Stacy that she wait before advancing funds to the borrower)?

(c) In what systems should you file evidence of her loan?

(d) Where (geographically) do you file?
Patent Act §261; UCC §§9-301(1), 9-307, 9-315(a)(1).

37.4. This week you have a meeting with your doctor client Tertius Lydgate, who recently purchased a patent on some new medical technology from Will Ladislaw Research (WLR). Just a few weeks later, Lydgate finds out that WLR (after the sale to Lydgate) also managed to borrow several hundred thousand dollars against the patent from Bulstrode Bank, which perfected by filing a financing statement in the UCC records. Lydgate tells you that he recorded his claim in the patent records immediately after he bought the patent. Is Lydgate's claim subject to Bulstrode's claim? Patent Act §261, UCC §9-322.

37.5. The day after your discussion with Stacy in Problem 37.3, she calls to tell you that she has a loan in her existing file that she has been meaning to discuss with you. On that loan, based on her understanding of *Peregrine*, she filed a notice of her interest only in the patent records. It now appears that a later creditor (Bulstrode Bank), acting with actual knowledge of her loan, made a later loan against the same patent, perfected by a filing in the UCC records. Who has priority, Bulstrode or Wessex Bank (Stacy's bank)? Patent Act §261; UCC §9-322(a) and comment 4.

37.6. While she has you on the phone, Stacy wants also to discuss an upcoming transaction in which her borrower is acquiring a competitor. To finance the transaction, her borrower wants to grant a security interest in all of the patents and patent applications of the company that it is acquiring. The acquired company has a large group of research scientists, coupled with a culture that strongly promotes patent filings, so it has several hundred patents and applications. Stacy wants to know if she has to file against each of the patents or whether she can make a single global filing against all of the patents. She is worried that the list of patents and applications that she has might be incomplete and wants to be sure that she has a security interest in all of the assets even if they do not appear on the list she has received. What do you tell her? UCC §§9-108, 9-502, 9-504; 37 C.F.R. §§3.11, 3.28, 3.31.

Assignment 38: Lending Against Other Forms of Intellectual Property

A. Trademarks

As Assignment 3 explains in some detail, protection for trademark draws partially on state law and partially on federal law. Traditionally, trademark rights have been regarded as arising in the first instance under state law, based on adequate use of the mark in commerce to generate secondary meaning. Acting under the Lanham Act, however, the federal Patent and Trademark Office has established a filing system, which gives nationwide protection for the mark, without regard to the actual scope of the mark's use in commerce.

In many respects, the law regarding transactions in trademarks is similar to the law for transactions in patents. Specifically, Lanham Act §10(a), 15 U.S.C. §1060(a), establishes a recording rule much like the rule in Patent Act §261:

> Assignments [of trademarks] shall be by instruments in writing duly executed. . . . An assignment shall be void against any subsequent purchaser for valuable consideration without notice, unless the prescribed information reporting the assignment is recorded in the Patent and Trademark Office within 3 months after the date thereof or prior to such subsequent purchase.

Although there is no definitive appellate interpretation of the trademark language like the *Cybernetic Services* case from the preceding assignment, the case that follows is representative: Courts interpreting the Lanham Act provision, like courts interpreting Patent Act §261, generally have concluded that filings in the federal system are neither necessary nor sufficient to perfect a security interest in trademarks.

In re Together Development Corporation
227 B.R. 439 (Bankr. D. Mass. 1998)

JAMES F. QUEENAN, Bankruptcy Judge.

This case presents the question of the proper method of perfecting a security interest in trademarks. The subject involves a trap for the unwary.

By previous order, the court authorized Together Development Corporation (the "Debtor") to sell substantially all its assets, including its trademark "Together Dating Service", free of the security interest of Horace Trimarchi ("Trimarchi"). . . . The order also set down an evidentiary hearing so the court could adjudicate the validity and perfection of Trimarchi's security interest. Set forth here are my findings of fact and conclusions of law following that hearing.

720

. . . Trimarchi is a former shareholder of the Debtor. By agreement dated May 13, 1986, the Debtor purchased all its shares owned by Trimarchi (and two others). The price for Trimarchi's shares was $200,000, which was represented by the Debtor's promissory note in that amount. . . . In consideration of other indebtedness owed Trimarchi, the Debtor gave him [another] promissory note in the sum of $30,372.12. . . . Both notes were secured by the Debtor's "accounts receivable, it's [sic] Trademark, Franchise Fees and Royalties." In furtherance of that security interest, the Debtor executed and delivered to Trimarchi a separate assignment which described the assigned property as the Debtor's "Trademark (Together Dating Service) . . . which is registered under Certificate Number 1,145,365 in the United States Patent Office transfer said mark [sic], along with the goodwill of the business connected with that mark. . . ." The Debtor also gave to Trimarchi a signed financing statement (UCC-1) covering the following described collateral: "All fixtures, office furniture, files, etc., accounts receivable, Franchise Fees, Royalties, License Fees, Franchise Agreements, License Agreements, and 'TOGETHER' Trademark–Registration number 1,145,365."

Trimarchi did not make a filing with the Secretary of State of Connecticut, where the Debtor's principal office was then located, nor with any other state. Instead, he filed the financing statement by mail with the United States Patent and Trademark Office ("PTO"), which sent back a written acknowledgment of the filing. There is no dispute that Trimarchi's security interest in items of property other than the trademark is unperfected for lack of recording with the appropriate state authority. The question is whether the filing with the PTO was sufficient to perfect his security interest in the trademark.

. . . If a federal statute contains filing requirements for particular collateral, [old] U.C.C. §9-302(3) defers to the federal statute. As in effect in New York, section 9-302(3) provides as follows:

> (3) The filing of a financing statement otherwise required by this Article is not necessary or effective to perfect a security interest in property subject to

> (a) a statute or treaty of the United States which provides for a national or international registration or a national or international certificate of title or which specifies a place of filing different from that specified in this Article for filing of the security interest. . . .

> (4) Compliance with a statute or treaty described in subsection (3) is equivalent to the filing of a financing statement under this Article, and a security interest in property subject to the statute or treaty can be perfected only by compliance therewith except as provided in Section 9-103 on multiple state transactions. Duration and renewal of perfection of a security interest perfected by compliance with the statute or treaty are governed by the provisions of the statute or treaty; in other respects the security interest is subject to this Article.

[Ed: See Revised UCC §9-311(a)(1).]

The "Lanham Act," chapter 22 of Title 15 of the United States Code, governs trademarks. Its provision on the transfer of an interest in a trademark reads in relevant part as follows:

> . . . An assignment shall be void as against any subsequent purchaser for a valuable consideration without notice, unless it is recorded in the Patent and Trademark Office within three months after the date thereof or prior to such subsequent purchase.

15 U.S.C. §1060.

The Lanham Act contains no definition of "assignment," thereby casting doubt on whether the term includes the grant of a security interest. The question therefore is this: Is its provision on transfer a statute which, in the words of U.C.C. §9-302(3), "specifies a place of filing different from that specified in this Article for filing of the security interest"?

I have been directed to no pertinent legislative history. In the abstract, the term "assignment" is broad enough to include the granting of a consensual lien. *See* BLACK'S LAW DICTIONARY 1342 (5th ed.1979) (defining term as "[a] transfer . . . of the whole of any property . . . or any estate or right therein."). It is helpful, however, to have some history in mind. The Lanham Act was passed in 1946, prior to the general passage by the states of the Uniform Commercial Code, which uses the phrases "security agreement" and "security interest" to describe the granting of a consensual lien in personal property. In 1946, a "chattel mortgage" or "conditional sale" was the vehicle through which most consensual personal property liens were granted. Outside the sales context, to describe the grant of a security interest it was then common to refer to the grant of a "mortgage" rather than an "assignment," the term used in the Lanham Act. The term "hypothecation" was often used with respect to receivables. Thus ordinary language usage points away from treating the grant of a security interest as an "assignment" under the Lanham Act.

Two other considerations indicate the statute does not apply to security interest filings. First, its reference to the "successor to the business" suggests Congress had in mind an outright assignment in the context of the sale of an entire business of which the trademark is a part. Second, and perhaps more persuasive, Congress has expressly included consensual liens in the copyright recording system, thereby demonstrating its awareness of the possibility of such liens and its inclination to make manifest an intention to require their recording when that intention is present. *See* 17 U.S.C. §205 (providing for recording of "transfer" of copyright); 17 U.S.C. §101 (defining "transfer" to include "mortgage" or "hypothecation").

I therefore conclude that Trimarchi's security interest in the trademark is unperfected. The case law appears to be in uniform agreement.

Pointing to the national filing requirement for security interests in copyrights, Trimarchi suggests that a similar requirement for trademarks makes a great deal of sense. He cites a copyright case, *National Peregrine, Inc. v. Capitol Federal Savings and Loan Association (In re Peregrine Entertainment, Ltd.),* 116 B.R. 194 (C.D.Cal.1990). In that case, in the process of holding that filing with the United States Copyright Office is the proper method for perfection of security interests in copyrights, the district court espoused the virtues of mandatory national filing of such security interests. Those virtues may also be present as to trademarks. A proposed purchaser or lender might well find it more convenient and reliable to have just one filing office at which to ascertain both the registered ownership of a trademark and the existence of encumbrances on it. But my job is to apply the statute as Congress has written it. The *Peregrine* court was careful to point out the absence of any reference to security interests in the trademark statute and the consequent irrelevance of trademark cases.

It is of course unfortunate that the trademark statute is sufficiently vague to require judicial interpretation. This produced the understandable mistake made here. Security interests in patents present the same difficulty. *See* 35 U.S.C. §261 (requiring recording for "assignment" of patents without furnishing definition of "assignment"). Not even the copyright statute is totally consistent with the Uniform Commercial Code. All three statutes should be amended to place them in better harmony with the Code. *See* Alice Haemmerli, *Insecurity Interests: Where Intellectual Property and Commercial Law Collide,* 96 COLUM. L. REV. 1645 (1996) (noting difficulties and various proposals for reform). The problem was emphasized long ago in a leading treatise. *See* 1 GRANT GILMORE, SECURITY INTERESTS IN PERSONAL PROPERTY §13.1 (1965) (stating statutes such as copyright and patent statutes "pose intricate and difficult problems with respect to the interrelationship of state and federal law and the jurisdiction of state and federal courts – problems which remain largely unsettled and indeed unexplored.").

Being unperfected, Trimarchi's security interest is "subordinate" to a "person who becomes a lien creditor before the security interest is perfected." U.C.C. §9-301(1) [Ed.: *See* Revised Article 9 §9-317(a)(2).] As debtor in possession, the Debtor "may avoid any transfer of property of the debtor . . . that is voidable . . . by a [lien creditor]." 11 U.S.C. §544(a)(1). Hence Trimarchi's security interest is subordinate to the Debtor's rights as a lien creditor, and the Debtor may avoid that security interest.

The most difficult thing about transactions involving trademarks relates to the ambiguous nature of the rights that they create. Unlike patents and copyrights, trademarks are not recognized as property, in that the owner of a mark does not have a free right to transfer the mark. As Assignment 3 explains, the fundamental basis for protection of the mark is the notion that it benefits consumers by identifying the source of goods and services. Working from that premise, it is said that the law bars the assignment of a trademark "in gross." What that means is that the trademark cannot be assigned without the business that it identifies.

In the Lanham Act, that rule is reflected in the first sentence of Section 10(a), which states that a "mark . . . shall be assignable with the good will of the business in which the mark is used, or with that part of the good will of the business connected with the use of and symbolized by the mark." 15 U.S.C. §1060(a). For financing purposes, that restriction limits the types of transactions for which trademarks can be used as collateral, because there can be no "asset-based" financing of a trademark standing alone. Rather, for a trademark to serve as collateral that a lender can take if the loan goes unpaid, the trademark must be given along with the business itself. That is not to say that trademarks are not useful collateral — there are, after all, quite a large number of loans for which the entire business is given as collateral. It is to say, however, that lenders' rights against trademarks are more circumscribed than their rights against more traditional assets.

B.   Trade Secrets

The last major category of asset commonly characterized as intellectual property is the trade secret. In almost all states, the applicable rules are codified in a local version of the Uniform Trade Secrets Act (UTSA). The subject matter is quite broad, any "information . . . that . . . derives independent economic value . . . from not being generally known to, and not being readily ascertainable by . . . other persons." UTSA §1(4). Thus, the protection extends to any form of information that is commercially valuable, without proof of novelty or uniqueness, and without any formal requirement that it be fixed or useful for any particular tangible process.

Like the trademark, the protection afforded the trade secret is so limited that it is not even clear that the trade secret qualifies as "property" in any conventional sense. Essentially, trade secret laws protect against the tort of misappropriation of confidential business information. See UTSA §1(2) (defining "Misappropriation" to mean "acquisition of a trade secret . . . by improper means" or "disclosure or use of a trade secret of another without . . . consent by a person who . . . used improper means to acquire knowledge of the trade secret"). On the other hand, because protections are limited to confidential information, protection is lost if the "owner" does not use reasonable precautions to maintain secrecy. See UTSA §1(4) (limiting the definition of "Trade secret" to information subject to "efforts that are reasonable under the circumstances to maintain its secrecy"). Because there is no formal registry or verification of the status of a particular trade secret — the information is secret — trade secrets do not have any particular term. Theoretically, at least, they could be protected forever.

Because there is no federal statutory protection of trade secrets (beyond statutes criminalizing certain forms of espionage that involve trade secrets), there is no doubt that security interests in trade secrets are governed by Article 9 of the Uniform Commercial Code. To the extent that they involve property of any kind (other than tort claims), they are protected by a security interest in general intangibles, perfected by a financing statement filed at the location of the debtor. UCC §§9-102(a)(42) (defining "[g]eneral intangible"), 9-301(1) (providing for filings in the location of the debtor), 9-310(a) (general rule requiring filing for perfection).

Two significant problems are involved in transactions that concern trade secrets. The first is the possibility (suggested above) that the lender's trade secret collateral might constitute (at least in part) a "commercial tort claim." Under the previous version of Article 9, tort claims generally were excluded as collateral. Old UCC §9-104(k). Under the revised version of Article 9, however, commercial tort claims are included. As defined in UCC §9-102(a)(13), that term includes any claim "arising in tort" where the plaintiff is a business (or the claim arises out of an individual's business), excluding damages for personal injury or death. Because claims for misappropriation of trade secrets arguably are nothing more than a specialized variety of tort claim, a lender's interest in the borrower's right to sue for violations of trade secret rights may constitute a commercial tort claim. Under Article 9, a security interest in a commercial tort claim requires a more specific description than other forms of collateral. See UCC §9-108(e)(1). That requirement could pose difficulty if the lender fails to notice that the collateral cannot be covered entirely by filings against "all general intangibles, including all trade secrets." See also UCC §9-204(b)(2) (security interest under an after-acquired property clause does not automatically attach to a commercial tort claim).

The other problem relates to the permutation of collateral. Federal intellectual property law does not protect trade secrets, but the concepts in trade secrets can be used to create protectable intellectual property: The company might decide to patent the ideas or use them to create a copyrightable software program (or both). If that happens, perfection in those derivative assets must come under the rules for patent and copyright lending discussed in the previous assignments. Again, a lender that sits on its rights as a perfected secured creditor claiming against "trade secrets" is likely to lose in those systems.

C. Web Sites and Domain Names

The last topic of this assignment involves assets that are unique to the new economy: the Web site and the domain name at which it is accessed. Not surprisingly, there is not any clear understanding of how lending transactions involving those assets will proceed. The pages that follow introduce the most salient problems that they raise.

A Web site itself is not protectable as intellectual property. Rather, it is a collection of software programs and data stored in a computer. Thus, a security interest in a Web site can be acquired by obtaining a security interest in the various components. For example, perfecting a security interest in the software requires attention to the issues discussed in Assignments 32 and 33. If some portion of the Web site involves patented technology (the shopping mechanisms, for example), the lender would want a security interest in that patent (as discussed in Assignment 34). To the extent that the name of the Web site has significance as a trademark (which often is the case), the lender would need to acquire a security interest in the trademark and related assets (following the rules discussed earlier in this assignment). Finally, an all-encompassing security interest under Article 9 would provide much protection for the remaining portion of the Web site.

The most difficult part relates to the domain name. The difficulty is that a domain name — however valuable it might be, and however much it might include the right to exclude others — is not property in any conventional way. Rather, it is a right to use that identifier under the system for allocating Internet addresses discussed in Assignment 3. Also, as discussed in Assignments 3 and 4, the domain name is distinct from the trademark: The right to a trademark does not include the right to use a domain name (although it might include the right to prevent certain uses of the domain name that confuse consumers or dilute the mark). Conversely, the right to a domain name gives no rights under trademark law at all.

To get an understanding of the problems, consider the following chronicle of the failed efforts of a creditor to get at a domain name. The creditor in this case is attempting to "garnish" a domain name. A "garnishment" is a proceeding in which an unsecured creditor attempts to collect a debt by (a) finding some person who owes money to the debtor (usually an employer, who owes salary to the employee); and (b) forcing the person who owes money to pay the money to the creditor instead of the debtor.

Network Solutions, Inc. v. Umbro International, Inc.

529 S.E.2d 80 (Va. 2000)

KINSER, Justice.

I. INTRODUCTION

In this case of first impression, we address the issue whether a contractual right to use an Internet domain name can be garnished. . . . [W]e . . . conclude that such a contractual right is . . . not subject to garnishment. Accordingly, we will reverse the judgment of the circuit court holding that the domain name registrations at issue in this appeal are garnishable.

II. FACTS AND PROCEEDINGS

In 1997, appellee Umbro International, Inc. (Umbro), obtained a default judgment and permanent injunction in the United States District Court for the District of South Carolina against 3263851 Canada, Inc., a Canadian corporation (the judgment debtor), and also against a Canadian citizen who owns the judgment debtor. That proceeding involved the judgment debtor's registration of the Internet domain name "umbro.com." In its order, the district court permanently enjoined the judgment debtor from further use of the domain name "umbro.com" and awarded judgment to Umbro in the amount of $23,489.98 for attorneys' fees and expenses. *Id.* at 8.

Umbro subsequently [had that judgment filed in the appropriate records in Virginia and then] instituted a garnishment proceeding that is the subject of this appeal.

In the garnishment summons, Umbro named Network Solutions, Inc. (NSI), as the garnishee and sought to garnish 38 Internet domain names that the judgment debtor had registered with NSI. Accordingly, Umbro asked NSI to place those domain names on hold and to deposit control of them into the registry of the circuit court so that the domain names could be advertised and sold to the highest bidder.

NSI answered the garnishment summons, stating that it held no money or other garnishable property belonging to the judgment debtor. Instead, NSI characterized what Umbro sought to garnish as "standardized, executory service contracts" or "domain name registration agreements." . . .

Umbro subsequently filed a motion for NSI to show cause why it had not deposited control of the judgment debtor's domain names into the registry of the circuit court. NSI opposed that motion . . . on the grounds that the . . . judgment debtor's domain name registration agreements with NSI are contracts for services and thus not subject to garnishment. . . .

In opposing the garnishment, NSI submitted an affidavit from its director of business affairs, who stated that domain names cannot function on the Internet in the absence of certain services being provided by a domain name registrar such as NSI. He further stated that NSI performs these domain name registration services pursuant to a standard domain name registration agreement.

After a hearing on Umbro's show cause motion, the circuit court determined that the judgment debtor's Internet domain name registrations are "valuable intangible property subject to garnishment." In a letter opinion, the court concluded that the judgment debtor has a possessory interest in the domain names registered with NSI. The court further found that there are no unperformed conditions with regard to the judgment debtor's contractual rights to use the domain names, that NSI is not being forced to perform services for entities with whom it does not desire to do business, and that the domain names are a "new form of intellectual property."

Accordingly, the court ordered NSI to deposit control "over all of the [j]udgment [d]ebtor's Internet domain name registrations into the [r]egistry" of the court for sale by the sheriff's office. Because of the intangible nature of the domain names, the court directed the sheriff's office to sell the domain names in whatever manner it "deem[ed] appropriate" after consultation with Umbro, and to notify NSI as to the name of the successful bidder for each domain name. According to the court's order, NSI then had to "transfer the domain name registration" to the successful bidder "as soon as commercially practicable following NSI's receipt of a properly completed registration application for the domain name from the winning bidder." This appeal followed.

Before analyzing NSI's assignments of error, we will discuss the Internet, the nature of domain names, and our statutory garnishment proceedings.

III.   THE INTERNET AND DOMAIN NAMES

The Internet, which began as a United States military computer network called ARPANET, is now a vast and expanding worldwide network of interconnected computers. Anyone connected to the Internet can access an exponentially expanding wealth of information through an array of communication methods such as electronic mail, electronic mailing list services known as listservs, chat rooms, newsgroups, and the World Wide Web (the Web). The Web is probably the most widely known and utilized method of communication on the Internet. In simple terms, the Web consists of information or documents presented on "pages". Pages may contain 'links' to other pages either within the same set of data files ('Web site') or within data files located on other computer networks.

Each method of communicating on the Internet depends on the use of a unique domain name . . . to locate a specific computer or network. Domain names have been compared to trademarks, addresses, or telephone numbers, but domain names, addresses, and telephone numbers, unlike some trademarks, are unique.

Each "host" computer that is "more-or-less permanently" connected to the Internet is assigned its own "Internet Protocol" (IP) number or address, which specifies the location of the computer. The IP number is comprised of four groups of numbers, with each group separated by a decimal point called a "dot." Because Internet users can more readily remember a name as opposed to a lengthy sequence of numbers composing an IP number, each individual computer or network also has an alphanumeric name called a "domain name." Reading from right to left, each portion of a domain name identifies a more specific area on the Internet, and as with IP numbers, is separated by a "dot." For example, in this Court's domain name, courts.state.va.us, "us" is the top-level domain, and is a country code or identifier which signifies that the domain name is registered in the United States. "[V]a," the second-level domain, indicates a sub-network used in the Commonwealth of Virginia; "state," the third-level domain, describes a sub-network used by the state government of Virginia; and "courts" further indicates a computer used by Virginia's judiciary.

If an Internet user knows the domain name for a particular Web site, such as this Court, the user can type the name into a Web browser and access that site directly without having to conduct what may be a time-consuming search. Even when a user does not know the specific domain name for a Web site, the user can often deduce the name and still find the site without performing a search. Most businesses on the Internet use the "com" top-level domain. Thus, a user could intuitively find a company's Web site by typing into a Web browser the corporate or trade name, such as "umbro.com." Because the second-level domain name, i.e., "umbro" in the example, must be exclusive, a company would obviously want to use its recognized name in the second level of its Internet domain name. The advantage of having such a domain name thus explains the value that is attached to some domain names and the reason why litigation has occurred between trademark owners and domain name holders.

NSI's role in the Internet domain name system is to manage certain domain name registrations. At one time, NSI held the exclusive right, pursuant to a contract with the National Science Foundation, to assign Internet domain names using the top-level domains "gov," "com," "org," "net," and "edu," *see id.,* but it now shares that right with other domain name registrars. . . .

In assigning the second-level domain names, NSI performs basically two services. NSI first compares applications with a database of existing domain names to prevent the registration of identical second-level domain names. NSI then matches the domain name to the corresponding IP number for the desired Web site. Domain names are available essentially on a first-come, first-serve[d] basis.

NSI performs these services pursuant to domain name registration agreements. NSI does not independently verify a registrant's right to use a domain name, but does require a registrant to make certain representations and warranties, such as certifying that the registrant has the right to use the domain name and that such use does not interfere with the rights of another party.

A registrant also agrees to be bound by NSI's "Domain Name Dispute Policy." In accordance with that policy, when litigation arises with regard to the registration and use of a domain name, NSI deposits control over the domain name into the registry of a court by furnishing the plaintiff in such litigation with a "registry certificate." In such instances, NSI agrees to be bound by the provisions of any temporary or final court orders regarding the disposition of a domain name without being named a party to the litigation, provided the domain name registrant is named as a party. The terms of the "Domain Name Dispute Policy" also authorize NSI, in its sole discretion, "to revoke, suspend, transfer or otherwise modify a domain name registration upon thirty (30) calendar days prior written notice, or at such time as [NSI] receives a properly authenticated order from a court . . . requiring the revocation, suspension, transfer or modification of the domain name registration."

NSI has also developed a procedure that allows a new domain name registrant to acquire a previously registered domain name with the consent of the former registrant of that name. The old registrant relinquishes its domain name registration, and the new registrant agrees to be bound by the terms of NSI's current

"Domain Name Registration Agreement" and "Domain Name Dispute Policy." NSI requires the old and new registrants to execute a form agreement titled "Registrant Name Change Agreement[,] Version 3.0 — Transfers" in order to effect this change.

IV. GARNISHMENT PROCEDURES

Under Virginia law, a judgment creditor can enforce a judgment for money by requesting the clerk of the court where the judgment was rendered to issue a writ of fieri facias and then by delivering that writ to a "proper person" of the court for execution. Code §8.01-466. The writ commands the officer "to make the money therein mentioned out of the goods and chattels of the person against whom the judgment is." Code §8.01-474. When property of a judgment debtor is not capable of being levied on, as in the case of intangible personal property, such property is nevertheless subject to the execution lien upon delivery of the writ to a sheriff or other officer.

Garnishment, like other lien enforcement remedies authorizing seizure of property, is a creature of statute unknown to the common law, and hence the provisions of the statute must be strictly satisfied. As pertinent here, a judgment creditor can institute garnishment proceedings if "there is a liability" on a third person to the judgment debtor. Code §8.01-511. "Liability" in this context means a "legal obligat [ion]", "enforceable by civil remedy," "a financial or pecuniary obligation," or a "debt." Black's Law Dictionary 925 (7th ed.1999).

"[A] proceeding in garnishment is substantially an action at law by the judgment debtor in the name of the judgment creditor against the garnishee, and therefore the judgment creditor stands upon no higher ground than the judgment debtor and can acquire no greater right than such debtor . . . possesses." *Lynch v. Johnson,* 196 Va. 516, 521, 84 S.E.2d 419, 422 (1954). A garnishment summons does not create a lien itself, but, instead, is a means of enforcing the lien of an execution placed in the hands of an officer to be levied.

V. ANALYSIS

In its first assignment of error, NSI asserts that the circuit court erroneously concluded "that Internet domain names are a new form of intellectual property, separate and apart from the domain name services provided by NSI, in which the judgment debtor has a possessory interest." NSI argues that the registration services agreement is the only source of rights acquired by a registrant and that a "registrant receives only the conditional contractual right to the exclusive association of the registered domain name with a given IP number for a given period of time." In NSI's words, a domain name is "simply a reference point in a computer database . . . [or a] vernacular shorthand for the registration services that enable the Internet addressing system to recognize a particular domain name as a valid address." Thus, NSI contends that such services are not subject to [a creditor's] execution lien.

In response, Umbro contends that, when NSI processes a registrant's application and assigns a specific domain name to the registrant under NSI's first-come, first-serve policy, that registrant acquires the right to use the domain name for an initial period of two years, to exclude others from using the name, and to effect a transfer of the name by using NSI's "Registrant Name Change Agreement." Thus, Umbro posits that NSI not only agrees to associate a particular domain name with an IP number, thus making the domain name an operational Internet address, but also grants to the registrant the exclusive right to use a unique domain name for a specified period of time. That contractual right, according to Umbro, is the intangible property in which the judgment debtor has a possessory interest and that is subject to garnishment. . . .

Irrespective of how a domain name is classified, we agree with Umbro that a domain name registrant acquires the contractual right to use a unique domain name for a specified period of time. However, that contractual right is inextricably bound to the domain name services that NSI provides. In other words, whatever contractual rights the judgment debtor has in the domain names at issue in this appeal, those rights do not exist separate and apart from NSI's services that make the domain names operational Internet addresses. Therefore, we conclude that a domain name registration is the product of a contract for services between the registrar and registrant. A contract for services is not "a liability" as that term is used in §8.01-511 and hence is not subject to garnishment. *See Sykes v. Beal,* 392 F. Supp. 1089, 1094-95 (D. Conn.1975) (analyzing garnishment of services and concluding that automobile insurer's duty to defend is not garnishable); *cf. J. Maury Dove Co., Inc. v. New River Coal Co.,* 150 Va. 796, 827, 143 S.E. 317, 327 (1928) (where "contract contains mutual obligations and liabilities, or involve[s] a relation of personal confidence," one party cannot assign it without consent of other party); *McGuire v. Brown, Guardian,* 114 Va. 235, 242, 76 S.E. 295, 297 (1912) (holding contract for personal services is not assignable).

If we allow the garnishment of NSI's services in this case because those services create a contractual right to use a domain name, we believe that practically any service would be garnishable. For example, if a satellite television customer prepaid the fee for a particular channel subscription, Umbro's position would allow garnishment of the subscription service. We also are concerned that a decision to uphold the garnishment at issue would be opening the door to garnishment of corporate names by serving a garnishment summons on the State Corporation Commission since the Commission registers corporate names and, in doing so, does not allow the use of indistinguishable corporate names. *See* Code §§13.1-630 and -631. *Cf. Gue v. The Tide Water Canal Co.,* 65 U.S. 257, 263, 24 How. 257, 16 L.Ed. 635 (1860) (a "franchise being an incorporeal hereditament, cannot . . . be seized under a [creditor's writ of execution]"). Without statutory changes, we are not willing to allow such results in Virginia simply because in today's case we are dealing with a unique and wholly new medium of worldwide human communication known as the Internet.

Nevertheless, Umbro attempts to draw a distinction between the judgment debtor's contractual right to use the domain names, which came into existence after NSI screened its database to guard against registering identical names and matched the judgment debtor's domain names to the corresponding IP numbers, and NSI's services that continue to make those domain names operational Internet addresses. We are not persuaded by Umbro's argument, although at least two jurisdictions have made a similar distinction with regard to telephone numbers.

[The court discussed cases permitting creditors to sell telephone numbers to repay unpaid debts, pointing out that the cases reach conflicting results.]

We are cognizant of the similarities between a telephone number and an Internet domain name and consider both to be products of contracts for services.

In our opinion, neither one exists separate from its respective service that created it and that maintains its continued viability.

Our view is not changed by the fact that NSI has developed a policy whereby control of Internet domain names is deposited with a court when the domain names are the subject of litigation and, as a part of that policy, agrees to abide by the terms of any court order regarding the domain names. That NSI routinely follows that procedure, in which the end result requires practically the same actions by NSI as those which would be required of it under the terms of the circuit court's order in this case, does not mean that NSI's Internet domain name services should be subject to garnishment. . . .

VI. CONCLUSION

Under Code §8.01-511, a garnishment summons may be issued with respect to "a liability on any person other than the judgment debtor.". . . In the present case, the only "liability" due on the part of NSI is the provision of its Internet domain name services to the judgment debtor. Code §8.01- 511. Although, as Umbro points out, domain names are being bought and sold in today's marketplace, we are not willing to sanction the garnishment of NSI's services under the terms of our present garnishment statutes. To do so would allow Umbro to step into the shoes of the judgment debtor. Even though the Internet is a new avenue of commerce, we cannot extend established legal principles beyond their statutory parameters.

For these reasons, we will reverse the judgment of the circuit court, dismiss the garnishment summons, and enter final judgment in favor of NSI.

Reversed and final judgment.

COMPTON, Senior Justice, with whom Chief Justice CARRICO joins, dissenting.

Relying heavily on decisions of federal trial courts, the majority concludes that a domain name registration is the product of a contract for services between the registrar and the registrant. The majority goes on to decide that such a contract is not subject to garnishment because it is not "a liability," as the term is used in Code §8.01-511. I disagree that the registration is a contract for services not subject to garnishment.

NSI, the garnishee, correctly acknowledges that the right to use a domain name is a form of intangible personal property. Code §8.01-501 clearly provides for an execution lien on intangible personal property, that is, property not capable of being levied upon. That lien attaches to the extent the judgment debtor has a possessory interest in the intangible property subject to the writ.

Therefore, the question becomes whether the judgment debtor has a possessory interest in the domain names it registered with NSI. In my opinion, the trial court correctly ruled that the judgment debtor, by virtue of the domain name registration agreements with NSI, has a current possessory interest in the use of the domain names, that is, a contractual right to the exclusive use of the names it has registered with NSI.

However, NSI contends that the judgment debtor's contractual rights are not subject to garnishment because they allegedly are contingent, dependent on unperformed conditions, or are like personal services. The majority erroneously has bought into this idea.

NSI's contractual obligation to the judgment debtor already is presently due, not contingent or akin to a personal service agreement. The judgment debtor has submitted its registration forms and paid the registration fees. NSI has completed the registration of the judgment debtor's Internet domain names under NSI's "first come, first served" policy, and the judgment debtor acquired the right to the exclusive use of the domain name for an initial period of two years.

Because NSI has received everything required to give the judgment debtor the exclusive right to use the domain names it registered, the contractual right, a valuable asset, is the intangible personal property in which the judgment debtor has a possessory interest. This right is a "liability" within the meaning of Code §8.01-511 and is subject to garnishment.

In my view, contrary to the majority's conclusion, this right exists separate and apart from NSI's various services that make the domain names operational Internet addresses. These services, as the trial court correctly ruled, are mere conditions subsequent that do not affect the garnishment analysis.

Consequently, I would affirm the judgment of the trial court.

The nature of rights in a domain name is a puzzling question. In some sense, it is much like a trademark: It is an exclusive right to identify a product (a Web site in this case) by an identifier that is unique to the particular product. Because it is often an asset of significant value to a business, it makes sense to think that a lender could use it as collateral, although it might be appropriate to include some "in-gross" restrictions similar to those that afflict trademark lenders. As the opinion suggests, however, there is no precedent or positive law specifically supporting such an approach.

And there certainly is something to the notion (prominent in *Umbro*) that a domain name in some respects is a right under a contract with the domain-name registrar. From that perspective, it would be natural to think of a domain name as a general intangible for which the domain-name registrar is the account debtor. See UCC §§9-102(a)(3) (defining "Account debtor" as "a person obligated on [a] general intangible"); 9-102(a)(42) (defining "General intangible"). It is difficult to see how that understanding would be burdensome on the registrar, because the services that the registrar provides are ministerial. Moreover, as discussed in Assignment 33, a loan that takes the borrower's interest in such a contract as collateral will not grant the lender any rights to force the registrar to recognize the lender unless the registrar's contract permits assignment of the domain name to a third party.

Thus, a lender taking an interest in a contract right normally takes several steps beyond the simple security agreement and financing statement. To the extent the domain name is a right under a contract with the registrar, the lender needs to do more than obtain the debtor's rights under that contract (the most that it could get from a security agreement and financing statement). It also needs to make sure that the steps are taken under those contracts to ensure that the asset retains its value. In this case, for example, the lender would like to make sure that the domain name is not lost for failure to pay the applicable fees or because of a technical failure to comply with some other requirement imposed by the registrar.

The ideal way to do that is to obtain a contractual arrangement with the contracting party (the "account debtor" for purposes of Article 9), in this case the registrar. In that arrangement, the contracting party would agree to give the lender a chance to resolve any problem before the contracting party terminates the contract that creates the lender's collateral. For example, the lender might try to persuade the registrar to provide five days' notice of a failure to pay fees (so that the lender could pay the fees) before terminating a domain-name registration. More aggressively, some lenders actually have the domain-name registration transferred into their names. That may sound odd, but it is not different from a traditional mortgage, in which the lender takes formal title to the collateral against which it advances a loan. In this context, it responds directly to the problem that a foreclosure under UCC §9-408 would not provide a right to use the name without the consent of the registrar.

At first glance, *Umbro* (and other cases like it) seem entirely unrelated to the problem discussed in the preceding paragraphs — how to perfect a security interest in a contract right. But the subtext of *Umbro* seems to be the notion that creditors should not be able to force the transfer of domain names. If that is the underlying impulse for the decision, then as applied to UCC transactions it would prevent creditors from obtaining an enforceable right to transfer the name. Ordinarily, a lender would respond to that problem by having the borrower agree in advance that the lender would have the right to transfer the name. Some lenders might have the borrower sign a power of attorney purporting to authorize the lender to sign the appropriate forms. Others might obtain such forms and have the borrower presign them at the time of the loan closing. Also, as the discussion above suggests, a lender might seek an agreement from the registrar at the time of the loan acknowledging the lender's authority to transfer the name.

The foregoing is offered only as an introduction to the problem. The design of these transactions is developing rapidly. Also, it is difficult at this point to predict how courts and legislatures will respond to those issues. The only thing that is clear is that lawyers, courts, and legislatures will confront them frequently in the years to come.

Relevant Glossary Entries

Internet Protocol (IP)
Protocol

Problem Set 38

38.1.   Stacy Vye calls to discuss the transaction involved in Problem 37.3 (a loan to fund the acquisition of a patent by Pheazer Pharmaceuticals). During the conversation, she comments that the pharmaceutical is marketed under the name EverHair. Does that comment prompt you to suggest any procedures for the transaction related to use of that name? Lanham Act §10(a), 15 U.S.C. §1060(a).

38.2.   Stacy has another transaction about which she wants to ask you. The borrower is a shipping company (Roadrunner Transit) that transports produce from farms in the southern part of Texas to Dallas, Houston, and San Antonio. The company has what it characterizes as a temporary cash-flow problem because a severe flood in Houston last week destroyed dozens of shipments that were en route through Houston. The total loss not covered by insurance exceeds a quarter of a million dollars.

The problem is that Roadrunner already has a lender with a security interest in "all inventory, all equipment, and all accounts receivables," so the only unencumbered asset on the balance sheet is the company's trademark. (It apparently did not occur to the existing lender, CountryBank, to take a security interest in the trademark.) Because the company has been in business for more than a hundred years and has a sterling reputation, Stacy believes that the trademark itself is worth several hundred thousand dollars. She believes that Roadrunner's underlying financial position is strong and would be perfectly willing to advance the money, but only if she could get control of the trademark. What is your advice? Lanham Act §10(a), 15 U.S.C. §1060(a).

38.3. Stacy calls you back one more time with regard to the Pheazer transaction from Problems 37.3 and 38.1. She says that she now believes that the "most valuable asset of all" is a production process that is used to manufacture EverHair. That process was not patented, largely because the existing manufacturer wants to keep it secret. The existing manufacturer has assured Pheazer that the process has been kept secret so that it has protection as a trade secret. What implications does this have for the loan transaction that you are planning?

38.4. Stacy's burgeoning IP-lending group has yet another loan under consideration. The borrower in this case is a company called Ecliptic Systems, Inc., which is working on software technology to help Web sites interact with mobile telephones and other wireless Internet-access devices. The company has been funded to date by a loan from Bulstrode Bank, for which Bulstrode took a security interest in all of the assets of the company, specifically including trade secrets. Bulstrode also filed a UCC-1, which specifically describes "all assets of the company, including present and future trade secret rights, patents, and patent applications."

Because of the dot-com bust of late 2000, Bulstrode has refused to advance any more funds to Ecliptic, bringing its work to a grinding halt. Stacy is impressed with the company's work and would like to advance funds, as long as she can get control of some of the products the company is developing (primarily software programs for sale to Web-site operators). Do you have any suggestions?

38.5. Your last matter of the day is a meeting with the developers of the renowned Web site *www.Textrade.com*. Because the site has been so successful, it has become quite valuable. The developers have decided to sell the site. The main question they have for you today is about how buyers will be able to finance the purchase. Because there is relatively little equity investment in Web sites these days, they expect that purchasers will need to borrow money from an institutional lender to pay for the purchase. They want to know if that will be feasible and, if so, how such a transaction would work.

A Note on Equity Financing of Startups

Many firms "bootstrap" their early operations using funds from friends or family, advances on credit cards, or funding from "angel" investors. However, at some point in time, most startup firms in the technology sectors (communications, software, and biotech) reach the stage of seeking institutional financing. Specialized lending institutions play an important role in financing the growth of technology startups. Because those firms are young and often have no revenues, the lenders generally require a security interest in the assets of the firm as a condition of the loan. The foregoing assignments discuss the legal rules that facilitate loan transactions using the assets of technology companies as collateral.

That lending, however, is not as important as equity financing, in which investors obtain an ownership interest in the firm, rather than a simple right to repayment of the funds loaned to the firm. The most important source of that equity financing is the venture capital firm. The role of the venture capitalist is important in understanding the material you have just read, because the venture capitalist and the technology lender have a symbiotic relationship, in the sense that backing from a venture capital firm generally makes banks more willing to extend credit to startups. From the bank's perspective, the principal source of repayment is likely to be a later round of funding by the venture capitalist. From the perspective of the venture capitalist, that lending is desirable because it provides an additional source of funds that can "lengthen the runway" of time that the firm can survive between rounds of venture capital funding. Because the return sought by the bank is lower than the return sought by the venture capitalist, bank lending also lowers the terminal value that the firm must attain for the venture capitalist to receive a suitable return. See Ronald J. Mann, *Secured Credit and Software Financing*, 85 CORNELL L. REV. 134, 153-165 (1999).

An understanding of the venture capital industry is important to an understanding of electronic commerce in this country, because venture capitalists have contributed to the development of most of the successful electronic commerce businesses (including Amazon.com, Apple Computer, Compaq, eBay, and Sun Microsystems). Even in 2003 (a very slow year), venture capitalists in the United States invested more than $18 billion in portfolio firms.

The leading role of the venture capital industry is an unusual — almost unique — feature of American entrepreneurial organization. The reasons why it has been so much more successful here than in other countries are not clear, but they probably involve some combination of the relative importance of capital markets and relative unimportance of banks in financing major corporations and also the rise of large pension funds (with assets that commonly are invested with venture capitalists). See Curtis J. Milhaupt, *The Market for Innovation in the United States and Japan: Venture Capital and the Comparative Corporate Governance Debate*, 91 NW. U. L. REV. 865 (1997); Bernard S. Black and Ronald J. Gilson, *Venture Capital and the Structure of Capital Markets: Banks Versus Stock Markets*, 47 J. FIN. ECON. 243 (1998). For comparative purposes, in 2003 venture capitalists in Japan (with an economy almost half as big as that of the United States) invested less than $2 billion in Japanese portfolio firms. Although there has been less discussion of the point, it also seems plain that the bank lending to technology startups is more common in this country than elsewhere, giving technology startups in the United States a considerable advantage.

Because this textbook focuses on how traditional commercial law topics apply in the context of electronic commerce, it is not practical to include an in-depth analysis of venture capital financing, which is driven by corporate and tax issues that cannot readily be covered in an abbreviated way. Nevertheless, a brief discussion of the basics of venture capital financing provides some context for the material in this text.

For present purposes, the most important point is the difference between the perspective of the bank making a traditional loan and the perspective of the venture capitalist. The commercial bank lender makes loans that provide short-term working capital or the purchase price for specific productive assets. In the first case, banks expect to be repaid out of future cash flow of the firm. In the second case, banks expect to be repaid out of the profits to be earned from exploiting the asset. In either case, banks rely heavily in underwriting their transactions on the historical performance of the firm as the best indicator of likely cash flow and profitability in the future.

Venture capitalists, by contrast, make investments in relatively early-stage firms based on predictions of future performance. Because venture capitalists rely on predictions rather than past success, many of the firms in which venture capitalists invest fail. Accordingly, venture capitalists can profit only if they receive a high return on the investments that are successful. They ordinarily invest by receiving stock (usually convertible preferred stock) in the firms in which they invest — often called "portfolio" firms because the typical venture capital fund invests in a sizeable portfolio of firms. Thus, traditional venture capital investment can be distinguished from angel financing, which often is less formal and usually precedes venture capital financing. See JOHN MAY AND CAL SIMMONS, EVERY BUSINESS NEEDS AN ANGEL (2001). It also is distinct from strategic investments by technology firms like Intel and Xerox that have tried to facilitate the growth of firms with technology complementary to their own. See HENRY CHESBROUGH, OPEN INNOVATION: THE NEW IMPERATIVE FOR CREATING AND PROFITING FROM TECHNOLOGY ch. 6 (2003).

A venture capital firm might receive hundreds of proposals a year from entrepreneurs seeking funding. Depending on market conditions and the quality of the proposals, they might meet with about one in ten of the entrepreneurs and seriously consider one in ten of those with whom they meet. For companies seeking funding for the first time, the process is likely to involve an intensive assessment of everything about the entrepreneur's prospects, including not only the quality of the technology, but also the plans for profiting from exploiting the technology, the past experience of the executive team, and references from other successful entrepreneurs and investors. Among other things, the venture capitalists focus on the potential size of the market in which the firm would operate, how much of that market the firm could expect to gain, how the firm would defend itself against competition (whether through IP protection, first-mover advantage, or the like), and how the firm might "exit" in a successful way (more on that topic below). Generally, the investors are looking for some special spark or "secret sauce" that would allow the firm to distinguish itself from competitors in a way that cannot readily be duplicated. In the last decade, venture capitalists in the

United States increasingly have focused on technology companies, as the most likely sectors in which to find the returns that can make their investments profitable.

Also, for obvious reasons, venture capitalists tend to specialize in particular technology sectors and in firms at particular stages: Very early startups face different problems than more mature firms closer to making and distributing products. For example, firms at the "seed" financing stage are likely to be largely devoted to research and development activities, and thus will receive financing tailored to the needs of those activities. Early-stage financing might focus more on revenue-generating activities, such as staff and expenditures for sales and marketing. Still further along, later-stage firms might be going into active production (depending on the nature of technology) and thus might require resources for manufacturing and distribution.

If the venture capitalist decides to invest, it will enter into a complex relationship with the portfolio firm. (You can see typical documents at www.nvca.org.) Generally, for the few firms that are selected following the evaluation process, a venture capitalist will make an offer of financing in the form of a nonbinding term sheet, which includes brief descriptions of such things as the amount to be invested, the capital structure the portfolio firm is to have, dividends to be required, liquidation preferences, various provisions to protect investors, provisions discussing the terms of future investments, and miscellaneous representations and warranties. The parties typically negotiate the term sheet extensively. When they have agreed on the basic terms in that document, they then will use those terms as the basis for drafting a set of longer and more formal closing documents, which will govern the relationship as the firm progresses.

Generally, the venture capitalist will receive a substantial ownership interest in the firm, based on the amount that the venture capitalist invests and the valuation that the parties agree upon for the portfolio firm. For example, if the parties agree that the portfolio firm has a value of $20 million and the venture capitalists invest an additional $5 million, the venture capitalists would receive a 20 percent interest in the firm ($5 million being 20 percent of $25 million). To ensure that the entrepreneurs retain a powerful incentive to make the portfolio firm succeed, it is important that the interests of equity investors not become too high. Aside from the quantity of equity ownership, the venture capitalists also are likely to exercise control directly through a variety of mechanisms. Among other things, at least one partner of the venture capitalist is likely to become a director of the portfolio firm; the financing documents will include protective covenants that limit the firm's business activities. Voting rules are likely to give the venture capitalist control over the timing and terms of any major decision such as a future round of investment, appointment and removal of key personnel, or a sale, public offering, liquidation, or the like.

For many reasons, including the need to maintain relatively close control over the direction of the portfolio firm, venture capitalists make their investments in stages called "rounds." Although there might be a "lead" investor in each round, there may be multiple venture capitalists in each round and often other investors as well (individuals or companies with strategic interest, perhaps as a future customer or supplier). The multiplicity of investors can be beneficial for the portfolio firm because of the different types of expertise different investors bring to the firm: potential customers, potential suppliers, individuals with important contacts or experience in a particular technology, venture capitalists with expertise in a particular market area, etc. It also is beneficial for the venture capitalists because they share risk and can take advantage of their differing strengths at different stages of the firm's development.

The timing between rounds differs based on the needs of the firm, but it is not unusual for a firm that succeeds to receive 3 to 5 rounds over the course of a five-year period of venture capital financing. Normally, investors in early rounds will retain a right to invest in all subsequent rounds. At each round, the firm will receive a new valuation. If the valuation is higher than it was at the preceding round, then the stock owned at a previous round will increase in value. If (as was often the case in the early years of this decade) the valuation falls from one round to the next — a "down" round — then the interests distributed at one round of financing often are diluted or even squeezed out by those who receive interests for investing in the down round.

The assets that venture capitalists invest typically are organized in separate funds, each of which has a relatively short life span (usually about a decade), at the end of which the fund is liquidated and the assets are distributed to the original investors from which the venture capitalists raised them (often pension plans and similar institutional investors). Thus, the ultimate aim of a venture capitalist is a successful exit in a relatively short time frame that will allow the venture capitalist to recoup its investment with a substantial profit.

The two methods of exit that are likely to be successful are an acquisition by an established firm in the industry or a public offering of securities in the portfolio firm. To use an example from Austin, a startup in the digital imaging sector might be so successful that Kodak decides it is easier to acquire the startup than to compete with it. Alternatively, as in the recent case of Google, a firm can develop products and a business model that are so successful that the firm can issue its own securities in the public markets. Ordinarily, the financing agreement will prevent the firm from being sold or issuing securities without the consent of the equity investors. If there is a successful exit, at that point the interest of the venture capitalist is likely to convert from preferred stock to common stock so that (after waiting periods established by contract and the securities laws) the venture capitalist can liquidate its interest, obtaining the profit that was the object of the investment in the first place.

In the more common scenario in which the firm languishes, venture capitalists effectively have considerable control over the decision to terminate the firm through the simple expedient of declining to invest in subsequent rounds. As discussed above, the agreements under which the venture capitalists invested also are likely to give them explicit control over the process by which any liquidation is to be conducted. In many cases the firm will be sold to a competitor that might have some use for the technology; IP protection is particularly important in that scenario because it makes it easier to identify and transfer specific assets. The potential for those transactions also is important to the lenders, because the ability to resell even failed technology helps to limit the losses the lenders incur when their portfolio borrowers fail.

When the firm is liquidated, it often will use an informal process called an assignment for the benefit of creditors (commonly called an ABC), which (in some states at least) tends to be cheaper and more expeditious than a bankruptcy proceeding. Generally, the choice between an out-of-court proceeding like an ABC and a bankruptcy proceeding will turn on some particular reason why bankruptcy would be useful. In some cases, creditors (often landlords) might insist on full payment of claims that would receive little in a bankruptcy proceeding. When important creditors take that view, those in control of the failing firm often will use bankruptcy to enforce a norm of equal loss-sharing among creditors. In other cases, the firm might have litigation involving its operations or about other matters related to its liquidation that can be most expeditiously conducted in a centralized bankruptcy forum. In cases that do not involve such disputes, however, the firm is likely to close its doors quietly, without any formal proceeding.

One of the most interesting aspects of the liquidation is the interaction between the entrepreneurs, the venture capitalists, and the lenders. In cases of failure, ordinarily the lenders are entitled to a claim on all of the assets of the firm before the equity investors (the venture capitalists and the entrepreneurs) can receive anything from the liquidation. It is regrettably the case that often liquidation will not even produce enough to repay the lender's debt — leaving the entrepreneur and the venture capitalists with nothing. In many lending contexts, those situations often become adversarial, as frustrations and tempers rise with the sinking fortunes of the borrower. In this context, however, it is much more common for the parties to cooperate in the shutdown of a failed portfolio firm. In this context, unlike in most types of lending, all of the parties are repeat players: The lenders depend on future business from future portfolio firms; the venture capitalists depend on the lenders to loan funds to their future portfolio firms and on the entrepreneurs to seek and accept venture capital financing; the entrepreneurs hope to obtain future funding from the lenders and the venture capitalists. Accordingly, all of the parties have an incentive to act cooperatively in the shutdown of failed portfolio firms. Those that deal sharply know that they will have difficulty in the future. Among other things, that means that the lender is much less likely to shut a firm down quickly than it might in other contexts. And it also means that a venture capitalist is much more likely to keep the lender well-informed about deteriorating conditions at a portfolio firm than an investor in a more conventional sector of the economy. Indeed, the solicitude often persuades venture capitalists to contribute additional funds in connection with the liquidation, solely to ensure that the liquidation goes smoothly. That is not to say that the venture capitalists protect lenders from losses on those transactions. It is to say, however, that they act much more carefully to limit those losses than borrowers that do not have the reputational and repeat-dealing ties that characterize this type of transaction.

Appendix A.   The History and Technology of Internet Addresses and Domain Names

A.   IP Addresses and the Domain-Name System

Computers, unlike humans, are quite happy to work with numeric addresses. Thus, as a technical matter, computers accessible by the Internet are identified by numeric IP addresses. As I write in 2004, IP addresses are still largely based on Version 4 of the IP protocol (IPv4), which uses IP addresses made up of twelve digits divided into four groups of numbers separated by decimals — e.g., 121.122.123.124. A total of about 4 billion unique IP addresses can be created using the IPv4 address-numbering system. The explosive growth in the number of computers connected to the Internet has led the Internet Engineering Task Force (an informal group that develops technical standards for the Internet), to come up with a new standard for IP addresses, known as Version 6 of the IP protocol (IPv6), or Next Generation IP (IPng). IPng will support many more IP addresses than IPv4, about 10^{36}. That will allow the number of computers and other devices (such as cellphones) that are connected to the Internet to continue increasing for years to come. Because there currently are about 6 trillion people on the earth (6×10^9), a shift to IPv6 would alter the number of available addresses per person from the current system of about 1 address for every thousand people to something on the order of 10^{27} available addresses per person.

It is not difficult to find out the IP address for any Internet-enabled computer that uses a recent version of the Windows operating system. The "Control Panel" (accessible from the settings menu on the Start button) provides information about network connections. By following the procedure outlined in the Help function accessible from the Control Panel, it is possible to determine whether the computer has a static or dynamic IP address. A static IP address is one that is permanently assigned to a computer. Because the number of IP addresses is limited, and because computers that access the Internet occasionally do not need to have a unique IP address, an Internet service provider often "dynamically" or "automatically" assign IP addresses. With dynamic IP addresses, a computer is assigned an IP number each time it accesses the Internet, which it surrenders when the session is complete. For example, AOL and Earthlink users use a different, randomly assigned IP address each time they log on to the Internet to check e-mail or surf the Web.

Because humans have a hard time remembering long strings of apparently random numbers, the domain-name system was devised to help humans locate resources on the Internet. Domain names uniquely identify computers connected to the Internet and are often recognizable as names or abbreviations. For example, *www.acm.org* is the domain name of the Web site of the Association for Computing Machinery, the oldest and one of the largest associations of computer professionals. This domain name includes an extension, known as a "top-level" domain, that is supposed to indicate something about the nature of the organization maintaining the Web site. In the *www.acm.org* example, the Association for Computing Machinery is a not-for-profit organization, ACM are its initials, and www identifies ACM's Web server, the particular computer within the ACM computer system that is providing the content.

Top-level domains (TLDs) currently include .com for commercial organizations, .edu for educational institutions, .mil for U.S. military agencies, .gov for U.S. government agencies, .net for network resources, and .org for other organizations. In addition to such "generic" top-level domains (gTLDs) there are also "country code" top-level domains (ccTLDs), such as .uk for the United Kingdom, .nl for the Netherlands, and .ca for Canada. In 2000, the decision was made to expand the number of gTLDs by seven: .aero for the air transport industry; .biz for businesses; .coop for cooperatives; .info for general unrestricted use; .museum for museums; .name for individuals; and .pro for professionals, such as attorneys, doctors, and accountants. Those domains are coming into effect as the second edition of this book goes to press.

A Uniform Resource Locator (URL) is the address of a particular resource, such as a Web page or particular graphic, on the Internet. For example, the URL *http://www.acm.org/education/overview.html* identifies the overview page of the education section of the Association for Computing Machinery Web site. The first part of the URL tells the browser software what application protocol to use. In this example, "http" identifies the Hypertext Transfer Protocol discussed above. (Addresses that begin with "ftp" refer to the File Transfer Protocol, another common application.) Next, the URL contains the domain name that identifies the particular computer on the Internet. In this example, that is the Web server used by the ACM. The next piece of information is the directory path, in this case the directory that holds files relating to education. Finally, the URL indicates which file on that computer is requested, in this example the overview page.

For all the computers connected to the Internet to translate domain names that are meaningful to humans into numbers that are meaningful to computers, there must be a standardized system for "resolving" domain names into IP addresses and vice versa. The Domain Name System (DNS) provides that mechanism. The DNS is distributed throughout the Internet. Within a domain, such as the ACM domain, there is a name server that stores information about where different computers and files within the ACM computer system can be found. When a message comes in from the Internet to the ACM system, the ACM system interprets the information in the URL and makes sure the data is sent to the proper location. The Internet in turn includes many lists of domain names and the IP addresses that correspond with them. When a computer needs to convert a domain name to an IP address, or vice versa, and it does not find the information within its own name server, it checks with one of the lists maintained on the Internet. So that the process of looking up domain names and IP addresses in these lists does not become unmanageable, the DNS is organized into zones. Most DNS directories only provide information about zones that physically are located near the computer hosting the directory. If a computer works through a series of directories in the prescribed order and is unable to find a DNS entry, it will report back that the DNS entry requested cannot be found or that the requested page cannot be displayed.

DNS directories are updated periodically to take account of new domain names and IP addresses and changes in existing entries. Because DNS directories are distributed around the world and because they are not maintained by a central authority but by various organizations helping to support the functioning of the Internet, changes in DNS entries may be made available to different Internet users at different times. At first glance that might seem to lead to a variety of difficulties. In practice, however, the lists are updated with sufficient promptness that it is a minor problem at best.

B. Governance of the Domain-Name System

When only a handful of computers were connected to the Internet, it was not difficult to keep track of the IP addresses assigned to each one. Dr. Jon Postel of the University of Southern California's Information Sciences Institute, was given responsibility for assigning blocks of IP addresses to computer networks. (Postel had been involved in the development of the Internet since its founding when he was a Ph.D. student in the computer-science department of the University of California at Los Angeles.) As the number of computers grew, however, it became apparent that a more formal system for managing IP addresses was needed. Thus, the DNS was created in 1985. The registration of domain names was handled first by the Stanford Research Institute and next by Network Solutions Inc. (NSI) under contracts with first the DoD and later the National Science Foundation (NSF). The Internet Name and Number Association (IANA), led by Postel, retained control over the process of allocating IP addresses even after the DNS was established.

The DNS was set up as a hierarchy, and generally continues to function as one. At the top of that hierarchy is the root-server system made up of thirteen root servers, and at the apex of the whole system is the central, or "A," root server. The root-server system maintains an authoritative list of the IP addresses of those computers that make up the DNS. In principle, control over the root-server system in general and over the A root server in particular carries with it the ability to control the DNS. Under the terms of its 1993 contract with the NSF, NSI was given responsibility for maintaining the A root server. In retrospect, it is clear that this was a sweeping grant of authority made without adequate consideration of its long-term political consequences. At the time, however, it seemed like a modest change, especially given that NSI had to cooperate with IANA to carry out its assigned role. In fact, much of the authority of NSI to carry out its function as domain-name registrar arose from its close working relationship with Internet old-timers such as Postel. Although the other twelve root-server operators were not legally bound to accept the authority of the A root server and conform the content of their files with that of the master copies maintained by Network Solutions, those operators in fact have done so.

By 1996, however, the relatively informal organization and operation of the DNS began to break down. NSF and NSI amended their agreement to permit NSI to charge a $50 annual fee to domain-name registrants, and NSI established a controversial "dispute resolution policy" that favored the owners of federally registered trademarks in disputes among parties interested in the same domain name. Postel and others associated with the Internet's early development responded to this growing controversy by suggesting that as many as 150 new generic top-level domains could be created, so that new registrars could be authorized to compete with NSI in the business of registering domain names. The owners of valuable trademarks resisted this approach because it would severely exacerbate the problem of "cybersquatting" they already had begun to face. Not surprisingly, NSI also fought hard against any diminution in its control over a franchise that was skyrocketing in value. Early in 1998, the United States government waded into the controversy first with a "green paper" and then with a "white paper" recommending the creation of a new, not-for-profit corporation that would manage domain names, IP addresses, and the root-server system. Later in 1998, the Internet Corporation for Assigned Names and Numbers (ICANN) was formed to take control of the system for managing domain names and IP address identifiers.

The legitimacy of ICANN's control over the DNS has been contested from its inception. The sudden and untimely death of Postel at exactly the moment that ICANN began operations in 1998 deprived it of whatever legitimacy it might have enjoyed from any association with him. ICANN's mandate as a not-for-profit organization is couched in terms of identifying or establishing a consensus among different constituencies of Internet users. Yet the procedures it has established to fulfill that mandate are at the same time too complex and too limited to achieve those objectives. As a result, many technologists and individual Internet users perceive ICANN as either woefully inept or the captive of special interests. Its harshest critics believe that it is a creature of multinational business interests trying to maximize the commercial value of their intellectual-property rights at the expense of the open, public character of the Internet.

Whether ICANN will be able to retain its position at the apex of the DNS hierarchy remains unclear. When ICANN finally authorized the creation of additional gTLDs in 2000, many members of the Internet community were unhappy with the limited number and appeal of the new gTLDs ICANN chose. Since 1997, when Postel and his colleagues first proposed expanding the number of gTLDs, individuals and businesses have been operating "alternative" unofficial domain-name systems outside the official hierarchy. Participants in that alternative DNS currently compete with ICANN-accredited domain-name registrars by offering a wider range of domain names than ICANN currently recognizes. To access domain names in that alternative system, such as .church, .family, .golf, or .kids, an Internet browser must be reconfigured by downloading and installing software that permits recognition of unofficial domain names. If those alternative DNS systems continue to grow in popularity, the monopoly granted to ICANN to control the official root-server system may eventually become irrelevant.

C.   Registration of a Domain Name

ICANN oversees registration of domain names for official gTLDs. The process for country-code top-level domains (ccTLDs) is less uniform; ICANN supervises them in some cases, and others are supervised through independent registrar entities selected by the country in question. Reflecting the concern about the monopoly over domain-name registration services held by NSI under the old system, ICANN was given a mandate to create competition in the market for domain-name registrations. Thus, ICANN already has accredited over 100 registrars. Those registrars each have the ability to take the relevant information for registering a domain name and then to cause the entry to be made in ICANN's master records. Those registrars essentially compete with each other on prices and service, acting collectively as intermediaries between the registrants and ICANN.

To register a domain name, an applicant must normally submit several pieces of information. That information is maintained in the "WHOIS" database. (The WHOIS database may be accessed from the Web sites of certain domain-name registrars, such as Network Solutions.) Searches of the WHOIS database provide information about who controls a particular domain name, including the name, postal address, and e-mail address of the registrant; the name and contact information for an "administrative contact" (so that the registrar knows to who it should submit bills when it is time to renew the registration); the name and contact information for a "technical contact" (so that people know who to call when experiencing problems caused by the computer system associated with the domain name); the dates the registration was granted and will expire; and the IP addresses of two different host computers used to maintain the Web site.

Because domain-name registrars do not undertake to check (much less update) the accuracy of the information they submit to that database, it has the potential to be wholly unreliable. On the other hand, in most serious disputes the information is likely to be relatively good, because the contending cybersquatter in fact wants very much to be contacted.

It is important to realize the distinction between the domain name and the Web site. The domain name is an identifier for the site, wherever the site might be maintained in the physical world. The Web site itself is a set of computer files to which the domain name gives access. Thus, even after a registrant obtains a domain name, the registrant must make separate arrangements to have the Web site hosted on a server connected to the Internet, and then advise its registrar of the IP addresses for those computers, so that Web browsers can locate the site by entering the alphabetic domain name.

Glossary

ACH: *See* Automated Clearing House

Active Server Pages (ASP): Web pages that include "scripts" or small programs that are processed before a server sends the page to the browser that requested it. For example, an ASP may combine data from a database with static Web-page content to create a customized page "on the fly" to display to the end user that requested the data.

ActiveX: a group of programming tools and technologies developed by Microsoft. Programs written for the ActiveX environment can perform functions similar to those of Java Applets.

American National Standards Institute (ANSI): a private, non-profit organization that administers and coordinates the United States voluntary standardization and conformity assessment system. ANSI is the United States representative to the International Organization for Standardization (ISO). *See* www.ansi.org.

API: *See* Application Programming Interface

Applet: a little "application" or small computer program that runs within another application, for example, in the browser application of a visitor to a Web site.

Application Programming Interface (API): a set of tools for building software applications that creates an interface between different programs or between a program and an operating system. Using APIs permits programmers to access information or functions provided by other programs or an operating system, thus streamlining the development and operation of the program making the requests of the other software programs.

Application Service Provider (ASP): a business that manages and distributes software and network services to its customers. Important because the software typically resides on the server of the ASP instead of the computers of the ASP's customers.

Archival Storage Media: digital storage media used to create and preserve highly reliable, secure copies of records that must be permanently stored.

ASP: *See* Active Server Pages or Application Service Provider

Asymmetric Cryptography: cryptography that uses two different but related "keys" or secret numbers. One is a "public key," which can be widely shared without compromising the security of the encryption, and the other is a "private key" that must be kept secret and under the control of a single individual or entity in order to avoid compromising the security of the encryption.

Authentication System: a system for confirming the accuracy or validity of something that is accessed by means of a computer network, most commonly the identity of an individual using a remote computer to communicate online.

Automated Clearing House (ACH): a financial services organization that provides secure electronic funds transfer services within the United States. Common types of ACH transactions include direct deposit of payroll and direct debit of regular monthly bills such as mortgage payments. Many regional ACHs work together to provide a nationwide electronic funds transfer system under the supervision of the National Automated Clearing House Association (NACHA). *See* www.nacha.org.

B2B: *See* Business to Business

B2C: *See* Business to Consumer

Backup System: permits electronic records to be copied so that they can be preserved in the event of equipment failure or other problem that makes the primary copies of the records unavailable. For backup systems to be useful, records must be copied to a backup system on a regular basis, such as daily or weekly.

Bandwidth: the term derives from "width of a band of electromagnetic frequencies," and is commonly used to describe the speed at which data can flow through a network. For example, a modem on a personal computer connected to conventional phone line may have a "bandwidth" of 28.8K (28,800) bits per second of data, which would be half the bandwidth of a modem that could send and receive 57.6K bits per second of data.

Bill of Lading: a document of title issued by a party in the business of transporting goods.

Bit: a measure of data stored within a computer, derived from "binary digit." A bit has a single binary value, which can be either "1" or "0" and is the smallest unit of information used by computers.

Biztalk: a registered trademark of Microsoft; the name of a proprietary standard for XML being developed and promoted by Microsoft. *See* www.biztalk.org; www.ebxml.org.

BOLERO: a project designed to replace paper bills of lading with an electronic equivalent. BOLERO is sponsored by SWIFT (Society for Worldwide Interbank Financial Telecommunication, an international electronic funds transfer service provider) and TT Club (Through Transport Club, a mutual insurance service for shippers). *See* www.bolero.net.

Bot: short for "robot" or machine that labors in the place of a human being; a computer program that acts on behalf of a human. The most commonly used bots are those used by search engines and others to search the Internet, copy relevant information and transmit copies back to the bot's source. The term robot first appears in Karel Capek's 1921 play *Rossum's Universal Robots;* he coined the term from the Czech "robota" meaning compulsory labor.

Brick and Mortar: a business that has a material world existence but not an on-line existence. Before the advent of networked computer systems and low-cost telecommunications, virtually all businesses were "brick and mortar" businesses.

Bricks and Clicks: a business that has both a material world "brick and mortar" existence and an on-line existence.

Brochureware: Web content based on the content of a paper brochure that has not been redesigned to take advantage of the new possibilities Internet communications offer.

Business Process Re-engineering: the analysis and design of work processes and information flows within an organization aimed at improving the efficiency of the organization.

Business to Business (B2B):   an Internet commerce model based on transactions between businesses rather than between businesses and consumers

(B2C). B2B commerce may include but is not limited to the traditional concept of "wholesale" (sale of goods in large quantities from one merchant to another that will resell them), which can be contrasted with "retail" (sale of goods or services in small quantities directly to the ultimate consumer). B2B commerce includes other types of transactions, such as procurement of raw materials for production, or "maintenance, repair, and operations" ("MRO") requirements.

Business to Consumer (B2C): an Internet commerce model based on transactions between a business and a consumer. B2C transactions are normally a "retail" transaction (the sale of goods or services in small quantities directly to the ultimate consumer).

Byte: a measure of data stored within a computer, derived from "binary term." A byte is equal to eight bits and is a unit of information more commonly used in programming than a bit.

CA: *See* Certification Authority

CA Root: the CA at the pinnacle of a CA hierarchy within a PKI (Public Key Infrastructure). A CA "certifies" a digital signature by signing a certificate containing a public key and information about the key; a party wishing to rely on that certificate needs to be able to validate the signature of the CA. The CA therefore includes a digital signature certificate to permit the relying party to validate its signature, but then the relying party needs to be able to validate the signature of the party that certified the CA's signature. The "root" CA is the CA for which no further validation is possible within a PKI.

CERT: a project once known as the "Computer Emergency Response Team" sponsored by the Software Engineering Institute of Carnegie Mellon University. The current name of this project is the CERT Coordination Center, and CERT is no longer an acronym. *See* www.cert.org.

Certificate Policy: a document describing the rules that apply to the members of a community participating in a PKI. A certificate policy may include rules applicable to different transaction types or communication procedures and may have a much wider scope than a certificate practice statement. The term "certificate policy" was originally defined by the IETF RFC 2527.

Certificate Revocation List (CRL): as part of its responsibilities in managing a PKI, the CA will publish a list of all certificates that have been revoked. Once a certificate has been revoked, then no one should rely on the contents of that certificate, for example, to associate a particular individual with a digital signature that can be validated using the public key in the revoked certificate.

Certification Authority (CA): a trusted third-party organization within a PKI that issues digital certificates used to create digital signatures and public-private key pairs.

Certification Practice Statement: a document describing the practices of a certificate authority in issuing and validating certificates and maintaining a PKI. Unlike a certificate policy, a certificate practice statement focuses more narrowly on computer security issues related to managing the use of certificates. The term "certification practice statement" was originally defined by the IETF RFC 2527.

CGI: *See* Common Gateway Interface

Cipher: a method of transforming text to disguise its meaning. The term derives from the Arabic "sifr," meaning empty or zero.

Ciphertext: as opposed to plaintext, ciphertext is transformed or encoded text. Until it has been decoded, ciphertext is unreadable.

Circuit Switching: a network technology that requires a complete circuit to be maintained in order for communications to take place. Circuit switching consumes more network resources than packet switching because the sender and the recipient must maintain a single, dedicated connection in order for communication to take place. Circuit switching produces much higher quality of service than packet switching, and so is used for voice telephone services. Although it is possible to make telephone calls using packet-switching technology, the result is poor sound quality, delays, and interruptions in communications as packets of data are reassembled for the listener.

Clickstream Data: information collected by an Internet commerce site about what content on its Web site visitors viewed, when it was viewed; how long it was viewed; whether a visitor is a new or repeat visitor; and the site that referred the visitor to the site collecting the data.

Clickwrap Terms: standard form contract terms presented to a visitor to an Internet commerce site to which the visitor manifests assent by "clicking" with a mouse on a graphical user interface. Clickwrap is derived from "shrinkwrap," a term that described the plastic wrapper placed around boxes of software distributed through bricks-and-mortar retail outlets; once a purchaser broke the "shrinkwrap," the purchaser was supposed to be bound by the terms of the software license contained within the box.

Closed PKI: a PKI in which the universe of all possible participants can be identified and access to the PKI can be limited to those participants.

Commercial off the Shelf (COTS):   ready-made products that can be easily obtained; the term is derived from U.S. military procurement systems. COTS software is software that provides electronic-commerce functions at a reasonable price but with limited customization.

Common Gateway Interface (CGI):   a method of passing information back and forth between an Internet site and its visitors; it is a "common" gateway interface because it can work with many different Web-programming languages and applications. CGI is part of the Hypertext Transfer Protocol (HTTP) that defines the World Wide Web.

Compiler: a program that converts statements written by human programmers in a specific programming language ("source code") into a form of software that is machine-readable ("object code").

Computer Database: a large collection of information organized in such a form that it can be readily stored and retrieved using a computer.

Computer Network: a system of computers connected by communication lines and common network protocols to permit the sharing of data.

CONTU: *See* National Commission on New Technological Uses of Copyrighted Works

Cookie: a text file stored on the hard drive of a visitor to a Web site that permits the Web site to recognize the visitor on a subsequent visit to the site; in some cases a cookie might also be used to identify the Web sites that the end user has visited recently.

Cookie-Cutter Software: software that will restrict the types of cookies a user's system will accept.

COTS: *See* Commercial off the Shelf

Cracker: an individual who uses his or her computer expertise maliciously to break into other people's computer systems.

Crawling: accessing a site by software robot or spider, normally in order to identify and copy information that is then transmitted back to the party that launched the spider.

Credit Header Information: information such as an individual's name, address, previous addresses, telephone number, and social security number that is included in the "header" section of a credit report. Credit header information is not protected by the Fair Credit Reporting Act in the same way that credit information included in a credit report is.

CRL: *See* Certificate Revocation List

Cross-Certification: The issuance by one CA of a certificate to another CA for use in the second CA's PKI; cross-certification permits digital signature certificates issued for use within one PKI to be used in a second PKI. The term "cross-certification" was originally defined by the IETF RFC 2527.

Cryptography: the process of ending and decoding messages whose meanings have been hidden.

Cryptosystem: a process that encrypts and decrypts text.

Cybersmear: an unsubstantiated charge or accusation made on the Internet.

Cybersquatting: bad faith, abusive registration and use of the distinctive trademarks of others as Internet domain names, with the intent to profit from the goodwill associated with those trademarks.

Database: a collection of data that is organized so that its contents can easily be accessed, managed and updated.

Data Mining: the analysis of data for relationships that have not previously been discovered.

Data Warehouse: a specialized database that is used to spot emerging market trends and relationships in customer data that would not otherwise be apparent to managers.

Decryption: the process of converting a coded message into intelligible form.

Deep Links: hyperlinks to a page deeper within a Web site than its main page or index page.

Deliverables: the items, usually intangible, to be delivered within the context of a business project; commonly used to describe the subject matter of a software development contract.

Denial-of-Service Attack: attack on a networked information system that deprives authorized users of access by forcing system resources to be allocated to responding to the attack.

Description Meta Tag: a meta tag that identifies a description of the site that can be displayed by a search engine written in a manner that will inform potential visitors of the character of the site.

Digital Signature: an electronic signature created using asymmetric cryptography.

DNS:　domain name system

Download:　transmission of information from one computer system to another, usually smaller one.

Dumpster Diving:　sorting through trash to find passwords or other sensitive information.

Dutch Auction:　a way of selling multiple, identical items in an auction. Items are sold to the highest bidders at the lowest successful bid price. For example, if a seller offered three gnomes for sale and there were four bidders that bid $1, $2, $3, and $4 respectively, then the gnomes would be sold to the three highest bidders for $2 each.

ebXML:　an open, public XML standard-setting effort sponsored by UN/CEFACT (United Nations Centre for Trade Facilitation and Electronic Business) and OASIS (Organization for the Advancement of Structured Information Standards). *See* www.ebxml.org; *cf.* www.biztalk.org.

Electronic Data Interchange (EDI):　a standard format for exchanging business data.

Electronic Signature:　a general term for any electronic equivalent of a manual signature; *cf.* Digital Signature.

Encryption:　the process of encoding a message so that its contents become unintelligible to any but the intended recipient.

Encryption Algorithm:　the procedure used to encrypt or decrypt a message; modern encryption algorithms are executed by computer systems.

End User:　the ultimate user of a finished product.

E-SIGN:　Electronic Signatures in Global and National Commerce Act, Pub. L. No. 106-229, 114 Stat. 464 (2000) (codified at 15 U.S.C. §§7001-7031).

eXtensible Markup Language (XML):　a system used to "mark up" content so that the structure and meaning of the content can be interpreted by machine processes. XML is a variation of HTML, the markup language used to format World Wide Web content so that it can be displayed in the end user's browser software. Like HTML, XML requires "tags" to be inserted in documents to permit different kinds of content to be distinguished. Unlike HTML, XML is not limited to document formatting, but is "extensible" so it can be expanded to permit many different kinds of information to be formatted in a way that can be interpreted by software programs. XML is also a variation of Standard Generalized Markup Language (SGML), a markup language developed in the 1980s to define document structures.

Fair Use:　a doctrine in copyright law that permits certain uses of copyrightable materials even though the uses infringe the exclusive rights that copyright law grants to authors. Less commonly, an analogous and still-nascent doctrine in trademark law.

Feature Creep:　a problem that arises once a supplier and its client have agreed on a project specification, when the client modifies the project specification to add new features not originally envisaged. Feature creep commonly results in delay, additional expense, or even the failure of a project.

FEDI:　*See* Financial EDI

File Transfer Protocol (FTP):　a communications protocol that permits files to be shared over the Internet. Other widely used Internet communications protocols include HTTP and SMTP.

Finance Lease: a transaction formally structured as a lease, but better characterized as a financing transaction designed to permit the lessee to acquire the leased asset over time; to be distinguished from a "true" lease, which grants temporary possession of a piece of personal property in return for lease payments to the lessor.

Financial EDI (FEDI): the electronic transfer of payments together with payment-related information, all in a machine-readable format.

Firewall: a software program installed at the gateway to a computer network that restricts communications to and from the computer network, permitting only those communications that are consistent with the security policies of the network administrator.

First-Sale Doctrine (also known as the rule of exhaustion): a copyright doctrine limiting the ability of the copyright owner to control the behavior of a purchaser of copyrighted materials after the sale is completed.

Five-Nines Uptime: a standard used in network services agreements to require that services will be available 99.999 percent of the time; the concept of "five nines" is widely discussed in marketing but rarely achieved in practice.

Frames: a method of presenting Web content from multiple sources. A Web page that contains frames provides links to other content in order to create a new combination of materials for the visitor to the framing site. Visitors to the framing site may not be aware that content being presented as an integrated whole is actually taken from disparate sources. Because early versions of Internet browser software cannot display content containing frames, Website developers may create two different versions of a single site—one that makes use of frames and one that does not.

FTP: *See* File Transfer Protocol

Functional Acknowledgment: a type of message sent by an EDI system, essentially an electronic acknowledgment of receipt of a message that does not contain a response to the contents of the message. Functional acknowledgments permit parties using EDI to verify that a message has been received.

Grantback Provision: a provision in a patent license that requires the licensee to grant back to the licensor patented improvements in the licensee's original technology; grantback provisions have generally been looked upon with hostility by U.S. antitrust enforcement agencies, especially where the grantback is exclusive.

Graphical User Interface (GUI) (pronounced "gooey"): a human-computer interface that makes use of graphics rather than exclusively text; a World Wide Web page viewed in a browser is one example of a GUI.

Hacker: originally, a clever programmer; the original meaning has been obscured by its use by journalists and others who are not themselves programmers as synonymous with "cracker."

Hash Function: a software program that turns one string of characters into another, shorter string of characters that represent the original string.

History File: a detailed list of Web sites recently visited, stored by browser software. The history makes it easy for the end user to access sites again; the contents of the history file can be viewed by anyone with access to the browser.

Horizontal Exchange: an online marketplace made up of direct competitors.

HTML: *See* Hypertext Markup Language

HTTP: *See* Hypertext Transfer Protocol

Hyperlink: an electronic link providing direct access from one electronic resource to another. The term is a contraction of "hypertext link." The use of hyperlinks is what makes the World Wide Web a web.

Hypertext: text that is organized by connected associations (hyperlinks) that do not require the use of an index. If electronic recourses other than text (such as graphics, audio, or video) are linked, the correct term is "hypermedia." The term seems to have been derived from "hyperspace," a science fiction term for space with more than three dimensions, because of the much more dynamic and intuitive manner in which information can be stored and retrieved using hyperlinks.

Hypertext Markup Language (HTML): a set of codes or "tags" that are used to "mark up" World Wide Web content to be displayed using a browser. HTML tags are generally limited to formatting, which limits their use in electronic-commerce applications. By contrast, eXtensible Markup Language (XML) tags permit files to be marked based on the meaning of the terms, e.g., permitting price and quantity terms in contracts to be identified without human intervention.

Hypertext Transfer Protocol (HTTP): an Internet communications protocol that permits files including text, graphics, sound, or video to be exchanged over the World Wide Web. Other widely used Internet communications protocols include FTP and SMTP.

IANA: *See* Internet Assigned Number Authority

IAP: *See* Internet Access Provider

ICANN: *See* Internet Corporation for Assigned Names and Numbers

ICP: *See* Internet Content Provider

Identity Manager: a feature of Microsoft Outlook Express that permits end users to create and maintain separate online identities with different security preferences or other attributes.

Identity Scrubber: software that allows individuals to remain anonymous while accessing Internet sites; Zero-Knowledge is a leading provider of such software. *See* www.zeroknowledge.com.

Identity Theft: misappropriation of someone's personal information in order to defraud creditors and others by assuming the identity of that person.

IETF: *See* Internet Engineering Task Force

Illusory Privacy Policy: a misleading document labeled "privacy policy" that does not provide any privacy protection to the individuals covered by it. For example, a privacy policy stating "We will make the fullest possible use of your personal information in order to serve you better" would be an illusory privacy policy.

Information Audit: a methodical examination or review by an organization of its policies governing the collection of information, the types of information it actually collects, and the uses to which that information is put.

Interface: point at which two independent systems meet and interact with each other.

International Organization for Standardization (ISO): a world-wide federation of national standards bodies from some 140 countries. ISO is a nongovernmental organization established to promote the development of open, voluntary standards in many fields. For example, if programmers had used the ISO 8601 standard for expressing dates (dd/mm/yyyy), Y2K problems with computer software could have been avoided. The name "ISO" is not an acronym but derives from the Greek prefix "iso-," meaning "equal" or "standard." The name ISO was adopted to avoid the creation of acronyms that would be different in different languages around the world. *See* www.iso.ch.

Internet: a network of networks of electronic communication systems and computers that can all share information with each other through the use of the TCP/IP standard.

Internet Access Provider (IAP): *See* Internet Service Provider.

Internet Alliance: a trade association and lobbying group established for Internet companies. *See* www.internetalliance.org.

Internet Assigned Number Authority (IANA): organization formerly charged with coordinating the process of assigning "Internet Protocol" (IP) addresses used to identify Internet domains; control of this process was transferred to ICANN in 1999.

Internet Content Provider (ICP): a party responsible for the creation or development of Internet content.

Internet Corporation for Assigned Names and Numbers (ICANN): a California not-for-profit corporation created in 1998 to take over administration of the domain name system, IP address allocations, and other technical functions essential to the administration of the Internet. *See* www.icann.org.

Internet Engineering Task Force (IETF): a voluntary standards-developing organization characterized by its openness and pragmatism. The task force requires two successful implementations before a proposed standard will be officially recognized. For an overview of the functions of the IETF, *see* IETF RFC 3160, issued August 2001, "The Tao of IETF—A Novice's Guide to the Internet Engineering Task Force." *See* www.ietf.org.

Internet Network Information Center (InterNIC): InterNIC is a registered service mark of the U.S. Department of Commerce. The name once referred to a joint venture among Network Solutions, Inc., General Atomics, and AT&T, which was established in 1993 to administer the domain-name system. Network Solutions later took exclusive control over the administration of the domain-name system from the joint venture, but in turn lost its monopoly over registration of .com, .org, and .net domain names when the Internet Corporation for Assigned Names and Numbers (ICANN) was created in 1998 to take over that function. ICANN now maintains the InterNIC Web site as a source of information about Internet domain-name registration services. *See* www.internic.com

Internet Protocol (IP): a network communications protocol that handles the address part of each data packet. The current version of the IP standard is known as IP version 4 or IPv4 and is contained in IETF RFC 791, written by Jon Postel in 1981. A revised IP standard is in the process of being implemented. That standard is known variously as IP version 6, or IPv6, or IP next generation, or IPng. That standard is contained in IETF RFC 1752, published in 1994. The change from IPv4 to IPv6 is needed because only about 4 billion IP addresses can be created within the framework of IPv4, but IPv6 will permit vastly more IP addresses to be created. (Specifically, it will support 2^{128} addresses, or 282, 366, 920 938, 463, 374, 607, 431, 768, 211, 456.)

Internet Service Provider (ISP): a party providing a connection between an end user's computer and the Internet.

InterNIC: *See* Internet Network Information Center

IP: Intellectual Property or Internet Protocol

IP address: In version 4 of the IP protocol (IPv4), an IP address identifies a computer connected to the Internet with a unique 32-bit number made up of 12 digits divided into four groups of numbers separated by decimals— *e.g.*, 121.122.123.124. In version 6 of the IP protocol (IPv6), an IP address will be a unique 128-bit number.

ISO: *See* International Organization for Standardization

ISP: *See* Internet Service Provider

Iteration: repetition of a procedure. In programming, iteration refers to a sequence of instructions; each time the computer executes the instructions is an iteration. In software development, iterative development refers to the process of building incrementally on selected elements of a project only after those elements have been tested. This is in contrast to more traditional software-development methods, in which an entire project is mapped out and built before substantial testing takes place.

Java: a programming language developed by Sun Microsystems that permits computer programs to operate in a networked or "distributed" environment. The programming language was originally created to develop software for interactive television and was named "Oak." The name was later changed to Java at a meeting at which many cups of coffee were sitting on the table in front of the developers. Programs written in Java can operate on any computer that is Java-enabled without regard to the operating system the computer runs, a feature known as "portability" that eliminates the need to write separate versions of programs for Microsoft, Apple, or Unix operating systems.

Java Applets: small programs that can be placed on a server as part of a Web site but that actually run on the computers of visitors to the Web site.

Just in Time (JIT) Inventory Control Systems: coordinate the production and delivery of parts so that only what is needed is made available just at the time it is needed; this is in marked contrast to traditional inventory systems, in which large stockpiles of parts are maintained by manufacturers to ensure their availability when and if they are needed.

Key: in cryptography, a long, seemingly random number combined with an encryption algorithm and applied to a plaintext to produce a ciphertext.

Keyword Meta Tag: a meta tag that identifies keywords that might be typed into a search engine; unlike description meta tags, keyword meta tags are not read by potential visitors but are only used by the search engine to gauge the likelihood that a site will contain contents of interest to a searcher.

Killer App: a wildly successful computer software application that produces fundamental changes in the way people use computers. Spreadsheet programs VisiCalc and then Lotus 1-2-3, Internet browsers Mosaic and Netscape Navigator, and the Word Perfect word-processing programs are all examples of "killer apps."

Legacy System: information systems using hardware, software, and data formats that are not the current version of those technologies.

Link: short form of "Hyperlink."

Local Registration Agent (LRA): a person or organization authorized to issue digital signature certificates to other persons or organizations already known to the LRA within a PKI. For example, if a company participates in a PKI established by a trade association, the company may designate an employee in its personnel department or information technology department to be the company's LRA and to its employee the digital signature certificates that are necessary for them to participate in the PKI.

Logic Bomb: a virus programmed to perform some destructive or security-compromising act whenever a specified set of conditions are present.

LRA: *See* Local Registration Agent

Maintenance, Repair, and Operations (MRO): general industrial products such as machine tools or cleaning supplies purchased on a recurring basis in a wide variety of industries.

Media Perils Insurance: insurance available to writers and publishers, covering liability for libel or intellectual property infringement.

Message Digest: a summary of a message; in cryptography, a summary of the electronic record signed using the private key. Message digests are produced using a "hash function," which is an algorithm that can take a message of any length and summarize it as a single number which is unique to that message. A one-way hash function can generate a digest of any message, but the message cannot later the recreated by analyzing the digest and the hash function algorithm.

Meta Tag: an HTML tag that describes the content of the Web site where it is found; meta tags are used by search engines to identify Web sites that may be of interest to searchers and to provide descriptions to searchers of those sites.

Middleware: software that permits two or more existing applications to share data or functions.

Model Electronic Data Interchange Trading Partner Agreement and Commentary (MTPAC): a form contract for use in negotiating and drafting EDI trading-partner agreements; developed by the Business Law Section of the American Bar Association and Published at 45 Bus. Law. 1717 (1990). The published version of the MTPAC was accompanied by a report explaining the function of EDI and the application of existing contract law doctrine to it. ABA Electronic Messaging Services Task Force, *The Commercial Use of Electronic Data Interchange—A Report*, 45 Bus. Law. 1645 (1990).

Mousetrapped: unable to exit a site without clicking on a succession of advertisements.

MRO: *See* Maintenance, Repair, and Operations

MTPAC: *See* Model Electronic Data Interchange Trading Partner Agreement and Commentary

National Arbitration Forum: an arbitration service made up of lawyers, law professors, and former judges. *See* www.arb-forum.com.

National Commission on New Technological Uses of Copyrighted Works (CONTU): created in 1978 by Congress to recommend changes in the Copyright Act to accommodate advances in computer technology; the report that it issued in 1979 outlined many of the issues that arise from the application of traditional copyright concepts to new information technologies.

National Infrastructure Protection Center (NIPC): federal project that provides a clearinghouse of information for private-sector organizations about current developments in computer security and information about appropriate responses to computer-security incidents (pronounced "Nip-see").

Network effect: if the value to one person of a product increases as the number of other people also using it increases, then the market for that product exhibits network effects.

NIPC: *See* National Infrastructure Protection Center

OASIS: *See* Organization for the Advancement of Structured Information Standards

Object Code: a form of software that is machine-readable. Decades ago, programmers wrote machine-readable code, but now object code is produced by running programs written in a form readable by humans ("source code") through a "compiler" to produce object code. While source code can readily be converted into object code, it is usually difficult or impossible to decompile object code back into source code.

OEM: *See* Original Equipment Manufacturer

On-line Privacy Alliance: an information-technology industry trade association and lobbying group that helps to define and advance the interests of U.S. business in the current debate regarding online privacy. *See* www.privacyalliance.org.

On-line Privacy Seal Program: voluntary programs that set up minimum privacy standards and provide Web sites that comply with such standards a seal that they can place on their site to demonstrate to visitors that they comply with the program's standards.

Online Service Provider (OSP): *See* Internet Service Provider (ISP)

Open PKI (Public Key Infrastructure): a PKI that is open to an unlimited number of possible participants.

Opt-In: a default rule for Internet privacy that would require an organization to first obtain an individual's express permission before direct-marketing materials could be sent to that individual. Privacy advocates opposed to direct marketing prefer opt-in to opt-out as a default rule.

Opt-Out: a default rule for Internet privacy that would require an individual to take some affirmative action in order to prevent unsolicited marketing from being sent to that person. Businesses that engage in direct marketing prefer opt-out to opt-in as a default rule.

Organization for the Advancement of Structured Information Standards (OASIS): and open, public standard-developing organization. *See* www.oasis-open.org.

Original Equipment Manufacturer (OEM): a company that combines the products of other companies to manufacture products that it markets under its own brand.

OSP: *See* Online Service Provider or Internet Service Provider (ISP)

Out-Link: a hyperlink that permits the viewer to move to another site on the Web.

Outsource: procuring from a source outside a firm a function that previously was performed inside a firm. For example, many small businesses now outsource the preparation of their payroll to a third-party vendor, while keeping all other bookkeeping functions in-house, because of the complexity of payroll calculations and the risk of liability for errors.

P3P: *See* Platform for Privacy Preferences

Packet: a unit of data sent from one computer system to another in a network system based on packet switching.

Packet Sniffer: software that monitors and analyzes network traffic. A network administrator may run packet sniffer software to detect bottlenecks or other problems with the network; sniffer software also may be installed and run by someone outside an organization without the knowledge or consent of the network administrator either for illicit purposes or to facilitate government surveillance.

Packet Switching: a network communication system that breaks data to be sent into smaller packets of data, each with a header to identify from where it is coming and to where it is going; the data is numbered before it is sent so that when all the packets are reassembled, they can be put back together in the right order. Packet switching consumes fewer network resources than circuit switching because the sender and the recipient do not need to maintain a single, dedicated connection. Rather, the packets of data may be routed over many different connections before they are reassembled at their destination.

Peripheral: any part of a computer other than those essential to functioning of the computer itself, such as a printer, a scanner, or a network connection.

Permission Marketing: marketing campaigns that are based on individuals "opting-in" or agreeing to participate.

Personal Digital Assistant (PDA): a small hand-held computer that provides information storage and retrieval functions, and that may also be networked. PalmPilot is a famous brand of PDA.

PET: *See* Privacy Enhancing Technologies

PKI: *See* Public Key Infrastructure

Plaintext: in cryptography, the text of the message before it has been encrypted or after it has been decrypted.

Platform for Privacy Preferences (P3P): an XML standard developed by the World Wide Web Consortium, which allows end users to set their browsers to remember their privacy preferences; if an end user tried to access a Web site that also uses P3P but that does not respect the end user's privacy preferences, the browser would alert the end user to the lack of adequate privacy protection.

Privacy Enhancing Technologies (PET): software or hardware designed to give an individual greater control over the personal information collected from that individual in online environments.

Protocol: a set of rules governing the processing and transmission of data shared among networked computer systems.

Proxy Bidding: the use of another as agent in a bidding process; in online auctions, proxy bidding is performed by software according to guidelines set by the individual bidder.

Proxy Server Software: directs outgoing and incoming data traffic through a centralized portal.

Public Key Infrastructure (PKI): distributes public keys reliably and provides a reliable source of information when the security of a private key has been compromised.

Puffer: *See* Shill

Pure Play: Internet company that has no off-line presence for dealing with its customers.

Relational Database: a database in which the information is organized according to predetermined categories; queries can be made and reports can be generated from the data in the database by taking advantage of the categories used to build it.

Remittance Advice Information: an EDI message sent to advise that payment has been sent.

Request for Comments (RFC): a formal document issued by the Internet Engineering Task Force (IETF) that has been reviewed by interested parties. Some RFCs are informational, but others contain technical standards that have been finalized. For example RFC 3160, issued in August 2001, is *The Tao of IETF–A Novice's Guide to the Internet Engineering Task Force*, a document that provides an overview of the functions of the IETF. All IETF RFCs are available at www.ietf.org.

Reserve Price: a price set by the seller at an auction as the minimum price that the seller will accept.

Reverse Auction: an auction in which the buyer sets the highest price that it is willing to pay and then permits various vendors to compete as to how far below that price they are willing to bid.

Reverse Engineering: the process of analyzing computer hardware or software for the purposes of understanding and/or recreating its design and structure.

RFC: *See* Request for Comments

Robot Exclusion Header: a message sent to computers programmed to detect whether the use of robots is authorized on a particular site.

Rule of Exhaustion: *See* First-Sale Doctrine

Safe Harbor: protection from liability based on compliance with specified objective requirements. For example, the Communications Decency Act, 47 USC § 230, protects OSPs from liability for defamatory content posted by another party. The Digital Millennium Copyright Act (DMCA) offers similar protection to OSPs with regard to protection against claims from copyright owners.

Schema: a structured framework; in XML programming, a framework that defines a group of XML tags (pronounced SKEE-ma).

Secure Sockets Layer (SSL): a communications security protocol that protects the privacy of communications between an Internet browser and a server. The browser and server first use public key encryption to establish a secure communication channel and then use symmetric key encryption to encrypt all information passed between the browser and server.

Self-Regulation: regulation of business entities by their own internal control procedures or by standards articulated by trade association or analogous organizations; an alternative to formal regulation by an agency or through binding contractual obligations.

SGML: *See* Standard Generalized Markup Language

Sham Bidder: *See* Shill

Shill: a person who appears to be a disinterested bidder at an auction, but who is actually making bogus bids on behalf of the seller in order to try to induce the other bidders to pay a higher price. Also sham bidder or puffer.

Shopping Bot or ShopBot: a software robot that acts as an agent on behalf of a human shopper in locating the best deal with regard to a particular item to be purchased.

Shrinkwrap Terms: standard-form contract terms that a software licensor wishes to make binding on the purchaser (licensee) of software, the premise being that the purchaser first sees the terms after it breaks the "shrinkwrap" that seals the box containing the software.

Silo: a large storage container; in business process reengineering, silos are created by internal divisions within firms that prevent sharing information and collaboration that would make the firm more efficient.

Simple Mail Transfer Protocol (SMTP): an Internet communications protocol that permits e-mail messages to be sent and received. Other widely used Internet communications protocols include FTP and HTTP.

Site License: Web-based contract that sets forth the expectations of a Web-site operator about the rights and obligations of visitors to the site.

SKU: *See* Stockkeeping Unit

Smart Card: a plastic card in which a microprocessor chip is embedded; smart cards are "smart" in comparison to plastic cards with magnetic strips, which provide only a limited storage media and no processing capacity on the card itself.

Smart Goods: tangible goods of which software is an essential element. For example, digital cellphones are smart goods, but rotary dial telephones are not.

SMTP: *See* Simple Mail Transfer Protocol

Sniffer: *See* Packet Sniffer

Sniping: shooting at someone from a hidden vantage point; in online auctions, placing a bid so close to the end of the auction that other bidders do not have time to react.

Social Engineering: low-tech attacks that successfully threaten computer security by tricking people into doing something that they should not.

Software Lease: the common name of a transaction for financing the acquisition of software, in which the lender ("lessor") makes a lump-sum payment to the licensor of the software, in return for the licensee's promise of a series of monthly payments to the lessor.

Software Robot: *See* Bot

Source Code: statements written by human programmers in a specific programming language that must be converted into machine-readable code ("object code") before a computer can run the program.

Source-Code Escrow: one of a variety of arrangements in which a software developer or licensor deposits a copy of a software program's source code with a third party. The third party agrees to deliver the source code to the sponsor or licensee in specified circumstances, such as a failure of the developer or licensor to conform to its obligations to develop, maintain, upgrade, or support the software.

Spam: a registered trademark of Hormel for luncheon meat; in a widely noted skit in the English television comedy *Monty Python's Flying Circus*, the word Spam is repeated to the point of absurdity in a restaurant menu; hence, by analogy, unsolicited commercial e-mail (UCE) which inundates Internet users to the point of absurdity.

Spamdexing: using meta tags to confuse or mislead search engines. For example, one Web site may copy the meta tags of a competitor into its own Web-site content. When a search engine provides a searcher with a link to the spamdexing site, it would appear to the searcher to be identical or nearly identical to the site whose meta tags it had copied.

Spider: a software robot that crawls the World Wide Web gathering information. Search engines commonly use spiders to identify and copy information that is then transmitted back to the search-engine system to be stored in a database and indexed.

Spoliation: the destruction or substantial modification of evidence, or the failure to preserve evidence that is relevant for the proof of an adverse party's case in litigation.

Spoof: to deceive in a good-natured way; creating a false network identity in order to gain unauthorized access or creating a false Web site that takes the place of the real one.

Spyware: a pejorative term that refers to any technology that permits information about an individual to be gathered without the knowledge of the individual.

SSL: *See* Secure Sockets Layer

Standard Generalized Markup Language (SGML):   a system used to "mark up" content so that the structure and meaning of the content can be interpreted by machine processes. SGML is used by online services such as Lexis-Nexis and Westlaw to mark up legal documents such as judicial opinions so that users of those online services can search by "segments" (which are created by inserting different SGML "tags" into legal documents). HTML and XML are subsets of SGML that have been developed for Internet applications. SGML is an open public standard issued by the ISO.

Stockkeeping Unit (SKU):   an inventory control number assigned by an organization for internal bookkeeping purposes (pronounced "Skew").

Streaming Media: media that can be displayed to the end user while it is still in the process of downloading. Video and audio files must be compressed before they can be sent over the Internet; in the early days of Internet multimedia, an end user first downloaded a file, then launched software that would decompress and play the media after downloading was complete. The advent of streaming media eliminated this two-step process, making it possible for the end user to begin enjoying the media file while it was still being transmitted and decompressed.

Supply Chain: every step in the process of producing and delivering a good or service, beginning with the raw materials and finishing with the retail distribution of the final product.

Supply Chain Re-engineering: analysis and design of work processes and information flows within a supply chain aimed at improving the efficiency of all the organizations that make up the supply chain.

Symmetric Cryptography: cryptography that uses the same key to encrypt and decrypt the information to be kept secret.

Tag: a generic term for labels applied to electronic content that permits the content to be processed automatically. SGML tags permit segment searching in Lexis-Nexis and Westlaw databases; HTML tags permit the browser to display the content correctly; XML tags can permit software to analyze the meaning of different terms in a legal document.

TCP: *See* Transmission Control Protocol

TCP/IP: the basic network communication protocol that defines the Internet; it consists of the Transmission Control Protocol and the Internet Protocol. The TCP/IP communication protocol works in combination with higher-level communication protocols such as HTTP, FTP, or SMTP to make Internet communications work.

Time Bomb: a software virus programmed to execute at a specific date or time.

TLS: See Transport Layer Security

Trademark Dilution: a cause of action in trademark law that does not require proof of consumer confusion, but instead provides liability for a competing use of the mark that reduces the capacity of a famous mark to identify and distinguish a product.

Trade Secret: valuable information belonging to a business that derives value from not being generally known or readily ascertainable by third parties.

Trading-Partner Agreement: an agreement between two firms using EDI technologies to form electronic contracts that sets out the mutual understandings of the parties with respect to their EDI communications.

Transmission Control Protocol (TCP): a network communications protocol that handles the breaking up of a message into data packets at its point of transmission and then their reassembly at their destination. The TCP standard is contained in IETF RFC 793.

Transport Layer Security (TLS): a communications-security protocol that protects the privacy of communications between an Internet browser and a server; the successor to the SSL protocol. The TLS protocol is contained in IETF RFC 2246.

Trojan Horse: malicious software code that is hidden within an apparently harmless software program.

Turnkey: a system that is delivered complete and ready to use.

Typosquatting: registering domain names that are intentional misspellings of distinctive or famous names.

UCE: *See* Unsolicited Commercial E-mail

UDRP: *See* Uniform Dispute Resolution Policy

UETA: Uniform Electronic Transactions Act; promulgated by the National Conference of Commissioners on Uniform State Laws (NCCUSL) in 1999 and adopted in 38 states by 2001. *See* www.nccusl.org.

UN/CEFACT: *See* United Nations Center for Trade Facilitation and Electronic Business

UN/EDIFACT: *See* United Nations Electronic Data Interchange for Administration, Commerce, and Transport

Uniform Dispute Resolution Policy (UDRP): policy issued by the Internet Corporation for Assigned Names and Numbers (ICANN) for the resolution of disputes between those registering domain names in the biz, .com, .info, .name, .net, and .org top-level domains and trademark owners that believe the domain names infringe or dilute their trademark. *See* www.icann.org.

Uniform Resource Locator (URL): the address of a file accessible on the Internet, such as www.acm.org (pronounced "You-Are-Elle" rather than "Earl").

United Nations Center for Trade Facilitation and Electronic Business (UN/CEFACT): an organization of the United Nations; participants include member states, intergovernmental organizations, and trade and industry associations that work to promote the growth of cross-border trade using electronic-commerce technologies. *See* www.unece.org/uncefact.

United Nations Electronic Data Interchange for Administration, Commerce, and Transport (UN/EDIFACT): a set of rules developed by various working groups of the United Nations Economic Commission for Europe (whose membership is open to all UN member states, not just European member states) and approved by the United Nations.

Universal Product Code (UPC): a 12-digit number provided by the Uniform Code Council that uniquely identifies a product in commerce. The first part of a UPC number identifies the company manufacturing a product, the second part identifies the product itself. UPC numbers appear in bar code labels that manufacturers place on the packaging of goods. *See* www.uc-council.org.

Unsolicited Commercial E-mail (UCE): junk e-mail sent to Internet users without permission; also known as "Spam."

UPC: *See* Universal Product Code

URL: *See* Uniform Resource Locator

User Agreement: a standard-form contract posted by a commercial Web-site operator that details the Web-site operator's interpretation of the rights and obligations of visitors to its Web site.

Use Tax: tax levied on residents of a state on goods purchased out of state for use within the state.

Value Added Network (VAN): data-network services provided to EDI trading partners that provided enhanced security and reliability.

Value Chain: a variation of "supply chain" that can apply to any vertical market in which the cooperation of a group of firms working together increases the value of a good or service. Value chain is meant to be a broader concept than supply chain. For example, companies that develop software that end users can run on personal computers form part of a value chain with the developer of the personal computer operating system and the manufacturers of the computers.

VAN: *See* Value Added Network

Vertical Exchange: an online marketplace composed of upstream (input) and downstream (output) producers in the same industry or economic sector.

Virtual Private Network (VPN): a private data network that uses public data networks for communications but maintains privacy by adding encryption and other security features to the communications.

Virus: malicious software code that enters a computer in a disguised form and then causes harm to the computer it has entered.

Web Bugs: a tiny file, often a transparent one-pixel by one-pixel graphic that is placed on a Web page or in an e-mail that can help the sender monitor the online behavior of the recipient; a variation of "cookie."

Web-Linking Agreement: an agreement between Web-site operators governing the use of hyperlinks between the two sites.

Web Server: the computer where the content of a Web site resides, or the software that permits the computer to deliver the content in response to requests from internal end users.

Wholesaling Domain Names: the practice of acquiring large numbers of domain names with the intent to profit from reselling them rather than using them to establish Web sites.

Wholesale Exception Clause: A revision to the Amazon.com privacy policy pejoratively characterized as creating a wholesale exception to its privacy commitments.

World Intellectual Property Organization (WIPO): a specialized agency of the United Nations responsible for administering various treaties dealing with intellectual-property law issues and for the further harmonization of intellectual property laws around the world. *See* www.wipo.org.

World Wide Web Consortium (W3C): a leading open, public standard-setting organization developing standards for the Internet; founded in 1994 by Tim Berners-Lee, the creator of the World Wide Web. *See* www.w3c.org.

Worms: malicious software code that harms the host computer by copying itself quickly, absorbing ever more system resources until the host computer crashes.

XML: *See* eXtensible Markup Language

Table of Cases

Case names and page numbers in italics indicate principal cases.

767

Index